An Introduction to American Archaeology   Volume Two: South America

Gordon R. Willey *Peabody Museum, Harvard University*

An Introduction to American

VOLUME TWO   **South America**

Prentice-Hall, Inc., Englewood Cliffs, New Jersey

Archaeology

Prentice-Hall Anthropology Series   *David M. Schneider, Editor*

An Introduction to American Archaeology
Volume Two: South America
Gordon R. Willey
© Copyright 1971 by Prentice-Hall, Inc.,
Englewood Cliffs, New Jersey.
Library of Congress Catalog No. 66–10096.
Printed in the United States of America.

Designed by Walter Behnke

Drawings by Avis Tulloch

Maps and Charts by Andrew J. Bennett, J & R Services

Current printing (last digit):

11   10   9   8   7   6   5   4   3   2   1

0–13–477851–0

To Julian H. Steward

This is the second of a two-volume work on American archaeology, written to introduce both the student and the layman to the subject. Like the first volume (which treats North and Middle America), this volume (on South America) is designed to serve the reader on two levels: First, the text is a narrative-descriptive account of New World prehistory. Although problems of interpretation and alternative opinions are frequently referred to, in this account the data of archaeology have been greatly compressed and simplified. Below this level is another, represented by the extensive footnotes and the Bibliography. This second level provides information for the student or general reader who wishes to delve deeper into the complexities and details of the history of Pre-Columbian culture. By interrelating these two levels, I have attempted to write a text that would "fit into" the extensive technical literature on the subject. That is, I have tried to use terminology that is the same as, or not at great variance with, that employed by the authors of specialized areal and regional monographs and papers; where I have been forced to depart from this terminology, I have called the reader's attention to it and explained the differences and their significance. Hence, as the reader refers from this book to the primary sources, he will not find himself in an unfamiliar world of bewilderingly different names for archaeological cultures, periods, and other data landmarks.

Most of this volume was written in the academic year 1968–1969, when I was on leave from Harvard University and in residence in Cambridge, England. Some changes and additions were made in 1969–1970 and, again, in 1970–1971. I am indebted to the President and Fellows of Harvard University and to the Bowditch Professorship, which I hold, for permitting me to take this year's leave. I am also indebted to the Master and Fellows of Churchill College, Cambridge University, for the privilege of an Overseas Fellowship in the college for the 1968–1969 terms.

Preface

As with the first volume, it would be unfair to single out by name professional colleagues who have helped me with advice and information: there have been so many. Most of them are referred to in appropriate footnotes to the text, but I offer them, collectively, my thanks. To those institutions and persons who have provided me with photographs or other illustrative material, I give special thanks and append their names to this Preface.

In the preparation of the book I have been helped immeasurably by the librarians and staffs of the Royal Anthropological Institute of Great Britain and Ireland, London (Miss B. Kirkpatrick); of the Department of Archaeology and Anthropology, Cambridge University (Mrs. Stella Clarke); and of the Peabody Museum, Harvard University (Miss Margaret Currier). I am most appreciative of this help.

A number of persons have been of great help in the preparation of the book. The manuscript was typed by Mrs. Margaret A. Doggett, of Milton, England, and Mrs. Maria von Mering Huggins, of Cambridge, Massachusetts. It was read critically by my wife, Katharine W. Willey. Miss Isabel Center prepared the Index. Miss Avis Tulloch, of Cambridge, prepared all the artifact and architectural drawings for this volume (except reproductions from other sources, which are so identified). The maps and charts were prepared by Andrew J. Bennett, J & R Services, under the direction of Walter Behnke of Prentice-Hall, Inc. Artists of Mr. Behnke's staff who have worked on the book include Rita Ginsburg, Ingeborg Schalkwyk, and Winifred Schneider. The editorial staff of Prentice-Hall who had charge of preparing the manuscript for the press was under the direction of David R. Esner; I wish especially to thank Norma Karlin and Arthur Vergara.

Gordon R. Willey

Acknowledgments

American Museum of Natural History
British Museum
Brooklyn Museum
Cambridge Museum of Archaeology and Ethnology
Carnegie Museum, Pittsburgh
Catamarca Museum, Argentina
Cura Collection, Catamarca, Argentina
Dumbarton Oaks Pre-Columbian Collection, Washington, D.C.
Ethnographic Museum, Buenos Aires
Ethnographical Museum, Goteborg
Field Museum of Natural History, Chicago
Harvard University Press, Cambridge
Inca Huasi Museum, La Rioja, Argentina

Instituto Cultura Puertorriquena
Instituto Venezolano de Investigaciones Cientificas
La Plata Museum, Argentina
McGraw-Hill Book Company, New York
Metropolitan Museum of Art, New York
Museo Arqueológico, San Pedro de Atacama, Chile
Museo Etnológico, Barcelona
Museo Nacional de Historia Natural, Santiago, Chile
Museo Nacional de Panamá
Museo del Oro, Bogotá
Museum of the American Indian, New York
Museum of the University of Tucuman, Argentina
Museum für Völkerkunde, Berlin
Museum für Völkerkunde und Vorgeschichte, Hamburg
National Gallery of Art, Washington, D.C.
Oxford University Press Inc., New York
Peabody Museum, Harvard University
Robert H. Lowie Museum, University of California, Berkeley
Servicio Aerofotográfico Nacional, Peru
Smithsonian Institution, Washington, D.C.
University of Chile, Santiago
University of Pennsylvania Museum
University of Puerto Rico Museum
University of Tokyo

Ricardo Alegría
Claude F. Baudez
Pierre Becquelin
R. E. Bell
W. C. Bennett
Elizabeth Benson
J. B. Bird
Warwick Bray
G. H. S. Bushnell
Allan Caplan
Donald Collier
E. M. Cigliano
W. M. Denevan
Don W. Dragoo
Dudley Easby
Gordon F. Ekholm
Frederic Engel
Emilio Estrada
Clifford Evans, Jr.
Edward Franquemont
Rosa Fung
A. R. Gonzalez
Wolfgang Haberland
D. E. Ibarra Grasso
Jorge Iribarren Charlín

Seiichi Izumi
Alfred Kidder II
Gerdt Kutscher
Rafael Larco Hoyle
Donald Lathrap
Jay C. Leff
Gustavo Le Paige
Ramiro Matos
Betty J. Meggers
Roberto Montandon
Grete Mostny
Mario Orellana
James J. Parsons
T. C. Patterson
George Plafker
Donald Proulx
Gerardo Reichel-Dolmatoff
Pedro Rojas Ponce
John Thacher
G. T. Trewartha
Bruce W. Trigger
L. E. Valcarcel
Henry Wassen
John Wise
Alberta Zucchi

Contents

5

6

An Introduction to American Archaeology   Volume Two: South America

Approach and Organization

This volume is devoted to the pre-Columbian culture history of South America. It follows as a sequel and second part to the first volume of this work which dealt with North and Middle America.[1] The objectives are the same—to relate the story of the native American prehistoric past from earliest times to the arrival of the Europeans. My method of doing this is also the same, and the reader is referred to the Introduction (Chap. 1) of that volume for a more detailed statement of both objectives and method. To recapitulate, the intent is to appraise the archaeological cultures of the New World; to define what we believe to be the principal lines of history—the major cultural traditions; and to plot out the development of these lines in their geographical settings and their chronological dimensions. The course of the presentation swings back and forth, from such abstractions as "major cultural traditions" to the specifics of individual archaeological sites and the man-made objects found within them. In other words, an attempt has been made to organize a narrative in outlines sufficiently bold to delineate the main currents of culture history, yet at the same time not to lose sight of man himself.

As in Volume One, the scheme of organization moves first to the early inhabitants and then takes up, in order, the later cultural traditions—here, of the Peruvian, South Andean, Intermediate (the

Introduction

1

northern Andes and lower Central America), Caribbean, Amazonian, East Brazilian, Chacoan, Pampean, and Fuegian areas. The geographic scope of the volume includes all the South American continent, the West Indies, and that portion of lower Central America which lies south and east of the frontier of Mesoamerica (see Vol. I, Chap. 3).

As with North and Middle America, the intention has been to review the archaeology of all parts of South America. In so doing we have taken into account available source material as well as extent of geographical area to be covered, so that an area such as the Peruvian, where there is a vast literature—comparable to Mesoamerica in Volume One—receives much more attention than the huge East Brazilian area about which archaeologists yet know very little. Throughout, we have been selective—sometimes severely so. Yet in making selections we have attempted to offer divergent opinions when these exist.

A summary word is in order about methodology and special terms although this largely duplicates the introductory remarks in Volume One. The *major cultural tradition* is our most inclusive classificatory unit. Major cultural traditions are abstracted from the concrete data of archaeological sites or components within sites. Such component and site data are classified or grouped by archaeologists into phases. The *phase*, as used here and, generally, in American archaeology, refers to a grouping of site components that share a very high degree of cultural similarity and that are restricted to relatively small territories and relatively brief periods of time.[2] Between the classificatory level of phase and the construct of major cultural tradition we will, on occasion, refer to "cultures" or "sub-traditions" that compose major cultural traditions. These constructs are of intermediate typological scope, between phase and major tradition. They have, as a rule, greater geographical and chronological dimensions than the phase, but in these dimensions they are of a lesser order than the major cultural tradition.

Culture areas are subdivided into *subareas;* these, in turn, are broken down into *regions;* and regions are made up of *localities* and *sites.*[3] As in Volume One, no systematic effort will be made to impose this formal geographical classification on all of the culture areas under consideration, at least with anything like completeness. Archaeological data are insufficient to do so in many—or most—places, and such careful and exhaustive geographical "pigeonholing" is not to our purpose. The orderly geographic frame of reference is, rather, to give the reader some idea of comparable spatial scale as we move from one part of the Americas to another.

In following out the lines of culture history we shall see that the American aboriginal cultures of the past did not adhere to strict geographic boundaries, that there was considerable shifting of regional and subarea borders through time within culture areas, and that even the boundaries of the major culture areas changed over the millennia. As a result, and to repeat what was said in Volume One, archaeological culture areas must be considered useful devices in the presentation of prehistory, but with the realization that they are also compromises. We define them as embracing significant cultural unity through significant spans of time (Fig. 1-1).

Archaeological *area chronologies* are the time scales or frames in which culture phases are plotted in local, regional, or subareal columns. They are a graphic means of following the histories of the major cultural traditions through time. These chronologies are marked off in *periods* and *sub-*

periods, and the lines so marking off these periods and subperiods are truly horizontal lines. That is, the archaeological period in an area chronology is defined strictly in terms of absolute years, centuries, or millennia. The dates placed upon it are arrived at in various ways—radiocarbon readings, glottochronological estimates, calculations from native histories, or various means of archaeological cross-dating or reckoning. To be sure, none of these has yet given full and accurate chronologies for any South American area; nor have all of them together; yet it is essential in historical or

Figure 1-1.

Archaeological
Culture Areas
of South America

archaeological reconstruction that the dimension of time be kept separate, or held constant, while we study cultural content and cultural events.

From the foregoing it should be clear that this is not a presentation of culture history by developmental stages.[4] The problem of American culture stages and a consideration of how the cultural traditions of South America may be fitted into a stage scheme are reserved for discussion only in a final chapter.[5]

It is emphasized again that this book is intended as a telling of specific culture histories. This intention is grounded in the belief that the substance of New World pre-Columbian history is worth knowing, both for its immediate and special value to the student of American archaeology and for the broader perspective it gives on human history as a whole. The intention derives further from the assumption that the findings of archaeology are cumulative and that, while new approaches and methods undoubtedly will give us new insights about these findings, the new methods and approaches may be most successfully applied in the fullest context of factual control that it is possible to obtain. This is not meant to imply that such a control may be obtained from a reading of this book. The work is, as the title indicates, an *introduction;* however, it is an introduction designed not only to give the student a wide overview of the subject but to lead the way for him into a study in depth of any part of it.

It is, of course, realized that the extent to which histories, or prehistories, of past human events can be made more meaningful depends on the success with which such things as the adaptations of cultures to natural environments, their relationships to their social settings, and their interrelationships among their various institutions or sub-systems are interpreted. And the degree of this success can only be measured by the reduction of the speculative and subjective in favor of the demonstrable and objective. In other words, a validation of hypotheses about the processes operative in past human and cultural behavior are to be sought in the interrelationships among the archaeological data.[6] But it should be borne in mind that for the past 50 years or more, the main trends of New World archaeological research have been descriptive ones —the describing of cultural forms and their arrangement in geographical and chronological

frames of reference. Only recently have American archaeologists begun to direct systematic attention to *understanding* as well as to *observing;* but studies of this nature have so far been undertaken only in relatively few places, and in South America they are very few indeed. Because of this, a history, or prehistory, of native America as told at the present time unavoidably overemphasizes the sheerly descriptive—the plotting of man's past by fragmentary bits that, aside from their spatial and temporal positions, are not well understood. If, as we hope, future archaeological research lives up to the promise of recent progress, the pre-Columbian histories of the future will offer us a more integrated and meaningful picture.

Natural Environment of South America[7]

Physiography. The Andes run the full length of the South American continent (Fig. 1-2). They are narrower in width than the North American western cordillera, but higher. Some peaks reach over 20,000 feet above sea level, and most passes are 10,000 feet or above. In the far south, the mountains descend to the Pacific Ocean, and the result is a series of drowned embayments or fjords. Coming northward, two long parallel ranges extend the length of Chile. These are separated by a narrow intermontane valley—the Central Valley of Chile—a structural counterpart of the long Sacramento–San Joaquin Valley of California. The higher of the two Chilean mountain ranges—the eastern one—is a part of the main chain of the Andes, and its eastern slopes and valleys descend into Patagonian and Pampean Argentina. At about 33 degrees south latitude the eastern Andes widen considerably, extending for 200 to 300 miles into the basin and range country of northwestern Argentina. Continuing northward, the Andes become still wider (over 400 miles) in Bolivia, a land of high intermontane plateaus. The total mass of the cordillera narrows again in Peru and Ecuador; and in these countries, once more, the principal ranges can be classified as either western or eastern Andes, with numerous high, intermontane basins in between. In Colombia, the Andes again widen, or rather splay out, into four distinct ranges. These ranges are separated by deep, wide valleys that provide marked

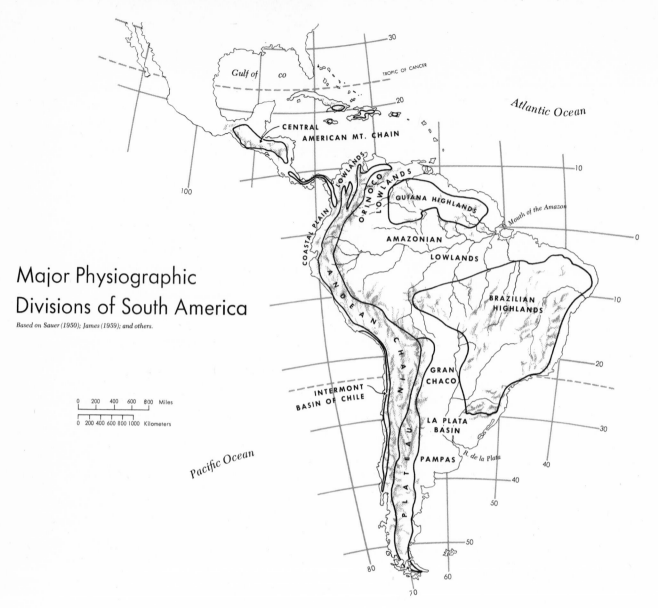

Major Physiographic Divisions of South America

Based on Sauer (1950); James (1959); and others.

0 200 400 600 800 Miles

0 200 400 600 800 1000 Kilometers

CENTRAL AMERICAN MT. CHAIN

COASTAL PLAIN

LOWLANDS

ORINOCO LOWLANDS

GUIANA HIGHLANDS

AMAZONIAN LOWLANDS

BRAZILIAN HIGHLANDS

ANDEAN CHAIN

INTERMONT BASIN OF CHILE

GRAN CHACO

LA PLATA BASIN

PAMPAS

PLATEAU

Gulf of co

TROPIC OF CANCER

Atlantic Ocean

Mouth of the Amazon

Pacific Ocean

R. de la Plata

Figure 1-2.

physiographic, climatic, and vegetational contrasts to the intervening ranges. The two western mountain ranges of Colombia are joined to volcanic ridges or chains that extend into Panama, Costa Rica, and Pacific Nicaragua, and these ridges abut on the Central American–Antillean mountain system in El Salvador and Honduras. Returning to Colombia, we see that the easternmost Andean Cordillera of that country extends in a north-easterly direction toward the Caribbean and then eastwards, along that sea, becoming the Venezuelan Maritime Andes.

Coastal lowlands, varying in width, border the Andes. In the far south of Chile these lowlands are negligible; but in northern Chile and Peru there is a narrow littoral cut by numerous small rivers that descend from the Andes to the Pacific. In Ecuador and Colombia the coastal lowlands widen into a plain 100 to 200 miles in depth. There is also a wide lowland plain along the Caribbean coast in northern Colombia; however, the Venezuelan Maritime Andes lie close to the sea, so the coastal strip here is, again, narrow.

The major islands of the West Indies are a part of the old east-west, Central American–Antillean mountain system which is partially submerged in the Caribbean. The smaller islands of the West Indies are either volcanic, as with the Lesser Antilles which extend northward from eastern Venezuela, or coralline, as with the Bahamas, which lie between Haiti and Florida.

The uplands of eastern South America are much older than the Andes, much more weathered, and considerably lower in elevation. Low mountains, hills, and plateaus occur in three principal sectors. North of the Amazon River they are most pronounced in the Guianas, but these hills also extend west of the Guianas, in a belt south of the Orinoco River, going as far as southeastern Colombia. The vast Brazilian highlands make up the second sector. Lying some distance south of the main course of the Amazon, they extend westward for 2000 miles, and from the Brazilian-Bolivian border their western margin runs south to Uruguay. Along the Atlantic this Brazilian tableland comes to within a few miles of the coast, and the narrow coastal zone is set off from the interior by a steep scarp. In the east, immediately back of this scarp, the terrain is hilly or mountainous; farther inland are tabular uplands; and in the west low hills drop off to the lowlands of the tributaries of the Upper Madeira River. Thus, in general, the contour of the Brazilian uplands is higher near the Atlantic with a gradual decline in elevation toward the west. The third eastern South American highland block is in Patagonia where a tabular upland or plateau slopes from the eastern edge of the Andes to the Atlantic. Throughout all of these eastern South American highlands the geological formations are, basically, ancient crystalline rocks. These have weathered differently: in the tropics they have decomposed, usually presenting a rounded, soil-covered outline; in Patagonia, on the other hand, weathering has been less rapid and the configuration is more rugged, the surface less soil-covered. Overlying the crystalline formations in many places are sedimentary beds—sandstones and limestones.

The lowland plains of interior South America may also be thought of in three sectors. In the north, the smallest of these lies along the Orinoco drainage, mostly to the north of that river and to the south and east of the Venezuelan Maritime Andes and the eastern cordillera of Colombia. In eastern Venezuela, at the delta of the Orinoco, this Orinocan lowland plain extends to the sea. To the south, the Orinocan lowlands are separated from those of the Amazon Basin by the uplands of southern Venezuela and southeastern Colombia. The Amazon Basin, or Amazonian lowlands, the second of the lowland plains, is vast, extending all the way from the eastern slopes of the Ecuadorian, Peruvian, and Bolivian Andes to the Atlantic. It is widest in the west, narrowing considerably from about the city of Manaos eastward to the delta, where it is bordered by the Guiana and Brazilian highlands. The third lowland plain sector is that of the Paraguay-Paraná-Plate system. Centering on that system, which drains southward into the Plate estuary between the Argentine Pampas and Uruguay, these lowlands connect, to the north, with those of the Amazon in eastern Bolivia.

Climate, Vegetation, Soils. Andean highland climates (H) (Fig. 1-3)—and soils and vegetation—are profoundly conditioned by altitude and are, accordingly, cool to cold in the higher elevations, even in the latitude of the equator.[8] The heights are, however, somewhat moderated by latitude and moisture so that, for example, in Colombia and Ecuador, forests reach to 10,000 feet and there is relatively abundant rainfall. Moving southward, away from the equatorial zone, high altitude climate becomes increasingly colder and drier in Peru, Bolivia, Chile, and northwestern Argentina. Here the vegetation is only a grass cover, but these grasses serve as food for llamas and alpacas. These animals were domesticated in the central Andean highlands in pre-Columbian times and were then a significant part of the economy; they are still so herded and domesticated by the highland Indians today. The principal crops of these dry uplands—at least in the basins and plateaus of 8000 feet or more of elevation—were the aboriginal domesticates, oca, quinoa, and the potato—all of which are still grown in the area, along with European-introduced wheat.

The narrow coastal shelf on the Pacific side of the Andes in Peru and northern Chile has an extremely dry (BWn) desert climate; however, the heat is moderated by winds off the cold Humboldt ocean current. Although this Peru-Chile coastal desert is almost rainless, and with little natural vegetation, there are a number of small rivers—especially in Peru—which descend the Andean slopes and fall to the sea. These streams,

Major Climatic Zones of South America

From Finch, Trewartha, Robinson, and Hammond (1957).

Types of Climate

A. Tropical Humid Climates
- TROPICAL WET (Rainforest, Af, Am)
- TROPICAL WET-AND-DRY (Savanna, Aw, As)

B. Dry Climates
- SEMIARID OR STEPPE (BS)
  Tropical and Subtropical Steppe (BSh)
  Middle Latitude Steppe (BSk)
- ARID OR DESERT (BW)
  Tropical and Subtropical Desert (BWh)
  Middle Latitude Desert (BWk)

C. Humid Mesothermal Climates
- DRY-SUMMER SUBTROPICAL (Mediterranean, Cs)
- HUMID SUBTROPICAL (Warm Summer, Ca)
- MARINE (Cool Summer, Cb Cc)

E. Polar Climates
- TUNDRA (ET)
- ICE CAP (EF)

H. Undifferentiated Highlands
- H
- EXTENSIVE UPLANDS SHADED

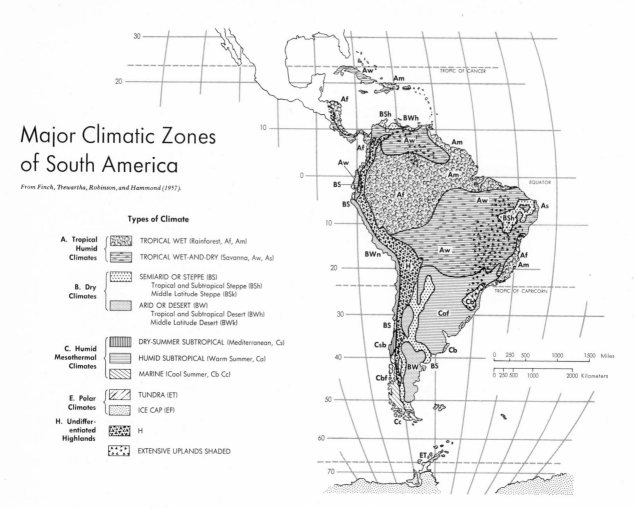

Figure 1-3.

fed by mountain rains and snows, create lush valley oases in the deep desert soils. As a consequence, the oases were formerly, and are still today, the settled human living zones of the region. Maize, lima beans, peanuts, a variety of vegetables and fruits, and cotton were the principal pre-Columbian crops.

Farther north, in Ecuador and Colombia, where the Pacific coastal shelf is considerably wider, climate and vegetation are either of tropical rainforest (Af, Am) or tropical savanna (Aw) type. The rainforest climate is marked by heavy, almost year-round rains and intense heat, with dense forest and vine cover. The tropical savanna climate has less rain and a noticeable annual dry season. Savanna vegetation cover is grassland with occasional stands of trees. Both the tropical savanna and rainforest soils are subject to leaching from the heavy rains and are low in mineral content. Thus, although there are rapid growing seasons—and two or three such seasons in a year—soils deteriorate rapidly under cultivation and must be left to lie fallow for several years between periods of farming. The usual method of cultivation in rainforest and savanna environments is of a swidden or slash-and-burn type. Maize is, of course, grown under these conditions, but such root crops as manioc also thrive.

Climates in southern Central America, north Caribbean Colombia, Venezuela, and most of the

West Indies are mainly of tropical rainforest or tropical savanna types. There are, however, some regional exceptions such as the dry, xerophytic strips (BSh, BWh) along the shores of the Caribbean and on both sides of the Gulf of Venezuela. Similar small zones also exist in portions of the Greater Antilles.

The middle and upper Amazon basin is tropical rainforest country, but the lower reaches of that basin, the Orinoco drainage, and much of the Guiana and Brazilian uplands are largely tropical savanna.

To the south, southern Brazil, Paraguay, Uruguay, and the Argentine Pampas have a humid subtropical (Caf) climate. These lands were for the most part grass-covered and had heavy soils that were difficult to cultivate by primtive means.

There is a long north-south strip of territory, reaching from the Gran Chaco in northern Paraguay to the southern extremity of the continent, and lying just to the east of the Andes, that is arid to semi-arid.

On the western side of the Andes in the far south, central Chile has a Mediterranean (Csb) climate with mixed grasslands, thorn bushes, and scrub; but below the 37th parallel these conditions give way to the beech and conifer forests of a humid marine (Cbf, Cc) zone. At the very tip of the continent, these marine forests diminish and fade out to open country.

The climatic conditions described pertain, of course, to the present day. It is also highly likely that they have pertained to South America over the past several millennia. The extent to which climate and vegetation was significantly different in late Pleistocene and early post-Pleistocene times will be discussed in Chapter 2 (pp. 33-34).

Peoples

Origins. The aboriginal populations of South America were American Indians; therefore the problem of their origins is essentially the same as that of the Indians of North and Middle America (see Vol. I, pp. 12-13).

American Indians were of a basic Mongoloid racial stock or else sprang from that line of human development at a time when it might best be considered as "Proto-Mongoloid." Their geographic source is believed to have been northeastern Asia, and these Mongoloids, or "Proto-Mongoloids," are presumed to have crossed from Siberia to Alaska in the vicinity of the Bering Strait and the Aleutian chain. From this point they gradually found their way south, through North America and, eventually, to South America.

The date of the arrival of the first Asiatic immigrants to the New World is a moot question. Archaeologists know for a certainty that man was in the Americas as early as 10,000 B.C., and it is generally believed that he may have been here for two or three millennia before that. His earliest definite appearances in South America are at about 9000 B.C., and again it may be surmised that he had arrived there at least a few thousand years in advance of this date. It should be stressed, however, that there are certain clues and lines of evidence that suggest—although they do not conclusively prove—that man came to the New World much earlier, perhaps as much as 20,000 to 40,000 years ago. These questions concerning the dating of the first migrations to the Americas are complex; they have been treated in some detail in Volume One, (pp. 29–37, 72); and they will be referred to again in our discussions of early man in this volume (see pp. 26–29).

Sub-races or Varieties of South American Indians. The American Indian, in both North and South America, presents a range of physical variation, and this variation has been classified and discussed under a number of groupings that physical anthropologists think of as sub-races or varieties. What is the history of these varieties? How did this variability come about? There are two principal theoretical positions on these questions. One is that the biological variations seen in the American Indian are the result of a series of migrations from the Old World to the New. According to some physical anthropologists, this variability in the American Indian is so great that it cannot be explained except by assuming that some of these migrations involved Old World peoples other than Mongoloids—especially Indo-Dravidian, Ainu, Australian, Melanesian, and other racial strains.[9] In general, those holding this position believe that these non-

Mongoloid migrations were the earliest and that they were followed by Mongoloid peoples who pushed the earlier groups back into refuge zones, in some cases interbred with them, and imparted an overall "Mongoloid cast" to the American Indian appearance.

The opposite theoretical position on the why and wherefore of American Indian physical variability is that it is a result of genetic drift and the separation of breeding populations within the

Americas after arrival from Asia. On this point of view it would be quite possible to derive all, or most, of the New World aborigines from a few early migrations of peoples from Asia to America in the late Pleistocene. M. T. Newman has developed this general hypothesis at some length. He has reasoned that selective adaptation to climatic zones has had an important influence on American Indian sub-racial differentiation and that this process could have taken place within the last 10,000 years or less.[10]

In choosing between the extremes of these two positions, I would tend to favor the Newman hypothesis;[11] but, whichever hypothesis is followed in the question of population origins, South American Indians do show somatological variation. Let us briefly review this variation. A number of authors have contributed to the subject, but Imbelloni has dealt with it more extensively, and more recently, than others. Imbelloni's classification[12] of American Indian sub-races or varieties was referred to in Volume One (p. 14), but in describing North American Indian physical variation we followed the scheme of George Neumann.[13] Imbelloni's classification is based on eleven varieties for the whole of the New World.[14] These are shown on the map reproduced from his study (Fig. 1-4). Six of the varieties concern us for South America.

The *Fuegides* variety of South American Indian is Imbelloni's term for peoples such as the Yahgan and Alacaluf of the Chilean Archipelago and southern Tierra del Fuego. Included also are groups along the Atlantic coast of Patagonia and a number of small enclaves found on the Chilean, south Peruvian, and Colombian coasts. In general, Imbelloni's physical descriptive data are drawn from measurements and observations on modern or late historic groups of Indians, although some cognizance is taken of archaeological skeletal material. Measurements and summary observations are offered for each sub-race or variety. Among the observations noted for the Fuegides are short stature, a dolichocephalic, low-vaulted cranium, a long face, and a long narrow nose.

The *Laguides* sub-race is based on the Lagoa Santa archaeological crania from eastern interior Brazil and on certain living or historic tribes found in that general region. The type is described as of short stature, dolichocephalic, high-vaulted, and wide- and low-faced.

Figure 1-4.

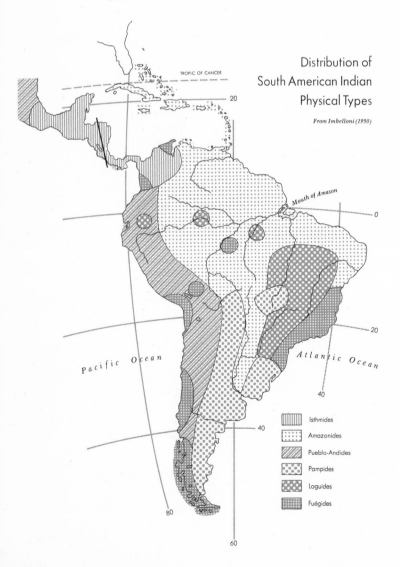

Distribution of South American Indian Physical Types

From Imbelloni (1950)

TROPIC OF CANCER

Mouth of Amazon

Pacific Ocean

Atlantic Ocean

- Isthmides
- Amazonides
- Pueblo-Andides
- Pampides
- Laguides
- Fuégides

The *Pampides* are the people of the Argentine Pampas, interior Patagonia, and the Gran Chaco. They are described as tall, heavy-boned, large Indians, with large heads and large, long faces. Both brachycephaly and dolichocephaly occur.

Amazonides, as the name suggests, are the peoples of the Amazon and Orinoco basins, the West Indies, the Guianas, the Atlantic coast of Brazil below the Amazon delta, and portions of interior eastern Brazil and the Bolivian lowlands. They are said to be Indians of medium stature, with well-developed torsos and arms, but rather short, small legs. The cephalic index is in the medium ranges.

Pueblo-Andides are found throughout the Andean areas, from Chiloé Island north to the Isthmus of Panama. In the northern Andes, however, they are intermixed with Isthmides. The Pueblo-Andides type is also found in central and northern Mexico and the southwestern and southeastern United States. They are listed as peoples of short stature and small brachycephalic skulls. The face is short. The nose has a broad base but is also prominent.

Isthmides are located in the northern Andes and lower Central America and are also found in southern Mesoamerica (including such peoples as the Maya). A listing of their salient physical characteristics reads much like that of the Pueblo-Andides—short stature (even shorter than the Pueblo-Andides) and high brachycephaly. Noses tend to be broad and flat (according to Imbelloni), although this is certainly not a satisfactory description of the Maya nose.

In a later statement, Imbelloni revised his distribution map of South American sub-races or varieties.[15] Among other changes, he eliminated the Isthmides type from the northern Andes, merging this part of their distribution with the Andides or Pueblo-Andides type. He also indicated a number of other distributional modifications resulting from what he considered to be blends of his major varieties. Most of these, such as a presumed merger of "Pampides over a Fuegides base," carry chronological implications. In fact, the Imbelloni scheme has throughout an intended chronological or historical dimension. Some archaeological data and inferences from geographical position are used to build this dimension. Thus, the Fuegides and Laguides, from their marginal

position (and also from their relatively non-Mongoloid morphology), are thought to represent earlier migrations or waves of population movement into South America, whereas the Pueblo-Andides and Isthmides are viewed as later arrivals. To date, there is little real information to back up these suppositions, for there are very few South American dated skeletal series, especially where long time spans are involved. By analogy with North America—as well as with other parts of the world—one might expect dolichocephaly to be, in a very general way, earlier than brachycephaly;[16] but even if this turns out to be true in South America, what does it mean? Is it to be related to ancient population separateness and different migrations into South America? Or are we dealing with forces of genetic drift?

The observations on racial variation among South American Indians have, however, some historical value, whatever their cause. Almost certainly they indicate areal and regional continuities of populations over long periods of time—a condition of consequence in the consideration of culture change and development. What is needed is more skeletal data from archaeology so that the histories of these South American physical variations can be more accurately plotted.[17] For the time being, the Imbelloni classification—imperfect and impressionistic as it may be—offers an overview of the physical variation in South American native populations.

Languages

Classification. In Volume One (Chap. 1) we considered the diversity of North and Middle American Indian languages. The situation in South America is comparable. At the time of the arrival of the first Europeans there were hundreds of mutually unintelligible languages spoken by the Indians of that continent. Research in the late nineteenth and early twentieth centuries arranged these into something less than 100 distinct language groups. Such groups were, roughly, of the order of the 55 language groups that Powell had proposed for native America north of Mexico in 1891. The best known recent classification of this kind for South American Indian languages is Mason's in the standard reference, *The Handbook of South American Indians.* He designates 65 language families or groups, plus a great many other languages that are simply placed on the map as being unaffiliated.[18]

Great difficulties confront the linguist in his attempts to further reduce these data of South American Indian languages in an historicogenetic synthesis. Many of the languages of the sixteenth century are now extinct, with extant vocabularies and other information about them exceedingly fragmentary and often unreliable. And even where languages are still spoken adequate recordings are sometimes lacking. In spite of these obstacles, a recent major attempt at genetic classification has been made by J. H. Greenberg.[19] Greenberg's methods are set forth simply and clearly. In his words: "Only those resemblances which involve both sound and meaning simultaneously are considered relevant for historical (linguistic) connections." Comparisons were both lexical and grammatical, and he found no contradiction in the results obtained. He advances his classificatory scheme with caution, as a tentative and trial beginning; nevertheless, it is the most up-to-date classification of South American Indian languages; it is accepted, in whole or in part, by many other linguists; and archaeologists must consider it as a background for the study of South American culture history.

It is Greenberg's underlying assumption that all South American native languages are related to each other and, moreover, that they are part of a great language phylum that includes all Middle and North American Indian languages with the exception of Nadene and Eskimoan. Greenberg's task, then, was to subdivide this great phylum. In doing this, he addressed himself to South and Central America and established eight super-stocks or linguistic super-families. These are constructs of the magnitude of the six super-stocks established by Sapir for North and Central America (see Vol. I, Chap. 1); and, in fact, in the Central American regions there is an overlap and coincidence between the two schemes.

The four Greenberg super-stocks that subsume the languages of the South American continent, the West Indies, and the southern portions of Central America are designated as: (1) Macro-Chibchan; (2) Andean-Equatorial; (3) Ge-Pano-Carib; and (4) Hokan.[20] In turn, these are subdivided into a total of 13 major language groups. These major groups are also still broadly inclusive constructs, each drawing together many distinct languages. By analogy with our summary of North and Middle American languages, these 13 language groups are the approximate scale equivalents of the 19 groups set forth by Driver.[21] In fact, one of the 13, Hokan, is also one of Driver's 19—a language group believed to be represented by enclaves in North, Central, and South America. The accompanying map (Fig. 1-5), which applies the Greenberg classification to the earlier Mason map, shows the distribution of these 13 South American major language groups.

The major language groups that Greenberg designates for the Macro-Chibchan are (1) Chibchan proper and (2) Paezan. They are both concentrated in northwestern South America and lower Central America, although some tribes of Macro-Chibchan affiliation are found in other parts of the continent.

(1) Among the Chibchan proper are such languages and tribes as the Chibcha of the Colombian highlands; the Cuna, Guaymi, Guetar, and others of Panama and Costa Rica; the Misumalpans (Mosquito, Sumo, and Matagalpa) of Nicaragua; and the Paya and Lenca of Honduras. More remote geographically are the Shiriana, on the Upper Orinoco in southern Venezuela and north-central Brazil.

(2) The Paezan major group includes Chocó and a great many other languages spoken in southern and central Colombia; the Colorado and Cayapá of Ecuador; and the Jirajara and others of western Venezuela. More distant geographically are the Warrau of the Orinoco delta, the Mura of the middle Amazon, the Yunca of the Peruvian coast, and the Atacameño of northern Chile and northwest Argentina.

The Andean-Equatorial super-stock of Greenberg subsumes: (3) the Andean; (4) Jívaroan; (5) Macro-Tucanoan; and (6) Equatorial major groups.

(3) The Andean languages are found in western and southern South America. They include the Sec of far north Peru, the Quechua and Aymará of Peru and Bolivia, and the various tongues of the south (Ona, Yahgan, Alacaluf, Araucanian, Puelche, and Tehuelche). They also embrace one other cluster of languages in the Ecuadorian-

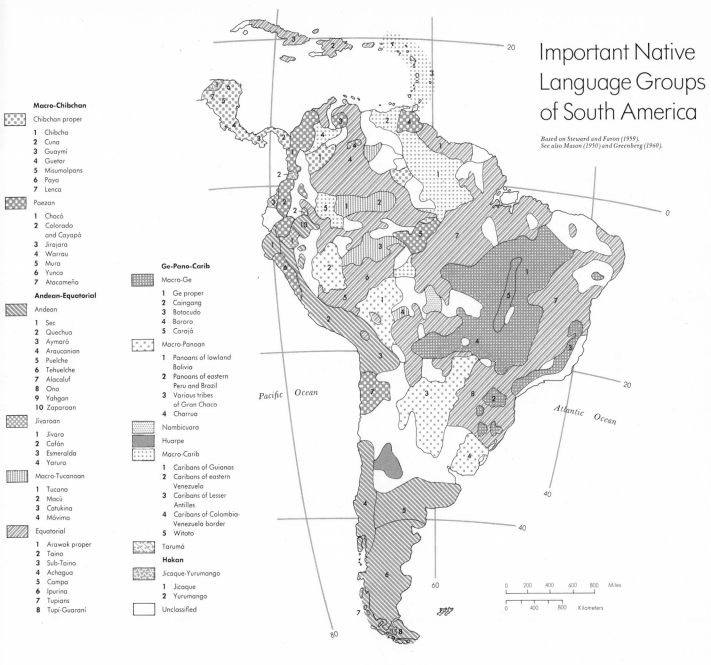

Based on Steward and Faron (1959).
See also Mason (1950) and Greenberg (1960).

Important Native Language Groups of South America

Macro-Chibchan

Chibchan proper

1 Chibcha
2 Cuna
3 Guaymí
4 Guetar
5 Misumalpans
6 Paya
7 Lenca

Paezan

1 Chocó
2 Colorado and Cayapá
3 Jirajara
4 Warrau
5 Mura
6 Yunca
7 Atacameño

Andean-Equatorial

Andean

1 Sec
2 Quechua
3 Aymará
4 Araucanian
5 Puelche
6 Tehuelche
7 Alacaluf
8 Ona
9 Yahgan
10 Zaparoan

Jívaroan

1 Jívaro
2 Cofán
3 Esmeralda
4 Yaruro

Macro-Tucanoan

1 Tucano
2 Macú
3 Catukina
4 Móvima

Equatorial

1 Arawak proper
2 Taino
3 Sub-Taino
4 Achagua
5 Campa
6 Ipurina
7 Tupians
8 Tupí-Guaraní

Ge-Pano-Carib

Macro-Ge

1 Ge proper
2 Caingang
3 Botocudo
4 Bororo
5 Carajá

Macro-Panoan

1 Panoans of lowland Bolivia
2 Panoans of eastern Peru and Brazil
3 Various tribes of Gran Chaco
4 Charrua

Nambicuara

Huarpe

Macro-Carib

1 Caribans of Guianas
2 Caribans of eastern Venezuela
3 Caribans of Lesser Antilles
4 Caribans of Colombia-Venezuela border
5 Witoto

Tarumá

Hokan

Jicaque-Yurumango

1 Jicaque
2 Yurumango

Unclassified

Pacific Ocean

Atlantic Ocean

Figure 1-5.

Peruvian montaña, to the east of the Andes, of which Zaparoan is the best known.

(4) Jívaroan languages are, principally, the Jívaro of the Ecuadorian-Peruvian montaña, the Cofán of the Ecuadorian montaña, and the Esmeralda of the Ecuadorian coast. They also include the Yaruro, a good distance to the east in interior Venezuela.

(5) Macro-Tucanoan languages were spoken by peoples of the Amazon basin, both to the south and to the north of the main course of that river, in Bolivia, Brazil, Colombia, and Venezuela. Among them are Tucano, Macú, Catukina, and Móvima.

(6) The Equatorial group is eastern South American, both lowland and Brazilian highlands as well as West Indian. It includes two large language families, Arawakan and Tupian. Among

the Arawakans are the Arawak proper of the Guiana coast, the Taino and Sub-Taino of the Greater Antilles, peoples such as the Achagua of lowland Colombia and Venezuela, and Campa and Ipurina of the Upper Amazon. Tupian includes a great many tribes of the Lower and Middle Amazon (south bank), of coastal and interior eastern Brazil, and the Guaraní, or Tupi-Guaraní, of southern Brazil and Paraguay. In addition, Greenberg includes a great many other tribes and languages as Equatorial that are not usually considered as either Arawakan or Tupian.

Ge-Pano-Carib subsumes: (7) Macro-Ge; (8) Macro-Panoan; (9) Nambicuara; (10) Huarpe; (11) Macro-Carib; and (12) Tarumá.

(7) Macro-Ge languages are those of the East Brazilian Highlands; the Ge proper, the Caingang, the Botocudo, and a good many others. Somewhat more apart from these linguistically are the Bororó and the Carajá.

(8) Macro-Panoan peoples are the various Panoan tribes of the Upper Amazon in lowland Bolivia, eastern Peru, and Brazil. They are also the numerous tribes of the Chaco, such as the Mataco, Lule, Abipón, and the Charrúa of Uruguay.

(9) The Nambicuara group includes only that language whose speakers lived in interior Brazil at the center of the South American continent.

(10) The Huarpe group is represented only by those peoples who lived on the eastern Andean slopes of central Argentina.

(11) Macro-Carib is an extensive group in northeastern South America and the Lesser Antilles. The principal component is the Cariban-speaking block of tribes of the Guianas, the eastern Venezuelan coast, and the Lesser Antilles. In addition, there are tribes of related speech along the Colombian-Venezuelan border south of Lake Maracaibo, as well as the Witoto on the Upper Amazon.

(12) The Tarumá group is represented only by that tribe, located on the Middle Amazon.

Hokan, for South and Central America, subsumes only: (13) the Jicaque and Yurumango. The Jicaque were in Honduras and the Yurumango on the Pacific coast of Colombia. As has already been noted, Hokan is also one of the major North American language groups, being represented by tribes in California, Baja California, and the Southwest.

Finally, as the map indicates, Greenberg's 13 major language groups may not cover all of the tongues of native South America. Thus there are a great many blank spots for which linguistic information was insufficient, inadequate, or as yet unanalyzed for the languages to be classified into the Greenberg scheme.

It must be remembered that this map (Fig. 1-5) is at best an approximation of linguistic reality. The territoriality of a language, especially in areas such as the vast Amazon basin, was often a fluid, changing dimension. Data vary chronologically, from the early sixteenth century down to the twentieth, so that there is no fixed synchronic plane at which we can say that such-and-such geographical distributions were maintained by the speakers of all the respective languages of South America. Also, there are classificatory disagreements among linguists. Such disagreements, for example, are to be seen between Mason and Greenberg, as a comparison of the present map and a reading of the Mason article will show.

Language and Culture History. In spite of all of these cautions, what clues to culture history can be read into Greenberg's sketch of the main lines of South American language affiliations? Some bold patterns seem to emerge. Thus, Andean languages link peoples of the central and the south Andes, and this linkage correlates with broad cultural relationships. Certainly this central and south Andean cultural block can be contrasted with the Amazon basin with its Equatorial and Ge-Pano-Carib languages. In the same way, the Chibchan and Paezan dominance of the northern Andes and lower Central America has general cultural correlates; and the Macro-Ge–speaking tribes of the highlands of eastern Brazil are to be contrasted culturally, as well as linguistically, with the surrounding Equatorial Tupians. On the other hand, there are, for the archaeologist, some strange affiliations. The cultural-historical significance of the Andean and Equatorial bracketing is obscure or, at best, equivocal. And what is to be made of the culturally and geographically distant Jicaque-Yurumango linguistic hookup?

It is, of course, expecting too much to be able to relate, immediately and satisfactorily, all of these linguistic affiliations to the very fragmentary archaeological and ethnohistorical records now available. Two major circumstances or conditions are obvious. One is that there has been a great amount of tribal movement, of the splitting up of peoples of the same speech, and the movement of one or more parties to such a separation to geographical regions remote from the others. This is seen especially in the linguistic patchwork of the map of the eastern part of South America, where tribes speaking the same or related languages are often separated from each other by great distances.

The other circumstance is that there must be great time differentials involved in the several separations of component members of language groups. Quite probably, some of these separations took place millennia ago while others may have occurred only a few centuries before the arrival of the Europeans. In general, it is assumed that the dimension of time, in such cases, correlates with similarity or dissimilarity in the languages compared. That is, two languages which split from a parent stock 500 years ago would show greater similarity to each other than two languages whose separation dated back to a thousand years. For example, with reference to Greenberg's scheme, one would expect the linguistic similarity shared by member languages of the Andean language group to be a measure of a relatively recent common history. In contrast to this, the member languages of the Andean group and those of the Equatorial group—despite the Andean-Equatorial linkage—would be expected to have had common beginnings much further back in time. The reader should be advised, however, that this assumption, while theoretically sound, has not yet been applied as a systematic principle to South American languages. This theory of glottochronology provides a method for such a systematic quantitative measurement of linguistic similarities and differences; and, in this way, it offers a means of measuring the time, in absolute years, of the separation of daughter languages from a parent stock (see Vol. I, pp. 17–19). Some glottochronological studies have been made of South American languages; and we shall have reference to some of these in the discussions of particular languages, areas, and cultures in the body of this book. For the most part, though, the method has not been widely applied in South America.[22]

South American Culture Origins

Early Cultures. We have already noted, in discussing the origins of the South American populations, that man was in the southern continent of the New World by 10,000 to 9000 B.C., and may have been there much longer than that. In any event, by the tenth millennium B.C. the early South American was equipped with chipped-stone tools and weapons—which enabled him to live as a hunter and forager. There can be little doubt that the cultural heritage of these first South Americans was ultimately of Old World Paleolithic inspiration, however crude or advanced this culture may have been originally or however much it had been modified before reaching South America. It also seems highly likely, as we have argued in Volume One (Chap. 2), that a good many early inventions in the fashioning of flint forms were made in the New World, quite probably in the North American High Plains and in the Pacific Northwest of North America. Therefore it would seem to follow—given the facts of geography and assuming a Northeast Asia-to-Alaska migration of man to the New World—that the early cultures of South America were at least partly derivative from those of North and Middle America. This does not deny, it should be added, that significant modifications, or inventions, in lithic technology could have taken place in South America.

The non-material cultural heritage that the earliest South Americans brought with them—from North America and, more remotely, from Asia—is largely a matter for speculation. Various life-crisis ceremonies and certain mythological concepts are possibilities. In general, these are practices and beliefs that are still shared by relatively primitive tribes in both the Old and the New World and that are presumed to be residues of very ancient beliefs and customs that might go back to common Paleolithic beginnings (See Vol. I, pp. 19–20).

The nature or frequency of contact between the early South Americans and the peoples of Middle and North America in the millennia following the late Pleistocene are still matters for conjecture. It is possible that the now dense jungle-cover of the

Panamanian Isthmus and the Pacific coast of Colombia—which is a barrier to land transportation or movement—was not in existence during the latter part of Pleistocene. Instead, those regions may have been covered by savanna growth,[23] a circumstance that would have made passage between the two continents much easier. Also, during a glacial maximum it is likely that the Isthmus was somewhat wider than it is today. However, with the glacial recession and the climatic changes set in train by that event, the Panama-north Colombia region probably developed the tropical forest and mangrove swamp vegetation for which it is now known. If this were the case, then it is almost certain that movement between North and South America became more difficult after 8000 or 7000 B.C.

The archaeological evidence on this question is not fully conclusive although, I think, it does tend to support a South American isolation or cultural independence for the several millennia between 7000 and 3000 B.C. In that span of time peoples and cultures in the Americas were becoming adapted to a number of regional environments. All were subsisting primarily by various forms of hunting, collecting, or fishing. In Middle America plant cultivation had begun; and, apparently quite independently, the same process was under way in parts of South America; but on neither continent was this yet the foremost means of subsistence. The hunting, fishing, and food-collecting gear, which makes up a large part of the archaeological inventories for either North or South American cultures of the period, reflects regional specialization. In North America, for example, we have the artifact assemblages of both the Archaic cultural tradition of the eastern part of that continent and of the Desert tradition of the western semi-arid lands and of upland Mexico. In South America, the best-known contemporaneous cultures were those of the Venezuelan, Peruvian, Chilean, and Brazilian coasts and the interior of Argentina. All of these cultures are distinctive and separable; and yet there are some items that are shared, and some of this sharing may also be extended to North American cultures. For instance, polished, bi-pointed, pendant-like stones were made by Californian and Brazilian shell mound dwellers of the same general era; and certain flint projectile point types were held in common by early post-Pleistocene peoples of Peru and Chile and those of North American Desert and Archaic cultures. To what extent is this independent development or convergence? To what extent may it be the result of contacts, however indirect or slow? I am inclined to think that most occurrences like this are unrelated and independent; but we cannot be sure. For the present, the best summary statement we can make is that for the era 7000 to 3000 B.C. South American cultures probably devloped in *relative* isolation from those of North America—or of any other part of the world.

Later Cultures. We must raise the question—previously referred to in Volume One (pp. 21–24)—whether by 3000 B.C. pottery was first introduced to the New World, via the Ecuadorian coast of South America, from the Jomon culture of Japan. This case has been laid before the archaeological world in great detail by the late Emilio Estrada and his colleagues, Betty J. Meggers and Clifford Evans.[24] These archaeologists approached the matter from the American side—from a series of excavations in sites of an Ecuadorian coastal culture known as Valdivia. The Valdivia sites are coastal shell mounds—as are Jomon sites—and, like Jomon, the Valdivia culture would appear to have been essentially a fishing and collecting one. Valdivia pottery, which is dated in Ecuador over a time range of about 3000 to 1500 B.C., is relatively simple but not crude. There are a number of close resemblances to Jomon pottery, which dates from about the same time to considerably earlier. In view of this dating, the postulated direction of the trans-Pacific migration of pottery-bearing voyagers is from Japan to the New World. We will return to the Jomon-Valdivia ceramic similarities in Chapter 5; but to summarize briefly here, my own opinion is that the similarities are very strong and that the whole situation does, indeed, suggest a relationship of the kind that Meggers, Evans, and Estrada have postulated.

The question of Asiatic-American trans-Pacific contacts following 3000 B.C., as these may bear upon cultural development of South America as well as of other parts of the New World, has been summarized briefly in the previous volume of this work. We will not reexamine the instances and arguments here but reserve them for some additional comment in the appropriate area contexts. Many of the most likely instances involve, again, the Ecuadorian coast, and some of them are highly suggestive of contact.[25]

Continuing upward in time to the second millennium B.C., there are a number of lines of evidence which, I think, demonstrate contacts between South American cultures and those of Middle America.[26] Some of these, such as the apparent diffusion of maize from Mesoamerica to Peru,[27] were of undoubted importance in the origins and developments of new patterns in South American cultures. Others refer to ceramic influences and interchanges between Mesoamerica and Colombia,[28] Ecuador,[29] and Peru.[30] These, too, we will discuss further along, as the story of South American prehistory is presented in its various geographical and chronological contexts.

Cultural origins in South America are also the story of the interrelationships between different cultures of that continent. This is, of course, the very substance of the culture history with which this book is mainly concerned. At this point, however, it seems advisable to offer the reader a quick overview of the nature of variation within South American culture, and this is best done by reviewing the concepts of culture types and culture areas as these have been developed and applied.

South American Culture Types and Culture Areas

J. M. Cooper. The viable beginnings for South American culture types and culture areas are those of J. M. Cooper.[31] He set forth three principal culture types: Sierral, Silval, and Marginal.

Sierral culture—taking its name from that major physiographic province of South America, the Andean sierras—was characterized by agriculture, with maize, beans, and white potatoes as the principal crops; cultivation was intensive, with the aid of irrigation and terracing. The llama and alpaca were domesticated. There was a sophisticated development in pottery, weaving, and metallurgy. Public buildings—temples, palaces, forts—

were constructed of stone or adobe and were of monumental proportions. In general, political institutions were complex, centralized, and geared to militaristic activities. Almost all of what Cooper designated as the Sierral area was, as of the time of the Spanish Conquest, a part of the Inca Empire.

Silval culture took its name from the forested lowlands of South America. It was defined as horticultural, but with swidden rather than intensive cultivation; manioc was the principal crop. Hunting and fishing were also of economic importance. Pottery was universal and weaving fairly well developed. Silval tribes were accomplished builders in wood and thatch, and with these materials they constructed large communal houses, chief's houses, and temples. Large villages or towns were known in some regions, and sometimes these were joined in loose political federations. In general, however, political organization was less complex and there were fewer material remains in the Silval type and Silval area than in the Sierral.

Marginal culture took its name from its position of geographic distribution in southern South America, in interior eastern Brazil, and in scattered enclaves within the Silval area. It was non-horticultural, with hunting, fishing, or gathering the means of subsistence. Pottery was sometimes lacking and when present was simpler in form and decoration than in the Silval cultures. Architecture was very primitive, and temples or other public buildings were lacking. The typical political unit was a small band of familial relatives.

Cooper's interest was not only in the geographical distributions of his three culture types but in their past histories. Peeling back the Incaic overlay on the Sierral area, the Silval penetrations into Marginal territory, and a number of other presumably late pre-Columbian migrations, he reconstructed a cultural map for South America as of circa A.D. 1000. The results of this (Fig. 1-7)[32] may be contrasted with the distributions that Cooper plotted for the early historic horizon (Fig. 1-6).[33]

Cooper's interests were evolutionary as well as historical. He saw Marginal culture as a simpler way of life, being replaced by the more advanced Sierral and Silval cultures; and he probably conceived a graded series of all three culture types

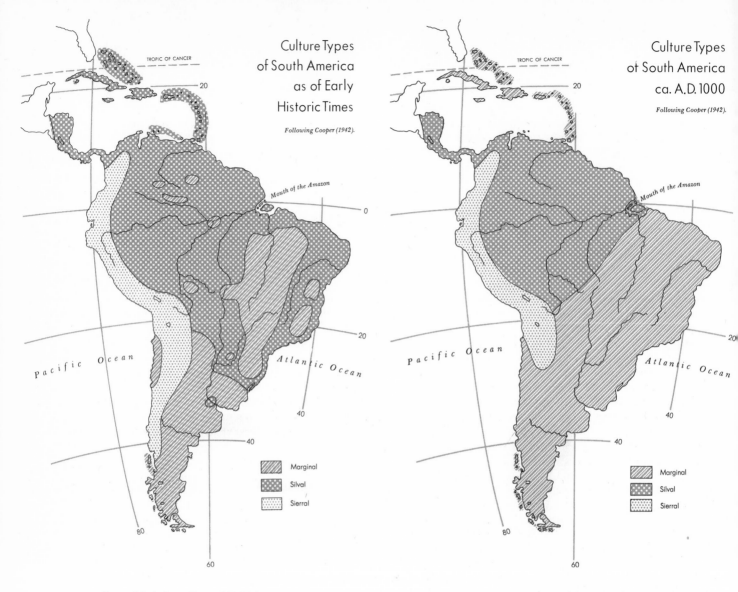

Figure 1-6. *Left.*   Figure 1-7. *Right.*

running in a developmental sequence from Mar ginal, through Silval, into Sierral. His scheme had both the advantages and disadvantages of com- bining culture history and cultural evolution. On the positive side, it offered a comprehensive view of the history and development of South American societies and cultures. The earliest populations had arrived with a Paleolithic-type culture; this way of life had persisted for many millennia; eventual- ly agriculture, ceramics, and weaving—a Neolithic condition—were either developed within or dif- fused to certain parts of South America; and at

the beginning of the fifteenth century this process had advanced, geographically, to the lines seen on Figure 1-6. On the negative side, Cooper's scheme obviously blurs or ignores many of the significant lines of history. To a large extent, what the cul- tures of any one of his major types shared was a basic similarity of developmental level rather than a very immediate common history.

J. H. Steward.   Steward's editorial organization of the *Handbook of South American Indians* grew out of Cooper's classification, but modifications and refinements of the scheme were developed by Steward early on in the course of this project. The first general map of South American cultures, published in Volume 1 of the *Handbook*, added a new culture type to Cooper's three (Fig. 1-8).[34] This is the Circum-Caribbean type, taking its name from its geographical location. Cultures so classified were separated out from those of the Tropical Forest or Silval type on two counts. First, they shared a number of traits in common that were not shared by other Tropical Forest cultures; second, a number of these distinctive traits were those that indicated Circum-Caribbean culture to be on a higher evolutionary threshold than the Tropical Forest level.

Steward made his first important theoretical statement on the culture-historical and developmental position of the Circum-Caribbean culture type in Volume 4 of the *Handbook*.[35] The gist of this theory is that Circum-Caribbean culture had its origins in a "Formative" or "Sub-Andean" level of development that in former times underlay the later Andean civilizations. Prior to the rise of these later civilizations such a Formative or Sub-Andean culture was carried eastward into the tropical lowlands of South America.[36] These diffusions set Circum-Caribbean culture at a higher level than that of Tropical Forest culture—as witnessed by such traits and institutions as a class-structured society, a hereditary nobility, slavery, and temple-idol religious cults. In some regions of the lowlands, however, according to Steward's hypothesis, these Formative or Sub-Andean diffusions failed to sustain themselves; in these regions the cultures declined or dropped back from a Circum-Caribbean level of development to a simpler Tropical adjustment.

Although Steward's Circum-Caribbean hypothesis of the sequence of culture development in lowland South America has not been borne out by archaeological research in some areas, such as the West Indies,[37] his insight is to be credited with conceiving the Circum-Caribbean and Tropical Forest developmental levels and in posing such problems. His views along these lines are forcefully presented by his mapping of culture types in Volume 5 of the *Handbook*. In this volume, devoted to topical and comparative treatments, he was no longer constrained by the editorial necessity of drawing a map that would serve as an index to tribal and cultural coverage within

Culture Types of South America

Following Steward, ed. (1946/a).

TROPIC OF CANCER

Mouth of the Amazon

Pacific Ocean

Atlantic Ocean

Andean

Circum-Caribbean

Tropical Forest

Marginal

Figure 1-8.

the volume; instead, the map (see Fig. 1-9) now becomes clearly developmental, eschewing the strict lines of culture history.[38] In a still later mapping of South American cultures, Steward—with Faron—continues in this developmental approach but with a terminology that has been altered in the direction of functional description (see Fig. 1-10).[39] Thus Central Andean culture is now designated as "Irrigation Civilization," Circum-Caribbean as "Theocratic and Militaristic Chiefdoms," and so on. There are also accommodations to historical, as opposed to strictly devel-

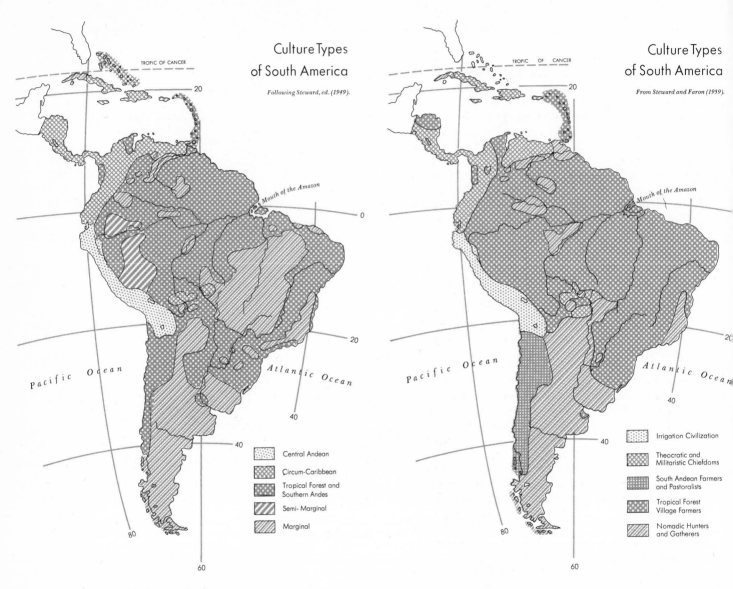

Culture Types
of South America

Following Steward, ed. (1949).

TROPIC OF CANCER

Mouth of the Amazon

Pacific Ocean

Atlantic Ocean

Central Andean

Circum-Caribbean

Tropical Forest and
Southern Andes

Semi- Marginal

Marginal

Culture Types
of South America

From Steward and Faron (1959).

TROPIC OF CANCER

Mouth of the Amazon

Pacific Ocean

Atlantic Ocean

Irrigation Civilization

Theocratic and
Militaristic Chiefdoms

South Andean Farmers
and Pastoralists

Tropical Forest
Village Farmers

Nomadic Hunters
and Gatherers

Figure 1-9. *Left.*   **Figure 1-10.** *Right.*

opmental, criteria. For instance, the South Andes, which on the Volume 5 *Handbook* map had been given the same symbol as the Tropical Forest cultures, is now listed as "Southern Andean Farmers and Pastoralists." However, even in making this concession to historical differences, the South Andean level of socio-political complexity is still considered as equivalent only to that of the "Tropical Forest Village Farmers."

Other Culture Area Formulations.
Clark Wissler[40] prepared a culture area map for South America as early as 1917, and his formulations must have influenced Cooper and, more indirectly, Steward. Wissler's map (Fig. 1-11) has five divisions, and it shows similarities to the later Steward and Cooper maps. Although Wissler makes some observations that carry either age-area or cultural evolutionary implications, he did not advance any very systematic arguments for

Culture Areas
of South America

Based on Wissler (1938).

Figure 1-11.

these points of view, and the overall result remained a descriptive one.

D. B. Stout,[41] writing after Cooper but before Steward, offered another South American culture area or "culture type" mapping. His map is more complex than Wissler's and dotted with "interior marginals" (Fig. 1-12). His classification is also more fine-grained than Steward's or Cooper's in the southern part of the continent where he has several divisions instead of one "Marginal" category.

Finally, the most detailed South American culture area breakdown is Murdock's[42]—which dates after Steward's *Handbook* maps. Murdock's data were ethnographically reported traits of all kinds, plus criteria of linguistic affiliation. He defines 24

areas (Fig. 1-13), and the reader may compare the correspondences and differences with the Cooper and Steward areas. Clearly, the Murdock areas have greater internal coherence as "diffusion spheres," at least for the historic-to-modern period.

Archaeological Culture Areas of this Book. As the reader will see, the archaeological culture areas that we will follow in this book have basic correspondences to the culture-area divisions of the *Handbook of South American Indians* and to some of the other culture-area schemes that we have just reviewed; however they follow none of

21

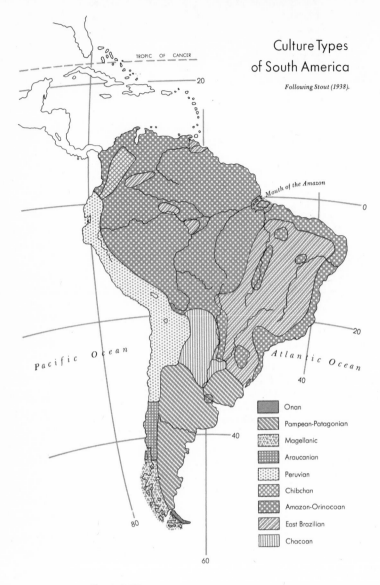

Culture Types
of South America

Following Stout (1938).

TROPIC OF CANCER

Mouth of the Amazon

Pacific Ocean

Atlantic Ocean

Onan
Pampean-Patagonian
Magellanic
Araucanian
Peruvian
Chibchan
Amazon-Orinocoan
East Brazilian
Chacoan

Figure 1-12.

them exactly.[43] The archaeological culture areas are, to paraphrase what has been said before, convenient devices for the presentation of culture interrelatedness over appreciable periods of time.

The following are the archaeological culture areas used in this volume (see Fig. 1-1):

(1) *The Peruvian, or Central Andean, area* consists of the coast and highlands of Peru and the adjacent Bolivian uplands.[44] The area definition derives from the Peruvian cultural tradition—a lifeway based on intensive agriculture. This was the area of the foremost South American native civilization, and the beginnings of the Peruvian

tradition go back about two millennia before the beginning of the Christian era. At the time of the Spanish Conquest this was the heartland of the Inca Empire. Quechuan and Aymaran languages were the dominant tongues of the area in late times; however, other languages (of the Paezan group) were known to have been spoken along the north and central Peruvian coasts.

(2) *The South Andes area*[45] appears to have developed as a southward extension of the Peruvian agricultural way of life into the mountainous regions of northwestern Argentina and the mountains and coast of northern Chile. However, the natural environmental setting differs from that of Peru in being generally drier, and the living spaces are notably smaller. There was a marked time-lag in the diffusion of traits from Peru to the South Andes; thus, farming can be dated only about as early as the beginning of the Christian era in the latter area. In late prehistoric times Inca control was extended over most of the South Andes. The principal languages of the area were, from north to south, Atacameño, Diaguitan, and Araucanian.

(3) *The Intermediate area* takes its name from its geographical position between the two areas of highest New World culture: Mesoamerica and Peru.[46] The area has a great many natural environmental zones: tropical coastlands, temperate upland valleys, savannas, and even semi-arid coasts. The Intermediate area shares many traits with Mesoamerica and with Peru; however, it differs from these in its somewhat lower profile of cultural development. Thus, architectural and monumental arts are less impressive, urbanism was less developed, and political formations not as advanced. In the sixteenth century a great many small tribes held petty states or chieftainships from Honduras to Ecuador. Most of these tribes were of Chibchan or Paezan linguistic affiliation.

(4) *The Caribbean area* embraces eastern Venezuela, northern Guiana, and the West Indies.[47] It, too, is an area of varied topography and vegetation, with mountains, savannas, and some rain forests. Climate is generally tropical. The Caribbean cultural tradition, which defines the area, was based on manioc cultivation and was established by about 1000 B.C. In historic times the peoples of the area were either Arawakan or Cariban-speaking.

Culture Areas
of South America

Following Murdock (1951).

Figure 1-13.

(5) *The Amazonian area* takes in most of the enormous Amazonian drainage system.[48] It is either tropical rainforest or tropical savanna country. The area has been agricultural—an agriculture of manioc and swidden cultivation—since well before the beginning of the Christian era. Tupian, Arawakan, Panoan, and Cariban languages are all represented in Amazonia.

(6) *Eastern Brazil* lies south of the main course of the Amazon and extends inland from the Atlantic coast to Bolivia and Paraguay.[49] This corresponds to a physiographical division of Brazil known as the Eastern Highlands, a rolling plateau

country of parkland savannas with some coastal rainforest fringes and some interior tropical steppe country. Toward the south there is a shading off into humid mesothermal climates. The older subsistence patterns in the area were hunting, fishing, and collecting. In many places these persisted even into historic times. In other places they were modified by some agriculture that was introduced to the area from Amazonia. It appears that Tupian peoples entered the area in relatively late prehistoric times. The older residents of Eastern Brazil appear to have been related to the Macro-Ge language group.

(7) *The Chaco* is little known archaeologically.[50] It lies in the lowland plains of southeastern Bolivia, northern Paraguay, and northeastern Argentina. Environment is that of a tropical savanna. The numerous tribes of the Chaco, mostly of Guaicuruan speech (Macro-Panoan), subsisted primarily by hunting and plant collecting, with but little agriculture.

(8) *The Pampean area*[51] subsumes the Argentine plains from Tierra del Fuego to the Paraná and Paraguay Rivers, the Republic of Uruguay, the southeastern tip of Brazil, and much of Paraguay. In the south, guanaco hunting was the basic way of life, and in the sixteenth century the Indian quickly adopted the horse as an aid in hunting. Although land hunting was pursued farther south, fishing was an even more important means of livelihood along the Paraná-Paraguay drainages. A distinctive ceramic tradition developed in the north and spread as far south as the Strait of Magellan. The Ona, Tehuelche, and Puelche tribes held the south, the Charrua were in what is now Uruguay,

and a number of now-extinct tribes, probably of Macro-Panoan linguistic affiliation, were found along the Paraná-Paraguay drainages.

(9) *The Fuegian area* is the coast and offshore islands of southern Chile and Tierra del Fuego.[52] This was the home of the Chono, Alacaluf, and Yahgan tribes, peoples who followed a marine subsistence pattern in this cold, wet, forested country. Available archaeological evidence suggests that this pattern dates back at least 5000 years.

These archaeological culture areas are phenomena of the geological Recent. This refers both to the culture developments which define the areas and to the natural environmental settings which helped condition the cultures. In the next chapter we shall go back in time to the late Pleistocene, and to the environments and cultural distributions which prevailed then, for a consideration of the very early inhabitants of South America. Only after we have prepared such a background will we come forward in time, once more, to consider in detail the great cultural and area diversity which has been outlined so sketchily above.

Footnotes

1 Gordon R. Willey: *An Introduction to American Archaeology: Volume One. North and Middle America.* Englewood Cliffs, N.J.: Prentice-Hall, Inc., 1966.

2 Willey and Phillips (1958, pp. 21–24).

3 Willey and Phillips (1958, pp. 18–21).

4 Willey and Phillips (1958, pp. 61–205).

5 Following the plan of Volume One, Chapter 8, of this work.

6 See Binford (1968 a) for a detailed discussion of this.

7 This summary of South American physiography and natural environment duplicates, with some expansion, the comments made in Volume One, Chapter 1, on "The Natural Setting of the Americas."

The reader is referred to summaries by Sauer (1950 a); James (1959); and Finch, Trewartha, Robinson, and Hammond (1957).

8 The letter designation (H), for Andean climates, and other similar climatic designation symbols used herein refer to the Koppen system of climatic classification, with modifications by Trewartha (1954).

9 Imbelloni's (1938) position on this is the most extreme; Hooton (1947) leaned toward this kind of interpretation; Birdsell (1951) and Coon (1965, p. 138) present more sophisticated views of non-Mongoloid elements entering into the New World populations.

10 M. T. Newman (1953, 1962; see also 1951, 1958).

11 This backs off from an argu-

ment in favor of separate migrations as an explanation of physical variability among American Indians which I proposed some years ago (Willey, 1950).

12 Imbelloni (1938, 1950 a, 1958). Imbelloni's work is, to an extent, an extension and refinement of that of Von Eickstedt (1933–34).

13 Neumann (1952).

14 Imbelloni (1950 a).

15 Imbelloni (1958).

16 See Cooper (1942) for a short summary of South American physical types, distributions, and broad chronological trends.

17 Newman (1947).

18 Mason (1950). For earlier linguistic summaries see also Rivet (1924) and Pericot (1936).

19 Greenberg (1960).

20 For the sake of consistency, in this volume we follow our terminology for Volume One (see Chap. 1), and refer to such classificatory categories as "super-stocks" or "super-families." Then, in descending order, we designate "major language groups" and, more informally, smaller groups of closely related languages or individual languages. Steward and Faron (1959, pp. 16–30), whom we follow in applying the Greenberg scheme to the Mason linguistic map, use a different and somewhat more formal terminology, referring to these same entities as "Families," "Subfamilies," "Groups," and "Languages."

21 Driver (1961, pp. 555–582, map 37).

22 The glottochronological method, while highly regarded in some quarters, particularly among linguists working with American Indian languages, has found less favor in others. See, for example, the differing points of view in Hymes (1960) and Bergsland and Vogt (1962).

23 Patterson and Lanning (1966 ms.).

24 Meggers, Evans, and Estrada (1965).

25 For various opinions and appraisals on this question, the reader is referred to: Nordenskiold (1931—a balanced evaluation of ethnographic evidence on Asian-American possible contacts); Heine-Geldern (1953, 1959, 1966—arguments favoring Asia-to-America diffusion, using mostly archaeological data); Estrada and Meggers (1961 —favoring Asia-to-America diffusion); Ekholm (1964—favoring Asia-to-America diffusion); Phillips (1966 —opposing Asia-to-America diffusion); and Heyerdahl (1952—favoring America-to-Asia diffusion).

26 See Willey (1955) and Meggers (1964) for general summaries.

27 Mangelsdorf, MacNeish, and Willey (1965).

28 Reichel-Dolmatoff, Gerardo and Alicia (1956); Reichel-Dolmatoff, Gerardo (1965).

29 Estrada and Evans (1963); Evans and Meggers (1966).

30 Porter (1953); M. D. Coe (1961); Lathrap (1966).

31 Cooper (1942); see also Cooper (1925, 1941) for earlier works on this and related topics.

32 Cooper (1942, fig. 2).

33 Cooper (1942, fig. 1) The Marginal enclave within the Sierral block, on the Chilean coast, represents a historic group known as the Chango. Little is known about them although in the eighteenth and early nineteenth centuries they were said to be living a nomadic or seminomadic fishing existence along this part of the Pacific (see Bird, 1946 a). The archaeology of the area, however, indicates a quite different type of life up to the mid-sixteenth century; it is most likely that the Chango were simply the surviving Indians of that part of the Chilean coast who were in a state of deculturation following Spanish settlement.

34 Steward, ed., (1946 a, map 1).

35 Steward (1948).

36 Steward (1948, p. 14).

37 Rouse (1953 a) has shown that in the West Indies the sequence of cultural development is from a Tropical Forest to a Circum-Caribbean type rather than the reverse.

38 Steward (1949 a, map 18).

39 Steward and Faron (1959, p. 13).

40 Wissler (1938, 3rd ed., fig. 58, pp. 247–259). The two earlier editions of this work are 1917 and 1922. Wissler was cited by Cooper in his 1942 article, and, apparently, Wissler's ideas on South American culture areas has some influence on Cooper's formulations.

41 Stout (1938). Also cited by Cooper (1942). Stout makes no definite mention of the West Indies or of Lower Central America. He may—or may not—have intended his Amazon-Orinocoan culture type to have extended into these areas.

42 Murdock (1951).

43 Wissler (1938, fig. 61, pp. 287–296) also suggests archaeological areas. These roughly approximate some of those used in this book.

44 This Peruvian area is the same as the Central Andes or "Central Andean Civilizations" of the *Handbook of South American Indians.* It corresponds closely to Murdock's (1951) "Peruvian" area except that he includes all of Ecuador that had come under Inca domination.

45 This area is the same as the South Andean culture area of the *Handbook* and is approximately what Murdock (1951) designated as the "Chilean" area.

46 The Intermediate area includes coastal and highland Ecuador, Murdock's "Colombian" and "Isthmian" areas, and the western part of his "Caribbean" area. The cultures within it are those considered as "Circum-Caribbean" type in the *Handbook.* For other definitions and mappings of the Intermediate area see Willey (1959) and Rouse (1962).

47 This Caribbean area definition follows Rouse (1962). It is also similar to Murdock's (1951) "Caribbean" area except that it does not embrace those parts of Colombia and western Venezuela that he includes. Our area also includes all of the West Indies, whereas he puts far-western Cuba into a "Floridian" area with that part of North America.

48 This is largely the area of Steward's Tropical Forest culture (see *Handbook of South American Indians,* especially Vol. 3). With reference to Murdock's (1951) map, it subsumes his Loreto, Montaña, Caquetá, Savana, Amazon, Juruá-Purus, Bolivian (lowlands), Pará, and most of his Guiana areas. The name "Amazonia" is taken from Rouse (1962), and the area approximates his.

49 Murdock's (1951) Xingú, Goyaz, Eastern Lowland, Paraguayan, and Atlantic areas approximately correspond to this area. With reference to the *Handbook of South American Indians,* the area as we have drawn it includes both Tropical Forest and Marginal type cultures.

50 This corresponds closely to Murdock's (1951) Chaco area. In the *Handbook* Chacoan tribes and cultures are considered as part of the Marginal grouping.

51 This is very similar to, or identical with, Murdock's (1951) "Pampean" area, and we have taken the name from him. The area is wholly within the Marginal culture type and area of the *Handbook.*

52 This follows Murdock (1951) exactly. The area is also wholly within the Marginal culture type and area of the *Handbook.*

The Early South Americans

The Antiquity of Man in South America

A Retrospective Look at North America. Any broad view of early man in South America must take into consideration what happened in the continent to the north and, at a further but still important remove, the whole problem of man's entry into North America from Asia in Pleistocene times. Let us begin, then, with such a North American review and, in so doing, also take the opportunity of noting some quite recent findings and comments that bear upon the general question of man's antiquity in the New World.

In Chapter 2 of Volume One (pp. 29–37) we indicated that there were strongly opposing views as to just when man had first crossed the Bering Strait to enter the Americas from Asia and as to the nature of the cultural heritage he brought with him. According to one view, the first Asians to arrive were not "big-game hunters," but subsisted rather by unspecialized hunting, gathering, and food foraging of whatever sort. They did not manufacture finely chipped bifacial projectile points but, instead, had a relatively crude stone-chipping technology, one believed to have been derived from the ancient Asian Chopper-Chopping Tool tradition. This "pre-projectile point" stage of development was thought to date back as much as 30,000 to 40,000 years ago in the New World;[1] and from this stage, it was further argued, all later American early lithic industries were developed. A number of archaeological discoveries, from all parts of the New World—South as well as North America—have been cited by the proponents of this view as supporting evidence for such a stage. Some of these discoveries were reviewed in Chapter 2 of Volume One, but it was emphasized there that, while suggestive of such an interpretation, none of them really offered convincing proof of such a "pre-projectile point stage." Recently, however, there have been new North American discoveries that seem to support the "pre-projectile point stage" hypothesis, and it is worth pausing here to consider them.

These new discoveries have appeared in Mexico. At Tlapacoya, in Estado de Mexico, man-made hearths and chipped-stone artifacts have been found in association with bones of Pleistocene animals. The context is that of an old lakeshore stratum now buried by deep volcanic ash. The radiocarbon dates from the volcanic ash are in the range of 24,000 to 20,000 years ago. The artifacts include a plano-convex discoidal scraper with definite edge chipping and a nicked obsidian flake blade.[2] The other Mexican discovery is at Valsequillo, in the state of Puebla, not far from Tlapacoya. Reference has already been made to the Valsequillo finds in Volume One (p. 33), but more recent excavations there by Cynthia Irwin-Williams and her associates have disclosed a number of rough chipped-stone tools beneath a layer of volcanic ash that dates by radiocarbon to 40,000 to 19,000 years ago.[3] Although a caution is in order concerning Valsequillo because the radiocarbon samples from the ash come from parts of the site at some distance from the loci of the artifacts, the findings appear to support those of Tlapacoya. In sum, Tlapacoya and Valsequillo appear to indicate that man was, indeed, present in southern North America as far back as 20,000 years ago if not earlier. They also indicate that his technical equipment at this time did not include bifacially flaked projectile points.[4] These are considerations to be borne in mind when we examine the story of early man in South America.

For the moment, though, let us return to our review of North America. It will be recalled that in opposition to the "pre-projectile point stage" hypothesis there was another view which held that the earliest immigrants to the New World were already specialized, Upper Paleolithic big-game hunters who followed the mammoth and other Pleistocene herd animals from Asia into the Americas. These hunters were possessed of a blade and bifacial-flaking technology that had its derivations in the Old World Levallois-Mousterian tradition. From these technological beginnings they developed the distinctive fluted point in the New World. Two variant interpretations then arise from this base. One is that the fluted point development took place on the Alaskan tundras during the time when the passage south into mid-continental North America was blocked by the closure of the Cordilleran and Laurentide ice fields. With the opening of the ice during the Two Creeks Interstadial, these fluted point hunters debouched southward onto the North American grassland plains to become the Clovis or Llano complex people whose artifacts and kill sites are securely dated at 9500–9000 B.C.[5] The other variant interpretation leading out of what we might call the "Levallois-Mousterian hypothesis" is that the blade and biface technology spread from Asia, through Alaska, into mid-continental North America prior to the Two Creeks interval, or well before 10,000 B.C. Here it served as the seed for the development of the Clovis-Llano industry on the North American Plains and in the Southwest.[6] Of these two variant interpretations, the first suffers from the lack of solid archaeological evidence to support the development of the fluted point in Alaska. While occasional fluted points have been found there,[7] and the recently discovered Sedna Creek and Utukok artifacts pertain to a blade technology,[8] none of these is securely dated; and, as A. L. Bryan has observed, it is incumbent upon proponents of the theory of the development of the Clovis point in Alaska to demonstrate the presence of such points there by 10,000 B.C. or earlier, for, failing this, the occasional undated fluted point in Alaska can be interpreted, with reason, as a marginal manifestation of the type from its presumed centers of origin farther south in North America.[9] The second variant interpretation is, to my way of thinking, the more likely. If Asiatic hunters crossed into Alaska by a land bridge, they could have done so after 26,000 B.C., the date assigned by geologists to the lowering of the sea level during the late Wisconsin glacial maximum.[10] After making this crossing, they then could have moved southward into mid-continental North America at any time before 21,000 B.C., the date after which the Cordilleran and Laurentide (Keewatin) ice sheets are presumed to have closed to inhibit such movement. Thus, a hunting people with a Levallois-Mousterian blade technology could have been on the North American mid-continent well before the Two Creeks Interstadial (ca. 10,000 B.C.) and the opening of the Cordilleran-Laurentide ice.[11] And there is, recently, one bit of evidence to support this. The lowest level of the Wilson Butte Cave, in south-central Idaho, has a radiocarbon dating of 12,500 to 13,000 B.C. Bryan and Crabtree have reassessed the artifacts from this lower level and have now identified a flint biface, a true blade, and a burin in the assemblage—in brief, the kind of Levallois-Mousterian-like assemblage one might postulate as ancestral to Clovis-Llano.[12]

In Volume One (p. 37) I stated my position with reference to the "pre-projectile point stage"

hypothesis and to what I am now calling the "Levallois-Mousterian hypothesis." At that time I said that I did not see why these two hypotheses necessarily should be mutually exclusive. This is still my feeling. In summarizing thus far, I would say that the appearance of man in North America, well south of Alaska, before 20,000 B.C. is highly likely. It is also likely that such men were possessed of only a crude, "pre-projectile point" technology. Later migrations, but still antedating 10,000 B.C., brought with them the rudiments of the Levallois-Mousterian heritage. Quite probably, there were various minglings and fusions between earlier and later immigrants and between their technologies. These, in brief, are the circumstances—and this the point of view—to be kept in mind as we turn to the South American data of early man.

A Brief Look at the South American Data. In Chapter 1 it was acknowledged that man had been in South America since 9000 B.C. This is a minimal, firmly supported estimate. In the foregoing review of the early-man data for North America I concluded by saying that I thought man's presence there as far back as 20,000 B.C. was highly likely. This being the case, it is a reasonable assumption that he entered the South American continent no more than a few thousand years after this, certainly prior to the minimal date of 9000 B.C. A very rapid glance at the South American evidence for his antiquity reinforces this assumption.

An interest in early man in South America is of long standing in the scientific world, and claims for antiquity have been advanced since the middle of the last century.[13] One of the most famous of these claims was that concerning the discoveries in the Lagoa Santa and Confins Caves of eastern Brazil (see Vol. I, p. 68).[14] Human bones, man-made stone implements, and the fossilized remains of mastodon, native horse, and ground sloth were reported as being found together in these caves. Additional discoveries, some years later, were those of human artifacts and extinct sloth remains in the Eberhardt Cave of southern Chile,[15] the human skull from Punín, Ecuador, said to have been found in a fossil-bearing stratum along with mastodon and native horse bones,[16] and the bone projectile points and Pleistocene faunal remains reported from the Gruta de Cadonga in the Argentine Province of Córdoba.[17] Although the validity of the Pleistocene associations has never been conclusively proven for these early discoveries, they nevertheless stimulated interest in the problem of man's age on the continent and also raised the question of the time of extinction of the Pleistocene mammals. Granted the genuineness of the man and faunal association: if such was the case, how much antiquity was indicated? More recent discoveries have begun to provide an answer to this question. In the 1930's J. B. Bird found artifacts together with native horse and sloth bones in cave sites on the Strait of Magellan, and a few years later radiocarbon analyses of specimens from these caves gave dates in the range of 8700 to 6600 B.C. for these associations.[18] This indicated a respectable, if not great, antiquity for man's early presence and also argued for the persistence of Pleistocene-type fauna into the early post-glacial period. Another Chilean find, this one from the Laguna de Tagua Tagua in the valley of the Rio Cachapoal, has pushed the record back a bit further in time.[19] This site is at a natural outlet of an old upland lake basin, once a favorable location for the hunting of animals as they came to the lake to drink. In the lowest occupation level were cracked, cut, and burned bones of native horse and mastodon together with chipped-stone and bone artifacts. A radiocarbon date from the level was 9400 B.C.[19a] But still another find of this sort takes us back even earlier. This one is from Muaco in northwestern Venezuela.[20] The site is a locality of old springs that are now deep mud beds and swamps. In the past this had been a watering place for large Pleistocene mammals and a hunting ground for man. Bones of mastodons and other extinct species that were found in the mud depths show splitting, breaking, and burning that appears to be the work of man. In addition, a few stone artifacts were taken from the mud along with the bones. Radiocarbon runs on the bones give results of 14,920 and 12,780 B.C. Although there are evidences of recent disturbances in the mud beds and it is possible that the stone artifacts may have sunk from relatively superficial depths down into association with the bones of the extinct animals, the markings and burnings of the bones are difficult to pass off as the results of natural, non-human agencies, and the chances favor man's presence in northern South America between 15,000 and 12,000 B.C.[21]

Besides these claims for antiquity which involve Pleistocene faunal association[22] there are others where the animal remains are lacking but where artifact-bearing strata have been assigned early radiocarbon dates, where there are geological clues to great age, or where artifact typology has seemed to indicate such age. Some of these have already been listed in Volume One (p. 33). They, and other findings, will be dealt with further on in this chapter. For the present it is sufficient to note that there are indications that carry man's history in South America back to the terminal Pleistocene, to an era and an environment significantly different from that of the present, and to a range in time of 9000 to, perhaps, 15,000 B.C.[22a]

Organization of the South American Data. If it follows from our previous discussions and tentative conclusions that man had appeared on the New World scene before 20,000 B.C., it is likely that at this time he was possessed of what we have been calling a "pre-projectile point" technology. Accordingly, we should see in the earliest South American industries clues to such a technology. It is my opinion that we do have such clues, and I shall attempt to synthesize and describe these as tool or technological traditions. I see three such technological traditions, and these will be referred to in the pages following as the *Flake tradition,* the *Chopper tradition,* and the *Biface tradition.* All are typologically "pre-projectile point" or non-projectile point industries, and all are characterized by percussion chipping and relatively crude and unspecialized forms. The Flake tradition is very widespread in South America; the Chopper tradition, as here defined, is known only from northern South America; the Biface tradition has an Andean chain distribution with some extensions to the east. As to chronological relationships among these three technological traditions, it seems most likely that the Flake tradition is the earliest, that it was followed by the Chopper tradition, and that the Biface tradition had the latest inception of the three. There was, however, considerable chronological overlap among the three, for it must be kept in mind that we are speaking of traditions rather than strict horizons.

Following these early technological traditions, I shall venture next a concept of an *Old South American Hunting tradition.* According to my

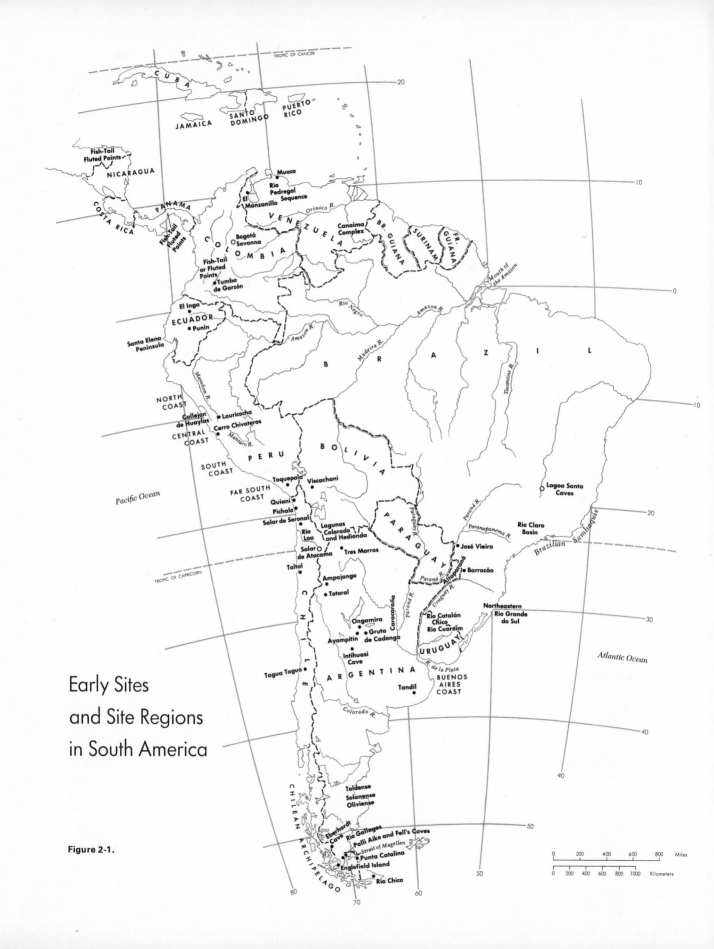

Early Sites
and Site Regions
in South America

Figure 2-1.

definitions, this tradition was characterized by game-hunting activities, especially the hunting of large game, including Pleistocene and early Post-Pleistocene species now extinct. Further diagnostics of the tradition are bifacially-flaked projectile points, generally of long, lanceolate form. With this, the first full cultural tradition I am attempting to examine, we are on firmer ground. The evidence is not abundant, but some of it is quite substantial. Remains of the Old South American Hunting tradition have been found in western and far southern South America. Its beginnings are believed to date from about 9000 B.C., and it persisted until about 7000 B.C.

Subsequent to this in my organization for tracing out the story of the early inhabitants of South America, we will consider two cultural traditions of the middle time ranges, the *Andean Hunting-Collecting* and the *East Brazilian Upland traditions.* The Andean Hunting-Collecting tradition,

Figure 2-2. Chronological chart of early phases or complexes and their affiliations with technological or major cultural traditions.

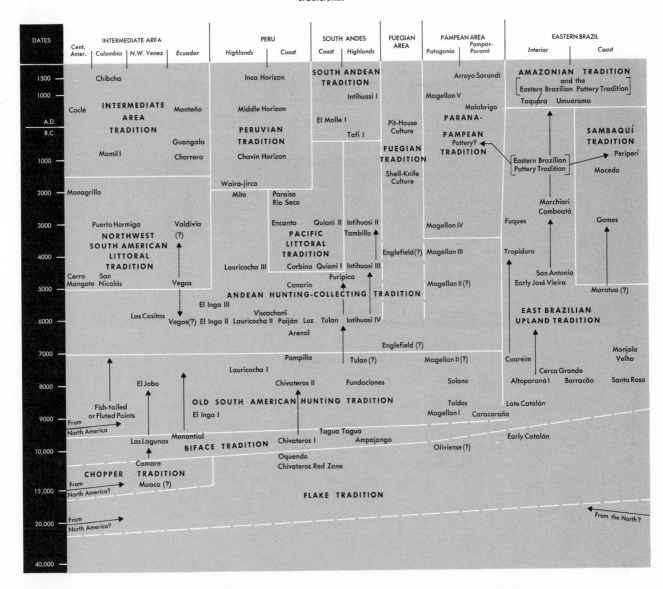

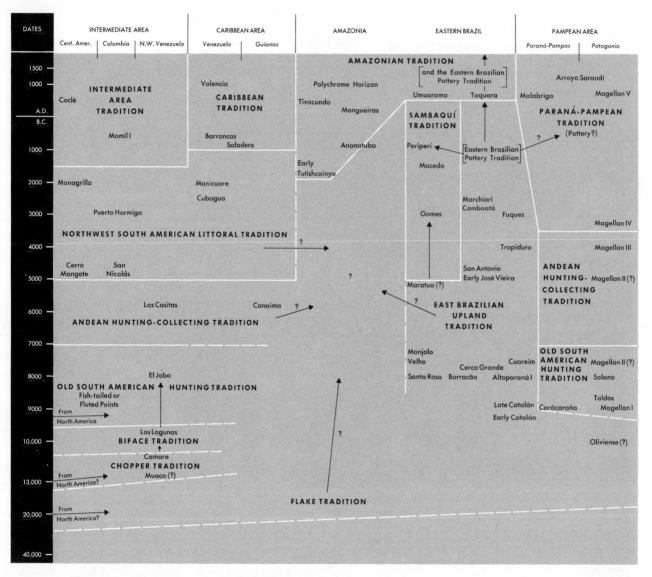

Figure 2-3. Chronological chart of early phases or complexes and their affiliations with technological or major cultural traditions.

as the name implies, was a hunting and food-collecting tradition that appears to have developed out of the earlier Old South American Hunting tradition. It is found in Andean and southern South America. In the upland valleys, where it appears to have its most characteristic adaptations,

it lasted as late as 3000 to 2000 B.C.; but along the Pacific coast it was superseded by coastal-adapted cultures by about 4000 B.C. The East Brazilian Upland tradition seems to have had its roots in the ancient Flake tradition technology. It persisted in the highlands of Eastern Brazil for several thousand years, being modified only in late prehistoric times by influences from agricultural traditions; however, along the Atlantic Coast it gave way to coastal-adapted cultures by about 4000 B.C.

Finally, in the course of this chapter we shall take note of a series of later South American cultural traditions, including some of the "coastal adaptations" to which we have just referred. These later traditions are, we believe, developments out of the Andean Hunting-Collecting and the East Brazilian Upland traditions, and all have their beginnings at some time after 5000 to 4000 B.C. These later cultural traditions will be introduced here only briefly, with an emphasis on their probable origins, in an attempt to provide a transition into the several geographic and culture area chapters, where they will be taken up in detail and where, as we shall show, they provide the foundations for the still later agricultural traditions.

With this conceptual-organizational structure outlined for the reader, there remains only one other preparatory step—a brief statement concerning the nature of the Pleistocene environments of South America.

Pleistocene Environments of South America

Pleistocene and early Post-Pleistocene environments in South America, as we have noted in the previous chapter, differed from those of the more recent past and of today. A glacial climate had a determining role in these earlier environments—in physiography, soil formation, vegetation, and fauna. Such a glacial climate for Pleistocene South America is inferred from glacial moraines, old ocean-strand lines, the deposition and erosion of sedimentary beds, the pollen residues in these beds, and the various fossil remains of former animal life.[23]

Late Pleistocene glacial chronology in South America is believed to parallel that of both Europe and the United States; that is, the major events—the glacial advances and retreats—are thought to have been essentially synchronous on all three continents.[24] Thus the last notable glacial advance in South America is presumed to date from about 9000 to 8000 B.C. and to correspond to the Valders Substage of the North American terminal Wisconsin stage (see Vol. I, p. 28) and to the European (or Scandinavian) Younger Dryas Substage of the Würm Stage. The preceding interstadial in both the Old and New World falls somewhere between 10,500 and 9000 B.C. and in North America is referred to as the Two Creeks, while in Europe it is the Alleröd. Prior to this interstadial, the late Pleistocene glacial maximum extends back in time to 18,000 B.C. or even earlier and is called the Mankato–Port Huron[25] in North America and the Older Dryas in Europe.

The extent of the glaciers in South America during the era of maximum advance is reasonably well known. Ice masses were located in the high Andes (above 10,000 ft., or about 3300 m.) in Venezuela, Colombia, Ecuador, and Peru, while farther south were the enormous glacial fields of southern Chile and adjacent Argentina. The fluctuations, or retreats and advances, of these glaciers during the subsequent Interstadial (Two Creeks equivalent) and the terminal Substage (Valders equivalent) are not well plotted; however, it is safe to say that the natural environment of South America was significantly influenced by glaciation down to 8000 or 7000 B.C.

The differences between the South American Pleistocene environments and those of today lie in the presence of lakes no longer in existence, in a formerly lower ocean level, and in significant contrasts in rainfall and vegetation patterns. There were glacial lakes in the mountains of Venezuela, Colombia, Ecuador, Peru, Bolivia, and Chile. On the Bolivian altiplano glacial drainage was responsible for two huge lakes, Minchin and Ballivián. The latter was, in fact, the ancestor of the present-day smaller Lake Titicaca. The late Pleistocene ocean level stood between 200 and 400 feet lower than it does today. This meant that additional large areas of the Atlantic shelf were exposed, all the way from southern Brazil down to Tierra del Fuego, as well as other smaller strips on the northeastern part of the continent. Similarly, on the Pacific side, land areas now inundated were exposed in Panama, Colombia, and Ecuador. In western South America there was more rain in Pleistocene times, temperatures were generally lower, and forests extended farther down the mountain sides. What are now desert wastes, such as the Santa Elena Peninsula of Ecuador and the Peruvian coastal strip, were then in grassy savannas with parkland stands of trees. In like manner, the semi-arid steppes of the Patagonian Plateau were also in lush grasses. In contrast, however, the eastern and lowland side of South America was drier. Thus, what are today the coastal rainforests and mangrove swamps of the Guianas and Brazil were then in open savannas.

These differences between the climate and terrain in the Pleistocene and in recent times must be kept in mind when we turn to consider man's early history in South America. For clearly, the presence of lakes, forests, and grasslands where none now exist, as well as a radically different fauna from that of today, would have conditioned his cultural adaptations. Nor can we overlook the presence of additional land areas, now submerged by the sea, in the tracing out of man's early movements in the continent. Such land strips as are believed to have existed along the Isthmus of Panama and the Brazilian coast would have been crucial avenues of migration for early hunters and food gatherers in their peopling of South America (see Fig. 2–4).

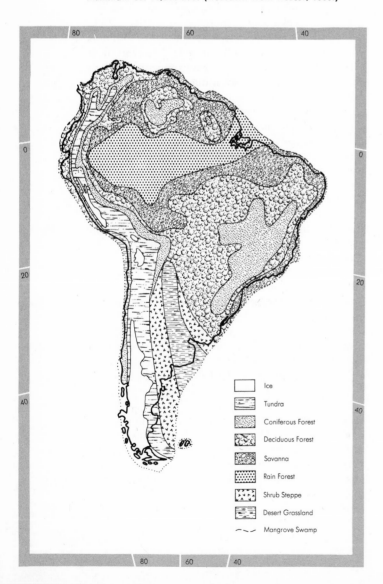

Figure 2-4. Estimated glaciation and vegetation zones, and larger land mass, of South America during Wisconsin glacial maximum ca. 18,000 B.C. (Redrawn from Hester, 1966.)

Ice

Tundra

Coniferous Forest

Deciduous Forest

Savanna

Rain Forest

Shrub Steppe

Desert Grassland

Mangrove Swamp

Clues to the Earliest Technological Traditions

The Flake Tradition. There are a number of lithic assemblages in South America—from Peru, Chile, Uruguay, and elsewhere—that appear to be of substantial age and that share the common characteristic of artifacts shaped almost entirely from crude primary stone flakes. To be sure, the use of such flakes in artifact manufacture is a feature of almost all stone-chipping industries of whatever place or period, but the complexes in question display no other technological mode. We subsume them here under the term and concept of the Flake tradition. The artifacts of this Flake tradition, which are very frequently of flint, are percussion chipped and generally show some simple retouch. Quite often this retouch confers a steep edge on these unifacial tools. Scrapers, punches, spokeshaves, picklike forms, and simple burins are typical. Significantly, bifacially chipped projectile points, or, for that matter, the clear and intentional bifacial-flaking of any implements, is absent in these Flake tradition industries.

The most securely dated of the Flake tradition complexes are those from the central coast of Peru.[26] These Peruvian complexes feature burins, and they have been referred to by E. P. Lanning and T. C. Patterson as "burin industries."[27] The sites in which these artifact assemblages are found are in the lower Chillón and Lurín Valleys, and the most important is Cerro Chivateros, a stratified workshop and quarry location in the former valley. At Cerro Chivateros the burin industry, or Chivateros Red Zone complex, artifacts are found in a basal stratum of red-brown eolian silt that lies to a thickness of about 40 centimeters over the

34

quartzitic bedrock of the hill. This red-brown silt is capped with a thin layer of salitre, or salt-impregnated silt, which also contains burin complex artifacts. Overlying this is another layer of dusty silt, this one of a gray color, which is again topped with a salitre crust. These two soil zones contain artifacts of the Chivateros I complex (see Vol. I, p. 67), which Lanning and Patterson assign to their "Andean Biface horizon" and which I discuss later in this chapter as a part of the Biface tradition.[28] There is, finally, a topmost layer at Cerro Chivateros, of gray-brown wind-carried silt, that contains implements of the Chivateros II, a complex transitional from the Biface tradition into the Old South American Hunting tradition.

The stratified Cerro Chivateros sequence is supplemented by findings at a nearby workshop and quarry called Oquendo where the artifacts from a single silt stratum are assigned to an intermediate chronological position between those of the Chivateros Red Zone and Chivateros I complexes, although these Oquendo tools lack the bifacial chipping of Chivateros I and are a part of the burin industries and the Flake tradition.

The dating of this Peruvian coastal sequence is keyed to two radiocarbon readings on wood fragments taken from the upper or salitre zone of the Chivateros I deposits at Cerro Chivateros. These give dates of 8420 and 8440 B.C. As the Chivateros I salitre is apparently to be correlated with a relatively moist and cool period on the Peruvian coast, the appropriate climatic phenomenon for this time would appear to be the Valders-equivalent glacial advance of the Andes.[29] Following this reasoning, the underlying silt, which also contains Chivateros I materials, has an Alleröd or Two Creeks equivalence, while the lower salitre layer and the Red Zone silts underlying it would correspond to the Mankato-equivalent advance and the fluctuations within it.[30] These two lowest strata are those that contain the burin complex materials.

This may be summed up, along with the Lanning-Patterson dating estimates, as follows:

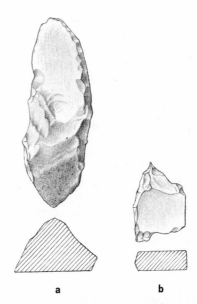

Figure 2-5. Chivateros Red Zone artifacts. *a*: Curved scraper. *b*: Small pointed implement. Length of *a*, 7.5 cm. (Drawn from specimens provided by T. C. Patterson.)

The Chivateros Red Zone artifacts are made of the local quartzite and are percussion-shaped (Fig. 2-5). Flakes were removed from unprepared cores, and most of the implements were made on these flakes. They include simple and right-angle burins, single- and double-pointed flake perforators, notched flakes or spokeshaves, and end- and side-scrapers. Edge retouch on the scrapers is notably steep, and there are a number of steep-sided pieces which probably served as cores. The Oquendo tools are similar but include also notched burins, burin-scrapers, and keeled denticulates. These latter link Oquendo with the succeeding Chivateros I complex.[31]

Quite probably these old Peruvian Flake tradition tools are "secondary" implements; that is,

Chivateros Red Zone complex—	prior to 10,500 B.C.	The Flake Tradition
Oquendo complex—	10,500–9500 B.C.	
Chivateros I complex—	9500–8000 B.C.	The Biface Tradition
Chivateros II complex—	after 8000 B.C.	

they were employed to make other, more directly used, things such as wooden spears and digging-sticks. The burin assemblages suggest wood working, and the Pleistocene Peruvian valleys were undoubtedly more wooded than they are today. The nature of subsistence of these early coastal peoples is almost wholly speculative. Shellfish from the sea, landsnails, and wild plants were probably a part of the diet. Whether they availed themselves of the Pleistocene camelids, mastodons, and other animals is unknown; but there is no direct evidence to this effect. Population groups must have been small, and camps were probably situated in the wooded valleys at some little distance from the hillside quarries and workshops.

Other Flake industry complexes are reported from along the Pacific Coast. In the Lurin Valley, a short distance south of the Chillon, explorations have revealed the Tortuga and Achona complexes which cross-date, respectively, with Chivateros Red Zone and Oquendo.[32] On the Santa Elena Peninsula of coastal Ecuador an Exacto burin industry has been defined by Lanning. This is a semi-arid region today although it was well watered in Pleistocene times. The Exacto sites are now on dry river courses that cut through old marine terraces immediately behind the present coastline. Exacto tools are right-angle and dihedral burins, perforators, scrapers, and nodule hammerstones or cores, all of which are made of a poor-quality chert. Resemblances are to both Chivateros Red Zone and Oquendo, although preponderantly to the latter. Lanning infers a date of a little before 10,000 B.C. as being in keeping with a pre-Alleröd moist climate.[33] In northern Chile there are Flake tradition sites along the course of the Rio Loa, the only stream of consequence in this now dessicated country. The complex is named the Chuqui, and the artifacts are burins, steep-edge scrapers, and various flakes that have resemblances to Chivateros Red Zone and Oquendo.[34]

Much farther afield, on the other side of the continent, there are other Flake tradition industries that show similarities to those of the Peruvian coast. Foremost among these is the Catalanian or Catalanense of northern Uruguay. This has been defined from a large series of chipped-stone artifacts gathered from the terraces of the Rio Catalán Chico, a tributary of the Rio Cuareim. Marcelo Bórmida estimates that this Catalanian industry

dates back to 9000 B.C.[35] His earliest phase, Catalán A, or Early Catalán, consists of large flake tools (Fig. 2–6). There is in the collection, however, one implement that is identified as a *bec burinant,* and this, together with the chipping techniques, suggests the relationship to the Peruvian burin industries.[36] Bórmida's work on the Catalanian materials also involves a stratigraphy; and it is significant that his Phase B, or Late Catalán, contains bifacially chipped implements whereas the Early Catalán collections do not. Also, it is of further importance to the Early Catalán dating that the stratum in which the artifacts are found is correlated with a torrential river flow and a lowered sea level, conditions suggesting terminal Pleistocene conditions.[37]

Figure 2-6. Early Catalán implements. *a*: Bec burinant. *b*: Knife with retouched edges. *c*: Plano-convex scraper. *d*: Perforator with retouched edges. *e*: Double perforator. Length of *a*, 8 cm. (Redrawn from Bórmida, 1964.)

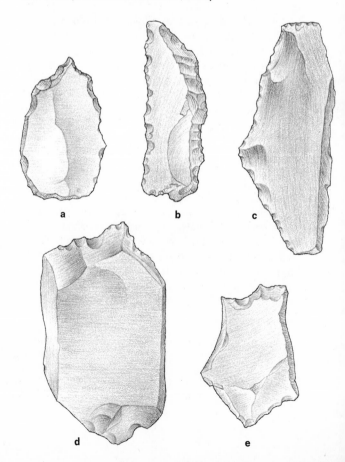

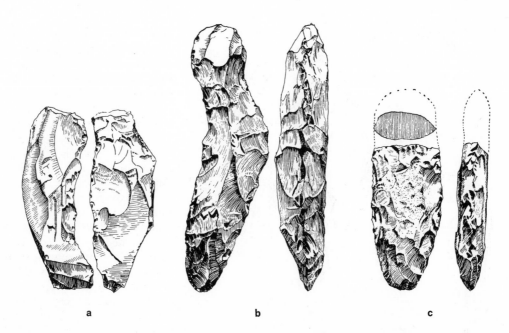

a					b					c

Figure 2-7. Altoparaná implements from Misiones, Argentina. *a*: Pebble with shaped cutting edge. *b*: Picklike, or hooklike, tool that shows bifacial percussion-flaking. *c*: Ovate or leaf-shaped bifacially chipped ax, suggestive of Biface tradition treatment. Length of *a*, 13.5 cm. (After Menghin, 1957.)

The 9000 B.C. date estimate for Early Catalán does not take us back into the chronological ranges one might anticipate for an ancient South American "pre-projectile point" industry. It is, of course, possible that Bórmida may have underestimated the age or that Early Catalán represents a late continuity of the Flake tradition. In fact, this latter possibility seems quite likely, for there are other clues which suggest that the Flake tradition persisted for a long time in eastern South America. One such clue is the Altoparaná or Altoparanense industry of the Paraná drainage in Paraguay and Argentine Misiones.[38] The characteristic artifacts of Altoparaná are rough picklike tools made on large plano-convex flakes (Fig. 2–7). The age of the complex is uncertain, although a terminal Pleistocene date has been suggested.[39] The dominant technology is certainly that of a rough-flake industry; however, it is probably a significant chronological indicator that bifacially chipped knives and other tools are also present.[40] From this I would suspect that the Altoparaná complex shows a conjunction of the Flake tradition and more recent Biface tradition elements. Such a hypothesis may also explain the contents of some of the eastern Brazilian lithic complexes. Humaitá and Camboatá of northeastern Rio Grande do

Sul,[41] Barracão of western Santa Catarina and Paraná,[42] Timburi of the Paranapanema Valley in northern Paraná,[43] and Santa Rosa of the Rio Claro Basin in the State of São Paulo[44] are all predominantly unifacial flake industries, and yet all show a few heavy bifacially chipped tools. For Santa Rosa (Fig. 2–8), which is the earliest horizon yet discovered in the Rio Claro region, T. O. Miller notes that most of the artifacts are manufactured from thick, irregular primary flakes of flint that have been unifacially worked on the convex face and sometimes retouched on the edges. Punches, beaks, spokeshaves, and scrapers were so fashioned. Such could almost be a basic description of the Flake tradition technology. But the complex of the Rio Claro also includes rare bifaces, and this suggests a persistence of the Flake tradition in the highlands of eastern Brazil into later times as well as into transitions to other traditions.

Finally, to the south, in the Argentine Pampas and Patagonia, there are a number of poorly

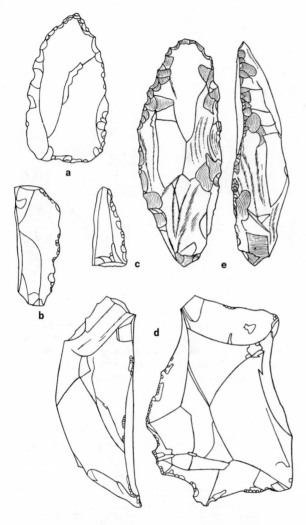

Figure 2-8. Santa Rosa chipped stone artifacts. *a*: Flake knife. *b, c*: Backed "penknives" (rare occurrences). *d*: Side and front views of beaked scraper. *e*: An Altoparaná-like implement. Length of *a*, 7.3 cm.; others to same scale. (Courtesy T. O. Miller, Jr.)

known complexes for which claims of great age have been advanced. Krieger has referred to these assemblages in his assessment of the "pre-projectile point" stage in South America.[45] Although descriptions and illustrations are lacking or inadequate, it is possible that some or all of these assemblages could pertain to the Flake tradition. Two of the

best known are the Oliviense[46] and the Rio Gallegos I[47] of Patagonia. Oliviense is defined from surface collections made in the regions of Caleta Olivia and Bahía Solano. These collections come from a series of old marine terraces which, according to Menghin, were occupied as active beach sites prior to 9000 B.C. and, perhaps, as far back as 18,000 to 25,000 years ago. The artifact range is meager—retouched flakes and crude scrapers for the most part. Rio Gallegos, farther south in Patagonia, is similar, and so is the Tandilense[48] assemblage found in rock shelter sites on the Buenos Aires pampas. The arguments for antiquity for all of these complexes or assemblages are clouded by the associated presence of technologically more advanced tools at both Caleta Olivia and Rio Gallegos sites. Such mixtures could, of course, be interpreted as I have done for the eastern Brazilian and Altoparaná finds; however, the data are so few here that we can do little more than make mention of them.[49]

The Chopper Tradition. The Chopper technological tradition is best known from northwestern Venezuela; in fact, it is only here that a case can be made out for the integrity of chopper tool complexes that also have indications of considerable age. Northwestern Venezuela is, today, a semi-arid country, but in Pleistocene times it was considerably wetter, cooler, and covered with either forests or grasslands. We know definitely that it was a land of the mastodon, small native horse, and giant sloth, for the bones of these animals have been recovered from the Muaco mud pits mentioned at the beginning of this chapter. Irving Rouse and J. M. Cruxent have defined a series of lithic industries from the region.[50] The collections in question come from the river terraces of the Rio Pedregal, and the seriation of the assemblages is based on both river terrace associations and similarity in typologies. It is assumed that collections from sites on the highest river terraces represent the oldest end of the series. The artifact complex of these highest terraces has been called the Camare. The complex of the terraces immediately below is the Las Lagunas, that of the next lowest the El Jobo, and that of the bottommost terraces the Las Casitas. At this point in our discussion it is the Camare complex with which we are concerned;

however, the problems of relative dating make it important that we view Camare in relation to the entire terrace series.

The Camare diagnostic implement (Fig. 2-9) is a large (about 11 × 5 × 3 cm.), crude chopper made by battering the edges and the sides of a quartzite boulder to produce a very rough tool that could be called "proto-bifacial." Associated with these heavy choppers are large trimmed flakes that were apparently used as scrapers or knives. No spear or projectile points were found on the Camare sites; such weapons, if they did exist, must have been made of fire-hardened wood.

The Camare complex is related to Las Lagunas, the next in the river terrace series, by a continuity of the Camare heavy choppers, although those in the Las Lagunas collections tend to be smaller. In addition, Las Lagunas is further distinguished by the presence of thinner, more carefully worked tools which can be considered as true bifaces. It is significant to our dating of the Venezuelan sequence that Las Lagunas is typologically close to Chivateros I of the Central Coast of Peru, and both may be classed in the Biface tradition, which we will describe next. Chivateros I, it will be recalled, is dated by radiocarbon at 8500 B.C. If we

assume this to be the approximate age of the Las Lagunas complex, then the preceding Camare and Manzanillo complexes of the Chopper tradition must be placed prior to this, or more or less to an age equivalence with the Peruvian coastal burin industries of the Flake tradition.[51]

The Biface Tradition. The Biface tradition is characterized by the first truly bifacially flaked tools in South America. Lanning and Patterson have argued that these bifaces developed out of the antecedent Chopper tradition form somewhere in the northern part of the continent, perhaps in northwestern Venezuela.[52] In the Rio Pedregal sequence the new Las Lagunas implement (Fig. 2-10) could have been used as a hand ax, a knife, or possibly as a thrusting spear tip.

Figure 2-10. Las Lagunas artifacts. Length of specimen at *left,* 8 cm. (After Rouse and Cruxent, 1963; courtesy Yale University Press.)

Figure 2-9. Camare chopper. Length, about 12 cm. (After Rouse and Cruxent, 1963; courtesy Yale University Press.)

Some of the Las Lagunas bifaces are ovoid-triangulate in outline and have a flat base; others are more of a diamond-shape although with one end of the diamond longer and more pointed than the other. An average length for a Las Lagunas biface is about 8 to 9 centimeters. All of the chipping is by percussion.[53]

Figure 2-11. *Above, left:* Large Andean bifaces, Chivateros I phase. Length is 16.5 cm. (Drawn from specimens provided by T. C. Patterson.)

Figure 2-12. *Above, right:* Two large bifacial implements of the Ampajango industry from Jujuy Province, Argentina. (Courtesy E. M. Cigliano.)

The bifaced tool of the Peruvian Chivateros I complex is also a heavy percussion-flaked tool, ovoid to triangulate in outline, keeled on one or both faces, and pointed at one end (Fig. 2-11). As in Las Lagunas, a few of the Peruvian Chivateros I bifaces are thin enough to be considered as knife-like, rather than hand ax, implements, and there are rare occurrences of long thin bifaces that might have been thrusting spear points.[54]

Heavy bifacial tools similar to the Venezuelan and Peruvian ones have been found on the Ecuadorian coast in the Manantial phase, which is believed to succeed the earlier Exacto phase of the Santa Elena Peninsula.[55] But it is in the southern rather than the northern Andes that we have the most substantial evidence for the Biface

tradition. The most publicized site and complex is the Ampajango (Fig. 2-12), described by C. M. Cigliano.[56] The site is in the Santa Maria Valley of Catamarca Province, in northwest Argentina. Here artifacts were found on the surface of an old river terrace and in the valley bottom of a small *quebrada* below the terrace. Most of these artifacts are rough bifaces made of a local andesite; some are thick and ax-like, while others are more slender. Resemblances to Venezuelan Las Lagunas and Peruvian Chivateros I are readily apparent.[57] Large unifaces and a variety of scrapers make up the complex. All tools were made by percussion flaking. The attempt to date Ampajango by its geological terrace association is unconvincing since the same bifacial tools are found both on the terrace and in the quebrada below it. Moreover, the situation is further complicated by the presence of an almost certainly later complex—one with pressure-flaked leaf-shaped projectile points—on a nearby higher and presumably older terrace, so that in this case position of terrace is not a good criterion of relative age.[58] Thus, any assignment of the Ampajango bifaces to a time period coeval with that of the Venezuelan or Peruvian biface industries must rest largely upon typological similarities.[59] But the whole argument is, however, bolstered by a number of other similar assemblages from the Argentine Andes which do have more convincing Pleistocene terrace associations than in the instance of Ampajango proper. Among these are the Punta del Agua finds of San Juan,[60] Totoral finds of La Rioja,[61] and the Turilari,[62] Zapagua,[63] Tres Morros, and Saladillo[64] complexes of Jujuy Province.

Biface tradition industries similar to those of northwestern Argentina are also found in north Chile. In the middle Rio Loa region, where he defined a Chuqui complex, Lanning also defines a Talabre industry which succeeds it.[65] A little farther south a great many early sites have been found around the Salar de Atacama, another *salinas* or dry salt basin which in earlier time was a lake valley with forests, grasses, and game. Le Paige has recognized a Ghatchi I, "pre-projectile point," phase among the materials collected around this *salar* (see Vol. I, p. 33).[66] Although questions have been raised about the validity of this complex, the diagnostic tool type is the Ampajango-type biface, so it seems probable that some of the Ghatchi zone artifacts represent the old Biface tradition even though Le Paige's assemblage may be a mixed lot.[67]

In the Argentine lowland Province of Santa Fe, Gonzalez and Lorandí have isolated a Caracaraña complex of heavy bifacial quartzite tools along the banks of a river of that name.[68] Various flakes and blade artifacts are associated but no projectile points. This would seem to be the easternmost complex that could be considered as pertaining fully to the Biface tradition. In Uruguay, as we have noted, the Late Catalán industry has some few heavy bifaces, but the full context is that of the Flake tradition; and this circumstance also pertains to Altoparaná and the several eastern Brazilian complexes that we have already mentioned.

The Problem of Traditional Continuities. In our discussions of these postulated early technological traditions we have already commented upon the problems of traditional continuities. For instance, it was noted that the Flake tradition probably had a late persistence in the

Figure 2-13. The Tres Morros and Saladillo sites, northwestern Argentina. *Top*: Tres Morros, along the edge of the site area which corresponds to an ancient lake playa or beach. *Bottom*: Saladillo, with Pleistocene terraces seen along *top* of the picture and Holocene terrace below. (Courtesy E. M. Cigliano; see also Cigliano, 1962.)

Catalanian industry and in some of the east Brazilian industries. This matter deserves some further comment.

To begin, let us take the other early technological tradition, the Chopper, and consider it in relation to a lithic complex that we have not yet mentioned, the Jabaliense.[69] Jabaliense is the name given by Bórmida to assemblages of rough pebble choppers found along the Buenos Aires Province Atlantic Coast. These choppers are, in fact, the same as those that Florentino Ameghino[70] once considered to be of such great age and that Hrdlička, Holmes, and Willis successfully refuted.[71] Bórmida would agree that they are of no notable antiquity.

Nevertheless, Bórmida sees their technological and generic affiliation with an ancient "Protolithic" tradition. In his words, Jabaliense is an "Epiprotolithic" manifestation, one derived from, or epigonic to, lithic tool beginnings that lie very remote in time. This brings us to the question of what the useful typological, spatial, and chronological limits of the tradition concept are. The same problem is posed about the rough pebble tools of Taltal in Chile. Krieger has suggested that they pertain to a "pre-projectile point stage" of technology,[72] while Bird rejected this, saying that the Taltal rough implements are found in full stratigraphic association with more advanced and clearly later stonework, with the whole dating at no more than 2000 to 4000 B.C.;[73] but as Krieger countered, the question is not one of age but of technological affiliation. Is there a relationship of traditional, generic continuity from early Chopper tradition beginnings down to these obviously later industries of Jabaliense and Taltal?

My opinion is that on the basis of the present scattered and sparse information we cannot be sure of a Chopper tradition affiliation for such industries as the Jabaliense and the Taltal. A relationship of all the pebble chopper complexes, so widely disparate in space and time, may have existed, but we cannot demonstrate it; also, other explanations seem as likely. The idea of using pebble choppers and pounders could have been hit upon, given the need for such implements, separately and independently, time and again. Or their isolation at certain sites may be a function of seasonal preoccupations with particular foods and subsistence practices—a likely possibility for the Jabaliense tools.

Summary. Three technological traditions in the working of chipped-stone tools appear to be the earliest artifactual evidences of man on the South American continent. These are the Flake, the Chopper, and the Biface traditions. Stratigraphy and radiocarbon dating from the Peruvian coast place the Flake tradition as antecedent to the Biface in that area and impute a date of 9500 B.C. or earlier for the Flake tradition industries there. Other Flake tradition complexes are known from various parts of South America: Ecuador, Chile, Uruguay, Paraguay, eastern Brazil, and, probably, the Argentine lowlands. For most of these complexes the evidence for dating is inadequate; however, there are some reasons to believe that the eastern manifestations of the tradition date somewhat later than those of Peru, perhaps in the range of 9000 to 6000 B.C. In this connection, it should be noted that Biface forms are found in association with some of these eastern South American Flake tradition complexes. There are also reasons to believe that the Flake tradition was the matrix of the later East Brazilian Upland tradition.

The Chopper tradition is known from northwestern Venezuela. The chopper tools are made from pebble cores or boulders. In their Venezuelan setting they have been placed in a river terrace and typological seriation that implies a date—through correlations with the Peruvian coastal radiocarbon dated sequence—of 9500 B.C. or earlier. The Chopper tradition is, thus, approximately coeval with the Flake tradition, insofar as there is evidence to bear upon this question; however, the more widespread and southerly distribution of the Flake tradition suggests that it may have the earlier beginnings. The Chopper tradition is succeeded in Venezuela by the Biface tradition, and there is a strong typological suggestion that the Biface tradition may have developed from the Chopper tradition.

The Biface tradition may represent the first introduction—or, conforming to what was said above, the first local development—of bifacial flaking in South America. The dating of the inception of the Biface tradition at 9500 B.C. hinges on the Peruvian radiocarbon date and the stratigraphy at the Cerro Chivateros site. The Biface tradition is essentially Andean in its geographical distributions, although the characteristic heavy bifacial tools have been found in small numbers in Flake tradition complexes in eastern South America. These eastern occurrences may be as old as the Biface tradition tools of the Andes, although there is a suspicion that they are somewhat later.

The patterns of life represented by these three traditions may be discussed only in the most general terms. Presumably, the people who made these various implements were hunters and food-gatherers, but the extent of their specializations in these directions is undetermined. Quite probably, many of the tools were "secondary" implements used in fashioning others of wood or bone.

Finally, it may be asked whether any of these three technological traditions—Flake, Chopper, or Biface—has identifiable counterparts in North America. If we assume a general north-to-south drift of peoples and basic flint technologies in the New World, this is a reasonable hypothesis for examination. Unfortunately, our answer must still be that we cannot be sure. Some of the debatable "pre-projectile point" industries of North America do have general similarities to these three traditions; but their very simplicity, together with the uncertainties of dating on both continents, allows us to do little more than speculate on this interesting question.

The Old South American Hunting Tradition

Some Definitions and Criteria. What we are here naming the Old South American Hunting tradition marks the earliest bifacial projectile point cultures in South America. The tradition has very definite "Paleo-Indian" aspects as this term is used in North America, and, as we shall see, there are a number of clues that strongly suggest that significant technological elements of the Old South American Hunting tradition did indeed derive from North American "Paleo-Indian" or "Big-Game Hunting" tradition cultures. For the first time in South America there is a clear emphasis on hunting—especially the hunting of herd animals, including Pleistocene species now extinct—reflected in the archaeological inventories. This does not mean that there were no other economic pursuits, but it does mean that the hunting of large land mammals, for food and for hides, was a major activity.

As in North America, the characteristic chipped-stone artifacts are lanceolate projectile points. These, as stated, are bifacially flaked, sometimes by pressure flaking. There are two distinctive forms or styles to these points. One we shall call the fish-tailed form, and we believe it to be the earlier of the two. It is a long, relatively broad-bladed shape with a stemlike tail that has an incurved base. It frequently has a slight to moderate basal fluting of this tail on one or both surfaces. As we said in Volume One (p. 68), these South American fish-tailed points are similar in outline and other details to the Clovis-derived Cumberland Points of the North American Big-Game Hunting tradition. The other basic point type that we are including in the Old South American Hunting tradition is an elongated leaf-shaped form (Vol. I, pp. 65–68). We feel that it defines a horizon a little later than the fish-tailed point. These are the two diagnostic forms of the tradition; in addition, there are other occasional lanceolates that we will mention in the course of the ensuing discussions. Besides the projectile points, other Old South American Hunting tradition artifacts are scrapers, knives, bone awls, and flaking tools—all items consistent with the projected picture of a hunting economy. The game hunted included deer, camelids, the giant sloth, the native horse, and, probably, the mastodon. Old South American Hunting tradition sites are found in the Andes and along the Pacific coastal strip, in far southern South America, and on the Argentine plains. There is a suggestion that during the latter half of the tradition there was a tendency to exploit higher Andean altitudes in the pursuit of the camelids and deer, and it will be my contention that such a trend led to the ecological adaptations of the later Andean Hunting-Collecting tradition. The general time span of the Old South American Hunting tradition is estimated at 9000 to 7000 b.c., the fish-tailed point horizon characterizing the earlier half of this span and the elongated leaf-shaped point horizon the latter half.

The Fish-Tailed Projectile Point Complexes. There are two well-documented fish-tailed point complexes: the Magellan I of far southern South America and the El Inga I of highland Ecuador. Besides these there are a few other assemblages and scattered finds that seem to pertain to this particular line of development within the tradition. Let us first consider the Magellan I complex or phase.

In our brief recounting of the indications of man's antiquity in South America, and especially with reference to Pleistocene faunal associations, we mentioned the Strait of Magellan discoveries of J. B. Bird. In his work in that region Bird had outlined a five-period culture sequence, of which Magellan I is the first phase or period.[74] The sites that Bird explored are old camping places that lie on the north, or mainland, side of the Strait of Magellan. The terrain is that of the eastern por-

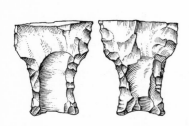

Figure 2-14. Obverse and reverse sides of two Magellan I–type projectile points from Fell's Cave. (Redrawn from Emperaire, Laming-Emperaire, and Reichlen, 1963.)

tion of the Strait, a windswept, treeless plain, similar in many ways to the High Plains of western North America. Those two sites in which Magellan I artifacts were found are cave or rock shelter locations. The Palli Aike Cave is in an old volcanic crater that rises above the surrounding plain, with the cave so situated that it faces away from the prevailing winds. The Magellan I phase artifacts were found in the lower refuse layers of the cave. These artifacts were the Magellan fish-tailed points, various flint scrapers, and simple bone tools. Associated with these were bones of native horse and ground sloth. Three partially cremated human burials also were associated with them. Higher in the cave stratigraphy, the upper depths of the refuse revealed, in successive order from lower to upper levels, the artifacts of the Magellan II through V phases.

The other principal site of the Magellan I phase is Fell's Cave, some 20 miles to the west of Palli Aike. The physical stratigraphy of Fell's Cave shows a deep layer of debris at the top which is underlain by a stratum of sandstone blocks that had fallen from the cave roof at some time in the distant past. Underneath this sandstone fall was another, and basal, layer of refuse. In the cultural stratigraphy, the basal refuse below the sandstone had Magellan I phase fish-tailed points (Fig. 2-14) and other artifacts together with native horse, sloth, and guanaco bones. Above the sandstone fall the upper refuse showed, from bottom to top, a succession of Magellan II, III, and IV phase artifacts, paralleling the sequence from Palli Aike. Since Bird's work in Fell's Cave, new excavations were made there by José Emperaire and Annette

Laming-Emperaire in the late 1950's.[75] Their detailed stratigraphic studies confirm Bird's sequence in general outline and especially in the details of the Magellan I phase.

The Magellan or Fell's Cave points range in size from about 4.0 to 6.5 centimeters in length, and they have a blade width in centimeters of 2 to 3. The blade is ovoid-triangulate in outline. The fish-tailed stem is eared or flared at the ends and may be as much as a third to a half of the total length of the point. At its narrow "waist" this stem is from 1 to 2 centimeters wide. The chipping of the Magellan fish-tailed points is well controlled, bifacial, and has been executed by both percussion and pressure flaking. On many of the specimens there is a short fluting of the fish tail. All in all, it is a specialized projectile form and quite distinct from the later points in the sequence. All of the points found in the lower occupation of Fell's Cave were of this fish-tailed type, with one exception. This is a long lanceolate with an incurved base, similar in many ways to the Plano points of North America. Accompanying artifacts in the Magellan I phase are unifacial flake scrapers of both side and end varieties, bone flaking tools and awls, and some cylindrical or disklike implements of lava which could have been used as depilators for hides.

The Magellan I phase of far southern South America supports our Old South American Hunting tradition construct in various ways. The sites in question are clearly camps of small bands of hunters who were pursuing large land game for food and hides. The game was of species now extinct, together with the guanaco; and these animals lived in a grassland environment different from that of the present. The diagnostic implement of the phase is a fish-tailed projectile point of chipped stone, a type reminiscent of points associated with similar cultures of late Pleistocene times in North America. From the limited physical anthropological observations on the Magellan I burials, we know that these people were dolichocephalic and, in general, of a physical type similar to the Brazilian Lagoa Santa population.[76] All of these considerations suggest the thesis of an early American hunting population of a long-headed physical type who had moved widely over the hemisphere by the end of the Valders glacial advance if not before (see Vol. I, pp. 12–16). The

44

radiocarbon date of 8700 B.C. from the Magellan I level of Fell's Cave tends to confirm this, and such a date brings the Magellan I hunters into approximate contemporaneity with the Cumberland and Folsom point Big-Game Hunters of North America. The other Magellan I radiocarbon date comes from the Palli Aike Cave and is about 6700 B.C. This date seems too late for such a correlation as we have been describing. It is, of

course, possible that it is the correct one, and it is also possible that both dates are valid and that they represent the early and late ends of the time range for the Magellan I phase; however, these two possibilities seem unlikely, and I am inclined to accept the earlier dating of Magellan I.[77]

Several thousand miles north of the Strait of Magellan is the site of El Inga in Ecuador where another early fish-tailed projectile point complex has been found.[78] The actual location is in the highlands a short distance east of the city of Quito. The setting is an Andean valley at an elevation of over 8000 feet (2600 m.) above sea level. Today the valley has a coarse grass and shrub cover, but in Pleistocene times it must have had a more verdant vegetation suitable for the grazing of large herbivores.

El Inga is on a small promontory. The depth of the site occupational debris is shallow, being only some 18 inches (45 cm.) at the deepest points, and this refuse zone rests on an underlying sterile zone of volcanic origin. Careful metrical excavation revealed a cultural stratigraphy in which three sequent phases have been distinguished. R. E. Bell, one of the excavators of El Inga, defines his earliest phase, the El Inga I, as being characterized by fish-tailed points very similar to those of the early Strait of Magellan culture (Fig. 2-15). If the El Inga fish tails show anything, it is a more pronounced fluting of the stem than the Fell's Cave points, a mode which brings them somewhat closer to the norm of the North American Clovis-derived forms. El Inga I points also have basal-edge grinding, another Clovis-Folsom-Cumberland characteristic. El Inga I is further linked to Magellan I by a particular type of large plano-convex scraper. Other El Inga I items are bifacially flaked knives, various flake and blade scrapers, and simple angle burins (Fig. 2-16).

The radiocarbon dates from El Inga—on charcoal samples—come from various depths and locations in the site. The earliest one from a deep provenience, is approximately 7000 B.C.[79] This would conform to the later of the two Magellan I dates, and, as in that case, it may be valid; however, I am inclined to think that it is too young. If we are to assume a relationship between the almost identical Magellan I and El Inga I projectile points,[80] and between these and the similar Clovis-derived points of North America, a date

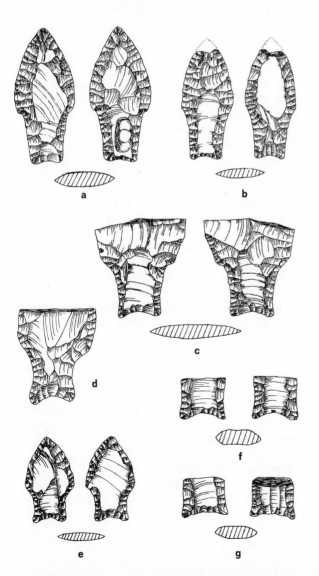

Figure 2-15. Magellan I or Fell's Cave fish-tail type points from El Inga, Ecuador. All of obsidian except *a*, which is chert. Length of *a*, 5 cm. (After Bell, 1965.)

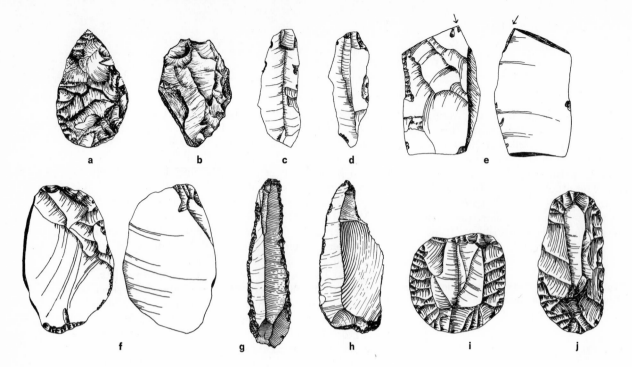

Figure 2-16. Various obsidian tools from El Inga, Ecuador. *a, b*: Biface knives. *c, d*: Flake knives. *e, f*: Flake scrapers. *g, h*: Bladelike scrapers. *i, j*: Plano-convex scrapers. Length of *a*, 4.6 cm. (After Bell, 1965.)

closer to 9000 B.C. would be more in keeping with the spread of this fish-tailed and fluted point form from north to south.

Although Magellan I and El Inga I are the only well-defined and stratigraphically isolated fish-tailed point complexes yet known from South America,[80a] there have been a number of scattered finds of such points. Some of these have already been alluded to in Volume One (pp. 66–68), and others can be added to the list. A pressure-flaked, fish-tailed point has been reported by Lanning from the Ecuadorian coastal complex of Carolina;[81] from Colombia, Reichel-Dolmatoff mentions and illustrates a fish-tailed Magellan-like point at Manizales in the Central Cordillera and another basally fluted stemmed point at Restrepo in the Western Cordillera;[82] Sanoja refers to "Folsomoid points" in north-central and southeast Venezuela;[83] and in Lower Central America fish-tailed and fluted points are described from Panama,[84] Costa Rica,[85] and Honduras.[86] To return to the main body of South America, there is a crude fish-tailed point in the early finds at the Eucaliptus Rock Shelter of eastern Brazil,[87] and others are also reported from the Brazilian Rio Claro region.[88]

Four fish-tailed points, said to be almost identical with those of Magellan I, are also known from southeastern Uruguay,[89] and this same point style is said to characterize the Toldos complex of the Rio Deseado caves in Patagonia.[90]

The Early Leaf-Shaped Projectile Point Complexes. I have used the qualifying term "early" here because in Volume One (p. 67) it was my suggestion that many of the leaf-shaped point complexes of South America—El Jobo, Chivateros II, Lauricocha II, Ayampitín, and others—were closely related and contemporaneous. I would now modify that opinion by saying that while such points are probably related in the sense of a continuity of a basic form over a long period of time, they are not all contemporaneous. Instead it now seems likely that there is a longer, narrower, heavier variety of the leaf shape which is earlier and which we have included here with the Old South American Hunting tradition while admitting that its appearance marks the beginning of a trend away from that tradition. These elongated leaf-shaped points precede the broader, willow-leaf shape that is a marker for the succeeding Andean Hunting-Collecting tradition and a somewhat later chronological horizon.[91]

What might be taken as the type specimen of the early, elongated leaf-shaped point is the El Jobo form. El Jobo points are found in northwest-

Figure 2-17. El Jobo points. Length of point at *left,* 9 cm. (After Rouse and Cruxent, 1963; courtesy Yale University Press.)

bifacial and flake, and unifacial scrapers. The sites are small, shallow, and badly eroded, and it is difficult to tell whether they were workshops, camps, or both. It seems reasonable to believe that El Jobo points were used for hunting, and a fragment of one was found in the Muaco mud deposits in general, but not specific, association with Pleistocene animal remains.

The fact that the El Jobo points follow the heavier Biface tradition tools in the Rio Pedregal terrace sequence suggests the possibility of a local development for this point form, perhaps in Venezuela or somewhere in the Andes; however, it is also a possibility that the early leaf-shaped point idea spread from North to Middle America via the Old Cordilleran tradition and Lerma points of Mexico (see Vol. I, pp. 51–55, 64–68).[93] An age of 8000 to 7000 B.C. is estimated for the El Jobo complex by means of comparisons to the Peruvian coastal sequence and radiocarbon dates to which we have already referred in connection with our discussions of the Flake and Biface traditions.[94]

Moving south of Venezuela, El Jobo-like points are reported from Ecuador, in the Manantial complex,[95] and they are also illustrated by collections from near Chordeleg in the southern Ecuadorian highlands.[96]

In the Central Peruvian coastal sequence, the Chivateros II long, keeled, and bipointed projectile points (Fig. 2-18) have their closest parallels in El Jobo points, although the Peruvian specimens do not seem to have been made by

ern Venezuela in the same Rio Pedregal terrace sequence that we have discussed in relation to the Chopper and Biface traditions. El Jobo complex artifacts are found, however, on the river terrace just below and younger than that of the Las Lagunas complex, which we described as a part of the Biface tradition. El Jobo points (Fig. 2-17) are generally made of quartzite, are elongated leaf-shape in outline, and lenticular in cross section. The basal end of the point is usually rounded, although it may be flat or even slightly concave.[92] Length varies from 5 to 10 centimeters. According to Cruxent and Rouse, El Jobo points were made from flakes on which both surfaces had been completely chipped. The edges were finely retouched, and this sometimes resulted in a serrated effect. Judging from their appearance, pressure flaking as well as percussion flaking were employed in the manufacture of some of them. Occasional El Jobo points also exhibit basal edge-grinding in a manner similar to the Magellan I-El Inga I fish-tailed points. Artifacts associated with El Jobo points on the terrace sites include knives, both

Figure 2-18. A Chivateros II chipped stone point. Length, 6 cm. (Drawn from Patterson, 1966.)

pressure flaking. A Pampilla complex is also defined from this region and placed chronologically as immediately after Chivateros II. Its projectile points are thinner and more finely chipped—although still percussion-made—than those of Chivateros II. Lanning dates both Chivateros II and Pampilla to the millennium between 8000 and 7000 B.C., the period at which the Pleistocene climate of the Peruvian coast was just beginning to dry.[97] It is this dating, based on the Cerro Chivateros stratigraphy, that is then extended to El Jobo as we have noted.

Besides the Peruvian coastal early leaf-shaped point complexes, there are a number of discoveries in the Peruvian and South Andean highlands that appear to be affiliated. One problem, however, is that many of these highland leaf-shaped point sites have multiple occupations, and it is difficult to separate the earlier leaf-shaped point phases from those of the willow-leaf point or Ayampitín-like horizon. One of the best-known sites is Lauricocha, in the Upper Marañón drainage. This, fortunately, was a stratified site and can be examined in its discrete levels of occupation. Lauricocha, or the Lauricocha zone of sites, is a series of caves which were occupied by man soon after the last glacial retreat.[98] Today, these caves are situated well above the active river channels of the Rio Lauricocha and the remnant of a glacial lake. Their cultural refuse contains numerous flint artifacts and debris and animal bone refuse, including deer and the South American camelids. No essential change in the way of life is reflected in the stratigraphic sequence, except in the final phases of occupation when pottery appears; and even at this juncture it would seem that the users of the caves were still exploiting them as summer hunting stations or camps. Augusto Cardich, the excavator, defines several occupational phases. Lauricocha I, the earliest, has an early radiocarbon date of about 7500 B.C. Lauricocha I projectile points are predominantly stemless, with a narrow triangulate outline (Fig. 2-19, *left, center*) that differs only slightly from the Chivateros II long, narrow leaf shape. Like El Jobo, but unlike Chivateros II, the Lauricocha I points are pressure-flaked. There are also some crudely chipped long and truly leaf-shaped points in the Lauricocha I collections together with a few diamond-shaped or vaguely stemmed points. The complex

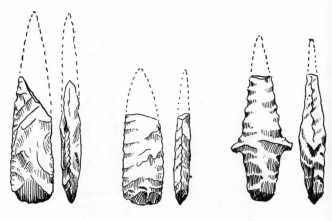

Figure 2-19. Lauricocha I projectile points. Length of point at *left,* 6.4 cm. (After Cardich, 1964.)

further contains some unifacial points and a number of flake scrapers. In my opinion, Lauricocha I represents a variant of the El Jobo–Chivateros II kind of development, but it probably lasts later in time, as is suggested by the triangulate outline of some of the points and by the stemmed diamond forms of others (Fig. 2-19, *right*). This would accord with Cardich's estimate, for he dates the phase from 8000 to 6000 B.C. Thus I think we can further visualize the Lauricocha I complex as being transitional between the Old South American Hunting tradition and the later Andean Hunting-Collecting tradition as represented by Lauricocha II.[99]

Before leaving Lauricocha we should note that a series of burials were found in Lauricocha I strata. Flint flakes, occasional chipped-stone artifacts, and bone and turquoise beads were placed with the dead.[100] The skeletons from these burials are referred to in the next chapter in a discussion of the early physical types found in Peru (p. 90); however, it can be noted here that they are of dolichocephalic head form and thus consistent with those other few cranial indexes we have for early man in South America.

Other clues to early leaf-shaped point complexes or assemblages are seen at Quishqui Puncu in the Callejón de Huaylas.[101] This site appears to have been a camp, workshop, and possibly a butchering station. According to Lynch, a square-based lanceolate point is the earliest point type at the site; however, Quishqui Puncu also has an occupation that lasts on into later horizons, and most of the points there are willow-leaf forms like those of Lauricocha II. Another Peruvian highland complex that seems to parallel the full Lauricocha I and II development is the Junín of the Mantaro drainage, well to the south of both the Callejón de Huaylas and the Upper Marañón.[102]

In northern Chile, Lanning has isolated a Talabre 5 subphase of his Talabre series, and this subphase is characterized by spear points and long, percussion-chipped leaf-shaped projectiles in much the same way that Chivateros II is so differentiated.[103] Another complex that appears to fit on this time level is the Fundaciones of the Chilean Salar de Atacama. Fundaciones projectile points are long leaf shapes or long lanceolates with incurved bases.[104] There is a strong suggestion that both Talabre 5 and Fundaciones represent a development out of the presumably earlier Biface tradition complexes of these same regions. Still a third north Chilean complex that may fall in this early leaf-shaped point bracket is the Tulan of the Salar de Atacama region; however with Tulan the picture is complicated by continuities onward and into the later willow-leaf point horizon.[105]

Northwestern Argentina also has indications of early leaf-shaped point complexes. Saladillo, in the Salinas Grandes region of Jujuy, would appear to be transitional from the Biface tradition into an early leaf-shaped point development;[106] and the same observation may be made with reference to Totoral, a complex found in La Rioja and Catamarca.[107]

To return to the Strait of Magellan and the long sequence of the Palli Aike and Fell's Caves, we have an interesting hint of the early leaf-shaped point horizon in the Magellan II phase. There are no radiocarbon dates for Magellan II, but the cave refuse of this phase, in which the sloth and native horse had given way to a modern fauna, suggests there was an environmental change from Magellan I times. Bird found no chipped-stone points at all, only bone projectiles;[108] but in later operations Emperaire and associates encountered what were described as "long points" of stone.[109] Such points—or point—were obviously not the distinctive Magellan fish-tailed type, and the de-

scription sounds more like those of elongated leaf-shaped form.[110] This point could possibly pertain to the early elongated leaf-shaped point horizon, but the evidence is extremely slight.

In the east, the Solano points of the Patagonian lowlands may pertain to the early leaf-shaped point group. The assemblage in question comes from the second highest terrace in the marine terrace sequence at Caleta Olivia.[111]

North of Patagonia in eastern South America occasional leaf-shaped points have been found—as in the State of Paraná, Brazil where T. O. Miller describes one from his early Santa Rosa phase of the East Brazilian Upland tradition and where Conceição de M. C. Becker illustrates some from collections of various point types.[112] It is also, however, possible that some or all of these particular leaf-shaped points are later than the time horizon with which we are here concerned. Thus they may link up with the later willow-leaf points of the Andean Hunting-Collecting tradition, which we will describe further on.[113]

Summary. In our ordering of the evidence for an Old South American Hunting tradition we have said that the early fish-tailed point complexes probably date to the millennium between 9000 and 8000 B.C. and those of the early leaf-shaped points to the millennium after this—in effect, to the period of the last major glacial advance and the immediate early post-glacial era. Neither this absolute nor relative dating is fully secure, but I prefer this interpretation of the evidence and offer the following as a schematic reconstruction of the events of those times.

In the millennium between 10,000 and 9000 B.C. the Biface tradition was the dominant technological tradition in Cordilleran South America. It was at this time, however, that nomadic hunters, coming from North America, brought the first bifacial *projectile point* technology into Andean South America in the form of a fish-tailed semi-fluted point. These new immigrants were specialized hunters of herd animals who had developed this pattern of life on the North American High Plains, and they stood in the ancient line of an Old World Levallois-Mousterian technology that had been brought to this hemisphere several thousands of years before. Their mode of life was in contrast to that of the older South American residents of the Biface tradition. In the pursuit of land game they were more mobile and more nomadic. Quite rapidly, they pushed to the southern end of the South American continent where we have a date for their presence by 8700 B.C. There is also an even earlier clue to their movements in the Central Chilean Tagua Tagua finds referred to at the beginning of this chapter. The Tagua Tagua artifacts—lamellar flakes, prepared cores, and bone flakers—suggest a technology in the Levallois-Mousterian tradition and one consistent with the preparation of bifacial points, even though none was found at this camp site where the remains of mastodon and other large animals were encountered along with these artifacts, and dated by radiocarbon to 9400 B.C.[114]

In their migrations southward it is unlikely that these new hunting peoples had any serious "displacing" effects on the old local populations; South America was too thinly populated at this time, and, moreover, the new arrivals were exploiting a series of environmental niches somewhat different from that of the peoples of the Biface technology. I would suggest, further, that the new projectile point technology of the immigrants had a stimulative effect on the Biface stone industries and that the first results of this were the hunting-adapted, elongated leaf-shaped projectile points of El Jobo, Chivateros II, and related complexes. This adoption of the leaf-shaped form could have been by analogy with, and in a sense a continuity out of, the old elongated bifacial tools—a thinning and shaping of these to produce spears and projectiles. So from this point of view, there is a local evolution of technology, but one given impetus and direction by diffused or introduced innovation.

An alternative hypothesis to this would be to see the early leaf-shaped points as a purely South American development out of the antecedent Biface tradition. The Magellan fish-tail point could then have been a later modification of the simpler leaf-shaped form or, perhaps, a later introduction from North America.

The Andean Hunting-Collecting Tradition

Some Definitions and Criteria. According to the thesis of this presentation, the Andean Hunting-Collecting way of life developed from the Old South American Hunting tradition somewhere in the central or south Andes, and we have already suggested that some of the trends toward this development were in evidence during the previous early leaf-shaped point horizon of the parent tradition. With the Andean Hunting-Collecting tradition this shift to high-altitude hunting of a modern fauna seems to have been complete. Thus, in a very definite sense, the Andean Hunting-Collecting tradition marks, for much of the Andean area, one of those major adaptive cultural changes of the New World that occurred in the early Post-Pleistocene millennia. It was characterized by a regional "settling in" and specialized subsistence exploitation of particular environments. It is comparable in this regard to such North American traditions as the Desert and the Eastern Archaic (Vol. I, pp. 55–64) ;[115] and, in a broader developmental sense, it is also like these North American traditions in being a part of a New World Archaic stage (see also Vol. I, p. 477). One of the characteristic features of such cultural traditions is a pattern of transhumance subsistence which is defined as, "the practice of changing abode in a regular and traditionally recognized way, as natural food crops are followed."[116] As will be seen further on, such a pattern was highly likely for many of the Andean Hunting-Collecting cultures.

The most characteristic projectile point style of the Andean Hunting-Collecting tradition is the willow-leaf shape. This basic shape is, of course, subject to various modifications, but it is, essentially, a broad, foliate form with a round-pointed to almost flat base. In the latter mode the specimens appear more triangular than leaf-shaped, but in the same complexes there is a very gentle gradation from one outline to the other. Lynch's description of the Andean willow leafs may be repeated:

Examples have been found made on many different kinds of stone, but they nearly always exhibit well-controlled flaking (and) are finished to the same general form and weight. Even the variations in the curvature of the base do not affect the overall proportions of the artifact as much as one might expect. In spite of the expert workmanship, they are usually rather thick in cross-section and frequently there are distinctive medial ridges resulting from collateral flaking; others are smoothly transverse-flaked on one or both sides, and have a lenticular cross-section. There are a few examples with serrated edges known, and a few cases of edge-grinding (basal end) have been identified...[117]

Lynch goes on to give size averages for the point as about 4 to 6 centimeters long, 1.5 to 2.0 centimeters wide, and 0.5 to 1.0 centimeter thick.

The other class of projectile point that is associated with some Andean Hunting-Collecting tradition complexes is the stemmed form. This is not so uniform in shape as the willow leafs and includes a number of types; it is usually of about the same general size as the willow-leaf points but differs in outline, which is slightly shouldered or stemmed.

Now besides these two principal classes of points that are characteristic of the earlier cultures of the Andean Hunting-Collecting tradition, there are a series of substantially smaller points that are marker types for the later cultures of the tradition. These too are of leaf-shaped, shouldered, and some other forms; we will describe them later.

All of the Andean Hunting-Collecting complexes have other chipped stone tools which vary somewhat as to place and time, and, significantly, many of them are distinguished by grinding and mortar stones suggestive of the preparation of seed and other food plants.

The sites of this tradition are of both cave and open varieties. They are usually small in area, reflecting small population bands and seasonal occupance.

The distribution of the Andean Hunting-Collecting complexes is in the Andes and along the Pacific Coast, from Ecuador to the south Andes. In addition, there are complexes in far southern South America and diagnostic projectile point types reported from Patagonia and the Argentine pampas. There are also some scattered clues to the tradition in the north Andes in Colombia and Venezuela.

The time range of the tradition is from about 7000 B.C. upward. A rather clear horizon can be defined between 6000 and 4000 B.C. by the large willow-leaf points. In some regions, particularly coastal ones, the Andean Hunting-Collecting tradition is replaced after 4000 B.C. by other traditions; but in the uplands it persists until much

later times. In its later persistence it is characterized by the smaller types of projectile points.

The Willow-Leaf Projectile Point Complexes. In presenting the foregoing hypothesis, we will begin with the Lauricocha cave sites, which, as mentioned in the foregoing section, are located on the Rio Lauricocha in the vicinity of Huánuco, Peru. The Lauricocha I complex was interpreted as representing a transition between the Old South American Hunting tradition and the Andean Hunting-Collecting tradition, and as dating to about 8000 to 6000 B.C. The Lauricocha II phase, with which we are now concerned, is dated from about 6000 to 4000 B.C.,[118] a period that corresponds to the horizon of the willow-leaf points. The Lauricocha II points are of this type, carefully flaked willow leafs of both the round-based and flat-based or triangular varieties (Fig. 2-20). The Lauricocha II tool kit also includes oval and asymmetrical bifaced knives, small thumbnail scrapers of a type well suited to hide dressing, and bone flakers, awls, and points. The

Figure 2-20. Lauricocha II projectile points. Length of point at *left,* 5 cm. (After Cardich, 1964.)

animal bones in the refuse are of the same species as those represented in the Lauricocha I levels of the caves: deer, llama, vicuña, and guanaco.

On the face of the evidence from Lauricocha alone, there seems little to justify a change in major cultural tradition between Lauricocha I and II; however, there are reasons for believing

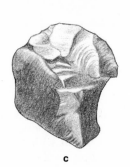

a b c d

Figure 2-21. Arenal chipped stone artifacts, Central Coast of Peru. *a, b*: Stemmed points (*a* is asymmetrically stemmed). *c*: Scraper. *d*: Pointed tool or perforator. Length of *a*, 5.6 cm. (Drawn from Lanning, 1963.)

that such a change was going on and that a new life-way had become well established by Lauricocha II times. On the Peruvian coast the "lomas culture" sites—camp locations on the low hills back from the shore that have a winter fog-vegetation—showed projectile points similar to those of Lauricocha I and Lauricocha II and the significant additions of milling and grinding stones suitable for seed and plant-food grinding. What is suggested here, following inferences drawn by both Lanning and Lynch,[119] is that these "lomas" complexes of the Central Coast of Peru are, in effect, the winter or fog-season settlements of the same peoples who also lived in the high-altitude hunting camps, such as the ones at Lauricocha, in the summertime.

In Arenal, the earliest of these coastal "lomas" phases, the milling stones are relatively rare. The site debris is shallow but contains a fair amount of wood and plant debris (preserved on the rainless Peruvian coast), land snails, a few seashells, fish and bird bones, some mammal bones, and cucurbit or squash rinds. The projectile points for this phase are not the leaf-shapes, but the diamond-shaped and vaguely stemmed (Fig. 2-21) forms that characterize Lauricocha I, and Lanning gives a correlation of Arenal with Lauricocha I and assigns it a date of about 6500 to 6000 B.C.[120] In the succeeding Luz and Canario phases of the "lomas" cultures, milling stones, mortars, pestles, and shaped and unshaped manos all appeared in substantial numbers. In chipped stone these phases bear close resemblances to Lauricocha II, especially Canario which features numerous willow-

leaf projectile points (Fig. 2-22). The Canario phase closes at about 4200 B.C.[121] It is the last of the Andean Hunting-Collecting tradition cultures of the coast, for the succeeding Corbina and Encanto phases mark a new adaptation, one that we are calling the Pacific Littoral tradition. In the highlands, however, the Lauricocha III phase, which can be dated from 4000 B.C. until the introduction of pottery at about 1800 B.C., represents the terminal continuation of the Andean Hunting-Collecting tradition.

But to continue with our survey of the willow-leaf point complexes of the 6000 to 4000 B.C. horizon, we return to the highlands. A short distance south of Lauricocha are the Ranracancha rock shelters[122] and the open terrace site of Ambo.[123] The Ranracancha deposits are stratified, with Lauricocha II and III levels underlying, and separated by a sterile soil zone from, an upper stratum with pottery. At Ambo, which was a workshop with available quartzite nearby for making implements, the predominant point form was the

Figure 2-22. Canario phase points. All from Chilca Valley. Not all to same scale: *a* is 5.7 cm. long; *b* and *c*, about 3.5 cm.; and *d*, 4.5 cm. (Courtesy Frederic Engel.)

a b c d

Lauricocha II willow leaf. To the north and west, in the Callejón de Huaylas, the previously mentioned Quishqui Puncu site has a substantial Lauricocha II and III occupation.[124] It has already been noted that well to the south of Lauricocha the Junín complex of the Mantaro Valley parallels both Lauricocha I and II in its development,[125] and the Callavallauri complex from the same valley can be placed in the small leaf-shaped and diamond-shaped projectile point bracket of Lauricocha III.[126] Still farther south, in the southern Sierra regions of Peru, around Moquegua and Arequipa, projectile point sequences seem to follow a similar course, with phases of the Toquepala sequence spanning the Lauricocha I through III range.[127] The later points of this sequence, small bi-points or diamond shapes and small leaf shapes, are also found in the late South Coast and Far South Coast complexes of Peru, such as Casavilca,[128] where an Andean Hunting-Collecting mode of life appears to have persisted longer than it did in the coastal regions to the north. Willow-leaf points are also well represented at sites on the Bolivian Altiplano. The best-known of such sites is the series of old beach terraces between La Paz and Oruro called Viscachani.[129] The leaf-shaped points that are found here are quite similar to those of Lauricocha II and the other willow-leaf horizon sites of the highlands, but there are also others that resemble the smaller points of Lauricocha III, Canario, and other complexes that date after 4000 B.C.

In this rapid survey of the willow-leaf point horizon we have been continuing the story beyond the 4000 B.C. date line in our mention of Lauricocha III and other complexes of what Lynch has called the "small point horizon."[130] This refers to the later small projectile points mentioned in our introductory definitions of the Andean Hunting-Collecting tradition. Lynch defines this horizon as being characterized by four principal point types: small leaf shapes, small diamond shapes or stemless-shouldered forms, bi-points, and small triangular forms with varying basal treatments. These points are between 2.5 and 3.2 centimeters in length and weigh only one-fourth or one-fifth as much as the large willow leafs of the preceding "willow-leaf horizon."

In considering this later "small point horizon," other questions arise concerning this continuation of the Andean Hunting-Collecting tradition in the highlands. Presumably, with the establishment of the Pacific Littoral tradition and the restriction of coastal population to locations near the shore after 4000 B.C., the transhumance of the earlier Hunting-Collecting tradition cultures came to an end. Thus, after this date, the highland populations must have remained in upland niches and modified their livelihood accordingly. Certainly by the end of preceramic times, or about 2000 B.C., there were sedentary communities at some places in the Peruvian Andes, communities in which the hunting mode of life had been changed to an agricultural one (see, for example, the Mito phase, this volume, pp. 102–104). Such changes would carry us beyond the definitions of our Andean Hunting-Collecting tradition; however, until we know more about these late preceramic cultures of the highlands, it is difficult to classify them as to traditional affiliation.

South of Peru, in the Chilean and Argentinian Andes, many sites have been reported that fall easily into the willow-leaf and small point horizons of the Andean Hunting-Collecting tradition. We have already mentioned the Chilean sites in the Salar de Atacama basin; both the Biface tradition (Loma Negra) and early leaf-shaped point (Tulan) complexes have been found there. The Tulan complex, as we have said, may embrace both the early leaf shapes and the willow-leaf points. The Puripica complex is known from sites that are situated on stream channels that enter the salar at its northeast corner. There are willow-leaf points, knives, and pointed implements on these sites, together with rough grinding stones; circular house foundations of dry stone masonry are also found on some of them. Two other complexes appear to be later; these are the Cebollar and the Tambillo, which feature small points. Those of the Cebollar sites, which are at the north end of the basin, are small triangulars with incurved bases. The Tambillo sites, on the eastern edge of the salar, have small triangular, leaf-shaped, and "winged" or slightly shouldered lozenge-form points. Stone mortars and pestles are also a part of this complex.[131] At the nearby Salar de San Martín, Barfield has identified both Puripica and Cebollar sites also. At one of the Puripica locations there are three rough, dry stone masonry foundations laid up of tufa blocks. The largest of the three buildings measures 22 feet (7 m.) in length and has three inter-connecting rooms within it. Significantly, the Puripica sites are situated 40 feet above the present floor of the salar, whereas the Cebollar sites are on the immediate margins of the salt flats. Not far from these Chilean sites, in southwestern Bolivia, are two groups of sites also explored by Barfield. These are located around the Lagunas Colorado and Hedionda. Puripica sites of the willow-leaf horizon occur in each group; but Cebollar and Tambillo sites are more common.[132] A little to the north of the Salar de Atacama, in the Calama oasis of the Rio Loa, Lanning tentatively defines a Chíuchíu complex of "foliate" points that appears to span both the willow-leaf and small point horizons;[133] and still farther north, in the Salares de Soronal and Huasco, back of Iquique, are similar sites.[134] All of these Chilean upland sites, both early and late, relate to the preceramic coastal cultures as defined by Bird at Quiani, Pichalo, and Taltal.[135] Lautaro Nuñez makes the suggestion that the highland hunters came down from the drying lake basins of the hills during the Altithermal and established a new kind of life along the sea coast,[136] and the projectile point evidence seems to bear this out. Quiani I, which is believed to date as early as 4200 to 4000 B.C., shows similarities to the large willow-leaf point horizon; and this would correspond, of course, to late Canario of the Peruvian coast. Quiani II points, on the other hand, resemble the late preceramic small-stemmed points of the Far South Coast of Peru.[137] But here in Chile, as in Peru, these late preceramic cultures are a part of the Pacific Littoral tradition.

In northwestern Argentina the willow-leaf points are found all through the highland valleys. Cigliano reports Ayampitín-like points from Jujuy and from near the Ampajango Biface tradition sites in Catamarca.[138] This style of point has also shown up in surface collections from various locations in the Provinces of La Rioja, Mendoza, Santiago del Estero, Córdoba, and San Luis;[139] and it has been found recently in a deep cave stratigraphy in San Juan.[140] There can be little doubt that the Andean Hunting-Collecting tradition was well established in these regions during the period of the willow-leaf point horizon. Our firmest data on the tradition come from sites in Córdoba and San Luis where the Ayampitín point was first de-

scribed and where its cultural contexts have been placed stratigraphically and dated by radiocarbon. The most important of these sites is Intihuasi Cave in northern San Luis, and the findings from this cave are supported by others from Ayampitín proper and Ongamira in northern Córdoba.

The sierras of San Luis and Córdoba are the southeasternmost outliers of the Andean chain in Argentina. They form a semi-isolated mountainous block that juts out toward the low pampean country to the east and south. They are lower in elevation than the main body of the cordillera in northwestern Argentina and consist of ranges of small mountains and hills and little valleys. The country is today semi-arid although there is a summer rainy season that produces a green grass cover and helps sustain a xerophytic vegetation with such scrub trees as the algarroba. In the past and until relatively recent historic times deer and guanaco roamed these regions, and the bones of such animals are found in the archaeological sites. Maize can be grown here when there is a good wet season, but conditions are by no means at an optimum for farming. In the late pre-Columbian past, the San Luis–Córdoba highlands were definitely marginal to the established farmers of the valleys to the north and west, and there is every reason to believe that a hunting-collecting subsistence lasted into relatively late times here and, in fact, was only partially replaced by the spread of Andean farming patterns. It is in this setting that the Intihuasi Cave is located, in a small valley some 70 kilometers northeast of the provincial capital of San Luis. The Intihuasi Cave is in one face of a small volcanic hill or "dome." Actually, it is a shallow cave or rock-shelter with a high outer "vestibule" and two inner, low-ceilinged caverns. Excavation revealed an average depth of about 1 meter of debris overlying sterile sedimentary beds. The uppermost crust of the debris was of recent origin and of no archaeological consequence, but the bulk of the debris was filled with traces of human habitation—old hearths, decayed organic material, kitchen refuse, and artifacts in a matrix of loess. Radiocarbon determinations on two charred animal bones from the very bottom of this thick layer of cultural refuse give dates of approximately 6000 B.C. This can be taken as the time of first occupancy of the cave. The immediately underlying sterile bed is a

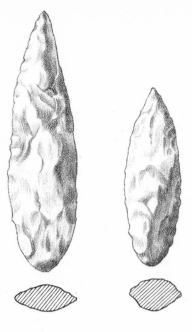

Figure 2-23. Two points of the Ayampitín type from Intihuasi Cave, phase IV. Longer is about 7 cm. in length. (Redrawn from González, 1960.)

loessial deposit of apparent Anathermal or Boreal age; and the period of the occupation, which was of considerable duration, is placed in the Climatic Optimum (Altithermal, Atlantic) and later climatic sub-stages.[141]

A. R. González defines his earliest cultural phase of the cave, the Intihuasi IV,[142] as possessing almond-shaped or willow-leaf points as the diagnostic projectile form (Fig. 2-23). Other chipped

stone implements are large end- and side-scrapers, cores, and flakes or blades retouched for use as knives. These are found with irregular milling stones and manos, occasional ground-stone simple ornaments, and bone awls. González considers the question of the degree of sedentism represented by this occupation and concludes that it is impossible to say that there was a year-round residence in the cave. He suggests the possibility of seasonal rounds of such activities as hunting and the gathering of such edibles as algarroba fruit. There is evidence in the cave, however, for a continuity of occupation over a long time range as his succeeding Intihuasi III phase, or subphase, shows a considerable carry-over of artifact types, including projectile points (Fig. 2-24). But this phase notably features large and medium-sized triangular points with straight or convex bases. These latter points also continue into Intihuasi II (see p. 212) where they are found along with smaller triangular forms and throwing-stick hooks of stone and bone. What appear to be bone projectile points of a blunt-tipped type are also a part of Intihuasi II. This Intihuasi IV-III-II sequence offers us a detailed stratigraphic look at one regional development of the Andean Hunting-

Figure 2-24. Intihuasi III and II phase projectile points. *Top, left,* 5.7 cm. long. (Courtesy A. R. González; see also González 1960.)

Collecting tradition, and it is estimated to span the millennia from about 6000 B.C. until the advent of pottery in the Intihuasi phase.

Two sites in Córdoba are also prominent in the literature and should be mentioned in connection with Intihuasi. The first of these is the open camp-site of Ayampitín proper, where a refuse layer overlying a loess stratum contained willow-leaf points, flakes, cores, milling stones, and manos. This is, of course, the Ayampitín-type site.[143] The Ongamira Cave (see p. 213) in the Córdoba highlands is another. The early levels of the deep refuse in this cave (Ongamira IV and III) are believed to cross-date with Intihuasi II, while the later, pottery-bearing, levels (Ongamira II and I) similarly correspond to Intihuasi I.[144]

We can conclude our survey of the willow-leaf points of the Andean Hunting-Collecting tradition with a look at the far south of South America and the Argentine Plains. Phase III of Bird's Strait of Magellan sequence shows a tool and weapon kit of a guanaco-hunting economy.[145] The projectile points are mainly of the straight-based willow-leaf variety (Fig. 2-25). Most are relatively broad although there are some proportionately long and narrow specimens. They are nicely pressure-flaked, and they compare quite closely with the Ayampitín points of the two lowest levels of the Intihuasi Cave.[146] Their predominantly triangular outline, however, suggests Intihuasi III rather than the earlier IV, and so a dating at about 4000 B.C. seems preferable to an earlier placement. There are end- and side-scrapers, and grooved bola stones, and two points with broad straight stems appear to anticipate the Magellan IV phase. This Magellan IV phase is considered as marking the beginning of the Paraná-Pampean tradition in the region; and, looked at from this point of view, Magellan III can be considered a transitional step from the older Andean Hunting-Collecting tradition in this direction of a plains-adapted hunting culture.

There is another archaeological complex in the Strait regions, that of Englefield Island,[147] which seems to show a quite different adaptive trend developing out of Andean Hunting-Collecting beginnings. Englefield Island is a small islet in the Bay or Sea of Otway. This almost entirely enclosed body of water lies just above the Peninsula of Brunswick. The area is that of the Chilean

Archipelago of numerous islands and a fjordlike coast. The artifacts of the site reveal a marine-adapted economy, one in which sea mammal hunting undoubtedly played an important part. The inhabitants had made and used unilateral-barbed harpoons of various types and bone projectile points. Land-hunting must also have been of some importance as bola stones are in the complex, and there is a rich complement of chipped flint and obsidian work. Among the latter are bifacially flaked willow leafs, similar in outline to those of Ayampitín and to the more triangulate Magellan III forms. There are also long narrow leaf shapes,

Figure 2-25. Projectile points of Magellan Period III. Longest point, *second row, right*, about 12 cm. long. (Courtesy American Museum of Natural History; see also Bird, 1938.)

and one long lanceolate blade or point with a tapered stem is shown. There are two radiocarbon dates for Englefield and these fall at about 7200 and 6500 B.C., with a 1500-year margin of error for each. These dates seem excessively early in view of the presence at Englefield of the grooved bola stones plus, moreover, a well-shaped, large ground-stone celt or ax. The interpretation of land-hunters in process of adaptation to a marine-hunting subsistence still stands, and seems quite reasonable; however, a dating after 4000 B.C.—and perhaps well after this—would fit better with what we know of the archaeology of the area. We will return to Englefield later, when we take up the question of the origins of the Fuegian tradition.

The Stemmed Projectile Point Complexes. In our definitions of the Andean Hunting-Collecting tradition we mentioned two principal styles of projectile points as occurring early within the tradition, the willow-leafed form and the stemmed form. We have reviewed the evidence and distributions of the former; let us turn now to the stemmed point complexes.

Long, lanceolate, stemmed points would appear to be as early as the leaf-shapes. Diamond points with vague shoulders and contracting stems—a point form that could indeed be a modification of a leaf-shape—are typical of the Peruvian coastal Arenal phase. This Arenal phase, to refer back a few pages, was a coastal lomas complex which we have considered as a seasonal manifestation of one of the early Andean Hunting-Collecting tradition cultures. Milling stones and other clues to a plant-gathering subsistence were found in the Arenal sites, and these lomas stations have been interpreted as complements to the highland hunting camps for the same societies living under a pattern of transhumance. Besides the vaguely stemmed, diamond-shaped points, another Arenal type is a single-shouldered form. Arenal is dated from 6500 to 6000 B.C., and is succeeded in the lomas localities of the Peruvian Central Coast by the Luz (6000–5500 B.C.,) and Canario (5500–4200 B.C.) phases.[148] We have already noted the presence of the typical willow-leafs in these phases, particularly the later Canario; however, the major point-type in Luz is a very definitely stemmed style known as the "Paiján Point" (Fig. 2-26). This Paiján Point

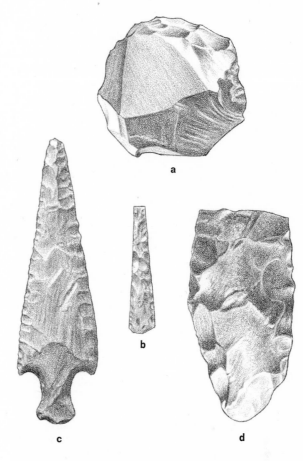

Figure 2-26. Luz chipped-stone artifacts, Central Coast of Peru. *a*: Scraper. *b*: Awl. *c*: Stemmed or Paiján point. *d*: Percussion-flaked blade fragment. Length of *c*, 10 cm. (Drawn from Lanning, 1963.)

is named after a complex found on the surface of old camp sites on the desert in the North Coast of Peru.[149] It is a large point with a long triangular blade and a long stem with an expanded basal end. After this Arenal and Luz appearance of stemmed points on the Peruvian coast they do not occur there again until we come to the relatively late stemmed points of the general small point horizon.

One of the best documented occurrences of the early stemmed points is at the El Inga site in highland Ecuador. These occur in both the El Inga II and III phases as these are defined by

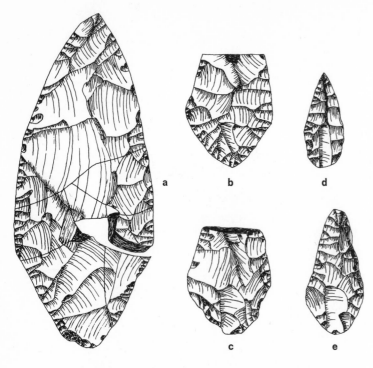

Figure 2-27. Ovoid or leaf-shaped points from El Inga, Ecuador. All of obsidian except *d*, which is basalt. Length of *a*, 12.5 cm. (After Bell, 1965.)

R. E. Bell.[150] El Inga II is actually a mixture of willow-leaf points and a broad-stemmed type. The leaf-shaped points are large to medium in size and distinctly ovoid or leaf-shaped (Fig. 2-27). They are made of obsidian but are otherwise very similar to the Lauricocha II or Ayampitín type.[151] The broad-stemmed type (Fig. 2-28, *c-e*) is also of obsidian or basalt. They average about 8 centi-

Figure 2-28. Stemmed points from El Inga, Ecuador. All of obsidian. Length of *a*, 5 cm. (After Bell, 1965.)

meters in length and are, proportionately, rather broad. The blade form is either triangular or ovoid-triangular. Some of the examples shown have a very slight incurvature of the base of the stem and just a suggestion of basal channeling or fluting.[152] This morphology is reminiscent, of course, of the earlier El Inga I fluted fish-tail points from the same site, and a development of the broad-stemmed type from the fish-tailed is a reasonable possibility. In this connection, the trait of basal-edge grinding occurs on most of the broad-stemmed points, and this, it will be recalled, is an Old South American Hunting tradition mode. As the name implies, the stem process on these points is relatively broad, and it tapers slightly to a flat base. The shoulders of the point are readily visible but not cleanly or squarely defined.

The El Inga III points are also stemmed. These are of about the same length as the broad-stemmed type, but they tend to be proportionately narrower (Fig. 2-28, *a, b*). They are also made of obsidian. The stems are narrow and tapering or contracting to a pointed or flat base. The shoulders are sharply and squarely defined. It is also possible that a few smaller, contracted stemmed and barbed points from El Inga belong to this late phase and are a variant of the contracted-stemmed type. Viewed developmentally, there is a likely local evolutionary series from the broad-stemmed form of El Inga II to the smaller points and the contracting-stemmed form of El Inga III.[153]

In the interpretation suggested here, the El Inga sequence is divided between the earlier El Inga I Old South American Hunting tradition complex and the El Inga II and III Andean Hunting-

Collecting tradition complexes, with a developmental implication running through the sequence. This may approximate the true history of what happened although it is admittedly speculative. It would suggest two lines of development for the Andean Hunting-Collecting tradition. One of these would be in Peru, where the willow-leaf points developed from the earlier elongated leaf shapes; the other is represented by this El Inga Ecuadorian sequence where stemmed types appear as an outgrowth of the earlier fish-tailed point technology. Whether the stemmed Arenal and Luz phase points of Peru, to which we have briefly alluded, have anything to do with the Ecuadorian appearance of early stemmed types must be left an open question. We are also at a loss to say whether El Inga II and III were hunting stations related to a coastal-highland transhumance pattern similar to that postulated for coastal Peru. This is a possibility, and we will mention it when we have an introductory look at the Northwest South American Littoral tradition; but there is no real evidence for it. The El Inga II and III complexes, besides the projectile points that we have described, have tool kits that appear to be completely oriented toward game-hunting pursuits. Flake knives and scrapers and plano-convex scrapers are abundant in both. Both had burins, and El Inga III had concave scraper-burin cores. In brief, the tools look like weapons with which to kill game, knives and scrapers with which to dismember it and to prepare hides, and, possibly, gravers with which to work bone or to aid in the production of wooden adjuncts to the chipped stone.

Lanceolate stemmed points may also be early in Colombia. Reichel-Dolmatoff mentions a flint point found near El Espinal, in the Tolima district, in a layer of clay overlain by deep sands and volcanic ash.[154] The situation suggests some antiquity, but just how much can only be a guess. The point in question is finely flaked, bifacial, of elongated ovoid-triangular outline with a short, straight, flat-based stem. Apparently this is a fairly common type of point for the district. It bears some resemblances to the El Inga III stemmed points, although the example shown appears to be larger and better made. There is also some hint of the Paiján form, although the El Espinal point does not have the expanded basal-end. Other stemmed points have been found on the Bogotá Savanna.

This is a large intermontane plain in the central part of the Eastern Cordillera of Colombia. Formerly an old Pleistocene lake basin, it was a favorable habitat for large game and for hunters 10,000 or more years ago. In 1967 W. R. Hurt and T. Van der Hammen explored some rock shelters in the limestone cliffs of a small valley in the savanna region known as El Abra. The deposits in the shelters proved to be 3.00 meters deep, with artifacts found to a depth of 2.25 meters, or possibly more, below surface. Pottery was found very superficially in the shelters but only chipped stone artifacts at lower depths, and it was clear from the nature of the deeper sands and clays that they had been deposited in more humid times. No full analysis of either the excavations or the artifacts has been published so far, but the latter are said to include both percussion- and pressure-flaked implements—knives, drills, perforators, and some triangular points and some contracting-stemmed points. There have been a number of radiocarbon dates for the levels with these points, and these average about 7000 B.C.[155]

Early stemmed points are also known in the Venezuelan Rio Pedregal sequence. These are found on the lowest of the terrace levels—those lower and later than the terraces of the El Jobo early leaf-shaped point assemblages. The complex with which they are associated is known as the Las Casitas. The Las Casitas points are of only medium length—notably shorter than the El Jobo points. They have a triangular or ovoid-triangular blade and a contracting stem, and in outline they are quite similar to the El Inga III points.[156] Similar or identical points are also found at the site of Canaima (Fig. 2-29), in the Venezuelan State of Bolívar, which is savanna country in the southeastern part of the Republic. Rouse and Cruxent suggest a dating for Las Casitas and Canaima at about 5500 B.C.[157]

Stemmed points, of both contracting-stemmed and squared-base forms, also occur in Eastern Brazil, but they will be discussed further on when we consider the East Brazilian Upland tradition.

Summary. The Andean Hunting-Collecting tradition was a Post-Pleistocene phenomenon, established primarily in the Andean regions of South America after 7000 B.C. It was essentially a hunting economy, based on camelids

Figure 2-29. Points of the Canaima complex. These are very similar to those of the Las Casitas complex. Length of point at *upper left*, about 5 cm. (After Rouse and Cruxent, 1963; courtesy Yale University Press.)

and deer, but smaller game and plant collecting were elements in the economy as well. In some places, such as Peru, an argument can be made out for an upland hunting and lowland collecting pattern of seasonal transhumance; and it may be that such a practice was quite widespread. At about 5000 to 4000 B.C. those Andean Hunting-Collecting cultures that had extended into the Pacific coastal lowlands and onto the Patagonian and Pampean plains became transformed, respectively, into the Pacific Littoral and Paraná-Pampean tradition cultures. It is also probable that the Northwest South American Littoral tradition cultures had roots in the Andean Hunting-Collecting tradition. In certain Andean upland regions, however, the original hunting-collecting mode of existence still persisted for a time after 4000 B.C.

A willow-leaf-shaped point is the typical and diagnostic artifact of the Andean Hunting-Collecting tradition, particularly in the central and south Andes and spreading eastward and southward into the South American plains. Through time, there is a tendency for this willow-leaf point to become smaller in size and to be modified to, or replaced by, a variety of forms—bi-points, triangulars, and stemmed types, all of relatively small size. Manos and milling stones are also typical artifacts of the tradition in many sites.

In Peru, Ecuador, Colombia, Venezuela, and British Guiana some large stemmed points appear in contexts of the tradition at its very beginning. As this geographical listing would indicate, there seems to be a more northerly distribution of the early stemmed points than of the leaf shapes. Peru and Ecuador would appear to be a meeting ground or a zone of overlap between the two basic forms.

Some of the origins of the tradition—perhaps most of them—appear to lie in the antecedent Old South American Hunting tradition. It can be argued that the willow-leaf points are Andean developments of the earlier elongated leaf-shaped points; and it is possible that the stemmed points of the Andean Hunting-Collecting tradition also derive locally from the stemmed fish-tailed points of earlier times. The El Inga sequence of Ecuador tends to support this latter contention. It is, of course, also to be entertained, as an alternative hypothesis, that North American Old Cordilleran and Plano projectile point influences impinged upon the Andean Hunting-Collecting tradition. This could have happened, perhaps, as far back as 8000 to 7000 B.C., before opportunities for north-south movement along the Panamanian Isthmus became impeded by the conditions of the onset of the climatic optimum.

The East Brazilian Upland Tradition

The concept of an East Brazilian Upland tradition is a hypothesis that is admittedly a "lumping" or "catch-all" category to enable us to take a broad overview of a great many lithic assemblages that are known from the plateau or upland country of southeastern Brazil and parts of the adjoining lowlands of northern Uruguay, Paraguay, and Argentine Misiones. Undoubtedly, a number of discrete industries are represented in this category or tradition, and these lines of development are only now being traced out by archaeologists working in this vast territory. It is my opinion, however, that these industries will be found to be interrelated and that eventually we shall see their adaptive relationships to what is for the most part the semi-tropical tableland of eastern South America. For the moment, the most satisfactory generalizations that we can make are that the industries of what we are calling the East Brazilian Upland tradition are characterized by a flake technology and that most of the tools are unifacial. These include scrapers, various beaked forms, punches, and cutting edges. Bifacially chipped implements, including projectile points, are either absent or rare, although their occasional occurrences appear to be significant in establishing evidences of contact with Andean or southern South American plains industries. Additional items that appear in some East Brazilian Upland tradition contexts are bone projectile points and ground- or partially-ground-stone celts or axes.

As we have indicated elsewhere, the origins of such an East Brazilian Upland tradition most probably lie in an ancient Flake technological tradition (see pp. 34–38). The documentation for these origins is, of course, poor or non-existent, as the case for an antecedent Flake tool tradition is similarly in the realm of speculation; yet the widespread presence and apparently long-term persistence of many lithic assemblages of the general appearance of those described in the preceding paragraph are facts of the archaeology of eastern South America, and the hypotheses advanced seem the most plausible explanations to account for these phenomena. To be specific about the dating of such an East Brazilian Upland tradition is clearly impossible. If an ancient Flake tradition antedated 9000 or 10,000 B.C., as we have suggested elsewhere in this chapter, then the East Brazilian Upland tradition followed some time after this date. If the Early Catalán industry of northern Uruguay, which is without bifacially chipped tools, dates to about 9000 B.C. (see p. 36), it may represent a terminal complex of the old Flake tradition and, if so, then Late Catalán, Altoparaná, and a number of the early Brazilian highland complexes—all of which show bifacial forms or bifacial projectile points—could be taken to mark an inception of the later industries with a predominantly flake technology that we are considering as the East Brazilian Upland tradition. Let us very tentatively set the beginnings of the tradition at about 9000 B.C. and continue it forward in time so that it parallels the Old South American Hunting tradition and the Andean Hunting-Collecting tradition. Such an East Brazilian Upland tradition is defined as lasting until late prehistoric or even historic times in certain parts of the Brazilian hinterland.

The life pattern of the East Brazilian Upland tradition is difficult to assess from the artifactual and refuse record that has come down to us in the archaeological sites. Concerning the flint artifacts, T. O. Miller has made an apposite remark: "They (the makers) were not concerned with patterned wholes, but rather with working edges and beaks, and knew how to get them."[158] In other words, the "patterned whole" that these craftsmen had in mind was not the functionally recognizable projectile point, obviously fashioned for hunting or as a weapon, but a step on the way to some other conceived goal such as a wooden implement or the proper preparation of some vegetable food. Looked at in this way, it is misleading to consider the chipped-stone work of the East Brazilian Upland tradition cultures as representing an "arrested" stage of technological development or a "decadence" from the fine pressure-flaking standards of the Old South American Hunting tradition. More likely, it was the product of an admirably adapted set of techniques for producing the numerous cutting and punching edges of stone that were necessary to the routine of economic life in the forest and savanna regions in which these peoples lived. It is highly possible that some of this routine involved the digging, cutting, and preparing of plant foods; and it has been suggested that certain of these industries could reflect a mode of food getting that was "incipient cultivation" although we can go no further than to note this speculation.[159] Hunting and fishing must also have played subsistence roles. Miller has made the point that a slightly warmer climate than that of today—and such a condition undoubtedly prevailed prior to 2000 B.C.—would effect surface-water depletion and change the vegetation type from the dense semi-tropical "mato" jungle to grasslands and gallery forests. Game would have been much more plentiful under the latter circumstance,[160] and the presence of both stone and bone projectile points in a number of sites supports this premise. However, as we said at the beginning of this section, there is considerable variety between industries; the area concerned is large and has internal regional-environmental differences; and the time span is long. Given all of these factors we must anticipate differentiation within the East Brazilian Upland tradition. One dimension of such differentiation might very well have been transhumance between settlements of the interior and those of the coast, such as has been proposed for the Andean Hunting-Collecting tradition in Peru.[161] Such, in fact, could have been the beginning of the process of change whereby the Sambaquí tradition became detached from the parent tradition of the interior.

Recent findings in the Rio Claro region of São Paulo, Brazil, offer details of the industries of the East Brazilian Upland tradition. The earliest horizon in the regional sequence is the Santa Rosa, to which we have referred earlier in this chapter (p. 37; Fig. 2-8). Artifacts of this horizon are found in river terrace deposits believed to date from the last Pleistocene advance. T. O. Miller, who has defined the horizon,[162] describes them as being made on heavy primary flakes, most of them only unifacially worked. Tools include spokeshaves, scraper-knives, beaked scrapers, prismatic flake knives made from prepared blades, long "needles," or punches, made from sub-quadrangular slivers of flint, and punches with expanding stems. Smaller tools include disk-shaped knives, backed "penknives," and a double-edged or bifacially worked "pruning hook." Miller also mentions one large

(15 cm. long) laurel-leaf blade or slender chopping tool.[163] Miller's tentative age estimate for Santa Rosa—based on geological context—is a terminal Pleistocene date of about 8000 B.C.

The second Rio Claro horizon is characterized by the Monjolo Velho complex and given a guess date of 7500–6000 B.C. Monjolo Velho implements (Fig. 2-30) are made of either quartz crystals or silty flint. Most are smaller than the Santa Rosa tools; for instance, in the collection from one site, Tira Chapéu II, over a third of the artifacts in the collection measured less than 4 centimeters on their greatest diameter. They were fashioned from small splinters, tabular pieces, flakes, blades, and cores by both percussion- and pressure-flaking. The majority are described as scrapers—end, side, and spokeshave forms. Knives, beaked tools, and "needles" also occur.

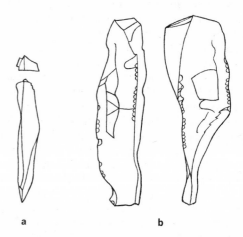

Figure 2-30. Monjolo Velho chipped-stone artifacts. *a:* "Needle." *b:* Two views of knife with irregular cutting edge. Length of *a,* 4.2 cm. (Courtesy T. O. Miller, Jr.)

The San Antonio phase follows Monjolo Velho. Again, artifacts were mostly worked by unifacial techniques. Scrapers are numerous and include heavy, footed forms not found in Monjolo Velho. Expanded-base punches are present but not the slender "needles." Flake knives and beaked flakes are common, and spent cores of polyhedral ball

Figure 2-31. Projectile point associated with San Antonio phase. Points of this general shape are occasionally found with earlier East Brazilian Upland tradition cultures. Length, 6.5 cm. (Courtesy T. O. Miller, Jr.)

shape were apparently used as bola stones. There are also some projectile points (Fig. 2-31). These are mostly unifacial, triangular, and with contracting stems; some few, however, are bifacial. The overall "miniaturization" of the industry that we saw in Monjolo Velho does not continue in San Antonio; instead, artifacts tend to be of various sizes, approximating a mean somewhere between Santa Rosa and Monjolo Velho.

Stone celts and small projectile points are markers for a later phase of the region, the Marchiori. These celts or ungrooved axes are either partially or fully ground and smoothed. The projectile points are bifacial, stemmed, and smaller than the San Antonio points. They tend to be long, narrow, and proportionately thick. The stems are long and contracting, the shoulders pronounced and, in some instances, barbed. However, the points are not numerous even in this late phase, and Miller suggests that their scarcity and thick-bodied, serrated form may be in imitation of a wooden or bone prototype. Flake knives, scraper flakes, beaked flakes and heavy and plano-convex scraper-planes or push-planes continue from San Antonio into Marchiori. The estimated end date for San Antonio is 2500 B.C., and Marchiori is believed

to have lasted to perhaps as late as the beginning of the Christian era.

Lack of published illustrations and differences in terminology between archaeologists working in Eastern Brazil render it difficult to make region-to-region comparisons of tools and complexes; however, the lithic finds in other southeastern Brazilian states certainly pertain to this East Brazilian Upland tradition. At the José Vieira site, a lithic complex beneath a pottery horizon presents a stone technology reminiscent of that of the Rio Claro sequence.[164] This complex lacks projectile points and has a radiocarbon date of about 3300 B.C. But in a still deeper level, one with a radiocarbon date of 4700 B.C. (see Early José Vieira on chart, Fig. 2-3), a well-chipped stemmed projectile point has been reported.[165] There is no further description of this point, although it may parallel those of the San Antonio phase of the Rio Claro sequence with which it should be approximately contemporaneous.

In the Paranapanema Valley Chmyz has defined two complexes of chipped-stone materials that also seem to fall in the same general tradition. These complexes are the Timburi, which Chmyz places as the earlier, and the Andirá.[166] Chmyz sees similarities between Timburi and both José Vieira and Barracão. The latter is a complex found at the junction of the Paraná, Santa Catarina, and Misiones (Argentina) borders, and it consists of flake knives, scrapers, and beaked tools, scrapers made on cores, and cores that have been bifacially chipped to produce something like the heavy tools of the Biface tradition (see pp. 39–41).[167] A bifacially chipped projectile point with a squared base is also present in the Barracão collection.[168]

In northeastern Rio Grande do Sul, E. T. Miller gives a chronologically seriated listing of three preceramic complexes.[169] The earliest, the Humaitá, is much like Barracão.[170] The second in the series, Camuri, continues the rough flake technology of Humaitá but is also characterized by unstemmed and stemmed projectile points. The former are of medium size and are reminiscent of the later triangular and leaf-shaped points of the Andean Hunting-Collecting tradition; the latter are small, sometimes with barbed shoulders, and more comparable to the small, stemmed Marchiori points of the Rio Claro sequence. The third member of the Rio Grande do Sul sequence is the

Camboatá phase. Sites of the phase show a variety of flake choppers and scrapers, but they are especially distinguished by sandstone abraders and semiground or fully ground and polished stone axes.[171]

The East Brazilian Upland tradition with its flake knives, scrapers, beaked forms, and other elements continues farther south than Brazil. We see it in Uruguay where, as Bórmida has pointed out, the northern third of that country lies within its range while the southern two-thirds lie within the geographic scope of the Paraná-Pampean and, probably, earlier hunting traditions.[172] We have already spoken of the Early Catalán culture, a complex that we suggested might fall within the postulated Flake tradition.[173] Late Catalán (see p. 36), with its continuity of the flake technology but its presence of some bifacially flaked implements, seems reminiscent of some of the East Brazilian complexes that we have just been reviewing. Still later phases of the Catalán industry continuum are Tropiduro—which has some leaf-shaped projectile points—and Fuqués—with small, roughly chipped points.[174] The small points of the latter suggest a correlation with the small point horizon of the Brazilian complexes, while the earlier leaf-shaped points may represent an influence from late Andean Hunting-Collecting or early Paraná-Pampean cultures farther south. I think that the Cuareim industry, from the same general drainage system as the Catalán, can also be placed in the East Brazilian Upland traditional context.[175] Early Cuareim (or Cuareim A) features large-size flake tools, with no bifaces and no points; Late Cuareim remains in the rough tool technology but shows a few triangular or convex-based lanceolates which are like those of Tropiduro. With these characteristics, Lanning and Patterson seriate the two Cuareim phases after Late Catalán and before Tropiduro, a placement with which I would agree.[176]

The Altoparaná industry of Paraguay and Misiones is another, like the Catalán, that can be interpreted as a late manifestation of the old Flake tradition or an early expression of the East Brazilian Upland tradition. The Altoparaná culture has been divided into three sequent preceramic phases on the basis of river terrace associations.[177] The industry is characterized by heavy, plano-convex flake tools, especially wedge-shaped,

slightly curved, picklike, implements. These were possibly used as hoes for digging. Heavy bifacial tools are present, however, in both phases I and II. The implements of these phases are found, uniformly, on the surface of an old, dark red, eolian soil stratum that is believed to correlate with late Pleistocene times. They are covered with recent reddish alluvium from the floods of the Paraná River. No conclusive dating can be drawn from these circumstances, but it is likely that the industry had beginnings more or less contemporaneous with the suggested early post-glacial dating of the Brazilian Santa Rosa horizon.[178]

Although most of our information on the East Brazilian Upland tradition comes from the southern end of its geographical range, there is another important set of finds from the north. These are the Lagoa discoveries of the State of Minas Gerais. They were mentioned at the beginning of this chapter (p. 28), and some of them have been known for a long time.[179] In his recent work in some of the Lagoa Santa caves or rock-shelters, W. R. Hurt was unable to demonsrate the associations of man and extinct Pleistocene fauna as given in the earlier reports on these sites; however, in the location known as "Rockshelter No. 6," Hurt isolated a cultural deposit and complex which he has named the Cerca Grande.[180] It features quartz crystal tools including projectile points of roughly chipped, triangular-bladed and squared-stem form. These points, which are like the squared or flat-based stemmed types from the State of Paraná rather than like the contracting stemmed points of the same region, are accompanied in the Cerca Grande complex by scrapers, spokeshaves, and rough percussion-flaked tools. Other projectile points in the complex are made of bone, and this material was used also for awls and beads. Olivella shell ornaments and partially chipped, partially ground, stone axes make up the inventory. A hunting subsistence, at least in important part, is verified by abundant bone scrap of a small modern-type fauna. Two radiocarbon dates from the Cerca Grande context are 7600 and 7000 B.C.[181] These dates seem too early for the semiground or polished stone axes; at least implements of this sort appear to be substantially later in the Paraná and Rio Grande do Sul sites mentioned above. On the other hand, the quartz crystal stemmed points are said to be of a size and shape that is more consistent with these dates,[182] and it may be that, in certain parts of the Brazilian interior, the partially ground stone axes had an earlier inception than we have estimated. The square-stemmed, Cerca Grande–type point has been found in the Marciano Cave in the same region; and at the nearby Eucaliptus Rock Shelter some large, contracting-stemmed points were recovered. These last were found together with a fish-tailed point (see p. 46).[183]

We can conclude this section with a short summary by saying that there is abundant evidence for a unifacial flake industry persisting over a very long period of time in the East Brazilian highlands and nearby regions to the south. This East Brazilian Upland tradition, as we have called it, cannot be dated very accurately, although we estimate it to have lasted from the time of the last glaciation until the beginning of the Christian era. It seems likely that many of the implements of the tradition were edge and cutting tools for use on wood or bone or, possibly, in the digging, cutting, or preparing of plant substances for food. The hunting of animal game was also a subsistence activity of the tradition, and projectile points were made of bone, probably of wood, and, to some extent, of stone. However, the stone points are relatively rare. They seem to have been locally made, and they probably result from imitative manufacture of forms from other South American areas. Thus, a few are fish-tailed types, others stemmed, and some leaf-shaped. Late in the Brazilian sequences stemmed and barbed small points appear. But through all this the fundamental flake scraper, flake knife, and rough stone tool technologies compose the main continuity of the East Brazilian Upland tradition.

An Introduction to Some Later South American Cultural Traditions

In following out the developments of both the Andean Hunting-Collecting and the East Brazilian Upland traditions we have noted their persistence in some regions, especially mountain valley or upland settings, until relatively late prehistoric times, while in other regions, notably coastal or lowland environments, these two traditions gave way to other major subsistence and life-way patterns. We have already mentioned these later cultural patterns in the preceding discussions, but, as a preliminary to their more detailed consideration in ensuing chapters, let us review them briefly at this point in the narrative.

The Pacific Littoral Tradition. One of the best known of these later traditions is the Pacific Littoral. Sites representative of it are found all along the Pacific coastal littoral from northern Peru down through northern and central Chile. Its early phases, such as Corbina[184] of the Central Coast of Peru or Quiani I[185] of the North Coast of Chile, date back to 4000 B.C. or slightly before. The tradition clearly had its origins in the Andean Hunting-Collecting way of life and in the lomas camps that were established near the shore as early as 6500 B.C. These camps are thought to have been the winter season plant-gathering stations of peoples who spent their summers as Andean valley game-hunters. From these locations, and with the onset of the climatic optimum, there was a steadily increasing utilization of marine resources—fish, shellfish, sea mammals, and birds—a shift from the lomas sites to actual shoreline locations, and, eventually, permanent settlement on the littoral. This new adaptation is reflected in assorted fishing gear—hooks, nets, floats, spears, harpoons—as well as in subsistence refuse and settlement pattern. The particular areal or subareal patterns within the larger pattern of the Pacific Littoral tradition vary, of course, as do the developmental configurations through time within these geographic divisions. For example, lithic elements differ between the Central Peruvian coastal cultures and those of the North Coast, and the Chilean phases of the tradition are distinguished by weapons suitable for sea mammal hunting, whereas these are lacking in Peru. Even more notable is the highly significant subsistence shift to plant cultivation and agriculture, a process that characterizes the Peruvian Pacific Littoral cultures but which is lacking or greatly retarded in those of Chile.

The Northwest South American Littoral Tradition. The early shoreline cultures of Ecuador, Colombia, Lower Central America, Venezuela, and the West Indies are drawn together under this category. Except for certain complexes in Venezuela[186] and the West Indies,[187] these cultures are much less well known than those of the Peruvian or Chilean coasts; however, data are now coming in from other areas.[188] Taken together, the information that we have indicates a variety of coastal collecting and fishing subsistence adaptations. They are all negatively characterized by the absence of chipped-stone projectile points and, for the most part, by an absence of skillful flint-chipping. Shell and bone artifacts are typical of some of the phases. The environmental settings are of a tropical forest, mangrove, or savanna type of coastal country; indeed, it is probable that some of these regions, which are today semiarid, were, in the periods with which we are here concerned, in heavier vegetation. It is estimated that some of these Northwest South American Littoral tradition cultures had their beginnings as early as 5000 B.C. The origins of the tradition are unclear. It is possible—perhaps likely—that they lie in the Andean Hunting-Collecting tradition of the highlands; and it may be that these Andean hunters came to the Pacific and Caribbean coasts in a transhumance pattern of seasonal occupancy in the way that we have hypothesized for the Peruvian and Chilean Andean hunters, although the evidence for this is slight to nonexistent in northwestern South America. Another possibility would be derivations from an old Flake tradition and East Brazilian Upland tradition continuum, one that had persisted in a forested Brazilian and Guiana Highland setting and from there had spread to the Caribbean lowlands and other coastal regions of northern South America. On the Ecuadorian coast, in the Caribbean lowlands of northern Colombia and northwestern Venezuela, and in Panama, the Northwest South American Littoral tradition shows modification with the introduction of pottery as early as the third millennium B.C. This occurs prior to the establishment of the Intermediate area and Caribbean agricultural traditions; however, these pottery phases of the latter part of the Northwest South American Littoral tradition are clearly transitional steps into these later traditions.

The Sambaquí Tradition. This is another littoral tradition of fishers and collectors. The name is the local Brazilian or Guaraní word for shell mound, and the sites are coastal shell middens from Uruguay to Rio de Janeiro and even farther north. The origins of the tradition can be traced back to the East Brazilian Upland tradition, and available radiocarbon dates suggest that the utilization of the shoreline and its resources began by about 5000 B.C.[189] Pottery of an Eastern Brazilian ceramic tradition was introduced into the context of the Sambaquí tradition in the first millennium B.C., and similar pottery was also assimilated into the later phases of the East Brazilian Upland tradition. It is uncertain whether agriculture was associated with this Eastern Brazilian pottery tradition; but if it was, it is most likely that this was at an "incipient" stage of development. Sometime later, at about A.D. 500, Tupiguaraní ceramics mark the introduction of the Amazonian cultural tradition into the East Brazilian area.[190]

The Paraná-Pampean Tradition. The Paraná-Pampean tradition was a hunting-fishing-collecting pattern of the Paraná-Uruguay drainage, the Argentine Pampa,[191] Patagonia, and northeastern Tierra del Fuego. Its origins appear to be twofold: the East Brazilian Upland tradition and the Andean Hunting-Collecting tradition. On the preceramic level the hunting patterns of the former seem to have gradually become dominant; on the ceramic level, the Lower Paraná drainage appears to have been a center of pottery development. The tradition began to take form as early as 4000 to 3500 B.C., probably for the most part in the south, in Patagonia, although there are indications of its emergence in the cave stratigraphies of San Luis and Córdoba, South Andean subareas that border on the Pampas. The Paraná ceramics probably derive from the Eastern Brazilian pottery tradition to the north. Just how early they are is a moot question, but it is estimated that they date back to at least 500 B.C. Even though pottery appears in the latter stages of the Paraná-Pampean tradition, the pattern of life remained largely non-agricultural. An exception to this was the presence of some farming in the Lower Paraná Valley cultures.[192]

The Fuegian Tradition. The far southern coast and archipelago of Chile and the western and southern portions of Tierra del Fuego were the setting of the Fuegian cultural tradition.

The tradition was adapted to the resources of the sea, especially sea mammals and shellfish. In late historic times the Fuegian tradition was represented by the Chono, Alacaluf, and Yahgan peoples. Just how far back in time the tradition may be pushed is uncertain; Bird's original estimate of the beginning of the Christian era seems too modest;[193] but the radiocarbon dates from the Englefield Island site—at 6500 to 7200 B.C.—appear excessively early.[194] Englefield Island probably shows the Fuegian tradition in its early formation, a development prompted by Andean Hunting-Collecting peoples adapting to a marine as opposed to a land hunting subsistence.[195]

Summary

This presentation of early man and early cultures in South America leaves us with a hypothetical model or reconstruction for the early human history of the continent. What is the model, in brief? And what are the evidences to support it? Our summary considers these two questions.

The reconstruction begins with the assumption that man has been in South America since before 10,000 B.C. and that he first entered the southern continent of the New World, by way of North and Middle America, with a lithic technology that can be described most generally as "pre-projectile point." That is, this early technology lacked well-finished bifacially chipped points or, for that matter, any carefully flaked bifacial implements. It was characterized instead by rough percussion-chipping and by heavy unifacial flake tools, such as scrapers, knives, beaks, and burins. We have referred to this technology as the Flake tradition and have presumed it to be of wide South American distribution.

Either developing from this Flake tradition or arriving anew to South America in these early times was a technique of making heavy, crude, bifacial choppers. This has been referred to as a Chopper tradition, and its distribution has been noted as essentially northern South American.

The Flake and Chopper traditions, to continue with this historical model, were followed at a somewhat later time by the Biface tradition. This tradition featured heavy bifacial chopping and

cutting tools. These could have been developed locally in South America from the cruder Chopper tradition antecedents, or there could have been new immigrants to South America bringing with them this more advanced technical skill.

At this point the story has been brought up to about 10,000 B.C., and the continent has already been populated from north to south, albeit thinly. The life-ways, even the basic subsistence, of these early inhabitants must remain most speculative although it seems highly likely that their stone tools were for fashioning other implements of wood or bone.

At about 10,000 B.C. important new introductions were made into South America by migrant hunters following large Pleistocene land game. These people are thought to have been related to the Clovis or Llano hunters of the North American Plains. Their technology was that of the finely chipped lanceolate projectile point, including the fluted point. Such a technology had remote Old World Levallois-Mousterian derivations, and peoples bringing it had entered the Americas and passed southward to the North American High Plains in advance of 10,000 B.C. In South America these hunters were characterized by what we have called the Old South American Hunting tradition. A diagnostic artifact of this tradition was a fish-tailed fluted projectile point. Another type of point was an elongated leaf-shaped lanceolate whose origins could have been in North America or locally in South America out of Biface tradition antecedents under stimulus from the new projectile point technology. The Old South American Hunting tradition lasted until about 7000 B.C. Like the Biface tradition, it was established largely in Andean South America although it spread to the southern tip of the continent and eastward into the Argentine Plains.

The Old South American Hunting tradition gave rise to the Andean Hunting-Collecting tradition, a cultural tradition in which subsistence was provided by the hunting of deer and South American camelids and by vegetable food collecting. One feature of this tradition was seasonal transhumance or a shifting of community residence as peoples pursued either highland hunting or coastal lowland collecting. Another feature was a trend toward specialization into regional environmental niches.

The Andean Hunting-Collecting tradition had its inception at about 7000 B.C., but by 4000 B.C. regional specialization had advanced to the point where new cultural traditions had come into being in some places. Along the Peruvian and Chilean coasts the seasonal collecting camps began to be replaced by permanent villages whose inhabitants depended primarily upon marine foods, although in Peru plant gathering remained an important economic activity and provided the basis for the rise of farming. This adaptation is the Pacific Littoral tradition. To the east, in the Argentine Pampas and Patagonia, the hunting of the guanaco remained paramount, but changes in artifact forms and the new ambience mark the beginnings of the Paraná-Pampean tradition. In the far southern Chilean archipelago country, sea mammal hunting replaced the primary land hunting dependence, and this has been termed the Fuegian tradition. Another coastal adaptation appears at about the same time in northern South America and Lower Central America, the Northwest South American Littoral tradition. It, too, may have descended from the Andean Hunting-Collecting tradition, although these antecedents are less clear than with the other developments. It is possible, instead, that its origins are to be found in the eastern areas of South America, and this leads us to that part of the continent.

During the period of the Old South American Hunting tradition, eastern South America north of the Argentine Plains was little affected by these new introductions. Here an East Brazilian Upland tradition arose out of the technology of the earlier Flake tradition. Implements of chipped stone were largely scraping-, cutting-, and punching-edges whose primary adaptation was for obtaining or processing plant foods or for making other tools of wood or bone. Hunting was undoubtedly of economic importance. Bone projectile points were used, and so, probably, were wooden ones; and a few chipped stone points were made by the peoples of these regions. These last appear to be in imitation of the point styles of the Old South American Hunting tradition and the Andean Hunting-Collecting tradition. Here, too, there was a settlement of the coast during the climatic optimum, and a coastal Sambaquí tradition came into being by at least 4000 B.C. as the result of an adaptive trend away from the Brazilian Upland tradition.

Such is a highly schematic model of the early prehistory of South America. How well can it be supported? To begin to answer this we have to go back to some of the things that were said about North America and Asia. According to geological opinion, northeast Asia and Alaska were a continuous land surface after 26,000 B.C., so that a land bridge would have been provided for man's movements from Asia to America at that time.[196] Such early immigrants could then have moved southward through the passage in the Canadian ice fields at any time before 21,000 B.C.[197] But did human beings actually arrive in the New World this early? As we have indicated, there are some clues that indicate that they may have (Tlapacoya, Valsequillo in Mexico). The Wilson Butte Cave finds of Idaho are a strong datum supporting man's presence in mid-continental North America prior to the last (10,000 B.C.) opening of the ice sheets, and, significantly, these Wilson Butte discoveries attest to the presence of a Levallois-Mousterian technology in this part of the New World by 13,000 to 12,000 B.C. In South America the Muaco discoveries and radiocarbon dates make man's presence in Venezuela by 15,000 to 12,000 B.C. quite probable. Such a man, and his relatives, could have been responsible for the Flake and Chopper traditions, but we certainly have no proof of this. The industries of these traditions are by no means securely dated to these early times, although the Peruvian coastal stratigraphy and radiocarbon dates are a good argument for the presence of the Flake tradition by 10,500 B.C. or earlier. This same stratigraphy, and the river terrace seriation from the Rio Pedregal region of Venezuela, imply that the Biface tradition has a later inception than the Flake and Chopper traditions and that it dates to approximately 9500 to 8000 B.C.

The Cachapoál or Tagua Tagua finds of a stone industry and associated mastodon bones in central Chile support the presence of a Levallois-Mousterian-derived technology in this part of South America as early as 9400 B.C., and this, in turn, tends to confirm the 8700 B.C. date for the Old South American Hunting tradition as represented in the Magellan I phase finds at the extreme southern tip of the continent. Well-documented components of the Old South American Hunting tradition are, however, few and far between; and there are ambiguities and differences of opinion about the datings of the fish-tailed point complexes and the early elongated leaf-shaped point complexes. That there were late Pleistocene big-game hunters living in South America and that they were related to the Clovis-Folsom-Plano groups of North America seem to be reasonably certain, but the specific developments and lines of connection to North America have yet to be clarified.

The camps of the Andean Hunting-Collecting tradition peoples in the highlands and on the coast of Peru are numerous, and we have a good idea of the artifact complexes of each. The hypothesis of their relationship in a pattern of transhumance subsistence needs much more testing. It appears to be a likely way to account for the trend toward coastal occupancy of a permanent sort, but one is left wondering just what happens to the highland components of the pattern once the sedentary marine subsistence and living has been established down on the ocean shore. For, clearly, the Andean basins continued to be occupied after 4000 B.C. and before the rise of settled agricultural life in the uplands. Did plant collection and incipient cultivation play a part here as they did on the coast? The idea that the coastal Pacific Littoral tradition developed out of the Andean Hunting-Collecting tradition is an economical hypothesis that seems to square with the facts as we know them now, and this process of development probably went on all along the Peruvian and north Chilean shore. When we come to Ecuador and Colombia, however, a development from the Andean Hunting-Collecting

tradition to the kinds of remains we are grouping together under the Northwest South American tradition seems a much less satisfactory explanation, and it must be admitted that our limited knowledge of preceramic cultures in the North Andean highlands is a serious handicap to hypothesis-building.

That the East Brazilian Upland tradition, for which we have substantial archaeological evidence, did arise out of an ancient Flake tradition base, for which we have little evidence, is obviously a tenuous part of our model structure. Alternatively, we might explain the East Brazilian Upland tradition and its distinctive lithic technology as a radical modification of Old South American Hunting tradition or Andean Hunting-Collecting tradition patterns that had occurred in the forested highlands of eastern Brazil; yet I am inclined to reject this because I see no good evidence for the lithic technologies associated with these hunting cultures in eastern Brazil. The occasional elements of them that we do find are rather scarce and appear as "strays" in the East Brazilian Upland tradition contexts. The relationships between the East Brazilian Upland tradition and the Sambaquí tradition are easily seen; in fact, the similarities between the two continue in a marked way until the later Sambaquí phases. No specific evidence can be cited to support the contention that the East Brazilian Upland tradition was in some way ancestral to the Northwest South American Littoral tradition, although there is a stronger typological resemblance between these two than either shares with the Andean Hunting-Collecting tradition.[198]

Footnotes

1 Krieger (1964) was at pains to point out that he was speaking of a "pre-projectile point *stage*" rather than a horizon or period for he quite rightly insisted that the concept should not be time-bound (see also Davis, 1966, p. 154); nevertheless, an integral part of the idea is that at some place in the Americas a "pre-

projectile point stage" of technology did characterize a time period or horizon that antedated any other New World technologies or industries. In Volume One we were concerned with both the horizon (Chap. 2, fig. 2–31, Chap. 8, figs. 8–1, 8–2, and p. 473, "Period I") and the stage (Chap. 8, p. 476, "Lower Lithic

Stage") aspects of the "pre-projectile point" concept.

2 Mirambell (1967); Haynes (1967).

3 Valsequillo was reported upon by Cynthia Irwin-Williams at the annual meeting of the Society for American Archaeology, Ann Arbor, Michigan, May 1967. J. L. Lorenzo

(1967) has since attacked the security of context and provenience of the Valsequillo artifacts, and Irwin-Williams (1969) has replied.

4 Unifacial chipping is generally held to be on an earlier stage of flint technology than bifacial chipping. The former is, thus, consistent with a "pre-projectile point" technology, possibly deriving from Old World Lower or Middle Paleolithic prototypes.

5 For example, Haynes (1964).

6 For example, Wormington (1961) or Wilmsen (1964).

7 Solecki (1950, 1951); Giddings (1961).

8 Schlesier (1967); Humphrey (1966). Sedna Creek and Utukok also resemble British Mountain (see Vol. I, p. 69, chart on p. 73).

9 A. L. Bryan (1967, ms.).

10 Müller-Beck (1966).

11 Wendorf (1966) has a similar argument but dates the Bering Land Bridge from 24,000 to 9000 B.C. and the closure of the Canadian ice from 18,000 to 11,000 B.C.

12 For Wilson Butte Cave see Gruhn (1961); however, the radiocarbon dates were released later (1965). The reanalysis of the artifact assemblage is by Bryan (1969) and Crabtree (1969).

13 The reader is referred to McCown (1950) for a review of the early literature on this subject.

14 Walter (1948).

15 See Bird (1946 b) and Gusinde (1921).

16 Sullivan and Hellman (1925).

17 Kirk Bryan (1945).

18 Bird (1938); for radiocarbon dates see Haynes (1965).

19 Montané (1968).

19a This early dating tends to be confirmed by a recent discovery (Lynch and Kennedy, 1970) in the Peruvian Callejón de Huaylas where the Guitarrero I complex has one radiocarbon date of about 10,600 B.C. The flake scrapers of Guitarrero I are said to correspond closely to those of Tagua Tagua.

20 Royo y Gomez (1960) first reported on Muaco. For more recent work see Rouse and Cruxent (1963, pp. 34–36).

21 Rouse and Cruxent (1963, p. 36) describe another similar site

nearby, called Taima Taima, in which comparable discoveries have been made although no radiocarbon dates are associated.

22 The Tumba de Garzon finds of Colombia (Burgl, 1958; Hammen, 1958) are not mentioned because I am unconvinced that the "artifacts" in question are truly man-made. These are objects of silicified wood which show chipping, but the chipping could be from natural causes. The presence of the Pleistocene megafaunal remains in the Pleistocene gravel layer are, of course, unquestioned.

22a Since the manuscript of this book went to press, R. S. MacNeish (1969) has brought out the first preliminary report on cave excavations in the Peruvian highlands near Ayacucho; and, still more recently, I have had the benefit of his personal communications of late 1970 on his second season of work in that region. To date, the earliest remains of the region, as based upon stratigraphic excavation, are those of the Pacaicasa complex. This complex is represented by an extremely crude series of tufa slab tools—implements made from fallen rock from a cave roof—hammers, choppers, spokeshaves, denticulates, scrapers. Following the Pacaicasa is the Ayacucho complex (see MacNeish, 1969), consisting of rough, unifacial flake tools, split pebbles, and pebble tools, and, finally, what appears to be a flake with burin blows. Following the terminology of this book, the Ayacucho complex might be grouped with our Flake tradition. The earlier Pacaicasa complex seems too amorphous for any kind of a tradition assignment. Significantly, bones of Megatheriidae and other extinct animals are associated with the Ayacucho complex; and a radiocarbon date on Ayacucho is 12,200 B.C. No dates are yet available on Pacaicasa, but, presumably, these would fall earlier than 12,000 to 13,000 B.C.

23 This section is based on articles by T. C. Patterson and E. P. Lanning (1967) and by J. J. Hester (1966). The reader is referred to the bibliographies of both these articles.

24 A working assumption of most authorities on the subject.

25 Perhaps the Cary and Tazewell Substages as well (see Vol. I, fig. 1–1, and p. 28).

26 Since this was written I would include the Peruvian highland Ayacucho complex in what I am calling the Flake tradition. Ayacucho complex is the next to earliest member of MacNeish's cave sequence and it dates to 12,000 to 13,000 B.C. (MacNeish, 1969, and personal communication, 1970). It is also possible that the Guiterrero I cave complex, of the Peruvian Callejón de Huaylas, should be included in the Flake tradition although the presence of a projectile point in the assemblage throws doubt on this interpretation. Guitarrero I has one radiocarbon date of about 10,600 B.C. (Lynch and Kennedy, 1970).

27 Lanning and Patterson (1967). In a more recent publication, Lanning (1970) refers to "Edge-retouched" and "Burin Traditions" for these industries. I have included both here as part of the Flake tradition.

28 Lanning and Patterson (1967). In Volume I (p. 67) we referred to Chivateros I. At the time of that writing the earlier Peruvian burin industries had not been discovered.

29 Salitre crusts form today in the coastal Peruvian deserts; however, under the arid conditions of the present they will form only fairly close to the actual seashore. Cerro Chivateros lies about a mile inland from the beach.

30 See several charts in Lanning and Patterson (1967).

31 Patterson (1966 b); Lanning (1967 a, ms.); Lanning and Patterson (1967).

32 Lanning (1967 a, ms.); see also Lanning (1970). It should be noted that Lanning's 1970 article, which appeared while this book was in galley proof, makes available a substantial portion of the data referred to in the Lanning manuscript references (1966, 1967 a, 1967 b).

33 Lanning (1967 b, ms.).

34 Lanning (1966, ms.).

35 Various archaeologists have written on the Catalán finds, but the present summary is based upon

Bórmida (1964 a, b) and on conversations with T. C. Patterson (1967). Another view, dealing more in terms of broad developmental stages than in technological traditions, is given by Campá-Soler (1967); see also Campá-Soler and Vidart (1962).

36 T. C. Patterson (personal communication, 1967).

37 Bórmida (1964 a); Lanning and Patterson (1967, ms.).

38 Mayntzhusen (1928, 1930); Menghin (1956, 1957 b), however, is responsible for the more recent interest in this complex.

39 Menghin (1956, 1957 b); Lanning and Patterson (1967, ms.) date the early phases of Altoparaná to about 8000 B.C.

40 A sequence has been developed within Altoparaná on the basis of river terrace associations. Of the three sub-complexes, the earlier two have the large biface implements whereas the latest does not (Menghin and Wachnitz, 1958).

41 E. T. Miller (1967).

42 Blasi (1965).

43 Chmyz (1967).

44 T. O. Miller, Jr. (1969).

45 Krieger (1964, pp. 49–50, map and list).

46 Menghin (1952).

47 Menghin (1957 a); A. R. Gonzalez (personal communication, 1966).

48 Menghin and Bórmida (1950) do not estimate Tandilense to be as early as Oliviense or Rio Gallegos I, but instead place it in terminal glacial times.

49 Oliviense, Rio Gallegos I, and Tandilense are not all of these debatably early Argentine or southern Chilean complexes. Vignati (1927) has reported on a Rio Chico shell midden in eastern Tierra del Fuego in which the lowest layer, with only rough flake tools and bola stones, is believed to be of great age. A middle layer at this site has stemless triangular points and bolas; and the upper layer, according to that author, has fish-tail and leaf-shaped points. However, the presence of bola stones in the two lower levels throws grave doubt on the validity of this stratigraphy which, in its implications, runs counter to all other early lithic chronological information in South

America. Emperaire and Laming-Emperaire have also excavated another midden in Tierra del Fuego, at Punta Catalina, where the lowest layer is without points and has only rough-flake tools; but I think it likely that this lowest layer corresponds to Bird's (1938) Magellan II horizon, for the upper layer at Punta Catalina corresponds to Magellan III (an interpretation derived from Rowe's [1960 b] comments).

50 Rouse and Cruxent (1963, pp. 27–37).

51 In dating Camare, or any other complexes of the El Joboid series of northwestern Venezuela, the radiocarbon dates from nearby Muaco are of little help. The only identifiable artifact found in the mud deposits (see this chapter, p. 47) was a projectile point fragment of what was probably an El Jobo point; however, the date of 12,000 to 15,000 B.C. seems much too early for El Jobo and would be more in keeping with what we would expect for Camare. As Rouse and Cruxent have indicated (1963, p. 36), the unreliability of the position of artifacts in the Muaco mud, with relation to the bone specimens used for radiocarbon dating tests, leaves any dating associations within the deposits open to considerable doubt. This stricture does not, however, apply to the bones themselves, which show what appear to be human cutting marks and burning.

52 Lanning and Patterson (1967).

53 Rouse and Cruxent (1963, p. 30 and pl. 3).

54 The Peruvian Biface industries are discussed in Lanning (1963 a, 1965, 1967, Chap. 4, 1967 a, ms.); Patterson (1966 b); Patterson and Lanning (1964); and Lanning and Patterson (1967, 1967, ms.). It should be noted also that a complex known as Conchitas, in the Lurín Valley, can be placed in the Biface tradition. Not all archaeologists agree with Lanning and Patterson on the early placement of these industries. For example, Lynch (1967 a, pp. 24–25) feels that these tool assemblages are much later. At the time of his writing, however, he had not yet reviewed the Chivateros Red Zone complex or Oquendo information (Lanning and Patterson, 1967).

55 Lanning (1967 b, ms.). Lanning places Manantial on the Chivateros II–El Jobo time level of 8000 to 7000 B.C. I have suggested on the chart (fig. 2–3) that it spans the Chivateros I–II time range.

56 Cigliano (1961, 1962 a, 1964).

57 As has been commented upon by several writers, for instance Lanning (1964).

58 Cigliano (1962 a, 1964) refers to this presumably later site and complex as being affiliated with the Argentine Ayampitín complex.

59 Lynch (1967 a, pp. 28–29) rejects a Pleistocene age for Ampajango. In his words: "Ampajango is located in a depression where large blocks of andesite, originally derived from the mountains, have been exposed by erosion of the Pleistocene deposit which had mantled the Pliocene terrace....The erosion, which opened the site for occupation, must have taken place...well before the onset of the Altithermal. Thus, occupation *could* have occurred during the Pleistocene, but it might equally well have taken place during postglacial times." And, again: "Given the presence in the area of sites from demonstrably recent times, the persistence through time of primitive non-projectile point industries, and the normal dominance of percussion and lack of projectile points at quarry sites of all ages, Cigliano's argument is likewise unconvincing." In support of the Cigliano and Lanning interpretations, which we are following in this chapter, I think the fortuitous or "quarry site" explanation of the Ampajango bifaced tools is greatly weakened by the numerous site occurrences in the South Andes of similar assemblages characterized by these tools and by the lack of points and pressure flaking.

60 Schobinger (1962); Gonzalez (1967).

61 Lanning (1963 c); Lanning and Patterson (1967).

62 Cigliano (1965, Site SII-T).

63 Cigliano and Calandre (1965).

64 Tres Morros and Saladillo are discussed by Cigliano (1962 b). Saladillo, however, has been known from the literature since Boman's (1908) time.

65 Lanning (1966, ms. and a letter to T. C. Patterson, dated 8 November 1967). The evidence for sequence in these middle Rio Loa industries—if other than typological—has not yet been presented. Similar biface tools have also been found farther north, in the vicinity of Tarapaca, in the Andean sub-Cordillera (True, Nuñez and Nuñez, 1970).

66 Le Paige (1959, 1960, 1964); Nuñez (1965); Orellana Rodriguez (1962, 1966); Barfield (1961).

67 For example, Orellana Rodriguez (1966) notes the presence of projectile points on the purported Ghatchi I sites, and Lynch (1967 a, pp. 14–16) voices similar misgivings about the isolation or typological purity of the Ghatchi I samples. In attempting to rearrange and resegregate the Ghatchi zone materials, Lanning and Patterson (1967) place a Loma Negra complex as contemporaneous with, and typologically closest to, Chivateros I; they then place a complex called Fundaciones as contemporary with Chivateros II. Le Paige (1964), to the contrary, sees Loma Negra as later than Ghatchi. Obviously, much more sorting out of the Ghatchi zone materials remains to be done; but for the present context of our discussion the important thing is that the Biface tradition technology is represented there.

68 Gonzalez and Lorandí (1959); Gonzalez (1966).

69 Bórmida (1962).

70 Ameghino (1911).

71 Hrdlička and others (1912).

72 Krieger (1964).

73 Bird (1965).

74 Bird (1938, 1964 b).

75 Emperaire, Laming-Emperaire, and Reinchlen (1963). Among other things, they report the presence of red paint on the Magellan I–type points.

76 Bird (1938).

77 See Haynes (1965) for radiocarbon dates. See also Bird (1970) for a new date for Fell's Cave which pertains to the Magellan I layer: 9050 B.C. ± 170. This confirms the dating preferred here. In the same article Bird discusses the later date from Palli Aike and gives his reasons for rejecting it.

78 The monographic treatment of El Inga is by Bell (1965).

79 Krieger (1964) does not accept this early dating of El Inga I and dates it as late as 3000 B.C.

80 It should be noted that the El Inga points are largely of obsidian, those of Magellan I of basalt.

80a A recent very important find pertains to the Old South American Hunting tradition and the fish-tailed point series. This is the discovery of the Huanta complex, by R. S. MacNeish, in his Ayacucho region cave stratigraphy in the Peruvian highlands. The Huanta complex lies stratigraphically between the earlier Ayacucho complex (non-projectile point) and the later Puente complex (leaf-shaped projectile points; MacNeish, 1969). Huanta points are similar to those of El Inga fish-tailed forms; various skin-working tools are associated; and extinct horse bones are present in the same level (MacNeish, personal communication, 1970).

81 Lanning (1967 b, ms.) dates his Carolina complex at about 7000 to 6500 B.C. and later than his Manantial complex with the elongated leaf-shaped points. I am inclined to feel that this single point is out of context in Carolina and that it is earlier. The reader's attention is called to Lanning's (1970) discussion of what he calls the "Fluted Point Tradition" in South America.

82 Reichel-Dolmatoff (1965 a, pp. 46–48).

83 Sanoja (1963). These are reported from the State of Carobobo and from Venezuelan Guiana.

84 Sander (1959, 1964).

85 Swauger and Mayer-Oakes (1952).

86 Bullen and Plowden (1963). Fragmentary bifacially flaked points are reported from a number of sites in northeastern Salvador (the Morazán complex) (Haberland, 1966–67); however, the data are insufficient to identify these with the fish-tailed points or, definitively, with the leaf-shaped or stemmed forms. They are believed to be preceramic.

87 Walter (1958).

88 Conceição de M. C. Becker (1966 a); Cruxent (1959). I am indebted to T. C. Patterson for calling these point occurrences to my attention.

89 Information from J. B. Bird as reported to T. C. Patterson in 1967.

90 Menghin (1952).

91 See Lynch (1967 a, pp. 72–73); T. C. Patterson (personal communication, 1967).

92 For a description of El Jobo finds see Cruxent and Rouse (1958–59, pp. 68–70, 239) and Rouse and Cruxent (1963, pp. 30–34).

93 The antiquity of the Old Cordilleran tradition in North America has been disputed by W. A. Davis (1966) and defended by Butler (1966).

94 Lanning and Patterson (1967).

95 Lanning (1967 b, ms.).

96 Carlucci de Santiana (1963).

97 Lanning (1967 a, ms., 1967, Chap. 4).

98 Cardich (1958, 1960, 1964).

99 MacNeish's (1969, and personal communication, 1970) Puente complex in the Ayacucho cave series presents an assemblage quite similar to Lauricocha I, with elongated leaf-shaped, diamond-shaped, and vaguely stemmed points. The radiocarbon date on terminal Puente is 6910 B.C., and MacNeish estimates the full range of the occupation as about 8000 to 7000 B.C. Significantly, Puente follows immediately out of the underlying Huanta (fish-tailed point) complex—both stratigraphically and, apparently, culturally. However, the recently discovered Guitarrero II complex (Lynch and Kennedy, 1970), from a cave in the Callejón de Huaylas, shows a surprising mixture of elongated leaf-shaped points, some that are vaguely stemmed (in the Lauricocha I manner), and a range of smaller willow-leafs and smallish ovate-triangular points with incurvate bases. These smaller points resemble those found elsewhere in the central and south Andes on a later time horizon. The Guitarrero II radiocarbon dates span from about 8500 to 5700 B.C.

100 Cardich (1964).

101 Lynch (1967 b).

102 Ramiro Matos (personal communication, 1967).

103 Lanning (letter of 8 November 1967).

104 Lanning and Patterson (1967) use this name for what has been referred to as Ghatchi II (Le Paige 1959, 1960); see also Nuñez (1965) for Ghatchi II.

105 There is frequent mention of Tulan in the literature (Le Paige, 1959, 1960; Barfield, 1961; Nuñez, 1965; Orellana Rodríguez, 1966; Lynch, 1967 a), but it is difficult to obtain a very clear typological impression. Most authors are inclined to date it at ca. 6000 B.C. and to relate it to the willow-leaf point horizon, which is later than the early leaf-shaped point group of complexes that we are concerned with here. Certainly, many of the Tulan points are the modified, triangular or flat-based leaf-shapes such as are seen in Ayampitín and Magellan III. Lanning and Patterson (1967, ms.), however, incline toward an earlier dating. Of special interest in connection with Tulan are some rough, circular house foundations of dry, pirca-type masonry that may date contemporaneously with the projectile points (Le Paige, 1959). Tulan points are also characteristic of the Early Toquepala complex of the southern Peruvian sierra (Ravines, 1967).

106 Cigliano (1962 b); Lanning and Patterson (1967).

107 Lanning (1963 c); Lanning and Patterson (1967).

108 Bird (1938, 1946 b).

109 Rowe (1960 b).

110 Emperaire, Laming-Emperaire, and Reichlen (1963, p. 214).

111 Menghin (1952).

112 T. O. Miller (personal communications 1968–69); Conceição de M. C. Becker (1966 a).

113 Bórmida (1964 a); Lanning and Patterson (1967, ms.).

114 Montané (1968).

115 Lynch (1967 a) also draws a parallel with the North American Old Cordilleran tradition. This somewhat controversial tradition was considered by me in Volume I (pp. 51–55) to be of comparable age to the Big-Game Hunting or "Paleo-Indian" cultures, at least in its earlier phases. Whether or not this turns out to be the case, it would appear to have persisted much longer, and in its later phases it does bear resemblances of a general developmental configuration to the Desert and Eastern Archaic traditions and also bears such resemblances, as well as more specific projectile-point typological ones, to the Andean Hunting-Collecting tradition.

116 E. L. Davis (1963, p. 202). I am, of course, indebted to Lynch (1967 a) for bringing several observations on transhumance to my attention.

117 Lynch (1967 a, p. 36).

118 My dating follows Lanning and Patterson (1967, ms.) and Lanning (1967, see chronology chart). Cardich, in his recent synthesis (1964), places Lauricocha II as 6000 to 3000 B.C. and Lauricocha III from 3000 to 2000 B.C. His Lauricocha IV is described as being characterized by "Chavinoid" pottery, although he is probably confusing this with early Initial Period incised pottery styles which do appear in the Peruvian highlands at about 1800 to 2000 B.C. Cardich also designates a Lauricocha V which he dates from about the beginning of the Christian era onward through the Inca horizon.

119 Lanning (1963 a, 1965, 1967, Chap. 4); Lynch (1967 a, pp. 45–47).

120 Lanning (1967, Chap. 4 and chronology chart) places Arenal chronologically at the very end of the Lauricocha I time span with this dating. This suggests that the interaction between coastal and highland sites began at the end of the Lauricocha I phase.

121 Luz, Canario, Corbina, and Encanto are described by Lanning (1967, Chap. 4) and Lauricocha III by Cardich (1964).

122 Cardich (1962).

123 Ravines (1965).

124 Lynch (1967 b).

125 Ramiro Matos (personal communication, 1967). This is also the place to note that MacNeish's (1969) Ayacucho cave sequence shows a number of preceramic complexes, estimated at dating between about 6000 B.C. and 1800 B.C., that show willow-leaf points (Jaywa complex) and smaller points (Piki, Chihua, and Cachi complexes).

126 Fung Pineda (1958). Callavallauri is the name of the complex to which H. Tschopik's (1946 b) Huancayo cave projectile points belong. See also Lynch (1967 a, p. 6).

127 Ravines (1967).

128 Vescelius (1963).

129 Menghin (1953–54) and Ibarra Grasso (1955) both feel that there is an early, "pre-projectile point" horizon represented at Viscachani (see Vol. I, p. 33—"Viscachani I"). This is a possibility, but only typological segregation of the surface collections has been adduced to demonstrate it. The comments on Viscachani presented here are derived from Patterson and Heizer (1965).

130 Lynch (1967 a, p. 37).

131 Le Paige (1959, 1960, 1963 a); but see, especially, Barfield (1961).

132 Barfield (1961).

133 Letter of 8 November 1967. Presumably, Chiu Chiu would correlate typologically and chronologically with Tambillo (3500–2000 B.C.) and Ascotan (2000 B.C.–A.D. 1) of the Salar de Atacama country (see Nuñez, 1965, chronology chart).

134 Nuñez (1965); Nuñez and Varela (1961–1964, 1966).

135 Bird (1943).

136 Nuñez (1965); True, Nuñez, and Nuñez (1970) describe willow-leaf point and smaller point complexes from the Tarapaca region.

137 Various writers have commented upon these similarities (see Lynch, 1967 a; A. L. Bryan, 1965; Patterson, 1963 b, c).

138 See Cigliano (1964, 1965).

139 González (1952); Lanning and Hammel (1961); Schobinger (1959).

140 Berberían, Calandra, and Sacchero (1966); González (1967).

141 The monographic reference to Intihuasi is González (1960).

142 González (1960) numbers the Intihuasi stratified phases from the top (latest) to bottom (earliest), so that Intihuasi IV is the earliest and Intihuasi I the latest. This is in contradistinction to most other sequences that we will review in this book, as, for instance, Bird's (1938) sequence at the Strait of

Magellan, which begins with the earliest phase as I and runs through the latest, which is V.

143 González (1952).

144 Menghin and González (1954).

145 Bird (1938, 1946 b).

146 See González (1960).

147 Emperaire and Laming (1961).

148 Arenal, Luz, and Canario are from Lanning (1967 a, ms., 1967, Chap. 4).

149 Lanning (1967, p. 54); see also Larco Hoyle (1948), who illustrates such a point from the "Pampa de Los Fosíles."

150 Bell (1965).

151 An opinion that I share with Lanning and Patterson (1967, ms.), but with which Lynch (1967 a) does not seem to agree.

152 Bell (1965, fig. 13, a, b, e).

153 Lanning and Patterson (1967, ms.) are inclined to lump Bell's El Inga II and III together as a single phase.

154 Reichel-Dolmatoff (1965 a, pp. 46–47).

155 Hurt (letter of 13 September 1968). One date is reported at 9000–10,000 B.C. This earlier date for the stemmed points is surprising and would seem to move them back into the chronological range of the Old South American Hunting tradition. But, pending further information, I have included the El Abra finds at this point of our presentation.

156 Rouse and Cruxent (1963, p. 33).

157 See Rouse and Cruxent (1963, pp. 42–43) for Canaima. Those authors date Las Casitas at just before 5500 B.C. (1963, chart, p. 30) but are inclined to place Canaima somewhat later as a "Paleo-Indian survival" into "Meso-Indian" times (see p. 42). Rouse and Cruxent also call attention to similar points at other Venezuelan Guiana sites near the Paragua River (Dupouy, 1958, 1960) and at sites still farther east in British Guiana (Evans and Meggers, 1960, pp. 21–24, pl. 8). See also Evans (1964).

158 Personal communication (1968).

159 Bórmida (1964 b) speculates that the Cuareim industry of north-

ern Uruguay and the Altoparaná of Paraguay-Brazil-Argentina may have been "proto-agricultural."

160 Personal communication (1968).

161 Meggers (1967).

162 T. O. Miller (1969).

163 Miller had earlier believed unifacial stemmed points to be associated with Santa Rosa; but he later revised this opinion and now sees the earliest Rio Claro points as belonging to the San Antonio phase. Stemmed points have been reported previously from the Rio Claro region. Conceição de M. C. Becker (1966 a, b) and Cruxent (1959) describe and illustrate these and other points from collections that also contained the fish-tailed points listed elsewhere in this chapter (p. 46). It is not clear, however, that these point collections represent a single archaeological horizon; on the basis of their typology I should think they did not.

164 Laming and Emperaire (1959 a, b).

165 Menghin (1962).

166 Chmyz (1967).

167 Blasi (1965). See also Laming and Emperaire (1959 a).

168 I am indebted to Lanning and Patterson (1967, ms.) for this information.

169 E. T. Miller (1967).

170 T. C. Patterson (personal communication, 1967).

171 Patterson (personal communication, 1967) would place Camboatá before Camuri in the seriation.

172 Bórmida (1964 b) makes this point, in effect, although his terminology is different.

173 Bórmida (1965 a).

174 Tropiduro and Fuqués are the names used by Lanning and Patterson (1967, ms.) for what Bórmida designated as Catalán c and d.

175 Bórmida (1964 b) apparently sees greater differences between Catalán and Cuareim than this.

176 Lanning and Patterson (1967, ms.).

177 This sequence is proposed by Menghin and Wachnitz (1958); for Altoparaná see also Mayntzhusen (1928, 1930).

178 T. O. Miller (personal communication, 1968) indicates implements from his Santa Rosa horizon that are like those of Altoparaná.

179 The Lagoa Santa discoveries date back to the work of P. W. Lund in the 1830's and 1840's (see Hrdlička and others, 1912, pp. 153–184). More recent excavations have been reported upon by Walter (1948). See also Lacerda (1882); A. Mattos (1946).

180 Hurt (1956, 1960, 1968). Evans (1950) describes assemblages similar to Cerca Grande from other Minas Gerais caves.

181 See Hurt (1964). In Volume One of this book (p. 68) these dates are given as 7600 and 8350 B.C. The latter date is in error.

182 The interpretation given by Lanning and Patterson (1967, ms.), who feel that there are similarities to some of the early stemmed points in the Andean areas.

183 Walter (1958). H. V. Walter's Lagoa Santa sequence, as published in this cited work, has four phases, the latter two of which have pottery. His earliest phase, the Mae Rosa, is characterized by stemmed bone points and completely polished stone axes, and his second phase by an increase in the number of polished axes. Although Hurt defined an upper level culture in the Rockshelter No. 6, the Lapa do Chapéu, that may correspond to Walter's earlier pottery phase, it is difficult to accommodate the Cerca Grande phase to Walter's early-level definitions.

184 Lanning (1967, Chap. 4).

185 Bird (1943, 1946 c).

186 Rouse and Cruxent (1963, pp. 44–46).

187 Rouse (1948 a, 1964); Alegría, Nicholson, and Willey (1955).

188 Lanning (1967 b, ms.); Meggers, Evans, and Estrada (1965); Reichel-Dolmatoff (1965 a, pp. 48–49, 51–60, 1965 b); Willey and McGimsey (1954); McGimsey (1956). Some of the cultural phases to which these citations refer are early ceramic complexes and have been described in considerable detail (e.g. Meggers, Evans, and Estrada, Reichel-Dolmatoff, Willey and McGimsey). This circumstance

of pottery appearing in some of the late phases of the Northwest South American Littoral tradition will be discussed at greater length in Chapter 5.

189 Laming and Emperaire (1959 b) cite dates from Maratua sambaquí of considerably more than this (approx. 5300 and 5800 B.C. plus-or-minus 1300 years). See also Laming and Emperaire (1957) for this site. See Hurt (1968) for general discussions of early sambaquís.

190 Some general references on the Brazilian sambaquís are Serrano (1946 a), Menghin (1962), and Altenfelder, Silva, and Meggers (1963).

191 Willey (1946 a).

192 For general references to the cultures of this tradition see Howard and Willey (1948).

193 Bird (1946 b).

194 See comments, this volume (pp. 477–478); Emperaire and Laming (1961).

195 Bird (1964 b) sees little possibility of the Fuegian tradition having arisen through diffusion from the Pacific Littoral tradition cultures of Chile.

196 A land connection was available, of course, at a much earlier substage of the Wisconsin when there had been a lowered sea level; and it is possible that people with a Lower or Middle Paleolithic type of technology crossed into the Americas then. The dating and the reasoning offered here, however, are those given by Müller-Beck (1965) and constitute his argument for bringing in peoples with a Levallois-Mousterian technology at some time after 30,000 B.C.

197 According to some geological opinion, there was never a complete closure of the Canadian ice fields that would have inhibited man's movements from Alaska to the south (T. C. Patterson, personal communication, 1967).

198 In connection with this summary, see Lanning (1970).

The Peruvian Culture Area

Fifteen hundred miles southeastward from Mesoamerica along the Pacific shore and in the Andes of South America is the other great center of native New World civilization: Peru. Like Mesoamerica, Peru is an area where these achievements of civilization climaxed a long cultural development, one beginning with early nomadic or semi-nomadic hunters and food gatherers and moving from this condition to the beginnings of sedentary life, to farming, to towns, cities, and empires. In this chapter we shall follow out this story of the rise of Peruvian civilization, looking back to its early antecedents which were described in Chapter 2 and taking up the narrative there to continue it forward to historic times.

The Natural Setting. The Peruvian culture area embraces highland and coastal Peru and a portion of the adjacent uplands of Bolivia (see Figs. 1-1, 3-1). Within this area are two great physiographic zones: the Andes and the coastal shelf.

The Peruvian Andes run from northwest to southeast (Fig. 3-2). In the north the three principal ranges, from west to east, are the Cordilleras Occidental, Central, and Oriental. In southern Peru these are reduced to only the Occidental and Oriental massifs (Fig. 3-2). They continue into western Bolivia but at a somewhat greater distance apart, bordering the high puna or altiplano that

Peru

3

lies between them. These Peruvian and Bolivian mountains are extremely high, rising to peaks of 15,000 to 20,000 feet; and the upland basins (Fig. 3-3) and plains that are surrounded by the ranges are also high, averaging 10,000 feet above sea level. Today the landscape is bleak. Below 5500 feet there is little vegetation cover, and above this there is mainly bush shrub and grass. In general, as one moves north in the highlands there is more rain, more vegetation, and vegetation at lower altitudes.

Peru lies, of course, in tropical latitudes, roughly between parallels 4 and 18 degrees south; but the highlands, because of their altitude, are temperate-to-cool, and nightly frosts are not uncommon in the southern basins and on the altiplano. Rains fall from November to May, the rest of the year being more or less dry.

A number of rivers rise in the Peruvian highlands and flow, eventually, eastward to the Amazon drainage. Among these are the Marañón, Huallaga, Mantaro, Apurímac, and Urubamba (Fig. 3-2). Except for the rivers of the Pacific coastal shelf, only the Upper Santa River, which flows out of a north-south rift valley known as the Callejón de Huaylas, empties westward into the Pacific. In the far south the altiplanos belong to an inland drainage system that centers on the great lake of Titicaca.

Man lives in, and has long occupied, the highland basins and altiplanos. They are regions of fertile soils and adequate rainfall, well suited to farming. The potato and the cereal quinoa were native to the very high basins and were probably first cultivated here. Other food plants, such as maize and beans, were introduced to altitudes up to 10,000 feet. Highland agriculture was supplemented by wild game—the guanaco, the vicuña, and deer—and by the domesticated camelids, the llama and alpaca.

The Peruvian coast—no more than a narrow shelf at the foot of the Andes—stands in strong environmental contrast to the highlands. It is a desert strip transected by 40 or more small river valleys that descend from the western slopes of the mountains to the sea. Between the valleys, rolling desert hills rise gradually to the Andes. Such hills, it will be recalled, were the locations of the lomas camps of the early hunters referred to in Chapter 2 (pp. 51–52). The Peruvian coastal valleys were once wooded with algarroba and similar trees—vestiges of which still remain in some places; but we know, however, that the valleys were cultivated for many centuries, back into the pre-Columbian past, as they are still cultivated. They are, in effect, a series of little green "Nile Valleys" relieving the otherwise dull-gray monotone of the surrounding desert sands and rocks (Fig. 3-4). Their soils are quite deep and rich, and wherever the life-giving waters of the rivers touch them they bloom with vegetation. All of the valleys hold ancient canals and garden plots—testimonies to their former years of intensive cultivation. And everywhere along the valley edges, or rising from the valley floors amidst present-day farms and fields, are rock and adobe mounds, house foundations, pyramids, and palaces—all relics of the markedly dense human occupance of

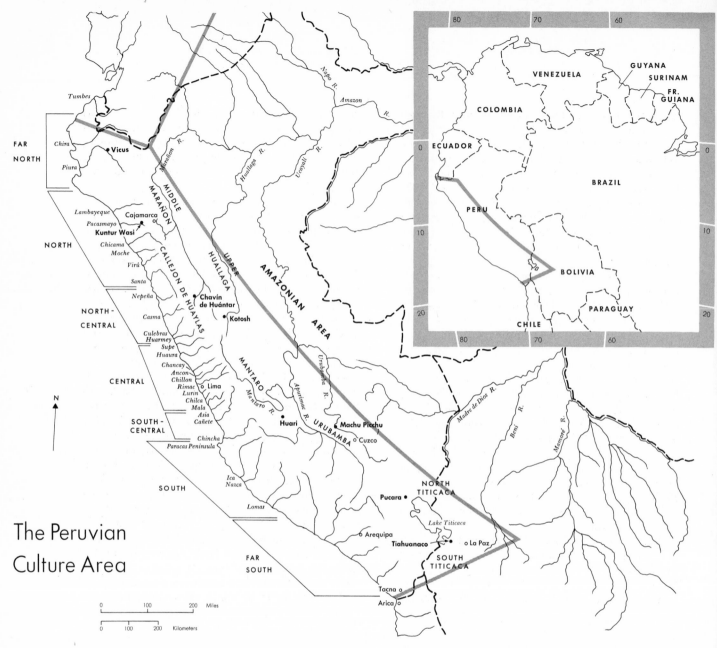

The Peruvian Culture Area

The map shows the following labeled regions and places:

Inset (South American setting):
VENEZUELA, COLOMBIA, ECUADOR, PERU, BOLIVIA, CHILE, BRAZIL, GUYANA, SURINAM, FR. GUIANA, PARAGUAY

Subareas (west side):
FAR NORTH, NORTH, NORTH-CENTRAL, CENTRAL, SOUTH-CENTRAL, SOUTH, FAR SOUTH, NORTH TITICACA, SOUTH TITICACA

Coastal valleys / places:
Tumbes, Chira, Piura, Vicus, Lambayeque, Pacasmayo, Kuntur Wasi, Cajamarca, Chicama, Moche, Virú, Santa, Nepeña, Chavín de Huántar, Kotosh, Casma, Culebras, Huarmey, Supe, Huaura, Chancay, Ancon, Chillon, Rimac, Lima, Lurin, Chilca, Mala, Asia, Cañete, Chincha, Paracas Peninsula, Ica, Nazca, Lomas, Huari, Machu Picchu, Cuzco, Pucara, Arequipa, Tiahuanaco, La Paz, Lake Titicaca, Tacna, Arica

Rivers / regions:
MARAÑON, MIDDLE MARAÑON, Napo R., Amazon, Huallaga R., Ucayali R., AMAZONIAN AREA, CALLEJON DE HUAYLAS, HUALLAGA, UPPER HUALLAGA, MANTARO, Mantaro R., Apurimac R., Urubamba R., URUBAMBA, Madre de Dios R., Beni R., Mamoré R.

0   100   200   Miles
0   100   200   Kilometers

N

Figure 3-1. *Above:* The map shows coastal and highland subareas, river valleys of the coast, some modern cities, and, in the highlands, certain archaeological sites. Inset shows the area in the larger South American setting.

Figure 3-2. (*Top*, p. 79)

Figure 3-3. The Peruvian Andes. *Right:* A modern village, with snowcapped mountains in background. (*Bottom*, p. 79) Panorama of the Cuzco valley. (Courtesy Peabody Museum, Harvard University.)

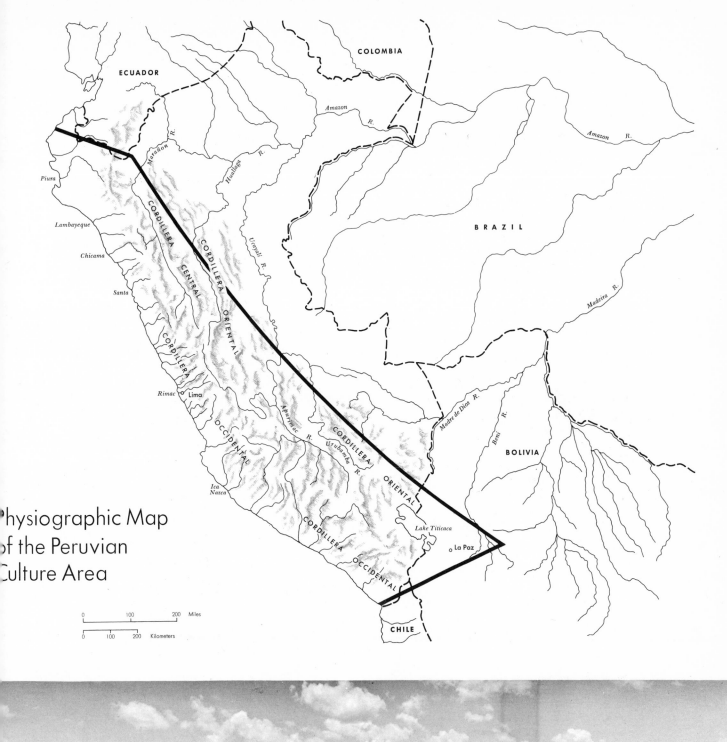

Physiographic Map
of the Peruvian
Culture Area

ECUADOR

COLOMBIA

Amazon R.

Amazon R.

Piura

Lambayeque

Chicama

Santa

Marañon R.

Huallaga R.

Ucayali R.

BRAZIL

Madeira R.

CORDILLERA CENTRAL

CORDILLERA ORIENTAL

Rimac Lima

Apurimac R.

Urubamba R.

CORDILLERA ORIENTAL

CORDILLERA OCCIDENTAL

Madre de Dios R.

Beni R.

BOLIVIA

Ica
Nazca

CORDILLERA OCCIDENTAL

Lake Titicaca

La Paz

0   100   200   Miles

0   100   200   Kilometers

CHILE

Figure 3-4. The Peruvian coast from the air. *Top:* Cerro Prieto de Guañape, Virú Valley, North Coast. The Cerro Prieto is a black, rocky outcrop connected to the mainland by a narrow spit of sand. The little protected bay thus formed provided a fishing place for the inhabitants of Huaca Negra, which was situated a short distance inland from the deep indenture of the bay. The white islets in the background are guano-covered. *Bottom:* The sea, the lower reaches of the cultivated valley (Virú), and a large lunate sand dune on the bordering desert. The line in the lower left is the Pan-American Highway, which now cuts through Virú and other coastal valleys. Prevailing winds from the south create the lunate dunes. (Courtesy Servicio Aerofotográfico, Peru.)

the aboriginal past. As a result of the exceptional aridity, the preservation of such ordinarily perishable items as basketry, cloth, wooden objects, and vegetable remains is almost as good as that of pottery or stone. Consequently, the archaeological record of the Peruvian coast is one of the richest and most complete in the world.

The extreme aridity of the Peruvian coast results from a combination of ocean currents, winds, and topographic features. The cold, northward-running Peruvian, or Humboldt, Current cools the prevailing winds that pass over it and strike the land. Because of the coolness these winds carry little moisture from evaporation; and what moisture there is does not produce rain over the land. Instead, the cold air and the warm land produce a fog. Near the shore the moisture from the fog is insufficient to sustain any vegetation, but higher up, on the coastal hills, it produces the seasonal growth of quick-flowering plants and grasses known as the lomas. We have seen in Chapter 2 that at one time in the distant past this lomas vegetation grew at somewhat lower elevations than it does today. From November to May the clouds and fog are less, the skies clear, and the air relatively warm. It is also in this period that the rivers run full as a result of the highland rains. On the whole, the climate and temperature of the Peruvian coast are remarkably uniform and mild. The average annual temperature at Lima is 66.7 degrees (F), and neither daily nor seasonal fluctua-

tions from this figure are great. The situation is, indeed, paradoxical: a desert frequently shrouded in mists but without rain[1] and a tropical land with a mild, rather non-tropical climate.

The fertile oasis valleys of the coast produced a great array of crops: maize, beans, manioc, squashes, peanuts, cotton, avocados, fruits—in fact, almost all of the plants that were grown in the highlands (Fig. 3-5), except those adapted to extremely high altitudes, together with a great many more fruits and vegetables that could not have withstood the colder upland climate. Wild land fauna offered some food resources; but the produce of the sea and seashore was tremendous and of great importance to the pre-Columbian

Figure 3-5. Agricultural terraces in the southern highlands of Peru. Still in use today, most or all of them date back to pre-Columbian times. In the distance, on the higher slopes (at top of picture), are the faint lines of additional ancient terraces. (Courtesy Peabody Museum, Harvard University.)

coastal dwellers. The cold Peruvian Current teemed with plankton and with the fish that fed upon the plankton. Gulls and cormorants fed on the fish, and the guano they deposited on rocky islets was an important source of agricultural fertilizer.

The Peruvian area has certain natural environmental limits. To the north, the coastal desert gives way to the savannas, mangroves, and forests of the southern Ecuador coast.[2] In the highlands, the Ecuadorian basins tend to be smaller than those of Peru, and there is more rainfall and a higher temperature. On the south, the Atacama desert of northern Chile is the most intensely arid section of South America. It is similar to the Peruvian coast, but a more extreme continuation of it. In interior Chile, northwestern Argentina, and western Bolivia, the basins and mountains are also extremely arid, with little or no rainfall except at the highest altitudes. Finally, on the east, the Peruvian area is bounded by the montaña country, a wet, cloud-forested transitional zone between the highlands and the jungle rainforest of the Amazonian lowlands.

The archaeological record shows that the heterogeneity of the environment and resources of the Peruvian area offered unusual opportunities for man to build one of the great pre-Columbian civilizations of the Americas and that he took advantage of these opportunities. Effective exploitation of the natural resources of small living niches (highland basins, coastal valleys) led to rapid population growth and a compression of these populations into relatively small territories. This concentration promoted an early development of social and cultural complexity, and this was further stimulated by contacts among the growing populations of the separate, but by no means completely isolated, habitable zones. The situation is not unlike that described for Mesoamerica (Vol. I, Chap. 3); but for Peru the relations between man and nature are seen even more clearly, perhaps, than in the former area.[3]

Archaeological Chronology. Archaeological culture sequences for the Peruvian area are projected for the occupancy of the area from earliest times—prior to the era of a Peruvian cultural tradition, through the millennia of that tradition, down to the Spanish Conquest.

A general sequence for Peruvian archaeology was first formulated by Max Uhle as the result of his excavations in the late nineteenth and early twentieth centuries.[4] The essence of the Uhle scheme was an "Early Period" of localized or regional cultures, a "Middle Period" of cultures reflecting stylistic similarities to the south highland Tiahuanaco culture, a "Late Period" of local or regional cultures once more, and, finally, a fourth period in which these regional cultures showed the stylistic and architectural influences of the expanding Inca empire. The area-wide synthesizing principles of this Uhle sequence were the broad spreads or diffusions of the Incaic and Tiahuanaco-like art styles, and such styles were later referred to as "horizon styles."[5]

Following Uhle, the field research of other archaeologists bore out his fourfold scheme and also supplemented it.[6] The supplementations or revisions resulted from the discovery and recognition of still earlier cultures. By the early 1940's it became clear that a Chavín stylistic horizon underlay Uhle's "Early Period."[7] Below this a still earlier ceramic period was marked off; and, finally, man's story in Peru was run back through a series of preceramic periods.[8] After 1950, chronology building in Peru was, of course, greatly abetted by the advent of radiocarbon dating. This dating has quite solidly confirmed the main outlines of the Uhle structure and the major additions to it.

In this presentation we shall follow the Peruvian archaeological chronology originally propounded by J. H. Rowe and recently elaborated upon by E. P. Lanning.[9] This is in accordance with our plan throughout both volumes of this book to adhere to archaeological periods that are defined strictly as time periods.[10] A number of other Peruvian sequence schemes have been employed by various authors over the past 20 years (Fig. 3-6). Although these are primarily chronological devices, their terminology—and, to some extent, their implications—have been those of developmental or evolutionary stages. In this ambiguity they have been comparable to the archaeological sequences and sequence terminology that have been in common use in Mesoamerica (see Vol. I, pp. 89–93). In our treatment of Mesoamerica we employed such a sequence and the terminology current for the area, although we made the stipulation that only chronological periodization was intended, with no developmental or functional connotations. For Peru, the Rowe scheme, with its noncommittal terminology, is well suited to our purpose.

The Rowe chronology was originally devised to subsume only the ceramic cultures of Peru. It was based upon stylistic seriations, stratigraphy, and radiocarbon dates from the Ica Valley of the south coast; and from here it was extended to other regions by stylistic and radiocarbon cross datings. In the last few years, with the greater attention paid to preceramic cultures, it has been necessary to supplement the chronological scheme by extending it downward, or back in time, so that it embraces all of the evidences of man in Peru, both on the coast and in the highlands. This has been done in the recent summary work by Lanning.[11]

Figure 3-6. Chart showing approximate correspondences between Rowe-Lanning chronological scheme used in this book and other chronological schemes for Peru.

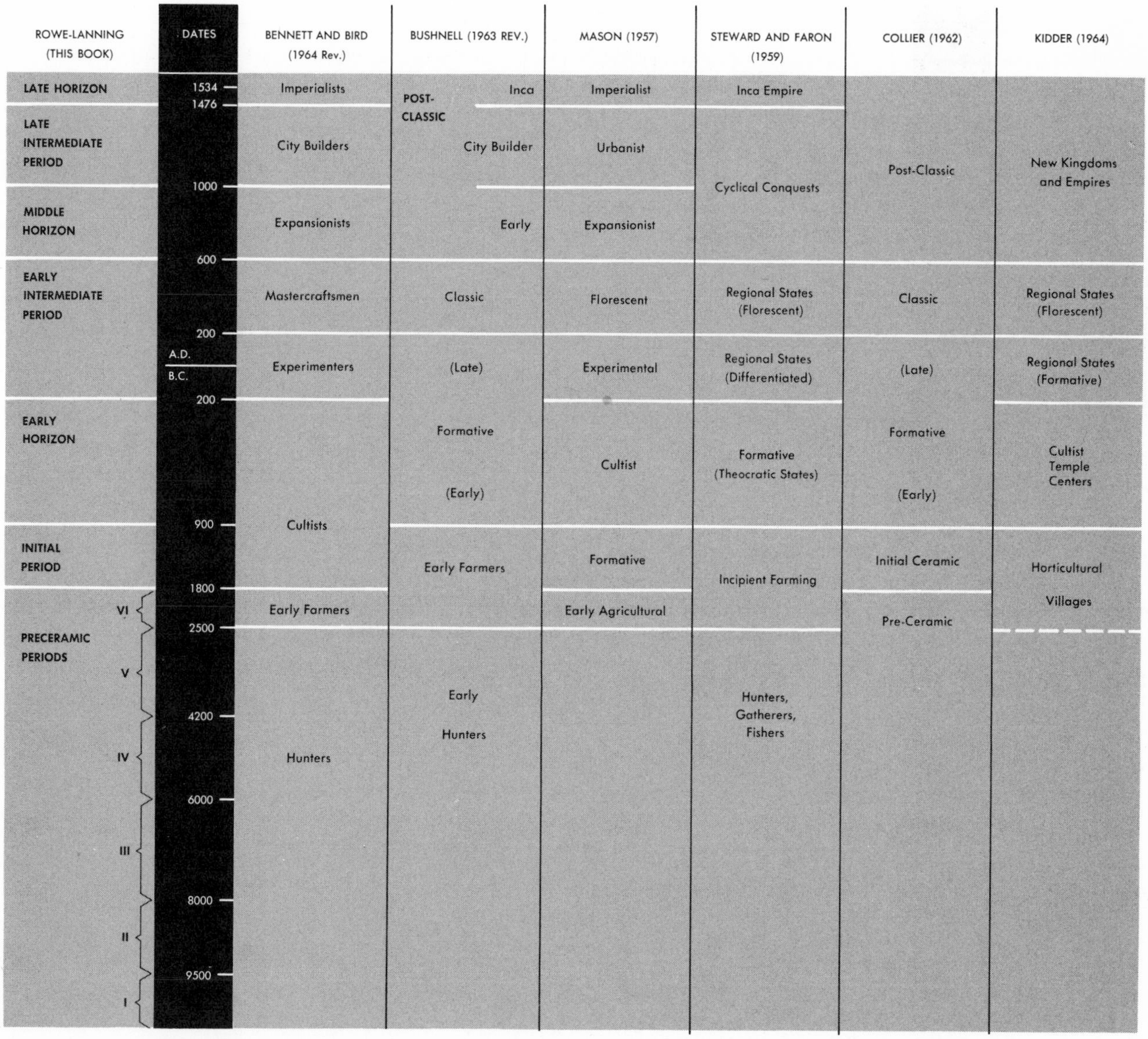

ROWE-LANNING (THIS BOOK)	DATES	BENNETT AND BIRD (1964 Rev.)	BUSHNELL (1963 REV.)	MASON (1957)	STEWARD AND FARON (1959)	COLLIER (1962)	KIDDER (1964)
LATE HORIZON	1534 / 1476	Imperialists	POST-CLASSIC — Inca	Imperialist	Inca Empire		
LATE INTERMEDIATE PERIOD	1000	City Builders	City Builder	Urbanist	Cyclical Conquests	Post-Classic	New Kingdoms and Empires
MIDDLE HORIZON	600	Expansionists	Early	Expansionist			
EARLY INTERMEDIATE PERIOD	200	Mastercraftsmen	Classic	Florescent	Regional States (Florescent)	Classic	Regional States (Florescent)
	A.D. / B.C.	Experimenters	(Late)	Experimental	Regional States (Differentiated)	(Late)	Regional States (Formative)
EARLY HORIZON	200	Cultists	Formative — (Early)	Cultist	Formative (Theocratic States)	Formative — (Early)	Cultist Temple Centers
INITIAL PERIOD	900 / 1800	Early Farmers	Early Farmers	Formative	Incipient Farming	Initial Ceramic	Horticultural Villages
PRECERAMIC PERIODS — VI	2500	Early Farmers		Early Agricultural		Pre-Ceramic	
V	4200	Hunters	Early Hunters		Hunters, Gatherers, Fishers		
IV	6000						
III	8000						
II	9500						
I							

The master chronological charts, shown as Figures 3-7 and 3-8, give the periods and dates[12] of the Rowe-Lanning chronology, with subarea columns and selected archaeological culture phases. There are 12 major periods: six preceramic and six ceramic. They are defined, and very briefly characterized, as follows:

(1) *Preceramic Period I (prior to 9500* B.C.). This is the time of the Flake tradition industries, represented by the Chivateros Red Zone and Oquendo complexes (see Chap. 2, pp. 34–36). The period is believed to correspond to the glacial era of the Mankato, Port Huron, or Older Dryas advance, and to the beginnings of the Two Creeks, or Alleröd, Interstadial.

(2) *Preceramic Period II (9500–8000* B.C.). This is the period of the Biface technological tradition as represented by the Chivateros I industry.

Figure 3-7. Chronological chart for the Peruvian coast, with subarea columns, major periods, and estimated dates.

PERIODS	DATES	FAR NORTH	NORTH	NORTH CENTRAL	CENTRAL	SOUTH CENTRAL	SOUTH	FAR SOUTH
LATE HORIZON	1534 / 1476	Inca Influences	Inca-Chimu	Inca-Chimu	Inca Influences	Inca Influences	Inca Influences	Inca Influences
LATE INTERMEDIATE PERIOD	1000	Chimu-Piura	Chimu	Chimu / Santa	Chancay Huancho	Chincha	Ica	Ilo
MIDDLE HORIZON	600	Piura	Tomaval	Pativilca	Epigonal Pachacamac Nievería	Cerro de Oro	Epigonal Atarco Pacheco	Loreto
EARLY INTERMEDIATE PERIOD	A.D. / B.C.		Moche / Gallinazo / Salinar	Patazca	Lima / Baños de Boza Mira-Mar	Estrella / Carmen	Nazca	San Benito Islay
EARLY HORIZON	200 / 900	Sechura / Paita	Cupisnique	Pallka	Colinas Garagay	Topará / Pozuelo	Paracas	Ichuña
INITIAL PERIOD	1800	Negritos / San Juan	Guañape	Cerro Sechín / Haldas	Curayacu / Florida / Chira		Hacha	
PRECERAMIC PERIODS VI	2500	?	Huaca Prieta	Culebras	Paraíso / Rio Seco	Asia Unit I	Casavilca	Ocoña / Toquepala III
V	4200	Honda			Encanto Chilca / Corbina		Cabezas Largas	
IV	6000	Siches	Paiján		Canario / Luz			Toquepala II
III	8000				Chivateros II			Toquepala I
II	9500				Chivateros I			
I					Oquendo / Chivateros R.Z.			

The presumed geological correlation is with the Two Creeks or Alleröd Interstadial equivalent and with the subsequent Valders or Younger Dryas glacial advance.

(3) *Preceramic Period III (8000–6000* B.C.*)*. The coastal complexes of this period are the Chivateros II, Pampilla, and Arenal. The first two belong to the Old South American Hunting tradition and are characterized by elongated leaf-shaped projectile points similar to those of the Venezuelan El Jobo complex. Arenal, on the other hand, is

assigned to the Andean Hunting-Collecting tradition, and its most common projectile point is a stemmed form. In the highlands the Lauricocha I phase is on this time level, and it is thought to mark a transition between the Old South American Hunting and Andean Hunting-Collecting traditions. The economy of the earlier tradition is

Figure 3-8. Chronological chart for the Peru-Bolivian highlands, with subarea columns, major periods, and estimated dates.

PERIODS	DATES	MIDDLE MARAÑON	CALLEJÓN DE HUAYLAS	UPPER HUALLAGA	MANTARO	URUBAMBA	NORTH TITICACA BASIN	SOUTH TITICACA BASIN
LATE HORIZON	1534 / 1476	Inca-Cajamarca	Inca Influence	Inca Influence	Inca Influence	Inca	Chucuito (Inca)	Inca Influence
LATE INTERMEDIATE PERIOD	1000	Cajamarca V	Aquilpo	Marabamba		Killke	Collao / Sillustani	Wancani
MIDDLE HORIZON	600	Cajamarca IV / Cajamarca III	Honco		Viñaque / Conchopata ▲ B	Viñaque	Tiahuanaco	Tiahuanaco
EARLY INTERMEDIATE PERIOD	A.D. / B.C.	Cajamarca II / Cajamarca I ↑	Recuay / White-on-Red	Higueras ↑	Chakipampa A / Huarpa / Aya Orjo	Huaru	Pucara	Qeya / Qalasasaya
EARLY HORIZON	200	Torrecitas / Kuntur Wasi	Chavín	San Blas / Sajara-Patac / Kotosh Chavín	Rancha / Wichqana	Chanapata / Marcavalle	Qaluyu	Late Chiripa
INITIAL PERIOD	900 / 1800		Toril ↑	Kotosh / Waira-jirca				Early Chiripa
PRECERAMIC PERIODS VI	2500			Mito				
V	4200	Lauricocha III			Callavallauri			↑
IV	6000	Lauricocha II		Ambo				Viscachani
III	8000	Lauricocha I			Junín			
II	9500							
I								

thought to have been more specialized in the direction of land hunting than that of the later tradition where a pattern of transhumance between highland hunting camps and coastal lomas plant-collecting stations is postulated. The climatic era corresponds to that of the terminal Valders or Younger Dryas and the Anathermal.

(4) *Preceramic Period IV* (*6000–4200* B.C.). In the highlands this period begins with the willow-leaf, or Ayampitín-type, projectile point horizon of the Andean Hunting-Collecting tradition. On the coast the contemporaneous Andean Hunting-Collecting tradition phases at first feature lanceolate stemmed points, but later in the period these tend to be replaced by the willow-leaf forms. The highland hunting-coastal plant-collecting transhumance subsistence continued, although toward the end of this period a new seasonal shifting of residence began between lomas plant-gathering camps and seashore fishing stations. In some of these latter sites we also have evidences of early plant domestication. Climatically and geologically this should have been the time of transition between Anathermal and Altithermal conditions.

(5) *Preceramic Period V* (*4200–2500* B.C.). This period was marked by Altithermal heat and dryness and the shrinkage of the lomas fog vegetation along the coast. Possibly as a result, coastal populations came to spend more time in lower valley and shoreline camps, and with these settlement shifts marine subsistence resources became of paramount importance. These sites, which we consider as the earliest stations of the new tradition—the Pacific Littoral tradition—are characterized by fishing gear and remains of domesticated plants, including squashes, chili peppers, guavas, and cotton (toward the end of the period). In the highlands, the Andean Hunting-Collecting tradition cultures persisted during this period.[12a]

(6) *Preceramic Period VI* (*2500–1800* B.C.). On the coast this period saw the continuity and enrichment of the Pacific Littoral tradition cultures. Populations increased. In the last centuries of the period the Pacific Littoral tradition began to be transformed into the Peruvian tradition. This transformation or transition was marked by the appearance of large habitation sites, sizable public or ceremonial constructions, and the first appearance of maize cultivation. The period closes with the appearance of pottery.[13]

(7) *The Initial Period* (*1800–900* B.C.). This is the first ceramic period in the Peruvian area archaeological sequence. It is also here considered as marking the emergence of the Peruvian cultural tradition.[14] As has already been noted, it begins with the appearance of pottery. It closes with the first appearances of the Chavín art style.

(8) *The Early Horizon* (*900–200* B.C.). The Early Horizon is the period of the Chavín style and its immediate derivatives. The Chavín style is not represented in all parts of the area, but cultures in subareas and regions where the style is not present may be assigned to the 900 to 200 B.C. period by cross dating.

(9) *The Early Intermediate Period* (*200* B.C.–A.D. *600*). This period opens with the various new subareal ceramic and art styles that replace Chavín and Chavín-influenced ones. It closes with the appearance of the Tiahuanaco and Huari horizon styles.

(10) *The Middle Horizon* (A.D. *600–1000*). The Middle Horizon is the time of the Tiahuanaco- and Huari-derived styles and their propagation throughout most of the Peruvian area. It closes with the emergence, once more, of subareal styles.

(11) *The Late Intermediate Period* (A.D. *1000–1476*). This period, intermediate between the Middle and Late Horizons, is characterized by a series of late ceramic and art styles—and by a series of corresponding late states or kingdoms.

(12) *The Late Horizon* (A.D. *1476–1534*). The Late Horizon begins with the expansion of the Inca style and culture—and with the expansion of Inca militarism and the Inca state—in the late fifteenth century. It closes with the downfall of this empire and the ascendancy of the Spanish conquerors under Pizarro.

As has been noted, other chronological or sequence schemes have been offered for Peru. Some of these are to be found in widely read sources on Peruvian archaeology. The chart in Figure 3-6 is an attempt to show the approximate correspondences, period by period, between the Rowe-Lanning scheme employed in this chapter and some of the well-known sequence schemes of other authors.[15]

Subareal Divisions. Following Lanning, with only minor modifications, we divide the Peruvian area into 14 such subareas (Fig. 3-1).[16]

Like the delimitation of the total Peruvian culture area, they are defined by cultures of relatively recent prehistoric times—in effect, by those dating from about the beginning of the Initial Period.

For the highlands these subareas are drainage basins. From north to south they are:

(1) *Middle Marañón.* This is the course of the river valley as it flows northward between the Cordilleras Occidental and Central, from the vicinity of Huamachuco to Cajamarca. The subarea is characterized by the distinctive Cajamarca "cursive" pottery styles.

(2) *Callejón de Huaylas (and the uppermost Marañón drainages).* The subarea lies largely within the Peruvian Department of Ancash. The Callejón de Huaylas is a narrow valley that runs northward in a rift of the Cordillera Occidental and, eventually, drains to the Pacific. Across the mountains, to the east of the Callejón, are numerous little tributaries that drain down into the Marañón. Chavín de Huántar, that important center of Chavín art and sculpture, is located in the subarea. The Callejón de Huaylas is noted for its Recuay, or Huaylas, painted pottery style as well as for the Aija stone sculptural style.

(3) *Upper Huallaga.* This northward-flowing river parallels the Upper Marañón but lies to the east of it, between the Cordilleras Central and Oriental. This, in the Department of Huánuco, is the subarea of the Kotosh site, of the early incised pottery styles of that site, and of Chavín-like pottery.

(4) *Mantaro.* The Mantaro River flows south through the central highlands, passing between the Cordilleras Occidental and Oriental.[17] It then doubles back north before turning sharply east to join the Apurímac-Ucayalí system. In the vicinity of Ayacucho is the great site of Huari, center of a Tiahuanaco-related pottery style that spread throughout much of Peru in Middle Horizon times.

(5) *Urubamba.* South and east of the Mantaro subarea is the Urubamba Valley. It drains northward between the converging Cordilleras Occidental and Oriental to reach, eventually, the Ucayalí. The principal site was Cuzco, center of Inca power in Late Horizon times.

(6) *North Titicaca Basin.* This is the Peruvian altiplano north of Lake Titicaca. The best known archaeological site is Pucará, the center of an Early Intermediate Period pottery style of that name.

(7) *South Titicaca Basin.* This is the Bolivian altiplano on the south shores of the lake. It is the subarea of the famed Tiahuanaco site.

For the Peruvian coast similar subareas consist of little groups of closely related river valleys. From north to south they are:

(8) *The Far North.* This includes the valleys of Chira and Piura.[18] In general, the subarea has an appearance of marginality to the cultural developments immediately to the south.

(9) *The North.* This includes the Lambayeque, Pacasmayo, Chicama, Moche, Virú, and Santa Valleys.[19] The subarea appears to have been the heart of the Early Intermediate Period Moche civilization and style; it seems also to have been the core territory of the Late Intermediate Period Chimu kingdom.

(10) *North-Central.* This includes the Nepeña, Casma, Culebras, and Huarmey Valleys. These are all small valleys compared to most of those of the Far North or North subareas. They are known for Early Horizon developments and strong Chavín influences. This is also the subarea of several notable preceramic and Initial Period sites.

(11) *Central.* This includes the Supe, Huaura, Chancay, Ancón, Chillón, Rimac, Lurín, Chilca, and Mala Valleys.[20] The subarea has a long preceramic sequence, as well as important Initial Period and Early Horizon sites. It is best known for the Lima style of the Early Intermediate Period and, in some of its valleys, for the Late Intermediate Period Chancay style.

(12) *South-Central.* This includes the Asia (Omas), Cañete, Topará, and Chincha Valleys .

(13) *South.* This includes the Paracas Peninsula and the Pisco, Ica, Nazca, and Lomas (Acarí) Valleys or regions. This is the center of the Paracas textiles and multi-color pottery and of the unusually handsome Nazca polychrome pottery style. Huari influence was strong in the subarea in Middle Horizon times, and the Late Intermediate Period is defined by the distinctive Ica style.

(14) *Far South.* This includes the territory south of Lomas to the Peruvian-Chilean border.[21] The subarea should also include the region of Arequipa, which lies some distance back from the coast in the lower reaches of the Cordillera Occidental. The archaeology of the region of Arica in far northern Chile might, at least in its later periods, also be considered within the subarea.

Within each subarea we shall, on occasion, refer to regions. A section of an upland valley or basin would be such a regional unit as would a single valley of the coast.[22]

The Peruvian Cultural Tradition. A number of years ago, the late W. C. Bennett defined what he termed the "Peruvian area co-tradition." This was, in his words, an "...overall unit of cultural history...within which the component cultures have been interrelated over a period of time."[23] He projected such a co-tradition back to what we are here designating as the Early Horizon in our time scale, and he set as his area the Peruvian or Central Andean area as we have defined it. This "co-traditional" definition is, essentially, our Peruvian culture sphere. As with Mesoamerica,[24] we define a Peruvian culture sphere as the geographical-culture area of Peru, the cultural tradition which defines that area, and the period of time during which the tradition persisted. As we have indicated, our spatial or geographic dimension is the same as Bennett's. On the temporal scale, we have revised his lower limit downward to include the Initial Period. Let us now briefly consider the third dimension of the Peruvian culture sphere, the content of the Peruvian cultural tradition itself.[25]

Basic to the Peruvian cultural tradition is the agricultural complex, with the foods maize *(Zea mays),* potatoes *(Solanum sp.),* lima beans *(Phaseolus lunatus),* kidney or common beans *(Phaseolus vulgaris),* squashes *(Cucurbita moschata, C. ficifolia),* quinoa *(Chenopodium quinoa),* sweet potatoes *(Impomoea batatas),* peanuts *(Arachis hypogaea),* manioc *(Manihot esculenta),* avocados *(Persea americana),* chili peppers *(Capsicum sp.),* and numerous other fruits and vegetables.[26] Cotton *(Gossypium barbadense),* gourds *(Lagenaria sp.),* coca *(Erythroxylon coca),* and tobacco *(Nicotiana tabacum, N. rustica)* were also cultivated for fibers, containers, and narcotics.

Irrigation, terracing, and the use of fertilizers were important parts of the Peruvian intensive agricultural economy. Irrigation was primarily a coastal technique and terracing a highland one. The archaeological record for the time of inception of these techniques is not yet an adequate one, but it seems likely that they were but little developed at the beginning of the Peruvian cultural

tradition. Certainly they were not fully exploited until much later.

Llama *(Lama glama glama)* and alpaca *(Lama pacos)* herding—and the use of these domesticated animals for meat, wool, hides, and beasts of burden—is an ancient part of the Peruvian cultural pattern, apparently for both highlands and coast. Other important domesticated animals were the guinea pig and the muscovy duck.

The sea was an important source of sustenance for the coastal peoples of the Peruvian tradition. Fish, shellfish, marine mammals, and seabirds (producers of guano) were the important elements. Fish were taken from the shore or from rafts with both hook-and-line and net techniques. The antiquity of these patterns goes back into the earlier Pacific Littoral tradition. There was, of course, a trend toward the replacement of these pursuits with those of an agricultural subsistence as the Peruvian tradition got under way; however, they remained of importance. The same is not true of land hunting, which probably was retained on the coast only as a sport and in the highlands as a minor food-getting activity.

The ancient Peruvians chewed coca leaves, with lime, as a narcotic. This was more prevalent than the use of tobacco, although the latter was also known.

The essential and characteristic elements of Peruvian clothing were the breech-clout, simple skirt, belt, slit-necked shirt, shawl, head-band (with some elaborations of head-gear), and the woven bag with strap.

Peruvian iconography from very early times featured felines, fish, serpents, birds, or rayfish designs, often rendered quite geometrically and stylized. A pattern of pairing, of the opposition of two similar figures, or of the concept of two-headedness (one head at each end of a body) was common. Condor designs, trophy human heads, and masked (human?) figures with capes were also characteristic.

Peruvian religion placed great emphasis upon ancestor reverence or worship. This is known definitely from the ethnohistoric horizon, but archaeological finds also suggest such attitudes for the past. There was also a pilgrimage pattern in religious observances, with people traveling for miles to visit and worship at famous sites or shrines or to consult oracles at these places.

Peruvian populations were large and densely concentrated into villages, towns, and cities. The phenomenon of the big town or the city is, as we shall see, as old as the tradition itself.

There were marked individual and class distinctions in old Peruvian society.

The organization of the territorial state also has a long Peruvian history. At the time of the Spanish Conquest the Inca state or empire was the largest in native America and, in fact, one of the largest political domains of the world of that era. There are clues in the archaeological record that strongly imply earlier empires for the area.

Reminiscent of Mesoamerica, the Peruvians built in adobe and stone, constructing massive public buildings of these materials—temples, palaces, fortifications, and other works.

The tradition is also characterized by monumental arts, such as the stone sculptures of Chavín, Pucará, Aija, and Tiahuanaco.

Again, as in Mesoamerica, Peruvian craft technology showed high competence or expertness. This is seen in pottery (from very early times), stone-carving (also old), metallurgy (including casting, alloying, and smelting), shellworking, wood carving, featherwork, and, above all, in weaving cotton and wool. Both the aesthetic qualities and the sheer quantitative volume of Peruvian craft goods are impressive.[27]

Unlike Mesoamerican culture, there was no Peruvian writing, and there are no records of complex mathematics or calendrics.

Individually, only a few of the traits or trait complexes that we have listed above are uniquely Peruvian. As with Mesoamerica, the completely unique is mostly stylistic or ideological, as seen or implied in the arts. But as the various Peruvian traits coalesce or adhere together in a grand pattern, they characterize the culture history of the area and compose a Peruvian cultural tradition that lasted for more than 20 centuries.

Peoples. The data of physical anthropology for Peru—those pertaining to archaeologically documented and dated skeletal series—are few. The earliest known skeletons are those from the Lauricocha Caves in the Upper Huallaga drainage of the highlands. These probably date back prior to 6000 B.C. or to the Preceramic Period III. They reveal a long-headed, high-headed,

rather broad-faced physical type—one, in fact, that corresponds to Imbelloni's "Laguides" group (p. 10).[28] On the Peruvian coast the earliest human remains are also long-headed. These come from Chilca[29] and Cabezas Largas.[30] They date appreciably later than the Lauricocha skeletons, falling in Preceramic Period V, or in a time range of about 3800 to 3000 B.C. Later, in Preceramic Period VI, or at some time after 2500 B.C., there are indications that a round-headed type may have replaced the earlier long-heads on the Peruvian coast. Findings from coastal Ecuador tend to support this hypothesis of a replacement. There, the earliest cranial series—associated with the Valdivia culture (see pp. 266–268) and dating to the third millennium B.C.—is notably brachycranic.[31] Were these Ecuadorians the ancestors of the Peruvian coastal brachycephalic "Pueblo-Andid" type[32] who had drifted south along the Pacific Coast?

Certainly by the time of the Early Horizon (ca. 900–200 B.C.) the basic Peruvian "Pueblo-Andid," or round-headed, physical type was found all along the coast, exhibiting only minor differences from valley to valley. M. T. Newman attributes these minor differences to the maintenance, over a long period of time, of semi-isolated breeding populations in each valley. In the Late Intermediate Period, however, these localized enclaves were leveled and the coastal population became more uniform than ever before.[33] In the highlands, although data are few, there always seems to have been more of a tendency toward dolichocephaly, and it could well be that the occasional long-heads who appear in the coastal populations after the Middle Horizon are highlanders. Such would seem likely in view of what we know of the social and political events of these late times.

The nature of Peruvian cranial indices is somewhat confused by the cultural practice of head deformation, and the question might be asked about the extent to which the appearance of the Peruvian round-headed type of the coast is an appearance of the trait of fronto-vertico-occipital deformation. Although cranial deformation has been known to mislead physical anthropologists in their appraisal of broad-headedness, it seems likely that in this case we can be fairly sure that the brachycephaly was genetic—even though in some instances it was exaggerated artificially.[34]

J. R. Munizaga has argued that the trait of

fronto-occipital deformation was brought to the Peruvian coast by the Machalilla peoples of Ecuador;[35] however, in supporting this argument, his dating of the Preceramic Period VI populations of the Peruvian coast at 1400 B.C.—to bring them into proper chronological alignment with Machalilla—is much too late. It is, of course, possible that cranial deformation was introduced to the Peruvian coast from the north sometime in Preceramic Period VI; but we also know that a fronto-vertico-occipital form of deformation was present in the Peruvian highlands, at Lauricocha, as early as Preceramic Period III.[36] It is an old and widespread trait; but, whatever its source and time of first origins, this kind of head deformation became the widespread custom on the Peruvian coast by Early Horizon times where a variant of it is actually known as the "Chavín type." It was produced by binding the head of the infant against the hard surface of a cradle-board and also so binding the child that the head invariably faced forward.[37]

Languages. When the Spaniards entered Peru in 1532 they found the country under the unified political control of the Inca. The Inca language was Quechua, one of the principal member languages of what Greenberg has designated as the Andean major language group (see p. 12). The Inca had made Quechua the official language of the empire and had enforced its use in regions where the local peoples spoke other tongues.

Besides Quechua, the most important other language, in the sense of being most widespread in the area, was Aymara, which was spoken by the peoples of the south Peruvian and adjacent Bolivian highlands. Aymara, too, was an Andean group language.

There were also the old regional languages of the kingdoms that had been overrun by the Quechua-speaking Inca. Sec and Tallan were recorded for the far north coast of Peru, and these are believed to have been remotely related to Quechua and Aymara in their common affiliation through the Andean major group. To the south of these were Yunca or Yunca-Puruhán languages. These are classified by Greenberg as Paezan rather than Andean. Paezan-affiliated languages are found mostly in Ecuador and Colombia, but the Atacameño of north Chile are also included in the

Paezan group. For the Peruvian central and south coasts there are no data on the old local languages although, presumably, they were not Quechua. It should be emphasized that the linguistic data for the coast—for the Tallan, Sec, and Yunca identifications—are extremely scanty. All of these tongues have long been extinct. Today Quechua and Aymara—with the minor exception of two small enclaves of Uru-Chipaya[38] speakers in Bolivia— are the only native languages still spoken in the area, and these are confined to the highlands.[39]

Considering the nature of the data, Peruvian area linguistics offer only the most tentative basis for culture-historical reconstructions. One possibility might be that an early population of Paezan speakers at one time held the Pacific coast from Colombia and Ecuador down as far as the territory of the Paezan-affiliated Atacameño of northern Chile. This Paezan distribution was later broken by the Tallan-Sec peoples and, still later, by the Incaic Quechua, both moving down to the coast from the highlands. But for now this must remain highly speculative.

The only sound glottochronological reconstruction that we have so far is more limited in geographic and chronologic scope. This is founded on changes within the Quechua language itself. The reconstruction postulates that mutually unintelligible dialects of that language had differentiated out and spread through the highlands between A.D. 850 and 1200.[40] This would mean that Quechua speakers were living throughout the Peruvian highlands before the Inca, with their particular dialect, began their expansion out of the Urubamba subarea. In other words, the pan-Peruvian aspects of Quechua—at least for all of its dialects—was not wholly a phenomenon of the Inca Empire.

Precursors and Foundations of the Peruvian Cultural Tradition

The Peruvian cultural tradition developed out of the cultures that immediately preceded it—the Pacific Littoral tradition of the coast and the Andean Hunting-Collecting tradition of the highlands. This story of local development can be traced back even further in time than this, as we have done in Chapter 2 and as is recapitulated in the Peruvian cultural-period resumé in this chapter; however it is in the Pacific Littoral tradition and the late phases of the Andean Hunting-Collecting tradition that we see the emergence of new trends that lead into the Peruvian cultural tradition. As we shall see, the archaeological record is notably uneven in this respect. The coast, with its rainless environment and amazing perservation, offers a much more detailed story for the Pacific Littoral tradition and its transition into the Peruvian cultural tradition than we have for the highlands and the later phases of the Andean Hunting-Collecting tradition.

The Pacific Littoral Tradition: Early Phases. A minimal and common-denominator definition of the Pacific Littoral tradition is based upon shoreline settlement, primary dependence on marine subsistence, and the use of certain fishing gear such as shell, thorn, or composite fishhooks; fishnets of sedges or cotton fibers; the use of gourds for net floats and for containers; and the making of basketry and mats. As so defined, the tradition will be considered in the chapter dealing with the South Andes area as well as in this one. It is in Peru, however, that the tradition acquires special traits, such as plant cultivation and permanent domestic and ceremonial architecture. As such, it becomes transitional to the Peruvian cultural tradition. In this section we will consider, first, the Pacific Littoral tradition as it is manifested in its earlier Peruvian phases—during Preceramic Period V—and, second, the tradition in its later phases—those of Preceramic Period VI.

Preceramic Period V (4200–2500 B.C.) probably coincided with the maximum glacial retreat in western South America. In western North America this was the Altithermal climatic era, and there are reasons to believe that a comparable era of increased heat and dryness also affected parts of South America. Along the Peruvian coast there is evidence that the lomas fog vegetation suffered a marked retreat and shrinkage at this time. This climatic change, which apparently came on gradually, must have provided an incentive for the establishment of more and larger camp sites along the littoral; and, finally, this trend resulted in the shifting of all activities to what became permanent, year-round villages of the shoreline. Climatic change need not, however, have been the only

factor working for settlement shift and cultural change. If the development of seashore subsistence pursuits was gradual, it may have taken some time before adequate fishing techniques were acquired in order to take advantage of the enormous "harvests" of the Peruvian Current. It should also be remembered that in Peru, as in Mesoamerica, the millennia of the Altithermal era were the important ones for the beginnings of crop domestication. As the valley floors near the rivers were the places along the Peruvian coast that were most suitable for farming,[41] a move to such locations—which were also nearer the sea—was in order.

By Encanto phase times (the latter part of Preceramic Period V), the shoreline summer camps were well established. One such summer camp on the shore is seen at Chilca, 67 kilometers south of Lima, in the Central Coast subarea. Chilca, which was excavated by Frederic Engel, is radiocarbon dated, in its earlier occupation, to a time range of 3800 to 2650 B.C.[42] Located 3 to 4 kilometers from the sea, it is a village refuse zone which has a number of well-preserved cane and grass house remains. Engel mentions no final house count but offers an estimate of a community of perhaps 100 families and 500 persons.[43] Subsistence was based on the sea: mesoderms (*Mesoderma donacium*), mussels (*Mytilus chorus, M. magellanicus*), and pectens (*Pecten purpuratus*) made up the bulk of the refuse. Fish bones and remains of the sea lion (*Arctocephalus australis* or *Octavia flavescens*) were also plentiful; but there was little evidence of land hunting. Gourds were cultivated and used for a variety of containers. In addition, Engel reports two species of beans, one wild, the other domesticated.[44] Various wild plants were utilized as foods and for fibers. Although the Chilca site is, today, on a dry quebrada, it is likely that at the time of its occupancy it was near a marsh fed by valley floor seepage or the river. This marshy area was a source of reeds and grasses from which matting and houses were made, and it is also likely that it provided garden locations for the raising of those few crops that were cultivated.

One house in the Chilca group has been described in some detail.[45] It had been constructed by first digging a circular hole 35 centimeters deep in the sandy soil. Postholes, each about 15 centimeters in diameter, were excavated in a circle within the hole. The posts, which served as the frame for the

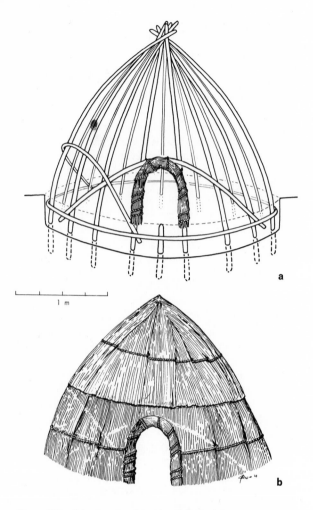

Figure 3-9. Construction features of Chilca house. *a:* Partially constructed house frame showing the kind of braces used and the method of attaching the door hoop. *b:* Completed house showing portion above surface. (After Donnan, 1964.)

1 m

house, were made up of several canes *(Gynerium sagittatum)* which were tied together with ropes made of junco *(Cyperus* sp.) grass. By staggering the canes in these bundles it was possible to make posts some 2 meters in length. These were placed in the holes and then bent inward and tied together over the center of the floor, forming a conical frame. The frame was strengthened by lashing horizontal cane bundles around its lower portion and also at higher elevations. A door was fashioned by a hoop of grass tied to two of the vertical posts and a cross-brace (see Fig. 3-9). Whale ribs—presumably obtained from the skeletons of stranded whales—were placed inside the structure as interior braces. The frame was then covered with bundles of junco grass which was laid horizontally around the lower part of the structure and covered with earth. The upper part of the frame was probably covered with vertically placed bunches of junco that were tied to the cane understructure with ropes. No evidences of fires were found inside the house; cooking, apparently, was done outside.

The house had, however, been used as a place of burial. This seems to have been customary as other Chilca houses also contained burials. In the house in question, seven people, ranging in age from 18 to 40 years and including two females and five males, had been wrapped in mats, in extended positions, and placed on the floor of the dwelling. The mats—perfectly preserved by the dry conditions of the Peruvian coast—were made of lengths of junco grass twined together with junco fiber string. From the situation of the bodies it would appear that the house had been intentionally collapsed over the dead; stones had then been used to weight down the flattened grass and cane structure that covered them. No signs of violence to the bodies were encountered.[46] But the range in age of the individuals and the clear inference that there was a single burial ceremony suggest that all had died at one time—perhaps of contagious disease or sudden illness.

The artifactual inventory of the Chilca site is meager. Limpet shell beads were found as a bracelet with one of the above-mentioned burials, and Engel refers to a bead of lapis lazuli with a burial in another house. This author also describes and illustrates bone needles (with and without eyes), bone spatulas, and other bone items. A few flint knives or projectile points are illustrated here, in addition to grinding stones. In Lanning's opinion these are definitely of the Encanto phase types, and they are typical of the time and phase that saw a dropping off in the ability or desire to fashion finely chipped points—probably as the result of a decline in the importance of hunting.

C. B. Donnan, who described the Chilca house construction, refers to a cactus-spine fishhook (Fig. 3-10, *a*) with a fragment of a fiber line attached; and Lanning also lists stone barb and bone barb hooks (Fig. 3-10, *b*) from Chilca. Engel identifies

Figure 3-10. Fishhooks and fishline sinker, preceramic periods. *a:* Cactus-spine hook, Chilca, Preceramic Period V. *b:* Bone hook, Chilca, Preceramic Period V. *c:* Bone linesinker, Chilca, Preceramic Period V. *d, e, f:* Shell and bone hooks, Asia, Preceramic Period VI. The cordage attached to all the hooks was found as shown. (Courtesy Frederic Engel.)

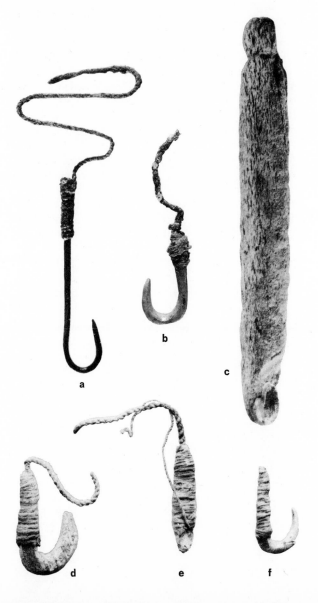

vicuña wool cordage at the site, but he is very definite that cotton was absent from the Chilca refuse and burials. In fact, it is his conception that the early Chilca occupation belongs to a stage of Peruvian coastal cultures best described as "preceramic but without cotton."[47]

Other Pacific Littoral tradition sites of Preceramic Period V include those at Cabezas Largas, the Ancón Yacht Club, and Ventanilla. Cabezas Largas[48] is in the Paracas region of the South Coast subarea, and we have referred to it already (this chapter, p. 89) in connection with early coastal long-headed populations. The Yacht Club site is at Ancón Bay on the Central Coast.[49] Burials at Cabezas, dated to about 3000 B.C., were found wrapped in rush or sedge mats, and were in either extended or flexed positions. They were accompanied by twined cloth, baskets (Fig. 3-11), nets, and looped bags, in addition to a few simple ornaments (beads of bone, shell, and stone), wooden spears, and other items of wood. At the Yacht Club site the burials were flexed and similarly wrapped. Here Lanning identifies the textiles as being of twined cotton.[50] Yacht Club fishing equipment included mussel-shell fishhooks and simple stone sinkers. Gourds, cotton, chili peppers, and guavas are all listed as plant domesticates found in refuse. At Ventanilla, not far from Ancón, the Pampa site is situated on a rocky point overlooking a shallow bay of the Pacific. The Pampa mussel-shell fishhooks and stone sinkers were the same as those from the Yacht Club site, but the tool inventory lacked milling stones and chipped points. Another significant difference was the presence at the Pampa site of domesticated squash *(Cucurbita moschata* and, possibly, *C. ficifolia)*.[51] These plants were undoubtedly used as food, although the diet was principally based on shellfish, fish, sea lions, and shore birds—the debris of which made up most of the site midden. Cordage was made of wild fibers, but no cotton is reported.

Such were the beginnings of the Pacific Littoral tradition in Peru during Preceramic Period V. The transition to the fully sedentary life of the littoral had not yet been completed. The lomas camps were still seasonally occupied. But the trend toward the new resources—those from the sea and from crop cultivation—was running strong. Preceramic Period VI (2500–1800 B.C.) would see communities of the

Figure 3-11. A twined basket and a textile fragment, from the Paracas region, Preceramic Period V. *Left:* Basket, about 30-35 cm. in diameter. *Right:* Twined reed textile fragment of a garment shown on a much smaller scale. (Courtesy Frederic Engel.)

Figure 3-12. Rough percussion-flaked objects of basalt from Huaca Prieta, Chicama Valley, Peru. These are found associated with Preceramic Period VI levels. *a–g:* Cores and/or choppers. *h:* Large flake tool. Height of *a*, 9.5 cm. (After Bird, 1965.)

Pacific Littoral tradition permanently established in coastal villages.

The Pacific Littoral Tradition: Late Phases. Huaca Prieta, a site on the shore of the North Coast Chicama Valley, is one such sedentary village of Preceramic Period VI.[52] At the time of its occupancy it must have been the dwelling place of several hundred people. These residents were living in well-made, "permanent" houses. J. B. Bird,[53] who excavated the site, discovered a number of these houses; they were small—one or two rooms —of subterranean or pit-house type. The walls had been lined with cobbles set in mud mortar, and the roofs were constructed of wooden or whalebone beams. Today the site appears as a great, black refuse hill. This refuse is ash, burned rock, fish bones, sea urchins, shells, sea lion and porpoise remains, and plant remains. In the absence of pottery, cooking was apparently done in twined baskets with stone roasting or stone boiling techniques. Such would account for the numerous cracked and fire-blackened stones in the midden.

Fishing, which was obviously an important part of subsistence, was done with nets that were fitted with stone sinkers and gourd floats.

Plant remains found in the debris included domesticated squash, peppers, lima beans, jack beans, gourds, and cotton.[54] Various wild tubers, roots, and fruits had also been gathered as food.

The chipped stone at Huaca Prieta shows none of the skill exhibited in the earlier preceramic periods. Coarse flakes, cores, and hammerstones were the typical implements (Fig. 3-12).

The cotton textile craft of Huaca Prieta was, however, surprisingly well developed. The commonest construction technique was twining with spaced wefts and exposed warps. Weaving, knotting, and looping were also employed. By careful

Figure 3-13. Double-headed design in twined cotton textile. From Huaca Prieta, Chicama Valley, Preceramic Period VI. Rock-crabs appear to be appended to the figures. Fabric detail indicated at *upper right*. The shaded background of the main figure is the extent of the surviving fragment, with the remainder of the design restored. Original length, about 40 cm. (Redrawn from Bird, 1963.)

study of a number of fragments Bird was able to plot a series of cloth textile designs that reveal to us a sophisticated art style and a very definite iconography. In some pieces the decoration consisted only of structurally contrasting areas, but in others it was possible to detect the fact that contrasting colors, with some dyed fibres, carried the designs. Besides geometric elements, birds, animals, and humans were depicted. Among these are such motifs as the paired, doubled, opposed, or interlocked beings, including fish or serpents, birds, and crabs (Fig. 3-13). The style of the designs is stiffly rectilinear, conditioned as it is by the weaving or twining techniques; but it is of great interest to see here, at this early time, the presence of motifs—as well as stylistic renderings of them—that were to become a part of the succeeding Peruvian cultural tradition and, as was noted earlier, to persist throughout much of that tradition.[55]

The art of Huaca Prieta was also exhibited through the medium of gourd-carving. One gourd bears a design of four faces (possibly human, possibly feline) disposed on the four sides of the vessel (Fig. 3-14, *right*). Another has a more complex and stylized design of what may well be humans and condors (Fig. 3-14, *left*). In both, the

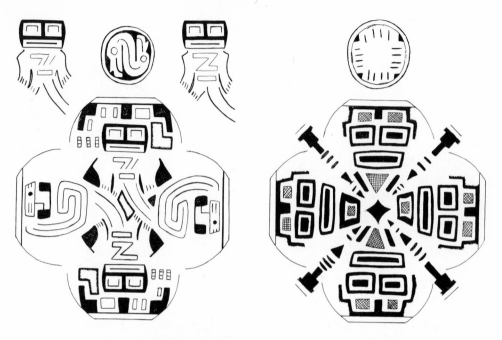

Figure 3-14. Two carved gourds from Preceramic Period VI levels at Huaca Prieta de Chicama. The respective carved lids are the disks shown above each gourd. The two other small figures above the gourd at *left* show the bottom details of that gourd with less distortion than in the "flattened-out" rendering of the design. (After Bird, 1963.)

quality of the style suggests the decorated textiles.[56] Both gourds showed techniques of careful cutting, with alternating uses of fine and broad-line incised areas cut into the epidermis of the gourd.

South of Chicama, in the North-Central Coast subarea, is Playa Culebras. This is a dwelling, refuse, and cemetery area situated on the south side of the Culebras River delta and the Bay of Culebras.[57] One of the largest sites of the Pacific Littoral cultural tradition, it occupies the entire slope of a large hill. The hillslope had been artificially terraced, and these terraces were faced with natural basalt blocks. On each terrace platform were several houses that were semi-subterranean, square or rectangular in outline, and from 1.5 to 3.0 meters on a side. They had two or three rooms, and in their lower, or subterranean, portions the walls of these rooms were lined with basalt blocks and mud mortar. The upper portions of the walls, which rose above ground level, are believed to have been of adobe or wattle-daub construction. The contemporaneous use of adobes is known, for

example, from the preceramic Huaca Negra (or Huaca Prieta de Guañape) site in the Virú Valley. Here, perhaps because of a local lack of suitable stone, subterranean houses were lined with rectangular adobe bricks. Poured clay was also used to make above-ground housewalls at the same site.[58]

To return to the Playa Culebras site, burials were found in the terraces, in the vicinity of the houses,[59] and also in a cemetery area at the top of the hill. These interments were tightly flexed and wrapped in cotton cloth and rush mats. Some of the individuals showed artificial occipital head flattening. Grave goods were both ornaments and utensils: rough chipped-stone tools, gourd vessels (some of which contained powdered lime, presumably for use in coca-chewing), baskets, shell pendants and beads, and mussel shell fishhooks.

Although fishing and shellfish-taking were apparently the principal modes of subsistence during most of the existence of Playa Culebras, the inhabitants of the site were also cultivators. And, most importantly, at least toward the end of the occupation, their cultivation included maize.[60] This Playa Culebras maize, together with that found at some other nearby coastal sites,[61] is the earliest known occurrence of the plant in Peru. If we assume that maize was of ultimate Mesoamerican origin, and that it diffused into western South America on a general north-to-south course, this presence of the plant in the North-Central valleys of the Peruvian coast, and its contemporaneous absence in sites farther north along the littoral, suggests a prior spread of the grain through the Peruvian Andes, with secondary upland-to-coastal diffusions.

The Preceramic Period VI sites farther south, in the Central Coast subarea, do not show maize; but they display an even greater emphasis on permanent architecture than those to the north. This emphasis is not only in domestic building but in the construction of what appear to be large public or ceremonial structures. At Rio Seco, north of Chancay Valley, houses (Fig. 3-15) were found to be compounds of several rooms, one such household unit accommodating perhaps as many as eight to ten persons. These were aboveground rather than subterranean or semi-subterranean dwellings. Two artificial pyramids or platforms were discovered at Rio Seco. These had been built by filling in an adobe-walled multi-room house compound with boulders and lump adobes. Another house compound was then constructed on top of this platform; and it too was subsequently filled.

The process was repeated. Finally, the whole was covered with a layer of sand, and several stone blocks or columns were set up on top of it.[62]

Much larger structures than those at Rio Seco are the ones at El Paraíso or Chuquitanta on the floodplains of the lower Chillón Valley.[63] The location, some distance from the sea and near fields that could have been cultivated at the time the site was occupied, suggests that the ancient community might have been concerned more with farming than with fishing. The ruins consist of eight large platforms. These lie within an area about 900 by 700 meters in extent. The constructions were built up primarily of roughly dressed or natural stone blocks set in mud mortar. Lanning describes one of the larger of the units as a possible temple complex. The contours of this structure give the impression of three platforms enclosing a patio, with the presumed "temple" facing toward the open end of this patio. This is a ceremonial arrangement that characterizes later structures of the Peruvian cul-

Figure 3-15. A building foundation at Rio Seco, Preceramic Period VI. (Courtesy Frederic Engel.)

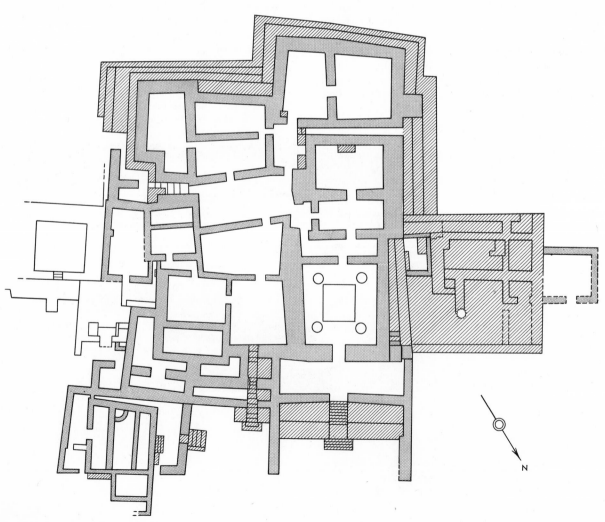

tural tradition. The two flanking mounds of the "temple" and patio are described as being honeycombed with rooms or apartments.

Another Paraíso structure has been excavated in some detail by Engel (Fig. 3-16). This is one of the smaller mounds, measuring about 50 meters square and being of rectangular-truncated or conical-truncated shape. Digging revealed it to have been constructed in five or six successive stages. Each stage consisted of a complex of conjoined rooms that were then filled with stone and earth to serve as the platform for the next stage. Engel cleared, mapped, and restored the some 25 rooms that compose the final stage. The ground plan could be that of a temple complex, a palace, or, perhaps, a series of living quarters (Fig. 3-17). No pottery or maize was found in any level of the excavation. Twined textiles were the most common although some woven pieces were also found. A few fabric-wrapped burials came from within and near the structure. Food debris included lima beans, possibly squash *(C. moschata),* various fruits such as pacae and lucuma, fish bones, shellfish, and sea lion and deer bones. A radiocarbon date, associated with the final building phase, falls in the 1800 to 1500 B.C. range. Although not all of the Chuquitanta-Paraíso ruins need have been built or occupied at the same time, it is evident that a sizable population must have maintained it as a town, a ceremonial center, or both. Engel's estimate of 1500 persons seems modest. The site was apparently abandoned just prior to the advent of ceramics on the Central Coast.

Not all the Central Coast sites of Preceramic Period VI had such ceremonial constructions. Lanning mentions two others—the Tank site, at Ancón, and another (Punta Grande) nearby at Ventanilla. He makes the suggestion that these were fishing stations that may have traded their catch for agricultural produce at Chuquitanta.[64]

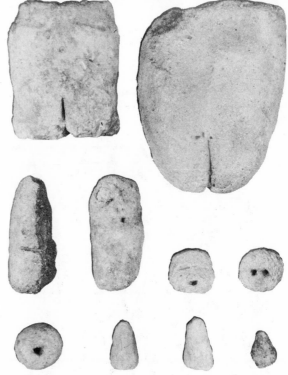

Figure 3-18. Figurines and miscellaneous items or fragments of unfired clay, Preceramic Period VI. *Top row:* From El Paraíso (Chuquitanta). Width of head is 6.5 cm. *Bottom:* From Rio Seco. (Courtesy Frederic Engel.)

Figure 3-16. *(Top,* p. 98) The restored Building Unit 1 at El Paraíso, or Chuquitanta. Preceramic Period VI. (Courtesy Frederic Engel.)

Figure 3-17. *(Bottom,* p. 98) The plan of Building Unit 1 at El Paraíso, or Chuquitanta. Total structure is about 50 m. in diameter. Hachure indicates terraces, steps, or platforms. Gray areas are restored walls. (Redrawn from Engel, 1966.)

Farther south, in the South-Central Coast subarea, there are no Preceramic Period VI sites as imposing as Chuquitanta, although there are large permanent villages. The Asia, or Omas, Valley site is one of these. Engel describes it as being composed of a series of small, refuse-covered hummocks.[65]

Figure 3-19. Foundations of walled compound at Asia Unit 1 site, Preceramic Period VI. (Courtesy Frederic Engel.)

One such hummock on careful excavation revealed a stone- and adobe-walled multi-room surface structure (Fig. 3-19). The other hummocks of the site presumably cover similar house foundations. Materials from the Asia Valley house include:

Figure 3-21. A small baked clay tablet or mirror-back. *Top:* Reverse side with incised design of double-headed bird or serpent. *Bottom:* Obverse side, concave and set (in an adhesive substance) with a bit of pyrite and small shell beads. The object measures 6.5 × 6.0 cm. (Courtesy Frederic Engel; see also Engel, 1963.)

Figure 3-20. Closeup view of twisted-looped cotton fabric, Asia Preceramic Period VI. (Courtesy Frederic Engel; see also Engel, 1963.)

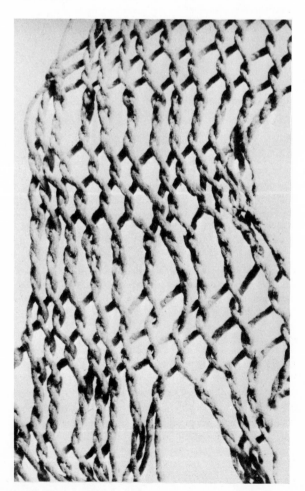

twined cotton textiles in great profusion (Fig. 3-20); some few woven textiles; bone implements and ornaments (bodkins, spatulas, needles, hairpins); shell fishhooks; spindles and spindle whorls; stone, shell, and bone beads; pendants of shell, bone, and animal teeth; wooden spear-throwers; rather crudely chipped stone points and knives; gourd dishes; and various mortars and milling stones. In general, the inventory is quite similar to the inventory for Huaca Prieta and Playa Culebras. Of special interest from the Asia site is a jet mirror set in a baked clay holder; the holder had been decorated

with an incised, double-headed bird or animal design on the reverse side (Fig. 3-21). An Asia twined textile also bore a multi-colored design of a two-headed serpent or fish in the same style as that of the Huaca Prieta textiles (Fig. 3-22).

South of Asia the sites of the Preceramic Period VI in the Paracas, Ica, and Nazca regions have

Figure 3-22. A double-headed serpent or fish design as reconstructed from the fragments of a polychrome twined cotton cloak. From Asia Unit 1, Preceramic Period VI. Detail of weave at right. (Courtesy Frederic Engel; see also Engel, 1963.)

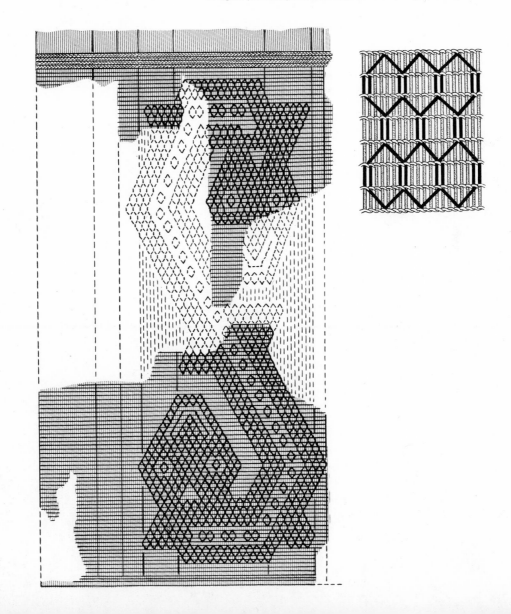

yielded cotton textiles and nets, gourds, squashes, cultivated fruits, and some artifacts similar to those found farther north;[66] however, these southern sites are smaller than, and do not have the architecture of, those of the Central and North Coasts. Lanning is of the opinion that in the South and Far South the Pacific Littoral tradition was never firmly established and that the populations of these subareas remained in the old Andean Hunting-Collecting condition of seasonal transhumance between lomas and shore for a much longer time than those farther north. Phases such as Casavilca or Ocoña would be representative of this.[67]

The Highlands. In the uplands significant changes were going on in the late Andean Hunting-Collecting phases toward the end of Preceramic Period VI. As we have suggested, maize farming probably became important in the highland valleys at this time, and the potato may also have been domesticated. Thus it is possible that agriculture was more advanced in the highlands than on the coast in Preceramic Period VI and that it sparked changes in highland population increase and in settlement size and stability.

Evidence for these changes comes from Kotosh in the Upper Huallaga subarea.[68] The Kotosh site is located on the bank of the Higueras River, a tributary of the Huallaga, a short distance above the modern town of Huánuco (Fig. 3-23). The elevation here is about 1950 meters (6000 ft.) above sea level. The climate is temperate to subtropical rather than the cold of the higher Andean

Figure 3-23. The ruins of Kotosh from the east. The archaeological site can be seen in the valley bottom, center (small light-colored area). (Courtesy Seiichi Izumi and University of Tokyo Expedition.)

Kotosh

basins, and the vegetation of the region is described as "tropical or sub-tropical thorn forest." There are two principal rock-covered mounds at the site. Nearby are other, smaller constructions, and still others—perhaps habitations—are a little distance away on a higher terrace of the river.

The University of Tokyo archaeologists who excavated Kotosh concentrated their initial efforts on the larger of the two big mounds (Mound KT). The mound proved to be a mass of superimposed constructions, some 13 meters in height and about 100 meters in diameter. Deep trenching revealed ten superimposed buildings. The deepest and earliest (discovered during the early work at the site and designated Construction J) was a special building or temple that was dubbed the "Templo de Las Manos Cruzadas" (or the "Temple of the Crossed Hands"; Fig. 3-24, *bottom*). The temple was a relatively small room (9.4 × 9.2 m. in exterior measurements) which had been constructed on a platform 8 meters in height.[69] Its thick walls were built of river stones laid up in mud mortar. These walls were then plastered with a clay coating, and the floor was similarly clay-covered. There were large niches in one wall, and beneath one such niche were a pair of crossed hands sculpted in clay (Fig. 3-24, *top*)—this is the feature from which the building takes its name. Llama bones were found in the niche. No pottery was encountered in the "Templo de Las Manos Cruzadas" nor in its underlying platform. The "Manos Cruzadas" had been covered, in turn, with a platform of boulders and pebbles, and on this platform was a second temple (Construction I), known as the "Templo de Los Nichitos" ("Temple of the Little Niches"; Fig. 3-25). Pottery was also absent from this structure.

In a later season's work at Kotosh the Japanese archaeologists uncovered additional structures similar in general form to the "Manos Cruzadas" and the "Nichitos." None of these contained pot-

Figure 3-24. The Temple of the "Manos Cruzadas," or "crossed hands," Kotosh. *Top:* Closeup view. Note the crossed hands sculptured in clay below the second niche from the right. Similar hands are also present below the corresponding niche on the opposite side of the large central inset. *Bottom:* The temple from a distance, with the valley in the background. (Courtesy Seiichi Izumi and University of Tokyo Expedition.)

Figure 3-25. The Temple of the "Nichitos," or "small niches," Kotosh. Detail of floor, bench, "nichitos," and wall interior. (Courtesy Seiichi Izumi and University of Tokyo Expedition.)

tery. In the oldest of these—one antedating the "Manos Cruzadas" and known as the "Templo Blanco"—there were, however, some unfired clay figurines and other small unbaked clay objects in a wall niche.

The Japanese archaeologists have designated this late preceramic, temple-building phase at Kotosh as the Mito phase, and they have characterized it by other traits. Among these are chipped-stone projectile points, polished stone axes, stone figurines, and various bone and antler items such as awls, pins, tubes, and ornaments (Fig. 3-26). A good many charred seeds were recovered from the debris in and around the temple buildings, but these have not yet been identified.

The dating of the Mito phase by stratigraphy places it as pre-Initial Period. The constructions and pottery of the Waira-jirca (Huairajirca) phase, an Initial Period manifestation, lie directly above the preceramic temples. The radiocarbon determinations so far available pertain to this Waira-jirca phase. They range from 1800 to 1150 B.C.[70] Acceptance of the earliest of these gives a late

Preceramic Period VI dating to the Kotosh Mito phase.

In spite of the good beginning at Kotosh, our information from the highlands for the crucial centuries of the Preceramic Period VI is still scanty.[70a] This is particularly true of our knowledge of food plants and agricultural beginnings, which is one of the greatest obstacles to our present understanding of Peruvian culture history. The situation is somewhat analogous to that in Mesoamerica although the environmental settings are reversed. For Mesoamerica, the record that spans the period of semi-sedentary to sedentary life, or from incipient to established farming, is from the uplands, from plant remains found in dry caves; almost nothing is known of contemporaneous happenings in the tropical coastal lowlands. In Peru we have the story in well-preserved vegetal debris from the deep middens of the rainless coast; but there are as yet no comparable data from the highlands. Still, for both Mesoamerica and Peru the interchange of cultigens between highland and lowland niches must have been one of the most dynamic factors in the rise to successful agriculture;[71] and until we know more about such micro-zonal interchanges our reconstructions of the culture history in either area will be seriously incomplete.

These digressions—into speculations about highland-lowland environmental relationships and the beginnings of agriculture—provide us with the opportunity of pausing still longer in our chronicle of Peruvian culture history and of considering the whole problem of agricultural origins for the area.

Agricultural Origins. Plants, because of their genetic makeup, lend themselves to genetico-historical reconstruction of their past. They have been, accordingly, an important means of tracing out the past histories of human societies and cultures, but the methods of this tracing are neither simple nor easy. For instance, the principle of monogenesis—the concept of a single wild plant ancestor, a single place, and a single time as the single source of a later domesticated plant—cannot always be taken for granted. Instead, as C. B. Heiser states: "It seems possible that wide-ranging diploid species might be brought into domestication in two different areas giving rise to similar cultivated plants which the botanist might place in the same species."[72] Or, it is also possible, in domesti-

Figure 3-26. Kotosh Mito phase artifacts and items. *Top: a:* Projectile points. *b:* Scraping implement. *c:* Stone figurine. *d:* Ax of ground stone. *e:* Seeds (as yet unidentified). *f:* Various bone and antler items (pins, flaking tools, awls, decorated tube, etc.). *g:* Unfired clay figurine fragments. *h:* Bone and antler scrap. *Bottom:* Various small bone pins, ornaments, and objects. (Courtesy Seiichi Izumi and University of Tokyo Expedition.)

cates, that two species could have a common ancestor: "...if cultivated species A were carried from Mexico to Peru, it might in time give rise to cultivated species B."[73]

Thus, a high mutation rate, artificial selection, and hybridization all could promote relatively rapid development of new species. Questions are also posed by the presence of a weed or wild species that is related to a cultigen of the same region. Is the wild species a progenitor of the cultivated plant, thereby indicating its natural habitat and region of origin? Or is it an "escapee" from cultivation that has "reverted" to the wild condition?[74] These are the kinds of considerations and qualifications that we must keep in mind as we review Peruvian domesticated plants and their relationships to those of other areas.

Although there is little that is absolutely certain in the history of Peruvian cultivated plants, it seems highly probable that three of the most important food crops, squash *(Cucurbita moschata),* maize *(Zea mays),* and the kidney bean *(Phaseolus vulgaris)* were brought or diffused from Mesoamerica. *Cucurbita moschata* antedates 5000 B.C. as a Mesoamerican domesticate,[75] and its Peruvian earliest occurrences are substantially later. It is also possible that its diffusion to Peru as a cultigen—at some time around 4000 B.C. or even earlier—not only effected the transfer of this one plant but, more importantly, "seeded" the very idea of crop cultivation among the semi-migratory lomas hunters and coastal fishers of the Peruvian coast. The *Cucurbita ficifolia,* the other squash reported from preceramic Peruvian coastal sites, may also have been introduced from Mesoamerica at this time, or it may have been a local domesticate.[76] The same is true for gourds *(Lagenaria siceraria)* and chili peppers *(Capsicum* sp.). Both of these are sufficiently ancient in Mesoamerica to have spread to Peru from there, but they are also plants with wide American distributions in both wild and domesticated forms.

Maize, that most important of plants, is much older in Mesoamerica than in Peru. It has been found in the wild state—or in the very earliest stages of domestication—in levels of Mexican cave sites that date at 5000 to 4000 B.C.; and it has been found as a very definite domesticate at about 3400 B.C. in these same caves.[77] As we have just seen, it does not appear on the Peruvian coast until the end of Preceramic Period VI, or at about 2000 to 1800 B.C. There is, of course, the possibility that the Peruvian highlands lay within the original natural habitat area of wild maize and that the grain was domesticated there independent of contacts with Mesoamerica.[78] It is also possible that Mesoameri-

can domesticated maize was, indeed, brought to the Peruvian highlands at about 2000 B.C. and that it crossed there with local wild forms of the plant, or with the related grass *Tripsacum.* Such hybridizations would help explain the explosive evolution and racial diversification that *Zea mays* underwent in Peru. Whatever happened, maize must have spread rapidly from the highlands down to the Peruvian coast. Subsequently—and this is well supported by botanical evidence—the rapid evolution of maize in Peru and other parts of the Andes resulted in a back-diffusion of new South American races of the grain into pre-Columbian Guatemala and western Mexico.[79]

The common bean, *Phaseolus vulgaris,* is substantially earlier in Mesoamerica (ca. 5000–3000 B.C.) than in Peru, and, as with maize, chances strongly favor its north-to-south diffusion. Again, however, there is a difficulty: *Phaseolus arborigeus,* which closely resembles *vulgaris,* is found wild from Peru to Argentina. Could *arborigeus* be a possible local ancestor of an independently domesticated *vulgaris*? Or is *arborigeus* merely an "escapee" from the domesticated and Mesoamerican-diffused *Phaseolus vulgaris*?[80]

The lima bean *(Phaseolus lunatus)* was probably first domesticated in South America and was the earliest important Peruvian coastal cultigen. Its cultivation dates much earlier in Peru than in Mesoamerica, and so chances favor a south-to-north diffusion. Still, botanists caution that the Mesoamerican variety is much smaller than the Peruvian and that separate domestication of a diploid species may be indicated.[81]

Other local primary domesticates of the Peruvian coast were the fruits, the pacae *(Inga* sp.), the lúcuma *(Lucuma bifera),* the ciruela del fraile *(Bunchosia armeniaca),* and probably, the guava *(Psidium guajava).*

The avocado *(Persea americana)* dates at the 7000 to 5000 B.C. time range in Mesoamerica;[82] it is early in Peru but nowhere this early. It may be a Mesoamerican import or it may represent an instance of separate domestication of widespread wild species.

The sweet potato *(Ipomoea batatas)* is a puzzle. There are good reasons for thinking it a South American tropical forest domesticate that spread, as early as preceramic times, to the Peruvian coast; and it may also have spread from South America to Mexico. Heiser cautions, however, that it may be a multiple domesticate from a widespread wild form.[83]

The circumstances surrounding cultivated cotton within the Americas are as complicated as those that frame the problem on a worldwide scale (see Vol. I, pp. 21–22). It was first cultivated in Peru at about 3000 B.C.[84] This was the species *Gossypium barbadense*. In southern Mesoamerica MacNeish reports the species *Gossypium hirsutum* still earlier, prior to 5200 B.C.[85] Mangelsdorf is of the opinion that the two species were separate domesticates.[86]

In the Andean highlands the grain quinoa *(Chenopodium quinoa)*, and the various roots, oca *(Oxalis tuberosa)*, arracacha *(Arracacia xanthorrhiza)*, and the potato *(Solanum* sp.) are all native. Quinoa was first domesticated in the Peru-Bolivia altiplano country, and the potato was originally cultivated either there or in nearby northern Argentina and Chile. We have no good evidence of when these domestications first took place; but in view of the nature of the cultural developments in these regions in the Initial Period (1800–900 B.C.), it is reasonable to suppose that both plants were cultigens by the end of Preceramic Period VI. It is also likely that potatoes were cultivated, or at least eaten wild, on the Peruvian coast in late preceramic times, although this is not clearly documented.[87]

At some time after the beginning of the Initial Period manioc *(Manihot esculenta)*[88] and peanuts *(Arachis hypogaea)* were added to the agricultural economy of the Peruvian coast. Neither plant was grown in the highlands; thus, it is possible that they were diffused from the upper Amazon to the Colombian Pacific coast and from there southward along the Ecuadorian and Peruvian coastal lowlands, rather than across the Peruvian Andes.[89] Manioc was the important starch root of the South American tropical lowland cultures. Probably first cultivated somewhere in the Amazon-Orinoco drainages,[90] its presence is inferred there as early as 1000 B.C. Some authorities have speculated that it is substantially older than this as a domesticate and that manioc-based societies of the tropical forest played an important role in influencing the growth of Peruvian cultures.[91] We shall return to this idea in a subsequent chapter.

So far, we have not commented on animal domesticates. According to Lanning, the guinea pig was the only domesticated animal for which we have evidence from the coastal preceramic periods. It was kept and bred for food.[92] The dog may have been present at this time although there is no definite evidence for it until later.[93] It is possible, or even probable, that the llama had been domesticated in late preceramic times in the highlands. Presumably, this domestication took place somewhere in south Peru, Bolivia, or the adjacent South Andean area from a wild guanaco-like ancestor.[94] However, the first evidence we have of llama domestication for both highlands and coast is from the Initial Period.[95]

The Initial Period

Emergence of the Peruvian Cultural Tradition. The Initial Period, dated at 1800 to 900 B.C., is marked by the first appearances of pottery and by the widespread use of woven (as opposed to twined or looped) cloth.[96] The latter implies the use of the heddle loom and the ability to produce cloth rapidly and with almost infinite varieties of technique. Yet, as Lanning has noted,[97] neither of these technologies—pottery-making or weaving—suddenly or radically transformed the life of the Peruvian preceramic coastal communities. A good many of the traits that we consider as characteristic of the Peruvian cultural tradition had already made their appearance in these coastal sites during the last centuries of Preceramic Period VI. The really significant change of the Initial Period was not so much that of radical innovation as that of propagation of ideas and elements that were present in the latter stages of the Pacific Littoral tradition. In Preceramic Period VI these ideas and elements were found rather spottily along the coast. For instance, sites of the North-Central subarea had maize, but those of other subareas did not; or sites of the Central Coast were the settings of large ceremonial or public buildings, but these were not found elsewhere along the littoral. However with the Initial Period, these traits and many others that had been quite restricted in their distribution were found over larger stretches of the coast. Another feature of the Initial Period was an increase in the number of sites. Peruvian coastal populations were doubling or tripling, and, undoubtedly, the same changes were also going on in the highlands.

Admittedly, the definition of the inception of an historical abstraction such as the "Peruvian cultural tradition" cannot be made chronologically precise, nor is this of great importance. In this instance, what we know is that at about the beginning of the second millennium B.C. important changes began to take place in Peruvian cultures. Within a few centuries these changes became widespread. The advent of ceramics coincides, chronologically but not necessarily functionally, with the successful spread of these changes throughout the culture area. This advent of pottery has a great practical advantage for the archaeologist and has been capitalized upon to define the beginnings of a period—and of a cultural tradition.

Earlier in this chapter we set down a list of traits and trait complexes that characterized the Peruvian cultural tradition. If we asume that this tradition can be dated from the Initial Period, how many of these traits and trait complexes were actually present in this period?

First and foremost was the agricultural complex. This has just been reviewed from the standpoint of origins. We have seen that a good many of the important plants were actually present on the Peruvian coast by the end of Preceramic Period VI. The major exceptions were the potato, manioc, and the peanut. The potato was of highland origin, and it is likely that it was under cultivation in the mountain valleys and on the altiplanos before the close of Preceramic Period VI. Almost certainly the potato was a highland domesticate by Initial Period times. Manioc and peanuts—as was noted before—were added to the coastal farming complex in the Initial Period. In brief, by the Initial Period all of the major food plants, and a good many minor ones, had been assembled.

Second, we have observed that the llama, the principal domesticated animal of the Peruvian tradition, was present in Initial Period sites of both highlands and coast.

Third, the Peruvian trait of chewing coca with lime as a narcotic is attested to even earlier than the Initial Period. It will be recalled that gourds filled with powdered lime came from the preceramic Playa Culebras site. Such lime-filled gourds are still a part of the Peruvian Indian's coca-chewing equipment.

Fourth, basic Peruvian clothing styles—the slit-necked shirt, shawls, carrying-bags with shoulder straps—were present in preceramic times.

Fifth, we have seen the complex textile designs and the similar designs on gourds from preceramic Huaca Prieta and from the Asia Valley. These double-headed and opposed fish, serpent, and bird designs suggest a common set of mythological concepts. It is likely that these concepts persisted into much later pre-Columbian times; at least the design motifs so persisted.

Sixth, it is a moot question whether "ancestor reverence" and "pilgrimage patterns" can be read into late preceramic and Initial Period burial practices and ceremonial-center-building, although the data could be so interpreted. With regard to ceremonial or public buildings, certainly the same general kind of massive adobe or stone structures that were later to serve as shrine or pilgrimage centers were being constructed at these times.

Seventh, large, settled communities—whether we call them towns or cities—were a feature of Peruvian life as early as the Preceramic Period VI and the Initial Period. On the other hand, there is nothing this early to suggest the large territorial states or political domains that we know of—or may reasonably infer—from later times.

Eighth, by the Initial Period the Peruvian crafts of cloth-weaving, ceramics, and shell-, wood-, and stone-carving were all established at a secure level of competence—if not on the level of elaborations and virtuosity that was to come in subsequent periods. Only metallurgy was still lacking.

Ninth, and finally, there is some evidence—as we shall see—that monumental art was beginning to develop in the Initial Period. This includes both stone- and clay-relief sculptures that were employed to embellish public buildings.

In sum, a Peruvian cultural tradition had coalesced by Initial Period times. Still to come were the technical, social, and artistic-intellectual achievements that would strengthen the internal cohesiveness of the tradition. Especially important in this regard would be the propagation of major art styles (and religious or political ideologies?) throughout much of the Peruvian area.

Pottery Origins. The date of 1800 B.C. would seem to correspond to the earliest pottery in the Peruvian area and, therefore, to the beginning of the Initial Period.[98] This radiocarbon mean date pertains to finds of the North-Central and Central Coasts, to the Far North Coast, the Callejón de Huaylas, and to the Upper Huallaga subarea.[99] Elsewhere, on the North Coast, on the South Coast, and in the southern highland subareas, the dates are a few centuries later, approximating 1400 or 1500 B.C.;[100] however, at this stage of investigation and radiocarbon dating it is unwise to place too much reliance on the 200- or 300-year differences in dates that occur from subarea to subarea, and it is probably safest to consider the first occurrences of Peruvian pottery to be more or less coeval until we have more dates and information. The only exception to this would be the Far South Coast subarea where there are some indications that pottery was appreciably later than in the rest of the area—not appearing, perhaps, until near the beginning of the Christian era.

The origins of Peruvian pottery are unknown, but, in view of the fact that all of the earliest Peruvian ceramics occur as well developed, it seems safe to say that the craft did not first develop there. Where pottery did develop is, of course, a general American problem rather than just a Peruvian one, and no ready answers are forthcoming. According to the present state of knowledge, the earliest New World pottery dates by radiocarbon to about 3000 B.C., and it comes from the Puerto Hormigas site on the Caribbean coast of Colombia.[101] Pottery dating from 2500 to 3000 B.C.—the Valdivia ware —has also been found in coastal Ecuador. These findings make it likely that Peruvian early pottery was derived from these northwestern South American beginnings, although it should be made clear that neither Puerto Hormigas nor Valdivia ceramics are closely related to the earliest Peruvian wares. The lines of relationship—whatever they may have been—are obscure or undiscovered to date.

The Coast. Coastal populations of the Initial Period were all settled town or village dwellers,[102] the only exception being, perhaps, those of the Far South subarea where a lomas-to-shore hunting existence probably still prevailed.

On the North Coast the Huaca Prieta and Huaca Negra sites of the Chicama and Virú Valleys—to which we have already referred in the discussion of Preceramic Period VI—continued to be occupied as Initial Period villages. At Huaca

Prieta the above-ground houses of the small village were now made of small cylindrical or biscuit-shaped adobes.[103] At Huaca Negra, in Virú, a feature of the Guañape phase—which is a regional manifestation of the Initial Period—was a temple or public building.[104] This was a simple affair. Only a rough stone foundation and floor plan remain; it is of rectangular outline, measuring 19 by 15.75 meters. A narrow, step-up entrance is centered on the eastern side. Inside, at the middle of the north wall, is a small platform, bench, or altar; at the west end, under a packed mud floor, were two llama burials which have the appearance of sacrifices. Guañape pottery, in the very earliest levels of the site, was a blackish plain ware, usually in the form of large, constricted-mouth, neckless jars. Decoration, when it occurred, was a rib-appliqué sort. Later in the stratigraphy other decoration techniques (incision, punctation, brushing) and surface polishing gradually became more frequent.[105]

On the North-Central Coast Las Haldas (or Las Aldas) is the outstanding site of the Initial Period. Located between the Casma and Culebras valleys, it had been a big Preceramic Period VI village of the Pacific Littoral tradition. In the Initial Period it became the site of an important ceremonial center, probably sustained by the farming populations of the two nearby valleys.[106] The ceremonial center is a great complex of platform mounds and plazas, estimated to span an area of 700 (640 m.) by 200 (185 m.) yards (Fig. 3-27). The contruction is of basalt blocks and mud mortar. Pottery relates to that of Huaca Prieta, although there is somewhat more vessel decoration in the form of incision, punctation, polishing, and black color zoning.[107] Two handmade pottery figurine fragments were also recovered from test excavations (Fig. 3-28).

These big ceremonial constructions are not rarities on either the North-Central or the Central Coasts. Playa Culebras, which, like Las Haldas, had been a large village or town in Preceramic Period VI, also had ceremonial construction in the Initial Period. The platform-and-plaza units here are smaller than at Las Haldas, although the site remained a sizable town or point of population concentration as well as becoming a ceremonial center. Other templelike constructions are reported from Huaricanga, in the Fortaleza (Supe) Valley,

Figure 3-27. The great temple or building complex at Las Aldas. *Top:* Looking from summit of structure down over lower terrace layout, with desert and hills in background. *Bottom:* View of main structure from below. (Courtesy Rosa Fung.)

Figure 3-28. *Right:* Pottery figurine from Las Aldas, Initial Period. (Redrawn from Ishida and others, 1960.)

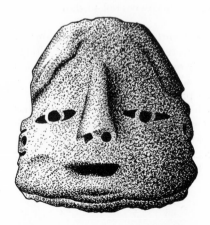

Figure 3-29. Two items from a late Initial Period tomb at Ancón (Tank Site sector). *Left:* A twined basket that was found inside the vessel shown at *right. Right:* Incised and red-painted pottery vessel. (Courtesy Ramiro Matos; photos courtesy A. Guillen.)

and at Ancón, on the hillslopes south of the bay (a location known as the "Tank Site"). In the latter, excavation has revealed large stone-faced Initial Period platforms deep beneath later refuse.[108] The Tank Site also offers us our best information on Central Coastal Initial Period pottery stratigraphy. A subphase A, defined by Ramiro Matos, has a radiocarbon date of 1825 B.C. and marks the introduction of pottery to the region. These earliest wares are plain or sometimes burnished or striated. Subphase B, dating to 1390 B.C., is said to resemble the Las Aldas pottery types and includes some incised decoration. Subphase C pottery is like the earliest ceramics at Curayacu, a site some distance to the south of Ancón. The most distinctive types of subphase C are bichromes of red-on-orange in which the red decoration has been zoned with incision. There are also zoomorphic and anthropomorphic jars. The date for subphase C is believed to be about 1200 B.C., and the buried platforms just noted are believed to date to about this time. Toward the close of subphase C the first Chavín stylistic influence—such as the incised jaguar or feline motifs—appear on some of the pottery, and the succeeding subphase D of the Ancon Tank Site sequence is fully Chavinoid and belongs to the Early Horizon.[109]

The largest of all the Initial Period constructions of the Central Coast, however, is at La Florida, near Lima in the Rimac Valley. It was built of angular fieldstones laid up in mud mortar.

A central pyramidal or platform mass is surrounded by outlying platforms and rooms. La Florida would appear to be an isolated ceremonial center or precinct, without immediate town or village dwelling units in the vicinity.[110]

No temple structures are reported for the South Coast Initial Period culture. This is a cultural phase known as Hacha and defined so far by pottery alone.[111] Hacha ceramics are interesting as they show elements such as double-spout-and-bridge jars and negative, or resist, painting. As we shall see, both these traits were to persist in great strength into later South Coastal Periods.

We have left until last one unusual temple complex of the North-Central Coast. This is Cerro Sechín, in the Casma Valley. Situated in the lower part of that valley, the site was built against a slope of an outcrop hill. The primary construction is a rectangular platform of earth faced with stones. Along its north, or front, side these stones or monoliths bear carvings. The facade measures 52 meters in length and is composed of 22 major, and more than twice that many minor, monoliths (Fig. 3-30). They had been evenly arranged on each side of a broad central stair that led to the top of

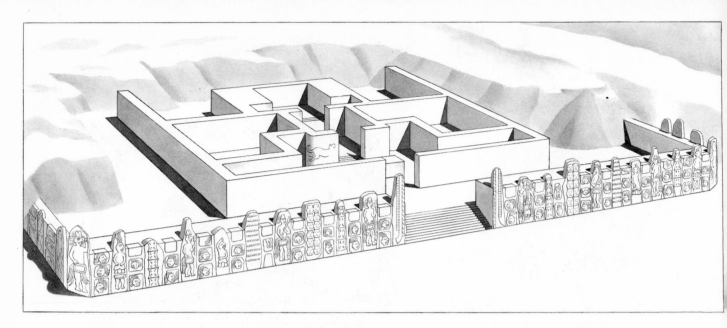

Figure 3-30. The temple of Sechín, Casma Valley—a reconstruction drawing. (Redrawn from Tello, 1943 and 1956.)

the platform, on which was a multi-roomed building of conical adobes. On the wall of one of the rooms of this building were painted feline figures. It is, however, the carved monoliths along the lower platform facade that are associated with the name of "Sechín art" or the "Sechín style."

The major Sechín monoliths average 3.0 to 3.5 meters in height (Fig. 3-31), somewhat less than 1 meter in width, and considerably less than that in thickness. The minor ones, which had been alternated with the major in the facade construction, were of lesser height but similar in width and thickness. All of the monoliths are natural, untrimmed granite blocks. On their facing surfaces they bear deep incised-line, rather than bas-relief, carving. The carvings represent: (1) warriors or dignitaries in regalia and carrying maces; (2) seminude dead or dismembered men, including a great many individual heads; and (3) serried geometric elements. The renderings are simple, economical of line, but not crude. The Sechín style has been compared to Chavín although the two have little in common in subject matter or line.[112] There are, however, certain associations or blendings of the two styles found in occasional artifacts from various places in Peru. For instance, a conch-shell trumpet (Fig. 3-32), from the Lambayeque Valley, bears an incised design of a man much like that of the Cerro Sechín sculptures, but this man-design is bordered by a very Chavín-like interlaced serpent

motif.[113] There is also a bone spatula from the Huaura Valley that combines Sechín and Chavín elements in a single anthropomorphized feline design.[114] These associations imply a connection, as does the temple building of conical adobes with the painted feline figures that surmounts the primary Cerro Sechín platform.

Unfortunately, the Cerro Sechín ceramic associations are confused, and the dating of the temple is uncertain. Tello placed the building and the monoliths as post-Chavín.[115] Donald Collier, on the other hand, prefers a pre-Chavín date, and both Lanning and I concur in this.[116] The Cerro Sechín style is of greatest importance, for, if it is correctly dated as Initial Period, it is testimony to the appearance of monumental art—and a major art style—that existed prior to Chavín art and that, perhaps, in some part was antecedent to that later great style.

The Highlands. In the highlands Initial Period ceramics are known from the Toríl phase of the Callejón de Huaylas, from Kotosh in the Upper Huallaga, from various phases in the Mantaro drainage, and from the early levels at Chiripa in the South Titicaca subarea. Of these, the Kotosh materials are the only ones that have been well described and illustrated.[117] We have referred to Kotosh previously as the location of preceramic temple structures. The earliest Kotosh pottery is associated with the badly battered remains of buildings (Constructions H and G) overlying the earlier preceramic Mito phase levels.[118] This early pottery

Figure 3-31. Relief carvings from Cerro Sechín. (Redrawn from Tello, 1956.)

phase (Fig. 3-33) is known as the Waira-jirca, ceramics of which tend to be dark brown in color and to have well-smoothed or polished surfaces. The neckless jar or subglobular bowl and the open-bowl forms predominate; however, some vessels were spouted or, apparently, double-spouted with a bridge connecting the spouts, as in the South Coast Hacha pottery. Decoration is largely by incision, and designs consist of nested panels of parallel lines and rectilinear bandings in which broad-incised lines form zones that are filled with fine-line hachure. Multi-colored post-fired pigments were sometimes applied to hatched areas. Dot and hollow-reed-end punctations were also employed. Designs are geometric and essentially rectilinear. The overall impression is that of more decoration, and somewhat more elaborate decoration, than is found in contemporaneous Peruvian coastal pottery. Upper Amazon basin influences, via the Ucayalí

113

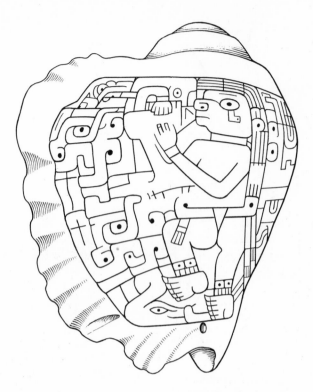

Figure 3-32. *Above:* The "Pickman Strombus," a large *Strombus* shell, which probably served as a trumpet, showing an incised design of a man blowing a shell trumpet (?). The man is rendered in a manner reminiscent of the Cerro Sechín carvings; the bordering elements of serpent, demons, etc., are in the Chavín style, however. Found in the Lambayeque Valley, near Chiclayo. The shell is about 25 cm. long. (Drawn from Larco Hoyle, 1941.)

Figure 3-33. *Below:* Kotosh Waira-jirca phase vessels, all Kotosh incised type. *a:* Post-fired polychrome painting in incised lines (diameter, 21.6 cm.). *b:* Post-fired application of red pigment in incised lines (diameter, 35.1 cm.). *c:* Incised hachure in incised zones and incision filled with post-fired applied red pigment. Diameter, 15.6 cm. (Courtesy Seiichi Izumi and University of Tokyo Expedition.)

Tutishcainyo complex,[119] are obvious, especially in the zoned hachure mode of incision. In my opinion there are also resemblances to Valdivia pottery of coastal Ecuador.[120] But whatever its affiliations, the Waira-jirca style is a distinctive one and cannot be described as representing early ceramic beginnings. It appears at Kotosh fully developed.

The nature of Waira-jirca economy is speculative. No artifacts, such as metates and manos, offer evidence of maize or cereal grinding; however, the building and maintenance of such a site seems unlikely—in this particular environment—without an agricultural economic base. Some chipped projectile points, ground-stone clubheads, pottery spindle whorls, and ground-stone and bone implements and ornaments were associated with the Waira-jirca levels of the site.

The Waira-jirca phase is succeeded by the Kotosh phase.[121] This phase is also marked by platform constructions (Construction F) within the big Mound KT. Associated radiocarbon dates are bunched consistently at about 1000 to 900 B.C.[122] These dates and the mound stratigraphy, which places these levels immediately below a Chavín phase, bracket the Kotosh phase in the latter part of the Initial Period. A Kotosh phase pottery bottle bears an incised design of what seems to be an ear of corn—an argument for maize cultivation. Kotosh phase artifacts are similar to those of Waira-jirca although the excavators comment on the increased number of pottery spindle whorls and then mention and illustrate a few pottery figurines. A number of new pottery vessel forms appear, including

b

a

c

Figure 3-34. Kotosh phase vessels. All Kotosh grooved type with black graphite paint added after firing (diameter, 18.9 cm.). *b:* Post-fired three-color paints in incisions and dots (diameter, 15.6 cm.). *c:* Bottle decorated with grooving and punctations (diameter, 14.8 cm.). (Courtesy Seiichi Izumi and University of Tokyo Expedition.)

effigies and stirrup mouths. Some few vessels bear small relief-modeled faces on the side. The most common decorative technique is still that of incising. Post-fired painting, including the use of black graphite (Fig. 3-34, *a*), on polished red surfaces is also characteristic and is usually applied in incised lines or in areas that are zoned by incised lines. In addition, some plain rocker stamping is noted. There are, in general, resemblances to the subsequent Chavinoid pottery complexes of Peru—especially in the stirrup-mouthed jars, polished black surfaces, color zoning (Fig. 3-34, *b*), and rocker stamping; however, no truly Chavín design motifs are recorded. The latter first appear, and in fact mark, the succeeding Chavín phase. Kotosh phase designs, apart from the maize ear and the little relief faces, tend to be rectilinear and geometric, much as were those of Waira-jirca. Wider relationships of Kotosh style pottery have been suggested with Ecuadorian Machalilla[123] and with Ucayalí Tutishcainyo.[124]

Reflections. The rapid burgeoning of the Peruvian cultural tradition during the Initial Period prompts the question, to what extent was this the result of an agricultural revolution? In answer, I think it is clear that some connection existed between early Peruvian cultural elaboration and farming. The concatenation of events—the appearance of the plants, the increase in number and size of sites, the ceremonial constructions, the florescence of arts and crafts—is too striking to deny a degree of causal relationship. Still, as we have seen, the story of development—at least on the coast—was not simple, and the causal relationships were not one-to-one equations of "agricultural economy equals rapid cultural growth." Sedentism, large communities, and ceremonial architecture have all been seen to precede the full establishment of agriculture. Thus, farming, while probably the single most important economic factor, was nevertheless not the only one in the crystallization of a

Peruvian cultural tradition. In the economic realm alone, fishing, shellfish taking, and llama herding also contributed. And there were other factors that were important to the process of civilizational growth. For example, I think it likely that centuries of settled living in concentrated villages and towns along the shore—long before the growing of crops became the principal economic mode of life—may have given the Peruvians a background of "social experience" that turned their interests relatively early toward politico-religious matters. These interests were to find still more elaborate expressions in the Early Horizon immediately following the Initial Period.

The Early Horizon: Chavín

Some Definitions. The Early Horizon has been defined as the time of the Chavín art style and its immediate derivatives—a period estimated as 900 to 200 B.C. Subsumed under the Early Horizon are those Peruvian cultures that are dominated by that style, those that show unmistakable strong influences of that style, and those that, although not Chavín or Chavinoid in their art forms, are nevertheless contemporaneous with the life of the style. That is, the Early Horizon is a period concept, defined primarily in terms of absolute time, but a period during which many of the existing cultures were pervaded by what we are calling the "Chavín Horizon Style."

In Peruvian archaeology a "horizon style" is one that is found widely throughout the area, one that interrupts or influences the local stylistic developments of regions or subareas, and one that thereby serves to align or coordinate chronologically these various regional or subareal sequences.[125] The assumptions behind this reasoning are that a complex entity such as an art style has a single point of origin, that if it occurs in two separate geographical locations it must have spread from one to the other, and that this spreading took place relatively rapidly, thereby indicating near-contemporaneity of the two occurrences.

The Chavín horizon style takes its name from the sculptures of the site of Chavín de Huántar, in the north highlands of Peru. The Chavín style is highly distinctive.[126] Its themes are anthropomorphic and animal: men, demons, jaguars, eagles, serpents, caimans, and other beasts. These are given fantastic renderings, and there is, especially, a conceit of giving jaguar or feline attributes (fangs and claws) to other animals and men or deities (Fig. 3-35). Serpent heads are also frequently disposed on all parts of the body of the principal animal or human represented in a sculpture. The style is graceful, flowing, essentially curvilinear, and intricately and rhythmically balanced. A characteristic mode is an eye with an eccentric pupil, and this, together with the grimacing, fanged mouths of the animals, demons, or gods, gives a somewhat sinister, baleful aspect to the Chavín figures. It appears to be an art well-adapted to, and perhaps developed in, the techniques of stone sculpture. Such sculptures are usually of a low-relief variety although full-round carvings are known. At Chavín de Huántar the style is known mainly from monumental sculptures—lintels, cornices, figures tenoned into massive stone masonry structures, and free-standing stelae. In its occurrence elsewhere, however, the style is often expressed in other media. Sometimes these are monumental clay sculptures associated with buildings; but more often they are smaller craft products such as sculpted and incised pottery, carved bone, small sculpted stone objects, hammered goldwork, and even textiles.

The origins of the Chavín style are obscure. J. C. Tello thought it to be trans-Andine and to have arisen in the tropical forests, the habitat of the great jaguar which is one of its principal motifs.[127] While it is possible that mythological concepts that may be expressed in the style have a tropical forest origin, there is, as yet, no real supporting evidence for the Chavín style as such in the montaña or the jungle. It is also possible that the origins of Chavín art lie on the coast. The presence of the Cerro Sechín style in the Casma Valley, as we have said, suggests a possible prototype here;[128] however, no definite transition from Sechín to Chavín has been documented, nor can we be sure that Sechín precedes Chavín. The other possibility, that of a highland origin, is supported by the fact that the type site of the style, and the place where it is known in its most spectacular monumental manifestations, is Chavín de Huántar in the north highlands; but there seem to be no earlier prototypical stages here or elsewhere in the highlands. Chavín art, as we know it, appears fully developed. About the best that we can say, at present, is that Chavín art is north Peruvian, beginning either on the coast or in the highlands.[129]

The dating of the Early Horizon, and the Chavín style, as falling between 900 and 200 B.C. has been confirmed by radiocarbon readings at various places in Peru.[130] The style did not remain static and unchanged through these seven centuries. Rowe has devised a chronology of Chavín stylistic evolution from a study of building-phase superimpositions at Chavín de Huántar and, similarly, from seriations of the art forms themselves.[131] The initial appearance and spread of the style must have taken place within a single century—from about 900 to 800 B.C.[132] Subsequently there were modifications, at Chavín de Huántar and elsewhere, and the style gradually lost its distinctiveness. In many places it became submerged in local styles that were, in part, derivative from it but that also reflected other influences. By 200 B.C. it had disappeared.[133]

The distribution of the Chavín style includes the Callejón de Huaylas (and Upper Marañón) and Upper Huallaga subareas of the highlands and the North, North-Central, and Central Coastal subareas. In all of these it is found in an essentially pure state, both in theme and in line. Its very definite influences are also to be seen in the South-Central and South Coast subareas, especially in ceramics of the Paracas culture. Elsewhere, in the subareas of central and southern highland Peru and Bolivia, and in the Far North and Far South Coastal subareas, it does not occur, or at least has not yet been discovered.

Chavín de Huántar. The ruins of Chavín de Huántar[134] are in what we have designated as the Callejón de Huaylas subarea; however they are not in the Callejón proper but instead lie to the east, on the other side of the Cordillera

Figure 3-35. Relief sculptures from Chavín de Huántar. *Top:* Feline being with serpent attributes. The technique is champlevé carving and incision. Length, 1 m. *Botto.n:* Serpent with feline attributes, carved on edge of same lintel as being at *top.* Length, 1 m. This stone was set in the southwest corner of the Castillo. (Redrawn from Bennett, 1942.)

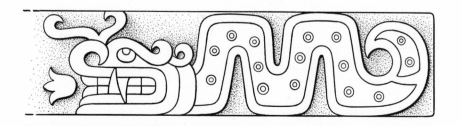

Blanca (a section of the Cordillera Occidental) in the Upper Marañón drainage. The immediate surroundings are those of a fertile valley that lies at some 10,000 feet (3700 m.) above sea level.

The central constructions of the site are a complex of stone masonry platforms that were originally ornamented with stone sculptures and clay reliefs. These several platforms cover an area about 210 meters square (Fig. 3-36). The height of artificial construction is more difficult to estimate as the main buildings rest on a hillslope (Fig. 3-37), but the southeast corner of the highest standing structure (the "Castillo" or "New Temple") rises about 13 meters above the surrounding terrace. The Chavín de Huántar masonry platforms are rectangular and they are arranged more or less in the cardinal directions. There are foundation evidences of stone buildings on the tops of the platforms, and these may have served as shrines or temples; but the platforms themselves are not solid masonry or fill. They are, in fact:

> ...honeycombed with stone-lined slab-covered galleries and rectangular rooms, forming at least three floors and perhaps more, many connected by stairways and inclines. Likewise the interior galleries are ventilated by a complex system of vent shafts, not only connecting galleries on the same floor but running vertically as well.[135]

These interior galleries varied in size. They ranged from 1.0 to 1.5 meters in width and from 1.5 to 3.0 meters in height. Rooms were 2 meters wide and 4 to 5 meters long. The galleries, rooms, and doorways were all roofed with stone slabs or lintels. The wall masonry of the interior rooms and

Figure 3-36. Plan of the structures at Chavín de Huántar. (Redrawn from Rowe, 1967; based on a survey by Rowe and Marino Gonzales Moreno; courtesy also Peek Publications, Palo Alto, California.)

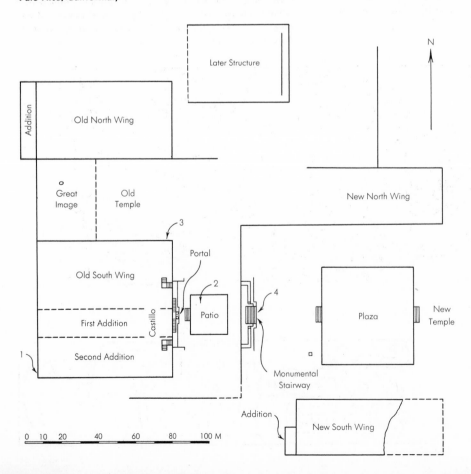

Figure 3-37. The "Castillo," or temple, at Chavín de Huántar. *Left:* View from a distance. *Right:* Closer view from another angle. (*Left:* Courtesy American Museum of Natural History; *right:* courtesy Donald Proulx.)

galleries, as well as the exterior masonry of the Chavín de Huántar buildings, follows a style of alternating horizontal rows of large and small stones. For the interior walls these were split but not carefully dressed stones; for the exterior walls they were well-dressed granite slabs. In construction, exterior facings and the interior walls were set against dirt and rubble fill. As Bennett concludes:

> Quite obviously, the Castillo was built up floor by floor with galleries, vents, facing, and fill carefully planned.[136]

The outside walls of the main temple building at one time were adorned with a row of great human and animal heads which were tenoned into the masonry.[137] A projecting cornice above the heads had been carved with relief figures, and various carved-stone slabs that must have been set into the masonry walls in a number of ways—as cornices, portal columns, lintels, panels—also have been found at the site although not usually in position. Among these are a number of large stelae or monoliths, which are the best-known sculptures of the Chavín style. One of these, the Great Image, or the Lanzón (Fig. 3-38), is still in its original place in a most dramatic setting.

In describing and analyzing the temple buildings, Rowe has postulated a sequence of original construction and successive enlargement. The first temple was a U-shaped structure consisting of a main building and two wings enclosing three sides of a rectangular court, the open side being on the

east. It is to be noted, in passing, that this temple form is not unlike the U-shaped or courtyard plan noted on the Central Coast at Chuquitanta, in Preceramic Period VI. Deep within the heart of this original temple at Chavín de Huántar, at the intersection of two galleries that bisect the building on its two central axes, is a carved shaft of white granite—the above-mentioned Great Image, or the Lanzón. The monolith is 14 feet 10 inches (over 4 m.) in height and is fastened to both the floor and the ceiling of the gallery. As Rowe states, this "setting in a dark passage gives it an awe-inspiring quality which can be felt even by a present day unbeliever."[138] The Great Image is prismlike in shape and pointed at the ends, presumably the more or less natural form of the slab selected for the purpose. The carving is bas-relief, but these carvings are on all faces of the monument. The figure is anthropomorphic, a standing man-form with a massive head and jaguarlike fangs and nostrils.[139] Hair is represented by serpents. Ear ornaments and a necklace are shown, and there is a girdle composed of serpent-jaguar faces. A similar chain of serpent-jaguar faces adorns the upper part of the Lanzón above the head of the figure. Tello has identified the being represented as Wira Kocha, the supreme divinity—a speculation based on projections from Inca ethnography; Rowe more

Figure 3-38. *Right:* The famed
"Lanzón" in the temple interior at
Chavín de Huántar. (Redrawn from
Tello, 1961, and from Rowe, 1962 b).

Figure 3-39. (*Left*, p. 121) Relief
carving on the famous "Raimondi
Stone," Chavín de Huántar. Height,
about 2 m. (Drawn from a photograph.)

conservatively designates it as a representation of the "Smiling God"—because of its large, notably upturned mouth.[140]

In later times the temple was enlarged, and the enlarged south wing became the "Castillo" or "New Temple." This newer portion also faced eastward over a new courtyard area, again flanked by wings (see plan, Fig. 3-36). The carvings and sculptures associated with the new were contrasted with those of the old, and this offered clues for Rowe's chronological seriation of Chavín art forms. In this seriation the general trend runs from curvilinear arrangements to greater use of straight lines, and from the employment of bandings of varying widths to those of more standardized dimension.[141] For instance, such a famous Chavín sculpture as the "Raimondi Stone" (Fig. 3-39) falls toward the end of the sequence, whereas the Great Image is early.

According to Rowe, Chavín de Huántar was not only a ceremonial center. He estimates that there was a contemporaneous settlement, indicated by Early Horizon ceramic refuse, which stretched for a kilometer to the north of the temple complex, and additional Chavín refuse is also found on the opposite side of the river from the site proper. A number of smaller contemporaneous sites have been located within a radius of a few kilometers of Chavín de Huántar.[142] The overall settlement picture, then, is that of a sizable town or small city, with its imposing ceremonial buildings, surrounded by outlying villages in the countryside.

Figure 3-40. Carved design on cornice slab, Chavín de Huántar. A condor or eagle with feline attributes. Width, 46.5 cm. (After Bennett, 1942.)

The ceramics at Chavín de Huántar (Fig. 3-41) share many characteristics with the Initial Period pottery of the coast, particularly those wares and styles found in the North Central subarea, such as at Las Aldas. It is, indeed, this ceramic similarity, together with the early presence of temple structures and the Cerro Sechín sculptural style, that suggests the North-Central Coast subarea as a hearth for the Chavín style.[143] Still, it is to be remembered that we know nothing of pottery antecedent to Chavín in the Chavín de Huántar region or the Callejón–Upper Marañón subarea; and at Kotosh, the closest highland location to Chavín de Huántar at which we have Initial Period ceramics, the pottery preceding the Chavín-influenced level has a number of traits in common with the Chavín wares. Thus there are also Chavín pottery prototypes in the highlands as well as on the coast.

In general, the pottery at Chavín de Huántar is a blackish or brownish, dark-fired ware, frequently polished and, when ornamented, bearing incised, punctate, brushed, or rocker-stamped decoration. Tello illustrates stirrup-mouthed jars, tall-necked bottles, subglobular bowls, simple bowls, and flat-bottomed bowls and beakers. Many of the incised designs are simple ones—circles, rectilinear figures—but there are also clear Chavín style faces with interlocked fangs and more stylized elements clearly recognizable as Chavín art. Some of these are executed in relief-modeling as well as incision.[144]

Fragments of bone spatulas, batons, or unidentified objects, which were handsomely carved in the Chavín style, came from Chavín de Huántar refuse, as did some stone mortars, ring-shaped club heads, some rather crude ground stone axes and knives or points of both chipped and ground stone. Axes were of full- and three-quarter-grooved and T-shaped types; knives were both stemmed and unstemmed.[145] Goldwork, with hammered Chavín-style designs, is also reported to have come from Chavín de Huántar, but this attribution is uncertain.[146]

Other Highland Manifestations of Chavín. Stone carvings, pottery, and other objects in the Chavín style are reported for all of the north highland subareas of Peru, although there is as yet little detailed information on specific sites. The best known, aside from Chavín de Huántar, is Kuntur Wasi (or La Copa), located in the upper Pacasmayo or Jequetepeque drainage on the border between the Middle Marañón and North Coast subareas. It is described as a stone-faced triple-terraced pyramid surmounted by a temple, or temples, now largely destroyed. Stone statues, heads, carved slabs, and lintels were found on and around the pyramid. A bird with feline attributes and a full-round sculpted head are those pieces among the sculptures that are like those of Chavín de Huántar. Other carvings seem less Chavín-like. While it is possible that all may be contemporaneous, there is a good chance that some monuments are later than the Early Horizon. The pottery from the site also appears to be a mixture of Chavín and later painted styles.[147]

Pacopampa and Yauya, in the Middle Marañón, also have Chavín affiliations. The former is known for its carved stone mortars, pestles, and bowls,[148] the latter for a stela with the relief carving of a standing monster, interpreted variously as a fish or caiman with feline attributes. Stylistically this Yauya monument is seriated toward the end of the Rowe sequence devised for Chavín de Huántar.[149]

At Kotosh, in the Upper Huallaga, a Chavín horizon and phase are represented by two constructions (E and D) in the main mound stratigraphy. The shapes of the pottery vessels are similar to those of Chavín de Huántar. The radiocarbon

Figure 3-41. Pottery vessel forms of Chavín style from Chavín de Huántar. (After Tello, 1960.)

dates for the Kotosh Chavín phase fall between 800 and 1000 B.C.[150]—the begining of the Early Horizon. This Kotosh appearance of Chavín is the southernmost highland appearance of the style now known.

The Pallka and Cupisnique Phases. The North-Central Coast, which we have noted as a subarea characterized by ceremonial constructions in the Initial Period, was also the setting for a number of important Early Horizon temple centers. One of the best known is Pallka (or Pallca) in the Casma Valley. The Pallka temple measures about 250 by 100 meters at the base. Upon this platform four main terraces rise, one above the other, pyramid-fashion. Construction is largely of mud and stone. The large ceramic sample is clearly Chavinoid, with vessel forms (stirrup-mouth jars, flat-bottomed bowls, tall-necked bottles), decorative techniques (incision, rocker stamping, punctation, appliqué, etc.) and designs (geometric and curvilinear bandings, stylized feline elements) duplicating those of Chavín de Huántar or Kotosh Chavín.[151] Mojeque (also Moxexe, Moxeke) is another Casma Valley temple. Approximately square (160 × 170 m. at the base), it rises to a total height of 30 meters, with the highest portions set toward the back of the structure as one ascends a front (northeast side) stairway. On an upper terrace, flanking the stairs on each side, are series of niches that contain adobe sculptures (now partially destroyed) of feline, serpent, and human forms, rendered in Chavín style. Both mud-and-stone and conical adobe bricks were used in the construction. The distinctive conical adobe form, it should be noted, is a characteristic Early Horizon trait of the north and central coastal sites.[152] The largest structure in the Casma Valley (250 × 300 m. at the base and 35 m. high), the gigantic Sechín Alto pyramid (not to be confused with Cerro Sechín) is also presumed to date largely from the Early Horizon. The structure is of conical adobes, stone, and clay mortar. On its summit platform smaller platforms were arranged to form a central court, enclosed on three sides and open on the fourth.[153]

In the Nepeña Valley, to the north of Casma, are two more temples that show Chavín elements in their clay sculptural facade decorations. Cerro Blanco is a stone platform in which the walls had been covered with mud or clay reliefs painted in multi-colors. The reliefs show Chavín-style eye and cross-fang elements, and the associated pottery is Chavinoid. The second Nepeña temple is Punkurí (Pungurí), also a stone platform with painted mud reliefs (Fig. 3-42). A wide stair that ascends to the platform of this temple has a huge, full-round, stone-and-mud feline head as a central ornament. An overlying constructional level was made of conical adobes, and an incised decoration on a plastered wall of this building is described as Chavín in style. Ceramic associations are not altogether clear, but it seems likely that both levels belong to the Early Horizon.[154] Tentatively, we group Cerro Blanco and Punkurí, together with the Casma sites just noted, into a Pallka phase of the North-Central Coast.

Figure 3-42. Feline sculpture in clay, painted; Chavín style. On the steps of the temple at Punkuri, Nepeña Valley, North Central Coast of Peru. (Drawn from Larco Hoyle, 1941.)

The overall settlement pattern of the Pallka phase has been studied in the Casma Valley by Donald Thompson, in conjunction with Donald Collier's pottery survey.[155] His investigations show residential communities at some little distance apart from the temple structures we have been describing. These residential units are closely clustered arrangements of rooms and buildings. One such large clustering extends over an area of 800

by 550 meters. It seems clear that both Casma and Nepeña were densely settled during the Early Horizon.

In the North Coast subarea the Early Horizon is best known for the Cupisnique phase,[156] named and defined for a tributary part of the big Chicama Valley. The name may temporarily be extended to cover a number of closely related sites and discoveries extending as far north as the Lambayeque Valley, although further research will undoubtedly specify and define regional and chronological distinctions.[157] A Cupisnique occupation is found at Huaca Prieta—the big midden accumulation near the valley beach where we have already traced man's activities in the Preceramic VI and Initial Periods. Maize and a full complement of other domesticated plants are present in this occupation together with the diagnostic Chavinoid pottery. Some subterranean dwellings were still in use, but in Chicama and Virú most of the Early Horizon houses were aboveground. They were constructed of either stone or conical adobes. Sometimes they were clustered or agglutinated units and sometimes small hamlets of one- or two-roomed buildings. Pyramids of conical adobes, such as the Huaca Pukuche in the Chicama Valley, must mark temple center sites.

Cupisnique is famous for its Chavín-like pottery. Much of it is the sombre gray-black or brown-black, highly polished ware that we associate with the Chavín horizon; however there is a clear stylistic seriation into chronologically ordered subphases. Vessels of the later subphases have more delicate stirrup spouts and feature combinations of red and black bandings separated by incised lines. Those of the earlier subphases have the heavier, thicker spouts, and decoration is wholly by plastic manipulation of the surface. Most of the Cupisnique vessels have come from graves where they had

Figure 3-43. *Top, left:* Magnificent specimen of modeled and incised blackware in the Cupisnique style. North Coast of Peru. The vessel is about 20 cm. high. (Drawn from Larco Hoyle, 1941.)

Figure 3-44. *Bottom, left:* Polished blackware bottle with incised Chavín style design and dentate rocker-stamped background. Top of orifice is broken. Cupisnique phase, North Coast of Peru. (Drawn from Larco Hoyle, 1941.)

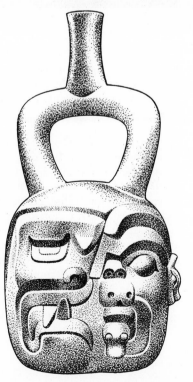

Figure 3-45. *Above:* Coast Chavín or Cupisnique pottery, North Coast. *Left:* Stirrup-mouth jar with surface-roughened (striation-pinching and dentate-stamping) and polished decoration. The ware is fired black. *Right:* Stirrup-mouth jar of grayware (low polish) with appliqué ridge and node decoration. Approximately half of the vessel has been left plain. These jars are about 20 cm. high. (*Left:* Courtesy Museum für Völkerkunde und Vorgeschichte, Hamburg; *right:* courtesy Museum für Völkerkunde, Berlin.)

Figure 3-46. *Left:* Dual feline-anthropomorphized feline concept. A Cupisnique (North Coast of Peru) modeled jar. The spout form suggests a relatively late dating within the Cupisnique phase. (Drawn from Larco Hoyle 1941.)

carefully been placed with the dead; as a consequence they are usually intact or nearly so. Many specimens are life-modeled, representing animals, humans, plants, and buildings (a small rectangular house with a gabled roof). In fact we see in Cupisnique the beginnings of that penchant for life-modeled ceramics that was to characterize the North Coast subarea for the next 2500 years.

Figure 3-47. *Left:* Cupisnique (late) stirrup-mouth jar. Ornamentation combines modeling, incising, red-slipping, and black painting. Specimen comes from Sausal, Chicama Valley, North Coast. Height, 23.5 cm. (Courtesy American Museum of Natural History.)

Figure 3-48. *Right:* Chavín-style gold crown, repoussé ornamentation. From Chongoyape, Lambayeque Valley. Height, 27 cm. (Courtesy Museum of the American Indian, Heye Foundation.)

It is also on the North Coast that we have the first good evidence of Early Horizon metallurgy. The objects in question are a series of magnificent gold items—crowns, ear spools, ornaments, tweezers, pins—all from a location known as Chongoyape (Fig. 3-48). The find was an accidental one, but the goldwork had apparently been placed as grave goods. Both pottery associations and the style of the designs on the gold itself relate it to Chavín. The metallurgical techniques involved in the manufacture of the articles include hammering and repoussé treatment, annealing, and soldering or welding.[158]

The Central Coast. Chavín influence was strong in the ceramics of the Central Coast subarea during the earlier part of the Early Horizon. At the Ancón Tank Site[159]—mentioned previously as an Initial Period temple and village location—a Chavín horizon phase (subphase D of the Matos sequence) can be linked to another at Curayacu,[160] a village site on the coast south of the Lurín Valley. A large temple construction, similar in plan and building materials to the Preceramic VI Chuquitanta temple, is known at Garagay in the Chillón Valley. It too dates from the initial spread of Chavín influences. In the

Figure 3-49. A feline-crab composite being, carved in low relief on a stone disk or plate. Cupisnique or Chavín style, North Coast of Peru. (Drawn from Larco Hoyle, 1941.)

Figure 3-50. Cupisnique knobbed stone mace-head. (Drawn from Larco Hoyle, 1941.)

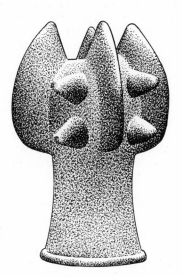

Central Coastal sites, as at Kotosh, there was a disappearance of distinctive Chavín stylistic motifs in the latter part of the Early Horizon.[161]

The South Coast. South Coastal pottery was also marked by Chavín influences although here the product showed more local features.[162] The culture involved is the Paracas,[163] which is best known from the Ica Valley. Menzel, Rowe, and Dawson have established a detailed seriation of the finer grave pottery of the general Paracas style.[164] Ten subphases plot the course of this seriation. The first eight of these show clear Chavín stylistic elements, and the nature of the style changes through these eight phases can be related to the sculptural seriation that Rowe devised for Chavín de Huántar. Thus it would appear that the South Coast was, by some as yet unexplained routes of trade or diffusion, in contact with Chavín de Huántar throughout much of the Early Horizon. This is in contrast to what happened at Kotosh, on the North Coast, the Central Coast, and the South-Central Coast,[165] where in each case, after its initial impact, Chavín influence became dilute and disappeared.

It should be explained that while the chronological seriation of the subphases of the Paracas style is based on a very tightly interlocked similary seriation,[166] this seriation is also further supported, and the series given time direction, by stratigraphic studies that place the entire Paracas style in a larger chronological frame of reference with relation to the Early Intermediate Period Nazca style.[167] Thus the tenth subphase of the Paracas series, which closely resembles the earliest Nazca pottery, may be presumed to be the latest in the Paracas series, for there is stratigraphic demonstration that places the Paracas style as a whole as earlier than the Nazca.

Paracas pottery is highly distinctive.

In spite of the evident importance of Chavín influence...the maintenance of local specialities makes the Paracas style in general...at all times a distinctive one, very different from the Chavín influenced styles in central and northern Peru. The double-spout-and-bridge bottle, one of the most distinctive south coast vessel types, has a prototype in the Hacha style, an Initial Period style of the Acarí Valley, as do red-slipped vessels and negative painting. Other important characteristics distinguishing

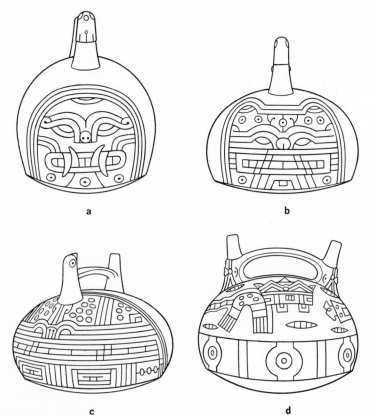

a

b

c

d

Figure 3-51. *Above:* Paracas vessels in the earliest subphase of the style, showing strong Chavín influence. Both are incised and bear post-fired resin painted designs. *Left:* Figure-bridge-and-spout jar. *Right:* Stirrup-mouth jar. Height of vessel at *left,* about 16 cm. (Courtesy American Museum of Natural History.)

Figure 3-52. *Left:* Vessel forms and designs of Paracas pottery. The incised areas were painted variously. *a:* Phase 4. *b:* Phase 6. *c:* Phase 7. *d:* Phase 8. Note the reduction of the feline motif. The term *phase* follows the Menzel, Rowe, and Dawson usage; this would be *subphase* in the terminology of this book. (After Menzel, Rowe, and Dawson, 1964.)

the south coast tradition from Chavín influenced pottery styles of other areas include single- and double-chambered whistling bottles, the variety of representational designs used in bowl as well as bottle decoration, and the emphasis on polychrome painting and color contrasts.[168]

Stirrup-mouthed jars, clearly Chavinoid in form, appear in subphase 1 (Fig. 3-51), but they are replaced in later subphases by the above-mentioned double-spout-and-bridge or spout-figure-and-bridge whistling jars (Fig. 3-52). The characteristic type of decoration is for the design (feline face, fox, bird, human, demon, geometric band) to be outlined in incision (usually rather fine-lined) and then for the zones between the incised lines to be filled in with bright-colored resin paint. This paint was applied after firing and so is not set in the same way that a fired pigment is set or fixed. Various shades of red, orange, yellow, blue, green, and brown resin paints were used in multi-color combinations on the vessels. Negative (resist) decoration was also effected with a dark over-color exposing a yellowish or lighter slip under-neath. In this negative technique the designs were simple—circles, dots, and lines.[169]

As would be anticipated from the inventories of the preceding Preceramic VI and Initial Period sites of the South Coast, the Paracas culture carried on the traditions of weaving, and it is evident that weaving techniques greatly influenced design formation and designs applied to Paracas pottery.

For most of Early Horizon times the people of the Paracas culture—inhabitants of the Ica, Nazca, and Acarí (Lomas) Valleys—did not build large temple structures and lived in villages or small towns along the edges of the valleys. But toward the end of the period, according to Rowe, there was a concentration of population into large towns or small cities. He describes two of these, Media Luna and Tajahuana, for the Ica Valley.[170] Both are about a kilometer in extent and show refuse, house foundations, and some adobe mounds. The latter may have been the sites of small temple structures. Interestingly, Tajahuana was fortified with multiple walls. This appearance of fortifications at the end of the Early Horizon and the beginning of the Early Intermediate Period is also noted for other subareas of the Peruvian coast.[171]

The Early Horizon and the Limits of Chavín Influence. Until quite recently it was thought that Chavín influence was missing or extremely faint in the Far North Coast subarea. Lanning's Piura and Chira surveys had defined Paita and Early Sechura phases for this time level, but Chavinoid elements in these were slight or dubious.[172] However, the recent excavations at the Vicus cemetery, in the Upper Piura Valley, have disclosed a substantial number of vessels that are either of Cupisnique style or very closely related to it.[173] Still farther north, Izumi and Terada define a Pechiche phase that shows a mixture of negative-

Figure 3-53. Pottery figurine in the Paracas style. Height, 7.5 cm. (Courtesy Ethnographical Museum, Göteborg.)

painted, white-on-red, and incised pottery types, and some of the latter bear definite Chavín feline designs. But, except for these few observations on pottery, little is known of the Early Horizon cultures of the Far North Coast.[174]

On the Far South Coast it is uncertain that settled life and pottery making had yet appeared in Early Horizon times.[175]

In the central and southern highlands of Peru and adjacent Bolivia we have evidence of Early Horizon population expansion and the settlement of many new sites. Life in these subareas was probably that of successful village and town farmers,[176] although Chavín style influences and temple architecture are absent. In the Mantaro subarea there are a number of phases that appear to date from the Early Horizon: Wichqana, Rancha, Kichka Pata, Atalla, Pirwapuquio, and Jurpac.[177] The best known and described of these Early Horizon phases, however, is Chanapata of the Urubamba subarea. Chanapata pottery is a dark-hued, incised, punctated and relief-modeled ware; in brief, it has the technical hallmarks of the Early Horizon but not the stylistic features of Chavín. Chanapata follows an earlier phase and ceramic style from which it was derived, the Marcavalle. Both these phases are defined from sites near Cuzco.[178] Farther south, in the North Titicaca subarea, a pottery style known as Qaluyu identifies a site and culture phase of the same name. Qaluyu ware is decorated either with incisions or with simple geometric designs in red-on-cream painting. The Qaluyu site refuse covers several acres.[179] Still farther south, in the South Titicaca subarea, in Bolivia, the Late Chiripa phase pertains to the Early Horizon. Here, at the Chiripa site, pottery found in a small cluster of individual house foundations is decorated in cream-on-red with the color zones separated by incised lines (Fig. 3-54).[180]

Reflections. The broader cultural antecedents and the context of the Chavín style are to be seen in the traditions of settled village or town life and in the rapidly expanding traditions of an agricultural economy that was being propagated throughout the Peruvian area all during the Initial Period. As Lanning has pointed out, Chavín influence moved within a context, or upon a base, of settled farming life, but it did not introduce that kind of life.[181] Chavín art—the pervasive power of the style as it is registered in many media and the frequent associations of this art with temples or special structures—can surely be interpreted as a visible symbol of a religion or ideology.[182] Was it spread by military force also? Is it, in effect, a sign of political power, imperial dominance? Such questions are difficult to answer from the data of archaeology, but the answers would appear to be negative.

Figure 3-54. Chiripa pottery. *Top:* Cream-on-red. *Bottom:* Yellow-on-red. Both from the Chiripa site, Bolivia. (Courtesy American Museum of Natural History.)

At the time of the greatest propagation of the style—during the earlier part of the Early Horizon—there were no obvious fortified sites in Peru; the ambience was not that of societies organized for war and accustomed to conquests, as was the case in later Peruvian periods. Nor are Chavín-style ceramics and other artifacts found only in contexts where they would appear to have been the possessions of a conquering elite. Except for monumental examples which are, of course, restricted to public buildings or temples, Chavín style items are found in all parts of dwelling or cemetery areas. These are not conclusive proofs of the peaceful dissemination of a religious cult, but they are most easily interpreted that way. Toward

130

the latter centuries of the Early Horizon the religion or cult of Chavín probably dimmed and died out; yet certain of its concepts must have continued in later Peruvian religions just as many of its symbolic themes and elements continued in later art.

The Early Intermediate Period: Early Kingdoms and Styles

Peruvian societies of the Early Intermediate Period (200 B.C.–A.D. 600) developed a series of brilliant subareal or regional civilizations and styles on the foundations of the Initial Period and the Early Horizon. Art styles of the period—reflected mainly in ceramics but also in other media—are strongly regionalized and in some cases intensely "nationalistic" in their iconographic content. They suggest separate states or kingdoms. Although we do not know the names or the ethnolinguistic composition of such kingdoms, it is highly likely that they did, indeed, exist. The story of the Early Intermediate Period is the tracing out of the rise, florescence, and rather sudden decline or transformation of these early regional styles and kingdoms.

It is quite probable that a maximum level of population was reached in the Peruvian area during the Early Intermediate Period. On the coast this was the time of the first great valley irrigation systems; for the highlands, although data are less secure, it was probably the period of the construction of the first large-scale agricultural terraces. In general, there is a marked increase in the number of sites.

The Early Intermediate Period seems also to have marked the first inter-regional wars. This is reflected in fortified sites and strongholds. Such constructions are one more element in the evidence supporting the contention of a militaristic "nationalism" on the part of the emerging states or kingdoms. Intensive craft specialization and marked social class distinctions are fully evident from the nature of manufactures, from the representative arts, from burials, and from architecture and settlement pattern.

Finally, and with reference to settlement pattern, it is important to point out that the Early Intermediate Period above all sees the rise of the first great Peruvian cities—clearly the loci of aristocratic power, both religious and military, as well as of specialized craft production and exchange.

Cities and Other Settlement Forms: A Digression. The reference to cities in pre-Columbian Peru takes us into questions of the sociological definitions of urban phenomena and into wider considerations of settlement types as these may be defined both sociologically and archaeologically. In our survey of Peruvian prehistory we can digress here only briefly, and the reader must be referred to other writings on the subject;[183] still, the importance of the topic, particularly at this juncture of our presentation, requires some definitions. Those that we offer follow the thinking of Rowe and Lanning, although with some modifications and comment.

Beginning at the lower, and essentially earlier, end of the developmental scale, the first settlement type is the *camp*. This is a locus of a temporary or semi-sedentary nature, presumably occupied only seasonally. Its population is estimated at less than 100 persons. In the earlier Peruvian periods, probably up through Preceramic Period V, such settlements were the only ones found in the area. In these times the camps were "achoritic," Rowe's term indicating that they were completely self-sustaining and in no way dependent upon, or related to, a system of satellite communities. In the later periods campsites were, of course, sometimes used for special purposes (for instance a fishing station along the shore) in conjunction with larger and sedentary sites; and in these conditions such camps would be parts of "synchoritic" (nucleus-and-satellite) systems.

Coming up the scale, the *village*, by definition is a sedentary site. It housed 100 to 1000 persons. Such permanent villages appeared on the Peruvian scene as early as Preceramic Period VI. In many instances, they probably were "achoritic," self-contained, and the functions of such village life were unspecialized. The village, however, could also be part of a "synchoritic" system, either as a nucleus community for satellite camps or, especially in later times, as a satellite to a town, city, or ceremonial center.

Town is the term used for a medium-sized permanent settlement, one with population limits between 1000 and 5000 persons. As we have seen, such towns appeared as early as Preceramic Period VI. Towns may be either "achoritic" or "synchoritic," although the latter pattern was the more common in pre-Columbian Peru. "Synchoritic" towns were political, religious, trade, or military centers supported by, and maintaining governance over, smaller satellite communities. In a word, such "synchoritic" towns were performing urban functions.

The *city* is the large, permanent, concentrated settlement of more than 5000 persons. As has already been stated, the earliest large cities date to the Early Intermediate Period. Probably all were "synchoritic." They show a magnification of the specialized functions noted for the "synchoritic" towns.

The concept of the *ceremonial center,* used throughout this chapter and elsewhere, is, to my mind, something apart from the *camp-village-town-city* typology and continuum. In terms of settlement, the ceremonial center is the actual locus of the specialized functions of religion, government, military power, and, probably, trade. Such a locus may occur unaccompanied by densely settled resident populations; that is, the ceremonial center may be, in effect, a "vacant" town or city with the supporting populations of its synchoritic system located some distance from it in scattered villages. Such a pattern is found in Peru, and both Rowe and Lanning appear to reserve the term and concept "ceremonial center" for it alone. However, in contrast to this, I have used the term "ceremonial center" for the phenomenon as it occurs incorporated within the massed residences of true towns and cities as well as under conditions of isolation.

This highly schematic listing of settlement forms by no means exhausts the subject.[184] There are a number of other types of which one of the most important is the *dispersed* community. This, for example, would be the residential component of a town or city that is strung out in widely separated individual house clusters for several kilometers along the sides of a valley. Apparently, Peruvian farming populations often were so settled, and the urban functions for such populations were taken care of in ceremonial centers placed in relative isolation from the residential zones. This kind of settlement appeared on the coast during and after the Early Intermediate Period. There are also other Peruvian settlement types that represent specialized functions of "synchoritic" systems: forts, garrisons, *tambos* (way stations on highways), and "manor houses" (country estates). These, too, date from the Early Intermediate Period and later.

The Rise of the Moche Civilization of the North Coast. The Moche[185] civilization represents the climax of aesthetic and architectural development on the North Coast during the Early Intermediate Period. A Moche State or kingdom—as we trace it in ceramics and architectural style—dominated the Pacasmayo, Chicama, Moche, Virú, Santa, and Nepeña Valleys. The dates for the Moche civilization are estimated at A.D. 200 to 700, or as spanning the latter part of the Early Intermediate Period and lasting on into the beginning of the Middle Horizon.[186] Apparently, the original heartland of the Moche style and of Moche political power was in the Moche and Chicama Valleys; both subsequently spread southward and northward from this hearth.

If, however, the Moche style and civilization is dated from A.D. 200 to 700, we are left with a gap in the North Coast sequence between the close of the Early Horizon at 200 B.C. and the date A.D. 200. These, it will be remembered, were the centuries following the Chavín-influenced cultures. What was taking place in this period, and in what ways was it antecedent to the Moche development?

The cultural phases assigned to these centuries of 200 B.C. to A.D. 200 are the Salinar and the Gallinazo, both well documented from excavations and surveys in the Chicama and Virú Valleys.[187] Salinar, which follows the last of the Cupisnique (Chavinoid) subphases, marks the shift from blackish, greyish, or brownish pottery (reduce-fired) to red wares (oxidized). New forms and decorative features also appear in Salinar pottery, but there is also some continuity of Cupisnique traits. Thus, Salinar introduces handle-and-spout (Fig. 3-55, *right*) and figure-handle-and-spout (Fig. 3-55, *left*) forms, but the old stirrup-mouth jar is also retained. Salinar decoration is most frequently in white painted bands or dots on a red slip or ground; and this color scheme, which is found elsewhere in Peru at the close of the Chavinoid ceramic styles, gives the name to the white-on-red pottery horizon.[188] But Salinar pottery also

Figure 3-55. *Above:* Salinar phase spout-and-handle jars in white-on-red style. *Left:* Owl effigy done in incision and white painting. *Right:* White-painted geometric decoration. (Redrawn from Larco Hoyle, 1944.)

Figure 3-56. *Below:* Salinar phase stirrup-spout jar with modeled decoration. This appliqué ornamentation is reminiscent of earlier Cupisnique style of the North Coast. (Redrawn from Larco Hoyle, 1944.)

continues incised line decoration, often with incision outlining the white-painted zones, and appliqué modeling combined with incision (Fig. 3-56). The designs, however, are relatively simple —lines, dots, and other geometric elements—and the Chavinoid feline motifs are gone. Life figure modeling is also met with in Salinar grave pottery. These pieces show humans, animals, and houses. The life renderings have neither the highly stylized sophistication of the Chavinoid Cupisnique modeled vessels nor the consummate naturalism of the later Moche wares; nevertheless, the Salinar ceramic complex, as a whole, offers significant elements of transition between Cupisnique and Moche.

Gallinazo pottery provides other elements of this transition between Cupisnique and Moche. It too is in an oxidized-ware tradition, ranging from reddish to orange or buff in color. Much of it is unpainted. There is some use of incision, and white band decoration links it with Salinar; however the main decorative technique is a negative or resist-dye painting (Fig. 3-57), in which a dull black pigment is used to contrast with the lighter ground colors. Vessel forms relate to those of

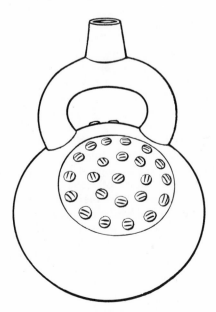

Figure 3-57. Gallinazo phase pottery, North Coast. The vessels at *left* and *center* show resist-painting designs. (Courtesy American Museum of Natural History.)

Salinar, but life figure modeling is even more common (Fig. 3-57). As indicated on the chronology chart (Fig. 3-7), Gallinazo succeeds Salinar; but there is a substantial overlap and association of the two styles. This is seen both in refuse stratigraphy and in grave lot collections. In general, however, there is a trend toward the replacement of white-on-red decoration with negative or resist painting.

The Salinar and Gallinazo styles, as indicated, seem to develop, in part, from the antecedent late Cupisnique styles; however, there are important new elements, and some of these may have their origins in the Far North Coast subarea. In our Early Horizon discussions we made brief mention of the Vicús site, in the Upper Piura Valley of the Far North Coast.[189] The Vicús assemblage of pottery comes from graves, and it is quite likely that a considerable range in time is represented by these. Some of the vessels suggest late Cupisnique forms and surface color; others are Salinar-like white-on-reds; but by far the largest number resemble Gallinazo modeled and negative-painted wares (Fig. 3-58). These latter pieces have been referred to as the "Vicús style." The several resemblances suggest that Salinar and Gallinazo

may have had Vicús, or Far North Coast, beginnings.

Whatever the ceramic origins of Salinar and Gallinazo, we know that these phases, as represented in the Chicama and Virú Valleys, were characterized by increased populations. They were also characterized by the expansion of the valley irrigation systems so that by the close of the Gallinazo phase the major canal lines were laid down.[190] Most of these continued in use throughout pre-Columbian times, and many of them are still in operation today as a part of modern Peruvian agriculture.

The average Salinar community was a smallish cluster of individual houses or a little complex of agglutinated rooms. Most of these had stone foundations or lower walls with the upper portions constructed of the same kind of conical-shaped adobes that were used by the Cupisnique people.

Figure 3-58. (P. 135) The Vicús style. *Top, left:* Negative-painted stirrup-mouth jar in shape of a puma (?). *Top, right:* Negative-painted effigy double-jar. *Bottom, left:* Warrior (?) figure, negative-painted decoration. The man wears a conical cap reminiscent of the Moche-style figures. *Bottom, right:* Double-jar with tubular connection and bridge-handle. Negative-painted decoration. The figure modeled at left appears to be a man within a building. (Courtesy Ramiro Matos; photos by A. Guillen.)

Flat-topped rectangular platforms were made of stone and conical adobes. These, dotted about the valley floors and valley edges, probably served as focal points of worship for the scattered populations. In addition, walled strongholds or places of refuge were built on the tops of natural hill outcrops. These—and others like them from other subareas—are the earliest fortified sites in the Peruvian North Coast sequence.

In Gallinazo times, the great site of Gallinazo proper (Fig. 3-59), on the plains of the lower Virú Valley, represents a kind of city.[191] The central nucleus is a ceremonial center, a complex of adobe[192] structures surmounted by a 25-meter-high mound or pyramid. Nearby are lesser pyramids and platforms and walled courtyards. In and around these structures, as well as in building units lying at some little distance from the main center, are apartmentlike clusters of adobe rooms. Such apartmentlike rooms were presumably made as dwellings, and excavations have shown that earlier ones have been filled with clay to provide the platform bases for later ones. W. C. Bennett, who excavated some of these dwelling units, estimates that there are some 30,000 top-level rooms in those clusters that lie nearest to the main ceremonial mound.[193] The total area involved in Bennett's estimate is about two square kilometers, so that the settlement is probably best described as "dispersed." Still, the main groups at Gallinazo indicate a concurrent population of at least 5000 persons, and if we enlarge the area to some six square kilometers—taking in additional Gallinazo phase structures—at least twice that many people would have been involved.[194] Other parts of the

Figure 3-59. Gallinazo constructions and architecture, Virú Valley. *Top to bottom:* 1. The main pyramid-construction complex at the Gallinazo site. This huge complex of adobe brick construction rises to a height of 25 m. above the valley floor. It has basal measurements of 200 m. It is located in lower Virú, a part of the valley formerly laced with irrigation canals and gardens but now arid and abandoned. 2. The Castillo de Tomaval, a pyramid-fortification complex situated on a rocky crag or spur on the north side of the middle valley. 3. An adobe frieze in a building of the Gallinazo site. 4. Detail of same. (Photos 1 and 3 courtesy W. C. Bennett; photos 2 and 4 courtesy Clifford Evans, Jr.)

136

Virú Valley were, of course, occupied at the same time as the Gallinazo "city." Such additional settlements were outlying farming communities, individual temples or shrines, and, significantly, four great forts or "castillos" guarding the upper reaches of the valley. Most probably, the Gallinazo "city," with its ceremonial center, was the valley capital during the phase and, as such, the head of a complex system of dispersed dwelling sites, lesser religious centers, fortifications, and canal systems.

With this sketch of Salinar and Gallinazo let us now return to the Moche civilization. Moche settlement and architectural types are similar to those of Gallinazo although there seems to be less evidence for city-type concentration of populations than in the earlier phase. In the Virú Valley, for instance, the Gallinazo site proper was abandoned in Moche times,[195] and in its place—although located at a distance of some kilometers

—a huge complex of adobe[196] pyramids, platforms, and enclosed courtyards was constructed. The four big "castillos" in the valley were enlarged by the Moche invaders and, apparently, continued in their military functions.

The greatest Moche ceremonial centers, however, are in the Chicama-Moche homeland regions, of which the most spectacular is the Moche site proper in that valley. The largest structure at that site, the Huaca del Sol, is a massive terraced and truncated pyramid (Fig. 3-60). The pyramid measures 228 by 136 meters at the base and rises to a height of 41 meters above the valley plain. Judging from a river that is cut along one side of the structure, the whole pyramid was built up of solidly packed adobe bricks. A short distance from the

Figure 3-60. The Temple of the Sun at Moche, North Coast. Modern cultivated fields of valley in background. The river (marked by line of trees) has cut along one side of the pyramid. (Courtesy Peabody Museum, Harvard University.)

Figure 3-61. *Above:* The Huaca de La Luna, Moche. This picture, taken many years ago, shows the famous "revolt of the weapons" mural on an adobe wall of the building. The mural, in polychrome, depicted animated axes, shields, and other weapons defeating and pursuing men. (Courtesy Peabody Museum, Harvard University.)

Figure 3-62. *Below:* Major irrigation canals cutting across the desert in the Santa Valley. These were identified by Rafael Larco Hoyle (personal communication, 1946) as Moche culture. (Courtesy Rafael Larco Hoyle.)

Huaca del Sol is the so-called Huaca de La Luna (Fig. 3-61).[197] This is a terraced platform built against a natural hillside and capped with large rooms and courtyards. Within the rooms of this palacelike complex are Moche-style wall paintings depicting anthropomorphized weapons and utensils revolting against their human masters.[198] Quite probably, the Huaca del Sol pyramid was the base for a major temple or temples, while the Huaca de La Luna palace complex housed the aristocratic leaders of the state.[199]

Moche cemeteries are found on pyramid platforms—such as the Huaca del Sol—and they are also found in open areas, often along the margins of the valleys that lie outside the irrigated lands. Graves are usually rectangular pits in which the bodies were placed in an extended position. Sometimes the pits have been lined and roofed over with adobes. Many elaborately furnished graves have been found, and the marked differentiation in the quality and quantity of grave goods indicates a highly developed social class system and complex divisions of labor and duties. These interpretations about old Moche society are, of course, reinforced by the portrayals of persons and activities in the ceramic art.

The outstanding Moche ceramic products are the famous stirrup-mouthed jars. Apparently a

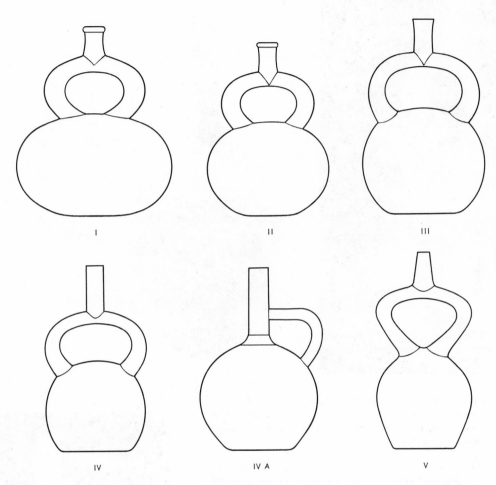

I   II   III

IV   IV A   V

Figure 3-63. Moche subphase vessel forms. *I:* Moche I subphase style. *II:* Moche II subphase style. *III:* Moche III subphase style. *IV:* Moche IV subphase style (this is the most frequent form seen in most museum Moche collections). *IVA:* Another Moche IV subphase form. *V:* Moche V subphase style. (After Rowe, 1957 ms.)

drinking vessel or water bottle, this form has a long history on the Peruvian North Coast; however it reaches its greatest refinement in the Moche civilization. Five Moche developmental subphases are marked by relatively slight changes in the spout form of these vessels. These are more easily illustrated than described (see Fig. 3-63);[200] however it is obvious that the Moche I spout with the beaded lip is a carryover from the preceding Salinar and Gallinazo modes of treatment and that in time the spout became longer and more slender. In the construction of these stirrup-mouthed jars, many of which are characterized by their realistic life modeling, the potter (certainly a craft specialist) first created a solid sculpture of the form desired and produced two halves of a mold over

this. The body of the intended vessel was then formed in these molds and its two halves were joined together. Finally, a base and the stirrup spout were added before firing.[201]

The naturalistic subjects of Moche ceramics— and these are rendered in three-dimensional modeling, low-relief modeling, and a red-on-white or red-on-buff painting—are amazingly varied. They include portrait heads of individuals (Fig. 3-64), animals, plants, anthropomorphized demons or

Figure 3-64. *Above:* Two Moche portrait vessels, Moche IV subphase. The one at *right* is 29.2 cm. high; the other is approximately the same size. (Courtesy Peabody Museum, Harvard University.)

Figure 3-65. *Right:* Moche stirrup-mouth jar (subphase IV) with painted scene of dignitary (seated in a house on a platform and holding a goblet) receiving courier. In the background (*right*) are nude prisoners and similar figures can be seen at *left*. Birds (vultures?) and animals (foxes, serpents) also inhabit the scene, perhaps as omens of doom or death for the captives. (Courtesy American Museum of Natural History.)

deities, and a great range of life scenes. These last constitute a rich prehistoric ethnography of the secular and sacred, the ordinary and the spectacular. The hunting of animals, fishing, war, the punishment of prisoners and criminals, the pomp of rulers seated upon thrones (Fig. 3-65), sexual acts and perversion are all shown. Architectural details—temples, pyramids, houses—are also disclosed in the ceramic art as are features of cloth-

Figure 3-66. Moche fantasy death scene in pottery; three views of the same vessel. In the modeling a large skeleton presides over the ceremony, and three small skeletons sit beside the body of the deceased(?). The body (?) would appear to be encased in a bundle or, perhaps, a wooden coffin. There is a human face painted on the top of the bundle or coffin at the end farthest away from the large skeleton. In the *bottom* picture we see the only living being in the scene, a small dog lying near the body (?) or coffin (?). It is, of course, possible that it is not a body or coffin that is represented and that the long object is a drum upon which the small skeletons are drumming. The painted scene below has a *danse macabre* quality about it. A small skeleton plays a drum. The larger ones hold maces and in some instances are shown with an obvious male member. This fascinating specimen is unusual although thoroughly in the Moche style. Spout form indicates a Moche IV subphase date. The vessel body, as can be seen, is rectangular. Total height, 18 cm. (Courtesy Peabody Museum, Harvard University.)

Figure 3-67. *Left:* A Moche stirrup-mouth jar fashioned as a house (or temple?) on what appears to be a circular, terraced mound or platform, Moche IV subphase. (Courtesy American Museum of Natural History.)

ing and adornment. For the latter, a breech-clout-skirt combination, a shirt, an elaborate belt, and a turban-like headdress are typical. Burial accoutrements preserved from graves verify such ceramic illustrations. Gold, silver, copper, and inlaid-bone nose and ear ornaments are among the finer objects

Figure 3-68. Moche V subphase vessel. The rather close-spaced, heavy-lined red painting is characteristic as is the sharp convergence of the base of the stirrup-spout at the point where it is attached to the vessel. (Courtesy British Museum.)

of personal jewelry that have been recovered from the Moche tombs.

In mentioning metals it should be noted that metallurgy on the North Coast of Peru had by now reached a stage of technical sophistication. It will be recalled that hammered and annealed gold were present on the Early Horizon in Chavinoid-style ornaments. Cast objects and gold-copper alloys were known in the Gallinazo phase. With Moche, there was not only casting (by simple and by "lost wax" methods), alloying, and gilding in the production of jewelry, but the use of copper for such utilitarian items as axes, spears, helmets, and agricultural implements.

The Far North Coast. The Far North Coast was a subarea that was influenced by both north Peruvian and Ecuadorian centers.[202] Quite probably, the earliest pottery—that of the San Juan and Negritos phases—derived from the Valdivia pottery tradition of Ecuador; and Ecuadorian influences seem to have continued in the succeeding Paita and early Sechura phases. These cross-date to the Early Horizon and the beginning of the Early Intermediate Period, and it is possible that the techniques of white-on-red and negative-painting were diffused from Ecuador to Peru at this time. Perhaps Vicús,[203] which is in the upper Piura Valley and to which we have made reference in the preceding section, represents a link in such an Ecuadorian-Peruvian relationship. In the later Sechura subphases there is an important change in pottery manufacture in the Far North Coast subarea, with a shift from coiling to a paddle-and-anvil technique; and it may be that this latter was a Far North Coast invention. In the still later Sechura phases there is Moche IV influence, with the introduction of pressed and moldmade wares; and for the remainder of the pre-Columbian sequence the Far North Coast showed successive Middle Horizon and Late Intermediate Period influences from farther south.

The Lima Style and the Central Coast. Immediately to the south of the Moche domain—in the valleys of Casma, Huarmey, Supe, and Huaura—there is little evidence concerning the events of the Early Intermediate Period; but in the principal valleys of the Central Coast subarea —Chancay, Ancón, Chillón, Rímac, and Lurín— the wide distribution of a pottery style known as the "Lima" suggests political unification and, perhaps, an inter-valley kingdom comparable in size and scope to that of Moche. This Lima style was in vogue in the latter half of the Early Inter-

Figure 3-69. *Above:* Pair of gold and stone-shell mosaic ear disks, Moche style. The settings are of gold, with the small, hollow ball framings. A gold rod or tube is attached to the center of each disk at the back. The mosaic consists of turquoise and other stones and of *Spondylus* shell pieces (red). The figures represent the running messengers, common to Moche art. Diameter of disks, 9.9 cm. (Courtesy Dudley Easby.)

Figure 3-70. *Left:* Moche I-style vessel from Vicús. (Courtesy Ramiro Matos.)

mediate Period and was essentially contemporaneous with the Moche style of the North Coast. Its antecedents—of the earlier half of the Early Intermediate Period, and contemporaneous with Salinar and Gallinazo—were in pottery styles and culture phases known as the "Baños de Boza" (Chancay Valley) and the "Miramar" (Ancón-Chillón valleys).

The Baños de Boza and Miramar[204] pottery styles of the Central Coast succeeded the late Chavinoid styles of that subarea; and their appearance is parallel—and undoubtedly in some way related—to the appearance of Salinar following

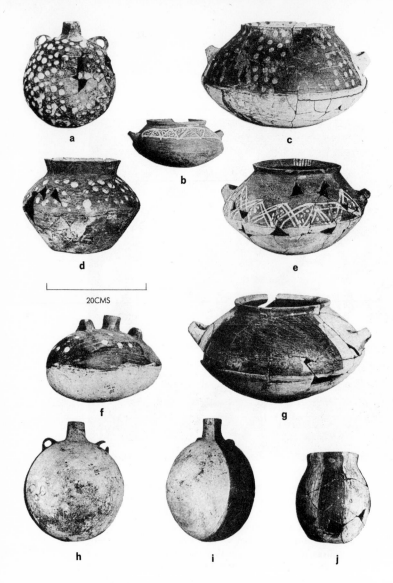

a

b

c

d

e

20CMS

f

g

h

i

j

Figure 3-71. Baños de Boza white-on-red pottery, Chancay Valley. (After Willey, 1943.)

the North Coastal late Cupisnique (Chavinoid) subphases. Both Salinar and Baños de Boza–Miramar feature red-fired, oxidized wares; both see the disappearance of Chavinoid iconography in their decoration and its replacement by relatively simple, geometric design elements; and both are characterized by the predominance of a white-on-red color scheme of decoration.[205] The Baños de Boza (Fig. 3-71) and Miramar pottery complexes —which though closely similar, are not identical— emphasize open bowl, olla, and some collared jar forms. In the Baños de Boza collections there are also a few double-spout-and-bridge and figure-spout vessels. The white-painted decoration has a

dull mat tone, and it is applied to both unslipped and red-slipped surfaces in pendant lines below bowl rims, in diagonal lines, concentric circles and semicircles, and in fields of dots. In the final subphases of the life of these styles there is an addition of black painted decoration that appears to be transitional into the succeeding Lima styles.

The Lima style is characterized by mat white and dull black painted decoration on a red ground color.[206] Decoration is, again, geometric but somewhat more sophisticated than in the Miramar–Baños de Boza patterns. A standard design is an interlocked fish or serpent motif rendered in a rigidly rectilinear fashion (Fig. 3-72). This design, it will be recalled, is a variant of an ancient Peruvian one that dates back to preceramic times in textiles. Two-color negative-painted pottery is also an element in the Lima complex.

Adobe platforms, or pyramids, were constructed in the Baños de Boza, and probably the Miramar, phases;[207] these presumably marked ceremonial centers. In the Lima phase these adobe pyramids were large and impressive.[208] Maranga or Aramburú, in the lower Rímac Valley in the area of the present city of Lima, was a multi-pyramid ceremonial center. Farming populations of the valleys were largely dispersed although there were one or two sizable villages or small towns. One of these, Playa Grande, near the coast at Ancón, offers an insight into burial customs of the time. The tombs at that site were roofed constructions of stone, adobe, and canes. A central burial, presumably a person of high status, was in each tomb, and this individual was accompanied by others who appear to have been buried alive. Baskets with human head skin coverings, necklaces of turquoise and lapis lazuli, pottery, textiles, and tropical birds were placed in the graves.[209] Cerro Culebra and Cerro de Trinidad, larger than Playa Grande and located in the Chillón and Chancay Valleys, respectively, appear as concentrations of dwellings grouped around pyramid-temple complexes. In both of these sites courtyard or palace enclosure walls have been found with multi-colored interlocking fish murals painted on them.[210]

The Nazca Style and the South Coast. The Nazca pottery style dominated the valleys of the South Coast during most of the Early Intermediate Period. Nazca pottery features polychrome painted decoration. It will be recalled that the antecedent pottery style of the Nazca and Ica Valleys was the Paracas, a polychrome style in which colors were "resin-painted" and not set by firing. The transition that archaeologists trace from Paracas to Nazca is in many ways a gradual one; but a key distinction is that the Nazca pigments are now set by firing. Colors include red, black, white, orange, gray, blue-gray and various shades of these; and it is not unusual for a single vessel to display four or five colors.

The seriational studies of L. E. Dawson, in combination with the stratigraphic digging carried out by W. D. Strong, have given us a chronological perspective on the development of the Nazca style.[211] Dawson has divided it into nine sequent subphases.[212] His subphase Nazca 1, which corresponds to Strong's "Proto-Nazca," has been found in the Ica and Nazca Valleys. In addition to the idea of setting the pigments of the polychromes by firing, Nazca 1 also features design elements that were not present in Paracas. Among these is a "cat-demon," which, although continuing the old feline theme of Paracas, is a new conception. Such "demons" are frequently depicted as wearing a gold mouth mask. There are also new bird, fish, fruit, and animal designs.

It is significant that the new designs on these Nazca 1 vessels are the same as some of those on the embroidered textiles and funerary garments of the "Paracas Necropolis" mummy bundles. These "Paracas Necropolis" mummy bundles are associated with the Topará pottery style of the South-Central Coast subarea. Topará pottery was roughly contemporaneous with the latter half of the Paracas-style pottery development, although its latest subphase lasted until Nazca 1 times. It is this late Topará subphase that is often referred to as "Paracas Necropolis" and that is associated with the famous mummy bundles. Topará pottery differs from Nazca in that it is monochrome. The slip has a high gloss and is usually cream-white or pale orange (Fig. 3-73). A melon-lobed jar with small double spouts connected by bridge handles is the familiar vessel form of the style. The "Necropolis" textiles associated with the late Topará pottery are woven of both llama wool and cotton. These textiles, made as special burial garments, have retained a jewel-like brightness in their colors. Backgrounds of black, dark red, or dark

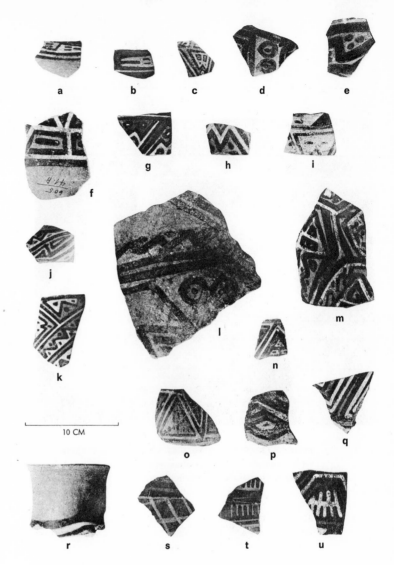

Figure 3-72. Lima-style pottery, Chancay Valley. Also known as "Interlocking style." The colors are red, white, and black. (After Willey, 1943.)

green are overlaid with embroidered polychrome designs of cat-demon figures, animals, and humans. The techniques of brocade, warp- and weft-stripe, gauze, lace, tapestry, and double-cloth were all known to the "Necropolis" or late Topará weavers. It was almost certainly from this source that many of the elements incorporated into the Nazca 1 pottery of the Ica and Nazca Valleys were drawn.

Nazca subphases 2, 3, and 4 have been named "Monumental Nazca" (Figs. 3-74, 3-75).[213] Open bowl and double-spouted jar forms were typical; their painted designs were bold cat-demon or vari-

Figure 3-75. *Above:* Typical Early Nazca polychrome double-spout-and-bridge jar with stylized fish designs. Height, 24 cm. (Courtesy American Museum of Natural History.)

Figure 3-76. *Below:* Typical Late Nazca polychrome jars or vases. (Courtesy American Museum of Natural History.)

Figure 3-73. *Above:* A Paracas Necropolis– or Topara–style white-slipped, double-spouted vessel. (Courtesy Peabody Museum, Harvard University.)

Figure 3-74. *Below:* Early Nazca polychrome vessels. Diameters of bowls are, respectively, 14.4 and 16.5 cm. (Courtesy Peabody Museum, Harvard University.)

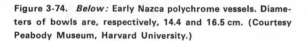

ous plant or animal figures drawn against dark red or white backgrounds that are free of small detail decoration—hence, the "monumentality" of the design. Nazca 5 saw design changes: bodiless human or demon heads and faces were common now, and tall goblet forms appeared.[214] Nazca subphases 6 and 7 have been dubbed "Proliferous." Recurved ray headdresses (Fig. 3-76) were a standard feature; backgrounds were crowded with small filler elements. These trends and others mark Nazca

Figure 3-77. *Above:* Two huge polychrome urns of the Nazca style. (Courtesy Brooklyn Museum and Jay C. Leff Collection.)

Figure 3-78. *Left:* Nazca-style figurines dating from the latter part of the life of the style. From the Chaviña site, South Coast. Figure at *left*, 5.5 cm. high. (Courtesy Peabody Museum, Harvard University.)

8—"Disjunctive" Nazca, so named for the use of disjointed human or demon figures. And with Nazca 9 the style moved from the Early Intermediate Period into the Middle Horizon and fusions with Tiahuanaco-Huari ceramic design elements.

This sketch of Nazca stylistic history pertains largely to Ica, Nazca, and Acarí, although the related Carmen and Estrella pottery styles of the South-Central valleys reflect some of the same trends. In general, these South-Central subarea valleys tended to vary in their stylistic affiliations. Perhaps they were most uniform in Early Horizon times with the Topará style; this style, as we have seen, even extended south into the Pisco-Paracas region. Then, as the Early Intermediate Period progressed, the South-Central valleys showed, variously, Nazca and Lima style affinities.[215]

There were large towns or cities in the South Coast subarea. Most notable of these is Cahuachi, in the Nazca Valley, which flourished during the epoch of the "Monumental" Nazca subphases. The site has a great temple constructed of handmade, wedge-shaped adobes; and the temple platform overlooks a flat-topped ridge covered with walled courts and large rooms. The debris of many smaller constructions, presumably dwellings, surrounds these central features. The temple complex served as a place for burials, for rows of adobe-walled and log-roofed tombs have been found within it.[216]

South Coastal metallurgy remained relatively undeveloped during the Early Intermediate Period.

Figure 3-79. Nazca-style hammered gold mask. Diameter, 22 cm. (Courtesy Museum of the American Indian, Heye Foundation.)

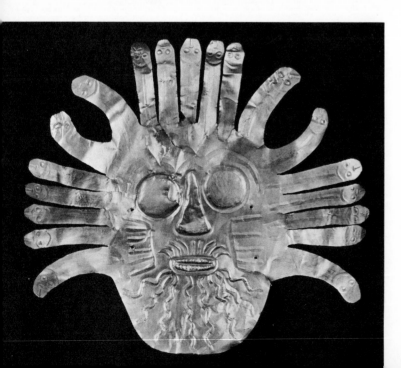

Beaten and cut-out gold ornaments, such as the "mouth masks" seen in textile and painted pottery designs, are found with Nazca burials (Fig. 3-79), but the uses of copper and evidences of casting are relatively late within the Nazca sequence and not numerous.

One other feature of the South Coast and of Nazca culture remains to be mentioned. This is the remarkable drawings or markings on the ground found in the vicinity of the Palpa tributary of the Nazca drainage. They occur on flat stretches of stony tableland where they were made by removing or sweeping the small stones from the surface of the land. This left a smoother, fresher surface that forms the drawings. Some of the drawings are long straight lines or paths that run parallel to each other, radiate out from centers, or are crisscrossed (Fig. 3-80). Others may be trapezoids, spirals, or figures of animals. Some of the latter include designs that resemble those of the Nazca pottery or the "Necropolis" textiles—elements, for instance, suggesting the whiskered or rayed mouth masks. The scale is large, many of the lines and figures spanning several hundred meters. Their identification as Nazca is based largely on the stylistic clues mentioned. According to Rowe and Menzel, these drawings were laid out by sighting from hilltops and by marking the ends and points of crossings with wooden posts. Various speculations have been offered concerning their use or significance. The most frequent is that some of them were astronomical or star-sighting lines; however, those of the animal figures could not have served this purpose. I would agree with Rowe and Menzel that the curious drawings of the Nazca desert are still a mystery.[217]

The Highlands: Northern Subareas. In the Middle Marañón subarea a Torrecitas or Torrecitas-Chavín pottery complex[218] dates to the Early Horizon or to the earlier half of the Early Intermediate Period.[219] Following the Torrecitas complex, which is monochrome incised pottery, there is a sharp stylistic change and the introduction of a new tradition called the Cajamarca. The ground slip of Cajamarca pottery is a light orange or cream, and the decoration is usually in red, although sometimes black is added to make a three-color combination. Decoration is characterized by small motifs: lines, wavy lines,

Figure 3-80. The strange markings on the desert, Nazca region, South Coast. (Courtesy Servicio Aerofotográfico, Peru.)

spirals, and elements that may be highly stylized animals. The decorated surface has a very "busy," cluttered appearance, and because of this and the frequency of wavy lines, it has been termed the "cursive" style. The tripod bowl is a frequent vessel form. This Cajamarca tradition can be traced through five stylistic phases.[220]

In the Callejón de Huaylas and the immediately surrounding regions, in the earlier half of the Early Intermediate Period, a white-on-red pottery style relates to those of the North and Central Coasts. Actually, the true colors of this highland white-on-red sometimes approach a very pale orange-on-dark maroon; but the vessel forms and simple geometric designs suggest those of the Central Coastal Baños de Boza style.[221] Graves containing this highland white-on-red ceramic are found intrusive at Chavín de Huántar and in the Callejón de Huaylas proper, near Huaraz.[222] The distinctive pottery style of the Callejón de Huaylas

during the latter part of the Early Intermediate Period, however, is the Recuay (also called Huaylas). Recuay pottery is negative or resist-painted, and it includes both two- and three-color types. For the two-color, the slip is white with designs blocked out by a grey-black pigment. For the three-color, the scheme is similar except that additional areas of the design have a red over-painting.[223] Designs are highly stylized felines, condors or other birds, serpents, and also geometric elements. One motif is the interlocking serpent or fish, quite similar to those painted positively on the contemporary Central Coastal Lima style. Many of the burial vessels are elaborately modeled, and this modeling shows clear relationships with the North Coast Gallinazo and Moche styles and with the Far North Coast Vicús style. Recuay modeling,

149

Figure 3-81. Recuay three-color negative pottery. *a:* Dignitary seated in a house, surrounded by retainers. There is a vessel orifice behind the man's head and a tiny spout before it. *b:* Vessel representing a house or palace, with figure of a man standing near a door at the top of stairs. Orifice is at the top, and there is a small spout above the head of another man looking out of a window. *c:* Seated warrior with shield and club. *d:* Large jar. *e:* Dignitary surrounded by retainers. The funnellike orifice is behind the man; the spout projects from the body of one of the servants. All these vessels have a white or whitish slip. The main features of the design are then outlined in black through a negative or resist process. Red pigment is then applied, apparently positively, over certain sections of the vessel. The designs on *a*, *b*, *e* feature the motif known as the "Recuay cat"; *c* has the "interlocking fish or serpent" design. The vessels vary in size, but *a*, *b*, *c*, and *e* average about 20 cm. in height; *d* is larger. (Courtesy Museum für Völkerkunde, Berlin.)

like that of Gallinazo or Vicús, is a less successful naturalism than that of Moche. Basic vessel forms include stirrup-mouth jars, head-bridge-spout jars, annular-based jars, and some tripod bowls. Modeling is most often that of a small attached figure of a man or an animal fastened to a vessel body, but there are also group modelings, or "scenes," with several figures.[224]

Recuay (or Aija) monumental stone carving is represented by columnar statues. Some of these show warriors holding clubs and shields, similar to the modeled figures depicted in pottery. In general, the sculptural style has a stiffness and angularity (Fig. 3-82) that characterizes all Peruvian highland stone carving except Chavín. Some human- and animal-head sculptures have been found with tenons, and these must have been masonry decorative elements attached to large stone temples in the manner of the earlier Chavín culture. Subterranean stone-lined galleries, or chambers, suggestive of Chavín are also identified with

Figure 3-82. Monumental stone carving, Recuay– or Aija–style. From the Callejón de Huaylas. (Redrawn from Bennett, 1944.)

the Recuay culture. Whether these underground constructions were used as temples or tombs is uncertain.[225]

In the Upper Huallaga subarea the refuse and constructional stratigraphy in the main mound at Kotosh showed an incised and a white-on-red pottery of the San Blas and Sajara-Patac phases following that of the Chavinoid styles. The succeeding phase, the Higueras, dating to the Early Intermediate Period, is known from red ware decorated with rather crude filleting and appliqué human faces. This Higueras style has some unusual vessel shapes, including tetrapod jars with llama-head effigy appendages. Furthermore, some of the pottery of the phase has negative or resist decoration. The phase is also noted for the first metalwork at Kotosh. This last is represented by pins and bells of copper.[226]

The Highlands: Central Subareas. For the Mantaro subarea, the Early Horizon Wichqana and Rancha phases, featuring incised ceramics, were replaced by the Early Intermediate Period Aya Orjo phase of combined incised-painted pottery decoration.[227] Little other data have been made available concerning the wider cultural contents or associations of these pottery complexes.[228] Aya Orjo gave way to the better-known Huarpa (Warpa) pottery complex and phase; and it was during this Huarpa phase that the great site of Huari (Wari) was established—or at least became important—in the Ayacucho region. The Huarpa pottery style is most frequently white-slipped with a mat white pigment and is usually decorated in black or black and red. Decoration often consists of geometric lines, spirals, zigzags, chevrons, checks, and cross-hatching, although some vessels bear more complex designs that clearly relate to the animal and demon figures of the Nazca 7 and 8 subphases of the South Coast. These relationships between Huarpa and the South Coast continued, as we shall see, into Middle Horizon times.[229]

The site of Huari is situated on a hill and covers several square kilometers.[230] It was obviously a ceremonial center and an extensive living zone as well. Some of the constructions are enormous rectangular compounds or enclosures, with high rough stone walls. In some instances these may have contained two- or three-storied buildings. Others are subterranean complexes of dressed

Figure 3-83.   Two general views of Pucará. *Top:* The ruins lie on the lower slope of the hill in the right foreground; in the middle distance is the modern town. *Bottom:* Closer view of main court. (*Top:* Courtesy Donald Proulx; *bottom:* courtesy Edward Franquemont.)

stone blocks. Unfortunately, relatively little architectural excavation has been carried out, and this limits both our knowledge of the city's form and content and our ability to assign proper dates to the various features. We know, however, that Huari was a great metropolis in the early centuries of the Middle Horizon during the Chakipampa and Viñaque phases. This was the time at which the Huari-generated pottery styles were diffused throughout most of Peru. For the Early Intermediate Period Huarpa phase, we cannot be sure of the extent of the site although it may have reached city proportions by then.

For the Urubamba subarea, centering on Cuzco, we have already mentioned the incised and simply painted pottery styles of the Early Horizon that belong to the Marcavalle and Chanapata phases. For the Early Intermediate Period we can do little more than add the name of the Huaru (Waru) phase, which follows Chanapata and precedes the Huari-influenced Middle Horizon cultures. This is a local pottery style that has some Pucará affiliations.[231]

The Highlands: Pucará. Pucará is the most impressive site in the North Titicaca Basin subarea. It was built and occupied in the earlier half of the Early Intermediate Period, rose to greatness, and then was abandoned probably before Huari became a major city. The central feature of the Pucará site is a ceremonial structure made of dressed stone blocks. This structure takes the form of an inner court partly surrounded by a horseshoe-shaped enclosure divided into small rooms (Fig. 3-83). Two subterranean burial vaults had been placed within the inner court. Farther out, extending for considerable distances from the central constructions, are the foundations of many smaller buildings, and Pucará pottery refuse is scattered over a wide area. In brief, Pucará was a major center, presumably political and religious; and it was also an urban aggregate.[232]

Pucará stone statues and stelae are all carved in relatively low relief (Fig. 3-84). They have the same columnar massiveness and stiffness that one sees in the Recuay sculptural style or in most of the monuments at Tiahuanaco. Statues frequently represent humans holding trophy heads. Serpents,

Figure 3-84. Pucará stone sculptures. The two pictures at *left* show front and side views of the same statue. Both it and the figure in the third picture are small (about 60 to 70 cm. in height). The figure at *right* is somewhat larger than the others. (Courtesy Edward Franquemont.)

Figure 3-85. Pucará pottery. (Courtesy Peabody Museum, Harvard University.)

fish (?), and geometric designs are carved on some of the slablike stelae.

Pucará pottery (Fig. 3-85) is a handsome black-and-yellow-on-red style. The colors are set by firing, but the zones of color are usually separated from one another by incised (or engraved?) lines. The designs include cat faces (some of which are also modeled in relief on the vessels), human heads, and llamas. Vessel forms are flat-bottomed jars and goblets that resemble those of the Tiahuanaco style. In fact, it is certain that Qeya and Tiahuanaco pottery styles of the South Titicaca Basin are related to the Pucará style, and they may be derivative from that style.

The Highlands: Tiahuanaco. On the bleak puna at the south end of Lake Titicaca in Bolivia is megalithic Tiahuanaco. The central constructions and monuments of the site lie within an area of about 1000 by 500 meters, but the extent of pottery refuse beyond this nucleus suggests that there may have been an extensive urban zone surrounding the center.[233] In fact, such a zone has been estimated at 2.5 to 3.0 square kilometers in extent and to have been a living area for a concentration of from 5000 to 20,000 people.

The city apparently had a key economic location as a point of exchange for produce from the eastern valleys, from the lakeshores of Titicaca, and from the puna. Furthermore, recent surveys have revealed new facts about the agricultural potential of the lands near Tiahuanaco. According to J. J. Parsons and W. M. Denevan,[234] some 200,000 acres of agricultural irrigation plots are dimly visible along the western shores of Lake Titicaca. Today these are alkaline-encrusted and are flooded only in years of exceptionally high water. The plots are described as earthen ridges several meters in width and 100 meters or more in length. The ridges rise a meter or so above the intervening drainage ditches and are arranged in ladderlike or checkerboard patterns. Such cultivation works suggest a farming productivity far beyond that maintained in the region at the present time.

The main constructions of the center of Tiahuanaco—which are laid up of dressed stone blocks and furnished with monoliths—are: (1) the *Acapana,* a big platform mound of earth (possibly built over a natural hill) faced with stones; (2) the *Qalasasaya* (Calasasaya, Kalasasaya; Fig. 3-86), a rectangular enclosure of monoliths with a sunken courtyard and a carved monolithic gateway (the famous "Gateway of the Sun"); (3) an enclosure, known as the *Palacio,* surrounded by double walls; and (4) numerous smaller buildings and features including semi-subterranean or subterranean stone-lined rooms, stairways, canals, and statues.[235]

The huge stone statues of Tiahuanaco are, as is the case with the smaller Pucará sculptures, great columns that have been modified with relief carving to resemble men. The head, headdress, face, arms, legs, and feet of these men were all stiffly blocked out. Careful attention was given to carving the details of clothing and ornament.

The dating of the buildings and sculptures at Tiahuanaco is not yet secure, and full results of the recent extensive excavations of the Bolivian archaeologist, Carlos Ponce Sangines, are awaited with interest. It is likely, though, that Tiahuanaco was a great center and city in the Early Intermediate Period. The earliest levels of the site have yielded pottery of a phase named "Qalasasaya,"[236] and this pottery is said to be closely related to the Pucará style. This pottery level is overlaid by that of the Qeya phase, and it was probably during this phase that most of the major buildings were

Figure 3-86. Views of the Calasasaya, Tiahuanaco. Pictures taken in the early 20th century before more recent excavations. *Top:* Overlooking the enclosure, with the bleak altiplano country in the background. *Bottom:* A closer view of the upright stones. (Courtesy Peabody Museum, Harvard University.)

Figure 3-87. Tiahuanaco monoliths. *Left* and *center* are views of same monument, now reset in a modern foundation. (*Left* and *center*: Courtesy American Museum of Natural History; *right*: courtesy Peabody Museum, Harvard University.)

constructed.[237] Qeya, which seems to be derived at least in part from the Pucará-like Qalasasaya pottery style, was ancestral to the succeeding Tiahuanaco pottery style proper. This latter style, however, belongs to the Middle Horizon. The dating of the statuary is uncertain: some of it may be of the Qeya phase while other pieces are Middle Horizon.

Qeya pottery (Fig. 3-88)—the ceramic style defined by Bennett as "Early Tiahuanaco"—is known from flat-bottomed beaker and bottle forms, the use of puma-head adornos, and a polychrome decoration.[238] All of these traits foreshadow the

Middle Horizon Tiahuanaco style (Fig. 3-89). In the latter style, the beaker has become a flaring-sided goblet, or *kero,* and various bottles, bowls, and vases abound. Designs are in black, white, yellow, gray, and brown on a dark red slip. In Qeya fewer colors were used and the surfaces had less lustre than in Tiahuanaco proper. Designs, which were more fully developed in the latter style, include human and divine representations, pumas or jaguars, raptorial birds, and step and scroll motifs.

The South Titicaca Basin was an important metallurgical center for the Peruvian area, and it is quite likely that this center developed for the most part independently of the North Coast focus of metalworking. In the late coastal Chavinoid and subsequent Gallinazo and Moche cultures the

156

Figure 3-88. *Above, left:* Early Tiahuanaco– or Qeya–style vessels. (Courtesy Cambridge Museum of Archaeology and Ethnology, England.)

Figure 3-89. *Above, right:* A classic Tiahuanaco polychrome beaker. This is an unusually fine specimen. Height, slightly less than 20 cm. (Courtesy Museum für Völkerkunde, Berlin.)

early work was in gold, and from this metal they progressed to gold-copper alloys (for ornaments) and copper (for tools and weapons). In the South Titicaca Basin metalworking begins with copper used in a utilitarian fashion—for tools and as clamps to fasten masonry blocks—in the Qeya phase of the Early Intermediate Period.

The Middle Horizon: Tiahuanaco and Huari

We have seen that by the close of the Early Intermediate Period Peruvian societies were enjoying the benefits of an agricultural production made possible by extensive irrigation and terracing systems. Population had increased during the period and true cities had come into being. These were the capitals of subareal or regional kingdoms, and such kingdoms shared a common heritage of technology and of ideology. At the same time these several kingdoms had diverged, one from the other. They had developed distinctive art styles and, almost certainly, different governments. The old Chavín-inspired religious unity had disappeared. These regional states were also in competition with each other for land and food resources; and their leaders must have vied

for power and prestige. In brief, the time was ripe for an imperial attempt. Such an attempt, or attempts, characterize the Middle Horizon.

The archaeological manifestations of these attempts at empire are seen in the widespread dissemination of the art styles of two of the great cities of the Early Intermediate Period: Tiahuanaco and Huari. The iconography and motifs of these styles—usually registered in pottery but also seen in textiles, metals, and other media—are found throughout most of the Peruvian area and, in some places, beyond the limits of that area. The story of their spread is a complex one. Trade, religious conversion, the movements of people, the exercise of military force, and the peaceful diffusion of ideas and elements may all have been involved. We will examine the evidence in different places and at different times in an attempt to interpret what did happen.

Although not all of the sculptures at the site may date to the Tiahuanaco phase proper, there is one that certainly does. This is the so-called "Gateway of the Sun," (Fig. 3-90) a monolithic work that bears, upon its upper part, a series of distinctive relief carvings. The central figure of these carvings, above the doorway, is an anthropomorphic figure, probably a god. This individual, who is shown facing toward the front, has a rectangular head and face, a jaguar mouth, and a serpent-ray headdress (Fig. 3-91). In each hand he holds a staff, or scepter. He is flanked by rows of smaller gods. These, too, are anthropomorphic, and they are depicted as winged running figures, all holding staves. There is no archaeologic or ethnohistoric reason to associate the gateway with the sun; the name is one of popular attribution; and Lanning has referred to the central figure of the carvings as the "Gateway God."[239] We will use this noncommittal name.

Figure 3-91. Details of carving of the "Gateway of the Sun." *Below:* Running figures, or "messengers." (*Bottom,* p. 159) Central figure in detail. The latter is about 45 cm. in height. (Courtesy Peabody Museum, Harvard University.)

Figure 3-90. The "Gateway of the Sun," Tiahuanaco, Bolivia. Pictures taken early in the 20th century, before restoration. *Top:* "Front," or ornamented side. *Bottom:* "Back," or opposite side. (Courtesy Peabody Museum, Harvard University.)

Tiahuanaco. Our tracing out of the story of the Middle Horizon empires begins at Tiahuanaco, that impressive site in the South Titicaca Basin subarea that we have just described in our discussions of the Early Intermediate Period. The city, as we said, had become an important center during the Qeya phase. This importance continued, and apparently increased, in the subsequent Tiahuanaco phase, at which point the Middle Horizon may be said to begin.

Figure 3-92. *Above:* Huge polychrome urn in Coastal Tiahuanaco style. This particular variant of the style is often called the Pacheco, after a Nazca Valley location. (Courtesy American Museum of Natural History.)

Lanning has suggested that this "Gateway God" may be a revival of the old Chavín "Staff God"; and, perhaps, Tiahuanaco symbolism and religion did have a revivalistic basis, awakening folk memories with the glories of a legendary past.[240] But, whatever the circumstances—a resurrected and refurbished god or a completely new one—the Tiahuanaco site and the Tiahuanaco phase appear as the place and time of origin for this motif.

The "Gateway God" motif, the "winged attendant" motif, jaguar figures, eagles, and other elements are the Tiahuanaco designs that are found so widespread throughout the Peruvian area. Max Uhle first noted them at Pachacamac, on the Central Coast of Peru,[241] and he made their appearance there and elsewhere serve as a major chronological reference point in his studies of Peruvian archaeology. For a long time after this it

159

was generally believed that the spread of Tiahuanaco-like art, religion, and political power stemmed directly from the Tiahuanaco site proper. More recently, however, as the result of the analyses of Menzel,[242] it has become apparent that there were two major centers of dissemination: Tiahuanaco and Huari. In its iconography—and quite probably its ideology—Huari was influenced by Tiahuanaco. Very early in the Middle Horizon Tiahuanaco ideas and symbolism were diffused or carried to Huari. This does not seem to have been a conquest, though, for, thereafter, each city rose quite independent of the other to a position of power as the center of its own empire.[243]

The Tiahuanaco Orbit of Influence. The Tiahuanaco orbit of influence, as opposed to that of Huari, was southern in its distribution. We know that early in the Middle Horizon, Tiahuanaco cultures dominated both the South and North Titicaca Basins; but, except for that special stimulus which they passed on to Huari, they and their influences did not reach farther north into Peru. Instead, they penetrated southward and southeastward. Strong Tiahuanaco horizon influence can be traced into Southern Bolivia as far as the Cochabamba region, on to the Far South Coast of Peru, and into the Atacama subarea of the South Andes. In all of these territories the implantation of Tiahuanaco remains is complete enough to imply actual colonization and, perhaps, conquest and dominance of local peoples. Beyond these limits, going still deeper into Southern Bolivia and into the provinces of northwestern Argentina, we find still other, although less clear and direct, influences of Tiahuanaco. But all of this, which is in fact the orbit of influence of Tiahuanaco proper, lies in the South Andean culture area and will be treated in Chapter 4. More germane to the Peruvian area is the influence of the other great center of the Middle Horizon, Huari.

Huari. As we have already observed, Huari (Wari) was an important site in the Mantaro Basin and probably the largest site in the subarea by the latter part of the Early Intermediate Period.[244] It had wide trade connections at that time, especially with the Nazca culture of the South Coast. Its resident ceramic style was one

known as Chakipampa A—a blend of Huarpa and Nazcoid influences. And, as we have said, the Huari region also had connections—whether through trade, religious pilgrimage, or whatever—with Tiahuanaco. The earliest implantation of Tiahuanaco influences dates from the beginning of the Middle Horizon, and it first occurs not at Huari proper but at another site nearby known as Conchopata.[245] Conchopata seems to have been the location of a religious shrine, and Tiahuanaco influences at the shrine are seen in the form of large beaker-shaped urns, which were made at Conchopata but whose polychrome decoration is a faithful depiction of the "Gateway God" from Tiahuanaco. However, the Conchopata style is a new style in its own right, with new local elements as well as borrowed Tiahuanaco designs, and it is a style that is not found at Tiahuanaco. The most likely interpretation is that missionaries had introduced Tiahuanaco ideas and iconography to the shrine city of Conchopata.

Within a short while the Conchopata style appeared at Huari proper and elsewhere in the Huari-Ayacucho region.[246] The context of the Conchopata urns is always one which suggests that they were votive offerings. Their size and nature precludes an everyday use. They were made in numbers, concentrated in one or a few locations at a site, and, apparently, were intentionally smashed.

A later result of the Tiahuanacoid Conchopata–local Chakipampa cultural fusion in the Huari-Ayacucho region was the rise of other styles, especially those known as Chakipampa B and Viñaque. These new styles are found in other Peruvian subareas. Notably, Chakipampa B occurs at Pacheco, in the Nazca Valley. It was further traded and imitated throughout the Mantaro and into the Callejón de Huaylas. Everywhere it occurred in contexts of politico-religious importance, and there can be little doubt that it carried high prestige and that the bearers of the style had access to the local aristocracies. Although we cannot be sure in every instance, this "access" must have often been brought about by force of arms. The Viñaque style was no longer specialized ritual ware, but included *keros* and beakers, bowls, face-neck and anthropomorphic jars, and spouted bottles. Such vessels were usually painted in glossy polychrome designs although some were in fewer colors and had a mat finish. The designs of the Viñaque style are the Tiahuanacoid mythological figures and associated animals and reductions of these. There are also the numerous variants in design that resulted from the combinations of the Viñaque stylistic tradition with the local pottery traditions of the various subareas and regions to which the style diffused.[247]

At the close of the Viñaque phase Huari was abandoned. This event occurred some little time before the close of the Middle Horizon.[248] Quite probably, the city fell before enemies, although there is no clear evidence of this. Whatever happened, with the abandonment of Huari the widespread empire also collapsed; but for the remaining two centuries of the Middle Horizon the impress of the Huari diffusion and conquest was still clearly apparent in numerous regional styles. However, these styles gradually became more modified and, in most instances, there were trends back toward the reestablishment of earlier regional traditions.

The Huari Orbit of Influence.   The Huari orbit of influence in the highlands eventually extended from the Urubamba Basin northward to the Middle Marañón subarea in the highlands. On the coast it reached from Ocoña north to Chicama.[249]

On the South Coast, Huari ceramic influences of the Chakipampa style blended with the Nazca tradition in the Nazca 9 subphase. They produced the subsequent Atarco style (Fig. 3-93). After the close of the Huari empire the South Coastal pottery styles are those generally referred to as "Epigonal."[250]

A similar sequence is seen on the Central Coast, where the first Huari impacts influenced the Nievería (Lima) style. This resulted in a Pachacamac style (Fig. 3-94), named for that site; situated in the Lurin Valley, the site must have been one of the most important of the Central Coastal subarea at the time. The Pachacamac polychrome style spread up and down the coast, and it may be that the site enjoyed some separate, semi-autonomous, or even autonomous, status within the Huari political sphere. Quite probably, the famed "Oracle of Pachacamac," known from Inca times and by the early Spanish conquistadors, was functioning during the Middle Horizon and

Figure 3-93. *Above:* Polychrome double-jar in the South Coast Huari-influenced Atarco style. (Courtesy British Museum.)

Figure 3-94. *Below:* Coast Tiahuanaco Pachacamac polychrome water bottle. The finish is hard and highly polished, the pigments bright. Height, about 20 cm. (Courtesy American Museum of Natural History.)

Figure 3-95. *Above:* Coast Tiahuanaco Epigonal polychrome beakers or keros, from Pachacamac, Central Coast. The finish is soft, the pigments dull. Such keros range from about 15 to 20 cm. in height. (Courtesy American Museum of Natural History.)

Figure 3-96. *Below:* Black-white-red Geometric style. (Courtesy American Museum of Natural History.)

even before that.[251] After the fall of Huari, the Pachacamac style was succeeded by derived "Epigonal" types (Fig. 3-95) and by a style known as the "Black-white-red Geometric" (Fig. 3-96).[252]

On the North Coast a Huari-like style of the Viñaque time horizon, and closely related to Viñaque, seems to represent the overthrow of the old Moche kingdom by highland invaders. It then gives way to derived or "Epigonal" styles.[253]

In the northern Peruvian highlands, the Wilkawain-Tiahuanaco, or Honco, style was the Huari-influenced pottery development in the Callejón de Huaylas, and farther north the tenacious Cajamarca "Cursive" tradition of pottery painting was also modified to some extent by Huari.[254]

This sketch of ceramic history of the Middle Horizon is bare of the substance of human events, and it is offered here only as a chronological guide to the monographic literature. But even this skeleton of pottery types and their changes through time offers us some insights into what was happening. L. M. Stumer has speculated on this in terms of the coast.[255] Using the terminology of "Coast Tiahuanaco I, II, and III" (although Stumer was actually referring to the Huari spread), he points out that his Epoch I was characterized by the arrival of the Tiahuanaco- (Huari-) style pottery and that these new ceramics were found associated with the old local Early Intermediate Period styles. In some instances, vessels of each were actually found associated in the same graves. In the Menzel outline this would correspond to the earlier part of the Middle Horizon (Menzel's I and II divisions). Stumer's "Coast Tiahuanaco II" then saw a drastic

upheaval and flux, with both the former local styles and the intrusive "Tiahuanacoid" (Huari) strain undergoing drastic modifications (Menzel's Middle Horizon III and IV divisions.) Finally, Stumer's Epoch III marked the threshold of the Late Intermediate Period with the appearance of new styles which, nevertheless, carried residues of both the old local and the Tiahuanaco (Huari) elements. In effect, the fusion was now complete. Although purely a pottery stylistic history, it is also a diagram

Figure 3-97. *Left:* Detail from a tapestry mantle. Middle Horizon, South Coast. (Courtesy John Wise.)

Figure 3-98. *Below:* Middle Horizon gold pieces from the Peruvian Coast (probably from either Central or North Coast subareas). *Left:* Thin, hammered, and soldered mask found attached to a mummy bundle. Height, 32.2 cm. *Right:* Kero or beaker, hammered and soldered and with polished stone inlays at top. Height, about 20 cm. (Courtesy Dumbarton Oaks pre-Columbian Collection.)

of culture change: the impact of forceful culture contact, disintegration and change, and the reintegration of new forms. The process can be observed in other aspects of culture.

We know, for instance, that the Huari impact on the North Coast set in motion a series of changes that went far beyond ceramic styles. We have already mentioned that pottery of the intrusive Huari style is frequently found in graves that have been made in or around former Moche centers of power. Those graves that Uhle discovered in the Pyramid of the Sun at the Moche site are an example, as are others, of the Tomaval phase of the Virú Valley.[256] In addition, there are important settlement changes in Tomaval. Moche military and political structures are abandoned, except as the cemeteries of the conquerors. Great walled rectangles of poured (tapia) adobe were constructed in the lower reaches of the valley. These may have been military garrisons, storehouses, palaces, or have served all such functions. Dwelling units were arranged in smaller walled quadrangles with interior rooms or houses symmetrically placed. The building of pyramids, while not completely abandoned, seems to have waned.[257] In the Rímac Valley of the Central Coast the Early Intermediate Period ceremonial centers are similarly occupied and used as Huari burial places. Planned urban compounds and cities—such as Pachacamac, Vista Alegre, and Cajamarquilla—follow.[258]

It seems very probable that the concept of the planned compound architecture—the great quadrangles divided into sections and rooms, which we first see on the North and Central Coasts in the Middle Horizon—was brought from Huari as a part of the Viñaque-phase imperial expansion. The idea was widely accepted, and almost certainly the great planned adobe cities of the succeeding Late Intermediate Period, such as Chanchan and Pacatnamú, of the North Coast, had either their actual physical beginnings or at least their conceptual antecedents in this Huari influence of the Middle Horizon.

One is led to wonder whether the very success of the Huari empire may not have rested on the planned urban idea. Had Peruvian society and culture reached that point in its development where urban planning—and the socio-political concomitants that it implies—had become a necessity? And yet not all of the Peruvian area became urbanized at this time. Curiously, the South Coast and the southern highlands, which had seen the early rise of small cities in the previous periods, reacted in opposite fashion.[259] Here, cities disappeared although "imperial" constructions, such as forts, garrisons, and other public buildings may have been established.[260]

The Significance of the Middle Horizon. The impress of the Huari empire radically changed the cultures of the Peruvian area. It was a social, political, and religious turning point rather than a technological one. Nevertheless, the economic effects were probably major ones. It is a reasonable guess that it was at this time that state control of the distribution of foodstuffs—on a wide territorial scale—came into being. This system, with its storehouses, highways, garrisons, and control stations, is well known from Inca archaeology and ethnohistory. The archaeology of the Middle Horizon suggests that the pattern was laid down then and that the later Inca were not the inventors.

The Late Intermediate Period: Late Kingdoms and Styles

New styles, cultures, and, undoubtedly, new kingdoms arose after the recession of the Huari and Tiahuanaco influences. These appear by about A.D. 1000, and this approximate date is taken as the beginning of the Late Intermediate Period. The chronicler Garcilaso de la Vega, a man of Inca-Spanish descent who wrote many years after the Spanish Conquest, describes four coastal kingdoms that had been taken over by the conquering Incas: Chimu, or Chimor of the North Coast; Cuismanu of the valleys of the Central Coast; Chuquismancu, farther south but also of the Central Coast; and Chincha of the South Coast.[261]

Chimu and the North Coast. The reality of a Chimu kingdom is attested to by chroniclers other than Garcilaso,[262] but its exact boundaries are open to some debate. It is possible that they extended from Tumbes to the Chillón Valley; however, a more conservative estimate—

Figure 3-99. Chanchan from the air, Moche Valley, North Coast. The sea lies off the bottom of the picture a kilometer or so distant. Some of the principal quadrangles of the site are seen in the foreground; other portions of the ruin have been encroached upon by present cultivation of the Moche Valley (off to right). In the background is a strip of desert, then the foothills of the Andes. (Courtesy Servicio Aerofotográfico, Peru.)

confirmed by the spread of Chimu pottery as the dominant style—embraces only the area from Chira to Supe.[263] The capital of the kingdom is known to have been in the north, at the site of Chanchan, in the Moche Valley.

Chanchan is situated in the valley plain near the sea. Its ruins cover an area of at least six square miles (Fig. 3-99). The nucleus of the site consists of ten major quadrangles, some of which are as much as 400 by 200 meters in extent. The enclosing or defining walls of these quadrangles are enormously thick and are made of tapia and brick adobe. In some places they still stand to a height of 12 meters or more. In spite of their formidable size, they have no parapets or other features that would suggest a defensive purpose. It has been suggested that they were *barrio* divisions of some sort, perhaps based on kinship, craft specialization, or both.[264] Within each quadrangle are large rooms, some of which have relief-orna-mented walls (Fig. 3-100), courtyards, sunken gardens or reservoirs, and numerous symmetrically arranged small rooms. Rich tombs have also been found within them.[265] These tombs had been furnished with large amounts of pottery, textiles, feather mantles, dishes and jewelry of gold and silver, bronze weapons and tools, and various carved items of wood. The lavish contents of the graves, together with the impressive architecture, leave little doubt that the ruling and upper classes of Chimu society occupied portions of the quadrangles.

165

Figure 3-100. Arabesque of the Huaca del Dragón, a small outlying building of the great Chanchan site. The style is very typically Chimu. (Courtesy M. D. Moseley and the Peabody Museum, Harvard University Chanchan Project.)

This kind of site, of which Chanchan is the outstanding Chimu example, has been called an "Urban Elite Center" by Schaedel[266]—with the functions of city life and political and religious administration imputed to such centers. Other Chimu "Urban Elite Centers" are Pacatnamú and Farfán, in the Pacasmayo Valley, and El Purgatorio, in Lambayeque.

Another type of site, the "Urban Lay Center," is also characteristic of Chimu civilization and is, in fact, even more common than the "Elite Center." The "Urban Lay Center'" has the enclosures and planned room arrangements but lacks the elaborate decorated courtyards and palace rooms of the "Elite Center." There are are many of these units in the Moche Valley, some of them on the edges of the Chanchan "Elite Center"; the implications are that these were dwelling com-

pounds housing the masses of the society. The overall settlement pattern for the Moche, and for other of the big North Coast valleys, was probably that of a concentrated capital, an urbanized "Elite Center." Tributary to this capital were several "Urban Lay Centers," while scattered up and down the sides of the valley were the still smaller dwelling units of a "dispersed community" pattern.

Other features of the total settlement would have been, of course, the canal systems—a heritage from earlier times—the various garrisons or fortified posts, and the inter-valley highways. It is also likely that the inter-valley highways—popularly thought of as the "Inca highways" because they were a prominent feature of that empire—were first established in Middle Horizon times and were maintained during the Chimu rule.[267] These highways imply widespread trade contacts and multi-valley political organization. Interestingly, there are indications that small valleys, such as Virú, lost population during the Chimu reign and became relatively minor "colonial" holdings of the central government. For instance, there are

166

no "Urban Elite Centers" of the Late Intermediate Period in Virú, only small "Urban Lay Centers" and dispersed dwellings.[268]

The Chimu pottery style continued in the old plastic or modeled tradition of the North Coast.[269] This tradition of figure and life modeling of vessels had begun in Cupisnique times, continued through the Salinar and Gallinazo phases, and reached an apogee of realistic art in the Moche civilization. The tradition then declined during the Middle Horizon but never perished; quite probably it was kept alive in the Pacasmayo and Lambayeque valleys, which lay to the north and beyond the strongest Huari waves of influence. But with the decline of Huari power, modeled pottery, reminiscent of the old styles, was revived in the heartland of the old Moche state, which had now become the center of the Chimu kingdom.

Chimu pottery (Fig. 3-102) is predominantly a mold-made blackware.[270] The stirrup-mouth jar, the figure-bridge-spout jar, and life themes of humans, animals, and houses all suggest the earlier

Figure 3-101. *Above:* Spouted vessel of the Cursive-modeled style from the North Coast of Peru. This is one of the styles that fall in the latter part of the Middle Horizon or the earlier part of the Late Intermediate Period. It reflects the modeling tradition of the North Coast but also shows elements of the North Highland "Cursive" painted tradition. (Courtesy British Museum.)

Figure 3-102. *Below:* Chimu blackware of the North Coast of Peru. Height of vessel *a*, about 18 cm. (*a, b, d, e:* Courtesy British Museum; *c, f:* courtesy Peabody Museum, Harvard University.)

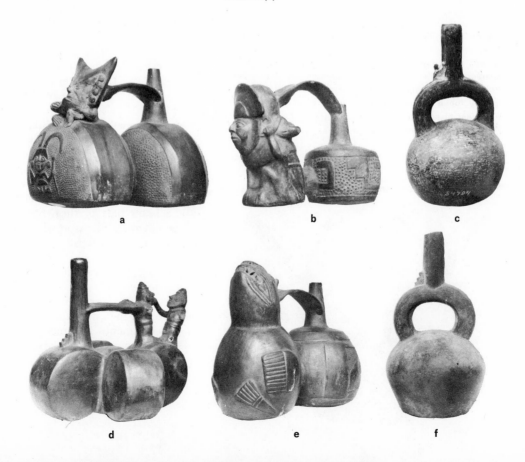

a   b   c

d   e   f

Moche style. Low relief decoration, effected by pressing in the mold, takes the place of the red-on-white scene painting of Moche times. Certain designs are of Huari inspiration; others, such as geometrically rendered birds and fish, are typical of Chimu art.[271] There is a drab sameness about Chimu pottery, a subtle lack of fine proportions, and a carelessness in the execution of the modeling that set it apart from its earlier Moche prototypes. It was turned out in enormous quantities, and one has the impression of mass production and a loss of interest in esthetic quality as opposed to earlier times.[272]

Chimu craft goods are perhaps more abundant in Peruvian archaeological collections than are those of any other culture of the area. In addition to pottery, we know tapestry and painted textiles, elaborate wood carvings, and items of metal. Among the wood carvings are figures, staffs, and such things as litters (Fig. 3-104)—presumably for carrying the distinguished nobility of the regime. Of the metals not only were silver and gold[273]

commonly used, but this was an age of bronze. The copper-tin alloy had been introduced into the Peruvian area from the south, probably from northwestern Argentina, and in the Late Intermediate Period it spread widely.[274] It was used not only for ornaments but for tools and weapons.

The Central Coast. There are two pottery style zones in the Central Coastal subarea during the Late Intermediate Period. The better known and northerly of the two is the Chancay (Fig. 3-105). Found in the Huaura, Chancay, Ancón, and northern Chillón Valleys, the style is often referred to as the "Chancay Black-on-white." It may have some prototypes in the "Black-white-red Geometric" style that preceded it in these same regions, and "Black-white-red Geometric" was in turn part of the "Epigonal" development of the latter part of the Middle Horizon. However, the Chancay Black-on-white is a highly distinctive style in its own right. It is white-slipped (although sometimes this white is almost a dirty lemon-yellow). The black line decoration is usually geometric, with a tendency to fill fields with parallel lines or checkered areas. Small appliqué-modeled figures of men and animals are used as additional embellishment. The most frequent forms are tall, collared, two-handled jars and large, rather crude hollow human figurines.[275]

In the southern Chillón, Rímac, and Lurín Valleys the Huancho style is the contemporary of

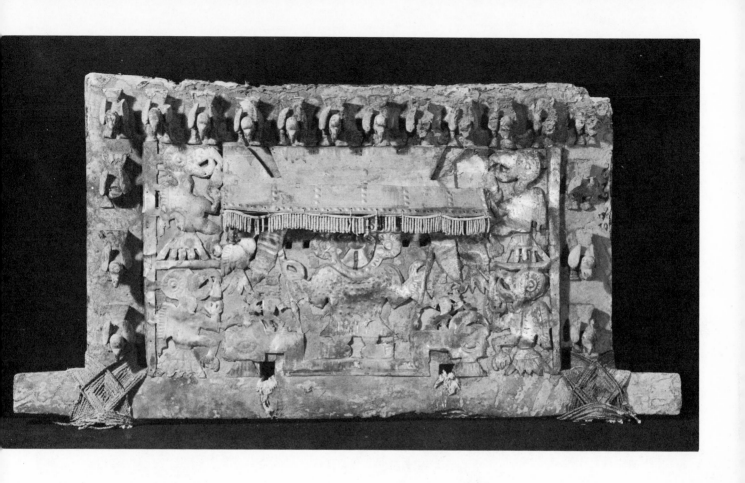

Figure 3-105. Chancay Black-on-white pottery. The "white" is usually a dirty yellow shade. Height, about 25 cm. This is relatively small; many such Chancay jars are 40–50 cm. high. (Courtesy American Museum of Natural History.)

Figure 3-106. Late Chancay–style figurines. The one at *right* was found "clothed" in the textiles wrapped around it. These figurines are usually hollow and quite large. The one at *right* is 29.3 cm. high; the others are approximately to this scale. (Courtesy Peabody Museum, Harvard University.)

Figure 3-107. The magnificent Fortaleza of Paramonga, near Supe, Central Coast. This Late Intermediate Period fort, constructed of massive adobe walls, has been nicely adapted, with its bastion features, to the contours of the small natural outcrop hill. Present-day cultivation surrounds and fills the valley in the distance. The sea lies off to the bottom and right of the picture, only a short distance away. The Pan-American Highway passes by the foot of the fortress, going toward Lima. (Courtesy Servicio Aerofotográfico, Peru.)

the Chancay.[276] Huancho pottery is related to the Chancay style, although its principal color scheme is a white-on-red painting. This sharp stylistic division within Garcilaso's "Cuismancu kingdom" is an argument against its reality as a political unit.

The late Central Coastal cities are, like those of the north, of great size and similar in their massive tapia adobe walls and planned layout. Cajamarquilla, in the Rímac Valley, and Pachacamac, in the Lurín, are, in their respective late phases, representative.

The South-Central and South Coasts.
The best-known Late Intermediate Period pottery styles of the South Coast subarea are those of Chincha and Ica. Both appear to have developed from the Middle Horizon "Epigonal" styles which, in turn, are derived from Huari and that secondary center of Huari influence on the coast, Pachacamac. In the Ica Valley this development has been plotted in a seriation of pottery complexes that runs from an Ica-Pachamac phase (contemporaneous with the Nazca Valley Atarco phase), through several "Epigonal" phases, into Ica subphase 1. After Ica-Pachacamac, there is a steady lessening of the old Huari iconography and a general trend toward simplification; but in Ica 1—which is the beginning of the Late Intermediate Period—this trend of simplification is reversed by a conscious archaism or revival of the old Ica-Pachacamac color schemes and designs.[277]

The Ica pottery style (Fig. 3-109), which has been traced through a series of ten subphases (the

170

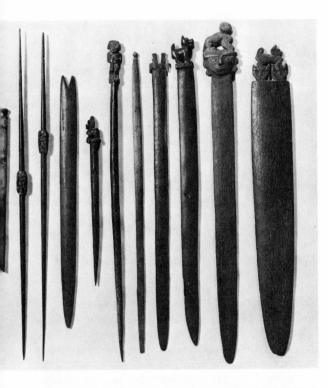

Figure 3-108. *Above:* Various wooden spindles, batons, and weave swords. The carving or decoration is Chimu or Chimu-related. Presumably from Late Intermediate Period graves of the North or Central Coast. Lengths vary from about 20–40 cm. (Courtesy Peabody Museum, Harvard University.)

Figure 3-109. *Below:* An Ica-style bowl. The design is black-and-white-on-red. Diameter, 13 cm. (Courtesy American Museum of Natural History.)

latter two corresponding to Inca Horizon and Spanish Colonial times), features an orange-red ground color with black and white designs. These designs are small and close-spaced, consisting of diamond forms, little rectangles, and highly stylized bird figures.[278]

The Chincha style, unlike the Ica, has not been traced in the earlier half of the Late Intermediate Period; consequently there is no record of a transition out of "Epigonal" forms into Chincha. The Chincha style is first noted at a point that would correspond to Ica subphase 5, or at about A.D. 1250. Much of Chincha pottery is a smoked black ware, but there are also polychromes. These latter, seen in bowls and various jars, have a chalky white or light cream slip with designs in purple or brick red outlined by black. These designs, which, as a rule, are also geometric or of bird figures, tend to be larger than those of the Ica style and not so closely spaced on the vessel surface. In the earlier Chincha subphases there is strong Ica influence, although this is reworked in a recognizably Chincha way.[279]

The interaction of the two styles is of interest and probably reflects the changes in prestige and power on the South Coast during the Late Intermediate Period. At first it would appear that Ica prestige was greater, but then, at a time equivalent with the Ica 8 subphase (ca. A.D. 1425), the currents of influence were reversed, and Chincha imitations are found in quantity in the Ica Valley. Menzel and Rowe do not interpret this as a conquest of Ica by Chincha, as no true Chincha imports are found in the former valley; but it is likely that this sudden popularity of the Chincha style corresponds to the increasing power and military force of Chincha. In this connection it is significant that the early colonial histories state that Chincha was something of a military power at the time of the Inca conquest and that the Chin-chans had, in fact, been raiding the southern Peruvian highland country; however these same early histories—in support of the archaeological record—do not indicate that Ica was a part of a Chincha kingdom and empire, or that such a kingdom extended much beyond the limits of the Chincha Valley itself.[280]

The South Coastal sites of this time were not large cities, although some of them were marked by large tapia adobe structures that could have served as administrative centers, garrisons, or shrines. La Centinela, in the Chincha Valley—together with the nearby La Cumbe and Huaca de Tambo de Mora—is such a complex, and it probably was the Chincha capital.[281] It was subsequently taken over by the Inca invaders.

The Highlands. A number of cultures from the highlands are assigned to the Late Intermediate Period although the details concerning most of them are sketchy.

In the north, the Cajamarca-Cursive ceramic tradition of the Middle Marañón continued;[282] and an Aquilpo phase, as yet undescribed, is listed for the Callejón de Huaylas.[283]

Farther south, we have the Killke or Killke-Inca, Sillustani, Collao, and Wancani phases. Killke is the name John H. Rowe has assigned to the developmental phase of the Inca culture, and Killke ceramics and other remains are confined to the vicinity of Cuzco. The phase clearly precedes the later imperial expansion of this culture and people. The pottery is a rather indifferently decorated red-white-black style. It has been found at Sacsahuaman, but in levels that antedate the building of the great fortress. Killke architecture proper is rather humble, being devoted mainly to dwellings of uncut fieldstone or to beehive-shaped tombs. Bone implements are common; a slate knife is a diagnostic trait; but metals are quite rare.[284]

Sillustani and Collao are pottery complexes of the North Titicaca Basin. They are presumed to date from the Late Intermediate Period but are known only from surface collections.[285] They include black-on-red, black-white-on-red, and other types that are distinct from either the Tiahuanaco or Inca styles of the same subarea. It is likely that they are the pottery remains of such Aymara-speaking tribes as the Cana, Colla, Lupaca, and Omasuyu who held this territory before they were overrun by the Incas in the first half of the 15th century. Both Sillustani and Collao pottery types are associated with the *chullpas*—burial towers of stone or adobe—which are characteristic of the southern Peruvian highlands. These towers also continued to be constructed and used by the Inca-influenced Chucuito and Taraco cultures of the subarea that followed Sillustani-Collao.

Wancani is another culture phase known from pottery samples alone. The distribution of this Wancani pottery complex is the South Titicaca Basin subarea. The name derives from a site some 30 kilometers south of Tiahuanaco. The principal feature of the Wancani site is a stone enclosure similar to the Qalasasaya at Tiahuanaco; but this structure dates to the Tiahuanaco culture and to Middle Horizon times, and does not concern us here. Rydén, who worked at Wancani, collected Tiahuanaco-, Wancani-, and Inca-influenced sherds from the surface of the site; and this would seem to be the sequence of occupation.[286] He segregated the Wancani pottery from the other two complexes on typological grounds, but his segregation is also supported by finding Wancani pottery in stratigraphic isolation at a nearby site called Pucará de Khonko. On the basis of the Pucará de Khonko evidence, Rydén assigns the Wancani complex (termed by him "Post-Decadent Tiahuanaco")[287] to a chronological position intermediate between Tiahuanaco and Inca, or consistent with the Late Intermediate Period. The Wancani pottery is described by Rydén as a black-on-brown style, featuring hemispherical bowl forms, and relating both to Tiahuanaco and to Inca in some of its design elements. Thus it may provide a transition between the two.

The Late Horizon: The Inca State

The Late Horizon, the briefest of our periods, dates from A.D. 1476 to 1534. This was the period of Inca imperial dominance in the Peruvian area and beyond. The beginning of the period is the date of the effective final consolidation of the Inca territorial conquests, and its close is the fall of that empire under the blows of the Spanish conquerors. This story of the Inca empire comes down to us through chronicles of the early Colonial Period, and it is also recorded in the material remains of archaeology.

The term *Inca* has been used to apply to the supreme ruler of that state, to the members of his lineage, to the small nucleus of the nation centered upon Cuzco, and to the full range of what has been called the Inca empire. The Incas spoke a Quechua language, and they imposed this language upon all of the subject peoples of the empire. Because of this, as was noted earlier in this chapter, Quechua is the principal native tongue of the central Andes today.

The Inca empire had its beginnings with the small tribal nation of the Urbamba subarea, and these beginnings, as we have noted, can be seen in the Killke archaeological phase of the Late Intermediate Period. From these origins the Inca state grew into the largest political formation, both in territory and population, that was ever known in native America. It may also lay claim to being one of the largest ever created anywhere in the world on the level of what we can consider as a "Bronze Age" technology. Dominating both coast and highlands, the Incas extended their power up and down the Andes for more than 2000 miles, or from south-central Chile to northern Ecuador. As such, the Inca state ran beyond the bounds of what had been the Peruvian culture area. It began, but never fully completed, the enormous task of welding all the peoples of this vast territory into a single society with one language, one set of values, and one culture.

Inca History. Inca archaeology, like that of the Aztecs, shades into the documents of ethnohistory. These documents, which are of great value not only for Inca history but for inferences about the whole Peruvian prehistoric past, include the accounts of sixteenth-century Spanish historians, and the works of native Peruvians—descendants of the Incas—who had become acculturated to European learning.[288] Thus they are based on firsthand observations of the Spanish Conquest, on later research into these early sources, and, to a degree, upon a continuity of word-of-mouth histories that had been passed down by Inca historians.

From the oral tradition of Inca history—a quasi-historical, semi-legendary view of the past—we learn of the Inca dynasty. Its first eight rulers, presumably dating in the span of A.D. 1200 to 1438, and probably pertaining to the small Killke Inca nation, are but dimly perceived and certainly to a degree mythic. It is with the ninth ruler, Pachacuti Inca Yupanqui (1438–1471), that we reach more solid fact, and it is also with him that the Inca started their imperial expansion. Pachacuti

gained control of the south highlands, dominating the neighboring Chanca, the Cana, Lupaca, Colla, and Omasuyu by 1463. Then, together with Topa Inca, his heir and eventual successor, he put much of the Peruvian coast and highlands and parts of Ecuador under Inca control by 1471. It was in these campaigns that their great North Coast rival, the Chimu, were subjugated.

Subsequently, Topa Inca Yupanqui, reigning from 1471 to 1493, added (as we noted in our discussions of the late Chincha kingdom) the southern Peruvian coast, as well as southern Bolivia, northwestern Argentina, and northern Chile. It is his South Coastal conquests of 1476 that consolidated and essentially completed the territorial domain of the empire and that also serve as the chronological base line for our Late Horizon.

Huayna Capac, who followed him (1493–1525),[289] spent most of his time in the north, in Ecuador. He slightly increased the imperial holdings in this quarter and established Quito as a kind of second capital. He died there of an epidemic disease, probably of European origin, which had by that time passed south from the Spanish settlements in Panama to reach Peru.

Huayna Capac's death left a problem in the succession. The role of imperial Inca was claimed by one son, Huascar, in Cuzco; but he was challenged by a half-brother, the governor of Quito, Atahuallpa. A bitter civil war ensued in which Atahuallpa's armies eventually bested those of Huascar in 1532. In one of those ironic moments of history, Atahuallpa, who was moving south in the wake of his victorious soldiers, and who had paused at Cajamarca, received the news of Huascar's defeat almost simultaneously with the tidings of Pizarro's landings on the Peruvian coast.[290]

The Inca Political and Social Order. In our full perspective of Peruvian culture history, we can appreciate the Inca achievement as a culmination of those trends in the Peruvian cultural tradition that were moving toward the formation of the all-powerful state. We saw the beginnings of these trends in the militaristic competition of the warring kingdoms of the Early Intermediate Period and their first climax in the Middle Horizon imperial domains of Huari and Tiahuanaco. Following this there was a recession in empire expansionism in the Late Intermediate Period; but this was then succeeded by the new and greater imperial resurgence of the Incas; and this time the empire phenomenon is documented from historical as well as archaeological sources.

The achievement of the Incas was essentially a military and an administrative one. Their cultural heritage was the same as that of their neighbors and contemporaries; or, if anything, they were somewhat marginal and rustic outlanders—certainly as compared with the highly civilized nations of the coast. Cuzco, in Killke times, could have been little more than a small mountain town when Chanchan was a glittering metropolis. Clearly, the Incas held no outstanding technological advantage over their rivals. Nor did they invent large-scale conquest, empire building, and statecraft; the earlier peoples of Huari and Tiahuanaco provided them with a model, one undoubtedly carried down in folk memory. The success of the Incas was a brilliant culmination of a trend. They proved to be masters of military and bureaucratic organization.

The Inca army was highly efficient; much of it, in fact, was of professional or "standing army" quality. Soldiers marched in regular ranks under strict discipline; they were armed with maces, spears, slings, and bolas. Probably more important than any of this, they were supplied by an excellent system of highways dotted with way stations and fortified posts. (These features are, of course, identifiable in the archaeological record as well as attested to by the chroniclers.) Communications also enabled the Incas to administer and incorporate conquered territories after the military victories. This incorporation was expedited and promoted by offering the rulers of defeated states positions of provincial governorships within the framework of the empire. In fact, many of the Inca "conquests" were accomplished through the pressure of psychological warfare leading to such "sellouts" on the part of beleaguered rulers. Revolt was also made difficult by the mass shifting of populations from their native regions to other parts of the empire (the "mitimae" system). That a revolt—Atahuallpa's—was eventually successful was probably due to the unwieldy size of the whole structure and to an intra-dynastic fight.

In these conquests the Incas prevailed every-

where in the densely settled Peru-Bolivia area and also in those regions of the North and South Andes where populations were living a similar, stable, town or village existence based upon intensive agricultural patterns similar to those of Peru. In contrast, their excursions into the tropical forests to the east were failures. Apparently, the strange terrain and the fact that the jungle tribesmen fought and ran (to fight again another day) were too much for the "'civilized'" and imperial Incas. Similarly, the resistance of the Araucanians of Chile, who were not a town and village people, was never broken by the Incas.

The Inca political order was ruled—and ruled absolutely—from the top. The *Inca,* or emperor, was considered divine, and succession passed to his male heirs by his principal wife. This wife, at least in the times of the later emperors, was also his sister. The actual successor among the sons was chosen by the ruler, a method that could lead to ambiguities about the rightful heir and that helped prompt the civil war between the half-brothers Huascar and Atahuallpa. The emperor lived in great pomp and ritual, and on his death was accompanied to an afterlife by immolated concubines and servants. As a ruler he was surrounded and supported by an aristocracy composed of blood relatives and those admitted to this status either because of their military or administrative abilities or owing to their position in the class of rulers of formerly independent states that had been made a part of the empire. The major administrators of the empire were drawn from this aristocracy and arranged in a strict hierarchy. At the top of the system, immediately below the emperor, were the four heads of the four major territorial divisions of the empire. Below these were the leaders of provinces, who, in turn and in descending order, supervised units of 10,000, 5,000, 1,000, 500, and 100 heads-of-families or taxpayers. On even lower rungs of the political ladder were nonnoble leaders who were responsible for units of 50 and of 10 taxpayers. All taxes were paid in labor, such service being either in agriculture—for the support of the state or of the state religion—public works, or military service.

The extent to which Inca society was kin-based is not definitely known. Today, a Quechua *ayllu* of the Peruvian highlands is, in effect, a village. Such villages are composed of a number of unrelated extended families living together and following common rules of crop rotation under informal leaders. The settlement pattern of the prehistoric Inca villages is the same as those of the modern *ayllus* or villages. In the latter each extended family occupies a walled rectangular compound within which are individual houses. Several compounds constitute the village. But were the Inca *ayllus* similar in their social makeup to those of the present Quechua? According to Rowe:

> ...the Inca *ayllu* was a kin group with theoretical endogamy, with descent in the male line, and without totemism. It was, therefore, not a clan in the classical sense at all. There is no historical or ethnological evidence to support the theory that the social group from which the ayllu developed was, in some prehistoric era, a true clan.[291]

Each Inca *ayllu* owned its own lands. Individuals within the *ayllu* cultivated these lands for their own living and also set aside a certain amount for the support of the *ayllu* chief or head. The Inca incorporated the *ayllus* into their system of imperial administration at the appropriate level of their particular population size.

Inca religion operated in the service of the state, and the Inca himself was, in effect, the head of "the church." Ritual and divination—for purposes of crop maintenance, curing, purification, and as guides to action—were of central importance. Viracocha, a creator and culture hero, was the supreme deity. Quite probably this was an ancient Andean concept, with prototypes represented in the Middle Horizon "Gateway God" of Tiahuanaco and Huari, and even before this in Chavín deities. However, the Inca conceived of Viracocha as a remote power, so that a lesser assistant, the Sun God, was more actively worshipped. The moon, the stars, thunder, the earth, the sea, and rocks, mountains, caves, and other natural phenomena of the landscape were also considered as gods or supernatural beings. Similarly, temples or shrines took on deep religious importance. All of this was undoubtedly in keeping with ancient Peruvian traditions, as for example the holy "oracle" city of Pachacamac (Fig. 3-110) on the Central Coast, which must have been thus revered

in Early Intermediate Period and Middle Horizon times, and which was maintained by the Incas as a shrine for pilgrims.

It was Inca policy to be tolerant of local religions in conquered territories and to allow worship of the old resident gods to continue, with, of course, the understanding that the imperial religion and the Sun God were supreme. It may be that this tolerance is reflected in the lack of any aggressively displayed iconographic theme in Inca art, in distinct contrast to the propagation of the "Gateway God" and associated themes that occurred in the old Huari empire.

An Inca calendar, based on lunar observations, was maintained and was an important adjunct to planting and harvesting, and thereby to religion. Writing, however, was lacking, as it is throughout all pre-Columbian Peru.[292] The lack is interesting, given the highly complicated bureaucracy of the Incas and the obvious need for a writing system. The Incas employed, however, a knotted-string device, the *quipu,* which served as a means of decimal recording (of goods, soldiers, census, or whatever) and as a mnemonic aid for their oral histories.

Other Aspects of Inca Culture. The Cuzco archaeological remains of imperial Inca times are notably different from those of the earlier Killke phase. The Late Horizon Inca ceramics are brightly painted in combinations of black-white-and-red. Designs are geometric bands or rows of diamonds, checks, serrations, and cross-hachures or, in some instances, animals, birds, fruits, or insects. As we have observed, there is nothing that would appear to be a central god theme. The pointed-based, long-necked, handled aryballoid jar (Fig. 3-112) is the most diagnostic vessel form. Goblets, pedestal-based beakers, pitchers, and plates are also typical.[293] Such vessels—which presumably are imports—are found throughout the Peruvian area, both highland and coastal. They usually occur in graves or in other contexts in or around major Inca public buildings that had been established, or taken over, in the conquered provinces. Quite clearly, Inca goods were being adopted by the local collaborating aristocracies, and Inca stylistic influences were being blended in with the resident traditions to produce new

Figure 3-110. Three air views of Pachacamac. *Top:* The Inca Temple of the Sun, crowning the highest point of the site. Terraces of the temple platform have been partially excavated and reconstructed. In left background is the cultivated Lurín Valley; off to the right is the Pacific Ocean with some guano islets. *Center:* Restoration of an Inca building, with multiple rooms and doorways, the so-called "Mama Cona." At a distance, in the desert, are remnants of other adobe buildings. *Bottom:* A general view of the site. The Inca Sun Temple is in the center foreground. Off to the left of this, and a bit farther back, are the eroded adobe walls of the Late Intermediate (and Inca) Period city. A tongue of the desert goes off to the left, and the Lurín Valley fields, backed by Andean foothills, are in the right distance. (Courtesy Servicio Aerofotográfico, Peru.)

176

Figure 3-111. *Above:* Inca settlement and architecture. *Top, left:* Ruined buildings and agricultural terraces at Pisac. *Top, right:* Agricultural terraces at Ollantaytambo. *Bottom, left:* Wall niches in room interior at Pisac. *Bottom, right:* Inca masonry, showing the amazing fitting of a stone of "12 angles" in a Cuzco wall. (Courtesy Peabody Museum, Harvard University.)

Figure 3-112. *Right:* Two large Inca polychrome jars. *Left:* Single-handled jar. *Right:* Aryballoid jar with characteristic "fern-pattern" design and banded neck. (Courtesy American Museum of Natural History.)

Figure 3-113. Two Inca-Chimu double vessels, one pre- and one post-Spanish Conquest. The vessel at *left* combines Chimu relief modeling and the double-jar idea with an Incaic (red-white-black) color scheme and Inca spout shapes. The one at *right* is very similar, but the Spanish trait of glazing (a light green) has been combined with the aboriginal traits. Heights, 18 cm. (Courtesy American Museum of Natural History.)

hybrid styles (Fig. 3-113). But old local styles also continued, in many cases little affected by Incaic influence; presumably, these traditions were maintained in the hands of the non-aristocratic members of the conquered provincial societies.

In the matter of pottery styles, it is of interest that the Incas, according to some historical accounts, brought potters from some of the newly incorporated lands back to Cuzco to practice their craft there. This would suggest that either subconsciously or purposefully there was an Inca policy of what we might call "stylistic homogenization"—an attempt to mix, blend, and absorb the various old regional stylistic lines of the past into a new unified body of Inca styles. The results of such a policy are varied. The hybridized styles of

the Ica and Chincha Valleys adhere rather closely to Inca modes, and one wonders whether this was purely technological—the harmonious merger of two predominantly polychrome traditions—or whether it reflected something in the social and political dynamics of this particular conquest. In contrast, the North Coast Chimu styles, which emphasized life modeling rather than polychrome painting, show less of a visible accretion of Inca influences; and, again, the question is raised about the extent to which this may have been simply a technological disharmony or one that had its roots deeper in the relations between Chimu and Inca.

Bronze tools (Fig. 3-114), weapons, and ornaments became area-wide under Inca sovereignty: digging-stick (or *taclla*—foot plow) heads, club heads, chisels, tweezers, and pins are typical objects. Silver, too, was more widely used than it was before (Fig. 3-115). Dishes, various maceheads, and llama figures were carved out of stone in the highlands and widely traded. Another characteristic Inca object is the wooden goblet or *kero*. This has a form similar to the Tiahuanaco-Huari pot-

Figure 3-114. *Above:* Bronze implements of Incaic date. Counting from *left*, the *first*, *fourth*, *sixth*, and *seventh* implements are crescentic knives, or *tumis*; the *second* and *third* are needles; the *fourth* is a star-shaped club head; the *eighth* is a chisel; and the *ninth* a spoonlike *topu*, or pin. (Courtesy American Museum of Natural History.)

Figure 3-115. *Left:* A silver alpaca in the Inca style, from the Island of Titicaca, Lake Titicaca. Height, about 19 cm. (Courtesy American Museum of Natural History.)

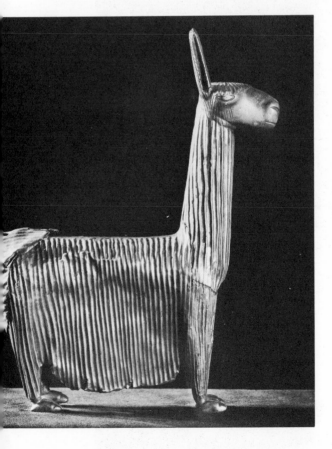

tery *keros*. Those of pre-Spanish times were usually decorated with carved designs; later, in the early Colonial Period, many were ornamented with lacquer figures.[294]

Inca architecture was typically of dressed stone. The stones were very carefully laid. Sometimes they were more or less of a uniform size and shape and were placed in even, ashlar-type rows; in other instances they were gigantic cyclopean boulders with their carefully finished polygonal sides fitted one to another. Examples of this latter type of stone masonry are to be seen in the mammoth foundations of the great fortress of Sacsahuaman (Fig. 3-116). The stone blocks, whether rectangular or polygonal, were usually shaped with slightly convex outer surfaces, so that the lines of the fittings were slightly depressed and shadowed, and

Figure 3-116. *Left:* The great fortress of Sacsahuaman, near Cuzco. (Courtesy Peabody Museum, Harvard University.)

Figure 3-117. *Below:* The ruins of Machu Picchu as seen from above. (Courtesy American Museum of Natural History.)

Figure 3-118. *Above:* Inca agriculture as seen by the Colonial Period historian Poma de Ayala. *Left:* Irrigating fields or garden plots. *Right:* Use of the taclla, or foot-plow, in planting. (After Poma de Ayala, 1936.)

Figure 3-119. *Right:* An Inca chullpa, or burial tower. (Courtesy Peabody Museum, Harvard University.)

this gave an extremely distinctive appearance to a wall. Doors, windows, and wall niches were made so that sides converged slightly near the top. On the coast Inca buildings were sometimes of stone and similar to those of the highlands; but more often the Incas followed in the local traditions of tapia adobe, and it was not unusual for them to take over, and sometimes remodel, a Late Intermediate Period structure. Cuzco, Ollantaytambo, Pisac, and Machu Picchu (Fig. 3-117) are Inca highland sites of the Late Horizon with well-known examples of military, governmental, and religious architecture; and on the coast the great "Sun Temple" at Pachacamac and the complex at La Centinela, in the Chincha Valley, are coastal Inca constructions.

Figure 3-120. Inca stone vessels. The exact size of these specimens is unrecorded, but vessels of the type shown at *right* are 20–30 cm. in diameter. (Courtesy British Museum.)

In settlement, the Inca were not primarily an urban people. Cuzco was an administrative and ceremonial center with only a small population; the sustaining farmers and herders lived in villages scattered throughout the surrounding valley. In their conquests the Inca often instituted regional resettlement programs, but these followed the Cuzco model of a politico-religious center and dispersed hamlet or village sustaining populations. Only in some of the old cities of the Central and North Coast was a truly urban way of life allowed to continue after the conquest; others in these same subareas were abandoned or semi-abandoned under Inca rule.

It is interesting to speculate whether this non-urban outlook of the imperial Incas was a reflection of their political outlook. The city—that is, the true urban city—is by its very nature a "forcing bed" of new ideas and culture change; or at least this has generally been so at other places and in other times in the world's history. The Incas were quite probably not amenable to "new ideas and culture change"—unless these were instigated and controlled by imperial policy. Certainly the distinctly "vertical" structure of the Inca socio-political system, with power and sanctions flowing only from the top downward through well-planned channels, would have been incompatible with much that could have gone on in the ferment of urban living conditions. In the Inca system one's

Figure 3-121. Inca wooden and lacquered kero of the Colonial Period. Note European clothing of individuals. Height, about 20 cm. (Courtesy British Museum.)

responsibilities were always to those immediately above or below in the power structure; "horizontal" intercommunication was discouraged. This kind of compartmentalization would have been much more difficult for the Inca to have maintained in an urban situation. If this analysis is correct, it would obviously not apply to the earlier Huari empire which, in contradistinction, appears to have had its beginnings in the urban center of Huari and to have promoted urban development on the North and Central coasts. And yet, should this paradox invalidate the above arguments about Inca urbanism or lack of urbanism? On the contrary, it seems quite probable that empires are phenomena that are functionally related to an urban precondition, even though the greatest "empire builders" may start from a position marginal to that urbanism, and even though the city contains within itself potential forces that may be antithetical to the monolithic state.

Spaniard and Inca

In 1532, the fateful year that Pizarro confronted Atahuallpa in the plaza at Cajamarca, the Inca empire had a population of at least 6,000,000 people.[295] Its geographical limits, as noted, reached from northern Ecuador to south-central Chile. The state was held together by a firmly established military bureaucracy under centralized control. How, then, did a few hundred Spaniards strike the blow that shattered this amazing monolith?

Lanning has called attention to four circumstances that favored the Spaniards.[296]

First, the Inca empire was just emerging from the throes of the devastating civil war between Atahuallpa and Huascar. For a pre-industrial society the direct effects of this "devastation" might not have been unduly severe; but, indirectly, they would have loosened the bonds of empire and given rise to doubts among many about the divine purpose of Inca leadership.

Secondly, and related closely to the above, the Spaniards—as did Cortez's men in Mexico—drew upon the great number of disaffected peoples in the conquered provinces. Their disaffection, and their hopes for independence, had undoubtedly been stimulated by the civil war.

Figure 3-122. A quipu, or knotted-string record. (Courtesy Peabody Museum, Harvard University.)

Thirdly, epidemics—smallpox and measles—resulted from diseases introduced by the Europeans into Central America a decade or two before, and these had spread south to the Inca domain by the 1520's. In fact, Huayna Capac probably died from one of these epidemics, which took their toll on the Indians both physically and psychologically.

Fourthly, the Spanish guile in appearing as "diplomats," when they were really plunderers bent on hard conquest, caught the Inca off guard, from Atahuallpa downward in the power structure.

And, added to all of these, there was the stern purpose of the conquistadors, pledged as they were to making Peru a part of Spain, and both goaded and bolstered by the knowledge that if they did not succeed, others would continue to come out across the seas until victory was won.

The story of the Spanish Conquest here, as in Mexico, is well known.[297] Pizarro took Atahuallpa by treachery, used him as a hostage to exact a golden ransom from his subjects, and then brutally murdered him. The monolithic structure of the state worked to the Spaniards' advantage. They took over the bureaucratic machinery and began to remake it to their own purpose. Pizarro appointed another royal Inca, Manco Capac, as a puppet emperor. Then in 1536 Manco Capac suddenly turned on the Spaniards to lead a bloody rebellion. Sensing now the enormity of the disaster that had befallen them, the Indians fought with ferocity and besieged their conquerors in both Cuzco and Lima. But the brief revolt failed, and Incaic Peru entered into the Colonial Period, with its destructions or radical transformations of the old native cultural traditions.

Footnotes

1 Rare and disastrous rains have occurred on the Peruvian North and Central coasts. These result from a lessening of the strong northward-flowing, cold Peruvian Coastal Current that, in turn, allows the warm, tropical waters off the Ecuadorian shore to form a southward-moving current known as "El Niño." The result is a southward shift of tropical warmth and precipitation which brings floods, landslides, scarcity of fish and guano birds, and a pestilence of insects. The last such major rain was in 1925.

2 On the central Ecuadorian coast there is a region of desert scrub, not entirely unlike the Peruvian desert coast. It too results from the effects of the cold Peruvian Coastal Current striking this westward-jutting portion of the continent at the end of its northern sweep; however, on the north coast of Ecuador the mangrove swamps and forests resume and continue from there northward into Pacific Colombia and Panama.

3 This section is based on James (1959, pp. 161–204), Sauer (1950 a), Bennett (1946 a), and Lanning (1967, Chap. 2).

4 Uhle (1903, 1913).

5 Kroeber (1944); Willey (1945).

6 See, for example, Kroeber (1926 a, b, 1927, 1930); Bennett (1934, 1939); Strong (1925); Strong and Corbett (1943); Willey (1943). In fact, the only chronological schemes for Peruvian archaeology that do not follow the basic Uhle structure are those of Means (1931) and Tello (1942), both of which are highly impressionistic and little supported by the hard facts of stratigraphy or stylistic seriations.

7 First credits for the realization of the early position of the Chavín style and the Chavín horizon are difficult to assign. Tello (1942, 1943, 1956, 1960) claims them; but a careful reading of his earlier published works (1923, 1929) does not bear him out. Larco Hoyle assigned a Cupisnique (a Peruvian north coastal Chavín ceramic complex) culture phase to a pre-Moche chronological position as early as 1941. Bennett actually formalized the Chavín horizon in 1943. See Willey (1951) for a history of the Chavín concept.

8 Bird (1948); Engel (1957 a, b, 1963 a, b); Lanning (1963, 1965, 1967, Chap. 4); Patterson and Lanning (1964).

9 Rowe (1960); Lanning (1967, Chap. 3).

10 Rowe (1962).

11 Lanning (1967).

12 As has been stated, the dates for these periods, except for that of the Late (Incaic) Horizon, which comes from historical sources, are derived from radiocarbon readings. These radiocarbon dates are not altogether consistent with each other. In fact, there tend to be two sets of dates, an "early" and a "late" set, which correspond to different radiocarbon laboratories and which thereby suggest differences in the processing or treatment of the organic samples by these laboratories. J. H. Rowe (1965) has discussed this at some length. For example, dates for the first appearance of pottery and the beginning of the Initial Period, on the South coast, cluster around 2000 to 1900 B.C. ("early" set) and 1450 to 1200 B.C. ("late" set). Dates for the beginning of the Early Horizon are clustered, similarly, at 1400 to 1200 B.C. ("early" set) and 800 to 600 B.C. ("late" set). For the beginning of the Early Intermediate Period these groupings are ca. 300 B.C. ("early" set) and A.D. 150 ("late" set); for the Middle Horizon they are, respectively, at A.D. 560 ("early" set) and A.D. 800 ("late" set); and for the Late Intermediate Period they group at A.D. 930 ("early" set) and A.D. 1100 ("late" set). Lanning (1967, Chap. 3) has compromised in various ways with this problem, as can be seen by comparing the dates on figures 3-2 and 3-3 with those listed here. The resolution of these dating difficulties will only come with more radiocarbon dates and more cross-checking of radiocarbon dates and archaeological stratigraphies and seriations. For the present, students and researchers can only be aware of the problem.

12a The Siches, Honda, and

Estero phases, all of Far North Peru (see chart, fig. 3-3) are more closely related to the Northwest South American Littoral tradition than to the Pacific Littoral tradition, and they are referred to in Chapter 5.

13 Lanning (1967, Chap. 3) arranges his chronology chart a little differently at this point. As there are indications that pottery did not occur at the same time in all Peruvian subareas, and that it may have been as late as the beginning of the Christian Era on the Far South Coast, he has indicated an overlap in time between Preceramic Period VI and the Initial Period, an overlap that ranges from 1800 B.C. (his compromise date from radiocarbon determinations for the first appearances of pottery) to A.D. 1. This arrangement violates our principle of adherence to strict chronological line as the bases of periods—a principle followed throughout this book. Therefore I have placed the line between Preceramic Period VI and the Initial Period at 1800 B.C.

14 This was, of course, the first period of the original Rowe (1960) scheme which was set up to treat only the ceramic periods.

15 The columns on the fig. 3–6 chart are taken from the most recent revised editions of several works or from the latest published opinions of the several authors concerned. See Bennett and Bird (1964); Bushnell (1963); Mason (1957); Steward and Faron (1959); Collier (1962); Kidder (1964). This is by no means all of the Peruvian chronological schemes. Means (1931) and Tello (1942) have already been referred to. Schemes similar to those on the fig. 3–6 chart have been offered by Larco Hoyle (1948), Strong (1948), and Willey (1948), among others.

16 Lanning (1967, Chap. 3). It should be noted that Lanning referred to these subdivisions of the Peruvian area as "regions." They are called subareas here in keeping with our overall culture-geographical scheme.

17 The intermediate Cordillera Central has disappeared at this latitude.

18 Lanning (1967, Chap. 3) included Tumbes in the Far North,

but his presentation was a consideration of the archaeology within the boundaries of modern national Peru. The archaeological cultures of Tumbes—at least on the basis of what is now known—group more easily with those of the El Oro subarea of Ecuador.

19 Lanning (1967, Chap. 3) does not list the Lambayeque and Santa Valleys, presumably for lack of adequate information. From what is known, however, I am inclined to group these two valleys in the North Coast subarea.

20 Supe and Huaura (on the north) and Mala (on the south) are not mentioned by Lanning. I tentatively place them in the Central Coast subarea.

21 Described as "Ocoña to Tacna" by Lanning (1967, Chap. 3). This would omit a stretch of about 225 kilometers between Lomas and Ocoña. I have placed this territory within the subarea.

22 The region concept follows Willey and Phillips (1958, pp. 18–21).

23 Bennett (1948 a). The area co-tradition concept has been reviewed by Rouse (1954), who interprets it as being not only an "overall unit of cultural history...within which the component cultures have been related over a period of time," but a unit of which all of the component parts have had a single common cultural ancestor. In this, Rouse rejects the idea that the area co-tradition is simply a culture area with time depth. I have never been convinced of the wisdom of the special definition that Rouse wishes to put upon the area co-tradition; and I do not believe it can be applied to the Peruvian area and cultures, especially as we can now see the lines of more than one antecedent cultural tradition converge in Preceramic Period VI and in the Peruvian Initial Period to produce what we are here calling the Peruvian cultural tradition. In sum, we here consider the Peruvian area as simply a culture area in time depth and without Rouse's qualification of cultural monogenesis.

24 Willey (1966, p. 85).

25 We shall use the term "Peruvian cultural tradition," which is

consistent with our terminology throughout this work. The term "co-tradition" is somewhat special and peculiar, and it can be left for the special definition and qualification Rouse (1954) puts upon it; however, as stated in the footnote above, I do not believe that a co-tradition so defined can be said to pertain to Peruvian culture history.

26 Lanning (1967, Chap. 2); Sauer (1950 b).

27 Bennett and Bird (1964, pp. 72–74) review these characteristics of Peruvian culture as a whole. See also Bennett (1948 a).

28 Imbelloni (1938, 1950 a).

29 Donnan (1964).

30 Hartwig (1961); Engel (1960). "Cabeza Larga," or "Cabezas Largas," is located on the Paracas Peninsula of the South Coast. The locality takes its name from the elongated and deformed crania found there which date to the Early Horizon and Early Intermediate Periods. These are not to be confused with the undeformed dolichocephalic skulls from preceramic levels to which we refer here.

31 Munizaga (1965).

32 "Pueblo-Andid" is Imbelloni's classification, referred to in Chapter 1, p. 11.

33 Such were Newman's opinions at that time (1948); however, as he has made clear, data are indeed few.

34 That brachycephaly of the coastal populations antedates fronto-vertico-occipital head deformation is supported by the Ecuadorian coastal data. There Munizaga (1965) found his earlier Valdivia populations to be round-headed but undeformed, while the succeeding Machalilla peoples were both brachycephalic and deformed.

35 Munizaga (1965).

36 Cardich (1964).

37 Munizaga (1965). There were also other types of cranial deformation in Peru. Sometimes the head of the infant was so bound as to produce an elongated, circular cranium. This is the so-called "Aymara type" and is best known from the south highlands. In fact, there was probably no other area in pre-Columbian America where as

much interest and virtuosity in manipulating the form of the skull was displayed as in Peru. See Stewart (1950); see also Imbelloni (1950 b) for a discussion of cranial deformation types (as based on South Andean materials, however).

38 The Uru-Chipaya belong to the Equatorial major language group.

39 For all of this, the reader is referred to Mason (1950, pp. 193–200, 224, and pocket map) and to Steward and Faron (1959, pp. 21–23.).

40 Parker (1963). I am grateful to D. W. Lathrap for calling this article to my attention.

41 There is the possibility that cultivation began in the lomas. M. E. Moseley (personal communication 1966) informs me that wild potatoes and other edible tubers are present in the lomas today and that in some places, as in the vicinity of Arequipa, these are cultivated with success.

42 Engel (1963 c, 1964); Donnan (1964); Lanning (1967, Chap. 4). Engel (1966 b) also reports an earlier date from Chilca, ca. 5000 B.C. This may refer to a Preceramic Period IV occupancy.

43 Engel (1964, 1966 b).

44 Engel (1964). These are identified further (Engel, 1966 b) as lima beans (*Phaseolus lunatus*).

45 Donnan (1964).

46 Donnan (1964) describes these individuals as dolichocephalic. It will be recalled that the crania from the Cabezas Largas site— dating at about 3000 B.C.—were also long-headed (see this chapter, p. 89).

47 Engel (1964). However, Lanning (1967, Chap. 4) mentions cotton textiles from the Chilca site. It seems likely that these cotton fabrics belonged to a later level in the site occupation than that dated in the 3800 to 2500 B.C. range and, therefore, later than the house and complex described above.

48 Engel (1960, 1964).

49 Lanning (1967, Chap. 4).

50 Lanning (1967, Chap. 4). Cotton from the Ancón Yacht Club site—assuming Lanning's cross dating of that site to Preceramic Period V to be correct—does not jibe with Engel's concept of a "preceramic but without cotton" stage. It may be a question of dating. Perhaps the Yacht Club site falls late in the period, near the 2500 B.C. line; or perhaps cotton occurred somewhat earlier on the Central Coast than on the South Coast. For the present, the best we can say is that cotton seems to appear around 3000 to 2500 B.C. and that, according to Lanning's definitions, it does occur in the latter part of Preceramic Period V (4200–2500 B.C.).

51 Lanning (1967, Chap. 4). Curiously, these plants were only in the lower levels of the site. Lanning does not classify the Pampa site as Encanto phase, as he does Ancón Yacht Club and Chilca; however, he recognizes it as contemporaneous. More recently, M. E. Moseley (personal communication, 1967), who has been working in the Ancón region, interprets the chronological position of the Pampa site as very late Encanto or post-Encanto—a dating that would put it at the close of Preceramic Period V or early Preceramic Period VI.

52 The radiocarbon dates from Huaca Prieta have been appraised by Bird (1951), who estimates the beginnings of the site to be at somewhere in the range of 2600 to 2300 B.C. See also Mason (1957, p. 31).

53 Bird (1948).

54 Towle (1961, pp. 104–105).

55 Bird (1963): "This limited evidence suffices to extend the known antiquity of artistic expression in Peru and indicates at least some continuity with the work of later times. It shows that an angular, highly conventionalized style can be an outgrowth of technique and does not have to fit into any theoretical sequence of art forms starting with naturalistic treatment There is as yet no basis for suggesting the origin or antecedents of this art style. As it is primarily a textile art, the chances of solving the questions of its origin are exceedingly remote and will, in any case, involve an understanding of the rise and development of twined fabric technology in various parts of the world" (p. 32).

56 Bird (1963). Lanning (1967, Chap. 5), however, points to simi-larities with designs of Valdivia phase pottery from the Ecuadorian coast.

57 Engel (1957 a); Lanning (1967, Chap. 5) refers to the site as "Culebras No. 1."

58 Strong and Evans (1952, pp. 19–20); Bird (1948); Willey (1953, pp. 41–42).

59 Engel (1957 a) describes some of these graves as intentionally constructed tombs; Lanning (1967, Chap. 5) seems to imply that they were burials in and under old house structures.

60 Lanning (1967, Chap. 5). Lanning also believes that the Playa Culebrans kept domesticated guinea pigs and that this animal was an important source of food.

61 Lanning (1967, Chap. 5) also lists the Huarmey Site No. 1 as a late preceramic community with maize and notes that Las Aldas, between the Casma and Culebras Valleys, probably had maize in association with preceramic levels. The Aspero site, at Puerto de Supe (located at the northernmost edge of the Central Coast subarea), also seems to have had a preceramic maize (Willey and Corbett, 1954).

62 Lanning (1967, Chap. 5). M. E. Mosely (personal communication, 1966) suggests that Rio Seco, which is at some distance from any well-watered valley, may have been sustained, in part, by cultivation in the nearby Lomas Lachay.

63 This description is based on Lanning (1965, 1967, Chap. 5), Patterson and Lanning (1964), and the most recent excavation report by Engel (1966 a).

64 Lanning (1967, Chap. 5).

65 Engel (1963 a).

66 Engel (1957 a); Strong (1957). Strong (1957) refers to these occupations under the name "San Nicolas"; Lanning (1967, chronology chart) uses the phase name "Casavilca."

67 Lanning (1967, Chap. 5).

68 Izumi and Sono (1963). I am also in receipt of correspondence from Professor Izumi (February, 1967) which adds details of results of the University of Tokyo 1966 expedition to Kotosh and nearby sites.

69 Terada (1964).

70 Izumi and Sono (1963, pp. 153–154); Yamasaki, Hamada, and Fujiyama (1966).

70a MacNeish's (1969) Ayacucho cave work has given us some information on the late preceramic cultures of the highlands; however, this work has not yet been reported in full.

71 M. D. Coe and Flannery (1966).

72 Heiser (1965, p. 934).

73 Heiser (1965, p. 934).

74 Heiser (1965).

75 See this work, Volume One, pp. 83–85, for a discussion of Mesoamerican agricultural beginnings.

76 Lanning (1967, Chap. 5) favors a Peruvian origin; Heiser (1965) questions the identification of *ficifolia* for Peru and believes it to be Mesoamerican.

77 This work, Volume One, pp. 83–85; see also Mangelsdorf, MacNeish, and Willey (1964, especially the "Addendum").

78 Grobman (Grobman and others, 1961) takes this position.

79 Mangelsdorf, MacNeish, and Willey (1964); see also Del Solar (1966).

80 Heiser (1965).

81 Heiser (1965); Mangelsdorf, MacNeish, and Willey (1964).

82 Mangelsdorf, MacNeish, and Willey (1964, especially "Addendum").

83 Heiser (1965).

84 In Volume One, p. 21, I gave the estimated date for Peruvian early cotton at "about 3000 B.C." Lanning (1967, Chap. 5) now extends this back another 500 years or so; but the question is still clouded. In this connection, see footnote 49, this chapter.

85 In Volume One, pp. 83–85, the Mesoamerican date of early cotton was put at "about 1700 B.C." MacNeish, in the "Addendum" to Mangelsdorf, MacNeish, and Willey (1964), moves this back to 5200 B.C.

86 Mangelsdorf, MacNeish, and Willey (1964).

87 Personal communication, T. C. Patterson (1965). See also footnote 42, this chapter.

88 Sweet manioc is also referred to as cassava or yuca.

89 Lanning (1967, Chap. 6).

90 This is the generally accepted opinion (see Sauer, 1950 b); however Rogers (1963) has challenged this, arguing that manioc probably originated in Central America or southern Mesoamerica. See also Bronson (1966).

91 Sauer (1952); Lathrap (1965).

92 Lanning (1967, Chap. 5—as at Playa Culebras).

93 See Appendix by Haag in Willey and Corbett (1954).

94 Lanning (1967, Chap. 6).

95 Llama bones are found as burials in temples in the coastal Virú Valley (Strong and Evans, 1952, pp. 27–34) and in the early temple at Kotosh (Izumi and Sono, 1963, p. 153).

96 Some woven cloth does appear in the latter part of Preceramic Period VI, but weaving does not predominate over twining until the Initial Period.

97 Lanning (1967, Chap. 6).

98 This is a compromise date, following Lanning (1967, Chap. 3). As has been previously noted (footnote 12, this chapter), there are some slightly earlier radiocarbon dates from the South Coast; but 1800 B.C. is the best round figure that we can give at the present time.

99 Trautman and Willis (1966, p. 197) give a date of 1825 B.C. for the earliest pottery levels at Ancón. Ramiro Matos (personal communication, 1967) assures me that this date pertains to the earliest Initial Period pottery at that site, not to "Chavinoid" pottery. Izumi and Sono (1963, p. 154) give a radiocarbon date of about 1800 B.C. for the earliest pottery level (Wairajirca) at Kotosh. There is also another date from this level of 1150 B.C. (Yamachi, Hamada, and Fujiyama). Lanning (1967, Chap. 6), however, quotes a date of 1450 B.C. as do Meggers, Evans, and Estrada (1965, pp. 173–174). Izumi and Terada (1966) give a radiocarbon date of about 1830 B.C. for San Juan (Far North Coast).

100 The reader is referred to Lanning's (1967) Chapter 6 and to his chronology chart and discussions in Chapter 3 for details of this.

101 Reichel-Dolmatoff (1961, 1965 b). There is also one date this early from Valdivia, in Ecuador (Meggers, Evans, and Estrada, 1965, p. 149).

102 This includes the coastal San Juan, Negritos, Guañape, Haldas, Cahuacucho, Gualaño, Florida, Curayacu, and Hacha complexes and the highland Wairajirca (or Huairajirca), Kotosh, Toríl, and Early Chiripa complexes. See, variously, Strong and Evans (1952), Collier (1962 b), Engel (1956), Izumi and Sono (1963), Izumi and Terada (1966), and Lanning (1959, 1963 b, 1967). Of these, only Guañape and the highland Waira-jirca and Kotosh complexes have been described in any detail.

103 Bird (1948).

104 See Strong and Evans (1952, pp. 27–34) for building and for description of the Guañape phase. This building dates to the Middle Guañape phase, which those authors then equated with the Chavín horizon. Lanning (1967, Chap. 6) equates this phase to just pre-Chavín times. This is based on his extensive comparisons of Initial Period and Early Horizon ceramics (Lanning, 1959 ms.), and I am following this interpretation here.

105 Strong and Evans (1952, pp. 34–38).

106 This important site has yet to be described satisfactorily. There is a brief account in Ishida and others (1960, pp. 444–447) who, incidentally, describe the layout of the complex as representing a mythical animal of some sort. Lanning (1967, Chap. 6) does not mention this. The site is currently under study by Rosa Fung, who supplied the photograph for figure 3-27.

107 Lanning (1967, chronology chart) indicates an Initial Period phase sequence for the subarea as: Haldas, Cahuacucho, and Gualaño in that order.

108 The Ancón "Tank Site" is the famous hillside shell heap that Uhle excavated many years ago (Strong, 1925) and in which I worked in 1941 (Willey and Corbett, 1954). T. C. Patterson (personal communication, 1966) tells me that my "Pit 1" narrowly missed

the edge of buried platform construction.

109 Matos (1968).

110 Lanning (1967, Chap. 6) and personal field notes of T. C. Patterson (1966).

111 Rowe (1956) refers to the Hacha style briefly. See also Menzel, Rowe, and Dawson (1964, p. 258) for an indirect but important reference to it. The Disco Verde Pottery style of the Paracas Peninsula, discovered by Engel (personal communication, 1960), may be of Initial Period date.

112 Kroeber (1944, pp. 49–50); Willey (1951).

113 Kroeber (1944, pp. 49–50), and see also that author (1944, pp. 49–50 and pl. 33) for a small stone vase from Chiclayo with a Sechín-Chavín design.

114 Lothrop (1951, fig. 74 d).

115 Tello (1943, 1956). The ceramics that Tello attributes to this post-Chavín, or "Sub-Chavín," level are, however, those of a style that he attributes to Teatino, in the Chancay Valley, and are of Tiahuanaco horizon date (see Willey, 1945, 1951).

116 Collier (1962 b); Lanning (1967, Chap. 6); Willey (1951). Donald Thompson (1964), however, dates Cerro Sechín to the Chavín horizon ("Middle Formative Period," in his terminology).

117 For Kotosh see Izumi and Sono (1963); for some others see Lanning (1967, Chap. 6). For the Mantaro information I am indebted to Ramiro Matos (personal communication, 1967).

118 Constructions H and G were two successive building levels in Mound KT, but their cultural contents were the same, so they were included in the same phase.

119 Lathrap (1958, 1965). Lanning (1967, Chap. 6) is inclined to discount these resemblances, but I think they are very strong.

120 Meggers, Evans, and Estrada (1965, pp. 173–174) refer to similarities between Waira-jirca and the "Valdivia-derived complexes of northern Colombia." By these they would presumably mean Puerto Hormigas, Barlovento, Malambo, etc. (See Chaps. 5 and 6 this volume).

121 The Izumi and Sono (1963) terminology utilizes double phase names: Kotosh Waira-jirca, Kotosh Kotosh, Kotosh Chavín, etc. That is, the name of the site precedes each phase name.

122 Izumi and Sono (1963, p. 154); Yamasaki, Hamada, and Fujiyama (1966).

123 Meggers, Evans, and Estrada (1965, pp. 173–174).

124 Izumi and Sono (1963, p. 155); see also Lathrap (1958, 1968 ms.).

125 Kroeber (1944); Willey (1945). The concept need not be restricted to Peru, of course. See Willey and Phillips (1958, pp. 29–34).

126 Willey (1951); Rowe (1962 b); Tello (1960). The best description and analysis of the style —as it is found at Chavín de Huantar—is the brief monograph by Rowe (1962 b).

127 As in Tello (1942).

128 Lanning (1967, Chap. 7) favors Sechín beginnings for the Chavín style.

129 For the question of possible Mesoamerican or Intermediate Area origins or affiliations of the Chavín style see Chapter 5 (pp. 350–351).

130 Rowe (1962 b) says 700 to 200 B.C. I follow the Lanning (1967) dating and interpretation of radiocarbon dates.

131 Rowe (1962 b) refers to seriations of Chavín-influenced Paracas pottery in this regard. These were carried out by L. E. Dawson and Dorothy Menzel but have not been published in any detail.

132 Lanning (1967, Chap. 7).

133 This is true except for occasional "archaisms" or "revivals" in later styles such as Moche pottery.

134 This section is based mainly on Bennett (1944), Tello (1960), and Rowe (1962 b); however, there are interesting earlier references to Chavín de Huántar in Middendorf (1895) and Roosevelt (1935). Rowe's 1962 article has also been revised and republished (Rowe, 1967).

135 Bennett (1944, p. 73).

136 Bennett (1944, p. 73).

137 The Chavín de Huántar ruins have been stone-robbed and desecrated by vandalism for years.

Recently, however, restoration has been undertaken.

138 Rowe (1962 b, p. 9).

139 Tello (1960, pp. 172–177).

140 Tello (1960); Rowe (1962 b).

141 Rowe (1962 b) has offered an interesting interpretation of the frequent use in Chavín art of multiple serpent or feline heads, mouths, fangs, eyes, etc., as these are disposed over a central figure. He refers to this as "figurative expression," or the use of metaphor in art, and he draws a comparison with the use of metaphors, or "kennings," in Old Norse court poetry.

142 Rowe (1963).

143 Lanning (1967, Chap. 7).

144 Tello (1960); see also Bennett (1944). L. G. Lumbreras (1968 ms.) has disclosed several new sub-styles of pottery from Chavín de Huántar and has suggested a sequence of phases, or subphases—Rocas, Ofrendas, Wacheqsa, and Mosna, in that chronological order.

145 Tello (1960).

146 The collection is described by Lothrop (1951). I think it more likely that this material came from the North Coast.

147 Carrion Cachot (1948). See also Willey (1951) for other possible Chavinoid highland finds.

148 Larco Hoyle (1946).

149 Tello (1923); Kroeber (1944); Rowe (1962 b). Another Early Horizon phase that probably shows Chavín influences is Torrecitas Chavín, near Cajamarca, between Pacopampa and Yauya (see map, fig. 3-1). The Reichlens (1949) describe pottery for the phase that has a general Early Horizon appearance.

150 Izumi and Sono (1963); Yamasaki, Hamada, and Fujiyama (1966).

151 Tello (1956, pp. 32–48); Thompson (1962, 1964). Previously (1951), I questioned the Chavín stylistic affiliation of Pallka, but this was before Tello had published more thoroughly on the pottery.

152 Tello (1956, pp. 49–66); Thompson (1962, 1964).

153 Tello (1956, pp. 79–83).

154 Tello (1943); Willey (1951).

155 Thompson (1962, 1964); Collier (1962 b).

156 Cupisnique is known best from the work of Larco Hoyle (1941, 1946).

157 As, for instance, the Guañape subphases for the Virú Valley region (Willey, 1953). The reader is also referred to this reference, especially the last three chapters, for general surveys of settlement and architecture for Peru as a whole.

158 Lothrop (1941)—and probably also Lothrop (1951)—deals with gold that came from the North Coast.

159 Willey and Corbett (1954). The deepest pit dug by us in the Ancón shell mounds, or "Tank Site," was largely involved with Early Horizon and Chavín-influenced pottery. Colinas is the name Lanning (1967) gives to a Chavinoid pottery phase in the Ancón Tank Site.

160 Engel (1956).

161 Patterson and Lanning (1964); Lanning (1967, Chap. 7).

162 Kroeber (1953) and I (1951, 1954) differed on this matter, and the argument has now been settled in his favor; however in self-extenuation I should like to point out that the Chavín-influenced Paracas vessels that I had seen in the early 1950's were those of the late Paracas subphases, in which Chavín influence was somewhat attenuated.

163 First described from the Paracas Peninsula and referred to as "Paracas Cavernas."

164 Menzel, Rowe, and Dawson (1964); see also Wallace (1962) and Sawyer (1966). It should be noted that Menzel and associates give absolute dates to the Early Horizon and its Chavín influences just a little later than those used by Lanning (1967) and followed here. The Disco Verde pottery style, discovered on the Paracas Peninsula by Engel (personal communication, 1960) probably precedes the Paracas series and belongs in the Initial Period (see footnote 111, this chapter).

165 On the South-Central Coast the little known Pozuelo phase is Chavín-influenced. This is succeeded by the Topará phase and style,

which continues from the latter part of the Early Horizon into the beginnings of the Early Intermediate Period. Topará ceramics, at least in their later time range, are those best known as "Paracas Necropolis" wares.

166 Similar seriation is the arrangement of series on the principle of similarity. That is, units are placed in the series next to those to which they bear the closest formal similarity. The assumption behind this, in cultural studies, is that culture change tends to be gradual.

167 Strong (1957). In Strong's sequence (according to Menzel, Rowe, and Dawson [1964, pp. 3–4]), his Early Paracas corresponds to the Paracas Phase 8 (or subphase 8 in the terminology of this book); Strong's Late Paracas then crossmatches, approximately, with Phases 9 and 10; and Strong's Proto-Nazca is equated with the Menzel-Rowe-Dawson Nazca Phase 1. Compare also the Menzel-Rowe-Dawson (1964, pp. 3–4) correlations with Wallace's (1962) Cerrillos work.

168 Menzel, Rowe, and Dawson (1964, p. 258).

169 No justice can be given to Paracas pottery in this very brief description. The reader is referred to the descriptions and beautiful illustrations (some in color) in Sawyer (1966).

170 Rowe (1963) classifies these as "achoritic" cities, or urban concentrations—those that are sustained wholly by peoples living within their confines. His "synchoritic" cities are those sustained—at least partially—by outlying satellite communities.

171 As, for example, the Chanquillo fortress in the Casma Valley (with a radiocarbon date of about 350 B.C.), Thompson (1964); or the Salinar (Puerto Moorin) fortresses on valley hilltops in the Virú Valley (Willey, 1953).

172 Lanning (1963 b, 1967, Chap. 7).

173 Larco Hoyle (1965); Matos (1967 ms.).

174 Izumi and Terada (1966). Lothrop (1948) describes large adobe mounds from the Far North subarea. Some of these seem to be identified with much later periods, and it is not certain if temple struc-

tures, pyramids, etc., were being constructed in the subarea during the Early Horizon.

175 Lanning (1967, chronology chart) lists a Preceramic Ichuña phase for the Far South Coast at this time level. Information on this subarea is very inadequate, however.

176 David Browman (personal communication, 1969) informs me that the nature of Pirwapuquio and Jurpac sites, in the Huancayo region, suggests a greater dependence upon hunting than upon plant cultivation.

177 These phases have been reported upon by Flores Espinoza (1960), Lumbreras (1960), Matos (1960), and David Browman (personal communication, 1969).

178 Rowe (1944, 1956).

179 Qaluyu and other related regional phases of the highlands are mentioned briefly by Rowe (1956, 1963). It should be noted that Rowe (1963) placed Qaluyu as Initial Period, but it seems more likely that it dates to the Early Horizon.

180 Bennett (1948 b).

181 Lanning (1967, Chap. 7).

182 See, for example, Willey (1948, 1951, 1962); Rowe (1962 b); Bennett and Bird (1964, pp. 91–102); Bushnell (1963, pp. 43–56); Lanning (1967, Chap. 7).

183 Rowe (1963); Lanning (1967, Chap. 3); Schaedel (1951); Willey, (1953); Kidder II (1956); Collier (1962 a); Thompson (1964 b). The reader will note that marked differences of opinion characterize these works. For example, Schaedel and Collier are inclined to see true cities or urbanism as occurring only after the advent of the Middle Horizon, while Rowe and Lanning talk of towns and cities as being much earlier.

184 See Lanning (1967, Chap. 3) for a more detailed discussion.

185 This is the civilization—and the pottery style—known also by the names: Proto-Chimu (Uhle), Early Chimu (Kroeber), and Mochica (Larco Hoyle). The term Moche (Rowe, Lanning), following the type station and the valley, is more non-committal with reference to ethnic identification (which is unknown). There are many sources on

Moche civilization: Kroeber (1926 b, 1930, 1944); Uhle (1913); Larco Hoyle (1938–40, 1945 a, 1946, 1966); Bennett and Bird (1960); Bushnell (1963); Mason (1957). This is only a sampling.

186 This follows Lanning's (1967) reconciliation of various radiocarbon dates.

187 See Larco Hoyle (1944, 1945 b); Bennett (1950); Strong and Evans (1952); Willey (1953). Salinar has been called "Puerto Moorin" in the Virú Valley; and Gallinazo has sometimes been referred to as the "Virú Culture."

188 Willey (1945).

189 Larco Hoyle (1965, 1966); Matos (1967 ms.).

190 This is demonstrated for Virú (see Willey, 1953, pp. 362–363).

191 Bennett (1950).

192 The Gallinazo adobe was rectangular, oblong, and had been poured and dried in a cane mold.

193 Bennett (1950, pp. 67–69).

194 Rowe (1963) and Lanning (1967) take the line that urban development, in the sense of true cities, did not appear on the North Coast until Middle Horizon times. While it is true that the Early Intermediate Period large settlement of the North Coast was less nucleated and compact, the evidence of Gallinazo suggests strong trends in this direction.

195 The Moche phase in the Virú Valley is referred to as "Huancaco."

196 The Moche adobe type, like the Gallinazo form, is oblong and rectangular; however, it appears to have been poured in a smooth-walled mold.

197 These names are of Hispanic attribution and have no known significance with relation to sun or moon.

198 Kroeber (1930, pp. 71–73). These murals have since been largely destroyed.

199 See Kroeber (1926, pp. 12–14). Although Uhle and others have excavated graves at Moche, this great site has never been properly excavated or explored in a large-scale, systematic manner.

200 This classification and these drawings come from a manuscript

prepared by John H. Rowe (1957). The spout-form seriation, however, was first suggested by Larco Hoyle (1948).

201 See Donnan (1965) for a detailed discussion of Moche pottery making.

202 Lothrop (1948); Lanning (1963 b).

203 I am indebted to Ramiro Matos for providing me with a manuscript covering his excavations at Vicús (Matos, 1967 ms.). The Vicús cemetery is located near Chulucanas, about 50 kilometers east of the city of Piura and well over 100 kilometers from the sea. The graves or tombs were found in earth or clay mounds, and there are also some deep-shaft-with-side-chamber graves. Unfortunately, many of the tombs had been destroyed before Matos's visit. Recent radiocarbon dates from Vicús (Disselhoff, 1969) fall in a range of about A.D. 200–700. These dates came from graves containing white-on-red and negative-painted pottery—the sort of material that is reminiscent of Salinar and Gallinazo. Thus, the dates seem surprisingly late when compared with our Chicama and Virú estimates.

204 Baños de Boza is the phase name associated with the Chancay White-on-red style (see Kroeber, 1926 a; Willey, 1943). Miramar is the contemporaneous and related style of the Ancón-Chillón regions which has been subdivided into four sequent subphases by Patterson (1966). Stratigraphic digging at Pachacamac, in the Lurín Valley, has also disclosed a white-on-red decorated pottery which is probably another regional variant of the Baños de Boza–Miramar series (Strong and Corbett, 1943). Patterson (personal communication, 1967) informs me that a Miramar-like style occurs even farther South in the Mala Valley.

205 Such phases have been grouped as a "White-on-red horizon" (Willey, 1945); however, it should be pointed out that such technological phenomena as red-fired or oxidized pottery and white-pigment painting do not have the same stylistic value—and chronological precision—as the true horizon

styles (Chavín, Tiahuanaco-Huari, and Inca).

206 The Lima style and phase has been known variously as "Proto-Lima," "Early Lima," "Maranga," "Playa Grande," "Interlocking Style," "Nievería," "Cajamarquilla." See Patterson (1966) for a discussion of these terms, some of which have embraced elements of the Middle Horizon Huari-influenced styles. In this discussion, following Patterson, we have limited the Lima style and phase to pre-Middle Horizon data.

207 Willey (1943). The Baños de Boza structure was of handmade hemispherical adobes. Conical adobes are known from Miramar sites (Patterson, personal communication, 1967). Apparently, there is considerable regional variation in adobe types in the Early Intermediate Period.

208 See Jijón y Caamaño (1949); Stumer (1954 a); Lanning (1967, Chap. 8). The Maranga constructions were laid up of rectangular mold-made adobes.

209 Stumer (1953).

210 Kroeber (1926 a) and Uhle (1926); Stumer (1954 b).

211 In this summary I am indebted to Dorothy Menzel for the use of a manuscript (Menzel, 1960, ms.) that summarizes and interprets South Coast and South-Central Coast ceramic history. Dawson's important studies have not been published but are reviewed by Menzel as are the recent important findings of Dwight Wallace. See also Strong (1957), Gayton and Kroeber (1927), and Kroeber (1937, 1956).

212 Dawson designated his seriation by "phases," but in keeping with the presentation of this book, these have been changed to "subphases."

213 "Monumental Nazca" would correspond to Gayton and Kroeber's (1927) "Nazca A" and to what Strong (1957) has defined as "Early Nazca" and, at least, to some of his "Middle Nazca."

214 This would correspond to some of what Gayton and Kroeber (1927) called "Nazca B." Part of their "B" would also be subsumed under the succeeding "Proliferous Nazca," although some of the "Proli-

ferous" may be within the Gayton-Kroeber "Nazca Y" concept. Dawson's Nazca 8 seems clearly to be "Nazca Y." The Nazca 9 sub-phase takes us into Tiahuanacoid influences.

215 This is a greatly simplified statement. In general, Cañete, the northernmost of these valleys, is more strongly influenced by the Central Coast and the Lima style, Chincha and Pisco-Paracas less so. The ceramic history on the Far South Coast probably begins in the Early Intermediate Period with the Islay and succeeding San Benito styles. At least no earlier pottery is yet reported for that subarea. Islay and San Benito are said to resemble the Pichalo pottery complexes of northern Chile and can be considered as much within the orbit of the South Andes as within the Peruvian culture area. Recent work in Far South Peru has been carried out by Gary Vescelius, and I am indebted to him and to T. C. Patterson for their observations on this subarea.

216 Strong (1957).

217 Kosok and Reiche (1947, 1949) present the "astronomical" interpretation of these lines. Rowe and Menzel (1964, ms.) disagree. Bushnell (1963, p. 91) cites a radiocarbon date of approximately A.D. 500 for a wooden post found at an intersection of the markings.

218 Reichlen and Reichlen (1949).

219 Lanning (1967) prefers to place Torrecitas in the early half of the Early Intermediate Period.

220 Lanning (1967) places Cajamarca I as Early Intermediate Period and Cajamarca II-IV as Middle Horizon. I am inclined to keep Cajamarca II, with its interlocking fish designs, in the Early Intermediate Period.

221 Some of light orange-on-dark red vessels were found by me (1943) in the Chancay Valley. T. C. Patterson tells me that he segregates these into a Lumbra style, which he believes was dominant in the upper part of the Chancay Valley, while the Baños de Boza style was the principal style of the lower valley (see also Patterson, 1966).

222 Bennett (1944).

223 It has generally been thought that this red "over-paint" was applied positively; however, the ceramic technologist Robert Sonin (personal communication, 1959) tells me that it too was probably applied by a resist method.

224 The Recuay style is well known and illustrated. See Bennett (1944, 1946 b); Bennett and Bird (1964); Bushnell (1963)—as a sampling.

225 *Ibid.*

226 Izumi and Sono (1963, pp. 156–158).

227 I am indebted to Ramiro Matos (personal communication, 1967) for information about Aya Orjo; it should be noted, however, that Lumbreras, at one time (1960), was inclined to date Aya Orjo as Middle Horizon or later.

228 From the Huancayo region, to the north of Ayacucho, but still in the Mantaro subarea. David Browman (personal communication, 1969) has defined a Huancayo phase which, presumably, is contemporaneous with Aya Orjo. He describes Huancayo sites as small hilltop locations—possibly selected as defensive locations. Dwellings were built of perishable materials on earth platforms. The economy is estimated to be mixed hunting-farming.

229 Bennett (1953) named and described the Huarpa phase but placed it as after the Middle Horizon Huari styles (Chakipampa and Viñaque). Its position now seems securely placed within the Early Intermediate Period; see Lumbreras (1960) and Menzel (1964). In the Huancayo region, Browman (personal communication, 1969) lists a Tinyari phase as being much like Huarpa in ceramic content. Middle Horizon influences were intrusive into Tinyari. It was somewhere at this approximate point of transition between Tinyari and the Middle Horizon that Huancayo region culture underwent profound change, with towns, stone architecture, ceremonial centers, and urban planning all appearing.

230 Bennett (1953) is the principal reference concerning the Huari site and its excavations; see also Rowe, Collier, and Willey (1950).

231 Rowe (1956).

232 Kidder II (1943, 1948); Bennett (1946 b); Rowe (1963).

233 Bennett (Bennett and Bird, 1964) considered Tiahuanaco as a ceremonial center, a "pilgrimage" center. It now seems that it was more of a city than that (see Rowe, 1963, and J. R. Parsons, 1968).

234 J. J. Parsons and Denevan (1967).

235 There are many sources for Tiahauanaco. The excavation report by Bennett (1934) is an important one. Posnansky (1945) shows excellent photographs, but his interpretations are very fanciful. See Ponce Sangines (1957, 1964) for results of his recent excavations. The reader is also referred to the various general works on Peru: Bennett and Bird (1964); Mason (1957); Bushnell (1963).

236 This is an unfortunate choice for a phase name if the Qalasasaya construction was built in Qeya times.

237 Lanning (1967, Chap. 8) says that the Acapana may be a Tiahuanaco proper or Middle Horizon structure.

238 Bennett (1934).

239 Lanning (1967, Chap. 9).

240 The Tiahuanaco "Gateway God" may also be a prototype of the Inca Viracocha, the creator god.

241 Uhle (1903).

242 Menzel (1964).

243 See Menzel's (1964) arguments.

244 This section derives largely from Menzel (1964) but is an extreme simplification of her complex study. See also Lanning (1967, Chap. 9). The other principal references on Huari are Rowe, Collier, and Willey (1950); Bennett (1953); and Lumbreras (1960 b, 1960 c). It should be noted that later work reversed Bennett's chronological arrangement of Huari (Chakipampa, Viñaque) and Huarpa.

245 This would be an event of what Menzel (1964) refers to as "Middle Horizon Epoch 1A."

246 An event of "Middle Horizon Epoch 1B" (see Menzel, 1964).

247 These events transpired in "Middle Horizon Epoch 2A and 2B" (Menzel, 1964).

248 According to Menzel (1964, pl. I), the abandonment of Huari and the close of "Middle Horizon Epoch 2B" would have taken place at about A.D. 950. Following the Lanning (1967) chronology, as we are doing in this chapter, the date would be about A.D. 800.

249 The Ocoña Valley is in the northern part of the Far South Coast subarea. To the north, Huari influence—at least as occasional pottery vessels—went as far as the Vicús site in the Piura Valley, and it can be argued that some Ecuadorian highland pottery styles show a vague Huari influence; it is, however, highly unlikely that Huari political power moved as far north as Ecuador.

250 This is a term originally used by Uhle (1903), with its meaning of "epigone," or "that which comes after." He used it in the sense of a post-Tiahuanaco and Tiahuanaco-derived style. On the South Coast, for example, Kroeber and Strong (1924) defined an "Ica Epigonal" style. See Menzel (1964) for a discussion of this.

251 See Uhle (1903) for the Tiahuanacoid or Huari influences as seen in the pottery of Pachacamac. I am indebted to T. C. Patterson (personal communication 1966) for his comments about the "Oracle of Pachacamac."

252 The "Middle Ancón II" and "Late Ancón I" styles (Strong, 1925) would pertain here. See also Kroeber's (1926 a) "Epigonal" and "Black-White-Red" styles from the Chancay.

253 The Huari-like style of the North Coast has been called Huari-Norteño A, or North Huari A, by Larco Hoyle (1966). The Tomaval style, or styles, of the Virú Valley subsume all of the Huari-influenced and Huari-derived pottery of the Virú Valley. See Ford (1949); Collier (1955).

254 For Wilkawain-Tiahuanaco see Bennett (1944) and for Cajamarca see Reichlen and Reichlen (1949).

255 Stumer (1956). Stumer's presentation of this is somewhat impressionistic, rather than documented in detail, but the case is, in general, convincing.

256 Uhle (1913). For the Tomaval phase see Ford (1949) and Collier (1955). The Tomaval phase brackets the time of the Huari expansion together with the subsequent derived styles of post-Huari times.

257 See Willey (1953, pp. 344–422).

258 For Rímac settlements see Stumer (1954 a); Patterson and Lanning (1964); Lanning (1967, Chap. 9). In the Middle Marañón subarea of the northern highlands the stone-walled city of Marca Huamachuco was probably built in the latter part of the Early Intermediate Period. It was subsequently overthrown by Huari invaders, who built the planned urban concentration at nearby Viracochapampa. See Mc-Cown (1945) for explorations of these two sites. The interpretation and dating, however, follow Lanning (1967, Chap. 9) and Menzel (1964).

259 Lanning (1967, Chap. 9).

260 This is uncertain, although see Willey (1953, p. 414) for structures of this type that may date this early.

261 Garcilaso de la Vega (El Inca, 1869–71).

262 Rowe (1948).

263 Lanning (1967, Chap. 10).

264 For descriptions and comment on Chanchan—in addition to the general sources cited for this chapter—see Squier (1877); Horkheimer (1944); Holstein (1927); Kroeber (1926 b, 1930).

265 Chanchan has been a treasure-hunter's paradise for the past 400 years, and the ruins have been looted relentlessly. Many splendid tombs have been discovered by "huaqueros" (pot hunters). Unfortunately, there is little record of their discoveries except the handsome specimens that have found their way into various collections.

266 Schaedel (1951).

267 Willey (1953, pp. 370–371).

268 Willey (1953, pp. 398–399 and 420–421).

269 See Willey (1964) for comments on this tradition.

270 Almost all Chimu modeled ware is reduced-fired, black, polished pottery. This reduce-fired, or "bucchero," ware was only a minor ele-

ment in the old Moche-modeled pottery.

271 Scheele and Patterson (1966) have presented a trial seriation of terminal Middle Horizon and Chimu pottery.

272 See Willey (1949, pp. 203–204).

273 There are stories of gold treasure buried in Chanchan and such treasure has, indeed, been recovered (see Lothrop, 1938, pp. 66–67).

274 Lanning (1967, Chap. 10).

275 For the Chancay style see Kroeber (1926 a); Strong (1925, "Late Ancón II"); Lothrop and Mahler (1957).

276 The Huancho style (Lanning, 1967, Chap. 10) is what has been referred to as "Sub-Chancay." Much of the pottery designated as "Inca-associated" at Pachacamac, by Strong and Corbett (1943), is Huancho.

277 Lyon (1966).

278 Kroeber and Strong (1924 b); Menzel (1966).

279 Kroeber and Strong (1924 a); Menzel (1966).

280 Menzel and Rowe (1966).

281 Menzel and Rowe (1966); see also footnote, this chapter.

282 Reichlen and Reichlen (1949). See Cajamarca V phase.

283 Lanning (1967, see chronology chart). Lanning (ibid.) also lists a Marabamba phase for the Huallaga in the Late Intermediate Period.

284 Rowe (1944, pp. 60–62).

285 Collao and Sillustani are described by M. H. Tschopik (1946), who dated them between Tiahuanaco and Inca. The chronological placement of Sillustani as the earlier of the two follows Lanning (1967, chronology chart). Another style of the North Titicaca Basin, Allita Amaya, may also belong in the Late Intermediate Period.

286 Rydén (1947, pp. 81–167, especially pp. 159–162 for the Wancani pottery style). The name Wancani, for this style and phase, has been given by Lanning (1967, chronology chart).

287 This follows Bennett's (1934) terminology of "Decadent" Tiahuanaco. Whether the Tiahuan-

aco materials are "Decadent" or "Classic" (see footnote 240, this chapter), the Wancani pottery complex in question is post-Middle Horizon. ·

288 See Rowe (1946, pp. 192–197) for a discussion of these sources. Among the more important are: Estete (1918) (an eyewitness account of the Conquest); Cieza de Leon (1554, 1880) (written in 1551); Toledo (1940) (written in the late 16th century); Cobo (1890–95) (written about 1653); and Garcílaso de la Vega (1869–71) (written in the early 18th century).

289 Rowe (1946, p. 203) gives the date of Huayna Capac's death as A.D. 1527; more recently (Rowe and Menzel, 1964 ms.) he has revised it to 1525.

290 See Rowe (1946) for this section and for further comments on the Inca.

291 Rowe (1946, pp. 253–256). See Zuidema (1962) for some other opinions.

292 Larco Hoyle (1938–40, 1945 a, 1966) maintained that the Mochicans (Moche phase of the North Coast of Peru) developed and used a system of "bean writing" (inscribing various simple markings on the lima bean), citing as his principal evidence the depiction of such beans in Moche vase painting; however, the beans in question are more likely counters or elements of a game. More recently, Barthel has claimed writing for the Incas (International Congress of Americanists, Lima, Peru, 1970); however, there is still no general acceptance of this claim.

293 Rowe (1944).

294 Rowe (1961).

295 This is Rowe's (1946) estimate. Kubler (1946) gives a figure of 4,000,000 persons. Means (1931), on the other hand, placed population at 16,000,000 to 32,000,000; and the recent computations of Dobyns (1966) are 30,000,000 to 37,500,000. I would favor Rowe's estimate, or one that is slightly higher.

296 Lanning (1967, Chap. 11).

297 The reader is referred, of course, to Prescott (1908) for the classic story of the conquest in all its drama; see Kubler (1946) for the history of the Indian in the Colonial Period. For modern Quechua or Aymara ethnography see Mishkin (1946) and H. Tschopik, Jr. (1946).

The Area

Natural Environment and Cultural Subareas. The South Andes area (Fig. 4-1) consists of the northern two-thirds of Chile, the southern highlands of Bolivia, and northwestern Argentina. It is a largely semi-arid country of high punas, mountain valleys, and coastal deserts. Broadly speaking, the area is composed of two great physiographic provinces: a narrow Pacific coastal shelf and a wider interior mountain upland.[1] Its natural environmental and cultural subdivisions may be considered together. There are twelve (Fig. 4-1) of these:

(1) *The Atacama.* The northernmost section of the Pacific coastal shelf of Chile, from the Peruvian border to the Rio Copiapó, is a land in which precipitation is so minimal as to be almost non-existent. This north Chilean desert is known as the Atacama, and in the sixteenth century it was the domain of the Atacameño people (Fig. 4-2). The shore of this part of Chile is rugged, with steep cliffs rising above the pounding seas to heights of 2000 to 3000 feet. Behind this awesome escarpment the desert lands rise gradually to the high cordillera of the Andes. The Rio Loa is the only major river to cross this interior wasteland, and its waters sustain a series of oases that since prehistoric times have been the principal places of settlement in the Atacama interior. A few other settlements were possible in smaller valleys. Archaeologically, the Atacama subarea

The South Andes

4

could be subdivided by setting the interior oases of the Rio Loa apart from the coast. Both Schaedel and Nuñez have done this in their rather detailed mappings of Chilean cultures;[2] however, for our more general presentation I have considered these as regions within the Atacama subarea.

(2) *The Valles Transversales.* South of the Atacama is a zone of less severe environment known as the "Valles Transversales," which stretches from the Rio Copiapó down to the Rio Choapa. Here there is some precipitation and, as the name suggests, several sizable river valleys that fall from the Andes to cross the interior desert shelf and enter the sea. These are the Rio Copiapó, the Rio Huasco, the Rio Elquí, the Rio Limarí, and the Rio Choapa. The subarea is sometimes referred to as the "Chilean Diaguita" after the sixteenth century inhabitants of this part of Chile who may have spoken the same language as the neighboring trans-Andean peoples of Argentina.[3]

(3) *The Central Valley.* This subarea extends from a point north of the Rio Aconcagua to the Rio Bío Bío and includes the northern portion of the Chilean Central Valley. In late prehistoric times it was held by the Araucanians until the Inca overran most of it in the fifteenth century. The Central Valley, which runs north-south, is drained by rivers that descend from the Andes to cut transversely through it, and through canyons in the coastal mountains, to go on to the Pacific. As a result, it is subdivided into a number of small basins. These enjoy a mediterranean-type climate, with mild, wet winters and cool, dry summers. The natural vegetation is an evergreen broadleaf woodland of scattered stands of trees and bush. The land has been intensively cultivated in modern times and was cultivated to a lesser degree in the prehistoric past.

(4) *The Araucanian.* The Central Valley continues south of the Rio Bío Bío; however, from this point southward, the climatic and vegetational change is radical, with the mediterranean conditions giving way to wet beech and cedar forests. Here the problem of the agriculturist, today and in the past, is the clearing of the forest so that the land may dry sufficiently for planting and cropping. These conditions continue to and include the Island of Chiloé, the southernmost point of native agriculture. Such an environment is obviously an exception to the arid and semi-arid climates that characterize the rest of the South Andes area. This was the Araucanian stronghold in Inca and Spanish Colonial times.

(5) *The Southern Bolivian.* The interior uplands of the Bolivian altiplano compose a high (11,000–13,000 ft., or 3200–4000 m. above sea level), dry plateau. Still higher mountain ranges divide this plateau into a number of intermontane basins drained by small, intermittent rivers. Irrigation agriculture was practiced here in the past, with potatoes and quinoa as the principal crops. The Southern Bolivian subarea embraces the Bolivian Departments of Oruro, Potosí, Cochabamba, Chuquisaca, Tarija, and a western edge of Santa Cruz. In the west this is true altiplano country, but on the east mountains and valleys descend toward the lowlands. In early historic

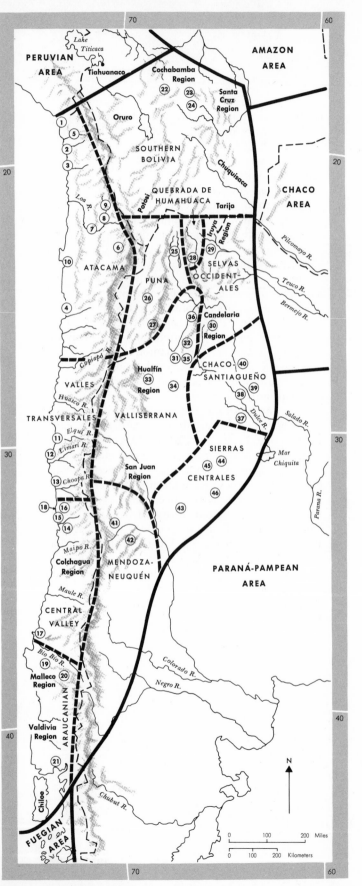

The South Andes Culture Area

with Archaeological Subareas,
Regions, Localities, and Sites

SUBAREAS

Atacama

1 Arica Region (Quiani, Chinchorro, Faldas del Morro, Playa Miller)
2 Pisagua Region (Pichalo, Pisagua Viejo)
3 Iquique
4 Taltal
5 Conanoxa
6 San Pedro de Atacama
7 Calama
8 Chiu Chiu
9 Lasana
10 Antofagasta

Valles Transversales

11 Coquimbo-La Serena Region
12 Huentelauquén
13 Guanaqueros

Central Valley

14 Las Cenizas
15 Concón
16 Longotoma 1
17 Concepción
18 Sitio Alacranes I

Araucanian

19 Angol, El Vergel
20 Cueva de los Catalanes
21 Puerto Montt

Southern Bolivian

22 Chullpa Pampa
23 Arani
24 Mizque

Puna

25 Sorcuyo
26 Tebenquiche
27 Laguna Blanca

Quebrada de Humahuaca

28 La Isla de Tilcara, Pucará de Tilcara, and Alfarcito

Selvas Occidentales

29 Titiconte
30 La Candelaria

Valliserrana

31 San José
32 Santa María
33 Belén, Aguada, Ciénega, Condorhuasi, Hualfín-the Hualfín Valley region
34 Alamito
35 Tafí
36 Pampa Grande

Chaco-Santiagueño

37 Las Mercedes
38 Sunchituyoj
39 Averías
40 Llajta Mauca

Mendoza-Neuquén

41 Agrelo
42 Viluco

Sierras Centrales

43 Intihuasi Cave
44 Ongamira Cave
45 Pampa de Olaen, including Ayampitín site
46 Villa Rumipal

Figure 4-1.

times the subarea was occupied by the Lipe and Chicha tribes.

(6) *The Puna.* The Argentine puna of Jujuy and Catamarca is much like the Bolivian altiplano. It was the seat of one of the "classic" manifestations of South Andean culture.[4] This is the "Puna Complex" of the Late Ceramic Period with its stone-walled houses and forts, metalwork, woodwork, and leatherwork. Llama herding was important, and people were Atacaman-speaking.

(7) *The Quebrada de Humahuaca.* This subarea is a narrow, trenchlike valley that lies just off to the east of the Argentine puna. In its high, northern end it has a punalike climate and scrub xerophytic vegetation; but its southern reaches, which are 9000 feet lower than its headwaters, enjoy a subtropical climate with luxuriant vegetation. Culturally, this subarea is closely related to the puna.[5] In early historic times it was occupied by the Humahuaca tribe.

(8) *The Selvas Occidentales.* To the east of the Quebrada de Humahuaca and the puna, in eastern Jujuy and Salta, are the Selvas Occidentales.[6] Structurally, these are composed of the eastward-facing edges of the puna together with some outlying Andean ranges. Broadleaf trees grow at higher elevations here, but at lesser altitudes these change to the kind of scrub growth that continues onward into the flatlands of the Gran Chaco. The most distinctive archaeological culture of the subarea is the Candelaria. Candelaria relates to the cultures to the west but also has tropical lowland connections. The Tonocoté lived here in early historic times, although their relationship to the Candelaria culture is obscure.

(9) *The Valliserrana.* To the south of the puna is the basin and range terrain that is sometimes referred to as the "Valliserrana" country. This takes in much of the Provinces of Tucumán and Catamarca and the Provinces of La Rioja and San Juan. Elevation here is between 4000 and 9500 feet (1200–3000 m.); rainfall is moderate. The terms "Argentine Diaguita" or "Calchaquí" are sometimes applied to this subarea.[7] The principal archaeological sequences of the South Andes have been developed here. It is the seat of the Barreales cultures (Ciénega and Aguada) and of the later well-known Belén and Santa María pottery styles. It was the historic territory of the Diaguita tribes.

(10) *The Mendoza-Neuquén.* This subarea is composed largely of these two Argentine provinces. In terrain it is similar to the Valliserrana; culturally, it was transitional between the South Andean and Pampean spheres. The protohistoric and historic peoples here were apparently the Huarpe, although Araucanians from Chile must have invaded a part of the subarea in proto-historic to early historic times. In any event, both archaeology and ethnohistory attest to a marginal Andean agricultural mode of life.[8]

(11) *The Chaco-Santiagueño.* The Valliserrana is bordered on the east by the Chacoan lowlands of the Province of Santiago del Estero. This is a deciduous scrub woodland with a subtropical climate. The subarea lies in the western or driest part of the Chaco where there is an annual rainfall of only about 20 inches; however, in ancient times the Indians farmed with flood-water irrigation along the courses of the Rio Dulce and the Rio Salado. Painted pottery styles of Middle and Late Ceramic Periods relate to those of the Valliserrana subarea but are also distinctive. Influences from the tropical lowlands are strongly indicated.[9] The Sanaviron seem to have been the principal group here in historic times.

(12) *The Sierras Centrales.* These mountains lie off to the southeast of Valliserrana in Córdoba and San Luis provinces. They are detached outliers of the Andes, composed of relatively low, north-south trending ranges and intermontane valleys. At higher elevations they are dry, rocky, and sparsely covered with a low grass vegetation; but the valley bottoms with their streams offered opportunities for irrigation farming. The subarea, like that of Mendoza-Neuquén, was marginal to the South Andes and transitional to the Paraná-Pampean patterns. Pottery quite probably arrived here much later than it did farther to the north or west; certainly it was never well established; and it may have been of Paraná River derivation rather than Andean. The agricultural patterns of the late prehistoric and early historic inhabitants were, however, clearly Andean. The subarea is sometimes referred to by the name of its historic tribe, the Comechingón.[10]

Ethnographic-Linguistic Sketch. The Spaniards first entered the South Andes area in the sixteenth century. There they met with native

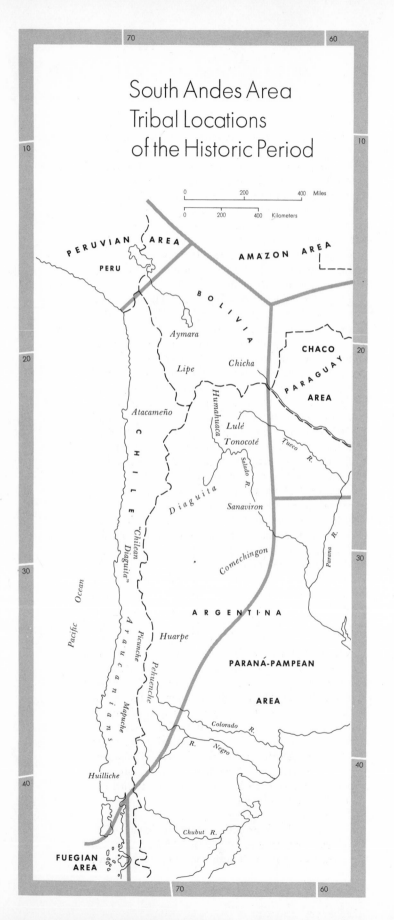

South Andes Area Tribal Locations of the Historic Period

peoples (Fig. 4-2) whose pattern of life was very similar to that revealed by the late prehistoric archaeological horizons of these regions. Along the Rio Loa in Chile and in the northwest Argentine highlands they found these natives living in villages or towns of stone-walled houses and practicing agriculture in the river valleys or on the hillsides with the aid of terracing and irrigation. Some of these towns were walled, hilltop strongholds, containing not only dwellings but special ceremonial buildings and cemeteries. Others were open villages, but the general pattern of settlement in many places was that of a central, fortified town with satellite hamlets. The Spaniards describe numerous small "states," presumably of this settlement type, and these are said to have coalesced under a more unified leadership only for warfare. Llama and alpaca herding was of economic importance, especially toward the north, and various items of harness gear for these animals were made of wood and other materials. The South Andean people were accomplished metalsmiths, working mostly in copper or bronze and casting club heads, tools, and ornamental plaques or breastplates. Woodcarving of various utensils was carried on with skill. The grinding and polishing of stone ornaments, dishes, and figurines was another notable craft, especially in the regions to the east and south. Weaving and pottery were well developed.

This was the pattern in the far north, especially in the Puna, Quebrada de Humahuaca, and interior Atacama subareas. There were variations of it. Along the Chilean desert coast the economy was divided between cultivation and fishing. In the Valliserrana subarea clay and adobe were frequently used in constructions, and towns and villages were smaller and somewhat more spread out than in the north. In the Argentine subareas to the east and southeast the pattern differed still further. Chaco Santiagueño houses were grass huts within wooden palisaded pueblos; and dwellings in the Sierras Centrales were, at least in some cases, pit houses with superstructures of perishable materials. In southern Chile the Araucanians followed a swidden or slash-and-burn method of

Figure 4-2.

cultivation in their forest homeland, with potatoes being a more important crop in some regions than maize. Araucanian houses were of wood and thatch and were dispersed in small settlements of a few dwellings each.[11]

Linguistic information for the South Andes is spotty and uncertain except for that pertaining to the Araucanians. In southern Bolivia the Lipe and Chicha may have been Aymara-speaking, like their neighbors to the north. The Atacaman-speaking Atacameño were the Indians of the Atacama and Puna subareas, as we have noted. This Atacaman language is grouped by Greenberg with the Paezan branch of the Macro-Chibchans (see Fig. 1-5). Their geographically closest relatives, according to this classification, would have been the Yunca language groups of the North Coast of Peru. Presumably, the separation here—if indeed such occurred—lies in the fairly distant past, as there is little in the archaeology of the ceramic periods to support such a relationship. The Humahuaca, or Omoguaca, of the Quebrada de Humahuaca may or may not have been of Atacaman speech. Farther south, supposedly in Chile as well as Argentina, were the Kakan (Cacan) or Diaguita language groups. Some authorities link these with Atacaman while others consider them unaffiliated languages. Other un-affiliated languages are represented by the marginal tribes to the east, or southeast, and south, such as the Tonocoté of the Selvas Occidentales, the Sanaviron of the Chaco-Santiagueña subarea, the Comechingón of the Sierras Centrales, and the Huarpe of Mendoza. In Chile, the Araucan-ians are also considered a separate language by some linguists; but Greenberg groups them with his Andean cluster.[12] One other group deserves mention in this rapid linguistic survey. This is the so-called Chango of the Atacama subarea. Chango refers to semi-sedentary fishermen who were reported along this coast as early as the mid-eighteenth century and continued into the nineteenth. They followed an existence reminiscent of that of the old Pacific Littoral, preceramic fishing periods. Although the Changos have sometimes been considered a separate ethnic group—and even linked to the Bolivian highland Uru—it is most likely that these small straggling bands were the impoverished descendants of the Atacameño.[13]

Cultural Traditions and Archaeological Chronology. In Chapter 2 we mentioned finds that indicated that several early traditions were represented in the South Andes area. The early Flake technological tradition was believed to be manifested in the Chuqui complex finds of northern Chile; the Ampajango complex, among others, was classed as a Biface tradition industry; and evidences of the Old South American Hunting tradition were seen in the early elongated leaf-shaped points reported from a number of places in the Chilean and Argentine highlands. It was then argued that an Andean Hunting-Collecting tradition was a development out of this earlier Old South American Hunting tradition and that, subsequently, a Pacific Littoral tradition had been evolved by Andean Hunters-Collectors who had moved from the uplands to the coast. The Andean Hunting-Collecting tradition, in its later phases in the uplands, and the Pacific Littoral tradition provided the base out of which a South Andean cultural tradition arose under stimuli from agricultural traditions to the north and east. This development took place in the latter centuries of the first millennium B.C.

In recent years Argentine and Chilean archaeologists have been moving toward the formation of an area chronology for the South Andes. I have followed their lead, especially for the ceramic periods within the South Andean tradition. For the preceramic era I have borrowed the preceramic scale used in the preceding Peruvian chapter. The line between preceramic and ceramic is usually placed by South Andean archaeologists somewhere between 500 B.C. and A.D. 1. I have set it at the earlier date. The preceramic and ceramic periods for the South Andes are as follows:

Preceramic Period I (prior to 9500 B.C.). This was the time of the Flake tradition. The Chilean Chuqui complex belongs on this horizon.

Preceramic Period II (9500–8000 B.C.). This was the time of the Biface and the earlier part of the Old South American Hunting tradition. The first is represented by Ampajango, Loma Negra, and related finds, the second by the Tagua Tagua discoveries and, perhaps, by some of the early leaf-shaped point complexes.

Preceramic Period III (8000–6000 B.C.). This was the time of the Old South American Hunting tradition and the beginnings of the Andean Hunting-Collecting tradition: Fundaciones, Tulan, and other complexes.

Preceramic Period IV (6000–4200 B.C.). The Andean Hunting-Collecting tradition lies largely on this horizon. Early Intihuasi or Intihuasi IV is the prime example of the tradition.

Preceramic Period V (4200–2500 B.C.). Intihuasi III and II show a continuation of the Andean Hunting-Collecting tradition. The Pacific

Littoral tradition has its inception with phases such as Quiani I.

Preceramic Period VI (2500–500 B.C.). This is the only deviation in dating from the Peruvian preceramic chronology. Here, the period lasts longer. The Andean Hunting-Collecting tradition continues in the highlands. On the coast this period is represented by later Pacific Littoral tradition phases.

Early Ceramic Period (500 B.C.–A.D. 600). The period begins with the estimated date for the first appearance of pottery in the South Andean area. The earliest radiocarbon date for this is about

Figure 4-3. Chronological chart, with subarea columns, phases, major periods, and estimated dates. Chile.

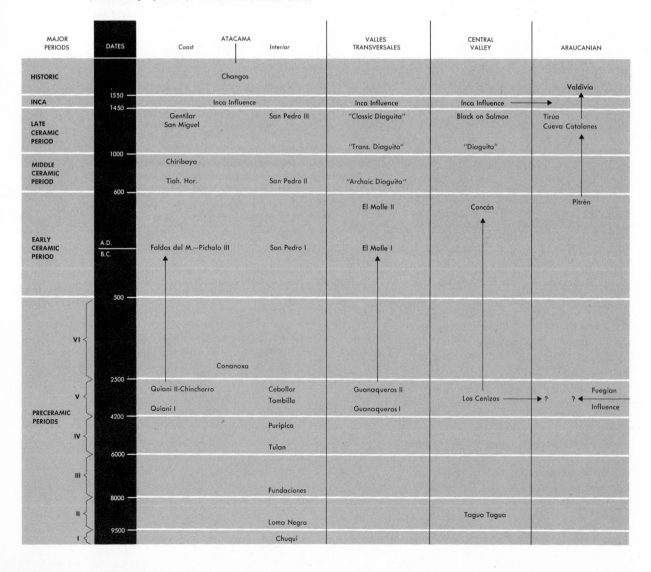

300 B.C., and this comes from the Tafí region of the Valliserrana subarea; however, Gonzalez allows for an earlier estimate of 500 B.C.[14] This, I think, is a conservative estimate, particularly if we assume that ceramics are probably earlier in the northern part of the area, especially the Southern Bolivian subarea. The styles of the Early Ceramic Period are predominantly monochromes or incised monochromes; however, painted styles make their appearance toward the end of the period. The terminal date line for the period is equally difficult to define. "Tiahuanacoid influences" are said to mark the beginning of the Middle Ceramic Period;

however, there is considerable amibiguity as to the nature of these influences. By strict definition, true Tiahuanaco horizon influence is known only from parts of the Southern Bolivian and Atacama subareas. Here Gonzalez and Núñez place the Early/Middle dividing line at A.D. 700, although on his chart Gonzalez indicated "Classic Tiahuanaco" influences in the Atacama subarea at about A.D. 600.[15] Elsewhere in the South Andes, what is

Figure 4-4. Chronological chart, with subarea columns, phases, major periods, and estimated dates. Southern Bolivia and northwestern Argentina.

MAJOR PERIODS	DATES	SOUTHERN BOLIVIA	PUNA AND HUMAHUACA	SELVAS OCCIDENTALES	VALLISERRANA	CHACO-SANTIAGUEÑO	MENDOZA-NEUQUÉN	SIERRAS CENTRALES
HISTORIC							Viluco	
	1550							
INCA	1450	Inca Influence	Inca Influence		Inca Influence		Inca Influence	
LATE CERAMIC PERIOD		Huruquilla, etc.	Puna Complex	Santa María	Santa María II – Belén II			
					Santa María I – Belén I	Averías		Villa Rumipal
	1000				San José – Hualfín			
MIDDLE CERAMIC PERIOD		Tiah.—Yampará II	"Middle Period"	Candelaria III	Aguada	Sunchituyoj		Intihuasi I
	600							
EARLY CERAMIC PERIOD		Yampará I		Candelaria II	Condorhuasi / Ciénega II		Agrelo (?)	
	A.D. / B.C.		Laguna Blanca		Ciénega I	Las Mercedes		
				Candelaria I	Tafí I			
		Cultura de los Túmulos						
	500							
PRECERAMIC PERIODS VI								
V	2500	L. Colorado / L. Hedionda						Intihuasi II
IV	4200							Intihuasi III
		Ayampitín	Ayampitín		Ayampitín			Intihuasi IV
III	6000							
	8000		Saladillo					
II			Tres Morros		Ampajango			
I	9500							

often called "Tiahuanacoid influence" is only vaguely related to the style and may be, in some instances, influence from Bolivian cultures that are actually pre-Tiahuanaco. For these, perhaps, a more appropriate term would be "Titicaca Basin influences". The date line of A.D. 600 has tentatively been selected for the close of the Early Ceramic Period.

Middle Ceramic Period (A.D. *600–1000*). The definition of the initial date for the period has been discussed above. In general, the period sees a considerable elaboration in material culture, including polychrome ceramics.

Late Ceramic Period (A.D. *1000–1450*). The period is characterized by localized pottery styles, most frequently featuring bicolor painting.

Inca Ceramic Period (A.D. *1450–1550*). Inca influence is found in all but the southern and southeastern subareas of the South Andes. It is seen in ceramics and, in some places, in metal objects and architecture. The period closes with the Spanish Conquest.

The Pacific Littoral Tradition of the Chilean Coast

It is the primary purpose of this chapter to describe the South Andean tradition; however, it is also important that we see it in its developmental settings, and for this reason we will turn first to the immediate local antecedents: the Pacific Littoral tradition and the later horizons of the Andean Hunting-Collecting tradition.

The Pacific Littoral tradition was in existence along the Chilean coast from about 4200 to 500 B.C., or for the duration of our Preceramic Periods V (4200–2500 B.C.) and VI (2500–500 B.C.). We have already defined the tradition as one characterized by a marine subsistence adaptation and further distinguished by certain specific traits pertaining to this subsistence pattern. This definition was outlined in the previous chapter in the context of the Peruvian area, where it was also noted that the Peruvian and Chilean manifestations of this tradition displayed some significant differences (p. 91). The most notable of these was that the cultures of the former had, from their inception, plant cultivation as an important secondary element in the economy, whereas those of the latter were more strictly oriented toward the sea. There were also other differences, especially in details of fishing gear. One reason for these differences may have been in the respective natural environments of the Peruvian and Chilean coasts. This would apply especially with regard to plant cultivation; the Chilean coastal valleys were tiny and less well favored with wild plants suitable for domestication than those of Peru. Another reason was probably the limitation of direct contact between the Peruvian Pacific Littoral tradition centers and those of north Chile. In Peru, these centers are largely on the North, Central, or South-Central Coasts. Below 14 degrees south latitude, typical Pacific Littoral tradition sites are rare (see p. 102). Here the southern Peruvian coast tends to be low and sandy and subject to the particularly heavy force of the ocean currents. As J. B. Bird has expressed it:

> ...as one travels south, Arica marks the beginning of a section of the coast which, from the standpoint of primitive coastal folk, offered more favorable habitation sites than the adjacent section to the north...[16]

This being the case, it is likely that Peruvian and north Chilean Pacific Littoral tradition communities were in semi-isolation from each other and tended to follow somewhat separate courses of development.

Certainly from Arica south the rocky inlets along the Chilean coast were ideal places for shellfish gathering and handline fishing. The marine resources were abundant and included not only fish and shellfish but porpoises, sea lions, and shore birds. Sea kelp that drifted ashore was also a boon for the old coastal dwellers for when dried it provided the only source for fuel in this land of scant vegetation. Finally, and crucially, many of these inlets along the coast were also near little oasis valleys with subterranean water. One such coastal oasis valley in the Atacama subarea is that of Azapa, near Arica; and it is from here that we have some of our most important data on the Chilean Pacific Littoral tradition.

The Arica Region: Quiani and Chinchorro. The city of Arica, in the valley of the Azapa, lies in the lee of the high headland of the Morro Arica. From the Morro Arica the coast-line curves slightly southeastward, and about 4 kilometers down the coast is the shell midden of Quiani. The immediate location is a hillslope that descends toward the beach from the high cliffs that back it. To the north, toward Arica, there is a considerable expanse of beach between the higher ground and the sea; but to the south the beach pinches out, and the rocky cliffs jut out into the ocean surf. Excellent shellfishing areas are found at the foot of these cliffs. Here the old Pacific Littoral peoples obtained the mussels that they brought to the nearest suitable camping ground on the low Quiani hillslope. The source of their water supply is something of a mystery, although it seems most probable that they had a well or spring, now no longer evident, in an ancient ravine that cuts through this hillslope.

The excavations at Quiani, carried out by J. B. Bird,[17] revealed a compacted layer of refuse 2 meters deep. This refuse was composed of mussels, whelks, sea urchins, crab remains, fish bones, bird bones, and—more rarely—porpoise and sea lion bones. The only bones of land mammals were those few that had been used to make artifacts. Chipped and ground stone were seen in abundance on and in the midden; manufactures of wood, shell, bone, and textiles were met with less frequently.

Stratigraphic separations of the Quiani materials indicate two chronological phases. The most characteristic artifact type of the earlier phase, the Quiani I (Fig. 4-5), is a shell fishhook, and the phase has sometimes been referred to as the "Shell Fishhook Culture." These hooks were cut from the choro mussel. They have a slightly curved shank and an incurving tip, but no barbs. A second fishhook type, also found in this earlier period, is a composite sinker-hook made of a curved barb of bone lashed to a piece of stone, bone, or shell. Harpoons (for sea mammals) with detachable forepieces fitted with bone barbs and stone points are another typical early-phase artifact.

In the Quiani II phase (Fig. 4-6), in contrast, thorn fishhooks are more common. It also has bone fish harpoon forepieces with thorn barbs, squid jiggers, and fishline sinkers. These Quiani II fish harpoon points were made of guanaco or vicuña bone and were fashioned with sharp tips and rounded butt ends. The two thorn barbs were lashed to the tip with cord. The squid jiggers probably had a wooden centerpiece to which three or four sharp bone barbs had been attached. The fishline sinkers were made of ground or polished stone in a cigar-shape form with grooves or notches at each end. Another Quiani II phase element—lacking in phase I—is the bola stone. Many of these appear to be natural pebbles that had simply been grooved for tying, but some had been shaped by pecking.

Chipped stone materials at Quiani include the heavy pebble choppers (Fig. 4-7) that are the same as the so-called "Paleolithic" tools of Taltal that we have previously discussed in Chapter 2 (see p. 42). There can be no doubt that at Quiani they are a part of the Pacific Littoral tradition inventories and are of no great age. They vary in length from 4 to 16 centimeters and are rather thick in cross section. Bird feels that they are chopping tools rather than cores since the numerous flakes struck from them were not used or worked. Furthermore, all of the points, knives, and scrapers at Quiani were made of chalcedonies and cherts rather than the coarse porphyry of the pebble tools. The most common projectile point of the Quiani I phase is, as we have said, the willow-leaf form (Fig. 4-5, b) derived from the early phases of the Andean Hunting-Collecting tradition. Stemmed and barbed points and triangular stemless forms with concave bases—reminiscent of those of the later phases of the Andean Hunting-Collecting tradition—are found in Quiani II levels.

Black lava bowl fragments, crude flat and conical mortars, small oval manos, and hammerstones were in use in both Quiani phases, although they were more common in the second.

Twelve burials were found at Quiani. Four of these were extended and had been placed upon, and covered with, twined totora reed mats. The bodies had been dressed in birdskin robes and leather pubic covers, and one adult male had a hairdress or headwrapping of wooden cords and a necklace of shell disk beads around his neck. A wooden spear-thrower and spear were found with one of the adults in this group. One of the four was a mummified infant that had been sewn tightly in a leather casing and then wrapped with woolen (vicuña, guanaco?) cords and bird skins.

The remaining eight burials were tightly flexed

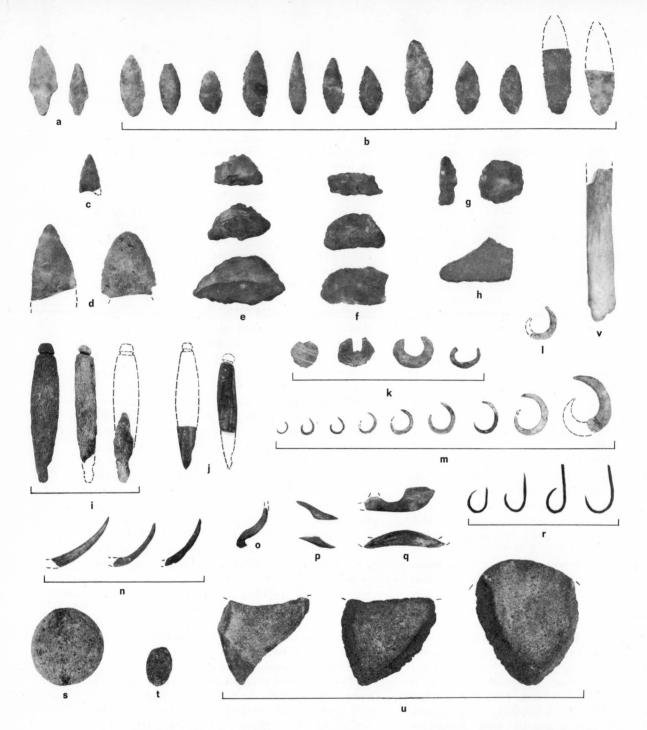

Figure 4-5. Various artifacts from Preceramic Phase I at Pichalo. These are identical or similar to those of Quiani I. *a:* Stemmed points, no barbs. *b:* Willow-leaf points. *c:* Triangular point. *d:* Knives (?). *e:* Double-edged side-scrapers, thick, with pointed ends. *f:* Double-edged side-scrapers, from thin flakes. *g:* End-scrapers (?). *h:* Stone saw. *i:* Composite sinker-hook of whalebone. *j:* Composite sinker-hook weights of mussel shell. *k:* Stages in the manufacture of shell hooks. *l:* Shell hook notched on outer shank. *m:* Mussel shell hooks showing range of size. *n:* Composite sinker-hook barbs of bone. *o:* Bone barb. *p:* Barbs for sea lion harpoon forepieces. *q:* Bone objects of unknown use. *r:* Thorn hooks, with shanks of two examples at left broken off. *s:* Naturally shaped pebble with incomplete pecked groove. *t:* Heavy stone bola weights without groove. *u:* Fragments of stone bowls. *v:* Chipping tool of sea lion rib. (After Bird, 1943.)

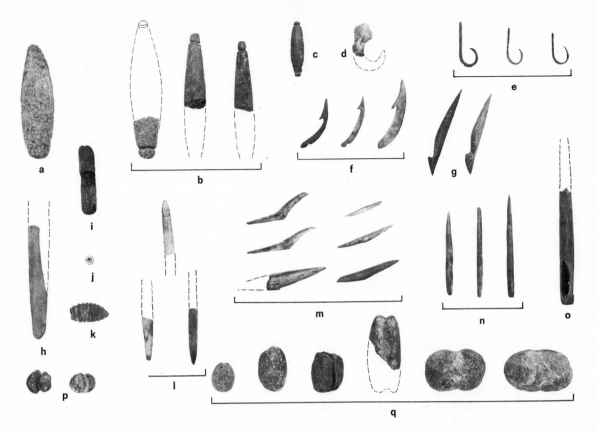

Figure 4-6. *Above:* Various artifacts from Preceramic Phase II at Pichalo, similar or identical to Quiani II. *a:* Unfinished stone sinker. *b:* Stone fishline sinkers. *c:* Composite sinker-hook weight of stone. *d:* Chipped-stone fishhook. *e:* Thorn fishhooks. *f, g:* Bone barbs of uncertain use. *h:* Chipping tool of bone. *i:* Fire drill hearth. *j:* Stone bead. *k:* Stone object of unknown use, grooved on both sides. *l:* Fragments of bone fish harpoon forepieces. *m:* Two types of bone barbs for sea lion harpoon forepieces. *n:* Bone barbs for squid hooks. *o:* Wooden central shaft of squid hook. *p:* Bolalike stone weights. *q:* Bolas. Length of *a*, 8.5 cm. (After Bird, 1943.)

Figure 4-7. *Left:* Rough percussion-flaked objects of basalt and other stone, from Quiani and Pichalo, Chile. These were found associated with preceramic levels. *a–e, g:* Quiani. *f:* Pichalo. Horizontal diameter of *a*, 13.4 cm. (After Bird, 1965.)

and had been placed on their sides on mats. Some of them had also been dressed in robes made either of bird skin or, possibly, of guanaco skin. Males wore twined woolen loincloths and, sometimes, woolen cord headbindings. Some of the bodies were also accompanied with harpoon forepieces, bone chipping tools, knotted woolen cord bags, and coiled baskets.[18] One had a spearthrower of a different style than that found with the extended burials.

205

Although it is difficult to relate the burials to the midden phases with precision, it is suggested by Bird that the extended interments were earlier and date to the Quiani I phase, while the flexed burials relate to Quiani II.

The Quiani burials lead us into the related problem of the "Chinchorro complex." The Chinchorro complex was first defined by Max Uhle, and it refers to burials found by him at the small site of Chinchorro, to the north of Arica, and to other burials from the slopes of the Morro de Arica.[19] Uhle called the peoples of these burials the "Aborígenes de Arica." They were long-headed individuals—similar to other early Andean populations (see p. 89)—and they deformed their heads by fronto-occipital flattening. In a recent publication Lautaro Núñez has noted the similarities between the Chinchorro burials, those from Quiani, and those from cemeteries at Pisagua Viejo and in the vicinity of Iquique.[20] From these similarities Núñez has drawn up a trait inventory for this Chinchorro "culture" or "complex." These traits include extended or flexed burial position, the mummification of infants, and the manufacture of little effigy mummy bundles or "momias estatuillas." The preparation of the infant bodies was rather elaborate, and it suggests a "cult of the dead." The corpses were first eviscerated; wooden sticks were thrust into the limbs; the bodies and limbs were sewn into leather casings; and the faces of the infants were coated with clay and painted. It is likely that the infant burial that Bird found at Quiani had been so treated. The "momias estatuillas" may be related to the same "cult of the dead." These little figures were constructed of sticks, clay, and bits of bone, then wrapped in textiles and placed in cemeteries along with adult burials.[20a] Grave furniture of the Chinchorro complex includes wooden spear-throwers and spears, harpoons, composite fishhooks, thorn fishhooks, small stone mortars, net textiles, coiled baskets,[21] woolen cord, bird and animal skin garments, twined mats, and leaf-shaped projectile points. Núñez also lists knotted cotton textiles and a cloth bag filled with quinoa among the various Chinchorro complex finds.

From these lists it is obvious that Chinchorro is hardly a single-phase assemblage; but how old is it, and what are the relationships to Quiani I and II? To attempt to answer the latter question

first: I think it is evident that the Chinchorro complex—or at least part of it—is simply the burial complex or burial aspect of the Quiani I and II phases. The site association of the burials in the Quiani midden argues for this as does the presence of both Quiani I and II traits in the Chinchorro complex as this has been defined by Núñez. As to absolute age, the Quiani I and II midden phases have been placed by radiocarbon dates at approximately 4200 and 3660 B.C. respectively.[22] The earlier date for Quiani I accords well with the willow-leaf point horizon in the South Andes, but the date of 3660 B.C. for Quiani II seems too early for the small projectile points that characterize the phase. There is, however, a radiocarbon date of about 3000 B.C. for the Chinchorro complex from the Pisagua Viejo site. This tends to support the Quiani II date in placing a Chinchorro–Quiani II burial complex at least as early as the latter part of the fourth millennium B.C. This has been compromised on the chart (Fig. 4-3) assignment by putting Quiani II at 3000 B.C.

How late did Quiani II last? In this connection, it is probably significant that the very uppermost levels of the Quiani midden contained cotton textile fragments, bits of gourd containers, and maize. In Peruvian Littoral tradition sites (see Chap. 2, fn. 50) cotton was certainly not a common commodity—if it was present at all—before 3000 to 2500 B.C., and maize does not make an appearance there until 2000 B.C. or perhaps a little later. This would suggest a persistence of a Quiani-Chinchorro type of culture in north Chile until after this latter date; and, so far as we know now, this kind of cultural pattern survived until the introduction of pottery and the firmer establishment of agriculture in such complexes as the Faldas del Morro and Pichalo III.[23] This takes us up to the threshold of the South Andean cultural tradition, and, according to the dating followed here (Fig. 4-3), this means that the Quiani II–Chinchorro phase spans the whole of Preceramic Period VI (2500–500 B.C.) and perhaps extends even a bit later. To subsume all of this as a Quiani II–Chinchorro phase is gross lumping; obviously, one of the tasks ahead in north Chilean archaeology is to segment this development so that we can appreciate in greater detail the important transition from the Pacific Littoral way of life to the "agroalfarero,"[24] or agriculture-pottery, horizon.

Pichalo. Punta Pichalo is 113 kilometers south of Arica. It is a steep, rocky spur which juts out into the Pacific to form the little-protected bay of Pisagua on its northern side. Like the cliffs near Quiani, this rocky promontory was an excellent shellfishing and fishing station. Shell and fishbone midden covers the northern slopes of the point above the sea, and J. B. Bird selected a large concentration of this debris for excavation.[25] Again like Quiani, there is no present-day fresh-water source nearby, and it is a matter of speculation whether the ancient fishers who camped here brought their water with them or knew of springs somewhere in the rocks.

The stratigraphic data from the Pichalo excavations confirm the Quiani sequence and the developments in the Pacific Littoral tradition that were observed in the Arica region. A Pichalo I and II phase division[26] can be made on much the same stratigraphic-typologic basis as that for Quiani I and II (Fig. 4-3). Shell fishhooks, composite sinker-hooks, detachable harpoon forepieces fitted with bone barbs and with leaf-shaped or double-ended chipped-stone points are the marker types for Pichalo I, and they correlate with Quiani I.[27] Thorn fishhooks, cigar-shaped stone lineweights, bone fish harpoons, bola stones, triangular stone points, and narrow-stemmed small points are the distinctive forms for Pichalo II. Continuity from Pichalo I to II is maintained in rough chopping tools, like those of Quiani, stone bowl fragments, and some double-ended or leaf-shaped points. A few burials were found in the Pichalo midden of extended form, but these had no grave goods accompanying them.[28] (See Figs. 4-5–4-7.)

Unlike Quiani, where maize and cotton appeared in the uppermost levels of the site, unaccompanied by pottery, Pichalo agriculture comes in simultaneously with ceramics and true weaving. Coiled baskets also occur here for the first time on this level.[29] The level is Pichalo III. It takes us into the South Andean cultural tradition, and we will come back to it later in this chapter.

Taltal. Taltal lies south of Pichalo. Two midden sites here excavated by Bird—the Cerro Colorado and Playa Morada (Playa Muelle de Piedra)—were essentially identical in cultural content.[30] Coarse percussion-flaked artifacts, like those of Arica and Pichalo, occur from top to bottom of both middens. These are the famous "Paleolithic tools" of Taltal (see p. 42). They are accompanied in the lower levels of the Taltal middens by pressure-flaked points of the leaf-shaped or double-ended type that we also saw in Quiani I and Pichalo I. In the upper Taltal levels pressure-flaked points are triangular and, at the very end of the sequence, small and stemmed. One distinctive feature of the Taltal flintwork is the end-scraper, suggesting a greater orientation here toward land hunting and the dressing of hides than at Pichalo or Arica. In this connection it is significant that Taltal is at the southern end of the Atacama subarea and in country that is transitional to the Valles Transversales subarea to the south, where there is more moisture and vegetation and, formerly, where there was more game in the interior. Taltal resembles Quiani I and Pichalo I in its possession of shell fishhooks, composite sinker-hooks, and harpoon barbs. For the most part, artifact types characteristic of Quiani II and Pichalo II, such as the cigar-shaped fishline weights, are not present in the Taltal middens; however, the changes in projectile points suggest a parallel to the developments farther north, and South Andean archaeologists usually recognize two phases: Cerro Colorado I and II.[31] These overall similarities in the trends of development for the Pacific Littoral tradition along the Atacama subarea coast are further indicated by some shell midden discoveries in the Antofagasta and Tocopilla regions, which lie intermediate between Taltal and Pichalo.[32]

The Taltal Pacific Littoral tradition sequence closes with the appearance of pottery in the upper midden levels at Cerro Colorado—which defines the Cerro Colorado III phase.[33]

Conanoxa: An Inland Adaptation. What was going on in the interior of the Atacama subarea at the same time that these Quiani and Pichalo "type sites" of the Pacific Littoral tradition were thriving on the shore? We know that late Andean Hunting-Collecting complexes, such as the Tambillo, Chíuchíu, and Ascotán were in existence in the uplands around the Salar de Atacama and along the oases of the upper Rio

Loa. But what of the interior of the coastal shelf? Certainly the only habitable places here would be the small valley oases, and it is in such a setting that we have the Conanoxa complex.

Conanoxa is in the Camarones Valley, which drains into the Pacific between Arica and Pichalo.[34] The archaeological sites are on old fluvial river terraces some 40 kilometers inland from the sea. These terraces are barren desert ground lying above the narrow valley bottom, which is in grasses and reeds, and which today is under modern cultivation. The old camps are small refuse areas with evidences of hearths, chipped-flint wastage, points, scrapers, drills, manos, and conical mortars or milling stones. The points are the small leaf shapes and stemmed types of Quiani II. Scrapers are of both end and side varieties. Fragments of coiled basketry, twined matting, hides, and netted textiles of vegetal fibres and guanaco-hair cord were also picked up in the refuse. A number of petroglyphs are also seen on large stone blocks or boulders near these sites. They may pertain to the Conanoxa complex, although later pottery horizon sites are also present on these terraces. From the nature of their trash it would seem that the Conanoxa complex peoples were hunters (guanaco, vizcacha), had some shellfish from the sea, and netted shrimp or camarones in the river. They must also have gathered wild plants and fruits from the river valley below the terraces.

Was Conanoxa a seasonal station, selected, perhaps, for plant gathering and camaron fishing by peoples who spent other parts of the year as Quiani or Pichalo shore dwellers? This, I think, is a good possibility. In our discussions of the Andean Hunting-Collecting tradition—especially with reference to Peru—we postulated such patterns of transhumance; and even after the establishment of the Pacific Littoral tradition in Preceramic Period V (4200–2500 B.C.), seasonal shifting between lomas camps and shore-edge villages is believed to have continued for a time in Peru. A similar situation may very well have obtained in the north Chilean deserts, where it could have continued later. In Peru, with good farmlands near many of the beach locations, the increasing importance of plant cultivation throughout Preceramic Periods V and VI would have worked for greater site stability on the shore; in Chile, where plant cultivation was not of importance until later, seasonal shifting from shore to interior oases may have continued longer. Consequently, it seems preferable to consider Conanoxa as a Pacific Littoral tradition manifestation rather than an Andean Hunting-Collecting one, even though it lacks the diagnostic fishing gear. Concerning cultural affiliation, we may note the only burial at Conanoxa, that of an infant. The child had been covered with a twined mat, and the mummified body was wrapped in bird skin and successive net and twined textile covers. A headdress had been fashioned of bird plumes, and a collar of shell beads and stones was around the neck. These elaborations are, of course, highly reminiscent of the Chinchorro burial complex. A Conanoxa radiocarbon date of 1790 B.C.[35] indicates a Quiani II or Preceramic Period VI chronological placement for the complex.

The Valles Transversales Subarea: Guanaqueros and Huentelauquén. Just south of Coquimbo,[36] on the Bay of Tongoy, is the archaeological site of Guanaqueros, or "Las Tacitas de Guanaqueros."[37] The immediate location is on the upper, or second, old marine terrace of the coast, some 12 to 15 meters above the present sea level. The site consists of an extensive shell midden, part of which was a cemetery area, but it takes the name "Las Tacitas" from the numerous circular pits or mortars that have been ground into the huge granite blocks that are partially buried in the surface of the terrace. These "tacas," or "tacitas," had been made by the aboriginal inhabitants presumably for the grinding of foodstuffs. Just what was ground or prepared in them is uncertain; it could have been plant or seed foods gathered from nearby valley bottoms, or, possibly, they were used for removing the shells from shellfish.[38] In any event, they are found not only here but at a number of other shell-midden locations along the Valles Transversales subarea coast, and they seem to be a standard feature of this subareal variant of the Pacific Littoral tradition. At Guanaqueros the individual mortars, or "tacitas," average about 14 centimeters in diameter and 9 centimeters in depth. They have more or less straight sides and are rounded at the bottom. Quite frequently many of them (6–12) will occur close together on the same large stone block. Their chronological and cultural association with the Guanaqueros shell-mound culture is secure, for some of the stone blocks with "tacitas" were found deep within the stratified refuse.

The Guanaqueros shell midden proved to be about 2 meters deep, and it contained numerous projectile points of chipped stone, including leaf shapes, triangular forms with straight bases, triangular forms with concave bases, and forms with broad tapered stems. Small end or thumbnail scrapers were also common, as were punches or perforators. The many manos and pebble hammers present probably had been used in connection with the "tacitas." Another Guanaqueros ground stone artifact is the "piedra horadada" or circular perforated "doughnut stone." In addition, some stone beads were recovered, and one cigar-shaped fishline sinker was spotted on the surface of the midden.

Bone fish harpoon points, bone barbs for composite harpoons of the sort used for hunting sea lions, and bone barbs for composite fishhooks are all Guanaqueros parallels to Quiani, as is, most significantly, the shell fishhook. The earlier phase of midden occupation appears to have been somewhat scattered in small, separated refuse deposits. The barbed harpoon and the shell fishhook are diagnostic of the phase, and these traits imply a correspondence to Quiani I and a Preceramic Period V dating.[39] The later phase refuse was deeper and more continuous, suggesting a larger population, a longer period of occupancy, or both.

A number of the burials in the cemetery were partially covered with colored pigments and had large, finely chipped knives in association. Such knives or blades were not found in the midden, and it is thought that they were solely of ceremonial function.[40] Other burials were without color pigments or grave goods of consequence. It has been suggested that the two types of burial correlate with the early and late phases of the midden occupation respectively.[41]

Other Guanaqueros-type sites have been explored at the mouth of the Rio Choapa where, in fact, the culture of the "tacitas" was first described.[42] Here, shell middens and the great stone blocks with the grinding pits are found among the sand dunes, and "piedras horadadas," or "doughnut stones," are associated. These latter average 5.5 centimeters in diameter, 2.5 centimeters in thickness, and are perforated with a centrally drilled biconcave or cylindrical hole. Originally flattish pebbles, they have been shaped by grinding. Their purpose is conjectural. They are not unlike perforated stones used by primitive societies in some parts of the world as digging-stick weights, and this may have been their function in the early coastal Chilean cultures in connection with digging for root plants. In general, the projectile points in the Rio Choapa midden sites are smallish and either stemmed or triangular and unstemmed. As such, they suggest a Preceramic Period VI horizon correlation.

It is also near the delta of the Rio Choapa that we have the puzzling Huentelauquén complex. The artifacts of the complex are found scattered over a series of salinas, or salt flats, between the village of Huentelauquén and the beach. This is at some little distance from the shell middens just described. Most of the artifacts in question have been recovered from the surface, although some were taken from shallow excavations. The most peculiar and characteristic ones are ground stone items (Fig. 4-8). These occur as smooth-edge disks, cog-edge disks, and quadrangular, triangular, and polygonal (as many as 12 sides) forms. They have been shaped from flattish pebbles or slabs of rock and range from 5 to 12 centimeters in diameter and from 2 to 3 centimeters in thickness. The larger surfaces are flat, concave, or convex. Some concavo-convex specimens are basinlike or cupiliform. A very few of the disks have central perforations, but these are quite distinct from the "doughnut stones" in that the total diameter of the disks is much greater and the central hole proportionately much smaller. This complex of geometric stones is as yet an isolate in Chilean archaeology, being known only from the Rio Choapa region.[43] It seems most probable that it is preceramic, and Gajardo Tobar,[44] who has studied the Huentelauquén materials, is inclined to date it earlier than the shell-mound culture of the nearby middens, although he makes clear that this is a very speculative placement. The other artifacts found with the geometric stones on the Salinas flats include a few crudely shaped ground stone axes or celts, some mano stones, a few "doughnut stones," and a number of chipped-stone projectile points. The stone axes are as anomalous in this Chilean coastal preceramic context as the geometric stones and offer little help in trying to relate Huentelauquén to other cultures.

Figure 4-8. Geometric stones from Huentelauqén. Respective diameters, from *left* to *right* are 15.0, 13.5, and 11.5 cm. Thicknesses from 5.5 to 6.0 cm. (Courtesy Grete Mostny and Museo Nacional de Historia Natural, Santiago, Chile.)

The manos are like those of the shell middens, but no milling stones, mortars, or "tacitas" are associated. The "doughnut stones" are the single most specific link to the shell-mound cultures; however, as these are surface finds, it is impossible to know whether they are true associations. This also applies to the projectile points, which, for the most part, are large leaf-shaped forms suggestive of a Preceramic Period V, or even earlier, date.

In searching for clues to the relationships of the Huentelauquén complex, one very surprising long-range comparison has turned up. Both Jorge Iribarren and Gajardo Tobar call attention to the similarity between some of the Huentelauquén geometric stones and the "cogged stones" of southern California.[45] Interestingly, the latter (see this work, Vol. I, p. 368) are found in non-agricultural, non-ceramic, coastal contexts that are believed to date somewhere in the range of 6000 to 3500 B.C. Eberhart, in commenting upon the Californian cogged stones, states: "...they are of such a nature that it is unlikely that they were invented more than once";[46] and Gajardo Tobar and Irribarren both feel that there is a historical connection between the Californian and Chilean occurrences. This is a possibility, but a direct contact at this early time level, over such a great distance and with no intervening traces along the coasts of Pacific America, is difficult to credit.

The Southern Subareas. The Pacific Littoral tradition is found in the Central Valley subarea. We know of Guanaqueros-like shell middens in the section between the Rio Petorca and the Rio Aconcagua. Like those farther north, these are all situated on the second, or higher, marine terrace of the coastline, some 12 or 15 meters above the ocean level.[47] At Sitio Alacranes I, near Las Ventanas, a "piedra tacita" was found half buried in a shell midden. Manos stones, "doughnut stones," and a number of flexed burials were also in the midden. Overlying the preceramic strata were pottery-bearing levels identified with the El Molle culture.[48] The Longotoma 1[49] site, on the Bahía de la Ligua, has no "tacitas"; but the midden here revealed pounding tools and manos, "doughnut stones," bone fish harpoons or spears, and leaf-shaped and triangular stone points intermixed with shells, bird bones, and fish bones. The physical type of the burials here was dolichocephalic, and this is consistent with observations on the human crania from similar early sites.[50]

Less information exists on the preceramic horizon farther south; however, it is clear that the Pacific Littoral tradition extends down through the Central Valley subarea to the vicinity of Concepción. One well-known site is Las Cenizas, which lies a few kilometers inland from Viña del Mar and Valparaíso. This is a sizable midden area with a great many bedrock and boulder mortars, called "tacitas." These tacitas are of various shapes and sizes, and in the immediate vicinity are the stones used in conjunction with them, flat-circular and oblong manos and cylindrical pestles. Perforated stones, or "horadadas," are also found in association with the "tacitas." The horadadas, manos, and chipped projectile points had been placed, in some cases, with burials.[51]

In addition to Las Cenizas, we know of scattered finds, such as those reported by Bird, that include composite sinker-fishhooks and stone bowls, occurring around or south of the Valparaíso-Santiago region;[52] and Berdichewsky has surveyed preceramic shell middens in the same stretch of the coast.[53] Ortiz Troncoso describes shell middens on the Río Reloca, in the Province of Maule, that show preceramic levels underlying superficial pottery deposits;[54] and, still farther south, Menghin, in his summary of the prehistory of the territory later occupied by the Araucanians, lists a preceramic shell-mound horizon with Ayampitín-like projectile points, "doughnut stones," manos, bone and shell artifacts, flexed burials, and a meso-to-dolichocranic physical type.[55]

It is less certain whether a comparable cultural horizon can be extended below Concepción and the Bío Bío into the different environment of the Araucanian subarea. Bird states that most of the pre-pottery midden sites in the Puerto Montt region and on the Island of Chiloé lack pressure-flaked points and display a chipped stone and shell tool technology that belongs to a Fuegian, rather than Pacific Littoral, tradition.[56]

Summary. The Pacific Littoral tradition was established along the Chilean coast at the beginning of Preceramic Period V, or at about 4200 B.C. This was more or less contemporaneous with the comparable and related developments on the Peruvian coast, and in both cases the evidence of the lithic and projectile point technology suggests that the cultural antecedents of the Pacific Littoral tradition are to be found in the earlier Andean Hunting-Collecting tradition. The new tradition is characterized by a marine subsistence adaptation, although this was supplemented in a minor way by seed gathering in some of the interior valleys.

Two major phases or periods can be distinguished in the Pacific Littoral tradition cultures in Atacama subarea. The earlier, featuring shell fishhooks and leaf-shaped projectile points, is estimated to have lasted until about 3000 B.C.

The later, which falls largely in Preceramic Period VI, is placed at 3000 to 500 B.C. and is distinguished by new fishhook forms and smaller projectile points. What is known as the Chinchorro burial complex probably falls in this second period. The individuals of the Chinchorro burials are of dolichocephalic type—as are almost all other human skeletons found in Pacific Littoral tradition sites—and this suggests that they are part of an ancient South American population stratum for which we also have evidences in the earlier cultural levels of the Peruvian sequences. Furthermore, as with some of the earlier Peruvian crania, the Pacific Littoral tradition peoples of Chile practiced fronto-occipital cranial deformation.

In the Valles Transversales subarea the greater moisture in the river valleys allowed for more dependence upon wild-plant foods and land hunting. This is seen in food-grinding implements, what are probably digging-stick weights ("doughnut stones"), and skin-dressing tools.

The Central Valley subarea has evidences of Pacific Littoral tradition cultures although here the pattern is attenuated, and the periodization into Preceramic V and VI is much less clear. For the Araucanian subarea still farther south there are only slight hints of the pattern. The preceramic cultures here, at least in the regions of Puerto Montt and Chiloé Island, appear to be of the quite distinct Fuegian tradition.

At some time during the latter part of Preceramic Period VI cotton and maize appeared on the Chilean coast; these plants were presumably brought into Chile from Peru. The art of pottery making came still later; again, the source of its introduction was probably Peru or the Peru-Bolivia area. With ceramics, we reach the "agricultural-pottery" threshold in Chilean coast prehistory at a date estimated at about 500 B.C.

Continuities of the Andean Hunting-Collecting Tradition

We have already made some references to these late Andean Hunting-Collecting phases in Chapter 2 (pp. 53–56; map, Fig. 2-1). They are known largely from their lithic industries; examples would be the Puripica and later Tambillo and Cebollar complexes of the Salar del

Huasco, the Salar de Soronal, the Salar de Atacama, Salar de San Martín, and the Lagunas Colorado and Hedionda regions of interior Chile and Bolivia. During these phases,[57] which apparently span the Preceramic V and VI periods, there was a shift from the larger willow-leaf points to smaller leaf-shaped triangular, and stemmed points (Fig. 4-9); stone mortars and pestles were in use; and rough stone masonry dwellings were constructed.

It will be recalled (pp. 55–56) that in the upper levels of the Intihuasi Cave—which is our

Figure 4-9. Generalized projectile-point form sequence for South Andes area. In this instance, it is based on a collection from the Chilean Salar del Huasco region; however, it also recapitulates the point sequence from the Intihuasi Cave as presented by A. R. Gonzalez (1960). (Redrawn from Núñez and Varela, 1966.)

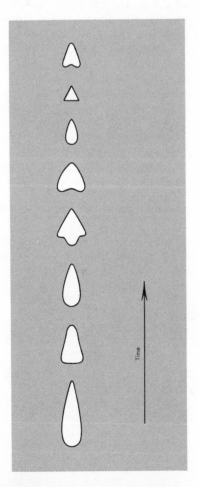

Time

primary datum for the Sierras Centrales—the Intihuasi II phase was dated to about 3000 B.C. and after, or to the Preceramic Period VI of our sequence. Intihuasi I (which followed it in time) was then placed at the pottery horizon—in this case at about A.D. 750. Intihuasi II shows a clear continuity out of the earlier III and a persistence of a hunting and plant-collecting economy.[58] The characteristic projectile point for the phase is a stemless triangular form with an incurved base; however, blunt-ended bone points, probably used for hunting birds or small game, are also typical. It is likely that most of the missiles were darts, and hooks of ground stone and bone for dart throwing-sticks were found in the cave. Chipped-stone scrapers were numerous and mostly of small —proportionately thick—end, side, and circular varieties. Sizable mammal bones were shaped into daggerlike implements, and smaller slivers of long bone fashioned as awls, punches, and needles. Bone tubes may have been used either as handles for implements or in shamanistic practices. Small ornaments were made of polished stone (double-ended or "fusiform" shaped pendants, beads), bits of cut mica, and shells. The animal bone scrap in the phase II levels, like that from the other levels of the cave, was largely from camelids (probably *Lama guanicoe* or guanaco) and deer (*Ozotoceros* sp. and *Hippocamelus* sp.), although the rhea (*Rhea* sp.) was also an important game source.[59] The plant or wild-seed aspects of the economy are reflected in the manos and milling stones, which were plentiful but little standardized in size and form.

It is not clear that Intihuasi I was a direct continuity out of Intihuasi II; however, even if an *in situ* development is not registered in the refuse of this particular cave, the ancestry of an Intihuasi II–type culture to an Intihuasi I–type must have taken place somewhere else in the South Andes. This is evident in the carryover of the modes of subsistence, with the same game animals, the same or similar implements for hunting and butchering them and for skin dressing, and the same or similar artifacts of other categories. The biggest change was in projectile-point size. The common Intihuasi I point measures 2.5 to 3.0 centimeters. It is triangulate, with convex sides and a markedly concave base and corner barbs. It seems highly likely that it was an arrow point and that by this time the bow and arrow had replaced the throwing-stick and dart. Manos and milling stones were similar to the earlier ones, although some few milling basins showed dressed edges. Bone awls and needles continued in use in skin working. Stone pendants and beads were the principal ornaments, and among the pendants the "fusiform," or elongated bi-pointed shape of Intihuasi II, is still present.

As we have noted, Intihuasi I is on the pottery horizon; however, there is no clear evidence that this was an agricultural phase. In fact, the pottery from the cave, which is of an extremely simple sort, could have come into the Sierras Centrales subarea from the Paraná-Pampean country to the east rather than from Andean South America. This could also have been the case with another Intihuasi I "neolithic" element, the polished stone ax. The Paraná-Pampean tradition was non-agricultural, so that these traits cannot in themselves be used to support the idea that plant cultivation had also arrived in Intihuasi I. Agriculture did eventually reach the Sierras Centrales from the northwest, for its presence is known from ethnohistoric records, and we will consider this later in the chapter; however there is no good evidence that Intihuasi I was agricultural, despite the estimated A.D. 750 date, and most of what we know about it suggests that it was not, at least in any very important economic way. It represents, instead, a very late phase of the Andean Hunting-Collecting tradition in a part of the South Andes that was marginal to, and late in receiving the influences from, the developing South Andean cultural tradition.

The situation in Ongamira Cave, another late Andean Hunting-Collecting tradition site in the Sierras Centrales, is similar to that at Intihuasi. The cave is located 300 kilometers northeast of Intihuasi in the highlands of Córdoba. Cave refuse of over 2 meters' depth allowed for the stratigraphic definition of four sequent phases. The two earlier phases (Ongamira IV and III) correspond most closely to Intihuasi II and the two later phases (Ongamira II and I) to Intihuasi I.[60] Blunt-ended bone projectile points belong to the earlier Ongamira levels, and these must have tipped throwing-stick darts, since stone throwing-stick hooks are associated with the same levels. Chipped-stone points and other flaked tools are

curiously absent, but otherwise the milling stones, manos, and other items are much the same as Intihuasi II. The later Ongamira levels had small triangular projectile points, with straight or concave bases, and a variety of small scrapers. Bola stones were an additional element of hunting gear found in Ongamira I. Both Ongamira II and I had pottery. In phase I (the latest) some of the sherds bore incised or basket-impressed markings, suggesting a relationship to the Paraná Valley. What appear to be either labrets or ear ornaments were also fashioned of pottery in this final Ongamira phase.

The South Andean Cultural Tradition: Early Ceramic Period

Diffusion was certainly one of the processes that sparked the agricultural South Andean tradition. In some places this diffusion may have been no more than a stimulus resulting from slight contact; in others it must have involved the implantation of ideas by direct and prolonged relationship. Such relationships might have involved the influx of new peoples into the South Andean area. The physical anthropological evidence from the Chilean coast could be interpreted to support such a hypothesis.[61] Pacific Littoral tradition Indians were dolichocephalic or mesocephalic, short, of slight build, and would appear to approach Imbelloni's Fuégid or Laguid physical types. By way of contrast, the later Indians of the area, as we shall see, were more rugged brachycephals of the Pueblo-Andid type (see Imbelloni's classification, this volume, pp. 9–11). Nevertheless, the archaeological story—whenever we have a reasonably complete record of the transition— is one of gradual cultural change, with the retention of many earlier traits in later contexts; and this is not altogether consistent with the idea of a major population replacement. Obviously, more data on the important period of transition are needed, not only from the Chilean coast but from the Argentinian interior, where we have virtually none.

The Atacama Subarea: Pichalo III, Faldas del Morro, San Pedro I. An "incipient cultivation" horizon, or at least a period characterized by the very first introduction of food plants, has been indicated in the Atacama subarea by the upper levels of the Quiani midden, where maize, cotton, and gourds were associated in the refuse with Quiani II–phase artifacts. Some burials of the Chinchorro complex were also accompanied by cotton textiles and, in one case, by a bag of quinoa.[62] But this agricultural, non-pottery horizon has not been dated to any but the widest chronological limits. The non-ceramic agricultural levels of Quiani were not, unfortunately, capped with an early pottery horizon; and there is every reason to believe that Chinchorro, as a burial complex, spans two or three millennia.

An early pottery horizon for the subarea is supported by a number of discoveries. The best of these is the Pichalo III–phase pottery. It has been described as consisting of:

> ...flaring-sided shallow bowls of a brownish, grit-tempered ware with red slip. The rims are two to four times as thick as the body sherds, the increase formed by a gracefully rounded bulge on the outer side, at the edge.[63]

A few polished black sherds were found in addition to the red ones, and the rest of the complex was made up of round-shouldered, flare-collared cooking pots of red or unslipped ware. The undecorated and relatively simple nature of all of this pottery makes comparisons difficult, but the red ware bowls are said to be closely similar to those of the Islay and San Benito styles of the Far South Coast of Peru. These are the earliest known ceramics in that neighboring subarea,[64] and Lanning dates them to the Peruvian Early Intermediate Period, or in the range of 200 B.C. to A.D. 600.[65] This estimation offers one rather general clue to the dating of Pichalo III. In these attempts at correlations it should further be pointed out that Pichalo III, together with Islay and San Benito, may be derived from the Southern Bolivan highlands rather than from farther north on the Peruvian coast; and, if so, the relationship would be to a monochrome tradition such as that represented in the pre-Tiahuanacoid Chullpa Pampa complex.

Pichalo III pottery occurs in an agricultural context, with maize, cotton, and calabashes, although it is unlikely that cultivation of plants was ever very important in the immediate setting. The continued importance of fishing in the economy of the phase is seen in harpoons, bone spears, stone linesinkers, and thorn or cactus spine fishhooks. Hooks were now also made of copper. True weaving is represented in woolen textiles, mostly plain, and fishlines were made of cotton. Potsherd spindle whorls had been used for the spinning of both of these fabrics. A Pichalo cemetery excavated by Bird apparently relates to the phase. The burials were in seated position, always accompanied by coiled baskets, and the graves were marked by wooden stakes.[66]

Another possible Early Ceramic Period complex for the Atacama subarea is the Faldas del Morro. The complex takes its name from a series of graves excavated by Uhle on the slope of the Morro Arica. These burials were similar in many respects to the Pichalo III burials, and they occasionally contained pottery. Both Núñez and Dauelsberg feel that this pottery is probably the same as the Pichalo III ware.[67] However the Faldas del Morro graves also had such items as gold plaques, copper spoons, and topu pins, so if an equation were to be effected it would suggest that the Pichalo III–Faldas del Morro horizon lasted up until the close of the Early Ceramic Period (A.D. 500).

There are other clues to what may be early pottery along the north Chilean coast. Berdichewsky suggests that the Copaca Red Polished ware of Tocopilla relates to Pichalo III–Faldas del Morro, as do the plain ceramics from the vicinity of Antofagasta and also the ceramics of the Cerro Colorado III phase of Taltal.[68] Burials from a site on the Rio Camarones, in the Conanoxa district, may also be a part of this horizon. The burials were accompanied by decorated baskets similar to those of Faldas del Morro and, also, with occasional plain pottery.[69]

The major Early Ceramic Period component for the Atacama interior is the San Pedro I phase of the Atacama Oasis. The Oasis is 2400 meters above sea level. It has sufficient water for maize, potatoes, quinoa, and fruit trees; and in ancient times it was a center for llama herders as well as farmers. As we have already seen, it was occupied in the remote past by early hunters; with the introduction of agriculture, it became one of the principal seats of settled populations.[70]

San Pedro I pottery, like the Pichalo III and Faldas del Morro styles, is a monochrome polished

a   b   c   d

Figure 4-10. Polished red ware of the San Pedro I phase. Height of *a*, about 16.5 cm. (Courtesy Gustavo Le Paige and Museo Arqueológico, Pedro de Atacama, Chile.)

red ware, but the vessel forms are quite different. San Pedro Polished Red (Fig. 4-10) features globular, flat-based jars with short, very narow necks. Some of these jars have tiny handles or perforated nodes attached to the sides, and some have low-relief modeled faces (probably human) on the neck. There are also large unslipped urns that have similar modeled faces. Some of the polished red ware is decorated with simple incised-line designs; and other minority types for the complex include San Pedro Polished Black and a black-on-red type. It is of chronological importance, however, that San Pedro Polished Black has

only its beginnings in San Pedro I, and is essentially a later type (Fig. 4-11). Most of the San Pedro I traits are known from grave lots, and these include, besides the pottery, winged or flanged labrets, polished stone axes, clay pipes, copper axes, rings, bracelets, gold plaquelike adornos, and

Figure 4-11. San Pedro II black ware vessels. (Courtesy Gustavo Le Paige and Museo Arqueológico, San Pedro de Atacama, Chile.)

wooden artifacts such as snuff tablets. The change from San Pedro I to II is gradual and accretive, with metalwork and wooden snuff tablets increasing in frequency along with the increase in polished black pottery and with the first appearances of pottery keros. This takes us right up to, and into, the appearance of Tiahuanaco horizon elements that mark the beginning of the Middle Ceramic Period. The final centuries of San Pedro I—or the transition from San Pedro I to II, whichever way it is designated—are believed to date at about A.D. 500–700,[71] and this is confirmed by the presence of Ciénega II and Condorhuasi trade pottery from the Valliserrana.

To sum up, the red wares of the Early Ceramic Period of the Atacama subarea are similar to each other and may be related within a common tradition. This tradition could have spread southward from the Peruvian Far South Coast, via the Islay and San Benito phases, or it could have come more directly from the Southern Bolivian highlands, via the Chullpa Pampa complex. A third possibility would be that two ceramic traditions are involved, one Peruvian coastal, which eventuated in Pichalo III–Faldas del Morro, and the other Bolivian highland, which gave rise to San Pedro I. The context in which this Early Ceramic Period pottery appears is an agricultural one—combining agriculture with fishing along the coast and agriculture with herding in the Atacama Oasis. We have evidence for an elaboration of the Early Ceramic Period cultures, seen in the addition of pottery traits, wood carving, and hammered copper and goldwork. This elaboration provides a transition to the Middle Ceramic Period, which sees the further addition of Tiahuanacoid stylistic elements.

The Valles Transversales Subarea: El Molle. The earliest pottery in the Valles Transversales of Chile is that of the El Molle culture. El Molle sites, largely cemeteries, are described in the Elquí and Hurtado Valleys;[72] however, El Molle-style pottery also has been found as far north as the Copiapó and south to the Rio Choapa and beyond. Direct radiocarbon dates are lacking, but from comparisons with the Valliserrana of Argentina an approximate date at the beginning of the Christian era is suggested for El Molle I.

The pottery of El Molle I is monochrome—gray, brown, black, or red—and sometimes the surfaces are burnished. There is also a limited amount of simple incised decoration. Vessels are small flat-bottomed jars, beakers, or bowls. Single vertical handles were occasionally used on beakers. Other characteristic El Molle artifacts are shaped and polished labrets of opal, jasper, and onyx (Fig. 4-12). Some of these are short and discoidal, others long and bottle-shaped; but both types have flared projections, or "wings," at one end which presumably would have been worn inside the mouth. Stone pipes are also an El Molle trait (Fig. 4-12). These are distinctive inverted T-shaped, or "monitor," pipes, with the bowl of the pipe centrally located on an equal-arm base. While the

Figure 4-12. El Molle stone pipes (*top*) and stone lip plugs, or tembetás (*bottom*). Length of pipe at top, about 25 cm.; other pipes to scale. Length of longest lip plug, about 8.5 cm.; other lip plugs to this scale. (Courtesy Jorge Iribarren Charlín.)

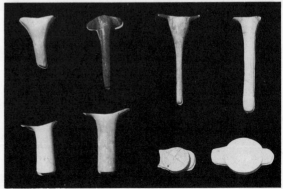

Figure 4-13. El Molle incised, engraved, and plain pottery. *a, d, e:* Incised. *b:* Engraved. *c:* Plain black. Diameter of *a*, about 11.5 cm. (Courtesy Jorge Iribarren Charlín.)

Figure 4-14. *Above:* El Molle painted styles. *Left:* Red-on-cream. *Right:* Negative-painted. Height of *left*, about 18 cm. (Courtesy Jorge Iribarren Charlín.)

pipes are found only in El Molle I, the lip plugs, or "tembetás," are in both phases; and copper ear pendants, bracelets, and rings are found in the graves of both phases.

El Molle II shows a trend toward elaboration. There is more pottery, and much of it is decorated. Incised-line designs of geometric and rectilinear layout were filled with fine-line incised hachure (Fig. 4-13). Such designs were often executed on polished black surfaces with white pigment rubbed into the incisions after firing. Similar rectilinear figures were also done in red-on-white painting (Fig. 4-14, *left*). The phase II vessel forms include double-spout jars with stirrup handles, stirrup-spout jars, and effigy forms (Fig. 4-15). One of the last—perhaps a representation of a llama—bears a negative-painted or resist-dye design (Fig. 4-14, *right*). In addition to the changes in pottery, new metal forms, including

Figure 4-15. *Below:* El Molle stirrup-spout (polished black) and effigy (red painted) vessels. Height of *left*, about 20 cm. (Courtesy Jorge Iribarren Charlín.)

Figure 4-16. El Molle metal objects. *Top row:* Tweezers and bracelets of copper. *Bottom row:* Copper pin, gold repoussé plaque, and copper T-shaped ax. (Courtesy Jorge Iribarren Charlín.)

gold and gold alloy plaques with repoussé decorations, were also put in the El Molle II graves (Fig. 4-16).

El Molle is judged to have had an agricultural economy—an estimate made largely on the basis of its chronological position and affiliations with other Early Ceramic Period cultures; however site location, in interior fertile valleys, supports this interpretation. Bedrock mortars, or "tacitas," are present at some sites, together with cylindrical pestles, shallow milling stones, and small manos.[73] These could have been used in the preparation of agricultural foods although, of course, we have already seen similar artifacts as a part of the earlier and non-agricultural Pacific Littoral tradition of the same regions. Hunting must also have been of some importance. Iribarren reports small and medium-sized triangular points, knives, and scrapers from the Elquí Valley.[74] Some marine dependence is also indicated by the presence of El Molle sherds in shell middens along the shore.

El Molle pottery relates to the early Atacama wares only in the way of general simplicity. More specific relationships are seen with the grey-black, incised wares of the Ciénega I phase of the Argentine Valliserrana subarea. These ties to the east are further reinforced in El Molle II times by the occurrence of vessels with designs similar to those of Condorhuasi Polychrome.[75] El Molle II also shares several rather complex features with the pre-Tiahuanacoid pottery styles of the Peruvian coast, such as the spout-with-bridge-handle, the stirrup-spout, and negative or resist-dye painting.[76] For these, it is difficult not to agree with Gonzalez that some coastwise contact (which bypassed, or has not been found in, the Atacama subarea) must have taken place between Peru and the Valles Transversales of Chile.[77]

The Valliserrana Subarea: Tafí, Ciénega, Condorhuasi. The earliest pottery of the Valliserrana subarea is the Tafí I complex of the Tafí Valley in Tucumán Province. The Tafí site proper has long been known in Argentine archaeology, and the pottery collections obtained there in earlier explorations appear to be mixed.[78] They include Incaic, Santa María, and other late types together with specimens that probably belong to the Tafí I complex.[79] More recent excavations, however, have isolated a monochrome pottery complex of red, black, and gray wares.[80] This complex is probably associated with some of the stone structures described from earlier explorations, and it has been dated by radiocarbon to a time range of 335 B.C. to A.D. 81.[81] A. R. Gonzalez is of the opinion that Tafí I pottery is representative of a widespread early tradition whose derivations lie in Southern Bolivia in the Cultura de los Túmulos and Chullpa Pampa complexes.[82] New traits that accompany this pottery in the Valliserrana are: an agricultural complex of the potato, quinoa, and, perhaps, maize; llama herding; mounds for burials or as platforms for structures; the urn burial of children; copper ornaments; and a settlement pattern of small scattered dwelling units each composed of a cluster of houses around a little patio. In brief, Tafí I is believed to mark the "agricultural threshold" and the inception of the South Andean tradition in northwest Argentina. Just how this complex was diffused or brought to the Valliserrana remains speculative, although it could have moved from Southern Bolivia across the Argentine Puna. If so, the same stream of influences could have spread from Bolivia to the Chilean Atacama at about the same time to result in the San Pedro I complex and, perhaps, in Pichalo III–Las Faldas.

The succeeding culture of the Valliserrana is the Ciénega. The Ciénega zone is in the Hualfín Valley in Catamarca, some little distance to the west of Tafí; however, a Ciénega culture—or at least a Ciénega pottery complex—is more widespread, being reported from the southern Puna subarea, from Salta, and from La Rioja and San Juan. In the latter province it is associated with the Calingasta culture and is dated by radiocarbon to about A.D. 400.[83] Ciénega pottery is most characteristically known from a gray-black incised or engraved type (Fig. 4-17). Gonzalez believes that its origins may also lie in Southern Bolivia but that it was spread to northwestern Argentina a little later than the Tafí complex.[84] As a pottery style, the incised gray-black ware has been known for a long time and was formerly lumped together with the Aguada styles into the "Barreales Culture."[85] Bennett, Bleiler, and Sommer recognized it as the type "Huilliche Monochrome"; however, this type grouped both the Ciénega I and II gray-black incised wares.[86] Gonzalez has separated these into a Ciénega I phase, in which the incised (or engraved?) decorations are all severely geometric and rectilinear, and a later Ciénega II phase in which some of these designs incorporate the feline motif.[87] These feline designs, or "Draconian" motifs, foreshadow a host of new influences that became predominant in the Aguada culture as it developed from the antecedent Ciénega; this development, however, moves us forward into the Middle Ceramic Period. To return to the Ciénega culture, other ceramics, found in both phases, include a red-on-buff type and a white-slipped type with black decorations. In all of these the decorations are simple and geometric. Both the red-on-buff and the gray-black incised types—and a variety of vessel forms—include burial urns as well as smaller bowls and jars. These urns were used for child burial, as in the Tafí culture, while adults were buried directly in cylindrical pit graves.

Ciénega stone carving was well developed, at least on the scale of modest manufactures such as anthropomorphic and zoomorphic mortars, soapstone vessels, masks, and polished stone axes. In addition, the Ciénegans made bola stones with noded or "grenaded" surfaces. These bola stones must have been used for guanaco hunting, and the further presence of camelid bones in the refuse and numerous small chipped stone projectile points and knives reflects an interest in this activity. Camelid bones, of course, must have also resulted from the butchering of the domesticated llamas for food and hides. Ciénega metalwork is mostly ornamental—copper bells, bracelets, rings; however, T-shaped axes and needles were also made of this metal. A few gold ornaments are also found, apparently pertaining to the phase.

Ciénega, fortunately, is one of the few Early Ceramic Period cultures for which we have settlement and architectural information. This comes from the site of Alamito, near Andalgalá, about halfway between the Hualfín and Tafí Valleys.[88] The Alamito dwelling units are scattered about, at some distance from each other, over a large area. From the surface they appear as oval "depressions"; however, upon excavation these "depressions" are revealed to be the former courtyards of

Figure 4-17. Ciénega pottery. The ware is polished black and decorated with incision or incision and punctation. (The whiteness of the decoration results from coloring for photography, not from aboriginal pigments.) Vessel at *left* is a burial urn for children. The other specimens are somewhat smaller. (Courtesy La Plata Museum, Argentina.)

little house circles. A typical dwelling unit measures about 40 to 50 meters in extent. Houses are arranged around three sides of the courtyard (see Fig. 4-18). On the fourth side—usually the western—is a refuse pile. The individual houses are of an elongated U-shape. The walls of these had been built up of earth reinforced by columns of stones. Floors were of packed earth, and roofs, which had been supported by the stone columns, must have been made of wood and grass or other perishable materials. The houses are about 20 meters long and less than half that in width. A narrow passage doorway opened from one end onto the courtyard. At the opposite end there may also have been a

Figure 4-18. Plan of dwelling site unit, Alamito, Ciénega culture. *1:* Refuse dump. *2:* Sustaining wall for dump. *3:* Stone platform structures. *4:* Passage between stone platform structures. *5:* Small earth mound. *6:* Central patio. *7:* Rectangular "houses," probably kitchens. *8:* U-shaped houses. *9:* Circles of stones at opposite ends of houses. *10:* Areas in which burials often found. *11, 12:* Retaining walls of earthen embankment. (After Gonzalez and Núñez Regueiro, 1958–59.)

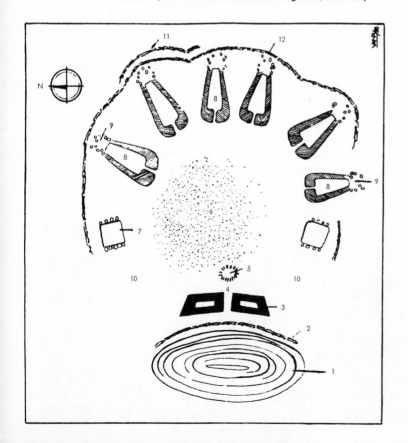

doorway, although this is less certain. Frequently at this end, however, there is a circle or semicircle of stones. In addition to the U-shaped houses there are also the remains of two smaller, rectangular structures near the west end of the courtyard. These buildings had the stone column supports but lacked the clay walls and may originally have been open-sided. Hearths, which had been lacking in the houses, were found in the buildings, and these, together with numerous milling and mano stones, imply kitchen functions. Between the courtyard and the west side refuse pile to which we have referred are two rectangular platforms. These are composed of earth and rock fill retained in stone slab and cyclopean masonry walls. Such platforms vary in size from 3 to 12 meters square and from 0.5 to 1.5 meters high. They may have had some ritual or sacred significance to the people who lived within a dwelling unit. In two instances sculptured stone figures were in the narrow passageway between the two platforms, and human bones have also been found in some of the platforms, although their primary function does not seem to have been for burial. Instead, burials were most often found in the floors of the houses themselves or in the open spaces between "ceremonial platforms" and the "kitchen" structures. Such burials were usually flexed, with the body placed on its side, and accompanied by pottery, ornaments, and utensils.

One of the most interesting Ciénega specimens comes from Alamito and is, in fact, a stone sculpture (Fig. 4-19) found in a dwelling unit passageway between the two "ceremonial platforms." It is a columnar statue of a female figure, almost a meter high. The peculiarly stiff style of the carving, in a bas-relief on the full round surface of the column, is fully at home on the Bolivian altiplano, and the figure is quite reminiscent of much of the sculpture that usually goes by the name of "Decadent Tiahuanaco."[89] This supposedly "Decadent Tiahuanaco" style is somewhat simpler than the principal Tiahuanaco monoliths of the Gateway of the Sun sculptural style seen at that site (pp. 158–159); but the Titicaca Basin–Tiahuanaco stylistic sequence in sculptures has never been fully and convincingly developed, and many of the so-called Decadent pieces may pertain to the Qalasasaya (Pucara-related) and Qeya

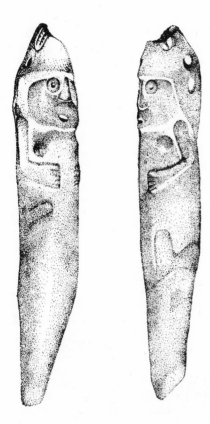

Figure 4-19. Two views of stone statue from an Alamito dwelling unit, Ciénega-Condorhuasi culture. The sculpture is 98 cm. high. (After Gonzalez and Núñez Regueiro, 1958–59.)

rather, a ceramic stylistic influence that is found mainly in Ciénega II grave pottery. It may signify the presence of foreign persons in Ciénega society who were individuals of special rank and prestige; or—and I think it more likely—the Condorhuasi grave pottery may be the hallmark of a rising local aristocracy who were becoming familiar, through trade contacts, with the more advanced and hierarchically structured societies of the Titicaca Basin.

Condorhuasi pottery comes from cemeteries in the Hualifín Valley, from Alamito, and from many other places in the Valliserrana subarea. The diagnostic types are white (or cream)-and-red, white-on-red, and red-white-black polychromes. Gonzalez believes the bi-color styles are a bit earlier than the polychrome,[90] and this, of course, would conform to the general sequence direction of Titacaca Basin styles where the earlier bi-color, red-and-cream Chiripa pottery is followed by later polychromes. Designs on Condorhuasi vessels are bold geometric step-forms that are similar not only to those of Tiahuanaco but also to other Titicaca Basin styles. The most distinctive vessel forms are tall beakers and modeled animal or human effigies (Fig. 4-20).

The Condorhuasi types are associated in the same graves with the incised gray ware of the Ciénega tradition. These graves are in the same cemeteries alongside graves that contain only Ciénega-style vessels. Burial customs are the same as those for the pure Ciénega graves, other artifacts are identical, and, presumably, dwellings and settlement patterns remain as they were.

There are four radiocarbon dates for Condorhuasi at Alamito, and these range from A.D. 300 to 399.[91] The dates help us to establish a time horizon for Ciénega II and El Molle II, where Condorhuasi influence is also found in strength. Such a dating would be contemporaneous with the Titicaca Basin Early Intermediate Period or the pre-Tiahuanaco horizon Qeya phase.

Other Argentinian Subareas. Evidences of an Early Ceramic Period occupation are still rather few for the Puna and the Quebrada de Humahuaca subareas. Gray-black, Ciénega-like pottery is said to be present at Laguna Blanca[92] and Tebenquiche[93] in the southern Puna; and in

phases (p. 154). Accordingly, we cannot safely project a Tiahuanaco "Expansionist" or Horizon dating to Alamito and the Ciénega culture on the basis of the statue in question. Moreover, as we shall see, the radiocarbon dates available for Alamito are too early for the post–A.D. 600 dating usually assigned to the Tiahuanaco horizon. Now this caution should not be taken to mean that Tiahuanacoid—or, at least, South Titicaca Basin—influences were not present in the Ciénega culture. On the contrary, they are registered very clearly, and this brings us to a consideration of what has been called the Condorhuasi complex.

The position taken here is that the Condorhuasi complex, as it is found in the Valliserrana subarea, is not a full culture or a phase. It is,

been diffused from Bolivia to the Valliserrana.[96] The Candelaria culture of the subarea[97] may cover a considerable span of time;[98] but there is general agreement that it has relatively early beginnings. Its early chronological position was suggested many years ago when Ambrosetti found Candelaria pottery stratigraphically beneath Santa María ("Diaguita") wares at the Pampa Grande site in southern Salta—a location near the border of the Selvas Occidentales and Valliserrana subareas.[99] This chronological position is confirmed by the close similarities between Candelaria incised pottery (Fig. 4-21) and the incised and hatched-zone Ciénega ceramics. The Candelaria ceramic assem-

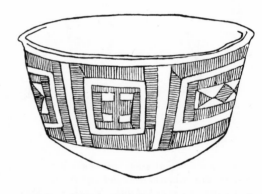

Figure 4-21. Incised pottery from Candelaria region. Assigned to Candelaria I phase and reminiscent of Ciénega incised style. (Redrawn from Rydén, 1936.)

Figure 4-20. Condorhuasi Polychrome. From the Belén region, Catamarca Province, Argentina. These vessels have a red slip and black decoration outlined with white. *Bottom, left* and *right* are side and front views of the same effigy vessel. Height of this piece, 30.5 cm. Note the double hole in lower lip of the woman, indicating use of double lip plugs. (Courtesy Catamarca Museum, Argentina.)

the Quebrada de Humahuaca, Lafon speaks of the Ciénega similarities of his earliest Quebrada complex[94] and reports a gray-black plain pottery from the Tilcara region.[95]

The Selvas Occidentales is the subarea through which a Ciénega-like kind of pottery may have

blages differ from those of Ciénega, however, in the presence of distinctive and numerous burial urns. These urns are usually decorated below the rim with heavy, broad incised-line patterns of zigzags or chevrons and are often ornamented with incised and low relief modeled human faces (Fig. 4-22). Pottery pipes of elbow form are also a distinctive Candelaria trait. Other frequent Candelaria artifacts are three-quarter grooved stone axes, stone adzes, pestles, mortars, milling stones, and flat manos. Metals, in contrast, were extremely scarce.

The Candelaria village sites are sizable areas and are usually covered with sherds and stone implements. The economy must have been sig-

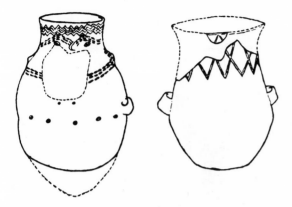

Figure 4-22. Candelaria burial urns with incised or relief decoration. (Redrawn from Rydén, 1936.)

nificantly agricultural; the various mealing devices suggest it, and scoring marks made with corncobs are a standard treatment on some of the plain pottery vessels. Rainfall in the subarea is seasonally heavy, and cultivation would have been quite feasible without the benefit of irrigation—for which there is no evidence.

The numerous Candelaria burial urns referred to above were used for the interment not only of children but also of adults. This custom suggests, in a very general way, the tropical forest and the country to the east. Gonzalez, in speculating on the origins of Candelaria pottery, says that it is reminiscent of the Paraná River cultures;[100] however there are no close resemblances between Candelaria styles and either the Guaraní burial urns or the modeled and incised-punctated wares of the Paraná.[101]

In the Chaco-Santiagueño subarea of the eastern lowlands the Early Ceramic Period is represented by a pottery type known as Bislín Incised—a gray-black ware with incised decorations much like those of the Ciénega culture. It is found together with a "Crude Urn" type at a number of sites along both the Rio Dulce and the Rio Salado.[102] This chronological assignment is based on crossties to other subareas and has not been backed up by stratigraphic excavation. The site name of Las Mercedes (Fig. 4-23) has been assigned to this presumably early, incised pottery-crude urn phase. It is a name originally given to one of three varieties or divisions of Chaco-

Santiagueño culture by Henri Reichlen—the other two divisions being called Sunchituyoj and Averías.[103] Although Reichlen did not specify these as three sequent phases, Gonzalez has since so arranged them, with Las Mercedes in the Early Ceramic Period and Sunchituyoj and Averías being placed, respectively, into the Middle and Late periods.[104]

The Southern Bolivian Subarea. We have been referring to the Chullpa Pampa culture and to the Cultura de los Túmulos as possible sources for the early ceramics of the subareas farther south. Chullpa Pampa is a habitation area—and probably a cemetery—some 30 kilometers to the west of the modern city of Cochabamba.[105] The pottery of Chullpa Pampa includes a gray ware that occurs in flat-bottomed beaker forms that are sometimes provided with plain or effigy handles. Some few pieces of this gray ware are incised. A second Chullpa Pampa type is a heavy-walled red or orange pottery, frequently red-slipped. This was made in large, deep bowl and shallower bowl forms. It is possible that the large bowls of this second ware group were used as urns for burial, although the evidence for this is not clear. Grooved stone axes and stone mortars and grinders are associated with the Chullpa Pampa complex. The origins of Chullpa

Figure 4-23. Las Mercedes phase incised and punctated vessels. One bowl fragment is shown inside another. Height of lower vessel, 8 cm. (Courtesy D. E. Ibarra Grasso; see also Ibarra Grasso, 1967.)

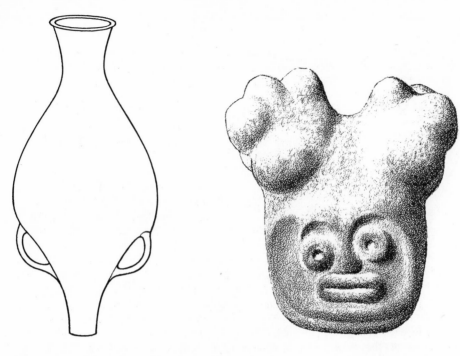

Figure 4-24. *Above, left:* Characteristic handled jar form purported to be associated with the Cultura de los Túmulos. (Redrawn from Ibarra Grasso, 1958–59.)

Figure 4-25. *Above, right:* Stone carving in the Cliza style. Believed to be associated with the Cultura de los Túmulos of Southern Bolivia. (Redrawn from Ibarra Grasso, 1958–59.)

Pampa are hazy, but D. E. Ibarra Grasso is almost certainly correct in assuming it to be of relatively early date and to be pre-Tiahuanaco.[106] I think it highly likely that it derives in part from the early pottery horizon of the South Titicaca Basin, possibly from a complex like Early Chiripa; however, Chullpa Pampa is probaly substantially later than Early Chiripa.[107] It is also possible that its burial urns—if, indeed, the large red or orange jars *are* burial urns—link it to Amazonian drainage cultures.[108] Whatever its beginnings, Ibarra Grasso groups Chullpa Pampa with a much more all-embracing concept: that of the Southern Bolivian "Cultura de los Túmulos" ("Culture of the Mounds"), or, as he sometimes refers to it, the "Cultura Megalítica" ("Megalithic Culture").[109]

This Cultura de los Túmulos is found throughout the Southern Bolivian subarea. The name derives from the rather compactly mounded dwelling (and burial) sites that characterize it. These vary from small, low hillocks to large (200 m. diameter) and high (6–8 m.) tumuli. These mounds show diverse strata of occupation and construction—clay floors, hearths, adobes, and stone foundations. Ibarra Grasso's definition of the Cultura de los Túmulos subsumes a gray incised pottery, other pottery styles with relief-modeled human faces, large amphora-like jars with vertical handles near a pointed base (Fig. 4-24), and true burial urns (in which adults were buried). Ground and polished stone traits are pipes, т-shaped axes with holes drilled in the base, socketed mace heads, finely carved stone basins, and large and small stone sculptures (Fig. 4-25). The stone sculptures are in the style that is clearly reminiscent of what has been called "Tiahuanacoid" but which, as we have indicated in our discussion of the Alamito sculpture from the Valliserrana, could well be earlier. It is from these sculptures that the term "Cultura Megalítica" derives. Copper and gold ornaments are also associated with some of the Cultura de los Túmulos phases. Further distributional and chronological studies are in order, but from the data at hand it would appear that the Cultura de los Túmulos horizon is one that could easily be ancestral to the Early Ceramic Period cultures that we have been describing in the

Valliserrana, the Selvas Occidentales, and else-where.

The Cultura de los Túmulos horizon was fol-lowed by one of bi-color and polychrome painted pottery which Ibarra Grasso divides into several regional cultures. These include Yampará I, Sauces, and Tupuraya. They are all dated in the range of A.D. 200 to 400, at least for their begin-nings. If this dating is correct it would mean that these painted pottery phases are contemporaneous with the Qeya phase of the South Titicaca Basin, that they are clearly prior to the Tiahuanaco expansive horizon that followed A.D. 600, and that they are thus in a chronological position to have influenced the later cultures of the Early Ceramic Period farther south. Significantly, some of these pottery styles are painted with bold black geo-metric designs outlined in white on a red ground color and with stepped design elements that are highly similar to those of the Argentinian Con-dorhuasi style.[110]

Summary Comment. The position taken here has been that the South Andean cul-tural tradition, with pottery and farming, devel-oped as the result of contacts with the Peru-Bolivian and Amazonian areas. Some of this early contact may have gone along the coast from southern Peru to northern Chile, although the more likely possibility is that the principal course of diffusion was from the Titicaca Basin through the Southern Bolivian subarea into the Chilean Atacama and the northwest Argentine subareas. It is believed that the culture, or cultural horizon, known as the Cultura de los Túmulos was the major vehicle for the transmission of these influ-ences to the south. This Cultura de los Túmulos is, admittedly, vaguely defined, and culture phases that have been grouped together under this gen-eral rubric were undoubtedly regionally diverse. It is quite likely that some of them, especially those to the east, were in contact with Amazonian cul-tures and that their Amazonian complexion, as seen in such traits as burial urns and smoking pipes, was so derived. This synthesis of Andean and Amazonian elements quite probably took place in the Southern Bolivian subarea. These dif-fusions from Southern Bolivia to the south began in the first millennium B.C., and by 500 B.C., or a few centuries thereafter, the principal subareas of

the South Andes had been profoundly affected by them and the South Andean cultural tradition had come into being, replacing the Andean Hunting-Collecting tradition in the highlands and the Pacific Littoral tradition on the coast.

The further position taken here is that at some time before A.D. 600 additional diffusions from the Bolivian highlands, by way of the Southern Bolivian subarea, effected a notable enrichment of the South Andean cultures. This is revealed espe-cially in the influences associated with the Con-dorhuasi complex as these are seen in the Valliser-rana and Valles Transversales subareas. Other influences from the north may also have come into the Valles Transversales subarea at about the same time, probably moving along the coast from south-ern Peru. Finally, all of these influences were climaxed by the irradiations of the Tiahuanaco horizon, which marks the beginning of the Middle Ceramic Period.

The South Andean Cultural Tradition: Middle and Late Ceramic Periods

Southern Bolivia and the Problem of Tiahuanaco Horizon Influences. A necessary preface to any discussion of the Tiahuanaco horizon influence in the South Andes is a con-sideration of the Tiahuanaco and South Titicaca Basin sequence. In Chapter 3 (pp. 130, 154, and Fig. 3-8) we followed a sequence that began with the Early and Late Chiripa ceramics, styles which, as I have just indicated, could have been at least in part ancestral to the Chullpa Pampa–Cultura de los Túmulos horizon pottery of Southern Bolivia. These were followed by the Early Inter-mediate Period Qalasasaya style, which relates closely to Pucará of the North Titicaca Basin, and to the Qeya style which is, in effect, Bennett's old "Early Tiahuanaco" phase.[111] Tiahuanaco is be-lieved to have become a great center during the Qeya phase. Qeya was followed by the Tiahuanaco phase proper, which marks the beginning of the Middle Horizon for the South Titicaca subarea— at a date estimated at A.D. 600. The ceramic con-tent of the Tiahuanaco phase proper still awaits proper definition, but it would presumably include most of what Bennett called "Classic Tiahuanaco." According to Bennett, the "Classic" was followed

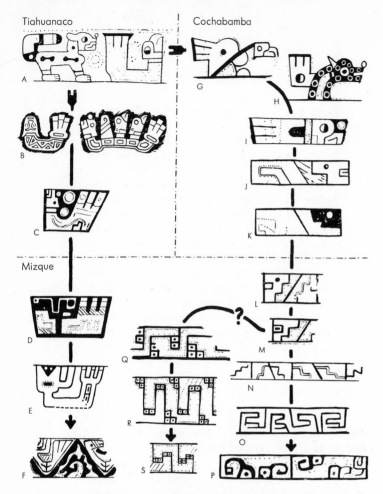

Tiahuanaco   Cochabamba

Mizque

Figure 4-26. Schematic diagram of design motif evolution in Tiahuanaco (Tiahuanacu) and Tiahuanacoid styles. *Top, left:* "Classic" Tiahuanaco motifs of Tiahuanaco proper. *Top, right:* "Derived" Tiahuanaco motifs of Cochabamba region. *Bottom:* "Derived" Tiahuanaco motifs of Mizque region; these are believed to have been derived from Tiahuanaco proper and from Cochabamba. (After Rydén, 1956.)

by a "Decadent" style that was maintained throughout the latter part of the Middle Horizon and that was the prototype of such Late Intermediate Period styles as the Wancani.[112]

There was another Tiahuanaco style, however, that Bennett defined and that is more pertinent to our concerns with the Southern Bolivian subarea of the South Andes. This was the "Derived Tiahuanaco" style (Fig. 4-26). Neither fully "Classic" nor matching the "Decadent," it was thought by Bennett to be chronologically intermediate between the two and to have arisen in southern Bolivia as a derivation of "Classic Tiahuanaco" influences.[113] It is well represented at Arani, Tupuraya, and Cayhuasi;[114] and it is found still farther east and

south in the Mizque, where Bennett referred to it as "Mizque-Tiahuanaco."[115] Ibarra Grasso differs from Bennett and sees "Derived Tiahuanaco" as *pre-* rather than *post-*"Classic Tiahuanaco."[116] I favor his interpretation here and so place such "Derived" styles as Yampará I (Fig. 4-27), Sauces, and Tupuraya as earlier than the Tiahuanaco Horizon and more or less contemporaneous with Qeya.

This does not mean that the Southern Bolivian subarea was not affected by Tiahuanaco horizon stylistic influences. According to Ibarra Grasso, the Tiahuanaco horizon, or "Expansionist Tiahuanaco," subsequently influenced the earlier painted pottery styles of Southern Bolivia, so that a Yampará II phase of the Cochabamba and Mizque Valley regions shows the true horizon affiliation.[117] This would presumably fall on a level with Bennett's Arani II, in contrast with the earlier Arani I, which would be pre-Tiahuanaco.[118] "Expan-

Figure 4-27. Southern Bolivian pottery styles. *a*: Yampará I (black designs, outlined in white, on a red ground). The others are all Late Period styles (including *e*: Huruquilla) painted, variously, red-black-white, red-black, or black-white. (After Ibarra Grasso, 1953.)

sionist Tiahuanaco" pottery is also found in Oruro and Potosí,[119] and it was apparently by this route that Tiahuanaco horizon influences entered the Atacama subarea oases of northern Chile, where they define the beginning of the Middle Ceramic Period as we shall see below.

After the Tiahuanaco horizon influences—which are strongest in Cochabamba, Oruro, and Potosí but much less manifest in Chuquisaca and Tarija—a number of local ceramic styles can be distinguished for the Late Period in Southern Bolivia. These include the Huruquilla (Fig. 4-27), Yuna, Chaqui, and others.[120] They feature red-and-black or red-black-white painting and, in general, can be related to the Titicaca Basin styles, for example, Colla and Wancani (p. 172). The cultures represented by these styles were farming-herding complexes. The peoples of these cultures were, without much doubt, the Chicha, Lipe, and others who were incorporated into the Inca State in the fifteenth century.

The Atacama: Tiahuanacoid and Later Styles. In the interior oases of the Atacama subarea, at San Pedro de Atacama and along the upper Rio Loa, we have observed (p. 216) a cultural continuity in the ceramics and other grave artifacts of the San Pedro culture that carried up from San Pedro I into San Pedro II (Fig. 4-28). With this transition we saw undeniable Tiahuanaco horizon traits. The most prominent of these were the polychrome keros (Fig. 4-29) or beakers painted in red, black, white, and orange. These were accompanied by carved wooden tablets (Fig. 4-30)—

a   b

c   d

Figure 4-28. *Above:* Incised and punctated ware of the San Pedro II phase. Height of *d*, about 11 cm. (Courtesy Gustavo Le Paige and Museo Arqueológico, San Pedro de Atacama, Chile.)

Figure 4-29. *Below:* Tiahuanaco-like pottery associated with San Pedro II phase, San Pedro de Atacama, Chile. Height of vessel at *left*, 12.5 cm. (Courtesy Gustavo Le Paige and Museo Arqueológico, San Pedro de Atacama, Chile.)

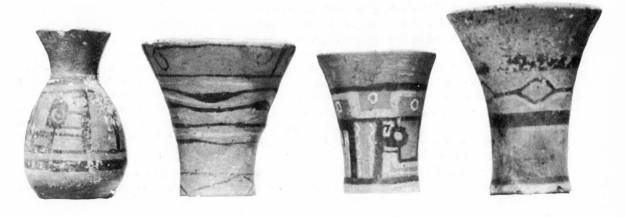

Figure 4-30. Elaborately carved wooden snuff trays. These date to San Pedro II. The man carved on *c* has inlaid shell eyes; and note the very striking Tiahuanaco design of the carving of *d*. Length of *b*, about 13 cm. (Courtesy Gustavo Le Paige and Museo Arqueológico, San Pedro de Atacama, Chile.)

usually associated with snuff taking—in which the handles had been fashioned as feline heads, by baskets and textiles with woven Tiahuanacoid designs, and by gold vessels and ornaments. The local pottery context into which these traits were intruded is that dominated by the type San Pedro Polished Black.[121] According to Orellana, agricultural terraces (Fig. 4-31) can be identified with this Middle Period or San Pedro II phase as can a settlement pattern of scattered stone-walled dwellings.[122] These Tiahuanaco horizon ceramic traits are also present on the coast, with the polychrome keros being associated with burials of the Cabuza and Sobraya phases. This is the same strong Tiahuanaco "expansion" that is also seen in the neighboring Loreto phase of the Peruvian Far South Coast.[123]

In the Late Preceramic Period, following the Tiahuanaco influence, the towns of the interior oases are those identified with the Atacameño peoples. In archaeological terms, this is the San Pedro III phase. The ceramics of the phase have some prototypes in the antecedent phase, particularly in the black wares (Fig. 4-32). A new type, however, is San Pedro Purplish-red, which is frequently represented in large, double-bodied vessels.[124] The important Atacameño ruins are mostly in the San Pedro Atacama–Rio Loa drainage and include the various sites around San Pedro

Figure 4-31. (*Top*, p. 229) View of agricultural terracing along the Rio Salado, a tributary of the Rio Loa, Atacama subarea. Such terracing probably dates from as early as Middle Ceramic Period times, and the old terrace plots are still maintained and used today. This picture captures the completely "river oasis" quality of the small north Chilean streams as they cut through the rocky and utterly barren desert. (Courtesy Mario Orellana and the Universidad de Chile.)

Figure 4-32. (*Bottom*, p. 229) Collection of San Pedro III pottery from a grave. (Courtesy Gustavo Le Paige and Museo Arqueológico, San Pedro de Atacama, Chile.)

Figure 4-33. Lasana. (Courtesy Roberto Montandon.)

together with Lasana, Chíuchíu, and Calama, which are in the Loa Valley. These little towns were built in the Late Ceramic Period, so that their pattern is generally of this time; however, they continued to be occupied in the Inca Period and probably received Incaic architectural additions. Lasana (Fig. 4-33) is very typical.[125] It was located in a narrow canyon valley, the floor of which was the agricultural sustaining area for the ancient population of the site. The immediate setting for the town is the spur of an old terrace that rises some 25 meters or so above the valley floor, and it obviously had been picked as a defensible location. This desire for defense is also seen in a wall that encircles the town. Within the wall are conjoined, somewhat irregularly arranged apartmentlike rooms. Most of these are quadrangular, although some are circular. They had been laid up of undressed stone and mud mortar. Doorways and windows were capped with stone

lintels; access to rooms was by winding alleys or narrow streets. The various dwellings had apparently been roofed with poles and thatch or other perishables.

Burials at Lasana were in cist graves made within the town under house floors or in the hillside outside the defense wall. Bodies were found in a flexed, or seated, position and wrapped in textiles. These were the remains of a sturdily built, round-headed people who had practiced fronto-occipital head deformation. The Atacameño were great wood carvers, and this was represented in the graves by the wooden snuff tablets, carved bone snuff spoons, spindle whorls, weaving implements, harness toggles and bells for llamas, spoons, spatulas, little statuettes and staff heads, and boxes. They were also leather workers. Some individuals had been buried in thick leather shirts and leather helmets and were accompanied by leather arrow quivers. Such, apparently, was the costume and gear for war.

The Atacameño townsmen were also metallurgists. Primitive smelters and stone molds for casting have been discovered in some sites, and axes, chisels, tweezers, and pendants of bronze are commonly found as burial furniture.

The agricultural-herding economy of the Atacameño towns is well demonstrated in the very settings of the oasis sites where such populations could only have been sustained by cultivation and where prehistoric agricultural terraces and irrigation features are still visible. In some places the dry climate has preserved the plant remains: maize, beans, squash, gourds, quinoa, and potatoes. These had been supplemented with wild fruits and algarroba pod beans. The llama and alpaca were an important source of meat, wool, and leather. The abundance of woolen textiles, leather goods, and the harness gear for these animals is a clear indication of their domestication and their importance to the Atacameños.[126]

This Late Ceramic Period Atacameño culture is also found in other interior valley oases of the Atacama subarea, at varying distances from the sea. There is a large settlement in the Conanoxa locality in the Camarones Valley,[127] a cemetery in the Pica region,[128] the walled Caserones I site (Fig. 4-34) in the Tarapacá Valley,[129] and the San Miguel site, some 20 kilometers inland from

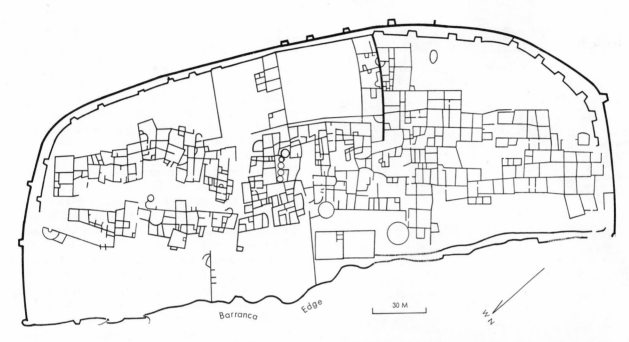

Barranca   Edge   30 M   N

Figure 4-34. Plan of the walled ruins of the Caserones I site, Valley of Tarapacá, Chile. The town was situated on the edge of the steep barranca of the Valley of Tarapacá. The large two-roomed structure at the center, near the barranca edge, may have been a political or ceremonial structure. The ruin probably dates from the Late Ceramic Period of walled Atacameño towns. (After Núñez, 1966.)

the sea.[130] All of these are in the northernmost Chilean Province of Tarapacá. They differ from the San Pedro de Atacama sites chiefly in pottery styles, for although they show some relationships to the San Pedro wares, they also share in a coastal pottery tradition.

This coastal pottery tradition is one that had its roots in the Tiahuanacoid influences that reached northern Chile and Far South Peru in the Middle Period. It is expressed in styles that feature three-color (red-black-white) painting and that still retain some recognizable Tiahuanacoid features, such as the kero or goblet vessel form. In the Arica region this style is known as the Chiribaya style. It gives rise to the Late Period San Miguel (Arica I) and Gentilar (Arica II) styles that Bird found at the Playa Miller site.[131] Both styles of painting are found on large, handled water jars, and the decorative designs are recti-curvilinear and geometric. There is a trend for the Gentilar designs to be somewhat smaller and more intricate than those of San Miguel (Fig. 4-35).[132] An additional common Gentilar vessel form is a small, single-handled pitcher, which sometimes also shows white paint.

These San Miguel and Gentilar styles are found as far south as the mouth of the Rio Loa although here they occur in connection with plain and modeled types that are more reminiscent of the Atacameño styles of the interior.[133]

The Puna, the Quebrada de Humahuaca, and the Selvas Occidentales. In these subareas the differentiation between Middle and Late Ceramic Period occupations is largely derived from typological inference.

With reference to the Middle Period, Gonzalez recognizes gold objects in the Tiahuanaco horizon style in the western Puna; and it is also likely that the wooden snuff tablets with feline and Tiahuanaco carvings that are found in the same regions date from this time.[134] In the Quebrada

Figure 4-35. Arica-style pottery from Tacna-Arica region. *a–e*: San Miguel (Arica I) Red-and-black-on-white. *f–j*: Gentilar (Arica II) Red-black-and-white-on-reddish-buff unslipped surface (*f* and *g* are opposite sides of the same jar). (After Bird, 1943.)

beginnings of agricultural terracing, and by stone and bone artifacts. These traits would be in contrast to the Late Period apartmentlike dwellings, extensive cultivation terraces, and wooden and metal objects.[136] In the Selvas Occidentales the Middle Ceramic Period is thought to be represented by the Candelaria III phase, in which the pottery resembles that of the Aguada phase of the Valliserrana Middle Period.[137]

On the Late Period level a typical site of the Puna is a fortified town, or a town near a fortified site. Sorcuyo, one of the late sites in the Rio Miraflores drainage, is representative.[138] The location is a natural hill capped by a fortress. Within the outer defense walls are a cluster of stone-and-mud rooms. Below the fortress, on the hillside, is another concentration of stone-walled buildings—apparently a contemporaneous dwelling site. Nearby are burial caves, the openings of which had been walled over with stone slabs and clay mortar. Late Period Puna pottery is either plain or black-on-red. The associated non-ceramic artifacts compose what has been referred to as the "Puna complex."[139] Wooden and leather objects, preserved in the dry climate, are especially diagnostic

Figure 4-36. Alfarcito Polychrome. (After Bennett, Bleiler, and Sommer, 1948; original sources, Debenedetti, 1910 and Bregante, 1926.)

de Humahuaca it is likely that La Isla de Tilcara was occupied this early; Bennett and others offer support for this supposition in stylistic seriations of grave lot pottery; for instance, the types Alfarcito Polychrome (Fig. 4-36) and La Isla Polychrome are assigned to the Middle Period.[135] Lafon suggests that the Middle Period complex at La Isla is characterized by individual stone houses, by the

of the complex and offer insights into various activities. Among the wooden artifacts are toggles for llama harnesses, spindle whorls, spindle shafts, weave swords, digging implements, arrow shafts and points, and war clubs. The ubiquitous carved snuff tablets are a part of the complex, as are incised wooden goblets, pyrograved gourds, and sandals, boxes, and bags of leather. As in the Chilean coastal Late Period cultures, basketry was made by coiling. Hoe blades were made of chipped-stone slabs, and axes, mortars, pestles, and ornaments were ground from stone. Most metalwork was of copper and included small tools and ornaments; but in some sites, as at Sorcuyo, gold bracelets and bangles were encountered. Contemporaneous sites of the Quebrada de Humahuaca are similar to those of the Puna. The well-known Pucará de Tilcara is an example.[140] Non-ceramic artifacts are essentially the same. Quebrada de Humahuaca pottery, however, includes a greater range of painted types than that of the Puna.

The Late Period sites of the Selvas Occidentales include those of the Iruya region of northwestern Salta. The Iruya towns are sometimes fortified; one of the best known is Titiconte, which has a defensible hilltop location with semi-subterranean, slab-lined rooms.[141] The most distinctive aspect of the Iruya phase or complex is the abundance of stone artifacts: hoes, spades, weapons, vessels, panpipes, and ornaments.[142] To the south and east the Late Ceramic Period is represented by ceramics that show an affinity to the late styles of the Valliserrana. These presumably succeed the Candelaria III phase in this part of the Selvas Occidentales.[143]

The Valliserrana: Aguada and the Argentine "Diaguita" Cultures. The Middle Period culture of the Valliserrana is the Aguada. It is known from La Aguada and other sites in the Hualfín Valley, from other regions in Catamarca, and from sites in La Rioja, San Juan, and southern Salta.[144] The ecological "niche" occupied by the Aguadans was the valley country just below 2500 meters (7500–8000 ft.). Sites of the culture are not found in the lower wooded valleys or in higher puna-type lands. The villages were located along river banks. Apparently, these villagers sometimes impounded water in dams, but there are no

signs of irrigation canals. Maize cultivation is verified, however, by the charred remains of the cereal. It is believed by the archaeologists who have studied the culture and its environmental setting that these valleys were somewhat better watered a thousand years or so ago—at the time of the Aguada culture—than they are today. In the last millennium they have suffered a progressive dessication.

In general, the settlements of the Aguada societies were scattered house arrangements, with the individual buildings made of clay and probably roofed with wood or straw. These buildings quite probably resembled those of the Alamito Ciénega dwelling units, with several houses grouped around a little central patio. Earth mounds are associated with the Aguada culture, and these may have been platforms for buildings, as hearth levels and stone foundations have been found in some of them. The dwellings were in all likelihood part of a pattern that also included structures of religious or political significance as represented by these mounds. Burials are found in the vicinity of the villages in deep (2–3 m.), stone-lined pits. Some are accompanied by trophy heads, and there is a notable differentiation in the amounts and richness of other goods from grave to grave that would indicate definite status ranking if not class distinctions. Children were usually buried in a manner similar to that of adults, with whom they sometimes shared graves; however, a few children were interred in urns in a manner like that of the earlier Ciénega phases.

The continuity of Ciénega-to-Aguada is clearly expressed in ceramics, with the plain gray and gray-incised tradition persisting. Some of the incised designs are now the stylized feline, however, and this same feline motif is seen on the painted wares. These are in black-on-yellow, black-and-purple-on-yellow, and black-and-red-on-white (Fig. 4-37). Additional motifs of design are those of humans, serpents, frogs, birds, and monstrous figures. Vessels are handled beakers, collared ollas, and various bowl pieces. Distinctive little handmade figurines and pipes were also produced of clay.

The feline motif also found expression in the other Aguada media. Steatite beakers had cats carved in relief on the sides; little bone spindle whorls were incised with feline figures; and bronze

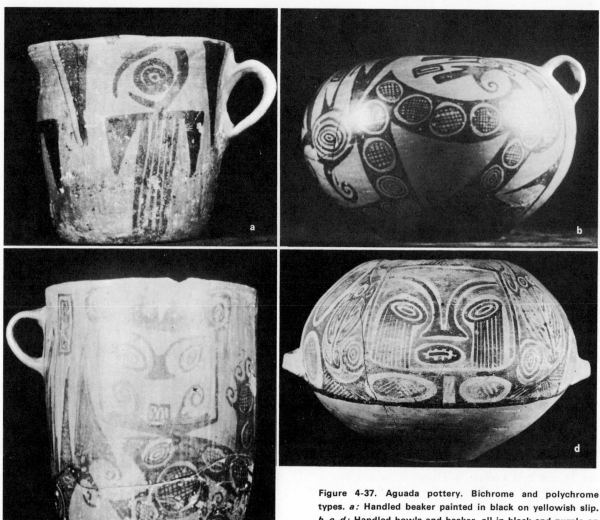

Figure 4-37. Aguada pottery. Bichrome and polychrome types. *a:* Handled beaker painted in black on yellowish slip. *b, c, d:* Handled bowls and beaker, all in black and purple on yellowish slip. *a* appears to have a stylized bird design; *b* and *c* show stylized felines; *d* may be anthropomorphic or animal. (Courtesy La Plata Museum, Argentina.)

axes were cast with jaguar or puma images on the portion of the ax opposite the cutting edge. Metals, in fact, were well represented in the grave materials: bronze or copper т-shaped axes, tweezers, needles, chisels, and bracelets.

Aguada stonework is much like that of northwestern Argentine ceramic-agricultural cultures in general. There are the usual mortars and milling stones, beads, and spindle whorls; the ax type is grooved; and the flint projectile points are common.

Gonzalez notes similarities between the Aguada feline iconography and that of the Peruvian Late Nazca polychrome pottery (pp. 145–148), and there is also a sharing of the treatment of trophy-head representations in the two styles. This suggests that the inspiration for Aguada art was derived from Peru before the era of the Tiahuanaco horizon; and this supposition is further supported by the ancient presence of the feline motif in the southern Peruvian highland and Lake Titicaca subareas. For example, it is found in the Pucará (Qalasasaya) style, and, of course, it has older beginnings in the Chavín horizon. Nevertheless, there is some imagery in Aguada art which is more specifically Tiahuanacoid, such as the human or demon figures with the squared heads who hold spears or spear-throwers at their sides;

and the radiocarbon dates for Aguada—ranging from A.D. 744 to 826[145]—allow for Tiahuanaco horizon contact. Thus, I would see Aguada art as being basically pre-Tiahuanacoid in its beginnings but also incorporating elements that could have been diffused to it from the Tiahuanaco horizon.

The Aguada culture came to an end at some time toward the close of the Middle Ceramic Period. It was replaced by a new culture that is often referred to as the "Diaguita," or the "Calchaquí." This "Diaguita" or "Calchaquí" culture

Figure 4-38. Bronze plaque or disk from northwest Argentina. Probably related to the Aguada phase. Height, 15 cm. (Courtesy La Plata Museum, Argentina.)

is especially distinguished by a new and distinctive pottery tradition.[146] This new tradition quite probably derived, at least in part, from the antecedent painted wares of Aguada; nevertheless, it displays a number of notable differences. The old feline iconography of Aguada has disappeared. In its place are a number of new motifs—highly stylized reptilian, avian, human, and other life forms, and these are incorporated into bold geometric design layouts that are quite unlike any of the previous South Andean styles.

The earlier stages of the new pottery tradition are represented in the little-known San José, Hualfín, and Early Angualasto phases,[147] dating from the end of the Middle Ceramic Period and to the beginning of the Late Ceramic Period, or what is estimated to be from about A.D. 900 to 1100. San José is in the Yocavil-Calchaquí region of northern Catamarca. Its burial urns (Fig. 4-39, e, f) are painted in a polychrome style—brownish-black and red on a yellow-orange ground color. The designs on the urns are composed of nested fields of triangles and zigzags, often combined with serpent figures. These designs are executed in a bold, careless manner typical of the new traditions. The urn form has a pointed base, a maximum diameter just above this base, slightly in-sloping walls, and a small flared collar. Horizontal strap handles are placed on each side of the vessel at the point of maximum diameter.[148] Hualfín urns, which are found in the Hualfín Valley to the south of the Yocavil-Calchaquí region, are similar although painted in a black-and-red-on-cream color scheme,[149] and the Angualasto style is said to resemble both San José and Hualfín.[150]

The latter stages of the "Diaguita" pottery tradition take us fully into the Late Ceramic Period, and the Belén and Santa María pottery styles are representative. In contrast to the San José–Hualfín horizon, the painted pottery is now largely bichrome. The urn form—a vessel used for the burial of children—is still typical, and those of Belén and Santa María have obvious prototypes on the preceding horizon. They too have the small, flattish base, a bulging midbody where the horizontal strap handles are attached, and, in contrast to the San José urns, a rather high collar with a flared rim.[151] The urns of Belén are painted in black-on-red (Fig. 4-39, a, b) and those of Santa

Figure 4-39. Painted urn styles, northwest Argentina. *a, b:* Belén style. *c, d:* Santa María style. *e, f:* San José style. (After Bennett, Bleiler, and Sommer, 1948; original source, Bregante, 1926.)

María in black-on-yellow (Fig. 4-39, *c, d*). Both styles employ highly abstract human face designs. These faces are often marked with what appear to be tear streaks and are called "weeping faces." Around these faces are geometric arrangements of stylized snakes, rheas, and other animals. Burial urns, though perhaps the most distinctive, are not the only Belén and Santa María pottery forms. Both cultures have a variety of bowl and plate shapes that bear designs similar to those on the urns.

On the San José–Hualfín horizon the settlement pattern was still the scattered one. This was replaced early in the Late Period by the fortified towns of the Santa María I phase.[152] Farther south, however, in the Hualfín Valley, the Belén I phase lacks stone architecture altogether, and the dwelling sites are small clusters of communal semisubterranean houses. Even in Belén II times, settle-

236

ment was still somewhat dispersed, although by now buildings were of pirca stone masonry. Not until Belén III does the fortified, concentrated town appear.[153] This suggests that the idea of the community as a fortified town was diffusing through the Valliserrana subarea from the north, presumably from the Puna, and that this mode of life did not reach the Hualfín until well after its establishment in the Yocavil-Calchaquí region.[154]

Several general comments can apply to all of these Late Period Valliserrana cultures that we associate with the "Diaguita" pottery tradition. They buried the adult dead in pit graves and surrounded the graves with low pirca masonry walls. Metals were found in all phases, but, as we have said, they became more common in the later ones. A number of tools were made of bronze: pincers, chisels, and axes. Cast gorgets or breastplates were the principal ornaments of this material. The wooden items were like those of the Puna and Quebrada de Humahuaca—mainly weaving implements and llama harness gear. Neither chipped nor ground stone was common in the "Diaguita" sites, but things like stone beads and arrowpoints are recorded.

The Valles Transversales: "Chilean Diaguita". Across the Andes from the Valliserrana, the Middle and Late Ceramic Period cultures of the Valles Transversales subarea are usually referred to as those of the "Chilean Diaguita." This is one of those ethnic identifications of an archaeological culture that has been debated endlessly and somewhat sterilely. According to some of the sixteenth century Spanish explorers, the Indians of the region of Coquimbo spoke the same language as those of the Argentine Diaguita or Calchaquí country;[155] and it may well be that the protohistoric inhabitants of the Valles Transversales were of the Diaguitan or Cacan language family. Certainly, to judge from their geographical position, this would not be too surprising. At the same time it should be emphasized that, although there are certain trans-Andine relationships in the archaeological cultures, Chilean and Argentine "Diaguita" cultures are significantly different.

The "Chilean Diaguita" tradition takes up in the Valles Transversales where the El Molle culture terminates. Although there is no easy transition from the one to the other, it is unlikely that there was any appreciable lapse of time between them. Actually, the ceramic style that has been taken to mark the inception of "Chilean Diaguita"—its "Archaic" phase—is very probably derived from Condorhuasi Polychrome influence (Fig. 4-40) that was brought into Chile from the Valliserrana of Argentina. The spread of this style into Chile most likely began in El Molle II times, following the paths of diffusion or trade that had been pioneered at the time of the earlier Ciénega–El Molle connections. Certainly by "Chilean Diaguita Archaic" times Condorhuasi, or Condorhuasi-imitated, pottery was a common feature of Valles Transversales grave furniture.[156] That the Condorhuasi style had spread by diffusion or trade rather than mass migration is supported by what little physical anthropological evidence we have. Although there are some differences between the El Molle and the "Chilean Diaguita" skeletons, the major change in physical type had come earlier, with the changeover from the Pacific Littoral to the South Andean tradition in Early Ceramic Period I.[157] The "Chilean Diaguita" Indians, like those of El Molle, were South Andean brachycephals.

Figure 4-40. Condorhuasi Polychrome vessel (white-and-black-on-red). From the Elquí Valley, Chile. Height, 20 cm. (Courtesy American Museum of Natural History.)

The "Chilean Diaguita" ceramic sequence runs through three sequent phases, as follows: "Archaic," "Transitional," and "Classic." This sequence was first advanced by Latcham,[158] and it has since been refined and verified by Cornely's[159] studies of grave collections and by the still more recent stratigraphic studies in coastal shell middens.[160] The Archaic phase is a boldly painted black-and-white-on-red style (Fig. 4-41, *top*). Sometimes the white is replaced by yellow pigment. The color scheme, the nature of the bold stepped geometric figures of the designs, and the vessel forms (including keros) are all reminiscent of the Tiahuanacoid styles, just as they are reminiscent of the Condorhuasi style. Cornely felt that the influence here was, indeed, that of the Tiahuanaco horizon proper, that Archaic "Chilean Diaguita" was, in effect, an "Epigonal" style. For reasons given in the course of the argument I have been following in this chapter, I would doubt this and, instead, identify the Condorhuasi influence in Archaic "Diaguita" as a part of a pre-Tiahuanaco horizon chain of influences.

The Transitional and Classic "Chilean Diaguita" phases are rather distinct from the Archaic. They have a white, rather than a dark red, slip, and they are decorated in rather small, tightly arranged, serried rows of geometric figures. Montane also says that there are significant paste and firing differences between Archaic, on the one hand, and Transitional and Classic on the other.[161] In spite of these differences, I think that the similarities are great enough to allow us to consider the Archaic phase pottery as the main prototype for the later phases. The other source of influence in the formation of the later styles was probably that of the Atacaman coastal San Miguel and Gentilar styles. These, it will be recalled, have a white ground color and also exhibit the chronological trend toward reduction in design size that we see in the Transitional and Classic "Chilean Diaguita" styles. The Transitional and the Classic styles (especially the latter) are noted for straight-sided bowl forms, spouted forms, narrow-necked jars with loop handles, shoe-shaped or duck-shaped pots, and bird effigy jars that have head-bridge-and-spout handles (Fig. 4-41, *center* and *bottom*).

"Chilean Diaguita" villages were neither as large nor as compact as the Late Period Atacama

Figure 4-41. Chilean Diaguita pottery. *Top:* Early or Archaic Diaguita. *Center:* Late or Classic Diaguita, but with retention of bold design reminiscent of Archaic Diaguita and of Condorhuasi Polychrome influence. *Bottom:* Typical Late or Classic Diaguita. Respective diameters: 20.5, 27.5, and 17 cm. (Courtesy Grete Mostny and Museo Nacional de Historia Natural, Santiago, Chile.)

Figure 4-42. Averías Polychrome, Chaco-Santiagueño sub-area. (After Bennett, Bleiler, and Sommer, 1948; original source, Wagner and Wagner, 1934.)

or Valliserrana subarea towns. The overall settlement pattern was dispersed, and individual houses were laid up of pirca stone walls and roofed with reeds. Some fortified hilltop sites are known, but just how they fit into the ceramic sequence is uncertain; it is possible that they are confined to the Inca horizon. Burials of the culture were direct inhumations in pit graves. In the Classic phase these were stone-lined cists. Most of our knowledge of "Chilean Diaguita" archaeology comes from grave materials and from cemeteries in inland valley sites; however, the Diaguita farmers also exploited the shoreline, and we have evidences of their occupancy in shell-midden sites there.

Metals were present in El Molle, and they continue in all "Diaguita" phases. Classic phase graves have yielded copper and bronze knives, axes, and wristguards; gold and copper bells; and a distinctive gold wire earring. Diaguita woodwork has resemblances to that of the Atacameño—snuff-trays and boxes—although the craft was probably less well developed. As with other Late Period cultures of the South Andes, the only chipped stone items of consequence in El Molle seem to be small triangular arrow points.[162]

The Chaco-Santiagueño. In our discussion of the Early Ceramic Period for the Chaco-Santiagueño subarea we noted that a gray incised pottery—related to that of the Ciénega culture—was diagnostic of the early pottery-agricultural horizon and that this horizon had been designated as the Las Mercedes phase. Following this gray incised pottery we have, much as in the Valliserrana, the introduction of polychrome and bichrome wares. Unlike the Valliserrana, however, there is no strong Condorhuasi Polychrome horizon in the Chaco-Santiagueño. Only an occasional specimen has been reported;[163] however, some Chaco-Santiagueño styles such as Averías Polychrome (Fig. 4-42),[164] are reminiscent of Condorhuasi in their stepped geometric figure designs. In

Averías Polychrome, though, the ground color is white rather than red; and this suggests a later chronological position than that assigned to Condorhuasi. Valliserrana and the Chaco-Santiagueño painted styles are in general closely related, as can be seen in the geometric designs and stylized life forms in such a Chaco-Santiagueño type as the Llajta Mauca Bicolor (Fig. 4-43).[165] In this relationship it is unlikely that the current of innovation and diffusion always ran from the Valliserrana eastward. For instance, the stylized bird, animal, and reptile forms, which are among the

Figure 4-43. Llajta Mauca Bicolor, Chaco-Santiagueño sub-area. (After Bennett, Bleiler, and Sommer, 1948; original source, Wagner and Wagner, 1934.)

most prominent characteristics of Late Period Valliserrana pottery, may very well have had their origins in the Chaco-Santiagueño and spread from there to the west.

These surmises about the direction of influences in the development of the northwest Argentine Middle and Late Period pottery styles are limited by our lack of knowledge about Chaco-Santiagueño culture sequences. A sequence has been proposed.[166] Las Mercedes, as we have said, refers to such types as Bislín Incised and to the Crude Urns. To Sunchituyoj, I would assign the polychromes, or most of them. The bi-color types would follow these in the Averías phase; and black-on-red pottery, which may show slight Inca influence, would close the sequence.[167]

Without attempting to be more specific about the chronological culture phases of the Chaco-Santiagueño, we may offer the following general cultural description. Sites are found along the courses of two rivers, the Dulce and the Salado.

These flow from the mountains of the northwest. The Dulce eventually empties into the Mar Chiquita, in Córdoba, while the Salado reaches the Río Paraná. The sites are marked by earth mounds and depressions. Mounds vary in size from 1 to 3 meters in height and from 10 to 150 meters in diameter. Some mounds may be of partly natural origin (eolian or dissected river terraces) and were selected as suitable places to live in a region seasonally flooded; however, all have been added to artificially, and in some instances they may be completely man-made. Excavation has revealed ash layers, debris, and house floors in them, and there can be little doubt that their primary use was as living sites, although burials were also made in them. The associated depressions may be natural, but it is more likely that they are "borrow-pits," whence earth was taken for mound construction. Many of the burials in the mounds were secondary interments in urns; this applied to both adults and children. Direct inhumations were also made in grave pits. Grave goods include pottery, a very distinctive style of pottery figurine known as the "ophidian" (Fig. 4-45) type, chipped-stone and bone arrowpoints,

Figure 4-44. Chaco-Santiagueña pottery types. *a, b*: Marías Polychrome. *c*: Represas Polychrome. (Redrawn from Bennett, Bleiler, and Sommer, 1948.)

a

b

c

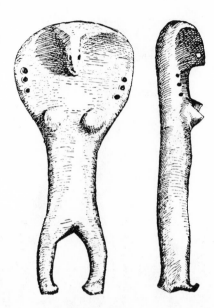

Figure 4-45. Chaco-Santiagueño pottery figurine in the "ophidian" style. (After Bennett, Bleiler, and Sommer, 1948; original source, Wagner and Wagner, 1934.)

and occasional metal objects of Valliserrana origin.[168]

As might be expected from its extreme eastern geographical position, the Chaco-Santiagueño subarea was influenced by—and undoubtedly had inter-influencing relationships with—the Paraná country to the east. The similarities of modeled bird adornos on some of the Chaco-Santiagueño vessels to those on Paraná River pottery have been commented upon.[169]

Summary Comment. The nature of the cultures of the Middle Ceramic Period was foreshadowed by changes that occurred toward the end of the Early Ceramic Period. These changes seem to have been set in motion by diffusions from Southern Bolivia. Condorhuasi Polychrome pottery was one result of these diffusions. Another was probably the rise of a more hierarchially ordered society. These diffusions were followed, according to our interpretations, by a continuing radiation of similar aesthetic, sociopolitical, and religious ideas that were carried by the Tiahuanaco horizon.

As might be expected from their geographical location, the northernmost subareas of the South Andes were most directly influenced by the highly specific iconography of the Tiahuanaco horizon. Farther south, the elaborations of the Valliserrana Aguada culture show less influence that can be classified as specifically Tiahuanacoid; here, rather, the feline "cult" as it is expressed in ceramic and other arts belongs to a style in its own right, and its ideological-aesthetic derivations are seen as relating to the feline motif as this belongs to the pre-Tiahuanaco Nazcoid or even Chavinoid cultures of Peru and Bolivia. In the Valles Transversales subarea, to the west of the Valliserrana, a style known as "Archaic Diaguita" is not specifically Tiahuanacoid but is, rather, derivative from Condorhuasi influences. East of the Valliserrana, in the Chaco-Santiagueño, the Condorhuasi is represented only weakly, although local polychrome styles of the Middle Period retain decorative elements reminiscent of it.

On the Late Ceramic Period level we are faced with a proliferation of subareal and regional styles. Those of Southern Bolivia are much like the various black-white-red or black-on-red pottery styles of the Titicaca Basin post-Tiahuanaco horizon period; and it is likely that the styles of San Pedro de Atacama, the Puna, and the Quebrada de Humahuaca are related to those of Southern Bolivia, both in the circumstance that all derive out of antecedent Tiahuanacoid origins and in the circumstance of their contemporaneous and interconnected developments. It is in these northern subareas that the concentrated and fortified town settlement came into being in the Late Period.

The Late Period pottery styles of the Atacama subarea coast are also Tiahuanaco-derived. Like the related styles of south Peru, they emphasize a white ground color with red and black decoration. The Atacama coastal styles had a strong influence on the development of the "Chilean Diaguita" white-slipped styles of the Valles Transversales. In the Valliserrana, local polychromes and then bichromes developed from the antecedent Aguada Polychrome pottery. Here the fortified town was known in the northern part of the subarea by the beginning of the Late Period. In the Chaco-Santiagueño the development of Late Period styles was interrelated with that of the Valliserrana. This subarea, on the eastern borders of the South Andes, shows some influences in its art forms from the Paraná area.

The South Andean Cultural Tradition: The Inca Horizon

In a sense, the South Andean cultural tradition could be said to end with the Inca horizon, for this horizon is a product of the Peruvian cultural tradition and was carried from that area to the South Andes by military might; however, Inca influences affected only certain aspects of local South Andean cultures, and, whatever the military and political aspects of this horizon might have been, the resident cultures seem to have continued without radical change.

The round date for the beginning of the Inca Ceramic Period in the South Andean chronology is set at A.D. 1450. Pachacuti had dominated the southern Peruvian highlands and adjacent Bolivia by about 1460; Topa Inca Yupanqui spread the Inca dominion throughout southern Bolivia, northwest Argentina, and northern and central Chile by A.D. 1490 (p. 173).

All of Southern Bolivia came under Inca domination, and Inca power and ceramic influence is seen as far south and east as the Incaic fortified sites such as Pucarilla near Santa Cruz.[170]

In the Chilean Atacama the Inca presence is reflected in the presence of the Cuzco Polychrome pottery style and in Inca local styles, such as the Saxamar Black-on-red. These are found both in the interior and on the coast.[171] Niemeyer has described an Inca cemetery from the Camarones Valley in which the circular, stone-lined Inca tombs contained Inca-style aryballoid jars, Saxamar vessels, carved wooden keros, little silver ritual objects, and other easily identified Inca-style items.[172]

Farther south, in the Valles Transversales (Fig. 4-46), Inca influence is, if anything, even stronger than in the Atacama region. One of the things that interested the Inca people in their domination of foreign areas was the extraction of metal ores. An Inca mining establishment—for gold, silver, and copper—has been found in the vicinity of Almirante Latorre, to the north of La Serena. The site is marked by evidences of the mining activities, Inca buildings, and artifacts.[173]

Figure 4-46. Inca aryballoid jar from Chilean Diaguita country. Height, about 22 cm. (Courtesy Cambridge Museum of Archaeology and Ethnology, England.)

The Inca are known to have held Chile as far south as the Rio Maule, which is in the southern part of our Central Valley subarea,[174] and Inca ceramic influence is found in Central Valley sites, including coastal shell middens[175] and inland cemeteries.[176] One rather spectacular Inca find was that of a sacrificial burial of a young boy on a high mountaintop shrine in the Chilean central Andes. A typical Inca stone crypt-tomb had been constructed, and the body was found with provincial-style Inca pottery, Inca textiles, and little ritual Incaic silver llama figurines.[177]

The presence of the Inca people can also be detected in many sites in both the Puná and Quebrada de Humahuaca subareas of northwestern Argentina. Inca roads and way stations were built here to consolidate the empire, and most of the fortified town sites show some indications of Inca influence. In fact, it is frequently a moot question to just what extent fortification features, temples, pavements, and other "public works" are Incaic or pre-Incaic. Undoubtedly, the Inca conquerors added some features to most of these sites—such as the Pucará de Tilcara;[178] however, it is also certain that the fortified-town concept definitely pre-dates the Inca expansion into northwestern Argentina. The nature of the Inca ceramic influence in these subareas is much like what it is in Chile; that is, there has been a synthesis of local and Inca traditions. The type Casa Morada Polychrome is a South Andean variant of Cuzco Polychrome, and vessel shapes, including the aryballoid jar and the little saucer-like plates, as well as polychrome painting, are overwhelmingly Inca. But Tilcara Black-on-red would appear to be a type that was in existence prior to the Inca invasion and which, in its later subvariants, assimilated certain Inca features.[179] The extent to which all this reflects imported Inca craftsmen and local imitators is of great interest, but the studies of the processes involved in the "Incaization" of South Andean pottery, or any other aspects of culture, remain to be made. Data are available for such studies, however. For example, Krapovickas has identified a small building in the Pucará de Tilcara as a shop in which an Inca, or Inca-trained, lapidary had made little stone llama and other typical Inca votive figurines, the buildings in question containing numerous partly finished and finished examples of the craft.[180]

Inca pottery and artifacts are also found in the Iruya region to the east of the Quebrada de Humahuaca. This would seem to mark an eastern limit for imperial expansion in this part of Argentina, for similar finds have not been reported from farther east in the Selvas Occidentales.[181]

The Valliserrana also has forts, roads, and tambos of Inca construction in addition to pottery and craft goods of all sorts that can be tied to the Inca expansion to the south.[182]

By about 1480 the Inca armies reached San Juan[183] and Mendoza. The fortress of Pucará del Inca, near the city of Mendoza, is, in fact, their southernmost Argentine outpost of consequence.[184] Beyond this, the remainder of the Mendoza-Neuquén subarea seems to have remained outside their perimeters.

In the southeast, the flatlands and the culture of the Chaco-Santiagueño were little affected by the Inca, and the Sierras Centrales of Córdoba and San Luis seem to have been untouched.

The South Andean Cultural Tradition: Marginal Developments

The Central Valley and Araucanian Subareas. El Molle II–type pottery has been found at the Sitio Alacranes I, only a short distance to the north of the Rio Aconcagua and well to the south of the Rio Choapa. This pottery includes distinctive complex effigy forms, and there can be no doubt of the identification.[185] A little farther south, at the mouth of the Aconcagua, Berdichewsky has found El Molle-like wares, including a possible negative-painted specimen, tembetás, monitor pipes, and copper pendants in the large Concón shell mound.[186] That author further remarks that such complexes are known from as far south as the Rio Maipo. He is of the opinion that they are all substantially later than in the Valles Transversales homeland for El Molle; but this, I think, is only a possibility, and we cannot be sure of it until we have radiocarbon dates to verify the degree of time lag.

Going farther south, to the Araucanian subarea, Menghin has suggested a "Pre-Araucanian" horizon that would subsume a number of scattered finds of plain pottery, tembetás, and monitor pipes, and that would date in a range of 0–A.D. 1000.[187] It may be that Menghin's Pitrén pottery complex, as reported from Valdivia Province, should be placed somewhere within this horizon.[188] Pitrén ceramics are largely monochromes, although there is one illustrated piece (Fig. 4-47) that looks suspiciously like a black-on-red negative-painted or resist-dye decorated specimen. Vessel forms are mainly collared and handled jars, but there are some effigy jars. In brief, the impression is that of an El Molle-derived assemblage. Berdichewsky's excavations in the "Cueva de Los Catalanes," in the Province of Malleco, a little to the north of Valdivia, may also pertain to the Pitrén complex, although in this cave he has a stratigraphy that carries onward into the historic period.[189]

Figure 4-47. *Above:* Pitrén vessel shapes, Province of Valdivia, Araucanian subarea. The vessel at *top, left* is described as having a black wash over a red ground color, with the black pigment notably eroded. The drawing and the description suggest a negative-painting technique. Height of vessel at *top, left*, about 16 cm. (After Menghin, 1959–60.)

Figure 4-48. *Below:* Huanehue pottery in the Valdivia style, Araucanian subarea. Painted in red-on-white. Vessel at *top, left*, about 16 cm. high. (After Menghin, 1959–60.)

On the later, painted-pottery horizon, we know that "Chilean Diaguita" pottery is found as far south as Colchagua Province, in the Central Valley subarea. Here, the Cahuil shell middens show "Transitional" and "Classic" "Chilean Diaguita" styles, in addition to terminal evidences of Inca influence.[190] These "Chilean Diaguita" painted wares appear to have been the inspiration for the development of the Araucanian styles. Latcham,[191] surveying the Araucanian styles very broadly, noted that those of the north (our Central Valley subarea) more frequently featured black-and-red-on-white decoration and, in general, were more closely related to the "Chilean Diaguita" styles in decorative motifs and vessel forms than the Araucanian styles of the south (our Araucanian subarea). The latter are bichromes, usually dark red or black-on-white. They are best represented in such phases as the Tirúa, which is believed to be fully pre-Columbian, and in the Valdivia (Fig. 4-48) and related phases, which date after A.D. 1550.[192]

Admittedly, this is an oversimplification of a much more complex ceramic history that is still far from clarified. For instance, on the late prehistoric and early historic time levels, a black-on-orange or black-on-salmon bichrome style is found widely in the Central Valley subarea, as far north as the Aconcagua;[193] in the south, the El Vergel culture, in Malleco Province, is known for its large, usually plain or simply incised burial urns.[194] Urn burial is not a historic Araucanian trait, so El Vergel seems definitely pre-Columbian; however, the association of small, bichrome-painted vessels with the urns suggests a late prehistoric placement. Another associated El Vergel trait is a small stone figure or idol representing a twin or two-headed human.[195] Interestingly, these figures are reminiscent of similar statues that are considered a part of the Cultura de los Túmulos complex at the far northern end of the South Andes area.

In the above, the assumption has been that the later, painted-ceramic styles and complexes of the Central Valley and Araucanian subareas were the work of Araucanian-speaking peoples.[196] Although there has been little historic site archaeology to support this assumption, the facts of archaeological and ethnographic distribution favor it very strongly. In the sixteenth century the Indians of both subareas were solidly Araucanians. In the north, the Picunche divisions of the Central Valley had been partially subjugated by the Inca, who held the line of empire on the Rio Maule; but the remainder of the Picunche and the Mapuche-Huilliche tribes to the south of them resisted the Inca. Although these Araucanians were never town dwellers—and this is consistent with the scattered household unit settlement pattern found by the archaeologists in these subareas—they were agriculturists who are estimated to have numbered at least half a million at the time of the European entry. Araucanian government was loosely federated and essentially democratic. Peacetime controls were decentralized and mostly nominal, but in time of war lineage chiefs selected a unified command. Although their pattern of warfare was of the "petty," feuding and raiding variety and in no way geared to imperialism, they were redoubtable warriors who were able to withstand the Inca armies and who, after being initially defeated by the Spanish conquistadors, rallied to keep the Europeans out of the country south of the Bío Bío until the late nineteenth century.[197]

The Mendoza-Neuquén Subarea. The Argentine "Diaguita"-type cultures stop short in San Juan; and Mendoza, the next Argentine province to the south, presents a clearly marginal picture of the South Andean tradition. What is known as the Agrelo culture probably marks the agricultural-pottery threshold in the subarea.[198] The Agrelo site is located about 20 kilometers

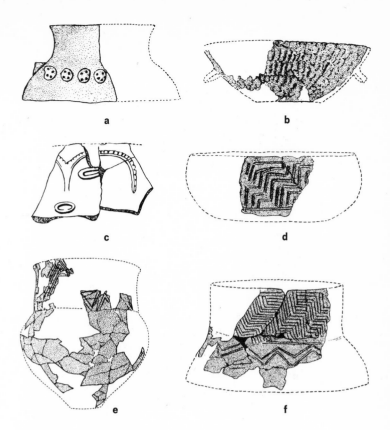

Figure 4-49. Agrelo pottery. *a:* Punched appliqué decoration. *b:* Fingernail-impressed decoration. *c:* Appliqué treatment of human face. *d–f:* Incised. (After Canals Frau and Semper, 1956.)

south of the city of Mendoza, and there are a number of other Agrelo phase sites in that general region. The country is semi-arid, and irrigation would have been necessary for farming, although we have no direct evidence of it. Agrelo ceramics are quite simple and crude (Figs. 4-49, 4-50). The ware is gray-black, roughly finished, and decorated only with incised lines, puncations, little appliqué nodes, or fingernail impressions. Vessels are mainly deep, wide-mouthed pots. These may be encircled on the upper portion of the walls with incised chevron patterns; others have human-face designs on the sides that have been made with the appliqué node technique. Spindle whorls and crude little figurines are also made of pottery. Other Agrelo traits include stone labrets, stone club heads, malachite and shell beads, and triangular projectile points of a medium size, suitable for darts. Agrelo burials were pit inhumations in which the grave location was marked by a circle of stones on the surface of the ground.

Figure 4-50. Vessel of the Agrelo culture. Height, 13 cm. (Courtesy D. E. Ibarra Grasso; see also Ibarra Grasso, 1967.)

In this review of Mendoza-Neuquén we should also note that a great many polished stone items have been found in the subarea.[202] These include both flat and spike-shaped lip-plugs, or tembetás; little stone "offertory basins" that may possibly be snuff tablets; engraved plaques ("placas grabadas"); т-shaped axes; and curious hooklike objects called "clavas insignias" (Fig. 4-51) that seem to be stylized birdheads.[203] Such artifacts do not seem to be part of the Viluco complex. Lip-plugs belong with Agrelo, but the other items do not. It is possible that they are traits of a pre-ceramic horizon, although it is more likely that they relate to cultures and peoples of the Pampean tradition who either occupied parts of the sub-area for a time or were in close contact with the resident groups in it.

The Sierras Centrales Subarea. Our survey of the South Andean tradition closes in the Sierras Centrales of Córdoba and San Luis—that marginal subarea of the South Andes where we have our best record of the terminal stages of the Andean Hunting-Collecting tradition. In Chapter 2 (pp. 54–56), and again in this chapter (pp. 211–213), we indicated that the transition between the Andean Hunting-Collecting way of life and a South Andean farming one occurred at a relatively late time. The latest Intihuasi and

Agrelo is difficult to place either culturally or chronologically; however, the nature of the pottery suggests a derivation from the incised Ciénega and El Molle styles, and the labrets and gravestone rings are also like El Molle. Assuming a Ciénega–El Molle derivation, we might expect that the pottery-making idea—and perhaps agriculture—reached Mendoza in the Early Ceramic Period; however, Agrelo ceramics may then have changed relatively little over the next several centuries, and the complex as it is now known may be considerably later.

In addition to Agrelo, there is a later ceramic horizon in Mendoza-Neuquén. It is seen at Viluco, which is a post-European contact settlement.[199] The graves here contain plain black and painted wares. The latter are little handled jars or kero beakers painted in black-and-white-on-red. The graves also contained European trade items. Viluco was probably under the control of the Inca in late prehistoric times. It seems most likely that it was a site of the Huarpe,[200] although Métraux held the opinion that it had been settled by Araucanians who had entered the region a century or so after the Inca.[201]

Figure 4-51. Polished stone "clavas insignias" from Neuquén. (After Schobinger, 1956.)

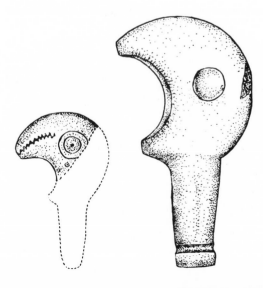

Ongamira Cave phases can be assigned a round estimated date of A.D. 750, and the introduction of agriculture may have taken place even after this date. We know that by the mid-sixteenth century, when the first Spaniards entered the Córdoba highlands, the Indians of the subarea— primarily the Comechingones—were valley farmers, raising maize and other crops with small-scale terracing and irrigation techniques. They are also described as living either in rock shelters or small, pit house villages and as having a relatively primitive political organization.[204] The archaeological record, although as yet offering little in the way of very specific dating, tends to support these early historic descriptions and to show that this kind of life dates at least a few centuries back into the pre-Columbian past.

The terminal Intihuasi and Ongamira phases had very little pottery. Two other sites from Córdoba, however, show considerably more pottery, as well as clay figurines and spindle whorls, and probably carry us later in time and into the agricultural transition. In fact, one direct clue to agriculture is the presence, at one of these sites, of pottery with what appear to be corncob surface striations. One of these sites, or site zones, is the Villa Rumipal in west-central Córdoba.[205] The zone consists of a series of old house or camp locations around the edges of a lake in the Rio Tercero Valley. These are marked by thin refuse, old hearths or pit ovens, and occasional rough alignments of large rocks. These latter may have served as foundations for dwellings of flimsy superstructure; however, clear evidence was found at Rumipal for rectangular, semi-subterranean pit houses. These had presumably been roofed with poles and grass in the manner described by the

Spanish conquistadors. Chipped-stone scrapers, knives, and small triangular or small-stemmed points were found in and around these dwellings, together with mano and milling stones, bola stones, bone artifacts, and pottery. Most notable among the bone artifacts were long, flat-bladed projectile points, some with straight bases and others stemmed and barbed. The pottery included incised and zone-punctated sherds, sherds marked with distinctive "drag-and-jab" incised-punctated decoration, net-marked, basketry-marked, and red-slipped and simple red-line painted types. The incised, punctated, and "drag-and-jab" decorated pieces point very definitely to the Paraná Valley and may indeed have been imports from there to the Córdoba hill country. On the other hand, the net-marked, basket-impressed, and red-painted specimens are more uniquely local and suggest a resident pottery tradition that was perhaps developing in the Sierras Centrales through stimulus diffusion from either the Paraná or the South Andean centers to the north. Pottery spindle whorls were numerous at Rumipal and were distinctively decorated with incisions and punctations. Pottery pipes are also present in the collections as are well-made little figurines with characteristic slit eyes and headdresses indicated by dot punctations. Villa Rumipal burials were simple, flexed interments with grave goods.

The other site zone is the Pampa de Olaen, in northwestern Córdoba.[206] The early Ayampitín-type site (p. 56) is one of the sites in this zone; however, other site locations there belong to the ceramic horizon. Both open villages and rock

Figure 4-52. Potsherd and figurine from the Córdoba–San Luis subarea. (Redrawn from Aparicio, 1946.)

shelters are represented. The artifacts from these are much the same as those from Rumipal. Although no Paraná-style incised-punctated sherds are reported, the red-line painted style is represented. Some of these painted sherds are large enough to indicate open bowl forms or narrow-necked bottles. The net-impressed ware is present as is the above-mentioned corncob-striated type.

The Sierras Centrales cannot be left without at least brief mention of the notable pictographs that are found in the northern part of the province of Córdoba on rock shelter walls. Some of these—painted in red-white-and-black and depicting animals and humans—are among the outstanding pictographs of South America or, for that matter, the New World.[207] Most likely, they are the work of the cultures herein described. That some of them date from relatively late times is assured by subject matter of battle scenes between Indians and Europeans.

The South Andes in Summary Perspective

The history of the South Andes and the South Andean cultural tradition as here construed visualizes the significant modification of ancient Andean Hunting-Collecting and Pacific Littoral cultures by diffusions—and perhaps migrations—primarily from the agricultural societies of the Peruvian area and secondarily from those of the southwestern Amazon Basin.[207a] These diffusions resulted in the establishment of farming and pottery-making cultures throughout most of the South Andes in what has been designated as the Early Ceramic Period—a span of time estimated at 500 B.C. to A.D. 600. Toward the end of this period additional diffusions from the Bolivian

altiplano and, perhaps, from the Peruvian coast helped transform the relatively simple "neolithic-type" cultures and societies of the Early Period into more complex ones. This complexity is expressed in new aesthetic-ideological forms and in signs of an emerging class structure. To be sure, the processes leading to these latter changes cannot all be classed as diffusion from "higher civilizations"; the local adaptation and spread of farming and herding technologies to new territories and the concomitant increases in population must have prepared South Andean societies to receive these foreign influences.

These new developments climaxed in the Middle Ceramic Period—from A.D. 600 to 1000—and a part of this climax was the extension of the Tiahuanaco "empire" into the northern subareas of the South Andes. Most of the South Andean area, however, seems to have remained culturally (and probably politically) autonomous. This Middle Period marks an esthetic florescence in its ceramics and other arts.

The Late Ceramic Period sees something of an aesthetic decline, although there is no general cultural decline. This was a period of concentrated towns and fortified towns. The latter trait, especially in the northern part of the area, was pronounced and surely indicative of an era of warfare and strong competition between small regional, or town, states. There is no good evidence, however, that any of these town states ever went on to become the nucleus of a larger territorial kingdom or empire—as happened in Peru. Imperial unification was to come to the South Andes only from the outside—by way of the Inca empire, which extended its influence by armed might through most of the South Andean area between A.D. 1450 and 1490.[208]

Footnotes

1 This section is based on various sources, but see, especially, James (1959—chapters on Chile and Argentina) and Bird (1943, pp. 183–186).

2 Schaedel (1957); Núñez (1965).

3 See Lothrop (1946).

4 See Casanova (1946). The "North" division of Bennett, Bleiler, and Sommer (1948, pp. 19–43) corresponds fairly closely to the Puna subarea (see their maps, pp. 14 and 20); however, I have fol-

lowed Gonzalez (1963 a, fig. 13) in extending it somewhat farther south.

5 Casanova (1946). This also falls within Bennett, Bleiler, and Sommer's (1948) "North" division.

6 The Selvas Occidentales subarea follows Gonzalez (1963 a, fig.

13), who would include within it the hilly Iruya-Victoria regions, which lie to the east of the Quebrada de Humahuaca; see Bennett, Bleiler, and Sommer (1948, p. 19). Much of the Selvas Occidentales corresponds to what Bennett, Bleiler, and Sommer (1948, map p. 14 and pp. 44–98) have called the Center division.

7 The Valliserrana subarea follows Gonzalez (1963 a, fig. 13). It would correspond to the "South" and part of the "Center" divisions of Bennett, Bleiler, and Sommer (1948, map. p. 14, and pp. 99–119 for "South"). See also Márquez Miranda (1946 a).

8 See Willey (1946 a); Boman (1920); Metraux (1929); Canals Frau (1946 a). Mendoza Neuquén is not included in the subareal divisions of the South Andes by either Bennett, Bleiler, and Sommer (1948) or Gonzalez (1963 a). My article (1946 a) treated Mendoza-Neuquén as a part of the "Greater Pampa." Now, however, I am more inclined to see it as South Andean.

9 This is Gonzalez's (1963 a, fig. 13) "Chaco-Santiagueño" subarea and, for Bennett, Bleiler, and Sommer (1948, map p. 14, and pp. 120–139), the "East" division. See also Márquez Miranda (1946 b).

10 See Gonzalez (1963 a, fig. 13); see also Aparicio (1946).

11 Secondary references pertaining to this short section may be found in Bennett (1946 c), Casanova (1946), Márquez Miranda (1946 a, b), Aparicio (1946), Canals Frau (1946), Willey (1946 b), Lothrop (1946), and Cooper (1946 a). These articles, all in *The Handbook of South American Indians,* Vol. 2, also contain primary references.

12 See Mason (1950) and Steward and Faron (1959, pp. 16–30); see also this volume, p. 12 and figure 1–5.

13 Bird (1946 a).

14 See Gonzalez (1961–64 b and 1963 a, fig. 14).

15 Gonzalez (1963 a); Núñez (1965). See also Orellana (1964) for indications of dating on the appearance of Tiahuanaco influences in the Atacama.

16 Bird (1943, p. 87).

17 See Bird (1943, 1946 c).

18 Bird (1943, p. 246) lists coiled basketry as accompanying the flexed burials; however, he says elsewhere (p. 249) that the trait was not present at Quiani. This latter statement may be due to his feeling that contemporaneity of midden levels and burials cannot be established (p. 249).

19 Carlos Munizaga (1957) has made a detailed analysis of the Uhle (1919) sequence for the Arica region and has compared this sequence, period for period and trait by trait, with that of Bird (1943). In general, Uhle's "Aborigenes de Arica" period corresponds to Quiani I and II and to the upper levels of the Quiani midden that showed incipient cultivation evidences. I would suggest, as I do in the discussions here, that Uhle's "Aborigenes de Arica" period probably lasts longer than the Quiani II phase as that is defined by Bird; and this later extension has been designated here as Quiani II–Chinchorro.

20 Núñez (1965, pp. 44–48).

20a See Núñez (1967–68) for details of these figurines.

21 Present with Chinchorro burials and with Quiani flexed burials, although not found in the Quiani midden.

22 These and other north Chilean radiocarbon dates are compiled by Núñez (1965, Appendix I).

23 Faldas del Morro refers to the burial complex, with pottery, from the slopes of the Morro de Arica where Uhle (1919, 1922) excavated; see Núñez (1965, pp. 55–59). Pichalo III is the phase designation now usually given to Bird's (1943) earliest pottery period at Pichalo.

24 A Spanish term widely used by Argentinian and Chilean archaeologists.

25 Bird (1943).

26 Bird (1943, 1946 c) originally used the terms "Pichalo I" and "Pichalo II" for his two pottery periods at Pichalo, referring to the earlier preceramic levels of the midden simply as the "first prepottery period" and the "second prepottery period"; however, general usage in late years has modified this to Pichalo I and II (both pre-

ceramic) and Pichalo III and IV (ceramic) periods.

27 Lanning and Patterson (1967, ms.) date Pichalo I as later than Quiani I. They see the projectile points of Quiani I as nearer the true willow-leaf or Ayampitín form, with those of Pichalo I as the smaller modification of this form. This is a possible interpretation; but I am inclined to rely on the shell fishhooks that the two phases share as a more reliable chronological guide in this instance.

28 Most of the burials that Bird (1943, pp. 273–275) recovered at Pichalo were not in the immediate midden excavation but in nearby cemetery areas. These he is inclined to date as contemporaneous with his two pottery periods (Pichalo III and IV).

29 Bird (1943, p. 276). With reference to this question of the first appearance of coiled baskets at Quiani, see p. 205 and footnote 18.

30 Bird (1943).

31 See, for example, Gonzalez (1963, fig. 14) and Berdichewsky (1965, chronology chart). The latter uses the names "Morro Colorado I and II."

32 Berdischewsky (1965) refers to the preceramic Caleta Chimba phase of Antofagasta and the Punta Blanca and Agua Dulce phases of Tocopilla.

33 Núñez (1965) refers to this Taltal pottery phase as Cerro Colorado II, as he recognizes only one preceramic phase at Taltal. In this, I have followed Gonzalez (1963, fig. 14), who designates it as Cerro Colorado III.

34 Niemeyer and Schiappacasse (1963).

35 For radiocarbon date see Núñez (1965, Appendix I).

36 Bird's (1943, pp. 301–306) surveys and test excavations had given clues to preceramic culture in the Coquimbo–La Serena region, including the Herradura site (Iribarren, 1960).

37 Schiappacasse and Niemeyer (1964); Iribarren (1956).

38 Iribarren (1962 a) cites evidence to suggest that the "tacitas" were also used by later agricultural peoples of the subarea and that they may have been used for the pre-

paration of cultivated plant foods. One circumstance that Schiappacasse and Niemeyer (1964) note is that the "tacitas" are not found in the Atacama subarea coastal sites, where extreme aridity precluded plant resources. This is a good argument for their employment in plant food preparation. A contrary argument is advanced, however, by Gajardo Tobar (1958–59), who feels that the "tacitas" had a ceremonial significance.

39 Schiappacasse and Niemeyer (1964) follow Bird (1943) in suggesting that the "shell fishhook" horizon may be later in the Valles Transversales subarea than in the north. This is a good possibility, but until more radiocarbon dates are available it is probably best to align the cultural phases on this horizon more or less contemporaneously, as we have done in Figure 4–2.

40 Similar blades were found with burials near Taltal but not in the middens (Bird, 1943).

41 Iribarren's (1956) burials are tentatively divided into two such phases by Schiappacasse and Niemeyer (1964).

42 Gajardo Tobar (1962–63).

43 The Rio Choapa region is the only one where these artifacts might be said to compose a "complex"; however, occasional geometric stones have occurred as far north as the northern limits of Coquimbo Province (Iribarren, 1961).

44 Gajardo Tobar (1962–63). Iribarren (1961) also seems inclined to this dating; however, in an earlier work, he suggested Huentelauquén to be later than the "shell fishhook" horizon (Iribarren, 1957).

45 Gajardo Tobar (1962–63); Iribarren (1962 b). For the California "cogged stones" see Eberhart (1961).

46 Eberhart (1961, p. 361).

47 Montane (1964) reviews this correlation of archaeological sites with the two Chilean marine terraces and discusses the question of rising and falling sea levels or shore lines. Almost certainly the height of the sea was considerably greater during Preceramic Period V—and probably much of Preceramic Period VI—than it is today. This would

appear to correlate with the climatic optimum; the lowering of the sea (or the rising of the land) would correlate with the Medithermal (after 2500 B.C.).

48 J. E. Silva (1964). Although preceramic sites are not found on the lower marine terrace, some ceramic sites do occur on the upper terrace where—fortunately for stratigraphic purposes—they often overlie the earlier pottery-less deposits.

49 Berdichewsky (1964).

50 Ericksen (1960 a) describes human skeletons from the "Shell Fishhook" cultures of the Herradura and Guanaqueros middens as being of short stature, gracile, and either dolichocephalic or mesocephalic.

51 Gajardo Tobar (1958–59).

52 Bird (1943, pp. 308–309).

53 Berdichewsky (1964).

54 Ortiz Troncoso (1964).

55 Menghin (1959–60).

56 Bird (1943, pp. 308–309, 1946 b).

57 The "Casas de Piedras" finds of stone foundations, lithic materials, and basketry from the Andean highland slopes of interior Coquimbo (Iribarren, 1949, 1957) probably should also be accommodated to the Andean Hunting-Collecting tradition.

58 Gonzalez (1960).

59 Pascual (1960).

60 Menghin and Gonzalez (1954); Gonzalez (1960, pp. 174–178). In the earlier reference a date for the beginning of Ongamira IV–III was estimated at about 3000 B.C.; in the latter reference Gonzalez suggests an upward revision to 1000–500 B.C. In the reconstruction given here I have preferred the first dating estimate. Another aspect of Ongamira IV should be mentioned. Owing to the lack of well-chipped stone artifacts, Gonzalez suggests the possibility of an ancient horizon in the cave—or, at least, a horizon characterized by a retarded pre-projectile point technology. Following this hypothesis, Ongamira III traits were then intruded into this horizon, either mechanically through strata mixture or culturally through influence. Gonzalez puts this forward, quite cautiously, as one variant interpretation. Alternatively, he also suggests limited sampling, or

some circumstance of local conditions, to explain the crude quartz implements in the lower levels. On the evidence presented, I should prefer these alternative explanations.

61 See, for example, Ericksen (1960 a, b, c).

62 Bird (1943).

63 Bird (1943, p. 265).

64 T. C. Patterson (personal communication, 1967).

65 Lanning (1967, chronology chart).

66 Bird (1943).

67 Núñez (1965); Dauelsberg (1963).

68 Berdichewsky (1965); for Cerro Colorado pottery see Bird (1943).

69 Niemeyer and Schiappacasse (1963).

70 Orellana Rodríguez (1964). The descriptions of San Pedro I presented here are based on this reference and on Orellana Rodríguez (1963) and Núñez (1965).

71 Le Paige (1963 b, c) has argued that this transition from San Pedro I to II is substantially earlier, and his argument is based on a radiocarbon date of A.D. 263 for a context in which San Pedro Polished Black pottery is present. See Orellana Rodríguez (1964). In Le Paige's opinion, Tiahuanacoid influence appeared in the Atacama at this early date. This, I think, is unlikely, and I follow Orellana Rodríguez's (1964) critique of Le Paige's use of this single date.

72 For El Molle see Cornely (1940, 1953, 1956 a, b, 1958); Iribarren Charlín (1957, 1962 a); Iribarren Charlín and others (1958); Montane (1962).

73 Iribarren Charlín (1962 a).

74 Iribarren Charlín (1962 c).

75 Mostny (1943, 1944) describes this Chilean Condorhuasi Polychrome as the "Fourth Style." See also Gonzalez (1963 a); Montane (1962); Iribarren Charlín and others (1958).

76 See Iribarren Charlín (1964) for a discussion of negative-painting in El Molle.

77 Gonzalez (1963 a). This author also points out that the polychrome and stepped motif idea could have been introduced into the Valley Transversales subarea in this

way, that is, from the Peruvian coast, where it is to be found in the Nazca styles. However, he favors—as I would—the introduction of these traits into northwestern Argentina from Bolivia and, ultimately, from Tiahuanaco or pre-Tiahuanaco levels in the Lake Titicaca region. From northwestern Argentina they then spread to Chile.

78 Ambrosetti (1897); Bruch (1913); Bennett, Bleiler, and Sommer (1948, pp. 82–83). Another site in the Tafí Valley is La Ciénega (see Quiroga, 1899; Bennett, Bleiler, and Sommer, 1948, pp. 82–83); however, this La Ciénega is not to be confused with the La Ciénega site zone of the Hualfín Valley in Catamarca Province, which figures importantly in the discoveries pertaining to Ciénega, Aguada, and Condorhuasi complexes.

79 Bennett, Bleiler, and Sommer (1948, pp. 89–90).

80 Gonzalez (1963 a).

81 Gonzalez (1961–64 b).

82 Gonzalez (1963 a). In this connection, Cigliano (1959–60) reports a stratigraphy from Molino del Puerto, two kilometers north of the city of Santa María (Catamarca), in which Santamariana, Aguada, Ciénega, and a polished black monochrome ceramic were found in that order, from the top downward. The black monochrome levels here may represent the Tafí I horizon or something closely related to it.

83 Gonzalez (1967) suggests a San Juan sequence of Calingasta I and II (Early Ceramic Period) and Calingasta III (Middle Ceramic Period). This is based on pottery observed at the Calingasta site (Debenedetti, 1917) and from excavations at the Volpianski site (the location of the radiocarbon date).

84 Gonzalez (1963 a).

85 Debenedetti (1931). Uhle (1912) also recognized this pottery as distinctive and believed it to be earlier than the painted wares of the Argentine "Diaguita" or "Calchaqui" styles.

86 Bennett, Bleiler and Sommer (1948, pp. 101–102).

87 Gonzalez (1961, 1963 a). In an earlier article Gonzalez (1955) had the Ciénega I and II phases reversed chronologically because, at that time, he believed Aguada preceded Ciénega and the indicated stylistic seriation was one that showed a loss rather than an elaboration of the feline motifs.

88 Gonzalez and Núñez Regueiro (1958–59); Núñez Regueiro (1970).

89 For example, see the sculptures illustrated by Bennett (1946 b, fig. 18, p. 135) from Mocachi, or that illustrated by Alcina (1965, fig. 518, p. 643).

90 Gonzalez (1956).

91 Gonzalez (1961–64 b); Núñez Regueiro (1970).

92 Gonzalez (1963 a).

93 Krapovickas (1958–59).

94 Lafon (1958–59).

95 Lafon (1957); see also Alcina (1965, p. 671, for comment).

96 Gonzalez (1963 a).

97 Rydén (1936) and Willey (1946 b) summarize this culture and also the archaeological literature pertaining to it.

98 Gonzalez (1963 a) indicates Candelaria I, II, and III phases on his chronology chart (fig. 14). Phases I and II are placed in the Early Ceramic Period; Phase III begins the Middle Ceramic Period and probably is intended to include some of the effigy pieces and two-color painted wares; however, this "phasing" of Candelaria is largely speculative and inferential.

99 Ambrosetti (1906).

100 Gonzalez (1963 a).

101 See Aparicio (1948) and Howard and Willey (1948) for summaries and illustrations of these styles. They are also discussed in this volume, pp. 465–467.

102 Bennett, Bleiler, and Sommer (1948, pp. 125–126, 136–139); see also Casanova (1942).

103 Reichlen (1940).

104 Gonzalez (1955, 1963 a, fig. 14). While there can be little doubt that a sequence does exist in the Chaco-Santiagueño subarea, it should be pointed out that the sites of Las Mercedes, Sunchituyoj, and Averías are probably all multiple occupation sites, and this makes it difficult to provide appropriate descriptions for the phases by using Reichlen's trait lists. Alcina (1965, pp. 681–683) runs into difficulty in this way by describing a Las Mercedes phase which has Bislín incised pottery but also takes in polychrome types that are probably later.

105 Rydén (1952).

106 Ibarra Grasso (1958–59, 1960) presents various arguments for the pre-Tiahuanaco position.

107 Ibarra Grasso (1958–59, 1960) feels there are clues to Chullpa Pampa (and his Cultura de los Túmulos) in the lower levels of the Tiahuanaco site. He may be referring to Qeya or Qalasasaya, although these styles seem too developed in their decorative treatment to be ancestral to Chullpa Pampa.

108 At Tiquipaya, Illuri, and Colcapirhua, Bennett (1936, pp. 375–412) found non-Tiahuanacoid burial urns, similar to Chullpa Pampa large vessels, underlying Tiahuanaco horizon pottery. I am indebted to T. C. Patterson (personal communication, 1968) for calling this to my attention and also for the use of his manuscript on this subject (Patterson, 1963 a, ms.).

109 Ibarra Grasso (1958–59, 1960, n.d.). Ibarra Grasso lists such regional variants as Cultura Megalítica de Oruro (sites in Oruro); Cultura Megalítica de Cochabamba (sites in Cochabamba, including Cliza and Chullpa Pampa, and sites in Chuquisaca and Potosí); Cultura Tarija Inciso (sites in Tarija); and Cultura Lípez Inciso (site in Potosí).

110 Ibarra Grasso (n.d., 1953 a, b, 1956).

111 Bennett (1934).

112 Rowe and Menzel (1964, ms.) and Menzel (1964) feel that Bennett's (1934) distinction between "Classic" and "Decadent" Tiahuanaco was a segregation based on relative fineness and elegance of the pottery and not one that could be demonstrated stratigraphically or chronologically. I am not fully convinced of this and think that there probably were time trends in the direction Bennett indicated between "Classic" and "Decadent"; however, the question of "Derived" Tiahuanaco and its chronological placement is another matter.

113 Bennett (1936, p. 505).

114 Ibarra Grasso (1953 a, 1958–59).

115 Arani is treated by Bennett

(1936), and Tupuraya and Cayhuasi by Rydén (1959).

116 Bennett (1936); Rydén (1956).

117 Ibarra Grasso (1953 a, 1958–59); Ibarra Grasso and Branisa (1955). At the Tupuraya site, in the Cochabamba region, Rydén (1959) found pottery that could be classified as "Classic" or "Decadent" Tiahuanaco, according to the Bennett definitions, without any cavil. This included polychrome keros, flaring-sided bowls, and necked jars. He also found "Derived Tiahuanaco" vessels. His inclination was to seriate these in a "Classic"-"Derived"-"Decadent" sequence running in that order. The other interpretation here, however, would be to put the "Derived" component—which Ibarra Grasso has called the Tupuraya style—as the earliest. It is then followed by the Tiahuanaco horizon pottery. Also, much of the pottery that Rydén (1956) illustrates from the Mizque Valley has designs that are Tiahuanaco horizon-derived. See especially, his Figure 43, p. 107.

118 Bennett (1936).

119 Ibarra Grasso (1958–59).

120 Ibarra Grasso (1953 a).

121 Núñez (1965); Orellana Rodríguez (1964).

122 Orellana Rodríguez (1968).

123 Dauelsberg (1959 a, b); Núñez (1965).

124 Núñez (1965); Orellana Rodriguez (1968); Spahni (1964).

125 Rydén (1944); Spahni (1964).

126 General sources on Atacameño archaeology are Latcham (1936 a, b) and Bennett (1946 c).

127 Niemeyer and Schiappacasse (1963).

128 Niemeyer (1962).

129 Núñez (1966). The architecture of this site is fully consistent with the Late Ceramic Period pattern for the Atacama subarea; however, this is the one site of those named here that has a very meagre ceramic component upon which to base a dating and cultural assignment. Núñez (1966) says that the few sherds found there resemble Pichalo III; but, if so, and if these sherds date the site, the settlement and architectural pattern is out of

line with everything else that we know about the Early Ceramic Period and the beginnings of agriculture in north Chile.

130 Núñez (1965).

131 Núñez (1965) offers a summary of Chiribaya and Maytas as well as San Miguel and Gentilar. The most adequate descriptions of the latter, however, are those of Bird (1943) in his discussion of the work at Playa Miller near Arica.

132 Uhle (1919) referred to the Gentilar style as "Chincha-Atacameño." In his opinion, the late Atacameño communities of the north Chilean coast had been brought under the cultural and political dominance of the Chincha "kingdom" of the South Coast of Peru. Archaeologists now see little in the way of Chincha stylistic relationships to Gentilar. The connection, which probably does exist, is a remote one in that the late South Coast Peruvian styles and the late Arica region styles both have an ancient common ancestry in the Tiahuanaco horizon. Both traditions, thereafter, follow the same trends toward reduction in design size, greater fine decorative complexity, and repetitive treatments (see Willey, 1954 b, for a commentary on this phenomenon).

133 Spahni (1967).

134 Gonzalez (1963 a). These influences of the Tiahuanaco horizon in the Puna would presumably fall in what Gonzalez has designated as a "Pozuelos" phase (1963 a, Fig. 14).

135 Debenedetti (1910, 1912); Bennett, Bleiler, and Sommer (1948, pp. 19–43).

136 Lafon (1958–59) dates this Middle Period complex as being on or after the Tiahuanaco horizon. In my dating (fig. 4–3) I have placed such a complex in the Middle Ceramic Period and thought it likely that it might date there; however, it could have been derived from earlier, pre-Tiahuanaco horizon diffusions into northwestern Argentina, just as I think that Condorhuasi Polychrome was so derived.

137 Gonzalez (1963 a).

138 Casanova (1938); Bennett, Bleiler, and Sommer (1948, p. 30).

139 Bennett, Bleiler, and Som-

mer (1948, p. 26); Krapovickas (1958–59 a).

140 Debenedetti (1930); Bennett, Bleiler, and Sommer, 1948, pp. 31–32. This is near, but separate from, the previously mentioned site of La Isla de Tilcara.

141 Debenedetti and Casanova (1933–35); Bennett, Bleiler, and Sommer, 1948, p. 37.

142 Bennett, Bleiler, and Sommer (1948, p. 26).

143 Gonzalez (1963 a, fig. 14).

144 Aguada culture is described by Gonzalez (1961).

145 Gonzalez (1961–64 b).

146 The ceramic tradition I am referring to would subsume the pottery of what Bennett, Bleiler, and Sommer call the Yocavil culture tradition—with its Calchaquí, Transitional, and Inca-influenced subdivisions (1948, pp. 90–95)—as well as their Belén and Aimogasta cultures (1948, p. 117).

147 Gonzalez (1963 a, fig. 14, 1967).

148 For a description of San José urns see Bennett, Bleiler, and Sommer (1948, pp. 54–56).

149 Gonzalez (1955).

150 Gonzalez (1967).

151 Santa María urns are described by Bennett, Bleiler, and Sommer (1948, pp. 50–54); however in their placement of them chronologically they assign them a position contemporaneous with that of the San José urns (1948, p. 98). In this presentation I follow Gonzalez's (1963 a, fig. 14) chronology instead. Belén urns are also described by Bennett, Bleiler, and Sommer (1948, p. 104).

152 Madrazo and Ottonello de Garcia Reinoso (1966, p. 52) indicate that they may even be as early as San José in this region.

153 Gonzalez (1955); Madrazo and Ottonello de Garcia Reinoso (1966).

154 Gonzalez (1967) says that the Angualasto culture of San Juan lacked the concentrated and fortified-town type of settlement until Inca times. San Juan is in the extreme southern portion of the Valliserrana.

155 Lothrop (1946).

156 Cornely (1950) places this Condorhuasi influence in the Classic

phase; however, Montane (1962) and Gonzalez (1956, 1963 a) put it with Archaic. See also Mostny (1943, 1944) for description of this Condorhuasi or "Fourth Style" pottery.

157 Ericksen (1960 a, b, c).

158 Latcham (1928 a, b).

159 Cornely (1950, 1951, 1956 b).

160 Montane (1960); Niemeyer and Montane (1960); Garjardo Tobar (1962–63).

161 Montane (1962).

162 Latcham (1928 b); Lothrop (1946).

163 Reichlen (1940).

164 Bennett, Bleiler, and Sommer (1948, pp. 128–129). There is an unfortunate terminological confusion here because the name Averías has also been selected to represent the Late Period phase of Chaco-Santiagueño culture; (see Gonzalez, 1963 a, fig. 14) but the type must be one of the earlier painted wares of the subarea.

165 Bennett, Bleiler, and Sommer (1948, pp. 126–128).

166 See my comments on this sequence as expressed in footnote 104, this chapter.

167 In this I disagree with the chronology and seriations suggested by Bennett, Bleiler, and Sommer (1948, pp. 136–139). The "Black-on-red" pottery phase follows the designation of Gonzalez (1963 a, fig. 14).

168 The principal references for Chaco-Santiagueño are Bennett, Bleiler, and Sommer (1948); Reichlen (1940); Casanova (1942). There is also the "classic" work of the Wagner brothers (1934).

169 Bennett, Bleiler, and Sommer (1948, p. 135).

170 Bennett (1936, pp. 393–394).

171 For example, Spahni (1964) reports Saxamar pottery at Lasana; see also Núñez (1965) and Orellana Rodríguez (1968).

172 Niemeyer (1963).

173 Iribarren and others (1962).

174 Latcham (1928 a); Menghin (1959–60).

175 Berdichewsky (1964 a).

176 Mostny (1946–47).

177 Mostny (1955); Medina (1958); Figueroa (1958); Reyes (1958).

178 Debenedetti (1930).

179 Bennett, Bleiler, and Sommer (1948, pp. 22–24, 62).

180 Krapovickas (1958–59 b).

181 Bennett, Bleiler, and Sommer (1948, p. 78).

182 Bennett Bleiler, and Sommer (1948, pp. 86–87, 94–95, 116).

183 The Angualasto-Inca phase (Gonzalez, 1967).

184 Canals Frau and Semper (1956).

185 J. E. Silva (1964).

186 Berdichewsky (1964 a, b). The identification of the negative-painted specimen, from the text description, is my own surmise and should not be attributed to Berdichewsky.

187 Menghin (1959–60, 1962 b).

188 Menghin (1959–60), however, estimates it as later (A.D. 1000–1200).

189 Berdichewsky (1968) follows Menghin in dating his lower cave levels, and Pitrén, at about A.D. 1200. His second and third phases lack any painted pottery, however, which is curious.

190 Montane (1960 b).

191 Latcham (1928 a).

192 Menghin (1959–60).

193 Berdichewsky (1964 a)—the Paraguas I and II styles at Potrero La Viña.

194 Bullock (1955).

195 Bullock (1936, 1955).

196 In this, I would follow Menghin's (1959–60) interpretation as opposed to Latcham's view (1928 b), in which the latter saw the Araucanians as late-comers from the Argentine Pampas.

197 See Cooper (1946 a), Canals Frau (1946 b), and Padden (1957) for summaries of Araucanian history and ethnography.

198 Canals Frau and Semper (1956). The pottery that Aparicio (1935) describes from Lake Lacar may also belong to Agrelo.

199 Boman (1920).

200 Boman (1920); Canals Frau (1964 a).

201 Métraux (1929).

202 See Willey (1946 a) for a summary of these.

203 The "clavas insignias" are known largely from Neuquén, Mendoza, and adjoining Chile (Schobinger, 1956).

204 These early accounts are summarized by Aparicio (1936, 1946).

205 Gonzalez (1943).

206 Gonzalez (1949).

207 Gardner (1931).

207a The reader's attention is called to the summary article on Chilean archaeology (Mostny, 1969), which appeared after this book had gone to press.

208 The parallelisms of South Andean and Southwestern North American pre-Columbian cultures have long attracted attention (see Meggers, 1967).

The Area

Definition and Setting. Between the areas of the great native American civilizations of Mesoamerica and Peru is a 1500-mile stretch of mountains, tropical valleys, and coastal plains that is referred to as the "Intermediate" area. The name derives from this geographic position—intermediate between the Mexican-Guatemalan and Peruvian centers. The territory of the Intermediate area includes the Ecuadorian Andes and Pacific coast, the Colombian Andes and Pacific Coast, the Colombian Caribbean coast, the Andes of western Venezuela and the adjoining Venezuelan coast, and all of Lower Central America up to a line that extends from the Gulf of Nicoya to the north-central Caribbean coast of Honduras (see map, Fig. 5-1). This latter line is the southern frontier of Mesoamerica as defined in Volume One (p. 85, Fig. 3-6).

The natural environment of the Intermediate area is internally diverse (Fig. 5-2). It is, as its latitude indicates, a tropical land. The climate and vegetation of its high Andean valleys are moderated by this latitude; the lowland valleys and coastal flats are hot and humid. As in Peru, there is a close juxtaposition of high, temperate basins to tropical lowlands. Unlike Peru, and in this regard more like Mesoamerica, the transition between these uplands and lowlands is gradual, with a great variety of "niches" for human habitation in this gradient.

The Intermediate Area

5

As might be expected from its geographical position between Mesoamerica and Peru, the story of cultural development within the Intermediate area is highly complex. Currents of influence from both Mesoamerica and Peru can be recognized; and the cultures of the Intermediate area, in turn, influenced those of the other two areas. This complexity is further compounded by a bewildering subareal and regional diversity in archaeological cultures—a diversity that certainly reflects to a large degree the natural environmental variation within the Intermediate area.

Archaeological Chronology. No area chronology of the kind formulated for Peru or Mesoamerica has yet been projected for all the Intermediate area, and we shall have to devise one for our purposes. This can be done by borrowing from neighboring areas and also by utilizing some of the schemes that have been employed for parts of the Intermediate area (see Figs. 5-4, 5-5, 5-6, 5-7).

For the preceramic periods we will borrow from the Peruvian chronology used in Chapters 2 and 3, although with some modifications.

(1) *Preceramic Period I (prior to 10,000 B.C.).* As with Peru, this period is based on the presence of Flake tradition industries. These have been described from the Ecuadorian coast as the Exacto complex. The Chopper tradition sites of northwestern Venezuela would also fall in this period.

(2) *Preceramic Period II (10,000–9,000 B.C.).* This is the period of the Andean Biface tradition, represented by Las Lagunas in northwestern

Venezuela and Manantial of the Ecuador coast. The beginning date for the period is estimated as some 500 years earlier than the Peruvian area Preceramic Period II, in keeping with the hypothesis that there was a general north-to-south diffusion of the Andean Biface tradition (see Fig. 2-2).

(3) *Preceramic Period III (9000–7000 B.C.).* This is the period of the fish-tailed, fluted projectile points, the El Jobo leaf-shaped points, and of the Old South American Hunting tradition, which subsumes such points.

(4) *Preceramic Period IV (7000–5000 B.C.).* The period is known from such complexes as the leaf-shaped and stemmed point assemblages of El Inga II-III and Las Casitas. It is the era of the Andean Hunting-Collecting tradition.

(5) *Preceramic Period V (5000–3000 B.C.).* The Northwest South American Littoral tradition of the coast dates from this period. Little is known from the interior highlands and valleys although, presumably, Andean Hunting-Collecting tradition societies carried on there.

The ceramic periods of the sequence are a modification of Meggers's Ecuadorian chronology.[1]

(6) *Early Ceramic Period (3000–1500 B.C.).* This period corresponds to the one that Meggers

Figure 5-1. (P. 256)

Figure 5-2. (P. 257)

Figure 5-3. (P. 258)

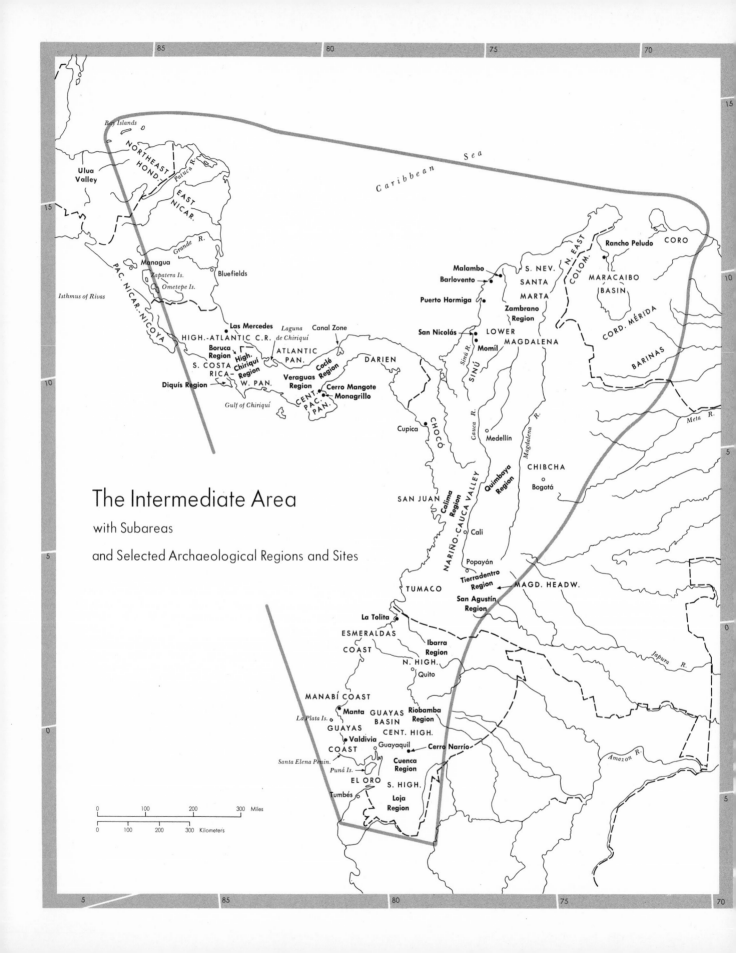

The Intermediate Area

with Subareas

and Selected Archaeological Regions and Sites

Bay Islands

NORTHEAST HOND.

Ulua
Valley

Patuca R.

EAST
NICAR.

PAC. NICAR.-NICOYA

Grande R.

Managua

Zapatera Is.

Ometepe Is.

Bluefields

Isthmus of Rivas

Las Mercedes

Laguna
de Chiriquí

Canal Zone

HIGH.-ATLANTIC C.R.

Boruca
Region

High.
Chiriquí
Region

ATLANTIC
PAN.

Coclé
Region

DARIEN

S. COSTA
RICA

W. PAN.

Veraguas
Region

CENT.
PAC.
PAN.

Cerro Mangote
Monagrillo

Diquís Region

Gulf of Chiriquí

Cupica

CHOCÓ

SAN JUAN

Calima
Region

NARIÑO-CAUCA VALLEY

Medellín

Cauca R.

Quimbaya
Region

Magdalena R.

CHIBCHA

Bogotá

Cali

Popayán

Tierradentro
Region

TUMACO

San Agustín
Region

MAGD. HEADW.

La Tolita

ESMERALDAS
COAST

Ibarra
Region

N. HIGH.

Quito

MANABÍ COAST

La Plata Is.

Manta

GUAYAS
BASIN

CENT. HIGH.

Riobamba
Region

GUAYAS
COAST

Valdivia

Guayaquil

Cerro Narrío

Santa Elena Penin.

Puná Is.

Cuenca
Region

EL ORO

S. HIGH.

Tumbés

Loja
Region

Caribbean Sea

Malambo

Barlovento

Puerto Hormiga

San Nicolás

Momíl

Simú R.

Sinú R.

S. NEV.
SANTA
MARTA

LOWER
MAGDALENA

Zambrano
Region

N. EAST
COLOM.

CORD. MÉRIDA

Rancho Peludo

CORO

MARACAIBO
BASIN

BARINAS

Meta R.

Japura R.

Amazon R.

0   100   200   300   Miles

0   100   200   300   Kilometers

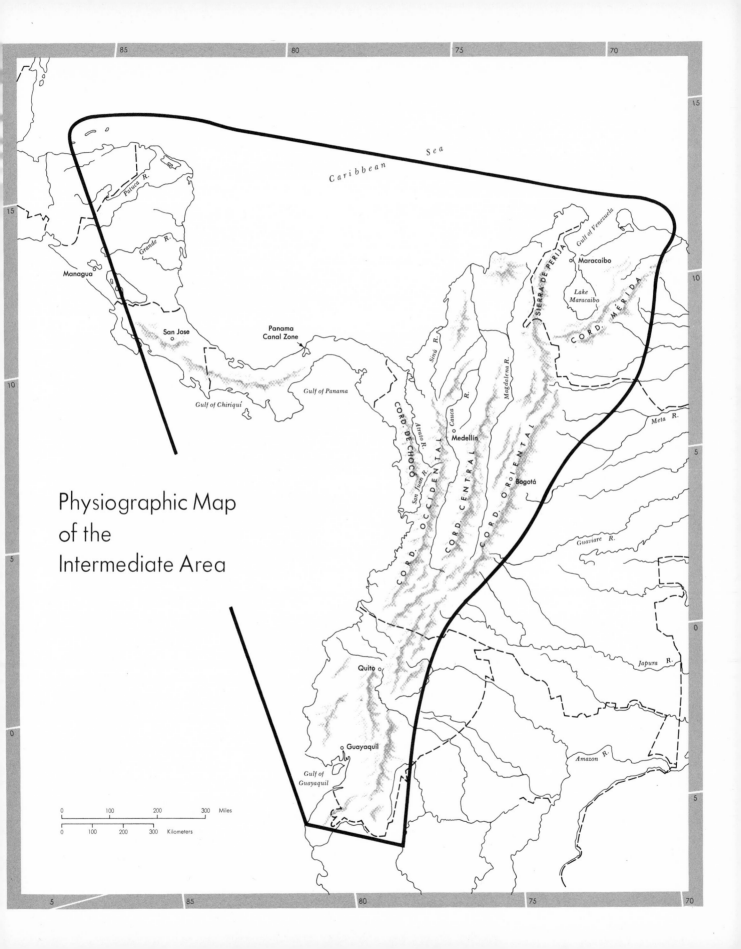

Physiographic Map
of the
Intermediate Area

Caribbean Sea

Managua

San Jose

Panama
Canal Zone

Gulf of Chiriquí

Gulf of Panama

Patuca R.

Grande R.

CORD. DE CHOCO

Atrato R.

San Juan R.

CORD. OCCIDENTAL

Sinú R.

Cauca R.

Medellín

CORD. CENTRAL

Magdalena R.

CORD. ORIENTAL

Bogotá

SIERRA DE PERIJA

Gulf of Venezuela

Maracaibo

Lake
Maracaibo

CORD. MÉRIDA

Meta R.

Guaviare R.

Quito

Guayaquil

Gulf of
Guayaquil

Japura R.

Amazon R.

0   100   200   300   Miles

0   100   200   300   Kilometers

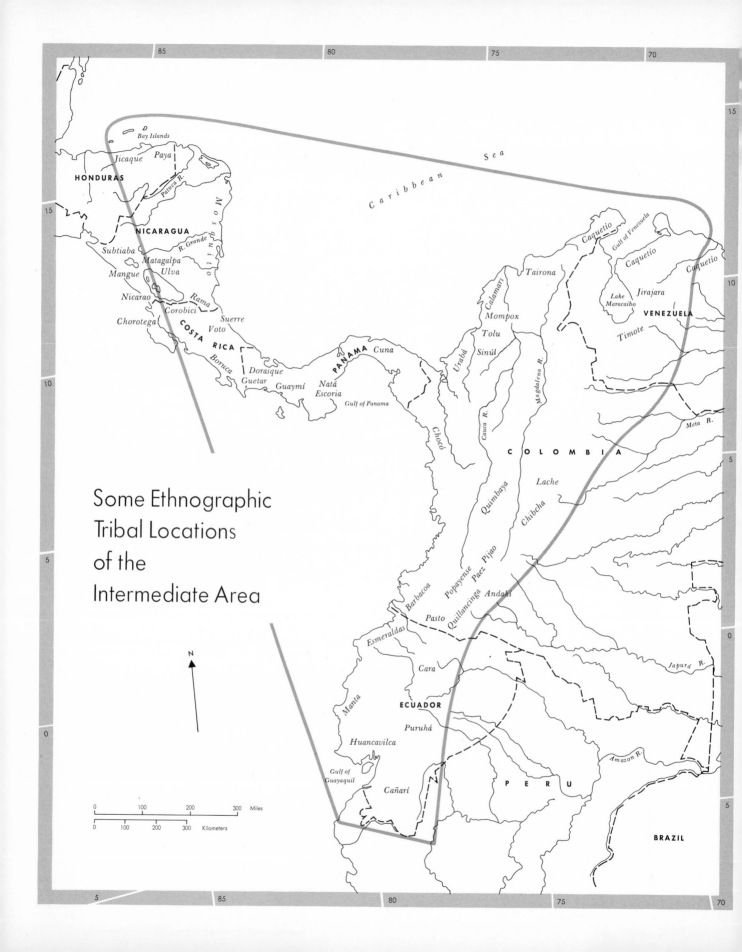

Some Ethnographic
Tribal Locations
of the
Intermediate Area

called "Early Formative." The name has been changed here because these early ceramic phases are considered to be within a different cultural tradition from those that follow. The period pertains to such early ceramic styles as the Valdivia and the Puerto Hormiga, which occur in a context of the late Northwest South American Littoral tradition. Although it is unlikely that pottery was known everywhere within the Intermediate area as early as 3000 B.C., it is highly probable that it had been so diffused before 1500 B.C.

(7) *Formative Period (1500–500 B.C.).* This period sees the establishment of the Intermediate area tradition—a way of life based on farming and, in a broad developmental sense, a way of life comparable to the Peruvian and Mesoamerican cultural traditions with which it is essentially synchronous. The origins of this tradition lay, partly, in the antecedent Early Ceramic Period and in the non-agricultural, or incipient agricul-

Figure 5-4. Chronological chart, with subarea columns, phases, major periods, and estimated dates. Ecuador.

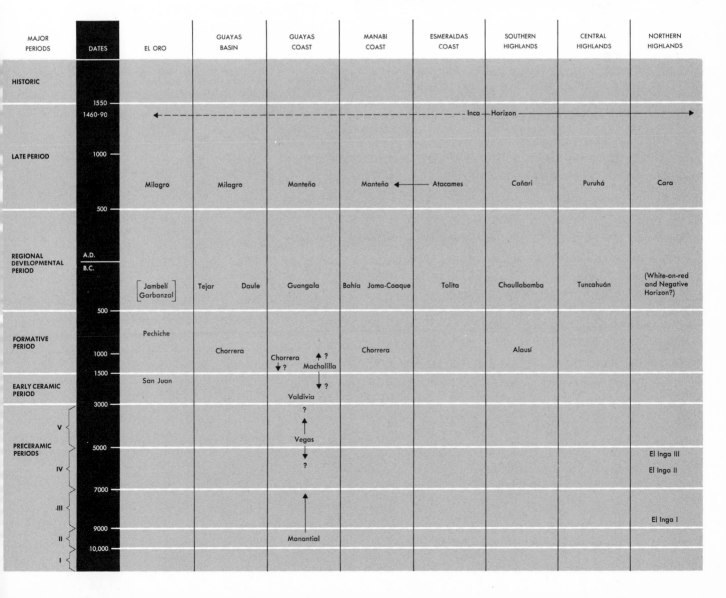

tural, late phases of the Northwest South American Littoral tradition. They also derived, in part, from contacts with the Mesoamerican and Peruvian traditions and the agricultural traditions of the South American tropical lowlands in the Orinoco and Amazon drainages. The period corresponds to Meggers's "Late Formative Period."

(8) *Regional Developmental Period (500* B.C.–A.D. *500)*. With reference to Ecuador, Meggers defines the period as a "...time of differentiation in sociopolitical organization, florescence in art style and elaboration in technology."[2] These characteristics can be extended to other parts of the Intermediate area.

(9) *Late Period (*A.D. *500–1550)*. In Ecuador there are indications of cultural fusions reflective of political unifications and larger territorial

Figure 5-5. Chronological chart, with subarea columns, phases, major periods, and estimated dates. Colombia.

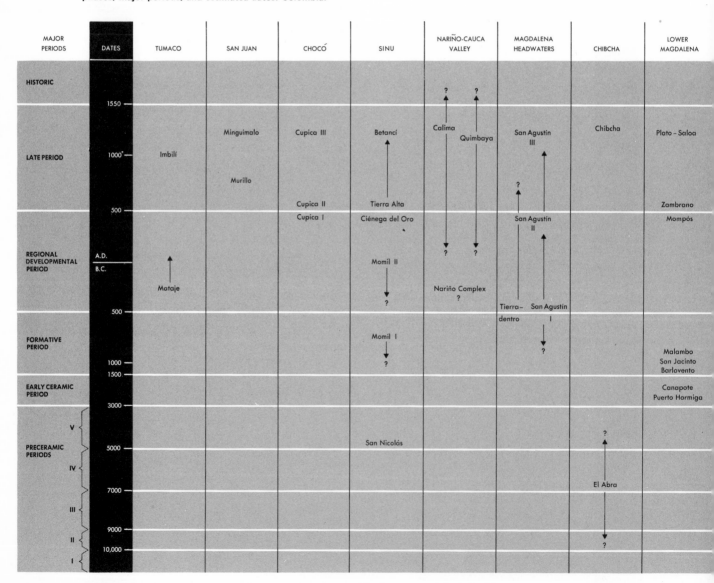

states in this period, and Meggers has applied the name "Integration Period" to it. In Colombia and Lower Central America this trend seems much less marked; in fact, in parts of Colombia there are some signs that the late centuries were characterized instead by political "fragmentation," although there are some moves toward integration, as in the Chibcha state. For the entire Intermediate area, however, the noncommittal term "Late Period" is offered for this time range.

The culture history of the Intermediate area is also plotted out in subareal divisions as well as chronological periods. These are given approximate location on the accompanying map (Fig. 5-1).

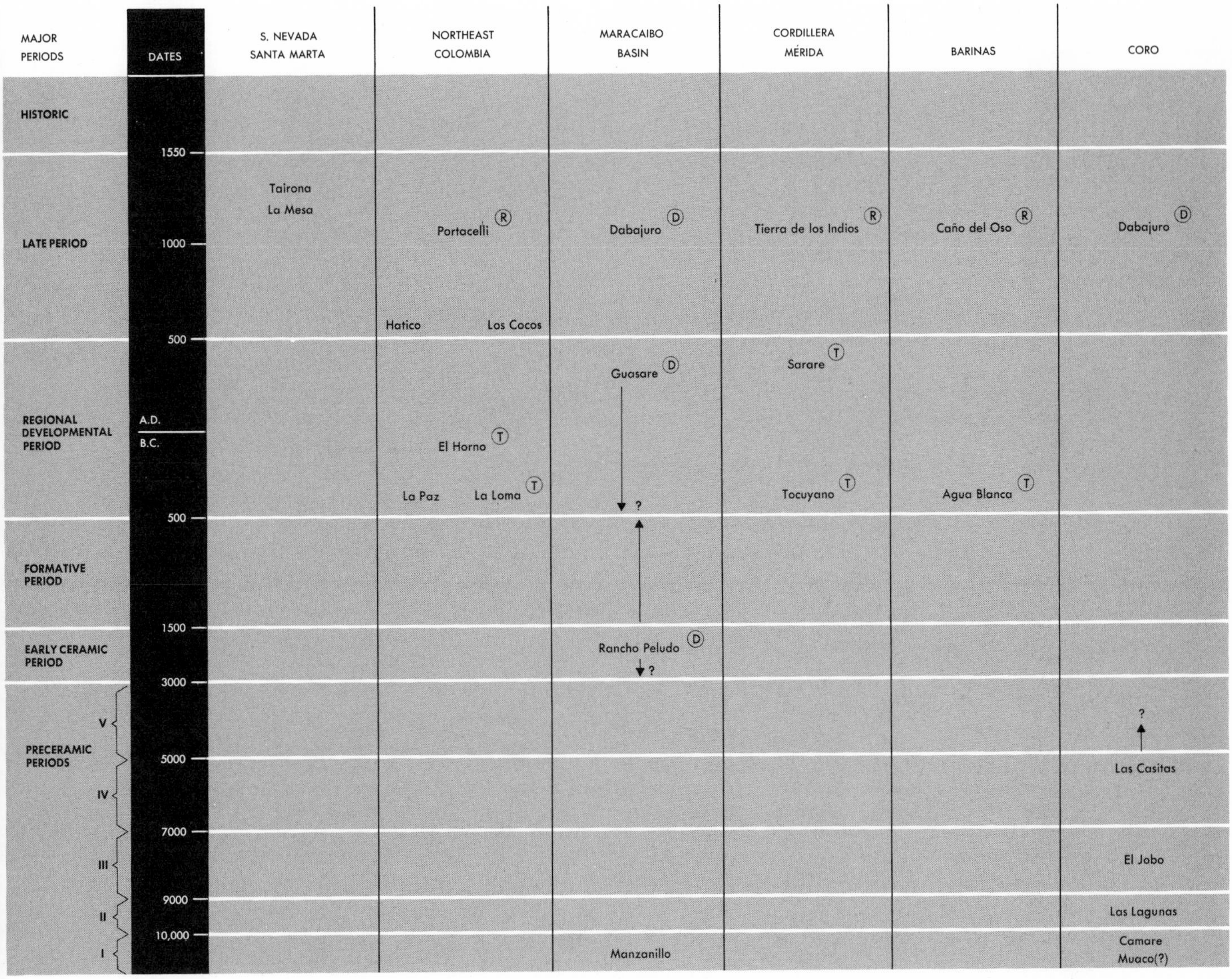

Figure 5-6. Chronological chart, with subarea columns, phases, major periods, and estimated dates. Northeastern Colombia and northwestern Venezuela. The small letters in the circles identify phases as to subtraditions: R, Tierroid; T, Tocuyanoid; D, Dabajuroid.

MAJOR PERIODS	DATES	S. NEVADA SANTA MARTA	NORTHEAST COLOMBIA	MARACAIBO BASIN	CORDILLERA MÉRIDA	BARINAS	CORO
HISTORIC							
	1550						
LATE PERIOD	1000	Tairona La Mesa	Portacelli ⓡ	Dabajuro ⓓ	Tierra de los Indios ⓡ	Caño del Oso ⓡ	Dabajuro ⓓ
	500		Hatico Los Cocos				
REGIONAL DEVELOPMENTAL PERIOD	A.D. B.C.		El Horno ⓣ	Guasare ⓓ ↓	Sarare ⓣ		
			La Paz La Loma ⓣ	?	Tocuyano ⓣ	Agua Blanca ⓣ	
	500			↑			
FORMATIVE PERIOD							
	1500						
EARLY CERAMIC PERIOD				Rancho Peludo ⓓ ↓ ?			
	3000						
PRECERAMIC PERIODS V	5000						? ↑ Las Casitas
IV	7000						
III	9000						El Jobo
II	10,000						Las Lagunas
I				Manzanillo			Camare Muaco(?)

Northwest South American Littoral Tradition: Preceramic Complexes

The Ecuador Coast: Vegas. Sites of Vegas complex have been found on the Santa Elena Peninsula of the Guayas Coast.[3] They are situated on the 10-meter terrace of the old shoreline or a bit farther inland on old stream channels that cut through the coastal terraces. The shoreline sites are shell middens—which offer our only direct evidence of marine subsistence—and Lanning suggests that the former midden dwellers might have followed a seasonal round of winter shellfishing at the beach and summer plant gathering and fishing along the streams. The Santa Elena Peninsula is now dessicated, but a few thousand years ago it is believed to have been in mangrove swamp vegetation; the shells in the middens are of mangrove species. All of the

Figure 5-7. Chronological chart, with subarea columns, phases, major periods, and estimated dates. Lower Central America.

MAJOR PERIODS	DATES	DARIEN	CENTRAL-PACIFIC PANAMA	WESTERN PANAMA–SOUTHERN COSTA R.	HIGHLAND–ATLANTIC C.R.	E. NICAR.–N.E. HONDURAS	S. PERIPHERY OF MESOAMERICA	
							NICOYA-NICAR.	ULUA VALLEY
HISTORIC								
	1550							
LATE PERIOD	1000	↑	Herrera Veraguas	Chiriquí Late Diquís	Las Mercedes	Cocal II		Naco
						Cocal I	Late Polychrome	Plumbate Horizon
			Late Coclé	San Lorenzo		Selin II	Middle Polychrome	
					Curridabat			Ulua Mayoid
	500	Darien Complex	Early Coclé	Burica Early Diquís		Selin I	Early Polychrome	
REGIONAL DEVELOPMENTAL PERIOD			Santa María				Linear Decorated	
	A.D.			Aguas Buenas			↑	
	B.C.		Pueblo Nuevo	La Concepción			Zoned Bichrome Horizon	
								Ulua Bichrome Eden
	500							
FORMATIVE PERIOD								Playa de los Muertos Jaral
	1500		Sarigua					Yarumela I
EARLY CERAMIC PERIOD			Monagrillo					
	3000							
PRECERAMIC PERIODS	V							
	5000		Cerro Mangote					
	IV							
	7000							
	III							
	9000							
	II							
	10,000							
	I							

Vegas artifacts are stone tools. A chert industry has a microlithic aspect, with little side- and end-scrapers, flake knives, gravers, denticulates, and spokeshaves. There are no bifacial pieces or projectile points. Besides the chipped stone implements, cobble choppers and pestles are frequently found in the shell middens, and it is thought that these were used for opening shellfish.

In Lanning's opinion, the Vegas assemblage is reminiscent of the Siches, the Honda, and the Estero complexes of the Far North Coast of Peru;[3a] and some of the rough pebble tools also are like those seen in the Peruvian North Coast Huaca Prieta phase, which we have classed with the Pacific Littoral tradition (pp. 94–96). The suggestion is made here that the boundary line between the Pacific Littoral tradition and the Northwest South American Littoral tradition falls somewhere in Far North Coast Peru and that this boundary was related to the environmental differences of the more abundant marine foods and desert coastal conditions to the south and the former coastal mangrove conditions to the north of the line. Lanning also relates Vegas to the Colombian Pomares and San Nicolás complexes and the Panamanian Cerro Mangote complex.

Colombia: San Nicolás and Other Finds. San Nicolás de Bari is not on the immediate coast but lies a short distance inland on a small eroded hill that is the first high ground met with as one proceeds up the Sinú River delta from the Caribbean coast of Colombia.[4] Numerous chert artifacts and scrap were collected from the hilltop, including flake scrapers, flake knives, and cores with prepared striking platforms. Similar materials were also discovered at Pomares, another river lowland site along the Canal del Dique; and Reichel-Dolmatoff reports still other comparable assemblages from riverbank sites along the Colombian Pacific coast.[5] In Reichel-Dolmatoff's words:

> The range of tools and the riverine or lagoonal environment suggest bands of food-gatherers and fishermen, but certainly not groups dependent upon hunting or cultivation. The emphasis upon scraping and cutting edges may well be connected with the daily task of scaling and cleaning fish, and with the manufacture of fishing gear or other wooden instruments.[6]

Panama: Cerro Mangote. Along the Gulf of Panama, on the Pacific side of that country, there is a stretch of coastal territory on the Azuero Peninsula which is lined with offshore mangrove-covered bars, salt flats, and grasslands. Behind these is the old coastline on which are shell midden sites of preceramic and early ceramic date. Cerro Mangote is one such site;[7] it is located on a hill a short distance back from the delta of the Santa María River. The shell refuse here covers a small area about 50 by 25 meters in extent and in some places is as much as 2 meters deep. Debris includes oyster shells, various mangrove or mud bank shellfish species, and crab remains. Presumably, this had been a shellfishing station at a time when the present-day salt flats between the old coast and the mangrove bar had been active lagoons rich in molluscs. The midden also contained a good many animal bones, especially deer, as well as bird and fish bones. Artifacts included a number of flakes and cores (unprepared) of petrified wood. These are even less specialized in form than those of the Vegas or San Nicolás complexes. Rough ground stone implements were very common. The most distinctive tool was a heavy edge-grinder, shaped only by use. Such grinders could have been used for seed foods prepared in shallow basin metates, of which several were found. A few bone awls, a shell bead, and a little shell pendant (this last possibly associated with a burial) make up the definite Cerro Mangote artifacts, although it is also likely that cut conch shells served as cups or vessels. Burials found in the midden were of two types. One was a secondary bundle form in which the scraped bones of the dead had been contained, apparently, in a small rectangular receptacle, probably a basket. The other was a primary flexed type of interment. The Cerro Mangote midden was potteryless, and its preceramic position is strongly implied by the resemblances in stone types between the Cerro Mangote collections and those from early pottery sites of the same region. There is a Cerro Mangote radiocarbon date of 4860 B.C.

Northwest South American Littoral Tradition: Ceramic Phases

The introduction of ceramics into the Northwest South American Littoral tradition at about 3000 B.C. marks the beginning of the Early Ceramic Period of our area chronology and the beginning of a transition from the old pre-agricultural way of life to the Intermediate area tradition. This transition spanned some 1500 years —from 3000 until 1500 B.C. The cultures of this transition were primarily dependent upon shellfish gathering and other food collecting and hunting, although in all likelihood they were partially or "incipiently" dependent upon plant cultivation.

Valdivia. The best known and most thoroughly documented of early ceramic cultures is the Valdivia.[8] Several Valdivia phase sites have been explored in the Ecuadorian Guayas Coast subarea, where the earlier Vegas complex finds were made. Today this is a semi-arid country of limited seasonal rainfall and xerophytic vegetation (Fig. 5-8). Conditions may have been some-

what more moist here a few thousand years ago, although it is unlikely that the ancient Valdivians found it a much more favorable environment for farming than do the present inhabitants. Subsistence then, as now, was largely from the sea. At that time, however, this part of the Ecuadorian coast was somewhat lower with relation to the level of the ocean, and there were a number of mangrove-fringed tidal lagoons offshore. These lagoons were excellent shellfish gathering places, and the Valdivia sites were situated along their edges. Now, with a rising coast, the lagoons have been transformed into sediment-filled, dry, salt flats or *salitres*.

The middens are made up of venus clams (*Anomalocardia* sp.) and other intertidal species, fish bones, crustacean remains, turtle carapaces, deer bones, and decayed organic matter. The fish were netted or caught with shell fishhooks. As some of the fish remains are those of deepwater species, boats must have been used for deep-sea fishing. Deer were either snared or hunted with spears or darts tipped with wooden points, as no chipped stone points are present in the sites. Finally, these coastal Ecuadorians may have depended to some extent on plant foods, since stone metates and manos are found in the refuse. Whether any of these plants was a domesticate is an open question; but, as Meggers, Evans, and Estrada point out, we know that contemporaneous coastal fishers from nearby Peru were growing

Figure 5-8. A view of the Ecuadorian coast of the Guayas subarea. The Valdivia site is in the immediate foreground; *below* it is the modern fishing village and the Bay of Valdivia. (Courtesy Clifford Evans, Jr. and B. J. Meggers.)

such things as lima beans, squashes, and chili peppers, so that their appearance in a similar situation in Ecuador would not be too surprising.[9] In other words, the principal difference between Peru and Ecuador in this regard may be no more than a condition of extremely favorable preservation for vegetal remains in the former.

Valdivia sites were composed of little clusters of houses. Bits of burned clay wattle-and-daub materials in the refuse give some slight hints concerning the nature of the dwellings. Evidences of fires and hearths also occur at various levels in the midden debris, but no floor or definite foundation evidence has been found. The Valdivia site proper is probably representative in size of settlement. The refuse here measures some 150 by 160 meters in extent, and in places it is as much as 3 meters or more in depth.

Valdivia chipped-stone tools are extremely rough forms—unspecialized, for the most part, and similar to those of the Vegas complex. The most definitely shaped item is a little perforator, or graver, a tool type that is not present in the earlier Vegas assemblages.[10] Ground stone, in addition to the food grinding implements, is represented by a few stone bowls, notched fishline sinkers, saws, hammerstones, pebble reamers apparently used to make shell fishhooks, and a few polished axes. One of the latter is of т-shaped form and is the only artifact definitely associated with a burial. Bone implements are extremely rare. Shell was used to make the fishhooks (Fig. 5-9), which are very similar to those of the Pacific Littoral tradition cultures in Peru and Chile. No spindle whorls of any material were recovered although it is possible that these were made of wood or gourd rind. Again, by analogy

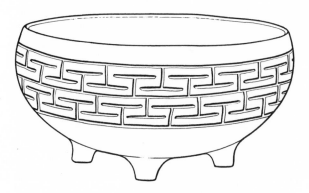

Figure 5-10. Valdivia red incised bowl with tetrapod supports. (Drawn from Meggers, Evans, and Estrada, 1965.)

with the contemporaneous cultures of Peru, it seems likely that the Valdivians had a knowledge of cotton, used it for nets and fishlines, and possibly wove it into textiles.

It is pottery, however, that is the most distinctive artifact of the Valdivia sites. Valdivia pottery is generally a gray fired ware, although a substantial portion of it has been red-slipped. The vessels have been built up by a coiling process, and the forms include open and incurved bowls and collared ollas, or jars. Some vessels have small, solid tetrapodal supports (Fig. 5-10). Surfaces are either smoothed or polished, and a high proportion of the ware is decorated. This decoration —usually confined to the upper portions of vessel exteriors—is carried out by incision, excision, punctation, rocker stamping, appliqué filleting, various kinds of finger manipulation, and pebble polishing or striating, as in Figures 5-11, 5-12, 5-13, 5-14. Except for a few instances where vessels contained the bones of infants or small children—in fact, urn burial of a sort—pottery was not placed with the dead, nor have whole vessels been found in any other contexts that would impute a ceremonial function to them. In brief, ceramics seem to have been essentially utilitarian in the Valdivia culture, and widely used.

Stratification in the Valdivia middens has allowed for subphase differentiation, especially in the pottery. Certain forms or decorative features characterize these subphases and show changes in occurrence or percentages of occurrence through

Figure 5-9. Shell fishhooks of the Valdivia phase. Height of hook at *left*, 3 cm. (Drawn from Zevallos and Holm, 1960.)

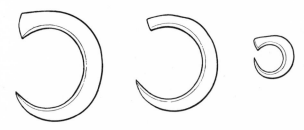

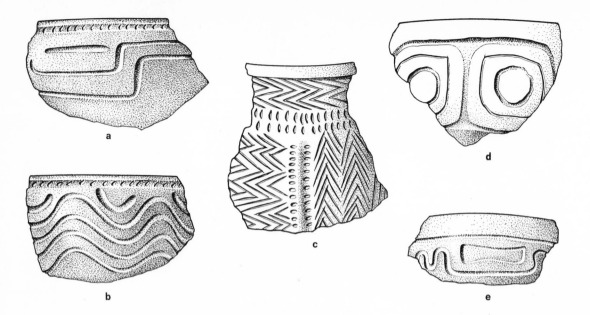

Figure 5-11. Valdivia potsherds. *a, b:* Broad-line incised. *c:* Modeled, incised, and punctated sherd, with red-painted lip. *d, e:* Excised sherds. Diameter of *a,* about 10 cm.; *b, c* also drawn to this scale. Diameter of *d,* about 7 cm.; *e* also drawn to this scale. (Drawn from Zevallos and Holm, 1960.)

time. Thus, for example, shell-edge stamping of vessel surfaces is a marker type for the earliest subphase, Valdivia A; the tetrapodal supports are typical of subphases A and B; markedly concave bases for jars are a mode for subphases B and C;

Figure 5-12. Valdivia potsherds. *a:* Brushed. *b, c:* Appliqué-fillet. *d:* Incised. *e:* Tetrapodal supports on base of polished red vessel fragment. *f:* Finger-punched (interior). *g:* Finger-punched (exterior). To varying scales. (Courtesy Clifford Evans, Jr. and B. J. Meggers.)

and appliqué-filleting decoration belongs to subphase D.

Stratigraphic change is also recorded in Valdivia figurines, one of the most distinctive traditions within the culture.[11] In subphase A, figurines are made of polished or ground stone (Fig. 5-15) and are peg-like little images of humans carved from elongated, rectangulate pebbles; arms and facial features are incised. There is no indication of sex. These are known as Palmar Incised figurines. In subphase B, Valdivia figurines are all of pottery and are handmade (Fig. 5-16). Only nude females appear to be represented. Considerable attention has been given to hairdress in these, with long "page-boy" coiffures shown in modeling and scoring. Eyes, mouth, and eyebrows are small slits in the clay. Types known as San Pablo, Buena Vista (Fig. 5-17), and Punta Arenas are found in subphases C and D. In these there has been a notable decline of realistic representation, with much less attention to facial features or hair detail. In general, all of the figurines are rather small, ranging in length from 4 to 10 centimeters in stone and a little bigger than this in pottery.

We have mentioned burials in passing. These were found within the midden areas, and the most typical form was a primary flexed interment. With the exception of the above-mentioned ⊤-shaped stone ax, no grave goods were associated with the burials, although the bones of infants or small children were found in pottery vessels.

A series of 13 adult skeletons from the Valdivia phase site of Buena Vista have been studied by

the physical anthropologist, J. R. Munizaga.[12] He observed a very high homogeneity within the series, such as might be expected in a small, endogamous group of peple. Cranial indices were markedly brachycephalic, and the skulls were undeformed. Another small skeletal series from the San Pablo site, however, showed much less homogeneity, with cranial indices ranging from dolicho- to brachycranic. Here, perhaps, the popu-

Figure 5-14. *Below, left:* Face design on Valdivia embossed sherd. The face is about 6 cm. in diameter. (Drawn from Meggers, Evans, and Estrada, 1965.)

Figure 5-15. *Below, right:* Valdivia figurine of stone. Height, 5 cm. (Drawn from Meggers, Evans, and Estrada, 1965.)

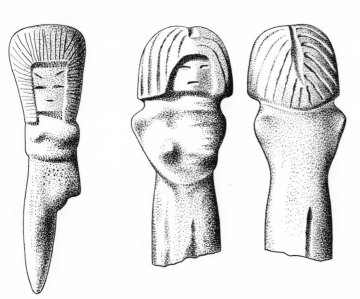
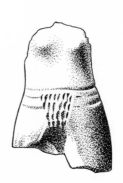

Figure 5-16. Valdivia pottery figurines. These are all solid, handmade specimens. All are females. Figurine at *left* measures about 9 cm. in height. (Drawn from Zevallos and Holm, 1960.)

Figure 5-17. The Buena Vista figurine style, Valdivia phase. (After Meggers, Evans, and Estrada, 1965.)

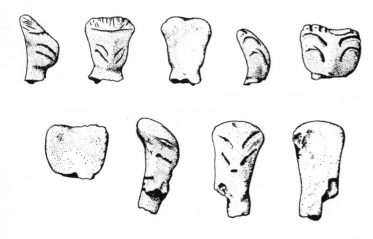

lation was of mixed physical origin. As yet, data are too few to provide a basis for firm conclusions concerning the physical nature of the old Valdivians—except to note that the Buena Vista group is the earliest well-documented round-headed series for western South America.

Puerto Hormiga. There is one other early ceramic complex in the Intermediate area that has radiocarbon dates placing it as early as Valdivia. This is Puerto Hormiga, from the northern lowlands of Colombia.[13] The Puerto Hormiga site is situated a short distance from the sea in the Department of Bolívar (see map, Fig. 5-1). It is near an old Colonial era canal known as the Canal del Dique. This canal drained the surrounding marshes and followed the course of a former river through these swamplands. Thus the site location is one that formerly would have been favorable for shellfishing, and the site debris indicates that it was such a shellfishing and fishing camp. The people who lived here presumably led a life much like that of the Valdivians of the Ecuadorian coast.

The conformation of the Puerto Hormiga site is interesting. The debris of the encampment—most of which is composed of oyster shells and shells of the genus *Pitar*—takes the form of a ring or oval measuring 77 meters north-south and 85 meters east-west. The width of the embankment of the ring varies from 16 to 25 meters, and the hollow or flat area within the ring is about 40 meters across. The embankment rises above the natural flat of the river bottom to a height of 1.2 meters. On excavation it was found that shells and cultural detritus were confined entirely to the ring embankment; the surrounding flats and the open space in the center of the ring were

devoid of any such materials. A natural stratigraphy of shell layers was observed. On the top
of at least one such layer were old fire pits and
the crushed packed shells and soil of an old living
surface. Reichel-Dolmatoff, the excavator, is of
the opinion that the ring represents the refuse
from a number of flimsy dwelling structures that
were once clustered in a circle in the swamp. In
his opinion, a community of 50 to 100 persons
had been established here, although occupancy
may only have been seasonal and intermittent.

Potsherds, stone, and shell artifacts were found
at all levels in the refuse, and there was little or
no stratigraphic change. Apparently, quartzite
flakes had been used for cutting fish, opening
shells, and other domestic chores. A good many
small, pitted anvil stones were recovered, and it
is surmised that these, together with the hammerstones found in the site, were used to crack
open the hard nuts of the coroso palms that grew
in the region. A few larger milling stones could
have been used in plant-food preparation. As with
Valdivia, the question of incipient plant cultivation is speculative. The bones of only small mammals were recovered from the midden, and these
were not numerous. Spears or darts, if they were
used, must have had wooden tips, and several
sandstone hones that were found in the refuse
could have been used in making and sharpening
such wooden spears. Shell was used to make axes
and what may be scrapers, as well as an occasional
pendant or perforated ornament. Baskets or mats
have left their plaited impressions in bits of burned
clay.

Again, as with Valdivia, the most common
artifact in the debris of the site was pottery, all
of it found in the form of sherd refuse. Puerto
Hormiga pottery is particularly notable for its
fiber tempering. This fibre aplastic included both
Spanish moss and flat grasses. The pottery was
not coiled but built up by a lump modeling
method. Besides the fibre tempered ware there
was other, sand tempered pottery in the Puerto
Hormiga complex. The vessels of this tempering
were better constructed than those of the fibre
ware and had probably been constructed by coiling. Both the fibre and sand tempered wares were
sometimes decorated with plastic techniques (Figs.
5-18, 5-19): incision, punctation, finger grooving,
modeling, rocker stamping, and shell-edge stamp-

**Figure 5-18. Puerto Hormiga potsherds. This stylistic strain
of the complex features somewhat simpler linear motifs
although there is clear overlap with the other strain shown in
Fig. 5-19. *e:* Rocker- or dentate-stamped. *j:* A vessel interior,
k: Plain. (Courtesy Gerardo Reichel-Dolmatoff.)**

Figure 5-19. Puerto Hormiga potsherds. This stylistic strain of the complex features very bold incised lines, heavy dot punctations, and modeled effigies (as in *c* and *g*) adornos. (Courtesy Gerardo Reichel-Dolmatoff.)

ing. Typical design elements are incised zones filled with punctations, with dentate rocker stamping, or with short, transverse incised lines that have terminal pit-punctations. The rims of the simple round or slightly oval bowls were sometimes ornamented with crudely modeled frogs, rodents, and, in one case, a human face. No burials were found in the ring; so we do not know whether pottery was placed with the dead.

Puerto Hormiga pottery is almost certainly related to that of Valdivia. It is true that the two styles have many differences; the Valdivia pottery is considerably better finished and decorated than that of Puerto Hormiga, and there is no fibre tempered ware in Valdivia. Nevertheless, there are similarities in vessel forms, in the plastic techniques of decoration, and in some of the design elements. Meggers, Evans, and Estrada list

some of these as: drag-and-jab punctation, finger grooving, broad-line incision, pit-punctations at the ends of lines, and incised zones filled with transverse parallel hachure.[14] In any effort to determine which complex may have been derivative from which, the radiocarbon dates do not offer much help. Twenty-one Valdivia dates range between 3200 and 1500 B.C.;[15] five dates from Puerto Hormiga span from 3090 to 2552 B.C.[16] The 3200 B.C. date from Valdivia is something of an isolate,[17] the next oldest of the series being 2670 B.C. At Puerto Hormiga there are four dates prior to 2800 B.C. It could be argued on general typological-developmental grounds that Puerto Hormiga is the parent complex as it is simpler and nearer to what we might imagine the early, experimental beginnings of pottery to have been. But, conversely, it could be argued that Puerto Hormiga represents a relatively crude replication of ceramic modes and ideas that had been derived from a source such as Valdivia. For the moment we will leave the question, to return to it in our summary comments on these early ceramic phases.

Canapote, Barlovento, and San Jacinto. A number of other early ceramic cultures in Caribbean Colombia are related to Puerto Hormiga and also date to our Early Ceramic Period. One of these is Canapote, described from a shell mound of that name on the eastern outskirts of the city of Cartagena. The site rises above salt flats on the edge of an old lagoon. Presumably, during site occupancy the lagoon was an active tidal basin.[18] Bischof, the excavator, defines three stratigraphically sequent phases from the excavations—Canapote, Tesca, and Barlovento—which provide the links in the development from Puerto Hormiga to Barlovento. The one radiocarbon date from an upper Canapote phase level of 1940 B.C. seems to bear this out.

The Barlovento phase of the Canapote site stratigraphy is better known from the Barlovento site, 10 kilometers north of Cartagena. It is a cluster of six shell mounds on a bar peninsula,

separated from the mainland by a swamp.[19] Quite probably the swamp was an active tidal basin a few thousand years ago. The mounds at Barlovento are in a semicircle, an arrangement reminiscent of the shell middens at Puerto Hormiga. Total area is about 100 by 100 meters in extent. Some of the midden piles proved to be as much as 6 meters deep; however there was little stratigraphic change in the cultural materials. Pebble choppers and fire-blackened stones were found at all depths. The latter were probably used for stone boiling in pottery vessels, which also were found in fragments throughout the midden (Fig. 5-20). These vessels were hemispherical or ovate bowls with incised, punctated, and hollow-reed impressed decorations; and, as has already been indicated, the designs, including parallel line arrangements, spirals, and other curvilinear elements, show a clear relationship to both Puerto Hormiga and Canapote. Radiocarbon dates for Barlovento range from 1550 to 1032 B.C. This takes us beyond the 1500 B.C. upper limit of the Early Formative Period of our area chronology; however, as we have said, the events of cultural growth and change were not synchronous throughout the Intermediate area, and the pattern of life as revealed at Barlovento almost certainly was of the same general fishing-collecting type as that of Valdivia, Puerto Hormiga, and Canapote. Reichel-Dolmatoff[20] notes that Barlovento phase sites are numerous along the coast, both to the northeast and to the south of the city of Cartagena; and there is also a closely related site in the interior at Isla de los Indios, on the Zapatosa Lagoon, at the confluence of the Magdalena and César Rivers.[21]

The San Jacinto complex is known from a site found on the Lower Magdalena River, about halfway between the coast and the confluence of the César.[22] The pottery is fibre tempered, like that of Puerto Hormiga, but the incised and punctated designs are more like those of Barlovento. Also, San Jacinto has pierced rim lugs and rim-channel spouts. There are no radiocarbon dates, but the nature of the pottery suggests an early date.[23]

Monagrillo. The Monagrillo shell mound is at the mouth of the Parita River on the Gulf of Panama.[24] The location is a tiny penin-

Figure 5-20. Barlovento potsherds. Diameter of *a*, 9 cm.; others to same approximate scale. (Courtesy Gerardo Reichel-Dolmatoff.)

a

b

c

d

e

f

g

h

sula of the old mainland, surrounded on three sides by a *salitre* that is flooded only by spring tides. A mile or so away is a mangrove-covered bar marking the present beach along the Pacific. There can be little doubt that when Monagrillo was occupied the present salitre was a lagoon well

stocked with shellfish. The conformation of the site itself is highly reminiscent of some of the Colombian ones we have just described. Shell ridges form an elongated oval, about 200 by 80 meters in extent, with a low depression in the center. Trenches into the refuse revealed bands of clam and oyster shells and stone and pottery artifacts to depths of about 2 meters. Some chipped stone was found and this included a few roughly flaked, unifacial, projectile points. The most common tool, however, was the pebble edge-grinder (Fig. 5-21) of the same type that characterized the earlier Cerro Mangote complex from

Figure 5-21. Monagrillo phase ground stone tools. These pebble choppers and chopper-grinders are almost identical with those of the Cerro Mangote phase from the same region. *a, b:* Choppers. *c, e:* Chopper-grinders. *d, f:* Grinders. *g, h:* Multi-faceted grinding stones, or manos. (After Willey and McGimsey, 1954.)

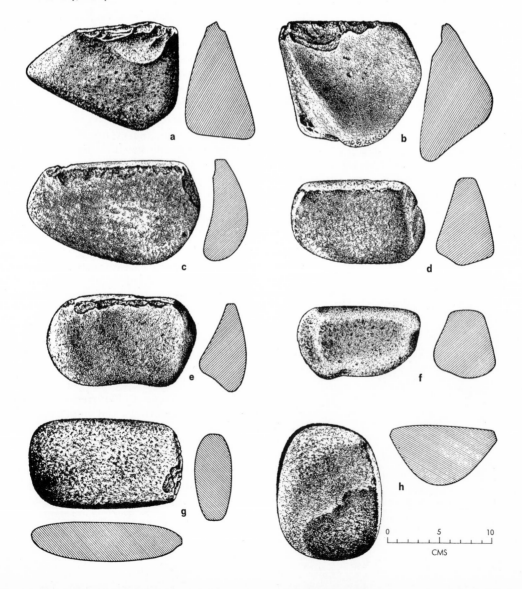

CMS

the nearby Santa María River delta. A few large milling stones were also recovered. The few burials found had little or no grave goods with them. Pottery (Fig. 5-22) was all in the form of potsherds—a gray fired or buff fired ware, sand tempered and smoothed or slightly polished. A relatively small percentage of it was decorated— by incision and punctation or by the painting of red bands around the rims of bowls. Vessels were all simple bowl forms. The incised and punctated decoration has some similarities to Barlovento and also to Valdivia. Evans, Meggers, and Estrada see, especially, links to their subphase C types; and the radiocarbon date from Montagrillo of 2140 B.C. is consistent with this.[25]

Rancho Peludo. The Rancho Peludo complex,[26] from northwestern Venezuela, stands quite apart from the others we have described. Valdivia, Puerto Hormiga, Canapote, Tesca, Barlovento, Monagrillo, and San Jacinto are all linked by a common tradition of simple bowl forms and incised and punctate decoration.[27] Rancho Peludo, in contrast, seems to belong to another tradition. On typological grounds alone, it is unlikely that archaeologists would have spotted Rancho Peludo as an early ceramic complex; however, it is associated with a number of early radiocarbon dates that span the period of 2820 to 445 B.C.[28]

The site is a riverbank one, on the Rio Guasare at the base of the Guajira Peninsula. The pottery is a thick, coarse, grit tempered ware made mostly in bowl or collared olla forms. Some of the bowls have tall annular bases, and at least one of these bowls contained the secondary burial of an infant. The basal portions of the collared ollas sometimes bear fabric impressions. The rare decoration of vessels is confined to appliqué strips or lumps that have been punctated or gashed.

Rouse and Cruxent place Rancho Peludo pottery in their Dabajuroid ceramic tradition, a tradition that persists until much later times. They note that fragments of two pottery griddles were found in the Rancho Peludo complex. This implies the use of manioc, although whether this was cultivated or wild is uncertain.

Machalilla. Machalilla is the other Early Ceramic Period phase from the Ecuador

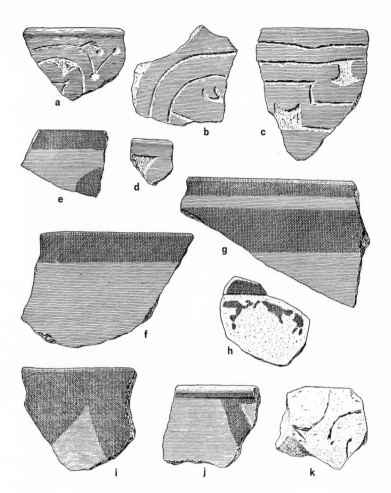

Figure 5-22. Monagrillo pottery. Incised-excised and red-banded. (After Willey and McGimsey, 1954.)

coast. It is known from sites in Guayas and southern Manabí. It is essentially later than Valdivia, although the chronological relationships between the two phases are controversial. Meggers, Evans, and Estrada, who did the excavation, feel that there was a substantial chronological overlap between the two cultures and that this is demonstrated by Machalilla trade sherds in Valdivia refuse deposits that date as early as Valdivia subphases C and D. They would further interpret this association as an indication that Machalilla culture had arrived on the Ecuador coast as a site-unit intrusion and that the peoples of the two cultures had lived together in the same general territory for several hundred years.[29] Other archaeologists, however, have been skeptical of this interpretation and prefer to see Machalilla as clearly and wholly later than Valdivia, with no

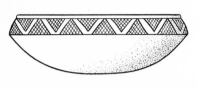
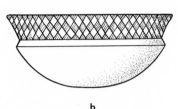

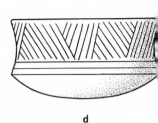

a   b   c   d

Figure 5-23. Machalilla phase vessel forms. *a, b:* Ayangue Incised, diameters, 24 and 22 cm. *c:* Embellished shoulder type, diameter, 18 cm. *d:* Machalilla incised, diameter, 15 cm. (Redrawn from Meggers, Evans, and Estrada, 1965.)

overlap.[30] The chronological chart (Fig. 5-4) is so drawn as to indicate this conflict of opinion.

Machalilla[31] presents a similar settlement and subsistence picture to that of Valdivia, although there is one change in settlement location that may be significant. Middens are situated not only on old lagoon inlets but also on cliffs overlooking the present active shore. This would be consistent with the later dating for Machalilla as it suggests that some settlements of the phase were made after shoreline changes had taken place. The economy, though, seems much the same as in Valdivia, with a continued strong dependence upon the sea. Machalilla shell fishhooks resemble those of Valdivia except that they are larger and slightly different in proportions. Chipped and ground stone cutting, grinding, and pounding tools are little changed. The Machalilla pottery (Fig. 5-23), however, is notably different from that of Valdivia. New forms include cylindrical spouted bottles, stirrup-mouthed jars, and bowls with carinate or angled shoulders and composite silhouettes. There is still some incised decoration, as is to be observed in the type Ayangue Incised, but incised lines now tend to be finer and sharper, with indications that they were drawn after the vessels had been thoroughly air-dried. Painted decoration appears. This last was done in red band designs in parallel geometric arrangements. Frequently, these red band designs were combined with incised or punctated lines setting color off from unpainted and unpolished portions of the vessel surface. A black-on-white type is also a part of the complex. Pottery figurines of Machalilla are quite rare, in contrast to Valdivia, and the few that do occur are of a crude, slablike style with "coffee-bean" eyes, beaklike noses, and no other features (Fig. 5-24). Machalilla burials are primary and flexed. Bodies are found in the shell middens where they may have been placed below or near dwellings; none was accompanied by grave goods. Only a few skeletons were sufficiently well preserved for study. The skulls of these had been markedly deformed in a fronto-vertico-occipital or tabular erecta manner, so that it was impossible to tell whether these Machalillans had been round-headed. The kind of deformation exhibited is the same as that seen on Early Horizon

Figure 5-24. Machalilla pottery figurine. Height, 6 cm. (Redrawn from Meggers, Evans, and Estrada, 1965.)

skulls from Peru, sometimes referred to as the "Chavín type" (see p. 90).[32]

Summary and Speculations. At about 3000 B.C. ceramics appear in a context of coastal shellfishing, fishing, and collecting cultures in the Intermediate area. It is likely, although not demonstrated, that these early ceramic cultures were minimally or incipiently horticultural and that they provide the transition from the Northwest South American Littoral tradition to the fully agricultural Intermediate area tradition. The period of these early ceramic cultures—and this presumes transition from fishing-collecting to farming—is from 3000 to 1500 B.C.

The ceramics in question are simple but by no means crude or experimental. Vessels are, for the most part, bowl or olla forms. Decoration is predominantly by plastic techniques of incision, punctation, finger manipulation, and appliqué element additions. Design motifs are strongly geometric—both recti- and curvilinear—and consist of triangular and rectangular panels, scrolls, and the like. Life-form elements—human and animal faces —occur but are not common. The use of red pigment is also noted, sometimes as a fired slip or as decorative bands, sometimes as a post-fired addition in the form of powder rubbed into incised or excised designs. In my opinion, such early ceramic phases as Valdivia, Puerto Hormiga, Canapote, Tesca, Barlovento, San Jacinto, and Monagrillo can together be related to a single pottery tradition. This tradition had its beginnings somewhere in the Intermediate area, and I would suggest that, through direct diffusion and more remote stimulus diffusion, this early pottery tradition of the Intermediate area ultimately became the source for the development of pottery for most of the Americas.

Where did this early pottery tradition originate? In the course of our previous discussions we posed this question with regard to our two earliest dated phases, Valdivia and Puerto Hormiga, and left it with the observation that as the radiocarbon dates were essentially the same, no incontrovertible chronological priority could be given to either. There are, however, other arguments that may be advanced to settle the question, and one line of these has been put forward by Meggers, Evans, and Estrada. It is their contention that the Ecuadorian coast was the American point of origin for this early pottery tradition and, at a further remove, that its ultimate origins can be taken across the Pacific to the Jomon culture of Japan.[33] There are many factors that favor their case. The Jomon pottery tradition in Japan dates back to 7000 B.C.; and by 3000 B.C. a series of sites on the island of Kyūshū show most of the decorative features of Valdivia subphase A pottery (Fig. 5-25). These features are the concentric rectangles and zones of parallel lines drawn in broad, squarish incised lines, the red-slipped vessels with interlocking rectilinear motifs, the little excised "dog-bone" and "hourglass" decorations, shell stamping, rocker stamping, and the spikelike castellations on vessel rims. The Jomon people were coastal fishers, shellfishers, and food collectors with a way of life not greatly different from that of the Valdivians; thus, a Jomon voyager stranded on the shores of Ecuador in the third millennium B.C. would have met with a "cultural threshold" similar to his own, his knowledge of the ceramic art would have been an acceptable technological contribution to improve the existence of the inhabitants. The Jomon fisherfolk made dugout canoes as early as 3000 B.C., and such a canoe could have been carried off in the clockwise ocean currents of the Pacific, so that a landfall in Ecuador, that western prominence of South America, would not have been out of the question.

Opponents of the Jomon-Valdivia connection cite the simplicity of the ceramic decorative techniques and motifs as vitiating the argument for a relationship. Such could have been duplicated quite independently—as has undoubtedly happened at other times and places in human history. Yet in the case of Jomon and Valdivia, these simple typological similarities are strongly reinforced by circumstances of chronology, cultural context, geography, and oceanography. It has also been pointed out that the Valdivia A complex is by no means duplicated in any single Jomon complex, that it has been necessary to reconstruct, by selecting from a number of Japanese sites of circa 3000 B.C., the appropriate assemblages to have served as the Valdivia prototype.[34] This is indeed an argument to be considered, yet it operates with the assumption that the Japanese archaeologists have established fully all of the regional and minor chronological variables of

Figure 5-25. Valdivia-Jomon ceramic resemblances. *a:* Valdivia "dog-bone" design. *b:* Same for Jomon. *c, d:* Valdivia broad-line incised designs. *i, j:* Same for Jomon. *e:* Valdivia heavy drag-jab punctation. *f:* Same for Jomon. *g:* Valdivia fine drag-jab punctation. *h:* Same for Jomon. (Courtesy B. J. Meggers and Clifford Evans.)

Figure 5-26. Rim projection, or castellation, on a Valdivia red incised sherd. (Drawn from Meggers, Evans, and Estrada, 1965.)

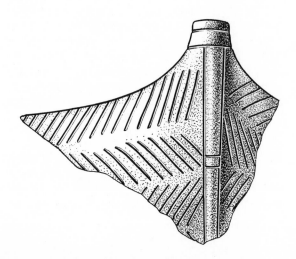

ceramic combinations that go to make up a complex.

If we reject the Jomon-Valdivia linkage, what then? Where did these early ceramics of the Intermediate area originate? The earliest pottery to the north, in southern Mesoamerica, is placed by radiocarbon at only 2300 to 2400 B.C. (see Vol. I, p. 83, fn. 6a). In Peru, pottery is no earlier than 1800 B.C. In the eastern Amazon it has been placed at 1800 to 2000 B.C.[35] The alternative answer would seem to be that it came into being as an independent invention somewhere in the Intermediate area. Beyond this, we are clearly up against the limits of our present archaeological knowledge and can only speculate. The Jomon-Valdivia linkage, while not proved beyond some reasonable doubts, is certainly a likely possibility to be kept in mind.

Rancho Peludo and Machalilla remain for summary and speculative comment. As noted, Rancho Peludo pottery is strikingly different from that of the Valdivia–Puerto Hormiga–Barlovento development. It may be, however, that it derives in some way from this development, through a process of stimulus diffusion.

Machalilla shares some features with Valdivia, and Lathrap has argued that it develops out of Valdivia—with some significant contacts with the Amazonian Basin Late Tutishcainyo culture, which he dates at about 1400 B.C.[36] Meggers, Evans, and Estrada, on the other hand, suggest that we look toward Mesoamerica for the new elements that are incorporated in Machalilla, although they admit that they can point to no specific region or complex in that area.[37] But whatever its relationships, Machalilla was beginning to reflect the emergent agricultural way of life that we will call the Intermediate area tradition.

The Concept
of an Intermediate Area Cultural Tradition

An Intermediate area cultural tradition took form in the Formative Period (1500–500 B.C.) with an economy based on plant cultivation. This change had not been sudden but gradual. It is likely that such phases as the Rancho Peludo and the Machalilla, which we have just reviewed, witnessed the beginnings of the change. In some subareas it must have occurred later than in others, and the date of 1500 B.C. is an approximation that is probably nearer the earlier than the later end of the gradient of this transformation. The change in subsistence was also accompanied by other cultural changes, some linked functionally to subsistence, some related historically to this spread of a new way of life through all of Nuclear America during the second millennium B.C. The listing below is an attempt to summarize and to generalize the salient features and conditions of the Intermediate area cultural tradition.

(1) First, as to subsistence, the principal crops of the Intermediate area cultural tradition were maize and manioc. Emphasis on one or the other varied according to region and, probably, according to time period. In tropical lowland riverine situations the root crop was usually the more important, with maize generally being favored in higher elevations. There are archaeological indications in northern Colombia that manioc pre-

ceded maize, suggesting that in this part of the Intermediate area ties with the Caribbean or Amazonian areas preceded those with Mesoamerica. Terracing, the construction of garden plots, and irrigation are recorded for some regions in Colombia and Ecuador; but for the most part, either "slash-and-burn" cultivation or the creation of somewhat more permanent agricultural fields through forest clearing was the prevalent mode.

(2) The characteristic units of settlement of the Intermediate area tradition were small hamlets and villages; however, towns and small cities came into being in some subareas in the later pre-Columbian periods.

(3) Historic period ethnography indicates that socio-political units tended to be small, ranging from the single autonomous community to the petty territorial state.

(4) Ceremonial sites or centers are known from many parts of the Intermediate area. Some were incorporated within towns; others appear to have been nuclei for dispersed settlements.

(5) Burial forms vary greatly. Urn burials are reported from Ecuador to Lower Central America although the distribution is spotty both geographically and chronologically. Deep shaft graves are found in many places, especially from Ecuador north to Panama. The immolation of retainers in the graves of chiefs and other mortuary evidences of kingly prestige are noted in, although not continuously throughout, the Intermediate area.

(6) Ceramics derive, in part, from the early pottery tradition of the Early Ceramic Period. Later, other techniques and forms link the Intermediate area with Mesoamerica, Peru, and lowland tropical South America. In general, the Intermediate area tradition emphasizes pedestal, annular-based, and tripod-based bowls and plates, negative painting, and appliqué decoration. The quality of craftsmanship in pottery is very good, the volume of production great.

(7) Metallurgical techniques—including casting, gilding, soldering, alloying, and repoussé work in gold, silver, copper, and alloys of these—are a prominent feature of the Intermediate area tradition. Such techniques are confined largely to ornaments or small tools. Metals are generally common in the Late Periods of the tradition; in the Regional Developmental Period, if present, they are rare.

(8) Monumental stonework—as slab carvings or column statues—is widely distributed throughout the Intermediate area. These carvings are rendered in many styles that, although individually distinctive, share a common level of competent although not outstanding craftmanship and a common bond of rather stiff or angular treatment of life forms.

(9) Small pottery manufactures, including figurines, spindle whorls, and musical instruments, are common. The figurine mold was known.

(10) Polished stone celts and small ornaments are also general; however, chipped stone tools are relatively rare and usually roughly executed.

(11) Technological features are widely shared in the tradition, but there are no horizon styles comparable in scope to those of the Peruvian area. The closest approach to such horizonal phenomena is seen in the gold work of Colombia and Lower Central America.[38]

(12) Language affiliation gives some historical unity to the Intermediate area—although probably one that lies remote in time. Only three principal language families are represented: Chibchan, Paezan, and Macro-Cariban (see Fig. 1–5).

As is obvious from this listing, the Intermediate area cultural tradition lacks those highly distinctive, areawide patterns that solidify such cultural traditions as the Mesoamerican, with its 260-day calendrical system, or the Peruvian, with its series of horizon styles.

On a general level of cultural development we see many common bonds with both Mesoamerica and Peru; however, an overall appraisal confirms the Intermediate area tradition in a developmental, as well as a geographical, "intermediateness" between the civilizations of Mesoamerica and Peru on the one hand and the simpler farming cultures lying outside Nuclear America on the other.

The Formative Period

Ecuador. The Chorrera[39] phase, named after a site in the Guayas River valley, marks the establishment of a farming economy on the Ecuador coast and in the Guayas Basin. There is a notable shift of settlement away from shore locations, with the new Chorrera sites being found at some distance inland in the coastal river valleys of Guayas and southern Manabí provinces and along the banks of the Daule and Babahoyo rivers in the Guayas Basin. Although some shell refuse is found in the Chorrera sites of the Santa Elena Peninsula region, there is a decline in the importance of the sea as a source of subsistence. Even more important as indicators of an agricultural economy are a series of traits in Chorrera—new to Ecuador—that are firmly associated with maize growing in Mesoamerica. Thus it has been speculated that maize was brought to Ecuador from Mesoamerica and that this occurred at about 1500 B.C. It was at this time that the Machalilla culture was transformed into the Chorrera culture[40]

Chorrera pottery, as might be expected, shows some carry-overs from Machalilla: stirrup-mouthed bottles, angular-shouldered, or carinate bowls, and the fine-line incision of the Machalilla Ayangue style. It also shows what is probably local evolution in the development of very thin-walled, highly polished ware, both unslipped and red-slipped.[41] But in addition there are new traits. Among these is an iridescent painted pottery type. This iridecent paint, which has a pinkish, glossy sheen, was probably applied as a thin clay film prior to firing. The designs, which are parallel line and dot arrangements, give a first impression of a negative or resist-dye technique although, apparently, the painting was done positively.[42] Another new mode of decoration is a burnished-line technique, in which the air-dried surface of the vessel was striated or marked with a pebble or round-ended instrument before firing. A third is the incised outlining of red or black painted zones. Still another is rocker stamping of a kind quite different from that of the earlier Valdivia phase. On the rather rare Chorrera type on which this technique occurs the stamping was done with a smooth-ended rather than a toothed implement, and the individual "rockings" or strokes are long and clearly separated. In addition to these decorative innovations there were new vessel shapes, including open bowls with outflared walls and low annular bases as well as spouted jars with bridge-handle and whistle attachments (Fig. 5-27).

Besides the innovations in pottery vessels, Chorrera ushers in a new figurine style, the so-called "Mate type" (Fig. 5-28). These make a clear

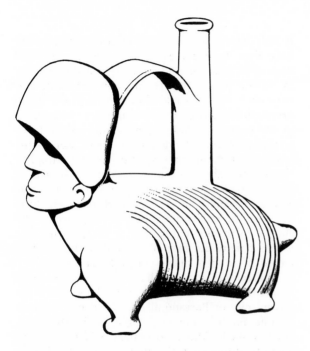

Figure 5-27. Chorrera vessel. A head-bridge-spout whistling jar in the form of a man-animal. The ware is a polished red with incised zones. Height to top of spout, about 7 cm. (Drawn from Estrada, 1962.)

Figure 5-28. Chorrera pottery figurines. *Left:* Estrada's "Mate Solido" (solid) type. *Right:* The same author's "Mate Hueco" (hollow) type. Height of pieces, about 7 cm. (Drawn from Estrada, 1962.)

break with the previous Machalilla figurines and are also quite different from the distinctive Valdivia type. They are handmade and may be either solid or hollow. The facial features are quite clearly modeled, and the headdresses either are smooth and cap-like or bear asymmetrically

arranged incised decorations. Another new ceramic item is a thin, finely made ear spool of "napkin ring" form.

Some of these new features may be local inventions. The spouted and bridge-handled jars, for example, could be derived from the earlier Machalilla stirrup-mouthed jar form. Others, however, suggest Mesoamerican origins. This is particularly true of the "napkin ring" ear spools and of the figurines, especially those with the asymmetrically incised hairdress ornamentations, which are much like the Preclassic Tlatilco figurines of Mesoamerica. Concerning this possibility of Mesoamerican connections, specific trait similarities are seen with an Early Preclassic Period Ocos culture of the Guatemalan Pacific coast. Ocos has the curious iridescent painting, the burnished-line designs, and a rocker stamping of the kind found in Chorrera. These may or may not be original Mesoamerican traits, but they strongly suggest a contact between Guatemala and Ecuador at this early time. The possibility of relationship is further bolstered by the presence of obsidian bladelets[43] in Chorrera, an artifact that had not been found in either Valdivia or Machalilla and that, like the "napkin ring" ear spools, is closely associated with Mesoamerican cultures, including Ocos.

In commenting upon these shared traits, M. D. Coe feels that:

> The homologies...are too close for the traits to have passed through an overland series of filters. The only explanation for such identities must be actual maritime contact between the peoples of the two areas, most certainly in the form of trading trips.[44]

This is to be kept in mind; yet we must remember that this was a time when a great many new ideas and techniques were being disseminated throughout all of Nuclear America—from Mesoamerica to Peru—and that we still know very little about regions of origin, directions of spread, and land, as well as sea, routes of diffusion.

Chorrera-like pottery—including the diagnostic Chorrera iridescent painted ware—has been found in the Southern Ecuadorian Highland subarea, although little is known of the actual site contexts. Meggers has referred to these manifestations by the collective name of the Alausí phase, after the upland basin of that name; but the phase also includes Chorrera-related materials from Cerro Narrío and the Cuenca and Loja Basins.[45] This Chorrera distribution in the southern highlands may mark a segment of a route along which ceramic ideas might have passed between the early Ecuadorian coastal cultures and those of the north Peruvian highlands (pp. 113–114) and the western Amazon Basin.[46]

Colombia. Chorrera-like pottery has not been traced to the North Ecuadorian highlands[47] or the Colombian Andes. Nevertheless in Colombia there are indications that village farming based on maize was established during the Formative Period. Reichel-Dolmatoff sees Mesoamerican voyagers landing on the south Colombian Pacific coast as early as 1200 B.C.[48] Following the Meggers hypothesis, this would have been at about the same time that similar Mesoamerican sailors brought maize and new ceramic traits to the neighboring Ecuadorian coast. From the Colombian coast the Mesoamericans made their way inland and by 500 B.C. had helped prepare the foundations of such cultures as San Agustín of southern Colombia. This is, of course, speculative. The Colombian archaeological record, as we now know it, is still sketchy, and most of it pertains to later periods. Still, I think it is likely that maize farming was propagated throughout much of Colombia during the Formative era. Whether this was done from the sea, by way of the Pacific coast, or else came by more gradual stages of diffusion through Lower Central America remains to be demonstrated.

We do have, however, some detailed archaeological information on the transition to maize farming from one part of Colombia, the northern Colombian lowlands. Let us take a look at that.

It will be remembered that the Barlovento phase of the northern Caribbean lowlands had a subsistence base of shellfishing, fishing, and food collecting, supplemented, perhaps, by some minor cultivation of plants. Of all of the plants that may have been ultilized, manioc (*Manihot esculenta*) was probably the most important. Foraging for manioc would have led coastal Indians some short distances inland into the lowland river bottoms that were the most favorable habitats for the plant.

A next logical step for such food collectors would have been to increase the crop by planting cuttings of it. Selection and planting probably resulted in genetic improvements and hybridizations, and improved yields would have encouraged these primitive farmers to devote more time to manioc, at the expense of other plant-gathering or food-getting systems.[49] Undoubtedly there were some brakes against this process: fish from the tropical rivers were abundant and a constant source of protein foods, and manioc itself is easy to grow and thus would have demanded relatively little time in its cultivation; but in any event, the change to manioc cultivation as the primary economic activity did take place, and we have a first record of it in a phase called Malambo.

Malambo is a large village refuse area situated on a freshwater lagoon a little to the south of the present city of Barranquilla.[50] Site debris contains organic matter, animal, reptile, and fish bones, but few shells. Malambo pottery, which occurs in quantity throughout the midden, is a sand tempered, polished ware with incised, punctated, and adorno-modeled decoration; and it clearly bears a relationship to the Puerto Hormiga–Canapote–Barlovento line of ceramic development for this subarea. Malambo also has typological affiliations with the Barrancoid phase of central and eastern Venezuela, and it has been reasoned that the Malambo peoples entered the north Colombian lowlands from the east, bringing with them a manioc subsistence pattern as well as a Barrancoid style of pottery. However, it is a good possibility that Venezuelan Barrancoid pottery and Colombian Malambo pottery both developed, in their respective regions, as separate branches of the old Puerto Hormiga–Barlovento tradition.

As no actual plant remains are found in Malambo, or other similar sites in the tropical lowlands, the primary basis of inference for a manioc economy is the presence of the pottery *budare,* or griddle. This is a flat pottery plate of the type used by modern Amazonian tropical forest Indians to prepare manioc flour or cassava cakes. As sweet manioc can be eaten roasted or boiled, in the manner of a potato, the pottery griddle is not a necessary piece of equipment for its utilization. The bitter manioc, on the other hand, must be ground, washed, and squeezed (usually in an elongated basket, or *tipití*) to free it of its prussic acid content before it can be eaten; and the final step in the preparation process is the toasting of the ground root on the *budare,* when it may also be pressed into thin cakes that can be stored. In historic times the Indians of northern Colombia and inter-Andean Colombia did not use the bitter manioc, nor did they possess the *budares;* but in Malambo times it is highly probable, in view of the common presence of this pottery griddle in the village middens, that bitter manioc was processed and eaten.[51] Malambo dates by radiocarbon from 1120 B.C. to A.D. 100 and so probably overlaps with the non-agricultural Barlovento phase at the lower end of its chronological scale and with a culture known as Momil at the upper end. The Momil culture is significant in that it shows the transition from manioc to maize farming in northern Colombia.

The site of Momil is on the lower Sinú, some distance inland, and situated on a small promontory in the river flatlands.[52] The Momil I levels have incised and dentate-roulette stamped pottery that, while showing some general relationships to Malambo, is nevertheless quite different from it (Fig. 5-29, *a-d, f*). The vessels include globular olla forms, various composite-silhoutte bowls, and, like Malambo—although stylistically different— large *budares* with thick, upturned edges. Momil I also has some painted pottery (Fig. 5-30): positive black-on-white, black-on-red, black-and-red-on-white, and a two-color negative, or resist-dye, type. In stonework, Momil I had a chipped stone industry, with pressure-flaked as well as percussion-flaked tools. Outstanding among the former are thousands of tiny little perforators or drills of the same sort that have been reported from the Valdivia sites.

In Momil II incised and dentate-roulette continue; but the painted wares become more prominent; a red-zoned incised type appears; and new vessel forms include tall tripod bowls and bowls with large solid or hollow mammiform supports. Other stratigraphic changes are those from a small, solid, rather crudely fashioned human figurine of phase I (Fig. 5-31) to a large, hollow and better-modeled style of phase II. There is also a time shift from flat stamps to cylindrical roller stamps and a phase II appearance of pottery spindle whorls. Momil II, most significantly, has trough-shaped, ground stone metates and loaf-

Figure 5-29. Momil I–II potsherds. (Sherd *e* dates only as Momil II.) *a, b, d:* Zoned dentated. *c:* A ridged-punctated sherd. *e:* Cross-hatched incised. *f:* Indented-appliquéd. Sherds not all to same scale. (Courtesy Gerardo Reichel-Dolmatoff.)

Figure 5-30. Polychrome and bichrome sherds, Momil I–II. *a, b:* Polychrome (red-and-black-on-white). *c:* Black-on-white. *d:* Black-on-red. Sherds not all to same scale. (Courtesy Gerardo Reichel-Dolmatoff.)

Figure 5-31. Pottery figurines, Momil I. (Courtesy Gerardo Reichel-Dolmatoff.)

shaped manos very much like the traditional corn-grinding implements of Mesoamerica.

It is on these artifact occurrences—the *budares* in the Momil I refuse and their absence in the Momil II levels and the introduction of the stone maize-grinding tools in Momil II—that the Reichel-Dolmatoffs base their case for the agricultural subsistence change in northern Colombia. Gerardo Reichel-Dolmatoff is quite properly cautious about this interpretation, pointing out that there is no one-to-one correlation of a maize economy with such stone implements;[53] however, as Reichel-Dolmatoff states, the metate and mano appear for the first time together with a series of new ceramic traits that suggest Mesoamerica—the home of maize cultivation.

There are no radiocarbon dates for Momil, but Reichel-Dolmatoff offers estimated datings of Momil I at 700 B.C. and Momil II at 100 B.C.[54] Assuming that the Momil I may have overlapped chronologically with Malambo, this first date seems a quite reasonable estimate; but if we assume that maize was introduced at the beginnings of Momil II, the 100 B.C. date for the inception of this phase may be too late. Certainly, it would be substantially later than the estimated date for the introduction of the cereal into southern Colombia. Now it may well be that this is the true picture and that maize did not find its way into the northern Caribbean lowlands until several centuries after it was known on the Colombian south Pacific coast and in the highlands. Indeed, in this case it might have been brought to Momil from the south rather than from the north. Southern

Panama and northwestern Colombia is swampy tropical mangrove country, an environment that would not readily have attracted maize farmers and that may have been bypassed in early Meso-american-to-South American movements.

Northwestern Venezuela. Formative Period remains from that part of northwestern Venezuela which lies within the Intermediate area have not been clearly defined. In a previous section we referred to Rancho Peludo pottery, from the Guajira region, which dated somewhere within the span of 2820 to 445 B.C. These dates suggest the possibility of a Formative Period, as well as an Early Ceramic Period, placement. In fact, judging from its appearance—which includes such features as pedestal bases and *budares*—I should think that the Rancho Peludo complex belongs to the later end of the chronological range offered by the radiocarbon dates. It is possible that maize agriculture had moved this far east in Rancho Peludo times, but there is neither direct nor good inferential evidence to back this up.[55]

Two other northwest Venezuelan pottery styles may possibly date to before 500 B.C. These are the La Pitia and the Santa Ana. Both are more developed in appearance than Rancho Peludo and feature painting combined with incised and modeled decoration. Rouse and Cruxent point to their general affinities with the La Loma and Tocuyano styles of northeastern Colombia and northwestern Venezuela.[56]

Lower Central America. If we adhere to our strict chronological definition of the Formative Period for the Intermediate area as a whole, there is little in Lower Central America that can be bracketed between 1500 and 500 B.C. The Sarigua complex may date to this period.[57] Sarigua is a small shell refuse site on the Gulf of Panama not far from Monagrillo;[58] its shoreline location, which lies farther out from the old mainland coastline than does the Monagrillo midden, suggests a more recent date than that given to Monagrillo. Also, a very few Sarigua sherds were found in a superficial level at Monagrillo, giving a stratigraphic hint of their relative age. Sarigua ceramics—thin, unslipped, and decorated by incision, punctation, shell-edge stamping, and appliqué ridges—bear a general resemblance to other early Nuclear American wares. All of these facts suggest a date somewhere intermediate between Monagrillo and the later Panamanian painted potteries. Still, the placement of Sarigua at 1000 B.C. must be regarded as highly tentative.

Other than Sarigua, early Lower Central American ceramic complexes which have a "Formative" cast are those of the Aguas Buenas (Fig. 5-32) and La Concepción ("Scarified Ware") (Fig.

Figure 5-32. Aguas Buenas pottery. (*Top, left*, courtesy Museum für Völkerkunde und Vorgeschichte, Hamburg; others courtesy Museo Nacional de Panamá and Wolfgang Haberland.)

Figure 5-33. Scarified Ware (Concepción phase). *Top, center,* is a type sometimes found in Aguas Buenas phase sites. *Top, right,* and *bottom, right,* are from the Solano site, near La Concepción; others from same general region but without specific provenience. (*Top, center,* and *bottom, left,* courtesy Museo Nacional de Panamá and Wolfgang Haberland; others courtesy Museum für Völkerkunde und Vorgeschichte, Hamburg.)

5-33) phases of northern Panama and the adjacent Costa Rican highlands,[59] the Early Diquís phase of southern Pacific Costa Rica,[60] and the Pueblo Nuevo[61] and Guacamayo[62] finds of Panama. These ceramics all emphasize combined incised or striated and red-zoned decoration—a decorative technique with an early and wide distribution in Nuclear America. However, the dates that can be assigned to these Central American phases through radiocarbon determinations fall within the range of 300 B.C. to A.D. 300.[63] What we may have, so far, in the archaeological record of Lower Central America, is a glimpse of the end of pottery traditions that have much earlier beginnings.

The Southern Periphery of Mesoamerica. The South Peripheral subarea of Mesoamerica takes us out of the Intermediate area and into another major cultural area. We have already considered this subarea in Volume One (pp.168–169); but as most cultural boundaries are to some degree arbitrary, and this one is especially so, it behooves us to have another look at it in connec-

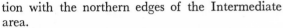

Figure 5-34. Vessels of the Zoned Bichrome Horizon from Pacific Nicaragua. *Left:* Upper portion of vessel red-painted; lower portion and interior of bottom rectangle left brown. Los Angeles, Ometepe Island. Diameter, about 9.5 cm. *Right:* Upper and lower portions red-painted; panel of incised design left brown. From Los Hornos, Ometepe Island. Height, about 20 cm. (Courtesy Museum für Völkerkunde und Vorgeschichte, Hamburg.)

tion with the northern edges of the Intermediate area.

Moving from south to north, we have three phases in northwestern Costa Rica all of which exhibit ceramic form and decorative features suggestive of Formative Period affiliations. These are the Chombo phase, located just to the north of the Nicoya Peninsula, the Monte Fresco phase, on the northern edge of that peninsula, and the Catalina phase, of the Tempisque River Valley. The ceramics are red- and black-zoned incised and painted types, similar engraved-painted combinations, and a zoned dentate rocker-stamped type.[64] Related phases—the Angeles and Avilés—have been found across the border in Nicaragua on the Isthmus of Rivas and on Ometepe Island. So far, however, the earliest radiocarbon dates for any of these phases are no earlier than the first or second centuries of the Christian era.[65]

It is not until we move still farther north that we have archaeological sequences that assure us that we are on a time level earlier than 500 B.C. These are the sequences established by Strong and his associates in the Ulúa Valley and Lake Yojoa regions (see Vol. I, Fig. 3-8).[66] Subsequent work has confirmed these sequences and their correlations with the body of Mesoamerican area Preclassic Period information.[67] Almost certainly these early Ulúa and Yojoa phases relate to those of the Zoned Bichrome Horizon of the Nicoya region. What remains puzzling is the chronological differences between them.[68]

Summary. Settled village life based on maize farming comes into being in the Ecuadorian coastal regions at the early part of what we have designated as the Formative Period (1500–500 B.C.). At the same time, a number of new ceramic and other traits appear. Not all of the latter are necessarily of Mesoamerican origin, but it is highly likely that some of them are. Transport of these new elements by sea from Mesoamerica also seems likely, although we need more archaeological information on the intervening Colombian and Lower Central American land areas.

In Colombia, our best knowldege of the 1500 to 500 B.C. period comes only from the northern lowlands of that country. There, a fairly continuous story of development can be traced from the older Early Ceramic Period cultures—which were primarily non-agricultural—into a stage of manioc horticulture at about 1000 B.C. At some time after this, maize farming was introduced; and here this event was also accompanied by the introduction of new Mesoamerican-like ceramic traits, although not all of them are the same new traits that we saw on the Ecuadorian coast. The date at which this introduction was made into northern Colombia is debatable. Reichel-Dolmatoff has suggested a time no earlier than 100 B.C. This may be too late, but, if so, it is unlikely that it occurred much before 500 B.C. It may well be that this introduction of maize and new ceramic forms did not enter the Colombian Caribbean lowlands directly from the north, by way of the Isthmus of Panama, but instead entered from the south, via the Ecuador-Colombia Pacific coast and the southern Colombian highlands.

This general hypothesis of a seaborne introduction of maize on the Ecuador-Colombia Pacific coast—of the spread of maize and its cultivation from there to the highland interior, and its subsequent diffusion to other parts of Ecuador and Colombia—gains some support from the absence of any clearly dated Formative Period remains in Lower Central America. Ceramic complexes have been found in Panama, Costa Rica, and Nicaragua that most probably are to be associated with corn cultivation, and some of these complexes relate to Preclassic (or Formative) Period developments in southern Mesoamerica; however, in their Lower Central American settings they date no earlier than about the beginning of the Christian era.

Ecuador: Regional Developmental and Late Periods

In the Intermediate area Regional Developmental Period, cultures take more specialized and "regionalized" turns in their development and, to a large extent, maintain this regionalization on through the Late Period to the Spanish Conquest. Because of this diversity, it is no longer feasible to treat them in an area-wide fashion. Moreover, archaeological research and synthesis has tended to follow along national boundaries, and it is within these somewhat arbitrary conventions that the lines of historical development have been most thoroughly pursued. In the succeeding sections of this chapter we shall treat groups or blocks of cultural subareas as these have been subsumed for Ecuador, Colombia, and Lower Central America. We begin with Ecuador.

Guangala. Guangala is the Regional Developmental Period for the Guayas Coast of Ecuador.[69] The two best-known sites are Guangala proper and La Libertad. Ecology is that of shoreline settlements or inland locations along the river valleys between the coast and the Colonche hills. These sites are little villages, or hamlets, situated with respect to advantages in farming or fishing. La Libertad, which is one of the largest, has a refuse zone 500 meters in diameter and includes low hummocks that may mark old house platforms. Burials were found within the village area and, in some instances, probably under house floors.

The Guangala maize agricultural economy is inferred from its sequence position following Chorrera, from the presence of interior valley sites, and from an abundance of stone metates and manos in the middens. The Guangala mano is of the long, "overhang" type; that is, the ends of the mano extended beyond the width of the flat floor of the metate—a type found in other parts of the Intermediate area but which was not common to Mesoamerica until the Postclassic (900–1520 A.D.) Period. Fishing appears to have been of some importance, however, as is indicated by the sites near the shore and by shell fishhooks (of a different style from those of the earlier Ecuadorian coastal periods) found in these. Some deer bones are also present in the middens, and the Guangalan are believed to have used the throwing-stick and the dart in hunting this animal. The throwing-stick is represented by hooks of shell, and the darts were probably tipped with stingray spines as no chipped-stone points are known from Guangala contexts. The few existing chipped-stone artifacts are rough percussion-flaked chopping or cutting implements, in addition to the little obsidian bladelets that were also noted for Chorrera.

Guangala ceramics relate back to Chorrera in such things as iridescent painting and some vessel forms, but they also show a number of innovations. One new type is a red-and-black-on-yellow polychrome (Fig. 5-35) with designs arranged as bands of geometric elements, stylized pelicans, or interlocking fish or serpents. The interlocking design is similar to the same motif in Peruvian styles. A bicolor black or brown-on-yellow is related to the polychrome. Vessel forms are usually bowls or cups. Another distinctive type has bur-

Figure 5-35. Guangala phase polychrome and zoned-engraved pottery. All sherds except *lower, right,* are of the red-and-black-on-buff La Libertad Tri-color type. The exception is red-on-buff with separating engraved lines. Diameter of sherd at *top, left,* about 10 cm. (Courtesy Cambridge Museum of Archaeology and Ethnology, England.)

nished-line designs on plate interiors (Fig. 5-36), and negative painting has now become an important ceramic decorative technique. In fact, negative painting together with the white-on-red positive painting may be considered as horizon markers for the Regional Developmental Period in Ecuador. Complex vessel forms are also very representative of Guangala and of the period as a whole. These include polypod bowls (usually three to five legs), tall annular-based compoteras,[70] and annular-based goblets. On the polypods a characteristic Guangala mode is an appliqué ornament of a stylized human face (Fig. 5-36).

Small ceramic, stone, and shell manufactures are typical of Guangala and, for that matter, other Regional Developmental cultures in Ecuador and the rest of the Intermediate area. These are pottery whistles, flat pottery stamps (Fig. 5-37) with geometric designs, beadlike spindle whorls (indicative of spinning and weaving), polished

stone and polished shell celts or chisels that would have been suitable for woodworking, and shell ornaments. It is possible to add pottery figurines to this list; most of those of Guangala are handmade, rather crude and stylized, and quite unlike the "mate type" of the preceding Chorrera phase. They depict humans wearing the ubiquitous nose rings, and sometimes they are painted with the negative technique. Another type resembles those handsome mold-made figurines that are the hallmark of the northern part of the Ecuador coast. They are hollow and quite large (20 cm. or more in height) and depict, in a very naturalistic manner, standing men or seated women.

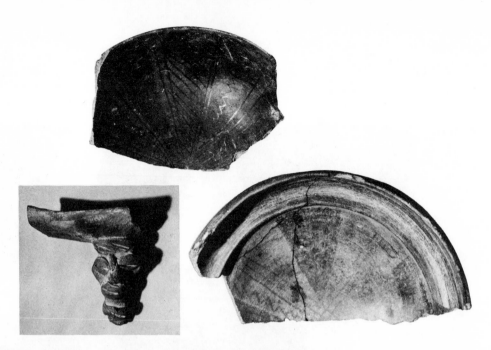

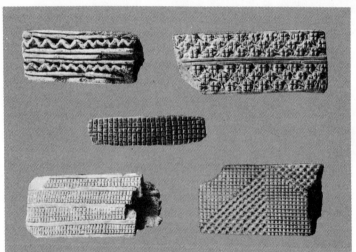

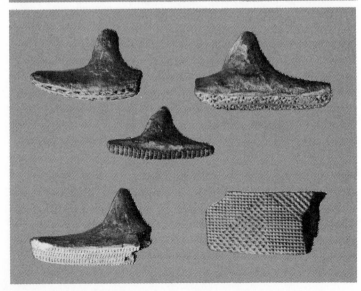

Figure 5-36. *Above:* Guangala phase pottery. *Top* and *bottom, right:* Pattern-burnished designs on bowl interiors. *Bottom, left:* Effigy leg from polypod vessel. Diameter of sherd at *top,* 12 cm. (Courtesy Cambridge Museum of Archaeology and Ethnology, England.)

Figure 5-37. *Left:* Pottery stamps of the flat variety. Guangala phase. *Top:* Stamping surfaces. *Bottom:* Same stamps from side, showing handles. Length of *top, left,* 3.5 cm. (Courtesy Clifford Evans, Jr. and B. J. Meggers.)

These individuals usually have a high, wide bulbous hairdress and, when viewed from the side, would appear to portray people with fronto-occipitally flattened heads. They are well polished and frequently decorated with panels of concentric incised lines and with paint (Fig. 5-38).

The Guangala phase marks the first definite appearance of metals in Ecuador. The objects are little eyed-needles, fishhooks, and nose rings. All have been fashioned by hammering.

Although Guangala has moved away from Chorrera norms in some elaboration of craft goods, there is still nothing in the culture to suggest any notable increase in ceremonial or religious activity. Large structures are lacking. Burials, which are found in village sites and are of flexed primary and secondary forms, show some differentiation in the presence of grave goods; however, this more clearly seems to correlate with age and sex than with the high status of individuals. In other words, there is nothing in the mortuary customs that would lead us to believe in either a stratified social

288

Figure 5-38. Guangala pottery figurine. The figure is painted a reddish-yellow, and the dark areas are from resist or negative coloring. The fine lines indicate engraving. (Drawn from Estrada, 1957 c. No scale given but figurine is probably between 15 and 20 cm. high.)

order or a "divine" kingship institution for Guangala.

Jambelí, Tejar, and Daule. Meggers, Estrada, and Evans define three other phases from the southern Ecuadorian coasts and Guayas Basin.[71] All are closely related to Guangala in their ceramic components. In Tejar and Daule this relationship is undoubtedly an expression of their common and parallel development out of the earlier Chorrera phase—in addition, of course, to some subsequent contacts. Jambelí, on the other hand, may be derived directly from early Guangala, as no Chorrera horizon has yet been found in the regions of Jambelí sites.[72]

The Jambelí phase sites are found in the El Oro subarea, if we include within that subarea those parts of Guayas Province that border the Gulf of Guayaquil and the Island of Puná. The name Jambelí comes from the Canal de Jambelí, which is the passage into the Gulf of Guayaquil between the eastern side of Puná Island and the mainland. Sites of the phase abound on both sides of the channel and are also found as far south as Tumbes, in Peru.[73] These are small, generally shallow shell middens, composed largely of a species of mangrove oyster. The El Oro coast is still in mangroves, but to the north and on the Island of Puná these mangroves are in process of drying up and giving way to salitres. Presumably, in the past—at the time of occupancy—the Jambelí sites were entirely in a mangrove environment, which would have been unsuited to cultivation; it is believed that subsistence was largely by fishing and shellfish collecting, despite the fact that the Jambelí people's immediate neighbors of the Guangala, Tejar, and Daule phases were farmers. The Jambelí culture is, however, more than just a series of fishing camps established by Guangala farmers. Manufactures, while similar, are not the same. A Jambelí figurine style is unique and quite different from anything in Guangala, Tejar, or Daule. These figurines appear to be handmade, are hollow, have vestigial arms and feet and a very broad, low head with incised and punctate facial features (Fig. 5-39). Non-ceramic items are generally scarce although there are some small, distinctive shell pendants, carved as bird and other figures, and a number of ground stone bark beaters used in the preparation of bark cloth.

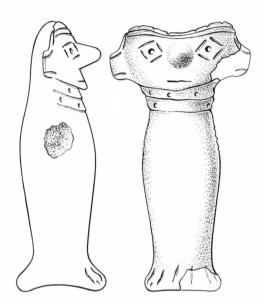

Figure 5-39. *Above, left:* Jambelí pottery figurine in profile and front view. Red-slipped, with some white paint, and with incised decoration. Height, about 13.5 cm. (Drawn from Estrada, Meggers, and Evans, 1964.)

Figure 5-40. *Above, right:* Jambelí white-on-red bowl. Diameter, about 20 cm. (Drawn from Estrada, Meggers, and Evans, 1964.)

Figure 5-41. *Right:* Jambelí Negative. Sherd at *left* is black over red; sherd at *right* has additional white positive painting. (Drawn from Estrada, Meggers, and Evans, 1964.)

Tejar and Daule sites are found in the Guayas Basin, located along the many tributaries of that river system. Those of Daule have a westerly distribution, those of Tejar are found on the east, with the two phases distinguished from each other by relatively minor features. Many of the sites are deep middens. Subsistence in the rich river-bottom lands was, we infer, largely agricultural, although fish from the rivers played a part in the economy. Like Guangala and Jambelí, there are no special sites or structures, nor are there other aspects of the cultural remains that would imply social and political stratifications or religious hierarchies. Pottery, like that of Jambelí and Guangala, features negative-painted and white-on-red wares, and there is some iridescent painting from the old Chorrera heritage. Vessel shapes, too, resemble those of the other cultures—compoteras, goblets—although polypods are relatively

rare and strap-handled bottles, including whistling jars, more common.

All of these cultures give indication of trade and contact with the others, and, in addition, all show items that can be referred to the Bahía culture of the Manabí subarea.

Bahía. The Bahía phase is found along the central coast of Manabí Province, from La Plata Island to the Bay of Caráquez.[74] This is a transition zone between the tropical forest coast to the north and the steppe and savanna country of Guayas. At the outset it should be noted that Bahía, although contemporaneous with Guangala, Jambelí, Tejar, and Daule, presents a quite different aspect with regard to elaborations that may be interpreted as signs of politico-religious development and the beginnings of a stratified society. Sites, for one thing, are larger. The big site of Manta reached its greatest proportions in the Late Period; however it is likely that it already was of large size in Bahía times.[75] A number of big platform mounds were found at Manta. Most of these have been destroyed by the expansion of the modern city, but some are said to have been terraced pyramid platforms—faced with rough stones or clay—measuring as much as 175 by 50 meters at the base. According to Meggers, some of these were built in the Regional Developmental Period, signifying not only a large town or city but an imposing ceremonial center.

There are both Chorrera and Machalilla survivals in the Bahía ceramics, seen in iridescent painting and zoned hachure designs discovered on angle-shouldered bowls, and the Regional Developmental Period horizon marker for Ecuador—negative-painting—is well represented. Much of the pottery is also painted with a positive red-on-buff decoration, and there is a red-and-black-on-white positive polychrome style. Life-modeled forms (spout-and-handle jars) are well developed, and sometimes these are embellished with post-fired pigments in reds, yellows, greens, white, and black (Fig. 5-42). One characteristic decorative mode for Bahía is an everted, cutout vessel rim.

The Bahía figurines include Bahía and Estero (Figs. 5-45, 5-46) types that are stylized, somewhat grotesque renderings of men and women; in fact, their grotesqueness suggests the larger pottery figures of the Ixtlán style of the Mexican Nayarit coast (see Vol. I, p. 173). They also have some general resemblances to the Guangala figurine style in that all are equally non-naturalistic. They are of special archaeological interest, however, in that they give some ideas about clothing and ornaments—the latter including the nose disk and little tusk-shaped engraved stone pendants (which are also found in Bahía sites in the original). The quite different and aesthetically much more pleasing La Plata figurine type is also

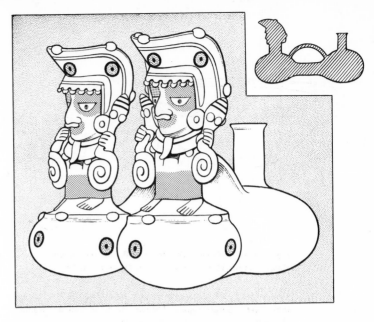

Figure 5-42. Bahía double-bodied-figure bridge-spout jar. There is iridescent fired painting on the body of the vessel, but the human figures have been painted (not all indicated in drawing) in red, yellow, pink, green, white, and black post-fired pigments. (Drawn from Estrada, 1962. See his Figure 50 for color detail. Scale is not given, but the vessel is apparently small, with height of about 15–20 cm.)

observed associated with the Bahía phase (Fig. 5-47). These are mold-made, frequently hollow, quite naturalistic, and they depict men—perhaps priests or dignitaries—with strange headgear, including point-shaped helmets.[76] This La Plata type —although recognizably different—is clearly related to the fine, mold-made, naturalistic figurines that are occasionally found in Guangala; and it is likely that Bahía influenced Guangala in this regard.

Figure 5-43. Bahía engraved and incised potsherds. a: Bahía engraved type. b, c: Bahía broad-line incised type. (Drawn from Estrada, 1962.)

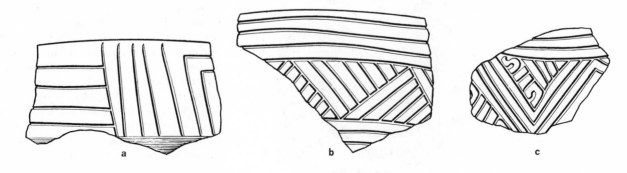

a   b   c

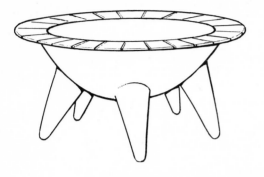  

Figure 5-44. *Above, left:* Bahía polished red polypod bowl. Height, about 15 cm. (Drawn from Estrada, 1962.)

Figure 5-45. *Above, right:* Bahía figurines of the Estero type. *Left:* "Estero type A." *Right:* "Estero type B." Height, about 7 cm. (Drawn from Estrada, 1962.)

Figure 5-46. *Right:* Bahía figure of pottery with multi-colored post-fired painting. From a tomb at Los Esteros, Bahía de Manta, Manabí. The man is wearing a headdress and a shell necklace. He holds what appears to be a coca bowl in one hand and has what may be a lime stick or spatula in his mouth. Height, about 50 cm. (Courtesy Museum of the American Indian, Heye Foundation.)

Figure 5-47. *Below:* Bahía pottery figurine, "La Plata type." (Drawn from Estrada, 1962.)

Among the ceramic manufactures of Bahía are little pottery house models. These are more or less vessel-sized items, some of which were containers—although not all of them were. They depict structures of double-sloped roofs with high front and rear gables and a curved or saddlelike roof. A door is usually shown open at the front end, sometimes with a little modeled figure of a person sitting within the house. Walls of the houses frequently have designs in various colored pigments applied after the firing of the piece. Another Bahía ceramic item is a head- or neckrest (Fig. 5-48). Such rests have a slablike base, usually columnar upright supports, and a curved head- or neckpiece. Sometimes the column supports are fashioned as humans, and sometimes a modeled human figure lies against the base.

292

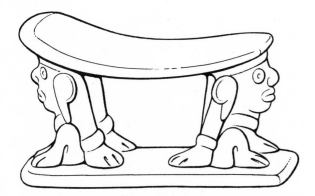

Figure 5-48. Bahía pottery headrest or neckrest with human figure supports. (Drawn from Estrada, 1962.)

These house models are of course quite "Oriental" in style and suggest not only Asiatic architectural styles but actual pottery house models of Asia. In the same way, the headrests are, in fact, thus designated on the basis of their close similarity to Asiatic, Oceanic, and African forms. Estrada and Meggers have called attention to these parallels and have suggested that they indicate that the Ecuadorian coast continued in sporadic contact with sailors from across the Pacific long after Jomon and Valdivia times.[77] By the Regional Developmental Period (500 B.C.–A.D. 500) the dugout canoes of the Far East would have been replaced by large Chinese trading vessels, and the same currents that are thought to have swept the Jomon voyagers across the Pacific to Ecuador may have done the same for the crafts of Chinese civilization some 3000 years later. To further strengthen the case, these authors add other traits:[78] panpipes with the tubes graduated toward the center, little pottery "golf-tee"-shaped earplugs, and a Bahía iconography rich in dragon and serpent themes as expressed in figurine and vessel modeling and painting.

We see in the Bahía phase a culture that, while having Formative Period antecedents in the earlier Chorrera, contains a number of exotic elements. Perhaps some of these elements were introduced by sea from distant Asian shores as has been suggested; others, without much question, were introduced from Mesoamerica, although possibly these diffusions were mediated by way of some of the

cultures that lay just to the north of Bahía—those known as Jama-Coaque and Tolita.

Jama-Coaque, Tolita, and the South Colombian Coast. The series of Regional Developmental Period coastal cultures which lay to the north of Bahía are closely interrelated. They are, from south to north, the Jama-Coaque of northern Manabí, the Tiaone of southern Esmeraldas, the Tolita of northern Esmeraldas, and the Mataje of the Tumaco subarea of the south Colombian coast. These cultures share a common tropical forest coastal environment; they were undoubtedly similar in a maize-manioc farming economy supplemented with river and coastal fishing; and they all show very definite Mesoamerican influences in ceramics and figurines. An underlying Formative Period Chorrera horizon has been determined for Jama-Coaque; north of this, however, there is no information on antecedent cultures.

Jama-Coaque sites are found from the Bay of Caráquez to Cape San Francisco. They seem to be mostly small refuse accumulations, with nothing rivaling the Bahía settlement at Manta in size. This modest settlement and the architectural nature of Jama-Coaque is curious in view of the considerable ceramic and aesthetic elaboration of the culture which rivals that of Bahía.[79] Jama-Coaque ceramics show the negative-painted and polished red-slipped and incised traditions of the cultures to the south; and the pottery house models (Fig. 5-49) and the pottery headrests of Bahía are also present. Pottery seals, of both cylindrical and flat forms, have complicated geometric and zoomorphic stamping motifs, and these—as well as little pottery masks (smaller than life-size)—are reminiscent of Mesoamerica. Moldmade figurines are notably Mesoamerican. One type frequently shows men dressed in feather or quilted suits and adorned with great fan-shaped headdresses in the Mexican manner.

The territory between Cape San Francisco and the Rio Esmeraldas is poorly known archaeologically. Data from various collections suggest, however, that a Regional Developmental Period culture here, while relating to its neighbors, may be distinguished from either Jama-Coaque or Tolita in ceramic and figurine types. Meggers has given it the name Tiaone.[80]

Figure 5-49. Pottery house model of the Jama-Coaque phase. (Drawn from Estrada, 1962. The scale and size of these models are not given in the publication, but it is assumed that they are in the range of 15 to 20 cm. in height.)

The Tolita culture[81] of northern Esmeraldas takes its name from the most famous site in Ecuador, the fabulous La Tolita, for years looted for its gold and figurines. Located on an island at the mouth of the Santiago River, it consists (or once consisted before its destruction) of 40 mounds, or "tolas," of earth and refuse. The larger of these were rectangular, flat-topped platforms and were arranged around a large open plaza. The tallest such mound is said to have been 9 meters high and 45 by 20 meters at the base. Other mounds at the site were of ovoid, circular, or irregular form. Little or nothing is known of their internal structure, but the flat-topped rectangular tumuli were probably erected as bases for temples or chiefs' houses while the others may have been burial places. All, however, were built up of refuse and contained thousands of figurines, fragments of these, potsherds, and gold and copper ornaments. Much of this material can be assigned stylistically to the Regional Developmental Period, so it may be that the mounds, or some of them, are of that date. But it is also possible that mound construction was largely—or entirely—restricted to the Late Period phase of the site and region—the Atacames.

Tolita ceramic manufactures include house models, and at least one of these is much like the saddle-roofed style of those of the Bahía and Jama-Coaque phases. Like Jama-Coaque, too, they include cylinder and flat stamps or seals, little pottery masks, and spindle whorls; and the Tolita figurines are outstanding in pre-Columbian America.[82] Mold-made figurines predominate although these have often been further embellished with hand modeling. Many of them are characterized by a considerably lifelike naturalism: they show women with short skirts and caplike hairdos and men dressed in loincloths, capes, turbans, and animal headdresses. A great many demonic figurines and anthropomorphic-animal combinations, while representing beings in the realm of fantasy or myth, have nevertheless a great naturalism of pose and gesture. All such mold-made figurines are generally referred to as the "Tolita type." For want of proper stratigraphy and study, little is known of the chronology of change within this flamboyant stylistic tradition of the Tolita figurines. There is also another distinctive style in the region, called the Cojimíes which refers to quite large handmade figurines or hollow pottery sculptures. These tend to be fantastic, frequently depicting monstrous or fanged men or gods.

Negative-painted pottery is common at Tolita. Uhle recognized it there many years ago and spoke of it as "Tuncahuán," as was the custom in referring to all negative-painted patterns in Ecuador 50 years ago.[83] There are also red-and-white, red-on-buff, red-zoned incised, and incised on polished red-slipped styles. Bowls with body flanges and mammiform supports appear;[84] and this could be the South American source for these features that come into the Momil II phase of northern Colombia, as Reichel-Dolmatoff has suggested. There are also polypods, such as we have seen farther south on the Ecuador coast, and tall pedestal composteras. One very typical Tolita form is a double-spout-and-bridge jar with divergent spouts.

The metalworking tradition of La Tolita is famous. It presumably extended through both the Tolita and Atacames phases. Rings, nose rings, pins, needles, bells, little masks, dangles, beads, and fishhooks were made of gold, copper, and tumbaga; and the techniques of hammering, welding, alloying, and simple smelting were all prac-

294

ticed by the Tolita smiths.[85] The style of the work shows some relationships to the Colombian highlands, but it is also distinctive and readily recognizable.

There is little information on burials at La Tolita; however the Stirlings recently have reported on "pottery tube" or "chimney" interment.[86] This type of burial, made in a mound or in flat ground, has a column of pottery tubes, or urns with the bottoms broken out, one above the other arranged in "chimney" fashion, with the burial made at the bottom of the "chimney" or pottery column. The one excavated by the Stirlings has a radiocarbon date of A.D. 267, placing it in the latter part of the Tolita phase according to our chronology; however this form of burial is also associated with the Late Period Atacames phase.[87]

Something very much like the Tolita phase is found across the Colombian border in the Tumaco subarea; figurines of the Tolita or Atacames styles have long been known from here.[88] These, like the Ecuadorian ones, show the strong Mesoamerican influences in representations of warriors, wrinkled grotesque faces, and gods or monsters. Pottery vessels from Tumaco include the double-spouted jars, like those of La Tolita, negative-painted wares, and bowls with mammiform supports. Reichel-Dolmatoff has described a three-phase sequence from the Mataje River that is dated by radiocarbon to indicate a Mataje I phase ending at about 300 B.C., a phase II falling between 300 B.C. and the beginnings of the Christian era, and a phase III immediately succeeding that. A continuity of the cultural tradition is also demonstrated from excavations in a Tumaco midden site, Imbilí, which has a Late Period radiocarbon date of about A.D. 1000.[89]

The Regional Developmental Period in the Highlands. Although the record for the Ecuadorian highlands is much less complete than that for the coast, a number of sites are known from the Cuenca Basin and the Cañar Valley. These are all village-sized concentrations of refuse, usually located on knolls or hill spurs overlooking rivers and valley bottom lands suitable for cultivation; and charred maize has been found in site debris dating from the Regional Developmental Period.[90] The Regional Developmental Period

ceramic complex of the South Highlands subarea was first referred to by Uhle as "Mayoid,"[91] on the somewhat fanciful notion that it bore a close resemblance and relationship to Maya pottery of Central America; Jijón y Caamaño, an associate of Uhle's, preferred the name Chaullabamba, after a site near Cuenca;[92] Collier and Murra designated a particular site component of it as Early Cerro Narrío;[93] and Bennett referred to another as Monjashuaico.[94] Meggers, in her summary of Ecuadorian archaeology,[95] has gone back to the term Chaullabamba and we will follow this usage.

The finer ceramics of the Chaullabamba phase —those, especially, which impressed Uhle—are thin, well polished, and frequently painted in a red-on-buff style with incised lines bordering the red bands. This Cerro Narrío Red-on-buff Fine, as it is called by Collier and Murra, is found in association with negative-painting, positive white-on-red painting, burnished-line decoration, and small amounts of iridescent painting—all horizon markers of the Regional Developmental Period. The vessel forms are largely bowls and jars, lacking the high pedestals and polypods of the related coastal complexes. Pottery figurines are rare in the South Highlands, although seals or stamps occur, as do pottery stools (which were met with in the Jama-Coaque phase). Those of the South Highlands are described as being about 10 centimeters high and 25 centimeters in diameter, with a circular, concave top, always perforated. They are painted in the pottery-painting color schemes of the phase—red-on-buff and white-on-red.[96]

For the Central Highland subarea, Jijón y Caamaño has put forward a long cultural sequence in the Riobamba Basin. This sequence terminated with the Puruhá and Inca phases; however, the earliest of Jijón's phases, Proto-Panzaleo I and II, have been questioned both as to their validity as complexes and as to their chronological position. Stratigraphic archaeology from both the South Highlands and the coast has failed to confirm them.[97] The third phase of the Jijón sequence is the Tuncahuán. It features negative-painted pottery (Fig. 5-50) and is somewhat better documented than Proto-Panzaleo. It was first described from a cemetery in Chimborazo Province, and the negative-painted wares in question include both two- and three-color types. The latter bear a general resemblance to the three-

Figure 5-50. A Tuncahuán three-color negative-painted bowl. *Left:* Exterior. *Right:* Interior. The colors are from a buff or light slip, a gray-black resist or negative application, and addition of red paint. Height of vessel, about 10 cm. (Courtesy Cambridge Museum of Archaeology and Ethnology, England.)

color negative style of Peruvian Recuay. Vessel forms are bowls and tall pedestaled compoteras. Besides the negative-painted types, the Tuncahuán complex also includes positive white geometric designs on a red-slipped ware. Small copper ornaments are found in Tuncahuán graves. Meggers has placed the Tuncahuán phase as the Regional Developmental culture of the Central Highlands on the basis of these negative-painted and white-on-red horizon markers.[98]

North Highland Ecuador comprises the Quito and Ibarra Basins of the Provinces of Cotopaxi, Pichincha, and Imbabura and the northernmost Province of Carchi. These are little-known regions from an archaeological standpoint. Mounds are found here—the only part of the Ecuadorean uplands in which they seem to be pre-Incaic. Some of them appear to have been used as burial places, whereas others were probably building platforms. Jijón has outlined sequences for both the Quito[99] and the Ibarra[100] basins, but both appear to be highly impressionistic and stylistically, rather than stratigraphically, grounded.

Manteño. In Ecuador, particularly along the coast, the cultures of the Late Period exhibit a number of trends that, in a general way, set them apart from those of the preceding Regional Developmental Period. Foremost among these is the development of towns. This appears to have been a correlate of overall population increase and functionally interrelated to the development of political chiefdoms or small kingdoms. A somewhat more imposing architecture, as contrasted to the earlier periods, was related to this trend. In technology, metals and metallurgy became common, with weapons and tools made of copper in addition to ornaments of copper, gold, and alloys. As in north coastal Peru, there is also a mass-produced quality to manufactures, including pottery, with an attendant aesthetic decline.[101]

The Manteño culture found in the Guayas and in the southern Manabí subareas displays these trends. Manteño appears to have had its hearth in southern Manabí, the old homeland of the Bahía culture, and it probably developed largely from Bahía, although the phases of transition have not been isolated. The peoples associated with the Manteño culture were the Manta or Manteño, supposedly a Yuncan-speaking tribe, who occupied this part of the coast in the early sixteenth century. Their principal site or city was Manta, in Manabí, which, as we have seen, had been an important site in earlier Bahía times. Quite probably, Manta was the political capital of a sizable domain ruled by a paramount chief who held dominion over lesser chiefs. It may have been, at least for periods of time, that the ruler of Manta was also the ruler of the entire Manteño territory; however, it is likely that such "kingdoms" were somewhat fluid affairs, with alliances shifting. The early ethnohistoric sources indicate that warfare was frequent.[102]

The stone foundations of houses and other buildings at Manta are said to have once covered several square miles,[103] although just how tightly packed these structures were as an urban mass has not been determined and, unfortunately, cannot be now, for much of this imposing ruin has been destroyed by the modern city. The house foundations were laid up of rough stone masonry. Superstructures must have been of wood, cane, and thatch. Individual houses usually had one or two rooms, but there were also some large, multi-roomed buildings within Manta that probably had temple or palace functions. The Spanish refer to such temples and to religious rites and priests. Palacelike buildings have been found outside Manta, a few miles inland in the coastal hill country. These buildings were associated with others of more ordinary domestic proportions, and such settlements were possibly residences of lesser chiefs and their subjects, all tributary to Manta. Another possibility is that these outlying sites were shrines or places of religious pilgrimage with the nearby dwellings of their attendants. M. H. Saville[104] explored a number of them, including Cerro Jaboncillo and Cerro de Hojas,[105] and it is from them that we have obtained most of our Manteño stone sculptures.

The Manteño stone sculpture[106] is the only monumental carving of the Ecuadorian part of the Intermediate area. The sculptures were found within the enclosures of stone foundations on the tops of raised rectangular earth and rock platforms. Foremost among them are the U-shaped stone seats (Fig. 5-51). These seats are monoliths carved with the figure of an animal or a crouching man as the support for the chair. Similar seats are represented in Manteño pottery figurines. Other sculptures are free-standing human or animal figures (Fig. 5-52), carved columnar pieces, and flat bas-relief stelae (Fig. 5-53). The stelae, sometimes as much as a meter in height, usually portray the seated or reclining figure of a

Figure 5-51. Stone seats from Cerro Jaboncillo, Manabí. Manteño culture. *a, b, c:* Side, front, and rear views of seat with crouching man support. *d:* Front view of another seat with puma or jaguar support. These stone seats average about 80–90 cm. in height. (*a, b, c;* drawn from Saville, 1907; *d;* drawn from Saville, 1910.)

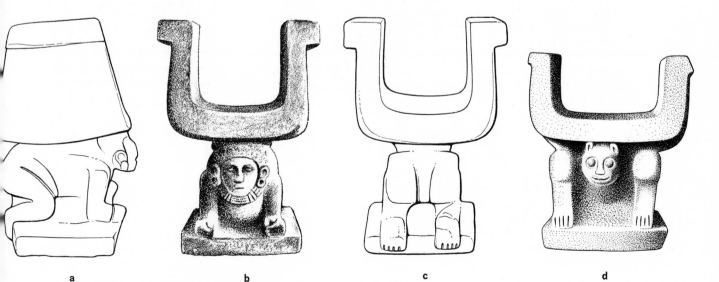

a   b   c   d

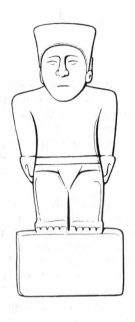 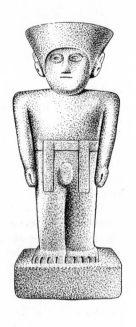

woman beneath a decorative frieze of geometric elements.

Manteño pottery shows the influence of its Guangala and Bahía prototypes.[107] Thus, repetitive pelican and geometric frieze designs of the Guangala painted wares occur on Manteño in-

Figure 5-52. *Left:* Stone figures, Manteño culture, Manabí. The figure at *right* is about 60 cm. tall; the other is not necessarily to this same scale. (*Left,* drawn from Saville, 1910; *right,* drawn from Saville, 1907.)

Figure 5-53. *Below:* Stone slab bas-relief carvings, Manteño culture, Manabí. (Drawn from Saville, 1910.)

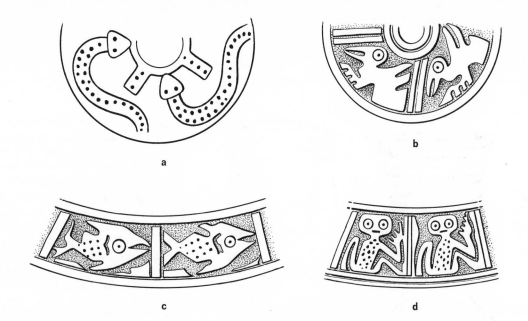

a

b

c

d

Figure 5-54. Pressed designs on pottery spindle whorls, Manteño phase. *a:* Serpents. *b:* Birds (pelicans?). *c:* Fish. *d:* Monkeys. (Drawn from Saville, 1910.)

cised-excised vessels or as engravings on Manteño clay spindle whorls (Fig. 5-54). One of the dominant Manteño styles is decorated with burnished-line designs (Fig. 5-55). This was as well a Guangala technique, but one confined to vessel interiors; in Manteño it is used on the exteriors of distinctively shaped jars. These jars have a low ring base, constricted neck, and flaring collar; a human or animal face, modeled in high relief,

Figure 5-55. Manteño burnished pottery. *Left:* Jar with face in color and burnished streaking on body. *Right:* Tall pedestal plate with burnishing on base. (*Left*, drawn from Estrada, 1957; *right,* from Estrada, 1962. No scales are given, but relatively large vessels are suggested.)

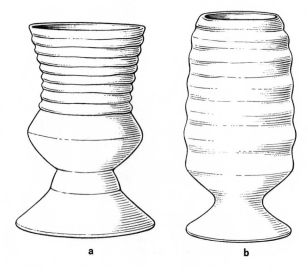

Figure 5-56. Fluted or horizontally channeled (*acanalado*) pedestal-based vessels of the Manteño phase. (*a*, drawn from Estrada, 1962; *b*, drawn from Saville, 1910.)

characteristically adorns the collar. Some Manteño pottery is decorative-stamped or mold-impressed. This technique developed on the Far North Coast of Peru in Middle Horizon and later times, and it is likely that Ecuador was influenced from Peru

Figure 5-57. Sketches of Manteño figure types. *a:* "Hueco" (hollow). *b:* "Solido" (solid). (Drawn from Estrada, 1962.)

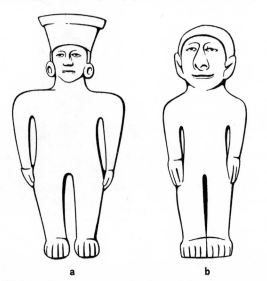

in this instance. A marker type for the northern or Manabí territory of Manteño culture, but not for Guayas and the south, is a red grater bowl or plate with deep, fingermade grooves on the interior. In general, Manteño pottery is monochrome, of black, grey, or brownish color. Some of it is red-slipped; much of it is well polished. Decoration, as we have noted, is by plastic techniques or burnishing. A small amount of negative painting occurs, but for the most part painted design is rare or absent.

Manteño figurines may be either hand or mold-made. Male figures (Fig. 5-57) are more common than are females, and the individuals represented have the same distinctive face, with the high, prominent nose, as those modeled on the collars of the pottery jars. Both sexes are usually shown with collarlike ornaments, a smooth headdress treatment, and the lower part of the body nude. Individuals are often represented as having broad, high heads, as though from fronto-occipital cranial flattening.

In metal, gold was most commonly used, but Bushnell found copper beads, bells, a gold-plated copper ring, and a silver earring with burials in the Santa Elena locality. A socketed copper chisel or digging-stick blade came from Manteño refuse at La Libertad, and casts for rectangular copper celts and T-shaped axes are similarly associated. One other copper form deserves special mention. This is the little "money ax," a T-shaped, thin, non-functional copper ax, believed to have been used in the way of a medium of exchange. These are more common in the contemporaneous and neighboring Milagro culture; however, they are reported from the Santa Elena region.[108] Quite similar objects were used as an exchange medium in prehistoric western Mexico (Vol. I, pp. 172–173).

The Manteño skill in textiles[109] is reported by the early Spanish, who describe peoples garbed in blankets, shawls, and skirts decorated with bird, animal, and fish designs and of many different colors. Quite probably, the flat and cylinder pottery stamps of the culture were used for decorating textiles, and the interest in spinning and weaving is further vouched for by the thousands of mold-made pottery spindle whorls.

Manteño burials have been recovered from the zone of the ancient city or town in Manta and in other Manteño sites along the Guayas and Manabí coasts. Possibly, separate cemetery areas were set aside for this purpose within the Manteño communities. At La Libertad, Bushnell found primary extended burials, urn burials, and mass secondary burials.[110] An urn burial was contained in a double urn, with one vessel placed mouth downwards to cover the other. The urns rested on a bed of ash about a meter below surface, and the lower urn appeared to have been heated by an *in situ* fire. The human bones inside, including at least an adult and five children, were calcined. The whole seems to represent secondary burial in an urn that was then subjected to partial cremation on the spot as part of the funeral ceremony. All burials at La Libertad were accompanied by such small items as shell beads, pottery spindle whorls, or copper beads. Urn burials with calcined bone or bone ash are also reported from Manta. At Olon, on the Guayas coast between La Libertad and Manta, Estrada mentions urn burials accompanied by additional burial pottery.[111]

The Manta were skilled sailors, participating in the traditions of boat building and coastwise navigation that characterized the north Peruvian and Ecuadorian coasts in the early historic period. S. K. Lothrop has described some of these native boats.[112] The most seaworthy and suitable for long voyages was the balsa log raft, the same kind of vessel, incidentally, that Thor Heyerdahl constructed and used in his trans-Pacific voyage.[113] These rafts were sail-driven and controlled by a system of centerboards that could be raised and lowered with ease. Such a raft was seen by the Spaniard Ruiz off the Ecuadorian coastal island of La Plata in 1527. It was loaded with passengers and produce and engaged on a trading mission. What appear to be pre-Columbian potsherds in Peruvian and Ecuadorian styles, found on the Galápagos Islands, some 600 miles off the Ecuadorian coast, indicate that such sailing craft sometimes ventured far out to sea.[114] A key feature of such a vessel as this was the centerboard. Now it is not known for certain whether the raft that Ruiz saw in 1527 possessed such a feature, although those of the 18th and 19th centuries, which form the basis of Lothrop's description, did have it. If the 1527 raft had the centerboard, it is a very good possibility that the idea was introduced to Ecuador from across the Pacific.

A centerboard-equipped raft would have facili-

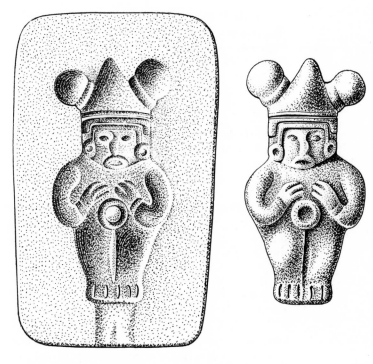

Figure 5-58. Pottery-figurine mold (of pottery), *left*, and cast from mold. Probably Manteño. (Drawn from Saville, 1910.)

tated coastwise sailing, and this kind of travel would have provided the means for long-distance trade between Mesoamerica and Ecuador. We have already mentioned some of the Mesoamerican-Ecuadorian trait similarities of the earlier periods. These similarities continue in the Late Period. For instance, the copper "money axes" would have been an ideal and expected element in such interchange.

This topic of sea trade raises interesting questions. Just what would its importance have been to the Ecuadorians? It seems unlikely that this was purely economic—at least as we use that word in reference to basic subsistence. There can be little doubt that the basic food staples for a community like Manta were grown locally or nearby; the presence of cultivation terraces in the hill country behind the Manabí coast suggests this and indicates an intensification of agricultural production in the Late Period to support the increasing population. Such populations could hardly have been fed by sea trade at that time. The importance of the long-distance trade was more likely of a different sort. Luxury goods and exotic items serve to distinguish and to consolidate a growing aristocracy, and with the class differentiation that was beginning to emerge in cultures like the Manteño it would have had this effect just as, at the other end of the trade routes in Mesoamerica, it was probably prized and maintained for the same reasons.

Milagro. In the old Daule and Tejar territory of the Guayas River Basin the Late Period Milagro culture was the contemporary and neighbor of the Manteño. This was rich agricultural country, and the large number of Milagro sites suggest a populous nation. Presumably, these people were the Huancavilca, linguistic relatives of the Manteño.[115] The Milagro sites are frequently marked by earth mounds. Some of these are small platforms, probably for ordinary dwellings in a country seasonally flooded; others, however, are large platforms, some of which measure as much as 100 by 30 meters in extent and 10 meters in height. These seem not to contain burials and are believed to have served as platforms for temples or other special buildings. Still others, of intermediate size and dome-shaped, must have been constructed especially for burials. Such burials are both direct inhumations and urn interments. Some of the latter are ordinary urn burials, with the burial urn capped by another jar, but some are of the "chimney" urn type (Fig. 5-59), where several urns, with the bottoms broken out, have been stacked one above the other to form a tube, sometimes as much as 5 meters in height.[116]

The Milagro pottery (Fig. 5-60) will tend to be thick and coarse, frequently black or brown in color, and often embellished with relief or appliqué designs of frogs, snakes, monkeys, and humans. Pedestal bowls or jars are frequently so treated. There is also some incision, some burnished-line decoration, some red-banding and slipping, and some negative-painting.[117]

The Milagro people were great metallurgists, and they evolved a distinctive ornamental style in gold, silver, and gilded-silver earrings and nose-rings. A distinctive feature of the style was the coiling or looping of the metal wires into attractive shapes, with an end of the wire then ham-

mered flat to produce a hooklike portion for attachment (Fig. 5-61). Dangles were often affixed to the coils of the ornament. They also manufactured rings, bracelets, and diadems or crowns, the latter equipped with silver or gold plumes. Profusions of these fine ornamental pieces accompanied some burials, clearly indicative of rank or social class. A good many tools were made of copper, including T-shaped or crescentic-handled knives or axes (Fig. 5-62), rectangular axes, tweezers, needles, knives, and fishhooks. The copper "money ax" (Fig. 5-62) is also present in Milagro, and many of these have been found in caches associated with burials.

Pottery figurines are lacking, but a very common Milagro item is a little carved stone amulet (Fig. 5-63) or figure—usually a frog, serpent, or a human-animal combination.

Manteño anthropomorphic jars are often found in Milagro graves, and Meggers suggests that the

Figure 5-59. Pottery vessels of a "chimney" burial. Milagro phase. (Courtesy Clifford Evans, Jr. and B. J. Meggers.)

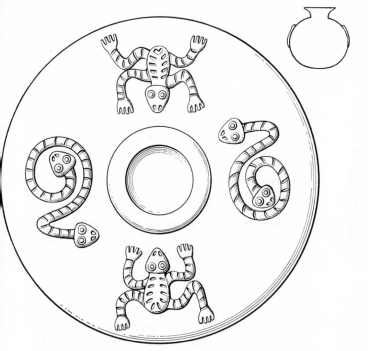

Figure 5-60. *Above:* Appliqué ornamentation on two Milagro phase pottery vessels. Vessel at *left* measures about 21 cm. in diameter. Vessel at *right* measures about 11 cm. in diameter. The rings in the noses of the human figures on this specimen are of copper—inserted, of course, after firing. (Drawn from Estrada, 1957 a).

Figure 5-61. *Left:* Gold nose ornament of the Milagro style. The piece was executed with a wire technique. (Drawn from Zevallos, 1958.)

Figure 5-62. *Below:* Copper axes. Milagro phase. The specimen at *right* is a heavy, functional ax. Height, about 12 cm. The others are thin "money axes." They are shown in stacks, as found. (Courtesy Clifford Evans, Jr. and B. J. Meggers.)

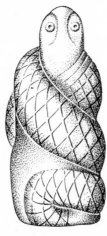

Figure 5-63. Milagro small stone carving. *Left:* Two views of a small human figure; height, about 11 cm. *Right:* Serpent figure; height, about 13 cm. (Drawn from Estrada, 1957 a.)

Guayas Valley people may have traded with the Manteño for salt.[118] Certainly, the two groups were in contact. Contact is also suggested with the Ecuadorian northern coast in the burial mound and "chimney" burial traits, both of which, as we have seen, were present in the Tolita phase.

Figure 5-64. Agricultural ridgings in the river bottom low-lands of the Guayas Basin, Ecuador. (Courtesy J. J. Parsons.)

If such trade did take place between the Milagrans and their coastal neighbors, it is possible that the valued goods of the former were food-stuffs. There are clues to suggest that the Milagro people were dedicated agriculturists. J. J. Parsons and William Denevan describe extensive earth-works in the savanna country of the Guayas Basin. These works consist of low ridges, 30 to 40 feet (approx. 9–12 m.) in width, some of them extending several kilometers in length. These ridges are particularly evident in the country about 20 to 25 kilometers north of the city of Guayaquil, between the Babahoyo and Daule drainages.[119]

Atacames. At the time of the arrival of the Spanish the territory north of the Bay of Caráquez—which had earlier been in the domain of the Jama-Coaque, Tiaone, Tolita cultures—was held by the Barbacoa (Atacames, Tacamez) and Esmeraldas tribes.[120] Meggers has given the name Atacames to the Late Period archaeological phase for all of these regions.[121] A similar culture seems to have existed on the other side of the Colombian border, and this would probably correspond to Reichel-Dolmatoff's Imbilí phase of the Tumaco subarea.[122] The Spaniards describe these Indians as town dwellers, with communities numbering from 1500 to 3000 houses. They were well organized for war; they had tem-ples for worship, and, best of all from the invader's point of view, they were rich in gold ornaments and emeralds—the latter circumstance, in fact, leading to the name given to the region and one of the tribes by the Spaniards.

The archaeological culture of the Atacames phase cannot be described satisfactorily as it has not been stratigraphically isolated from the earlier Jama-Coaque, Tiaone, and Tolita cultures; how-ever, mound construction in the town sites and "chimney" burial are two of the traits associated with the Late Period in the Esmeraldas subarea. It is not known to what extent the rich and elaborate figurine cult of earlier times persisted into the Atacames phase.

The Late Period in the Highlands. At the time of the Spanish Conquest the Inca were in control of the Ecuadorian highlands, and in some places they had begun their shifting and reorganizing of local populations that character-

304

ized their regime; however, some knowledge of the principal Late Period Ecuadorian tribes has come down to us from the Spanish accounts. The Cañari were in the South Highlands subarea of the Cuenca, Cañar, and Alausí basins; in the Central Highlands were the Puruhá, centering in the Riobamba Basin; and in the north, in the Quito and Ibarra basins, were the Cara. The Cañari and Puruhá are believed to have been of the Yuncan speech family; the Cara probably spoke a Chibchan-affiliated tongue. In all three subareas subsistence and the general pattern of life were similar. Maize, potatoes, and quinoa were the principal crops; the llama and guinea pig were kept as domesticates; and settlements were in valley floors along river courses. Political organization was generally that of small chieftainships, with individual chiefs venerated as supreme rulers. In the South and Central Highlands this political pattern seems to have prevailed right up to the time of the Inca Conquest; and, in fact, such fragmentation must have contributed to the Inca success in subjugating these people. In the North Highlands the Cara are reputed to have been organized into somewhat larger territorial states or, at least, to have so operated in times of war. Their resistance to the Inca was considerably tougher than that of their southern neighbors, but, eventually, they too succumbed.

The somewhat more evolved state organization of the Cara may be reflected in settlement pattern and architecture. As we have already noted, the North Highlands is the only part of the Ecuadorian sierra where large mound constructions occur. Some of these are huge, flat-topped, ramp-approached platforms that look like the bases of temples or palaces and are indeed the visible signs of former centralized power. The dating of these is not certain, but it is probable that both large mound construction and the elaborate burials found here belong to the Late Period. Meggers has subsumed these in a Cara archaeological phase.[123] The elaborate burials are deep shaft-and-chamber graves. Some have multiple side chambers at the bottom of the entrance shaft and contain the remains of more than one individual as well as large quantities of grave goods, suggesting the interment of an important lord with his wives and retainers. Other burials in the same localities—in fact, the majority—are of pit and simpler shaft-and-chamber forms, usually with a single individual and small or modest amounts of burial artifacts. These differentiations indicate status differences of individuals and support the ethnographic observations with reference to the importance of a ruling class.

Cara phase ceramics are often negative-painted, usually combined with positive red painting, and a most characteristic form is observed to be a large, tall, amphoralike jar with a high neck. Tall tripods, compoteras, annular-based jars, and anthropomorphic relief modeling and decoration on jars are all common in the complex. Metals are not particularly plentiful but include some copper tools and ornaments and some gold ornaments. The latter are stylistically closer to those of southern Colombia than to the metals of the Ecuadorian South Highlands. Ground stone axes and celts and ring-shaped and star-shaped maces of stone are also found in the Cara graves.

The Puruhá phase (following the Meggers terminology)[124] of the Central Highlands is known from such sites as Guano and Elenpata.[125] The pottery follows general Late Period trends in Ecuador, especially in the modeling and painting of stylized anthropomorphic jars (Fig. 5-65). Metals are relatively scarce, ground stone axes and mace heads frequent. Burials are of simple pit and shaft-and-chamber types; but the grave elaboration of the Cara phase to the north is not encountered. There is domestic architecture in stone and mud masonry and tapia adobe, but no mounds.

The Cañari phase[126] of the south presents a similar picture in the widespread use of anthropomorphic jars—although in a local style quite unlike that of Puruhá. Ground stone weapons are similar. Here, however, there is a much greater development in metalwork, with copper tools and ornaments much like those of the Milagro culture. The subarea is best known, however, from the contents of shaft tombs, such as those of Sigsig and Chordeleg.[127] These contained gold hoards, apparently the wealth of important chiefs that had been buried with them: gold disks, nose and ear ornaments, bells, crowns (Fig. 5-66), and throwing-sticks wrapped in sheet gold.

The Inca in Ecuador. Between 1463 and 1493 the Inca armies overran the Ecuadorian highlands, pushing north through the Cara

country to what is now the Colombian border. In the course of this and afterwards these empire builders proceeded with their usual administrative measures. They shifted peoples about under the *mitimae* system of colonization, and they constructed major forts and imperial centers. The great highland highway was extended from Peru north through the country. Inca religion was established and the Quechua language promulgated.

Figure 5-65. *Left:* Two vessels of the Puruhá culture. The taller one is 44 cm. high. (Courtesy Museum of the American Indian, Heye Foundation.)

Figure 5-66. *Below:* Gold crown with plumes and bangles from Sigsig, South Highlands of Ecuador. The style is very reminiscent of the Chimu crowns of north Peru. Height, about 35 cm. (Courtesy Museum of the American Indian, Heye Foundation.)

Their penetration of the Ecuadorian coast was much less effective. Apparently, they held some sort of sway over at least the southern portion of the coast, but the full weight of the imperial machinery was never brought to bear even there.[128] The tropical savanna and forest environment of the coast and the Guayas Basin was undoubtedly not to their liking. But even in the highlands the impress of the Inca presence is only slightly reflected in archaeology. Some architectural traces remained around Tomebamba, where they had one of their most important administrative centers;[129] but at Quito, another former provincial capital, these have disappeared. Inca ceramics, especially the aryballoid jar, are found in small quantity in the highlands and, rarely, in the lowlands. Apparently, some of them were made locally, either in imitation or by craftsmen who had been moved into Ecuador from Peru.

Colombia-Northwest Venezuela: Regional Developmental and Late Periods

Setting, Cultural Pattern, and Ethnography. Colombia and northwestern Venezuela compose the largest segment of our Intermediate area, and environmentally it is the most internally diverse segment. On the Pacific Coast are tropical forests and mangrove swamps extending to the westernmost part of the Caribbean coast. Farther east are the savannas and scrub-growth country of the Caribbean lowlands. In the interior of Colombia a low range of hills, the Cordillera de Chocó (Serranía de Baudó) separates the Pacific coastal swamplands from the tropical San Juan and Atrato River Valleys. East of these valleys is the Cordillera Occidental, and between this cordillera and the Cordillera Central is the great Cauca River Valley. The Cauca begins at an altitude of 6000 feet and flows northward to join the other major Colombian river, the Magdalena, which has its trough between the Cordillera Central and the massif of the Cordillera Oriental. On the eastern slopes of the latter are the upper tributaries of the Orinoco and Amazon systems, which lead out of the Intermediate area into the eastern South American lowlands. In the north, the Sierra de Perijá and the Cordillera de Mérida extend northward and northeastward to frame the

Maracaibo Basin of northwestern Venezuela; and just back of the sea, at the base of the Guajira Peninsula, is the steep, isolated mass of the Sierra Nevada de Santa Marta, (see Fig. 5-2). This juxtaposition of tropical coasts and river valleys, temperate valley stretches and upland basins, and high, colder basins provided an almost endless variety of microgeographic and microclimatic niches for human habitation; and this diversity has been an important factor in the semi-isolated cultural development of a great many Colombian tribal groups.

After the original spread of maize farming in the Formative Period, this new mode of subsistence allowed for the opening up of new lands for substantial human settlement, especially those of the highlands. In general, swidden cultivation was practiced; however, this was significantly modified from region to region by such things as the presence of alluvial soils in valley bottoms or favorable exposures of certain mountain slopes to seasonal rains. In these cases there was a more or less permanent maintenance of fields without annual shifting and new clearing. In others, irrigation, agricultural terracing, or both were maintained. Maize was the primary crop virtually everywhere. It was seconded by yuca (sweet manioc), the sweet potato, yams, racacha, beans, and, at higher elevations, potatoes and quinoa. Agricultural produce was further supplemented by various fruits and vegetables. All tribes are said to have maintained some food surpluses, and these were used for trade, for the sustenance of men engaged largely in military pursuits, and for the consumption of upper classes not primarily concerned with food production.

The general Colombian cultural pattern, which Reichel-Dolmatoff has called the "Sub-Andean,"[130] was characterized by small, class-structured chiefdoms. All such chiefdoms were extremely authoritarian, with the chief having a quasi-deified status. Near-constant and attritive warfare was an expression of his power. Although it would be an exaggeration to say that anything so permanent as the "standing armies" of the Inca were maintained by these Colombian tribesmen, nevertheless an inordinate amount of time was devoted to campaigning and fighting. Its purposes were territorial control, loot, tribute, head hunting, the capture of slaves, and cannibalism. Religion was maintained in these Sub-Andean chiefdoms through a priest-temple-idol cult in reference to which, for some groups, the term "organized priesthood" could be used appropriately. There was an exceedingly active trade among chiefdoms and regions. Gold, cotton cloth, salt, dried fish, and agricultural foodstuffs were all a part of this commerce.

This Sub-Andean cultural pattern is known to a very large extent from ethnohistoric sources. Sebastián de Belalcázar (Benalcázar) directed the first expedition of conquest into the southern part of the country and the Cauca Valley in the 1530's. He found the Indians farming the slopes of the Cauca Valley; both men and women were engaged in the work. Their settlements were small hamlet clusters of dwellings or dispersed individual houses dotted over the mountainsides. Houses were made of poles and thatch. Chiefs' dwellings served as rallying points for warriors, and the burials of chiefs are described as being made in deep shaft tombs into which the bodies of immolated wives and retainers were also placed, along with pottery and gold, to accompany the great man. The tribes to which such descriptions pertained were the Pasto, the Quillacinga, the Andaquí, the Popayense, the Moguex, Paez, Coconuco, Pijao, and the Quimbaya and their many minor neighbors along the middle reaches of the Cauca (Fig. 5-3). These tribes were quite probably all affiliated with the Paezan language group of the Macro-Chibchan superstock (see p. 12).[131]

To the north and east of these tribes listed above were the Chibcha—in the country of what is now the Colombian Departments of Cundinamarca, Boyacá, and Santander. Here are the cold, high basins of the Cordillera Oriental. Politically and militarily the Chibcha were the most impressive of the Colombian Indians, and they had moved somewhat beyond the threshold of the warring Sub-Andean tribesmen; but in spite of this they were subdued by Jiménez de Quesada less than two years after his entrance into their country in 1538.[132]

On the Pacific Coast were the Chocó, and in the north Colombian lowlands of the Sinú and Magdalena drainages the Spaniards met with such peoples as the Urabá, the Sinú (Cenú), Tolú, Calamari, Mompox, and Tamalameque.[133] These tribes may have been Paezan, too, although some

authorities see closer affinities with Cariban-speaking peoples. These farmers and fishers lived in villages and towns, often stockaded. They had wooden temples, constructed burial mounds, and made and wore gold ornaments. The latter two features have for a certainty been confirmed by archaeology.

In northeastern Colombia the important early historic period nation was the Tairona, living in the mountain mass of the Sierra Nevada de Santa Marta.[134] Their language is not definitely known, although it may have been of Paezan or Macro-Chibchan affiliation. Their pattern of life, which has been verified by archaeology, was organized on a town or even urban basis, with terracing, irrigation, and stone architecture—features more consistent with a true Andean or Peruvian-type level of development, in contrast to their Sub-Andean neighbors.

In western and northwestern Venezuela the Sub-Andean pattern prevailed with tribes like the Timote (probably of Chibchan language affiliation), the Chaké (Cariban), and the Lache (unidentified linguistically). All were village and town agriculturists; some practiced irrigation; temples and chiefs' houses are reported from the sixteenth century. Along the coast and near Lake Maracaibo were the Arawakan-affiliated Caquetio and Jirajara. These were the tribesmen seen in 1527–28, some of them living on pile dwellings around the lake, and it was from them that the region—and later the country—took the name of Venezuela, or "little Venice."[135]

This brief sketch offers an ethnographic background against which the archaeological findings of the Colombian Regional Developmental and Late Period findings may be better appreciated.

Nariño-Cauca Valley. This is a highly tentative subarea. Most of the archaeological data are from grave collections. There is little chronological information.

What has been called the Nariño complex may or may not be a single complex or phase. The pottery comes from graves in the highlands of that Department. It features two-color and three-color negative painting which is rather like that of the North Highlands of Ecuador, including some of that of the Cara phase. The painted decoration is applied to olla exteriors and plate

Figure 5-67. Funerary ware of the Quebrada Seca complex. Vessel at *left* is about 40 cm. high. (After Ford, 1944.)

(including pedestal-plate) interiors. The graves in question are shaft-and-side-chamber affairs which contained direct primary and urn interments. The little clay manufactures, so typical of the Ecuadorian Regional Developmental and Late Periods —whistles, ocarinas, spindle whorls—are common in these graves, and there is some hammered and cast goldwork.[136]

From around Popayán we have scraps of information that cannot be tied together into complexes, much less be given chronological arrangement. Lehmann illustrates a large figurine type from the region, a chief seated on a bench, holding a shield and wearing an elaborate headdress.[137] His legs have the curious bulging shape that appear to depict leg ligatures, a trait that is generally associated with the tropical lowland cultures of eastern South America. Figurines similar to these are associated with the so-called "Quimbaya" culture, found some distance north along the Cauca, and this kind of human figure modeling is also seen on the Lower Magdalena Valley burial urns.[138] We also know that there is a huge artificial mound construction near Popayán, made of adobes; however the potsherds from it have not been dated or culturally related.[139]

In the Cali region three grave complexes—the Rio Pichindé, Rio Bolo, and Quebrada Seca—have been defined by Ford from the valley hillslopes around that city. All the complexes have shaft-and-chamber graves, and such graves are found near the small, scattered hillside house platforms of the region. None of the pottery from the graves

is particularly well painted or ornamented. The vessel forms of the Quebrada Seca phase (Fig. 5-67) include tall pedestal bowls, and small gold ornaments have also been found in the Quebrada Seca tombs.[140]

North of Cali, at Buga, Warwick Bray has defined two complexes, Yotoco and Sonso.[141] Remains of both are found in the alluvial flats of the river valley. Bray's Yotoco phase has a radiocarbon date of A.D. 1175. Its ceramic traits include negative or resist-dye overpainting in circle and spiral patterns, bridge-and-spout vessels, low incurved rim bowls, and pedestal forms. There is some embossed goldwork; and one covered urn burial of a child was recovered from the phase.

The Sonso phase dates by radiocarbon to about A.D. 1550 in the Buga region; however Sonso shows trade relations and close connections with the Calima Valley culture which is found just to the west of Buga, and these Calima sites have been dated by radiocarbon to A.D. 1250. Perhaps the Sonso phase spans most of the Late Period, or it may be that the Buga region date on Sonso is too late. With reference to the A.D. 1550 date it should be noted that no European trade items were found. The Sonso refuse contained milling stones, ground stone axes, pottery spindle whorls, a black-on-red negative-painted style, and incised and relief-modeled types. In general, the pottery is somewhat more crudely made than that of Yotoco.

Figure 5-68. Yotoco and Sonso phase pottery from the Cauca Valley. *Top, left:* Yotoco pedestal bowl. Upper portion and pedestal have white slip with black negative decoration; central portion is red-slipped with black negative patterns. There are similar negative designs in interior. Height, 8.7 cm. *Top, right:* Yotoco bowl. Red rim and orange exterior with black negative decoration. Interior red-slipped with black negative designs. Height, 6.5 cm. *Bottom, left:* Sonso three-handled jar with black negative decoration on red slip. Height, about 20 cm. *Bottom, right:* Sonso three-handled jar, brownish slip. Height, about 22 cm. (Courtesy Warwick Bray.)

Some vessels are large, have three loop handles, and are of composite-silhouette forms. In spite of its contemporaneity with Calima, Sonso lacks the effigy jars of that culture and, apparently, the fine goldwork.

To the west of the Buga region is Calima. The Calima River drains west into the San Juan, and in its upper courses it flows through the hills of the Cordillera Occidental. Reichel-Dolmatoff is of the opinion that the Calima Valley was a main route for the movements of people between the Pacific Coast and the Colombian highlands, and

the ceramics of the Calima region appear to bear this out.[142] Calima pottery features a sub-globular jar that has a smaller hemisphere on its top and two small divergent spouts protruding from this hemisphere, the spouts connected by a high-arching bridge handle. The form is reminiscent of jars from Tolita and Tumaco on the coast. The finer Calima wares also include a number of distinctive human effigies. These are seated or crouching figures, with the container part of the vessel in the form of a basket on the back of the individual. There is something in the posture and style of these figures that suggests similar forms from the Mexican west coast, and we are reminded, again, of Reichel's hypothesis that Mesoamerican traits were brought to the Ecuadorian–south Colombian coast and from there diffused inland. Other effigies are animal and bird forms. Decoration runs to red-and-white positive painting and negative-painting. Other types, of less careful finish, are heavy globular jars with necks or collars and three loop handles. This last form, of course, is a link to the Sonso phase that Bray described from the

Buga region. As we have said, a radiocarbon date from Calima places this culture at A.D. 1250. We may be dealing with a cultural tradition, however, that has much earlier beginnings. This is suggested by the Calima links with Tolita and Tumaco.

The Calima settlement pattern seems to be that of the scattered hillside house platforms, similar to what has been observed in the Cauca Valley; however there are evidences of extensive old cultivated plots in the region, plots marked by earth ridges or grids that cover a considerable territory and indicate some intensification of agricultural production.[143] The Calima pottery is found in shaft-and-side-chamber tombs, and along with the pottery is some of the outstanding goldwork of pre-Columbian America.[144] These gold ornaments have been fashioned as breastplates, masks, crowns, and various body ornaments. Both casting and hammering techniques were employed, and an especially gaudy effect was created by hanging the principal pieces of the objects with numerous dangles. In style and design there are resemblances in the Calima goldwork to the fang-toothed monster or feline faces of San Agustín, and there are also close resemblances to the even more famous Quimbaya gold style from the Middle Cauca Valley.

This Quimbaya gold style—and a more broadly defined "Quimbaya culture"—takes its name from a historic tribe who occupied a small area between the Cauca River and its eastern tributaries, the Micos and Guacaya. These Quimbaya were exceptionally talented goldsmiths—an occupation well calculated to arouse Spanish interest. They were quickly disposed of in the early Colonial period, but their name has been extended to a style of gold artifacts and a pottery style (or tradition) that is found from Zarzal to Medellín and beyond, along the Cauca River and in the Cordillera Central to the east of that river. We shall use the term *Quimbaya* in this more general archaeological sense, with the stipulation that its reference be much broader geographically and much deeper chronologically than the sixteenth century Quimbaya tribe. With reference to time, it seems highly probable that what has been called Quimbaya in the archaeological sense spans both our Regional Developmental and Late Periods and has many regional expressions.

The gold ornaments of the Quimbaya style that dazzled the Spanish conquistadors are among the most splendid metallurgical accomplishments of native America. They were manufactured by *cire-perdue* ("lost-wax") casting, soldering, annealing, and hammering; and they include many of the same general forms that we saw in the Calima style: masks, breastplates, crowns, helmets, earrings, and nose rings. There are also small animal or human figure pendants, and—above all—flasks, or bottles. These last, made of gold or gold-copper (tumbaga) alloy, are graceful fluted forms with narrow necks. [145]

The goldwork has been found in graves and tombs, most of which have been looted, without proper record, in the past century. These graves, like those of Calima and the general southern Colombian highland pattern, are often of shaft-and-side-chamber form; but some are large under-

Figure 5-69. Quimbaya-style gold flasks. *Left:* Height, 16.7 cm. *Right:* Height, 23.4 cm. An analysis of the contents of the flask on the right revealed lime powder, a substance used with the chewing of coca. Vessels similar to these are shown suspended from the necks of human figurines. (*Left*, courtesy National Gallery of Art, Washington, D.C., and Museo del Oro, Bogotá; *right*, courtesy Dudley Easby and Museo del Oro, Bogotá.)

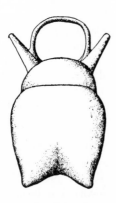

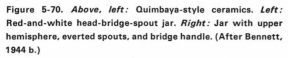

Figure 5-70. *Above, left:* Quimbaya-style ceramics. *Left:* Red-and-white head-bridge-spout jar. *Right:* Jar with upper hemisphere, everted spouts, and bridge handle. (After Bennett, 1944 b.)

Figure 5-71. *Above, right:* Quimbaya negative-painted pottery. These vessels are about 25 and 23 cm. high. (Courtesy American Museum of Natural History.)

Figure 5-72. *Right:* Bowl of the so-called Quimbaya Brown Incised ware. Diameter, 18 cm. (Courtesy American Museum of Natural History.)

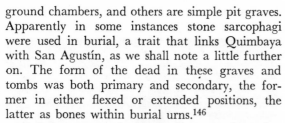

ground chambers, and others are simple pit graves. Apparently in some instances stone sarcophagi were used in burial, a trait that links Quimbaya with San Agustín, as we shall note a little further on. The form of the dead in these graves and tombs was both primary and secondary, the former in either flexed or extended positions, the latter as bones within burial urns.[146]

Quimbaya ceramics—and the term here has been used very broadly—have general resemblances to Calima, Tumaco, and Ecuadorian Tolita. The finer grave pottery occurs in the double-spouted jar form described for Calima, that is to say, the one with the little upper hemisphere on top of the globular main body (Fig. 5-70, *right*), the two little divergent spouts, and the high-arching bridge handle. There are also double jars and whistling jars. In these, one side is modeled as an animal or bird and has the whistle feature; the other side is a plain jar form. The two are then connected by a tubular body and a bridge handle. Tall pedestal bowls occur, but a more

definitive Quimbaya form is a tall jar with a high shoulder and constricted orifice (Fig. 5-71, *left*). Another widely recognized Quimbaya type is a large, hollow male or female figure with relief-appliqué features, a rather vaguely shaped body, and negative-painted decoration (Fig. 5-71, *right*). Negative-painting, in either two-color or three-color negative-positive combinations, is the most typical surface decoration. Colors vary but are most often a whitish or yellowish underslip, a blackish resist paint, and additions in positive red painting. In addition, there is a considerable amount of incision and incision-excision. A well-recognized type in the latter technique is the so-called Quimbaya Brown Incised (Fig. 5-72). This is a brownish-fired pottery in which very large exterior surface areas have been cut out to form the decoration, along with incised lines.[147] In addition to vessels, the Quimbaya ceramists made flat and cylindrical stamps, spindle whorls, and other small artifacts. Polished stone ornaments have been found in the tombs, including polished obsidian mirrors.

This Nariño-Cauca Valley section is sorely in need of a summary statement, but no very meaningful one can be prepared with what we know at present. Settlements were small and scattered; but the lack of ceremonial sites, other than the cemeteries with their rather elaborate tombs, seems curious in view of the very high craft level of most of the cultures in the subarea. This may have been the true situation, although there are some hints, such as the mound near Popayán, that this was not everywhere and always the case. Pottery on the whole is related to the negative-painting traditions of the Ecuadorian cultures. This is seen not only in this kind of decorative treatment but in the total complex of certain vessel forms and features. There are also resemblances of a general sort to both Peruvian and Mesoamerican pottery styles. Metallurgy was advanced, and the products were aesthetically spectacular.

The Magdalena Headwaters: San Agustín and Tierradentro. The San Agustín region is in the highland Magdalena headwaters to the east of the Nariño-Cauca subarea. The elevation is about 5000 feet, with climate, rainfall, soils, and drainage all favorable to cultivation. The evidences of this former cultivation can be seen in fields, irrigation ditches, and terracings; similarly, numerous archaeological sites with deep refuse reflect the substantially large populations that formerly lived here. But the most notable features of San Agustín are the mounds and stone monuments. These archaeological attractions have been known since the eighteenth century and were first explored in the early part of the twentieth.[148] The name *San Agustín,* taken from a small modern town, applies, in an archaeological sense, to a region of several hundred square kilometers. Within this region there are at least 30 sites or ceremonial centers of mounds and sculptures. The rest of the general settlement pattern is not well known, but Reichel-Dolmatoff feels that it was a dispersed one.[149]

The mounds, which were made of earth, contain interior chambers of stone that served as burial places and, apparently, also as shrines. The largest of the mounds measure 30 meters or so in diameter and 5 meters in height and may have several such stone crypts or chambers. Smaller tumuli usually have only one. These interior chambers were constructed of great unworked slabs of andesites and basalts, some placed upright on their edges and others laid across beamwise to form roofs. The interiors of some of the chambers had been painted in red, black, white, and yellow geometric patterns. Many of the chambers were entered by stone-lined passageways or tunnels.

The San Agustín stone sculptures are the largest and most spectacular of the Intermediate area. Some are found within the mound chambers, giving rise to the interpretation that these are shrines; others are found near the mounds or at some distance apart from them. The sculptures show a considerable variation in technique of carving, ranging from the full round to bas-relief. The tallest is more than 4 meters in height, although most of them are somewhat smaller. They stand free and are, in effect, carved stelae. A human-animal being, or a man with feline fangs, is a frequent conception. There are also animals and birds of prey. Two other themes in the art are the alter-ego motif, that of an animal being on the back of a man, and that of a man or god holding a child in front of its body. Besides the stelae, San Agustín carving is represented by monolithic sarcophagi, altars or thrones, and bedrock outcrop carvings of channels and pools that may have been sacred baths.

The dating of San Agustín sculptures is only beginning to be attacked on a systematic basis; however it is obvious that there is a long cultural sequence in the region, one that probably antedates and postdates the period of the carvings. Luis Duque Gomez, Reichel-Dolmatoff, and T. C. Patterson have all advanced tentative ceramic chronologies. These are somewhat complex, and it is not possible to make a fully satisfactory correlation of them on the data that have been presented so far. Apparently, however, the earliest ceramic horizon in the region was one characterized by rather simple vessel forms, incised and punctate designs, and a white, pastelike pigment in the incised lines (Fig. 5-75). This horizon quite possibly dates back as early as 500 B.C. The second horizon for the region is probably the one of the mounds, mound chambers, and most of the stone sculptures. The pottery of this horizon is more

a   b   c

d   e   f

Figure 5-73. San Agustín monumental stone sculptures. *a:* A demonic or god figure. This figure combines both human and jaguar attributes and was found in a stone-walled and roofed crypt in a mound. *b, c:* Similar figures, which were found near mounds. *d, e:* Warriors with animal "alter-ego" or tutelary-deity headdresses. *f:* Owllike hawk; this sculpture holds a serpent in its beak and claws. (Courtesy Gerardo Reichel-Dolmatoff.)

Figure 5-74. Monolithic sarcophagus at San Agustín. At the sides are the fallen slabs of a tomb. (Courtesy Gerardo Reichel-Dolmatoff.)

Figure 5-75. The presumably early incised and modeled pottery of the San Agustín and Tierradentro regions. Sherds *d, e, f* have white paste in the incised lines and dots. (After Bennett, 1944 b.)

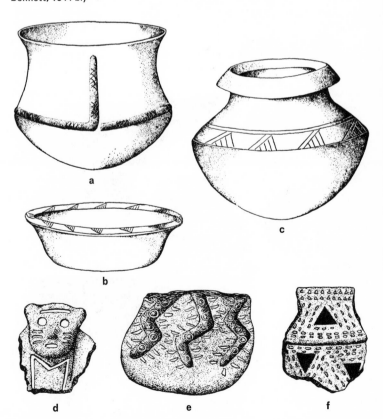

complex in form, including double-spout-and-bridge jars and pedestal-based plates, and also features negative painting. Gold ornaments were also known at this time. In general, the horizon seems comparable to the Calima and Quimbaya complexes; however, this gives us little aid in dating. These complexes, as we have said, seem to span relatively long periods of time. The third horizon sees a new pottery tradition in the Magdalena Headwaters, one that probably derives from the Late Period cultures of the Lower Magdalena. By this time the apogee of the great stone carving was passed. The reader is referred to an extended footnote for more details on the San Agustín sequences.[150]

The other archaeological region of the Magdalena Headwaters subarea is Tierradentro,[151] to the north and west of the San Agustín region. It has long been known for its large underground burial chambers. Carved out of the soft rock of the region, they probably should be considered as an elaboration or specialization of the more general north Andean shaft-and-chamber grave type. They show no surface markings whatsoever. Entrances are stepped or spiraled shafts. The chambers are large and circular or oval in floor plan; roofs are domelike; and around the walls are pilasters separating niches that have benches or banquettes within them. Walls and columns are painted in reds, blacks, whites, and yellows—bold geometric designs of triangles, diamond shapes, and the like, plus stylized human faces. Apparently, the Tierradentrans cremated their dead, put the remains in urns, and buried the urns in the floors of such chambers. The form of the chambers suggests that they were also used for gatherings or ceremonies, possibly at the times of burials.

The pottery found in the Tierradentro chambers is a thick ware ornamented with raised ridges and with incised and punctate designs that have white paste pigment fill. According to Patterson,[152] this pottery can be seriated to the earliest phase in the Tierradentro region, and it is also very similar to the early incised pottery at San Agustín. This suggests that the Tierradentro burial chambers are earlier than the San Agustín mounds and mound chambers. Previously, it was customary to place Tierradentro as later than San Agustín.[153] In Patterson's Tierradentro seriation the later ceramic phases resemble our second San Agustín pottery horizon and are associated with the more usual shaft-and-side-chamber grave type rather than the large underground chambers. There is also a stone sculptural style in the Tierradentro region—with smaller, more naturalistic human figures than those of San Agustín—that remains unplaced chronologically.

Figure 5-76. Tierra Alta potsherds. Diameter of *a*, 4.5 cm. All others to this scale except *d*, which is 13 cm. (Courtesy Gerardo Reichel-Dolmatoff.)

a

b

c

d

e

f

g

The Northern Colombian Lowlands: Sinú and Lower Magdalena. The northern part of Colombia was culturally quite distinct from the Nariño-Cauca Valley and Magdalena Headwaters subareas during the Regional Developmental Period. The underlying Formative culture here was that of Momil, which in its earlier phase was oriented toward manioc cultivation but in its later phase assimilated maize farming. This later Momil phase continued on into the Regional Developmental Period, and sites pertaining to it have a wide distribution in the tropical lowland river bottoms of both the Sinú and Lower Magdalena subareas. The Ciénega de Oro phase, which succeeds Momil II in the Sinú subarea, has a similar site ecology to that of Momil. Continuities are also seen in ceramics, with an emphasis on incision and on other such plastic decorative techniques.[154] The neighboring Mompós phase of the Lower Magdalena subarea differs from Ciénega de Oro in that its ceramics emphasize painting rather than incision and modeling.[155] In this, Mompós is more like the cultures of the Ranchería-César subarea to the northeast, where painting was established early in the La Loma phase. What appears to have happened is that the Momil Formative Period ceramic heritage tended to diverge in the Regional Developmental Period, with the cultures of northwestern Colombia following in incision-modeling modes, while those of the northeast retained painting.

After Ciénega de Oro and Mompós there was a definite movement of some populations out of the lowlands into the higher country of the Middle and Upper Sinú drainage. This is represented by the Tierra Alta phase of those regions.[156] This would be the beginning of the Late Period, and there must also have been a parallel southward movement of populations on the Magdalena. This did not mean, however, that northern river lowlands were abandoned. Some groups remained, and these are represented by the numerous village settlements in the Zambrano region.[157]

There are stylistic differences between the Sinú and Lower Magdalena cultures of the Late Period, and there are also stylistic differences from phase to phase within the culture sequences of each subarea; however certain broad trends characterize the whole of these northern lowlands. Ceramic decoration is very nearly all by incision or plastic techniques; annular bases and pedestal bowls have now become common; and there are some animal and human effigy vessels. There is, of course, a great deal of culinary pottery of bowl and olla forms. Gold ornaments were possessed. Settlements were generally small, although refuse accumulations were of a depth to indicate a high degree of permanency of settlement. These settlements varied according to terrain. Those of the Zambrano type were more concentrated, and some houses apparently were constructed on artificial mound platforms along the rivers. In Tierra Alta and in some of the foothills of the Lower Magdalena, country houses were dotted along hillsides and were located near small agricultural terrace plots.

In the latter part of the Late Period the most impressive culture of the northern lowlands was the Betancí (or Betancí-Viloria).[158] This is the culture phase that can be identified with the sixteenth-century Sinú tribe, and sites representing it are found in both the Sinú and San Jorge drainages. In the lowlands along the San Jorge, agricultural ridges and earthworks, similar to those described for the Guayas Basin of Ecuador, have been reported over an extensive area. These are parallel and checkerboard ridge arrangements, with the individual ridges a meter or a little less in height, 6 to 7 meters in width, and, in some instances, more than a kilometer in length.[159] They have not been culturally identified, although they may pertain to the Sinú culture or the Betancí phase. Again, as with the Guayas ridges, it is uncertain exactly what kind of crops were grown in these plots; but perhaps they included manioc.

The Spaniards referred to the Sinú (or Cenú) as accomplished goldsmiths and described some of their towns. These were marked by mounds, some of them definitely burial places; others, judging from their size and shape, may have served as temple platforms. At the Marcayo site in the Middle Sinú the largest mound is 60 by 40 meters at the base and 8 meters high. It was surrounded by an earthen wall enclosure. The burials found in the Betancí mounds are primary and extended and furnished with pottery and gold and shell ornaments. Betancí ceramics (Fig. 5-78) extend the tradition of incision and modeling, and some of the tall jars ornamented with high-relief human figure modeling are of outstanding artistic quality;

but black-on-red painting is also a Betancí pottery mode, suggesting influence from the east. Betancí goldwork (Fig. 5-79), like that of Quimbaya to which it is related, was done by *cire perdue* casting, and it includes crowns, pendant-figurines, and various other body ornaments.

On the Lower Magdalena, the Plato and Saloa phases [160] are related to Betancí, as is the Crespo phase[161] of the Caribbean coast. These cultures, however, all have urn burial as a feature. As it would be expected from the ecological zone in which Crespo sites are found, this phase had a combined fishing and farming basis, and Reichel-Dolmatoff suggests that it represents a line of development directly from the old Malambo–Momil I fishing and manioc economy.[162]

The Pacific Coast. Pacific coastal Colombia can be considered in a framework of three subareas. In the south is Tumaco. This was the most favorable subarea of this coast for native agriculture, and it is here that we have the Mataje and Imbilí cultures, which we referred to in connection with the Tolita and Atacames developments of the Ecuadorian Esmeraldas subarea. North of Tumaco is the San Juan subarea, centering on the delta of that river and the city of Buenaventura, and north of this is the very dense tropical forest coast of the Chocó.

Reichel-Dolmatoff refers to two Late Period complexes in the San Juan subarea, the Murillo and the Minguimalo.[163] The Murillo, which is the earlier of the two, is estimated to date at around A.D. 800 to 900. The remains suggest a minimal tropical forest agricultural adjustment. There are no stone implements suitable for maize grinding, and the economy may have been based on manioc. Ground T-shaped-type axes are the principal stone artifact, and these were probably used in coping with the forests in land clearing. The ceramics are undistinctive—globular cooking pots, for the most part, with very simple incised-line designs. The wider relationships of Murillo are unknown. Minguimalo has metates—and, by inference, had maize. Sites are numerous. The land-clearing implements are trapezoidal ground stone celts rather than the T-shaped axes. The pottery is simple in form and design but different from that of Murillo. The most characteristic surface treatment was the creation of bosses by

Figure 5-77. Agricultural ridged fields, San Jorge River Basin, Lower Magdalena subarea, northern Colombia. *Above:* High-altitude photograph showing thousands of ridges lying at right angles to drainage channels. *Left:* Photograph taken at lower elevation of a sector of these ridges. (Courtesy James J. Parsons.)

Figure 5-78. Betancí vessels. *a, b:* Two views of the same incised jar (the neck is broken). *c:* Pedestal base (the plate or bowl section has been broken) with human figures modeled in high relief. *d:* Painted olla (black-on-red). *e:* Tall pedestal plate. These vessels are not all to the same scale. (Courtesy Gerardo Reichel-Dolmatoff.)

Figure 5-79. A Sinú or Betancí nose pendant of gold. Length, 23 cm. (Courtesy Museum of the American Indian, Heye Foundation.)

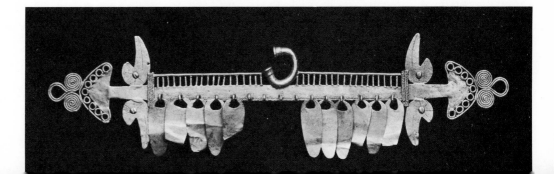

punching outwards from the inside of the unfired vessel with a stick.

What little is known of the Chocó region comes largely from the recent work of the Reichel-Dolmatoffs.[164] This was done in the Cupica region, where a large burial mound was excavated. Several phases were defined, all of which had secondary burials. Pottery vessels and other goods accompanied the human remains. The earliest phase, Cupica I, had sub-globular cooking vessels. These were incised and dentate-stamped and resemble the wares of the Momil and Ciénega cultures of the Sinú subarea. Cupica II has been linked to Tierra Alta; and Cupica III shares traits with Betancí. This latter phase has a much more elaborate ceramic complex than the others. Vessels include pedestal plates, fancy modeled decoration, and polychrome painting. This last is similar to that of the Panamanian Coclé style and points to ties in this direction. There is also a component of the bossed ware of Minguimalo in Cupica III, linking it to the San Juan subarea. A radiocarbon date of A.D. 1227 for the phase is consistent with these various relationships.

Northeastern Colombia: Ranchería-César. What I have designated here as the Northeast Colombian subarea takes in the valley of the Rio Ranchería, a stream that empties into the Caribbean near the base of the Guajira Peninsula, and the upper drainage of the Rio César, which flows southwestward along the Colombian-Venezuelan border, eventually to reach the Magdalena River. The Rio Ranchería region is now dessicated, but there is reason to believe that it was formerly much less so. The sequence begins with the La Loma and El Horno phases. These date largely to the Regional Developmental Period (Fig. 5-6). Sites of these phases are deep midden accumulations along the banks of the river. La Loma and El Horno mark what Reichel has called the "First Painted Pottery Horizon" for Northeast Colombia. The painting scheme is a red-and-black-on-white (or cream). Designs are pleasingly bold and curvilinear, with scrolls, wavy bands, and running notched or comblike patterns. An associated style is a black ware, highly polished and decorated with incised lines filled with white pigment. Vessel forms of the La Loma and El Horno are dishes, pedestal cups, and multiple-

support bowls. A large, hollow human figurine is especially characteristic of El Horno. The Los Cocos and Portacelli phases follow, in that order, and see a reduction in the decorative color scheme, with painting now in black-on-white, red-on-white, or black-on-red. The latter is most typical of Portacelli, a style that features rows of little stylized bird figures painted in solid black on a red ground. Los Cocos and Portacelli are sometimes referred to as the "Second Painted Pottery Horizon."

The Portacelli culture seems to have suffered a decline before the Spanish Conquest, perhaps to be correlated with an increasing aridity of the Ranchería region. The key factor in this dessication may have been the rise of the Tairona culture in the Sierra Nevada de Santa Marta subarea, where the headwaters of the Rio Ranchería lie. Land clearing and deforestation in that upland block could have initiated an erosion cycle that had disastrous effects on the lower valley.

The Rio Ranchería sequence is duplicated in the upper drainage of the Rio César, although in this valley, as one moves west, the earlier cultures of La Paz and Hatico belong more in the Lower Magdalena subarea orbit.[165] By Portacelli times, however, the painted wares of the Ranchería region predominate here as well.

Northwestern Venezuela. We have referred to Northwestern Venezuela in our surveys of both the Early Ceramic and the Formative periods of the Intermediate area, and on both occasions we had reference to an early pottery complex of the Maracaibo Basin known as Rancho Peludo. Rancho Peludo is believed to date somewhere in the wide range of 3000 to 500 B.C., and it was succeeded by another phase known as the Guasare. Both are grouped by Rouse and Cruxent within their Dabajuroid pottery series or subtradition.[166] Guasare presumably dates to the Regional Developmental Period (500 B.C.–A.D. 500) and perhaps a bit later; unfortunately there are no radiocarbon dates on the phase, so this placement must remain provisional.

Guasare continues the Rancho Peludo traits of fabric impression, appliqué decoration, and annular-based vessels, adding to them somewhat more elaborate appliqué-incised decoration and some red-painting. Guasare, in its turn, is replaced by the Dabajuro phase, the best-known member of the Dabajuroid pottery subtradition. The Dabajuro phase is represented in sites in the Maracaibo Basin and Coro subareas,[167] and the phase dates from the latter part of the Late Period, or from A.D. 1000 until the Spanish Colonial Period.[168] In addition to the earlier traits of Rancho Peludo and Guasare, Dabajuro has acquired such things as black, white, and red polychrome painting, zoomorphic rim lugs, and large, hollow tripod legs. These new features can be derived from another pottery series or subtradition, the Tocuyanoid series.

This Tocuyanoid series[169] is distinguished by its black-and-red-on-white decoration and its scroll pattern and other curvilinear designs, which link it very closely with the La Loma–El Horno horizon ("First Painted Pottery Horizon") of Northeast Colombia. Earlier in this chapter (p. 282) we have referred to two Venezuelan pottery styles, both of which featured polychrome painting and show some relationships to La Loma and Tocuyano. These were the La Pitia, of the Maracaibo Basin, and the Santa Ana, of the Trujillo region of the Cordillera de Mérida subarea. Neither has been dated, but it is possible that either or both are prototypes to La Loma–Tocuyano.[170]

Tocuyano phase proper is named for a site in the Barquisimeto region of the Cordillera de Mérida, and there is a radiocarbon date on the phase of 295 B.C. The site is a village refuse zone, buried under some 2 meters of sterile soil. The pottery bears the characteristic curvilinear black-and-red-on-white designs, and a typical vessel form is a bowl with bulbous hollow tripod legs which extend up the sides of the vessel almost to the rim. The Tocuyanoid series or subtradition continues in the Barquisimeto region into the Sarare phase, which is estimated to last until about A.D. 1000. There are also related Tocuyanoid phases in other Cordillera de Mérida regions, in the Barinas subarea (Agua Blanca), and in eastern Venezuela.

After A.D. 1000 the Tocuyanoid subtradition gave way to another that in large part developed from it. This was the Tierroid subtradition, named after the Tierra de los Indios site, also in the Barquisimeto region.[171] Tierra de los Indios pottery is stratigraphically later than Tocuyano at the Tocuyano site, and the dating of the Tierroid series is further aided by a radiocarbon

date of A.D. 1350 from a site in the Trujillo region. Tierra de los Indios pottery is red-black-white painted, but the trend toward reduction in the number of colors that we saw in the Late Period phases of northeastern Colombia is also observed here. This relationship to Colombia is further exemplified in the Tierroid use of little bird figure designs like those of Portacelli. Tierra de los Indios tripods have shorter legs than those of Tocuyano, and they frequently have a diagnostic rodlike handle. The Tierroid styles are widespread in the Cordillera Mérida and the Barinas subarea. In the latter they are represented by the Caño del Oso and La Betania phases. The La Betania phase is known for its little platform mounds and some ceramics that bear an amazing resemblance to El Hatillo or Herrera style types from the late periods of Central-Pacific Panama (see p. 332).[172]

Figure 5-80. Tierroid series or subtradition pottery. From the Trujillo region, Cordillera de Mérida subarea, Northwest Venezuela. This style is called Carache or Mirinday. Decoration is in red-on-white. Diameter of *c*, about 16 cm. (After Kidder II, 1944.)

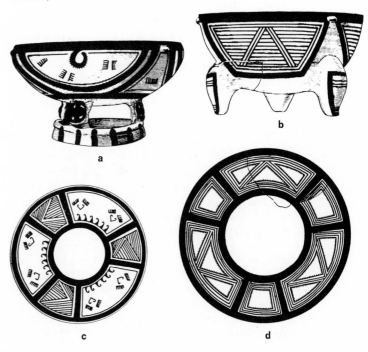

Figure 5-81. Figurine in Tierra de los Indios style from Northwestern Venezuela. Height, 21.5 cm. (Courtesy Museum of the American Indian, Heye Foundation.)

Northeastern Colombia: Tairona. Returning to northeastern Colombia, another sub-area claims our attention on the Late Period level. This is the Tairona or Sierra Nevada de Santa Marta. It is an upland country, a detached mountain block that lies just back of the coast and below the base of the Guajira Peninsula.

Although the origins of the Tairona culture are not definitely known, it seems most likely that they are to be found in the Lower Magdalena in the phases of the Zambrano development. The Lower Magdalena burial urns bear some resemblance to those of Tairona, and what may be a transitional step between the lowland Magdalena

cultures and Tairona proper is a complex known as La Mesa,[173] represented by sites on the southern flanks of Sierra Nevada.

The Tairona were village dwellers, and each village seems to have had some degree of local control of political and religious affairs. A frequent central feature of the villages was a special temple or palace building placed on a mound or terrace. But the villages were united, however, under powerful chiefs who lived in important towns; and Reichel-Dolmatoff has referred to the Tairona nation as a "village federation," a level of sociopolitical development more advanced than that of the Sub-Andean societies and cultures that characterized most of the rest of Colombia during the Regional Developmental and Late Periods.[174]

The archaeological ruin of Pueblito was one of the "important towns" of the Tairona.[175] Pueblito has some 3000 house foundations, and it has the remains of other, more elaborate buildings that probably functioned as temples or palaces. The streets of the town were paved with stone slabs (Fig. 5-82, *top*); streams within the town were spanned with stone-slab bridges. Remains of water reservoirs, irrigation canals, and extensive terrace cultivation systems are to be seen on all sides. The individual house rings are seen archaeologically only as foundations. In these, stone slabs were placed on the ground in a circular arrangement and flanked and held in place by other slabs placed on edge. Characteristically, they had two doorways, on opposite sides of the ring or circle, and these were marked with sill stones. Frequently, these house foundations were placed on low earth platforms or on hillside terraces, and some of the houses were as much as 20 meters in diameter. Within was a fireplace. Walls and roofs were presumably of wood and thatch. Temple or other special buildings were larger than the houses, although they too had been made of wood set upon stone foundations. Such structures were usually on high platforms and had stone stairway approaches.

Culinary pottery, celts, stone metates, pestles, and handstones—and other implements—are found on the house floors. The dead were sometimes placed beneath the floors in stone-lined tombs, although urn burial outside of the dwellings was perhaps the more common mode of disposal. Special pottery caches were placed beneath the

Figure 5-82. Tairona archaeology. *Top:* Section of pavement. *Bottom:* Typical burial urn. (After Mason, 1931–39; courtesy Field Museum of Natural History, Chicago.)

"treasure jars," or lidded vessels, which are in the subfloor caches and which often contain pebbles or beads.

The most common Tairona ceramics are red-ware cooking vessels and polished black household and special pieces. Many of the latter are modeled in life forms—animals, humans, gods or demons—and there is also a great variety of other shapes, including pedestal-based jars, basket-handled trays, the lidded cylinder, or "treasure," jars, stirrup-mouthed jars, and vessels with bulbous, hollow tetrapodal supports (these last often combined with zoomorphic modeling). Such pottery was placed in quantity with the dead, along with the relief-modeled burial urn in which the secondary remains were placed. Polished stone pendants of a wing-shaped form and cast gold pendants were other items of grave equipment.

Tairona culture has a great many elements that suggest Mesoamerican affiliations. Among these would be the great emphasis on ritual caches, pottery representations of beings with protruding tongues in the manner of Tlaloc, and figurines and ocarinas in which a head of a man protrudes from the jaws of a jaguar or serpentlike monster. The suggestion of affiliation with Mesoamerica becomes stronger when we see that the modern Cogui have such concepts as the number nine as a sacred number, deities in quadruplicate, and

Figure 5-83. Tairona treasure jars. (After Bennett, 1944 b.)

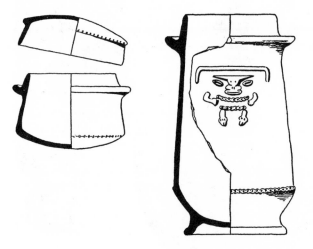

house floors; and, in this connection, Reichel-Dolmatoff notes the interesting custom among the Kogi (Cogui), the modern descendants of the Tairona, of placing pottery vessels beneath floors at the time of house construction. Pebbles were put in these vessels, one for each of the members of the family who occupied such a house, and upon the birth of a child the vessel was exhumed and another pebble added. Such would coincide with the archaeological findings of the Tairona

colors associated with the four world quarters. Some of these could possibly come from an ancient common Nuclear American heritage, of a Formative Period level or earlier; however, some of them suggest the Mesoamerican Postclassic Period, an era contemporaneous with the Tairona culture. Reichel-Dolmatoff suggests that such ideas were brought quite directly from Mesoamerica to northern Colombia at this time by voyagers coming across the Caribbean.

Chibcha. The Chibcha domain, in what is now the departments of Cundinamarca and Boyacá, was first seen by the Spanish in 1537.[176] The early conquistadors were impressed by the large populations and the numerous palisaded towns and villages in these old lake basins of the Cordillera Oriental, and they described the civil and military government of the Chibcha in glowing terms. They also referred to palaces and temples, gold and emeralds, a prosperous agriculture, and a thriving trade within the territory. The Chibcha government actually appears to have been a dual one. One major chiefdom, ruled over by a leader known as the Zipa, had its seat at old Bogotá; the other, under a chief called Zaque, was centered in a town in the Tunja region of the northern part of the Chibcha or Muisca lands. The stability of their nascent states is somewhat questionable. Wars were going on within them at the time of the Spaniards' first visit. The Chibcha religion was centered on sun worship, with temples, idols, and a trained body of priests. They also worshipped a culture hero deity, a being called Bochica who was visualized as a bearded man. This concept, so much like that of the Mexican culture hero Quetzalcoatl, was accompanied by rituals of human sacrifice in which there are further Mesoamerican parallels. Chibcha farming was concerned with potatoes,

324

Figure 5-86. Gold or tumbaga figures of the Tairona style. These apparently represent a crocodile god and were probably worn as pendants. That on the *right* is known to be tumbaga (copper-gold alloy) but with the surface copper removed to leave only the gold. *Left:* Height, about 12 cm. *Right:* Height, about 15 cm. (*Left,* courtesy Allan Caplan; *right,* courtesy Dumbarton Oaks Pre-Columbian Collection.)

quinoa, maize, and other crops; and Chibcha trade involved the exchange of salt, emeralds, and cotton cloth for gold and other luxury items. Such were the Chibcha as represented by the sixteenth century Spanish.

Chibcha archaeology is still not very well known, but its finds, to date, have been somewhat disappointing. Some archaeologists, like Haury and Cubillos, have felt that the Spanish accounts of the prowess of these people were exaggerations;[177] others, like Broadbent, have countered with the argument that most of the developments that the Spanish emphasized in their chronicles, such as complex political organization, do not necessarily leave archaeological traces.[178] One of the puzzling things, however, was what appeared to be an almost complete lack of settlements on the valley floors. In fact, it had been surmised that the valley floors of the Bogotá and Tunja basins had been too marshy for ancient cultivators and that most of the farming and settlement must have been on the surrounding hillsides. But the recent discovery of a huge site called La Ramada, on the Sabana de Bogotá, near Funza, forces revision

of this thesis. Sylvia Broadbent, who excavated at this site, estimates midden refuse to cover a zone of 2 square kilometers. The debris is as much as 1.5 meters deep in some places. It consists of organic soil, potsherds of Chibcha type, manos and milling stones, flint chopping and scraping tools, polished stone axes, and pottery spindle whorls— in brief, the detritus of household occupation. A number of small test excavations were conducted, with no large exposures, but even in the small tests the basal clay beneath the refuse was seen to be marked with post molds indicative of former structures. Broadbent considers this site to be the remains of the Chibchan Bogotá, the former capital of Zipa.[179] Thus it is now certain that the valley floors were occupied and that the main towns were probably so located.

It is also likely that the valley floors were farmed as well as occupied. The Bogotá sabana is 60 by 40 kilometers in extent. As the La Ramada site is located at its heart, the distances from the town to the surrounding hills would have been too great to be traveled on foot for ordinary farming chores; the flatlands closer to home must have been cultivated, and this appears to be verified by the presence of ridged fields—similar to those seen in the San Jorge Valley—on the Bogotá sabana. But the hillsides bordering the Bogotá sabana were also tilled by the Chibcha. The Spaniards say that the Indians practiced terrace agriculture on them, and pre-Columbian stone-faced terraces have been identified near the Chibchan sites of Facatativá and Tocancipá.[180]

The Chibcha architecture that is known from archaeology seems to be that of temples or public buildings. The Spaniards had described such temples as consisting of circular or rectangular wooden post buildings with cane and mud walls and thatched roofs. The post molds of the outer ring of posts and a large central supporting post were discovered at Sogamoso, the site of a "Temple of the Sun" which had been burned by the Spanish.[181] Occasionally, rough stone columns were used in these buildings, presumably combined with wood and cane building materials. Ten such stone columns were found in a circle at Goranchacha.[182]

Chibcha burials have been found in or near villages or houses, usually in simple pit graves. The individuals in these graves had been placed in either extended (in the southern part of the sub-area) or flexed (in the northern part) positions. The dead have also been found in caves where the bodies had been especially prepared for mummification and wrapped in textiles. It is largely from these cave burials that the major collections of Chibcha pottery and other complete artifacts have been recovered. It is also probable that certain Chibcha burials were made in hillside chambers or artificial caves. These chambers were constructed either by hollowing out the earth from beneath a large *in situ* rock or by capping an excavation with stone slabs.[183]

So far, no real archaeological sequence has been developed for the Chibcha subarea. Pre-Columbian "classic" Chibcha ceramics and other artifacts have been identified, as have those of an early Spanish Colonial phase; but there are no well-defined earlier archaeological phases,[184] and Chibchan prototypes are unknown. To be sure, there are a number of general similarities with the Colombian Sub-Andean cultures as a whole, but nothing that would single any of them out as a definite ancestor. In attempting to explain this, it has been suggested that the high Tunja and Bogotá basins were not occupied by farming peoples until the Late Period; but, given the suitability of these regions for farming, this seems unlikely.

Chibcha pottery runs to slipped monochromes: oranges, dark reds, and browns. A small portion of it shows painted decoration, usually red-on-orange or red-on-cream. The painted designs are fine parallel lines, fields of small dots, and spirals. Some types are decorated either with incisions or with incisions combined with painting. Most vessels are utility ollas and pots, but there are also pedestal bowls, double-jars, and large anthropomorphic forms (Fig. 5-87). These last kinds are the most distinctive Chibcha vessel. The facial and body modeling is stiff and stylized, and the individual represented would appear to be a warrior or dignitary wearing a large, crossed, beltlike necklace of what look like long tubular beads.

Such beads as those represented on the anthropomorphic jars are known from burial and other collections. They may be made of bone, stone, or shell. Little figurines, rather crudely done of stone, wood, and pottery, are also in these collections; and Chibcha human figure sculpture is also represented in a few larger stone statues. In general, the conceptions and rendition of Chibcha carving are stiff, augular, and aesthetically far below the style and skill of San Agustín monumental work. We have mentioned manos, milling stones, axes, and spindle whorls from the La Ramada site. Other Chibcha artifacts are stone spear-thrower hooks, stone net weights (for fishing in the lakes), and gold, copper, and tumbaga ornaments. Most of these metal objects are cast figurine pendants (Fig. 5-88). The style is less handsome than that of Quimbaya or Calima and is easily recognizable from its applications of soldered wire embellishments to the flat, unpolished backgrounds of the figures. Its relationships are also much more restricted than those of Quimbaya or Calima. These styles show links to Panamanian–Costa Rican goldwork; Chibchan does not.

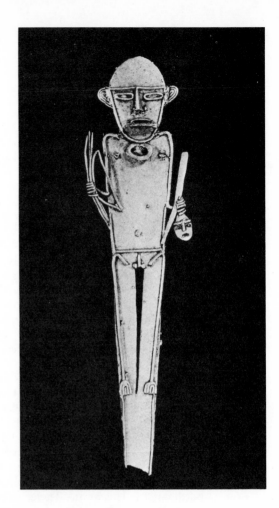

Figure 5-87. *Above, left:* A Chibcha effigy vessel with the typical "bandelero"-type necklace or ornamentation. Height, about 19 cm. (Courtesy Cambridge Museum of Archaeology and Ethnology, England.)

Figure 5-88. *Above right:* A Muisca- or Chiocha-style gold pendant representing a man with bow and arrow and trophy head. Height, 12.4 cm. (Courtesy Dudley Easby and Museo del Oro, Bogotá.)

Lower Central America: Regional Developmental and Late Periods

Setting, Cultural Pattern, and Ethnography. South Panama or Darien is a tropical rainforest, much like that of the Colombian Chocó; and as one moves north from here through Central America the Atlantic slopes and coast tend to retain this tropical forest setting and climate all the way to Northeastern Honduras and beyond. In the highlands and on the Pacific slopes, however, there is a pronounced winter dry season, and temperatures and vegetation are somewhat moderated from tropical rainforest norms. These conditions prevail from central and western Panama northward through Costa Rica and Nicaragua and into Mesoamerica proper.

The general cultural pattern throughout Lower Central America was comparable to that described by Reichel-Dolmatoff for Colombia under the rubrics of "Sub-Andean cultures" and "Lowland Chiefdoms";[185] it is known from sixteenth century ethnography and from archaeology. With reference to the latter, however, it should be kept in mind that most of our knowledge comes from the Pacific slopes and coast and that the cultures of the typical rainforest zones are not well represented in our sampling.[185a]

In the sixteenth century the Cuna and Cueva Indians lived in southern Panama or what we shall call the Darien subarea. The Spaniards described numerous native settlements along both coasts, and one of the things that caught the eye of the

327

explorers was the great skill of these people in wood carving, as expressed in house ornamentation and artifacts.[186] Unfortunately, none of this remains to us from archaeology. The Cuna and Cueva were of the Chibchan language group as are their presumed descendants, the San Blas, who live in parts of the Darien subarea today.[187]

West and north of Darien the Spaniards met with a number of autocratic chiefs—Natá, Escoria, Parita, Paris—each supreme in his small domain and each enormously wealthy in gold ornaments. Some of these rulers and their warriors put up a valiant resistance against the Europeans;[188] but within a few decades they were either decimated or driven back into the mountains. The Chibchan-speaking Guaymí may be the descendants of some of them.[189]

Tribes of Chibchan speech—including the Dorasque, Boruca, Talamanca, Guetar, Suerre, Voto, Corobici, and Rama—held Pacific and interior Costa Rica,[190] while the lowlands of Atlantic Nicaragua were occupied by the Sumo, Matagalpa, Ulva, and Mosquito tribes who represent the northernmost extension of that language family.[191] The Paya, Jicaque, and Lenca were in northeastern Honduras. These tribes are sometimes thought of as belonging to independent language groups (see pp. 12–14); however, it has been argued that they affiliate linguistically either with Chibchan or with the Otomanguean stocks.[192]

On the Nicoya Peninsula of Costa Rica and extending north along the Pacific coast of Nicaragua we pass over into a zone of interpenetration and contact between Lower Central American and Mesoamerican cultures. In the early sixteenth century the principal groups in Pacific Nicaragua-Nicoya were the Subtiaba (of possible but very remote Hokan affiliation), the Mangue, Orotiña, and others (who are grouped as Chorotega and into the larger classification of Otomanguean speech), and the Nicarao, Bagaces, and Nahuatlato (of Nahuatl Uto-Aztecan speech). It seems likely that the latter were latecomers to these regions, probably moving south in the Postclassic Period (of the Mesoamerican chronology) or the Late Period (of the Intermediate area chronology). The Nicarao, for example, are reported to have had a number of distinctively Mesoamerican traits, including writing and calendars (see Vol. I, p. 169).[193]

Darien. Darien archaeology is still known largely from the surveys of Sigvald Linné, who explored both coasts by boat in the 1920's.[194] In general, the pottery of Darien has likenesses to that of the Chocó (Late Cupica phase) and Sinú (Betancí phase) subareas of northern Colombia in its emphasis on incision and modeled decoration; however, some ties are also seen with Central Panamanian styles such as the Coclé. For example, at Utive, on the Rio Chepo, Stirling reports pottery on which the design motifs are like the stylized life forms of the Coclé polychrome wares except that they are executed in incisions.[195] On the Pearl Islands, Linné has evidence that Coclé-inspired wares are later than some rather simple incised and punctated types.[196] It is possible that these latter are quite early, as Linné has suggested; however, there is no proof of this.

Central Pacific Panama. Central Pacific Panama extends along the Pacific coast and drainage from the Panama Canal west to the beginning of the Gulf of Chiriquí. The countryside is semi-open, with grassy hills and savannas dotted with patches of jungle. There are a number of fertile river valleys. The coastline shows some semi-arid stretches, some mangrove. The subarea subsumes the Veraguas region on the western side of the Azuero Peninsula, the Parita Bay and Coclé regions on the eastern side of that peninsula, and the territory between Coclé and the Canal Zone.

The Central Pacific Panama sequence begins in the Parita Bay region with preceramic Cerro Mangote, runs through the Early Ceramic Period Monagrillo phase, and continues in the Formative Period Sarigua phase.[197] Another Formative period phase was the Pueblo Nuevo of the Veraguas region.[198] The marker type of Pueblo Nuevo is the "Scarified Ware"—usually florero-shaped vases with long, vertically arranged parallel scorings on the sides. These vessels are found in shaft graves, along with intricately carved three-legged metates. The Pueblo Nuevo radiocarbon date is 340 B.C.,[199] indicating an overlap here from Formative into Regional Developmental times. Scarified Ware is also known from the Chiriquí country, to the west of Pueblo Nuevo,[200] and at sites in the Coclé Province, to the east.[201] One of the latter is the Girón site, a shell midden on the banks of the lower Santa Maria River,[202] which site brings us to the next major phase in the Central Panama sequence, one designated as the Santa María.

Girón is at the foot of some small hills overlooking the rich alluvial valley of the river. The characteristic pottery type is a black-and-red on a natural buff ground color, with designs that combine curvilinear and rectilinear geometric elements in bold compositions. One of the most usual of these designs is an hourglass-shaped panel of cross-hachure placed on the upper half of large, necked ollas. Open plates have red-slipped interiors with black-line markings on the lips. S. K. Lothrop found such pottery at Sitio Conte,[203] and John Ladd's later analysis on the stratigraphic trench material from that site disclosed the lower portion of the refuse to pertain to this Santa María phase.[204] At both Girón and Sitio Conte a number of sherds associated with the Santa María phase levels suggest the Scarified Wares.[205] The most reasonable interpretation, I think, is that Santa María phase chronologically followed the Scarified Ware horizon and that there was some continuity between them.

The Santa María phase and its influence seem almost as widespread as the Scarified Ware horizon. The Black-line Geometric type (Escotá Polychrome), which is one of its best markers, is found in Veraguas region graves,[206] and the complex is present at two sites in the vicinity of Parita.[207] In these Parita sites, as at Girón and Sitio Conte, the Santa María pottery is succeeded by the later polychrome styles that we associate under the generic term of "Coclé," with some of the Black-line and Red-line or Red-daub types providing a continuity between Santa María and the later complexes. This is very clearly seen at the Venado Beach site in the Panama Canal Zone region, where Lothrop found a mixture of Black-line and Red-line Santa María types associated with pottery bearing the "scroll patterns and a few zoomorphic motifs as seen on the oldest Coclé Polychrome from Sitio Conte."[208]

Although the Coclé pottery styles appear to have some derivations in Santa María, they also bring forth a number of new elements, especially the highly stylized life forms that are so flambuoyantly executed in polychrome painting. The Coclé horizon is also associated with a rich metallurgical tradition, one most likely derived

Figure 5-89. Black-line Geometric ware of the Santa María phase. *Left:* Bowl rim and interior. The rim is natural buff with black designs; the bowl interior is red. Diameter, about 17.5 cm. *Right:* Necked olla with black hourglass design on buff ground and red base. Height, about 22.5 cm. From Sitio Conte. (After Lothrop, 1942.)

from the Colombian traditions in goldwork and tumbaga. Lastly, the Coclé and affiliated cultures would seem to mark a point of some important changes in the Panamanian cultures. For at this time level—which probably corresponds to our Late Period of the Intermediate area chronology—we get the first appearances of elaborate tomb offerings indicative of notable differences in wealth and status.

The great Coclé type site is Sitio Conte, which is near Penonomé. Both the Early and the Late Coclé phases are well represented in the site. These are estimated to span from about A.D. 500 until 1000.[209] Before the Early Coclé phase, as we have just noted, there was a Santa María occupation at the site. The location is a river valley a few miles from the coast. Burials here, accompanied by gold and pottery, were first brought to attention by the cutting back of the river bank in flood times. The site had obviously been of some importance and was also probably the village residence of a chief or lineage of chiefs.

Coclé pottery is extraordinarily handsome (Fig. 5-90). Much of it has a white slip, and over this are designs in black filled with red and purple. The finest examples are flat plates that have bold, rhythmic life designs: alligators, birds, humans and monsters. Elegant jars and carafes are often painted with panel and scroll designs. Vessels of

Figure 5-90. Coclé-style polychrome pottery. All from Sitio Conte, Early subphase. *a:* Bird and crab patterns; diameter, about 26 cm. *b:* Tray form. *c:* Bottle. *d:* Stylized crab patterns; diameter, 32.4 cm. *e:* Deer head; diameter, 29.2 cm. Specimens *b* and *c* fall in the same general size range as indicated for other vessels. (After Lothrop, 1942.)

the Early phase have large areas of free space around large design figures, whereas those of the Late phase show increased filling of the area decorated and reduction in design unit size.

Coclé pottery was found in profusion in the graves. These were deep rectangular pits that contained the bones of a central or otherwise important person, together with his numerous wives and retainers who, we believe, had been immolated and interred with the deceased personage. Much of the pottery in such graves had been intentionally broken, apparently at the time of the funeral ceremony. Gold and tumbaga pendants (Fig. 5-91), breastplates, crowns, and ear and nose ornaments bedecked the individuals found in the graves and were, of course, the particular pre-

Figure 5-91. Coclé-style gold pendant or pectoral. The figures are leaf-nosed bats dressed and equipped as warriors; the object has been cast as a single piece. Maximum width, 10.5 cm. (Courtesy Dudley Easby and Metropolitan Museum of Art, New York.)

Figure 5-92. Small bone carvings, Coclé style, Sitio Conte. Representations of the crocodile god. Figure at *left* identified as whale ivory; others probably manatee bone. Length of central figure, 14.6 cm. (After Lothrop, 1937.)

rogative of the "personage." The helmets, breastplates, and other flat pieces had been fashioned by hammering and embossing, while the pendants —alligators, frogs, humans, bats—had been cast by the *cire perdue* method over clay and charcoal cores. Both techniques and the style are especially reminiscent of Colombian Quimbaya gold—so much so that there can be no doubt that the metallurgical industries of Panama and the Cauca Valley were closely related. Among the most splendid Coclé pieces are gold pendants set with uncut Colombian emeralds. Other pendants and ornaments from the Coclé graves were finely cut or carved from whale tooth ivory, from manatee bone (Fig. 5-92), or from agate. Some of the latter are wing-shaped and similar to the wing-shaped polished stone pendants of the Late Period Tairona culture of northern Colombia.

Although Sitio Conté was probably not occupied or in use as a burial ground as late as the early sixteenth century, the tradition represented here was one that persisted in the Coclé and Parita Bay regions until early historic times. The first conquistadors to enter this country—in 1519— tell of the burial ceremony of the ruler, Parita, who was to have been accompanied to the grave with several hundred pounds of golden treasure as well as sacrificed slaves. The Spaniards' appearance on the scene saved the intended victims of immolation—as well as the gold—from being interred with this chief. Such a description certainly accords with what Lothrop found in the burial pits at the Sitio Conté as well as with similar evidences among the burials at Venado Beach in the Canal Zone region.[210]

There are a series of Coclé-related pottery styles in the Parita Bay region and in the interior of the Azuero Peninsula. These have been referred to by various regional and site names, such as El Hatillo, Azuero, Parita, and Macaracas.[211] Insofar as these styles can be placed chronologically, they appear to be either contemporaneous with Late Coclé or a little later. John Ladd has described some of them from the El Hatillo site, which is located between Parita and Pese.[212]

El Hatillo consists of a group of ten small mounds that are clustered in a roughly circular arrangement over an area about 100 meters in diameter. The purposes for which the mounds were built are not altogether clear. They are relatively small, circular or ovoid, flat tumuli, the largest being approximately 20 meters in diameter and between 2 and 3 meters in height. Excavation revealed horizontal banding of ash- and clay-fill layers in some of them, and it may be that they were used as house platforms. Some were places of burial. Either these burials were in the fills of the mounds, or the graves had been dug from various levels within the mounds down deep into submound soils. Both suggest that burial had been made through house floors. Grave goods, especially pottery, were abundant.[213] There were also cases of pottery caches or deposits in mounds that had no burials in association.

The ceramic stratigraphy within the mounds and in the flat ground surrounding the mounds showed that the El Hatillo site had first been occupied in Late Coclé times; but the later and heavier occupation, and probably the one to be associated with most of the mound construction, has been designated as the Herrera phase. Herrera-phase pottery looks like a development out of Coclé. It has a glossy cream-to-orange slip—in contrast to the white slip of Coclé; however, designs are outlined in black and then filled with red or purple in much the same manner as Coclé. But decoration tends to be more intricate, and there is a much more stylized rendering of life forms. The Herrera-phase styles also show much more rectilinear geometric fretwork and paneling than the Coclé-phase styles. Vessel forms, too, differ. Those most common to Herrera are bowls or plates on tall pedestal bases. Many of these pedestal bowls have the modeled heads, tails, and wings of bird effigies. Small ollas and pedestal plates—miniatures, in fact—are another Herrera trait. These were probably specially made as mortuary ware. Artifacts other than pottery that were found at the El Hatillo site and can be associated with the Herrera phase include some finely carved manatee bone batons that are ornamented with alligator and frog figures executed with amazing delicacy. They are comparable both in style and workmanship to some of the bone carvings from Sitio Conte. Goldwork, curiously, was rare at the El Hatillo site, although two gold disks were recovered with a burial.

To the east, Coclé-related gold and ceramic styles have been found at the large burial site of Venado Beach in the Canal Zone.[214] We have already noted that Santa María–like pottery is present at this site, but the Coclé influences are perhaps more pronounced. There are two radiocarbon dates from Venado Beach burials: A.D. 210 and 960. According to Ladd,[215] these came from almost identical burials, presumably both of Coclé rather than Santa María affiliation. I would be inclined to agree with that author's acceptance of the later date as being closer to the true age. The bulk of the pottery at Venado Beach, however, is not predominantly polychrome and Coclé-like but is rather in another tradition of an incised and modeled polished brown ware. This incised and modeled pottery undoubtedly links southward into Darien and beyond to the Cupica culture of the Chocó subarea of Colombia. Apparently, two ceramic decorative traditions, the incised and modeled wares of the south and the polychromes of Central Pacific Panama, were meeting and blending in the cultures of the Canal Zone region. Biese's pottery collection from the Panama Viejo site shows this mixture but, I would estimate, on a somewhat later time level than that seen at Venado Beach.[216] The fusion of the two traditions on single pieces can be seen in the Panama Viejo incised and modeled zoomorphic designs.[217] This is the same fusion that Stir-

Figure 5-93. Veraguas pottery. *Left:* Jar from Soná with looped tripod legs and small appliqué ornamentation. Height, 27.6 cm. *Right:* Red ware jar from Bubí with face modeling on neck. Height, 27 cm. (After Lothrop, 1950.)

Figure 5-94. Veraguas-style gold pendant. An eagle (?). Height, 15 cm. (Courtesy Dumbarton Oaks Pre-Columbian Collection.)

ling noted in the Rio Chepo pottery a little farther to the south in Darien.[218]

To the west of Coclé and Parita Bay is the Veraguas region.[219] The Veraguas ceramic style dates from the Late Period and is known almost entirely from deep shaft-and-side-chamber graves in the hill country from around Soná. Most of it is monochrome or unslipped, of a buff color, and looped tripod legs are typical (Fig. 5-93). The decorative emphasis is on modeling. Tall pedestal-based bowls and tripod bowls are rather lavishly ornamented with frog, alligator, and other adornos. In these features there are certain similarities to some of the modeled pedestal bowls of the incised-modeled brown ware tradition as seen in the Canal Zone region, especially at the Panama Viejo site just mentioned; and it is entirely possible that this penchant for modeled ornamentation spread among groups on the little-known Atlantic coast of Panama, from Darien north, and then inland over the continental divide, bypassing the Coclé polychrome enclave of Central Pacific Panama. Large basket-type handles and loop legs are other distinctive features. In addition, Veraguas graves are noted for their goldwork (Fig. 5-94). While related to Coclé gold, the Veraguas styles differ in that they are most frequently rendered in gilded copper rather than solid gold. The gilding was *mise en couleur,* a process whereby the gold of a tumbaga (or gold-copper alloy) piece was "floated" to the surface with acids. Stone metates

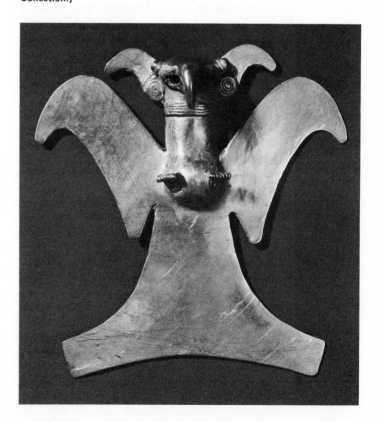

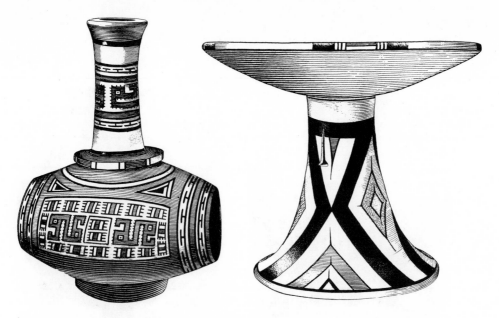

Figure 5-95. Herrera phase polychrome pottery found in Veraguas contexts. Height of both vessels, about 22–24 cm. (After Lothrop, 1950.)

also come from Veraguas graves. These are of both the four-legged jaguar-effigy type and the three-legged type with an underfretwork of carved birds or animals. It will be recalled that this last type was present in an earlier Scarified Ware grave at Pueblo Nuevo, so we know that there is a substantial tradition for the carved metate in the region. The great care with which these have been made, the almost delicate structure of some of them, and their obvious lack of use would indicate ceremonial rather than utilitarian purposes.

Lothrop reports early Spanish iron axes and knife blades in shaft tombs in association with typical Veraguas ceramics.[220] Significantly, some Veraguas graves also contain Coclé-related ceramics. These are almost always of the Macaracas, Parita, or El Hatillo styles—that is, those styles that are associated with Late Coclé or with the Herrera phase (Fig. 5-95).[221] These facts, taken together, allow us to extend the historic horizon into the Parita Bay and Coclé regions and to assume, with good reason, that the Herrera phase, or something very similar to it, must have lasted up until the early sixteenth century.[222]

Not surprisingly, considering its geographical position, the Veraguas culture and the Veraguas region as a whole shows relationships to cultures of western Panama and adjacent Costa Rica, and this brings us to our next section.

Western Panama–Southern Costa Rica. This subarea includes the Gulf of Chiriquí, highland Chiriquí, and the adjacent Costa Rican Boruca and Diquís regions. It is best known for the Chiriquian archaeological complex.[223] This Chiriquian complex or phase pertains to the late pre-Columbian Period and can probably be attributed to tribes of the sixteenth century, like the Doraces (Dorasque) and their neighbors.[224] Recently, however, archaeological research has revealed earlier archaeological phases in this subarea, phases that are the forerunners of the Chiriquí horizon, and we will take up the story with them.

Our survey of the Formative Period mentioned La Concepción (see Fig. 5-33) and Aguas Buenas (see Fig. 5-32) as the earliest pottery complexes of the subarea. The La Concepción phase is known from grave sites in the lowlands and foothills of central Chiriquí Province, around David and Concepción.[225] The pottery is purely that of the Scarified Ware horizon. The most typical vessels are open bowls with ring bases and alternating exterior panels of red painting and unpainted scored or scarified zones. There are also casuela bowls similarly decorated and having three small solid feet and head- and taillike nubbins as though in imitation of a bird. The tall, flat-bottomed "florero" vase, which we described for the more easterly Pueblo Nuevo and Guacamayo manifestation of Scarified Ware, is not present in La Concepción, although there is a tall, cylindrical tripod jar.

Aguas Buenas sites lie along the Panama–Costa Rican border from Puerto Armuelles inland to the Volcán country of the highlands.[226] As such, their distribution is a little to the west of those of the La Concepción phase, although there is some territorial overlap. The principal pottery types are red-slipped or red-rimmed, and the most common forms are ollas, or collared jars, with short tripod slab feet. Rather crudely modeled animals or birds are attached to the sides and rims, and sometimes there is punctation or Scarified-like incision below the rims. The complex includes some true Scarified Ware types, which suggests continuity between the La Concepción and Aguas Buenas phases. Wolfgang Haberland, who defined both phases, has suggested their contemporaneity; but the modeling and the form of some of the tripod legs of Aguas Buenas seem to be moving in the direction of the modes of the later Chiriquí style, and I follow Coe and Baudez in suggesting a date somewhat later (see Fig. 5-7).[227]

The Barriles site should be mentioned before we leave the Aguas Buenas phase. It is in the Panamanian highlands, just to the southwest of the town of El Volcán, and the ceramics that have been found there are like those of Aguas Buenas. Barriles was a ceremonial center of some importance, as is indicated by a number of sculptures, which are among the largest in Lower Central America. They include life-size statues of chiefs or warriors usually represented as holding an ax in one hand and a trophy head in the other. Such dignitaries are often shown as being carried in "piggyback" style on the shoulders of other men. Besides the statues, there are huge, obviously ceremonial stone metates or tables several feet high and several feet in length. Assuming the Barriles sculptures to be dated by the associated pottery, we have here an earlier—and more elaborate—aspect of the style of sculpture that has always been associated with the Chiriquí phase.

The time interval between Aguas Buenas and the Chiriquí horizon has been filled in the Gulf of Chiriquí region by the excavations of Olga Linares de Sapir.[228] Her earliest phase, the Burica, has plain wares that are like some of those of the Scarified Ware and Aguas Buenas complexes; and it seems likely that Burica as a whole is a development out of these styles. A maroon slipped class of pottery is typical, both in large urns (probably for burial) and in smaller vessels decorated with appliqué ridges and pellets. The time horizon would appear to be that contemporaneous with Early Coclé—a correlation made on the basis of trade sherds. This would place Burica at about A.D. 500. The next phase, the San Lorenzo, has a red-banded style that is probably a prototype of the Red-line wares that have been mentioned in connection with Coclé and that are also common to "classic" Chiriquí. The trade sherds are those of Late Coclé; the terminal phase is Chiriquí. In this region it is represented in the well-known Armadillo ware (or "Biscuit ware"), a light-buff, very thin-walled pottery that is decorated in appliqué techniques and that occurs in numerous vessel forms, especially tripod bowls and small ollas.

Highland Panamanian Chiriquí sites, graves, and ceramics are, as we have noted, well known from the excavations of a half-century or more ago.[229] The graves are shallow, stone-lined pits, sometimes marked with stone columns. They usually contain a single burial and are capped with surface stone slabs or boulders. The pottery includes the Armadillo (Figs. 5-96, 5-97, *a*) and Red-line wares and two painted styles. These last are the so-called "Alligator ware" (Fig. 5-97, *b*, *c*), which is named for its highly stylized alligator designs rendered in red and black on a white or buff slip—a style that has some connections with the Coclé-Herrera alligator designs—and a two-color negative-painted type (Figs. 5-97, *g*, *h*,

Figure 5-96. Armadillo ware from Panama. *Left:* **Diameter, 16.5 cm.** *Right:* **15 cm. (After MacCurdy, 1911.)**

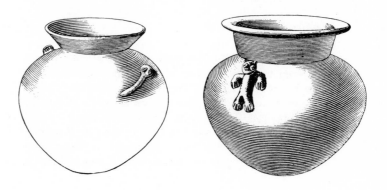

Figure 5-97. Chiriquí pottery. *a:* Armadillo ware. *b, c:* Alligator ware (positive painting in red-and-black-on-buff or white). *d, e, f:* Tripod ware. *g, h, i, j:* "Lost-color" ware (a negative or resist technique). These vessels are all rather small—25 to 15 cm. in height. (Courtesy Peabody Museum, Harvard University.)

i, j, 5-98). Besides pottery, graves contain the jaguar effigy metates (Fig. 5-99) and what may be round metates (or stools?) that are sometimes carved with little human figures as Atlantean supports. These stone items, and small (50–75 cm. in height) stone statues of men and women, which also come from the tombs, relate to very similar or identical forms from farther north in the Costa Rican highlands. The Chiriquí cemeteries of the highlands are also known for their little gold and tumbaga pendants. These are similar or identical in style to the metalwork of Veraguas.

No complete survey of Chiriquían regional cultural variation is possible here. Suffice it to know that such does exist. For instance, in the Boruca region of the General Valley of southern upland Costa Rica, Haberland has distinguished a Buenos Aires phase,[230] in which grave shafts tend to be deeper with the burial placed in a little centrally located subpit within the floor of the larger pit, and in which there are some variations of the ceramic pattern we have described so briefly.

Another distinctive region within our subarea is the Diquís Delta. The Rio Diquís flows into the Pacific out of the Terraba Plain, which lies between the two ranges of the Costa Rican cordillera. The flat delta country of the river was once densely occupied: remains of numerous house platforms are reported, although most of these have now been destroyed by recent large-scale agricultural operations. These mounds, or platforms, were constructed of earth with river boulder retaining walls; some were as much as 3 meters or more in height. A ceramic sequence in the region can be subsumed in two phases.[231] The earlier phase features a Brown ware and a Fugitive Red ware. Perhaps at the beginning of the earlier phase there was little or no decoration, or decoration was limited to very simple incised and appliqué pellet designs (Fig. 5-100); but much of the Brown ware shows modeling and, especially, modeled adornment on tripod vessel legs. Small pottery figurines, apparently hand-made, are also associated with the earlier phase. Later phase pottery is another expression of "classic" Chiriquí: negative painting, Alligator ware, and related types.

The Diquís delta is especially well known for its stone carving. These carvings include the jaguar metates that have been mentioned for other regions, but the more notable sculptures are small limestone and granite statues. These are mostly human figures, male or female, done with a cer-

Figure 5-98. Chiriquí negative-painted pottery. *Left:* Diameter, 10.5 cm. *Right:* 12.5 cm. (After MacCurdy, 1911.)

Figure 5-99. Typical jaguar metate. This one is from the Chiriquí country of Panama. Length, about 50 cm. (After MacCurdy, 1911.)

Figure 5-100. Incised Brown ware and Fugitive Red ware figurines from the Diquís region. Diameter of vessel, 38 cm. Figurine heads, between 3 and 4 cm. in height. (After Lothrop, 1963.)

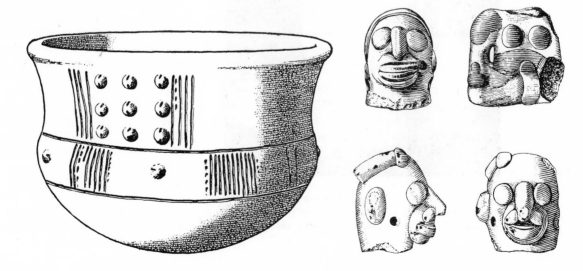

Figure 5-101. Heads of Diquís anthropomorphic deity sculptures. Picture at *bottom* shows the back of a head. Respective widths: 17, 25, and 16 cm. (After Lothrop, 1963.)

tain realism of depiction in facial features, genitals, arms, and legs, although the style is stiff and not naturalistic. Some are rather flat in appearance, and these figures frequently have the arms partially freed from the body; others are more lumplike in contour. They vary in length from 30 to 60 centimeters.[232] Gods or individuals combining human and animal qualities are among the representations, especially a being with pronounced teeth, and a serpent, or serpents, dangling from his mouth (Fig. 5-101). The region is further noted for the curious large stone balls that range from 30 centimeters to more than 2 meters in diameter. Some of the largest are estimated to weigh as much as 16 tons. Their purpose of function is unknown although, presumably, it was ceremonial or ritualistic. Some are said to have been on the mound platforms; others seem to have been placed in alignments near mounds.[233] It is believed that both the carved stone statues and the stone balls date from the later of the Diquís Delta phases. This later phase equates with the Chiriquí phase in the Gulf of Chiriquí sequence and with similar manifestations elsewhere in the subarea. The earlier Diquís phase, that of the Brown and Fugitive Red ware, has been aligned variously, but I have followed Linares de Sapir in equating it with the Burica phase.[234]

Atlantic Panama West of the Canal Zone. A recent archaeological reconnaissance made by the Stirlings[235] describes small sites in the region around the Chiriquí Lagoon and Almirante Bay. They found such items as modeled tripod vessels and jaguar metates—similar to those of Late Period Chiriquí culture assemblages. It was somewhere near Almirante Bay that the Aztec Sigua colony was established at some time before 1540.[236] The Sigua are known from ethnohistory, but their presence in Caribbean Panama suggests the kind of mechanism by which Mexican traits may have been carried to the Tairona culture of Caribbean Colombia. However, Stirling's search for archaeological traces of this colony yielded no positive result.

Highland and Atlantic Costa Rica. This subarea takes in most of the Republic of Costa Rica except the Diquís and Boruca regions of the south and the Nicoya and Tempisque regions of the northeast. In the sixteenth century it is purported to have been held by the Guetar tribe, and the subarea has sometimes been referred to under that name. Our archaeological information comes largely from two regions within the subarea, the Central Plateau around Cartago and San José and the "Old Line" region of the Atlantic watershed in the vicinity of such modern towns as Germania and Toro Amarillo.

platforms, flank this largest structure on three sides, forming courtyards or plazas. The whole group measures about 100 by 75 meters, and the orientation of the mounds conforms, at least approximately, to the cardinal directions. In the immediate vicinity of these principal structures are low mounds or stone circles filled with refuse. These are believed to have been house sites, and graves are found in them, suggesting burials made through the floors of dwellings. Such would con-

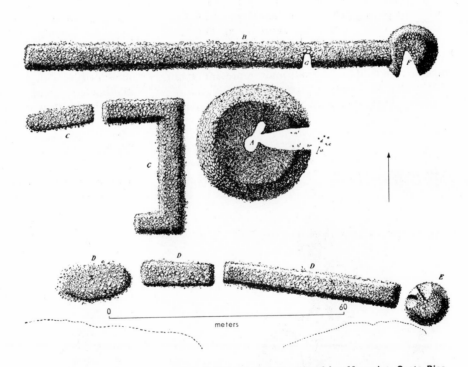

Figure 5-102. Plan of the site of Las Mercedes, Costa Rica. (After Hartman, 1901.)

The best known site in the subarea is Las Mercedes, a mound group on a tributary of the Reventazón River in the "Old Line" region.[237] The mounds are laid out in a formal arrangement (Fig. 5-102). The central feature is a large circular platform 30 meters in diameter and 6.5 meters in height. The facing of the mound is a circular wall of boulders and mud mortar, and the interior is earth fill. Long, low mounds, or

form to the early sixteenth-century descriptions of houses and burial practices along the Atlantic coast of Costa Rica.[238] The graves in question were of rectangular or oval shape, the walls lined with boulders, and the floors and roofs of stone slabs. Grave goods were frequently in large supply; these included pottery, carved jaguar metates, human statues, the so-called "altar slabs," and gold ornaments.

The Las Mercedes stone statues and carvings are related to those of the Diquís and Chiriquí regions but nevertheless have distinguishing characteristics. The small statues, which are invariably found in graves, average 30 to 60 centimeters in length. They are much more realistically done than those of the Diquís style, although perhaps less accomplished in this regard than the big Barriles figures. Mercedes figures are usually shown standing, with separated legs, arms bent and partially separated from the body, and heads and faces carved in greater detail than those of Diquís. Both men and women are represented (Fig. 5-103). Men sometimes carry trophy heads; and there are also single sculptured heads, somewhat smaller than life-size, that may represent such trophies; there is also a larger size statue, one of life-size. These presumably, were placed around

the site. Some of these were of purely human form, but the three that Mason describes would appear to be deities of some sort. One is a standing, nude human male with a ferocious alligator head (Fig. 5-104), another a human female body with a bird head, and the third a man-bird being reclining on his back with a receptacle in his stomach—after the manner of a Mesoamerican Chac Mool.[239]

In addition to the statues, the carved stone slabs of Las Mercedes are worthy of special mention. These seem restricted to the "Old Line" region. They are sometimes referred to as "altars," although there is nothing except the elaborateness of their carving that suggests such a function. A carved slab of average size is approximately 1.4 meters long and approximately one-half to one-third as wide as that. It is quite thin (a few centimeters) and bears small figures of men, animals, or birds carved on the ends or the sides, either free standing or in bas-relief. Some slabs also have relief geometric ornamentation. The quality of the carving is very good, and the slabs are among the finest examples of art from Lower Central America. They are found in tombs; and, on the basis of ethnographic information, Mason held the opinion that they may once have served to mark primary burial places for the dead— places in which the body was left exposed for a

Figure 5-103. Small stone statuary from Las Mercedes. Heights, respectively 25 and 16 cm. (After Mason, 1945.)

Figure 5-104. Large stone statue, purportedly from Las Mercedes. Height, 1.55 m. (After Mason, 1945.)

period of time before the remains were gathered up and given secondary burial in a proper tomb. At this latter time the carved slabs were then interred along with the bones.[240]

The ceramic complex of Las Mercedes—and this general description can be extended to the "Old Line" region—includes appliqué-decorated types (Lothrop's "Applique" group). Among these

there is the "Stone-Cist type," named for its occurrences in the stone-cist graves. The type features ollas and tripod bowls or jars that are heavily ornamented with appliqué ridges, pellets, and little animal effigies—the last being rather crudely modeled and difficult to identify as to species. This "Stone-Cist type" is obviously closely related to another, the "Tripod type," which is also similarly decorated, although not quite so flambuoyantly, and in which the vessel forms are very tall tripod jars with the legs large, hollow, and fashioned as very stylized fish or alligators. Both the "Stone-Cist" and "Tripod" types show some resemblances to the Armadillo ware of the Chiriquí regions to the south. Other wares of the Las Mercedes complex are brown or maroon incised monochromes, simple painted ones, and polychromes. The simple painted styles include Red-line, Black-line, and negative-painted decoration—all of which are related to similar types from the Chiriquí regions. The polychromes, however, show significant new influences from Pacific Nicaragua and Nicoya and, specifically, to a style known as Nicoya Polychrome.[241]

The Las Mercedes occupation ended at sometime in the sixteenth century; this is attested by the presence of European glass beads in some of the graves.[242] These cross date with similar finds in graves from the Central Plateau region. The Orosí site is a case in point.[243] Incidentally, the Central Plateau sites—Santiago, Chircot, Los Limones, Orosí, Curridabat, and others—all show a similar complex to that observed in the ceramics of Las Mercedes. At one of them, Curridabat, there is evidence for an earlier period. Hartman found what he designated as a Curridabat style (Fig. 5-105) in unlined graves from the lower levels of the site.[244] Overlying these graves were others of the stone-lined type that contained vessels of the "Stone-Cist" (Fig. 5-106) and "Tripod" (Fig. 5-107) types. This Curridabat style, which is also discussed by Lothrop,[245] occurs in globular ollas with a shoulder ridge and with appliqué strip and button decorations. These appliqué features are sometimes combined with red painting on the natural buff surface of the ware. It is a style that is obviously related to the later "Tripod" and "Stone-Cist" styles and is probably a forerunner of them. To date, it is the only ceramic complex of the Highland and Atlantic Costa Rica subarea

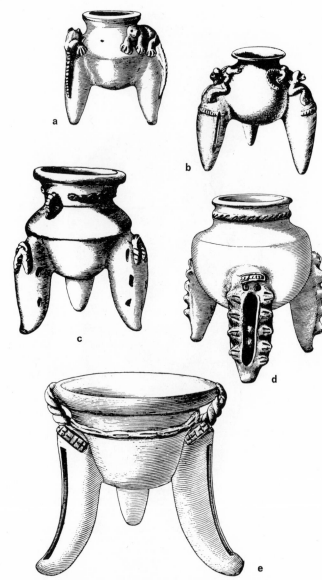

Figure 5-105. *Above, left:* Curridabat ware from Costa Rica. Diameter range, about 15–20 cm. (After Lothrop, 1926.)

Figure 5-106. *Left:* Stone-Cist ware from the Chircot cemetery, Costa Rica. Height of pot at *top*, about 12 cm. (After Hartman, 1901.)

Figure 5-107. *Above, right:* Tripod ware from Costa Rica. *c, d, e:* These have vaguely fish effigy legs, a frequent feature of the style. *a–d:* These range from about 10–18 cm. in height. *e:* About 12 cm. high. (*a–d:* After Lothrop, 1926; *e,* after MacCurdy, 1911.)

that can be dated earlier than the prevailing Las Mercedes–Chircot styles.[246]

Eastern Nicaragua-Northeastern Honduras. This subarea includes the Atlantic watershed of Nicaragua and Northeastern Honduras, between the Segovia and Aguan Rivers.

The jungles and swamps of eastern Nicaragua are almost unknown archaeologically. Spinden visited this territory a good many years ago and reported upon it in a brief article in 1925;[247] Strong drew upon this in his survey statement of 1948;[248] but there has been no significant archaeological work there since. From what little we do know, eastern Nicaragua seems to provide a geographical continuity in Late Period ceramic styles from Atlantic Costa Rica to Honduras. Spinden found modeled and appliqué-decorated tripod vessels in shell mounds near Bluefields that apparently belong to the same tradition as those of the "Tripod" and "Stone-Cist" types of Costa Rica. Animal-head metates are also reported from this same locality. A mound site is reported from the confluence of the Yasica and Tuma Rivers; large stone statues were found here, and one of them is described as a man with an alligator on his back.

Northeastern Honduras is essentially the same as what Doris Stone has termed the "Paya region";[249] there are many mound sites in the subarea that are reminiscent of those of Mesoamerica. Some mound sites are enclosed with earth or stone walls. In some instances these may have been ceremonial features, but in others they appear to be fortifications and, as such, suggest the Late Postclassic fortified sites of southern Mesoamerica. Stone statuary does not seem to be typical; however there are plain monoliths or stelae at some sites, as at Plan Grande, on Bonacca, in the Bay Islands.[250] Lesser stone carvings of Northeast Honduras are metates, tables, and handsomely fashioned cylindrical bowls. These are often found in votive caches—deposits of ceramics and of carved stone that have been incorporated into the tops of hills, with the presumed purpose of functioning as ceremonial offerings.

Ceramics are known from two major phases, both of which date from our Late Period. This is based on stratigraphic digging from the Eighty-Acre site on Utila Island, but the sequence has pertinence for the mainland regions of Northeastern Honduras as well.[251] The earlier phase, the Selin, can be divided into two subphases. Selin I pottery is of the stylistic groupings that have been referred to as "Ulúa Mayoid" and "Ulúa Bold Geometric" in the Ulúa Valley region of the Mesoamerican Southern Periphery and that can be related farther to the west to the Maya Late Classic Period Tepeu 1 and 2 styles (ca. A.D. 600–800).[252] Selin II sees a cessation of this Late Classic Mayoid influence and the beginnings of another pottery tradition—one that Strong has called the "North Coast Appliqué style."[253] Apparently, Selin II cross dates with Tepeu 3 and the beginnings of the Postclassic Period (ca. A.D. 800–1000). The succeeding phase is the Cocal I, in which the dominant pottery is the North Coast Appliqué style. Its derivations are obviously from the south—that is, from the "Stone-Cist" and "Tripod" appliqué wares of Highland and Atlantic Costa Rica. Its influences are also seen in another Cocal type, Bay Island Polychrome. This type has retained the black-and-red-on-orange color scheme of the Ulúa Mayoid styles, but the appendages and vessel forms link it to the North Coast Appliqué wares. In addition there are also elements in Bay Island Polychrome that are similar to those in the Pacific Nicaragua–Costa Rica Nicoya Polychrome style: for instance, plumed serpent motifs and a pear-shaped jar with an annular or tripod base. These elements in turn suggest Mesoamerica and, particularly, Mesoamerica of the Early Postclassic Period. The presence of Plumbate pottery in Cocal I as a trade ware confirms this dating. Cocal II shows minor changes, but the North Coast Appliqué and Bay Island Polychrome styles remain dominant up until the Spanish entry.

Nicoya–Pacific Nicaragua: The Southern Edge of Mesoamerica. Our consideration of Eastern Nicaragua-Northeastern Honduras carried us up to the borderlands of Mesoamerica on the Atlantic side of Central America. In turning to Nicoya–Pacific Nicaragua we also enter this frontier but on the Pacific side. Nicoya–Pacific Nicaragua can be considered either as part of Mesoamerica (as we did in Vol. I, Ch. 3, pp.

Figure 5-108. Pacific Nicaraguan pottery types. *Left:* Monkey-effigy vessel in black-and-cream-on-red. The black paint has a characteristic metallic lustre. This is a late variety of the type Tola Trichrome. This type is more commonly seen in the Linear Decorated Period but lasts into Early Polychrome times. Height, 15.2 cm. *Center:* Bowl with low-relief animal effigy. Rim red, animal red and brown, background brushed. Placed as Early-to-Middle Polychrome. Diameter, 50 cm. *Right:* Polychrome (black-and-red-on-cream) anthropomorphic vessel with bowl in back of figure. The date is Early-to-Middle Polychrome. Height, 10.1 cm. All specimens from Los Angeles site, Ometepe Island, Nicaragua. (Courtesy Museum für Völkerkunde und Vorgeschichte, Hamburg.)

168–169), or as a subarea of the Intermediate area.[253a]

In our Formative Period discussions we have already made reference to what Coe and Baudez have termed the "Zoned Bichrome Horizon" (see Fig. 5-34).[254] There are a few radiocarbon dates on the horizon, and from these and other considerations Baudez and Coe estimate a date of about 300 B.C. to A.D. 200. The ceramics of the horizon bear a number of similarities to those of the Scarified Ware horizon farther south, particularly in the matter of color zoning with incision. Sites of the Zoned Bichrome Horizon are few and small. These seem to be simple villages, marked by stone metates and manos and potsherds.

The succeeding period for the subarea is the Linear Decorated, a name derived from the appearance of geometric line painting of pottery.[255] This painting is usually done in black-on-red or black-and-white-on-red (Fig. 5-108, *left*). It may be related to such linear geometric styles as the Santa María of Panama—a suggestion put forward by Baudez and Coe. At least, it holds a contemporaneous position in the chronology. The dating estimate is A.D. 200 to 450.

The Early Polychrome Period is estimated at A.D. 450 to 800, and this is the horizon of the beginning of the Nicoya Polychrome style. This is a handsomely painted pottery. The ground color is usually a light orange or cream-white (Fig. 5-108, *right*). Designs are carried out in red, darker orange, black, and brown. The motifs include monkeys, birds, people, serpents, and other life forms, as well as geometric ones. There are relationships between early Nicoya Polychrome and the Ulúa Mayoid styles (Fig. 5-109) that we have just described under the Selin phase of Northeastern Honduras; and both relate to the Maya Classic Tepeu phase.

These traditions of Nicoya Polychrome painting and the associated small stone carvings continue into the Middle Polychrome Period, placed at A.D. 800 to 1100, and this period marks a kind of cultural climax for the subarea. This was the time of the later and the most typical Nicoya Polychrome style (Fig. 5-112),[256] that of the pear-shaped, pedestal-based jars or the pear-shaped tripod jars with animal effigy heads and tails. The period saw a population peak, with sites larger and more numerous than before. Oddly, this was also the time of the greatest exploitation of marine shellfish resources in the coastal sites; however, this may not have been primarily a subsistence measure. Coe and Baudez note that the most common shell in the coastal shell middens is the *Murex*, a genus used for making purple dye, and it may have been that such a luxury activity and trade, linked to the civilizations of Mesoamerica, was responsible for a degree of the prosperity on this southern periphery.

This was also the time of the most notable ceremonialism in Nicoya–Pacific Nicaragua. The well-known Isthmus of Rivas style[257] sculptures

Figure 5-109. *Above:* Cylinder jar of white-on-red decorated pottery with modeled monkey form. From the Nicoya Peninsula. The pseudo-glyphic arrangement of white lines around the upper border is reminiscent of Mayan glyph bands on cylinder jars. Probably Early Polychrome Period, although the colors are more suggestive of Linear Decorated Period. Height, 16.3 cm. (Courtesy Peabody Museum, Harvard University.)

Figure 5-110. *Below:* Two jadeite ceremonial or "votive" axes from the Nicoya subarea, Costa Rica. Height of specimen at *left*, 17.2 cm. (Courtesy Dumbarton Oaks Pre-Columbian Collection.)

Figure 5-111. *Above:* Lidded vessel or incense burner of Modeled Alligator Ware. In more recent terminology this type is called Potosí Appliqué: Respiradero Variety. The figure of the anthropomorphic alligator or crocodile seated on the lid and the body of the lid and vessel are rough, unpainted (buff-colored), and adorned with appliqué pellets. There are red bands at base and rim and on the lid base and at top. Such specimens have been dated by Haberland (personal communication, 1969) to the Gato phase of Ometepe Island and to the transition from Early Polychrome to Middle Polychrome Periods. The specimen shown comes from Ometepe Island, Nicaragua. Height, 36 cm. (Courtesy Peabody Museum, Harvard University; see also Lothrop, 1926, Vol. II.)

345

Figure 5-112. Nicoya Polychrome style, Middle Period. Height of vessel in *center*, about 37 cm. (Courtesy British Museum.)

appear to date to the period (Fig. 5-113). These sculptures usually represent a human male figure, seated or standing, with an animal or animal head on the back or head of the man. The concept is that of the so-called "alter ego" (or man and tutelary animal spirit) to which we have referred previously in this chapter as being seen in other Intermediate area stone statuary. In at least two instances in the Nicaraguan figures the man wears a duckbill mask, which is a form of symbolism that points northward to Mesoamerica and to Preclassic styles.[258]

In general, the Isthmus of Rivas type statue is large (although usually somewhat less than life-size) and has either a plain base or a tenon at the top, depending how it was set into or attached to the masonry of the platform mounds. These mounds, and the statues, are the principal features of the Nicoya–Pacific Nicaragua ceremonial centers. Such centers are known from Zapatero Island in Lake Nicaragua, on the Isthmus of Rivas, and in the Nicoya regions. Mounds consist of earth and stone facings. Some are described as circular;

others appear to be rectangular.[259] One other type of stone sculpture should be mentioned here: the Chontales style (Fig. 5-114). It is found on the eastern side of Lake Nicaragua, a region very little known and one that may be appropriately placed more with Eastern Nicaragua rather than with Nicoya–Pacific Nicaragua. This Chontales style of statue is carved in a much lower relief than the Isthmus of Rivas style. A man, presumably a warrior, is depicted holding a spear or club; headdress and textile designs of his clothing are portrayed in the carving.[260] We have no clues to the dating of this style, and it is mentioned at this point in our survey only to contrast it to the Isthmus of Rivas style.

The Middle Polychrome Period can be correlated in time with the Early Postclassic Period of Mesoamerica—with, in effect, the Toltec horizon and the spread of Tohil Plumbate and X-Fine Orange pottery. Late Nicoya-type polychrome vessels are found in the Maya subareas—both Highland and Lowland—and in contexts with Tohil and Fine Orange associations.

The Late Polychrome Period of Nicoya-Pacific Nicaragua is placed between A.D. 1100 and the Spanish Conquest. One polychrome pottery type of the period, known as Vallejo Polychrome, shows

Figure 5-113. Isthmus of Rivas style statuary, Pacific Nicaragua. *a, b:* These show top "tenons," but *b* also has man's head in jaws of animal. *c, d, f–h:* These show seated human figure with animal or bird headdress. All appear to have been shortened by recent museum mountings in concrete bases (not shown). Figures *g* and *h* are front and side views of the same statue, apparently a woman. *e:* Standing human figure with animal crouched on back and head. *a, b, e:* From Zapatero Island in Lake Nicaragua; Bovallius (1886) has illustrated *a* and *e. c, d, g, h:* From Ometepe Island, Lake Nicaragua, and *f* probably comes from there. The figures are a little less than life size. (Courtesy Wolfgang Haberland.)

a   b   c   d

Figure 5-114. Statues of the Chontales style, Nicaragua. *a:* Upper fragment of stone figure. This apparently male figure had a breast ornament and was holding something in his hand. A very weathered animal figure was on the head. Length of piece, 1.37 m. Said to come from the Sierra de Amerisque but photographed in Juigalpa, Chontales. *b:* Upper part of figure. Length, 1.05 m. Provenience data same as *a. c:* Near-complete statue, probably a female. Length, 2.4 m. Purported to have come from Sierra de Amerisque but photographed in Jinoteque, Chontales. *d:* Upper part of figure. Length, 93 cm. Purported to have come from Sierra de Amerisque but photographed in Juigalpa, Chontales. (All courtesy Wolfgang Haberland.)

strong Mexican influences in painting and design motifs like those of the Mixteca-Puebla styles. Another type, however, Luna Polychrome (Fig. 5-115), lacks these typically Mesoamerican features. It is a distinctive style with a white or very light cream slip and rather fine line painting designs of geometric or much reduced life forms. There is also modeled and appliqué decorated pottery in the Late Polychrome Period—an expectable occurrence in view of its predominance in Eastern Nicaragua and Northeastern Honduras at this same time. Baudez and Coe cite some evidence for a population decrease in this period. Certainly, there seems to have been a decline in ceremonial activities, for it would appear that the sculptures and the mounds of the Middle Polychrome Period

do not continue into the Late Polychrome Period. Perhaps this reflects a disruption of contacts with Mesoamerica.

Summary and Nuclear American Perspective

We began the chapter by describing how an Intermediate area cultural tradition had its foundations in an earlier one designated as the Northwest South American Littoral tradition. This tradition was a lifeway based upon shoreline collecting and fishing in a coastal lagoon and mangrove environment. It seems to have had its beginnings here in the Intermediate area at about 5000 B.C., and evidences of it are recognized from Ecuador to Panama. Quite probably this pattern of life also extended even farther north into southern Mesoamerica. For instance, the preceramic finds of Islona de Chantuto, on the Chiapas coast (Vol. I, p. 84), may be a manifestation of it.

At about 3000 B.C. pottery was added to the scanty material inventory of the Northwest South American Littoral tradition. This was a simple, but competently made, pottery, generally unpainted but decorated by incision, punctation, and other plastic treatment. Such pottery is found from the Ecuadorian coast north to the Caribbean low-

Figure 5-115. Luna Polychrome bowls, Pacific Nicaragua. Late Polychrome Period. White slip with red and black decorations. (*Left*, courtesy Museum für Völkerkunde und Vorgeschichte, Hamburg; *right* (3 vessels), Courtesy British Museum.)

lands of Colombia and on to Panama. For the most part it dates in the time range of 3000 to 1500 B.C., persisting a few centuries later in some places. We have referred to it as the "Valdivia," or "Valdivia–Puerto Hormiga–Barlovento," pottery

Figure 5-116. Comparative chart of major chronologies of Nuclear America (Mesoamerica, the Intermediate Area, and Peru).

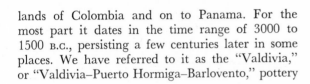

DATES	MESOAMERICA	INTERMEDIATE AREA	PERU
1500	POSTCLASSIC PERIOD	LATE PERIOD	← INCA HORIZON
			LATE INTERMEDIATE PERIOD
1000			
	CLASSIC PERIOD		MIDDLE HORIZON
			EARLY INTERMEDIATE PERIOD
A.D. / B.C.	LATE PRECLASSIC PERIOD	REGIONAL DEVELOPMENT PERIOD	
			EARLY HORIZON
	MIDDLE PRECLASSIC PERIOD		
		FORMATIVE PERIOD	INITIAL PERIOD
1000	EARLY PRECLASSIC PERIOD		
2000		EARLY CERAMIC PERIOD	PRECERAMIC PERIOD VI
3000	FOOD-COLLECTING AND INCIPIENT CULTIVATION PERIOD		PRECERAMIC PERIOD V
		PRECERAMIC PERIOD V	

tradition. According to one hypothesis, this pottery tradition was first introduced to the Ecuadorian coast from Japan. If so, we are dealing in this instance with an extra-Nuclear American diffusional occurrence. It may have been the first pottery in the New World; certainly, the radiocarbon dating evidence favors this interpretation. Early on, however, other American ceramic traditions sprang up, perhaps by way of stimulus diffusion from this Valdivian one. One such tradition was the Rancho Peludo of Northwest Venezuela, a second the early Upper Amazonian pottery of Tutishcainyo (pp. 401–402) and the related early Waira-jirca complex of the Peruvian Andes (pp. 112–115), and a third the southern Mesoamerican ceramic beginnings that we see in the Pox and Purron pottery complexes (Vol. I, pp. 83 and 175).

Almost certainly, the peoples of the later stages of the Northwest South American Littoral tradition were experimenting with food plant cultivation. In the north Colombian lowlands this experimentation must have involved manioc, and the Ecuadorian coastal populations were probably growing such things as lima beans and squash in the manner of their Peruvian contemporaries. But at some time in the second millennium B.C. maize was introduced to the Ecuadorian coast, and this resulted in the important changes that mark the end of the Northwest South American Littoral tradition and the beginning of the Intermediate area cultural tradition. It will be recalled (see p. 106) that maize was also introduced to Peru at about this same time. Because of its long developmental history in Mesoamerica we assume that this area was the homeland of maize and that maize spread from there to Ecuador and Peru. Certain ceramic traits also appear in Peru and Ecuador more or less contemporaneously with the introduction of maize, and these traits have a very definite Mesoamerican "feel" about them. In Peru, these are collarless subglobular ollas, or *tecomates,* and pottery figurines—both quite similar to types from the Early Preclassic Period of Mesoamerica.[261] In coastal Ecuador, the carinated or angle shouldered bowls and the incised color zoning of the Machalilla phase suggest the Mesoamerican area Preclassic cultures, and widespread Nuclear American relationships are also implied by other Machalilla traits which may be local inventions, such as the stirrup-spout jar, which is found in

Mesoamerica and Peru at about this same time. Very definite Mesoamerican evidences are also seen in the Ecuadorian Chorrera culture, which follows Machalilla and is the earliest Ecuadorian coastal phase that can be said to be agricultural. These are pottery figurines (similar to those of the Mexican Preclassic Tlatilco phase), napkin ring ear spools, and obsidian bladelets. Moreover, there are other traits, such as the highly specific iridescent pottery painting technique, which link Chorrera with Pacific Guatemala; but, in this case, the trait may be an Ecuadorian invention that passed from south to north.

That such diffusions may have taken place by sea rather than by land receives support from the patterns of geographical distribution of these traits in Nuclear America. Thus, maize and the early Mesoamerican pottery traits that often accompany it may not make an appearance in northern Colombia and Lower Central America until about the beginning of the Christian era,[262] suggesting that these subareas were bypassed in the early diffusions of these elements from Mesoamerica to Ecuador and Peru. Furthermore, we have such phenomena as the striking similarities between the Mesoamerican Tlatilco ceramic complex (Vol. I, pp. 103–105) and that of the Peruvian Cupisnique complex (pp. 123–126).[263] These are so close and numerous that it is difficult not to suspect a Mesoamerican-Peruvian contact that skipped the Intermediate area.

These Tlatilco-Cupisnique similarities lead one to a related question. Was there a connection between the Olmec sculptural style of Mesoamerica (with which Tlatilco ceramics can be associated) and the Chavín sculptural style of Peru (with which Cupisnique is associated)? However, this question may involve the Intermediate area—by way of the sculptural style of San Agustín. All three styles have some similarities in thematic content, particularly in the jaguar motif or in the attribution of the jaguar qualities of fangs and claws to humans or deities; but as styles—that is, systems of line, design, and iconographic expression—they are quite dissimilar.[264] What they do in fact hold in common may have resulted from contact; but if this is so, what was imparted in this relationship must have remained abstract— the essence of a religious or mythological idea— for the expressions of it as art forms are very different. Olmec and Chavín appear to be about contemporaneous and, interestingly enough, to have analogous roles in the cultural developments of their respective areas, marking as it were the first great iconographic horizons in these areas and, perhaps, the first great, areawide religious systems.[265] San Agustín is possibly as early as the other two—at least in its beginnings—although this is uncertain. We do not yet know enough about the archaeology of southern Colombia to appraise the developmental significance of the style.

After 500 B.C., with the beginning of the Regional Developmental Period, Intermediate tradition cultures show amazing diversity; however, there are certain ceramic traits that are widespread in the area and tend to typify it. Tripod vessels, tall pedestal bases, high annular bases, and negative or resist-dye painting are some of these. The histories of these traits are difficult to trace, both within and without the Intermediate area.[266] Tripods and annular bases are early in both Mesoamerica and Peru, but they may be as early in the Intermediate area—for instance, in Northwestern Venezuela. Tall pedestal plates seem to be earlier in the Intermediate area (as in Momil I of northern Colombia) than anywhere in Nuclear America. Negative painting, on the other hand, dates to the Initial Period in southern Peru (Hacha phase; see p. 111), and the chances seem to favor it as having been passed to the Intermediate area from the south. Once within the Intermediate area, however, it achieved a vogue in both temporal duration and spatial distribution that outstripped it in other parts of Nuclear America. Another distinctively Intermediate area trait complex is gold and gold-copper metallurgy. Like negative painting, the original technology probably derives from Peru. So far, at least, it has not been satisfactorily dated to early periods in the Intermediate area.[267] Some of the southern Ecuadorian styles relate to Peru, but the others, particularly the famous gold styles of the Cauca Valley, are unique local developments that spread northward to Lower Central America.

The cultures of the Intermediate area continued to be influenced from other parts of Nuclear America, especially Mesoamerica, through the Regional Developmental and Late Periods. This is, again, highlighted in Ecuador, and the sea-

borne trade hypothesis seems the most satisfactory explanation of the similarities. The cultures showing the strongest Mesoamerican influence are the Jama-Coaque, Tolita, and Atacames. Their mold-made figurines have very clear Mexican-Mayoid parallels: warriors in feather cloaks, human heads emerging from animal jaws, bat and jaguar figures, old men with wrinkled and grotesque faces, and human figures tied to beds or racks.[268] To these figurine resemblances can be added a three-pronged incense burner, a specialized device characteristic of certain southern Mesoamerican cultures that is also found in coastal Ecuador.[269] These trait parallels cannot all be traced to one region or one brief time period in Mesoamerica. In general, southern Mesoamerica seems to be involved. Evans and Meggers propose a dating to the first half-millennium A.D. These dates would be appropriate for some of the traits; others suggest a somewhat later time range into the Toltec horizon. For Ecuador the dating would fall in the latter half of the Regional Developmental Period with an extension into the Late Period. This would suggest that contacts were more or less continuous over a considerable period of time, a reconstruction that would fit with the hypothesis of a more or less regular sea trade between Mesoamerica and the Ecuador coast.

Another sphere of Mesoamerican–Intermediate area contact seems to have been on the Caribbean side of the continents, and, again, it may have been through the medium of sea travel. We have referred to Tairona pottery representations of human heads emerging from jaguar or serpent jaws and of Tlaloc-like figures; and both Tairona and Chibchan ethnography reveal many mythological and cosmological elements that suggest Mesoamerica. We have also seen archaeological evidences of contact between northern Colombia and Lower Central America. In these latter cases we seem to be observing more gradual diffusion, of the sort expressed by general similarities in complete pottery complexes. As examples, I refer to the probability of relationships between the early painted wares of Momil II and La Loma of Colombia with those of the painted geometric styles of Panama and Costa Rica–Nicaragua. In fact, it may be that the idea of polychrome painted ceramics first reached southern Mesoamerica at this time (the beginning of the Christian era) and by this gradual diffusional means and route from northern South America. A few hundred years later the Late Period ceramic appliqué and modeling tradition—particularly that of the modeled tripod vessels—must have had its beginnings in the cultures of the Lower Sinú and Chocó coasts and have spread from there all the way up to the borders of Mesoamerica in Northeast Honduras.

To return to the Pacific coast: we can note other clues to long-range contacts in addition to the figurine traits of northern Ecuador; they involve territories all the way from Peru to the Nayarit coast of Mexico. These contacts were not all one-way; in fact, in these later times it may be that the south and the Intermediate area was more a donor than a receiver. Resemblances have long been noted between the life-modeled pottery of Nayarit and Jalisco (Vol. I, pp. 172–173) and that of the great life-modeling tradition of the North Coast of Peru. Further, the modeled pottery of some Intermediate area subareas, such as the Quimbaya style of the Cauca Valley, is also similar to some of the ceramics of western Mexico. Cauca Valley shaft-and-chamber graves of Colombia are also very much like those of western Mexico.[270] This latter parallel gains significance when we note that deep shaft-and-chamber burials are not a typical Mesoamerican way of disposing of the dead; in Central America they are found no farther north than the Veraguas region of Panama. Thus their west Mexican presence suggests South American influences as do the ceramics found in the graves.

We have mentioned the spread of the Colombian gold styles north through Panama and Lower Central America. This was one way gold techniques were introduced into southern Mesoamerica; but the more important route seems to have been along the Pacific coast, from Peru and Ecuador north to Oaxaca and beyond. This was the way that copper metallurgy, with casting and other advanced techniques, reached Mesoamerica. Smiths and merchants must have made the introduction, bringing with them the skills and the goods, and even the incipient currency that was a part of their trading operations—the copper "ax-money."

Footnotes

1 Meggers (1966, fig. 3).

2 Meggers (1966, p. 67).

3 Lanning (1967 b ms.).

3a The chronological positions of Siches, Honda, and Estero are indicated on the Far North Coast column of the chronological chart in Chapter 3, figure 3-7. Siches is radiocarbon dated to 6000–4000 B.C., and Siches sites contain mainly mangrove mollusks. The Siches industry is characterized by unifacial chipped-stone implements (gravers, denticulates, spokeshaves), ground stone mortars, and a few T-shaped axes. Honda dates are around 3000 B.C., and Honda artifacts are similar to those from Siches. Estero artifacts are in the Siches-Honda tradition, but there are numerous T-shaped ground stone axes, mortars, and stone bowl fragments. A single radiocarbon date for Estero is about 4000 B.C., but Richardson questions this, and, in general, the technology suggests a later date. The Estero site was first described by C. Barrington Brown in 1926; the summary of the region follows J. B. Richardson III (1969 ms.).

4 G. and A. Reichel-Dolmatoff (1958).

5 Reichel-Dolmatoff (1955 a, pp. 48–50). The Colombian Pacific coastal drainage finds come from the Catrú and Juridivá rivers. Angulo Valdés (1963) describes these as including more formally finished artifacts (scrapers, perforators, burins, knives) than San Nicolás.

6 Reichel-Dolmatoff (1965 a, p. 50).

7 McGimsey (1956, 1958).

8 The Valdivia phase is reported on in full in the Meggers, Evans, and Estrada (1965) monograph. See also Meggers (1966, pp. 34–42); Evans and Meggers (1958); and Zevallos and Holm (1960).

9 Meggers, Evans, and Estrada (1965, p. 107).

10 Lanning (1967 b ms.) refers to this as a "micro-chisel"; Meggers, Evans, and Estrada (1965, p. 28) point to the virtual identity of these little tools with the "Jaketown perforators" of the south Louisiana Poverty Point culture of the Lower Mississippi Valley (see Vol. I, p. 291).

11 Meggers, Evans, and Estrada (1965, pp. 95–106, 108–109).

12 J. R. Munizaga (1965); see also this volume, pp. 89–90.

13 Reichel-Dolmatoff (1961 a, 1965 b, 1965 a, pp. 53–58).

14 Meggers, Evans, and Estrada (1965, p. 168).

15 Meggers, Evans, and Estrada (1965, p. 149).

16 Reichel-Dolmatoff (1965 b).

17 It is also out of stratigraphic alignment.

18 Bischoff (1966), who exca-

vated Canapote, is cautious about this geological interpretation. For Canapote see also Reichel-Dolmatoff (1965 a, p. 58).

19 Reichel-Dolmatoff (1955, 1965 a, pp. 58–59).

20 Reichel-Dolmatoff (1965 a, pp. 59–60).

21 Reichel-Dolmatoff (1954).

22 Reichel-Dolmatoff (1965 a, p. 59) refers to this as Bucarelia; there is a brief description of the pottery in Cruxent and Rouse (1958–59, Vol. I, p. 36).

23 Angulo Valdés (1963, fig. 8).

24 Monagrillo was excavated in 1948, and a preliminary report was presented in 1949 (Willey, 1951 b). The final monograph is by Willey and McGimsey (1954) and describes not only Monagrillo but another nearby site, Zapotal, which belongs to the Monagrillo phase.

25 Meggers, Evans, and Estrada (1965, p. 168).

26 Rouse and Cruxent (1963, pp. 48–49).

27 Rouse and Cruxent (1963, pp. 48–49) mention that Patrick Gallagher found pottery at the bottom of the great shell heap of La Pitía, not far distant from Rancho Peludo, and that he describes this pottery as being similar to that of "Meso-Indian sites of Colombia and Panama." This, presumably, would mean similar to such styles as Barlovento and Monagrillo; if so, this would extend such a tradition eastward into Venezuela. Unfortunately, there is no further information available on these La Pitía discoveries at the present time.

28 Rouse and Cruxent (1963, pp. 48–49).

29 Meggers, Evans, and Estrada (1965, pp. 147–156).

30 See, for instance Lathrap (1967), who has challenged the Meggers-Evans-Estrada interpretation with the counterargument that the apparent contemporaneity of Machalilla and late Valdivia ceramics is based on inverted cultural stratigraphy. He cites, in particular, the Buena Vista site (Meggers, Evans, and Estrada, 1965, pp. 18–21) where, in his opinion, a deep and extensive Valdivia midden had been capped by a thinner and more localized Machalilla occupation.

This Machalilla refuse was, in turn, buried under slope wash containing redeposited Valdivia sherds. In brief, Lathrap (1967, 1968 ms.) would see Machalilla as wholly later than Valdivia and, contrary to the Meggers-Evans position, as a development out of Valdivia rather than an intrusive culture into the Guayas subarea from the outside. He would draw the chronological dividing line between Valdivia and Machalilla at about 1400 B.C., and it may be significant that the three Machalilla radiocarbon dates all fall after this date, whereas all of the Valdivia dates fall before it (see dates, Meggers, Evans, and Estrada, 1965, p. 149). The situation is obviously a complex one—involving stratigraphy, radiocarbon dates, and stylistic appraisals. The possibility of reversed or inverted stratigraphy is difficult to judge because the shell middens in question showed, in Meggers, Evans, and Estrada's (1965, p. 15) words: "no significant natural stratigraphy"; and the radiocarbon dates, as is often the case, are susceptible to various interpretations (1965, pp. 149–152).

31 Meggers, Evans, and Estrada (1965, pp. 110–146); Meggers (1966, pp. 47–51; Meggers and Evans (1962).

32 J. R. Munizaga (1965).

33 Meggers, Evans, and Estrada (1965, pp. 157 ff.) have presented this case in great detail—and very amply illustrated.

34 Lathrap (1967).

35 Lathrap (1968 ms.); however, in this article Lathrap seems to imply that South American ceramic origins will be found somewhere in the Amazon lowlands.

36 Lathrap (1968 ms.).

37 Meggers, Evans, and Estrada (1965, pp. 173 ff.).

38 Another partial exception would be the Late Period Dabajuro pottery style of northwestern Venezuela (Rouse and Cruxent, 1963, p. 63).

39 For Chorrera see Evans and Meggers (1957); Estrada (1958); Meggers (1966, pp. 55–62). It would also appear that Bushnell's (1951) Pre-Guangala and Engoroy phases belong within Chorrera as it is now defined.

40 Meggers (1966, p. 62) notes the development of Chorrera out of a Machalilla context and asks the question why the new Chorrera traits failed to take root in late Valdivia culture which, according to the chronological interpretation she favors, had a late persistence contemporaneous with Machalilla. If, however, we follow the other interpretation—of Machalilla being wholly later than Valdivia—then the question is voided, as Valdivia would no longer have been in existence at the time of the arrival of maize and the new traits.

41 Michael P. Simmons, in reporting on recent work in the Santa Elena Peninsula region (Annual Meeting of the Society for American Archaeology, Santa Fe, New Mexico, May 1968, and in a letter dated October 1968), indicates that a polychrome type—probably a development out of the earlier Machalilla type, Cabuya Black-on-white—occurs in what appears to be a Machalilla-to-Chorrera (Engoroy) transition.

42 It has been suggested that this iridescent painted pottery may have been the prototype for negative painting (Evans and Meggers, 1957). Michael P. Simmons (letter of October 1968) mentions true negative-painted pottery as appearing after iridescent painting in a late Chorrera context on the Santa Elena Peninsula.

43 Obsidian hydration dating has played an important part in dating estimates for the Chorrera phase (see Meggers, Evans, and Estrada, 1965, pp. 152 ff.).

44 M. D. Coe (1960 b). Coe also suggests that the sea trip could have been made by sail-driven rafts or canoes by taking advantage of the prevailing winds in the proper seasons of the year and that the round-trip journey, with layovers for the seasonal wind changes, could have been accomplished in just a year. A stop-off in the vicinity of the Azuero Peninsula in Panama is postulated as necessary, and a small campsite of the Sarigua phase, on Parita Bay, is further suggested as a clue to Ocós travelers. Sarigua pottery, which follows the Monagrillo ware chronologically but bears no typological relationship to it, is

similar to certain Ocós phase types.

45 Meggers (1966, pp. 62–65).

46 Lathrap (1968, ms.).

47 Meggers (1966, p. 65).

48 Reichel-Dolmatoff (1965 a, p. 115).

49 A process suggested by Flannery (1968) in his hypotheses about the shift from incipient to full cultivation in the Valley of Oaxaca.

50 Angulo Valdés (1962); Reichel-Dolmatoff (1965 a, pp. 64–66).

51 Reichel-Dolmatoff (1965 a, pp. 63–64).

52 G. and A. Reichel-Dolmatoff (1956); Reichel-Dolmatoff (1965 a, pp. 68–79).

53 Reichel-Dolmatoff (1965 a, p. 73).

54 Reichel-Dolmatoff (1965 a, chronology chart, fig. 5).

55 Rouse and Cruxent (1963, p. 60).

56 Rouse and Cruxent (1963, pp. 75–79). Sanoja (1965) reports Santa Ana pottery as being associated with Tocuyano, implying that the two styles are approximately contemporaneous and dating from the Regional Developmental Period.

57 See, for example, Baudez (1963, fig. 6).

58 Willey and McGimsey (1954, pp. 105–110).

59 Haberland (1955, 1962).

60 Lothrop (1963). Baudez (1963) suggests Early Diquís dates within this group of complexes, but Linares de Sapir (1968 a, p. 90) thinks it is later.

61 Lothrop (1959).

62 Harte (1958).

63 Baudez (1963, fig. 6); Lothrop (1966); Haberland (1966 b); Linares de Sapir (1968, p. 88).

64 Coe and Baudez (1961); Baudez (1963, 1967).

65 See Norweb (1964) for the Isthmus of Rivas sequence and Haberland (1960) for that from Ometepe. With particular reference to the matter of the age of these early complexes, Haberland (1966 a) has described a small collection of pottery found below his Angeles phase (Zoned Bichrome Horizon) in a deep deposit on Ometepe Island. This earlier collection came from a stratum separated from those above it by sterile volcanic debris.

The pottery from this earlier deposit is either plain or bears deep-dot punctations and incised line decoration. Some rim sherds have been painted red. It is difficult to place culturally within the range of Central American or Mesoamerican ceramic styles. Haberland offers a guess date of 1500 B.C. If such turns out to be correct, this pottery, which has been designated as the Dinarte complex, could be of unusual importance and could mark a truly early Formative Period manifestation in Pacific Nicaragua. Until it is more fully described and more definitely dated we can only footnote its presence. See also Haberland (1969 b).

66 Strong, Kidder, and Paul (1938).

67 Canby (1951). Baudez and Becquelin (1969) have recently defined a ceramic sequence at Los Naranjos, Lake Yojoa region, Honduras. Their earliest phase, the Jaral, has incised designs with roughened areas enclosed in the zones. An Olmec figurine and an ax and a cinnabar offering are associated with the phase, and these Olmec traits affiliate the phase with the Middle Preclassic Period of Mesoamerica. The Eden phase, which immediately overlies the Jaral, has Late Preclassic markers such as Usulutan ware, and also red zone incised decoration. Apparently, the Eden complex cross dates with the Zoned Bichrome Horizon, but the Jaral is clearly earlier. See also Willey (1969).

68 Baudez (1966) would narrow this chronological difference a bit. In his revisions of a Ulua-Yojoa sequence, he correlates what he terms a "Pre-Usulutan Period" with the Mesoamerican Middle Preclassic and the earlier part of the Late Preclassic. That is, he dates it as prior to 100 B.C. He then dates a "Usulutan Period" from 100 B.C. to A.D. 575. I am not yet convinced by this shortening of the chronology for the Ulua-Yojoa.

69 This section on Guangala is derived from Bushnell (1951) and Meggers (1966, pp. 70–78). Disselhoff (1949) describes some Guangala cemetery wares.

70 The tall compotera form

seems to have an earlier South American history, however, as it occurs on the Peruvian Coast in the Initial Period (1800–900 B.C.).

71 Evans and Meggers (1957); Estrada (1957 b); Estrada, Meggers, and Evans (1964); Meggers (1966, pp. 78–85).

72 Estrada, Meggers, and Evans (1964, especially pp. 540–542).

73 Ishida and others (1960—Garbanzal sites). Estrada, Meggers, and Evans (1964) note that there are two sites at Garbanzal but that only one on the lower alluvial terrace fits with the Jambelí phase.

74 Ishida and others (1960) discuss Garbanzal sites. Evans and Meggers (1964), in discussing these, note that there are two sites at Garbanzal but that only the one on the lower alluvial terrace fits with the Jambelí phase. Izumi and Terada (1966) also treat Garbanzal. Their radiocarbon dates for it appear too late (ca. A.D. 1000); its more likely chronological position is 500 B.C.–A.D. 500. They also have a radiocarbon date in the vicinity of 1830 B.C. for San Juan (see chronology chart for Far North Coast in Chapter 3 of this volume). Another complex of this same northernmost strip of the Peru coast is Pechiche—with white-on-red and negative-painted pottery—and its radiocarbon dates are circa 370 and 850 B.C. Pechiche may precede Garbanzal and Jambelí.

75 Jijón y Caamaño (1930, 1951) has referred to a stratification at Manta which, in his terminology, ran from Proto-Panzaleo I and II through the "Cylinder-Seal Period," through Tuncahuán, and terminated in Manteño. Estrada's more recent work has failed to verify this. He identified Proto-Panzaleo at Manta and elsewhere in Ecuador as relatively late pottery that cannot be defined as a phase on the basis of valid contexts or stratigraphy. The "Cylinder Seal Period" he places with Manteño—implying a confusion in Jijón's stratification. On the other hand, the Tuncahuán element of the Jijón sequence was probably an identification made on the basis of negative-painted pottery, and it is likely that this referred to a Bahía phase component. A Bahía

354

component was discovered recently at Tarquí just east of the city of Manta (Stirling and Stirling, 1963). A radiocarbon date on this component is 213 B.C.

76 Estrada (1962) believes that the hollow La Plata figurines were manufactured over cloth, or cloth-covered, molds. The name "La Plata figurine" derives from the Island of La Plata off the Manabí coast. A large deposit of figurines was found there in a Bahía site (Dorsey, 1901; Carluci de Santiana, 1966).

77 Estrada and Meggers (1961).

78 Another possible Old World linkage here might be the little stone rectangles, found in a Bahía context on La Plata Island, which, Dorsey's (1901) objections notwithstanding, look very much like the "boards" for a patolli game—an oft-debated Old World–New World trait. Although it has a wide American distribution, patolli may have been introduced to the New World via trans-Pacific contacts to Ecuador.

79 Meggers (1966, pp. 96–102) makes no mention of mounds for Jama-Coaque although Estrada (1957 c) shows mounds, or "tolas," on his map of the Coaque type site. These do not seem to be of any great size, and it may be that they are refuse piles rather than architectural platforms. It is also possible that they date from the Late Period, not the Regional Developmental.

80 Meggers (1966, pp. 107–108).

81 Meggers (1966, pp. 102–107).

82 D'Harcourt (1947) presents many of these figurines.

83 Uhle (1927).

84 Corbett (1953).

85 Bergsoe (1937).

86 Stirling and Stirling (1963).

87 Meggers (1966, p. 141). These "chimney" or "tube" burials are another Regional Developmental trait from Ecuador that suggests Old World parallels.

88 Rowe (1949).

89 Reichel-Dolmatoff (1965 a, pp. 111–115, and 132). Cubillos (1955) has excavated on the Tumaco coast and defined a two-period ceramic sequence that pertains to the Regional Developmental and Late Periods, or the Mataje-Imbilí time range.

90 Collier and Murra (1943, p. 38).

91 Uhle (1992 b).

92 Jijón y Caamaño (1927, 1930).

93 Collier and Murra (1943).

94 Bennett (1946 d).

95 Meggers (1966, pp. 108–110).

96 Meggers (1966, p. 109).

97 Jijón y Caamaño's (1927) Proto-Panzaleo I was defined by him as agricultural, with the domesticated llama, rough mud-and-stone architecture, and plain or comb-incised, pedestal-based pottery. Developmentally, this is not necessarily inconsistent with either the Ecuadorian Formative or the Regional Developmental picture; but there is no stratigraphic support, and from what is known elsewhere in Ecuador it does not seem to accord with established sequences. Proto-Panzaleo II, which also lacked stratigraphic reference, is similar to I but also has two-color negative- and positive-painted wares. The sequence has been criticised by Collier and Murra (1943) and Estrada (1957 a).

98 Meggers (1966, pp. 111–112).

99 Jijón y Caamaño (1951) outlines a sequence for the Quito Basin but does not go into details. See Jijón y Caamaño (1914) and Bennett (1946 d, pp. 72–73) for comment on the Quito region.

100 In the Ibarra region of Imbabura Province, Jijón (1914, 1920) defines a sequence. Phase I has burial mounds, red-on-cream and incised pottery in jar, bottle, and tripod forms, and copper objects. Phase II lacks mounds but has burials of deep shaft type, pottery more complex in form than before, and relief decoration. Phase III has mounds as platforms for buildings with burials only incidentally placed in them, ceramics like the preceding phase, and goldwork similar to that of the coastal Esmeraldas subarea. It is difficult to appraise this sequence. Perhaps the later two phases pertain to the Late Period and Phase I to the Regional Developmental Period.

101 Meggers (1966, pp. 119–122).

102 Chroniclers of the Ecuador coast include: Estete (1918); Sama-

nos (1884); Xérez (1872); Cieza de Leon (1864).

103 See Meggers (1966, pp. 122–131) for this and other comments on Manteño; Saville (1907–1910) is the primary source on the archaeology of Manta, but I am skeptical of his estimate of the size of the ruins.

104 Saville (1907–1910, Vol. 2, pp. 32 ff.).

105 Stirling and Stirling (1963) excavated in one of the stone-walled structures or "corrals" at Cerro de Hojas. A charcoal sample from these excavations gave a radiocarbon date of A.D. 1397. See Meggers (1966, p. 27) for other Manteño radiocarbon dates that fall in the range of A.D. 850 to 1390.

106 Bushnell (1952).

107 Estrada (1957 c); Bushnell (1951).

108 Bushnell (1951, pp. 115–118 and 72–73).

109 Meggers (1966).

110 Bushnell (1951).

111 Estrada (1957 c).

112 Lothrop (1932 a); see also Estrada (1957 b, pp. 47–56) for descriptions of these sailing craft as they are made today. The reader is also referred to West's (1961) article on aboriginal Middle American–South American navigational contacts.

113 Heyerdahl (1952).

114 Heyerdahl and Skjösvold (1956).

115 Estrada (1954, 1957 a) prefers to identify the Milagro culture with the Colorado, a tribe, like the Esmeraldas and Barbacoa of the northern Ecuadorian coast, who spoke a Chibchan-affiliated language. He sees their entrance into the Guayas Valley as a movement from the coast, presumably at the beginning of the Late Period. I think, however, that the Huancavilca identification is the more likely (see Meggers, 1966, pp. 140–141).

116 See Meggers (1966, pp. 131–141) for a summary of the Milagro phase.

117 Estrada (1957 a, p. 8) originally proposed two phases, Quevedo and Milagro, with Quevedo as the earlier. According to him, the presence of negative painting was one of the traits that distinguished Quevedo

from Milagro; metal objects were more common in Milagro. In this general survey I have followed Meggers in treating these as a single phase.

118 Meggers (1966, p. 140).

119 Parsons and Denevan (1967); J. J. Parsons (1969).

120 These tribes were probably affiliated with the Chibchan language group (see Mason, 1950, pp. 180, 187; Bushnell, 1951; Jijón y Caamaño, 1919, for discussion and conflicting views on these affiliations and the territorial extent of these tribes).

121 Meggers (1966, pp. 141–142).

122 Reichel-Dolmatoff (1965 a, p. 132).

123 Meggers (1966, pp. 142–148).

124 Meggers (1966, pp. 148–151).

125 Jijón y Caamaño (1927).

126 Meggers (1966, pp. 151–154).

127 Gonzalez Suarez (1878); Uhle (1922 c); Saville (1924).

128 One of the rare Ecuadorian coastal Inca archaeological discoveries comes from La Plata Island, off the Manabí shore. We have previously referred to the island as a special shrine for the Bahía people; but an Inca grave also was found there (Dorsey, 1901), containing typical Inca pottery and the little Inca gold and silver figurines, much like those referred to in Chapter 4 (p. 242) in far-distant Central Chile.

129 Uhle (1923).

130 Reichel-Dolmatoff (1961 b, 1965 a, pp. 80 ff.). The term and concept Sub-Andean was also used by Steward (1948) in a similar way.

131 Hernandez de Alba (1946 a, 1948 a) gives a summary account of these tribes and explorations. Language affiliations are discussed by Mason (1950), but see also Steward and Faron (1959, pp. 21 ff.). There is considerable uncertainty and argument about these affiliations as data are few.

132 Kroeber (1946); Restrepo (1895).

133 Hernandez de Alba (1948 b). For language affiliations see Mason

(1950) and Steward and Faron (1959, pp. 21 ff.).

134 Tribes like the Cágaba (Park, 1946) or Kogi (Cogui) (Reichel-Dolmatoff, 1949–51) seem to be the present descendants of the Tairona nation.

135 For summaries of the ethnography of these regions see *Handbook of South American Indians*, Vol. 4, especially Hernandez de Alba (1948 c) and Metraux and Kirchoff (1948).

136 Bennett (1944 b, 1946 e).

137 Lehmann (1946).

138 Bennett (1946 e, pl. 171).

139 Cubillos (1959).

140 Ford (1944).

141 Bray (1965); Bray and others (1968); Bray (personal communication, 1969).

142 Reichel-Dolmatoff (1965 a, pp. 99–101). In this connection, Reichel (1965 a, p. 85) mentions the Catanguero site, in the middle reaches of the Calima Valley, which appears to be a link between Tumaco and Calima.

143 Reichel-Dolmatoff (1965 a, pp. 99–101).

144 The standard work on Calima gold is by Perez de Barradas (1954).

145 Perez de Barradas (1965–66); see also Perez de Barradas (1958) for the Tolima gold style, which is related to Quimbaya.

146 Reichel-Dolmatoff (1965 a, pp. 101–110).

147 Reichel-Dolmatoff (1965 a, pp. 101–110); Bennett (1944 b); Duque Gomez (1963).

148 Some of the principal earlier works on San Agustín are Preuss (1931); Perez de Barradas (1937); Duque Gomez (1947, 1963).

149 Reichel-Dolmatoff (1965 a, pp. 85–95) summarizes San Agustín; see also Reichel-Dolmatoff (1966).

150 Luis Duque Gomez (1963) has advanced a scheme of three phases. The earliest, Lower Mesitas, is posited as lasting from 550 B.C. (a radiocarbon date) until A.D. 425. According to Duque, the pottery with this phase is like that which I have referred to in the text as "the second horizon." The burials of Lower Mesitas were of the shaft-and-side-chamber type, and the phase was believed to antedate the

mounds, mound chambers, and sculptures. Middle Mesitas (A.D. 425–1180) remains in the "second horizon," but this was the time of the mounds, chambers, and sculptures. Upper Mesitas (following A.D. 1180) saw the stone sculptural tradition in its dying phase and a new pottery tradition ("third pottery horizon").

The Reichel-Dolmatoff (1967) sequence runs, from earliest to latest, with accompanying radiocarbon dates: *Primavera* (incised and appliqué wares); *Horqueta* (incised wares; A.D. 20–50); *Isnos* (slipped wares of fine quality, double-spouts, bridge handles, painting; A.D. 100–330); *Matanzas* (continuation of same tradition—black-on-red, black-on-cream types); *Mesetas* (spelled differently from Mesitas; new pottery tradition, coarse corrugated wares, incised decoration, heavy-legged tripods; A.D. 1410–1630). From the descriptions, Duque's Lower Mesitas would seem to correspond with Isnos, although Duque's radiocarbon date is earlier than Reichel's radiocarbon dates. Duque's Middle Mesitas would seem to correspond with Reichel's Isnos and Matanzas, while Duque's Upper Mesitas probably parallels Reichel's Mesetas.

The Patterson (1965) sequence, essayed on a seriational analysis of the published pottery, has six phases. The earliest phase, significantly, has only incised decorated pottery (with white paste pigment in the lines), and Patterson associates this with the shaft-and-side-chamber graves. The next two phases, with more elaborate and painted wares, are still associated with shaft-and-side-chamber graves. Not until Patterson reaches the fourth phase of his sequence does he establish a correlation with the San Agustín mound chambers; however, the pottery of this fourth phase probably would be subsumed within the "second pottery horizon" referred to in the present text.

151 For Tierradentro see Perez de Barradas (1937); Bennett (1944 b); Hernandez de Alba (1946 b); Nachtigall (1955); Reichel-Dolmatoff (1965 a, pp. 95–99).

152 Patterson's (1965) Tierra-

dentro seriated phases, in chronological order, from earliest to latest, are: *Segovia* (incised ware with white pigment, from burial caves of region); *La Montaña* (incised types with white pigment plus some double-spout-and-bridge forms, from the classic burial chambers); *Belalcázar* (painted wares, double-spout-and-bridge forms, Quimbaya resemblances—all from short-shaft-and-side-chamber graves); and *Calderas* (modern native pottery—lying outside the range of our interests here).

153 For an example, see Bennett (1946 e).

154 Reichel-Dolmatoff (1954 a).

155 Reichel-Dolmatoff (1954 a and see also 1965 a, pp. 122–124).

156 G. and A. Reichel-Dolmatoff (1958).

157 Reichel-Dolmatoff (1965 a, pp. 122–125); G. and A. Reichel-Dolmatoff (1953).

158 G. and A. Reichel-Dolmatoff (1958).

159 Parsons and Denevan (1967); J. J. Parsons and W. A. Bowen (1966).

160 G. and A. Reichel-Dolmatoff (1953, 1954). These would be later phases within the Zambrano development (see Reichel-Dolmatoff, 1965 a, pp. 122–124).

161 Alicia Dussan de Reichel-Dolmatoff (1954).

162 Reichel-Dolmatoff (1965 a, p. 129).

163 Reichel-Dolmatoff (1965 a, pp. 129–132); G. and A. Reichel-Dolmatoff (1962).

164 G. and A. Reichel-Dolmatoff (1961); Reichel-Dolmatoff (1965 a, pp. 129–132); see also Linne (1929) for archaeological survey notes of the Chocó coast.

165 G. and A. Reichel-Dolmatoff (1951).

166 Rouse and Cruxent (1963, pp. 61–67). More recently, Erika Wagner (1965, 1967 a, b) has defined a Miquimú phase from near Carache. Miquimú shows Dabajuroid affinities, especially to Guasare. Wagner would date both Guasare and Miquimú to A.D. 300–1000.

167 I have divided Northwest Venezuela into four subareas. These, and the way they correlate with the "areas" of the Cruxent and Rouse

(1958–59) and Rouse and Cruxent (1963) geographical-culture groupings, are: (1) Maracaibo Basin subarea ("Maracaibo area"); (2) Coro subarea ("Coro area"); (3) Cordillera de Mérida subarea ("San Cristobal, Merída, Trujillo, Barquisimeto, and San Felipe areas"); and (4) Barinas subarea ("Barinas area").

168 Dabajuro sites in the Maracaibo Basin and Coro subareas have been excavated by Osgood and Howard (1943, pp. 128–131, 63–74). Related and contemporaneous phases (Capacho, La Mulera) are also known from the Cordillera de Mérida subarea and from farther east in Venezuela (Rouse and Cruxent, 1963, fig. 9, pp. 61–64).

169 Rouse and Cruxent (1963, pp. 67–71).

170 Yet if all this is correct, it is curious that this line of painted pottery development seems to have had little interrelationship with the other early ceramic tradition of these same subareas, that of the Rancho Peludo–Guasare wares. The blending of these two lines, as we have just seen, did not take place until the Late Period Dabajuro phase. However I can see little evidence to support Reichel-Dolmatoff's suggestion that the La Loma–El Horno painted pottery development derives from Panama.

171 Rouse and Cruxent (1963, pp. 71–75); see Osgood and Howard (1943, pp. 90–91) for the Tierra de los Indios type site; see also Kidder II (1944, pp. 91–92) for related sites. Wagner (1967 a) describes a Mirinday phase (A.D. 1000 to historic) as succeeding Miquimú in the Carache sequence and as being a part of the Tierroid series.

172 Zucchi (1966, 1967) dates the inception of Caño del Oso somewhat earlier than Rouse and Cruxent (1963). She also suggests withdrawing Caño del Oso and La Betania from the Tierroid series and placing them in a new classificatory group.

173 G. and A. Reichel-Dolmatoff (1959).

174 For a summary of Tairona culture, see Reichel-Dolmatoff (1965 a, pp. 142–158).

175 Mason (1931–39); Reichel-Dolmatoff (1954 b, c).

176 For the Chibcha see Kroeber (1946); Reichel-Dolmatoff (1965 a, pp. 158–168); Broadbent (1965 a). For a review of early historic sources see Broadbent (1966).

177 Haury (1953); Haury and Cubillos (1953).

178 Broadbent (1965 a).

179 Broadbent (1966). It is known that modern Bogotá was not located on the site of old Chibchan Bogotá. The La Ramada site, near Funza, is some distance from modern Bogotá.

180 These ridges were reported upon by S. M. Broadbent at the annual meeting of the Society for American Archaeology, Santa Fe, New Mexico, May 1968. The hillside terraces are also described by her (Broadbent, 1964). Another type of hillside ridge or ditch, as seen at Chocontá, is believed to be of Colonial date.

181 Silva Celis (1945).

182 Hernandes de Alba (1937).

183 Broadbent (1965 b).

184 Broadbent (1962, 1969) has isolated ceramic components at several sites that are antecedent to "classic" Chibcha; however, it is not yet clear as to whether or not these earlier phases are ancestral to the better-known Chibcha types. For a discussion of the problem of Chibcha origins see Silva Celis (1964–65).

185 Reichel-Dolmatoff (1965 a).

185a A recent summary of Lower Central American archaeology has been provided by Baudez (1970). He subsumes Lower Central America proper under the heading of "Zone of South American Tradition" (pp. 158–218), and this corresponds to all but our "Nicoya-Pacific Nicaragua" section. This latter portion of Lower Central America is treated by Baudez under "Zone of Mesoamerican Tradition" (pp. 36–157).

186 Lothrop (1948 b).

187 Stout (1948).

188 Lothrop (1948 c).

189 F. Johnson (1948 a).

190 F. Johnson (1948 b, pp. 53–56).

191 Kirchhoff (1948). These languages have been grouped together under the Misumalpan stock of the Macro-Chibchan phylum by

F. Johnson (1940); see also Mason (1950, pp. 176 ff.).

192 Mason (1950, p. 174).

193 F. Johnson (1948 c); Lothrop (1926, Vol. 1, pp. 30–89). The reader is also referred to Stone (1966) for a general summary of the ethnohistory of all of Lower Central America.

194 Linné (1929).

195 Stirling (1950).

196 Linné (1929, pp. 134–138), in fact, says that this incised and punctated pottery was similar to that of Ancón, Peru, which would suggest a Formative Period date; however, the comparisons seem too general to be of much value.

197 The reader is referred to the chronological charts in Haberland (1969) for a temporal organization of Panamanian and other Lower Central American subareas.

198 Lothrop (1959); Baudez (1963) refers to the site, but there is a misprint in which it reads as "Puerto Nuevo" rather than Pueblo Nuevo.

199 Ladd (1964, p. 12). Lothrop (1966) gives a Pueblo Nuevo radiocarbon date of 230 B.C. The difference is due to a "Suess effect" correction made by Ladd.

200 Scarified ware was first described and named from the Chiriquí country (Holmes, 1888, pp. 87–89); see also Haberland (1962).

201 Stirling and Stirling (1964a).

202 Willey and Stoddard (1954); Ladd (1964).

203 Lothrop (1942, see figs. 237, 234) called this "Black-line Geometric ware."

204 Ladd (1957).

205 Ladd (1964, pl. 14).

206 Lothrop (1966). Linares de Sapir (1968, chart on p. 88) indicates a Mariato phase for the Veraguas region that is placed as contemporaneous with Santa María; and Baudez (1963) refers to a "white-slipped polychrome phase" in Veraguas for this same time bracket. These references apparently pertain to work of C. R. McGimsey, which has not yet been published.

207 Ladd (1964, the He-1 and He-2 sites).

208 Lothrop (1966, p. 203). Lothrop here also identifies Black-line style pottery from Linné's

(1929) published illustrations from the Pearl Islands; and I feel that some of the pottery that the Stirlings (1964 b) found on Taboga (for instance, their Figures 50 and 51) is related to the Santa María phase.

209 Lothrop (1937–42) originally felt that the Coclé culture dated in the last few centuries before the Spanish Conquest. This dating has been revised now—largely on the basis of radiocarbon datings on Coclé-associated finds at Venado Beach in the Canal Zone and on stratigraphy at the El Hatillo site in the Parita Bay region (Ladd, 1964)—and most authorities would place Early and Late Coclé within the range of A.D. 500 to 1000 (see, for example, Ladd, 1964, pp. 13 and 221–225; Baudez, 1963; and Linares de Sapir, 1968, p. 88).

210 Lothrop (1954).

211 See Lothrop (1942, figs. 461–464 and 1950, fig. 132) for Macaracas and Parita styles; see Stirling (1949) for El Hatillo style; and see Ladd (1964, pp. 18–23) for summary of all these Coclé-related styles.

212 Ladd (1964).

213 Some of the burials at El Hatillo may have been in urns, although this is not certain; however, the Herrera phase can be associated with urn burial, for Biese (1964, p. 19) mentions the presence of El Hatillo Polychrome (a Herrera type) in association with urn burials in the Azuero Peninsula.

214 Lothrop (1954, 1966).

215 Ladd (1964, p. 222).

216 Biese (1964, p. 49), however, feels that his Panama Viejo ceramics may be slightly earlier than Venado Beach.

217 Especially as shown by Biese (1964, pls. 12a and 13). There are also resemblances between the Panama Viejo pedestal bird effigy bowls (1964, pl. 6), decorated in incision and modeling, and the Herrera phase pedestal effigies, decorated in polychrome painting and modeling. Oddly, too, the Panama Viejo modeled pottery shows some resemblances to the geographically very distant incised and modeled pottery of Santarém, on the Amazon.

218 Stirling (1950).

219 Lothrop (1950).

220 Lothrop (1950, pp. 88–89).

221 Ibid. (Lothrop 1950, pp. 81–84).

222 The La Mula complex (see Willey and McGimsey, 1954) of the Parita Bay region should probably be subsumed under the Herrera phase. The El Tigre complex (Willey and McGimsey, 1954) is believed to be Colonial but probably of later Colonial date than the sixteenth century.

223 Holmes (1888); MacCurdy (1911); see also Osgood (1935).

224 Linares de Sapir (1968 a, pp. 75–81).

225 Haberland (1962).

226 Haberland (1955, 1962).

227 Coe and Baudez (1961).

228 Linares de Sapir (1968 a, b).

229 Holmes (1888); MacCurdy (1911); Osgood (1935); Lothrop (1948 b).

230 Haberland (1957, 1959 a, b). Another regional variant of the highlands can be seen in the materials excavated by Laurencich de Minelli and Minelli (1966) at San Vito de Java, Costa Rica, near the Panama border.

231 Lothrop (1948 b, pp. 109–111) lists it as three; however, his earliest phase is weakly defined from relatively few sherds of plain Brown and Fugitive Red wares taken from the lowest levels of stratigraphic cuts, and, for the present, I would bracket it with the second phase.

232 See Lothrop (1948 b, pp. 25 ff.); see also Stone (1958) on the Diquís region and Mason (1945) on Costa Rican stone sculpture.

233 Lothrop (1948 b, pp. 15 ff.); Stone (1958).

234 Linares de Sapir (1968 a, pp. 88–90); Baudez (1963) favors a placement that would align Early Diquí with the Scarified Ware horizon.

235 Stirling and Stirling (1964 c). This report gives an account of the observations of the 1502 voyage of Columbus and the 1536 voyage of Gutierrez (reported on by Oviedo).

236 Lothrop (1942).

237 Explorations were carried out here in the last century by

Minor C. Keith, and the collections from this work have been reported upon by Lothrop (1926) and Mason (1945); however, the first careful reporting of fieldwork at Las Mercedes was that of Hartman (1901). All three of these sources have been consulted in the preparation of this section. See also Strong (1948 b) and Stone (1958, pp. 15 ff.).

238 As reported by Las Casas who accompanied Columbus on his fourth voyage (cited from Mason, 1945, p. 204).

239 Mason (1945, pp. 256–274).

240 Mason (1945, pp. 247–256).

241 This ceramic summary is based primarily upon Lothrop (1926, Vol. 2, pp. 295–355); see also Stone (1958, pp. 20–24).

242 Hartman (1901).

243 Hartman (1901).

244 Hartman (1907 b); see also Rowe (1959).

245 Lothrop (1926, Vol. 2, pp. 332 ff.). In this connection, Rowe (1959) cautions that Lothrop's definition of Curridabat probably encompasses a much greater range of material than that found in the stratigraphic context by Hartman. Rowe also notes that additional proof for the earlier age of Curridabat was found at Orosí, where Hartman discovered "Stone-Cist" ware graves in Curridabat rubbish.

246 I have followed Rowe (1959) on the chronological chart (fig. 5-7) in designating these late styles as the Chircot phase; Baudez (1963) uses the term *Cartago*. This statement in the text should not be taken to mean that we have no clues whatsoever to other pre-Chicot or pre-Cartago finds in Highland or Atlantic Costa Rica. For instance, Stone and Balser (1965) describe a slate disk or mirror back from a grave at La Fortuna, in the north central region of Costa Rica, which is a Maya manufacture with hieroglyphs carved in a fifth century A.D. style. This grave probably predated the Chircot-Cartago horizon and perhaps that of the Curridabat wares as well. Ceramics from other graves of the La Fortuna cemetery are dated by Coe and Baudez (1966) as contem-

poraneous with their Linear Decorated (Early Polychrome A) Period of the Nicoya–Pacific Nicaragua subarea. As yet, however, there is no full definition of these earlier phases from Highland or Atlantic Costa Rica.

247 Spinden (1925).

248 Strong (1948 c).

249 Stone (1941, pp. 19–52). See also Strong (1948 c) for the "Northeast Coast Region" of Honduras. This part of Honduras "fell between the stools" in the *Handbook of Middle American Indians*, Vol. 4 (1966, R. Wauchope, G. F. Ekholm, G. R. Willey, eds.) as it was omitted by Glass (1966; see footnote, p. 159) and not picked up by Lothrop (1966).

250 Strong (1935, 1948 c). This section on Northeastern Honduras also draws on Stone (1941) and Spinden (1925).

251 Epstein (1959).

252 Strong, Kidder, and Paul (1938); Glass (1966).

253 These and other pottery types are described in Strong (1948 c, 1935) and Strong, Kidder, and Paul (1938).

253a Lange (1970) makes the point that the dominant subsistence pattern and the bulk of the ceramic influence—as seen in the Rio Sapoa Valley of northwestern Costa Rica—is southern rather than Mesoamerican. The reader's attention is called to Lange's paper and a series of other papers published with it, which deal with recent excavations in the Rio Sapoa region.

254 Coe and Baudez (1961). This Nicoya–Pacific Nicaragua section is based largely upon this reference and Baudez and Coe (1962), M. D. Coe (1962), Haberland (1960), and Norweb (1964).

255 Formerly called "Early Polychrome A Period" (Baudez and Coe, 1962); see Baudez (1963) for the present terminology.

256 See Lothrop (1926, Vol. 1, pp. 89 ff.) for descriptions and illustrations of this pottery style.

257 See, primarily, Richardson (1940); see also Strong (1948 b, fig. 17 b and pl. 13, a, b, d, e) and Bovallius (1886, pls. 1–32). This and other Central American sculp-

tural styles have been classified and described by Haberland (1970).

258 For instance, the famous Tuxtla Statuette, of Veracruz, which is Olmec-affiliated. It should also be noted that tenoned statues, similar to the Isthmus of Rivas style, have been found at Kaminaljuyu, Guatemala and that their associations appear to be with the Preclassic cultures.

259 Baudez and Coe (1962). I have visited the Zapatero Island and other Nicaraguan sites with mounds and statues. The mounds tend to be rather small (2–3 m. in height), flat-topped, and of indefinite outline.

260 Richardson (1940).

261 Lothrop (1966) reviews these early Peruvian-Mesoamerican similarities. It should be noted that incised color-zoning and tall compotera forms appear in Peru as early as the Initial Period (Matos, 1968).

262 Recent pollen core studies from the Atlantic side of the Panama Canal Zone, by Alexandra S. Bartlett, show maize pollen associated with a radiocarbon date of 2250 B.C. (personal communication, A. S. Bartlett, 1969). This is an important finding, and, if this pollen represents cultivated maize, this would push the date of maize farming for this region back much earlier than we have estimated.

263 Porter (1953).

264 Olmec-Chavín resemblances have been discussed by many archaeologists. See Kidder II, Lumbreras, and Smith (1963) for a view expressing a definite relationship between the styles. See also the dispute between M. D. Coe (1962 b, 1963) and Lanning (1963 d).

265 Willey (1962).

266 See Willey (1955 a); Lathrap (1966); Meggers and Evans, eds. (1963, Appendix, Table 2).

267 Meggers and Evans, eds. (1963, Appendix, Table 2). Just how early the *cire perdue* casting at San Agustín may be is open to question.

268 Evans and Meggers (1966) treat of these parallels with excellent illustrations.

269 Borhegyi (1959, 1960).

270 Evans and Meggers (1966).

We consider two major culture areas in this chapter: the Caribbean and the Amazonian. Both lie within tropical latitudes and both are essentially "lowland"—at least in contrast to the Andean half of South America. Each reflects these lowland tropical conditions in its basic culture patterns, especially in those that relate to agricultural subsistence. We shall deal first with the Caribbean area and then with the Amazonian.

The Caribbean Area

The Setting. The Caribbean area includes central and eastern Venezuela, northern Guyana (British Guiana), Trinidad, and the West Indies (Figs. 1-1, 6-1)[1] Most of this Caribbean area is suited to agriculture and will sustain either root crops or maize. Favorable places on the mainland are the valleys and basins in the Caribbean Cordillera and the gallery forest strip along the Orinoco. There are also indications that in the past the Venezuelan llanos were cultivated in many places, although today this country is given over largely to cattle. In the islands, the Lesser Antilles have good soils and adequate rainfall and can be farmed. The same is generally true of the larger islands. Their northern and eastern portions tend to receive their heaviest rains, have a lush vegatation, and are well adapted to crops; their southwestern sections get less precipitation and are drier and not as well situated for cultivation. The Bahamas are stony and have little or no surface water; however they have a good annual

The South American Tropical Lowlands

rainfall, and it is possible to carry on gardening activities there.[2]

On a pre-agricultural or non-agricultural level, the resources of the Caribbean area were most ample along the coasts and courses of the major rivers, with subsistence based on shellfish, fish, aquatic animals, and plants. The best country for land hunting was probably the Guiana highlands and savannas and parts of the Venezuelan llanos.

Cultural Traditions. We recognize three cultural traditions in the area. The earliest of these is, to be sure, very tentatively identified. It is based largely on the Canaima finds of the savanna country of the Venezuelan state of Bolívar and other scattered projectile-point finds in Venezuela and Guyana (see p. 59 and fn. 157). The Canaima points are of the triangular stemmed class that we have grouped, along with the Casitas complex points of Northwestern Venezuela, in the Andean Hunting–Collecting tradition.

The second tradition is one that we have already referred to in the foregoing chapter, the Northwest South American Littoral tradition. It is known from both the mainland and the islands of the Caribbean area, and it is, as we have already defined it, a lifeway based on fishing and collecting in a tropical shoreline environment.

Our third cultural tradition is the Caribbean—the cultural tradition that, in effect, defines our culture area. It is an agricultural tradition with a primary emphasis on manioc cultivation but with a secondary emphasis upon maize. The Caribbean cultural tradition shows a high level of competence in the ceramic arts, with a number of distinctive styles that helps define the tradition. Other neolithic level crafts, such as weaving and stone carving, reveal a similar development. Unlike the Intermediate area, metallurgy was not developed, and the few metals found in Caribbean tradition sites appear to be trade items from the west. Ceremonialism was less advanced than in the Intermediate area—at least insofar as we can measure this in archaeological remains and ceremonial-center sites. Most of the people sharing in the Caribbean cultural tradition were of Arawakan or Cariban speech.

Archaeological Chronology. The area chronology that we shall follow in this chapter is that developed by Rouse and Cruxent for Venezuela and by Rouse for the Antilles (Figs. 6-2, 6-3).[3]

(1) *Paleo-Indian Period (?–5000* B.C.*).* The Canaima complex is believed to date from the latter part of this period and the beginning of the next.

(2) *Meso-Indian Period or Period I (5000–1000* B.C.*).* The Northwest South American Littoral was the dominant tradition. Although known best from complexes that date toward the end of the period, it probably has beginnings in the mainland part of the area as early as 5000 B.C. The period closes with the introduction of pottery making and the realization of an agricultural economy. These events took place at about 1000 B.C. on the mainland; however they did not occur in the West Indies until the next period.

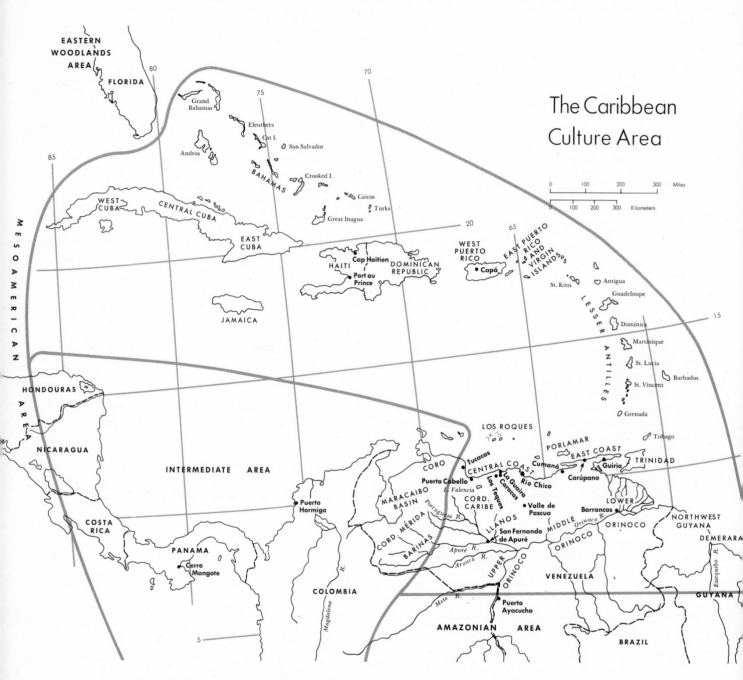

The Caribbean Culture Area

Figure 6-1. The area is shown in relation to other areas (the Intermediate, the Amazonian, the Mesoamerican, and the Eastern Woodland of North America). Archaeological subareas are indicated, together with the neighboring subareas of Northwestern Venezuela. Archaeological regions are designated, and as these frequently take their names from modern cities, they are placed on the map. Only a very few actual site locations are given, but sites discussed in the text can be placed approximately by subareal and regional reference.

(3) *Period II (1000 B.C.–A.D. 300)*. By the close of this period almost all parts of the area were agricultural and possessed pottery. The one major exception was the western end of Cuba, which remained non-agricultural and non-ceramic down to historic times. The Period is divided into

subperiods IIA (1000 B.C.–0) and IIB (0–A.D. 300).

(4) *Period III (A.D. 300–1000)*. This and the subsequent pre-Columbian period are defined largely on the basis of ceramic changes. It is divided into subperiods IIIA (A.D. 300–700) and IIIB (A.D. 700–1000).

(5) *Period IV (A.D. 1000–1500)*. This was the period of the florescence of the Caribbean cultural tradition.

(6) *Period V or Indo-Hispanic Period (A.D. 1500–present)*. This period saw the rapid extinction or drastic modification of the native cultures. These processes were most swift in the islands, less so in some mainland interior regions.

Some 20 archaeological subareas may be distinguished within the Caribbean area. For the most part, these have been defined by Rouse and Cruxent.[4] We will not review them here (see map, Fig. 6-1), but will refer to them in the course of the discussions.

Figure 6-2. Chronological chart, with subarea columns, phases, major periods, and estimated dates. Venezuela and Guyana. The small letters in the circles identify phases as to subtraditions: V, Valencioid; O, Ocumaroid; T, Tocuyanoid; S, Saladoid; G, Guayabitoid; B, Barrancoid; M, Memoid; A, Arauquinoid. It should be noted that the early Canaima phase or complex is not in the Middle Orinoco subarea proper but is near there, in the savannas of Bolívar.

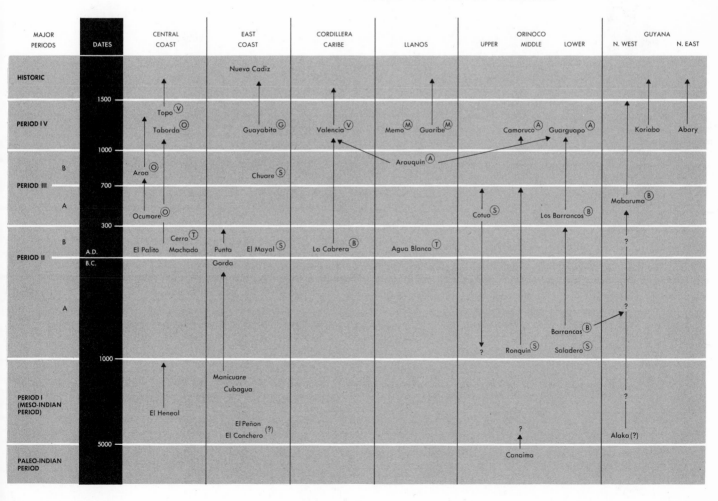

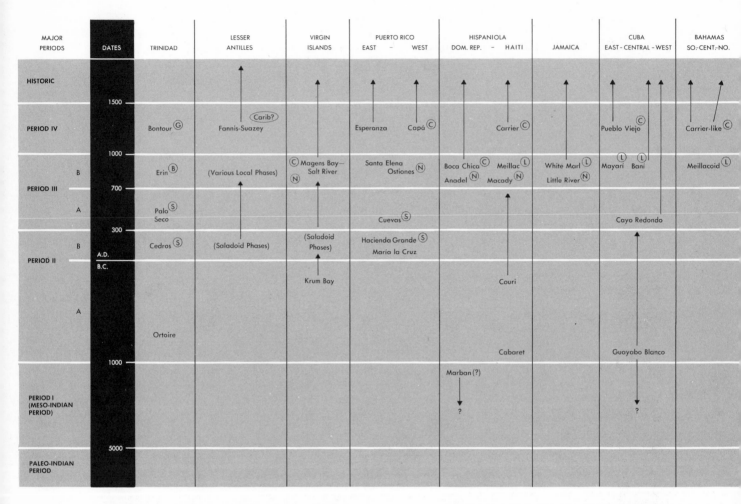

Figure 6-3. Chronological chart, with subarea columns, phases, major periods, and estimated dates. Trinidad and the West Indies. The small letters in the circles identify phases as to subtraditions: G, Guayabitoid; B, Barrancoid; S, Saladoid; C, Chicoid; N, Ostionoid; L, Meillacoid.

Northwest South American Littoral Tradition

Preliminary Comment and a Hypothesis. The following presentation of the Northwest South American Littoral tradition is guided by a hypothesis about its development and spread that can be stated very simply. It assumes that the earliest manifestations of the tradition are characterized by rough chipped-stone implements—cutting edges, scrapers, choppers—that were used for sundry purposes by early coastal dwellers: cutting and scraping fish, opening shellfish, processing plant foods, and making wooden implements. Later, ground stone utensils were added to this inventory of the amorphous chipped ones and, in time, came to replace them. Similarly, depending upon environmental circumstances, bone and shell were also utilized for artifacts. These technologies and simple tool types were taken from the Caribbean mainland shore out into the West Indies by the earliest inhabitants of those islands. The hypothesis assumes that the most likely route of their migration would have been from the mainland to Trinidad and from there, island by island, through the Lesser Antilles and on to the Greater Antilles. Admittedly, no evidences of these early preceramic cultures have yet been found in the Lesser Antilles. As one moves north and east, they first appear in the Virgin Islands and Puerto Rico. Nevertheless, there can be little doubt that the Lesser Antillean route was the one followed by most of the later agricultural and pottery-making Indians; and it is likely that it was also the route of the first Caribbean islanders. It is, of course, also possible, in view of some of the evidence that we will review, that there were additional preagricultural contacts between some of the Greater Antilles and mainland areas other than South America.

The order of review to be followed below is conditioned by the above hypothesis. We will begin by describing the simpler, less specialized artifact assemblages and go on from these to the more specialized ones. This is, it should be pointed out, a developmental reconstruction of a time order. We have little absolute or relative chronological information on the assemblages in question.

El Peñon and El Conchero. Both of these sites are in the Venezuelan East Coast subarea. El Peñon is a shell mound in the Cumaná region and El Conchero (El Conchal) is a similar site on the Paria Peninsula in the Güiria region.[5] Both sites show no artifacts other than stone chips and flakes, serviceable as cutters or scrapers of a simple sort. Although some of this debris could be wastage, these sites are not primarily workshops but, apparently, habitation places. The extent to which these may or may not be total cultural assemblages, fully representative of the tool kit of the former inhabitants, must remain as a doubt; however, it is probably significant that such assemblages are quite similar to those of Vegas and San Nicolás of the Ecuadorian and Colombian littoral zones (pp. 262–263).

No dating is available for either El Peñon or El Conchero. On typological grounds, however, I would anticipate that they date from early in the Meso-Indian Period.

Alaka and Ortoire. Along the mangrove shore of the Northwest Guyana subarea are numerous shell mounds—debris heaps composed of oyster, clam, and mussel shells, crab carapaces, fish and animal bones, ash, and fire-cracked stones. Some of these are no more than a few meters in diameter, perhaps the detritus from a single dwelling or camp; others are as much as 80 by 30 meters in extent and relatively deep. These mounds are the sites of what Evans and Meggers have dubbed the Alaka culture or phase.[6] The bottom levels of some of these middens reveal only chipped-stone artifacts—hammers, choppers, scrapers, and picks—in addition to a few rubbing stones. Above these are levels in which celts, mortars, pestles, handstones, and milling slabs have been added to the inventory. Perhaps, as Evans and Meggers speculate, cultivated food plants made their appearance at this time. A few potsherds then come into the sequence. Some of these are probably trade wares, but there is also the beginning of the manufacture of a local plain pottery. Finally, contacts with the west are seen in the appearance of Mabaruma (a Barrancoid style) trade sherds. But by this time, however, the Alaka culture is horticultural, ceramic making, and must be considered a part of the Caribbean cultural tradition.

The Ortoire phase has been defined from the Ortoire and St. John sites on Trinidad.[7] Like Alaka, El Peñon, and El Conchero, it features a chipped-stone component of crude tools; and, like the later Alaka levels, it has stone grinders and milling slabs. In addition, there are notched stone net sinkers, a stone paint mortar, and bone points and bone barbs.

Ortoire has a radiocarbon date of about 800 B.C. No radiocarbon dates are available for Alaka, but I would suspect that its earliest levels are older than this, although its later pottery levels may be more recent than 800 B.C. Evans and Meggers give no firm estimate for Alaka beginnings but place its termination at about A.D. 500 on the basis of an equation with Mabaruma.

Ortoire and Alaka—and especially the stratification within Alaka—are, I think, important in our understanding of the development within the Northwest South American Littoral tradition within the Caribbean area. They reveal the modification of the earlier rough chipped-stone complexes, such as we see in El Peñon and El Conchero, by the addition of the grinding stones and a few other implements. In the case of Alaka, development goes on beyond this point into the agricultural-pottery condition.

El Heneal. A phase known as El Heneal is represented by sites in the Venezuelan Central and East Coast subareas. El Heneal and Cerro Iguanas, of the Tucacas region, are the best known of these shell-mound sites.[8] The distinctive artifact type of the phase is a pebble edge-grinder, a fist-size boulder or pebble on which a narrow edge, rather than a larger flat surface, has been used for grinding or chopping. The implement is, in fact, identical to the edge-grinders associated with the Northwest South American Littoral tradition in Panama—as seen in both the Cerro Mangote and Monagrillo cultures (pp. 263 and 271). Hammer-stones and anvil stones were also found at the El Heneal site and crude celts and a bone pin at Cerro Iguanas. The stone flake tools of Alaka or Ortoire, however, are lacking.

There is an El Heneal radiocarbon date of 1550 B.C. and three Cerro Iguanas dates in the range of 3800 to 3400 B.C. All fall in our Period I, or Meso-Indian Period. These dates suggest that the rough stone flake aspect of the tradition drops out earlier in the west than in the east. In line with this, we may recall the Cerro Mangote date of about 4850 B.C. Cerro Mangote had some chipped flints, but the edge-grinders were the principal implement.

The Manicuare Phase. Another Northwest South American Littoral tradition culture phase is the Manicuare.[9] The site of Manicuare is on the Peninsula of Araya in the Cumaná region of the East Coast subarea. Another site of the phase is Punta Gorda, on Cubagua Island, in the Margarita group of islands off the Venezuelan coast (Porlamar subarea). Still a third site is in the Carúpano region. The phase can be broken down into three chronological subphases. The earliest of these, the Cubagua, is placed in Period I (with a radiocarbon date of 2325 B.C.); the next is Mani-cuare, in Period I and IIA (with radiocarbon dates of 1730 and 1190 B.C.; and the last is the Punta Gorda subphase dated to Period IIB through trade sherd associations. During the two earlier subphases the sea level off the Venezuelan coast was somewhat lower than it is today—a finding that would be consistent with old shoreline associations of Northwest South American Littoral tradi-

tion sites of the Intermediate area. In the Cubagua subphase we have bi-pointed stones (perhaps used in slings), flat milling stones, and hammers and cups made from conch shells. In the Manicuare subphase the shell gouge, a rather specialized wood-working tool made from the wall of a conch, is the important addition; and shell was also used for making beads and pendants. In Punta Gorda there are the further additions of shell projectile points and shell celts. By this time, however, pottery-making and farming cultures of other parts of Venezuela were in existence, and a few pottery specimens are present in these Punta Gorda sites. Interestingly, these fragments come from water bottles—a desirable item to the Manicuare peoples—and not manioc griddles, for which, presumably, these beach dwellers had no use.

The whole cast of the Manicuare culture is that of one adapted to the sea. Its peoples were fishers and shellfishers; their use of canoes is implied in their exploitation of the offshore islands; and that they could have manufactured canoes finds support in the presence of the shell gouges. I would assume that the Manicuare culture succeeded the El Peñon–El Conchero culture in the Venezuelan East Coast subarea and that it represents a subtraditional specialization in the direction of a more itensified marine dependence. Quite probably it was contemporaneous with El Heneal, which lay to the west of it, but through subsistence adaptations (harpooning of fish, canoe travel) and environmental resources (use of conch shells for dishes and heavy tools) it had moved in a different direction of development within the general framework of the Northwest South American Littoral tradition.

Krum Bay and Puerto Rico. A midden at Krum Bay, on St. Thomas, in the Virgin Islands, is one of the most thoroughly and carefully explored preceramic stations in the West Indies. The site had been known for some years from earlier excavations;[10] recently, R. P. Bullen and F. W. Sleight have carried out intensive work there.[11] It is a shell midden on a protected bay on the south side of the island. Cultural refuse averages a little less than 50 centimeters in depth and, in addition to shells, contains fish and turtle bones, burned rocks, and stone chips, fragments, and dust. It had presumably been a living and shellfish collecting location as well as a workshop for making stone artifacts.

The Krum Bay artifacts are made of igneous rocks, basalt, gabbro, and diorite. The most distinctive tools are designated as "large blades," "blade-like" tools, and "celts." All of these were made by bifacial chipping; subsequently, however, they were pecked and ground to varying degrees. The "large blades" and "bladelike" tools appear to be, on stratigraphic grounds, the earliest forms. Most of them are of axlike or celtlike outline—long, proportionately narrow, and with a relatively narrow or pointed end and a broader butt end. In fact, the "large blades" really appear to be a type of celt or adze. Some of the "bladelike" tools also have this celt form; others, however, are asymmetrical, and the long sides may have been used for cutting. The "celts," which occur higher up in the Krum Bay refuse, are quite narrow, thick in cross section, and show considerably more grinding

Figure 6-4. Couri large flint knives made from prismatic flakes. *Left*: About 9 cm. long. (Redrawn from Rouse, 1941.)

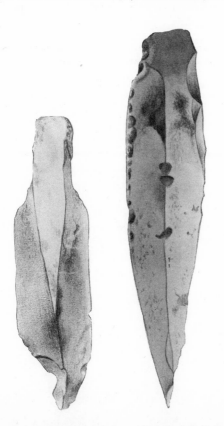

of the chipped surfaces than do the earlier "large blades." It should be noted that all of these forms are large, ranging from 20 to almost 30 centimeters in length; and they would have served well as heavy-duty axes and adzes in the manufacture of canoes or in other woodworking. The remainder of the Krum Bay tools are not particularly distinctive: hammerstones of the elongated battered-pebble variety, disc-shaped hammerstones with pitted flat sides, utilized flakes of the Ortoire-Alaka sort, and a few bone pin or awl fragments.

In line with the hypothesis offered here, I would see Krum Bay as fully consistent with the developmental trends of the Northwest South American Littoral tradition, with the "large blades" and celts paralleling the appearances of the celts in the latter part of the Alaka phase. Two radiocarbon dates from Krum Bay, of 225 and 450 B.C., fall easily into this interpretation.

In Puerto Rico, a preceramic complex known as the María de la Cruz has hammerstones and used flakes similar to those of Krum Bay; however, it lacks the "large blades" and celt forms of that site. Instead, the characteristic María de la Cruz artifacts are the pebble edge-grinders and edge-choppers like those of El Heneal. The radiocarbon dates on this complex are in the first century A.D.[12]

The Couri Cultures. The Couri phase of northern Haiti differs from all of the other West Indian or mainland Northwest South American Littoral tradition cultures that we have discussed so far. Diagnostic artifacts are lamellar flakes fashioned as knives and daggers with a distinctive unifacial retouching (Fig. 6-4). These flints are accompanied by ground stone dishes, double-bitted axes (Fig. 6-5, *a*), peg-shaped pendants (Fig. 6-5, *b*), shell pendants (Fig. 6-5, *c*), and stone mortars and pestles. The less specialized hammerstones and miscellaneous crude implements that we have been listing for other preceramic phases are also a part of Couri; however, it is the first-mentioned artifacts that distinguish the culture.[13] A similar complex, the Cabaret, is reported from near Port-au-Prince,[14] and on the Dominican side of the island the Marban complex can be added to the same Couri series.

The Couri unifacially chipped knives and daggers are of unusual interest. In searching for simi-

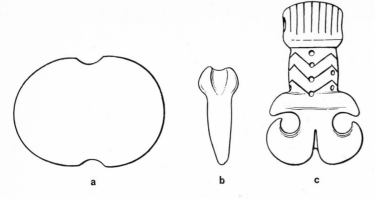

Figure 6-5. Couri ground stone and shell artifacts. *a:* Double-bitted stone ax. *b:* Stone peg. *c:* Carved shell pendant. Height of *a*, about 9 cm.; height of *b*, about same; height of *c*, about 7 cm. (Redrawn from Rouse, 1941.)

larities we find the closest ones in Central America. Comparable implements occur in both Maya Highlands and Lowlands, where they date to the Preclassic Period (ca. 2000 B.C.–0).[15] They also come from farther south, in Panama,[16] so they can be said to have an association with the general territory of the Northwest South American Littoral tradition. Bullen suggests that they, and perhaps the edge-grinders of Puerto Rico, were carried into the Antilles directly from Central America.[17]

The only one of these Couri complexes that has a radiocarbon date is Marban. This date is the earliest from the West Indies—2190 B.C. If accepted, it indicates an occupation of the islands a thousand years or so earlier than previously had been supposed.[18] I belive this single date should be viewed with caution. Certainly, the relative elaboration of the Couri cultures is somewhat inconsistent with it.

Cayo Redondo and Guayabo Blanco. These two preceramic or non-ceramic cultures of Cuba are distinguished by shell implements.[19] In Guayabo Blanco, which may be the earlier of the two, these are shell vessels made from conchs; in Cayo Redondo they include gouges (Fig. 6-6), celts, and cups. Roughly ground stone tools are shared by both, and Cayo Redondo has peg-shaped stone pendants like those of Haitian Couri.

It is unknown how early these complexes may date. A radiocarbon date is available for Cayo Redondo, and this falls in the tenth century A.D.; however this is not surprising as we know from historic Spanish sources that cultures of a Cayo Redondo type continued in far western Cuba until the sixteenth century. This part of the West Indies never became agricultural, and pottery was unknown here. The Spanish referred to these non-farming Indians as "wild men" and "cave dwellers"—the Ciboneys.

Oddly, the closest parallels to Cayo Redondo and Guayabo Blanco are to be seen in the Venezuelan coastal Manicuaroid cultures.

Recapitulation. We have argued for the division of the Northwest South American Littoral tradition into at least two main stages of development. The earliest of these stages is believed to have been characterized by roughly chipped stone tools, as we see in the El Peñon, El Conchero, and early Alaka complexes. The absolute dating of such a stage is largely a guess, but I would estimate its beginnings at 5000 B.C. In some places, in both the Intermediate area and in the Caribbean area, the tradition may have been modified soon after this; in others such a technology was retained for a longer time. During this earlier stage all of the Northwest South American Littoral tradition populations were on the South American or Central American mainland.

Figure 6-6. Shell gouge of Ciboney culture, eastern Cuba. (Courtesy Museum of the American Indian, Heye Foundation.)

The subsequent stage is marked by the appearance of various grinding stones, pounding stones, or ground stone artifacts. In it we can group all of the other complexes that we have discussed. The chronological range is from at least 3500 B.C. to 1000 B.C. on the South American mainland; in parts of the West Indies the stage lasted much later. It was during this stage that peoples first moved from South America into the West Indies.

Admittedly, there are weaknesses in this hypothesis. For one thing, no preceramic sites have yet been found in the Lesser Antilles, the presumed "stepping-stones" in the postulated migration from the South American mainland out to the larger islands of the Caribbean. For another, there is the lack of any consistent geographical pattern in the distribution of the more diagnostic artifact forms. While such simple things as hammerstones are found in almost all the phases, the more specialized edge-grinder is reported only from El Heneal and Puerto Rico. Stone celts or axes are known from the middle Alaka levels, the Virgin Islands, and the Couri cultures of Hispaniola, but not elsewhere. Shell gouges and other implements made from conch shells belong to the Manicuare and Cayo Redondo phases, but are not shared by the others. This lack of pattern would support Rouse in his belief that the earliest inhabitants of the West Indies came haphazardly from several different mainland areas as boats and rafts were accidentally carried from these shores and brought by currents and winds to one or another of the islands.[20] In this hypothesis, South American, Central American, and North American points of departure are all possible. Thus the shell gouges of Cuban Cayo Redondo might be explained either by drifting voyagers from Venezuelan Manicuare or by Archaic Period peoples from Florida.[21]

Yet, despite all the objections, I prefer the hypothesis of a single main line of development for the Northwest South American Littoral tradition cultures of the Caribbean area, both mainland and island. The Lesser Antilles were the principal route of migration from the mainland to the West Indies in later times, and considerations of geography strongly favor them for the earlier route as well. The randomness of artifact distributions could be due to environmental setting, such as the littoral site ecology of both Manicuare and Cayo Redondo, where large conch shells were more plentiful and suitable for the fashioning of cutting implements than was stone. Of course there may be exceptions. The Couri flintwork stands out strangely not only in the West Indies but in the whole Caribbean area, and this particular trait may be the result of a direct contact between Central America and Hispaniola.[22]

An Ethnographic Sketch of the Caribbean Area

At this point, before going on with the later cultures of the agricultural Caribbean cultural tradition, let us break into our archaeological presentation with a brief ethnographic outline of the area as it was known in early historic times and later (map, Fig. 6-7; see also Fig. 1-5). This will give us some background against which to view the archaeological data.

First, we can begin by noting the historic presence of several tribes who are reported as living on a hunting-fishing-gathering level and who might, at least in the sense of basic subsistence, be considered as maintaining the Northwest South American Littoral tradition way of life—which we have just viewed archaeologically—into the sixteenth century and later. In describing the Cayo Redondo–Guayabo Blanco cultures of the West Cuban subarea, we mentioned the Ciboney, the historic period non-agricultural peoples of this part of the West Indies. A culturally related group was also known from the southwestern tip of Hispaniola. Little is known of either of these peoples, and their language is unidentified.[23]

Other non-agricultural tribes were found on the Venezuelan and Guyana mainland in the sixteenth century. They may have been descendants of old hunting-fishing peoples who had never changed over to agriculture; or, possibly, they descended from former farmers who for one reason or another had given up or modified their mode of subsistence. Among these were the Guahibo and Chiricoa of the Upper Orinoco—essentially grassland hunters and gatherers.[24] The Guahibo made pottery, apparently in imitation of some of their agricultural neighbors. Their language, Guahiban, is distinct from either Arawakan or Cariban.

North and east of the Guahibo were several tribes who depended on river game and fishing

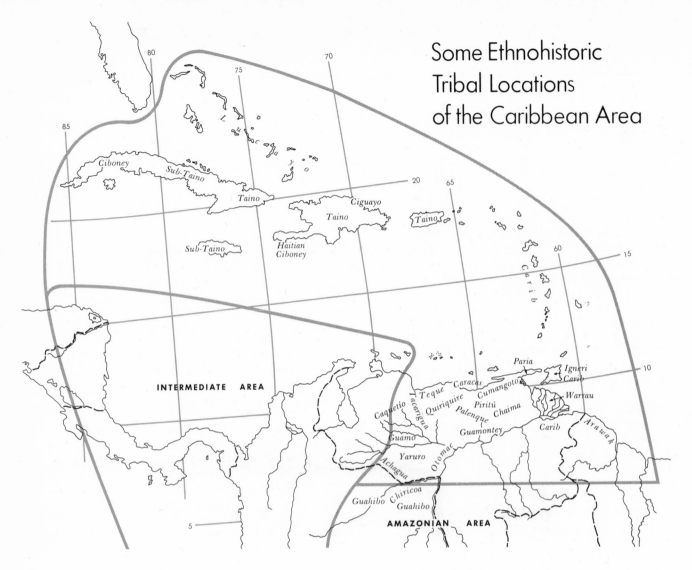

Some Ethnohistoric Tribal Locations of the Caribbean Area

Figure 6-7.

rather than land hunting. Among these were the Yaruro, Guamontey,[25] and Warrau.[26] These tribes also cultivated manioc on a small scale, probably as the result of Arawak influence.[27] By historic times all were making pottery. All spoke independent languages.

On the agricultural level—that of the Caribbean cultural tradition to which we will turn next in our archaeological account—a number of Cariban-speaking tribes held central Venezuela between the coast and the Orinoco River: the Tacarigua, Teque, Caracas, Piritú, Cumangoto, and Paria.[28] One important Arawak village, Araucay, was located near the distributary point of the Orinoco River;[29] and there were both

Arawaks and Caribs on the island of Trinidad and in northern Guyana. Bitter manioc was the staple food of these people, but sweet manioc, sweet potatoes, chilis, and fruits were also raised. Cultivation was by slash-and-burn system, occasionally supplemented with small-scale irrigation. Hunting, fishing, and plant collecting were also of some importance in the economy. Villages are described as being fortified with wooden palisades. Small states were ruled over by paramount chiefs. These rulers were carried about on litters, had harems, and possessed treasures of gold.[30] Such descriptions would probably apply to the Period IV archaeological cultures of this part of Venezuela—especially to the Valencia phase (see below).

The Arawakan Achagua lived in the Venezuelan Llanos subarea, together with neighbors of a similar culture.[31] They too had palisaded villages, with the palisades surrounding large communal houses. Two other Llanos tribes deserve special mention: the Otomac and Guamo. They were linguistically distinct from the Achagua, nor did they speak Carib. They had many Mesoamerican-like traits.[32] Maize was more important to them than manioc, and they made it into bread as well as beer. But most striking of all was the trait of a ball game, played with a rubber ball on a prepared court by two teams. Such a game is met with, again, in some of the West Indies, but the Otomac occurrence is the only geographically intermediate instance of the game betwen Mesoamerica and the Greater Antilles.

A number of early accounts give a fairly detailed picture of aboriginal life in the West Indies in the early sixteenth century.[33] The main population of the islands was Arawakan: Igneri (Lesser Antilles and Trinidad), Taino and Ciguayo (Puerto Rico, Hispaniola, and eastern Cuba), Sub-Taino (central Cuba and Jamaica), and Lucayo (Turks, Caicos, and Bahamas). In the Lesser Antilles, however, the Caribs were in process of overruning the Arawak at the time of Columbus's voyages.

Puerto Rico and Hispaniola (Dominican Republic and Haiti) were the centers of elaboration of the Caribbean tradition in the West Indies. Taino agriculture was highly productive. Cultivation was by slash-and-burn techniques for the most part, although there is one early mention of ditch irrigation in Haiti.[34] Bitter manioc was the most important crop. There were six varieties of it, and it was grated, squeezed, and baked into bread on pottery griddles. The sweet potato (*Ipomoea batatas*) was second in importance and maize third. The latter was not made into bread but eaten green or parched. Other domesticates were peppers, beans, peanuts, pineapples, tobacco (*Nicotiana tabacum*), gourds, and cotton (*Gossypium hirsutum*).

Taino villages or towns had as many as a thousand houses and populations up to 5000 persons. Houses were made of poles, cane, and thatch and were grouped around central plazas, which were also used as courts for the ball game. This apparently was the same general kind of ball game played by the Otomac of the mainland. Town or village chiefs owed allegiance to paramount chiefs in Taino government. On Hispaniola, for example, there were five such territorial paramount chiefs. Such individuals were accorded great homage. They and their immediate retainers made up an aristocracy that dominated commoner and slave classes.

Taino religion was animistic and based upon ghosts of the departed dead or upon the spirits of natural phenomena. These were controlled by the manufacture of zemis, or idols, which became residences of the spirits, and each household had at least one such zemi. The idols were usually carved of wood or stone in the form of grotesque men or women with emphasized sexual organs. Some were simply represented as three-pointed stones, an object frequently found archaeologically. The zemis of the chief had special powers and were worshipped in a temple on the outskirts of the town, where they were propitiated with food offerings, songs, dances, and self-induced vomiting.

The Taino were first-rate potters and carvers of stone and wood. We shall see samples of their products in the archaeological record of what will be called the Chicoid subtradition.

The other Arawaks had cultures that were less intensified versions of the Taino—populations were smaller, political domains less firmly organized, ceremonialism abated. For instance, the ball court has not been found in Trinidad, the Lesser Antilles, Cuba, Jamaica, or the Bahamas.[35]

The Caribs of the Lesser Antilles were also farmers, although they may have depended somewhat more on fishing than the Arawak. Carib men are said to have lived in a special men's house apart from the dwellings of the women, and it is reported that they spoke a different language from their wives. It has been surmised that this last peculiar fact results from the relatively late pre-Columbian conquest of the Lesser Antilles by the Carib men who had then married with Arawak women. Carib villages were small by Taino standards, and, except for war, the villagers were not organized into larger political units. The Carib were noted as fierce warriors and cannibals who devoured their defeated dead.[36]

The West Indian peoples wilted rapidly under the hands of the Europeans. It was in the Bahamas that Columbus had his first landfall, and on his second voyage he explored all of the major islands, establishing a permanent settlement in the northern part of what is now the Dominican Republic side of the Island of Hispaniola. Tributes in gold were exacted from the leading chiefs for a time, but this scarce source of revenue was soon exhausted. In 1502 the repartimiento system was established whereby Indians were indentured to Spanish plantation and mine owners. By 1535 most of the Indians on Hispaniola were dead, and Puerto Rico and Jamaica suffered a similar fate soon after. Some Carib continued in the Lesser Antilles until the mid-eighteenth century; on the larger island of Cuba the Indians survived the repartimiento in greater numbers than in Hispaniola, and a few of them maintained an ethnic identity down to the nineteenth century.[37]

The Caribbean Cultural Tradition in Venezuela and Guyana

In our review of the Northwest South American Littoral tradition we saw occasional signs of contact with pottery-using, agricultural peoples in the later cultural phases. The agricultural pattern of the Caribbean area, which we are calling the Caribbean cultural tradition, was the source responsible. Presumably, it had its centers of origin in the interior of Venezuela along the Orinoco and its tributaries. In the previous chapter we have suggested that manioc farming possibly began in these regions. Ceramics, on the other hand, probably diffused to the Orinoco from the Intermediate area. But whatever the nature of and sources for the synthesis that produced the Caribbean cultural tradition, the plenitude of manioc pottery griddles—or budares—in the village middens points unmistakably to manioc cultivation as a major source of livelihood by the beginning of the first millennium B.C. or the Period II of our area chronology.

The earliest of these Period II sites of the Caribbean cultural tradition are known from the Lower Orinoco subarea. They manifest two quite distinct ceramic and cultural subtraditions: the "Saladoid" and the "Barrancoid."[38]

The Saladoid Subtradition. The Saladoid would seem to be the earlier of these two basic subtraditions; at least it is the earlier in the Lower Orinoco subarea. The Saladero site is one of several in the Barrancas site zone—at the main distributary junction of the Orinoco River.[39] Here Saladero refuse was found underlying that of the Barrancas phase. The site, essentially like all others of either the Saladoid or Barrancoid subtraditions, was composed of living debris—organic matter, fish bones, a little flint scrap, numerous potsherds and griddle fragments, and a few other simple bone or ground stone tools or ornaments. There were neither architectural or artifactual remains that could be readily interpreted as having special ceremonial or socio-political significance. The dead were buried near the village area with little or no grave furniture.

Saladero pottery is a thin, finely made, grit tempered ware. Sometimes it is decorated with red painted designs over the natural ground color of the vessel; sometimes it has been red slipped and decorated in white pigments. A flat-based, bell-flared bowl is the diagnostic vessel form, and strap handles, sometimes noded, are the only appendages.

The radiocarbon dates on Saladero indicate a placement in the earlier part of Period IIA—that is, between 1000 and 700 B.C. There are no obvious prototypes in the Intermediate area or anywhere else in South America. Perhaps the Saladero style arose through stimulus diffusion contact with early potters of the Intermediate area—a not altogether satisfactory hypothesis, but the best that we can frame with the information now available.

Although Saladoid origins are obscure, the later history of this ceramic style series—and cultural subtradition—is better known. In the Lower Orinoco subarea it is replaced by the Barrancas style of the Barrancoid subtradition and at about the same time, the Ronquín phase of the Middle Orinoco[40] undergoes strong Barrancoid modification. At its inception Ronquín was much like Saladero (Fig. 6-8), but in its life-span it displays an increasing trend away from Saladero shape and decorative norms toward those of the Barrancoid subtradition. White-on-red decorative techniques are, for example, replaced by those of modeling and incision.[41] This process of Barrancoid modification is also seen in other Saladoid phases: the Cotua of the Upper Orinoco and the El Mayal, Irapa, Chuare, and El Agua of the East Coast and Porlamar subareas.[42] All date from Periods

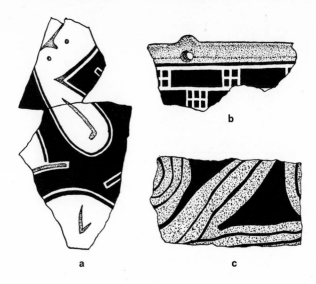

Figure 6-8. Ronquín-style (Saladoid subtradition) pottery. *a, b*: Red-and-white on natural color of ware; *c*: Red on natural color of ware. (After Howard, 1943.)

IIB and III. In passing, we should note that it was from such Saladoid phases as the Mayal that the Saladoid subtradition must have been carried to Trinidad and on to the West Indies in these same periods, and that all of the West Indian Saladoid phases show the beginnings of this Barrancoid influence.

The Barrancas replacement of the Saladero phase in the Lower Orinoco subarea and the "Barrancoidization" of the Saladero styles in other subareas has prompted Rouse and Cruxent to see a significant population change throughout much of eastern Venezuela in Period II times. Apparently, Saladerans were driven out or subjugated by Barrancans.

The Barrancoid Subtradition. We have already suggested in Chapter 5 (p. 280) that the remote origins of the Barrancoid subtradition were western, deriving from the Valdivia–Puerto Hormiga–Barlovento ceramic tradition in the lowlands of northern Colombia;[43] but a more geographically immediate Venezuelan center of distribution remains to be found. Rouse and Cruxent think that such a center may have been in the Llanos subarea and further postulate that the Barrancas style and its carriers spread from there in two directions: eastward down the Orinoco and northward via the Rio Portuguesa to the Valencia Basin and the Venezuelan Central Coast.[44] This would account for the geographical distribution of the Barrancoid styles into their eastern and western groupings; however, to date, no Barrancoid style has been reported from the hypothesized center in the Llanos of Apure.

The Barrancas phase proper, of the Lower Orinoco, is probably the earliest known manifestation of the Barrancoid stylistic series.[45] Barrancas pottery is thicker and coarser than Saladero ware; however it is often smoothed to a polish and decorated by incision and modeling. Designs tend to be curvilinear. Incisions are used to outline and adorn modeled figures; the figures may be human faces done in low relief on vessel walls or human or animal lugs attached to vessel rims. The most common Barrancas vessel is a bowl with a low, solid annular base, vertical sides, and a flanged rim. There are also double-spout jars with bridge handles. These remind one of the double-spout jars of the Colombian Regional Developmental cultures; however, in a Barrancoid fashion, the spouts are heavily modeled to represent human or animal figures. Some increments of the Saladero style, such as white-and-red painting and strap-handles, are also found in Barrancas—apparently the result of cross influence between the two styles.

The Los Barrancos style (Fig. 6-9), which succeeds the Barrancas in the Lower Orinoco subarea, is the classic manifestation of the Barrancoid ceramic series. Saladero holdover traits are gone by this time. The ware is more finely polished than previously, and incised designs have a closer spacing of the lines and are more often combined with terminal punctations than in Barrancas. Los Barrancos adorno modeling shows more variation; annular bases are less common, and double-spout jars have disappeared. The complete rim flange of Barrancas is no longer so typical but has been replaced by flangelike lugs that are usually incised. Nevertheless, in spite of all of these minor differences, Los Barrancos and Barrancas are very much alike and are readily distinguished only by the expert. The Barrancoid series thus displays a remarkable conservatism, for while the Barrancas phase was dated at 700 B.C. to A.D. 300, the Los Barrancos persists through Period III, or until A.D. 1000.

Other Barrancoid phases of the eastern group are Mabaruma,[46] of the Northwest Guyana subarea, and Erin,[47] of the island of Trinidad. Both are remarkably close to the Barrancas–Los Bar-

Figure 6-9. *Above:* Los Barrancos style incised monkey head adorno and vessel rim flange. Such adornos range from about 4 to 7 cm. in height. (Redrawn from Osgood and Howard, 1943.)

Figure 6-10. *Right:* Mabaruma adornos, sherds, and vessel. Height of *a*, about 5.5 cm.; diameter of vessel, about 16 cm. (After Evans and Meggers, 1960.)

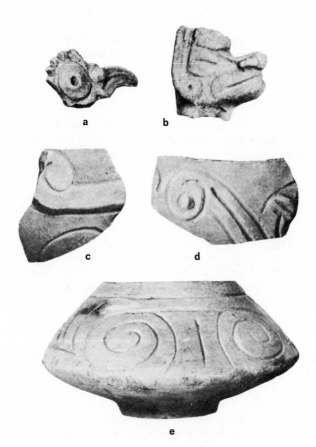

rancos continuum as seen in the Lower Orinoco subarea. Rouse has dated Erin to Period IIIB, or an equivalence with Los Barrancos.[48] Mabaruma is also contemporaneous with this; however, the beginnings of Mabaruma may date back as early as Barrancas and Period II,[49] and the latter part of the phase appears to go on through Period IV.

Barrancoid phases of the western group include La Cabrera (Lake Valencia region, Cordillera del Caribe subarea), El Palito, and Taborda (both of Puerto Cabello region, Central Coast subarea). Of these, La Cabrera is the best known, being documented from the stratigraphic digging of Kidder II.[50] Two cultural levels were clearly defined in this digging, an earlier Barrancoid La Cabrera and a later Valencia phase. La Cabrera ceramics (Fig. 6-11) include the double-spout jars that we have described for the Lower Orinoco Barrancas phase, thus arguing for an early equation in the Barrancoid series; however, there are also incised designs and modeled and incised adornos that correlate with the later Los Barrancos phase. Western ceramic influences are seen in leg-ring bases, perforated annular bases, and rod handles. La Cabrera burials were primary and had little in the way of grave goods with them. Artifacts of the phase other than pottery included polished stone celts, stone pendants, bone and shell beads, clay earplugs, and clay pipes of an oblique angle elbow form. Some La Cabrera houses may have been constructed on piles while others were on low earth platforms. Thus Kidder reports that pottery refuse of the phase was found in the lower levels of such platforms on the east side of Lake Valencia;[51] however, most of the platform mounds around the edges of Lake Valencia appear to pertain to the Period IV Valencia phase occupation of the site.

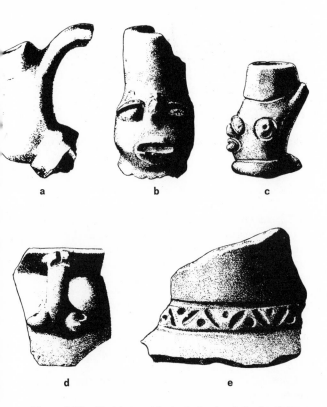

Figure 6-11. Modeled and incised sherds of the La Cabrera phase, Barrancoid subtradition. *a–c* **are spouts. (After Kidder II, 1944.)**

El Palito, of the Central Coast, is ceramically very much like La Cabrera, and radiocarbon dates of A.D. 260 and 290 for this phase help date the Barrancoid spread north to this coastal subarea.[52]

The Ocumaroid Subtradition. The Ocumaroid subtradition is centered in the Venezuelan Central Coast subarea, and its origins would seem to lie in a fusion of the Northwest Venezuelan Tocuyanoid series cultures with those of the Barrancoid subtradition. The earliest Ocumaroid phases are the Ocumare proper, of the Puerto Cabello region, and the Boca Tacagua of the La Guaira region.[53] Both date to Period III. The Aroa and Palmasola phases continue the subtradition into Period IV.

The Ocumaroid sites are simple shell middens and other refuse accumulations. Pottery manioc griddles, common to all of them, establish this kind of agricultural subsistence; and the dominant western strain in the other ceramics at least suggests that maize agriculture had also been introduced. Ocumare ceramics feature two-color and three-color painting: red-on-white, black-on-white, and red-and-black-on-white. They also show such Northwest Venezuelan Tocuyanoid traits as perforated annular bases and tripod legs. Fused together with these are eastern pottery elements—modeled and incised rim flanges and modeled adornos—almost certainly borrowings from the Barrancoid cultures.[54]

Recapitulation for Periods II and III. The three subtraditions—Saladoid, Barrancoid, and Ocumaroid—subsume almost all that we know about the development of the Caribbean cultural tradition during Periods II and III. The first two have their hearths in the east, along the Orinoco River and, perhaps, in the Llanos. Their remote origins, at least as far as ceramics go, are probably to be derived from the Intermediate area although at a time prior to the first millennium B.C. Both are grounded in a manioc farming economy. The third subtradition, the Ocumaroid, derives from Northwest Venezuela, via a Tocuyanoid line of development, at a much later time. Its growth, however, was clearly influenced by the Barrancoid tradition.

These three subtraditions—Saladoid, Barrancoid, and Ocumaroid—gave rise to a number of new subtraditions in Period IV, and it is to these that we turn now.

The Guayabitoid Subtradition. This ceramic series or subtradition is a Period IV derivation from the antecedent Saladoid subtradition cultures.[55] Sites classified as Guayabitoid are located in the East Coast subarea. Those of the Guayabita style proper are in the Güiria region, and those of the related El Morro style are in the Carúpano region. The Period IV Bontour phase from the nearby island of Trinidad is also included in the subtradition.

Guayabitoid sites are thin shell middens near the shore, containing sherds, clay griddle fragments, polished stone celts, and a few other stone or shell artifacts. The pottery consists largely of collared olla forms. Decoration is skimpy—by incision and appliqué features and a few effigy lugs. The interpretation of Guayabitoid derivations from the earlier Saladoid styles is supported by stratigraphy and seriation in the East Coast sub-area where the Saladoid Irapa and Chuare phases underlie Guayabita and El Morro. The radiocarbon dates for the Guayabitoid cultures range from A.D. 1210 to 1650.

The Arauquinoid Subtradition. The Arauquinoid cultures developed primarily from the Barrancoid subtradition.[56] They are found along the Orinoco, including Camoruco on the Middle Orinoco and Guarguapo on the Lower Orinoco, and in the Llanos, including Arauquín proper and Matraquero. They date essentially as Period IV, although Arauquín proper may have Period IIIB beginnings.

Arauquinoid pottery is tempered with freshwater sponge spicules that give it a characteristic gray color and softish feel. The Barrancoid ancestry is revealed in incised designs (often on the interior of the beveled rim of a bowl) and in modeled lugs. The strongest Barrancoid similarities are seen in the collections from the Arauquín site, and in the San Fernando de Apure region of the Llanos.[57] It is for this reason that it has been suggested that Arauquín proper had somewhat earlier beginnings than the other phases; hence, the San Fernando region may have been the origin point for the style. There are also some western traits in Arauquinoid, such as modeled human faces on jar collars and pottery cylinder stamps, both being traits that suggest northern Colombia. In general, the incised decoration of the Arauquinoid styles (Fig. 6-12) is quite distinct from that of the Barrancoid styles. The incised lines are sharply cut rather than rounded; portions of the decoration are actually cut out of the vessel surface; and designs are rectilinear bands of running zigzags or triangles confined between lines. Clay griddles, pot rests, clay spindle whorls, stone celts, and stone metates and manos are other Arauquinoid traits.

Sites in the San Fernando region have mounds, or *calzadas*. These are generally thought to be earth platforms that were raised for living areas in lands seasonally flooded or, perhaps, raised as agricultural plots.[58] Many are quite large, extending for several kilometers in length, being as much

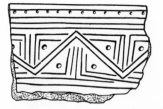

Figure 6-12. Arauquinoid incised sherds. (Redrawn from Howard, 1947.)

as 25 meters in width, and standing 1 to 3 meters in height. Such calzadas are found throughout the Llanos of the States of Barinas, Portuguesa, and Apure,[59] and not all of them can be associated with the Arauquinoid cultures;[60] however, some do appear to be so associated. On the Middle Orinoco there is an artificial mound associated with the Camoruco phase;[61] its function is uncertain, but it may be comparable to those of the Llanos. No such mounds occur in the Lower Orinoco Guarguapo phase.

Camoruco deposits overlie those of the earlier Saladoid Ronquín phase and Guarguapo materials are found above those of the earlier Barrancoid Los Barrancos phase. The suggestion is made by Rouse and Cruxent that the Arauquinoid styles were carried from the Llanos to the Middle Orinoco, where the Camoruco phase settlement was established.[62] From here, their further spread down river by diffusion influenced the Los Barrancos pottery makers, and this resulted in the Guarguapo phase.

The Memoid Subtradition. The Memoid subtradition has Northwest Venezuelan antecedents, probably in the Tocuyanoid line. We have seen that one branch of this Tocuyanoid expansion went to the Central Coast subarea, where it is known as the Cerro Machado phase and where it gave rise to the subsequent phases of the Ocumaroid subtradition. Another branch can be traced to a Period IIB phase of the Llanos subarea known as the Agua Blanca. Agua Blanca was probably the forerunner of the Memoid styles.

The principal Memoid phases are the Memo and Guaribe of the Valle de Pascua region of the Llanos subarea.[63] They date to Periods IV and V.

The ceramics show some painting that is similar to Ocumaroid pottery—in this case, red-on-white geometric design arrangements—and some appliqué ridges and dots that are reminiscent of the Period IV Dabajuro culture of Northwestern Venezuela. Although the ceramic decorative features of Memoid are western, the agricultural pattern would appear to be eastern: manioc griddles are common on the sites.

The Valencioid Subtradition. The Valencia culture is the best-known archaeological complex in Venezuela. The little pottery figurines with the broad, flat, triangular ("canoe-shaped") heads—typical of the Valencia phase (Fig. 6-13) —are indeed the pre-Columbian hallmark of the country. The Valencia phase is known mainly from a number of mound sites at the eastern end of Lake Valencia, Cordillera del Caribe subarea.[64] Bennett and Osgood dug two of these, one at La Mata and one at Tocorón.[65] Apparently, pole-and-thatch dwellings had been placed on artificial earth mounds to raise them above the marshy lakeshore edges. These mounds were also used for burial purposes, and urn burials are found in

them. Both the burial urns and other Valencia phase pottery are rather rough surfaced. Except for an occasional red slip, there is no painting, and decoration is in very simply arranged incision or in small relief features. These last may be adornos, ornamented handles, or appliqué elements on the vessel walls. Arauquinoid influence is seen in the appliqué human faces with coffee-bean eyes and arching eyebrows on the necks of jars. Vessel shapes are mostly ollas and jars, although there are some annular-based bowls, including annular bases that have cutout or perforated portions. There are also occasional spout-and-bridge-handle jars.

Kidder's stratigraphy on the La Cabrera Peninsula, to which we have already referred in our summary of the Barrancoid subtradition, helps place the Valencia phase in time. The antecedent La Cabrera phase dates to Periods II–III, Valencia

Figure 6-13. *Below, left:* Valencia figurine from Tocorón, Venezuela. Height, about 17 cm. (Redrawn from Osgood, 1943.)

Figure 6-14. *Below, right:* Valencia phase vessel forms. (After Bennett, 1937, and Osgood, 1943.)

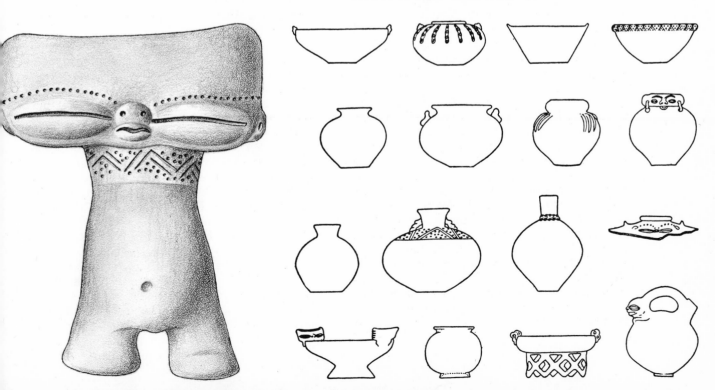

to Period IV. This is corroborated by three radio-carbon dates from La Mata that cluster between A.D. 920 and 940. This falls a few years short of the round-date beginning of Period IV at A.D. 1000, but there are other indications that the Valencioid cultures range through Period IV and even into Period V.

Other phases of the Valencioid subtradition are the Las Minas and El Pinar from other regions of the Cordillera del Caribe subarea, the Topo, Rio Chico, and Cementerio Tucacas of the Central Coast subarea, and the Krasky of the Los Roques Islands subarea. All show a somewhat reduced version of Valencia proper. None has mounds; some have urn burials. All are linked by pottery similarities, but the adorno and relief modeling so characteristic of the Valencia complex is largely missing from them. Some generally held traits for the subtradition are clay griddles, stone metates and manos, rectangular and bat-wing pendants of polished stone, stone beads, shell beads and pendants, and stone and shell celts.

It seems likely that the Valencioid subtradition had its beginnings and center of dispersal in the Lake Valencia Basin region. The resident population of the earlier La Cabrera phase quite probably evolved the Valencia style. There are some carryovers from the Barrancoid subtradition, and there is an obvious influence from the Arauquinoid. The mound idea may have been diffused into the Valencia Basin from the Llanos. Traits such as figurines and stone bat-wing pendants look like later pre-Columbian imports from the west.[66]

Koriabo and Abary of Guyana. The Koriabo and Abary phases of northern Guyana (British Guiana) relate to, but nevertheless stand outside, the main subtraditions of Caribbean Venezuela. Koriabo sites are located on high ground along the Barima and Waini Rivers in the Northwest Guyana subarea.[67] These are simple habitation areas, with organic debris, stone tools, and potsherds. No shellfish remains are found in them, although, as Evans and Meggers point out, the Koriabo sites are located in the same regions as those of the earlier Alaka phase sites in which shell refuse was typical. This, together with the abundance of clay griddle fragments in Koriabo middens, implies a manioc agricultural base for the phase.

Koriabo pottery is predominantly plain and sand tempered; there is, however, a minor percentage of cariapé-tempered ware.[68] Decorated Koriabo types bear either a sharp lined incision, with designs in very simple patterns, or scraped or striated markings. Both of these modes of surface treatment are sometimes combined with low appliqué ridges, little nubbins, or nubbins with modeled faces.

Late Mabaruma sherds occur in Koriabo sites, and Koriabo sherds are found in late Mabaruma sites. Thus, Koriabo probably dates no earlier than Period IV, and there are hints that it might extend on into Period V.[69] However, in spite of these Mabaruma trade sherds, the Koriabo style does not link closely with it. Instead, it is likely that Koriabo origins lie to the east, along the Surinam, French Guiana, and Brazilian Guiana coasts. In this connection, Evans and Meggers note the similarities of Koriabo wares to pottery from the Charlesburg site near Paramaribo,[70] and they further state that Koriabo-like pottery continues to be found eastward to the northern part of the Territory of Amapá in Brazil. In brief, the Koriabo phase would appear to be one that pertains essentially to the Amazonian area and cultural tradition.

The Abary phase is represented by a group of sites on the Abary River in the Northeast Guyana subarea.[71] The sites are small in area, but depth of refuse is greater than in sites of the Koriabo phase, a circumstance that may indicate longer periods of occupation. Clay griddles—those archaeological markers of a manioc cultivation tradition—were rather rare in Abary sites, but stone manos and metates are noted. This may indicate a reliance on maize cultivation. Site refuse also yielded burned clay wattle fragments of the kind that would be left by mud-plastered pole dwellings—structures of greater permanence than very simple bush huts. Abary stone artifacts are much like those of Koriabo—and of Mabaruma—axes, adzes, celts, and beads.

Abary pottery is over 99 per cent plain ware. Early in the phase this was largely cariapé tempered, but later the cariapé wares were replaced by sherd- and sand-tempered ones. What little local Abary decorated pottery there is has simple incised and incised nubbin ornamentations or, occasionally, red painted bands; however,

Mabaruma trade is represented by finer incised and modeled pieces. The only evidence for Abary disposal of the dead comes from one cemetery site, which was filled with large urn burials.

Evans and Meggers are of the opinion that the Abary peoples passed through the Northwest Guyana subarea in the early part of Period IV, or between A.D. 1000 and 1300. This is based on the assimilation of Mabaruma traits into Abary pottery and on the dating within the Mabaruma internal sequence of the traits assimilated. Apparently, they see little relationship between Abary and Koriabo, although on their summary chronological chart these are indicated as almost exact contemporaries (between A.D. 1300 and 1600).[72] Such a relationship might have been avoided, however, if the Abary group had passed through Mabaruma territory and established themselves in Northeastern Guyana before the Koriabo arrived on the scene.[73] But if this were the case, it is curious that the earlier movement of Koriabo culture, from the eastern Guianas coast to the west, had not brought it into contact with Abary.[74] It may be worth noting that Abary and Koriabo share the trait of Cariapé temper, and in this and

in other ways both stand somewhat apart from the Caribbean area tradition and closer to the Amazonian cultures.

Recapitulation—General. The earliest farmers and pottery makers of which we have knowledge date to the beginning of Period II. They have been identified as the peoples of the Saladoid and Barrancoid cultural subtraditions. In the Lower Orinoco subarea the Saladoid group was the earlier of these two. They were overrun, apparently, by the Barrancoid groups, who must have had an equally early history as farmers and potters somewhere along the reaches of the Middle and Upper Orinoco or in the Llanos. Both the Saladoid and Barrancoid cultures were manioc cultivators. Maize may have been known this far east at this early time, but, if so, it must have been of less importance than manioc.

At some time in Period II, cultures in Northwest Venezuela were becoming familiar with maize. These cultures also had pottery, but of a notably different kind from those of central and eastern Venezuela. Whereas the Saladoid phases featured relatively simple vessel forms and white-and-red painting, and the Barrancoid phases a distinctive incision and modeling, the Northwest Venezuelan cultures, like those of neighboring Colombia, were distinguished by black-and-red-on-white polychrome and rather complicated annular-based and footed forms. The earliest clearly defined Northwest Venezuelan subtradition so characterized was the Tocuyanoid. It would appear that peoples bringing a Tocuyanoid pottery style came into the Caribbean area, moving both along the coast and into the Llanos, in the latter part of Period II. A fusion of these Tocuyanoid influences with the Barrancoid subtradition resulted in the Ocumaroid subtradition of the Venezuelan Central Coast subarea.

Period III was dominated by Saladoid, Barrancoid, and Ocumaroid cultures, their geographical distributions running generally in that order from east to west.

In Period IV we have the appearance of the Memoid subtradition in the Llanos, another outgrowth of the Tocuyanoid cultures. Along the Orinoco, as far east as the delta, were the Arauquinoid cultures, a subtraditional line of development that is traced back largely to Barran-

Figure 6-15. Abary phase pottery adornos, showing Mabaruma influence. (After Evans and Meggers, 1960.)

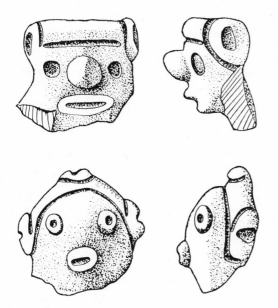

coid prototypes and that probably had its origins on the upper courses of the river or in the adjacent Llanos. In the East Coast subarea the Guayabitoid subtradition developed from the earlier Saladoid. The Valencioid subtradition seems to have had its center in the Lake Valencia Basin and to have spread from there to other Cordillera del Caribe regions and to the Central Coast subarea. It seems to be a blend of Arauquinoid elements and western influences, the latter probably mediated through the Ocumaroid and Memoid styles.

At the extreme eastern edge of the Caribbean area, the Barrancoid Mabaruma phase persisted through Period IV and, in so doing, exercised important ceramic influences on two other Period IV phases that are found in sites to the east of the Mabaruma country. These are the Koriabo and Abary. Except for their Barrancoid influence, they stand apart from any of the subtraditions described for Venezuela. The origins of Koriabo probably lie to the east—in Surinam, French Guiana, and Brazilian Amapa—and thus may be thought of as Amazonian rather than Caribbean. The origins of Abary are obscure, although these too may be eastern.

All during Period IV there was a steady process of "westernization" going on in the Caribbean area cultures. This occurred through Northwestern Venezuela, which is really a part of the Intermediate area (see pp. 320–321). This "westernization" brought not only changes in ceramic styles but, undoubtedly, a greater reliance on maize agriculture and the beginnings of socio-political and ceremonial forms that were more evolved than any that had been seen in central and eastern Venezuela prior to this time. We have noted mound constructions in the Llanos and in the Lake Valencia Basin. Although these were built for agricultural purposes, as ordinary dwelling foundations or for modest burials—rather than as temple or palace platforms—they nevertheless bespeak a degree of labor organization that one associates with hierarchically structured societies. Certainly the Lake Valencia Basin was a very densely settled region in Period IV times, approaching, perhaps, an urban condition.[75]

Spanish-Indian Cultural Fusion. Columbus sighted Trinidad in 1498 and entered the Caribbean to sail northward to Hispaniola.

He took back knowledge of pearl fisheries on the coastal Venezuelan islands, and this led to the exploration and settlement of these islands and, subsequently, of the mainland. The Indians of the Caribbean area were under the encomienda system throughout much of the sixteenth century. After the abolition of this system many grouped around Spanish missions, especially in the Llanos. These resettlement procedures hastened deculturation from Indian ways and acculturation to a new Spanish-American mestizo culture, much as in other parts of Latin America.

Rouse and Cruxent note three kinds of Indo-Hispanic Period (Period V) sites in the area.[76] First, there are sites that are essentially aboriginal in nature but in which trade items from Spanish culture occur. We have already referred to this condition in our mention of the Period V continuities of Venezuelan and Guyanese native subtraditions. Such sites may date all the way from the sixteenth into the nineteenth centuries. Second, there are mission-Indian sites, dating largely from the seventeenth and eighteenth centuries. None of these has been thoroughly explored, although surface collections from some of them indicate products of a fusion of Caribbean and Spanish traditions. Third, there are sites that were built under Spanish direction, as Spanish towns, but to which Indians were brought as slaves.

The Caribbean Cultural Tradition in Trinidad and the West Indies

The Saladoid Subtradition. The first farmers and pottery makers of the Caribbean cultural tradition to enter Trinidad and the West Indies were peoples of the Saladoid subtradition. It will be recalled that early in Period II the Saladoid peoples were displaced from the Lower Orinoco by a Barrancoid invasion and that some of them moved north to establish the El Mayal, Irapa, and Chuare phases on the East Coast in Periods IIB and III. These northward movements did not apparently stop at the Venezuelan coast but continued on into Trinidad and the West Indies. It is surmised that the Saladoid farmers, on reaching the Venezuelan coast, made contacts with the resident peoples of the Manicuaroid cultures—fishers and canoe people—and acquired from them the crafts of canoe making and seafaring. Equipped with these new skills they then set out to the islands at about the beginning of the Christian era (Period IIB) (see chart, Fig. 6-3). In Periods IIB and IIIA (A.D. 0–700) they established themselves on Trinidad, in the Lesser Antilles, the Virgin Islands, and Puerto Rico. This represents the full spread of the Saladoid subtradition in the West Indies.[77]

It is generally assumed that these first Saladoid emigrants to Trinidad and the West Indies were Arawakan-speaking Indians. As we saw in our ethnographic sketch, Arawakans dominated the West Indies when Columbus discovered them at the close of the fifteenth century. This fact, together with the very strong cultural continuity that can be traced from Saladoid subtradition cultures into those of the historic period, supports the assumption. So too does the glottochronological estimate of the time of the separation of Igneri Arawak from the mainland language. This is placed at about the beginning of the Christian era, or at the time when archaeological and radiocarbon dating fix the movement of the El Mayal peoples from the Venezuelan coast to the islands.[78]

The remains of the Saladoid cultures in Trinidad and the Indies accord well with the evidence that we have of this subtradition from the mainland. Sites are middens of modest village size, but there is usually a depth of refuse of a half meter or more, which would indicate some stability of residence. There are no special constructions such as artificial platforms or mounds, and burials are simple and without grave goods. Clay griddle fragments of the manioc complex are abundant in all sites; diagnostic pottery is the thin, hard, well-fired ware made in inverted bell-shaped bowl forms and jars, and D-shaped strap-handles are a common feature of these vessels. Some specimens are red-slipped and bear white painted decorations of circles, spirals, and straight lines; red paint had been used on others to produce similar designs. As on the mainland, incised and modeled decoration is rare; however, simple zoomorphic head lugs do make an appearance, and these represent the signs of Barrancoid influence, which, it will be remembered, was beginning to affect the Saladoid styles before their first spread to the islands.

The earliest Saladoid phase on Trinidad is the Cedros.[79] The pottery complex is such as described above. Importantly for cross-dating purposes, there is a percentage of the pottery that bears a fine line crosshatched incised decoration. This is a distinctive element of the Mayal phase style of East Coast Venezuela, and its presence in Cedros helps narrow down the time at which Saladoid pottery was first taken to Trinidad. In the succeeding Trinidadian Palo Seco phase these crosshatched motifs have disappeared. Other changes have also taken place. Palo Seco ware is thicker and coarser than that of Cedros. White-on-red painting has become rare, being supplanted with red monochrome, and a number of vessels have rim flanges, some with broad line incisions. As we shall see as we move farther out into the West Indies, these are general trends of development for the Saladoid subtradition in the island subareas. Although perhaps originally set in motion by Barrancoid influence on the mainland, the evolution seems to run a course of its own on the Antilles.

There are a number of Saladoid phases recognized in the Lesser Antilles.[80] Apparently, Grenada was the next stop—by logic of geography—northward from Trinidad.[81] Three successive phases represent the subtradition there: Black Point Beach, Pearls, and Salt Pond. Salt Pond, the latest of the three, sees the dying out of crosshatched fine incision and white painting and the trend to thicker pottery, modeling, heavy incision, and rim flanges.[82]

Interestingly, the Saladoid subtradition middens on Grenada—and elsewhere in the West Indies—show less shell than the middens of the later subtradition, suggesting that these first farmers to invade the islands were more set in an agricultural way of life than their descendants who succeeded them and who turned to marine resources to supplement cultivation. This may reflect minor climatic changes. Increasing rains and storms might very well have been damaging to maize crops, leading to some abandonment of farming practices—as Bullen speculates.[83] On the other hand, one wonders whether population expansion in the new island niches did not lead to more varied subsistence pursuits. Protein foods would have been scarce on the islands, which have no large mammals, and oysters and conchs could well have supplied this lack. That there was population expansion seems indicated by an increase in the number of sites in the later periods. Rouse notes this, for instance, between the Cedros and Palo Seco phases in Trinidad, with the latter being represented by many more sites than the former.[84]

The course of the Saladoid subtradition can be plotted north of Grenada with an A.D. 490 radiocarbon date for a phase on St. Lucia and one of A.D. 180 for another on Martinique.[85] Guadalupe, Antigua, St. Kitts, and Saba–St. Eustatius all have the horizon. From here we can go to the Coral Bay or Coral Bay–Longford phase of the Virgin Islands.[86]

On Puerto Rico, a Hacienda Grande phase correlates with the Cedros of Trinidad, with its fine line crosshatched incised marker type and a radiocarbon date of A.D. 120. There is a radiocarbon date also for the later Puerto Rican Cuevas phase of A.D. 510.[87]

Thus, the archaeological tracing out of the Saladoid subtradition, from the mainland to Trinidad and from there on through the Lesser Antilles to Puerto Rico, is extraordinarily neat and well documented—an outstanding example of the archaeological plotting of space-time relationships. As we have presented it here, it is also somewhat abstract—places, dates, ceramic marker types, a beautifully articulated skeleton; but *still* a skeleton. To give it a little more substance, let us take a good sample site—the Cuevas site proper on Puerto Rico—and have a closer look.

The Cuevas site is situated on the bank of the Rio Grande de Loiza in northeastern Puerto Rico;[88] it is about 10 kilometers back from the coast. The surroundings are those of a river flood plain, in extremely fertile soils, country today planted in sugar cane. The only surface indications of an ancient Indian village were a few potsherds, although a railroad cut through the site revealed more pottery and deep refuse. The extent of the refuse measures about 100 meters in diameter, and excavations revealed that it has an average depth of 2.5 meters. The physical strata were multiple and interbedded, with light brown and dark brown (refuse-impregnated) loam alternating. The location of the old community had been on the slope of a hill. The dark strata must have been habitation levels, while the lighter ones, with less cultural debris, seem to represent the results of flooding and soil wash. The

occupation pertains largely to the Cuevas phase of the Saladoid subtradition; however, sherds of the later Ostiones phase were found in the upper levels. These gradually increased in quantity toward the top, giving the impression of a slow replacement of Cuevas styles by Ostiones styles. The flexed burial of a child and portions of an adult skeleton were found in the refuse. Neither had grave goods. In addition to the 3000 and more potsherds taken from four 2-meter-square test pits, the associated artifacts included 51 clay griddle fragments, a chipped-stone ax, stone chisels or adzes, hammerstones, polishing stones, a stone slab, a stone and a bone bead, a bone pick, shell dishes, and miscellaneous cut conch shell scrap. Food refuse included bird, fish, rodent,

Figure 6-16. Cuevas phase white-on-red pottery from Puerto Rico. No exact size information, but such bowls range from about 25–35 cm. in diameter. (Courtesy University of Puerto Rico Museum.)

iguana, manatee, and turtle bones, and a few marine shells.

The Ostionoid Subtradition. The Ostionoid subtradition is clearly a Greater Antillean development. It appears to have originated in Puerto Rico at the beginning of Period IIIB (A.D. 700) and to have spread from here to the Virgin Islands (early Magens Bay phase), the Dominican Republic (Anadel phase), Haiti (Macady phase), and Jamaica (Little River phase).[89] On Puerto Rico and the Virgin Islands the stratigraphic position of the Ostionoid cultures is above that of the Saladoid cultures.[90] In the Dominican Republic and in Haiti the Ostionoid cultures compose the first pottery horizon and overlie the earlier preceramic Couri cultures. On the island of Jamaica the Ostionoid Little River phase appears to represent the earliest level of human occupation.

In appraising archaeological sequences one is often inclined to dub certain phases or complexes as "transitional." Frequently, this is because they are discovered after an earlier and a later phase of the chronology have been established and fixed in the mind as points of reference. The new intermediate phase is then seen to resemble both and to form a sequential link between them so that, in a sense, "transitions" are a device of the archaeologist. With Ostiones, however, this "transitional" designation seems exceedingly apt. We see styles very obviously in the flux of change. The clear patternings of the white-on-red pottery types of the Saladoid subtradition melt away into the nondescript plain and monochrome wares of the Ostionoid styles. The monochromes are red slipped and smooth finished, and the distinctive inverted-bell-shaped bowls give way to straight-sided or incurved-sided casuelas. Even the Barrancoid modeling and incising, with which the West Indian Saladoid styles were tinged, is reduced in Ostionoid ceramics; and plain tab lugs are the only rim modifications.

Now although the styles that Rouse has defined as being within the compass of the Ostionoid series are only the ones that we have just listed, it should also be noted that similar trends in the reduction of the Saladoid style were going on elsewhere in the West Indies and in Trinidad. In the latter island, as we have previously said, the changes in the Cedros–to–Palo Seco sequence

Figure 6-17. Ostiones phase pottery bowl from Puerto Rico. No exact size information, but such bowls range from about 25–35 cm. in diameter. (Courtesy University of Puerto Rico Museum.)

were not unlike those observed in the Cuevas-to-Ostiones developments. Both show reduction in design elements and, especially, loss of two-color painting. In Trinidad, however, there was some reason to believe that these changes were involved with the increasing "Barrancoidization" of the Saladoid styles—as witnessed by the presence of incision and modeling. In Puerto Rico, on the contrary, Ostionoid ceramics are not particularly Barrancoid; they have simply moved off on a course of change of their own. This course of change is also recognized in the Lesser Antilles. Rouse has not designated any of the Period IIIB phases there as Ostionoid, but they reflect the same breakdown in the Saladoid styles that is seen farther north and east.[91] As Bullen says, it seems to be a "Pan-Antillean process." I do not think that it represents another invasion of the islands from the mainland; it is rather an internal West Indian development.

Although I have spoken of a "breakdown" of the Saladoid styles and of reduction and simplification of pattern, this should not be further construed to mean general cultural deterioration or collapse. Quite the contrary; the Ostionoid horizon, in the earlier part of Period IIIB, was a time of expansion, vitality, and innovation. The Ostionoid subtradition carried the pattern of the Caribbean farmers to other islands in the Greater Antilles. Populations must have increased in numbers. New artifact types appeared, such as the "petaloid" celt, carved pottery stamps, and little carved stone idols and three-pointed stones—these last, the evidences of the inception of the "zemi cult." It is also probable that ball courts first appeared in Puerto Rico in the Ostiones phase,

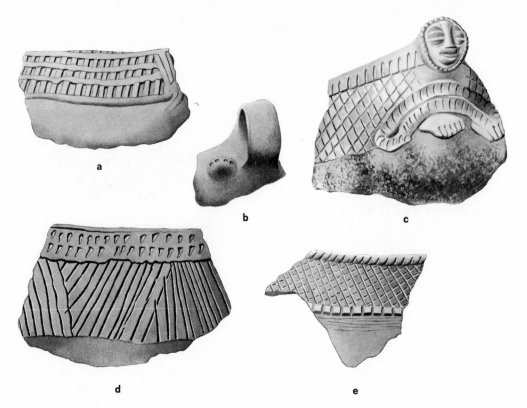

Figure 6-18. Meillac potsherds. *a:* Incised and appliqué-strip decoration. *b:* Strap handle. *c:* Incised and appliqué with effigy lug. *d:* Incised and punctated. *e:* Incised and appliqué. (Redrawn from Rouse, 1941.)

heralding a major element in the rise of West Indian ceremonialism.[92] What the ceramic record reveals to us, rather, is that the old styles and modes of the Venezuelan mainland heritage were being forgotten in the semi-isolation of the islands, and the new styles that were to replace them had not yet fully emerged.

The Meillacoid Subtradition. Eventually, two new stylistic subtraditions did emerge from Ostionoid. These were the Meillacoid and Chicoid. Both appear to have had their origin on Hispaniola: the Meillacoid in Haiti, the Chicoid in the Dominican Republic. They first appear in the latter half of Period IIIB, or between A.D. 850 and 1000. The Meillacoid is the simpler, the more "primitive" of the two subtraditions. It looks to be completely Antillean in its origins, and its spread was from Haiti to the west and north. We will consider it first.

Meillacoid sites are principally village middens, usually shell-refuse deposits, although these are almost always near suitable farming land. In Haiti these sites have been grouped in the Meillac phase,[93] and the Meillacoid sites of the Bahamas are also subsumed under this name.[94] In the latter subarea a good many Meillac sites are known from caves and from petroglyph locations. In the Eastern Cuba subarea the Meillac phase is the Mayarí;[95] in Central Cuba it is the Baní;[96] and on the island of Jamaica it is referred to as the White Marl phase.[97] Jamaica, too, has cave sites, which seem to have been used for burials and perhaps ceremonies, and petroglyph sites as well as open villages. Nowhere, however, do Meillacoid sites have ball courts.

As has been indicated, the original Meillacoid time horizon is between A.D. 850 and 1000. However, in Central Cuba the Baní phase then lasts on through Period IV; in Jamaica the White Marl phase has a comparable time span; and the same is true for the Meillac-type culture in the northern region of the Bahamas.[98]

Meillac pottery in Haiti, where it is seen to best advantage, is thin, hard ware; but surfaces are rough rather than smoothed or polished as was the case with Ostiones. All vessels were bowls, either round or boat shaped, of an inturned-rim or casuela class. Loop handles are common. Decoration is most frequently incised; the lines are fine and sharp and are usually arranged in crosshatch patterns on the shoulders of the vessels. Sometimes little appliqué strips are combined with the incised designs. Although the vessel forms—and, indeed, the idea of making pottery—are almost certainly taken from the Ostionoid cultures, the designs are reminiscent of the simple engravings on some of the stone and shell ornaments of the earlier Haitian preceramic cultures. There are also other signs of continuity from preceramic times in both Haitian and Cuban Meillacoid cultures. Thus in Haiti the Couri flint knives and daggers carry over into the Meillac phase, and in Cuban Mayarí there are celts and shell gouges that look like inheritances from a Cayo Redondo horizon. These cultural continuities hint at some continuity of peoples, and increments of the old preceramic and pre-agricultural populations may have been involved in the development of the Meillacoid subtradition, in addition to Ostionoid groups.

To sum up, the Meillacoid subtradition is a distinctively local one, confined to the Western Greater Antilles and the Bahamas. It combines features of the Ostionoid subtradition with those of the earlier insular cultures of the Northwest South American Littoral tradition. The thrust of its expansion was to the west and the north, not to the east, for in the east it had a more powerful rival in the Chicoid subtradition.

Erin, a Barrancoid Phase in Trinidad. Before moving on to the Chicoid subtradition, we must pause for a paragraph on the Erin phase of Trinidad.[99] The pottery found in Erin sites is typically Barrancoid: open bowls with thick rim flanges, incised designs on these flanges and on effigy adornos, and the adornos fashioned as elaborately stylized animal head lugs. Rouse dates Erin to Period IIIB.[100] This correlates with the end of the Los Barrancos phase of the mainland. In other words, toward the end of its lifespan the Barrancoid subtradition was carried into Trinidad. It seems to have gone no farther out into the Caribbean than this. However, occasional Barrancoid ceramic traits do occur in some of the Period IIIB styles of the Lesser Antilles, the Virgin Islands, and in late Ostiones of Puerto Rico. This is interesting in view of the fact that, as Rouse says, "the Chicoid series is distinguished by a renewed interest in modeled incised lugs and incised designs. Its designs look Barrancoid, and it may be no accident that, at the time the Chicoid series was arising in the Dominican Republic, Barrancoid people were expanding into Trinidad..."[101] This is a fairly recent comment. It is cautiously worded. The resemblances between the Barrancoid and Chicoid styles are marked.

The Chicoid Subtradition: Cultural Climax of the West Indies. The Chicoid subtradition can thus be seen as a development out of the Ostionoid subtradition in the Dominican Republic, with strong Barrancoid influences. It will be recalled that the earlier Saladoid subtradition was spread continuously from Trinidad to Puerto Rico. In this migration, Puerto Rico was the first sizable island to come under its influence, and it was here that the Ostionoid subtradition was later generated. Ostionoid spread west, and it is on the next large island, Hispaniola, that the succeeding Meillacoid and Chicoid subtraditions were born. The Meillacoid, being farther away from the mainland sources of new cultural stimuli, developed as the simpler and more "provincial" of the two. The Chicoid, in eastern Hispaniola, or the Dominican Republic, was closer to these sources, and it evolved the most flambuoyant of the insular art styles and the most elaborate ceremonial life. This history suggests, then, a kind of balance between demographic potential (as offered by the large islands of the Greater Antilles) and cultural stimuli (as provided by the cultures of the South American mainland) as the requisites for cultural florescence.

The parent phase of the Chicoid subtradition is the Dominican Boca Chica, which had its beginnings in the latter part of Period IIIB (A.D. 850).[102] From here the Chicoid subtradition spread back eastward to form the Capá and Esperanza phases of Puerto Rico[103] and the late Magens Bay development in the Virgin Islands.[104] The spread westward and northward included the Carrier phase of Haiti,[105] the Carrier-derived phase of the Southern and Central regions of the Bahamas,[106] and the Pueblo Viejo phase of the Eastern Cuba subarea.[107] These "spreads" of the Chicoid subtradition appear to be cultural diffusions. Their result was to transform the Ostionoid and Meillacoid cultures into the various subareal versions of the Chicoid culture that we

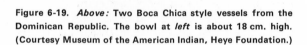

Figure 6-19. *Above:* Two Boca Chica style vessels from the Dominican Republic. The bowl at *left* is about 18 cm. high. (Courtesy Museum of the American Indian, Heye Foundation.)

Figure 6-20. *Right:* A Tainan (Boca Chica phase) hollow pottery figure from Santo Domingo. Height, about 40 cm. (Courtesy Museum of the American Indian, Heye Foundation.)

know from Period IV. In the western and northern Antilles only the Central and Western subareas of Cuba, the island of Jamaica, and the Northern region of the Bahamas were not affected by these Chicoid diffusions.

Chicoid pottery, as we have said, has a resemblance to the Barrancoid styles of the mainland. It varies recognizably from subarea to subarea; however, the broad, round-bottomed incised lines, dot punctations terminating the ends of lines, and biomorphic adornos delineated in incision are general characteristics. In the Puerto Rican Capá style an incised circle with a punctate dot in the center is a standard motif; in Carrier this has been changed to an oval enclosing a horizontal line. Inturned-rim bowls are the most frequent vessel forms, but other shapes occur, such as the bottles that are seen in Boca Chica.[108]

Chicoid manufactures, other than pottery vessels, are the "classic" Taino artifacts.[109] Some of these artifacts are not confined to the Chicoid cultures but are widespread and earlier. The West Indian polished stone "petaloid" celt would be one of these; others would be polished stone chisels, net sinkers of pottery or stone, bone awls, gouges, and picks made from manatee bones, and stone, shell, or pottery beads, pendants, earplugs, and various ornaments. Restricted to Chicoid and Taino are the heavily carved stone "collars," "three-pointed stones," and "elbow-stones"—all presumably ritual or religious objects. These may be associated with the ball game, and we will return to them later. Other well-known items are carved wooden snuff tubes, bone and wooden spatulas to induce ritual vomiting, wooden stools in anthropomorphic form (Fig. 6-21), and wooden idols. Some of the latter are inlaid with mother-of-pearl eyes or teeth, and occasionally this inlaying is in gold. Although the Spanish frequently referred to the gold of the Tainos, very little of it has been found archaeologically. What metalwork there was—as in the case of the rare inlays referred to—was simple hammered gold.

Chicoid sites are numerous; archaeological surveys have turned up hundreds in the Greater Antilles. Like those of the earlier agricultural subtraditions, they are mostly small midden areas— sometimes heaps of shell debris near the sea, sometimes refuse areas without shell located in the interior valleys of the islands. There are also cave sites. The most impressive sites, however, are midden areas that also embrace stone-lined plazas or ball courts. Such sites must have been the important seats of chiefdoms where the ball game was played and other ceremonies were performed.

The most famous of these Chicoid villages or towns with the stone-bordered plazas is Capá, or Utuado, in west-central Puerto Rico. It was excavated in 1915 by J. A. Mason, and the pottery collection from these excavations was later studied by Rouse and identified as belonging to the Capá variant of the Chicoid stylistic[110] series. It is easily the largest aboriginal site on the island. Whereas the stone-lined plazas or ball courts are usually found as single structures in villages, Capá has at least nine of these (see Fig. 6-22). The site is on the end of a small spur of land surrounded on three sides by fairly deep ravines. On the remaining side the spur probably had been fortified at a narrow point, thus isolating some six or seven

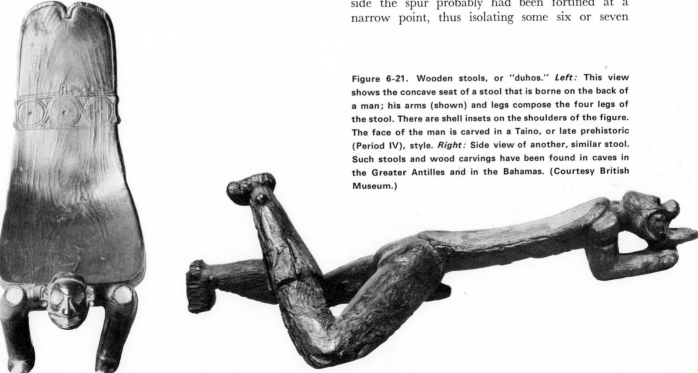

Figure 6-21. Wooden stools, or "duhos." *Left:* This view shows the concave seat of a stool that is borne on the back of a man; his arms (shown) and legs compose the four legs of the stool. There are shell insets on the shoulders of the figure. The face of the man is carved in a Taino, or late prehistoric (Period IV), style. *Right:* Side view of another, similar stool. Such stools and wood carvings have been found in caves in the Greater Antilles and in the Bahamas. (Courtesy British Museum.)

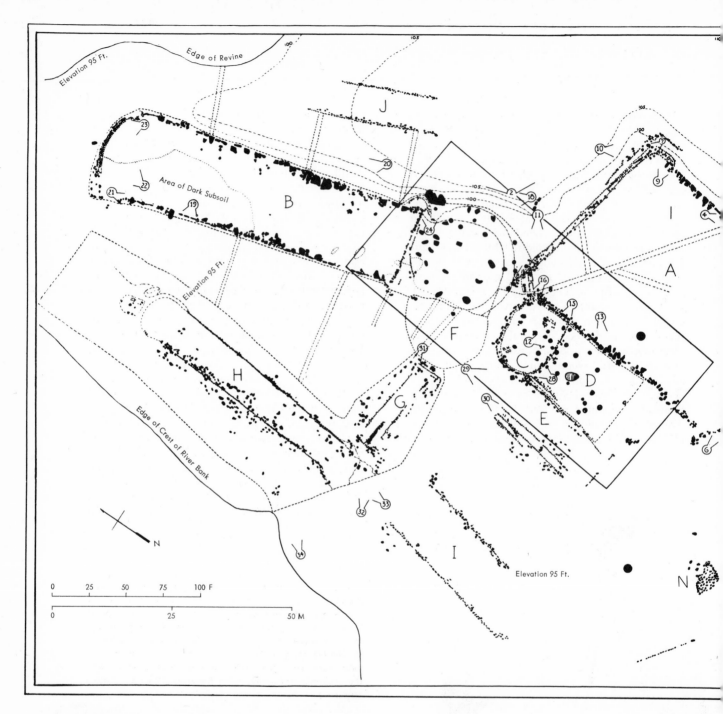

Figure 6-22. Ground plan of the Capá, or Utuado site, Puerto Rico, showing stone alignments that form rectangular courts and other enclosures. Some of these must have been used in ball games. (After Mason, 1941.)

acres. This plot of ground was leveled by the Indians in their preparation of it as a major ceremonial center.

The most imposing Capá structure (Structure A) is a rectangular enclosure measuring about 160 by 120 feet (approx. 50 × 37 m.; Fig. 6-22).

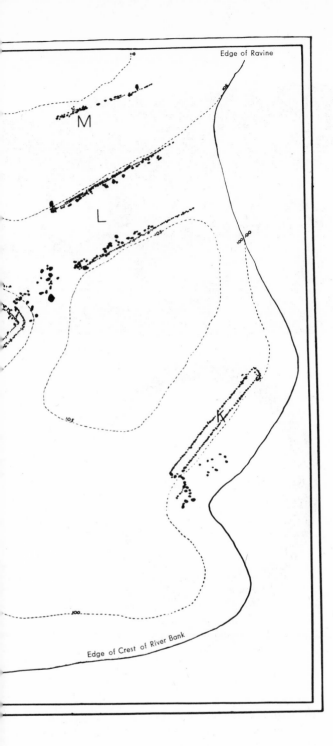

It is oriented with the longer axis north-south. The leveling of the area for this court had been done by excavating the north, east, and south sides so that a natural banquette of 1 to 2 meters in height partially surrounded it; only on the west side was it more or less level with the natural ter-

rain. The east side of the enclosure had been formed with large, irregular limestone slabs, each slab being about 2 meters in diameter and about 15 centimeters in thickness. These had been stood on their edges in a small trench dug to receive them and were braced with smaller stones. Subsequently, many of them had fallen forward into the court. Relief carvings can still be seen on some of these slabs—the typical zemilike faces, with the deep, cuplike eyes and stylized nose and mouth that adorn most stone artifacts and wood carvings of the Chicoid or Taino culture. They are also the faces that are represented on the pottery adornos—sometimes human, sometimes monkey-like, sometimes a blend of both. In Mason's opinion, all the limestone slabs along this side of the great plaza had once been so carved, although many have since lost the carvings through erosion. The west wall of the Structure A enclosure is composed of huge granitic boulders, some of which weigh more than a ton. These were presumably hauled up from the ravines several hundred meters away—a not inconsiderable task and one that must have involved an organization of manpower and man-hours. The north and south ends of the Structure A enclosure are of less monumental size. At each end there are two rows of relatively small boulders placed slightly more than a meter apart, thus giving the appearance of a little bordered path or walkway.

We cannot be certain, of course, that the Capá Structure A enclosure was used as a ball court. It could have been so used, or it could have served as a place for congregation or dancing. It is interesting, however, that the enclosure is of somewhat different proportions and construction from those of the other courtlike enclosures at the site. These others are proportionately much longer in relation to their width. For example, Structure B, the largest of the others, is about 200 by 55 feet (approx. 70 × 17 m.). Its one narrow end is straight and consists of a double row of small stones, as in the case of the narrow ends of Structure A; but its opposite narrow end is a rounded, or arclike, arrangement of stones. As can be seen from Mason's map, reproduced here (Fig. 6-22), Structures H, J, G, E, I, L, and K, although smaller, all have this same elongated outline with, in some instances, the one rounded end. Perhaps these elon-

Figure 6-23. *Above:* Ball courts at Capá, or Utuado, west-central Puerto Rico. The courts have been excavated and some of the stones set upright. (Courtesy Instituto Cultura Puerto-rriqueña.)

Figure 6-24. *Right:* Stone yoke, or "collar," Puerto Rico. These objects measure about 40–45 cm. on the longer diameter. (Courtesy University of Puerto Rico Museum.)

gated enclosures were the ball courts, and Structure A was a plaza of other functions; or perhaps Structure A was simply a grander, more differently designed court.

There are also other structures at Capá, and these are clearly not ball courts (see plan, Fig. 6-22). The elongated oval space C and the rectangular space D are framed by stone alignments. These abut on the big court of Structure A and on each other. Wooden posts were found within D, indicating a building of some sort—perhaps a temple. The area F was an artificial mound.

Undoubtedly, Capá was the "capital" of a very important paramount chief, and it was quite probably taken and destroyed by the Spanish in the early sixteenth century. It provides us with our best archaeological information on the size, layout, and megalithic construction of a Period IV Taino ceremonial center.

The finest examples of Taino or Chicoid art are the sculptures of wood and stone to which we have already referred. There are a great many of these in museum collections. Wooden idols and the carved wooden stools, or *duhos*, come from caves

—some, notably, from Turks Island in the Southern Bahama region. But fine stone sculptures, especially the "collars" and "elbow stones," have yet to be found, at least as complete specimens, in a controlled archaeological excavation. It seems probable that they, too, had been cached away in mortuary and ceremonial caves and thus were among some of the first West Indian archaeological materials to find their way into the hands of collectors. However in recent archaeological excavations at the Capá site—a good many years

390

after Mason's first work there—Rouse did find several stone "collar" fragments in one of the plaza structures.[111] This association has helped prompt the speculation that the "collars" were in some way related to the ball game that was played in the plazas or courts. Another circumstance that has suggested this function for them is their general resemblance to the U-shaped stones, or "yokes," of Veracruz, in Mesoamerica, which are believed to have been associated with a similar game there (Vol. I, p. 143). Ekholm has developed this hypothesis for both the Mesoamerican and the West Indian stone objects.[112]

The West Indian ball game, which we have referred to in our "ethnographic sketch" (p. 371), was described by Oviedo shortly after the Conquest.[113] It was played in courts or plazas by two teams of players pitted against each other. A heavy, resilient ball was bounced and kept in the air, without the use of the hands or feet. As in Mesoamerica, this was done by striking the ball with the hips. Ekholm is of opinion that the so-called stone "collars" either represent, or actually were, devices that were worn around the hips of the players for protection in striking the ball. That they were replicas of wooden prototypes is highly probable. Thomas Joyce noticed that they had been carved as though to indicate a slender trunk-and-branch section of a small sapling tree of which the two ends had been bent around and lashed so that it formed an oval loop.[114] Such wooden "belts" may have been the original, functional, gear for the game, with the stone versions as memorials, trophies, or prizes, although Ekholm considers the possibility that the stone "collars" or "belts" were worn by the players. The more slender of the stone "belts" weigh about 10 pounds. Their external dimensions are 35 to 40 centimeters on their longer axis and a little less on the shorter; internal measurements seem to be very much standardized and average about 32 by 21 centimeters. They are carefully smoothed on the interior surfaces, and experiments have shown that they can be fitted comfortably over the hips of a relatively slender man. On the exterior surface they have a thick point or boss at the end of one of the points of the oval. This corresponds to the knot or fork of the branch-and-trunk of the simulated wooden tree specimen. It would also have been the point of contact with the ball. A decorated panel is situated near the boss, and this is carved in much the same style as the incised and modeled adornos of the Chicoid pottery styles. There is usually a zemi or deity head in the panel, and this is bordered with geometric and rather intricate relief carvings that may indicate stylized arms and legs of the anthropomorphic-zoomorphic zemi being. Other stones—the "elbow stones" (Fig. 6-25)—appear to represent only the boss and decorated sections of the complete "collars" or

Figure 6-25. "Elbow stones" from Puerto Rico. These are similar to the yokes and are probably stone replicas of ball-game paraphernalia. "Elbow stone" at *top* measures about 30 cm. across; the one at *bottom* is approximately the same size. (*Top:* Courtesy Peabody Museum, Harvard University. *Bottom:* Courtesy University of Puerto Rico Museum.)

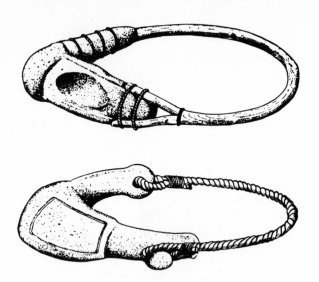

Figure 6-26. Puerto Rican elbow stones with reconstructed wooden and rope belts. (After Ekholm, 1961; courtesy Harvard University Press.)

"belts." These have grooves, holes, or knobs at the ends; thus, they could have been worn also as belts if equipped with a wooden or rope attachment to complete the loop (Fig. 6-26).

Ekholm has gone even further in his speculations about these stones, suggesting that the West Indian "three-pointed stones" may also have been related to the game (Fig. 6-27). These are the triangular stones, varying from a few centimeters to as much as 20 centimeters in length. Sometimes

Figure 6-27. Puerto Rican zemi stones. The one at *right* is about 12.5 cm. long. (Courtesy Museum of the American Indian, Heye Foundation.)

they are plain or very simply incised; however, the Chicoid ones are carved with zemi heads. In these, the head is at one end; the hindquarters of the human, animal, or demon are at the other; and a steep hump or point rises in the middle. The underside of the stone is curvate and slightly hollowed. According to Ekholm's reconstruction, this curvate side was lashed to a wooden belt, and the three-pointed stone served as the striking point of the belt in much the same manner as did the carved boss of the stone "collars."

This hypothesis, or series of hypotheses, about the game and its associated features is of unusual interest both functionally and historically. In the first place, if correct it would indicate an extraordinary integration of most of the Taino or Chicoid subtradition high art with the ball game. This, together with the prominence of the plazas or courts in the major sites, would seem to elevate the game to the status of the principal ceremonial-religious and social integrative force in late pre-Columbian West Indian society. Second, this interpretation of the stone paraphernalia would help in throwing light on the historical origins of the game in the Antilles. Ekholm opts for a direct relationship between the islands and Mesoamerica, the other area where the game had great prominence and where it, too, became "memorialized" in stone—both courts and equipment. Yet the real development of the West Indian game is not in those islands closest to Mesoamerica but in Puerto

Rico. It is also in Puerto Rico that the "three-pointed" stones are earliest, dating back to Period III. At this first appearance they are plain or simply carved. As Rouse has said, their presence offers an early beginning for one of the central themes in West Indian art.[115] It may also be evidence of the early beginning of the ball game in the eastern Greater Antilles and of the slow development of the game in the Puerto Rican subareas, along with the rise of the indigenous West Indian zemi art as it is expressed in "three-pointed stones" and other stone carvings. Such a view tends to divorce the elaboration of the game, and its attendant art, from Mesoamerican sources.

The Question of Carib Archaeology. When Columbus came to the Caribbean, the Carib had perhaps recently begun to conquer and raid the Arawak. Such may have been the course of events, although we cannot be certain, and it is possible that the Carib occupancy of the Lesser Antilles was of somewhat longer duration. Bullen is of this latter opinion, and he has argued for an identification of the Carib with a Period IV archaeological culture known as the Suazey phase. Suazey has been described from both Grenada and Barbados.[116] The pottery is a coarse, grit tempered, uneven-surfaced ware, frequently bearing scratched or striated decoration; a characteristic rim is finger indented. Footed pottery griddles are found in association. Just how far north this pottery complex is to be found is as yet uncertain; however, the Fannis phase, a Period IV complex on St. Lucia, is very similar.[117]

Bullen places the Suazey and Fannis phases in Period IV, an assignment that receives some support from a radiocarbon date of A.D. 1100 on a site in Barbados. Bullen notes that the Suazey phase is more fully represented—in number of sites, depth of sites, and range of materials—on Barbados than on any other island. This suggests to him that the Carib carriers of the Suazey culture first came to Barbados and, after establishing settlement there, moved on to Grenada and the other islands. He further speculates that these Carib migrants came from the Surinam coast, for this accords with Carib traditions concerning origins. This hypothesis gathers some additional strength from the scratched and striated pottery of the Surinam coast, which, as we have mentioned

earlier (pp. 378–379), may also have been the prototype of the Guyana Koriabo phase.

West Indian archaeologists are by no means agreed on this identification of a Carib archaeological complex. In referring to the time when the Carib reached the Lesser Antilles, Rouse says:

> ...pottery may not be a good indicator of this event...when...the Carib killed the Arawak men and married their women, it was the women's language which survived. Since the women were the potters, their ceramics should also have survived.[118]

Haag observes that the Suazey-Fannis pottery has old, presumably Arawak, prototypes in the Lesser Antilles, calling attention to the finger impressed rims, which, he says, go back to Periods IIB and III.[119] But Bullen counters with the argument that this antiquity of the finger impressed rim is just what one might expect:

> ...assuming women were the pottery makers, one would expect some Arawak ceramic traits to be added to or blended with the pottery traits introduced by the Carib women.[120]

There the question stands for the moment. One barrier to its solution is that the Period IIIB and IV developments in the Lesser Antilles are still not well known. After the Saladoid subtradition cultures had died out in those islands in Period III, the subsequent developments followed a somewhat different course from those of the Greater Antilles. The degrees to which these developments were derivative of the antecedent Saladoid horizon, were influenced from the Greater Antilles, or were influenced from the South American mainland are still to be plotted; and until this is done, the task of isolating the archaeological evidences of a Carib migration will not be an easy one.

Recapitulation. The first farmers to enter Trinidad and the West Indies were peoples of the Saladoid cultural subtradition—presumably Arawakans—who came from the East Coast of Venezuela at the beginning of Period IIB (A.D. 1). They brought with them an agricultural complex that surely included manioc and may have included maize, the sweet potato, and other domesticates. The characteristic ceramics of this Saladoid subtradition were white-on-red painted styles. Saladoid cultures spread north and east as far as Puerto Rico by the Middle of Period IIB (A.D. 150). They then persisted in these subareas until the close of Period IIIA (A.D. 700).

The Ostionoid subtradition rose from the Saladoid in Puerto Rico in the early part of Period IIIB (A.D. 700–850) and was carried from there to the Virgin Islands, Hispaniola, and Jamaica. This was a time of rapid change for the Arawakans of the Greater Antilles. Old mainland ceramic styles were drastically modified, new territories were opened up to the farming cultures, and the seeds of a new, distinctively West Indian art and ceremonial life began to emerge. These last were integrated around the zemi cult and the ball game.

The Meillacoid subtradition developed out of the Ostionoid in Haiti and spread west from there in late Period IIIB. In its origins we see, however, not only Ostionoid traits but traits of the earlier preceramic cultures that had continued a relatively late existence in Haiti and Cuba. In fact, in Western Cuba these preceramic cultures—identified ethnically as Ciboney—persisted throughout pre-Columbian times.

The Chicoid subtradition also developed out of the Ostionoid, but this occurred in the east, in the Dominican Republic, which was more readily accessible to the Barrancoid diffusions out of Venezuela via the Erin phase of Trinidad. As a consequence, the Chicoid subtradition incorporated many Barrancoid elements in its art style; however, Chicoid art was a new and vital entity in itself. Radiating out of the Dominican Republic in Period IV, it dominated Puerto Rico, the Virgin Islands, Haiti, Eastern Cuba, and parts of the Bahamas. This Chicoid art was closely linked to the ball game in the ornamentation of its paraphernalia, and the art style and the ball-game ceremonial must have reflected the ideological core of Taino culture.

The Chicoid florescence in art and in the development of the ball game raise the possibility of cultural stimuli entering the West Indies at this time directly from Mesoamerica. This comes to our attention especially with regard to the stone-walled courts and with what may be the stone "belts" that were used in the game. We must

regard this as a possibility but no more than that. An alternative explanation posits an ancient common heritage that includes the game, the spread of the game in a simpler or archaeologically untraced form through the northern South American mainland, and its later separate elaboration in the Chicoid cultures of the eastern Greater Antilles.

The Lesser Antilles and Trinidad lay outside the Chicoid sphere of strong influence. On Trinidad peoples of the Guayabitoid subtradition, identified in the Bontour phase, may have been Arawakan descendants of the old Saladoid line of development. They may have competed with Caribs for control of that island; but Carib archaeological remains have not been identified on the Lesser Antilles. However from historic sources we know that Carib peoples were in those islands in the late fifteenth century. The Suazey-Fannis pottery styles of some of those islands may be the ceramic component of a Carib culture that was brought from Surinam in late pre-Columbian times.

The Amazonian Area

The Setting. The vast Amazonian area (Figs. 1-1, 6-28) centers on the drainage system of the Amazon, plus some additional bordering lands. It includes the Brazilian states of Pará, Amazonas, and northern Mato Grosso, and the territories of Amapá (Brazilian Guiana), Rio Branco, Acre, and Guaporé. Beyond the Brazilian borders it takes in north Bolivia, eastern Peru, eastern Ecuador, southeastern Colombia, southern Venezuela, southern Guyana, Surinam, and French Guiana.

The terrain is mostly low-lying and flat. At the Atlantic coast the Amazon valley lowlands extend the full width of the area; in the west they are 800 miles across; only in an intermediate stretch of the river course, between the Guianan and

Figure 6-28. (P. 395) The area is shown in relation to other areas (Caribbean, Intermediate, Peruvian, South Andes, Chacoan, and East Brazilian). Archaeological subareas are indicated. Archaeological sites or regions are designated, for the most part, by names of modern cities or towns referred to in the text.

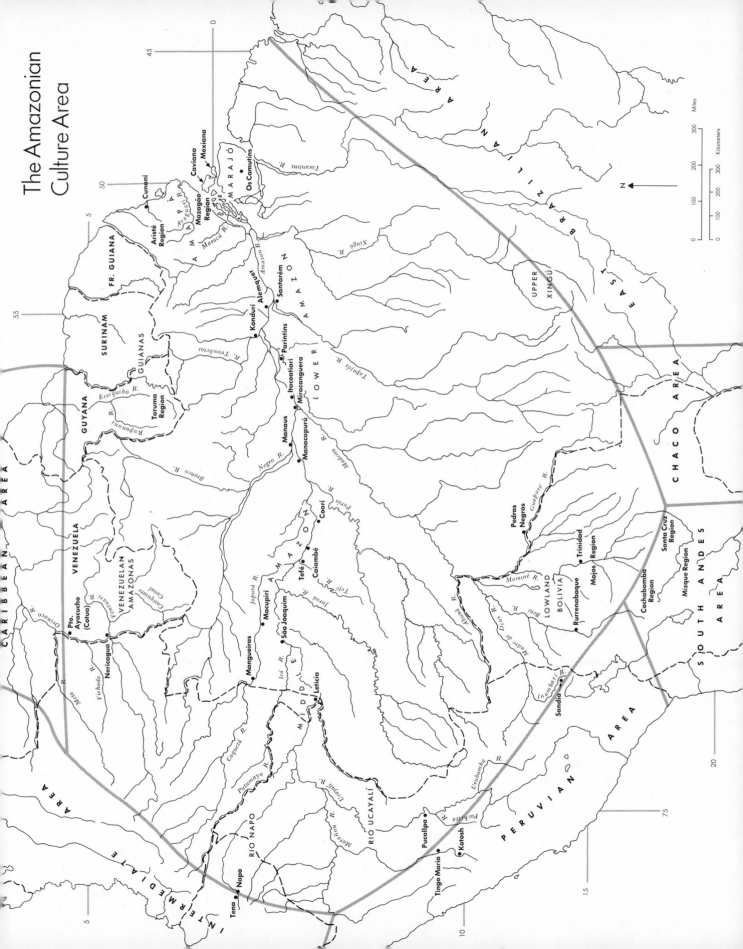

The Amazonian
Culture Area

CARIBBEAN AREA

INTERMEDIATE AREA

VENEZUELA

VENEZUELAN
AMAZONAS

Pto.
Ayacucho
(Cotua)

Nericagua

Orinoco R.

Meta R.

Vichada R.

Casiquiare Canal

Ventuari R.

GUYANA

SURINAM

FR. GUIANA

GUIANAS

Taruma
Region

Aristé
Region

Essequibo R.

Rupununi R.

Branco R.

R. Trombetas

Cunaní

Caviana
Mexiana

Os Camutins

MARAJÓ

Mazagão
Region

Araguari R.

Maracá R.

Amazon R.

Konduri
Alemquet
Santarém

Parintins

Itacoatiara
Miracanguera

Manaus
Manacapurú

Negro R.

Tapajós R.

Xingú R.

LOWER

**UPPER
XINGÚ**

AMAZON

EAST

BRAZILIAN

AREA

A M A Z O N

Coari

Calambé
Tefé

Macupiri

São Joaquim

Mangueiras

Japurá R.

Juruá R.

Teté R.

Purús R.

Madeira R.

Pedras
Negras

Guaporé R.

CHACO AREA

Santa Cruz
Region

**SOUTH ANDES
AREA**

Mizque Region

Cochabamba
Region

**LOWLAND
BOLIVIA**

Trinidad

Mojos Region

Rurrenabaque

Mamoré R.

Beni R.

Abuná R.

Madre de Dios R.

Sandia

Inambari R.

**PERUVIAN
AREA**

Urubamba R.

Pachitea R.

Pucallpa
Kotosh

Tingo Maria

RIO UCAYALÍ

Ucayali R.

Marañón R.

Putumayo R.

Icá R.

Caquetá R.

M A D D E

Leticia

RIO NAPO

Napo

Tena

M A D E I R A

0

45

50

55

5

15

20

75

10

5

N

Miles

Kilometers

300

200
300

100
200

100

Brazilian Uplands, are these lowlands narrowed. Within the larger Amazon Valley setting, the actual floodplain of the river is a considerably narrower band—20 to 60 miles in width—a seasonally inundated strip over which the great stream frequently changes course, creating oxbows, natural levees, and lagoons, and carving into the banks of the cliffs that border it. These conditions are similar, if on a smaller scale, in the tributary river valleys. The main tributaries of the north bank are, from east to west, the Trombetas, the Negro, the Japurá, and the Putumayo; in the far west the Napo, Marañón, and Ucayalí converge to form the Amazon proper; on the south, from west to east, are the Juruá, Purús, Madeira, Tapajós, Xingú, and Tocantins.

Amazonian vegetation cover and climate are mostly those of a tropical forest, and the area is largely in *Af* or *Am* climatic-vegetation zones (Fig. 1-3). Toward the south this changes to tropical savanna (*Aw*) country, and the same is true in the north, in southern Venezuela and the Guianas. Rainfall is heavy, although it exceeds 80 inches only in parts of the Upper Amazon. Most precipitation falls in the January-to-June period; however the remainder of the year is a "dry" season in only relative terms. Temperatures are not unbearably hot. Readings at Manaus, in the heart of the area, show an annual average of only 81 degrees. There is no significant seasonal variation, although there is a day-night fluctuation of several degrees.

The Amazon Basin is not an area that abounds in land game. The largest animals are monkeys, tapirs, and big water rodents, such as the capybara. The rivers, however, are a great source of food, with fish and turtles extremely numerous. Edible wild flora includes fruits and nuts, the Brazil nut being an outstanding example. A hunting-fishing-gathering existence is thus possible in the area, and we know that various groups have followed such a way of life in historic times; however, the Amazon is not as favorably situated for this sort of subsistence as are some other American areas.

Farming, especially root-crop farming with manioc, is feasible in the Amazonian area, and it is the mode of subsistence that was most prevalent in the area in pre-Columbian times and provided the basis for what we are calling the Amazonian

cultural tradition. The most suitable soils for such cultivation were in the floodplains, seasonally replenished, as they were, with silts and minerals. The better drained soils of the area, like those of all tropical rainforests, suffered from heavy leaching and loss of mineral content; however, they too were cultivated under a fallowing or rotation system of swidden agriculture.[121]

Languages and Tribes. Hundreds of tribes are recorded for the Amazonian area,[122] and we can mention only a sampling here (Fig. 6-29; see also Fig. 1-5). The first Europeans arrived on the Atlantic coast in the sixteenth century. Native groups were found there and missions and settlements established among them. As a result, these Indians were decimated rather rapidly. Further into the interior, contact was made first with those peoples along the major rivers. Remote regions—in the Upper Amazon, along some of the southern tributaries, and in the Guianas—served as "refuge areas" for many tribes even until the nineteenth and twentieth centuries. The sketch that follows attempts to approximate sixteenth-century distributions.

The main language stocks found in the Amazonian area were the Arawakan, Tupian (Tupí-Guaraní), Cariban, Panoan, and Tucanoan. In general, the Arawakan and Tupian tribes were fully agricultural in their subsistence patterns, and they held the prime agricultural lands along the major rivers; in contrast, tribes speaking Cariban, Panoan, and Tucanoan languages were more often found in what could be described as "hinterland" positions; however there are indications that in late prehistoric and early historic times some of these latter peoples were beginning to expand at the expense of the more settled Arawakans.

Arawakan tribes were found principally at the Amazon delta (Aruã), in the Middle Amazon (Manao), and to the north of the Amazon in Venezuela (Achagua, Caquetío—also referred to in the Caribbean area) and in the Guianas (Arawak proper). Another Arawakan bloc lies to the southeast, in Lowland Bolivia (Ipuriná, Mojo, Baure) and eastern Peru (Campa).

Tupian tribes were found essentially to the south of the main course of the Amazon. They include the Tembé, Shipaya, Mundurucú, Maué, and Parintintin. They were also present in great strength in the East Brazilian area. In fact, this was the homeland of the Tupí proper, the Tupinamba, and the Guaraní, as we will see in the next chapter.

Cariban-speaking tribes were mostly to the north of the Amazon (Apalai, Waiwai, Macusi, Galibí, Makiritare); however, one large group, the Carijona, were in eastern Colombia, and other tribes

are reported from scattered locations south of the Amazon.

The Panoans were interior tribes of the western Amazon. The main body (including the Shipibo, Conibo, Amahuaca, Catukina) were in eastern

Figure 6-29.

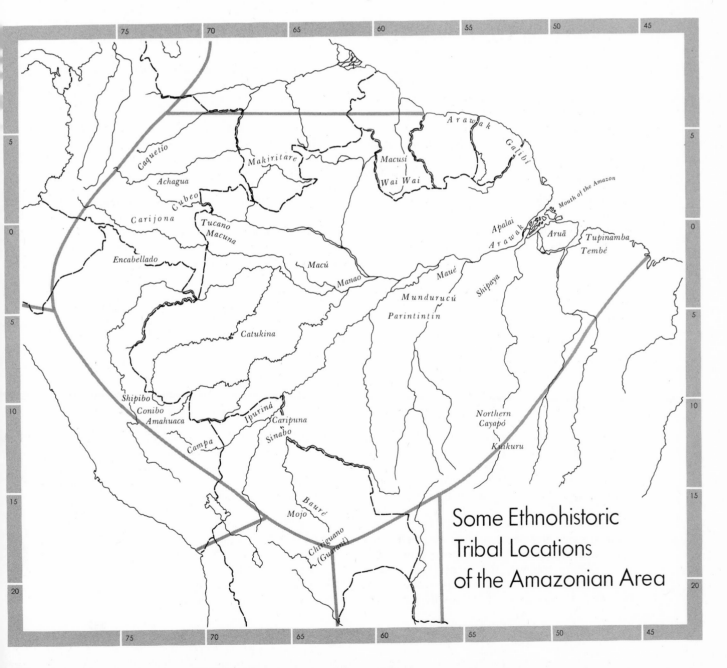

Some Ethnohistoric Tribal Locations of the Amazonian Area

Peru and adjacent Brazil, where some of them still remain today. Another group (Sinabo, Carapuná) were in the northern Bolivian lowlands. The Tucanoans were in southeastern Colombia (Tucano, Cubeo, Macuna, Encabellado, Macú). The Ge-speaking peoples—whom we have not mentioned up to this point—were centered in the East Brazilian area; however, one branch of them, the Northern Cayapó, extended northward into the Amazonian area.

The Amazonian Cultural Tradition and Tropical Forest Culture. What we are here defining as the Amazonian cultural tradition is based to a very large degree on what Steward called South American "Tropical Forest Culture" (see pp. 18–20). In other words, we assume a historic continuity from a pre-Columbian Amazonian area past to an ethnographically known "Tropical Forest Culture."

The basic food staple of Tropical Forest Culture was manioc, and its cultivation and preparation form a complex of traits central to the pattern. As an example, Robert Carneiro has given us a present-day picture of manioc cultivation among one small tribe, the Kuikuru (Guicuru) of the Upper Xingú.[123] The Kuikuru are a Cariban-speaking people who, in the 1950's, numbered about 145 persons. They lived in a single village composed of nine large, wooden-post, thatched, multi-family houses. They farmed in a zone described as a four-mile radius around this little village—a total of about 13,500 acres of which only 95 were in use at any one time. The period of actual use was only a few years, after which the fields were allowed to lie fallow for a good many years. Planting was done by the slash-and-burn technique, the trees being cut at the beginning of the dry season, burned at the end of it, and the manioc cuttings planted at the beginning of the rainy season. These plantings were made in little hillocks, some 1500 of such hillocks being heaped up in an area of an acre and a half. Yield of manioc tubers was from 4 to 5 tons per acre per year. The tubers could be harvested after 5 to 6 months in the ground; however they were often left for 18 to 20 months to allow them to grow considerably larger. After cropping, the manioc was peeled, ground, and freed of poison by washing and squeezing. It was then made into flour or cakes that could be eaten immediately or stored for use at other times.

Fishing was probably the second most important food source for peoples of a Tropical Forest Culture pattern. Carneiro estimates that it made up 15 per cent of Kuikuru subsistence; with other groups it was even more significant. Amazonian techniques used in fishing were hook-and-line, nets, basket traps, shooting with bow and arrow, and poisoning. In the latter method, plants containing drugs were crushed in the water; this stupefied the fish so that they could be gathered on the surface of the stream.

Bows and arrows were used for land hunting, although the more distinctive Tropical Forest area weapon was the blowgun. This was a hollowed cane or wooden tube; the darts were palm-wood slivers often tipped with poison, the latter including the fast-acting and famous *curare*. For the most part hunting was not as widespread or as economically important in the Amazon area as fishing.

Tropical Forest settlements were generally small —from a hundred persons or so up to a thousand. There were probably exceptions to this, and we will return to this question later; however it is fair to say that the general ethnographic picture is one of small and, often, shifting communities. There was considerable variation in the house types. Some were small, flimsy shelters, others well built, wooden-post houses with thatched roofs. Small buildings—whether flimsily or sturdily built —housed single families; large structures—of necessity well put together—were multi-family dwellings within which each nuclear family had its own hammocks slung around its separate cooking fire. The Arawakan multi-family dwellings were usually circular with conical roofs; those of the Tupians were usually rectangular with gable roofs. Both types were found among the Caribs.

Pottery was common among Tropical Forest peoples—or nearly so—in historic times. Vessels were employed for cooking, food and water storage, ritual purposes, and as household utensils. The craft has a long history in the Amazonian area, as we shall see in our archaeological review. Ground stone celts and grooved axes were widely used and of various styles and shapes. In general, though, stone artifacts tended to be rare owing to the scarcity of stone in many parts of the Amazonian lowlands. Arrowpoints were most often made from wood or bone. Although clothing was scanty, weaving was sufficiently developed for the production of wild fibre and domesticated cotton textiles—including such articles as hammocks, baby slings, waistbands, and loincloths. Both twined and twilled basketry techniques were employed, the latter more common in the making of the various containers, mats, fans, and the all-important *tipitís,* or manioc presses.

Lastly, one important fact about Tropical Forest or Amazonian area culture was the facility of movement among its peoples by means of the river systems. Dugout canoes were manufactured and used in streams where portage was not necessary; in regions where there were rapids the bark canoe was preferred because of lightness.[124]

This Tropical Forest Culture, then, forms the core of our definition of an Amazonian cultural tradition. It was a lifeway based on the slash-and-burn cultivation of manioc. Communities tended to be small and were frequently shifted; the socio-political unit was usually the single community; and political authority was weakly developed. But given this Tropical Forest culture type as a sort of base-line condition, there were also some deviations from it, and we will expand our definition to include these within the Amazonian cultural tradition. For the differences are developmental rather than culture-historical. For example, some Amazonian cultures and societies were probably "below" the developmental level of Tropical Forest agricultural village life. From ethnography we know that certain tribes of the Upper Amazon, the Juruá, and Purús tributaries were only minimal farmers and that they led a semi-nomadic existence.[125] Likewise, from archaeology, it has been argued that the earliest pottery makers of the Amazon delta were incipient rather than fully established Tropical Forest farmers.[126] At the other end of the scale some of the sixteenth-century chiefdoms of the Bolivian Lowlands appear to have gone "above" the Tropical Forest village level in community and socio-political development,[127] and there are indications, as we shall see, that this could be said about some of the archaeological cultures of Amazonia.[128]

Archaeological Chronology and Geographical Subdivisions. No areawide Amazonian chronology is yet employed by archaeologists; but a system of four major pottery horizon styles has been devised by Meggers and Evans, and this has served for some archaeological phase correlations between subareas.[129] These horizon styles have been named after distinctive ceramic decorative characteristics and are:

(1) *The Zoned Hachure Horizon Style,* dating prior to A.D. 500.

(2) *The Incised Rim Horizon Style,* estimated as dating from 0 to about A.D. 900.

(3) *The Polychrome Horizon Style,* placed at A.D. 600 to 1300.

(4) *The Incised and Punctate Horizon Style,* dated at A.D. 1000 to historic times.

As has been indicated, these horizon styles represent chronological horizons that "slope" significantly and overlap to a substantial degree. Accordingly, they cannot be treated as major periods of a chronology in the sense that we have set up such chronologies for other culture areas in this book; however we will have frequent recourse to them in discussing relationships between subareas. For our strictly chronological frame of reference we will not formally name or number periods but simply use calendrical dates arrived at by estimate and with the aid of some radiocarbon determinations. The chronology chart (Fig. 6-30) is thus divided into the second and first millennia B.C., the first millennium A.D., the final pre-Columbian time bracket of A.D. 1000 to 1500, and the subsequent historic era.

This chronology is believed to pertain only to the Amazonian cultural tradition. At least we have no firm archaeological evidence of earlier cultural traditions within the Amazonian area, with the exception of scattered surface finds in the Guiana savannas that have been referred to under the Andean Hunting-Collecting tradition (Chap. 2, fn. 157).[130] It seems probable that preceramic sites will eventually be found within the Amazon drainage proper, but, to date, none have been reported.[131] This circumstance, however, is not surprising in view of the deep alluvial deposits, the shifting river channels, and the dense tropical vegetation—all conditions that would militate against the easy discovery of early remains. Moreover, stone materials for tools are lacking in many parts of the Amazon Basin, so even if it had been populated prior to the introduction of pottery, it is likely that many of these early inhabitants would have had few or no manufactures of imperishable materials.

The date of the inception of the Amazonian cultural tradition is put as coterminous with the first appearance of pottery in the area, and this is estimated as early as the second millennium B.C. I consider this estimate to be somewhat early; however, the reasons for and against such a dating take us into the archaeological problems of the area, and these reasons will be discussed as we proceed through the chapter.

Subareal divisions of the huge Amazonian area are extremely approximate. They are based on a few pinpoints of information dotted over an enormous expanse of territory; but we will be referring to the following:

(1) *Marajó Island* (which includes that great island and the smaller neighboring ones).

(2) *The Lower Amazon* (the lower course of that river up to Manaus and including the lower courses of its numerous tributaries in that stretch).

(3) *The Middle Amazon* (the course of that river westward from Manaus to the confluence of the Rio Napo, together with the lower courses of the tributaries of this stretch).[132]

(4) *The Rio Napo* (including the drainage of that river westward to the Ecuadorian Andes).

(5) *The Rio Ucayalí* (including the drainage of that river southward for an undesignated distance).

(6) *Lowland Bolivia* (including the northeastern portion of that country drained by the Madeira and its tributaries).

(7) *Amapá* (or Brazilian Guiana).

(8) *The Guianas* (French Guiana, Surinam, and southern Guyana).

Figure 6-30. Chronological chart, with subarea columns, phases, and estimated dates. The Amazonian area. The small letters in the circles identify phases as to horizon styles (or subtraditions): Z, Zoned Hachure Horizon; R, Incised Rim Horizon; P, Polychrome Horizon; I, Incised and Punctate Horizon.

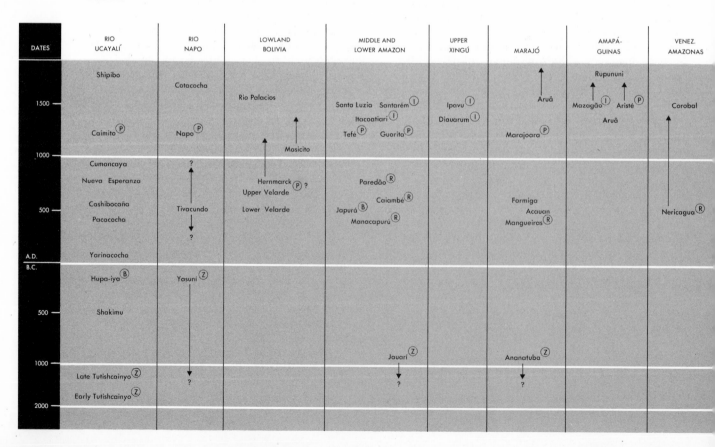

DATES	RIO UCAYALÍ	RIO NAPO	LOWLAND BOLIVIA	MIDDLE AND LOWER AMAZON	UPPER XINGÚ	MARAJÓ	AMAPÁ-GUINAS	VENEZ. AMAZONAS
	Shipibo	Cotacocha	Rio Palacios			Aruã ↑	Rupununi ↑	
1500				Santa Luzia Santarém (I)	Ipavu (I)		Mazagão (I) Aristé (P)	Corobal
				Itacoatiari (I)	Diauarum (I)		Aruã	
	Caimito (P)	Napo (P)		Tefé (P) Guarita (P)		Marajoara (P)		
1000		? ↑	Masicito ↑					
	Cumancaya		Hernmarck (P) ?	Paredão (R)				
	Nueva Esperanza		Upper Velarde	Caiambé (R)		Formiga		
500	Cashibocaña	Tivacundo	Lower Velarde	Japurá (B)		Acauan		Nericagua (R)
	Pacacocha			Manacapurú (R)		Mangueiras (R)		
A.D.	Yarinacocha	? ↓						
B.C.								
	Hupa-iya (B)	Yasuní (Z)						
500	Shakimu							
1000		? ↓		Javari (Z)		Ananatuba (Z)		
	Late Tutishcainyo (Z)			?		?		
2000	Early Tutishcainyo (Z)							

**Figure 6-31. The Peruvian Amazon country near Caballococha.
(Courtesy Donald W. Lathrap.)**

(9) *Venezuelan Amazonas* (including the Orinoco and its tributaries in south-central Venezuela).

(10) *The Upper Xingú* (a vaguely defined zone on the uppermost tributaries of that river).

The Amazonian Cultural Tradition

The Rio Ucayalí Sequence. Lake Yarinacocha is an oxbow lake in the Ucayalí River near Pucallpa, in the tropical lowlands of eastern Peru. The present Shipibo Indian town of San Francisco de Yarinacocha is located on the lake, around which are a number of ancient sites. Excavation at two of these sites by Donald W. Lathrap in the mid-1950's led to the beginning of the formulation of a long cultural sequence, and subsequent work by Lathrap and his associates at Yarinacocha and other Ucayalí regions have added to this sequence (see chart, Fig. 6-30).[133] According to Lathrap's estimates, it runs from about 2000 B.C. to historic or, actually, to present times.

The earliest phase is the Tutishcainyo, divided into Early and Late subphases. The Tutishcainyo site was a high knoll some little distance from the present lake shore. It was covered with a mantle of occupational refuse. The later phases of Yarinacocha, Pacacocha, and modern Shipibo were represented in the upper levels of this refuse, and the Tutishcainyo materials were at the bottom. Early Tutishcainyo ceramics are most typically large shallow bowls, frequently with composite profiles. The quite definite break between vessel sides and base is marked with a ridge or flange, and the typical rim has a broad horizontal extension. A high percentage of the sherds are decorated. This is characteristically with incision. Step-fret and step-scroll designs are outlined with deep incision and filled with fine line hachure, cross-hachure, punctation, or occasional red painting. Temper of the pottery was either sand or shell.

In Late Tutishcainyo the horizontally expanded rims disappeared, incised designs became less well executed, and the texturing of the incised zones was frequently by dentate roulette rather than hachure.[134]

The absolute dating of the Tutishcainyo phases depends upon cross comparisons with Peruvian sequences and indirect applications of radiocarbon dates. In Chapter 3 (pp. 112–115) we dealt with the Peruvian Initial Period Waira-jirca phase, the earliest ceramic complex of the Upper Huallaga subarea as determined in the stratigraphy at the Kotosh site, and it was noted that Waira-jirca pottery resembled that of Tutishcainyo. Lathrap

Figure 6-32. *Above:* Early Tutishcainyo potsherds. (Courtesy Donald W. Lathrap.)

Figure 6-33. *Below:* Late Tutishcainyo potsherds from lowest component at Cashibocano site. *Top:* Collared vessel with strap handle and vertical ridges or flanges. *Bottom:* Top view of an incised medial flange from a bowl. (Courtesy Donald W. Lathrap.)

spells out these resemblances as the sharing of: zoned hatched incision, carinated composite-silhouette bowl forms, post-fired painting with a hematite pigment made with a resin base, and occasional double-spout-and-bridge jars.[135] Waira-jirca is dated by radiocarbon at 1800 B.C. (p. 104 and Fig. 3-3), and Lathrap extends this date to Early Tutishcainyo.[136] This crossdating is bolstered by Late Tutishcainyo resemblances to the Kotosh phase, which succeeds Waira-jirca at the Kotosh site and is placed at about 1300 to 900 B.C. (Fig. 3-3).[137]

The Shakimu phase follows Late Tutishcainyo in the Ucayalí sequence. It was isolated stratigraphically over Tutishcainyo at another site on Lake Yarinacocha. Shakimu pottery appears to be a development out of Tutishcainyo. Much of it bears simple incised decoration, but the most distinctive specimens have a glossy finish and rather elaborate incised-excised scroll and step decorations. These usually occur on flat-bottomed bowls. Lathrap sees general Peruvian Early Horizon similarities in Shakimu, and a Shakimu radiocarbon date of 650 B.C., the earliest actual date in the Ucayalí sequence, bears this out. Lathrap is of

402

the opinion that by this time all influences were running from the Peruvian highlands to the montaña lowlands, whereas earlier, in Tutishcainyo times, he feels that the Ucayalí cultures were cast in the role of donor, rather than receiver, of ceramic traits.[138]

Following Shakimu, the subsequent phases of the Ucayalí sequence show little resemblance to anything in the Peruvian Andes. The Hupa-iya phase, which overlies Shakimu, is a dense occupation, implying a larger community than any of those of the previous phases. Hemispherical and oval bowls and plates are decorated in broad incised lines, with the lines usually ending in punctated pits; design is flowing, curvilinear, and on all parts of the vessel; modeled adornos and strap handles are additional features. As such, the complex looks very Barrancoid, suggesting influence from down the Amazon and over to the Orinoco in the Caribbean area. There are no associated radiocarbon dates, but earlier Shakimu and later Yarinacocha phase dates bracket a placement of about 200 B.C. to 0 for Hupa-iya. A primary extended burial was found in probable association with the phase. Modeled pottery spindle whorls make their first appearance at this point and continue through the Ucayalí sequence. Those of the earlier phases had been the perforated potsherd type. Stone axes, of the T-shaped or eared form, belong to Hupa-iya also; however, these were found in all phases of the Ucayalí chronology.[139]

The Yarinacocha phase, which follows Hupa-iya, has a radiocarbon date of A.D. 90. It represents a complete break with the Hupa-iya, Barrancoid pottery. It is a heavy, sherd tempered ware, and it is the first member of the Ucayalí sequence that has what may be thought of as a typical "Amazonian" appearance. This is seen in large, flat-bottomed, vertical-sided urns. It seems likely that such vessels were used for urn burial, although

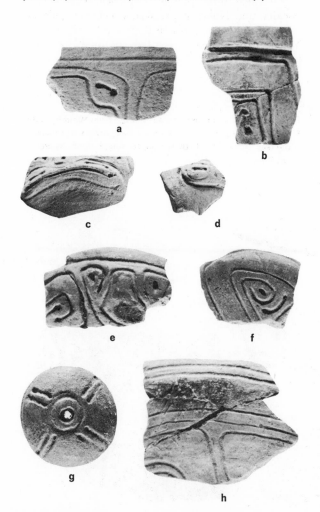

Figure 6-36. A Yarinacocha pottery bowl. (Courtesy Donald W. Lathrap; photo by Pedro Rojas Ponce.)

there is no direct evidence of this. Other forms are large, flat, circular platters. Most of the ware is undecorated, but some sherds are painted red, black, or white on a plain base.

The next three phases—the Pacacocha, Cashibocaña, and Nueva Esperanza, which are believed to occur chronologically in that order—differ from Yarinacocha in particulars but continue the large, heavy urn forms. Those of Pacacocha are huge

Figure 6-37. Cumancaya phase sherds from Caimito site. Sherd at *lower right* is finger-impressed; others are incised. (Courtesy Donald W. Lathrap; photo, *lower right*, by Pedro Rojas Ponce.)

flowerpotlike affairs, ornamented with crude adornos. Clay "fire-dogs," probably pot-rests but possibly pestles, are a Pacacocha feature. Cashibocaña vessels tend to be orange slipped, and some of them have corrugations below the rim. In Nueva Esperanza corrugation is more common, and the modeled adornos on the urns are carefully modeled bat heads. Nueva Esperanza has a radiocarbon date of A.D. 770.

The Cumancaya phase is named after the type site that is located on another Ucayalí oxbow lake some 20 miles upstream from the Pachitea confluence. The site is on relatively high ground, but is sometimes flooded; Lathrap and his associates found the midden layer under a thin layer of silt. The midden extends along the lakeshore for a third of a mile. A stratigraphy of Shakimu, Hupa-iya, Cumancaya, and Caimito were represented in the refuse, chronologically in that order. Pottery was either sherd or cariapé (bark ash) tempered. Some of it was overall corrugated, some brushed surface, and some decorated with fine line incised scroll and fret red-zoned designs. Cumancaya has a radiocarbon date of A.D. 810.

The Caimito complex, which overlies Cumancaya at the latter type site, is also well represented by sites on Lake Imaríacocha, 70 miles upstream from Pucallpa. The Caimito style of pottery is highly distinctive. It includes black-and-red-on-white polychrome, polychromes combined with broad line incision, incision-excision combinations, and fine line incision made through a white slip. The style is, in fact, that of the Polychrome Horizon of the Marajoara phase of the Amazon delta and the Napo phase of the Rio Napo subarea. Dates of A.D. 1320 and 1375 place Caimito at the end of the pre-Columbian sequence in the Ucayalí subarea. It is believed that the style continued until about A.D. 1500 and that it is the prototype for historic-to-modern Cocama and perhaps, Shipibo pottery.[140]

The Rio Napo Sequence. In the vicinity of Tena and Napo the Rio Napo descends rapidly from the Ecuadorian Andes to the lowlands. A recent archaeological survey along the Rio Napo and its tributaries has located a number of midden sites between Napo and the Peruvian frontier. Two such sites, on the lower section of this span of the river valley, pertain to a phase which

404

Evans and Meggers have named the Yasuní.[141] Both are small, thin refuse spreads on high spots of ground on or near the river banks. Yasuní pottery is sand or cariapé tempered; a common vessel form is a carinated bowl. Horizontal rim flanges or sublabial flanges are a typical feature, and the most distinctive decorative unit is an incised zone filled with fine line incised cross-hachure. The similarities to Tutishcainyo pottery are close. The one radiocarbon date for Yasuní, however, is 50 B.C., which is a thousand years or so later than Lathrap's estimate for Late Tutishcainyo.

The next Rio Napo phase, the Tivacundo,[142] is also represented by small and thin refuse accumulations. The pottery is sand, grit, or cariapé tempered, with open bowl, subglobular olla, and necked olla forms. One olla form has a very low basal angle and a constricted and flattened conical base. Decoration is in fine, incised, and red painted zones, arranged in a complex curvilinear and rectilinear pattern. A few griddle fragments were found, although these imply a quite small circular griddle, perhaps unsuited for bitter manioc flour

Figure 6-38. Caimito phase vessel. Top view of a squared plate. (Courtesy Donald W. Lathrap.)

preparation. There is a single radiocarbon date of A.D. 510 that Evans and Meggers believe pertains to the latter part of the Tivacundo phase. It is difficult to relate Tivacundo to the Ucayalí sequence, although the presence of "fire-dogs," or pot-rests, suggests a parallel to their first appearance in the Pacacocha phase of the Ucayalí, which Lathrap places at about A.D. 400. The red zoned, fine line incised decoration of the pottery sounds something like that described by Lathrap for his Cumancaya phase (which, however, has a radiocarbon date of A.D. 800).

Figure 6-39. *Left:* Some Yasuní phase vessel forms. Largest vessel has a diameter of about 40 cm. (After Evans and Meggers, 1968; drawings by Marcia Bakry.)

Figure 6-40. *Below:* Tivacundo phase incised and zoned red sherds. (After Evans and Meggers, 1968; drawings by George Robert Lewis.)

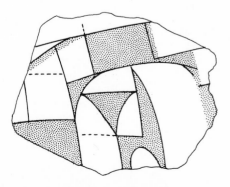

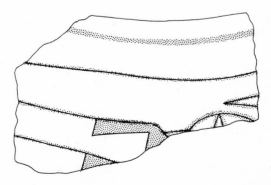

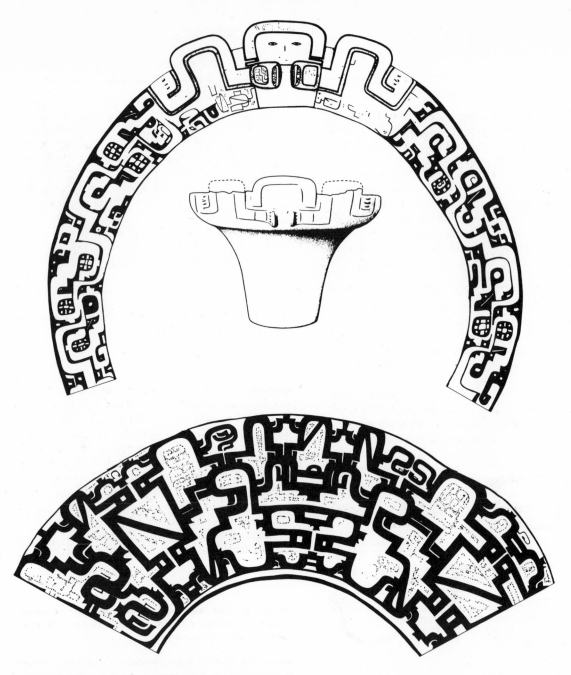

Figure 6-41. A Napo phase painted burial urn. The upper, black-on-white design encircled the upper portion of the vessel, which was also ornamented with anthropomorphic modeling. The lower design, in red-and-black-on-white, was on the lower portion of the vessel. This lower design banding, with the fine line red elements (indicated in stippling) and bold black bands, is in the tradition of the Polychrome Horizon style of painting. (After Evans and Meggers, 1968; drawings by George Robert Lewis.)

Napo phase sites are much larger than those of the previous phases of the subarea.[143] Two of them extended for more than 500 meters along the river bank; however, they are all relatively thin, implying brief occupation. They contain large griddle fragments and mano stones so that bitter manioc is definitely indicated and maize suggested. Pottery—cariapé, charcoal, or sand tempered—occurs in a number of forms: large basin shapes, bowls with a low angle or shoulder and a flattened-

Figure 6-42. Pottery of Rio Napo style, Ecuador. *Left:* Height, about 17 cm. *Right:* Height, about 30 cm. (Courtesy B. J. Meggers and Clifford Evans, Jr.)

conical base, bowls with an expanded upper portion and a flattened-conical base, and squared vessels. There is much plain ware; but incised, excised, painted, and modeled decoration was also used on household pieces as these were found in great quantity. These decorative techniques were often combined. Thus a vessel would be incised or excised, then slipped, and then the areas in incision or excision would be touched up in a contrasting colored paint. Red and white are the most frequent colors, and white the most usual slip. Black-and-red-on-white polychrome and red-on-white and black-on-white dichromes were typical. The design pattern is highly complicated and continuous or interconnected. Perhaps the best way to describe it is to say that it relies on the juxtaposition of very bold line and fine line elements. The motifs probably are highly stylized life forms. Burials were apparently made in urns; these are sometimes found in the habitation zones and sometimes in isolated localities. Such urns probably contained secondary interments or, perhaps, incompletely cremated remains;[144] the urns themselves were modeled and painted with human figures. Other Napo phase items are clay pot-rests, side notched and eared stone axes, chisels, and miscellaneous grinding stones. Three radiocarbon dates were obtained from the Napo phase sites. Two of them, at A.D. 1168 and 1179 are accepted by Evans and Meggers; the third, at A.D. 1480, seems too late.

We have already mentioned the similarities among Caimito, Napo, and Marajoara pottery. This Polychrome Horizon can be extended to a number of Middle Amazonian finds, which we will come to presently; however a very recent discovery may be mentioned at this point. Near Leticia, a Colombian border town where Brazil, Peru, and Colombia come together, Lathrap and colleagues designate a Yanayacu phase that they describe as very similar to Napo and that can be included in the Polychrome Horizon network.[145]

The early Spanish explorers found no Indians along the Rio Napo in 1541 or, later, in 1651. However, there is a historic period pottery complex represented at a few sites along the river, one that Evans and Meggers have named the Cotacocha.[146] The pottery is very simple, being plain, fingernail-impressed, or red banded. It is believed to pertain to Quechua Indians who moved down from the highlands after 1651.

The Marajó Island Sequence. The earliest phase here is the Ananatuba, the sites of which are located on the north-central portion of the island.[147] These sites are small midden areas of circular or oval outline, comprising from 300 to 700 square meters. Quite probably they represent the locations of single large communal houses that served as the dwellings for 100 to 150 people. It is likely that such houses were built on piles, and they may have been fairly substantial constructions, for numerous clay wattles are present in the refuse. The site refuse is quite deep—averaging from 0.6 to 1.0 meter—which suggests relatively stable and long-term residence. The ecological situation of the Ananatuba sites is at the edges of patches of forest, overlooking open savanna land. Streams that are large enough for a dugout canoe are usually a kilometer or so distant from the sites. Evans sees in this settlement choice an economy that was probably oriented a little more toward hunting and gathering than were the later culture phases of the Marajó sequence, and in a developmental ranking he places Ananatuba as "Incipient Agricultural" rather than on the full "Tropical Forest Agricultural" stage.[148] Potsherds were extremely abundant in the Ananatuba middens. These are fragments of sherd tempered plain, brushed, and incised wares; and, most significantly for wider correlations, the latter technique includes incision outlined zones filled with hachure —much as we saw in the Early Tutishcainyo and Yasuní phases. There is a radiocarbon date of 980 b.c.[149] This is the earliest actual date on the Zoned Hachure Horizon, falling about midway between Lathrap's Early Tutishcainyo dating estimate and the Yasuní radiocarbon date from the Rio Napo.

The next Marajó Island phase is the Mangueiras.[150] Sites of this phase are also found on the neighboring smaller island of Caviana. The individual locations are ten times as large as those of Ananatuba sites, and it is thought that they represent groups of large communal houses with correspondingly larger populations than those of the earlier phase. The Mangueiras sites are situated in forested land close to navigable streams. These changes in site size and ecology suggest to Evans a more productive economy than that of the Ananatubans, and he places Mangueiras fully on the "Tropical Forest Agricultural Stage."[151]

Mangueiras ceramics show a notable acculturation to Ananatuba modes, and this is interpreted as the result of conquest and assimilation of the Ananatubans by the Mangueirans.[152] Most Mangueiras pottery is rather simple, with brushed or scraped surface treatments; but as has been indicated, some of it has incised motifs similar to those of Ananatuba. Mangueiras also has an incised rim mode —a wide, flat-topped rim with broad incised lines on its top—that links it to the Incised Rim Horizon Style.[153] Besides potsherds, Mangueiras sites also yielded a few other clay items: tubular pipes, human figurines, and labrets.

Two other Amazonian delta phases, the Acauan and the Formiga, appear to be approximately contemporaneous with Mangueiras. One Acauan site is reported from Marajó, but most of them are on the smaller nearby island of Mexiana.[154] Acauan ceramics show simple plastic treatments of corrugation, incision, and scraping. Formiga pottery, much of which is brushed, shows evidence of contact with Mangueiras; and Formiga sites are found in the same region of Marajó Island as the Mangueiras.[155] There is an important difference in the settlements of the two cultures,

Figure 6-43. Potsherds of the Ananatuba phase, Marajó Island. Incised and brushed decorative techniques. (Courtesy B. J. Meggers and Clifford Evans, Jr.)

Figure 6-44. Mangueiras phase potsherds. Incised decorative technique. (Courtesy B. J. Meggers and Clifford Evans, Jr.)

however, in that Formiga sites are situated in savanna or *campo* country. It is just possible that this reflects some difference in agricultural practices and so it may be that Formiga foreshadows the pattern of the next phase, the Marajoara.

Marajoara phase sites are marked by artificial mounds and are located on the open *campos* of Marajó Island. They are usually found on the shores of lakes or streams, and a number of them are concentrated in the expanse of plains east of Lago Ararí.[156] The mounds are of two types: habitation and burial. At the Os Camutins site there are 18 habitation mounds and two burial mounds. The former average something like 50 by 35 meters in extent and may be as much as 6 meters in height. They contain a core of clean, artificially piled clay that was apparently put down to raise the dwellings above the seasonal floodings of the island. Evidences of house floors and hearths, superimposed, attest to long usage. The larger Os Camutins burial mound measures 255 by 30 meters and has a height of 10 meters. It was constructed in stages, as though to meet the needs of periodic interments. The urn burials within are of both secondary and cremation types. In the earlier sub-

phase of the culture the secondary form was in vogue.[157] The bones were placed in large jars that were plain, painted, or excised and that were covered with bowls as lids. Inside with the human remains were other pottery vessels, pottery *tangas,* or pubic covers, and animal, bird, and crocodile bones. In such burials there are indications of status differentiation. For example, the bones of a single individual were found in a large polychrome anthropomorphic jar that was flanked by several plain jars containing the remains of other persons. Cremation was the mode in the later subphase. The burial urns were smaller and less ornate, and tangas were never associated. Some of the later burials were also made directly in the earth.

Although much of the Marajoara pottery is plain, the decorated wares are of unusual interest. These are slipped, incised, excised, modeled, and painted in a series of combinations. In polychromes the background is frequently white, with red and black as the decorative colors. In one kind of Marajoara decoration the design background has been deeply excised to allow the motifs to stand out in relief. The style is very similar to the style of the far-distant Napo phase of the Upper Amazon that we have just reviewed. There is the characteristic disposition of bold line and fine line elements into an intricate overall pattern. Vessel shapes include anthropomorphic burial urns, a variety of jars and bowls, and pedestal-based plates. Other ceramic manufactures of the Marajoara style are observed to be tangas, pedestal stools, seated human figurines, earplugs, labrets, and spindle whorls.

Meggers and Evans feel that the Marajoara culture was intrusive into the Amazon delta country and had been developed elsewhere with the support of more intensive agricultural methods. On the Marajó Island savannas, according to these writers, this culture gradually withered and died.[158] We will return to these problems of origins and decline a little later; but, for whatever reasons, the Marajoara phase came to an end at some time before A.D. 1500.

When the first Portuguese arrived in this part of Brazil at the beginning of the sixteenth century they found the Arawakan-speaking Aruã Indians in control of Marajó Island. Aruã culture was strikingly different from that of Marajoara.[159] The Aruãns had presumably come over to Marajó

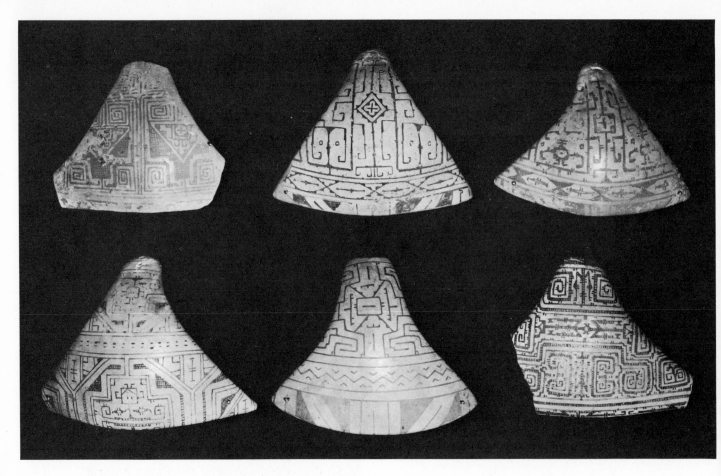

Figure 6-45. *Above:* Pottery *tangas,* or pubic covers. Marajoara phase. (Courtesy American Museum of Natural History.)

Figure 6-46. *Below:* Marajoara phase pottery. Ollas and bowl of the type Joanes Painted. Vessel in center is about 22 cm. high. (Courtesy B. J. Meggers and Clifford Evans, Jr.)

and the delta islands from the mainland of Amapá or Brazilian Guiana. They lived in very small communities, probably of single communal house size. These sites, marked by small, thin middens, are located on navigable stream banks in the forests. Cemeteries, found apart from the dwelling loca-

Figure 6-47. *Above, left:* Marajoara phase pottery. *Left:* Pottery "stools" of the types Anajás Plain and Arari Plain Excised. *Right:* Urn of type Arari Red Excised, White Retouched. Maximum diameter of "stool" at *top left* is about 14 cm.; other "stool" to same scale. Urn is about 29 cm. high. (Courtesy B. J. Meggers and Clifford Evans, Jr.)

Figure 6-48. *Above, right:* Marajoara burial urn with modeled and red-and-black-on-white painted decoration. Type: Joanes Painted. Height is about 45 cm. (Courtesy B. J. Meggers and Clifford Evans, Jr.)

tions, are collections of urns that had been left on the surface of the ground or only partially buried. These Aruã urns, which contained secondary burials, are plain or else bear rows of impressed rings or appliqué strips. Other Aruã pottery is usually plain, although some is brushed. Burial goods are not plentiful or usual; but smaller pottery vessels, simple pottery figurines, polished nephrite axes, and European glass beads are sometimes found with the urn cemeteries. Aruã phase culture apparently persisted for two or three centuries after the first European contact.

Sequences of the Lower and Middle Amazon. In the 1950's and 1960's P. P. Hilbert carried out a number of stratigraphic tests in the Lower and Middle Amazon subareas, and the results of his surveys provide a chronological framework for these parts of Amazonia. Although in no one region does Hilbert have as long a continuous sequence as those of Marajó or the Ucayalí, it is possible to piece together a number of site stratigraphies.

The earliest known Lower Amazon subarea phases are found at Ponta do Jauarí, just west of the town of Alemquer.[160] The location is an old oxbow lake, on the north side of the Amazon, a little upstream from the mouth of the Tapajós, and the site is on a little tongue of land that is seasonally inundated. The site surface is covered with stone scrap, all of which must have been brought in from the nearest rock outcrops, which are some little distance either to the north or to the

south. Stone artifacts, including polished T-shaped and notched axes, manos, and mullers, have also been found on the site surface. At two places there are shell refuse concentrations, and on and around these concentrations—which look as though they could have been pile-house locations—are potsherds. Ponta do Jauarí must have been an excellent fishing and river hunting location, for bone refuse is also present near the shell middens—including tapir, wild pig, alligator, turtle, and fish remains. Hilbert has evidence for two pottery phases. The earlier, which he calls the Castalia, is characterized by shell tempered pottery, mostly plain. The later, the Jauarí, has cauixí (freshwater sponge spicule) tempered pottery; and this Jauarí phase style is similar in vessel forms and in incised zoned hachure decoration to the pottery of Ananatuba. Jauarí thus provides a geographical link between Early Tutishcainyo and Yasuní, at one end of the Amazon, and Ananatuba at the other. So far, it is the only Zoned Hachure Horizon Style manifestation to be reported from

411

this vast intervening stretch of the Amazon Basin. But the Jauarí style also differs from the others of the horizon in incorporating modeled zoomorphic lugs or adornos. Tubular pottery pipes also are associated with the Jauarí phase. These are made with flattened mouthpieces and are decorated with incision and modeling. One illustrated by Hilbert bears a typical zoned hatched design on the barrel. In the Marajó Island sequence, it will be recalled, tubular pottery pipes were a feature of the later Mangueiras phase but not of Ananatuba.

On the next later chronological horizon are a series of phases that have been related to the Incised Rim Horizon. Hilbert defines these phases from three Middle Amazon subarea sites, in all of which the phases in question represent the earliest site occupation. The Paredão phase is named after a site on the left bank of the Rio Negro, a few kilometers east of Manaus.[161] The location is a steep river bank, above flood waters. Like many Amazonian sites it is a "terra preta," or black-earth zone—the name given to the black organic midden soil of prehistoric sites.[162] The midden is said to be spread over several hectares, so that Paredão is much larger than the Jauarí site. The characteristic pottery of the phase is an open-bowl form in which a wide everted rim has been incised with a paneling of nested hatched triangles or chevrons; however, there are also other forms, including jars, bowls with arching basketlike handles, and numerous manioc roasting plates or *budares*. Decoration also includes red slipping, fine line red painting in rectilinear panels, and adorno modeling. Secondary burials in large burial urns were recovered from within the site zone. These were big, round-bodied, straight-collared shapes that were plain except for large hemispherical biomorphic adornos. Pottery beads and modeled pottery spindle whorls are other Paredão traits. Two radiocarbon dates from Paredão fall at A.D. 870 and 880,[163] and relative chronological placement is aided by an overlying stratum of sherds that are assigned to the Guarita phase, an affiliate of the Polychrome Horizon style.

The Manacapurú phase is named from a large "terra preta" on the north bank of the Solimões (or Middle Amazon) near the town of Manacapurú.[164] This extensive midden is said to extend for more than 2 kilometers along the river bank and for 400 meters inland, indicating a former sizable village or town. The midden, which is 80 centimeters deep, pertains largely to the earlier Manacapurú phase, the Guarita phase being represented only by a superficial showing of pottery. Manacapurú pottery is linked to Paredão by the incisions on the inner sides of large everted bowl rims; however, the complex also shows types of a freer, more curvilinear, and widely spaced incised decoration in which the incised lines were made with a broad-ended, double-toothed tool. Rim adornos and lugs are also more ornate than was the case with Paredão. Burial urns, like those of Paredão, were probably used in Manacapurú, as fragments of the big biomorphic adornos have been found—although no actual urn interments were discovered. The radiocarbon date for Manacapurú is A.D. 425.

The Caiambé phase comes from near that community, a short distance below the town of Tefé, on the south bank of the Solimões.[165] Again, some of the pottery has the rim incisions, relating it to the two previously described phases; but, judging from Hilbert's illustrations, much of the incision is of the broad-lined toothed-tool inscribed variety like that of Manacapurú. Typical Caiambé designs are close-spaced, interlocking key frets. In this decoration and design the Caiambé phase shows certain ties with the later, similarly incised wares of the Polychrome Horizon. This horizon is represented at the Caiambé site by an overlying stratum of Tefé phase pottery. The Caiambé phase radiocarbon dates are A.D. 630 and 640.

As the above-mentioned site stratigraphies all indicate, phases of the Polychrome Horizon follow those of the Incised Rim Horizon. To Guarita and Tefé can be added the São Joaquim and Pirapitinga phases, located farther up the Middle Amazon;[166] and to all of these we can add a series of scattered burial urn finds of the Amazon: Manaus, Miracanguera, Macupirí (on the Rio Japurá), and others on the Rio Purús and Rio Madeira.[167] The most impressive site of the Guarita phase is La Refinaria, near Manaus and not far from the Paredão site. At this section of the Amazon and Lower Rio Negro the escarpment of the Guiana highlands lies close to the river drainages; in fact, the high clay walls of this escarpment, which are some 40 to 60 meters above the low-water mark of the river, are the banks of the active streams. La Refinaria (now the location of an oil refinery some 6 kilometers below Manaus) was a big "terra preta," said to cover 4 hectares and to be as much as 3 meters deep at places.[168] Unfortunately, most of this huge site was destroyed by bulldozers in the construction of the refinery in the 1950's, but Hilbert was able to make some test excavations in a small portion of it. Great quantities of potsherds came from the midden. This was either painted in black-and-red-on-white or red-on-white or ornamented with a deep grooved incision.

The decoration and design elements of the Guarita phase, and of the closely related Middle Amazon phases, show many resemblances to both Marajoara and Napo; however there are differences. For one thing, the grooved incision of the Middle Amazon styles is a much deeper, bolder type of treatment than the incision or excision techniques of either Marajoara or Napo; for another, these Middle Amazon styles feature vessel flanges and a substantial amount of adorno modeling, while neither of these modes is typical for Marajoara or Napo. Thus, oddly, the two members of the Polychrome Horizon style that are found at its easternmost and westernmost extensions have more in common than either does with the geographically intermediate Middle Amazon phases.

The painted and modeled burial urn relates all of these Polychrome Horizon phases, however; and,

as we have noted, most of the earlier finds of Amazonian burial urns can be drawn into this general classificatory grouping. These urns seem always to have been placed in cemeteries or special mortuary places. On Marajó Island, as we have seen, these places were artifically constructed mounds. On the Middle Amazon the urns were left in cemetery fields, apparently on the surface of the ground or only partially buried. The Middle Amazon urns, like those of Marajoara and Napo, were anthropomorphic. Heads and faces were modeled in relief on either the urn wall or else a removable urn lid. Arms were only vaguely fashioned, but legs were more carefully made and frequently stood free from the vessel walls. The individuals were depicted in a seated or squatting position, and the legs were nearly always portrayed as being bound by ligatures below the knee and at the ankle. Although information concerning most of the urn finds is rather scant, it would appear that secondary treatment of the dead, cremation, or both were practiced in connection with the urns.

There is but a single radiocarbon date on the

Figure 6-49. Amazonian burial urn styles. *Left:* Maracá (height, about 40 cm.). *Center:* Miracanguera (height, about 43 cm.). *Right:* Aristé phase or Cunaní style (height, about 39 cm.). (Courtesy B. J. Meggers and Clifford Evans, Jr.)

Middle Amazon Polychrome Horizon style. This comes from the Coarí I site, a Guarita phase component on the river between Tefé and Manaus. It is A.D. 1150, or very close to the Napo phase dates.[169]

The latest of the horizon styles for the Amazon area is the Incised and Punctate. Hilbert refers to one phase, the Itacoatiari.[170] It is represented in overlying strata at the Refinaria site and is also found at Itacoatiari in the Lower Amazon subarea. The distribution of the components of the horizon tends to be eastern. Thus it is known from Santarém, at the mouth of the Rio Tapajós, from Kondurí, on the Rio Trombetas, and from the Mazagão phase in the Territory of Amapá. There are no radiocarbon dates, but the stratigraphy in the Lower Amazon sites places the horizon after the Polychrome Horizon, implying a date of after A.D. 1200 or 1300.

Figure 6-50. Elaborately modeled pottery of the Santarém style. The three specimens at the top have caryatid bases. Vessel at *top left* is 18.5 cm. high. (Courtesy University of Pennsylvania Museum; see also Palmatary, 1960.)

Itacoatiari is linked to the Incised and Punctate Horizon by fine line incisions and punctations arranged in bands on shallow bowl interiors or jar exteriors. These traits had presumably been introduced to the Lower Amazon from Venezuela, through the Arauquinoid subtradition by way of the Rio Negro. There is also a great preference for modeled adorno treatment in Itacoatiari, and this, too, tends to relate it to Arauquinoid styles of Venezuela.

The best-known phase of the Incised and Punctate Horizon, however, is the Santarém. Large collections of Santarém pottery were taken from a site in the location of the modern city.[171] It is probably the most flambuoyantly modeled pottery style in pre-Columbian America. Bowls, jars, and composite-silhouette forms are lavishly elaborated with adornos in human, crocodile, jaguar, monkey, bird, and frog forms. Such ware would have had to have been ceremonial in function, for the fantastic bric-a-brac attached to the vessels would have been an impediment to ordinary household use. Many of the composite-silhouette pieces have pedestal or caryatid bases; handles and flanges are

Figure 6-51. Santarém modeled and relief modeled vessels. The bowl at *left* has a "gutter rim." Specimen at *left* is 15 cm. high; *center*, 12 cm. high; *right*, 19.5 cm. high. (Courtesy University of Pennsylvania Museum; see also Palmatary, 1960.)

common; and specimens often show "gutter" or double rims—as though one bowl or dish had been fashioned inside another, slightly larger, one. The Santarém ware may be tempered with either cauixí or cariapé.[172] Surfaces are usually a natural light tan or buff color, although a small proportion of Santarém pottery is painted. Hollow and solid handmade pottery figurines are associated with the phase, and these tend to be rather crude and grotesque. The most typical representation is a seated, spread-legged female—a figurine type that both in pose and in treatment suggests the Chiriquí figurines of Panama and Costa Rica (p. 337). Elbow-type pottery pipes are also life-modeled in a style reminiscent of the figurines. These are pipes that would need a reed stem for insertion into the bowl for smoking.

Santarém is located fairly near stone outcrops of the lower Tapajós River, and boulders and pebbles of porphyry, quartzite, shale, jadeite, sandstone, and limestone have been used to make artifacts. The most typical Santarém stone artifact is a little polished pendant called a *muiraquita*

Figure 6-52. Santarém figurines, male and female. The male figure at *left* is represented carrying another individual on his back. Height of *left*, 14 cm.; height of *right*, 14.2 cm. (Courtesy University of Pennsylvania Museum; see also Palmatary, 1960.)

(Fig. 6-53). A stylized frog or toad is the most common theme for these muiraquitas, although some are fashioned as birds. Plain celts, notched axes, and eared axes are all represented in the collections obtained at Santarém. Spindle whorls were also made of stone. Coarser manufactures were mortars, pestles, and various pounding and milling implements. These last appear to be relatively rare, although sampling may be distorted, as collectors are likely to ignore such crude items.

There are no data on Santarém nor Itacoatiari burials, and there seem to be no burial urns. In view of this, there has been speculation that these peoples disposed of their dead in another manner. Early travelers to this part of Brazil reported that the Tapajós Indians—a Tupian-speaking tribe who probably are to be associated with Santarém culture—followed secondary burial customs and, afterward, ground up the bones of the deceased, mixed them with beer, and drank them at funeral ceremonies. This may account for the absence of burial remains; and it may also account for the elaborately

Figure 6-53. Santarém stone frog pendants. One at *right* is about 6 cm. long. (Courtesy Museum of the American Indian, Heye Foundation.)

modeled vessels that could have been special receptacles reserved for such ceremonies.

Before leaving the Lower and Middle Amazon subareas, a word should be said about two other phases that appear on the chronology chart (Fig. 6-30): Santa Luzia and Japurá. Hilbert found Santa Luzia pottery above the Polychrome Horizon São Joaquim phase at a site near São Joaquim.[173] In this stratigraphic position it must approximate the Incised and Punctate Horizon phases in time; however it is quite different in ceramic content. Big, flat, concave-sided bowls are usually painted in simple red designs on a white ground, although there is some incised decoration. From the illustrations, I should suspect it to be a localized descendant of the Polychrome Horizon styles, developing in the west and out of the range of Incised and Punctate Horizon influence.

Japurá pottery is found in the Japurá drainage at a site called Mangueiras (not to be confused with the phase of the same name from Marajó Island).[174] It is not placed stratigraphically, but there is an associated radiocarbon date of A.D. 635. In Hilbert's opinion, this style, with broad line incision and zoomorphic adornos, is closer to the Barrancoid subtradition than it is to the Arauquinoid; and the date is more in keeping with the former. In fact, Japurá should have been about contemporaneous with the Incised Rim Horizon phases; however it is typologically distinct from them. It will be recalled that Lathrap's Hupa-iya phase of the Ucayalí was also described as Barrancoid in appearance. Lathrap's estimated date for Hupa-iya is 200 B.C., which is much too early to fall in line with the Japurá phase date. Still, we know that the Barrancoid subtradition had a long history—one that more than spans both of these dates—and it may be that there was more than one Barrancoid diffusion into the Middle and Upper Amazon.

Amapá and the Guianas. The terrain of Amapá Territory varies from seasonally flooded lowlands, like those of nearby Marajó Island, to small mountains and plateaus of the interior. The earliest known archaeological culture is the Aruã phase, which is found throughout the subarea. Aruã sites, it will be recalled, were also found on Marajó and the neighboring islands of the delta, and it is believed that the Aruã tribe

416

migrated from Amapá to these islands at about A.D. 1500. Presumably, they had occupied Amapá for a somewhat longer time. Aruã culture of the mainland is similar to that of the islands, with small, thin midden sites that contain only crudely made and predominantly undecorated pottery;[175] but burial urns and cemeteries have not been reported for the mainland Aruã, and their burial customs remain unknown. Some crude stone alignments are found on the mainland. These consist of rough-hewn, undressed columns and slabs of local granites which had apparently been stood in rows, circles, or triangles; but no burials or finds of consequence have been found nearby.

In southern Amapá, following the Aruã Phase, the dominant archaeological culture is the Mazagão.[176] Mazagão dwelling and cemetery sites are found on hilltops. Burials are of secondary form in large urns. Mazagão pottery (Fig. 6-54) is decorated with incision, and there are design resemblances to the Venezuelan Arauquinoid subtradition and, thus, to the Incised and Punctate Horizon Style of the Amazon. Occasional European glass beads encountered in some Mazagão burials place the phase as late prehistoric–to–early historic.

Apparently contemporaneous with the Mazagão culture is the Maracá phase, sites of which are found along the Maracá River in southern Amapá. Maracá burial urns, which were found in caves, are human effigy forms representing individuals seated upon stools. Arms and legs are in high relief or free standing; the head and face of the man is a pottery lid. Red, black, white, and yellow pigments are used in additional decoration.[177] This Maracá urn form has similarities to the burial urns that have been reviewed in connection with the Polychrome Horizon in the Middle Amazon subarea and elsewhere.[178] In some instances these similarities persisted down to historic times, as in the case of Maracá.

In northern Amapá, north of the Rio Araguarí-Amaparí, the Aristé archaeological phase follows the Aruã.[179] Aristé pottery resembles that of the Mazagão phase, particularly in its earlier period; but later on, Aristé ceramics tend to be decorated with painted designs rather than incisions or scrapings. These painted designs relate to those of the Polychrome Horizon, so in a sense Aristé sees a very late prehistoric-to-protohistoric

Figure 6-54. Potsherds of the Mazagão phase, Territory of Amapá, Brazil. Incised decorative technique. (Courtesy B. J. Meggers and Clifford Evans, Jr.)

fusion of the Polychrome and Incised and Punctate Horizon influences. Aristé villages are on hilltops, and burials are in urns, either secondary or cremated. Sometimes the urns were placed in caves, but there are Aristé cemeteries in open ground in which simple pit or deep shaft-and-chamber graves were excavated. The well-known Cunaní River site had such shaft tombs and the painted Cunaní pottery is typical of the Aristé phase.[180]

North and west of Amapá we come to the Guianas and to the peripheries of the Caribbean area. Earlier in this chapter (p. 378) we noted that the northern Guyana Koriabo phase probably linked to cultures in Surinam and, more remotely, to Aristé. We also saw that some Barrancoid influences were found as far east as Surinam, and, in fact, these can be traced onward into French Guiana.[181] These observations, however, pertain to the coast. There is reason to believe that inland in the Guianas an occupation by Tropical Forest–type farmers was a relatively late event, occurring largely after A.D. 1500. These interior savannas and forests, which in very early times had been occupied by hunting peoples (Chap. 2, fn. 157), had apparently long been abandoned, and it may be, as Evans suggests, that their protohistoric-to-historic occupancy was the result of an inland retreat of Indian groups occasioned by the arrival of the Europeans.[182] Evans and Meggers define a Rupununi phase from the savanna of the same name in central Guyana.[183] Thin refuse village locations covered from 1000 to 5000 square meters, and the slash-and-burn agriculture that sustained these people was probably carried out on the forest hillslopes that alternate with savanna flats. Crude, undecorated pottery is typical, including large burial jars and pottery griddles. The burial jars were found with secondary remains in rock shelters. Stone hoes and axes were, apparently, used in farming. The phase is related to the Macushi (Macusi) Indians, whose presence is documented in the region in the late eighteenth and early nineteenth centuries. A Taruma phase is based on sites from the headwaters of the Essequibo. The archaeological residue of this phase— particularly the pottery—is somewhat more distinctive than that of the Rupununi. Incised, stamped, and red-on-white wares are recorded, as well as griddles, pot-rests, and spindle whorls. The absence of burial urns seems to correlate with the ethnographic information that the Taruma Indians practiced cremation. But Rupununi and Taruma, in somewhat different ways, thus preserved some of the cultural heritage of the Amazonian tradition into virtually modern times.[184]

Venezuelan Amazonas. The Amazonas Territory is in south-central Venezuela. It is known archaeologically from work in regions along the Orinoco, between Puerto Ayacucho and the mouth of the Ventuari, and on the Ventuari and its tributaries.[185] These drainages border and descend from the western edges of the Guianas highlands. Most of the terrain surveyed is flat or rolling country, with gallery forests backed by savannas. Two archaeological phases have been defined. One, the Nericagua, centers along the Lower Ventuari and the Orinoco. Sites are rather small. In one instance a circle of refuse mounds was grouped around an open plaza. The individual mounds are from 40 to 80 meters long, 8 to 10 meters wide, and 1.25 to 3.00 meters in height. They are composed of stratified refuse and could be the kind of accumulations that build up under pile houses. In most sites, however, there is no such visible refuse patterning. No Nericagua cemeteries have been located, and nothing is known of burial practices. Nericagua pottery is both cariapé and cauixí tempered; in this case, the cauixí temper is the later, gradually replacing the cariapé in the refuse sequences. Simple bowls have wide, outsloped rims, and the upper sides of these rims bear the zigzag and zoned parallel incised lines that are associated with the Incised Rim Horizon.[186] Modeling, however, tends to replace incision toward the end of the phase. This modeling is in the form of rather sloppily made biomorphic adornos. There is also an increment of negative or resist-painted pottery in the complex, with fine, wavy-line designs. This negative-painting, together with cylindrical pottery stamps, hints at affiliations to the west with Colombia. Pot-rests, pottery griddles, some percussion-fashioned choppers, and some polished celts make up the inventory. Radiocarbon dates—which are consistent with the stratigraphy —indicate a span from at least A.D. 761 to 1339, and Evans suggests a beginning date for the phase of about A.D. 500.[187] This conforms to the general dating for the Incised Rim Horizon. There are some similarities to the Venezuelan Cotua phase, located in the Puerto Ayacucho region on the northern Amazonas border. Cotua has been dated by Rouse and Cruxent as A.D. 300–700.[188] However, these similarities refer largely to certain incised rim decorations; otherwise, Cotua, which is in the Venezuelan Saladoid subtradition, does not closely resemble Nericagua.

The other phase, the Corobal, comes from sites higher up on the Ventuari and its branches.[189] Sites are small and refuse is thinner than in Nericagua sites. Pottery is mainly sand tempered, plain, or decorated with appliqué nubbins, fillets, and anthropomorphic adornos. Griddles, flat stamps, spindle whorls, and stone axes, polished and percussion-chipped, belong to the complex. There are no radiocarbon dates, and there are few specific resemblances between Corobal and Nericagua, so that dating is difficult. The adorno elaboration and one little frog pendant of polished stone hint at relationships with Santarém, although Corobal as a whole has a much simpler artifact inventory. Thus it appears to be relatively late—that is, to have its beginnings somewhat later than those of Nericagua.

Lowland Bolivia. A consideration of this subarea takes us to another corner of the Amazonian area. Lowland Bolivia is drained by the Madeira and its tributaries. It is situated next to the southeastern edge of the Peruvian area and to the northeastern edge of the South Andes area; thus the prehistoric cultures here might be expected to show relationships to these other areas, and this seems to have been the case, although the specific nature of these relationships remains largely speculative. Little systematic archaeological research has been executed in this Amazonian subarea, but the surveys and excavations made by Baron Nordenskiold, more than 50 years ago, give a tantalizing glimpse of the cultural complexities of Lowland Bolivia, and any summary of the subarea is based largely on his work.[190]

Nordenskiold's principal excavations in the Mojos region were in three mound sites, Velarde, Hernmarck, and Masicito, all located near the town of Trinidad, which is situated on the Rio Mamoré.[191] This is flat, seasonally flooded, savanna country; however, the mound sites are frequently in slightly higher forest patches, and this was the case with Velarde mound. The mound measured 45 by 25 meters and was about 5 meters in height. It is difficult to say to what extent it was simply a refuse accumulation and to what extent it may have been purposefully constructed. Quite probably, it started out as a debris heap from a pile house or houses; later it probably was intentionally added to in order to construct a house platform, a burial place, or both. Two distinct cultural layers were observed in the refuse in and around the mound. These two layers—or their contents—have been designated as Lower and Upper Velarde, and they represent distinct culture phases. Lower Velarde pottery decoration is by painting in a purplish-brown-on-buff or a polychrome red-and-purple-on-cream. Designs are short spirals, triangles, hooks and areas of cross-hachure. These were apparently worked into larger patterns of some intricacy. Vessel forms are flat-based bowls with wide, open orifices and slightly incurved rims; ollas; and collared ollas. Many vessels have four small, solid feet, and some have low annular bases. There are no handles, but human head rim adornos are common. Pottery pestles or grinders, pottery ladles, a pottery whorl, and a female figurine were associated with Lower Velarde, as were two primary extended burials.

Both Nordenskiold and Bennett have seen vague Tiahuanacoid similarities in the Lower Velarde pottery.[192] This too has been my impression,[193] particularly with reference to the purplish pigment and to some of the painted designs; however, it should be emphasized that the resemblances are

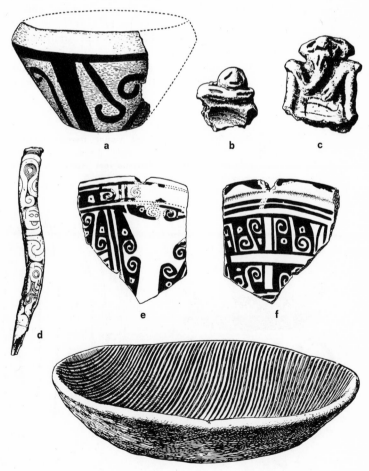

Figure 6-55. Lower Velarde complex artifacts, Mojos region. *a:* Painted vessel. *b, c:* Pottery adornos. *d:* Carved bone. *e, f:* Painted sherds. *g:* Vessel with deeply scored interior. Diameter of *a* is 16 cm., and *b* and *c* are to this scale; length of *d* is 17.5 cm., and *e* and *f* are to this scale; diameter of *g* is about 53 cm. (After Nordenskiold, 1913.)

slight and that they cannot be taken to establish a firm connection. Therefore the important question of whether or not this Amazonian lowland complex was derived from the Bolivian Andes cannot now be answered. It is a possibility, nothing more. Certainly, Lower Velarde cannot be linked to any specified point in the Tiahuanacoid, or pre-Tiahuanacoid, developments of the highlands; and Bennett's correlation of Lower Velarde and the Arani I phase of the Cochabamba region of Southern Bolivia must remain highly speculative.[194] I have, however, followed this correlation in the tentative alignment proposed on the chronology chart (Fig. 6-30), together with the estimated date of A.D. 500.[195]

Upper Velarde pottery is painted in either monochrome or bichrome designs—a purplish-brown on a buff or orange ground color. (It is not definitely stated whether the ware was slipped). Painted designs occur in horizontal bands on bowl exteriors, as crudely traced lines in interiors, and as vertical bands on large burial urns. Checker patterns, crosses, cross-hatchings, pyramid steps, triangles, s-shapes, and other geometric elements were employed. There was a tendency to juxtapose heavy lines or zones with lighter lines—a general

characteristic, it will be recalled, of the styles of the Amazonian Polychrome Horizon. Vessels, including both bowls and large burial urns, have tripod supports. The urns contained secondary burials and had bowls used as covers. Other objects of discoidal shape surmounted by a large handle may have served as urn covers. Other Upper Velarde items are large clay platters with interior grooves or ribs and ribbed clay cylinders. These were perhaps used as grinding sets, and manioc may have been prepared in them—in place of the wooden boards set with small stones that are used in other parts of the Amazon.[196] In this connection it should be observed that Lowland Bolivia is a stoneless country. Stools were also made of pottery, and one was painted in the same style as the pottery vessels. A few polished stone axes, miscellaneous bone artifacts, and a pottery figurine make up the collection for the phase.

There are some ceramic continuities—largely in the use of painted decoration and in some design elements—between the Lower and Upper Velarde wares, and it may be that Upper Velarde is a development out of Lower; however, the differences in the two styles clearly indicate a break or a hiatus in the Velarde mound occupancy so that if we are dealing with the same pottery tradition, the intermediate stages of its development are missing. There is little by which to essay a date for Upper Velarde, and the placement on the chart (Fig. 6-30), between A.D. 500 and 1000, is sheer guess-

Figure 6-56. Upper Velarde and Mound Hernmarck complexes, Mojos region. *Left* and *right*: Hernmarck. *Center*: Upper Velarde. All have small tripod feet. Height of *center*, about 64 cm. (After Nordenskiold, 1913.)

work. Such a date, however, would not be completely out of keeping with the chronological range of the Amazonian Polychrome Horizon that Meggers and Evans have bracketed between A.D. 600 and 1300,[197] although it would be somewhat earlier than any of the radiocarbon dates that are now available for that horizon.[197a]

Mound Hernmarck, Nordenskiold's second mound, is near Caimanes, between the Mamoré and Itonama Rivers. It, too, is in a forested high spot; it is 225 by 85 by 3 meters; and there is a large depression nearby that may have been a borrow pit. This implies purposeful construction, probably to provide a living site safe from the floods. An interesting feature of the site is a long causeway that passes through the Hernmarck mound on its way across the savannas.[198] These artificial causeways are a prominent feature of the Bolivian savannas, and we will mention them and other "earthwork" features further on. Nordenskiold found river shells, fish and animal bones, potsherds, ribbed clay platters and grinders, spindle whorls, figurines, and a polished T-shaped stone ax in this tumulus. He also uncovered 43 burial urns with secondary burials. Hernmarck pottery resembles that of Upper Velarde in that decoration is by painting in one or two colors, and bowls, ollas, and urns have the little tripod feet seen on the Upper Velarde specimens. Painted designs are similarly intricate arrangements of spirals, s-shaped elements, and small interlocked motifs. They suggest high stylization of life forms, although what these forms may have been is lost in the abstraction. Like Upper Velarde—and the Amazonian Polychrome Horizon—the general impression of the designs is that of juxtaposed use of heavy and fine line elements. The dating of Hernmarck follows that of Upper Velarde—on the basis of fairly close typological correlation—although I will surmise that Hernmarck is slightly later. Its style impresses one as more in the mode of such Polychrome Horizon styles as Napo and Marajoara, and this suggests a position of A.D. 1000 or after.

Nordenskiold's third Mojos mound, Masicito, is near the course of the Mamoré, 25 kilometers southwest of Loreto. The immediate location is open, low savanna. It is an extensive platform, almost certainly built up as a living and burial place. Like the other mounds, it contained living refuse, sherds, and urn burials. Unlike the other two mounds, the Masicito pottery is decorated primarily by incision. The incisions form parallel diagonal lines, chevrons, and hatched triangles, and there are also lines encircling bowls. Punctation is often combined with the incisions. Vessels typically have tripod supports that are modeled as stylized animal feet. The grooved platters and grooved or ribbed clay cylinder grinders, like those of Upper Velarde and Hernmarck, were also found at Masicito. The tripod feet and the grooved platters suggest a dating more or less comparable with that of Hernmarck and Upper Velarde, although Bennett has estimated Masicito to be slightly later.[199]

Mounds like these three—or at least mounds similar in size and appearance—are common throughout the Mojos region. They indicate a substantial pre-Columbian population and also one that was organized to a degree that can be considered over and above the level of the usual Tropical Forest society. Some of the mounds are considerably larger than the ones described. W. M. Denevan reports one as much as 15 meters high and 100 meters long.[200] In addition to the mounds there are the causeways. These would appear to be former means of travel between mounds or between mounds and patches of high ground. Usually less than a kilometer in length, they are raised about a meter above the surrounding flats and are from 2 to 8 meters in width. But even more impressive are the prepared fields. These cover many square miles of savanna land and include ancient furrow rows, raised rectangular platforms 25 to 50 centimeters in height, and fields filled with regularly spaced little circular hillocks.[201] Such extensive works were almost certainly for agriculture. They would have aided in drainage, and the digging and piling up of earth in the various furrows, platforms, and hillocks would have mixed the sod and grass through the soil and improved its texture and fertility. Unfortunately, there is little ethnohistoric information about the actual technical use of these fields, although farming on the savannas, with the digging of drainage canals and the building of causeways, was reported by early sixteenth-century Spaniards. The Indians occupying the region at this time were the Arawakan-speaking Mojo and Baure who lived in villages numbering as many as 400 houses and had a class-structured society and a well-developed institution of chieftainship.[202] Mounds like those of

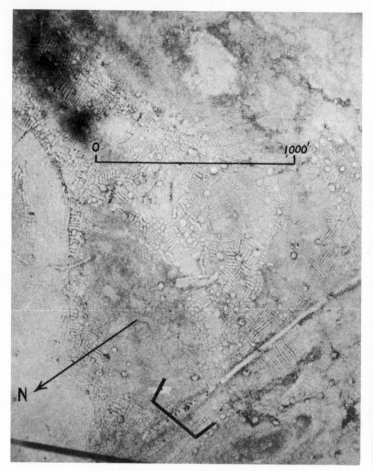

Figure 6-57. Views of the ridges, fields, and causeways in the Mojos region of Lowland Bolivia. Air photos. *Left:* Vertical shot. Note scale line of 1000 m. *Right:* Oblique shot (not of same locality). (Courtesy W. M. Denevan and George Plafker; see also Denevan, 1966.)

Hernmarck, Velarde, and Masicito were presumably constructed by the ancestors of peoples like the Mojo and Baure.

The Mojos region is the only one in the Bolivian Lowlands subarea for which we have substantial information. Elsewhere there are a few scattered findings. North of the Mojos, on the Rio Guaporé, at the Brazilian border, burial urns and three-footed vessels are reported, although here the principal pottery decoration is an incised style that would appear to be more like the Acauan complex of the Amazon delta than any of those we have just described.[203] On the Upper Rio Beni, to the west of the Mojos, Nordenskiold dug a village midden at Chimay in which he found primary extended burials, no burial urns, and four-footed pottery.[204] These features suggested a relationship to the Lower Velarde phase; but as there was no polychrome, and only incised and modeled decoration, Bennett felt that Chimay was later, perhaps more comparable to Masicito.[205] At Rurrenabaque, downstream from Chimay, Nordenskiold reported both tetrapodal and tripodal pottery and painted decoration with hook-element designs. This sounds like Lower Velarde pottery. But a modeled pottery urn was also in the collection, an anthropomorphic representation, suggestive of those found on the Middle Amazon and stylistically associated with the Polychrome Horizon.[206]

Amazonian Area Margins. Moving outside the Bolivian Lowlands and considering the adjacent Andean areas, we note what appear to be essentially Andean cultures descending down to about 2000 meters above sea level in the vicinity of Sandia, Peru, on the Upper Inambari River. The Upper Inambari is a tributary of the Madre de Dios, which in turn joins the Beni. These cultures have fieldstone or stone block houses that are associated with cultivation terraces, and in some cases Inca influences have been identified. Below 2000 meters the stone terraces still continue, although today only shifting Tropical Forest–type agriculture is practiced by the tribes here. These tribes are Amazonian in their general cultural affiliations.[207]

To the south of the Bolivian Lowlands is the Southern Bolivian subarea of the South Andes area. To recapitulate briefly, the earliest pottery horizon here, one variously referred to as Chullpa Pampa, "La Cultura de los Túmulos," or "La Cultura Megalítica," is estimated to date to as early as 500 B.C. This horizon probably presents many regional variations, but as it is known in the Cochabamba region it is a ceramic complex of gray, flat-bottomed beakers in addition to deep bowls or burial urns of a thick orange or red-slipped ware (see pp. 223–225). It has been conjectured that this complex shows a blend of early or pre-Tiahuanaco highland influences and unidentified lowland influences. Whatever these lowland influences may have been remains obscure, for as we move east from the Cochabamba region, into the Mizque and Santa Cruz regions, we find nothing that throws light on the problem. Nordenskiold's Mizque region excavations at sites such as Pererereta, Peres, Sapaina, and Pulquina reveal direct inhumations and not urn burials, and all sites show clear Tiahuanaco horizon influences in kero-shaped vessels, polychrome painting, and designs of running demon or god figures and puma heads. There does, however, seem to have been some blending of lowland ceramic traits in these Mizque-Tiahuanaco complexes; for instance, many vessels have tripod supports.[208] There are also plain and incised wares in these sites, and Bennett saw such wares as representing a horizon, one intermediate between the Tiahuanaco horizon influences and the still later Inca influences.[209] It is a pure surmise, however, to consider such a horizon of plain and incised wares as "Guaraní," as Nordenskiold was inclined to do. The Inca sites of the Mizque region include places like Incallacta and Batanes, with their adobe and stone houses, temples, and fortifications.

Going still farther east, to the Santa Cruz region, takes us to the extreme limits of the South Andes area and perhaps beyond them. Rio Palacios, north of the city of Santa Cruz, yielded urn burials.[210] These urns are globular-bodied, high-collared forms with finger-impressed scallops or corrugations on the collars. It is the style of urn that is associated with Guaraní sites to the south and east, in the Chaco and in Eastern Brazil; and this style represents an important subtradition or offshoot of the Amazonian cultural tradition, one that has an eastern and southerly distribution in South America. In late prehistoric and early historic times this Guaraní urn subtradition was a strong influence along the South Andes–Amazonian frontier, and it is likely that it corresponds to the expansion of Guaraní peoples in this direction at these times.[211] Other Rio Palacios pottery is largely plain or appliqué-strip decorated, and vessels often have tripod legs. Copper and silver ornaments were found at Rio Palacios, and these may indicate Inca influence. The Santa Cruz region was known to be the easternmost outpost of the Inca, who established a fort at Pucarilla and another site at Samaipata. In the latter were found the little gold and silver llama and human figurines, essentially identical in style with those found on the far marches of the Inca empire in Ecuador (Chap. 5, fn. 128) and in Central Chile (p. 242).

Comment on the Bolivian Lowlands and Its Borders. We have reviewed cultures at variance with those seen along the main course of the Amazon and in the Ucayalí and Napo subareas. The closest link would seem to be in the resemblances that are seen between Upper Velarde and Hernmarck and the Amazonian Polychrome Horizon.[212] On an earlier level, the Lower Velarde complex stands essentially unrelated. Possibly it shows slight contact with Tiahuanaco-related cultures of the Andes; however as a culture phase it appears to be lowland-adapted. The modeling and incision of the Masicito pottery bears only general resemblances to the Amazonian cultures with these traits; certainly no clear "horizon-type" affiliations can be pointed to. It would seem that such pottery is relatively late in Lowland Bolivia, and what are probably related manifestations of it appear to be on a post-Tiahuanaco horizon in the adjacent Mizque and Cochabamba regions of Southern Bolivia. In very late times in the Santa Cruz region

—at that point where the Bolivian Lowlands, Southern Bolivia, and the Chaco borders converge—what is called Guaraní pottery and Inca materials are found together.

The Upper Xingú. Except for the Bolivian Lowlands, the country of the great southern tributaries of the Amazon is archaeologically almost unexplored. Some preliminary items of information come from the Upper Xingú. These result mainly from work at a group of sites on the Upper Xingú proper and at another group on the tributary Culuene (Kuluene) River. Sites are small riverbank midden areas, a hundred meters or so in diameter and averaging a half meter in depth, although in some sites the refuse is substantially deeper. The immediately surrounding country is that of gallery forests, with savannas lying farther back from the streams. This is, of course, the same region from which Carneiro has described the twentieth-century Kuikuru Indian tribe referred to earlier in this chapter.

The Upper Xingú group of sites have been designated the Diauarum phase, those of the Culuene, the Ipavu phase. The ceramics of both phases have been linked to the Incised and Punctate Horizon. There are, however, some differences in the two phases. Diauarum pottery is cariapé tempered, that of Ipavu cauixí tempered. In the former phase red-on-white painting is reported as more common. Both phases have manioc griddles, sherd disks, pot-rests, and chipped and semi-polished stone axes.[213]

Farther north on the Xingú, Curt Nimuendaju has reported both Santarém-like pottery (which would align with the Incised and Punctate Horizon) and urn burials (which, unlike Santarém, might align with the Polychrome Horizon).[214]

Recapitulation: Amazonian Horizon Styles or Subtraditions. In attempting to summarize the archaeology of the Amazonian cultural tradition we will start with the four major horizon styles to which we have had reference in the above discussions. Although these styles are horizon phenomena and thus have a utility in plotting cultural relationships in a "horizontal" or period-by-period fashion, they also have a "vertical," or traditional, dimension in that each persisted over a relatively long period of time and overlapped chronologically with one or more of the others. From this latter point of view, it is appropriate to think of them as subtraditions of the Amazonian cultural tradition, in much the same way that we spoke of the various Caribbean area subtraditions.

The earliest of the horizon styles is the Zoned Hachure. Pottery of the horizon is characterized by step-fret and other simple geometric designs that have been drawn with deep incised lines and then filled with fine line hachure or cross-hachure. Pottery of this style is found in the Tutishcainyo phase of the Ucayalí subarea, in the Yasuní phase of the Rio Napo subarea, in the Anantuba phase of the Marajó Island subarea, and in the Jauarí phase of the Lower Amazon subarea. In the Tutishcainyo context this zoned hachure decoration is associated with composite-silhouette bowls, vessels with rim and body flanges, and a few double-spout-and-bridge jars. Yasuní pottery is close to Tutishcainyo, particularly Late Tutishcainyo, in the presence of carinated bowl forms and flange features; but Anantuba and Jauarí both have simpler vessel forms than these. In the case of Jauarí there are additional decorative features in modeled adornos that are not seen in the other phases of the Zoned Hachure Horizon Style.

As to the cultural context of the Zoned Hachure Horizon Style, Lathrap is inclined to view the Tutishcainyo phases as fully agricultural—at least in the sense of a Tropical Forest level of agricultural development—while Evans thinks that Anantuba may be only incipiently agricultural. None of the phases in question has manioc griddles, and this may be significant as indicating that none processed bitter manioc. As to settlement, all of the sites that pertain to the horizon are of modest size, although an appreciable duration of occupancy is indicated. There is no evidence for any specialized or ceremonial architecture.

The Zoned Hachure Horizon is estimated to have begun as early as 1800 B.C. This is based upon the cross dating of Early Tutishcainyo with the Waira-jirca phase of the Peruvian highlands, which has such a radiocarbon date. A direct radiocarbon date on Yasuní, however, is only 50 B.C., and the radiocarbon date for Anantuba is 980 B.C. If all of these dates are accepted, the Zoned Hachure Horizon would have a "traditional" persistence of almost 2000 years; thus, it should be emphasized that this conclusion is by no means a firm one.

There are two principal hypotheses about the origins and connections of the Zoned Hachure Horizon complexes. Lathrap sees Early Tutishcainyo as one of the earliest of the New World pottery complexes.[215] He feels that it shares a common ancestry with the Valdivia pottery of the Ecuador coast (see pp. 264–266) and that this ancestry probably lies somewhere to the north, perhaps in such a complex as Puerto Hormiga (pp. 268–270). Further, he thinks that the diffusion of this zoned hatched pottery moved southward from Colombia to Peru by a lowland route that lay to the east of the Andes. Early Tutishcainyo thus contributed to the development of the Andean Waira-jirca complex of Kotosh rather than the reverse so that, if anything, Early Tutishcainyo is earlier, instead of later, than Waira-jirca. Presumably—although Lathrap has not yet spelled out all of these ideas in print—the other Zoned Hachure Horizon complexes then derive from a spread or diffusion of Tutishcainyo to other parts of the Amazonian area.[215a]

The other hypothesis is that of Evans and Meggers.[216] They too recognize the Tutishcainyo relationships to Puerto Hormiga,[217] but they would see the diffusion southward from Colombia to be by an Andean route, so that Kotosh Waira-jirca was established before Tutishcainyo and was in fact ancestral to the latter. In keeping with this interpretation they believe that there was a substantial time lag between Waira-jirca and Tutishcainyo and that in this way Tutiscainyo is substantially later than Lathrap's estimate. In their reconstruction Yasuní is a late manifestation of Tutishcainyo. Ananatuba and Jauarí could then be the results of an Amazonian downstream movement of peoples carrying the Zoned Hachure stylistic ideas; or these phases could have resulted from diffusions or migrations that went from Puerto Hormiga in northern Colombia eastward through the Caribbean area and from there to the Lower Amazon. In this latter connection we recall that one important decorative element in the Saladoid subtradition, as represented at El Mayal on the Venezuelan coast and at Cedros on Trinidad (see pp. 372 and 381), is a form of incised zone cross-hatching that is similar to the zoned hachure styles of the Amazon; however, El Mayal and Cedros are dated at about the beginning of the Christian era, and this is a millennium too late for the Ananatuba radio-carbon date of 980 B.C. It is clear that the problems centering around the origins, dispersals, and relationships of the Zoned Hachure Horizon are far from settled, but my own feeling is that the Tutishcainyo ties to Waira-jirca, in addition to the Ananatuba radiocarbon date at the distant mouth of the Amazon, argue strongly for an inception of the horizon well before 1000 B.C.

The phases of the Incised Rim Horizon Style are linked by a wide, flat-topped rim on an open-bowl form that bears incised line designs. These designs are usually rectilinear, parallel-line arrangements, such as chevrons or triangles. The horizon is recognized in the Mangueiras phase of Marajó, the Paredão, Manacapurú, and Caiambé phases of the Middle Amazon, and the Nericagua phase of Venezuelan Amazonas. There is considerable diversity among all these phases. Thus Mangueiras pottery is simple in form and decoration, that of Paredão more elaborate, with basket-handled vessels and modelled adornos; Manacapurú ceramics also have adornos together with a different kind of incised designs; and the other phases show their peculiarities. In fact, it is only the rim decoration mode, in addition to a general emphasis on incision as a decorative technique, that establishes the horizon. The cultural context is assumed to be that of Tropical Forest agriculture. This is suggested either by the presence of manioc-roasting plates or by site ecology. Such things as pottery pipes, labrets, and spindle whorls are found in the sites; and urn burial is reported from one, or perhaps two, of the phases.

The radiocarbon dates of the Incised Rim Horizon phases fall mostly between A.D. 400 and 900; but Meggers and Evans have suggested a beginning date in the first century A.D., so the approximate range may be estimated as more or less the first millennium A.D.

The origins for the Incised Rim Horizon are uncertain. It is possible that they may be in the Caribbean area. The linking of the Cotua phase to the horizon suggests this. Cotua is a Saladoid phase that also shows strong Barrancoid influences. The presence of two Barrancoid phases in the Amazon area—Hupa-iya in the Ucayalí sequence and Japurá in the Middle Amazon—indicates contact from a Caribbean or Orinocan direction. A local evolution of the Incised Rim Horizon Style is another possibility. In this event, the earlier Zoned

Hachure Horizon complexes could have been the setting in which the mode of incised decoration on a wide, flat-topped rim developed in some one subarea and spread from there to the others. Little more than these speculations can be offered about this horizon at the present time.

The Polychrome Horizon is distinguished by black-and-red-on-white painting, by incision and excision techniques combined with painting, by anthropomorphically modeled burial urns, and by a design style that is most briefly characterized as one in which large and highly stylized motifs are composed by the juxtaposition of broad line and fine line elements. The horizon is represented by the Marajoara phase of Marajó, the Guarita and related phases of the Middle Amazon, the Napo and Caimito phases of the Upper Amazonian subareas, and the Aristé phase of Amapá. Beyond these, horizontal similarities are probably to be seen in the Maracá style of Amapá and in the Upper Velarde and Hernmarck complexes of Lowland Bolivia. There is a high degree of similarity in ceramic forms and decoration among many of these complexes. There are also differences among them, as, for instance, the tendency to a deeper, grooved-type incision and the adorno modeling in the Middle Amazonian phases.

The developmental level of the cultures of the Polychrome Horizon is clearly higher and more complex than that of the cultures of the two previous horizons. This is first seen in the size and depth of the sites. Many of the Polychrome Horizon middens are of dimensions that suggest small towns of 1000 to 2000 persons. It is also seen in special mortuary places—cemetery areas or mounds built for burials—and in differential treatment of the dead indicating status or class differences. In some subareas, such as Marajó Island or the Bolivian Lowlands, large habitation mounds were also constructed.

There are not many radiocarbon dates on the Polychrome Horizon, but the ones available range from A.D. 1150 to 1375. These are too few and the dating span is too brief to allow us to draw conclusions about localities of origin or directions of spread. Evans and Meggers interpret the horizon as a cultural complex that was introduced into Amazonia from elsewhere.[218] In looking for a hearth of origin they pick the Colombian

highlands and inter-Andean valleys, singling out the Quimbaya and San Agustín regions for special mention; however, the traits that the Amazonian Polychrome Horizon shares with these regions are of rather a general nature, and Evans and Meggers admit that the closest actual stylistic parallels are to some of the anthropomorphic urns of the Lower Magdalena Valley Plato and Saloa phases (p. 317, Fig. 5-5).[219] This Lower Magdalena section of Colombia is a tropical lowland similar to the environmental settings of the Amazonian area where the Polychrome Horizon cultures are found. Thus, while a Colombia-to-Amazonia movement of such cultures is a possibility, it is also possible that the spread could have been in the other direction. It is true that an origin of the Polychrome Horizon cultures on Marajó Island seems highly unlikely. The Marajoara phase appears full-blown there. The same is also true of the appearance of the Napo phase at the other end of the Amazon. The Middle Amazon may be a better possibility. Here the Guarita and related phases show features of incising and modeling that could be continuities out of earlier local cultures. To these could have been added polychrome painting and burial urn traits to produce an essentially Amazonian lowland climax culture. The burial urn and polychrome ideas may have come from Colombia, but other good possibilities are the Ucayalí drainage, where painted wares and burial urns are as early as the Yarinacocha phase (A.D. 90), and the Bolivian Lowlands, where polychrome painting is found in the Lower Velarde phase.

This consideration of the origins of Polychrome Horizon cultures takes us directly into the matter of the potentialities of the lowland tropical forest country for culture development. The Meggers-Evans opinion on this, which is linked to their strong feeling that cultures such as Marajoara and Napo must have been formed outside the Amazon area, is that a tropical forest environment and a system of slash-and-burn cultivation set a very definite ceiling on culture growth and that the elaborations of the kind displayed by the Marajoara phase were precluded by these conditions.[220] To their way of thinking, such a form of agriculture simply was not productive enough to sustain the population concentrations necessary for what Steward has called a "Circum-Caribbean" or "Sub-

Andean" (see pp. 18–20) level of development. Others have disagreed about this, insisting that slash-and-burn, root-crop agriculture can be highly productive.[221] Without attempting to settle this ecological argument here, I should like, however, to offer one observation about the Amazonian situation. The two most elaborate Amazonian cultures—Marajoara and the Upper Velarde-Hernmarck development in Lowland Bolivia—have savanna rather than tropical forest settings. This prompts us to ask whether savanna cultivation might not be more productive than that of the forest. Or—and this is more important—does successful savanna land cultivation necessitate a higher level of social and political organization? The various cultivation "works" of the Bolivian Lowland savannas—the furrowed fields, the raised fields, the fields of hillocks, the drainage ditches, and the associated mounds and causeways—look as though they would have demanded the co-ordinated efforts of rather large-scale labor groups. It all stands in striking contrast to the garden-plot, digging-stick cultivation of the individual farmer of the forests. Apparently there are no such cultivation "works" on the Marajó savannas; at least they are not reported. Perhaps their absence is a clue to the Marajoara "failure"; for, if the Marajoara culture failed for reasons of environmental non-adaptiveness, it should be pointed out that this failure occurred in a savanna rather than a forest ecological niche.

The last of the four Amazonian horizon styles is the Incised and Punctate. Diagnostic features are incised and punctated banded designs on wide-rim interiors and on jar exteriors. The incised lines tend to be finer than those of the earlier Incised Rim Horizon, and this, together with the punctations and the application of designs to portions of vessels other than rim tops, distinguishes the later from the earlier horizon. The phases of the Incised and Punctate Horizon are concentrated in the Lower Amazon subarea. The best known are Itacoatiari, Santarém, and Kondurí. Mazagão of Amapá Territory and Diauarum and Ipavu of the Upper Xingú are also grouped with the horizon. The level of cultural development seems to have been that of Tropical Forest village agriculture for the most part; however the size of the sites and the degree of ceramic elaboration in the Santarém phase suggest a somewhat more complex socio-political and ceremonial organization. Radiocarbon dates are lacking, but stratigraphy and European contact associations with some phases indicate a dating for the Incised and Punctate Horizon sites just prior to and after A.D. 1500.

The origins of the Incised and Punctate Horizon phases are probably in the Arauquinoid subtradition of Venezuela. Meggers and Evans include Arauquín in the horizon; but these authors also include Mabaruma, and this raises the question whether the Incised and Punctate Horizon has Barrancoid as well as Arauquinoid relationships. Of course, in the Orinocan development of styles, the Arauquinoid subtradition derives in large part from the Barrancoid, so that there would be an indirect relationship in this way; however it is also possible that there was a parallel Barrancoid-to-Arauquinoid development in the Amazon Basin. For instance, at Santarém there are sherds that look more Barrancoid than Arauquinoid, and such specimens also occur in Kondurí.[222] They suggest that there may be a Barrancoid horizon on the Lower Amazon, although Hilbert's surveys in that subarea have not yet disclosed it.

This horizon summary leaves a number of Amazonian phases unmentioned. In the Ucayalí subarea the Shakimu phase, with a radiocarbon date of 650 B.C., seems to be a development out of Tutishcainyo and influences from the Peruvian area. The subsequent Hupa-iya phase is thought by Lathrap to be a distant relative of the Venezuelan Barrancoid subtradition, and Hilbert has made the same observation about the Japurá phase of the Middle Amazon. In the Ucayalí the subsequent series of phases—Yarinacocha, Pacacocha, Cashibocaña, Nueva Esperanza, and Cumancaya, bracketed between radiocarbon dates of A.D. 90 and 770 —precede and, perhaps in a developmental sense, lead up to the Polychrome Horizon Caimito phase. In the Rio Napo subarea the Tivacundo phase, with a date of A.D. 510, may be linked to Cumancaya by means of its incised technique and its red zoned decoration.

At the other end of the Amazon, on Marajó and nearby islands, the Acauan and Formiga phases seem to be approximately contemporaneous with, and in some ways similar to, Mangueiras, although they do not share the Incised Rim Horizon mode.

The later Aruã phase of Marajó and the Amapá mainland looks like a reduced end product of the Polychrome Horizon (and subtradition); and in the Middle Amazon subarea the same can be said about the Santa Luzia phase. This reduction and impoverishment of the old Amazonian cultures is seen carried even later into the Rupununi and Taruma phases of the interior of the Guianas and, probably, in the Cotacocha phase of the Rio Napo, despite the identification of the latter with Quechua groups.

Corobal, in Venezuelan Amazonas, seems fully prehistoric. It may show Santarém influences, although in a much debased form.

The Lowland Bolivia Lower Velarde complex has polychrome painting and tetrapodal supports. Its ancestry and affiliations are obscure; the Tiahuanacoid resemblances, if present at all, are slight. As already indicated, I have suggested a relationship between Upper Velarde and Hernmarck and the Polychrome Horizon, although these complexes do deviate from the other phases of that horizon in a number of ways, such as in the use of tripod supports for urns. Masicito is a burial-urn culture that features incised decoration. These incised modes are just possibly a geographically remote expression of the Barrancoid subtradition; however, Masicito appears to have a very late pre-Columbian date.

Finally, along the Lowland Bolivian-Southern Bolivian frontier we have phases such as the Rio Palacios, which were contemporaneous with the Inca expansion of the fifteenth century but which, in their corrugated and fingernail-impressed burial urns, relate very specifically to the Guaraní cultures of the Chaco and the East Brazilian area.

Footnotes

1 See Rouse and Cruxent (1963) and Rouse (1964 a) for a definition of the Caribbean area.

2 Sauer (1950 a); James (1959, pp. 63–99, 739–856); Sleight (1965).

3 Rouse and Cruxent (1963). Rouse has presented the West Indian chronology many times, but see his recent summary (1964 b).

4 Rouse and Cruxent (1963); Cruxent and Rouse (1958–1959); Rouse (1964 b). These authors refer to these geographical divisions as "areas." I have occasionally combined some of their "areas" into subareas.

5 Cruxent and Rouse (1958, pp. 113–114 and 128–129); Rouse (1960).

6 Evans and Meggers (1960, pp. 25–64); Osgood (1946, pp. 49–50, the Barambina shell mounds).

7 Rouse (1953 b, 1960).

8 Cruxent and Rouse (1958, pp. 75–76). See also same reference for the Cabo Blanco site, Central Coast subarea, Guaíra region and the Pedro García site, East Coast subarea, Barcelona region. See Rouse and Cruxent (1963, p. 47) for Cerro Iguanas.

9 Cruxent and Rouse (1958, pp. 46–55 and elsewhere); Rouse and Cruxent (1963, pp. 44–46).

10 De Booy (1917, 1919); Hatt (1924).

11 Bullen (1962); Bullen and Sleight (1963).

12 Alegría, Nicholson, and Willey (1955); Alegría (1965).

13 Rouse (1941); Rainey (1941).

14 Rouse (1960).

15 W. R. Coe (1957). Based also on my own knowledge of Maya Highland and Lowland occurrences.

16 Bullen (1962).

17 Ibid.

18 Ortoire, in Trinidad, dating at about 800 B.C., had been thought to mark the beginning of the first movements from the mainland to the island chain (Rouse, 1953, 1960). Rouse (1964 b) expresses some doubt about the validity of the single Marban date.

19 Rouse (1942, 1960, 1964 b); Osgood (1942); Cosculluela (1951).

20 Rouse (1960) follows G. G. Simpson's lead on this. Simpson proposes the origins of West Indian faunal populations as the result of such accidental "rafting" from the mainland areas. This apparently gave a randomness to the distribution of certain species throughout the islands.

21 Rouse (1960). In this same reference Rouse mentions a collection of large, stemmed flint projectile points said to be from Jamaica. These have the closest resemblances to Southeastern United States Archaic Period cultures. They are the only supposedly "preceramic" remains reported from that island; they are not well documented as to provenience; and I think that there is a good chance that they may not be from Jamaica. Lovén (1935, pl. XIII) illustrates these points.

22 See Bullen (1962 a).

23 Rouse (1948 a).

24 Kirchhoff (1948 d).

25 Kirchhoff (1948 d).

26 Kirchhoff (1948 d).

27 The reader is referred to Leed's (1961) paper on Yaruro cultivation as affording an insight

into the nature of minimal Tropical Forest horticulture and its cultural correlates.

28 Hernandez de Alba (1948 c, d).

29 This is the location of the Barrancas site zone, and its terminal Guarguapo phase may pertain to these Arawaks.

30 Gold must have been rare in the Caribbean area. True metallurgy was not known, and the gold of the Spanish descriptions was probably trade material from Colombia.

31 Hernandez de Alba (1948 e).

32 Kirchhoff (1948 c). Murdock (1951) tends to discount this alleged Mesoamerican affiliation. Perhaps it has been overstressed, but the ball-game similarity is notable.

33 Taino ethnography and ethnohistory have been summarized by Rouse (1948 b); H. W. Krieger (1930); and Loven (1935). The notable primary sources are Columbus (1893, 1930); Las Casas (1951); Benzoni (1857); Oviedo (1851–1855).

34 Taino agriculture has been described from the sources by Sturtevant (1961).

35 Rouse (1953 a).

36 Rouse (1948 c).

37 Rouse (1948 b).

38 Rouse and Cruxent (1963) and Cruxent and Rouse (1958) use the term and concept "series" to refer to a set of ceramic complexes or phases that are related to each other and that can be plotted in space and in time. Following the scheme of presentation in this book, I have considered these as ceramic traditions, or cultural subtraditions within the larger, inclusive Caribbean cultural tradition.

39 Cruxent and Rouse (1958, pp. 213–223); Rouse and Cruxent (1963, pp. 112–125).

40 Howard's (1943) "Early Ronquín" phase is now called simply Ronquín (Rouse and Cruxent, 1963, pp. 112–125). This "Early Ronquín," or Ronquín, is overlaid at that site by the "Late Ronquín," or Camoruco phase (Arauquinoid subtradition).

41 Rouse and Cruxent (1963, pp. 112–125).

42 The Rio Guapo style of the Central Coast subarea (Rio Chico region) is also to be considered as a Barrancoid influenced style of the Saladero subtradition (Rouse and Cruxent, 1963, pp. 108–110).

43 Favored by Sanoja (1965).

44 Rouse and Cruxent (1963, pp. 89–90).

45 Cruxent and Rouse (1958, pp. 223 ff. on Barrancas and other Barrancoid styles); Rouse and Cruxent (1963, pp. 81–90). The radiocarbon dates on the Barrancas phase fall between 985 and 930 B.C. This is an overlap with the Saladero radiocarbon dates from the lower levels of the same site. However, we follow Rouse and Cruxent here in giving the stratigraphic evidence priority over the radiocarbon dates. The Barrancas phase is thus placed at 700 B.C. to A.D. 300.

46 Evans and Meggers (1960, pp. 65–123).

47 Rouse (1953 b).

48 Rouse (1964 b).

49 The cross dating of Mabaruma with the Barrancas–Los Barrancos sequence of the Lower Orinoco is a matter of some dispute. Evans and Meggers (1960, 1964) prefer a derivation from, and a chronological equivalence to, Los Barrancos. Lathrap (1964, 1966 b) takes the view that the Mabaruma phase was derived from Barrancas and that it dates, in its beginnings, as early as 800–700 B.C. Lathrap's case for a Barrancas cross dating is supported by the presence of complete rim flanges in the lower Mabaruma levels—a Barrancas trait; however, the other good Barrancas marker—the double-spouted vessel —is absent from Mabaruma. The question obviously bears on the terminal dating of the earlier Alaka phase of Guyana, for if Mabaruma can be dated back to the early part of Period II, then the Alaka culture must have been assimilating to ceramics and agriculture at about this time rather than a thousand years or so later. The chronology chart (fig. 6–30) expresses this ambiguity. Both Evans, Meggers, and Lathrap agree that Mabaruma lasts on until historic times.

50 Kidder II (1944, pp. 27–85, 1948 b); Rouse and Cruxent (1963, p. 87).

51 Kidder II (1948 b, p. 421).

52 Rouse and Cruxent (1963, pp. 87 ff.).

53 Cruxent and Rouse (1958, pp. 80–83); Rouse and Cruxent (1963, pp. 101–105).

54 Rouse and Cruxent (1963, pp. 68 and 105).

55 Cruxent and Rouse (1958, pp. 131–133); Rouse and Cruxent (1963, pp. 125–127); Osgood and Howard (1943, pp. 115–121).

56 Cruxent and Rouse (1958, pp. 190–194, 209–210, 230–234); Rouse and Cruxent (1963, pp. 90–95).

57 Petrullo (1939).

58 They would not only have had a drainage advantage; the heavy, grass-covered soils would have been turned and loosened in their construction, rendering them more suitable for farming. Extensive ridged fields, presumably for cultivation, have also been reported west of San Fernando Apure (personal communication, W. M. Denevan, 1969).

59 See Cruxent (1966) for a discussion of "calzadas," especially in the State of Barinas.

60 Some are associated with the Caño del Oso phase of Northwest Venezuela (Rouse and Cruxent, 1963, pp. 71–75).

61 Howard (1943) referred to the Camoruco phase as "Late Ronquín."

62 Rouse and Cruxent (1963, pp. 71–75).

63 Cruxent and Rouse (1958, pp. 103, 196–199); Rouse and Cruxent (1963, pp. 105–108). The La America phase of the Central Coast also belongs to the Memoid subtradition. It is dated as Period V.

64 Cruxent and Rouse (1958, pp. 42, 78, 97, 102, 169–178, 180–182); Rouse and Cruxent (1963, pp. 95–101).

65 Bennett (1937); Osgood (1943).

66 The recently defined Zancudo phase (Sanoja, 1965) from the southern part of the Lake Maracaibo subarea of Northwest Venezuela is a likely source of "western" influences for the Valencia phase. The Zancudo ceramics include the anthropomorphic modeling on vessel

necks and the coffee-bean eye treatment. It is, of course, evident that "western" influences were already making themselves felt in the Lake Valencia region in the earlier La Cabrera phase.

67 Evans and Meggers (1960, pp. 124–153).

68 Cariapé temper is an ash that comes from a tropical tree bark. It is a characteristic aplastic of Amazonian area pottery and, in the present instance, would appear to be introduced with the Koriabo phase from the east. However cariapé temper also occurs in minor amounts in early Mabaruma phase pottery, and Evans and Meggers (1960, p. 152) speculate that in this instance it results from diffusion from the Upper Orinoco subarea.

69 These are given indirectly through the presence in late Mabaruma (and late Koriabo) of a pottery style known as Apostadero. Apostadero would appear to be the final expression of the Barrancoid tradition (Evans and Meggers, 1960, pp. 152–153). Apostadero pottery occurs in the Lower Orinoco subarea, apparently contemporaneous with the Arauquinoid Guarguapo phase, and it is sometimes associated with eighteenth- and nineteenth-century trade goods (Cruxent and Rouse, 1958, pp. 234–237).

70 The Charlesburg site was explored by P. Goethals, whose work is cited by Evans and Meggers (1960, p. 150).

71 Evans and Meggers (1960, pp. 154–190).

72 Evans and Meggers (1960, p. 334).

73 Evans and Meggers (1960, p. 338). This seems to be indicated in their general conclusions.

74 Evans and Meggers (1960, pp. 188–189) suggest the Mayo site complex from Trinidad as a possible Abary prototype; however Rouse believes this to be a seventeenth- and eighteenth-century Hispano-Indian site.

75 Sanoja (1963, 1965).

76 Rouse and Cruxent (1963, pp. 130–139).

77 Rouse's most recent summary of this is his 1964 b article; but see also Rouse (1948 b, 1951).

78 Taylor and Rouse (1955).

79 Rouse (1947); Bullbrook (1953).

80 See Rouse (1964 b) for a listing of these.

81 In this connection, it is interesting that the Saladoid subtradition is very weakly represented on Barbados, which lies off to the east of a Trinidad-Tobago–to–Grenada route. The Bullens suggest that Barbados was bypassed in the main Saladoid migration into the West Indies and only received Saladoid influences later from Grenada (Bullen and Bullen, 1968).

82 Bullen (1964, 1965). Bullen is hesitant about the Arawak identification of the Saladoid subtradition in the West Indies and prefers to refer to it as "Pre-Arawak," reserving the Arawak identification for the later subtraditions.

83 Bullen (1965).

84 Rouse (1947).

85 Haag (1965).

86 Bullen (1962 b).

87 Alegría (1965).

88 Rouse (1952, pp. 413–417).

89 See Rouse (1964 b). For more details on the Ostionoid culture of Puerto Rico see Rouse (1952); for the Virgin Islands see Bullen (1962 b); for Jamaica see Howard (1965) and DeWolf (1953).

90 In Eastern Puerto Rico there is a phase known as Santa Elena, which dates from the latter half of Period IIIB and which Rouse does not include in the Ostionoid or any other of his principal West Indian ceramic series (Rouse, 1964 b). From the descriptions, however, Santa Elena would appear to be a subareal variant of Ostionoid—at least it is more like Ostionoid than it is like any of the other Puerto Rican styles.

91 See Rouse (1964 b); Bullen (1965, 1962 b). For instance, the Grenada styles most comparable to Ostionoid would be those of the Caliviny Period (Bullen) or, presumably, what Rouse calls Westerhall on his chart.

92 Rouse (1948 b).

93 Rouse (1941, 1948 b).

94 Granberry (1956).

95 Tabío and Rey (1966); Tabío and Guarch (1966).

96 Rouse (1942).

97 R. R. Howard (1956, 1965).

98 Rouse (1964 b).

99 Rouse (1947).

100 Rouse (1964 b).

101 Rouse (1964 b, p. 11).

102 Rouse; (1964 b, p. 11) see also H. W. Krieger (1929, 1931).

103 Rouse (1952).

104 Bullen (1962 b).

105 Rouse (1941).

106 Granberry (1956).

107 Rouse (1942); Tabío and Rey (1966).

108 Chicoid pottery descriptions and illustrations are to be found in Rouse (1941, 1948 b, 1952) and H. W. Krieger (1929, 1931).

109 Rouse (1941, 1948 b, 1952); Lovén (1935); Joyce (1916); Fewkes (1907).

110 Mason (1941); this includes an appendix by Rouse on the pottery and artifacts. Mason used the name Capá; however, the nearest small community is Utuado, and this is the better-known name in Puerto Rico. The site is now a Commonwealth park area.

111 Rouse (1952, p. 477).

112 Ekholm (1946, 1961).

113 Oviedo y Valdés (1851–55); see Alegría (1951) for a recent summary of the game from ethnohistoric sources.

114 Joyce (1916, pp. 186–193).

115 Rouse (1961).

116 Bullen (1964, 1965); Bullen and Bullen (1968).

117 Rouse (1964 b).

118 Rouse (1964 b, p. 14).

119 Haag (1965).

120 Bullen and Bullen (1968, p. 143).

121 This section is based on James (1959, pp. 539–554); Sauer (1950 a); Gilmore (1950); Levi-Strauss (1950).

122 See Mason (1950, especially linguistic map).

123 Carneiro (1961). Levi-Strauss (1948) mentions this tribe with the spelling "Guicuru."

124 See Lowie (1948) for a summary of Amazonian Tropical Forest ethnography.

125 Steward and Faron (1959, pp. 346–349).

126 Evans (1964).

127 Steward and Faron (1959, pp. 254–257).

128 Evans (1964).

129 Meggers and Evans (1961).

It has been used by Hilbert (1968) in his monograph. The dates that I have given here have been modified slightly from the original Meggers-Evans estimates as the result of new radiocarbon dates.

130 These finds (see Evans and Meggers, 1960, pp. 21–24; Evans, 1964) probably relate to the Canaima complex of Venezuela (Rouse and Cruxent, 1963, pp. 42–43).

131 Hilbert (1968, p. 255) mentions possible preceramic shell mounds on the Atlantic coast south of the Amazon delta and also in the Amazon Valley at Santarém and Alemquer; however these are not discussed further. Lathrap and associates (1967) refer to a site (Primera Altura) on an eastern tributary of the Ucayalí, in which the lower levels of a midden are without pottery; however no definite artifacts were found in these levels.

132 Hilbert (1968) refers to all of the Amazon, from just above Marajó to the Peruvian border, as the "Middle Amazon"—as in the title of his book; however in other places he seems to restrict the "Middle" designation to the section above Manaus, sometimes called the Rio Solimões. Thus, "Der rund 1400 km lange Amazonaslauf zwischen Manaus an der Rio Negro-Mundüng und der Atlantikküste wird im allgemeinen als Unterlauf bezeichnet. An der Rio Negro-Mundüng beginnt der Mittellauf des Amazonas..." (1968, p. 41).

133 Lathrap (1968 ms.). Since this book went to press, Lathrap (1970) has brought out a summary of his research and interpretations which should be consulted by all serious students. Compare his chronology chart with that offered here.

134 Lathrap (1958). Lathrap's Yarinacocha work is presented in great detail in a Ph.D. thesis (1962).

135 Lathrap (1968 ms.).

136 Lathrap (1968 ms.) argues for Early Tutishcainyo as being slightly earlier (2000–1800 B.C.) than Waira-jirca (1800 B.C. and immediately after); however at the present stage of our knowledge this seems to be shaving it a little too fine, and I have chosen to regard both as nearly contemporaneous.

137 One other indirect radiocarbon cross-reference bearing on the dating of Tutishcainyo comes from the Alto Pachitea sequence. This region is a tributary valley of the Ucayalí, which descends from the Andean foothills on the west; thus it is a transitional zone between our Peruvian and Amazonian areas. The sequence has been developed through the work of William Allen, an associate of Lathrap's, and to date has only been reported upon in a very preliminary way (Lathrap and associates, 1967 ms.). It runs through six sequent phases, the earliest of which, Cobichaniqui, is dated by radiocarbon to 1778–1418 B.C. Neither Cobichaniqui nor the second phase, Pangotsi (1275 B.C.) show close resemblances to Early Tutishcainyo or the Ucayalí sequence, although they do feature carinated and composite-silhouette bowls and incised decoration. The third phase, Nazaratequi, continues in the same tradition as the first two but does have some Late Tutishcainyo vessel-form features. The radiocarbon date on Nazaratequi is 670 B.C. This sequence and these dates—in spite of the lack of close Tutishcainyo ties—would indicate the presence of pottery in the immediate neighborhood of the Ucayalí subarea at the beginning of the second millennium B.C.

Another Late Tutishcainyo link to the west is seen in the pottery from the Cave of the Owls, near Tingo María, on the Huallaga River, again a location of the very border of the Peruvian and Amazonian areas (Lathrap and Roys, 1963).

138 Lathrap (1968 ms.).

139 This and other Ucayalí phase descriptions are based on Lathrap (1958, 1968 ms.) and Lathrap and associates (1967 ms.).

140 Lathrap (1968 ms.) suggests Cumancaya as the most likely prototype for modern Shipibo pottery and Caimito as the principal prototype for Cocama. However, modern Shipibo ware, with its black-and-red-on-white designs, is clearly in the same closely related tradition as Caimito.

141 Evans and Meggers (1968, pp. 7–18).

142 Evans and Meggers (pp. 19–31).

143 Evans and Meggers (pp. 32–82).

144 The doubt expressed over the nature of the urn remains results from many of the urn finds being casual discoveries of the past century.

145 Lathrap and associates (1967 ms.).

146 Evans and Meggers (1968, pp. 83–87, 106–107).

147 Meggers and Evans (1957, pp. 174–193 and 1956); Evans (1964).

148 "The earliest pottery-producing sites in the Amazon drainage show characteristics of village refuse accumulation that differ from sites typical of the Tropical Forest slash-and-burn complex, suggesting a slightly different subsistence base." (Evans, 1964, p. 424). This is a change from the earlier interpretation (Meggers and Evans, 1957, p. 589), in which it was felt that the Ananatuba phase initiated the "Tropical Forest Pattern."

149 Evans and Meggers (1968, p. 89).

150 Meggers and Evans (1957, pp. 194–221).

151 Evans (1964).

152 Meggers and Evans (1957, p. 591).

153 Meggers and Evans (1961).

154 Meggers and Evans (1957, pp. 429–456).

155 Meggers and Evans (1957, pp. 222–241).

156 This section is taken largely from Meggers and Evans (1957, pp. 259–424); however there is an extensive earlier literature on Marajoara, or the "Marajó style" of pottery (see, for example, Hartt, 1885; Steere, 1927; Palmatary, 1950).

157 The Meggers-Evans sequence of Marajoara subphases has been challenged by Joanna Harris (1966 ms.), who feels that the sequence that they have presented runs the other way. This would imply a cultural elaboration, rather than a deterioration, through time.

158 Meggers and Evans (1957, see summary on pp. 593–594).

159 Meggers and Evans (1957, pp. 37–44 and 158–159).

160 Hilbert (1968, pp. 69–71, 87–90).

161 Hilbert (1968, pp. 91–122).

162 Debate over the origin of the black soil seems settled by recent analyses; see Hilbert (1968, p. 262); it is decayed organic matter from human occupation.

163 Hilbert (1968, pp. 258–259), for this and other radiocarbon dates.

164 Hilbert (1968, pp. 122–136), also see Hanke (1959).

165 Hilbert (1968, pp. 136–148).

166 Hilbert (1968, pp. 149–193).

167 Hilbert (1968, pp. 193–206), see also Meggers (1948, "Maraca," "Miracanguera," "Manaos," "Teffé," "Japurá") and Evans and Meggers (1968, pp. 95–104).

168 Hilbert (1968, pp. 149–151).

169 Hilbert (1968, p. 262).

170 Hilbert (1968, pp. 207–224 and 265–266).

171 The principal collections from this site were obtained by Curt Nimuendaju in 1922 but never fully published by him. The most thorough description of the style is Palmatary's (1939, 1960); see also Nordenskiold (1930).

172 The chronological value of these two temper types is unclear. There is now some evidence that cauixí (sponge) is the earlier, being associated with the Incised Rim Horizon; cariapé is more commonly associated with the Polychrome Horizon. However, there is a late reintroduction of cauixí in some places in the Amazon. While recognizing that temper type does show chronological changes in some sequences, we advise caution in applying such a chronology for the Amazon area as a whole. See Evans, Meggers, and Cruxent (1959, p. 368).

173 Hilbert (1968, pp. 239–254 and 266–267).

174 Hilbert (1968, pp. 225–238 and 267).

175 Meggers and Evans (1957, pp. 37–44).

176 Meggers and Evans (1957, pp. 44–103).

177 Meggers and Evans (1957, pp. 75–78); see also Howard (1947), Ferrerira Penna (1879), and Goeldi (1905) for accounts of this famous urn style.

178 For example, Hilbert (1968, pp. 193–206) and, for even more widespread tracings, Imbelloni (1950 c).

179 Meggers and Evans (1957, pp. 103–167).

180 Goeldi (1900).

181 See Reichlen and Reichlen (1947). It is of interest that ancient cultivation ridges have been reported near the shore in Surinam (Parsons and Denevan, 1967). There is reason to believe that these date to the first millennium A.D., and that they relate to Mabaruma-like cultures.

182 Evans (1964).

183 See Evans and Meggers (1960) for details on the Rupununi and other interior Guiana phases; see also Evans (1964).

184 In the twentieth century the Wai Wai Indians have replaced the Taruma in the Upper Essequibo region (Evans and Meggers, 1960). A phase similar to some of these, especially to the Rupununi, is the Taponaiké of interior French Guiana (Reichlen and Reichlen, 1947).

185 Evans, Meggers, and Cruxent (1959).

186 Meggers and Evans (1961).

187 Evans (1964).

188 Rouse and Cruxent (1963, p. 114). Meggers and Evans (1961) include Cotua in the Incised Rim Horizon.

189 Evans, Meggers, and Cruxent (1959).

190 Results of Nordenskiold's principal excavations, which were in the Mojos region, were published in 1913. Nordenskiold also worked in the Beni region (Nordenskiold, 1906, 1924 a, b). In addition, he investigated and published on several regions in southern Bolivia: Mizque (Nordenskiold, 1917, 1924 a); Chuquisaca (Nordenskiold, 1924 a); Tarija (Nordenskiold, 1924 a); and Santa Cruz (Nordenskiold, 1911, 1913, 1924 a). These southern Bolivian regions are subsumed in the present book under the "Southern Bolivian subarea" of the South Andes (see pp. 223–225 and 225–227); however, they present transitional cultural features linking the Peruvian, South Andean, and Amazonian areas. The reader is referred to Bennett (1936, pp. 341–412) for a summary of both the Bolivian Lowland and Southern Bolivian regions. Bennett worked in the latter himself, and although he did not go into Lowland Bolivia proper, he summarized Nordenskiold's Mojos and Beni results and attempted to relate them to Southern Bolivia. A still later analysis of the Nordenskiold data, together with those of Bennett, is given by Howard (1947, pp. 60–75).

191 Nordenskiold (1913).

192 Nordenskiold (1917); Bennett (1936).

193 Willey (1958).

194 Bennett (1936, Table 2, opposite p. 413).

195 The difficulties in this estimated dating are great. Even if we assume a Lower Velarde–Arani I correlation, we are left with the dating, both relative and absolute, of Arani I. Bennett, of course, dated Arani I as "Derived Tiahuanaco," but, as I have pointed out in Chapter 4 (pp. 225–227), there is considerable controversy and uncertainty as to the proper relative and absolute dating of "Derived Tiahuanaco." Can "Derived Tiahuanaco" be considered as marking a relatively brief span of time? And is "Derived Tiahuanaco" a derivation of the Tiahuanaco horizon, or is it (or some of it) a pre-horizon development? As we have noted in Chapter 4, Ibarra Grasso has taken the latter position, and I have favored this. Thus I have equated Arani I with Ibarra Grasso's Yampará I, with an estimated date of ca. A.D. 200 to 600 (see Fig. 4–3); and, following this, I place Lower Velarde toward the end of this time range, or at A.D. 500.

196 Rydén (1964).

197 Meggers and Evans (1961).

197a Lathrap's (1970) dating of the Bolivian Lowland cultures is about the same as mine.

198 Denevan (1966) made these observations on Hernmarck many years after Nordenskiold's work there. Denevan also reports that causeways and an apparent "borrow pit" are in the vicinity of Mound Velarde.

199 Bennett (1936); Howard (1947).

200 Denevan (1963) also heard of a Mojos region mound that was said to be over 30 meters in height.

201 These features are described by Plafker (1963) and Denevan (1963, 1966). They are seen to best advantage from the air, which probably explains why it has been only in recent years, since the development of aerial photography, that they have come to attention.

202 Steward and Faron (1959, pp. 254–257) describe these tribes.

203 Becker-Donner (1956).

204 Nordenskiold (1924 b).

205 Bennett (1936, pp. 399–400).

206 Nordenskiold (1924 b). See also Imbelloni (1950 c).

207 Lathrap and associates (1967 ms.).

208 Nordenskiold (1917 a, 1924 a, b).

209 Bennett (1936, pp. 387–389).

210 Nordenskiold (1913); Bennett (1936, pp. 392–394).

211 Nordenskiold (1917 b).

212 Evans (1964) notes similarities between Hernmarck–Upper Velarde and the Polychrome Horizon but is hesitant to include them within the horizon.

213 Simoẽs (1967); PRONAPA (1970). Dole (1961–1962) has also reported on excavations in two localities in the Culuene country, and from the descriptions of the pottery it seems likely that it pertains to what Simoẽs is calling the Ipavu phase. Dole describes extensive "ditches," which she believes may have been dug by the Indians as defensive works, near some of these sites. Simoẽs (1967) cautions that these may be natural river channels, former stream courses.

214 Nimuendajú (1948).

215 Lathrap (1968 ms.).

215a The reader can now be referred to Lathrap's views in his 1970 book.

216 Evans and Meggers (1968, pp. 88–92).

217 Evans and Meggers see Puerto Hormiga as derived from Ecuadorian Valdivia (as has been explained here, pp. 275–276). Lathrap would be more inclined to see Valdivia as derived from Puerto Hormiga or from some Colombian lowland complex. This disagreement, however, does not bear upon the present argument, as both parties suggest Puerto Hormiga as the source for Tutishcainyo.

218 Evans and Meggers (1968, pp. 93–106).

219 These are the same burial urns that Bennett (1946 e, p. 850, pl. 171, f) refers to as the "Mosquito" style.

220 Meggers and Evans (1957); see also Meggers (1954).

221 Ferdon (1959), Dumond (1961), and Carneiro (1961) all argue for the positive productiveness of tropical forest swidden farming. Nevertheless I am inclined to agree with Meggers and Evans in that I think the tropical forest and slash-and-burn agriculture do set limits on social and cultural growth. My difference with them would be that I think these limits are somewhat higher than they are willing to allow. I would not see the "Sub-Andean" or "Circum-Caribbean" developmental level as being precluded by these conditions. In fact, we have abundant evidence from both South American and Meso-american lowlands to the contrary. What probably is precluded by a tropical forest setting and slash-and-burn cultivation is the truly urban level of development. For instance,

Tikal, the largest of the Maya "cities" and probably the largest tropical forest site in native America, had an estimated resident population of about 10,000 (W. R. Coe, 1965). This is to be contrasted with the closely packed habitation pattern of Teotihuacán in the Mexican uplands, for which a population of 85,000 has been estimated (Sanders and Price, 1968).

Carneiro (1961), although arguing that slash-and-burn farming was highly productive, feels that Amazonian communities remained small for another environmental reason. This was that cultivable land was present in almost limitless quantities. As population grew there was no necessity for peoples to stay together but, rather, every inducement for fission and dispersal into the ever-available new forest terrain. The political power to insist on tribal cohesion was lacking, and the system fed back into itself, in that the numerous small, autonomous villages precluded the rise of chiefly power. It is Carneiro's further hypothesis that it is only in regions where cultivable lands are clearly circumscribed by natural environmental limits that a significant build-up of population numbers and their enforced concentration into single communities occurs and allows for the attendant rise of political controls and general cultural advance. This is an extremely interesting idea, but it does not help us much with the archaeological facts of the Marajoara and other Polychrome Horizon cultures, which show a level of advance beyond that of the Tropical Forest village.

222 E. K. Easby (1952) has noted such pottery in Santarém and referred to it as "Unrelated Ware." For Kondurí see Hilbert (1955).

Eastern and Southern South America embraces four major culture areas:

(1) the East Brazilian; (2) the Chaco; (3) the Pampean; and (4) the Fuegian (see pp. 23–24 and Fig. 1-1). We shall consider them in this order.

The East Brazilian Area

The Setting. The East Brazilian culture area includes almost all of eastern and southern Brazil (Figs. 1-1, 7-1). The line separating it from the Amazonian area is an environmental as well as cultural boundary. It approximates the northern edge of the Brazilian plateau and the southern edge of equatorial climates; it also approximates the southern boundary of typical Amazonian tropical forest vegetation.[1] The western boundary of the area, from the Mato Grosso south to Uruguay, follows the western edge of the uplands and hills where these descend to the flats of the Gran Chaco and the Paraguay Valley. In the south there is a gradual transition from the highlands into the pampas of Uruguay.

In Eastern Brazil the highlands rise sharply behind the Atlantic coast to an elevation of over 2000 feet. Climate ranges from tropical in the north to temperate in the south. Rainfall is generally less than in the Amazonian area. In the northeast, where there is more precipitation along the coast, there are fringes of forest vegetation, but the interior, which is drier and has poorer

Eastern and Southern South America

soils, sustains only a scrub cover. In the south there are subtropical forests and a moderate rainfall.[2]

The rivers of Eastern Brazil, like those of the Amazonian area, are well stocked with fish, and along the Atlantic Coast there are—or were—shellfish resources. The interior offered better hunting lands than those of the Amazonian area. Thus we can say that the East Brazilian area provided a number of different but suitable settings for non-agricultural peoples, and the archaeological record shows the occupancy of these settings going back to very early times, as we have seen in Chapter 2. Farming is, of course, feasible in many parts of the area, especially along the coast and in the interior.valleys. We have records of such farming from ethnography, and, before that, there is indirect testimony to it from archaeology.

Languages and Tribes. A glance back at the general linguistic map for South America (Fig. 1-5) will show two major language groups in the East Brazilian area: the Macro-Ge and the Tupian.[3] Tribes of the Macro-Ge group are clustered in two main blocks, one of which lies inward from the Atlantic Coast, along the crest of the Brazilian Plateau. The land here is generally less well suited for farming than that of the immediate coastal strip or the north-south interior valley of the São Francisco. The tribes in question (Fig. 7-2) are the Botocudo, Guaitacá, Purí-Cororado, Patashó, Camacan, and, in scattered enclaves farther south, the Caingang.[4] The other and larger block lies well to the interior. Here

were—and in some cases still are the Central Ge, the Southern Cayapo, the Timbirá, the Carajá, the Bororo, and others.[5]

Tribes of the Tupian language group (Tupí, Guaraní, Tupinamba, Tupinikin, Potiguara, and others) held the Atlantic coastal strip, the interior country between the Macro-Ge-speakers of the Atlantic ridge and the Ge proper, and much of far southern Brazil.

The subsistence of the Macro-Ge peoples of the Atlantic ridge was, in some cases, based entirely on hunting and plant collecting; in other instances these pursuits were supplemented by farming—most frequently of sweet potatoes and maize. Some tribes made rather simple pottery; others, like the Botocudo, made none at all. Villages consisted of either single-family or large multi-family houses. The construction of these was much the same as in the Amazonian area. In the interior, the Central Ge and their neighbors were more often dependent upon agriculture than were the tribes of the Atlantic ridge group, and, in general, they appear more like the Tupian Tropical Forest farmers.[6]

The Tupians of Eastern Brazil were typical Amazonian-like Tropical Forest cultivators, dependent primarily upon bitter manioc. This was supplemented by sweet potatoes, maize, peanuts, lima beans, kidney beans, and other cultigens. The Tupians were also hunters and, to a lesser extent, fishers. They made and used dugout canoes, lived in large multi-family houses, and were potters and weavers. Among the vessels made and used by these people were burial urns that are obviously

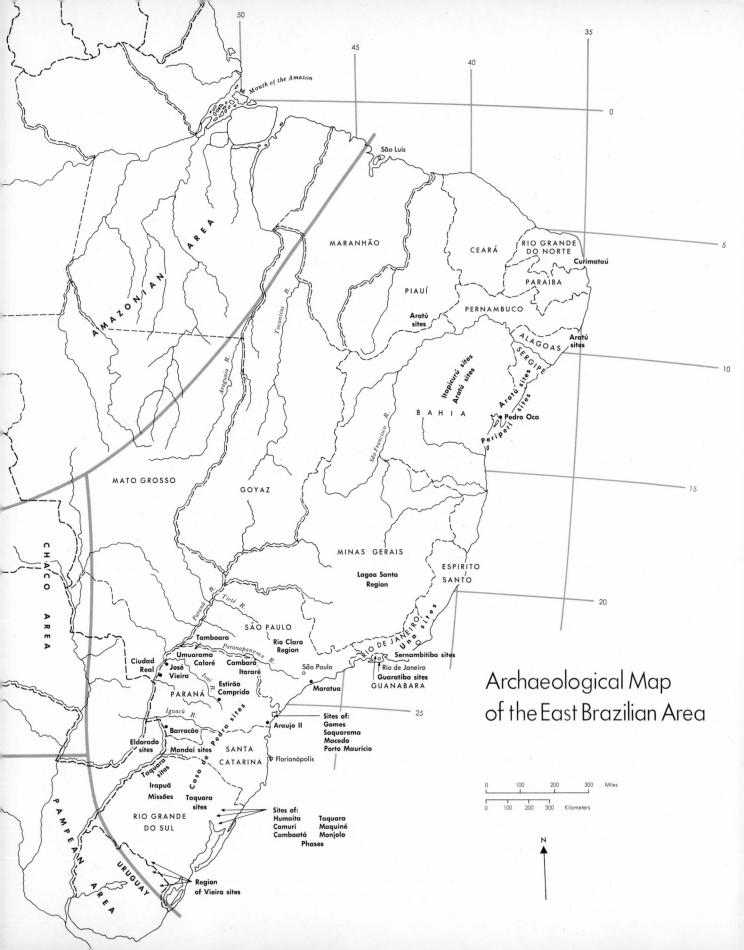

Archaeological Map of the East Brazilian Area

Mouth of the Amazon

50
45
40
35
0
5
10
15
20
25

São Luis

AMAZONIAN AREA

MARANHÃO

CEARÁ

RIO GRANDE DO NORTE

Curimataú

PIAUÍ

PARAIBA

PERNAMBUCO

Aratú sites

Aratú sites

ALAGOAS

SERGIPE

Itapicurú sites

Aratú sites

Aratú sites

Periperi sites

B A H I A

Pedro Oca

Araguaia R.

Tocantins R.

São Francisco R.

MATO GROSSO

GOYAZ

CHACO AREA

MINAS GERAIS

ESPIRITO SANTO

Lagoa Santa Region

SÃO PAULO

Rio Claro Region

Paraná R.

Tietê R.

Paranapanema R.

Tamboara

Umuarama

Caloré

Cambará

Itararé

Ivaí R.

Ciudad Real

José Vieira

Estirão Comprido

PARANÁ

São Paulo

Maratua

RIO DE JANEIRO

Una sites

Sernambitiba sites

Rio de Janeiro

Guaratiba sites

GUANABARA

Iguacú R.

Araujo II

Sites of:
Gomes
Saquarema
Macedo
Porto Mauricio

Barracão

Eldorado sites

Mondaí sites

SANTA CATARINA

Casa de Pedra sites

Florianópolis

Taquara sites

Irapuã

Missões

Taquara sites

RIO GRANDE DO SUL

Sites of:
Humaita   **Taquara**
Camuri   **Maquiné**
Camboatá   **Monjolo**
     Phases

Region of Vieira sites

PAMPEAN AREA

URUGUAY

| 0 | 100 | 200 | 300 | Miles |
| 0 | 100 | 200 | 300 | Kilometers |

N

Figure 7-1. (*Left*, p. 436) The map shows some site locations specifically; others are indicated in a more approximate regional manner.

Figure 7-2.

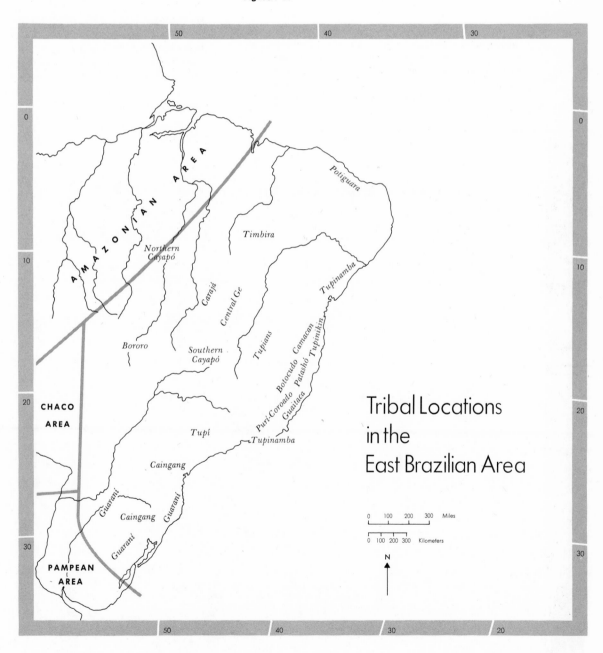

Tribal Locations in the East Brazilian Area

related to the styles (and to the mortuary practices) of the Amazon area.[7]

Steward's interpretation of this Macro-Ge and Tupian linguistic and cultural dichotomy in Eastern Brazil was that the Macro-Ge represented the earlier populations of the area who had been non-agricultural and, at least in some instances, non-pottery making.[8] They were subsequently overrun by Tupian peoples of an Amazonian cultural tradition who brought in a Tropical Forest, manioc-agricultural pattern of life. The newcomers occupied the more favorable agricultural lands, especially those that approximated the tropical coasts and river valleys of their original Amazonian homeland. The Macro-Ge peoples were left as enclaves in interior highlands where, subsequently, they acculturated, in varying degrees, to the modes of an agricultural existence. Donald Lathrap has

Figure 7-3. Chronological chart of East Brazilian area, showing both interior and coastal cultures by approximate subareas. Key for small letters in circles: U, East Brazilian Upland tradition; S, Sambaquí tradition; B, Eastern Brazilian pottery tradition; T, Tupiguaraní subtradition of the Amazonian tradition; N, Neo-Brazilian pottery tradition; ?, unidentified pottery complex.

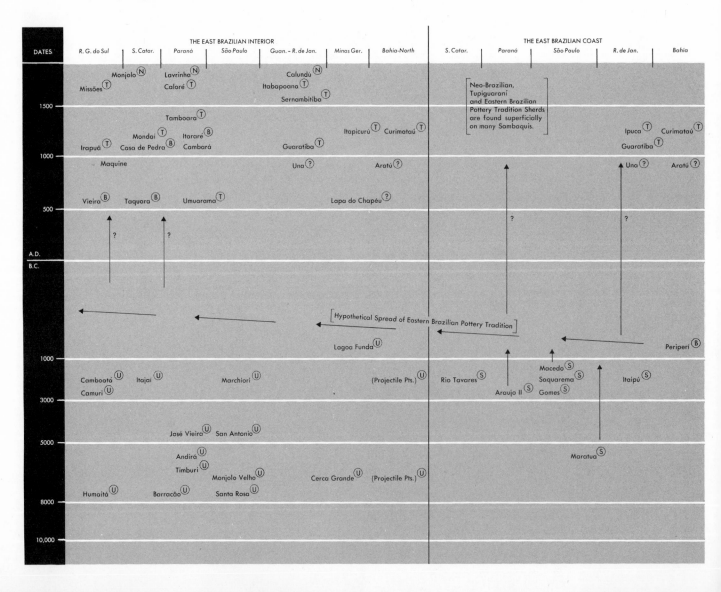

Figure 7-4. A sixteenth-century representation of the Tupinamba Indians of the coast of Brazil. The artist shows a stockaded village with long houses (note the hammock beds in the houses). Indians are fighting in the foreground (*right*) and participating in a ceremony (*left*). In the center (*right*) some Indians are torturing captives and displaying cannibalism, and others (*left*) are constructing a house. In the distance is a long house with a skull over the door—perhaps the building where the dead were kept prior to secondary inhumation in burial urns. The rendering is highly stylized; the land's end in the distance (at top of picture) is labeled, "Strait of Magellan." (From the Jean Rotz Atlas of 1542, courtesy Manuscript Room, British Museum.)

taken issue with Steward's interpretation—at least in part—arguing that the Macro-Ge and other similar so-called "marginal" peoples of Eastern Brazil were once full-fledged riverine farmers. He would see their historic period dependence on hunting and collecting as a result of their having been pushed back into interfluvial uplands and other less favorable agricultural terrain by the expansion of the Tupi-Guaraní.[9] This poses a major problem for archaeology: how old was agriculture in the area, and can it be attributed to the early non-Tupi-Guaraní populations? We shall refer to these questions again. For the moment we can note that both the Steward and Lathrap interpretations place the Macro-Ge as the early residents of the East Brazilian area, the Tupi-Guaraní as later comers.

Cultural Traditions and Chronology. The cultural traditions of the East Brazilian area are:

(1) the East Brazilian Upland tradition; (2) the Sambaquí tradition; (3) the Eastern Brazilian pottery tradition; (4) the Amazonian cultural tradition as represented by its Tupiguaraní branch or subtradition; and (5) a Neo-Brazilian pottery tradition.

We have discussed the East Brazilian Upland tradition in Chapter 2 (pp. 61–65), where we noted that its inception was as early as 9000 to 8000 B.C., that its technological beginnings may have derived from an ancient South American Flake tradition, and that it was characterized by a hunting-collecting way of life and a percussion-flake industry that produced cutting edge, scraper, and punch forms. The occasional bifaces and projectile points found in some of the East Brazilian Upland assemblages were interpreted as the results of diffusion from other early South American traditions. This East Brazilian Upland tradition persisted in the interior of Brazil for a very long time, perhaps as late as A.D. 500, although it is likely that it began to undergo important modifications some centuries before this date.

On the Brazilian coast the Sambaquí tradition arose as a littoral adaptation of the East Brazilian Upland tradition. This occurred at about 5000 B.C. The Sambaquí tradition was a shellfish-collecting, fishing, hunting, and collecting way of life. It too may have lasted until as late as A.D. 500

although, again, there are some qualifications about this date, and this leads us to a consideration of the Eastern Brazilian pottery tradition.

The Eastern Brazilian pottery tradition is the collective name that I have given to a series of "regional traditions" that have been defined, on the basis of pottery assemblages, by Brazilian archaeologists.[10] Most of them appear to date in the centuries following A.D. 500; however, at least one of these "regional traditions" is substantially earlier, dating back, as it does by radiocarbon, to the early part of the first millennium B.C. I am hehitant to describe this Eastern Brazilian pottery tradition as a "full cultural tradition." It is possible that its appearance marks a new life pattern—specifically, that agriculture appeared in the East Brazilian area with this pottery. But there is no proof of this. If verified, this possibility would conform with Lathrap's hypothesis of an early agricultural population in the area. Alternatively, it may be that the ceramics of this Eastern Brazilian pottery tradition were simply grafted onto the resident hunting, collecting, fishing, and shellfish-gathering economies of the East Brazilian Upland and Sambaquí cultural traditions.[10a]

It is with the appearance of the Tupiguaraní pottery complex, at about A.D. 500, that we have the first definite introduction of an agricultural economy to the East Brazilian area.[11] This Tupiguaraní complex and cultural subtradition was an offshoot of the Amazonian cultural tradition. It is associated with a Tropical Forest riverine agriculture and with pottery styles that link clearly to those of Amazonia and especially to those of the Polychrome Horizon of that area. The Tupiguaraní term is well established in the archaeological literature, and there is little doubt that this complex was associated with the movements of Tupí-Guaraní tribes into the East Brazilian area.

Finally, a Neo-Brazilian pottery tradition represents the early acculturation of the Indians of the area to European customs and to ways of making pottery. The tradition dates from the mid-sixteenth century through the next 200 years or so.

Our chronological scheme for dealing with the East Brazilian area will be the same as that used for the Amazonian; that is, there will be no reference to formal area periods. Instead, the chronology chart (Fig. 7-3) will simply be ruled with the absolute dating estimates of millennia, together with the fixed points of A.D. 500 (the earliest Tupiguaraní pottery) and A.D. 1500 (the European entry).

No formal subarea divisions are established. We will refer, for the most part, to modern Brazilian states in discussing site and regional locations, especially to the southern states of Rio Grande do Sul, Santa Catarina, Paraná, São Paulo, Guanabara, and Rio de Janeiro. In addition, the northern coastal states of Bahía, Pernambuco, and Rio Grande do Norte come into the discussions, as well as interior Minas Gerais.

The East Brazilian Upland Tradition: Retrospect and Continuity. Two gross horizons are suggested for the East Brazilian Upland tradition:

(1) An earlier one that dates from its beginnings until about 3000 B.C. and that is characterized by percussion-flaked choppers, scrapers, perforators, and various cutting edges; (2) A later one, which continues this earlier technology but also features semi-polished and polished axes and bifacially chipped projectile points.

If, further, we assume that Eastern Brazilian tradition pottery was assimilated into the old way of life with little other cultural change, a third horizon would be characterized by this pottery.

On the earliest horizon we have mentioned several phases of the Rio Claro region sequence of São Paulo State: Santa Rosa, Monjolo Velho, and San Antonio. The chronological estimates for these phases, in the order given, is from about 8000 to 3000 B.C. (see chronological chart, Fig. 7-3).[12] The José Vieira complexes of western Paraná State also pertain to this earliest horizon. The earliest levels in that site have a radiocarbon date of 4700 B.C. A later level, with a date of 3300 B.C., shows a continuation of the rough technology.[13] The Timburi and Andirá phases of the Paranapanema Valley[14] and the Barracão phase[15] of western Paraná also appear to belong to this horizon, as does Humaitá of northeastern Rio Grande do Sul.[16]

On the later horizon, the Marchiori phase succeeds the San Antonio in the Rio Claro sequence, and Marchiori is dated as beginning at about 2500 B.C. Marchiori features both polished celts and numerous small projectile points of chipped stone.[17] In the Santa Catarina State a number of

open sites in the Itajaí Valley, a drainage that runs from the uplands down to the Atlantic Coast, show collections of artifacts including medium-sized or small stemmed points and stone pestles.[18] These sites are without pottery and may be relatively early. The typology of the points suggests a dating somewhere in the later horizon of the East Brazilian Upland tradition. In the northeastern Rio Grande do Sul sequence E. T. Miller's Camuri and Camboatá complexes may both date to the later horizon.[19] Camuri has a number of unstemmed points and stemmed points, all of which look relatively late, some of them resembling those of Marchiori. Miller places it earlier than Camboatá. The latter has no points but has, instead, semi-polished and polished axes, suggesting a late dating. I have indicated Camboatá as about contemporaneous with Marchiori, which also has the polished axes; Camuri may be either a little later or a little earlier.

There are, however, some data that do not appear to conform to this early and late horizon division—a division based essentially on the absence or presence of polished stone axes. As we have already noted (pp. 64–65), the Cerca Grande complex of the Lagoa Santa region of Minas Gerais displays an assemblage of roughly chipped implements, stemmed projectile points, bone points, and partially ground and polished

Figure 7-5. Typical projectile point found in later (post-2500 B.C.) cultures of the East Brazilian Upland tradition. Length, 5.7 cm. (Courtesy T. O. Miller, Jr.)

stone axes. The radiocarbon dates on Cerca Grande are 7700 and 7000 B.C. This dating would definitely place the complex in the earlier horizon of the East Brazilian Upland tradition, despite the stone axes. Thus it may be that the partially polished stone ax is not a reliable late versus early chronological indicator—although it seems to be in the south—or it may be that the Cerca Grande complex as now defined spans several millennia. A radiocarbon date from one cave in the Lagoa Santa region, Lagoa Funda, is 1000 B.C., and this suggests a considerable chronological span for cultures like that of Cerca Grande.[20]

Still farther north, in the Middle São Francisco Valley, are various surface finds that appear to pertain to the East Brazilian Upland tradition. In some cases these are large stemmed or unstemmed lanceolate projectile points that appear, from their typology, to be relatively early; that is, they would be comparable to the Cerca Grande points or some of the occasional leaf-shaped points that were mentioned in Chapter 2 as being found in early East Brazilian Upland contexts. Other points are of the smaller stemmed and barbed types, those more closely resembling the later horizon forms of southern Brazil.[21]

The Sambaquí Tradition of the Coast. The Sambaquí tradition takes its name from the local term for shell mound. These mounds are found in great number along the southern coast of Brazil; north of Rio de Janeiro they are less frequent, but they continue on northward along the entire coast of the East Brazilian area. Not all shell mounds pertain to what we are calling the Sambaquí tradition; some such deposits are the remains of later cultures; however, by far the greater number of the shell heaps of the coast are sites of this Sambaquí tradition. The tradition was obviously littoral-adapted, with a subsistence primarily based upon molluscs and fish. The mounds are found on old strand lines, and many of them date to a period when the level of the sea stood higher than at present. The earliest Sambaquí date goes back to 5000 B.C., although most of the radiocarbon dates that have been obtained for the coastal shell mounds fall between 3000 and 1500 B.C.

We have stated that the Sambaquí tradition derived from the East Brazilian Upland tradition.

This is a hypothesis based, in part, upon an analogy with what seems to have been the general trend of culture history on the South American continent. There is evidence from Peru, Chile, and elsewhere that interior land hunters and gatherers began to exploit coastal environments in an intensive way at about 5000 B.C., or with the onset of the climatic optimum following the early post-Pleistocene. The hypothesis is also based upon close technological and artifactual similarities between East Brazilian Upland and Sambaquí tradition cultures. Indeed, it could be argued that the distinction we are making between an East Brazilian Upland tradition and a Sambaquí tradition is simply an expression of seasonal food pursuits of the same peoples, or, in other words, that the data reflect a pattern of transhumance—similar to that referred to in Peru (pp. 50–52, 91)—in which several months of highland hunting was followed by a season of shellfish and plant collecting at coastal sites. The relative ease of movement along the east-west valleys of the Brazilian Uplands—which rise on the scarp of the plateau just back of the coastal plain and flow inland—lends plausibility to such a pattern; and I think it likely that such semi-nomadism did take place. At the same time, it is also probable that, as in Peru and Chile, some groups tended to remain year-round in the littoral settings and to specialize in this maritime subsistence at the expense of their inland foragings. Certainly there are some cultural differences between East Brazilian Upland and Sambaquí cultures—such as the presence of a more elaborated polished stone art in the coastal sites—that are not directly explainable as expressions of food-getting techniques and that do suggest a significant divergence in cultural traditions.

The Brazilian sambaquís are compact concentrations, usually less than 100 meters in diameter, but many of them are of great depth—15 meters or more being not uncommon. Because of this depth, some authorities have doubted whether they were man-made accumulations of shellfish refuse, concluding, rather, that they were natural formations created by tidal action.[22] This question can now be set aside, for the archaeological research of the last 20 years indicates very clearly that man-made artifacts, burials, and fire hearths are to be found at all depths within the sambaquís.

Many of the sambaquís show a flattened top

or central portion, and this has been confirmed by excavations that have shown the bedded strata near the centers of the mounds to be horizontal. This supports the suggestion that there were living areas—with huts and hearths—on the mound summits. Such raised living sites would have offered several advantages in the Brazilian coastal lagoon terrain. The elevation of only a few meters would have given exposure to cooling breezes and kept the inhabitants of the mound tops above the worst swarms of the mangrove-swamp mosquitos. Further, the mound heights would have provided vantage points from which to observe schools of fish swimming toward the shore.[23]

The first significant archaeological research on the sambaquís was carried out by Ricardo Krone at the beginning of this century.[24] Krone was of the opinion that those located farther inland, on old beach lines, were of greater age than those located nearer the present shore; he also referred to stratigraphical changes of artifact types within the middens, although he presented no systematic results or conclusions on this stratigraphy. Later Serrano outlined a general chronological sequence of artifact forms for the sambaquís. In this chronology he refers to an "Archaic" phase, represented by middens located at some distance inland, in which the typical artifacts are said to be crudely chipped stone axes with ground and polished bits and various picks, crude points, scrapers, hammerstones, and bone points.[25] Later phases, which he designates as "Middle" and "Southern" (terms of geographical reference on the Brazilian coast), were then characterized by the addition of polished stone inventories, including fully polished axes, lip plugs, pendants (or "fusos"), and finely carved and polished stone "zooliths," or effigy trays (or basins). But Serrano cites no specific site stratigraphies to support this sequence, and the carefully controlled digging of recent years has not given conclusive verification of it.

The earliest radiocarbon dates from a sambaquí come from the lowermost excavated level of the Maratua midden near Santos, in the State of São Paulo.[26] Two readings fall in the sixth millennium B.C. (about 5800 and 5300 B.C., with a 1300-year margin of error). The only artifacts in association with these dates were a few battered bits of quartzite that look as if they had been used for pounding. In the overlying levels of the mound were rough choppers and axes and bone projectile points. Using Serrano's criteria, all of this material could be assimilated to his earlier, or "Archaic," horizon.

A number of other recent excavations have been undertaken in sambaquís to the south of Maratua, especially in Paraná State. The Gomes sambaquí, on the Bay of Antonina, an arm of Paranaguá Bay, is one of these.[27] The radiocarbon dates here span the centuries from 3000 to 2500 B.C., and the midden rests on an old beach line separated from the present shore by a mangrove swamp. Most of the shells in the midden are oysters (*Ostrea* sp.), indicating that they had been taken from an active lagoon that probably once occupied the area of the mangrove swamp when the sea stood at a somewhat higher level than it does today. There is no stratigraphic separation of artifacts, which are listed as percussion-flaked axes, roughly chipped scrapers, knives, and stone points, and bone points. Burials in the midden were extended. All were associated with red ocher, and one had a perforated shark-tooth pendant. Gomes possibly correlates with the later layer described for Maratua; the artifact assemblages are similar.

Saquarema is a large sambaquí near Gomes. Excavation here demonstrated a refuse depth of at least 10.5 meters.[28] Radiocarbon dates range from about 2500 to 2100 B.C. The lowest levels contain mostly oyster shells and the middle and upper levels *Anomalocardia brasiliana* and *Modiolus brasiliensis*. These latter are species that are most frequent in the open sea rather than in lagoons.[29] The lowest levels had only percussion-flaked axes, whereas the uppermost ones had chipped and semi-polished specimens. Artifacts found throughout included stemmed points, roughly fashioned like those of the Cerca Grande complex of the interior uplands, and the usual sambaquí lot of rough choppers, scrapers, knives, hammerstones, and fish vertebrae perforated for use as beads or ornaments. Burials were both extended and flexed, and tear-drop stone pendants were found with two of these interments. These last are probably comparable to Serrano's pendants, or "fusos."[30]

Sambaquí Macedo,[31] dug by Hurt and Blasi, is a short distance east of Gomes and Saquarema. The base of this mound rests on an old beach

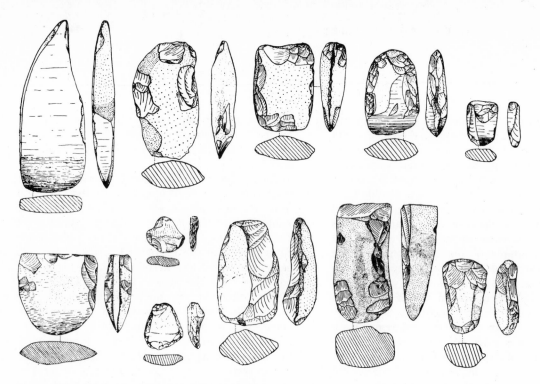

Figure 7-6. Typical chipped and chipped-and-polished stone axes from the sambaquís. From Sambaquí Macedo, State of Paraná, Brazil. Ax at upper *left* is 22 cm. long. (After Hurt and Blasi, 1960.)

which is 1.6 meters above the present ocean level. The sambaquí was roughly of truncated pyramidal form, 55 by 34 meters in extent and 8 meters deep. In the center of the mound the shell and ash strata lay in horizontal bedding, and hearths were found on these horizontal strata. Oyster shells were found only at the bottom of Macedo, the upper levels being composed of alternating bands of *Anomalocardia* and *Modiolus*. Semi-polished axes were present in the bottommost levels, together with bone and shell ornaments, various chipped tools, and flexed burials. These artifacts also continued through to the upper levels, but in these a fully polished stone ax and some bone points can be added to the inventory. These Macedo levels have radiocarbon dates that are stratigraphically consistent and that range from about 1700 to 1350 B.C.[32] The Macedo surface was capped with a humus layer that contained Neo-Brazilian pottery and porcelain fragments.[33]

The radiocarbon dates, shell debris, and artifact typology of Gomes, Saquarema, and Macedo all suggest a chronological series running from earliest to latest in the order given. Such a series would indicate a Sambaquí cultural tradition, changing

very little from about 3000 until 1500 B.C. One indicator of change in this series would seem to be greater frequency of appearance of semi-polished stone axes.

To the south of the Paranaguá, the Orssichs have described excavations at the Araujo II mound on an old shore of Guaratuba Bay in Paraná State.[34] Three cultural phases were noted stratigraphically. In the earliest were partially ground–partially chipped celts, huge picklike implements, and pestles. Above this assemblage was another that featured well-shaped, fully ground and polished celts or axes of rectanguloid outline. In the topmost artifact series these well-made celts were missing, although the partially ground ones were again present, together with bifacially chipped adzes and axes, various rough knives, scrapers, stemmed projectile points, and a bone labret. The remains of a structure were indicated by what appeared to be old post holes filled with concretions of conglomerate shell. These suggested a building or shelter 3 meters wide and at least 5 meters long. Level, compacted, superimposed ash strata within the post pattern probably were old floors, and burials had been made under these floors. There are no radiocarbon dates on Araujo II, but the artifacts and shell species suggest a contemporaneity toward the end of the Gomes-Saquarema-Macedo sequence. The odd celt or ax sequence—with the partially ground specimens

444

being replaced by the fully ground and polished ones, and these, in turn, being succeeded by the partially ground forms—must be explained either as a sampling anomaly or the seasonal use of the mound location by varying groups of somewhat different technological traditions.

The same Sambaquí cultural tradition is represented elsewhere and by many sites, and we cannot attempt to review all of them here.[35] On the Guanabara and Rio de Janeiro coasts Dias has defined an Itaipú phase.[36] Most of the sites are small sambaquís; some show little or no shell refuse; but the flake tools, various pounding and anvil stones, crude points, and semi-polished axes fall in the pattern we have been describing. South of Paraná other sambaquís are known in Santa Catarina and Rio Grande do Sul.[37]

Any discussion of the sambaquís must make some reference to the highest examples of sambaquí art—the polished stone effigies, or "zooliths." These are the artifacts that Serrano refers to in his "Southern" phase of the sambaquís. Quite possibly they represent a late horizon in the Sambaquí tradition, as that author has stated; however, there is little provenience information on the zooliths. Their general distribution would appear to be mainly in Paraná and Santa Catarina States. Most of them are in private or museum collections. The zooliths usually represent fish or birds, although sometimes mammals and, possibly, insects are portrayed. They are carved and polished from fine-grained stones—diabase, schist and andesite. They vary in length from 5 to 40 centimeters, with most of them somewhere near the middle of this size range. All share the common feature of an oval, round, or rectangular concavity on one of the large flat surfaces of the effigy. Occasionally red pigment is found in these concavities, and it is possible that the zooliths were used to grind mineral colors; however it is just as frequent for the entire object to bear traces of the red pigment, and this suggests that the paint may have been applied in burial ceremonies. We have noted from other places in South America, especially in the South Andes, the use of stone trays for the preparation of snuff. We also know that snuff taking was practiced in many parts of eastern and lowland South America. Thus it is possible that the zooliths served such a function, in connection with wooden or bone snuff tubes that have perished.

Figure 7-7. Typical stone fish effigy with basinlike depression. Sambaquí tradition. (Redrawn from Serrano, 1946.)

Whatever their use, their elaboration implies that they were important ritual objects in the Sambaquí culture, and the skill and artistry with which they were made hints at a much richer artistic tradition—perhaps in wood carving—that has not come down to us in the archaeological remains. Tiburtius presents specific data on the discovery

Figure 7-8. Stone bird effigy with basinlike concavity. Brazilian Sambaquí tradition. Length, about 37 cm. (Redrawn from Tiburtius and Bigarella, 1960.)

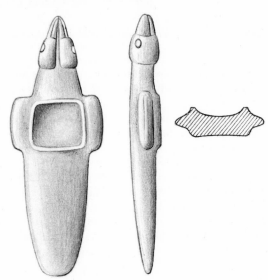

of a few zooliths. These were in sambaquís, as burial accompaniments. In one case a bird effigy had been placed in a cache of small stones found beneath a flexed burial. In another, bird, fish, and mammal effigies were found at the side of the skeleton along with other, simpler grave objects.[38]

The Eastern Brazilian Pottery Tradition. The earliest of the "regional pottery traditions" of Eastern Brazil is the Periperí. Periperí pottery is found in shell mound sites on the Bahía coast. This is a location that is well to the north of the sambaquí sites that we have been describing in the preceding section; however, the nature of the sites and their contents—with the exception of the pottery—fall easily within the compass of the Sambaquí cultural tradition. Only one Periperí site has been thoroughly excavated. This is the Pedro Oca midden on the east side of the bay of Todos Santos.[39] The midden here was composed of *Anomalocardia,* oyster shells, ash, and sand. Some postmolds were noted. The artifact assemblage sounds much like those of the sambaquís from farther south, although perhaps with more emphasis on rough pounding and grinding tools (hammers, anvils, grinders) than on the roughly chipped chopping and cutting implements. Fish vertebrae beads and perforated shell beads or pendants were also present. The Periperí pottery is a plain, dark brown-to-black, sand-tempered ware. One rim sherd had unobliterated coils on its exterior. The vessels are rounded bowl forms of simple outline. A radiocarbon date from the site is 880 B.C., or more than 1000 years earlier than any other pottery we know of in Eastern Brazil. The northern geographical position of Periperí and its early date suggest the possibility that this pottery might be derived from the early and approximately contemporaneous pottery of the Marajó Island sequence at the mouth of the Amazon (pp. 407–408); however if this was the case, the stimulus was remote and indirect as the Periperí ceramics are much simpler than those of Ananatuba.

The other "regional pottery traditions" which concern us here appear to be substantially later than Periperí, although the dates of some are not known. It should also be kept in mind that the beginnings of any of these "regional traditions" may be considerably earlier than the dates that

are now known, and that the chronological gap between them and Periperí may be less than it appears to be.[40]

The Vieira "regional tradition" (not to be confused with the José Vieira site of the East Brazilian Upland preceramic tradition) is the southernmost of these pottery groups considered here in the inclusive category of the Eastern Brazilian pottery tradition. Vieira sites are known from southeastern Rio Grande do Sul and adjacent Uruguay.[41] It is a country of lagoons and marshes, frequently inundated in the rainy season, and the sites are small mounds—20 to 100 meters in diameter and 0.3 to 3 meters in height. Such mounds, which are found in groups of from two to eight, are composed of fish- and animal-bone refuse, other organic debris, chipped stone artifacts and scrap, ground stone artifacts, and potsherds. The chipped stone artifacts include stemmed points and flakes, while those of ground stone are grooved axes, bolas, and pitted anvil stones. The pottery is sand tempered, predominantly plain, of simple flat-based and insloped-wall forms. When it does bear surface decoration this is in rows of punctations or dentate-stamping impressions. The pottery is fairly close in appearance to that of the Lower Paraná and Lower Uruguay Rivers and to that of the northern part of the Argentine pampas and probably is related to it.

Sites of the Taquara "regional tradition" are found in western Rio Grande do Sul (Taquarucú phase), northeastern Rio Grande do Sul (Taquara phase), and southwestern Santa Catarina (Xaxim phase).[42] They are located on high ground or hilltops, and there are two types of sites. One type consists of a cluster of pit houses—as many as 36 have been counted in a single site location—and such pit house sites are said to occur by the hundreds on the planalto from northern Rio Grande do Sul to southern Paraná. Individual pit houses have diameters of from 1 to 13 meters and are from 2.8 to 5.0 meters in depth. It has been noted that their upland distribution corresponds to the habitat of the Araucária pine, and it is possible that they were occupied mainly in the season of pine-seed harvests.

The second type of Taquara site is marked by small, low mounds. These tumuli are no more than 50 centimeters high, and several are frequently enclosed by a low earth wall. It seems likely that these mounds were for burials. Menghín has described such mounds and enclosures from the Argentine Province of Misiones,[43] which borders on Rio Grande do Sul and Santa Catarina; the Eldorado culture in which he places these earthworks could be considered another of the Taquara series of phases. At one site the earthwork enclosures were quite complicated, with a large circle of 160 meters in diameter in addition to other, smaller circles tangent to the larger one, as well as long embankment-bordered passageways leading into the circles. A mound, 20 meters in diameter and 3 meters height, was in the center of the larger circle. Excavations within the enclosure disclosed rock chips, polished axes, and a few sherds of pottery, but no burials. Menghín also mentions another mound site at which the tumulus was completely excavated by amateur archaeologists. No burials were found here either; however, as Menghín points out, the Caingang Indians, who occupied this same region in historic times, made such mounds for burial. Within them they placed the bodies of their chiefs in wooden tombs or crypts, and the dead were accompanied with textiles, bows and arrows, and other perishables. Such burials and such grave goods might leave little or no trace. Certainly, the presence of such burial customs among the Caingang—presumably one of the old pre-Tupí-Guaraní tribes of southern Brazil—suggests the possibility of a continuity of tradition between them and the earlier mound-builders, a continuity that was never completely broken by Tupí-Guaranian peoples or the Tupiguaraní culture.

The Taquara pit house sites and the mound sites of the Taquara and the Misiones phases are linked by a pottery style of brown, smoothed, sand-tempered pottery that has been decorated with punctations, fingernail impressions, and incisions. Vessels are small shallow bowls, deeper bowls, and cylindrical jars. Other Taquara artifacts are all implements that could have been carried over from the antecedent East Brazilian Upland tradition—bifacial and unifacial choppers, retouched and used flakes, hammerstones, cores, and bone projectile points. There are two radiocarbon dates on the Taquara phase of A.D. 570 and 760; and, excepting Periperí, these are the earliest dates on any of the regional pottery traditions. Like the Vieira pottery tradition, the Taquara ceramics

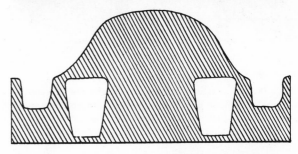

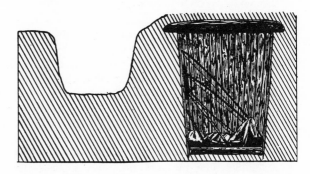

Figure 7-9. Drawings of a Caingang burial mound, southern Brazil. *Top:* The mound with its surrounding borrow trench. *Center:* Cross-section diagram showing position of burial chambers. *Bottom:* Wood-lined chamber with burial of chief accompanied by bows and arrows. (After Metraux, 1946.)

are reminiscent of the Paraná-Pampean tradition wares farther south.

Two other rather simple pottery series are associated with the Casa de Pedra and Itararé "regional traditions." Casa de Pedra sites are found in northeastern Rio Grande do Sul, southern Santa Catarina, and central and western

Figure 7-10. Taquara pottery. *a:* Punctations in rows. *b:* Irregularly spaced punctations. *c:* Drag-and-jab punctations. *d:* Dentate stamped. *e, f:* Fingernail marked. *g:* Incised. Height of *a,* about 5 cm. (After PRONAPA, 1970.)

tions" are interrelated and that they represent an old resident pottery-making tradition in the East Brazilian area—the one referred to here as the Eastern Brazilian pottery tradition.

As for the two other "regional pottery traditions" that the Brazilian archaeologists describe—Una and Aratú[46]—I should be inclined to see their basic relationships as outside our Eastern Brazilian pottery tradition. Una sites are in the vicinity of Rio de Janeiro, and there is one radiocarbon date of A.D. 890; sites are both on the coast and in the interior. Refuse areas are relatively large, measuring up to 100 meters in diameter. Burial urns have been found in some of these sites and in rock shelters. In general, the vessels of the Una tradition are much larger than those of the southern "regional traditions" that we have reviewed. Their decoration is, however, scanty, consisting of minor incisions and polishing striations. Aratú sites are located farther north, in coastal and interior Bahía, Goyaz, Sergipe, and Alagoas. Some are reported to be large habitation

Paraná.[44] There is some territorial overlap with Taquara sites. Pit houses, like those described with Taquara, are found in Casa de Pedra territory, although it is not clear whether these are to be associated with the Casa de Pedra pottery and culture. The pottery is plain—large bowls of brownish ware. Itararé pottery comes from sites in eastern Paraná and perhaps from the Santa Catarina coast.[45] A radiocarbon date of A.D. 1070 is available. The sites are small areas, from 15 to 30 meters in diameter and with thin refuse. The pottery is a thin, sand tempered, smoothed and red slipped ware, with vessels of smallish size.

The Vieira, Taquara, Casa de Pedra, and Itararé ceramics can be described generally as being simple in form and surface treatment. Incision, punctation, fingernail marking, and related plastic techniques link Vieira and Taquara to each other and both to the ceramics from farther south, especially to the Paraná drainage in Argentina and Uruguay. Casa de Pedra and Itararé are more difficult to relate in a wider frame of reference because of their extreme simplicity; and the same can be said of the Periperí pottery. I think it likely, however, that all of these "regional tradi-

Figure 7-11. Aratú pottery vessel forms. The large burial urn *a* is about 90 cm. high; all other vessels range in height from about 12 to 50 cm. (After PRONAPA, 1970.)

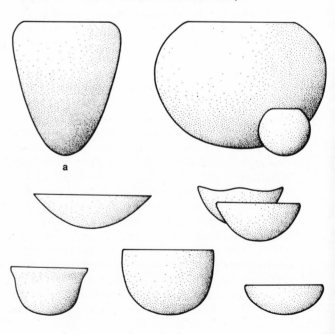

areas, with refuse of almost a meter deep, and one cemetery is said to have yielded more than 100 burial urns. One site in Bahía has a radiocarbon date of A.D. 870. The Aratú burial urns are large, high-shouldered jars; other vessels are bowls and globular jars. Decoration of all this pottery is rather limited, incision, corrugation, and relief modeling being the principal techniques.

The presence of burial urns, large vessels, the larger sites, and the generally northern geographical position of these two "regional traditions" suggest that their affiliations are ultimately to be found in the Amazonian cultural tradition. They may be the results of Tupiguaraní stimuli—the surface treatment of the pottery is distinctly non-Tupiguaraní—or they could result from other Amazonian stimuli prior to the Tupiguaraní influx.

The Amazonian Tradition in Eastern Brazil: Tupiguaraní. The Tupiguaraní subtradition is defined by a very distinctive ceramic complex that features black-and-red-on-white painting, corrugation, and surface brushing techniques of decoration. Lesser techniques are rim nicking, incision, punctation, and various kinds of fingernail marking. In the painted wares the slip is frequently white, and this is painted with black (or brown), red, or black-and-red designs. These designs, on bowl interiors or urn exteriors, are linear, fine lined, and complex, and their stylistic affinities to the Polychrome Horizon potteries of the Amazonian area (discussed in Chap. 6) are obvious. The corrugated decoration is produced by pinching, finger pressing, or stick pressing the unsmoothed and unfired surfaces of the coiled vessel. Other vessels show rough surfaces which have been brushed, scored, or striated before firing. The Tupiguaraní vessel forms include deep, pointed-bottomed urns with wide shoulders and restricted orifices (which were used for urn burial) and various open and casuela bowls. Some of the bowls were of oval or rather square forms instead of circular. These vessel forms again recall the Amazonian styles.[47]

Tupiguaraní artifacts other than pottery include clay pipes, stone lip plugs (or tembetás), celts that were fully polished, and various rough-chipped and ground-stone tools—scrapers, flakes, choppers, pounders, abraders, and the like—

reminiscent of those of the East Brazilian and Sambaquí preceramic cultures.

Tupiguaraní sites usually are in low-lying, forested regions or in an ecological setting that appears to be favorable to Tropical Forest agriculture; and it is assumed that such agriculture was the basic subsistence. This assumption is supported by the comparative data from the Amazonian area, by the presence of manioc griddles in some Tupiguaraní sites, and by the early historic ethnography of the area. Secondary urn burials are found in or near the habitation areas.

Figure 7-12. Tupiguaraní painted sherds from Eastern Brazil. *a, b:* Red-on-white. *c:* White-on-red. *d–g:* Polychrome or red-and-black-on-white. Height of *a*, about 6 cm. (After PRONAPA, 1970.)

Figure 7-13. Tupiguaraní fingernail marked, brushed, and corrugated sherds from Eastern Brazil. *a:* Irregular fingernail marked. *b:* Fingernail ridged. *c:* Regular fingernail marked. *d, e:* Brushed. *f–h:* Corrugated. Height of *a,* about 5.5 cm. (After PRONAPA, 1970.)

In Brazil, Tupiguaraní sites are known from Rio Grande do Sul north to Rio Grande do Norte, both in the interior and along the coastal front. They are also reported from nearby Misiones,[48] in Argentina; and, as we shall see later in this chapter, they are found outside the East Brazilian area in the Paraguay, Paraná, and Uruguay River drainages, going as far south as the mouth of the Plate.[49] In Brazil the occurrences of Tupiguaraní pottery in the upper levels of old coastal Sambaquí tradition sites and old East Brazilian Upland tradition sites of the interior give a general guide to the dating of the subtradition. Radiocarbon dates make this more precise by providing absolute readings on the earliest Tupiguaraní sites of about A.D. 500. Later radiocarbon dates then extend almost to the historic era, and indeed, European artifacts in Tupiguaraní contexts indicate a continuation of the subtradition up to A.D. 1500 and later. Within this time span of about 1000 years a great many Tupiguaraní regional phases can be defined. These have been classed into three typological groups by the archaeologists of the Brazilian National Archaeological Program.[50] Each group is characterized by a dominant ceramic stylistic technique: (1) painting; (2) corrugating; or (3) brushing. Such decorative techniques do not occur in pure component form; most Tupiguaraní sites show pottery of all three decorative classes, although with a tendency for an emphasis on one or another technique from site to site. Seriation of site collections, together with some radiocarbon dates, has further indicated that these three techniques have a chronological ordering, with painting as the oldest, corrugating next, and brushing the most recent. For instance, the painted wares have their earliest radiocarbon date in Paraná, with the Umuarama phase; then Guaratiba, Itapicurú, and Curimataú are all later, as one moves north. For the corrugated wares, the earliest phase is the Maquiné, in Rio Grande do Sul. Other southern occurrences of corrugation are later than Maquiné, and northern occurrences are much later. Brushed ware complexes do not occur north of Guanabara, a circumstance that prompts Brochado and his colleagues to speculate that there had not been sufficient time for this technique to diffuse all the way from south to north before the European conquest.[51]

This pattern of Tupiguaraní ceramic occurrences in space and in time supports the argument that the Tupiguaraní subtradition had its origins in southern Brazil; but this is not to say that the key elements in the subtradition are not Amazonian. I would speculate that the Tupiguaraní complex, as we now know it, was synthesized somewhere in southern Brazil and that the Amazonian influences that went into this synthesis were blended with the older resident tradition, namely, the Eastern Brazilian pottery tradition.[52] Subsequent to this synthesis, both the Tupiguaraní subtradition and the Eastern Brazilian tradition con-

450

tinued on in contemporaneity for several centuries; for, as the Brazilian archaeologists have shown, there is abundant evidence of interchange between the two.

The Neo-Brazilian Pottery Tradition. This is the name given to the ceramic complexes—and to the general culture—of the Indian populations of Eastern Brazil subsequent to the first effects of Portuguese acculturation. Sites of the Neo-Brazilian tradition date from the mid-sixteenth century and are of various types—towns, missions, trading posts, farming hamlets. The three principal phases that have been defined are the Monjolo (northeastern Rio Grande do Sul), the Lavrinha (southeastern Paraná), and the Calundú (Rio de Janeiro).[53] Related remains have also been reported from Bahía. Neo-Brazilian ceramics are largely decorated by brushing, corrugation, finger pressing of appliqué ridges, punctation, and deep incision (often over unobliterated coils). Painting is absent, and the burial urn seems to have disappeared, probably as the result of Christian influences. Shoulder lugs and flat pedestal bases on some vessels are attributed to European influences, and site collections often include porcelain sherds and iron tool fragments. The pottery elbow pipe, which had an aboriginal beginning, seems to enjoy a florescence of elaboration in modeling in the Neo-Brazilian tradition.

The Spanish also influenced the Indians of the area, establishing towns and missions up the Paraná River from a main base in Asunción. The town of Ciudad Real,[54] at the confluence of the Rio Piquiry and the Paraná, in western Paraná State, was founded in 1556 and abandoned sometime in the mid-17th century. This was an administrative center for the control of thousands of Guaraní Indians who were agricultural laborers under the encomienda system. Pottery picked up at Ciudad Real is largely that of the Tupiguaraní tradition as we have defined it here—polychromes, corrugated wares, fingernail marked types. There are also some pottery fragments of European type although the degree to which an actual fusion of ceramic traditions took place is unclear.[55]

Summary. The earliest substantial evidence of aboriginal occupancy in East Brazil is that of the East Brazilian Upland tradition.

Figure 7-14. Potsherds of the historic period or the Neo-Brazilian pottery tradition. *a, b:* Incised. *c–e:* Zoned punctate. *f:* Incision over unobliterated coils. *g:* Pinched over unobliterated coils. *h:* Pinched and incised over brushing. *i:* Finger pressed lug. Height of *a*, about 5 cm. (After PRONAPA, 1970.)

The remains are those of the hunters of the Brazilian plateau and interior hills. The technology exhibited in the stonework is of a rough percussion sort; most of the tools are cutting, perforating, scraping, or chopping edges. They are made from flakes and are predominantly unifacial, although some bifaces are present. Stone projectile points are either absent or very rare in these East Brazilian Upland assemblages. In the earlier millennia of the tradition—between 9000 B.C. and 3000 B.C.—the points that do occur are reminiscent of early point types in other parts of South America: fluted fish tails, leaf shapes, and large, stemmed types. But within the East Brazilian Upland tradition contexts these are rather crudely made. Apparently, to judge from finds in a number of places, bone points were widely used in hunting, and wooden ones may also have been employed. After 3000 B.C. smaller chipped-stone points appear—usually stemmed and barbed forms —and these become quite common in some regions. Another innovation is the polished celt or ax; sometimes these are partially chipped and partially polished, sometimes fully polished. Although this sequence of developments seems to hold for most subareas, there do seem to be some exceptions—that is, localities in which polished axes occur prior to 3000 B.C.—and it must be stressed that the stratigraphic data and the radiocarbon dates on the East Brazilian Upland tradition are still very few.

Along the Brazilian shore a shellfish-collecting and fishing culture came into being by about 5000 B.C. Its rough chipped stone technology is very similar to that of the East Brazilian Upland tradition, and it seems quite likely that this new cultural tradition—the Sambaquí—was a development out of the uplands. Perhaps this came about through seasonal transhumance between interior and coast. The Sambaquí cultural tradition sites are shell mounds or sambaquís—enormously deep concentrations of refuse, many of which are located on old shore lines that were active when the sea stood at a higher level than it does today. They contain relatively few artifacts—mostly choppers, scrapers, and flake tools, plus a few polished, or partially polished, axes, anvil stones, grinding and pounding stones, simple shell or bone beads, bone points, and an occasional rare polished stone ornament or ceremonial object. Among the latter category are the "zooliths," or stone effigy basins. These are fashioned as fish or birds that have a traylike concavity in the side; they may have been used as snuff tablets. There are some hints in sambaquí stratigraphies that polished axes and other polished stone items succeed a horizon of chipped and hammered stone; but this still has to be satisfactorily demonstrated.

What is probably the earliest pottery of the East Brazilian area is subsumed under the heading of the Eastern Brazilian pottery tradition. It is known from a number of subtraditions: Periperí, Vieira, Taquara, Casa de Pedra, and Itararé. The Periperí pottery, which is extremely simple, is found in a coastal sambaquí context and dated by radiocarbon from 900 to 800 B.C. The other subtraditions that are dated by radiocarbon come considerably later in time; however, there is speculation that these, as we know them, are the later expressions of earlier beginnings and that there is an old pottery horizon in the East Brazilian area that relates to the earliest ceramics of the Paraná Valley farther to the south. It is further thought that the general drift of this old pottery horizon was from north to south and that this spread of pottery came into the later phases of the East Brazilian Upland and Sambaquí tradition cultures. Whether or not this pottery was accompanied by agriculture and significant economic changes in the way of life of the East Brazilian Upland and Sambaquí tradition peoples is unresolved.

At some time around A.D. 500 a Tupiguaraní ceramic complex appeared in the East Brazilian area. Present information would indicate that it first arose in the southern part of the area, but many of the key elements in it are of Amazonian area origin. There was presumably some cultural synthesis between an Amazonian-type culture, brought by Tupí-Guaraní invaders, and the resident cultures of the older East Brazilian populations. This is reflected in ceramics, and the result of this synthesis was the Tupiguaraní subtradition. A Tropical Forest agricultural economy is associated with the subtradition. Between A.D. 500 and 1500 Tupiguaranian and East Brazilian pottery tradition cultures occupied the East Brazilian area, and the distribution of the two is notably intermingled. There is, however, some evidence to lead us to believe that the Tupiguaraní archaeological sites are found on lands more suitable to farming than is the case with the Eastern Brazilian tradition sites.

After the arrival of the Portuguese on the east coast there was an Indian-European cultural fusion that is reflected in ceramic manufactures. This is known as the Neo-Brazilian pottery tradition. It arose in the mid-sixteenth century and persisted for the next two centuries.

The Chaco Area

The Setting. The Chaco culture area centers on the natural physiographic depression of the Gran Chaco and on that part of the

Paraguayan Republic which lies west of the Paraguay River. To this may be added bordering portions of surrounding countries (see Figs. 1-1, 7-15). For the most part, it is a vast alluvial plain of deep, clayey soils, essentially stoneless. Wet and dry seasons are marked. The Pilcomayo and Bermejo, the major rivers that cross the Chaco, flow from the Andes to the Paraguay, shifting their courses after each seasonal flood. During the dry, parched months patches of alkali crusts appear on the ground, and water supply is a problem for all living things. The Paraguay River is a vegetational boundary. To the east of it are the savannas dotted with stands of palms and strung with river gallery forests, while to the west, in the true Chaco, tough grass savannas occur only in patches and much of the land is covered with a scrub xerophytic growth.[56]

The definition of the Chaco archaeological culture area is a highly tentative projection; we know very little of its prehistory. To a considerable extent it is a residual territory that is left over after we have extended the boundaries of the South Andes cultures to their northern and eastern limits, those of the Amazonian area to their southernmost extent, those of East Brazil as far west as they can be taken, and those of the Pampean area to their northern peripheries. In historic times, however, the tribes of the Chaco did present certain cultural similarities that linked them to each other and that set them off from the peoples of the neighboring areas, and this culture area identity of the Chaco has been recognized by various ethnographers (see culture area discussions, pp. 17–24). Such ethnographic recognition of the cultural distinctiveness of the Chaco prompts us to consider it as an archaeological area. First, however, let us make a quick review of the ethnographic and linguistic data.

Languages and Ethnography. The South American linguistic map (Fig. 1-5) will show that most of the tribes of the Chaco belong to the Guaicuruan division of the Macro-Panoan major language group. This division includes most of the linguistic families that Metraux lists in his ethnographic summary of the Chaco:[57] The Guaicuruan proper, the Mascoian, the Lule-Vilelan, the Matacoan, and the Zamucoan. Only the Tupí-Guaranian and Arawakan families would

be excepted. In a still more inclusive classification of languages, Greenberg places his Macro-Panoan major group with a Ge-Pano-Carib super-stock.[58] The languages of this super-stock stand apart from those of the Andean-Equatorial super-stock to which both Tupian and Arawakan belong. These linguistic considerations, together with the geographical distributions of the tribes involved, suggest that the Macro-Ge and Macro-Panoans were the ancient populations of Eastern Brazil and the Chaco and that the Arawakans and Tupians had moved south from the Amazonian area to overrun them. As we have seen, there is archaeological evidence in the East Brazilian area to support this hypothesis, and the few available prehistoric data from the Chaco also hint at it.

Important historic tribes of the Chaco (Fig. 7-15)—of which remnants of some still exist— were: the Abipón, Mocoví, Pilagá, Tobá, Payaguá, Mbayá, and Caduveo (all of the Guaicuruan linguistic family proper); the Mascoian and related tribes (Mascoian linguistic family); the Lule and the Vilela, with their many sub-tribes (Lule-Vilelan linguistic family); the Matará (linguistically unidentified); the Mataco, Choroti, and Ashluslay (Matacoan linguistic family); and the Zamuco, Chamacoco, and their neighbors (Zamucoan linguistic family). In linguistic contrast to these were the Chiriguano in the northwestern Chaco, and the Guaraní, in the southeastern Chaco, both of whom are, of course, Tupian in speech, and the Chané and Guaná, of the northwestern and northern Chaco, who are Arawakan.[59] These Tupí-Guaranian and Arawakan tribes, it will be noted, hold somewhat marginal positions on the edge, or else just outside, the physiographic zone of the Gran Chaco proper; and, significantly, the lands that they held were those along river courses that were suitable to agriculture.

The basic culture pattern of most of the Chaco tribes was one in which wild food plants were of major economic importance.[60] The algarroba bean —collected on the pod from a xerophytic tree— was a dietary staple in historic times. These beans contain sugar, starches, and proteins. They were ground in wood mortars, the flour mixed with water and eaten as a paste, or used for making beer or chicha. Palm seeds, shoots, and hearts were eaten, and the palm sap was made into a fer-

Archaeological and Tribal Map
of the Chaco Area
Archaeological Locations, and a few Modern Cities
and Tribal Locations, Indicated

15

AMAZONIAN AREA

B R A Z I L

Santa
Cruz ○

B O L I V I A

Chané

20

SOUTH ANDEAN AREA

Chiriguano

Chané

Zamuco
Guaná

Chamacoco

Caduveo

EAST BRAZILIAN AREA

20

Chané

P

*Mbayá
Guaná*

Payaguá

Mbayá

Tobá

A

Mataco

Orán ○ ○ Embarcación

R

Choroti

Monte Lindo R.

○ Concepción

● **Olmedo**

A

Pilcomayo R.

Ashluslay

Lengua

● **Quirquincho** ●

**Las
Lomitas**

G

Naranjo ●

Pilagá

Tobá

Lule

U

[CANDELARIA
CULTURE]

● **Pocitos**

25

Vilela

Bermejo R.

A

Asunción ○

25

Mocoví

Paraguay R.

Guaraní

Y

Paraná R.

[CHACO-
SANTIAGUEÑO
CULTURE]

Abipón Matará

N
↑

Resistencia ● ○ Corrientes

Uruguay R.

0   50   100   150   Miles

PAMPEAN   AREA

0   50   100   150   Kilometers

Figure 7-15. (*Left*, p. 454)

mented drink. Additional resources were wild fruits, tubers, honey, and roasted locusts. Fishing was seasonally important to tribes near rivers. Fish were taken in nets, scooped up from shallow pools with baskets, speared, and shot with bows and arrows. The Amazonian technique of fish poisoning seems to have been unknown. Catches were dried for storage and for trade with groups without access to streams. Rheas, deer, and peccaries were hunted. These were stalked on foot with bow and arrow; but after the arrival of the Europeans, many of the Chacoan tribes acquired the horse, and hunting drives or surrounds by mounted hunters became a typical and profitable method of pursuing game.

By A.D. 1800, if not before, nearly all the Chaco tribes practiced some agriculture. Generally, it was rather casually or indifferently conducted. Maize, sweet manioc, beans, pumpkins, tobacco, and cotton were all grown, but it is difficult to estimate just how long these crops had been of importance in the tribal economy. There can be no question that natural conditions made crop cultivation extremely difficult in most parts of the Chaco. As Metraux has stated:

> Dryness of soil, lack of chemicals, and excessive floods are not the only factors handicapping farming in large parts of the Chaco; crops are also threatened by blights, locusts, tordo birds, parakeets, peccaries, and (today) by cattle and other domesticated animals.[61]

Thus, I think it unlikely that farming was ever well established in the pre-Columbian Chaco. Many groups probably continued as collectors and hunters until historic contact times; others may have assimilated some cultivation practices through contact with the Tupi-Guaraní and Arawakan tribes. In this connection, it is undoubtedly significant that the most capable and intensive farmers reported from the early historic era were the Arawakan Guana. This, incidentally, proved to be to their disadvantage when the semi-sedentary Mbayá acquired the horse, subjugated the Guana, and enslaved them as agricultural laborers.

Typical Chacoan communities were small bands composed of members of related extended families. These usually numbered 50 to 200 inhabitants, although some were as large as 1000. Location of the village was often changed, apparently in response to seasonal economic activities and also for religious reasons (following a death). Some houses were small circular or oval huts of poles and palm-leaf or grass thatch roofs. Sometimes these were linked together to form long communal dwellings. Other houses were of an even more flimsy and temporary nature, being simply shelters of rush mats laid on a framework of sticks. Heavier built post and gable-roof dwellings were constructed by some tribes, but this, apparently, was under Mestizo influences. In general, the dwellings of a village were arranged in semi-circular fashion around an open plaza, and sometimes the whole was protected by thorn fencing.

There was little political unity among the Chacoans. Raid warfare was constant among tribes, and the introduction of the horse led to larger-scale fighting on the part of some tribes, especially the Abipón, Mocoví, and Mbayá, who took captives as slaves and whose social rank system was strengthened by the war complex. As mounted fighters, these Indians proved formidable foes to the Spanish.

Chaco tribes made nets for bags and rush mats; basketry, however, seems to have been known only by a few groups, and Metraux was of the opinion that the technique had been introduced by tribes of Amazonian heritage. Textiles for clothing were made of twined fibres from wild plants and from cotton. The latter, as well as loom weaving, was apparently introduced in pre-Columbian times from either the Amazonian or the Andean area. Deer and rhea hides were used for bags and garments but were not tanned. Gourds served as vessels and containers and were sometimes engraved. Bows, arrows, spears, clubs, mortars, and other utensils were made of wood, and because of the scarcity of stone, arrow and spear tips were of hardened wood or bamboo or bone. In later historic times points were made of iron or cow horn. Stone appears to have been imported from surrounding areas in aboriginal times, and this was used to make ground stone axes, including T-shaped forms. The use of metals was entirely post-Columbian.

Figure 7-16. Mbayá-Caduveo painted pottery plates. The style is reminiscent of the Amazonian area. (After Metraux, 1946 a.)

Pottery—which offers the best hope of linking Chaco archaeology with Chaco ethnography—is reported from almost all Chacoan tribes. It was made by coiling, and vessel forms were simple—cooking pots, narrow-necked water jars, and open bowl forms.[62] Much of it was plain, but some painted decoration was done by applying a resinous gum to the hot, freshly fired surfaces of pots. Prefired decoration was all of a plastic nature, including fingernail impression and pellet appliqué work; however, the most distinctive technique —in fact, the only distinctive Chacoan ceramic technique—was that of cord impressions. Individual cords or strings were pressed into the surface of the wet, unfired clay of the vessel wall. The Mbayá and Caduveo ornamented pottery with these cord impressions. They also painted the zones between the cord-marked lines red and black. These designs on Mbayá vessels are extraordinarily sophisticated, being composed of curvilinear and complex scrolls and volutes. Metraux states that this ceramic accomplishment of the Mbayá is to be attributed to the captive Guaná women who introduced such a tradition to the Mbayá, although he sees Andean and European influences in the designs themselves. I would suggest that design layout and overall style of these pieces is as much Amazonian—in the manner of some of the fine painting of the Polychrome Horizon—as it is Andean or European.

Archaeology. There is precious little archaeology known from the Chaco, and what there is might be better understood if we approached it from outside the area proper. Let us

begin with the Selvas Occidentales subarea of the South Andes (see p. 222). Nordenskiold investigated a series of sites on the Rio San Francisco, which is a northward-flowing tributary of the Bermejo.[63] It joins the latter stream just below the city of Oran, in the Province of Salta, Argentina. He found burial urns and other vessels in these sites. The urns had incised and modeled faces on the necks, and the flat-bottomed bowls bore nested diagonal line and circle-and-dot incised designs. The complex suggests the Candelaria culture that is known from southern Salta, especially the Candelaria I phase (see p. 223) and, in general, the early incised ware complexes from other parts of the South Andes, such as the Las Mercedes of the Chaco-Santiagueño subarea.[64]

Now, moving out toward the Chaco from the Selvas Occidentales, we come to Lomas de Olmedo. This is a site 75 kilometers southeast of the town of Embarcación. It is in Salta Province and very near the line we have drawn between the South Andes and Chaco areas. The location is that of some springs a little to the south of the present course of the Teuco (Upper Bermejo) River. Niels Fock found urn burials of children here and direct burials of adults. The urns were collared and the collars decorated with incisions, punctations, and cord impressions. These latter were single-line impressions of the sort just described for the modern or historic Mbayá pottery. Flat-bottomed, open bowls, similarly decorated, were associated with the urns, as were polished, T-shaped stone axes.[65]

From Lomas de Olmedo, Fock continued his survey, going now into the true Chaco as he followed the direction of the course of the Teuco-Bermejo to the east. At Quirquincho, 60 kilometers east-southeast of Lomas de Olmedo, he found another site, this one on an old dry channel of the Bermejo. He describes the pottery from this location as incised, punctated, and fingernail-impressed, being much like that of the Lower Paraná Valley. Similarities were also noted to the Las Mercedes phase of the Chaco-Santiagueño subarea of the South Andes. With the pottery were T-shaped axes and pottery figurines, or "dolls." These last, again, are said to be like those of the Lower Paraná as well as those of the early Chaco-Santiagueño cultures.

At Naranjo, near a small permanent lake some 70 kilometers east-southeast of Quirquincho, Fock reports pottery much like that of Lomas de Olmedo—that is, collared burial urns with cord-impressed decorations on the neck. Bowls, used as urn lid covers, were also cord-impressed and finger-impressed.

Still continuing on in a southeasterly direction for another 70 kilometers, Fock came to Pocitos, so named for its rows of little depressions and small (4 m. diameter) mounds. These may have been dug for catching rainwater, or they could have been used for cultivation. The pottery here was noted as either plain or incised.

Most of our other archaeological information on the Chaco also comes from this southern part of the area, along the Bermejo and Pilcomayo drainages. At Pozo de Maza, in Formosa, near the Pilcomayo course, Rydén found sherds with cord impressions, some with markings that looked like cord-wrapped-stick impressions, and some with fingernail markings.[66] In central Formosa, at Las Lomitas, Márquez Miranda described a complex that featured geometric band designs in incisions, a possible cord-impressed sherd, and basketry-impressed and net-marked pottery.[67] Biró de Stern's work, a little farther to the south, concerns incised and fingernail-impressed materials.[68] Continuing still farther east, to the eastern edge of the area, we have other examples of the cord-impressed decoration from the Upper Paraguay River, at Puerto 14 de Mayo, where Boggiani noted it in shell and refuse mounds along the river many years ago.[69]

This survey across the Chaco gives us only a scant idea of its archaeology, but even with this limited information it is obvious that several lines of influence are involved. The burial urns and some of the incised decoration influences probably come from the South Andes, that is, from the

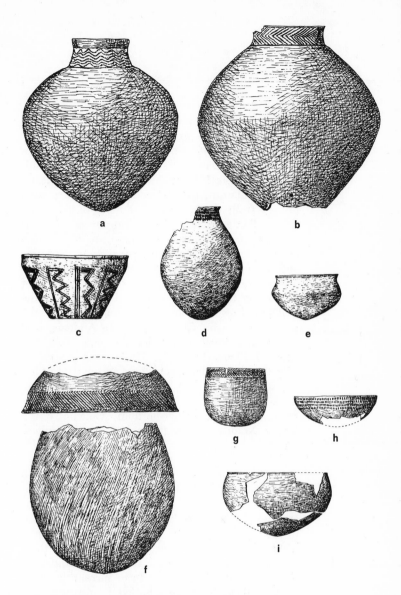

Figure 7-17. Chacoan pottery. *a:* Burial urn, Lomas de Olmedo, with cord-impressed decoration on neck. *b:* Burial urn from Naranjo, similarly decorated. *c:* Incised bowl, Lomas de Olmedo. *d:* Small burial urn (for fetus) with finger-pinched marks on neck. *e:* Bowl used as lid for Naranjo urn—also has cord-impressed decoration on rim. *f:* Urn and bowl lid, with incised and punctate decorations on latter, from Quirquincho. *g–i:* Vessels from Quirquincho, with incised and punctate (*g*) and punctate (*h*) decoration. Height of *b*, about 55 cm. (After Fock, 1961.)

Selvas Occidentales and Chaco-Stantiagueño cultures.[70] On the other hand, some of the incision and the fingernail-marking techniques point in the opposite direction: to southern Brazil and the Eastern Brazilian pottery tradition and to the

Paraná Valley. However, the cord-impressed decorative technique seems uniquely Chacoan.

Tupiguaraní influences appear in the eastern Chaco. Max Schmidt[71] and Vellard[72] have both described typical Tupiguaraní ceramic complexes, with burial urns, painted pottery, and corrugated pottery from the vicinity of the city of Asunción on the Paraguay River; and Metraux noted similar styles from Paraguay.[73] There are no definite dates, although we know that such pottery continued to be made after Spanish contact. Other Tupiguaraní-like pottery has been found, of course, on the opposite side of the Chaco, in the Bolivian Lowlands around Santa Cruz, at the point where the Chacoan, South Andean, and Amazonian area boundaries converge (see pp. 422–424, "Guaraní sites"). This pottery was probably that of the late prehistoric and early historic Chiriguano, and one would surmise that these Tupí-Guaranians had crossed from the Upper Paraguay, through the northern Chaco, to the Upper Madeira drainages in late pre-Columbian times.

Summary: The Question of Cultural Traditions. What are the cultural traditions of the Chaco? We have no clues to very early hunters or gatherers. Such peoples, if they once hunted in the Chaco, must have used weapons and implements of materials other than stone, and these would have perished. Or, if stone points and tools were brought into the area from surrounding territories, these have been buried in silts or have not been found.

The earliest occupancy of which we have record is that of the pottery-using peoples who lived along the Bermejo and Pilcomayo Rivers. These people were apparently influenced in their ceramic manufactures by both South Andean and Eastern Brazilian–Paraná River cultures. But they also developed a pottery tradition of their own—the one characterized by the cord-impressed wares. We have seen that this form of decoration ran from prehistoric times down to the present-day ethnographic horizon. This Chacoan pottery tradition can be conceived of as being embodied with a broader Chacoan cultural tradition—one about which we know very little archaeologically but which is seen in the ethnographic record. This Chacoan cultural tradition was based primarily

upon plant collecting. Hunting and fishing were adjuncts to the economy. It is unlikely that it was ever significantly agricultural, although a minimal, incipient horticulture may have been present in some places well back into prehistory. Communities were small, dwellings flimsy. The socio-political structure lacked hierarchical features.

The other cultural tradition of the Chaco area is the Tupiguaraní subtraditional branch of the Amazonian cultural tradition. Its manifestations are similar to what we have seen in the East Brazilian area. In the Chaco it appears to have been established in the lands suitable for farming along the Paraguay River. Without much question it can be identified with the Guaraní tribes of the area.

We have no archaeological chronology for the Chaco area. From what we know of time relationships in southeastern Brazil, we would not expect the Tupiguaraní subtradition to have appeared along the Paraguay River until A.D. 500—and probably some time after that date. If our hypothesis about a Chacoan pottery tradition is correct, it would have been formed from early South Andean stimuli (Las Mercedes, Candelaria I, etc.) and from Lower Paraná Valley stimuli. Such a synthesis would have taken place prior to the arrival of the Tupiguaraní culture.

The Pampean Area

The Setting. The Pampean or "Campestral" culture area (see p. 24) is so defined as to include Uruguay, the Argentine Provinces along the Middle and Lower Paraná Rivers, the Argentine Pampas proper, Patagonia, and eastern and northern Tierra del Fuego (Figs. 1-1, 7-18). Three kinds of country are thus embraced. The river lowlands of the north are alluvial plains and savannas, broken occasionally by rolling hillocks and smaller valleys. The Pampas are flat and grass covered, humid in the east with tall grasses and ample rainfall, drier in the west and covered with a scrub tree or "monte" vegetation. Patagonia is a land of arid plateaus and is intersected at wide intervals by west-to-east–flowing streams; in the

Figure 7-18. (*Right*, p. 459)

458

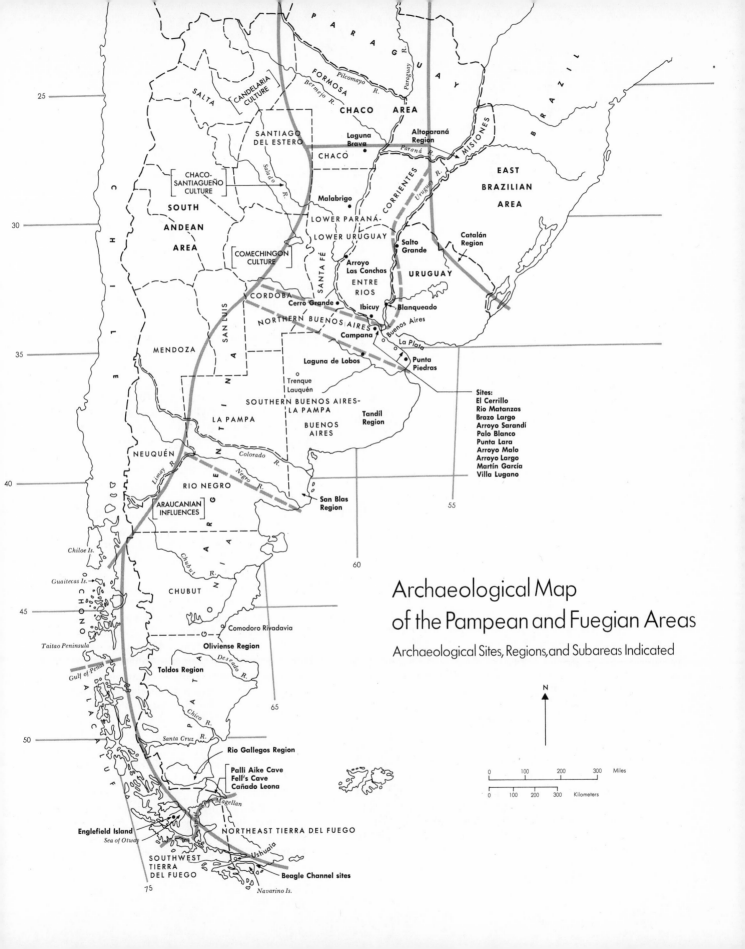

Archaeological Map of the Pampean and Fuegian Areas

Archaeological Sites, Regions, and Subareas Indicated

N

Sites:
El Cerrillo
Rio Matanzas
Brazo Largo
Arroyo Sarandí
Palo Blanco
Punta Lara
Arroyo Malo
Arroyo Largo
Martín García
Villa Lugano

0   100   200   300   Miles

0   100   200   300   Kilometers

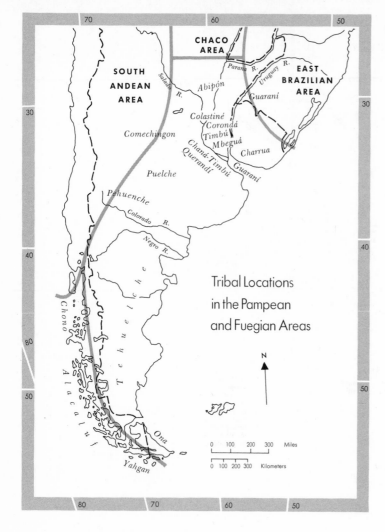

Figure 7-19.

bleak far south and on Tierra del Fuego the climate is perpetually cold and windy.[74]

From late Pleistocene times to the historic present, Patagonia and the Pampas were favorable lands for game hunters—with the guanaco and the rhea plentiful. In the north, too, there was game as well as the fish of the Paraná and Uruguay River systems; and farming was possible: we know that some tribes along the Paraná practiced it in historic times, and perhaps they did so earlier. The Pampas grasslands, although destined to become one of the great agricultural areas of the world in modern times, were resistant to primitive digging-stick farming, and farther south the arid plateaus of Patagonia were completely unsuited for the growing of crops.

Languages and Tribes. According to the Greenberg classification (see map, pp. 12–14, Fig. 1-5), Pampean area languages fall into three major divisions: (1) those which can be shown to be affiliated with the Macro-Panoan group; (2) those which have been unidentified as to affiliation; and (3) those affiliated with the Andean group. Under the Macro-Ge heading come the Charrua and related tribes of Uruguay. The "unidentified" tongues were the Chaná-Timbú, Chaná-Mbeguá, Timbú, Mbeguá, Corondá, Colastiné, and others of the Lower Paraná-Lower Uruguay subarea, and the Querandí of northern Buenos Aires Province. Linguistic data are few or nonexistent on these tribes; the logic of geography suggests that they may all have belonged to the Macro-Panoan group, but there is no proof. To the south were the Puelche of the Pampas, the Tehuelche of Patagonia, and the Ona of Tierra del Fuego—all well-known tribes in the historic period ethnographical literature. All are classed in the Andean major language group. Two other languages remain to be mentioned: Tupian and Araucanian. Guaraní peoples moved into the northern part of the area, along the Paraná drainage, in late prehistoric times. Araucanians crossed the Andes from Chile into the western edge of Patagonia and the Pampas in historic times.[75]

An ethnographic summary of all of these peoples divides conveniently into two major sections. The northern river tribes of the unidentified language groups subsisted primarily by fishing, secondarily by hunting and plant gathering, and, in some degree, by farming.[76] This last trait is of particular interest. It may be that tribes like the Timbú acquired hunting in relatively late times from the invading Guaraní; however in view of our arguments about the possibility of pre-Tupiguaraní farming in the East Brazilian area, there is at least the same possibility that the Timbú and related tribes had a long history of cultivation even though this cultivation was not their primary means of livelihood. The Timbú seem to have been fairly sedentary, and their villages were composed of large rush-covered houses that were divided into family compartments. They knew cotton and used it for clothing, and, although pottery is not mentioned in the early historic account, the archaeological record from the area

460

makes it certain that these people were also potters.

The other cultural pattern seen from ethnography is that of the Charrua, Querandí, Puelche, Tehuelche, and Ona. These people were primarily plains hunters, although the Charrua and Querandí, who lived near rivers, were also fishers. They were not agricultural, but they made pottery (the Ona being the only non-potters). Their sites were of a semi-sedentary nature. Dwellings were mats supported by poles or skin windbreaks. The guanaco, rhea, and deer were taken with bolas or with bow and arrow, the latter being tipped with chipped-stone or bone points. Clothing was made entirely of hides. Life was lived in small exogamous bands, each of which usually had its own circumscribed hunting territory. After the advent of the Europeans these groups became horsemen, and for a time there was a native florescence, with an increase in the Indian populations as they became more effective huntsmen; however, with the decimation of game and the steady encroachments of the white settlers, Indian peoples and their culture declined rapidly in the nineteenth century.[77]

Of the two late intrusive groups, the Guaraní of the Paraná River were, of course, agricultural and pottery making, and they lived a sedentary life in well-made thatched houses.[78] The Araucanian Pehuenche probably began moving into Argentina in the early historic period,[79] and we have already referred to possible Araucanian influences in Mendoza (pp. 245–246). Pottery of undoubted Araucanian affiliation is found in the Rio Limay region of the Neuquén-Patagonian border, attesting either to their presence on this periphery of the Pampean area or to their cultural influence.[80]

Cultural Traditions, Subareas, and Chronology. As we have seen in Chapter 2, an ancient Flake tradition may have once characterized the Pampean area, and elements of the Andean Biface tradition were also observed in northern Argentine and Uruguayan early industries (Caracaraña, Altoparaná, Early Catalán). The Old South American hunting tradition was represented by the Magellan I fish-tail point complex of far southern Patagonia, by the similar Toldos finds of the Rio Deseado, and by the

Solano complex of leaf-shaped blades and points. This tradition was followed by the Andean Hunting-Collecting tradition as seen in the Magellan III phase and in the willow leaf and stemless triangular points found elsewhere in Patagonia and to the north. We then argued that a Paraná-Pampean tradition developed in the area at about 4000 to 3000 B.C. It is with this Paraná-Pampean cultural tradition that we will be concerned primarily in this section.

The Paraná-Pampean cultural tradition is the result of a cultural synthesis that began some time after 4000 B.C., one involving southern hunters of an Andean Hunting-Collecting background and northern riverine fishers, collectors, and hunters of an East Brazilian Upland tradition background. The synthesis quite probably proceeded very slowly at first; but here we are handicapped by our lack of specific knowledge about the preceramic horizon in the north. Later, with the diffusion of pottery from the Paraná drainage to the Strait of Magellan, the Paraná-Pampean tradition is more easily appreciated; however, it should be emphasized that the northern-southern dichotomy persisted throughout the life-span of the tradition into historic times.

The only other cultural traditions that concern us in this section—and these but briefly—are the Amazonian, in the form of a late prehistoric-to-historic Tupiguaraní intrusion into the Lower Paraná and Lower Uruguay Rivers, and the South Andean, in the form of late intrusions into western Patagonia and La Pampa.

We will refer to six subareas in our discussion of the Paraná-Pampean tradition:

(1) Lower Paraná–Lower Uruguay; (2) Uruguay; (3) Northern Buenos Aires; (4) Southern Buenos Aires–La Pampa; (5) Patagonia; and (6) Northeast Tierra del Fuego (see map, Fig. 7-18).[81]

As with East Brazil and the Chaco, there will be no formal chronology for the Pampean area; we will refer simply to absolute dating estimates (see Fig. 7-20).

The Paraná-Pampean Tradition: Preceramic Horizon. As we have already observed, the preceramic beginnings of the Paraná-Pampean tradition are seen to best advantage in the site stratigraphies at the Strait of Magellan.

The Magellan IV phase succeeded the Magellan III willow leaf and stemless triangular point horizon both at Fell's Cave (pp. 43–44) and at another site called Cañadon Leona.[82] The latter is a site on the eastern shore of Laguna Blanca, a residual glacial lake, about 60 miles west of Palli Aike. The original occupation (Magellan III) was in the sandy soil of a disintegrating tufa bed.

Some 8 to 9 feet (a little less than 3 meters) of wind-blown soil covered this original occupation, and in this soil were the stemmed dart points that are identified with the Magellan IV phase levels in Fell's Cave. The characteristic stemmed points of Magellan IV (Fig. 7-21) are 3 to 5 centimeters long, the blade is triangular or triangulate, and the stem is proportionately broad, straight, and basally indented. They are of a size most usually associated with use as darts; however, the smaller ones could have been accommodated to the bow and arrow. Other Magellan IV artifacts

Figure 7-20. Chronological chart for the Pampean and Fuegian areas. With subarea columns and principal cultures and culture phases.

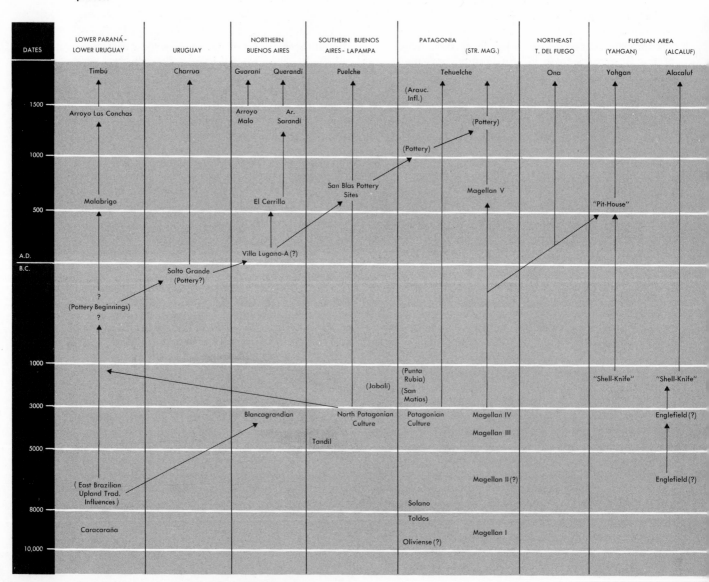

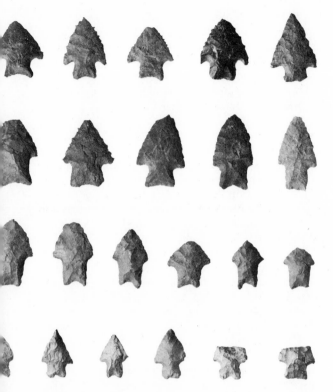

Figure 7-21. Projectile points of Magellan Period IV. Point at *upper left* is about 3.5 cm. in length. (Courtesy American Museum of Natural History; see also Bird, 1938.)

are little end-scrapers, side-scrapers, bone chipping tools, grooved bolas stones of a larger size than those of Magellan III, and simple bone and stone beads. Guanaco and rhea bones were met with frequently in the refuse. At the top of the Cañadon Leona site were the smaller Phase V points (Fig. 7-22) that can be identified with those used in historic times by the Ona.

These data from far southern Patagonia give us a good beginning for our tracing out of the history of the Paraná-Pampean tradition. How can we move on from here? To do so, we must turn to the findings and conclusions of several Argentine archaeologists who have been concerned with the various lithic complexes and industries of Patagonia and the Pampas over the past several years—especially to the works of Menghín and his followers, Bórmida, Sanguinetti de Bórmida, and others.[83] These prehistorians incorporate the Magellan IV complex into what they have called a Patagonian (Patagoniense, Tehuelchense) culture. This culture is found throughout Patagonia[84] and in Northeastern Tierra del Fuego. Its beginnings are estimated by Sanguinetti de Bórmida at about 2000 B.C.; however, following my dating estimate of Magellan IV, I would suggest a date of a millennium or so earlier. The Patagonian

Figure 7-22. Projectile points of Magellan Period V. These are significantly smaller than those of earlier periods. The point at *upper left* is about 2 cm. in length. (Courtesy American Museum of Natural History; see also Bird, 1938.)

culture tool kit includes stemmed points like those of Magellan IV (and III as well), together with the scrapers, knives, and various skin-dressing and skin-working tools of a hunting culture. It would appear that the Patagonian culture extends north as far as the San Blas region of the Southern Buenos Aires–La Pampa subarea, for Magellan IV and III style projectile points are found on sites there, together with ground stone items, such as "sobadores," or hide depilators, and grooved bolas.[85] These sites carry the Patagonian cultural continuity on into later times and, eventually, to the ceramic horizon.

Farther north, however, the Patagonian culture is replaced by a North Patagonian (or Norpatagoniense) culture that is found in parts of the Southern Buenos Aires–La Pampa subarea. Its projectile points are stemless, and this could indicate a greater antiquity, linking to Magellan III rather than IV. Or it could signify a chronological lag in the diffusion of such points from south-to-north—an explanation more in keeping with Sanguinetti de Bórmida's dating estimate of 1000 B.C.

In the Northern Buenos Aires subarea there are several industries of crudely flaked tools. A Blancagrande (or Blancagrandense) culture has only unifacial points and knives.[86] The Argentine prehistorians relate it back to the earlier Tandíl industry of the same subarea and from there extend the line of development back still further to the putatively early Flake tradition industries of Oliviense and Rio Gallegos in Patagonia.[87] This raises the whole complex question of the late survival of early technologies—a matter discussed at some length in Chapter 2 (pp. 41–42) and brings our attention to the well-known rough percussion-flaked complexes of the Pampean and Patagonian Atlantic coasts. One of these, the Jabalí (Jabaliense), was mentioned in Chapter 2; it is the rough pebble tool industry for which claims of great age were made by Ameghino, which Holmes and others rebutted. San Matías (Sanmatiense) and Punta Rubia (Puntarrubiense) are the other two, the former featuring denticulates and scrapers, the latter cores and bi-polar forms. Jabalí is found on the Southern Buenos Aires coast, and San Matías and Punta Rubia are known from there and from farther south. San Matías is believed to date as early as 3000 B.C.,

while Punta Rubia and Jabalí are estimated at a millennium or so later. As such, they would all parallel, chronologically, the interior Patagonian, North Patagonian, and Blanca Grande cultures, and one wonders to what extent the coastal complexes may not be some sort of seasonal expressions of the inland industries.[87a]

The Paraná-Pampean Tradition: The First Appearance of Pottery. For a good many years it was conventional to think of pottery as a relatively recent arrival to the Pampean area. This, for example, is reflected in a speculative survey of South American cultures, ceramics, and dating estimates that I published in 1958.[88] In this, a guess-date of about A.D. 400 was offered. More recent estimates of Argentine scholars have been more liberal. Thus, Sanguinetti de Bórmida suggests the round figures of 1000 B.C., 500 B.C., and A.D. 0 for the first appearances of ceramics in Northern Buenos Aires, South Buenos Aires, and Patagonia, respectively.[89]

Unfortunately, there are no radiocarbon dates that are of much assistance to us in the matter of dating the inception of Paraná-Pampean pottery.[90] There are, however, culture-historical relationships that may bear on the problem, and these also lead us to questions of the affiliations and origins of the Paraná-Pampean pottery tradition. I have previously favored an Amazonian-East Brazilian line of descent for Paraná-Pampean pottery and still do.[91] Thus I would interpret the foundations of pottery making in the Paraná-Pampean tradition as deriving out of the Eastern Brazilian pottery tradition. As we have seen, there is evidence (the Periperí phase) that this tradition had its beginnings as early as 800 to 900 B.C. Although the Vieira and Taquara subtraditions of this Eastern Brazilian pottery tradition probably date considerably later than this, they provide us with some clues to what such an early Brazilian pottery stratum may have contained. Much of the ware was undoubtedly plain, but some of it was probably decorated with incisions, punctations, and linear punctation. These techniques are present in the Paraná-Pampean pottery of the Lower Paraná–Lower Uruguay subarea.

In keeping with the Brazilian dating that we have so far, I am hesitant to accept a date prior to 1000 B.C. for the Lower Paraná–Lower Uruguay pottery. To be consistent with my thesis of a north-to-south spread of the idea of ceramics in eastern South America, I offer the rough estimate of 500 B.C. for the beginning of the ceramic horizon on the Lower Paraná (see chronology chart, Fig. 7-20).

Although the Eastern Brazilian pottery tradition probably had the major role in the synthesis of a Paraná-Pampean pottery tradition, there is a good possibility that elements from the South Andean area went into this synthesis. As Ibarra Grasso has reasoned, some such elements may have come from the Chaco-Santiagueño and Sierras Centrales cultures, which fronted along the western edge of the Pampean area;[92] however, it must also be considered that the course of diffusion ran as much from east-to-west as *vice versa* and that the life-modeled adornos on Chaco-Santiagueño pottery (p. 223) could have had their beginnings on the Lower Paraná. Our control of the dating is too tenuous to resolve such a question at the present time.

The Paraná-Pampean Tradition: The Ceramic Horizon on the Lower Paraná-Lower Uruguay. What we may tentatively call the Malabrigo phase seems most representative of the full development of the ceramic art in the Lower Paraná–Lower Uruguay subarea. The Malabrigo group of sites is located on the Santa Fé Province side of the Paraná River near the town of Reconquista.[93] The sites appear to be midden accumulations on little natural knolls in the river flood plain. There has been some debate in the past over whether Malabrigo and similar sites were artificial mounds or natural eminences. A survey of the published data would indicate that they were refuse accumulations on natural high spots that rose above the seasonal floodwaters. Although burials are found in them, they do not appear to be artificially constructed "burial mounds." Refuse in the Malabrigo sites averaged a litttle less than a meter in depth. This refuse contained shells, fish bones, bird bones, reptilian and animal remains, and charred palm nuts. The human burials found in the refuse were all of the secondary type. In some instances bones had been painted with red ocher and boulders placed with the burials. Bolas were the only stone artifacts found in these sites. The pottery was in subglobular and hemispherical

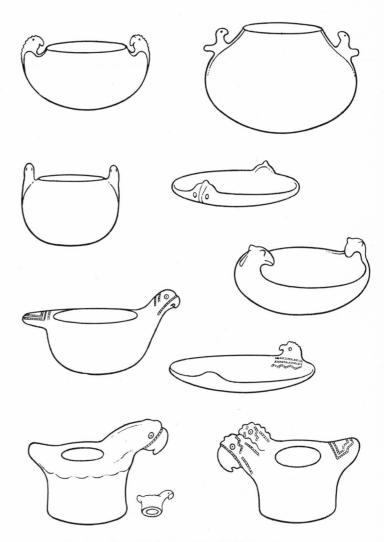

Figure 7-23. Pottery vessel forms of the Malabrigo phase. (Redrawn from Badano, 1955.)

bowl forms (Fig. 7-23). These bowls had been decorated with drag-and-jab punctation (Figs. 7-24, 7-25), incisions, rows of punctate dots, and fingernail impressions. Motifs or decoration arrangements were parallel straight or zigzag lines as well as other simple schemes. Modeled adornos were a common trait (Figs. 7-23, 7-25). These are affixed to the bowl rim, are either hollow or solid, and most frequently represent a bird's head, apparently that of a parrot. The adornos are large,

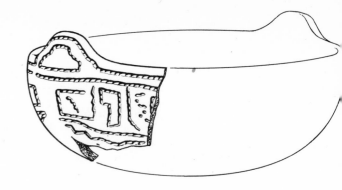

Figure 7-24. *Right:* Linear-punctated or drag-and-jab punctated vessel. From Arroyo Las Mulas, Provincia de Entre Rios. (Redrawn from Serrano, 1946 b.)

Figure 7-25. *Below:* Malabrigo phase sherds. *Left:* A parrot-head "plastic representation" (height, about 8 cm.). *Right:* A drag-and-jab decorated sherd. (Redrawn from Aparicio, 1948.)

sometimes being as much as 10 centimeters in diameter, and are almost always decorated with drag-and-jab punctated lines. Some of them are painted, and many vessel body sherds bear red band designs.

A number of fragments at Malabrigo came from what are known as "campanas," or "alfarerías gruesas." These are either bell-shaped or tubular-shaped objects of thick-walled pottery. Many are made with a bird-head adorno similar to the adornos found on the regular pottery vessels (Fig. 7-26). The "campanas," or "alfarerías gruesas," are not vessels, however, as they are open at both the bottom and the top or else open at the bottom and equipped with side vents. Various speculations have been made as to their functions. Some archaeologists have suggested that they were pot-rests or "fire dogs," used to hold cooking vessels upright in the fire. They average 9 to 12 centimeters in diameter and are frequently as tall as, or taller than, this. Ibarra Grasso thinks that they were employed in connection with fire, but in a ritual or ceremonial, rather than a utilitarian, manner, arguing that they were placed with the dead to cover small sacred fires or incense.[94] Whatever their function, they were obviously an integral part of the Malabrigo complex; most of them

Figure 7-26. Complete "campana," or bell-shaped pottery object, Lower Paraná. (Courtesy D. E. Ibarra Grasso; see also Ibarra Grasso, 1967.)

bear the typical drag-and-jab linear-punctated designs on the effigy head.

Malabrigo-like assemblages are found both to the south and north of Reconquista. At Ibicuy,[95] Campana,[96] and Cerro Grande[97]—all refuse hillock sites in the river flats of the Lower Paraná—and at Blanqueado[98]—on the Lower Uruguay—the drag-and-jab punctated pottery is present as are the biomorphic adornos. In addition, Cerro Grande, the northernmost of these sites, has the "campanas," or "alfarerías gruesas." These last seem to have a more northerly distribution, being restricted to a "Middle Paraná" division of the Lower Paraná.[99] At Las Tejas the characteristic Malabrigo phase traits are found associated with child urn burials, the only non-Tupiguaranian occurrence of urn burials in the Lower Paraná–Lower Uruguay subarea.[100] The adult burials at the site were secondary but not in urns. A northernmost occurrence of Malabrigo-type biomorphic adornos is Laguna Brava, some 25 miles west of Resistencia, in the Territory of the Chaco, and on the border of the Paraná-Pampean and Chaco areas. Here, appropriately, the adornos were decorated with cord impressions, in the Chacoan mode, rather than with the more usual drag-and-jab punctations.[101]

There is little or no chronological information on these sites that we have grouped together as a tentative "Malabrigo phase." I would suspect, however, that such a "phase" could be broken down into a series of phases spanning a considerable time range. All that we know for certain is that most of the Malabrigo-like sites are prehistoric but that a few of them persist until the early historic period. At Arroyo Las Conchas, near the city of Paraná, in Entre Rios Province, Venetian glass beads came from a context of drag-and-jab pottery and biomorphic adornos.[102]

The Paraná-Pampean Tradition: The Ceramic Horizon in Northern Buenos Aires. In the Northern Buenos Aires subarea, including the shores of the delta of the Plate, the ceramic complexes relate to, but also show certain differences from, those of the Malabrigo phase. A number of tentative phases can be recognized in the subarea. One is known from a type site called El Cerrillo, a low mound of detritus, ash, and hearth remains on the edge of a swampy tributary

of the Plate known as the Paraná Guazú. Both Torres and Lothrop found burials and artifacts here.[103] The burials for the most part were secondary interments although not urn burials. The bundled bones of the dead had apparently been placed in shallow graves in which food and fire offerings had first been made. Red pigment was sometimes applied to the bones, and a number of skeletons were accompanied by artifacts. Site debris included both fish bones and animal bones and a good many artifacts made from bone: awls, points, and pins that had been decorated by carving. The El Cerrillo pottery (Fig. 7-27) is a brownish ware, similar to that of Malabrigo although completely unslipped and unpainted. Decoration was also similar to Malabrigo in that drag-and-jab punctations were used in linear designs, along with wavy and straight incised lines. Designs also included short, parallel, incised lines or semilunar punctations placed hachure-fashion within rectilinear incised zones. Simple bowls were the characteristic shapes; the adornos and "alfarerías gruesas" of the Malabrigo phase were lacking.

Several other sites on the Plate estuary are similar to El Cerrillo. One of these, Brazo Largo, has secondary burials, drag-and-jab decorated ceramics, and numerous bone implements.[104] In fact, it probably could be included in the El Cerrillo phase, although it does show one difference, the presence of a few corrugated sherds. These last could indicate Tupiguaraní contact, and this suggests a possibly later chronological position than El Cerrillo. Two other sites, Rio Matanzas[105] and Punta Piedra,[106] have the El Cerrillo ceramic complex, with the drag-and-jab punctated, incised, and zoned semi-lunar punctated decorations; however, both sites lack the extensive bone tool and weapon inventory of El Cerrillo. Rio Matanzas had small, unstemmed triangular arrow points of chipped stone, Punta Piedra a single dart-sized stemmed point of the Magellan IV class. The El Cerrillo–type ceramic complex is also reported at Laguna de Lobos, a lakeshore site some 150 kilometers southwest of the city of Buenos Aires.[107]

A related but somewhat different ceramic complex of the Northern Buenos Aires subarea is that represented at Arroyo Sarandí[108] and other sites. This complex includes the drag-and-jab (Fig. 7-29) punctated incised types similar to those of El Cerrillo but in addition has red slipped, white

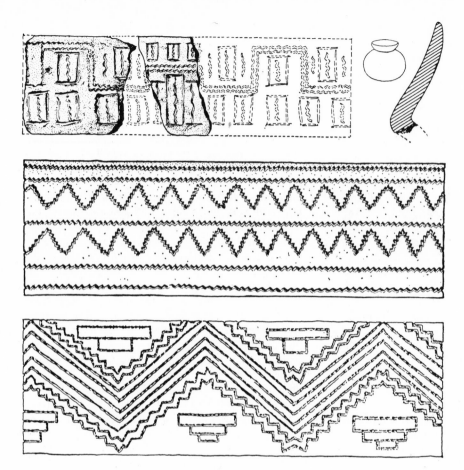

Figure 7-27. *Above:* Drag-and-jab punctated or incised designs, El Cerrillo. *Top:* Design on rim interior of jar. *Center* and *bottom:* Varieties of design arrangements. (After Lothrop, 1932 b.)

slipped, and red band decorated wares. This painted pottery is in no sense in the Tupiguaraní style, but one cannot help wonder if it resulted from Tupiguaraní stimulus. As we shall see further on, Tupiguaraní sites are present in the same region as Arroyo Sarandí and El Cerrillo; at least one of these Tupiguaraní sites has early Spanish trade materials; and indirectly we may

Figure 7-28. *Below:* Potsherds from the northern Buenos Aires subarea. *a:* Elongated punctations in incised zones. *b:* Fingernail-impressed or "imbricated" ware. *c:* Linear-dot punctations. (Redrawn from Howard and Willey, 1948.)

a   b   c

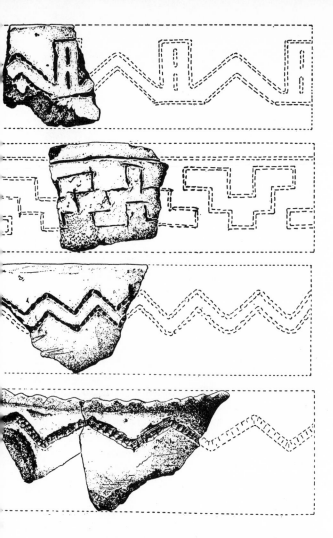

Figure 7-29. Drag-and-jab or linear-punctated pottery designs. Sherds from Arroyo Sarandí. (After Lothrop, 1932 b.)

reason—or at least suspect—that Arroyo Sarandí, with its red and white painted pottery, is later than El Cerrillo. In fact, the Arroyo Sarandí midden contained the remains of iron artifacts and cow bones, and if these were in true association with the aboriginal artifacts, the site must be dated to the early historic period. Quite possibly it was a Querandí village. Arroyo Sarandí burials were about equally divided between those of primary and secondary form. Bone artifacts were common—awls, punches, fish stringers, lance points, arrowpoints, and throwing-stick hooks. Bola stones were present as was a chipped-stone arrowpoint. Shell had been used for beads and pendants. One additional trait from Arroyo Sarandí is worth special mention. This is the hollow pottery tube (Fig. 7-30), referred to in Argentine archaeology as a "tubular." These tubes have also been found at some of the inland sites in Northern Buenos Aires.[109] They are sometimes referred to as "fire dogs," and it has been suggested that they were so used in cooking. Although much simpler than the Malabrigo "campanas" or "alfarerías gruesas," they may be related.

Figure 7-30. *Below, left:* Pottery "fire dog" or "tubular" from Arroyo Sarandí. Height, 18 cm. (Redrawn from Lothrop, 1932 b.)

Figure 7-31. *Below, right:* Pottery pendants from Arroyo Sarandí. The figurinelike pendant (reminiscent of Chaco-Santiagueño figurines) is 5 cm. high. (After Lothrop, 1932 b.)

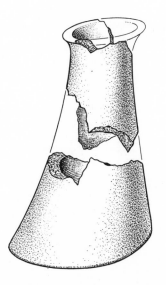

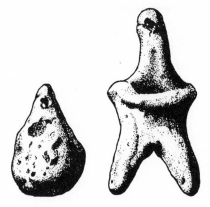

Figure 7-32. Potsherds from San Blas region, Southern Buenos Aires–La Pampa subarea. (After Howard and Willey, 1948.)

Other Northern Buenos Aires sites that seem to fall into the suggested Arroyo Sarandí phase pattern are Punta Lara and Villa Lugano–Site B. Punta Lara, on the estuary below Buenos Aires, is a midden capping a shell "cordon."[110] The site appears to be a double occupation for there is horizontal—and perhaps some vertical—stratigraphy separating a later Tupiguaraní complex from an earlier Arroyo Sarandí-like complex. The Arroyo Sarandí-like sherds include red band and incised red zoned painting and fragments of "tubulares." Villa Lugano–Site B is within the environs of the city of Buenos Aires.[111] The pottery complex includes red banded, red slipped, and red zoned types. These were found with small stemless points, bolas, fragments of iron tools, and pipes, one of which seems to show European influence.

Although the artifact variations among all of these Northern Buenos Aires sites cannot be properly appraised from present evidence—lacking chronological and distributional information as we do—a gross ceramic sequence of El Cerrillo (earlier) to Arroyo Sarandí (later) is indicated, with the Arroyo Sarandí-type sites lasting into European contact times and into contemporaneity with Tupiguaraní sites.

The Paraná-Pampean Tradition: The Ceramic Horizon in Other Subareas. Southern Buenos Aires–La Pampa is classed by Argentine archaeologists as lying within the scope of a North Patagonian, or "Norpatagoniense," culture that has preceramic beginnings. Also, on the coast of Southern Buenos Aires Province are remains of the crude pebble-tool Jabaliense culture. Just how these cultures relate to the appearance of pottery is not altogether clear, although it is implied that the North Patagonian stoneworking traditions were the context for the subarea into which pottery was diffused. Most of the archaeology in the subarea centers on the coastal San Blas Peninsula region. Outes described chipped-stone artifacts from a site at the foot of a sand dune near Puerto San Blas:[112] knives and scrapers of both unifacial and bifacial workmanship and large stemless (Magellan III–like) and stemmed (Magellan IV–like) projectile points. Mullers, mortar stones, and pitted hammerstones were associated, as well as polished and engraved stone plaques. These last,

the "placas grabadas," are flat, rectangular stones with rows of engraved rectilinear designs. The Puerto San Blas pottery was unpainted ware, in quality and appearance much like that from farther north. The designs on it, however, are different. They feature fine line incision and little dot punctations, including incised triangles and other figures filled with such punctations (Fig. 7-32). The heavy lined, drag-and-jab punctation, seen in the Northern Buenos Aires or Lower Paraná–Lower Uruguay subareas, is rare or absent. Whether the collection from Puerto San Blas represents a single phase or several phases is uncertain; quite possibly both preceramic and ceramic horizon occupations are reflected in the materials.

Torres mentioned other San Blas sites.[113] These have the large points, like those just mentioned, but also small stemless and stemmed types that could have served as arrow tips and that resemble those of the pottery horizon at some of the Northern Buenos Aires sites. It should be emphasized, however, that points—and flintwork in general—are much more common in Southern Buenos Aires–La Pampa than farther north. Torres also noted the engraved plaques, some polished stone lip plugs, and fine line incised and punctated pottery. He suggested a pottery sequence for the region, with earlier fine line incised types being succeeded by those with somewhat deeper linear-punctated line designs—these last apparently being rather similar to the drag-and-jab decorated types of the north; however, he did not explain his evidence for such a sequence.

The San Blas fine line incised pottery is known inland in the subarea as well. Outes reported it from a sand dune site at Hucal, in La Pampa Province, where it was associated with small unstemmed and stemmed points.[114]

The ceramic horizon in the Patagonian subarea is represented only by scattered finds; however, a knowledge of pottery—if not of pottery making—extended as far south as the Strait of Magellan.[115] Plain, simple pottery is present in Phase V of the Magellan sequence, which is also known for its small (3- to 2-centimeters-long) arrowpoints. These have triangulate or long triangulate blades, short and straight stems, and pronounced barbs.[116] Known as the "Ona points," they are found in the Northeast Tierra del Fuego subarea, where they are associated with the historic Ona tribe. Bird states that they are also found as far north as the Rio Negro, the northern boundary of Patagonia.[117] Other Magellan V items are bolas, bone flaking-tools, what may be bone implements for removing bark from trees, and bone combs. Clay pipes and European metals also come in at the close of Magellan V, taking us into the historic period.

It is likely that the various polished stone artifacts—celts, perforated club heads, the engraved "hachas insignias," or "tokis" (which are obviously related to the "clavas insignias," Fig. 7-33, that occur in Neuquen and were mentioned on p. 246), as well as the engraved plaques (like

those of the San Blas region, Fig. 7-34)—that are found throughout Patagonia all pertain to late pre-Columbian and early historic times.[118] And it is also likely that the rock paintings of the Comodoro Rivadavia region date similarly. Menghín notes that many of the rock painting designs look like the engraved decorations on the stone plaques.[119] Guanaco hunts are also depicted in the rock paintings.[120]

This survey of the ceramic horizon has omitted one subarea: Uruguay. This subarea subsumes most of that country, with the sole exception of the Lower Uruguay Valley. The ceramics of the Uruguay subarea are unlike those of the Lower Paraná–Lower Uruguay or of Northern Buenos Aires in that they show relatively little decoration, and what there is consists of a few zigzag incised lines, dot punctations, and fingernail markings.[121] Serrano has remarked that it resembles the pottery of Southern Buenos Aires–La Pampa.[122] This raises the possibility that the Southern Buenos Aires and Uruguayan styles may represent an

Figure 7-33. *Below, left:* Typical stone "clava insignia," or "toki." (Redrawn from Schobinger, 1956.)

Figure 7-34. *Below, right:* Engraved stone plaque ("placa grabada") from the Rio Negro country, Patagonia. (Redrawn from Willey, 1946.)

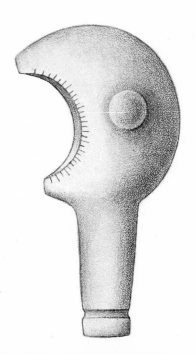

Figure 7-35. Petroglyph from Patagonia. A guanaco. Como-doro Rivadavia region. Overall length, about 50 cm. (After Vignati, 1950.)

earlier and simpler stratum in the pottery evolution for the Pampean area; however, this has not been demonstrated stratigraphically.[123] Another interpretation of the situation would be that the nomadic Uruguayan and Southern Buenos Aires grassland hunters had let the ceramic art decline in comparison to the condition of the craft among the more sedentary river dwellers.

Guaraní Sites. Guaraní sites are known from the Northern Buenos Aires subarea—in the same region of the Plate Delta as Arroyo Sarandí and El Cerrillo.[124] The contents of these sites are very similar to those of the Tupiguaraní subtradition sites that we have described from the Upper Paraná River in Misiones and southeastern Brazil. Arroyo Malo, one of the Guaraní sites excavated by Lothrop, was an extensive, although not deep, midden with secondary urn burials. The urns were the familiar pointed-bottomed, high-shouldered forms, capped by inverted bowls. Pottery decoration was by fingernail marking and corrugation in addition to painting (red-and-black on a light slip, Fig. 7-36) and red slipping. Glass beads and sherds of Spanish origin show that Arroyo Malo continued to be occupied into historic times. Two other sites of the delta, Arroyo Largo[125] and Martín García,[126]

have pottery very similar to that of Arroyo Malo but lack the European trade items; thus it is likely that the Guaraní sites were established in the Plate Delta country prior to the arrival of the Spanish but continued to be occupied into early historic times. The early Spanish chroniclers reported communities of both the agricultural Guaraní[127] and the non-agricultural Querandí[128] in the region.

Araucanian Influences. Although the Araucanian descent into Argentina is known largely from historic sources,[129] excavations along the Rio Limay, on the Neuquén-Patagonian border, revealed Araucanian pottery in the uppermost levels of a sequence.[130] The Araucanian pottery of Neuquén—which is known mainly from collections of uncertain provenience—consists of collared, handled jars and simple effigy forms.[131] Its exact dating is unknown, but it probably belongs to the historic period.

Summary. At some time around the beginning of the fourth millennium B.C. an Andean Hunting-Collecting tradition technology—or peoples with such a technology—began spreading into the Pampean area. It may be that this spread came mostly by way of the south, beginning in southern Patagonia and gradually moving northward, although it is also possible that there were movements from the San Luis—Córdoba hills directly into the Pampas from the west. The arti-

472

Figure 7-36. Painted Guaraní pottery from the Plate Delta. From Arroyo Malo. *Top:* Sherd of casuela bowl. *Bottom:* Polychrome (red-and-black-on-light slip) burial urn. Height of urn, about 45 cm. (Redrawn from Lothrop, 1932 b.)

ing tradition to one that we are calling the Paraná-Pampean tradition. This latter is a plains-adapted, guanaco-hunting tradition.

The Paraná-Pampean tradition—as the double name implies—also had another line of ancestry, one that can be traced back into the East Brazilian Upland tradition. In this line, bifacial tools are generally lacking. Cutting edges, scrapers, and other unspecialized-appearing implements are unifacial and made from flakes or battered pebbles. In southern Brazil, Uruguay, and Argentine Misiones this technology is represented by such industries as the Santa Rosa, the Catalán, the Cuareim, and the Altoparaná; in the Argentine Pampas it may be represented by the Blancagrandian and certain coastal facies such as the Jabalí. These industries reflect another kind of food-getting pattern, one less dependent on the pursuit of large animals in open terrain. Although the nature of these subsistence activities is speculative, they probably included plant gathering and fishing, as well as some hunting. It is our hypothesis that these two lines of ancestry—an Andean Hunting-Collecting tradition from the west and south, and an East Brazilian Upland tradition from the north and east—blended to produce the Paraná-Pampean tradition.

The Paraná-Pampean tradition was not fully amalgamated, however, until after the appearance and wide diffusion of ceramics. It has been speculated that these ceramics came to the Pampean area from the north, via the Eastern Brazilian pottery tradition, and that the idea of pottery making was implanted in the Lower Paraná Valley as early as 500 B.C. The Lower Paraná became the main center of pottery development in the Pampean area, and from there this development spread southward into the Pampas and Patagonia.

Although the Paraná-Pampean tradition must be characterized as essentially a hunting one, it is possible that agriculture played some part in its development, especially in its ceramic florescence along the Lower Paraná River. Here environmental conditions were more favorable for crop cultivation. We know that in late prehistoric times a Tupiguaranian people and culture moved down the Paraná Valley. They were farmers, and it may be that they were responsible for introducing a knowledge of agriculture to peoples of the Lower Paraná, such as the Timbú, who we know were

facts that provide the evidence for this spread of an Andean Hunting-Collecting technology are the stemless leaf-shaped and triangular projectile points of the Magellan III and Ayampitín types. On the Patagonian Plains a new cultural tradition began to take form, and new projectile points appear. These are medium-sized, triangular-bladed, straight-stemmed dart points—the Magellan IV points—and their appearance, along with a complement of knives, scrapers, bone implements, and bola stones, has been taken to mark the transition from the Andean Hunting-Collect-

farming in the sixteenth century. But the very good possibility also exists that the Lower Paraná peoples had been made aware of agriculture much earlier, perhaps at the time that pottery was first introduced from Eastern Brazil.

The Fuegian Area

The Setting. The Fuegian area extends from the Guaitecas Islands, just below the Island of Chiloé, southward along the shore to include the numerous islands of southern Chile and the western and extreme southern portions of Tierra del Fuego (Figs. 1-1, 7-18). The terrain is rugged with mountains descending into the sea to form deep and narrow fjords, hilly islets, and rocky beaches. It is a cold, wet land, with fogs, rain, and even snowfalls. It is also a heavily forested country.[132]

Mammals are scarce in the area and the terrain is too rugged for successful land hunting. Berries, various plants, and fungi are all edibles, but the main source of food for the native populations was the sea. It abounded in mussels, limpets, sea urchins, crabs, and snails. Seals and sea lions and flocks of birds lived along the shore.[133]

Tribes. The three principal tribes (Fig. 7-19) of the Fuegian area were the Chono,[134] the Alacaluf,[135] and the Yahgan.[136] The Chono occupied territory from the Guaitecas Islands south to the Gulf of Peñas. The Alacaluf were found from this point down to the Straits of Magellan. The Yahgan were the aboriginal people of the south coast and southern and western offshore islands of Tierra del Fuego. The language of the Chono is unknown; the Alacaluf and Yahgan languages are classed with the major Andean group.[137]

The culture of these three tribes was much the same. They gathered shellfish and crustaceans in the intertidal zone, and they harpooned seals and sea lions. They were good swimmers and canoeists. Their utensils were baskets, skin or bark buckets, chorro mussel shell scrapers and knives, bone wedges for removing the bark from trees, crude percussion-flaked axes, and anvil stones for cracking shellfish. Their weapons of the hunt or catch were bows and arrows, spears, barbed bone points or harpoons, chipped-stone projectile points, wooden leisters, clubs, and nets. Dwellings were small dome-shaped sapling frames covered with bark, sealskins, or ferns. They lived in small extended family bands of six to eight persons, and these little bands usually moved to a new beach location every few days.

Many ethnographic accounts of the Yahgan and Alacaluf have emphasized the ruggedness of life in this environment, and, to be sure, the climate is a miserable one. But as Steager has pointed out, it has its compensations.[138] The enormous productivity of the littoral zone has made food getting relatively easy, demanding only a simple technology and a degree of mobility. These archipelagic tribes had adapted to a very specific ecological niche, and this adaptation tended to preclude cultural change. They were not so much "refugees" pushed off into an undesirable corner of the continent as peoples who lived there because of a cultural heritage that demanded such an environment. This, of course, is another way of saying that the cultural heritage was fashioned in this environment—the only one of its kind in South America—and that the heritage has a great antiquity. Let us have a look at this antiquity.

The Fuegian Tradition. The Fuegian cultural tradition characterizes the Fuegian area throughout its history. We have described its apparent beginnings in Chapter 2 (pp. 66–67) in connection with the Englefield Island site.[139] This is a shell midden in the Sea of Otway, at the southern end of the Alacaluf subarea. The inhabitants of Englefield were seamammal hunters and shellfish gatherers; barbed harpoons (Fig. 7-37) and the bones of these animals were found in the refuse. But the Englefield peoples also possessed elements of the Andean Hunting-Collecting tradition, such as finely flaked willow leaf points (Fig. 7-38) and bola stones (Fig. 7-37). These findings suggest that Englefield represents the beginnings of a divergence between the Andean Hunting-Collecting tradition and the sea-oriented Fuegian tradition.

The Englefield findings thus support a hypothesis advanced by Frederik Barth.[140] Previously, J. M. Cooper had surmised that the Alacaluf, Chono, and Yahgan were the descendants of north

474

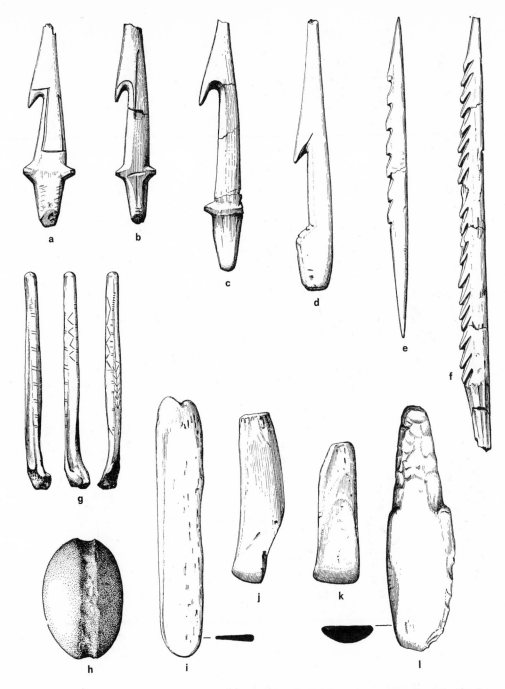

Figure 7-37. Bone artifacts and bola stones from the Fuegian area. *a–c:* Double-tenon, single-barbed harpoon heads from Englefield Island. *d:* Single-tenon, single-barbed harpoon head of late prehistoric style. *e, f:* Multi-barbed harpoon heads or spear points from Englefield Island. *g:* Bone awls with incised decorations from Englefield Island. *h:* Longitudinally grooved bola stone from Englefield Island. *i–l:* Spatulas or wedges (?) from Englefield Island. Length of *a*, 11.6 cm. (From Emperaire and Laming, 1961.)

Chilean fishers—presumably peoples of a Chilean Pacific Littoral tradition—who had made their way down the Pacific Coast in early times.[141] Barth countered with the suggestion that the Yahgan and Alacaluf were originally Pampean-Patagonian peoples and that their historic cultures were maritime adaptations of ancient land-hunting patterns. He cited in evidence the fundamental sameness of religion and ceremonial life between

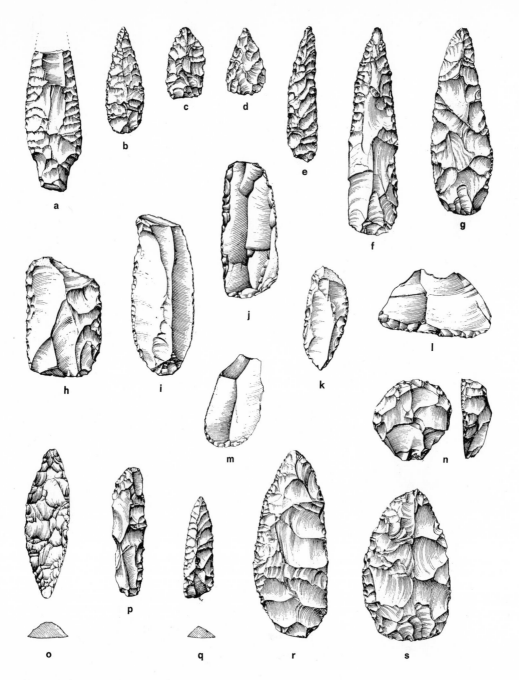

Figure 7-38. Chipped obsidian artifacts from Englefield Island. *a:* Bifacially flaked stemmed point. *b–g:* Various bifacially flaked leaf-shaped points. *h–m:* Flaked blades dressed as scrapers. *n:* Turtle-backed scraper. *o:* Double point. *p:* Knife. *q:* Single point. *r, s:* Large flakes dressed as knives. Length of *a,* 8 cm. (After Emperaire and Lanning, 1961.)

Yahgan-Alacaluf and the historic land-hunting Ona-Tehuelche, noting that the main differences between the Fuegian and the Paraná-Pampean peoples were traits associated with subsistence activities. I have modified this reconstruction only in referring to the ancient land-hunting patterns as the Andean Hunting-Collecting tradition—a terminology in keeping with the date at which it now seems that the sea-mammal hunting versus land-hunting separation took place.

Later archaeological cultures in the Fuegian area suggest that there was a progressive divergence of the Fuegian tradition away from the land-hunting cultures for a time. Thus the earlier of Bird's two phases in the Beagle Channel region of southern Tierra del Fuego and Navarino Island has an inventory of chorro mussel shell knives, barbed harpoon points of bone (Fig. 7-39), and rather crude percussion flintwork. This is Bird's "Shell-Knife Culture," and as a complex it almost duplicates the preservable material culture of the modern Alacaluf Indians, well to the north of Beagle Channel.[142]

This divergence becomes less apparent, however, in the Yahgan subarea in later prehistoric—and, indeed, in historic—times. Bird's later Beagle Channel phase, the "Pit-House Culture," has circular pole-and-brush dwellings with excavated floors. Chorro knives and harpoons continue, but there are new items, such as pressure-flaked points (Fig. 7-40) and knives.[143] Other explorations along Beagle Channel, in the vicinity of Ushuaia, confirm this picture of the Fuegian tradition. Here the Fuegian way of life was modified by important borrowings from the Paraná-Pampean tradition cultures of Patagonia; Vignati found

Magellan IV and V type points in shell middens there, along with bone harpoons,[144] and Sanchez-Albornoy reports similar assemblages—in one of which he found a Patagonian polished ceremonial stone or "clava insignia."[145]

It remains to say something about the chronology of these Fuegian tradition developments. As we said in Chapter 2, the Englefield radiocarbon dates of 7200 and 6500 B.C. (plus or minus 1500 years) are surprisingly early. In general, coastal adaptations of the Andean Hunting-Collecting tradition did not begin to come into being until about 4000 B.C. Thus, this later date would seem more appropriate for the emergence of many of the Englefield traits and, thereby, for the inception of the Fuegian tradition. For the "Shell-

Figure 7-39. *Below, left:* Single-barbed bone harpoon points. This general type was used by both "Pit-House" and "Shell-Knife Culture" peoples. Length of longest harpoon, about 35 cm. (Courtesy American Museum of Natural History; see also Bird, 1938.)

Figure 7-40. *Below, right:* Projectile points of the southern Chilean "Pit-House Culture." Point at *top left*, about 7 cm. in length. (Courtesy American Museum of Natural History; see also Bird, 1938.)

Figure 7-41. Navarino Island, off southern Tierra del Fuego, on Beagle Channel. A "Pit-House Culture" site in the foreground with a "pit" location. (Courtesy Museum of the American Indian, Heye Foundation.)

Knife Culture" of Beagle Channel, Bird has offered an estimate of about 1800 years ago, or approximately the time of Christ, an age appraisal made on rising shoreline phenomena.[146] However, as Bird's original shoreline age estimates on the Magellanic Strait cultures have proven much too recent in the light of radiocarbon dating, I have hazarded an earlier date for the beginning of the "Shell-Knife Culture"—one of 2000 B.C. The placement of the "Pit-House Culture" (see chronology chart, Fig. 7-20) is simply an intermediate one between the "Shell-Knife Culture" and the historic Yahgan.

Summary. The Fuegian tradition has been viewed as an offshoot of the Andean Hunting-Collecting tradition. This came about through the changes in technology that occurred in adaptations to the shoreline subsistence of the Fuegian area. The Englefield Island site in the Sea of Otway appears to represent the point of divergence between the Andean Hunting-Collecting and the Fuegian traditions. Englefield has been dated in the range of 7200–6500 B.C.; for various reasons this seems too early, and an alternative dating of about 4000 B.C. is suggested. The "Shell-Knife Culture" is believed to be later than that of Englefield and definitely more shoreline-adapted. This "Shell-Knife Culture"—at least in its material artifacts—was preserved in historic Alacaluf culture in the Alacaluf subarea, perhaps because subsistence there was more strictly maritime and chances for later borrowings from land hunters were fewer. In the Beagle Channel country, however, which is the historic Yahgan territory, the stratigraphically later "Pit-House Culture" shows a more equal division between land-oriented and sea-oriented equipment, a circumstance attributed to their greater proximity to land-hunting zones and to the Ona. As these references to historic tribes imply, the Fuegian cultural tradition persisted well into the historic period.

Footnotes

1 PRONAPA (1970). This article, which will be cited throughout the section on Eastern Brazil, is a joint effort of the group of the Brazilian National Program of Archaeological Research, and the name "PRONAPA" is the abbreviation for this program, which, begun in 1965 and projected for five years, was instigated by Clifford Evans and B. J. Meggers of the Smithsonian Institution. Collaborators have been drawn from various Brazilian institutions. The authors of the present summary paper, written at the close of the third field season, are: J. P. Brochado, Valentin Calderón, Igor Chmyz, O. F. Dias, C. Evans, Silvia Maranca, B. J. Meggers, E. T. Miller, N. A. de Souza Nasser, C. Perota, W. F. Piazza, J. W. Rauth, M. F. Simões.

2 James (1959, pp. 383–534); PRONAPA (1970).

3 See also Mason (1950, linguistic map).

4 Murdock (1951) refers to this block in his conception of an "Atlantic area" (see also this volume, fig. 1-13).

5 This block is the basis for Murdock's (1951) "Goyaz area" (see also this volume, fig. 1-13).

6 For a summary of the ethnography of these tribes see Lowie (1946).

7 For the ethnography of these Tupian tribes see Metraux (1948 a, b).

8 Steward (1949, pp. 678–679); also Steward and Faron (1959, pp. 362–373).

9 Lathrap (1968).

10 PRONAPA (1970).

10a Hurt (1968) seems to give no credence at all to such an Eastern Brazilian pottery tradition. He places the first pottery in the sambaquís at about A.D. 1000 and attributes it to Tupí-Guaraní influence.

11 This term is taken from the "Tupiguaraní tradition" of PRONAPA (1970). This has been modified to "subtradition" in keeping with our general scheme of the book. Brochado and others use the spelling "Tupiguaraní" to refer to the archaeological tradition or subtradition to distinguish it from the linguistic and tribal designation, "Tupí-Guaraní."

12 T. O. Miller, Jr. (1969 ms.); see also Silva (1967).

13 Laming and Emperaire (1959 a, b); Menghín (1962 a).

14 Chmyz (1967).

15 Blasi (1965); Laming and Emperaire (1959 a).

16 E. T. Miller (1967).

17 T. O. Miller (1969 ms.).

18 Piazza (1967).

19 E. T. Miller (1967).

20 For Lagoa Santa and the Cerca Grande complex see Hurt (1960, 1964, 1968); see also Walter (1948, 1958) and Evans (1950).

21 Calderón (1967).

22 Serrano (1946 a) was inclined to believe that the sambaquís were largely natural formations that had been occupied rather superficially. For a historical summary of sambaquí investigations, including references to earlier writers on the subject, see Laming and Emperaire (1957); see also Menghín (1962 a) for a summary of sambaquí investigations to that date.

23 Alan R. Bryan, who has worked in sambaquí archaeology, tells me that such schools of fish are still spotted offshore by local Brazilian fishermen (personal communication, 1969).

24 Krone (1914).

25 Serrano (1946 a) further identifies his "Archaic" phase with the presence of the marine shell *Azara prisca*, said now to be extinct in these Brazilian waters.

26 Laming and Emperaire (1957, 1959 b). Laming and Emperaire (1957) also discuss several other sambaquís that they explored.

27 Hurt (1962, 1964, 1966, 1968).

28 Rauth and Hurt (1960); Hurt (1962, 1964, 1966).

29 Blasi (1957).

30 Serrano (1946 a).

31 Hurt and Blasi (1960); Hurt (1964); Blasi (1963).

32 Hurt (1964) gives these dates as about 1450–1350 B.C.; Blasi (1963) gives a dating average of about 1700–1600 B.C.

33 See also Rauth (1967) for a description of excavations at Porto Mauricio, in the Paranaguá-Antonia region. This is a mound similar to Macedo.

34 Orssich and Orssich (1956).

35 See Menghín (1962) for a more detailed discussion of the sambaquís.

36 Dias (1967).

37 Rohr (1960). Alan R. Bryan (personal communication, 1969) has also excavated a big sambaquí at Fort Marechal Luz on the Santa Catarina coast. In the lower levels he found only bone and a few ground stone implements, with rough chipped stone artifacts occurring in the upper levels. Fort Marechal Luz has radiocarbon dates running from 1700 B.C. to A.D. 1100 (Hurt, 1968).

38 Tiburtius and Bigarella (1960).

39 My comments on Periperí are derived from PRONAPA (1970). Calderón (1964) has published an article on the Pedro Oca site, but I have not seen it.

40 These regional pottery tradition descriptions are based largely on PRONAPA (1970).

41 In addition to PRONAPA (1970) see also Schmitz and others (1967).

42 PRONAPA (1970); E. T. Miller (1967).

43 Menghín (1957 b).

44 PRONAPA (1970).

45 PRONAPA (1970); Chmyz (1967).

46 PRONAPA (1970); Calderón (1967).

47 Tupiguaraní pottery descriptions and other aspects of culture are based on PRONAPA (1970); for pottery see also Simons (1966).

48 See, for example, Ambrosetti (1895) or Menghín (1957 b).

49 Howard and Willey (1948) summarize some of these southern Tupiguaraní occurrences.

50 PRONAPA (1970). Although I have depended to a large degree on this recent summary of the Brazilian National Archaeological program, there are a number of other articles on Brazilian Tupiguaraní ceramics and pottery; for example: Pereira de Godoy (1952), F. A. Silva and Blasi (1955), Rohr (1966), Piazza (1965), Chymz (1967), F. A. Silva (1961–1962, 1967), Calderón (1967), Souza Nasser (1967), E. T. Miller (1967).

51 PRONAPA (1970).

52 Some stratigraphic support is given to this hypothesis of Tupiguaraní Amazonian influences intrusive into earlier resident styles at the site of Estirão Comprido, on the Rio Ivaí, a tributary of the Rio Paraná, in the State of Paraná. Here, according to F. A. Silva and Oldemar Blasi (1955), pottery at the lowest levels of an 85-centimeter-deep refuse deposit was essentially plain; fingernail marked, corrugated, and incised types were in the middle levels; and the characteristic polychromes were found at the top.

53 PRONAPA (1970); E. T. Miller (1967).

54 Watson (1947).

55 Blasi (1966) also describes the Jesuit mission site of Santo Inácio Mini in northern Paraná.

56 James (1959, pp. 283–286).

57 Metraux (1946).

58 Greenberg (1960).

59 See also Mason (1950, especially linguistic map).

60 These descriptions are drawn from Metraux (1946).

61 Metraux (1946, p. 251).

62 Nordenskiold (1919) offers descriptions of pottery making from the Ashluslay and Choroti.

63 Nordenskiold (1902–1903).

64 Fock (1961) does not believe Candelaria to be as early as other authorities (including myself in this volume, fig. 4-4) have indicated it to be. Although admitting that

some pottery that has been designated as La Candelaria may overlap with the Diaguitan styles in time, I still feel that Candelaria I is about as early as we have shown it on the chart in Chapter 4.

65 Fock (1961, 1962).

66 Rydén (1948).

67 Márquez Miranda (1942).

68 Biró de Stern (1944).

69 Boggiani (1900).

70 The question of the origin of the burial urn takes us back to Chapter 4 (see p. 223). There it was observed that some authorities had suggested that the burial urn had diffused to the La Candelaria culture of the Selvas Occidentales from the Lower Paraná—presumably along this Pilcomayo-Bermejo route across the Chaco; but the burial urn is rare in Lower Paraná cultures prior to the Tupiguaraní invasion. In fact, it is reported from only one site, Las Tejas, in eastern Santa Fe (Howard and Willey, 1948, p. 19; see also Serrano, 1922, 1930, 1931).

71 Schmidt (1932, 1934).

72 Vellard (1934).

73 Metraux (1946); Metraux quotes Grubb (1913, p. 73) and Pride (1926).

74 James (1959, pp. 294–296).

75 Consult also Mason (1950, especially linguistic map).

76 See Lothrop (1932 b, 1946 b) for ethnographic summaries of these river tribes.

77 Serrano (1946 c); Lothrop (1928, 1932 b, 1946 b); Cooper (1946 b, c).

78 Metraux (1948 b); Lothrop (1932 b).

79 Cooper (1946 a).

80 Schobinger (1959 b).

81 These subareas differ in some details from those employed by Willey (1946 a) and Howard and Willey (1948). For one thing, certain portions of the Willey (1946 a) "Greater Pampa" have been shifted to the South Andean area (see Ch. 4); for another, I have placed somewhat different interpretative emphasis on the ceramics than in the Howard-Willey summary.

82 Bird (1938).

83 Menghín (1952, 1956, 1957 a); Menghín and Bórmida (1950); Menghín and Wachnitz (1958); Sanguinetti de Bórmida (1965). See Ibarra Grasso (1967, pp. 525–559) for a summary.

84 A good example would be the Monte Leon site, on the Santa Cruz coast (Gradin, 1961–1963).

85 Outes (1907); Torres (1922); Daguerre (1934).

86 The Trenque Lauquen site, in northwestern Buenos Aires Province, has a late Blancagrandian component (Trenque Lauquen A). This is succeeded by a later component (Trenque Lauquen B), which pertains to a Blancagrandian-derived industry, the Bolívar (Bolívarense) with which pottery is associated (Sanguinetti de Bórmida, 1961–63). For Trenque Lauquen see also Palavecino (1948) and Marquez Miranda (1954). The Paradero García, also in the Northern Buenos Aires subarea, is probably another preceramic station of the Blancagrandian-Bolívarian line of development (Bonaparte and Pisano, 1950).

87 Bórmida (1962 a, b).

87a There are various syntheses and interpretations of the lithic industries of the Pampas and Patagonia that have been published in recent years. The interpretation offered here, quite tentatively, relies essentially on Bórmida (1962 a, b, 1968) and Sanguinetti de Bórmida (1965). Somewhat different terms and concepts are used by other authors (see Austral, 1968). One has the impression that most of the Pampas-Patagonian lithic interpretations are based almost entirely on typology.

88 Willey (1958).

89 Sanguinetti de Bórmida (1965); see also Ibarra Grasso (1967, pp. 525–559).

90 Cigliano (1966 a, b) has recently announced radiocarbon dates on pottery from the Northern Buenos Aires coast that are surprisingly early. A determination of 2810 B.C. was obtained from a shell ridge in the locality of Palo Blanco. This ridge, now humus-covered, *may* be a true shell midden. It is on an old coastline, and it is said to consist of alternate bandings of complete shells and crushed shells and sand. A few badly eroded plain pottery fragments were found in one of the strata of whole shells, and it was from shells of this context that the early date was obtained. If accepted, it stands as one of the earliest dates on pottery in the New World, comparable, in fact, to the early Valdivia and early Puerto Hormiga pottery dates from Ecuador and Colombia that have been referred to in Chapter 5 (see p. 270). As such, this Buenos Aires date may seem unacceptable in the light of what we know of the history of pottery in pre-Columbian America. So far, the earliest ceramic dates from the Atlantic coast of South America have been in the area of 1000 to 800 B.C. These are the dates from the early Ananatuba phase of the Marajó Island (p. 408) and from the Periperí phase of the coast of Bahía (p. 446). The Palo Blanco date exceeds these by almost 2000 years. That the new Buenos Aires date does not harmonize with the others—or with our working ideas on the ages and diffusions of ceramics in South America—is not sufficient reason to discard it out of hand, but it does justify caution. Cigliano, who made the Palo Blanco finds, has also provided two other dates, these on a similar shell ridge or old beach-line "cordon" at Los Talas, a short distance south of Palo Blanco. There were no sherds in this ridge, but its shell content and strata and estimated geological history were the same as for the Palo Blanco ridge. Again, the dates were very early, 2040 and 2300 B.C., not as old as the Palo Blanco reading but still far in excess of the expectable. Thus it seems likely that the shell ridges are truly this old; but whether the potsherds were contemporaneous inclusions may still be open to some doubt. Perhaps germane to this question is the fact that the overlying humus of the ridges contained a good many potsherds, these of the incised and punctated types characteristic of the Paraná-Pampean cultures. We must, I think, accept the possibility that the Palo Blanco pottery may be as old as the dates indicate; but for the time being I prefer to hold these dates in abeyance as only a *possibility* and to turn to other kinds of evidence for providing us with a dating esti-

mate for the beginnings of pottery in the Pampean area.

91 Willey (1949, 1958).

92 Ibarra Grasso (1967, pp. 591–597) opposes the Amazonian–East Brazilian derivation of Lower Paraná and Pampean pottery. He sees the Lower Paraná styles, especially the plastic or modeled elements and the "campanas," as deriving from the Chaco-Santiagueño; the simpler pottery of Buenos Aires Province and Patagonia he would derive separately from South Andean styles such as the Comechingón (Sierras Centrales) and the Agrelo (Mendoza).

93 Frenguelli and Aparicio (1923). For general discussions of the Lower Paraná River cultures see Aparicio (1948), Serrano (1954), and Badano (1955).

94 Ibarra Grasso (1967, pp. 591–597).

95 Aparicio (1928).

96 Torres (1907, pp. 60–89).

97 Gonzalez (1939, 1947).

98 Freitas (1942); see also Arredondo (1927). There are a number of sites in the Lower Uruguay Valley, especially on the tributary Rio Negro, in the southwestern corner of the Republic. La Blanqueada was a refuse hillock, 2 meters high and 60 by 25 meters in extent. Drag-and-jab decorated pottery was typical, and there was also some red and white painting, much as at Arroyo Sarandí. A few bird-head adornos and vessel handles were also present, reflecting influence from the Malabrigo pattern.

99 See Palavecino (1948) and Ibarra Grasso (1967, p. 592) for distributions of these Paraná pottery styles. The El Cerrillo complex ("Entrerriana") is found in the Lower Paraná–Lower Uruguay subarea; the Malabrigo in the Middle Paraná subarea; the "alfarerías gruesas" occupy a somewhat middle geographic position, overlapping both, although the stylistic affinities of the "alfarerías gruesas" are clearly with the modeled biomorphic adornos, the Malabrigo hallmark.

100 Serrano (1922, 1930, 1931).
101 Outes (1918).
102 Serrano (1934).
103 Lothrop (1932 b, pp. 146–162); Torres (1911, pp. 97–184); see also Howard and Willey (1948) for a summary of this and other sites discussed in this section.
104 Gatto (1939).
105 Villegas Basavilbaso (1937).
106 Vignati (1931).
107 Márquez Miranda (1934).
108 Lothrop (1932 b, pp. 162–182).
109 As at Punta Lara (Maldonado Bruzzone, 1931); see also Willey (1946 a) for reproductions of pictures of both the Arroyo Sarandí and Punta Lara examples.
110 Maldonado Bruzzone (1931).
111 Rusconi (1928).
112 Outes (1907).
113 Torres (1922).
114 Outes (1904 a).
115 Outes (1904 b).
116 Bird (1938).
117 Bird (1946 b).
118 Bird (Ibid.); Outes (1905, 1916 a); Vignati (1923 a, b, 1931 b).
119 Menghín (1952 b).
120 Vignati (1950).
121 Serrano (1932, 1946 c); see also the general Uruguayan archaeological summaries of Fontana Company (1951), Figueira (1962), and Muñoa (1965).
122 Serrano (1931).
123 Such stratigraphic evidence has not yet been forthcoming; however, there is a hint of a "horizontal" stratification in Villa Lugano, in the outskirts of Buenos Aires. We have mentioned the Villa Lugano–Site B and identified it as a typical Northern Buenos Aires complex, similar to that of Arroyo Sarandí, with drag-and-jab decoration, painting, etc. Only a short distance from this site Rusconi (1928) located another, Villa Lugano–Site A. The pottery from this site is much simpler than that from Site B; it is decorated with fine incised lines and is reminiscent of the Southern Buenos Aires–La Pampa, or the Uruguayan, types. Does it represent

an earlier horizon in the heart of the Northern Buenos Aires subarea?

Another explanation for the difference between Northern Buenos Aires and Lower Paraná pottery versus that of Southern Buenos Aires–La Pampa and Patagonia is that of Ibarra Grasso (1967), who sees the contrasts as resulting from different South Andean derivations: the first, from the Chaco-Santiagueno, the second, from the Sierras Centrales and Mendoza.

There is no area in South America where fine-grained studies in ceramic stratigraphy and seriation would be so helpful as in the Pampean.

124 Lothrop (1932 b); see also Howard and Willey (1948).
125 Outes (1918 b).
126 Outes (1916b).
127 Metraux (1948 b).
128 Lothrop (1946 b).
129 Cooper (1946 a).
130 Vignati (1944).
131 Schobinger (1959 b).
132 James (1959, pp. 269–271).
133 Steager (1965).
134 Cooper (1946 d).
135 Bird (1946 b).
136 Cooper (1946 e).
137 See also Mason (1950, especially linguistic map).
138 Steager (1965).
139 Emperaire and Laming (1961).
140 Barth (1948).
141 Cooper (1942 a, b). It is to be noted, though, that the southern end of the Araucanian subarea shows some indications of blending of Pacific Littoral and Fuegian traditions (see this volume, p. 211).
142 Bird (1938, 1946 b).
143 Compare the points that Bird (1938, 1946 b) shows for Magellan V (Ona) and those for the later period of Beagle Channel ("Pit-House Culture").
144 Vignati (1927).
145 Sanchez-Albornoy (1958).
146 Bird (1938); Lothrop (1928) computes a similar age on the basis of the volume of shell in the midden sites of this culture.

**Cultural Traditions:
The Lines of History in South America**

In the concluding chapter of Volume One, we reviewed the cultural traditions of North and Middle America. We propose now to do the same for the major cultural and technological traditions with which we have been concerned in this survey of South American prehistory.

The Flake Tradition. This name was given to a series of South American lithic assemblages in which all the artifacts were fashioned from primary flakes and in which this fashioning had been done by percussion flaking (Figs. 8-1, 8-2, 2-2, 2-3). Bifacial flaking and projectile points are absent. Artifacts are scrapers, punches, picks, and in some instances simple burins. These implements of the Flake tradition appear "secondary" in that they look as though they had been used largely for the making of other tools from wood or, perhaps, bone.

The subsistence pattern of the Flake tradition cultures probably varied according to environmental circumstances. Shellfish were utilized to a small extent along the Pacific coast, and wild plant foods may have been gathered. It is unknown to what extent Flake tradition peoples were hunters; the stone technology gives no positive indication.

The tradition is known from assemblages in coastal Peru, highland Peru, coastal Ecuador,

Summary and Perspective

8

interior north Chile, Uruguay, and, possibly, Patagonia. As we defined it, there are putative beginnings before 20,000 B.C., but these cannot be proved. Stratigraphic and indirect radiocarbon datings on Flake tradition complexes in Peru do, however, indicate an age in excess of 10,000 B.C., and geological correlations in Uruguay suggest a date in the vicinity of 9000 B.C. The dating of the tradition leads to the vexing problem of possible technological continuities into much later times. In Argentina there are assemblages, or "cultures," which date from relatively late times (5000–1000 B.C.) but which seem to be characterized only by the crudest percussion tools. Are these survivals of the Flake tradition? Or are they partial assemblages—for instance, the remains of seasonal food pursuits—of technologically much more advanced cultures? The interpretation followed here has been to consider many of them as "partial assemblages" rather than full traditional survivals.

It is suggested that the Flake tradition is related to some of the unnamed "pre-projectile point" assemblages of North and Middle America and that all of these are, in turn, derived from Asiatic Lower and Middle Paleolithic technologies that were brought to the Americas from the Old World by the first immigrants to the western hemisphere at some time before 20,000 B.C.

The Chopper Tradition. The Chopper tool tradition (Figs. 8-1, 2-2) takes its definition from northwestern Venezuela, where a seriation of lithic assemblages has been correlated with river terraces. The earliest complex of the seriation is the Camare, which features crude pebble choppers made by battering the edges and sides of boulders. These implements are vaguely or haphazardly bifacial. They are associated with flake scrapers and knives. The next later assemblage in the northwestern Venezuelan series has true bifacial choppers or thick bladelike tools; thus the Camare complex has been considered as prototypical to, and a developmental step toward, the true biface. The chronological position of the Chopper tradition is suggested as 13,000 to 11,000 B.C. in northern South America. It may have originated here from an antecedent Flake tradition beginning, or it may have been introduced to northern South America from North and Middle America.

The Biface Tradition. This tradition is characterized by percussion-flaked but well-shaped bifacial implements (Figs. 8-1, 8-2, 2-2, 2-3). Some appear to be axes; others are slender enough to have been spear points. These bifaces are frequently accompanied by similarly shaped and sized unifaces, by flakes struck from prepared cores, by denticulates, by spokeshaves, and by large end-scrapers. As with the Flake tradition, we can say little about the larger cultural context of the Biface tradition.

The Biface tradition, which has been referred to as the "Andean Biface Horizon" by Lanning and Patterson, is best known from the Las Lagunas complex of northwestern Venezuela, the Chivateros I of Peru, and the Ampajango complex of the northwest Argentine highlands. Compara-

483

ble assemblages have been found in coastal Ecuador, in northern Chile, and at many locations in northwestern Argentina. Occasional implements of the same type have also turned up in Uruguayan and East Brazilian cultures of the East Brazilian Upland tradition.

The firmest dating of the Biface tradition comes from the upper part of the Chivateros I stratum in Peru. This is a radiocarbon determination of 8500 B.C. Elsewhere an early dating is supported by the Venezuelan river terrace sequence and by geological terrace and lakeshore correlations in Argentina. A continent-wide dating estimate of

Figure 8-1. Schematic diagram of the major cultural traditions of South America, viewed diachronically. The Intermediate Area–Peru–South Andean–Fuegian–Pampean–East Brazilian line. Compare with Fig. 2-2.

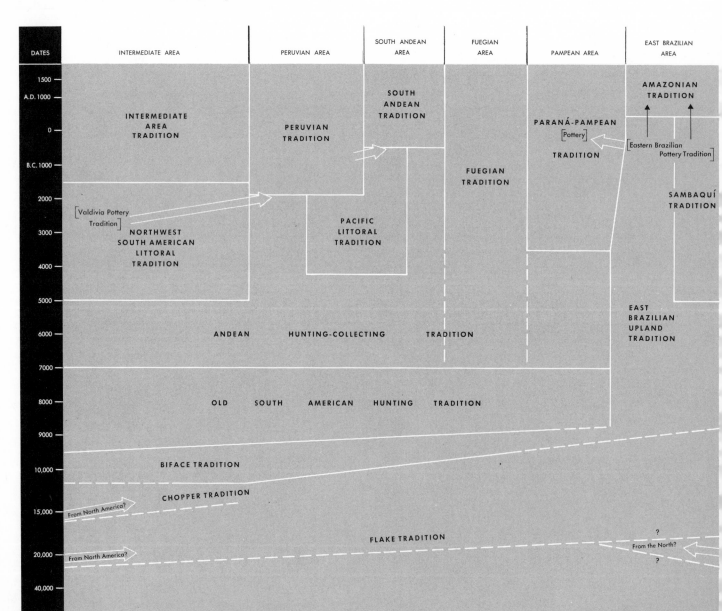

10,500 to about 8500 B.C. is given here, with the estimate placed earliest in Venezuela in keeping with the hypothesis that the Andean Biface tradition developed from the preceding Chopper tradition in northern South America and diffused south from there.

The Old South American Hunting Tradition. This is the earliest South American tradition with bifacially flaked projectile points (Figs. 8-1, 8-2, 2-2, 2-3). There is a clear emphasis on hunting reflected in the artifact inventories. This included the hunting of animals now extinct

Figure 8-2. Schematic diagram of the major cultural traditions of South America, viewed diachronically. The Intermediate Area–Caribbean–Amazonian–East Brazilian–Pampean line. Compare with Fig. 2-3.

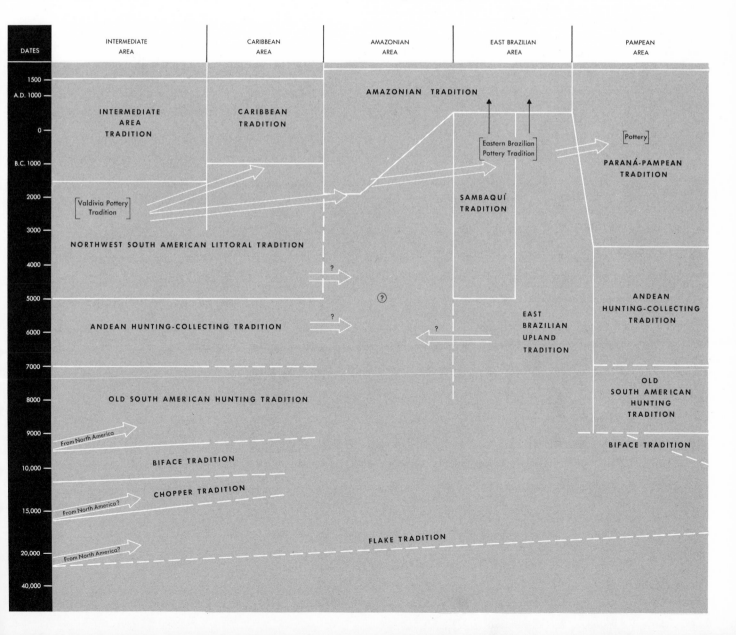

as well as the deer and the Andean camelids. Two types of points characterize the tradition: fishtails and elongated leaf shapes. The fishtailed points resemble the Clovis-derived points of North America. They are known from the Magellan I phase of far southern South America, from the El Inga I phase of highland Ecuador, and from scattered finds in the North Andes, Lower Central America, Eastern Brazil, Uruguay, and Patagonia. In the Magellan I phase these fishtailed projectile points are associated with flint scrapers, bone flaking tools and awls, and bones of the now extinct native horse and sloth.

It is our contention that the fishtailed point horizon marks the earliest phases of the Old South American Hunting tradition and that this tradition was derived from the North American Big-Game Hunting tradition. At Tagua Tagua, in central Chile, a lamellar-flake and prepared-core industry has been dated by radiocarbon to 9400 B.C. Although no points were found at Tagua Tagua, this lamellar-flake–prepared-core complex is the appropriate technological context for the production of the fishtailed points. This suggests that the Old South American Hunting tradition dates back to the tenth millennium B.C. in southern South America. The earliest radiocarbon date for Magellan I is 8700 B.C.

The elongated leaf-shaped points are best known from the El Jobo complex of northwestern Venezuela, from the same river terrace sequence in which we found the Camare and Las Lagunas complexes. In fact, El Jobo follows Las Lagunas in this sequence, and the similarity of the elongated leaf-shaped points to some of the thinner bifaces of Las Lagunas can be interpreted as a local evolution of the elongated leaf-shaped projectile from the Biface tradition. This same sequence is found, again, in the Peruvian coastal Chivateros I–Chivateros II stratigraphy. Other early leaf-shaped points are known from Ecuador, from the Peruvian highland Lauricocha I phase and other sites in the upland Peruvian basins, from northern Chile and northwestern Argentina, and from scattered occurrences in eastern South America. It has been our argument that the elongated leaf-shaped points date from about 8000 to 7000 B.C.

Although the elongated leaf-shaped points may well have evolved out of the earlier Biface tradition, it has been speculated that this development was stimulated by the arrival of North America hunters with a Big-Game Hunting, bifacial projectile-point technology and that the first results of this stimulation were the hunting-adapted El Jobo points of northern South America. This would account for the contemporaneity of the two types of points in some regions.

The East Brazilian Upland Tradition. The tools of the East Brazilian Upland tradition—or at least those of its earlier phases—seem much like those of the Flake tradition: a flake technology, unifaces, scrapers, beak forms, punches, cutting edges. There are, however, occasional chipped-stone projectile points in some of the East Brazilian Upland complexes, and these suggest contact and contemporaneity with the Old South American Hunting and later Andean Hunting-Collecting traditions. Thus, the East Brazilian Upland tradition is estimated to have fairly early beginnings, going back perhaps to 8000 B.C. (Figs. 8-1, 8-2, 2-2, 2-3). It also had a long persistence in the East Brazilian area. Changes mark this long history, however, and polished or partially polished axes become common after 3000 B.C., and small stemmed and barbed projectile points begin to make their appearance.

We must raise the question of when argriculture appeared in the East Brazilian area and at what date we can terminate the East Brazilian Upland tradition. It is possible that some cultivation practices did come into the area in the first millennium B.C. along with the first pottery. This earliest pottery of the area has been referred to under the term "Eastern Brazilian Pottery tradition." If cultivation did not become established this early, we know that it was introduced by A.D. 500, the date at which we have the first definite evidences of a Tropical Forest–type economy and culture in the East Brazilian area—one derived from the Amazonian cultural tradition. The terminal date of the East Brazilian Upland cultural tradition must be left, then, as somewhere between about 1000 B.C. and A.D. 500.

The territorial extent of the East Brazilian Upland tradition includes the upland portions of the East Brazilian area, the upper drainages of the Paraná River, and probably the northern perimeters of the Pampean area. It may have extended northward as far as the Guianas.

486

The Andean Hunting-Collecting Tradition. The Andean Hunting-Collecting tradition developed from the Old South American Hunting tradition in Andean South America at some time after 7000 B.C. (Figs. 8-1, 8-2, 2-2, 2-3). It was an early post-Pleistocene adaptation to changing environmental conditions, especially to conditions of the Andean upland valleys. Subsistence was based both on the hunting of the llama, alpaca, vicuña, guanaco, and deer and on the collecting of plant foods. In some areas there are clues to a transhumance pattern of seasonal highland hunting and coastal or lowland collecting. Sites are small camp locations—either open sites or cave shelters.

The tradition is characterized by some distinctive projectile-point styles, especially by a stemless, willow leaf form. This willow leaf point is proportionately broader than the elongated leaf-shaped point of the Old South American Hunting tradition. Through time, within the history of the tradition, there is a tendency for the willow leaf point to become smaller in size and to be replaced by smaller triangular, bi-pointed, and stemmed forms. These points of the Andean Hunting-Collecting tradition are usually well made, pressure-flaked, and finely retouched. Most of them are of a size to have served as dart or spear tips, although it is possible that the decrease in size in the later ones signals the use of the bow and arrow. Other artifacts of the tradition are scrapers, knives, drills, and—in many cases—milling and mortar stones.

The principal willow leaf point complexes of the Andean Hunting-Collecting tradition are: the Lauricocha II and III of the Peruvian highlands; those phases of the Peruvian coast, such as the Canario, which could have represented a segment of a transhumance pattern in association with Lauricocha II-III; the Tulan and Puripica complexes of northern Chile; and the numerous Ayampitín point phases of northwestern Argentina, especially the Intihuasi IV and III of the cave of that name in the Province of San Luis. Dating evidence, where available, indicates that these willow leaf point complexes tend to assemble along a horizon of 6000 to 4000 B.C. After 4000 B.C. the smaller and more varied projectile points appear. Along the Pacific shore this carries us later than the Andean Hunting-Collecting tradition—into a Pacific Littoral tradition—but in the

Andean highlands the Andean Hunting-Collecting tradition has been conceived as continuing on until the advent of established agricultural communities, that is, until 2000 B.C. or even later.

Besides the willow leaf projectile-point form and its derivatives, there is another principal projectile-point form that can be said to characterize some of the Andean Hunting-Collecting cultures. This is a stemmed point. We refer now not to the smaller stemmed points that appear after 4000 B.C. but to larger lanceolate-stemmed types. For instance, a diamond-shaped point, with vague shoulders and a contracting stem, is found in the Arenal phase of the Peruvian coast. Arenal is dated at 6500 to 6000 B.C. and is thought to be a coastal component of a highland-coastal transhumance pattern. Another Arenal point is a single-shouldered form. Both the diamond-shaped and single-shouldered points are found in the Lauricocha I phase of the Peruvian highlands, a phase that is estimated to have persisted from 7500 to 6000 B.C. (Fig. 2-2). Another early stemmed-point type is the Paiján of the Peruvian coast, which is placed at about 6000 B.C. Apparently, both willow leaf and large stemmed points were being used along the Peruvian coast at about the same time, probably originating with groups of somewhat different cultural heritages; however, the early stemmed types seem to have a more northerly distribution in Andean South America than do the willow leafs. They are found in El Inga II and III, in highland Ecuador, although here they occur along with willow leafs. Lanceolate-stemmed points also appear to be quite early in Colombia. In northwestern Venezuela they belong to the Las Casitas phase, which is dated after 6000 B.C.

If the Andean Hunting-Collecting tradition developed out of the Old South American Hunting tradition, then it seems likely that the willow leaf point evolved from the earlier elongated leaf-shaped form while the stemmed points had an ancestry in the fish-tailed form. These are the hypotheses favored in this book; however, an alternative theory is to be entertained. This would be that the willow leafs and stemmed points of the Andean Hunting-Collecting tradition are descendants of Old Cordilleran and Plano (derived Big-Game Hunting) points of North America. This second hypothesis would envisage continued migrations of hunters from North to South America after 8000 B.C.

The Pacific Littoral Tradition. Sites of the Pacific Littoral tradition are found along the Peruvian and Chilean shores (Figs. 8-1, 2-2). The tradition is presumed to have come into being at the end of the fifth millennium B.C. as a stabilized adaptation of Andean Hunting-Collecting peoples to the environment of the littoral.[1] The steps that led up to such an adaptation were those of seasonal transhumance, for Andean Hunting-Collecting groups apparently not only moved from coastal lowlands to highland valleys, as they alternated between plant collecting and game hunting, but they shifted as well between the coastal "lomas" and the actual shoreline of the Pacific as they supplemented their diet with shellfish and fish. At about 4000 B.C., or a little before, foods from the sea became the most important part of their diet. Of course, such a transition was probably gradual, and it must have varied from region to region; but what emerged was a mode of life that was more sedentary than before, one lived for the most part in shell midden fishing stations along the coastal edge.

In many ways, the Pacific Littoral tradition—as one geared to marine subsistence—is best viewed in Chile. Here a series of phases, dating from about 4200 to 3000 B.C. (Fig. 4-2), reveals its Andean Hunting-Collecting heritage in leaf-shaped projectile points. A characteristic new item of equipment was a shell fishhook. Other fishhooks were made of bone barbs lashed to stone or shell. The importance of sea mammal hunting is reflected in detachable harpoon forepieces fitted with bone barbs and stone points. Stone bowls, mortars, and manos are also found in these early phases. Later Chilean phases are distinguished by smaller and more varied projectile points, thorn fishhooks, fish harpoons, and a greater abundance of, and variety in, ground stone utensils. These early Chilean peoples of the Pacific Littoral tradition had not given up land hunting altogether; for instance, garments were made of camelid hides and wool. Nor was plant gathering of no account, as some sites are located in the small river valleys at some distance inland from the coast. Nevertheless, the peoples of the Pacific Littoral tradition were primarily dependent upon the sea. Sites of the tradition date to as late as 500 B.C.

In contrast to the Chilean situation, the Pacific Littoral tradition in Peru does not appear ever to have been quite so specialized toward a sea economy. Between 4200 and 2500 B.C. there was still seasonal occupancy of the camps in the lomas vegetation a few kilometers from the actual shore; and the continued exploitation of this particular environmental niche must have been a major factor in the development of plant cultivation, which distinguishes the Peruvian branch of the Pacific Littoral tradition from that of the Chilean coast. For although the Peruvian Littoral tradition sites have shell, thorn, and composite fishhooks similar to those of Chile—as well as grinding stones, basketry, mats, and nets—these Peruvian sites show the domesticated lima bean, domesticated squash, and, later, cotton and other plants. With the continued drying up of the lomas vegetation, Pacific Littoral tradition settlement in Peru moved completely to the shoreline and became fully sedentary after 2500 B.C. The plant cultivation that probably began in the lomas locations was now continued in the lower river-valley bottoms. A permanent pit-house and above-ground architecture developed utilizing both rough stone-and-mud masonry and adobe. Sites were much larger than those of Chile, and overall population for the Peruvian coastal regions must have been much greater than that of the Chilean ones. Twined cotton appeared. The complex designs seen in the twining of some of these textiles, as well as on carved gourds, introduced a distinctive art style and iconography that was to be an important part of the heritage of the later Peruvian cultural tradition. This cultural build-up continued in the very last stages of the tradition—between 2000 and 1800 B.C.—with the appearance of maize, monumental ceremonial architecture, and pottery. The last trait is taken to mark the point of transition into the Peruvian cultural tradition.

The Northwest South American Littoral Tradition. A Northwest South American Littoral tradition is approximately contemporaneous with the Pacific Littoral tradition (Figs. 8-1, 8-2, 2-2, 2-3); however, aside from the fact that both traditions represent an adaptation to shoreline life and shellfish collecting, with apparent beginnings during the climatic optimum, they have little in common. Whereas the Pacific Littoral tradition showed an early specialized adaptation to the coastal environment in fishing gear and marine hunting equipment, this is lacking in the Northwest South American Littoral tradition. Furthermore, the environmental settings of the two traditions are radically different. The desert coasts and small valleys of Peru and Chile with their cold offshore waters are in sharp contrast to the mangrove and tropical coasts of the areas of the Northwest South American Littoral tradition.

Northwest South American Littoral tradition remains are found along the Ecuadorian coast (Vegas complex; Fig. 5-4), in the north Colombian lowlands (San Nicolás complex), in Lower Central America (Cerro Mangote complex), along the Caribbean coast of Venezuela (El Peñon, Alaka, El Heneal, and Manicuare complexes or cultures), and in Trinidad (Ortoire phase) and the West Indies (Krum Bay, Couri, Cayo Redondo, and other phases). On the Ecuadorian coast they may date as early as 6000 to 5000 B.C.; in Panama a radiocarbon date of about 4800 B.C. pertains to such remains; and in the Caribbean area radiocarbon dates and various estimates range from 3800 up to 1000 B.C. and later. In fact, the Northwest South American Littoral tradition can be said to last on to early historic times in western Cuba with the Cayo Redondo phase of the Ciboney culture (Fig. 6-4).

The origins of the Northwest South American Littoral tradition are uncertain. Possibly, they lie in the contemporaneous Andean Hunting-Collecting tradition cultures of the northern Andes. Another possibility is that the Northwest South American Littoral tradition cultures are related to the East Brazilian Upland tradition.

It is thought that the earliest stages of the Northwest South American Littoral tradition are represented by the collections of scrapers, denticulates, flake knives, cobble choppers, and miscellaneous flakes, such as are found in the shell midden sites along the Ecuadorian coast or in the San Nicolás refuse site. To this kind of technology were then added grinding stones and handstones of various types, including pebble edge-grinders or pounders. Still later there were a number of sub-

areal specializations as seen in the use of shell adzes, bone points, chipped-and-ground axes, large lamellar flake knives, and polished stone and small shell ornaments. For example, such variants characterize the cultures of Venezuela and the West Indies.

Late in its history the Northwest South American Littoral tradition provided a matrix for an important set of cultural changes that are heralded by the appearance of the Valdivia pottery tradition.

The Valdivia Pottery Tradition. As the name implies, the Valdivia pottery tradition is not a major, or "full," cultural tradition but a technological tradition. It is the name given to a series of ceramic complexes (Figs. 8-1, 8-2, 5-4, 5-5, 5-7) that occur in the Intermediate area between about 3000 and 1000 B.C. The series includes Valdivia, on the Ecuadorian coast; Puerto Hormiga; Canapote; Barlovento; San Jacinto, in northern Colombia; and Monagrillo, in Panama. A good many radiocarbon dates imply that this pottery of the Valdivia tradition is the earliest in South America or, for that matter, in the New World. The vessel forms of the tradition are simple bowl forms, the decoration almost entirely by plastic techniques—incision, punctation, scoring, dentate impressions, and the like. Design motifs, although varying considerably from phase to phase, are uncomplicated and geometric.

The origins of the tradition are open to debate. One line of thought on the matter is that the inspiration for the Valdivia tradition was brought across the Pacific by Japanese voyagers of the Jomon culture and that the tradition was first established on the Ecuadorian coast in what we know as the Valdivia phase. Opponents of this idea have pointed to the very early radiocarbon dates for the Colombian Puerto Hormiga complex and have suggested an ancient zone of indigenous pottery development running from the northern lowlands of Colombia down along the eastern side of the Andes as far south as Peru.

Occurring as it does in the context of the Northwest South American Littoral tradition, the Valdivia pottery tradition is a correlate of the transition from the Northwest South American Littoral tradition into the agricultural Intermediate area tradition. This latter tradition has its inception at 1500–1000 B.C., probably in both manioc —which was most likely first cultivated in the Venezuelan or Colombian lowlands—and in maize —which was diffused from Mesoamerica. Assuming this to have been the case, then we can say that during the last 1500 to 1000 years of its history the Northwest South American Littoral tradition, as it was represented in the Intermediate area and in the mainland portions of the Caribbean area, was probably in a condition of incipient agriculture, a condition comparable to the Pacific Littoral tradition of Peru at approximately the same time.

The Valdivia pottery tradition undoubtedly had a wide influence on the development and spread of the idea of pottery making in South America and in the New World. In Peru, pottery first appears at about 1800 B.C. Although this earliest Peruvian pottery does not closely resemble that of Valdivia, it shares some common features in general simplicity of form and incised decoration. Influences could have passed from Ecuador southward along the coast to Peru; they could have been carried from the Colombian-Ecuadorian highlands to the Peruvian highlands; or the route of diffusion could have been from Valdivia tradition centers in the north Colombian lowlands southward through the Upper Amazon Basin and from there to the Peruvian highlands. In this last connection, it may be that the earliest pottery of the Amazonian area, that of the Zoned Hachure Horizon, is of ultimate Valdivia tradition inspiration. To the east, early Caribbean ceramics, especially those of the Barrancoid subtradition, could easily have had a Valdivia–Puerto Hormiga ancestry. And to all of these we might add, as well, the early pottery of Eastern Brazil and the Paraná drainage.

Looking in the opposite direction, to Middle and North America, the earliest pottery known for the Mesoamerican area is that of the Purrón and Pox complexes of southern Mexico (Vol. I, pp. 93–94, fn. 6a), which dates at 2400–2300 B.C. This is some centuries later than the beginnings of the Valdivia pottery tradition, so that it could be argued that Mesoamerican pottery beginnings were stimulated from the south. The Purrón and Pox ceramics are undecorated, and the simple forms suggest local stone vessel prototypes so that

any claimed connection with the Valdivia tradition would have to rest on no more than stimulus diffusion. However somewhat more specific resemblances and claims have been put forward for Eastern North American ties with the Valdivian complexes, and these indirectly raise other questions about a Valdivia-Mesoamerican linkage.

These latter claims have been advanced by J. A. Ford, who points to similarities between the early fibre-tempered wares of the Southeastern United States (Vol. I, pp. 257–258) and those of Valdivia, Puerto Hormiga, and Barlovento.[2] The fibre-tempered pottery of Georgia and Florida appears to be the oldest ceramic of the Eastern Woodlands. Dated by radiocarbon at 2000 to 1000 B.C., it antedates the cord-marked and fabric-marked pottery of the northern part of the Woodlands area by almost 1000 years. Ford notes the similarities of fibre tempering in Georgia-Florida and in northern Colombia, and, more specifically, he indicates the decorative technique and design parallels between Valdivia proper and the coastal Georgia Stallings Island phase vessels. In both cases a drag-and-jab linear-punctation method has been used, and in both, lines are arranged in horizontal rows and geometric panels. Simple arrangements of dot punctations and rows of dashed lines are also shared. Still other Southeastern United States–Valdivian parallels are seen in the incised scroll and punctate designs of the Florida Tick Island type and the Barlovento incised types of Colombia. In Ford's opinion these resemblances are not chance convergences but are the results of contact and colonization. He hypothesizes that seafarers from the Caribbean coast of Colombia must have been carried northward and eastward, being swept through the Florida Straits by the Gulf Stream, eventually making a landfall on the Atlantic coasts of north Florida and Georgia.

I am inclined to agree that there is a connection between the Valdivia pottery tradition and the Georgia-Florida fibre-tempered wares; however I would prefer to reserve judgment on the Caribbean–Gulf Stream voyages as the means by which such a connection was effected. As Ford himself details,[3] there are many clues to ceramic affiliation between the Intermediate area, Mesoamerica, and the Southeastern United States on a somewhat later chronological level. For instance, he cites the resemblances that are to be found between Ecuadorian Machalilla pottery (which succeeds that of the Valdivia phase), pottery from the Veracruz Preclassic, and the early Burial Mound Period of the Mississippi Valley. In view of these Nuclear American ties that involve Mesoamerica, I think it too early to rule out an east coastal–Mesoamerican passage for a gradual diffusion that would explain the Valdivian–Eastern North American resemblances.

The Peruvian Tradition. The Peruvian cultural tradition has one extremely clear matrix in the Pacific Littoral tradition (Figs. 8-1, 2-2, 3-3). Here the archaeological record is a straightforward one—aided by the unusual preservative conditions of the Peruvian desert coast—in which the cultural build-up of the fishers and incipient farmers of the coastal valleys leads directly into the Peruvian tradition. One of the dynamic elements in this transition was the appearance of maize in the coastal valleys. There are reasons for believing that this maize, which was probably of ultimate Mesoamerican origin, may have spread to the Peruvian coast from the highlands. This consideration, together with what we know of the Peruvian highlands in late preceramic times, indicates that the highlands also contributed significantly to the emergence of the Peruvian cultural tradition.

In the highlands this matrix culture, according to our scheme, would have been the Andean Hunting-Collecting tradition. We have reviewed this tradition in the Peruvian highlands in such phases as the Lauricocha II and III; however it is obvious that the tradition was undergoing radical change in its later phases. These changes can be seen for example in the Mito phase, which underlies the earliest pottery-bearing stratum at Kotosh (pp. 103–104). The clearly sedentary condition of the Mito phase and its association with permanent public architecture show that the late developments of the Andean Hunting-Collecting tradition were paralleling those that were occurring in the Pacific Littoral tradition just prior to 1800 B.C.

The Peruvian tradition begins with the inception of the Initial Period at 1800 B.C. This threshold is marked by the appearance of pottery and the widespread use of woven, as opposed to twined, cloth. The tradition is also further char-

acterized by a number of other traits and trait complexes. Many of these were already present—at least in an incipient form—in the matrix cultures.

As we have seen, the Peruvian agricultural complex had preceramic period antecedents, but by the Initial Period it included maize, the potato, lima beans, kidney beans, manioc, peanuts, a variety of other foods, the narcotic coca, and the fibre cotton. The complex was eventually to involve huge irrigation and agricultural terracing works; however the extent to which these were present or in process of development in the Initial Period of the tradition is uncertain. Agriculture was supplemented by llama and alpaca herding, and the domestication of these animals goes back at least to the Initial Period. Fishing and shellfish collecting, which continued to be of economic importance along the coast, were, as we have seen, already fully developed in the Pacific Littoral tradition.

Peruvian tradition crafts included weaving, ceramics, metallurgy, and carving in stone, shell, and wood. These, of course, are (with the exception of metallurgy) the basic neolithic-level skills; but in the Peruvian tradition they were elaborated further than anywhere else in South America. Weaving was in both cotton and wool, and the Peruvian industry came to excel in embroidered cloths, gauzes, tapestries, and other techniques. Ceramics were elaborately modeled and painted. The use of the mold became common in the later centuries of the tradition, especially in the northern part of the Peruvian area, resulting in a virtual mass-production of vessels. Metallurgy had its beginnings on the Early Horizon, 900 to 200 B.C., with casting, soldering, smelting, alloying, and plating techniques appearing as widespread during the Early Intermediate Period (200 B.C.–A.D. 600). Copper tools and weapons were manufactured this early in parts of the north, and bronze was similarly employed in the south. In general, the use of metals for ornaments, receptacles, tools, and weapons became more frequent during and after the Middle Horizon, A.D. 600 to 1000; and with the Inca Horizon (A.D. 1476 to 1534) bronze and silver were widely propagated as well as gold and copper.

We have already noted that sizable communities of permanent architecture were a feature of the Peruvian area—in both highlands and on the coast—prior to the advent of the Peruvian tradition. These developments continued—and, in general, were expanded—during the history of the tradition. By the Early Intermediate Period, closely packed communities that must have housed more than 5000 persons can be called cities. Such cities performed the urban functions of serving as bases for politico-religious leadership, as centers for trade, and as the nuclei for the developments of crafts and arts. By Middle Horizon and Late Intermediate Period times, cities were even larger, and the great multi-compound city of Chanchan, on the north coast, probably numbered several thousand resident inhabitants and drew upon the support of 50,000 to 100,000 persons living in the very immediate vicinity of the same small valley. The development of this Peruvian urbanism was linked to both demographic and cultural factors. There was a rapid increase of population in Initial Period and Early Horizon times, a growth to be correlated with the expansion of intensive agricultural techniques. After this there was probably little total population increase, and the grouping of this population into cities was a cultural and political choice.

Public architecture was of impressive size throughout the Peruvian tradition. It had its beginnings late in the Pacific Littoral and Andean Hunting-Collecting traditions, and these were continued in the great platform constructions of the Initial Period (Las Haldas), the temples of the Early Horizon (the Castillo at Chavín de Huántar), the enormous adobe pyramids of the Early Intermediate Period (Pyramid of the Sun at Moche), and the numerous great constructions of the Late Intermediate and Inca Horizon times. Monumental art developed within this context of temple and palace architecture and was executed on a notable scale as early as the Early Horizon.

The elements and iconography of Peruvian tradition art can be traced, in some cases, back to preceramic times, where they are found in woven textile or carved gourd designs. Such motifs then continue on in the pottery, metalwork, textiles, and monumental stone-carving of the Peruvian tradition proper. These motifs or themes include humans with feline attributes, condors, two-headed birds or fish, serpents, masked human figures, and anthropomorphic god representations.

The Peruvian tradition and area was marked by a series of three major art styles or horizon styles. On the Early Horizon this was the Chavín art style, and its spread has been interpreted as the propagation of a religious cult, in many ways analogous to the spread of Olmec art in Mesoamerica. Its center was presumably somewhere in the northern part of the area, perhaps at the site that gives the style its name, Chavín de Huántar. In Middle Horizon times the Tiahuanaco-Huari style blanketed Peru and extended south into the South Andean area for a distance. The content of Tiahuanaco art as well as the contexts in which it moved imply a proselytizing, military-driven conquest of the area, one emanating from the important site of Huari in the highlands. As such, it seems to presage the later, and historically documented, Inca Horizon and Conquest in which military power directed from one center—that of Cuzco—brought the rest of the area, as well as lands beyond, into the compass of a single political authority. Thus, this sequence of horizon styles reflects unifying religious, social, and political forces that helped to form the Peruvian cultural tradition as we know it. The achievement of the Inca Empire, which the Spanish saw and conquered in the early sixteenth century, was the culmination of this singularly unified cultural tradition—a tradition that, in the last few decades of the Inca power, had been extended in a superficial way over most of the neighboring South Andean area and a part of the neighboring Intermediate area.

The view expressed here is one in which the Peruvian cultural tradition was fundamentally an indigenous cultural growth, one arising from antecedent cultural traditions; but, at the same time, it has also been made clear that certain external influences had an important formative role. During the Initial Period and the Early Horizon these influences appear to have come into the Peruvian area from the north, from the Intermediate area, and, in some cases, from Mesoamerica—either directly by sea or via the Intermediate area. There were apparently also important contacts and interchanges with the western Amazon Basin at about the same time. These early influences must have been of a basic, determinative nature in many instances, bringing as they did such things as maize, a knowledge of pottery making, and, prob-

492

ably, certain religious concepts. Later, from the Early Intermediate Period onward, Peruvian cultures became more firmly set in their own patterns. Contacts with the areas to the north undoubtedly continued, probably by the medium of sea trade; however, these later contacts seem to have had less of a "formative" influence on basic Peruvian cultural developments. Indeed, in the later periods the Peruvian cultural tradition had a radiative, rather than a receiving, function. This was exercised particularly strongly to the south, so that the Peruvian cultural tradition may rightfully be said to have had the primary "formative" influence on the cultural developments of the South Andean area.

The South Andean Tradition. The South Andean cultural tradition, like the Peruvian tradition, had its local roots in the Pacific Littoral tradition and in the late continuities of the Andean Hunting-Collecting tradition of the highlands (Figs. 8-1, 2-2, 4-2, 4-3). In the South Andes area, however, the Pacific Littoral tradition did not experience the increasingly important modifications of incipient cultivation from the fifth millennium B.C. onward, as was the case in Peru; nor were the Andean Hunting-Collecting cultures of the South Andean mountain valleys and plateaus influenced by agriculture until a much later time than was the case in the north. Accordingly, the picture of development in the South Andes area is one in which these earlier precursor traditions continue on in their characteristic non-agricultural form for some centuries after their extinction in Peru, and the threshold of the South Andean cultural tradition, when we finally see it, appears primarily derivative from a fully developed Peruvian agricultural tradition. Thus the economic basis of the South Andean cultural tradition was irrigation agriculture and llama-alpaca herding—the general pattern of the Peruvian tradition although in a reduced form.

The Early Ceramic Period (500 B.C.–A.D. 600) is taken as the formal beginning of the South Andean cultural tradition. From evidence now available, it would appear that the earliest ceramics of the tradition are found in the Southern Bolivian subarea and are associated with a culture known as the "Cultura de los Túmulos." These ceramics are largely plain. Some forms

suggest derivations from the early cultures of the South Titicaca Basin; others, especially large urns, point to possible Amazonian ties. Farther south, the early pottery of the Selvas Occidentales, the Chaco-Santiagueño, the Puna, the Valliserrana, and the Atacama subareas show relationships to this early pottery complex of Southern Bolivia and may be derived from it. The Early Ceramic Period must have been the time at which agriculture was diffused or carried to most of the area. Communities were for the most part small, with overall population sparse but growing.

In the later part of the Early Ceramic Period there is evidence of population increase and general cultural elaboration. Some of the pottery styles, such as those of the Valliserrana subarea, are decorated with motifs that suggest the feline designs of Peruvian tradition cultures; however such clues of contact with Peruvian art styles are of a general, vague, and non-specific nature. For example, the South Andean Condorhuasi Polychrome style has stepped-fret designs reminiscent of Qeya and Tiahuanaco, but the similarities are not definite enough to enable us to say that Condorhuasi is a clear result of Tiahuanaco Horizon influence.

The problems of these relationships between the South Andean and Peruvian area styles are complicated, however, by the fact that true Tiahuanaco Horizon influences do appear in the Southern Bolivian and Chilean Atacama subareas at about A.D. 600, and their presence is taken to mark the beginning of the South Andean Middle Ceramic Period. They presumably correlate with the Tiahuanaco cultural and political expansion out of the south Titicaca Basin at a time more or less the same as that of the Huari expansion over much of highland and coastal Peru.

In the Late Ceramic Period (after A.D. 1000) the cultures of the South Andean tradition are characterized by a number of new pottery styles. Most of these look as though they have been derived from those of the preceding period, but there are also new elements in these Late Period styles, especially the burial urn, which is now widely used for child burial. The most probable source for the latter is the Chaco-Santiagueño subarea, which had enjoyed a quasi-separate development from that of the highland subareas and which had from early times been exposed to Amazonian influences. Late Preceramic Period sites also show important changes from earlier periods. The late sites are usually concentrated town settlements, often walled or situated in defensive positions. Although the trends toward the fortified town predate Inca influences, they continue after the establishment of Inca dominance over the area (i.e., after A.D. 1450).

In general, the South Andean cultural tradition lacked great ceremonial or politico-religious centers or constructions. Monumental art was similarly undeveloped, and there are no true South Andean areawide horizon styles as in Peru. The partial exception to this last is the extension of the Peruvian horizon styles of Tiahuanaco and Inca to the area.

The Intermediate Area Tradition. The heritage of the Intermediate area tradition was somewhat different from that of either the Peruvian or South Andean tradition cultures (Fig. 8-1, 8-2, 5-4, 5-5, 5-6, 5-7). It shared with these a background in the Andean Hunting-Collecting past of the uplands, but its precursor on the coasts of the Pacific and Caribbean was the mangrove-shore–adapted Northwest South American Littoral tradition. As we have already outlined, the Northwest South American Littoral groups assimilated the idea of pottery making at about 3000 B.C. This early pottery tradition—the Valdivia pottery tradition—marks the transition from the Northwest South American Littoral tradition to the Intermediate tradition, and this transitional period was probably a time of incipient agriculture with a shift away from the shore-side pursuits of shellfish collecting to those of cultivation.

The sixteenth-century picture of the Intermediate area tradition cultures that the Spanish explorers saw in Ecuador, Colombia, and Lower Central America was one of both cultural richness and cultural diversity. The landscape varied from tropical river bottoms to temperate mountain basins. The natives were, also variably, manioc cultivators and maize growers. Some practiced terrace and irrigation agriculture; some did not. Small villages contrasted with large, permanently built towns. Throughout, there was a high level of craft skill in pottery, weaving, and metallurgy. The latter industry was particularly well devel-

oped in gold and gold-alloy casting. There was strong regionalism in artifact styles, a circumstance that was probably a correlate of the relatively petty size of most political territories. Except for the Chibcha and, to a lesser extent, the Tairona, the nations of the Intermediate area were small. Almost everywhere, however, chiefs or rulers had great power and were venerated as semi-divine. Generally, the social order was tightly class-structured. Religions were run by organized priesthoods of which the members maintained temples and idols in ceremonial centers. The construction of these centers was, for the most part, less impressive than in the Peruvian area or in Mesoamerica. Temples were usually made of wood, although sometimes on stone foundations, and earthen mounds were used both for temple bases and for burial of the distinguished dead.

The development of the Intermediate area culture is traced in three major periods. A Formative Period, from 1500 to 500 B.C., was the time of the establishment of a fully agricultural way of life. This agriculture seems to have had multiple beginnings, one line of the development of which was through the manioc cultivation of the north Colombian lowlands; another was through the maize farming that was diffused to the Intermediate area from Mesoamerica. The routes of this maize diffusion are open to debate. Some authorities have surmised that maize was brought from Mesoamerica by sea to the Ecuadorian coast. This would account for the seemingly later occurrence of maize, and of certain ceramic traits believed to have been associated with its diffusion, in the intervening regions of northern Colombia and Lower Central America. Reichel-Dolmatoff takes this position and holds, further, that both maize and these associated ceramic traits were then carried inland from the Ecuadorian–south Colombian Pacific coast to the highlands. After this, they diffused northward in Colombia, eventually fusing with the Malambo line of ceramic development and with manioc agriculture. Such is a possibility; however, it will be recalled that maize appears as early as 2000 B.C. in Peru and that there are reasons to believe that in this area it was initially introduced into the highlands, and that from there it found its way to the coast. This would seem to imply that there had been an Andean land route for its initial spread. It is, of course, possible that both things happened, that maize came by an overland route down the Andes and that, later, it was introduced by sea to the Ecuador coast along with certain Mesoamerican pottery traits. Clearly, the problems are complex and the data bearing upon them still few. What we can be fairly certain of, however, is that by 500 B.C. a village agricultural pattern had been established throughout the Intermediate area, that the pattern had (with suitable regional environmental restrictions) both manioc and maize, and that it shared with Mesoamerica and with Peru many basic ceramic features.

The Intermediate area Regional Developmental Period (500 B.C.–A.D. 500) saw, as the name implies, the development of marked regional styles. These developments arose out of the Formative Period heritage, which was also enriched by further seaborne diffusions from Mesoamerica. These are apparent in figurine styles and in specialized elements, such as the three-pronged incense burner, that are found on the Ecuadorian coast in the Jama-Coaque and Tolita cultures.

The Late Period (A.D. 500–1550) in the Intermediate area was characterized, to some extent, by cultural and, possibly, political integration, although this integration does not approach what we have seen in the Peruvian area on either the Middle Horizon (Tiahuanaco-Huari) or Late Horizon (Inca) levels. Sea trade with areas to both north and south continued. This is attested to by early Spanish accounts of such native trading missions and by continued clues in the archaeological record. Among the latter is the presence of "ax-money," small, non-ultilitarian T-shaped copper axes that we know, from Mesoamerican ethnohistoric accounts, were used as a medium of exchange. These little "money-axes" are found in both Ecuador and on the Pacific coast of Mexico. In the Late Period there also must have been contact and exchange with Mesoamerica along the Isthmus of Panama and across the Caribbean. Such contacts are needed to explain the iconographic (archaeological) and mythic (ethnographic) evidences of Mesoamerican influences in such cultures as the Tairona.

The Caribbean Tradition. The Caribbean tradition is an agricultural tradition with a primary—and an older—basis in manioc

farming and a secondary—and more recent—basis in maize farming (Figs. 8-2, 6-3, 6-4). The core zone of the tradition was probably the Orinoco Valley, and it may be that this was the original hearth of manioc cultivation. Maize was diffused into the Caribbean tradition from the west, *i.e.* from the Intermediate area, after manioc cultivation was already under way. As to the chronology of these events, we can be fairly sure that manioc was under domestication on the Lower Orinoco as early as 1000 B.C.—a date that is taken as the beginning of the Caribbean tradition. Maize arrived at some time after this, and there are indications that it became more important economically as time went on.

The Caribbean tradition exhibits a development in ceramics nearly comparable to that of the Intermediate area, but metallurgy was of little or no consequence. From what we know of the historic period, the political organization of Caribbean tradition cultures was, in some instances, comparable to that of the petty chieftainships and class-stratified societies of the Intermediate area; in other instances it approached more nearly to the mode of the less class-structured societies of the Amazonian Tropical Forest villages. Settlements were generally small and ceremonial centers little developed. There were some few exceptions to this in late prehistoric-to-historic times; for example, the large towns and ball-court ceremonial centers on some of the Greater Antilles.

The Caribbean tradition has been segmented chronologically into the latter four periods of the five-period Caribbean area chronology. (Period I of this chronology pertains to the pre-agricultural and preceramic Northwest South American Littoral tradition.) The Caribbean tradition begins with Period II (1000 B.C.–A.D. 300), during which the archaeological record is carried by two principal subtraditions. Both date back to near the beginning of the period. One, the Saladoid subtradition, is known from white-on-red painted pottery, combining some incision. The other, the Barrancoid subtradition, featured deep, broadlined incision and adorno modeling. It is likely that these subtraditions had their origins in the Valdivia pottery tradition of the Intermediate area. Sites of both subtraditions are simple village areas along the Orinoco drainage, and manioc-griddle fragments are associated with both.

During the first millennium B.C. the Saladoid and Barrancoid subtraditions spread throughout eastern Venezuela, including the northeast coast opposite the Island of Trinidad. From this coast both Saladoid and, later, Barrancoid, ceramic complexes were carried on to Trinidad, out into the Lesser Antilles, and eventually to the Greater Antilles. The first spread of Saladoid subtradition pottery in this manner may be taken to mark the movement of the Caribbean tradition into the West Indies, and this movement was almost certainly effected by Arawakan peoples.

On the mainland Saladoid-Barrancoid fusions gave rise to later Caribbean tradition branches or subtraditions. This cultural mixing and blending was further complicated by the spread of the Tocuyanoid culture from northwestern Venezuela. This spread occurred toward the end of Period II (0–A.D. 300), and it is possible that in addition to new ceramic introductions, the Tocuyanoid cultures also brought maize to the Caribbean area at this time.

The subsequent developments of Periods III (A.D. 300–1000) and IV (A.D. 1000–1500) can be broadly summarized by saying that the mainland Caribbean area cultures were characterized by a progressive "westernization"—a process that resulted from contacts with the northwestern Venezuelan subareas of the Intermediate area. That this "westernization" occurred in the West Indies seems less likely. The late changes there— the florescence in art and in the ball-game ceremonialism—seem more likely to have been the end products of a local social and cultural evolution in the Greater Antilles.

The Amazonian Cultural Tradition. The dominant subsistence mode of the Amazonian cultural tradition (Figs. 8-2, 6-5) was that known as "Tropical Forest Agriculture"—essentially manioc farming carried out in the vicinities of small, more or less sedentary villages. These villages averaged a few hundred people and consisted frequently of long pole-and-thatch multi-family houses. Characteristic manufactures of the tradition included hammocks for sleeping, dugout or bark canoes for river travel, cotton textiles, basketry, pottery, bows and arrows, and spears. Stone tools were relatively rare; the most frequent

was a polished celt or ax. Spears and arrows were commonly tipped with hardened wood or bone and were used in hunting and fishing. The latter activity was often of considerable economic importance, and fish were also taken in nets, traps, and with fish poisons.

The origins of the Amazonian tradition are obscure; we have virtually no data on earlier culture patterns from the area. It seems most probable that the earliest pottery of the Amazonian tradition derived from that of the early Valdivia tradition of the Intermediate area and that this pottery was carried down the Amazon drainage, from west to east, by small immigrant groups of farmers.

The development of the Amazonian tradition can be plotted in gross outline by a series of pottery style horizons or subtraditions. The earliest of these is known as the Zoned Hachure Horizon, after a distinctive mode of pottery decoration in which geometric zones outlined with very deep incised lines were then filled in with finer lined plain or crosshatched incision. Phases of this Zoned Hachure Horizon are reported from the Upper Amazon Ucayalí and Napo tributaries, from the Lower Amazon course, and from the Amazon Delta islands. The dating on the earliest of these phases, that of Early Tutishcainyo in the Ucayalí, is inferred as about 1800 B.C., and this date is taken as the inception of the Amazonian tradition in the west. Dates for other Zoned Hachure phases range later—1000 B.C. and 50 B.C. —so that the "horizon" as defined has considerable time depth and can be viewed equally as a subtradition.

An Incised Rim Horizon is dated, broadly, to the first millennium A.D. The distinguishing ceramic feature is rectilinear incised designs on the flat-topped rim of a bowl form. With this horizon the more characteristic Tropical Forest level of culture emerges, with pottery manioc-roasting plates, pottery urns for burials, spindle whorls, and labrets. The sites representing the horizon are found mostly along the Lower and Middle Amazon and at the delta; Mangueiras, Manacapurú, and Paredão are typical phases. These developments of the Incised Rim Horizon may be linked to the Caribbean tradition, especially to the early Saladoid and Barrancoid subtraditions of that tradition. Pottery typology and geographical distribution both suggest this; however, the cultures have a definite Amazonian "cast" about them that suggests local area developments.

The Polychrome Horizon is next in time. Many of its phases date from A.D. 1000 to 1300; but there are suggestions that it may have earlier beginnings in the Upper Amazon drainages and in Lowland Bolivia that go back a few centuries before A.D. 1000, so that there is probably some chronological overlap with the Incised Rim Horizon. Distinctive ceramics are painted red, black, and white—quite frequently with a white slip or ground color. Further diagnostics are large burial urns. These are often polychrome painted and are anthropomorphically modeled.. The well-known Marajoara phase of Marajó Island belongs on this horizon, and there are a number of other phases on the Lower, Middle, and Upper Amazon. Some complexes of Lowland Bolivia are also affiliated. Authorities agree that the horizon had its origins in the west, in the Upper Amazon, although there is difference of opinion on just where, with suggestions ranging from Colombia down to Lowland Bolivia. It is to be questioned, however, whether these polychrome urn styles were derived fully formed from these edges of the Amazonian area. Arguments can be made that many of the incised and relief-modeled features of some of the styles can be brought out of the earlier Incised Rim Horizon of the Middle Amazon.

Some of the cultures of the Polychrome Horizon mark a clear florescence of the Amazonian cultural tradition in which the tradition is taken from a simple Tropical Forest agricultural level to a level of "Sub-Andean" cultures. Sites are large. Those on Marajó Island and those in Lowland Bolivia are associated with huge habitation mounds and burial mounds, and it has been suggested that the societies involved were stratified "chiefdoms" of the sort that the Spanish discovered in the Bolivian Mojos region in the sixteenth century. This level of cultural development has raised questions about basic economy, and it seems likely that a more productive and complexly organized type of agriculture was practiced than simple forest root-crop cultivation. Perhaps significantly, some of the regions in which Polychrome Horizon cultures are found are riverine savanna lands rather than typical jungle bush, and

in the Bolivian Mojos the mound sites are surrounded by extensive savanna fields of artificial cultivation ridges.

An Incised and Punctate Horizon dates as prior to and immediately after A.D. 1500, and it is known mainly from Lower Amazon sites. The Santarém pottery style is a part of this horizon. Relationships to the Arauquinoid subtradition of the Caribbean are suggested.

An important southern branch of the Amazonian tradition has been designated as the Tupiguaraní subtradition. The Tupiguaraní archaeological complex has polychrome burial urns, which bear some relationships to the urns of the Polychrome Horizon. It also has distinctive corrugated and fingernail-marked wares. Tupiguaraní is found throughout the East Brazilian area, both coast and interior, in the Chaco area, and as far south as the Paraná Delta. Apparently, its spread began as early as A.D. 500, and some of its sites date as late as the historic horizon of the sixteenth century.

The use of the name Tupiguaraní for an archaeological subtradition implies an ethnic connection, and the linkage between this particular complex and the Tupí-Guaraní tribes is well established. The ethnic identifications of other Amazonian subtraditions or horizons are more speculative; however, the Amazonian tradition was principally in the hands of Arawakan and Tupian peoples and was probably the creation of their ancestors. In the sixteenth century groups like the Arawakan Aruã, around the mouth of the Amazon, still followed in an Amazonian traditional way of life.

The Sambaquí Tradition. This tradition pertains to the shell midden sites of the Brazilian coast and lagoonal embayments. They are composed mostly of molluscs but also of fish and animal bones and ash. Many are of great depth, and they indicate a degree of sedentism—perhaps for long seasonal periods of each year—of the non-agricultural peoples who formerly occupied them.

Most of the artifacts that have been found in the sambaquís are rough percussion-flaked axes, scrapers, picks, coarsely flaked stemmed points, and bone points; however there are also some polished stone items, both tools and ornaments or ceremonial objects. Sambaquí tradition burials are primary—either flexed or extended—and are as a general rule wholly or partially covered with red ocher.

It has been speculated that the Sambaquí tradition came into existence at about 5000 B.C. and that its origins lay in the East Brazilian Upland tradition, which displays a similar lithic technology (Figs. 8-1, 8-2, 7-3). The separation of the two traditions could have begun as a result of seasonal transhumance between the interior plateau and the littoral zone, eventually with some shellfish gatherers electing to live more or less permanently along the shore.

Although the Sambaquí way of life may be as old as 5000 B.C., most of the radiocarbon dates that we have fall in the range of 3000–1000 B.C. Within this range there is evidence that suggests a gradual technological change to more ground and polished stone tools and also the development of definitive Sambaquí ceremonial patterns. These last are particularly reflected in polished stone effigy dishes or basins. These are usually fashioned as fish or birds, and their function is unknown.

The Sambaquí tradition probably began to decline after 1000 B.C., and this seems to have been correlated with the lowering of the sea level and an increasing scarcity of shellfish; however, Sambaquí sites continued to be occupied to a much later time. We have set an end-date of A.D. 500 for the close of the Sambaquí tradition, and its replacement by the Amazonian Tupiguaraní culture. Quite probably, the Tupí-Guaraní tribes, who were the bearers of Tupiguaraní archaeological culture, drove the Sambaquí tradition peoples away from the coastal strip. Although the newcomers may have exploited fishing and shellfish collecting to some extent, they were primarily Tropical Forest farmers. Along with agriculture they brought their pottery into the area—the pottery of the distinctive Tupiguaraní subtradition referred to in our summary of the Amazonian cultural tradition. However it seems that this Tupiguaraní pottery was not the first pottery to be introduced to the Sambaquí tradition. An earlier pottery was known in the East Brazilian area, and this brings us to a consideration of what has been called the Eastern Brazilian pottery tradition.

The Eastern Brazilian Pottery Tradition. The Eastern Brazilian pottery tradition is a technological rather than a "full" cultural tradition, but, like the Valdivia pottery tradition, it warrants separate consideration. Its context or contexts are those of the East Brazilian Upland and Sambaquí traditions—although in the terminal stages of those traditions (Figs. 8-1, 8-2). Like the Valdivia pottery tradition, it is uncertain that this Eastern Brazilian pottery tradition was accompanied by plant cultivation; however if it was, the likelihood is that it was cultivation of a minimal, or "incipient," sort.

There is only one radiocarbon date for the Eastern Brazilian pottery tradition that is appreciably earlier than that of Tupiguaraní pottery (Fig. 7-3). This is the date of approximately 900 B.C. for the Periperí ceramic complex of the Bahía coast. The Periperí pottery is found in a sambaquí midden and Sambaquí tradition context. It is extremely simple, undecorated ware, and its wider relationships are as yet speculative; but the interpretation has been put forward that it is a stimulus derivative of the early (ca. 1000 B.C.) Zoned Hachure Horizon pottery of the mouth of the Amazon.

Other pottery complexes that have been grouped with the Eastern Brazilian pottery tradition are known from the southern states of Brazil, both near the coast and in the interior. These southern manifestations differ from Periperí pottery in being more developed examples of the potter's art. Although vessel forms are simple, there is surface decoration in incision, punctation, and fingernail marking. The earliest radiocarbon date for any of these complexes is approximately A.D. 500, which is essentially contemporaneous with the first appearances of Tupiguaraní pottery in the same subareas.

Eastern Brazilian tradition pottery continued until historic times—as did Tupiguaraní pottery—and the co-existence of the two, with ample evidence of interchange and contact between the traditions, can be viewed as archaeological evidence of the interspersal of Macro-Ge and Tupian peoples that was found in the East Brazilian area in historic times.

The Chacoan Tradition. Our ethnographic knowledge of the tribes of the Chaco area suggests that the basic pattern of life there was one closely adapted to the semi-arid and peculiar natural environment of the Chaco Depression. Subsistence in this pattern was primarily by wild-plant collecting supplemented with hunting and fishing. This was the likely mode of existence of the Guaicuran-speaking tribes who would appear to be the earlier inhabitants of the area. In later prehistoric times Guaraní tribes, with a Tupiguaraní agricultural economy, occupied the eastern regions of the Chaco area along the Paraguay River.

The archaeology of the area, except for Tupiguaraní sites of the Paraguay, is known from only a few locations along the Teuco-Bermejo and Pilcomayo drainages in the Argentine Provinces of Formosa and Chaco. These sites have yielded little except pottery and polished stone axes. The pottery includes burial urns and other vessels. The burial-urn trait—which seems to antedate the Tupiguaraní burial urns in the area—may be derived from the west, that is, from the Selvas Occidentales and Chaco-Santiagueño subareas of the South Andean area. On the other hand, the vessel decoration is more suggestive of the Eastern Brazilian pottery tradition in its incisions, punctations, and fingernail markings. Most typical of the Chaco pottery, however, is a cord-impressed type of ornamentation—apparently a unique local development.

The Paraná-Pampean Tradition. The Paraná-Pampean tradition of the Pampean area is believed to have had two precursors: the Andean Hunting-Collecting tradition cultures of the southern part of the area and the East Brazilian Upland tradition cultures that influenced the northern part of it (Figs. 8-1, 8-2, 7-7). In the south, at least, the transition from the Andean Hunting-Collecting cultures to those of the Paraná-Pampean tradition is dated to about 3500 B.C., or at a time somewhere between the Magellan III and Magellan IV phases of the Strait of Magellan sequence. Between 3500 and the first millennium B.C. the pattern of a guanaco hunting culture, with triangular, stemmed dart points and appropriate skin-dressing tools, apparently spread northward, coming into contact with such cultures as the North Patagonian (Norpatagoniense) and the Blancagrandian (Blancagrandense). The

fusion of these traditions resulted in the later period developments of the Pampas proper. These developments were further influenced by the introduction of the bow and arrow (the small stemless and stemmed points) and by the introduction of pottery.

The pottery of the Paraná-Pampean tradition seems to have developed along the Lower Paraná Valley and as such could be referred to as a "Paraná pottery tradition."[4] Subsistence in the Paraná Valley had probably always been somewhat different from that farther south, with a greater dependence on fishing and riverine collecting. It was here, we have hypothesized, that the Eastern Brazilian pottery tradition influences, moving southward along the Paraná River from Brazil, provided the stimulus for this new ceramic development. An estimated beginning date for the Lower Paraná pottery has been given as 500 B.C. It is possible, also, that some plant cultivation of an incipient level sort was also introduced from southern Brazil at about the same time. The Lower Paraná Valley pottery is distinguished by bowl forms and by curious open-ended cylinders or bell-shaped manufactures of uncertain use. Both the vessels and the cylinders were frequently adorned with bird-head effigies and with a linear-punctate or drag-and-jab type of punctation-incision. Later, some use of red slipping and red zoning appeared in the tradition. This Paraná pottery tradition must have been the work of the Timbú and other tribes of unknown linguistic affiliation who held the Lower Paraná when the Spaniards first arrived there early in the sixteenth century, for the tradition continues up to the historic horizon in that subarea. With some modifications—generally in the direction of simplicity— the tradition was passed from the Lower Paraná peoples southward to the Querandí of Northern Buenos Aires, to the Puelche of the Southern Buenos Aires–La Pampa subarea, and eventually to the Tehuelche of Patagonia. Only the Ona of Northeastern Tierra del Fuego remained without pottery in historic times.

In what must have been very late prehistoric times the Guaraní established a few small settlements near the mouth of the Plate Delta. The archaeological remains of these settlements are those of the Tupiguaraní subtradition of the Amazonian agricultural tradition, and the early

Spanish explorers of the sixteenth century report that these Guaraní were farmers.

The Fuegian Tradition. The cold, wet Fuegian area provided the setting for the unique cultural adaptation that we have called the Fuegian tradition (Fig. 8-1). These peoples of the Fuegian area—in historic times the Chono, Alacaluf, and Yahgan—were shellfish collectors and sea mammal hunters who led a semi-nomadic existence.

The earliest archaeological complex pertaining to the tradition is that of Englefield Island, from the Sea of Otway (Fig. 7-7). Interestingly, the Englefield Islanders were both land hunters and sea mammal hunters. They possessed the willow leaf projectile points of the Andean Hunting-Collecting tradition as well as the barbed bone harpoons of the typical later Fuegian tradition cultures. This suggests that Englefield may mark the time of divergence between the two traditions or the point at which a Fuegian marine adaptation was beginning to separate away from an Andean Hunting-Collecting land-based culture. The radiocarbon dates on Englefield are ca. 7000 B.C., and if these dates are correct then this divergence between the two patterns occurred surprisingly early; however there are reasons for thinking that the Englefield dates are too early, and a later date—of about 4000 B.C.—has consequently been suggested.

Following Englefield—whatever the date of Englefield may be—we next pick up the story of the Fuegian tradition in the "Shell-Knife Culture" of Beagle Channel. The implements of the complex are bone harpoons, mussel-shell knives, and percussion-chipped stonework. The finely chipped points of the Englefield complex have disappeared; the Fuegian sea-oriented culture has come into existence. The date of the "Shell-Knife Culture" has been estimated at 2000 B.C., but this kind of artifact inventory continued until historic times—as, for instance, in the Alacaluf subarea. Farther south, in southern Tierra del Fuego, the "Shell-Knife Culture" was succeeded by the "Pit-House Culture," in which well-chipped points again make their appearance and in which a mixed land-hunting and sea-collecting economy implies influences from the Pampean Ona.

Correlation of Cultural Traditions and Area Chronologies: South America

One way to summarize the correlations between South American cultural traditions and the area chronologies in which they have been examined is to compare the charts on which the cultural traditions have been plotted (Figs. 8-1, 8-2) with the charts of archaeological area chronologies (Figs. 8-3, 8-4).

The Peruvian Area. The Peruvian area *Preceramic Period I* (prior to 9500 B.C.) correlates with the Flake tradition complexes of Chivateros Red Zone and Oquendo;[4a] *Preceramic Period II* (9500–8000 B.C.) pertains to the Biface tradition Chivateros I phase; and *Preceramic Period III* (8000–6000 B.C.) was the period of the Old South American Hunting tradition cultures on the coast (Chivateros II, Pampilla) and in the highlands (Lauricocha I). By *Preceramic Period IV* (6000–4200 B.C.) the Andean Hunting-Collecting tradition had come into being, and this was the time of probable coast-highland transhumance within that tradition. *Preceramic Period V* (4200–2500 B.C.) saw the inception of the Pacific Littoral tradition on the coast and the continuation of Andean Hunting-Collecting cultures in the sierra. *Preceramic Period VI* (2500–1800 B.C.) marked the climax of both the Pacific Littoral tradition and the late Andean Hunting-Collecting tradition cultures, and, in its final centuries, it saw the advent of maize farming and the beginnings of large permanent architecture. These developments of Preceramic VI led directly into the Peruvian cultural tradition; the next six periods—*Initial* (1800–900 B.C.), *Early Horizon* (900–200 B.C.), *Early Intermediate* (200 B.C.–A.D. 600), *Middle Horizon* (A.D. 600–1000), *Late Intermediate* (A.D. 1000–1476), and *Late Horizon* (A.D. 1476–1534) —all pertain to the development of this tradition, terminating with the arrival of the Spanish under Pizarro.

The South Andes Area. The South Andes area has the same set of preceramic periods as the Peruvian area, with the same dates, except for *Preceramic Period VI,* which runs from 2500 to 500 B.C. The culture tradition correlations are also the same as those for Peru except for the Pacific Littoral and Andean Hunting-Collecting traditions lasting on until 500 B.C. The ceramic periods of the South Andes area are the *Early Ceramic* (500 B.C.–A.D. 600), the *Middle Ceramic* (A.D. 600–1000), the *Late Ceramic* (A.D. 1000–1450), and the *Inca* (A.D. 1450–1550). These ceramic periods all pertain to the development of the South Andean cultural tradition.

The Intermediate Area. The Intermediate area *Preceramic Period I* (prior to 10,000 B.C.) is thought to be represented by some Flake tradition industries of the Ecuadorian coast and by the Camare complex of the Chopper tradition in Northwest Venezuela; *Preceramic Period II* (10,000–9000 B.C.) brackets the Biface tradition, as is seen in the Las Lagunas complex of Northwestern Venezuela; *Preceramic Period III* (9000–7000 B.C.) is conceived of as the period of the Old South American Hunting tradition of the leaf-shaped El Jobo points and the fishtail points of El Inga I; *Preceramic Period IV* (7000–5000 B.C.) pertains to the Andean Hunting-Collecting tradition and its Ecuadorian El Inga II-III and Venezuelan Las Casitas complexes; in *Preceramic Period V* (5000–3000 B.C.) the coastal cultures of the Northwest South American Littoral tradition had their beginnings in Ecuador, Colombia, Panama, and Venezuela, while in the highlands the Andean Hunting-Collecting tradition cultures carried on. The *Early Ceramic Period* (3000–1500 B.C.) is known for the Valdivia pottery tradition, a ceramic tradition carried in the later stages of the Northwest South American Littoral tradition. The well-known phases of the period are Valdivia, Puerto Hormiga, Barlovento, and Monagrillo. The *Formative Period* (1500–500 B.C.) saw the establishment of the agricultural Intermediate area cultural tradition, and this tradition persisted through the *Regional Developmental Period* (500 B.C.–A.D. 500) and the *Late Period* (A.D. 500–1500). Inca influences are seen in the latter part of the Late Period.

The Caribbean Area. The Caribbean area *Paleo-Indian Period* is placed prior to 5000 B.C., and is represented by projectile-point complexes that are ascribed to the Andean Hunting-Collecting tradition. The succeeding *Meso-Indian Period (or Period I)* (5000–1000 B.C.) is still fully preceramic. The coastal and island cultures are those of the Northwest South American Littoral tradition, while in the interior there may have been a continuity of the Andean Hunting-Collecting cultures. *Period II* (1000 B.C.–A.D. 300) introduces the Caribbean cultural tradition to the Venezuelan-Guiana mainland. Toward the end of this period the Caribbean tradition is carried into the Antilles, where it begins to replace the Northwest South American Littoral tradition. By the end of *Period III* (A.D. 300–1000) the Caribbean tradition had spread to all of the West Indies except western Cuba. This situation continued in *Period IV* (A.D. 1000–1500), with the Northwest South American Littoral tradition being maintained only in the West Cuban subarea.

The Amazonian Area. The Amazonian *Zoned Hachure Horizon* has estimated dates ranging from about 1800 B.C. to 0. It is considered to be earlier in the west (at least in the Ucayalí Basin) than in the east. An *Incised Rim Horizon* is thought to span the 0 to A.D. 1000 range. This is followed by a *Polychrome Horizon* placed at about A.D. 600 to 1300, so that there is some overlap with the preceding horizon. An *Incised and Punctate Horizon* is dated at about A.D. 1300 to 1600.

The East Brazilian Area. Prior to 8000 B.C. the Early Catalán culture represents a probable transition from the Flake to the East Brazilian Upland tradition. East Brazilian Upland cultures such as Santa Rosa and Cerca Grande date in the 8000 to 5000 B.C. range; and this tradition continues in the 5000 to 3000 B.C. bracket with San Antonio, Early José Vieira, and other complexes. It continues on in the span from 3000 to 1000 B.C. with the polished stone ax and small projectile-point cultures, such as the Marchiori. Running parallel with the East Brazilian Upland tradition, after 5000 B.C., is the Sambaquí tradition. At about 1000 B.C. both the East Brazilian Upland and Sambaquí traditions are believed to have been influenced by an Eastern

Brazilian pottery tradition (although there is only a single radiocarbon date to support this interpretation). By A.D. 500 pottery was known widely in Brazil, and this pottery pertains to both the Eastern Brazilian pottery tradition and the Tupiguaraní subtradition within the Amazonian tradition.

The Chaco Area. Pottery was probably not introduced into the area until after 500 B.C.; the Chacoan cultural tradition is thought to begin at about the time of the introduction of pottery. Later, Tupiguaraní ceramics and culture were brought into the eastern part of the area.

Figure 8-3. A correlation of major area chronologies for South America. The Intermediate Area–Peru–South Andean–Fuegian–Pampean–East Brazilian line.

MAJOR PERIODS	DATES	INTERMEDIATE AREA	PERUVIAN AREA	SOUTH ANDEAN AREA	FUEGIAN AREA	PAMPEAN AREA Patagonia	Paraná	EAST BRAZILIAN AREA Interior	Coast
VII		HISTORIC	HISTORIC	HISTORIC				Calundú	
	1500	LATE PERIOD	LATE HORIZON	INCA	Alacaluf Yahgan	Tehuelche (Pottery)	Arroyo las Conchas	Curimataú	
	A.D. 1000		LATE INTERMEDIATE PERIOD	LATE CERAMIC PERIOD					
			MIDDLE HORIZON	MIDDLE CERAMIC PERIOD	"Pit-House"	Magellan V	San Blas	Taquara	Una Umuarama
VI	0	REGIONAL DEVELOPMENTAL PERIOD	EARLY INTERMEDIATE PERIOD	EARLY CERAMIC PERIOD			Malabrigo		
			EARLY HORIZON				(Pottery?)		
	B.C. 1000	FORMATIVE PERIOD	INITIAL PERIOD						Periperí
	2000	EARLY CERAMIC PERIOD	PRECERAMIC PERIOD VI	PRECERAMIC PERIOD VI	"Shell-Knife"	Jabalí Punta Rubia		Marchiori	Macedo
	3000		PRECERAMIC PERIOD V	PRECERAMIC PERIOD V	Englefield (?)	San Matías			Gomes
V	4000	PRECERAMIC PERIOD V				Magellan IV North Patagonian Magellan III	Blanca Grande		
	5000		PRECERAMIC PERIOD IV	PRECERAMIC PERIOD IV				San Antonio	Maratua
IV	6000	PRECERAMIC PERIOD IV							
	7000		PRECERAMIC PERIOD III	PRECERAMIC PERIOD III					
	8000	PRECERAMIC PERIOD III			Englefield(?)			Cerca Grande Santa Rosa	
	9000	PRECERAMIC PERIOD II	PRECERAMIC PERIOD II	PRECERAMIC PERIOD II		Magellan I		Early Catalán	
III	10,000					Oliviense (?)			
	15,000	PRECERAMIC PERIOD I	PRECERAMIC PERIOD I	PRECERAMIC PERIOD I					
II	20,000								
I	40,000								

The Pampean Area. Prior to 8000 B.C. there are claims for Flake tradition complexes (Oliviense, etc.). There are also firm evidences of the Old South American Hunting tradition as seen in its Magellan I phase. The Magellan III phase is placed at 4000 B.C., and this phase is considered to be within the Andean Hunting-Collecting tradition. The changes between Magellan III and Magellan IV (3500 B.C.) are taken to mark the transition between the Andean Hunting-Collecting and the new Paraná-Pampean tradition. A number of lithic industries are dated in the range of 3000 to 1000 B.C. These have been considered within the scope of the Paraná-

Figure 8-4. A correlation of major area chronologies for South America. The Intermediate Area–Caribbean–Amazonian–East Brazilian–Pampean line.

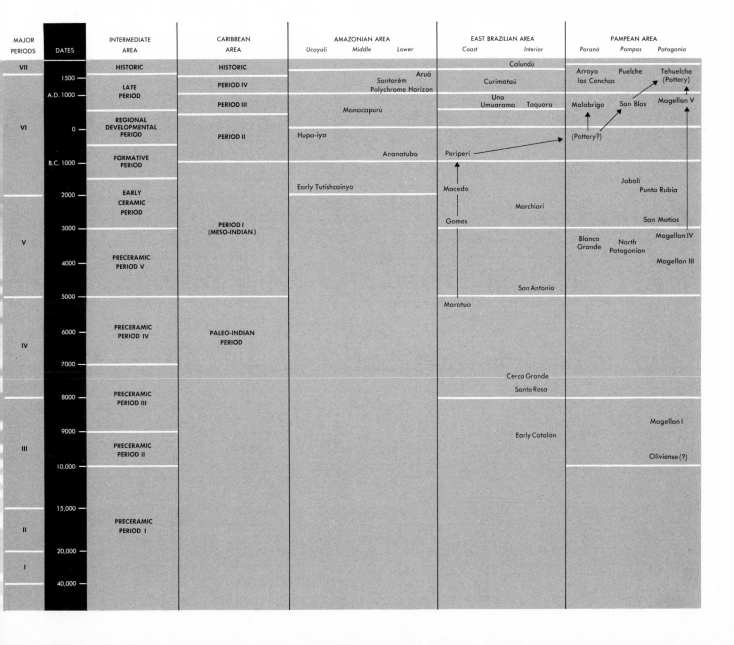

Pampean tradition, although the more northerly ones present special technological aspects. It has been estimated that pottery made its first appearance in the area at about 500 B.C., along the Lower Paraná River; the pottery spread from there southward through the Paraná-Pampean tradition cultures, arriving in southern Patagonia at about the historic horizon.

The Fuegian Area. It is possible that the Englefield Island complex, which is believed to be the transition from the Andean Hunting-Collecting to the Fuegian tradition, dates as early as 7000 B.C., but a more likely date is about 4000 B.C. By an estimated date of 2000 B.C. the Fuegian tradition was fully developed and is represented in the "Shell-Knife Culture." In some parts of the Fuegian area this "Shell-Knife Culture" persisted until historic times; in other parts it was modified through contacts with the Paraná-Pampean tradition to produce the "Pit-House Culture," dated at about A.D. 500. This "Pit-House Culture" continues into historic period Yahgan culture with little change.

A Summary Listing of New World Cultural Traditions and Culture Areas

For the convenience of the reader we have set down below a listing of all the major cultural and technological traditions and all the major archaeological culture areas that we have treated in both volumes of this book.

The cultural traditions begin with those of North and Middle America and are arranged essentially as they were presented in Volume One:

1 *An Unnamed Technological Tradition or Traditions.* (This pertains to the putatively early rough percussion industries. Technologically, they are similar to the Flake and Biface traditions of South America.)
2 *The Big-Game Hunting Tradition.*
3 *The Old Cordilleran Tradition.*
4 *The Desert Tradition.*
5 *The Archaic Tradition.*
6 *The Mesoamerican Tradition.*
7 *The Southwestern Tradition.*

8 *The Woodland Tradition.*
9 *The Mississippian Tradition.*
10 *The Plains Village Tradition.*
11 *The California Coast and Valley Tradition.*
12 *The Northwest Coast Tradition.*
13 *The Northwest Riverine Tradition.*
14 *The Northwest Microblade Tradition.*
15 *The Arctic Small-Tool Tradition.*
16 *The Eskimo Tradition.*
17 *The Denetasiro Tradition.*

Those of South America, as presented in Volume Two, continue the list:

18 *The Flake Tradition.*
19 *The Chopper Tradition.*
20 *The Biface Tradition.*
21 *The Old South American Hunting Tradition.*
22 *The East Brazilian Upland Tradition.*
23 *The Andean Hunting-Collecting Tradition.*
24 *The Pacific Littoral Tradition.*
25 *The Northwest South American Littoral Tradition.*
26 *The Valdivia Pottery Tradition.*
27 *The Peruvian Tradition.*
28 *The South Andean Tradition.*
29 *The Intermediate Area Tradition.*
30 *The Caribbean Tradition.*
31 *The Amazonian Tradition.*
32 *The Sambaquí Tradition.*
33 *The Eastern Brazilian Pottery Tradition.*
34 *The Chacoan Tradition.*
35 *The Paraná-Pampean Tradition.*
36 *The Fuegian Tradition.*

The culture areas are similarly arranged, beginning with North and Middle America in Volume One:

1 *The Mesoamerican Area.*
2 *The Southwest Area.*
3 *The Eastern Woodlands Area.*
4 *The Plains Area.*
5 *The Northeast Mexico-Texas Area.*
6 *The Great Basin Area.*
7 *The Baja California Area.*
8 *The California Area.*
9 *The Northwest Coast Area.*
10 *The Interior Plateau Area.*

11 *The Subarctic Area.*
   (a) *Western Subarctic.*
   (b) *Eastern Subarctic.*
12 *The Arctic Area.*

And continuing in Volume Two for South America:

13 *The Peruvian Area.*
14 *The South Andes Area.*
15 *The Intermediate Area.*
16 *The Caribbean Area.*
17 *The Amazonian Area.*
18 *The East Brazilian Area.*
19 *The Chaco Area.*
20 *The Pampean Area.*
21 *The Fuegian Area.*

The map shown in Figure 8-5 is included as a further schematic summary of all of the New World culture areas together with the major cultural and technological traditions in each.

Some Synchronic Perspectives of Major American Periods

In Volume One (pp. 473–476) we offered a series of synchronic perspectives, or time horizons, on a continental scale for North and Middle America. Let us continue this kind of examination here for South America (with reference to Figs. 8-1, 8-2, 8-3, 8-4). In so doing, however, we shall extend the perspectives for the hemisphere, recapitulating, to an extent, what was said in Volume One.

Period I: 40,000–20,000 B.C. Man may or may not have been in the Americas this early. If he was, he was a recent arrival from Asia and he most likely had traveled over the Bering land bridge toward the close of this period. Traces of North American percussion industries like those of Lake Manix in the Great Basin, Lake Chapala in Baja California, Lewisville in Texas, and Valsequillo in Mexico have been advanced as possibly pertaining to this period. Such industries would fall within our concept of the "Unnamed Technological Tradition" of North America. In South America it is possible that man had arrived

this early. If so, his industries would pertain to what we have called the Flake tradition, although no definite assemblages or complexes can be placed for this period.

Period II: 20,000–15,000 B.C. This period was marked off in our North American survey to bracket a time at which the idea of the bifacially flaked lanceolate point or knife may have been brought to the New World. It was suggested that the British Mountain complex of the Arctic might fall into this period, but it was also emphasized that the dating of British Mountain was far from secure. As we have noted in Chapter 2 of this volume, the earliest radiocarbon-dated evidence for this technology is that from Wilson Butte Cave in Idaho. However the dates here are, at the earliest, about 13,000 B.C. or somewhat later than those set for Period II. In South America there is nothing that corresponds to this "Levallois-Mousterian" technology that dates as early as Period II. We have speculated that the crude percussion Flake and Chopper tradition industries were spreading through the southern continent at this time.

Period III: 15,000–8000 B.C. The beginning date for the period is speculative. In North America the Wilson Butte finds are to be incorporated into the earlier part of Period III. In South America the Flake tradition is diagramed as persisting into it, and the Chopper and Biface traditions are placed within it.

In the latter part of the period we have the North American evidences of the Big-Game Hunting and Old Cordilleran traditions, and in South America these are matched with the Old South American Hunting tradition complexes such as the Magellan I, El Inga I, El Jobo, and Tagua Tagua. In fact, it is only with the latter part of Period III that we are on firm ground—with distinctive artifact complexes, definite stratigraphic-geologic contexts, and a number of radiocarbon dates—and some archaeologists would prefer to begin the story of man in the New World on this period level; however I have indicated my reasons

Figure 8-5. (Pp. 506–507)

WESTERN ARCTIC AREA

TRADITIONS

Eskimo Trad.
Arctic Small-Tool
Northwest Microblade
Old Cordilleran
Big–Game Hunt (?)
Unnamed Tech. Trad.

TIME

EASTERN ARCTIC AREA

TRADITIONS

Eskimo
Arctic Small-Tool
Boreal Archaic (?)

TIME

EASTERN SUBARCTIC AREA

TRADITIONS

Boreal Archaic
Unnamed Tech. Trad. (?)

TIME

CARIBBEAN AREA

TRADITIONS

WESTERN SUBARCTIC AREA

TRADITIONS

Denetasiro
Northwest Microblade
Old Cordilleran

TIME

EASTERN WOODLANDS AREA

TRADITIONS

Mississippian
Woodland
Archaic
Big–Game Hunt
Unnamed Tech. Trad.

TIME

NORTHWEST COAST AREA

TRADITIONS

Northwest Coast
Old Cordilleran
?

TIME

INTERIOR PLATEAU AREA

TRADITIONS

N. West Riverine
Old Cordilleran

TIME

PLAINS AREA

TRADITIONS

Plains Village
Woodland
Plains Archaic
Big–Game Hunt
Unnamed Tech. Trad.

TIME

**N. EAST MEXICO-
TEXAS AREA**

TRADITIONS

Desert-Archaic
Big–Game Hunt.
Unnamed Tech. Trad.

TIME

GREAT BASIN AREA

TRADITIONS

Desert
Old Cordilleran
Unnamed Tech. Trad.

TIME

CALIFORNIA AREA

TRADITIONS

Calif. Coast-Vall.
Desert + Old
Cordilleran
Unnamed Tech. Trad.

TIME

SOUTHWEST AREA

TRADITIONS

Southwestern
Desert
Big–Game Hunt.
Unnamed Tech. Trad.

TIME

BAJA CALIFORNIA AREA

TRADITIONS

Desert
Unnamed Tech. Trad.

TIME

MESOAMERICAN AREA

TRADITIONS

Mesoamerican
Desert
Big–Game Hunt
Unnamed Tech. Trad.

TIME

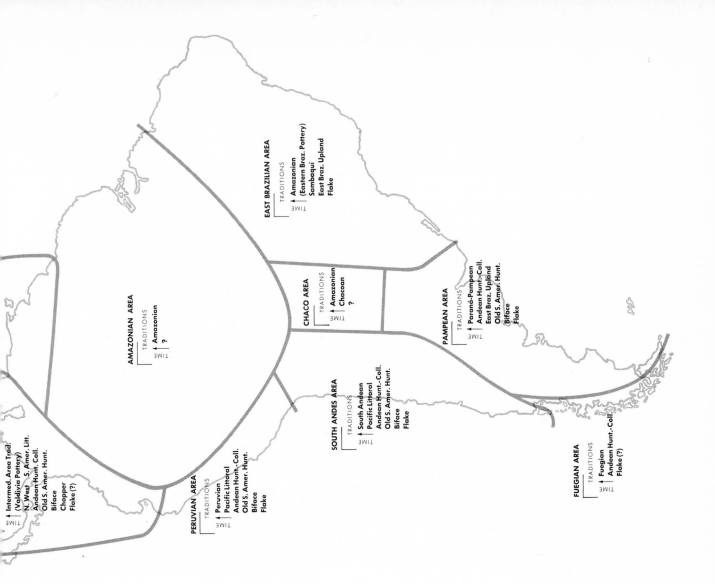

New World Culture Areas
and Major Cultural
or Technological Traditions

throughout this volume (and in Vol. I as well) for thinking that Period I and Period II presences of man in the Americas are to be given serious consideration.

Period IV: 8000–5000 B.C. This was the time of the amelioration of terminal Wisconsin Pleistocene conditions in North and South America. The Archaic tradition of the Eastern Woodlands and the Desert tradition of western North America came into being as adaptations to changing environments in the northern continent, and in the south we have the beginnings of the Andean Hunting-Collecting and East Brazilian Upland traditions. In parts of North America, of course, the Big-Game Hunting tradition and the Old Cordilleran tradition persisted.

Period V: 5000–2000 B.C. In North America the Archaic tradition developed its specializations in this period; the California Coast and Valley tradition appeared in the far west; and, possibly, the Northwest Riverine and Northwest Coast traditions began to emerge before the end of the period. In the Arctic a technological tradition known as the Arctic Small-Tool, apparently derived from the Siberian Mesolithic, spread from west to east. In the west, of course, the Desert tradition persisted in some areas, and in upland Mexico this Desert tradition underwent significant modification with the appearance and gradual increase in plant cultivation that we have frequently referred to as a condition of "incipient cultivation."

In South America this was the period of the "littoral" traditions, the coastal shellfish-collecting, fishing, and maritime cultures of the Pacific Littoral, Northwest South American Littoral, Sambaquí, and Fuegian traditions. All seem to have arisen in response to coastal adaptations beginning with the climatic optimum. Another contemporary modification of the old hunting cultures—in this case a plains-adapted one—was the Paraná-Pampean tradition.

A notable development of the last millennium of Period V was the appearance of pottery. This occurred in the context of the Northwest South American Littoral tradition. The origins of this pottery are debated; perhaps they resulted from a transpacific introduction. In any event, this Valdivian pottery tradition, as we have chosen to call it, developed and spread over the next 1000 years and was probably responsible for the "seeding" of the pottery idea in Peru, the western Amazon Basin, southern Mesoamerica, and even the southeastern United States.

Period VI: 2000 B.C.–A.D. *1500.* For North and Middle America the beginning date of this period was taken as the threshold of successful village agriculture in Mesoamerica and the beginnings, thereby, of the Mesoamerican cultural tradition. Farther afield the period saw the origins and rise of the Southwestern, Woodland, Mississippian, and Plains Village traditions—all fully or partially agricultural—and the full establishment of the Northwest Riverine, Northwest Coast, Denetasiro, and Eskimo traditions—all non-agricultural. In some areas, the non-agricultural Archaic (Boreal Archaic, Desert-Archaic), Desert, and California Coast and Valley traditions continued into or through the period.

In South America Period VI is the time horizon of the beginnings and development of the Peruvian, South Andean, Intermediate Area, Caribbean, and Amazonian traditions—all agricultural and founded on patterns of sedentary life. The later cultures of the East Brazilian Upland and Sambaquí traditions also belong to the period, as do those of the Paraná-Pampean and Fuegian traditions.

Period VII: A.D. 1500–Present. This is the European historic period in the New World. Its dominant theme is the breakup of pre-Columbian cultural traditions and their replacement by European ones. Native cultural traditions that were extant in A.D. 1500 persisted for varying lengths of time into the period and with varying results of acculturation. Among the last peoples of the western hemisphere to maintain cultures of essentially native patterns were certain Eskimo and northern North American groups and South American tribes of the Brazilian interior forests and of the Fuegian area; but by the last third of the twentieth century even these patterns were dying or changing rapidly.

Observations. It was observed at this same place in Volume One that our major

American periods are not ready devices for general hemisphere-wide cultural description, for there is a non-synchroneity about many important cultural changes when we view the entire New World as a whole. Nevertheless, the alignment of these synchronic perspectives is a preparatory step for the formulation of culture stage concepts.

Major American Culture Stages

Culture stages are defined by general similarity in cultural content and general level and intensity of cultural attainment. They are not formulations that explain culture process.[5] They are, rather, intended to describe points on a scale of culture change that can serve as a basis for inquiries into the whys and hows of culture development.

In Volume One (pp. 476–478) we projected a scheme of culture stages for the entire New World and indicated how the various cultural traditions of North and Middle America might be accomodated to such a scheme.[6] In what follows we will summarize what was said there and add to it the data of South America.

Lower Lithic Stage. This stage, like the Major Period I of our synchronic perspectives, treats of the putatively early rough percussion artifact assemblages of North and Middle America —the ones grouped under the term "Unnamed Technological Traditions" in our listing. In South America it pertains to the Flake, Chopper, and Biface traditions—again, putatively early. The overall time range thus begins at some point after 40,000 B.C. and continues to 20,000 B.C. or later. Just how much later raises the question of the technological lag or retention of such traditions. It has been my position in treating this problem in Chapter 2 that the demonstrably later pebble or cobble industries of the Argentine (Jabalí) and Chilean (Taltal) coasts, and other similar manifestations should not be included within these traditions because I doubt whether they are fully representative assemblages of the cultures concerned. Following this reasoning, they should not be included with the Lower Lithic stage.

It is assumed that the cultures of the Lower Lithic stage were those of hunters and gatherers whose food quest must have been relatively unspecialized.

Upper Lithic Stage. This stage was one of hunters equipped with bifacially chipped lanceolate projectile points and specialized butchering and skin-dressing tools. The hunters were those of the North American Big-Game Hunting and Old Cordilleran traditions and the Old South American Hunting tradition. It is also possible that the early beginnings of the East Brazilian Upland tradition should fall in this stage, although most of the stone technology seems more easily accommodated to the Lower Lithic.

If we use the criteria of prepared cores, blades, and the bifacial knife or point—in brief, the "Levallois-Mousterian" technology—as a marker for the Upper Lithic stage, and if we further ascribe such a technology to the Major American Period II, then we might argue that the Upper Lithic dates back to 20,000 B.C. in the New World. This, however, is a hypothetical reconstruction. The earliest well-dated complexes that belong to the stage are those of the hunting traditions referred to above, and these belong in the 10,000 to 8000 B.C. range. After 8000 B.C. the Upper Lithic stage began to give way to the Proto-Archaic.

We have argued that there were wide historical relationships among the cultural traditions of this Upper Lithic stage and that, for instance, the Old South American Hunting tradition was probably derived, via migrant hunters, from the North American Big-Game Hunting tradition.

Proto-Archaic Stage. Proto-Archaic peoples were, variously, hunters and gatherers, depending to a great extent upon environmental setting. A technological criterion of the stage is that of ground stone implements. Many or most of these are domestic utensils shaped from use— milling stones, handstones, mortars, pestles. The stage began during Major Period IV (8000–5000 B.C.) with the North American Archaic and Desert cultural traditions. In South America the earlier part of the East Brazilian Upland, Andean Hunting-Collecting, Sambaquí, and Northwest South American Littoral traditions belong to this stage. The earlier ranges of the Paraná-Pampean tradition would probably also fit best here, and all of the Fuegian tradition could be accommodated to it.

There were also some late persistences of the stage in North America, with the Great Basin and Baja California Desert tradition cultures and the Desert-Archaic cultures of Northeast Mexico–Texas lasting on until historic times with little change of technology or subsistence.

Although diffusion or migration contacts between North and South America cannot be ruled out, it is likely that the development of the South American Proto-Archaic stage traditions are largely independent of those of North America.

Full Archaic Stage. This stage represents a more settled existence than known heretofore in the Americas. For the most part, life was probably still semi-nomadic, but long portions of the year were spent in certain localities, especially in coastal lagoon and riverine sites that were well situated for shellfish collecting. Ground and polished stone implements, vessels, and ornaments are characteristic of the stage.

Full Archaic stage developments date to the beginning of the climatic optimum—to 5000 B.C. and after. The latter part of the North American Archaic tradition belongs on this stage as do the later cultures of the California Coast and Valley tradition, the Northwest Riverine tradition, and the Northwest Coast tradition. In South America the Pacific Littoral tradition, the latter part of the Northwest South American Littoral tradition, the later Sambaquí cultures, and the later Paraná-Pampean cultures can also be assigned to the stage. In general, the time span for the stage is 5000 to 2000 B.C., or our Major Period V; however, as is obvious from the traditions listed, there are continuities of the stage to historic times in both North and South America.

Pottery is found in a number of Full Archaic stage cultures. The Valdivia tradition pottery in the Northwest South American Littoral tradition context, the fibre-tempered pottery of the southeastern United States, and the Eastern Brazilian and Paraná tradition potteries are examples.

In some places we also have definite evidence that Full Archaic stage cultures were partially horticultural. Cultigens are commonly found in Pacific Littoral tradition levels in Peru; and in the uplands of Mesoamerica the later phases of the Desert tradition cultures show similar possession of domesticated plants. Elsewhere, as in the North-

west South American tradition cultures, Sambaquí tradition cultures, or Lower Paraná Valley cultures, such incipient cultivation is highly likely if not clearly demonstrable.

The degree to which certain stoneworking technologies are historically related among cultures of the Full Archaic stage is unknown. Those of western and eastern North America are not clearly linked, and there is even less to show for ties between North and South America. Consequently, the general assumption in this book has been that there is little or no relationship between the Full Archaic of the two continents; however, the possibilities of contacts cannot be completely discounted, for there is evidence that early pottery from northwestern South America may have stimulated pottery in eastern North America.

Agricultural Stage: Formative. This stage is defined by a threshold of subsistence agriculture.[7] Sedentary village life and ceramics occur as concomitants to the Agricultural stage although, as indicated above, they also appear during the previous stage in some instances.

The Mesoamerican, Southwestern, Mississippian, Plains Village, and Woodland traditions have all been cited as pertaining to the Agricultural stage. Of these, some earlier Woodland cultures and some marginal ones may be more appropriately assimilated to the Full Archaic tradition, depending upon interpretations of their agricultural status. For South America, the stage can be extended to include the Intermediate area tradition, the Peruvian tradition, the South Andean tradition, the Caribbean tradition, and the Amazonian tradition. Of these, the latter two featured manioc cultivation. The others, and all of the above-mentioned North and Middle American traditions, were primarily maize agricultural.

The stage generally dates from our Major Periods VI and VII, or from about 2000 B.C. into the historic period.

The basic plant elements of the Agricultural stage were widely diffused, so that there is a historical interconnection among the cultural traditions of the stage. However there are also indications that many of the same food plants may have been separately domesticated in Mesoamerica and Peru, two of the principal primary traditions in the origination of New World agriculture.

Manioc cultivation probably arose in the Caribbean tradition.

The Formative level of the Agricultural stage has been projected to subsume a wide range of settlement type and cultural intensity—from cultures with small permanent villages to those with sizable towns. Ceremonial architecture may vary from none to huge and elaborate structures, and art may vary from minor regional styles to styles of wide geographic range and monumental productions.[8]

Agricultural Stage: Classic. In Mesoamerica and in Peru the criterion of urban life has been used to define a Classic stage that in both areas begins at about the opening of the Christian era. The extent to which phenomena of this class and order are to be found in other area and cultural traditions is a moot point; however it is probable that this stage can be extended to Intermediate area tradition cultures of the Ecuadorian coast after A.D. 500.

Agricultural Stage: Postclassic. This stage is an epiphenomenon of the Classic, and it is characterized by further developments in urban forms, by an increase in large-scale warfare and empire building, and by a secularization of political control as opposed to earlier religious leadership. In Mesoamerica the changes heralding this stage come into being at about A.D. 700 with the collapse of the city of Teotihuacán and the rise of militaristic Toltecs. In Peru the chronology is about the same as the Tiahuanaco-Huari empire overran the Early Intermediate Period civilizations.

Concluding Remarks

In this chapter, as in the concluding chapter of Volume One, we have closed with a recapitulation of the major cultural and technological traditions whose histories we have followed in detail. In this case these traditions have pertained to South America. We have summarized their correlations with culture areas and with culture area chronologies. For this latter we have viewed the South American cultures from the perspective of a series of "Major American Periods," combining this view with the similar perspective offered by these same periods for North and Middle America. The reader is referred to Volume One (Chap. 8) and to the summary charts of cultural traditions and area chronologies for a comparison of the North and Middle American data with those of South America. Finally, a series of culture stages was projected for South America —and for the New World as a whole. These stages crosscut cultural traditions, culture areas, and chronological periods; they deal, instead, with general cultural types that may also be considered as levels of cultural development. We have not previously referred to these stages in this volume— just as we did not refer to them in the body of Volume One—but they are offered here as still another perspective on New World culture history and as a broad frame of reference for the consideration of problems of culture process.

As we observed at the outset, this book was written in the belief that the substance of New World culture history, imperfectly as we may know or interpret it, is of value as a part of the broader human history of the world at large. Archaeology in America, as elsewhere, is now at the point of an important reassessment of its goals and methods. With this reassessment will come a much greater understanding of the events of the buried past than we have ever had before. This book is intended to be a narrative summary of what we know now; its author hopes that it will serve as a point of departure for what we may yet come to know.

Footnotes

1 See Binford (1968 b) for an interesting worldwide comparative discussion of post-Pleistocene cultural changes and littoral adaptations. The Pacific Littoral tradition beginnings, as well as those of the other South American "littoral cultures," can be viewed in the light of his thesis.

2 Ford (1966, 1969).

3 Ford (1966, 1969).

4 As I did some time ago (Willey, 1949).

4a The newly discovered early complexes from the Ayacucho region caves (MacNeish, 1969, personal communication, 1970; see this volume, Chap. 2, fn. 22a) would fall in this period also.

5 See Willey and Phillips (1958, p. 200): "The stages are not formulations which *explain* culture change. Explanation, we believe, lies in the complex interplay of the multiple factors of natural environment, population densities and groupings, group and individual psychologies, and culture itself. Our culture-stage constructs are fashioned for the infinitely simpler purpose of describing types of cultures and the arrangement of these types in sequential order in the various parts of the New World." See Binford (1968 a, pp. 14–16) for a further and more detailed discussion of this; Binford, however, seems to feel that the Willey-Phillips scheme of stages did lay claim to "explanation."

6 A single scale of cultural stages for the entire New World—as outlined here and as previously proposed in Willey and Phillips (1958)—suggests a unilinear evolution of culture into which all cultures can be placed. Now it is quite evident that this does violence to the histories of New World cultures and that in one sense it would be more meaningful if such a stage classification, or classifications, were projected to assume a multilinear evolution of culture, taking into account the various natural environmental settings of the New World, their productive capacities, and the cultural ecologies that evolved within these settings. See, for example, J. J. Hester (1962). On the other hand, there are certain comparative advantages to the single-scale ranking. For still another consideration of the single-scale kind see Beardsley et al. (1956).

7 In connection with this definition see Volume One, Chapter 8, footnote 14. It is also to be noted that the term and concept "Formative" as used here differs from that of Ford (1966, 1969). Ford states that the Willey-Phillips definition of a Formative stage based on a neolithic-type food-production level, as applied to the Americas, "...is self-defeating, for it automatically excludes the coast-dwelling, seafaring people, who seem to be the prime agents of the spread of advanced culture traits." In his way of thinking, the "American Formative" is more usefully defined "...as the 3000 years preceding the Christian Era, during which Neolithic-level cultural elements were being diffused and added to the Paleolithic-level cultures that already existed" (Ford, 1966, p. 782). I would agree that this is a more useful definition if the problems to be considered are simply those of inter-American trait diffusion; however, the food-producing level definition, as offered in Willey and Phillips (1958) and in this present work, is equally useful for other purposes of cultural comparison of a functional rather than a strictly historic-diffusional sort. The reader is referred to Reichel-Dolmatoff's (1959) distinction between the "Developmental Formative" concept (the Willey-Phillips one) and the "Correlative Formative" concept (similar to Ford's).

8 For example, Hester's subdivisional treatment of the Formative.

Alcina Franch, José (1965), *Manual de Arqueología Americana,* Aguilar, S.A., Madrid.

Alegría, R. E. (1951), "The Ball Game Played by the Aborigines of the Antilles," *American Antiquity,* Vol. 16, pp. 348–352, Menasha, Wisconsin.

Alegría, R. E. (1965), "On Puerto Rican Archaeology," *American Antiquity,* Vol. 31, No. 2, pp. 246–249, Salt Lake City.

Alegría, Ricardo, H. B. Nicholson, and G. R. Willey (1955), "The Archaic Tradition in Puerto Rico," *American Antiquity,* Vol. 21, No. 2, pp. 113–121, Salt Lake City.

Ambrosetti, J. B. (1895), "Los cementerios prehistóricos del Alto Paraná, Misiones," *Boletín del Instituto Geográfico Argentino,* Vol. 16, pp. 227–263, Buenos Aires.

Ambrosetti, J. B. (1897), "Los monumentos megalíticos del Valle de Tafí," *Boletín del Instituto Geográfico Argentino,* Vol. 18, Nos. 1–3, pp. 105–114, Buenos Aires.

Ambrosetti, J. B. (1906), *Exploraciones arqueológicas en Pampa Grande,* Publicaciones de la Sección Antropológica, No. 1, Facultad de Filosofía y Letras, Universidad de Buenos Aires, Buenos Aires.

Ameghino, Florentino (1911), "Une nouvelle industrie lithique. L'industrie de la pierre fendue dans le Tertiare de la région littorale au sud de Mar del Plata," *Anales, Museo Nacional de Buenos Aires,* Vol. 20, pp. 189–204, Buenos Aires.

Angulo Valdés, Carlos (1962), "Evidence of the Barrancoid Series in Northern Colombia," in *The Caribbean: Contemporary Colombia,* A. C. Wilgus, ed., pp. 35–46, University of Florida, Gainesville.

Angulo Valdés, Carlos (1963), "Cultural development in Colombia," in *Aboriginal Cultural Development in Latin America: An Interpretative Review,* B. J. Meggers and C. Evans, eds., pp. 55–66, Smithsonian Miscellaneous Collections, Vol. 146, No. 1, Smithsonian Institution, Washington, D.C.

Aparicio, Francisco de (1928), "Notas para el estudio de la arqueología del sur de Entre Ríos," *Anales, Facultad de Ciencias y Educación,* Vol. 3, pp. 1–63, Paraná, Argentina.

Aparicio, Francisco de (1935), "Viaje preliminar de exploración en el territorio de Santa Cruz," *Publicaciones, Museo de Antropología y Etnografía,* Ser. A, Vol. 3, pp. 37–92, Buenos Aires.

Aparicio, Francisco de (1936), "La antigua provincia de los Comechingones," *Historia de la Nación Argentina,* La Junta de Historia y Numismática, eds., Vol. 1, pp. 389–428, Buenos Aires.

Aparicio, Francisco de (1946), "The Comechingón and Their Neighbors

Bibliography

of the Sierras de Córdoba," in *Handbook of South American Indians,* J. H. Steward, ed., Vol. 2, pp. 676–686, Bureau of American Ethnology, Bulletin 143, Smithsonian Institution, Washington, D.C.

Aparicio, Francisco de (1948), "The Archaeology of the Paraná River," in *Handbook of South American Indians,* J. H. Steward, ed., Vol. 3, pp. 57–68, Bureau of American Ethnology, Bulletin 143, Smithsonian Institution, Washington, D.C.

Arnold, B. A. (1957), *Late Pleistocene and Recent Changes in Land Forms, Climate, and Archaeology in Central Baja California,* University of California Publications in Geography, Vol. 10, No. 4, Berkeley and Los Angeles.

Arredondo, Horacio (1927), "Informe preliminar sobre la arqueología de la boca del Río Negro," *Revista Sociedad "Amigos de Arqueología,"* Vol. 1, pp. 7–45, Montevideo.

Austral, A. G. (1968), "Prehistoria del Sur de la Región Pampeana," *37th International Congress of Americanists,* Vol. 3, pp. 325–338, Buenos Aires.

Badano, V. M. (1955), "Carácteres del arte plástico indígena del Paraná inferior," *31st International Congress of Americanists,* Vol. 2, pp. 777–800, São Paulo.

Barfield, Lawrence (1961), "Recent Discoveries in the Atacama Desert and the Bolivian Altiplano," *American Antiquity,* Vol. 27, No. 1, pp. 93–100, Salt Lake City.

Barth, Frederik (1948), "Cultural Development in Southern South America: Yahgan and Alakaluf vs. Ona and Tehuelche," *Acta Americana,* Vol. 6, pp. 192*ff.*, Sociedad Interamericana de Antropología y Geografía, México, D.F.

Baudez, C. F. (1963), "Cultural Development in Lower Central America," in *Aboriginal Cultural Development in Latin America: An Interpretative Review,* B. J. Meggers and C. Evans, eds., pp. 45–54, Smithsonian Miscellaneous Collections, Vol. 146, No. 1,

Smithsonian Institution, Washington, D.C.

Baudez, C. F. (1966), "Niveaux céramiques au Honduras: une reconsidération de l'évolution culturelle," *Journal de la Société des Américanistes,* Vol. 55, No. 2, pp. 299–342, Paris.

Baudez, C. F. (1967), *Recherches Archéologiques dans la Vallée du Tempisque, Guanacaste, Costa Rica,* Travaux et Mémoires de l'Institut des Hautes Etudes de l'Amérique Latine, No. 18, Paris.

Baudez, C. F. (1970), *Central America,* Archaeologia Mundi, Nägel, Geneva, Paris, and Munich.

Baudez, C. F. and Pierre Becquelin (1969), "La Séquence Céramique de Los Naranjos, Honduras," *38th International Congress of Americanists,* Vol. 1, pp. 221–228, Stuttgart and Munich.

Baudez, C. F. and M. D. Coe (1962), "Archaeological Sequences in Northwestern Costa Rica," *Akten, 34th International Congress of Americanists,* pp. 366–373, Vienna.

Baudez, C. F. and M. D. Coe (1966), "Incised Slate Disks from the Atlantic Watershed of Costa Rica: A Commentary," *American Antiquity,* Vol. 31, No. 3, pp. 441–444, Salt Lake City.

Beardsley, R. K., et al. (1956), "Functional and Evolutionary Implications of Community Patterning," in *Seminars in Archaeology: 1955,* R. Wauchope, ed., Memoir No. 11, pp. 129–157, Society for American Archaeology, Menasha, Wisconsin.

Bell, R. E. (1965), *Archaeological Investigations at the Site of El Inga, Ecuador* (bound together with Spanish version), Casa de la Cultura Ecuatoriana, Quito.

Bennett, W. C. (1934), *Excavations at Tiahuanaco,* Anthropological Papers, Vol. 34, Pt. 3, pp. 359–494, American Museum of Natural History, New York.

Bennett, W. C. (1936), *Excavations in Bolivia,* Anthropological Papers, Vol. 35, Pt. 4, American Museum of Natural History, New York.

Bennett, W. C. (1937), *Excavations at La Mata, Maracay, Venezuela,* Anthropological Papers, Vol. 36,

Pt. 2, American Museum of Natural History, New York.

Bennett, W. C. (1939), *Archaeology of the North Coast of Peru,* Anthropological Papers, Vol. 37, Pt. 1, pp. 1–153, American Museum of Natural History, New York.

Bennett, W. C. (1943), "The Position of Chavín in Andean Sequences," *Proceedings of the American Philosophical Society,* Vol. 86, pp. 323–327, Philadelphia.

Bennett, W. C. (1944 a), *The North Highlands of Peru: Excavations in the Callejón de Huaylas and at Chavín de Huántar,* Anthropological Papers, Vol. 39, Pt. 1, American Museum of Natural History, New York.

Bennett, W. C. (1944 b), *Archaeological Regions of Colombia: A Ceramic Survey,* Yale University Publications in Anthropology, No. 30, New Haven.

Bennett, W. C. (1946 a), "The Andean Highlands: An Introduction," in *Handbook of South American Indians,* J. H. Steward, ed., Vol. 2, pp. 1–60, Bureau of American Ethnology, Bulletin 143, Smithsonian Institution, Washington, D.C.

Bennett, W. C. (1946 b), "The Archaeology of the Central Andes," in *Handbook of South American Indians,* J. H. Steward, ed., Vol. 2, pp. 61–148, Bureau of American Ethnology, Bulletin 143, Smithsonian Institution, Washington, D.C.

Bennett, W. C. (1946 c), "The Atacameño," in *Handbook of South American Indians,* J. H. Steward, ed., Vol. 2, pp. 599–618, Bureau of American Ethnology, Bulletin 143, Smithsonian Institution, Washington, D.C.

Bennett, W. C. (1946 d), *Excavations in the Cuenca Region, Ecuador,* Yale University Publications in Anthropology, No. 35, New Haven.

Bennett, W. C. (1946 e), "The Archaeology of Colombia," in *Handbook of South American Indians,* J. H. Steward, ed., Vol. 1, pp. 823–850, Bureau of American Ethnology, Bulletin 143,

Smithsonian Institution, Washington, D.C.

Bennett, W. C. (1948 a), "The Peruvian Co-Tradition," in *A Reappraisal of Peruvian Archaeology,* W. C. Bennett, ed., Memoir No. 4, pp. 1–7, Society for American Archaeology, Menasha, Wisconsin.

Bennett, W. C. (1948 b), "A Revised Sequence for the South Titicaca Basin," in *A Reappraisal of Peruvian Archaeology,* W. C. Bennett, ed., Memoir No. 4, pp. 90–92, Society for American Archaeology, Menasha, Wisconsin.

Bennett, W. C. (1950), *The Gallinazo Group, Virú Valley, Peru,* Yale University Publications in Anthropology, No. 43, New Haven.

Bennett, W. C. (1953), *Excavations at Wari, Ayacucho, Peru,* Yale University Publications in Anthropology, No. 49, New Haven.

Bennett, W. C. and J. B. Bird (1964), *Andean Culture History,* 2nd and rev. ed., American Museum of Natural History and The Natural History Press, Garden City, New York.

Bennett, W. C., E. F. Bleiler, and F. H. Sommer (1948), *Northwest Argentine Archaeology,* Yale University Publications in Anthropology, No. 38, New Haven.

Benzoni, Girolamo (1857), *History of the New World,* W. H. Smith, trans. and ed., Hakluyt Society, No. 21, London.

Berberían, E. E., H. A. Calandra, and Pablo Sacchero (1966), "Primeros secuencias estratigráficas para San Juan (Rep. Argentina), La cueva de El Peñoncito, Dto. Jáchal," mimeogr. and distr., *37th International Congress of Americanists,* Mar del Plata, Argentina.

Berdichewsky, Bernardo (1964 a), "Arqueología de la desembocadura del Aconcagua y zonas vecinas de la costa central de Chile," in *Arqueología de Chile Central y Areas Vecinas,* Publicación de los Trabajos Presentados al Tercer Congreso Internacional de Arqueología Chilena, pp. 69–107, Imprenta "Los Andes," Santiago.

Berdichewsky, Bernardo (1964 b),

"Informe preliminar de las excavaciones arqueológicas en Concón," *Antropología,* Vol. 2, pp. 65–86, Centro de Estudios Antropológicos, Universidad de Chile, Santiago.

Berdichewsky, Bernardo (1965), "Exploración arqueológica en la costa de la Provincia de Antofagasta," *Antropología,* Vol. 3, No. 1, pp. 3–30, Centro de Estudios Antropológicos, Universidad de Chile, Santiago.

Berdichewsky, Bernardo (1968), "Excavaciones en la 'cueva de los Catalanes,'" *Boletín de Prehistoria de Chile,* Vol. 1, No. 1, pp. 33–84, Departmento de Historia, Facultad de Filosofía y Educación, Universidad de Chile, Santiago.

Bergsland, Knut and Hans Vogt (1962), "On the Validity of Glottochronology," *Current Anthropology,* Vol. 3, No. 2, pp. 115–153 (including various readers' comments), University of Chicago, Chicago.

Bergsøe, Paul (1937), "The Metallurgy and Technology of Gold and Platinum among Pre-Columbian Indians," *Ingeniorvidenskabelige Skrifter,* Nr. A 44, Copenhagen.

Biese, L. P. (1964), "The Prehistory of Panama Viejo," *Anthropological Papers,* No. 68, pp. 3–51, Bureau of American Ethnology, Bulletin 191, Smithsonian Institution, Washington, D.C.

Binford, L. R. (1968 a), "Archaeological Perspectives," in *New Perspectives in Archaeology,* S. R. and L. R. Binford, eds., pp. 5–32, Aldine Publishing Co., Chicago.

Binford, L. R. (1968 b), "Post-Pleistocene Adaptations," in *New Perspectives in Archaeology,* S. R. and L. R. Binford, eds., pp. 313–341, Aldine Publishing Co., Chicago.

Bird, J. B. (1938), "Antiquity and Migrations of the Early Inhabitants of Patagonia," *The Geographical Review,* Vol. 28, No. 2, pp. 250–275, New York.

Bird, J. B. (1943), *Excavations in Northern Chile,* Anthropological Papers, Vol. 38, Pt. 4, American Museum of Natural History, New

York.

Bird, J. B. (1946 a), "The Historic Inhabitants of the North Chilean Coast," in *Handbook of South American Indians,* J. H. Steward, ed., Vol. 2, pp. 595–598, Bureau of American Ethnology, Bulletin 143, Smithsonian Institution, Washington, D.C.

Bird, J. B. (1946 b), "The Archaeology of Patagonia," in *Handbook of South American Indians,* J. H. Steward, ed., Vol. 1, pp. 17–24, Bureau of American Ethnology, Bulletin 143, Smithsonian Institution, Washington, D.C.

Bird, J. B. (1946 c), "The Cultural Sequence of the North Chilean Coast," in *Handbook of South American Indians,* J. H. Steward, ed., Vol. 2, pp. 587–594, Bureau of American Ethnology, Bulletin 143, Smithsonian Institution, Washington, D.C.

Bird, J. B. (1946 d), "The Alacaluf," in *Handbook of South American Indians,* J. H. Steward, ed., Vol. 1, pp. 55–80, Bureau of American Ethnology, Bulletin 143, Smithsonian Institution, Washington, D.C.

Bird, J. B. (1948), "Preceramic Cultures in Chicama and Virú," in *A Reappraisal of Peruvian Archaeology,* W. C. Bennett, ed., Society for American Archaeology, Memoir No. 4, pp. 21–28, Menasha, Wisconsin.

Bird, J. B. (1951), "South American Radiocarbon Dates," in *Radiocarbon Dating,* F. Johnson, ed., Memoir No. 8, pp. 37–49, Society for American Archaeology, Salt Lake City.

Bird, J. B. (1963), "Pre-Ceramic Art from Huaca Prieta, Chicama Valley," *Ñawpa Pacha,* Vol. 1, pp. 29–34, Institute of Andean Studies, Berkeley.

Bird, J. B. (1965), "The Concept of a 'Pre-Projectile Point' Cultural Stage in Chile and Peru," *American Antiquity,* Vol. 31, No. 2, pp. 262–270, Salt Lake City.

Bird, J. B. (1970), "Paleo-Indian Discoidal Stones from Southern South America," *American Antiquity,* Vol. 35, No. 2, pp. 205–208, Salt Lake City.

Birdsell, J. B. (1951), "The Problem of the Early Peopling of the Americas As Viewed from Asia," in *Papers on the Physical Anthropology of the American Indian,* W. S. Laughlin, ed., pp. 1–68, The Viking Fund, New York.

Biro de Stern, Ana (1944), "Hallazgos de alfarería decorada en el Territorio del Chaco," *Relaciones, Sociedad Argentina de Antropología,* Vol. 4, pp. 157–161, Buenos Aires.

Bischof, Henning (1966), "Canapote — An Early Ceramic Site in Northern Colombia. Preliminary Report," *Actas y Memorias, 36th International Congress of Americanists,* Vol. 1, pp. 484–491, Seville.

Blasi, Oldemar (1957), "Notes on the Shell Mounds of the Coast of Paraná, Brazil," *Museum News,* Vol. 18, No. 10, Vermillion, South Dakota.

Blasi, Oldemar (1963), "Cronología absoluta e relativa do Sambaquí do Macedo-Alexandra 52.13-Paraná-Brasil," *Arquivos do Museu Paranaense, Arqueología,* No. 1, Curitiba, Paraná, Brazil.

Blasi, Oldemar (1965), "Os indícos arqueológicos do Barrãcao e Dionísio Cerquerira, Paraná-Santa Catarina," *Arquivos do Museu Paranaense, Arqueología,* No. 2, Curitiba, Paraná, Brazil.

Blasi, Oldemar (1966), "Investigações arqueológicas nas ruinas da Redução Jesuita de Santo Inácio do Ipaumbucu ou Mini, Paraná, Brasil-Nota Previa," *Actas y Memorias, 36th International Congress of Americanists,* Vol. 1, pp. 473–480, Seville.

Boggiani, Guido (1900), "Compendio de etnografía Paraguaya moderna," *Revista Instituto Paraguayo,* Vol. 3, Nos. 23–25, 27, 28, Asunción.

Boman, Eric (1908), *Antiquités de la Région Andine de la République Argentine et du Désert D'Atacama,* Vols. 1, 2, Paris.

Boman, Eric (1920), "Cementerio indígena en Viluco (Mendoza) posterior a la conquista," *Anales, Museo Nacional de Historia Natural,* Vol. 30, pp. 501–560, Buenos Aires.

Bonaparte, J. F. and J. A. Pisano

(1950), "Dos nuevos paraderos indígenas neolíticos de la cuenca del Rio Julan," *Arqueología,* No. 1, Museo Popular de Ciencias Naturales, Buenos Aires.

Bonavía, Duccio (1966), "Excavations of Early Sites in South Peru," *Current Anthropology,* Vol. 7, p. 97, Wenner-Gren Foundation, Chicago.

Borhegyi, S. F. (1959), "Pre-Columbian Cultural Connections between Mesoamerica and Ecuador," *Middle American Research Records,* Vol. 2, No. 6, Tulane University, New Orleans.

Borhegyi, S. F. (1960), "Pre-Columbian Cultural Connections between Mesoamerica and Ecuador: Addenda," *Middle American Research Records,* Vol. 2, No. 7, Tulane University, New Orleans.

Bórmida, Marcelo (1962 a), "El Jabaliense, una industria de guijarros de la Península de San Blas, Provincia de Buenos Aires, Republica de Argentina," *Trabajos de Prehistoria del Hombre de la Universidad de Madrid,* Vol. 6, pp. 7–54, Madrid.

Bórmida, Marcelo (1962 b), "El Epiprotolítico Epígonal de la Pampa Bonaerense," *Jornadas Internacionales de Arqueología y Etnografía,* No. 2, pp. 113–132, Universidad de Buenos Aires, Buenos Aires.

Bórmida, Marcelo (1964 a), "Las industrias líticas pre-cerámicas del Arroyo Catalán Chico y del Río Cuareim," *Rivista di Scienze Preistoriche,* Vol. 19, Fasc. 1–4, Stamperia Editoriale F.lli Parenti di G., Florence.

Bórmida, Marcelo (1964 b), "El cuareimense," in *Homenaje a Fernando Márquez-Miranda,* pp. 105–128, Ediciones Castilla, S.A., Madrid and Seville.

Bórmida, Marcelo (1968), "Arqueologia de las Altas Cotas de La Costa Norpatagónica," *37th International Congress of Americanists,* Vol. 3, pp. 345–374, Buenos Aires.

Bovallius, Carl (1886), *Nicaraguan Antiquities,* Kongl. Boktryckeriet, Stockholm.

Bray, W. M. (1965), "Archaeology of the Middle Cauca Valley, Central Andes, Colombia," in *Year*

Book of the American Philosophical Society, 1965, pp. 485–487, Philadelphia.

Bray, W. M., J. W. L. Robinson, and A. R. Bridgman (1968), "The Cauca Valley Expedition 1964," *Explorer's Journal,* Vol. 46, No. 1, New York.

Bregante, Odilla (1926), *Ensayo de Clasificación de la Cerámica del Noroeste Argentino,* Angel Estrada Cia., Buenos Aires.

Broadbent, S. M. (1962), "Excavaciones en Tunjuelito: Informe Preliminar," *Revista Colombiana de Antropología,* Vol. 10, pp. 343–346, Bogotá.

Broadbent, S. M. (1964), "Agricultural Terraces in Chibcha Territory, Colombia," *American Antiquity,* Vol. 23, No. 4, pp. 501–504, Salt Lake City.

Broadbent, S. M. (1965 a), "Investigaciónes arqueológicas en el territorio Chibcha," *Antropología,* Estudios de la Universidad de los Andes, No. 1, Bogotá.

Broadbent, S. M. (1965 b), "Stone-Roofed Chambers in Chibcha Territory, Colombia," *Nawpa Pacha,* No. 3, pp. 93–106, Institute of Andean Studies, Berkeley.

Broadbent, S. M. (1966), "The Site of Chibcha Bogotá," *Nawpa Pacha,* No. 4, pp. 1–13, Institute of Andean Studies, Berkeley.

Broadbent, S. M. (1969), "Prehistoric Chronology in the Sabana de Bogotá," *Kroeber Anthropological Society Papers,* No. 40, pp. 38–51, Kroeber Anthropological Society, Berkeley.

Bronson, Bennett (1966), "Roots and the Subsistence of the Ancient Maya," *Southwestern Journal of Anthropology,* Vol. 22, No. 3, pp. 251–279, University of New Mexico, Albuquerque, New Mexico.

Brown, C. Barrington (1926), "On Stone Implements from Northwest Peru," *Man,* No. 26, pp. 97–101, London.

Bruch, Carlos (1913), "Exploraciones arqueológicas en las Provincias de Tucumán y Catamarca," *Revista del Museo de La Plata,* Vol. 19, pp. 1–209, La Plata, Argentina.

Brush, C. F. (1965), "Pox Pottery: Earliest Identified Mexican Ceramic," *Science,* Vol. 149, pp. 194–195, Lancaster, Pennsylvania.

Bryan, A. L. (1965), *Paleo-American Prehistory,* Occasional Papers, No. 16, Idaho State University Museum, Pocatello, Idaho.

Bryan, A. L. (1969), "Early Man in America and the Late Pleistocene Chronology of Western Canada and Alaska," *Current Anthropology,* Vol. 10, No. 4, pp. 339–367, Wenner-Gren Foundation, Chicago.

Bullbrook, J. A. (1953), *On the Excavation of a Shell Mound at Palo Seco, Trinidad, B.W.I.,* Yale University Publications in Anthropology, No. 50, New Haven.

Bullen, R. P. (1962 a), "The Preceramic Krum Bay Site, Virgin Islands, and Its Relationship to the Peopling of the Caribbean," *Akten, 34th International Congress of Americanists,* pp. 398–403, Vienna.

Bullen, R. P. (1962 b), *Ceramic Periods of St. Thomas and St. John Islands, Virgin Islands,* W. L. Bryant Foundation, American Studies, Report No. 4, Maitland, Florida.

Bullen, R. P. (1964), *The Archaeology of Grenada, West Indies,* Contributions, Florida State Museum, Social Sciences, No. 11, Gainesville, Florida.

Bullen, R. P. (1965), "Archaeological Chronology of Grenada," *American Antiquity,* Vol. 31, No. 2, pp. 237–241, Salt Lake City.

Bullen, R. P. and A. K. (1968), "Barbados Archaeology: 1966," in *Second International Congress for the Study of Pre-Columbian Cultures in the Lesser Antilles,* mimeogr., pp. 135–146, Barbados.

Bullen, R. P. and W. W. Plowden (1963), "Preceramic Archaic Sites in the Highlands of Honduras," *American Antiquity,* Vol. 28, No. 3, pp. 382–386, Salt Lake City.

Bullen, R. P. and F. W. Sleight (1963), *The Krum Bay Site, A Preceramic Site on St. Thomas, United States Virgin Islands,* W. L. Bryant Foundation, American Studies, Report No. 5, Central Florida Museum, Orlando, Florida.

Bullock, D. S. (1936), "Dos estatuas de piedra de Angol," *Revista Chilena de Historia Natural,* Vol. 40, pp. 259–264, Santiago.

Bullock, D. S. (1955), *Urnas Funerarias Prehistóricas de La Región de Angol,* Boletín, Museo Nacional de Historia Natural, Vol. 26, No. 5, Santiago.

Bürgl, Hans (1958), "Artefactos paleolíticos de una tumba en Garzón (Huila)," *Revista Colombiana de Antropología,* Vol. 6, pp. 7–28, Bogotá.

Bushnell, G. H. S. (1951), *The Archaeology of the Santa Elena Peninsula in South-West Ecuador,* Occasional Papers, No. 1, Cambridge Museum, Cambridge, England.

Bushnell, G. H. S. (1952), "The Stone Carvings of Manabí, Ecuador," *Proceedings, 30th International Congress of Americanists,* pp. 58–59, Royal Anthropological Institute, London.

Bushnell, G. H. S. (1963), *Peru,* rev. ed., in Ancient Peoples and Places Series, G. Daniel, ed., Frederick A. Praeger, New York.

Butler, B. R. (1961), *The Old Cordilleran Culture in the Pacific Northwest,* Occasional Papers, No. 5, Idaho State University Museum, Pocatello, Idaho.

Butler, B. R. (1962), *Contribution to the Prehistory of the Colombia Plateau,* Occasional Papers, No. 9, Idaho State University Museum, Pocatello, Idaho.

Butler, B. R. (1965), "The Structure and Function of the Old Cordilleran Concept," *American Anthropologist,* Vol. 67, No. 5, pp. 1120–1131, Menasha, Wisconsin.

Butler, B. R. (1966), "Comments on Prehistory," in *The Current Status of Anthropological Research in the Great Basin: 1964,* W. L. d'Azevedo *et al.,* eds., pp. 299–304, Desert Research Institute, Social Sciences and Humanities Publications No. 1, Reno, Nevada.

Calderón, Valentin (1964), *O sambaquí da Pedra Oca,* Instituto de Ciencias Sociais, No. 2, Universidade da Bahía, Salvador (cited from PRONAPA, 1970).

Calderón, Valentin (1967), "Noticia preliminar sobre as seqüencias arqueológicas do médio São Francisco e da Chapada Diamantina, Estado da Bahía," *Programa Nacional de Pesquisas Arqueológicas; Resultados Preliminares do Primeiro Ano 1965–1966,* Museu Paraense Emílio Goeldi, Publicações Avulsas, No. 6, pp. 107–120, Belém do Pará, Brazil.

Campá-Soler, Raúl (1967), "Antecedentes y relación sintética de los trabajos conducentes a la localización de los estratos culturales básicos de prehistoria Uruguaya," *Revista Mexicana de Estudios Antropológicos,* Vol. 21, pp. 363–397, Sociedad Mexicana de Antropología, México, D.F.

Campá-Soler, Raúl, A. Taddei, and J. Chebataroff (1959), "Horizontes precerámicos en El Uruguay," *Actas, 33rd International Congress of Americanists,* Vol. 2, pp. 378–381, San José, Costa Rica.

Campá-Soler, Raúl and Daniel Vidart (1962), "La cultura precerámica del Catalán," *Amerindia,* No. 1, pp. 85–113, Montevideo.

Canals Frau, Salvador (1946 a), "The Huarpe," in *Handbook of South American Indians,* J. H. Steward, ed., Vol. 1, pp. 169–176, Bureau of American Ethnology, Bulletin 143, Smithsonian Institution, Washington, D.C.

Canals Frau, Salvador (1946 b), "The Expansion of the Araucanians into Argentina," in *Handbook of South American Indians,* J. H. Steward, ed., Vol. 2, pp. 761–766, Bureau of American Ethnology, Bulletin 143, Smithsonian Institution, Washington, D.C.

Canals Frau, Salvador and Juan Semper (1956), "La cultura de Agrelo (Mendoza)," *Runa,* Vol. 7, Pt. 2, pp. 169–187, Archivo para la Ciencia del Hombre, Universidad de Buenos Aires, Buenos Aires.

Canby, J. S. (1951), "Possible Chronological Implications of the Long Ceramic Sequence Recovered at Yarumela, Spanish Honduras," *Selected Papers, 29th International Congress of Americanists,* Vol. 1, pp. 79–85, University of Chicago Press, Chicago.

Cardich, Augusto (1958), *Los Yacimientos de Lauricocha: Nuevas*

Interpretaciones de la Prehistoria Peruana, Studia Praehistorica I, Centro Argentino de Estudios Prehistóricos, Buenos Aires.

Cardich, Augusto (1960), "Investigaciones prehistóricas en los Andes Peruanos," in *Antiguo Peru: Tiempo y Espacio,* pp. 89–118, Librería-Editorial Juan Mejía Baca, Lima.

Cardich, Augusto (1962), "Ranracancha: un sitio prehistórico en el Departamento de Pasco, Perú," *Acta Praehistorica,* Vols. 3–4, pp. 35–48, Centro Argentino de Estudios Prehistóricos, Buenos Aires.

Cardich, Augusto (1964), *Lauricocha, Fundamentos para una Prehistoria de los Andes Centrales,* Studia Praehistorica III, Centro Argentino de Estudios Prehistóricos, Buenos Aires.

Carluci de Santiana, M. A. (1963), "Puntas de proyectil. Tipos, técnica, y áreas de distribución en El Ecuador andino," *Humanitas,* Boletín Ecuatoriano de Antropología, Vol. 4, No. 1, pp. 5–56, Quito.

Carluci de Santiana, M. A. (1966), "Recientes investigaciones arqueológicas en la Isla de La Plata (Ecuador)," *Humanitas,* Boletín Ecuatoriano de Antropología, Vol. 6, No. 1, pp. 33–66, Quito.

Carneiro, R. L. (1961), "Slash-and-Burn Cultivation Among the Kuikuru and Its Implications for Cultural Development in the Amazon Basin," in *The Evolution of Horticultural Systems in Native South America, Causes and Consequences,* J. Wilbert, ed., pp. 47–68, Sociedad de Ciencias Naturales La Salle, Carácas.

Carrión Cachot, Rebecca (1948), "La Cultura Chavín, Dos Nuevas Colonias: Kuntur Wasi y Ancón," *Revista, Museo Nacional de Antropología y Arqueología,* Vol. 2, No. 1, pp. 97–172, Lima.

Casanova, Eduardo (1938), "Investigaciones arqueológicas en Sorcuyo (Puna de Jujuy)," *Anales, Museo Argentino de Ciencias Naturales,* Vol. 39, pp. 423–456, Buenos Aires.

Casanova, Eduardo (1942) "Exégsis. Los aborígenes de Santiago del Estero," *Relaciones de la*

Sociedad Argentina de Antropología, Vol. 2, pp. 171–182, Buenos Aires.

Casanova, Eduardo (1946), "The Cultures of the Puna and the Quebrada de Humuhuaca," in *Handbook of South American Indians,* Vol. 2, pp. 619–632, Bureau of American Ethnology, Bulletin 143, Smithsonian Institution, Washington, D.C.

Chard, C. S. (1959), "New World Origins: A Reappraisal," *Antiquity,* Vol. 33, No. 129, pp. 44–49, London and Tunbridge.

Chard, C. S. (1963), "The Old World Roots: Review and Speculations," *Anthropological Papers, University of Alaska,* Vol. 10, No. 2, Fairbanks.

Chmyz, Igor (1967), "Dados parciais sôbre a arqueologia do vale do río Paranapanema," *Programa Nacional de Pesquisas Arqueológicas; Resultados Preliminares do Primeiro Ano 1965–1966,* Museu Paraense Emílio Goeldi, Publicações Avulsas, No. 6, pp. 59–78, Belém do Pará, Brazil.

Cieza de Leon, Pedro de (1864), *The Travels of Pedro de Cieza de Leon, A.D. 1532–1550, Contained in the First Part of His Chronicle of Peru,* Hakluyt Society, No. 33, London.

Cieza de Leon, Pedro de (1880), *Segunda Parte de la Crónica del Perú,* Biblioteca Hispano–Ultra Marina, Vol. 5, Madrid.

Cigliano, E. M. (1959–60), "Nuevos aportes sobre las primeras culturas alfarero-agrícolas del Valle de Santa María," *Acta Praehistorica,* Vols. 3–4, pp. 150–152, Centro Argentino de Estudios Prehistóricos, Buenos Aires.

Cigliano, E. M. (1961), "Noticia sobre una nueva industria precerámica en el Valle de Santa María (Catamarca): El Ampajanguense," *Anales de Arqueología y Etnología,* Vol. 16, pp. 169–179, Facultad de Filosofía y Letras, Universidad Nacional de Cuyo, Mendoza, Argentina.

Cigliano, E. M. (1962 a), *El Ampajanguense,* Publicación No. 5, Instituto de Antropología, Universidad Nacional de Litoral, Rosario, Argentina.

Cigliano, E. M. (1962 b), "Indus-

trias precerámicas de la Puna Argentina," *Ampurias,* Vol. 24, pp. 1–34, Barcelona.

Cigliano, E. M. (1964), "El precerámico en el N.W. Argentino," in *Arqueología de Chile Central y Areas Vecinas,* Publicación de los Trabajos Presentados al Tercer Congreso Internacional de Arqueología Chilena, pp. 191–198, Imprenta "Los Andes," Santiago.

Cigliano, E. M. (1965), "Dos nuevos sitios precerámicos en la Puna de Argentina: Turilar, Departamento de Susques, Provincia de Jujuy," *Etnía,* No. 2, Article 11, pp. 6–8, Museo Etnográfico Municipal "Dámaso Arce," Olavarría, Buenos Aires.

Cigliano, E. M. (1966 a), "La cerámica temprana en America del Sur. El yacimiento de Palo Blanco (Partido de Berisso, Prov. de Buenos Aires, Argentina)," *Ampurias,* Vol. 28, pp. 163–170, Barcelona.

Cigliano, E. M. (1966 b), "Contribución a los fechados radiocarbónicos Argentinos (I)," *Revista, Museo de La Plata* (n.s.), Vol. 6, pp. 1–16, La Plata, Argentina.

Cigliano, E. M. and H. A. Calandre (1965), "Hallazgos arqueológicos en La Quebrada de Zapagua, Departamento de Humahuaca, Provincia de Jujuy," *Anales de Arqueología y Etnología y Etnología,* Vol. 20, pp. 27–36, Facultad de Filosofía y Letras, Universidad Nacional de Cuyo, Mendoza, Argentina.

Cobo, Bernabe (1890–95), *Historia del Nuevo Mundo,* Sociedad de Bibliófilos Andaluces, Seville.

Coe, M. D. (1960 a), "A Fluted Point from Highland Guatemala," *American Antiquity,* Vol. 25, pp. 412–413, Salt Lake City.

Coe, M. D. (1960 b), "Archaeological Linkages with North and South America at La Victoria, Guatemala," *American Anthropologist,* Vol. 62, pp. 363–393, Menasha, Wisconsin.

Coe, M. D. (1961), *La Victoria, an Early Site on the Pacific Coast of Guatemala,* Peabody Museum Papers, Vol. 53, Harvard University, Cambridge.

Coe, M. D. (1962 a), "Costa Rican

Archaeology and Mesoamerica," *Southwestern Journal of Anthropology,* Vol. 18, No. 2, Albuquerque, New Mexico.

Coe, M. D. (1962 b), "An Olmec Design on an Early Peruvian Vessel," *American Antiquity,* Vol. 27, No. 4, pp. 579–580, Salt Lake City.

Coe, M. D. (1963), "Olmec and Chavín: Rejoinder to Lanning," *American Antiquity,* Vol. 29, No. 1, pp. 101–104, Salt Lake City.

Coe, M. D. and C. F. Baudez (1961), "The Zoned Bichrome Period in Northwestern Costa Rica," *American Antiquity,* Vol. 26, No. 4, pp. 505–515, Salt Lake City.

Coe, M. D. and K. V. Flannery (1966), "Microenvironments and Mesoamerican Prehistory," in *New Roads to Yesterday,* J. R. Caldwell, ed., pp. 348–360, Basic Books, Inc., New York.

Coe, W. R. II (1957), "A Distinctive Artifact Common to Haiti and Central America," *American Antiquity,* Vol. 22, No. 2, pp. 280–282, Salt Lake City.

Coe, W. R. II (1965), "Tikal: Ten Years of Study of a Maya Ruin in the Lowlands of Guatemala," *Expedition,* Vol. 8, No. 1, pp. 5–56, University of Pennsylvania Museum, Philadelphia.

Collier, Donald (1955), *Cultural Chronology and Change as Reflected in the Ceramics of the Virú Valley, Peru,* Fieldiana: Anthropology, Vol. 43, Chicago Natural History Museum, Chicago.

Collier, Donald (1962 a), "The Central Andes," in *Courses Toward Urban Life,* R. J. Braidwood and G. R. Willey, eds., Viking Fund Publications in Anthropology, No. 32, pp. 165–176, Wenner-Gren Foundation, New York.

Collier, Donald (1962 b), "Archaeological Investigations in the Casma Valley, Peru," *Akten, 34th International Congress of Americanists,* pp. 411–417, Vienna.

Collier, Donald and J. V. Murra (1943), *Survey and Excavations in South Ecuador,* Anthropological Series, Vol. 35, Field Museum of Natural History, Chicago.

Columbus, Christopher (1893), *The Journal of Christopher Columbus (During His First Voyage, 1492–93), and Documents Relating to the Voyages of John Cabot and Gasper Corte Real,* C. R. Markham, trans. w. notes and intro., Hakluyt Society, No. 86, London.

Columbus, Christopher (1930), *The Voyages of Christopher Columbus, Being the Journals of His First and Third, and the Letters Concerning the First and Last Voyages, to Which Is Added the Account of His Second Voyage Written by Andrés Bernáldez,* Cecil Jane, trans., Argonaut Press, London.

Conceiçao de M. C. Becker, Maria da (1966 a), "Quelques données nouvelles sur les préhistoriques de Rio Claro, État de São Paulo," *Actas y Memorias, 36th International Congress of Americanists,* Vol. 1, pp. 445–450, Seville.

Conceiçao de M. C. Becker, Maria da (1966 b), "Établissement de critères discriminatifs pour les pièces fausses et authentiques de la collection de préhistoire brésilienne G.M.," *Actas y Memorias, 36th International Congress of Americanists,* Vol. 1, pp. 451–458, Seville.

Cooper, J. M. (1925), "Culture Diffusion and Culture Areas in Southern South America," *Proceedings, 21st International Congress of Americanists,* Vol. 1, pp. 406–421, Göteborg, Sweden.

Cooper, J. M. (1941), "Temporal Sequence and the Marginal Cultures," *Anthropological Series,* No. 10, Catholic University of America, Washington, D.C.

Cooper, J. M. (1942 a), "Areal and Temporal Aspects of South American Culture," *Primitive Man,* Vol. 15, Nos. 1–2, pp. 1–38, Catholic Anthropological Conference, Washington, D.C.

Cooper, J. M., (1942 b), "The South American Marginal Cultures," *Proceedings, 8th American Scientific Congress,* Vol. 2, pp. 147–160, Washington, D.C.

Cooper, J. M. (1946 a), "The Araucanians," in *Handbook of South American Indians,* J. H. Steward, ed., Vol. 2, pp. 687–760, Bureau of American Ethnology, Bulletin 143, Smithsonian Institution, Washington, D.C.

Cooper, J. M. (1946 b), "The Ona," in *Handbook of South American Indians,* J. H. Steward, ed., Vol. 1, pp. 107–126, Bureau of American Ethnology, Bulletin 143, Smithsonian Institution, Washington, D.C.

Cooper, J. M. (1946 c), "The Patagonian and Pampean Hunters," in *Handbook of South American Indians,* J. H. Steward, ed., Vol. 1, pp. 127–168, Bureau of American Ethnology, Bulletin 143, Smithsonian Institution, Washington, D.C.

Cooper, J. M. (1946 d), "The Chono," in *Handbook of South American Indians,* J. H. Steward, ed., Vol. 1, pp. 47–54, Bureau of American Ethnology, Bulletin 143, Smithsonian Institution, Washington, D.C.

Cooper, J. M. (1946 e), "The Yahgan," in *Handbook of South American Indians,* J. H. Steward, ed., Vol. 1, pp. 81–107, Bureau of American Ethnology, Bulletin 143, Smithsonian Institution, Washington, D.C.

Corbett, J. M. (1953), "Some Unusual Ceramics from Esmeraldas, Ecuador," *American Antiquity,* Vol. 19, No. 2, pp. 145–152, Salt Lake City.

Cornely, F. L. (1940), "Nuevos descubrimientos arqueológicos en la Provincia de Coquimbo," *Boletín, Museo Nacional de Chile,* Vol. 18, pp. 9–14, Santiago.

Cornely, F. L. (1950), "Prehistoria del territorio Diaguita-Chileno," *Publicaciones del Museo y la Sociedad Arqueológico de La Serena,* Boletín No. 5, pp. 3–18, La Serena, Chile.

Cornely, F. L. (1951), *Cultura Diaguita-Chilena,* Revista Chilena de Historia Natural, Vols. 51–53, pp. 119–262, Santiago.

Cornely, F. L. (1953), *Cultura de El Molle,* Museo Arqueológico, La Serena, Chile.

Cornely, F. L. (1956 a), "The El Molle Culture of Chile," *Archaeology,* Vol. 9, No. 3, pp. 200–205, Archaeological Institute of America, Cincinnati.

Cornely, F. L. (1956 b), *Cultura Diaguita Chilena y Cultura de El Molle,* Editorial del Pacífico, S.A., Santiago.

Cornely, F. L. (1958), "Cultura de 'El Molle,'" *Arqueología Chilena,* Centro de Estudios Antropológicos, Pub. No. 4, pp. 9–12, Universidad de Chile, Santiago.

Cosculluela, J. A. (1951), "Cuatro años en la Ciénega de Zapata," *Revista de Arqueología y Etnología,* Vol. 6, No. 12, pp. 31–168, Havana.

Crabtree, Donald (1969), "A technological description of artifacts in Assemblage I, Wilson Butte Cave, Idaho," *Current Anthropology,* Vol. 10, No. 1, Wenner-Gren Foundation, Chicago.

Crook, W. W. and R. K. Harris (1957), *Hearths and Artifacts of Early Man near Lewisville, Texas, and Associated Faunal Material,* Bulletin, Vol. 28, pp. 7–97, Texas Archaeological and Paleontological Society, Abilene.

Crook, W. W. and R. K. Harris (1958), "A Pleistocene Campsite near Lewisville, Texas," *American Antiquity,* Vol. 23, No. 3, pp. 233–246, Salt Lake City.

Cruxent, J. M. (1952), "Notes on Venezuelan Archaeology," *Selected Papers, 29th International Congress of Americanists,* S. Tax, ed., Vol. 3, pp. 280–294, University of Chicago Press, Chicago.

Cruxent, J. M. (1959), "Noticia sobre litos de sílex del Brasil," *Boletín del Museo de Ciencias Naturales,* Vols. 4–5, Nos. 1–4, pp. 7–46, Carácas.

Cruxent, J. M. (1966), "Apuntes sobre las Calzadas de Barinas—Venezuela," *Boletín Informativo, Instituto Venezolano de Investigaciones Científicas,* No. 4, Carácas.

Cruxent, J. M. and Irving Rouse (1958–59), *An Archeological Chronology of Venezuela,* 2 Vols., Social Science Monographs, Pan American Union, Washington, D.C.

Cubillos, J. C. (1955), *Tumaco: Notas Arqueológicas,* Ministerio de Educación, Departamento de Extensión, Cultural, Bogotá.

Cubillos, J. C. (1958), "Pubenza. Arqueología de Popayán, Cauca, Colombia, S.A.," *Boletín Antropológico,* No. 1, pp. 7–39, Instituto Etnológico de la Universidad del Cauca, Popayán, Colombia.

Cubillos, J. C. (1959), "El Morro de Tulcán. Pirámide Prehispánica," *Revista Colombiana de Antropología,* Vol. 8, pp. 217–357, Bogotá.

Daguerre, J. B. (1934), "Nuevos paraderos y enterratorios en el Litoral de Carmen Patagones (Provincia de Buenos Aires)," *25th International Congress of Americanists,* Vol. 2, pp. 21–24, Buenos Aires.

Dauelsberg, Percy (1959 a), "Una tumba encistada de Playa Miller (Arica)," *Boletín, Museo de Arica,* No. 1, Arica, Chile.

Dauelsberg, Percy (1959 b), "Contribución a la arqueología del Valle de Azapa," *Boletín, Museo de Arica,* No. 3, Arica, Chile.

Dauelsberg, Percy (1963), "Complejo arqueológico Faldas del Morro," *Actas del Congreso Internacional de Arquelogía en San Pedro de Atacama,* Anales, No. 12, Universidad del Norte, Antofagasta, Chile.

Daugherty, R. D. (1956), "Archaeology of the Lind Coulee Site, Washington," *Proceedings, American Philosophical Society,* Vol. 100, No. 3, Philadelphia.

Davis, E. L. (1963), "The Desert Culture of the Western Great Basin: A Lifeway of Seasonal Transhumance," *American Antiquity,* Vol. 29, pp. 202–212, Salt Lake City.

Davis, W. A. (1966), "Theoretical Problems in Western Prehistory," in *The Current Status of Anthropological Research in the Great Basin: 1964,* W. L. d'Azevedo et al., eds., pp. 147–166, Desert Research Institute, Social Sciences and Humanities Publications No. 1, Reno, Nevada.

Debenedetti, Salvador (1910), *Exploración Arqueológica en Los Cementerios Prehistóricos de la Isla de Tilcara (Quebrada de Humahuaca, Provincia de Jujuy),* Publicaciones de la Sección Antropológica, No. 6, Facultad de Filosofía y Letras, Universidad de Buenos Aires, Buenos Aires.

Debenedetti, Salvador (1912), "Los cementerios prehistóricos de La Isla de Tilcara (Provincia de Jujuy)," *17th International Congress of Americanists,* Vol. 1, pp. 502–509, Buenos Aires.

Debenedetti, Salvador (1917), *Investigaciones arqueológicas en los valles preandinos de San Juan,* Publicaciones de la Sección Antropología, No. 15, Facultad de Filosofía y Letras, Universidad Nacional de Buenos Aires, Buenos Aires (cited from González, 1967).

Debenedetti, Salvador (1930), *Las Ruinas del Pucará, Tilcara, Quebrada de Humahuaca (Provincia de Jujuy),* Archivos del Museo Etnográfico, No. 2, Pt. 1, Universidad Nacional de Buenos Aires, Buenos Aires.

Debenedetti, Salvador (1931), *L'Ancienne Civilisation de Barreales,* Ars Americana, Vol. 2, Paris.

Debenedetti, Salvador and Eduardo Casanova (1933–35), *Titiconte,* Publicaciones del Museo Etnográfico de la Facultad de Filosofía y Letras, Vol. 3, pp. 7–35, Universidad Nacional de Buenos Aires, Buenos Aires.

De Booy, Theodoor (1917), "Archaeological Investigations in the Virgin Islands to Solve the Riddle of the Origin of Their Aborigines," *Scientific American Supplement,* Vol. 84, pp. 232–234, New York.

De Booy, Theodoor (1919), *Archaeology of the Virgin Islands,* Indian Notes and Monographs, Vol. 1, No. 1, Museum of the American Indian, Heye Foundation, New York.

Della Santa, Elizabeth (1959), "Les Cupisniques et l'origine des Olmeques," *Revue de l'Université de Bruxelles,* Vol. 5, pp. 340–363, Brussels.

Denevan, W. M. (1963), "Additional Comments on the Earthworks of Mojos in Northeastern Bolivia," *American Antiquity,* Vol. 28, No. 4, pp. 540–541, Salt Lake City.

Denevan, W. M. (1966), *The Aboriginal Cultural Geography of the Llanos de Mojos of Bolivia,* Ibero-Americana, No. 48, University of California Press, Berkeley and Los Angeles.

Del Solar, Daniel (1966), "Interrelation of Mesoamerica and the Peru-Ecuador Area," *Kroeber Anthropological Society Papers*, No. 34, pp. 31–52, University of California, Berkeley.

De Wolf, Marian (1953), "Excavations in Jamaica," *American Antiquity*, Vol. 18, pp. 230–238, Salt Lake City.

D'Harcourt, M. R. (1947), "Archéologie de la Province d'Esmeraldas, Equateur," *Journal de la Société des Américanistes*, Vol. 34, pp. 61–200, Paris.

Dias, O. F., Jr. (1967), "Notas prévias sôbre pesquisas arqueológicas nos Estados da Guanabara e do Rio de Janeiro," *Programa Nacional de Pesquisas Arqueológicas; Resultados Preliminares do Primeiro Ano 1965–1966*, Museu Paraense Emílio Goeldi, Publicações Avulsas, No. 6, pp. 89–106, Belém do Pará, Brazil.

Disselhoff, H. D. (1949), "Grabungen und Funde im Canton Sta. Elena, Ecuador," *Mexico Antiguo*, Vol. 7, pp. 343–410, México, D.F.

Disselhoff, H. D. (1969), "Seis Fechas Radiocarbónicas de Vicús," *38th International Congress of Americanists*, Vol. 1, pp. 341–345, Stuttgart and Munich.

Disselhoff, H. D. and Sigvald Linné (1960), *The Art of Ancient America. Civilizations of Central and South America*, Art of the World, Crown Publishers, Inc., New York.

Dobyns, H. F. (1966), "Estimating Aboriginal American Population," *Current Anthropology*, Vol. 7, No. 4, pp. 395–416, Wenner-Gren Foundation for Anthropological Research, Utrecht.

Dole, G. E. (1961–62), "A Preliminary Consideration of the Prehistory of the Upper Xingú Basin," *Revista do Museu Paulista*, No. 13, pp. 399–423, São Paulo.

Donnan, C. B. (1964), "An Early House from Chilca, Peru," *American Antiquity*, Vol. 30, No. 2, pp. 137–144, Salt Lake City.

Donnan, C. B. (1965), "Moche Ceramic Technology," *Nawpa Pacha*, Vol. 3, pp. 115–134, Institute of Andean Studies, Berkeley.

Dorsey, G. A. (1901), *Archaeological Investigations on the Island of La Plata, Ecuador*, Anthropological Series, Vol. 2, No. 5, Field Columbian Museum, Chicago.

Dumond, D. E. (1961), "Swidden Agriculture and the Rise of Maya Civilization," *Southwestern Journal of Anthropology*, Vol. 17, pp. 301–316, Albuquerque, New Mexico.

Dupouy, Walter (1958), "Dos piezas de tipo Paleolítico de la Gran Sabana, Venezuela," *Boletín del Museo de Ciencias Naturales*, Vols. 2–3, pp. 95–102, Carácas.

Dupouy, Walter (1960), "Tres puntas líticas de tipo Paleo-Indio de la Paragua, Estado Bolívar, Venezuela," *Boletín del Museo de Ciencias Naturales*, Vols. 5–6, pp. 7–14, Carácas.

Duque Gomez, Luis (1947), "Los últimos hallazgos arqueológicos en San Agustín," *Revista de las Indias*, Vol. 96, pp. 387–418, Bogotá.

Duque Gomez, Luis (1963), *Reseña Arqueológica de San Agustín*, Instituto Colombiano de Antropología, Imprenta Nacional, Bogotá.

Easby, E. K. (1952), "The Pre-Conquest Art of Santarém, Brazil," M. A. thesis, Faculty of Philosophy, Columbia University, New York.

Eberhart, Hal (1961), "The Cogged Stones of Southern California," *American Antiquity*, Vol. 26, No. 3, pp. 361–370, Salt Lake City.

Ekholm, G. F. (1946), "The Probable Use of Mexican Stone Yokes," *American Anthropologist*, Vol. 48, pp. 593–606, Menasha, Wisconsin.

Ekholm, G. F. (1961), "Puerto Rican Stone Collars as Ball-Game Belts," in *Essays in Pre-Columbian Art and Archaeology*, S. K. Lothrop *et al.*, eds., pp. 356–371, Harvard University Press, Cambridge.

Ekholm, G. F. (1964), "Transpacific Contacts," in *Prehistoric Man in the New World*, J. D. Jennings and E. Norbeck, eds., pp. 489–510, Rice University Semi-Centennial Publication, University of Chicago Press, Chicago.

Emperaire, José and Annette Laming (1954), "La Grotte du Mylodon (Patagonie Occidentale)," *Journal de la Société des Américanistes*, Vol. 43, pp. 173–206, Paris.

Emperaire, José and Annette Laming (1961), "Les gisements des Iles Englefield et Vivian dans la Mer D'Otway, Patagonie Australe," *Journal de la Société des Américanistes*, Vol. 50, pp. 7–75, Paris.

Emperaire, José, Annette Laming-Emperaire, and Henri Reichlen (1963), "La Grotte Fell et autres sites de la Région volcanique de la Patagonie Chilienne," *Journal de la Société des Américanistes*, Vol. 52, pp. 167–252, Paris.

Engel, Frederic (1956), "Curayacu, a Chavinoid Site," *Archaeology*, Vol. 9, No. 2, pp. 98–105, Archaeological Institute of America, New York.

Engel, Frederic (1957 a), "Early Sites on the Peruvian Coast," *Southwestern Journal of Anthropology*, Vol. 13, pp. 54–68, Albuquerque, New Mexico.

Engel, Frederic (1957 b), "Sites et établissments sans céramique de la côte Péruvienne," *Journal de la Société des Américanistes*, Vol. 46, pp. 67–155, Paris.

Engel, Frederic (1960), "Une groupe humaine datant de 5000 ans à Paracas, Pérou," *Journal de la Société des Américanistes*, Vol. 49, pp. 7–35, Paris.

Engel, Frederic (1963 a), *A Preceramic Settlement on the Central Coast of Peru: Asia, Unit 1*, Transactions, Vol. 53, Pt. 3, American Philosophical Society, Philadelphia.

Engel, Frederic (1963 b), "Notes relatives à des explorations archéologiques à Paracas et sur la côte sud du Pérou," *Travaux de l'Institut Français d'Etudes Andines*, Vol. 9, pp. 1–72, Paris and Lima.

Engel, Frederic (1963 c), "Datations à l'aide du radiocarbone 14, et problèmes de la prehístoire du Pérou," *Journale de la Société des Américanistes*, Vol. 52, pp. 101–132, Paris.

Engel, Frederic (1964), "El precerámico sin algodón en la costa del Perú," *Actas y Memorias*,

35th International Congress of Americanists, Vol. 3, pp. 141–152, México, D.F.

Engel, Frederic (1966 a), "Le complexe précéramique d'El Paraíso (Pérou)," *Journal de la Société des Américanistes,* Vol. 55, No. 1, pp. 43–96, Paris.

Engel, Frederic (1966 b), *Geografía Humana Prehistórica y Agricultura Precolombina de La Quebrada de Chilca. Tomo I, Informe Preliminar,* Universidad Agraria, Lima.

Epstein, J. F. (1959), "Dating the Ulua Polychrome Complex," *American Antiquity,* Vol. 25, No. 1, pp. 125–129, Salt Lake City.

Ericksen, M. F. (1960 a), "Antropología física de los restos oseos encontrados en La Herradura y Guanaqueros, cultura del anzuelo de concha," *Publicaciones del Museo y la Sociedad Arqueológica de La Serena,* Boletín No. 11, pp. 15–27, La Serena, Chile.

Ericksen, M. F. (1960 b), "Antropología física de restos oseos encontrados en cementerios pertenecientes a la cultura de El Molle," *Publicaciones del Museo y la Sociedad Arqueológico de La Serena,* Boletín No. 11, pp. 29–40, La Serena, Chile.

Ericksen, M. F. (1960 c), "Antropología física de restos oseos encontrados en cementerios de la cultura Diaguita," *Publicaciones del Museo y la Sociedad Arqueológico de La Serena,* Boletín No. 11, pp. 41–52, La Serena, Chile.

Estete, Miguel de (1918), *El Descubrimiento y la Conquista del Perú,* Boletín, Sociedad Ecuatoriana, Estudios Históricos, Vol. 1, No. 3, Quito.

Estrada, Emilio (1954), *Ensayo Preliminar Sobre la Arqueología del Milagro, Guayaquil,* Museo Víctor Emilio Estrada, Guayaquil.

Estrada, Emilio (1957 a), *Ultimas Civilizaciones Pre-Históricas de la Cuenca del Río Guayas,* Publicación del Museo Víctor Emilio Estrada, No. 2, Guayaquil.

Estrada, Emilio (1957 b), *Los Huancavilcas. Ultimas Civilizaciones Pre-Históricas de la Costa del Guayas,* Publicación del Museo Víctor Emilio Estrada, No. 3, Guayaquil.

Estrada, Emilio (1957 c), *Prehistoria de Manabí,* Publicación del Museo Víctor Emilio Estrada, No. 4, Guayaquil.

Estrada, Emilio (1958), *Las Culturas Pre-Clasicas, Formativas, o Arcaicas del Ecuador,* Publicación del Museo Víctor Emilio Estrada, No. 5, Guayaquil.

Estrada, Emilio (1962), *Arqueología de Manabí Central,* Publicación del Museo Víctor Emilio Estrada, No. 7, Guayaquil.

Estrada, Emilio and Clifford Evans (1963), "Cultural Development in Ecuador," in *Aboriginal Cultural Development in Latin America: An Interpretative Review,* B. J. Meggers and C. Evans, eds., Smithsonian Miscellaneous Collections, Vol. 146, No. 1, pp. 77–88, Smithsonian Institution, Washington, D.C.

Estrada, Emilio and B. J. Meggers (1961), "A Complex of Traits of Probable Transpacific Origin on the Coast of Ecuador," *American Anthropologist,* Vol. 63, pp. 913–939, Menasha, Wisconsin.

Estrada, Emilio, B. J. Meggers, and Clifford Evans (1964), *The Jambelí Culture of South-Coastal Ecuador,* Proceedings of the United States National Museum, Vol. 115, No. 3492, Smithsonian Institution, Washington, D.C.

Evans, Clifford, Jr. (1950), "A Report on Recent Archaeological Investigations in the Lagoa Santa Region of Minas Gerais, Brazil," *American Antiquity,* Vol. 15, No. 4, pp. 341–343, Salt Lake City.

Evans, Clifford, Jr. (1964), "Lowland South America," in *Prehistoric Man in the New World,* J. D. Jennings and E. Norbeck, eds., pp. 419–450, University of Chicago Press, Chicago.

Evans, Clifford, Jr. and B. J. Meggers (1957), "Formative Period Cultures in the Guayas Basin, Coastal Ecuador," *American Antiquity,* Vol. 22, pp. 235–246, Salt Lake City.

Evans, Clifford, Jr. and B. J. Meggers (1958), "Valdivia—An Early Formative Culture on the Coast of Ecuador," *Archaeology,* Vol. 11, pp. 175–182, New York.

Evans, Clifford, Jr. and B. J. Meggers (1960), *Archaeological Investigations in British Guiana,* Bureau of American Ethnology, Bulletin 177, Smithsonian Institution, Washington, D.C.

Evans, Clifford, Jr. and B. J. Meggers (1964), "British Guiana Archaeology: A Return to the Original Interpretations," *American Antiquity,* Vol. 30, No. 1, pp. 83–84, Salt Lake City.

Evans, Clifford, Jr. and B. J. Meggers (1966), "Mesoamerica and Ecuador," in *Handbook of Middle American Indians,* R. Wauchope, G. F. Ekholm, and G. R. Willey, eds., Vol. 4, pp. 243–264, University of Texas Press, Austin.

Evans, Clifford, Jr. and B. J. Meggers (1968), *Archaeological Investigations on the Rio Napo, Eastern Ecuador,* Smithsonian Institution Contributions to Anthropology, Vol. 6, Washington, D.C.

Evans, Clifford, Jr., B. J. Meggers, and J. M. Cruxent (1959), "Preliminary Results of Archaeological Investigations Along the Orinoco and Ventuari Rivers, Venezuela," *Actas, 33rd International Congress of Americanists,* Vol. 2, pp. 359–369, San José, Costa Rica.

Ferdon, E. N., Jr. (1959), "Agricultural Potential and the Development of Cultures," *Southwestern Journal of Anthropology,* Vol. 15, pp. 1–19, Albuquerque, New Mexico.

Ferreira Penna, D. S. (1879), "Urnas do Maracá," *Archivos, Museu Nacional de Rio de Janeiro,* Vol. 2, pp. 69–71, Rio de Janeiro.

Fewkes, J. W. (1907), "The Aborigines of Porto Rico and Neighboring Islands," *25th Annual Report, Bureau of American Ethnology,* pp. 1–220, Smithsonian Institution, Washington, D.C.

Figueira, J. J. (1962), "Relaciones etnográfico-arqueológicas entre Argentina y Uruguay," *Jornadas Internacionales de Arqueología y Etnografía,* No. 1, pp. 69–82, Sociedad Argentina de Antropología, Universidad de Buenos Aires, Buenos Aires.

Figueroa, Gonzalo (1958), "Cerámica de los sitios arqueológicos

'Piedra Numerada' y 'Cerro El Plomo,' " *Arqueología Chilena*, No. 4, pp. 73–83, Centro de Estudios Antropológicos, Universidad de Chile, Santiago.

Finch, V. C., G. T. Trewartha, A. H. Robinson, and E. H. Hammond (1957), *Elements of Geography: Physical and Cultural*, McGraw-Hill, New York.

Fitting, J. E., Jerry Devisscher, and E. J. Wahla (1966), *The Paleo-Indian Occupation of the Holcombe Beach*, Anthropological Papers, Museum of Anthropology, No. 27, University of Michigan, Ann Arbor.

Flannery, K. V. (1968), "Archaeological Systems Theory and Early Mesoamerica," *Anthropological Archaeology in the Americas*, B. J. Meggers, ed., pp. 67–87, Anthropological Society of Washington, Washington, D.C.

Flores Espinoza, Isabel (1960), "Wichqana, Sitio Temprano en Ayacucho," in *Antiguo Peru, Espacio y Tiempo*, pp. 335–344, Librería-Editorial Juan Mejía Baca, Lima

Fock, Niels (1961), "Inca Imperialism in North-West Argentina and Chaco Burial Forms," *Folk*, Vol. 3, pp. 67–90, Copenhagen.

Fock, Niels (1962), "Chaco Pottery and Chaco History, Past and Present," *34th International Congress of Americanists*, pp. 477–484, Vienna.

Fontana Company, M. A. (1951), "Arqueología del Uruguay," *Revista de la Sociedad "Amigos de Arqueología,"* Vol. 11, pp. 153–221, Montevideo.

Ford, J. A. (1944), *Excavations in the Vicinity of Cali, Colombia*, Yale University Publications in Anthropology, No. 31, New Haven.

Ford, J. A. (1949), *Cultural Dating of Prehistoric Sites in Virú Valley, Peru*, Anthropological Papers, Vol. 43, Pt. 1, American Museum of Natural History, New York.

Ford, J. A. (1966), "Early Formative Cultures in Georgia and Florida," *American Antiquity*, Vol. 31, No. 6, pp. 781–799, Salt Lake City.

Ford, J. A. (1969), *A Comparison of Formative Cultures in the Americas: Diffusion or the Psychic Unity of Man?*, Smithsonian Institution Contributions to Anthropology, Vol. 11, Washington, D.C.

Freitas, C. A. (1942), "Alfarería del delta del Río Negro," *Revista Historia*, segunda epoca, año 36, Vol. 13, Nos. 38–39, pp. 363–418, Montevideo.

Freitas, C. A. (1953), "Algunos aspectos de la arqueología del Rio Uruguay," *Revista de la Sociedad "Amigos de Arqueología,"* Vol. 12, pp. 53–100, Montevideo.

Frenguelli, Joaquin and Francisco de Aparicio (1923), "Los Paraderos de la margen derecha del Río Malabrigo," *Anales, Facultad de Ciencias y Educación*, Vol. 1, pp. 7–112, Paraná, Argentina.

Fung Pineda, Rosa (1958), "Informe preliminar de las excavaciones efectuadas en el abrigo rocoso No. 1, de Tschopik," *Actas y Trabajos del II Congreso Nacional del Perú*, No. 1, pp. 253–272, Lima.

Gajardo Tobar, Roberto (1958–59), "Investigaciones acerca de las Piedras con Tacitas en la zona central de Chile," *Anales de Arqueología y Etnología*, Vols. 14, 15, Facultad de Filosofía y Letras, Universidad Nacional de Cuyo, Mendoza, Argentina.

Gajardo Tobar, Roberto (1962–63), "Investigaciones arqueológicas en la desembocadura del Río Choapa (Prov. de Coquimbo, Chile): La cultura de Huentelauquén," *Anales de Arqueología y Etnología*, Vols. 17–18, pp. 7–57, Facultad de Filosofía y Letras, Universidad Nacional de Cuyo, Mendoza, Argentina.

Garcilaso de la Vega (el Inca) (1869–71), *The First Part of the Royal Commentaries of the Incas*, 2 Vols., Clements R. Markham, trans., Hakluyt Society, Vols. 41, 45, London.

Gardner, G. A. (1931), *Rock-Paintings of North-West Córdoba*, Clarendon Press, Oxford.

Gatto, Santiago (1939), "El paradero cementerio de Brazo Largo, Delta del Paraná. Noticia preliminar," *Physis*, Vol. 16, pp. 365–376, Buenos Aires.

Gayton, A. H. and A. L. Kroeber (1927), *The Uhle Pottery Collections from Nazca*, University of California Publications in American Archaeology and Ethnology, Vol. 24, No. 1, Berkeley.

Giddings, J. L. (1961), "Cultural Continuities of Eskimos," *American Antiquity*, Vol. 27, No. 2, pp. 155–173, Salt Lake City.

Gilmore, R. M. (1950), "Fauna and Ethnozoology of South America," in *Handbook of South American Indians*, J. H. Steward, ed., Vol. 6, pp. 345–464, Bureau of American Ethnology, Bulletin 143, Smithsonian Institution, Washington, D.C.

Glass, John B. (1966), "Archaeological Survey of Western Honduras," in *Handbook of Middle American Indians*, R. Wauchope, G. F. Ekholm, and G. R. Willey, eds., Vol. 4, pp. 157–179, University of Texas Press, Austin.

Goeldi, E. A. (1900), *Excavações archeológicas em 1895. Primeira Parte, As Cavernas Funerarias Artificiaes dos Indios Hoje Extinctos no Rio Cunany e Sua Ceramica*, Memorias do Museu Goeldi, Belém do Pará, Brazil.

Goeldi, E. A. (1905), *Excavações archeológicas em 1895 Executadas Pelo Museu Paraense no Littoral Guyana Braziliena*, Memorias do Museu Goeldi, Bélem do Pará, Brazil.

González, A. R. (1939), "Excavaciones en el túmulo del Paraná Pavón," *Revista Geografía Americana*, Vol. 12, pp. 151–153, Buenos Aires.

González, A. R. (1943), "Arqueología del yacimiento indígena de Villa Rumipal (Prov. de Córdoba)," *Publicaciones del Instituto de Arqueología, Linguistica y Folklore "Dr. Pablo Cabrera,"* No. 4, Universidad Nacional de Córdoba, Argentina.

González, A. R. (1947), "Investigaciones arqueológicas en las nacientes del Paraná Pavón," *Publicaciones del Instituto Arqueología Linguistica y Folklore "Dr. Pablo Cabrera,"* No. 17, Universidad Nacional de Córdoba, Argentina.

González, A. R. (1949), "Nota sobre la arqueología de Pampa de Olaen (Córdoba)," *Notas del Museo de La Plata*, Vol. 14,

Antropología, No. 56, La Plata, Argentina.

González, A. R. (1952), "Antiguo horizonte precerámico en las Sierras Centrales de la Argentina," *Runa*, Vol. 5, pp. 110–133, Buenos Aires.

González, A. R. (1955), "Contextos culturales y cronología relativa en el área central del noroeste Argentino," *Anales de Arqueología y Etnología*, Vol. 11, pp. 7–32, Facultad de Filosofía y Letras, Universidad Nacional de Cuyo, Mendoza, Argentina.

González, A. R. (1956), "La cultura Condorhuasi del noroeste Argentino," *Runa*, Vol. 7, Pt. 1, pp. 37–85, Buenos Aires.

González, A. R. (1960), "La Estratigrafía de La Gruta de Intihuasi, (Prov. de San Luis, R.A.) y Sus Relaciones con Otros Sitios Precerámicos de Sudamerica," *Revista del Instituto de Antropología*, Vol. I, Universidad Nacional de Córdoba, Argentina.

González, A. R. (1961), "The La Aguada Culture of Northwestern Argentina," in *Essays in Precolumbian Art and Archaeology*, S. K. Lothrop *et al*, eds., pp. 389–420, Harvard University Press, Cambridge.

González, A. R. (1961–64 a), "La cultura de La Aguada del N.O. Argentina," *Revista del Instituto de Antropología*, Vols. 2–3, pp. 205–253, Universidad Nacional de Córdoba, Argentina (Spanish version of González, 1961).

González, A. R. (1961–64 b), "Nuevas fechas de la cronología Argentina obtenidas por el método del radiocarbón (V)," *Revista del Instituto de Antropología*, Vols. 2–3, pp. 289–296, Universidad Nacional de Córdoba, Argentina.

González, A. R. (1963 a), "Cultural Development in Northwestern Argentina," in *Aboriginal Cultural Development in Latin America: An Interpretative Review*, B. J. Meggers and C. Evans, eds., Smithsonian Miscellaneous Collections, Vol. 140, No. 1, pp. 103–118, Smithsonian Institution, Washington, D.C.

González, A. R. (1963 b), "Las tradiciones alfareras del período temprana del N.O. Argentino y sus correlaciones con las áreas aledañas," *Actas del Congreso Internacional de Arqueología en San Pedro de Atacama*, Anales, No. 2, Universidad del Norte, Antofagasta, Chile.

González, A. R. (1966), "Las Culturas Paleoindias o Paleolíticas Sudamericanas: resumen y problemática actual," *Actas y Memorias, 36th International Congress of Americanists*, Vol. 1, pp. 15–41, Seville.

González, A. R. (1967), "Una excepcional pieza de mosaico del N.O. Argentino," *Etnia*, No. 6, pp. 1–28, Museo Etnográfico Municipal "Dámaso Arce," Olavarría, Buenos Aires.

González, A. R. and A. M. Lorandí (1959), "Hallazgos arqueológicos a las orillas del Río Carcarañá," *Revista del Instituto de Antropología*, Vol. 1, pp. 161–222, Facultad de Filosofía, Universidad Nacional del Litoral, Rosario, Argentina.

González A. R. and Victor Núñez Reguero (1958–59), "Apuntes preliminares sobre la arqueología del Campo del Pucará y alrededores (Depto. Andalgalá, Prov. Catamarca)," *Anales de Arqueología y Etnología*, Vols. 14–15, pp. 115–162, Facultad de Filosofía y Letras, Universidad Nacional de Cuyo, Mendoza, Argentina.

González, A. R. and J. A. Pérez (1966), "El área Andina meridional," *36th International Congress of Americanists*, Vol. 1, pp. 241–265, Seville.

González Suarez, Federico (1878), *Estudio Histórico sobre los Cañaris, Antiguos Habitantes de la Provincia del Azuay, en la Republica del Ecuador*, Imprenta del Clero, Quito.

Gradin, C. J. (1961–63), "Concheros y materiales líticos en Monte León (Provincia de Santa Cruz)," *Acta Praehistorica*, Vols. 5–7, pp. 53–72, Centro Argentino de Estudios Prehistóricos, Buenos Aires.

Granberry, Julian (1956), "The Cultural Position of the Bahamas in Caribbean Archaeology," *American Antiquity*, Vol. 22, No. 2, pp. 128–134, Salt Lake City.

Greenberg, J. H. (1960), "The General Classification of Central and South American Languages," in *Men and Cultures, Selected Papers, 5th International Congress of Anthropological and Ethnological Sciences*, A. F. C. Wallace, ed., pp. 791–794, University of Pennsylvania Press, Philadelphia.

Grobman, Alexander, W. Salbuana, R. Sevilla, and P. C. Mangelsdorf (1961), *Races of Maize in Peru*, Publication 915, National Academy of Sciences and National Research Council, Washington, D.C.

Grubb, W. B. (1913), *An Unknown People in an Unknown Land; an Account of the Life and Customs of the Lengua Indians of the Paraguayan Chaco*, H. T. Morrey Jones, ed., Seeley and Co., London.

Gruhn, Ruth (1961), *The Archaeology of Wilson Butte Cave, South-Central Idaho*, Occasional Papers, No. 6, Idaho State University Museum, Pocatello, Idaho.

Gruhn, Ruth (1965), "Two Early Radiocarbon Dates from the Lower Levels of Wilson Butte Cave, South-Central Idaho," *Tebiwa*, Vol. 8, No. 2, Idaho State University Museum, Pocatello, Idaho.

Haag, W. G. (1965), "Pottery Typology in Certain Lesser Antilles," *American Antiquity*, Vol. 31, No. 2, pp. 242–245, Salt Lake City.

Haberland, Wolfgang (1955), "Preliminary Report on the Aguas Buenas Complex, Costa Rica," *Ethnos*, Vol. 20, pp. 224–230, Ethnographical Museum of Sweden, Stockholm.

Haberland, Wolfgang (1957), "Excavations in Costa Rica and Panama," *Archaeology*, Vol. 10, No. 4, pp. 258–263, Brattleboro, Massachusetts.

Haberland, Wolfgang (1959 a), *Archaeologische Untersuchungen in Südost-Costa Rica*, Acta Humboldtiana, Ser. Geographica et Ethnographica, Nr. 1, Franz Steinen Verlag GMBH, Wiesbaden.

Haberland, Wolfgang (1959 b), "A Re-Appraisal of Chiriquían Pottery Types," *Actas, 33rd Interna-*

tional Congress of Americanists, Vol. 2, pp. 339–346, San José, Costa Rica.

Haberland, Wolfgang (1960), "Secuencia estratigráfica de la cerámica Nicoyana según Baudez y Coe, Congreso Americanista de Vienna, Austria, Julio 1960," *Informe Semestral, Instituto Geográfico de Costa Rica,* pp. 73–74, Ministerio de Obras Publicas, San José, Costa Rica.

Haberland, Wolfgang (1962), "The Scarified Ware and the Early Cultures of Chiriquí (Panama)," *34th International Congress of Americanists,* pp. 381–389, Vienna.

Haberland, Wolfgang (1966 a), "Early Phases on Ometepe Island, Nicaragua," *Actas y Memorias, 36th International Congress of Americanists,* Vol. 1, pp. 399–403, Seville.

Haberland, Wolfgang (1966 b), "El sur de Centroamerica," *Actas y Memorias, 36th International Congress of Americanists,* Vol. 1, pp. 193–200, Seville.

Haberland, Wolfgang (1966–67), "Morazán, a Non-Ceramic Complex in Northeastern Salvador," *Folk,* Vols. 8–9, pp. 119–126, Copenhagen.

Haberland, Wolfgang (1969 a), "Die Kulturen Meso- und Zentral-Amerika," in *Die Kulturen Alt-Amerikas, Handbuch der Kulturgeschichte,* pp. 1–192, Akademische Verlagsgesellschaft Athenaion, Frankfurt-am-Main.

Haberland, Wolfgang (1969 b), "Early Phases and Their Relationship in Southern Central America," *38th International Congress of Americanists,* Vol. 1, pp. 229–242, Stuttgart and Munich.

Haberland, Wolfgang (1970 ms.), "On Stone Sculpture from Southern Central America," paper presented at Metropolitan Museum Symposium, October, 1970, New York.

Hammen, Thomas van der (1958), "Las terrazas del Río Magdalena y la posición estratigráfica de los hallazgos de Garzón," *Revista Colombiana de Antropología,* Vol. 6, pp. 261–270, Bogotá.

Hanke, Wanda (1959), "Archä-

ologische Funde im oberen Amazonasgebiet," *Archiv für Völkerkunde,* Vol. 14, Vienna.

Harris, Joanna (1966 ms.), "Seriation of Marajoara Ceramics," mimeogr., Department of Anthropology, University of Illinois, Urbana.

Harte, E. M. (1958), "Mountaintop Burials," *Panama Archaeologist,* Vol. 1, pp. 29–31, Balboa Heights, Canal Zone.

Hartman, C. V. (1901), *Archaeological Researches in Costa Rica,* Royal Ethnological Museum, Stockholm.

Hartman, C. V. (1907 a), *Archaeological Researches in the Pacific Coast of Costa Rica,* Memoirs, Vol. 3, No. 1, Carnegie Museum, Pittsburgh.

Hartman, C. V. (1907 b), "The Alligator as a Plastic Decorative Motif in Costa Rican Pottery," *American Anthropologist,* Vol. 9, No. 2, Menasha, Wisconsin.

Hartt, C. F. (1885), "Contribuições para a Ethnología do Valle do Amazonas," *Archivos, Museu Nacional de Rio de Janeiro,* Vol. 6, pp. 1–174, Rio de Janeiro.

Hartweg, Raoul (1961), "Les squelettes de sites sans céramique de la côte du Pérou, II, Étude descriptive de documents nouveaux," *Journal de la Société des Américanistes,* Vol. 50, pp. 111–133, Paris.

Hatt, Gudmund (1924), "Archaeology of the Virgin Islands," *Proceedings, 21st International Congress of Americanists,* Pt. 1, pp. 29–42, The Hague.

Haury, E. W. (1953), "Some Thoughts on Chibcha Culture in the High Plains of Colombia," *American Antiquity,* Vol. 19, pp. 76–78, Salt Lake City.

Haury, E. W. and J. C. Cubillos (1953), *Investigaciones Arqueológicas en La Sabana de Bogotá, Colombia (Cultura Chibcha),* University of Arizona Social Science Bulletin, No. 22, Tucson.

Haynes, C. V. (1964), "Fluted Projectile Points: Their Age and Dispersion," *Science,* Vol. 145, pp. 1408–1413, Lancaster, Pennsylvania.

Haynes, C. V. (1965), "Carbon-14 Dates and Early Man in the New

World," *Interim Research Report No. 9, Geochronology Laboratories,* University of Arizona, Tucson.

Haynes, C. V. (1967), "Muestras de C14, de Tlapacoya, Estado de México," *Boletín, Instituto Nacional de Antropología e História,* No. 29, pp. 49–52, México, D.F.

Heine-Geldern, Robert von (1953), "Die Asiatische Herkunft der Südamerikanischen Metalltechnik," *Paideuma,* Band 5, pp. 347–423, Frobenius-Institut–J. Wolfgang Goethe-Universität, Frankfurt-am-Main.

Heine-Geldern, Robert von (1959), "Representations of the Asiatic Tiger in the Art of the Chavín Culture: A Proof of Early Contacts Between China and Peru," *Actas, 33rd International Congress of Americanists,* pp. 321–326, San José, Costa Rica.

Heine-Geldern, Robert von (1966), "The Problem of Transpacific Influences in Mesoamerica," in *Handbook of Middle American Indians,* R. Wauchope, G. F. Ekholm, and G. R. Willey, eds., Vol. 4, pp. 277–295, University of Texas Press, Austin.

Heiser, C. B., Jr. (1965), "Cultivated Plants and Cultural Diffusion in Nuclear America," *American Anthropologist,* Vol. 67, No. 4, pp. 930–949, Menasha, Wisconsin.

Heizer, R. F. and Richard Brooks (1965), "Ancient Campsite or Wood Rat Houses?" *Southwestern Journal of Anthropology,* Vol. 21, pp. 155–165, Albuquerque, New Mexico.

Hernández de Alba, Gregorio (1937), "El Templo del Sol de Goranchacha," *Revista de las Indias,* Vol. 2, No. 7, pp. 10–18, Bogotá.

Hernández de Alba, Gregorio (1946 a), "The Highland Tribes of Southern Colombia," in *Handbook of South American Indians,* J. H. Steward, ed., Vol. 2, pp. 915–936, Bureau of American Ethnology, Bulletin 143, Smithsonian Institution, Washington, D.C.

Hernández de Alba, Gregorio (1946 b), "The Archaeology of San Agustín and Tierradentro," in *Handbook of South American Indians,* J. H. Steward, ed., Vol. 2, pp. 851–860, Bureau of American Ethnology, Bulletin 143, Smithsonian Institution, Washington, D.C.

Hernández de Alba, Gregorio (1948 a), "Sub-Andean Tribes of the Cauca Valley," in *Handbook of South American Indians,* J. H. Steward, ed., Vol. 4, pp. 297–328, Bureau of American Ethnology, Bulletin 143, Smithsonian Institution, Washington, D.C.

Hernández de Alba, Gregorio (1948 b), "Tribes of the North Colombia Lowlands," in *Handbook of South American Indians,* J. H. Steward, ed., Vol. 4, pp. 329–338, Bureau of American Ethnology, Bulletin 143, Smithsonian Institution, Washington, D.C.

Hernández de Alba, Gregorio (1948 c), "The Tribes of Northwestern Venezuela," in *Handbook of South American Indians,* J. H. Steward, ed., Vol. 4, pp. 469–474, Bureau of American Ethnology, Bulletin 143, Smithsonian Institution, Washington, D.C.

Hernández de Alba, Gregorio (1948 d), "The Tribes of North Central Venezuela," in *Handbook of South American Indians,* J. H. Steward, ed., Vol. 4, pp. 475–480, Bureau of American Ethnology, Bulletin 143, Smithsonian Institution, Washington, D.C.

Hernández de Alba, Gregorio (1948 e), "The Achagua and Their Neighbors," in *Handbook of South American Indians,* J. H. Steward, ed., Vol. 4, pp. 399–412, Bureau of American Ethnology, Bulletin 143, Smithsonian Institution, Washington, D.C.

Hester, J. J. (1962), "A Comparative Typology of New World Cultures," *American Anthropologist,* Vol. 64, No. 5, pp. 1001–1015, Menasha, Wisconsin.

Hester, J. J. (1966), "Late Pleistocene Environments and Early Man in South America," *The American Naturalist,* Vol. 100, No. 914, pp. 377–388, Lancaster, Pennsylvania.

Heyerdahl, Thor (1952), "Aboriginal Navigation in Peru; Objects and Results of the Kon-Tiki Expedition; Some Basic Problems in Polynesian Anthropology," *Proceedings, 30th International Congress of Americanists,* pp. 72–85, Royal Anthropological Institute, London.

Heyerdahl, Thor and Arne Skjölsvold (1956), *Archaeological Evidence of Pre-Spanish Visits to the Galápagos Islands,* Memoir No. 12, Society for American Archaeology, Salt Lake City.

Hilbert, P. P. (1955), "A cerâmica arqueológica da região de Oriximiná," *Publicación,* No. 9, Instituto de Antropología e Etnología do Pará, Belém do Pará, Brazil.

Hilbert, P. P. (1968), *Archäologisch Untersuchungen am Mittleren Amazonas,* Marburger Studien zur Volkerkunde, Bd. 1, Dietrich Reimer Verlag, Berlin.

Holmes, W. H. (1888), *Ancient Art of the Province of Chiriquí, Colombia,* Bureau of American Ethnology, 6th Annual Report, Smithsonian Institution, Washington, D.C.

Holstein, Otto (1927), "Chan-Chan: Capital of the Great Chimu," *Geographical Review,* Vol. 17, pp. 36–61, New York.

Hooton, E. A. (1947), *Up from the Ape,* rev. ed., The Macmillan Co., New York.

Horkheimer, Hans (1944), *Vistas Arqueológicas del Noroeste del Perú,* Librería e Imprenta Moreno, Trujillo, Peru.

Howard, G. D. (1943), *Excavations at Ronquín, Venezuela,* Yale University Publications in Anthropology, No. 28, New Haven.

Howard, G. D. (1947), *Prehistoric Ceramic Styles of Lowland South America, Their Distribution and History,* Yale University Publications in Anthropology, No. 37, New Haven.

Howard, G. D. and G. R. Willey (1948), *Lowland Argentine Archaeology,* Yale University Publications in Anthropology, No. 39, New Haven.

Howard, R. R. (1956), "The Archaeology of Jamaica: A Preliminary Survey," *American Antiquity,* Vol. 22, pp. 45–58, Salt Lake City.

Howard, R. R. (1965), "New Perspectives on Jamaican Archaeology," *American Antiquity,* Vol. 31, No. 2, pp. 250–255, Salt Lake City.

Hrdlička, Aleš, *et al.* (1912), *Early Man in South America,* Bureau of American Ethnology, Bulletin 52, Smithsonian Institution, Washington, D.C.

Humphrey, R. L. (1966), "The Prehistory of the Utukok River Region, Arctic Alaska: Early Fluted Point Tradition with Old World Relationships," *Current Anthropology,* Vol. 7, No. 5, pp. 586–588, Wenner-Gren Foundation for Anthropological Research, Utrecht.

Hurt, W. R. (1956), "The Lagoa Santa Project," *Museum News,* Vol. 18, Nos. 9–10, W. H. Over Museum, University of South Dakota, Vermillion, South Dakota.

Hurt, W. R. (1960), "The Cultural Complexes from the Lagoa Santa Region, Brazil," *American Anthropologist,* Vol. 62, pp. 569–585, Menasha, Wisconsin.

Hurt, W. R. (1962), "New and Revised Radiocarbon Dates from Brazil," *Museum News,* Vol. 23, Nos. 11–12, pp. 1–4, W. H. Over Museum, University of South Dakota, Vermillion, South Dakota.

Hurt, W. R. (1964), "Recent Radiocarbon Dates for Central and Southern Brazil," *American Antiquity,* Vol. 30, No. 1, pp. 25–33, Salt Lake City.

Hurt, W. R. (1966), "Additional Radiocarbon Dates from the Sambaquís of Brazil," *American Antiquity,* Vol. 31, No. 3, pp. 440–441, Salt Lake City.

Hurt, W. R. (1968), "The Pre-Ceramic Occupations of Central and Southern Brazil," *37th International Congress of Americanists,* Vol. 3, pp. 275–297, Buenos Aires.

Hurt, W. R. and Oldemar Blasi (1960), *A Sambaquí do Macedo. A. 52.13-Paraná, Brasil,* Arqueología No. 2, Departamento de Antropología, Universidade do Paraná, Curitiba, Paraná, Brazil.

Hymes, D. H. (1960), "Lexicostatistics So Far," *Current Anthro-*

pology, Vol. 1, No. 1, pp. 3–44 (including various readers' comments), University of Chicago, Chicago.

Ibarra Grasso, D. E. (1953 a), "New archaeological cultures from the departments of Chuquisaca, Potosí, and Tarija, Bolivia," *American Antiquity,* Vol. 19, No. 2, pp. 126–129, Salt Lake City.

Ibarra Grasso, D. E. (1953 b), "Un nuevo panorama de la arqueología Boliviana," *Cuadernos Americanos,* Vol. 71, pp. 143–167, México, D.F.

Ibarra Grasso, D. E. (1955), "Hallazgos de puntas paleolíticas en Bolivia," *Anales, 31st International Congress of Americanists,* Vol. 2, pp. 561–568, São Paulo.

Ibarra Grasso, D. E. (1956), "Una civilización pre-Tiahuanaco," *Cuadernos Americanos,* Vol. 88, pp. 139–154, México, D.F.

Ibarra Grasso, D. E. (1958–59), "Los primeros agricultores de Bolivia," *Anales de Arqueología y Etnología,* Vols. 14–15, pp. 205–228, Facultad de Filosofía y Letras, Universidad Nacional de Cuyo, Mendoza, Argentina.

Ibarra Grasso, D. E. (1960), "Esquema arqueológico de Bolivia y relaciones con el Perú," in *Antiquo Perú, Espacio y Tiempo,* pp. 301–308, Librería-Editorial Juan Mejía Baca, Lima.

Ibarra Grasso, D. E. (1967), *Argentina Indígena y Prehistoria Americana,* Tipográfica Editora Argentina, Buenos Aires.

Ibarra Grasso, D. E. (n.d.), *Mapa Arqueológico de Bolivia,* Ministerio de Educación y Bellas Artes, La Paz.

Ibarra Grasso, D. E. and Leonardo Branisa (1955), "Nuevos estilos en la cerámica prehispánica de Bolivia," *31st International Congress of Americanists,* Vol. 2, pp. 727–760, São Paulo.

Imbelloni, José (1938), "Tabla clasificatoria de los Indios, regiones biológicas y grupos raciales humanos de America," *Physis,* Vol. 12, No. 44, pp. 230–249, Buenos Aires.

Imbelloni, José (1950 a), "La Tabla clasificatoria de los Indios a los trece años de su publica-

ción," *Runa,* Vol. 3, pp. 200–210, Buenos Aires.

Imbelloni, José (1950 b), "Cephalic Deformations of the Indians in Argentina," in *Handbook of South American Indians,* J. H. Steward, ed., Vol. 6, pp. 53–56, Bureau of American Ethnology, Bulletin 143, Smithsonian Institution, Washington, D.C.

Imbelloni, José (1950 c), "La extraña terracotta de Rurrenabaque," *Runa,* Vol. 3, Pts. 1, 2, Buenos Aires.

Imbelloni, José (1958), "Nouveaux apports à la classification de l'homme américain," *Miscellanea Paul Rivet Octogenario Dictata, 31st International Congress of Americanists,* pp. 109–136, Universidad Nacional Autónoma de México, México, D.F.

Iribarren Charlín, Jorge (1949), "Casa de piedra en San Pedro Viejo," *Publicaciones del Museo y la Sociedad Arqueológico de La Serena,* Boletín No. 4, La Serena, Chile.

Iribarren Charlín, Jorge (1956), "Investigaciones arqueológicas en Guanaqueros," *Publicaciones del Museo y la Sociedad Arqueológico de La Serena,* Boletín No. 8, pp. 10–22, La Serena, Chile.

Iribarren Charlín, Jorge (1957), "Las poblaciones indígenas en el área de la Provincia de Coquimbo," *Publicaciones del Museo y la Sociedad Arqueológico de La Serena,* Boletín No. 9, pp. 26–29, La Serena, Chile.

Iribarren Charlín, Jorge (1960), "Yacimientos de la cultura del anzuelo de concha en el littoral de Coquimbo y Atacama," *Publicaciones del Museo y la Sociedad Arqueológico de La Serena,* Boletín No. 11, pp. 8–14, La Serena, Chile.

Iribarren Charlín, Jorge (1961), "La cultura de Huentelauquén y sus correlaciones," *Contribuciones Arqueológicas,* No. 1, Museo Arqueológico de La Serena, La Serena, Chile.

Iribarren Charlín, Jorge (1962 a), "Correlaciones entre las piedras tácitas y la cultura de El Molle. La Tortorita, sitio arqueológico en el Valle de Elquí," *Publica-*

ciones del Museo y la Sociedad Arqueológico de La Serena, Boletín No. 12, pp. 39ff., La Serena, Chile.

Iribarren Charlín, Jorge (1962 b), "Correlations between Archaic Cultures of Southern California and Coquimbo, Chile," *American Antiquity,* Vol. 27, No. 3, pp. 424–425, Salt Lake City.

Iribarren Charlín, Jorge (1962 c), "Material lítico en la cultura de El Molle — hallazgos arqueológicos en el Parque-Elquí," *Publicaciones del Museo y la Sociedad Arqueológico de La Serena,* Boletín No. 12, pp. 55–60, La Serena, Chile.

Iribarren Charlín, Jorge (1964), "Decoración con pintura negativa y la cultura de El Molle," in *Arqueología de Chile Central y Areas Vecinas,* Publicación de los Trabajos Presentados al Tercer Congreso Internacional de Arqueología Chilena, pp. 29–51, Imprenta "Los Andes," Santiago.

Iribarren Charlín, Jorge, et al. (1958), "Nuevos hallazgos arqueológicos en el cementerio indígena de La Turquía-Hurtado," *Arqueología Chilena,* Centro de Estudios Antropológicos, Pub. No. 4, pp. 13–40, Universidad de Chile, Santiago.

Iribarren Charlín, Jorge, et al. (1962), "Minas de explotación por los Incas y otros yacimientos arqueológicos en la zona de Almirante Latorre, Depto. de La Serena," *Publicaciones del Museo y la Sociedad Arqueológico de La Serena,* Boletín No. 12, pp. 61–72, La Serena, Chile.

Irwin-Williams, Cynthia (1969), "Comments on the Association of Archaeological Materials and Extinct Fauna in the Valsequillo Region, Puebla, Mexico," *American Antiquity,* Vol. 34, No. 1, pp. 82–83, Salt Lake City.

Ishida, Eiichiro, et al. (1960), *Andes 1: University of Tokyo Scientific Expedition to the Andes,* Kadokawa Publishing Co., Tokyo.

Izumi, Seiichi and T. Sono (1963), *Andes 2: Excavations at Kotosh, Peru, 1960,* Kadokawa Publishing Co., Tokyo.

Izumi, Seiichi and Kazuo Terada

(1966), *Andes 3: Excavations at Pechiche and Garbanzal, Tumbes Valley, Peru,* Kadokawa Publishing Co., Tokyo.

James, P. E. (1959), *Latin America,* 3rd ed., Cassell, London.

Jijón y Caamano, Jacinto (1914), *Contribución al Conocimiento de los Aborígenes de la Provincia de Imbabura en la República del Ecuador,* Estudio de Prehistoria Americana, II, Blass y Cía., Impresores, Madrid.

Jijón y Caamano, Jacinto (1919), "Ensayo provisional. Contribución al conocimiento de las lenguas indígenas que se hablaron en Ecuador," *Boletín de la Sociedad Ecuatoriana de Estudios Históricos Americanas,* Vol. 2, No. 6, Quito.

Jijón y Caamano, Jacinto (1920), "Nueva contribución al conocimiento de los aborígenes de la Provincia de Imbabura," *Boletín de la Sociedad Ecuatoriana de Estudios Históricos Americanas,* Vol. 4, pp. 1–120, 183–244, Quito.

Jijón y Caamano, Jacinto (1927), *Puruhá. Contribución al Conocimiento de los Aborígenes de la Provincia de Chimborazo, de la República del Ecuador,* 2 Vols., reprinted from *Boletín de la Academia Nacional de Historia de Ecuador,* Vol. 3, No. 6; Vol. 5, Nos. 12–14; Vol. 6, Nos. 15–17; Vol. 7, No. 19; Vol. 9, Nos. 24–26, Quito.

Jijón y Caamano, Jacinto (1930), "Una gran marea cultural en el noroeste de Sudamérica," *Journal de la Société des Américanistes,* Vol. 22, pp. 107–197, Paris.

Jijón y Caamano, Jacinto (1949), *Maranga: Contribución al Conocimiento de Los Aborígenes del Valle del Rimac, Perú,* La Prensa Católica, Quito.

Jijón y Caamano, Jacinto (1951), "Las civilizaciones del sur de Centro América y el noroeste de Sud América," *Selected Papers, 29th International Congress of Americanists,* Vol. 1, pp. 165–172, University of Chicago Press, Chicago.

Johnson, Frederick (1940), "The Linguistic Map of Mexico and Central America," in *The Maya and Their Neighbors,* C. L. Hay

et al., eds., pp. 88–114, D. Appleton-Century Co., Inc., New York.

Johnson, Frederick (1948 a), "The Caribbean Lowland Tribes: The Talamanca Division," in *Handbook of South American Indians,* J. H. Steward, ed., Vol. 4, pp. 231–252, Bureau of American Ethnology, Bulletin 143, Smithsonian Institution, Washington, D.C.

Johnson, Frederick (1948 b), "Central American Cultures: An Introduction," in *Handbook of South American Indians,* J. H. Steward, ed., Vol. 4, pp. 43–68, Bureau of American Ethnology, Bulletin 143, Smithsonian Institution, Washington, D.C.

Johnson, Frederick (1948 c), "The Meso-American Division," in *Handbook of South American Indians,* J. H. Steward, ed., Vol. 4, pp. 199–204, Bureau of American Ethnology, Bulletin 143, Smithsonian Institution, Washington, D.C.

Joyce, T. A. (1912), *South American Archaeology,* G. P. Putnam's Sons, New York.

Joyce, T. A. (1916), *Central American and West Indian Archaeology,* G. P. Putnam's Sons, New York.

Kidder II, Alfred (1943), *Some Early Sites in the Northern Lake Titicaca Basin,* Peabody Museum Papers, Vol. 27, No. 1, Harvard University, Cambridge.

Kidder II, Alfred (1944), *Archaeology of Northwestern Venezuela,* Peabody Museum Papers, Vol. 26, No. 1, Harvard University, Cambridge.

Kidder II, Alfred (1948 a), "The Position of Pucará in Titicaca Basin Archaeology," in *A Reappraisal of Peruvian Archaeology,* W. C. Bennett, ed., pp. 87–89, Memoir No. 4, Society for American Archaeology, Menasha, Wisconsin.

Kidder II, Alfred (1956), "Settlement Patterns — Peru," in *Prehistoric Settlement Patterns in the New World,* G. R. Willey, ed., pp. 148–155, Viking Fund Publications in Anthropology, No. 23, Wenner-Gren Foundation, New York.

Kidder II, Alfred (1964), "South American High Cultures," in *Prehistoric Man in the New World,* J. D. Jennings and E. Norbeck, eds., pp. 451–488, University of Chicago Press, Chicago.

Kidder II, Alfred, L. G. Lumbreras, and D. B. Smith (1963), "Cultural Development in the Central Andes — Peru and Bolivia," in *Aboriginal Cultural Development in Latin America: An Interpretative Review,* B. J. Meggers and C. Evans, eds., Smithsonian Miscellaneous Collections, Vol. 146, No. 1, pp. 89–102, Washington, D.C.

Kirchhoff, Paul (1948 a), "The Caribbean Lowland Tribes: The Mosquito, Sumo, Paya, and Jicaque," in *Handbook of South American Indians,* J. H. Steward, ed., Vol. 4, pp. 219–230, Bureau of American Ethnology, Bulletin 143, Smithsonian Institution, Washington, D.C.

Kirchhoff, Paul (1948 b), "Tribes North of the Orinoco River," in *Handbook of South American Indians,* J. H. Steward, ed., Vol. 4, pp. 481–494, Bureau of American Ethnology, Bulletin 143, Smithsonian Institution, Washington, D.C.

Kirchhoff, Paul (1948 c), "The Otomac," in *Handbook of South American Indians,* J. H. Steward, ed., Vol. 4, pp. 439–444, Bureau of American Ethnology, Bulletin 143, Smithsonian Institution, Washington, D.C.

Kirchhoff, Paul (1948 d), "The Food-Gathering Tribes of the Venezuelan Llanos," in *Handbook of South American Indians,* J. H. Steward, ed., Vol. 4, pp. 445–468, Bureau of American Ethnology, Bulletin 143, Smithsonian Institution, Washington, D.C.

Kosok, Paul and Maria Reiche (1947), "The Mysterious Markings of Nazca," *Natural History,* Vol. 56, No. 5, pp. 200–207, 237–238, American Museum of Natural History, New York.

Kosok, Paul and Maria Reiche (1949), "Ancient Drawings on the Desert of Peru," *Archaeology,* Vol. 2, pp. 206–215, Cambridge, Massachusetts.

Krapovickas, Pedro (1958–59 a),

"Arqueología de La Puna Argentina," *Anales de Arqueología, y Etnología,* Vols. 14–15, pp. 53–113, Facultad de Filosofía y Letras, Universidad Nacional de Cuyo, Mendoza, Argentina.

Krapovickas, Pedro (1958–59 b), "Un taller de lapidario en el Pucará de Tilcara," *Runa,* Vol. 9, Pt. 2, pp. 137–151, Buenos Aires.

Krieger, A. D. (1964), "Early Man in the New World," in *Prehistoric Man in the New World,* J. D. Jennings and E. Norbeck, eds., pp. 23–81, University of Chicago Press, Chicago.

Krieger, H. W. (1929), *Archaeological and Historical Investigations in Samaná, Dominican Republic,* United States National Museum, Bulletin 147, Smithsonian Institution, Washington, D.C.

Krieger, H. W. (1930), "The Aborigines of the Ancient Island of Hispaniola," in *Annual Report, Smithsonian Institution for 1929,* pp. 473–506, Smithsonian Institution, Washington, D.C.

Krieger, H. W. (1931), *Aboriginal Indian Pottery of the Dominican Republic,* United States National Museum, Bulletin 156, Smithsonian Institution, Washington, D.C.

Kroeber, A. L. (1926 a), *The Uhle Pottery Collections from Chancay,* University of California Publications in American Archaeology and Ethnology, Vol. 21, pp. 265–304, Berkeley.

Kroeber, A. L. (1926 b), *Archaeological Explorations in Peru. Part I: Ancient Pottery from Trujillo,* Field Museum of Natural History, Anthropological Memoir, Vol. 2, No. 1, Chicago.

Kroeber, A. L. (1930), *Archaeological Explorations in Peru. Part II: The Northern Coast,* Anthropological Memoir, Vol. 2, No. 2, Field Museum of Natural History, Chicago.

Kroeber, A. L. (1937), *Archaeological Explorations in Peru. Part IV: Cañete Valley,* Anthropological Memoir, Vol. 2, No. 4, Field Museum of Natural History, Chicago.

Kroeber, A. L. (1944), *Peruvian Archaeology in 1942,* Viking Fund Publications in Anthropology, No. 4, Wenner-Gren Foundation, New York.

Kroeber, A. L. (1946), "The Chibcha," in *Handbook of South American Indians,* J. H. Steward, ed., Vol. 2, pp. 887–910, Bureau of American Ethnology, Bulletin 143, Smithsonian Institution, Washington, D.C.

Kroeber, A. L. (1948), *Anthropology,* Harcourt, Brace and World, New York.

Kroeber, A. L. (1953), *Paracas Cavernas and Chavín,* University of California Publications in American Archaeology and Ethnology, Vol. 40, No. 8, Berkeley.

Kroeber, A. L. (1956), *Toward Definition of the Nazca Style,* University of California Publications in American Archaeology and Ethnology, Vol. 43, No. 4, Berkeley.

Kroeber, A. L. and W. D. Strong (1924 a), *The Uhle Collections from Chincha,* University of California Publications in American Archaeology and Ethnology, Vol. 21, No. 1, Berkeley.

Kroeber, A. L. and W. D. Strong (1924 b), *The Uhle Pottery Collections from Ica, with Three Appendices by Max Uhle,* University of California Publications in American Archaeology and Ethnology, Vol. 21, No. 3, Berkeley.

Krone, Ricardo (1914), "Informações ethnographicas do Valle do Ribeira de Iguapé," *Boletín, Comision Geographia e Geologia do Estado de São Paulo,* São Paulo.

Kubler, George (1946), "The Quechua in the Colonial World," in *Handbook of South American Indians,* J. H. Steward, ed., Vol. 2, pp. 331–410, Bureau of American Ethnology, Bulletin 143, Smithsonian Institution, Washington, D.C.

Lacerda, A. (1882), "Documents pour servir a l'histoire de l'homme fossile du Brésil," *Mémoires de la Société d'Anthropologie de Paris,* 2me Ser., Vol. 2, No. 4, Paris.

Ladd, John (1957), "A Stratigraphic Trench at Sitio Conte, Panama," *American Antiquity,* Vol. 22, pp. 265–271, Salt Lake City.

Ladd, John (1964), *Archaeological Investigations in the Parita and Santa María Zones of Panama,* Bureau of American Ethnology, Bulletin 193, Smithsonian Institution, Washington, D.C.

Lafon, C. R. (1957), "Nuevos descubrimientos en el Alfarcito (Depto. de Tilcara, Prov. de Jujuy)," *Runa,* Vol. 8, Pt. 1, pp. 43–59, Buenos Aires (cited from Alcina, 1965).

Lafon, C. R. (1958–59), "Ensayo sobre cronología e integración de la cultura Humahuaca," *Runa,* Vol. 9, pp. 217–230, Buenos Aires.

Laming, Annette and José Emperaire (1957), "Les sambaquis de la côte méridionale du Brésil (campagnes de fouilles, 1954–1956)," *Journal de la Société des Américanistes,* Vol. 45, pp. 5–163, Paris.

Laming, Annette and José Emperaire (1959 a), "A jazida José Vieira; um sitio guarani e pre-cerâmico do interior do Paraná," *Arqueología,* No. 1, Secção 1, pp. 1–142, Universidade do Paraná, Curitiba, Paraná, Brazil.

Laming, Annette and José Emperaire (1959 b), "Bilan de trois campagnes de fouilles archéologiques au Brésil méridional," *Journal de la Société des Américanistes,* Vol. 47, pp. 199–212, Paris.

Lange, F. W. (1970), "Culture History in the Rio Sapoa Valley, Costa Rica," *Archaeological Research in the Rio Sapoa Valley Area: Report on the Second Season of Archaeological Research in Northwestern Guanacaste Province, the Republic of Costa Rica,* pp. 124–134, Ibero-American Studies Program, University of Wisconsin, Madison.

Lanning, E. P. (1959), "Early Ceramic Chronologies of the Peruvian Coast," mimeogr., Berkeley, California.

Lanning, E. P. (1963 a), "A Preagricultural Occupation on the Central Coast of Peru," *American Antiquity,* Vol. 28, No. 3, pp. 360–371, Salt Lake City.

Lanning, E. P. (1963 b), *A Cera-*

mic Sequence for the Piura and Chira Coast, North Peru, University of California Publications in American Archaeology and Ethnology, Vol. 46, No. 2, Berkeley.

Lanning, E. P. (1963 c), "Highland South America," in "Current Research," *American Antiquity*, Vol. 28, pp. 419–421, Salt Lake City.

Lanning, E. P. (1963 d), "Olmec and Chavín: Reply to Michael D. Coe," *American Antiquity*, Vol. 29, No. 1, pp. 99–101, Salt Lake City.

Lanning, E. P. (1964), review of "El Ampajanguense," by E. M. Cigliano, *American Antiquity*, Vol. 30, No. 2, pp. 233–234, Salt Lake City.

Lanning, E. P. (1965), "Early Man in Peru," *Scientific American*, Vol. 213, No. 4, pp. 68–76, New York.

Lanning, E. P. (1966 ms.), "Early Man in the Andean Area," project proposal submitted to National Science Foundation, Columbia University, New York.

Lanning, E. P. (1967), *Peru before the Incas*, Prentice-Hall, Inc., Englewood Cliffs, New Jersey.

Lanning, E. P. (1967 a ms.), "Preceramic Archaeology of the Ancón-Chillón Region, Central Coast of Peru," report to National Science Foundation, Columbia University, New York.

Lanning, E. P. (1967 b ms.), "Archaeological Investigations on the Santa Elena Peninsula, Ecuador," report to National Science Foundation, Columbia University, New York.

Lanning, E. P. (1970), "Pleistocene Man in South America," *World Archaeology*, Vol. 2, No. 1, pp. 90–111, Routledge and Kegan Paul Ltd., London.

Lanning, E. P. and E. A. Hammel (1961), "Early Lithic Industries of Western South America," *American Antiquity*, Vol. 27, No. 2, pp. 139–154, Salt Lake City.

Lanning, E. P. and T. C. Patterson (1967), "Early Man in South America," *Scientific American*, Vol. 217, No. 5, pp. 44–50, New York.

Lanning, E. P. and T. C. Patterson

(1967 ms.), "Early Man in South America."

Larco Hoyle, Rafael (1938–40), *Los Mochicas*, 2 Vols., Casa Editora "La Crónica y Variedades," S.A. Ltda.

Larco Hoyle, Rafael (1941), *Los Cupisniques*, Casa Editora "La Cronica y Variedades," Lima.

Larco Hoyle, Rafael (1944), *La Cultura Salinar*, Sociedad Geográfica Americana, Buenos Aires.

Larco Hoyle, Rafael (1945 a), *Los Mochicas*, Sociedad Geográfica Americana, Buenos Aires.

Larco Hoyle, Rafael (1945 b), *La Cultura Virú*, Sociedad Geográfica Americana, Buenos Aires.

Larco Hoyle, Rafael (1946), "A Culture Sequence for the North Coast of Peru," in *Handbook of South American Indians*, J. H. Steward, ed., Vol. 2, pp. 149–175, Bureau of American Ethnology, Bulletin 143, Smithsonian Institution, Washington, D.C.

Larco Hoyle, Rafael (1948), *Cronología Arqueológica del Norte del Perú*, Hacienda Chiclín, Trujillo, Peru.

Larco Hoyle, Rafael (1965), *La Cerámica de Vicus y sus Nexos con las Demás Culturas*, 2, Santiago Valverde, Lima.

Larco Hoyle, Rafael (1966), *Peru*, Archaeologia Mundi, Nägel, Geneva, and The World Publishing Company, Cleveland.

Las Casas, Bartolomé de (1951), *Historia de Las Indias*, Edición Agustín Millares Carlo, Fondo de Cultura Economica, México, D.F.

Latcham, R. E. (1928 a), *La Alfarería Indígena Chilena*, La Comisión Oficial Organizadora de la Concurrencia de Chile a la Exposición Ibero-Americana de Sevilla, Santiago.

Latcham, R. E. (1928 b), *La Prehistoria Chilena*, La Comisión Oficial Organizadora de la Concurrencia de Chile a la Exposición Ibero-Americana de Sevilla, Santiago.

Latcham, R. E. (1930), "Influencias Atacameñas en la antigua alfarería Diaguita-Chilena," *Revista Chilena de Historia Natural*, Vol. 34, pp. 346–349, Santiago.

Latcham, R. E. (1936 a), "Indian Ruins in North Chile," *American*

Anthropologist, Vol. 38, No. 1, pp. 52–58, Menasha, Wisconsin.

Latcham, R. E. (1936 b), "Atacameño Archaeology," *American Anthropologist*, Vol. 38, No. 4, pp. 609–619, Menasha, Wisconsin.

Lathrap, D. W. (1958), "The Cultural Sequence at Yarinacocha, Eastern Peru," *American Antiquity*, Vol. 23, pp. 379–388, Salt Lake City.

Lathrap, D. W. (1962), "Yarinacocha: Stratigraphic Excavations in the Peruvian Montaña," Ph.D. thesis, Department of Anthropology, Peabody Museum, Harvard University, Cambridge.

Lathrap, D. W. (1964), "An Alternative Seriation of the Mabaruma Phase, Northwestern British Guiana," *American Antiquity*, Vol. 29, No. 3, pp. 353–359, Salt Lake City.

Lathrap, D. W. (1965), "Origins of Central Andean Civilization: New Evidence," *Science*, Vol. 148, pp. 796–798, Lancaster, Pennsylvania.

Lathrap, D. W. (1966 a), "Relationships between Mesoamerica and the Andean Areas," in *Handbook of Middle American Indians*, R. Wauchope, G. F. Ekholm, and G. R. Willey, eds., Vol. 4, pp. 265–276, University of Texas Press, Austin.

Lathrap, D. W. (1966 b), "The Mabaruma Phase: A Return to the More Probable Interpretation," *American Antiquity*, Vol. 31, No. 4, pp. 558–565, Salt Lake City.

Lathrap, D. W. (1967), "Review of 'Early Formative Period of Coastal Ecuador: Valdivia and Machalilla Phases,'" *American Anthropologist*, Vol. 69, No. 1, pp. 96–98, Menasha, Wisconsin.

Lathrap, D. W. (1968), "The 'Hunting' Economies of the Tropical Forest Zone of South America: An Attempt at Historical Perspective," in *Man the Hunter*, R. B. Lee and Irven DeVore, eds., pp. 23–29, Wenner-Gren Foundation and Aldine Publishing Co., Chicago.

Lathrap, D. W. (1968 ms.), "The Tropical Forest and the Cultural Context of Chavín," mimeogr. ms. presented to the Dumbarton

Oaks Conference on Chavín, University of Illinois, Urbana.

Lathrap, D. W. (1970), *The Upper Amazon*, Ancient Peoples and Places Series, No. 70, Glyn Daniel, ed., Thames and Hudson, London.

Lathrap, D. W., *et al.* (1967 ms.), "Report on the Continuing Program of Research on the Culture History of the Upper Amazon Basin," Department of Anthropology, University of Illinois, Urbana.

Lathrap, D. W. and Lawrence Roys (1963), "The Archaeology of the Cave of the Owls in the Upper Montana of Peru," *American Antiquity*, Vol. 29, pp. 27–38, Salt Lake City.

Laurencich de Minelli, Laura and Luigi Minelli (1966), "Informe preliminar sobre excavaciones alrededor de San Vito de Java," *Actas y Memorias, 36th International Congress of Americanists*, Vol. 1, pp. 415–427, Seville.

Leeds, Anthony (1961), "Yaruro Incipient Tropical Forest Horticulture, Possibilities and Limits," in *The Evolution of Horticultural Systems in Native South America, Causes and Consequences*, J. Wilbert, ed., pp. 13–46, Sociedad de Ciencias Naturales La Salle, Carácas.

Lehmann, Henri (1946), "The Archaeology of the Popayán Region, Colombia," in *Handbook of South American Indians*, J. H. Steward, ed., Vol. 2, pp. 861–864, Bureau of American Ethnology, Bulletin 143, Smithsonian Institution, Washington, D.C.

Le Paige, Gustavo R. P. (1959), "Antiguas culturas atacameñas en la cordillera chilena: época Paleolítica," *Revista Universitaria, Universidad Católica de Chile*, Vol. 43, pp. 139–165, Santiago.

Le Paige, Gustavo R. P. (1960), "Antiguas culturas atacameñas en la cordillera chilena: época Paleolítica," *Revista Universitaria, Universidad Católica de Chile*, Vols. 44–45, pp. 191–206, Santiago.

Le Paige, Gustavo (1963 a), "Ghatchi y su zona," *Revista Universitaria, Universidad Católica de Chile*, Vol. 48, pp. 177–193, Santiago.

Le Paige, Gustavo (1963 b), "Continuidad o discontinuidad de la cultura atacameña," *Actas del Congreso Internacional de Arqueología en San Pedro de Atacama*, Anales, No. 2, Universidad del Norte, Antofagasta, Chile.

Le Paige, Gustavo (1963 c), "La antiguedad de una tumba comprabada por carbono 14 y el ambiente que la rodea," *Revista Universitaria, Universidad Católica de Chile*, Vol. 48, pp. 167–176, Santiago.

Le Paige, Gustavo (1964), *El Precerámico en la Cordillera Atacameña y Los Cementerios de Periodo Agro-Alfarero de San Pedro de Atacama*, Anales, No. 3, Universidad del Norte, Antofagasta, Chile.

Lévi-Strauss, Claude (1948), "The Tribes of the Upper Xingú River," in *Handbook of South American Indians*, J. H. Steward, ed., Vol. 3, pp. 321–348, Bureau of American Ethnology, Bulletin 143, Smithsonian Institution, Washington, D.C.

Lévi-Strauss, Claude (1950), "The Use of Wild Plants in Tropical South America," in *Handbook of South American Indians*, J. H. Steward, ed., Vol. 6, pp. 465–486, Bureau of American Ethnology, Bulletin 143, Smithsonian Institution, Washington, D.C.

Linares de Sapir, Olga (1968 a), *Cultural Chronology of the Gulf of Chiriquí, Panama*, Smithsonian Contributions to Anthropology, Vol. 8, Washington, D.C.

Linares de Sapir, Olga (1968 b), "Ceramic Phases for Chiriquí, Panama, and Their Relationship to Neighboring Sequences," *American Antiquity*, Vol. 33, No. 2, pp. 216–225, Salt Lake City.

Linné, Sigvald (1929), *Darien in the Past*, Göteborgs Kungl. Vetenskaps-och Vitterhets-Samhalles Handlingar, Femte Foljden, Ser. A, Bd. 1, No. 3, Göteborg, Sweden.

Lorenzo, J. L. (1967), "Sobre metodo arqueológico," *Boletín, Instituto Nacional de Antropología e Historia*, No. 28, México, D.F.

Lothrop, S. K. (1926), *Pottery of Costa Rica and Nicaragua*, 2 Vols., Contributions, Vol. 8, Museum of the American Indian, Heye Foundation, New York.

Lothrop, S. K. (1928), *The Indians of Tierra del Fuego*, Contributions, Vol. 10, Museum of the American Indian, Heye Foundation, New York.

Lothrop, S. K. (1932 a), "Aboriginal Navigation of the West Coast of South America," *Journal of the Royal Anthropological Institute*, Vol. 62, pp. 229–256, London.

Lothrop, S. K. (1932 b), "Indians of the Paraná Delta, Argentina," *Annals of the New York Academy of Sciences*, Vol. 33, pp. 77–232, New York.

Lothrop, S. K. (1937–42), *Coclé, An Archaeological Study of Central Panama. Pts. I and II*, Memoirs, Vols. 7, 8, Peabody Museum, Harvard University, Cambridge.

Lothrop, S. K. (1938), *Inca Treasure as Depicted by Spanish Historians*, Publications of the Frederick Webb Hodge Anniversary Publication Fund, Vol. 2, Southwest Museum, Los Angeles.

Lothrop, S. K. (1941), "Gold Ornaments of Chavín Style from Chongoyape, Peru," *American Antiquity*, Vol. 6, pp. 250–262, Menasha, Wisconsin.

Lothrop, S. K. (1942), "The Sigua: Southernmost Aztec Outpost," in *Proceedings, Eighth American Scientific Congress*, Vol. 2, pp. 109–116, Washington, D.C.

Lothrop, S. K. (1946 a), "The Diaguita of Chile," in *Handbook of South American Indians*, J. H. Steward, ed., Vol. 2, pp. 633–636, Bureau of American Ethnology, Bulletin 143, Smithsonian Institution, Washington, D.C.

Lothrop, S. K. (1946 b), "Indians of the Paraná Delta and La Plata Littoral," in *Handbook of South American Indians*, J. H. Steward, ed., Vol. 1, pp. 177–190, Bureau of American Ethnology, Bulletin 143, Smithsonian Institution, Washington, D.C.

Lothrop, S. K. (1948 a), "Pariñas-Chira Archaeology: A Preliminary Report," in *A Reappraisal of Peruvian Archaeology*, W. C.

Bennett, ed., Memoir No. 4, pp. 53–65, Society for American Archaeology, Menasha, Wisconsin.

Lothrop, S. K. (1948 b), "The Archaeology of Panama," in *Handbook of South American Indians,* J. H. Steward, ed., Vol. 4, pp. 143–168, Bureau of American Ethnology, Bulletin 143, Smithsonian Institution, Washington, D.C.

Lothrop, S. K. (1948 c), "The Tribes West and South of the Panama Canal," in *Handbook of South American Indians,* J. H. Steward, ed., Vol. 4, pp. 253–257, Bureau of American Ethnology, Bulletin 143, Smithsonian Institution, Washington, D.C.

Lothrop, S. K. (1950), *Archaeology of Southern Veraguas, Panama,* Memoirs, Vol. 9, No. 3, Peabody Museum, Harvard University, Cambridge.

Lothrop, S. K. (1951), "Gold Artifacts of the Chavín Style," *American Antiquity,* Vol. 16, pp. 226–240, Menasha, Wisconsin.

Lothrop, S. K. (1954), "Suicide, sacrifice, and mutilations in burials at Venado Beach, Panama," *American Antiquity,* Vol. 19, pp. 226–233, Salt Lake City.

Lothrop, S. K. (1959), "A Re-Appraisal of Isthmian Archaeology," *Amerikanistische Miszellen, Mitteilungen,* No. 25, pp. 87–91, Museum für Völkerkunde, Hamburg.

Lothrop, S. K. (1961), "Early Migrations to Central and South America: An Anthropological Problem in the Light of Other Sciences," *Journal of the Royal Anthropological Institute,* Vol. 91, pp. 97–123, London.

Lothrop, S. K. (1963), *Archaeology of the Diquís Delta, Costa Rica,* Papers of the Peabody Museum, Vol. 51, Harvard University, Cambridge.

Lothrop, S. K. (1966), "Archaeology of Lower Central America," in *Handbook of Middle American Indians,* R. Wauchope, G. F. Ekholm, and G. R. Willey, eds., Vol. 4, pp. 180–208, University of Texas Press, Austin.

Lothrop, S. K. and Joy Mahler (1957), *A Chancay-Style Grave at Zapallán, Peru,* Papers of the Peabody Museum, Vol. 50, No. 1, Harvard University, Cambridge.

Lovén, Sven (1935), *Origins of the Tainan Culture, West Indies,* Elanders Boktryckeri Aktiebolag, Göteborg, Sweden.

Lowie, R. H. (1946), "Eastern Brazil: An Introduction," in *Handbook of South American Indians,* J. H. Steward, ed., Vol. 1, pp. 381–396, Bureau of American Ethnology, Bulletin 143, Smithsonian Institution, Washington, D.C.

Lowie, R. H. (1948), "The Tropical Forests: An Introduction," in *Handbook of South American Indians,* J. H. Steward, ed., Vol. 3, pp. 1–56, Bureau of American Ethnology, Bulletin 143, Smithsonian Institution, Washington, D.C.

Lumbreras, L. G. (1960 a), "Algunos problemas de Arqueología Peruana," in *Antiguo Peru, Espacio y Tiempo,* pp. 129–148, Librería-Editorial Juan Mejía Baca, Lima.

Lumbreras, L. G. (1960 b), "La cultura de Wari, Ayacucho," *Etnología y Arqueología,* Año I, No. 1, pp. 130–227, Universidad Nacional Mayor de San Marcos, Lima.

Lumbreras, L. G. (1960 c), "Esquema arqueológico de la sierra central del Perú," *Revista del Museo Nacional,* Vol. 28, pp. 64–117, Lima.

Lumbreras, L. G. (1968 ms.), "Para una revaluación de Chavín," presented to the Dumbarton Oaks Conference on Chavín.

Lynch, T. F. (1967 a), *The Nature of the Central Andean Preceramic,* Occasional Papers, No. 21, Idaho State University Museum, Pocatello, Idaho.

Lynch, T. F. (1967 b), "Quishqui Puncu: A Preceramic Site in Highland Peru," *Science,* Vol. 158, pp. 780–783, Lancaster, Pennsylvania.

Lynch, T. F. and K. A. R. Kennedy (1970), "Early Human Cultural and Skeletal Remains from Guitarrero Cave, Northern Peru," *Science,* Vol. 169, pp. 1307–1310, Lancaster, Pennsylvania.

Lyon, P. J. (1966), "Innovation through Archaism; the Origins of the Ica Pottery Style," *Nawpa Pacha,* No. 4, pp. 31–62, Institute of Andean Studies, Berkeley.

MacCurdy, G. G. (1911), *A Study of Chiriquían Antiquities,* Memoir No. 3, Connecticut Academy of Arts and Sciences, New Haven.

MacNeish, R. S. (1959), "A Speculative Framework of Northern American Prehistory as of April 1959," *Anthropologia,* Vol. 1, pp. 7–23, Canadian Research Center for Anthropology, University of Ottawa.

MacNeish, R. S. (1969), *First Annual Report of the Ayacucho Archaeological-Botanical Project,* Robert S. Peabody Foundation, Andover, Massachusetts.

Madrazo, G. B. and Marta Ottonello de García Reinoso (1966), *Tipos de Instalación Prehispánica en la Región de la Puna y su Borde,* Monografías, No. 1, Museo Etnográfico Municipal "Dámaso Arce," Olavarría, Buenos Aires.

Maldonado Bruzzone, Rodolfo (1931), "Notas arqueológicas. Breve reseña del material recogido en Punta Lara," *Notas Preliminares, Museo de La Plata,* Vol. 1, No. 3, pp. 329–354, La Plata, Argentina.

Mangelsdorf, P. C., R. S. MacNeish, and G. R. Willey (1964), "Origins of Agriculture in Mesoamerica," in *Handbook of Middle American Indians,* R. Wauchope and R. West, eds., Vol. 1, pp. 437–445, University of Texas Press, Austin.

Márquez Miranda, Fernando (1934), "Arqueología de la Laguna de Lobos, Provincia de Buenos Aires," *25th International Congress of Americanists,* Vol. 2, pp. 75–100, Buenos Aires.

Márquez Miranda, Fernando (1942), "Hallazgos Arqueológicos Chaqueños," *Relaciones, Sociedad Argentina de Antropología,* Vol. 3, pp. 7–27, Buenos Aires.

Márquez Miranda, Fernando (1946 a), "The Diaguita of Argentina," in *Handbook of South American Indians,* J. H. Steward, ed., Vol. 2, pp. 637–654, Bureau of American Ethnology, Bulletin 143, Smithsonian Institution, Washington, D.C.

Márquez Miranda, Fernando (1946 b), "The Chaco-Santiagueño Culture," in *Handbook of South American Indians,* J. H. Steward, ed., Vol. 2, pp. 655–660, Bureau of American Ethnology, Bulletin 143, Smithsonian Institution, Washington, D.C.

Márquez Miranda, Fernando (1954), *Región Meridional de America del Sur,* Program of History of America, Vol. 1, No. 10, Pan-American Institute of Geography and History, México, D.F.

Mason, J. A. (1931–39), *Archaeology of Santa Marta, Colombia,* Anthropological Papers, Vol. 20, Nos. 1–3, Field Museum of Natural History, Chicago.

Mason, J. A. (1941), *A Large Archaeological Site at Capá, Utuado, with Notes on other Porto Rico Sites Visited in 1914–1915,* Scientific Survey of Porto Rico and the Virgin Islands, Vol. 18, Pt. 2, New York Academy of Sciences, New York.

Mason, J. A. (1945), *Costa Rican Stonework,* Anthropological Papers, Vol. 39, Pt. 3, American Museum of Natural History, New York.

Mason, J. A. (1950), "The Languages of South American Indians," in *Handbook of South American Indians,* J. H. Steward, ed., Vol. 6, pp. 157–318, Bureau of American Ethnology, Bulletin 143, Smithsonian Institution, Washington, D.C.

Mason, J. A. (1957), *The Ancient Civilizations of Peru,* Penguin Books, Harmondsworth, England.

Matos, Ramiro (1960), "Informes sobre Trabajos Arqueológicos en Castrovirreyna," *Antiguo Perú, Espacio y Tiempo,* pp. 313–324, Librería-Editorial Juan Mejía Baca, Lima.

Matos, Ramiro (1967 ms.), "Notas preliminares para el estudio de Vicús," to be published in *Revista de Etnología y Arqueología,* No. 2, Universidad de San Marcos, Lima.

Matos, Ramiro (1968), "A Formative-Period Painted Pottery Complex at Ancón, Peru," *American Antiquity,* Vol. 33, No. 2, pp. 226–232, Salt Lake City.

Mattos, Anibal (1946), "Lagoa Santa Man," in *Handbook of South American Indians,* J. H. Steward, ed., Vol. 1, pp. 399–400, Bureau of American Ethnology, Bulletin 143, Smithsonian Institution, Washington, D.C.

Mayer-Oakes, W. J. (1963), "Early Man in the Andes," *Scientific American,* Vol. 208, No. 5, pp. 116–128, New York.

Mayntzhusen, Frederico (1928), "Instrumentos paleolíticos del Paraguay," *Annals, 20th International Congress of Americanists,* Vol. 2, Pt. 2, pp. 177–180, Rio de Janeiro.

Mayntzhusen, Frederico (1930), "Funde altsteinzeitlicher Werkzeuge im Alto-Paraná-Gebiet," *Proceedings, 23rd International Congress of Americanists,* pp. 346–350, New York.

McCown, T. D. (1945), *Pre-Incaic Huamachuco. Survey and Excavations in the Region of Huamachuco and Cajabamba,* University of California Publications in American Archaeology and Ethnology, Vol. 39, No. 4, Berkeley.

McCown, T. D. (1950), "The Antiquity of Man in South America," in *Handbook of South American Indians,* J. H. Steward, ed., Vol. 6, pp. 1–10, Bureau of American Ethnology, Bulletin 143, Smithsonian Institution, Washington, D.C.

McGimsey III, C. R. (1956), "Cerro Mangote: A Preceramic Site in Panama," *American Antiquity,* Vol. 22, No. 2, pp. 151–161, Salt Lake City.

McGimsey III, C. R. (1958), "Further data and a date from Cerro Mangote, Panama," *American Antiquity,* Vol. 23, No. 4, pp. 434–435, Salt Lake City.

McKern, W. C. (1939), "The Midwestern Taxonomic Method as an Aid to Archaeological Study," *American Antiquity,* Vol. 4, pp. 301–313, Menasha, Wisconsin.

Means, P. A. (1931), *Ancient Civilizations of the Andes,* Charles Scribner's Sons, New York.

Medina, Alberto (1958), "Hallazgos arqueológicos en el 'Cerro Plomo,'" *Arqueología Chilena,* No. 4, pp. 43–63, Centro de Estudios Antropológicos, Universidad de Chile, Santiago.

Meggers, B. J. (1948), "The Archaeology of the Amazon Basin," in *Handbook of South American Indians,* J. H. Steward, ed., Vol. 3, pp. 149–166, Bureau of American Ethnology, Bulletin 143, Smithsonian Institution, Washington, D.C.

Meggers, B. J. (1954), "Environmental Limitation on the Development of Culture," *American Anthropologist,* Vol. 56, pp. 801–824, Menasha, Wisconsin.

Meggers, B. J. (1964), "North and South American Cultural Connections and Convergences," in *Prehistoric Man in the New World,* J. D. Jennings and E. Norbeck, eds., pp. 511–526, University of Chicago Press, Chicago.

Meggers, B. J. (1966), *Ecuador,* in Ancient Peoples and Places Series, No. 49, G. Daniel, ed., Frederick A. Praeger, New York.

Meggers, B. J. (1967), "Considerações gerais," *Programa Nacional de Pesquisas Arqueológicas; Resultados Preliminares do Primeiro Ano 1965–1966,* Museu Paraense Emílio Goeldi, Publicações Avulsas, No. 6, pp. 153–158, Belém do Pará, Brazil.

Meggers, B. J. and Clifford Evans, Jr. (1956), "The Reconstruction of Settlement Pattern in the South American Tropical Forest," in *Prehistoric Settlement Patterns in the New World,* G. R. Willey, ed., Viking Fund Publications in Anthropology, No. 23, pp. 156–164, Wenner-Gren Foundation, New York.

Meggers, B. J. and Clifford Evans, Jr. (1957), *Archaeological Investigations at the Mouth of the Amazon,* Bureau of American Ethnology, Bulletin 167, Smithsonian Institution, Washington, D.C.

Meggers, B. J. and Clifford Evans, Jr. (1958), "Identificação das Areas Culturais e dos Tipos de Cultura na Base da Ceramica das Jazidas Arqueológicas," *Arquivos do Museu Nacional,* Vol. 46, pp. 9–33, Rio de Janeiro.

Meggers, B. J. and Clifford Evans, Jr. (1961), "An Experimental Formulation of Horizon Styles in the Tropical Forest Area of South America," in *Essays in Pre-Columbian Art and Archaeology,*

S. K. Lothrop *et al.,* eds., pp. 372–388, Harvard University Press, Cambridge.

Meggers, B. J. and Clifford Evans, Jr. (1962), "The Machalilla Culture: An Early Formative Complex on the Ecuadorian Coast," *American Antiquity,* Vol. 28, No. 2, pp. 186–192, Salt Lake City.

Meggers, B. J. and Clifford Evans, Jr., eds. (1963), *Aboriginal Cultural Development in Latin America: An Interpretative Review,* Smithsonian Miscellaneous Collections, Vol. 146, No. 1, Smithsonian Institution, Washington, D.C.

Meggers, B. J., Clifford Evans, Jr., and Emilio Estrada (1965), *Early Formative Period of Coastal Ecuador,* Smithsonian Contributions to Anthropology, Vol. 1, Smithsonian Institution, Washington, D.C.

Menghin, O. F. A. (1952 a), "Fundamentos cronológicos de la prehistoria de Patagonia," *Runa,* Vol. 5, pp. 23–43, Buenos Aires.

Menghin, O. F. A. (1952 b), "Las pinturas rupestres de la Patagonia," *Runa,* Vol. 5, pp. 5–22, Buenos Aires.

Menghin, O. F. A. (1953–54), "Culturas precerámicas en Bolivia," *Runa,* Vol. 6, Pts. 1–2, pp. 125–132, Buenos Aires.

Menghin, O. F. A. (1956), "El Altoparanaense," *Ampurias,* Vols. 17–18, pp. 171–200, Barcelona.

Menghin, O. F. A. (1957 a), "Das Protolithikum in Amerika," *Acta Praehistorica,* No. 1, Centro Argentino de Estudios Prehistóricos, Buenos Aires.

Menghin, O. F. A. (1957 b), "El poblamiento prehistórico de Misiones," *Anales de Arqueología y Etnología,* Vol. 12, pp. 19–40, Facultad de Filosofía y Letras, Universidad Nacional de Cuyo, Mendoza, Argentina.

Menghin, O. F. A. (1959–60), "Estudios de prehistoria Araucana," *Acta Praehistorica,* Nos. 3–4, pp. 49–120, Centro Argentino de Estudios Prehistóricos, Buenos Aires.

Menghin, O. F. A. (1962), "Los sambaquís de la costa atlántica del Brasil meridional," *Amerindia,* No. 1, pp. 53–81, Montevideo.

Menghin, O. F. A. and Marcelo Bórmida (1950), "Investigaciones prehistóricas en cuevas de Tandilia, Provincia de Buenos Aires," *Runa,* Vol. 3, pp. 5–36, Buenos Aires.

Menghin, O. F. A. and A. R. González (1954), "Excavaciones arqueológicas en el yacimiento de Ongamira, Córdoba (Rep. Arg.)," *Notas del Museo de La Plata (Eva Perón),* Vol. 17, No. 67, pp. 215–274, Universidad Nacional de La Plata (Eva Perón), La Plata, Argentina.

Menghin, O. F. A. and Hermann Wachnitz (1958), "Forschungen über die Chronologie der Altoparanákultur," *Acta Praehistorica,* Vol. 2, pp. 138–145, Centro Argentino de Estudios Prehistóricos, Buenos Aires.

Menzel, Dorothy (1960 ms.), "Results of Archaeological Research Done under the Fulbright Program in Peru in 1957, 1958, and 1959: Studies of the South Coast in the Ica, Pisco, Chincha, and Cañete Valleys," typescript, Berkeley.

Menzel, Dorothy (1964), "Style and Time in the Middle Horizon," *Nawpa Pacha,* No. 2, pp. 1–106, Institute of Andean Studies, Berkeley.

Menzel, Dorothy (1966), "The Pottery of Chincha," *Nawpa Pacha,* No. 4, pp. 77–144, Institute of Andean Studies, Berkeley.

Menzel, Dorothy (1966), "The Role of Chincha in Late Pre-Spanish Peru," *Nawpa Pacha,* No. 4, pp. 63–76, Institute of Andean Studies, Berkeley.

Menzel, Dorothy, J. H. Rowe, and L. E. Dawson (1964), *The Paracas Pottery of Ica, A Study in Style and Time,* University of California Publications in American Archaeology and Ethnology, Vol. 50, Berkeley.

Métraux, Alfred (1929), "Contribution à l'ethnografie et à l'archéologie de la Province de Mendoza," *Revista del Instituto de Etnología de la Universidad Nacional de Tucumán,* Vol. 1, No. 1, pp. 5–73, Tucumán, Argentina.

Métraux, Alfred (1946 a), "Ethnography of the Chaco," in *Hand-book of South American Indians,* J. H. Steward, ed., Vol. 1, pp. 197–370, Bureau of American Ethnology, Bulletin 143, Smithsonian Institution, Washington, D.C.

Métraux, Alfred (1946 b), "The Caingang," in *Handbook of South American Indians,* J. H. Steward, ed., Vol. 1, pp. 445–476, Bureau of American Ethnology, Bulletin 143, Smithsonian Institution, Washington, D.C.

Métraux, Alfred (1948 a), "The Tupinamba," in *Handbook of South American Indians,* J. H. Steward, ed., Vol. 3, pp. 95–134, Bureau of American Ethnology, Bulletin 143, Smithsonian Institution, Washington, D.C.

Métraux, Alfred (1948 b), "The Guaraní," in *Handbook of South American Indians,* J. H. Steward, ed., Vol. 3, pp. 69–94, Bureau of American Ethnology, Bulletin 143, Smithsonian Institution, Washington, D.C.

Métraux, Alfred and Paul Kirchoff (1948), "The Northeastern Extension of Andean Culture," in *Handbook of South American Indians,* J. H. Steward, ed., Vol. 4, pp. 349–368, Bureau of American Ethnology, Bulletin 143, Smithsonian Institution, Washington, D.C.

Middendorf, E. W. (1895), *Peru,* Vol. 3, *Das Hochland von Peru,* Oppenheim (Gustav Schmidt), Berlin.

Miller, E. T. (1967), "Pesquisas arqueológicas efetuadas no nordeste do Río Grande do Sul," *Programa Nacional de Pesquisas Arqueológicas; Resultados Preliminares do Primeiro Ano 1965–1966,* Museu Paraense Emílio Goeldi, Publicações Avulsas, No. 6, pp. 15–38, Belém do Pará, Brazil.

Miller, T. O., Jr. (1969), "Pré-História da região de Río Claro, S. P.: Tradições em Divergenia," *Cadernos Rioclarenses de Ciencias Humanas,* No. 1, pp. 22–52, Faculdade de Filosofía, Ciências e Letras de Río Claro, Brazil.

Mirambell, Lorena (1967), "Excavaciones en un sitio pleistocénico de Tlapacoya, México," *Boletín, Instituto Nacional de Antropología e Historia,* No. 29, pp. 37–41, México, D.F.

Mishkin, Bernard (1946), "The Contemporary Quechua," in *Handbook of South American Indians,* J. H. Steward, ed., Vol. 2, pp. 411–470, Bureau of American Ethnology, Bulletin 143, Smithsonian Institution, Washington, D.C.

Montane, J. C. (1960 a), "Arqueología Diaguita en conchales de la costa. Punta de Teatinos," *Publicaciones del Museo y la Sociedad Arqueológica de La Serena,* Boletín No. 11, pp. 68–75, La Serena, Chile.

Montane, J. C. (1960 b), "Elementos precerámicos de Cahuil," *Notas del Museo de La Serena,* No. 8, La Serena, Chile.

Montane, J. C. (1962), "Cuatro cerámicos Molle de Copiapó," *Publicaciones del Museo y la Sociedad Arqueológica de La Serena,* Boletín No. 12, pp. 33–37, La Serena, Chile.

Montane, J. C. (1964), "Fechamiento tentativo de las ocupaciones humanas en dos terrazas a lo largo litoral Chileno," in *Arqueología de Chile Central y Areas Vecinas,* Publicación de los Trabajos Presentados al Tercer Congreso Internacional de Arqueología Chilena, pp. 109–124, Imprenta "Los Andes," Santiago.

Montane, Julio C. (1968), "Paleo-Indian Remains from Laguna de Tagua Tagua, Central Chile," *Science,* Vol. 161, pp. 1137–1138, Lancaster, Pennsylvania.

Mostny, Grete (1943), "Un nuevo estilo arqueológico," *Boletín del Museo Nacional de Historia Natural de Chile,* Vol. 20, pp. 91–96, Santiago.

Mostny, Grete (1944), "Un nuevo estilo arqueológico," *Boletín del Museo Nacional de Historia Natural de Chile,* Vol. 22, pp. 191–196, Santiago.

Mostny, Grete (1946–47), "Un cementerio Incásico en Chile Central," *Boletín del Museo Nacional de Historia Natural de Chile,* Vol. 23, pp. 17–41, Santiago.

Mostny, Grete (1955), "El Niño del Cerro 'El Plomo,'" *31st International Congress of American-* *ists,* Vol. 2, pp. 847–863, São Paulo.

Mostny, Grete (1969), "Estado Actual de los Estudios Prehistóricos en Chile," *38th International Congress of Americanists,* Vol. 1, pp. 443–456, Stuttgart and Munich.

Müller-Beck, Hansjürgen (1965), "10,000 Jahre Steinzeitliche Sammler und Jäger in Südamerika," *Umschau,* Vol. 18, pp. 568–572, Frankfurt-am-Main.

Müller-Beck, Hansjürgen (1966), "Paleohunters in America: Origins and Diffusion," *Science,* Vol. 152, pp. 1191–1210, Lancaster, Pennsylvania.

Munizaga, Carlos (1957), "Secuencias culturales de la zona Arica. Comparación entre las secuencias de Uhle y Bird," *Arqueología Chilena,* No. 2, pp. 77–122, Universidad de Chile, Santiago.

Munizaga, J. R. (1965), "Skeletal Remains from Sites of Valdivia and Machalilla Phases," Appendix 2, in *Early Formative Period of Coastal Ecuador, the Valdivia and Machalilla Phases,* E. Estrada, B. J. Meggers, and C. Evans, eds., Smithsonian Contributions to Anthropology, Vol. 1, pp. 219–233, Smithsonian Institution, Washington, D.C.

Munoa, J. I. (1965), "Los pueblos prehistóricos del territorio Uruguayo," *Cuadernos Antropológicos,* No. 3, Centro de Estudios Arqueológicos y Antropológicos Americanos, Montevideo.

Murdock, G. P. (1951), "South American Culture Areas," *Southwestern Journal of Anthropology,* Vol. 7, No. 4, pp. 415–436, University of New Mexico Press, Albuquerque, New Mexico.

Nachtigall, Horst (1955), *Tierradentro: Archäologie und Ethnographie einer Kolombischen Landshaft,* Mainzer Studien zur Kultur und Völkerkunde, Bd. II, Origo Verlag, Zürich.

Nasser, N. A. de Souza (1967), "Notas preliminares sobre a arqueología da foz do sistema Curimataú-Cunhaú," *Programa Nacional de Pesquisas Arqueológicas; Resultados Preliminares do Primeiro Ano 1965–1966,* Museu Paraense Emílio Goeldi, Publi- *cações Avulsas,* No. 6, pp. 107–120, Belém do Pará, Brazil.

Neumann, G. K. (1952), "Archaeology and Race in the American Indians," in *Archaeology of Eastern United States,* J. B. Griffin, ed., pp. 13–34, University of Chicago Press, Chicago.

Newman, M. T. (1947), *Indian Skeletal Material from the Central Coast of Peru: An Archaeologically Oriented Study in Physical Anthropology,* Peabody Museum Papers, Vol. 28, No. 1, Harvard University, Cambridge.

Newman, M. T. (1948), "A Summary of the Racial History of the Peruvian Area," in *A Reappraisal of Peruvian Archaeology,* W. C. Bennett, ed., Memoir No. 4, pp. 16–19, Society for American Archaeology, Menasha, Wisconsin.

Newman, M. T. (1951), "The Sequence of Indian Physical Types in South America," in *Papers on the Physical Anthropology of the American Indian,* W. S. Laughlin, ed., pp. 69–97, The Viking Fund, New York.

Newman, M. T. (1953), "The Application of Ecological Rules to the Racial Anthropology of the Aboriginal New World," *American Anthropologist,* Vol. 555, pp. 311–327, Menasha, Wisconsin.

Newman, M. T. (1958), "A Trial Formulation Presenting Evidence from Physical Anthropology for Migrations from Mexico to South America," in *Migrations in New World Culture History,* R. H. Thompson, ed., Social Science Bulletin No. 27, pp. 33–40, University of Arizona, Tucson.

Newman, M. T. (1962), "Evolutionary Changes in Body Size and Head Form in American Indians," *American Anthropologist,* Vol. 64, pp. 237–257, Menasha, Wisconsin.

Niemeyer, Hans (1962), "Nuevos excavaciones en Pica, cementerio de Santa Rosita," *Boletín, Museo y Sociedad Arqueológica de La Serena,* No. 12, pp. 7–17, La Serena, Chile.

Niemeyer, Hans (1963), "Excavación de un cementerio Incaico en la Hacienda Camarones (Prov. de Tarapacá)," *Revista Universitaria,* Vol. 48, pp. 207–233, Universidad Católica de Chile, Santiago.

Niemeyer, Hans (1964), "Petroglifos en el curso superior del Río Aconcagua," in *Arqueología de Chile Central y Areas Vecinas,* Publicación de los Trabajos Presentados al Tercer Congreso Internacional de Arqueología Chilena, pp. 133–149, Imprenta "Los Andes," Santiago.

Niemeyer, Hans (1968), "Petroglifos del Río Salado o Chuschul (San Pedro de Atacama, Depto. del Loa, Prov. de Antofagasta), Chile," *Boletín de Prehistoria de Chile,* Vol. 1, No. 1, pp. 85–92, Departamento de Historia, Facultad de Filosofía y Educación, Universidad de Chile, Santiago.

Niemeyer, Hans and J. C. Montane (1960), "Arqueología Diaguita en conchales de la costa," *Publicaciones del Museo y la Sociedad Arqueológica de La Serena,* Boletín No. 11, pp. 53–67, La Serena, Chile.

Niemeyer, Hans and Virgilio Schiappacasse (1963), "Investigaciones arqueológicas en las terrazas de Conanoxa, Valle de Camarones (Prov. de Tarapacá)," *Revista Universitaria,* Vol. 48, pp. 101–166, Universidad Católica de Chile, Santiago.

Nimuendajú, Curt (1948), "Tribes of the Lower and Middle Xingú River," in *Handbook of South American Indians,* J. H. Steward, ed., Vol. 3, pp. 213–244, Bureau of American Ethnology, Bulletin 143, Smithsonian Institution, Washington, D.C.

Nordenskiold, Erland von (1902–03), "Präcolumbische Wohn- und Begräbnisplätze an der Südwestgrenze von Chaco," *Kongliga Svenska Vetenskapsacademiens Handlingar,* Vol. 36, No. 7, pp. 1–21, Stockholm.

Nordenskiold, Erland von (1906), "Ethnographische und Archäologische Forschungen im Grenzgebiet zwischen Peru und Bolivia 1904–1905," *Zeitschrift für Ethnologie,* Jahrg. 38, pp. 80–99, Berlin (cited from Bennett, 1936).

Nordenskiold, Erland von (1911), *Indianer och Hvita i Nordöstra Bolivia,* Stockholm (cited from Bennett, 1936).

Nordenskiold, Erland von (1913), "Urnengräber und Mounds im Bolivianischen Flachländer," *Baessler Archiv,* Vol. 3, pp. 205–255, Leipzig and Berlin.

Nordenskiold, Erland von (1917 a), "Die Östliche Ausbreitung der Tiahuanaco-kultur in Bolivien und ihr Verhältnis zur Aruakkultur in Mojos," *Zeitschrift für Ethnologie,* Jahrg. 49, pp. 10–20, Berlin.

Nordenskiold, Erland von (1917 b), "The Guarani Invasion of the Inca Empire in the Sixteenth Century: An Historical Indian Migration," *Geographical Review,* Vol. 4, pp. 103–121, New York.

Nordenskiold, Erland von (1919), *An Ethno-Graphical Analysis of the Material Culture of Two Indian Tribes in the Gran Chaco,* Comparative Ethnographical Studies, No. 1, Göteborg, Sweden.

Nordenskiold, Erland von (1924 a), *Forschungen und Abenteuer in Sudamerika,* Strecker und Schröder, Stuttgart.

Nordenskiold, Erland von (1924 b), "Finds of Graves and Old Dwelling-Places on the Río Beni, Bolivia," *Ymer,* Vol. 2, pp. 229–237, Stockholm.

Nordenskiold, Erland von (1930), *L'Archéologie du Bassin de L'Amazone,* Ars Americana, No. 1, Paris.

Nordenskiold, Erland von (1931), *Origins of the Indian Civilizations in South America,* Comparative Ethnographical Studies, No. 9, Göteborg, Sweden.

Norweb, A. H. (1964), "Ceramic Stratigraphy in Southwestern Nicaragua," *35th International Congress of Americanists,* Vol. 1, pp. 551–563, México, D.F.

Núñez, Lautaro (1965), "Desarrollo cultural prehispánica del norte de Chile," *Estudios Arqueológicos,* No. 1, pp. 37–115, Universidad de Chile, Antofagasta, Chile.

Núñez, Lautaro (1966), "Caserones-I, una aldea prehispánica del norte de Chile. Nota preliminar," *Estudios Arqueológicos,* Vol. 2, pp. 25–29, Universidad de Chile, Antofagasta, Chile.

Núñez, Lautaro (1967–68), "Figurinas tempranas del Norte de Chile (Provincia de Tarapacá)," *Estudios Arqueológicos,* Vols. 3–4, pp. 85–105, Universidad de Chile, Antofagasta, Chile.

Núñez, Lautaro and Juan Varela (1961–64), "Un complejo preagrícola en el Salar del Soronal (Cordillera de la Costa, Norte de Chile)," *Revista del Instituto de Antropología,* Vols. 2–3, pp. 189–204, Universidad Nacional de Córdoba, Argentina.

Núñez, Lautaro and Juan Varela (1966), "Complejo preagrícola en el Salar del Huasco (Provincia de Tarapacá)," *Estudios Arqueológicos,* No. 2, pp. 9–24, Universidad de Chile, Antofagasta, Chile.

Núñez Regueiro, V. A. (1970), "The Alamito Culture of Northwestern Argentina," *American Antiquity,* Vol. 35, No. 2, pp. 133–140, Salt Lake City.

Orellana Rodríguez, Mario (1962), "Descripción de artefactos líticos de Ghatchi, el problema del precerámico en el norte de Chile," *Notas del Museo de La Plata, Antropología, No. 79,* Vol. 20, pp. 75–123, La Plata, Argentina.

Orellana Rodríguez, Mario (1963), "La cultura de San Pedro," *Arqueología Chilena,* No. 3, Universidad de Chile, Santiago.

Orellana Rodríguez, Mario (1964), "Acerca de la cronología del complejo cultural San Pedro de Atacama," *Antropología,* Vol. 2, pp. 96–104, Centro de Estudios Antropológicos, Universidad de Chile, Santiago.

Orellana Rodríguez, Mario (1965), "Informe de La Primera Fase del Proyecto Arqueológico Río Salado," *Antropología,* Vol. 3, pp. 81–117, Centro de Estudios Antropológicos, Universidad de Chile, Santiago.

Orellana Rodríguez, Mario (1966), "Prehistoria de la Puna y Salar de Atacama, Norte de Chile (Pre-Agro-Alfarero)," *Actas y Memorias, 36th International Congress of Americanists,* Vol. 1, pp. 165–171, Seville.

Orellana Rodríguez, Mario (1968), "Tipos alfareros en la zona del Río Salado," *Boletín de Prehistoria de Chile,* Vol. 1, No. 1, pp. 3–31, Departamento de Historia, Facultad de Filosofía y Educación, Universidad de Chile, Santiago.

Orssich, Adam and E. S. Orssich (1956), "Stratigraphic Excavations in the Sambaquí of Araujo

II," *American Antiquity,* Vol. 21, pp. 357–369, Salt Lake City.

Ortiz Troncoso, O. R. (1964), "Investigaciones en conchales de Reloca (Prov. Maule, Chile)," in *Arqueología de Chile Central y Areas Vecinas,* Publicación de los Trabajos Presentados al Tercer Congreso Internacional de Arqueología Chilena, pp. 59–62, Imprenta "Los Andes," Santiago.

Osgood, Cornelius (1935), "The Archaeological Problem in Chiriquí," *American Anthropologist,* Vol. 37, pp. 234–243, Menasha, Wisconsin.

Osgood, Cornelius (1942), *The Ciboney Culture of Cayo Redondo, Cuba,* Yale University Publications in Anthropology, No. 25, New Haven.

Osgood, Cornelius (1943), *Excavations at Tocorón, Venezuela,* Yale University Publications in Anthropology, No. 29, New Haven.

Osgood, Cornelius (1946), *British Guiana Archaeology to 1945,* Yale University Publications in Anthropology, No. 36, New Haven.

Osgood, Cornelius and G. D. Howard (1943), *An Archaeological Survey of Venezuela,* Yale University Publications in Anthropology, No. 27, New Haven.

Outes, F. F. (1904 a), "Arqueología de Hucal, Gobernación de La Pampa," *Anales, Museo Nacional de Buenos Aires,* Vol. 10, pp. 1–15, Buenos Aires.

Outes, F. F. (1905), "La edad de la piedra en Patagonia," *Anales, Museo Nacional de Buenos Aires,* Vol. 12, pp. 203–575, Buenos Aires.

Outes, F. F. (1907), "Arqueología de San Blas, Provincia de Buenos Aires," *Anales, Museo Nacional de Buenos Aires,* Vol. 14, pp. 249–275, Buenos Aires.

Outes, F. F. (1916 a), *Las Hachas Insignias Patagónicas,* privately printed, Buenos Aires.

Outes, F. F. (1916 b), "El primer hallazgo arqueológico en la isla de Martín García," *Anales, Sociedad Científica Argentina,* Vol. 82, pp. 265–277, Buenos Aires.

Outes, F. F. (1918 a), "Nuevo jalon septentrional en la disperción de las representaciones plásticas de la cuenca Paranaense y su valor indicador," *Anales, Sociedad Científica Argentina,* Vol. 85, pp. 53ff., Buenos Aires.

Outes, F. F. (1918 b), "Nuevos rastros de la cultura Guaraní en la cuenca del Paraná Inferior," *Anales, Sociedad Científica Argentina,* Vol. 85, pp. 153–182, Buenos Aires.

Outes, F. F. (1940 b), "La alfarería indígena de Patagonia," *Anales, Museo Nacional de Buenos Aires,* Vol. 11, pp. 33–41, Buenos Aires.

Oviedo y Valdés, Gonzalo Fernández de (1851–55), *Historia General y Natural de Las Indias, Islas y Tierra Firme de la Mar Oceano,* 4 Vols., Editorial José Amador de los Ríos, Madrid.

Padden, R. C. (1957), "Cultural Change and Military Resistance in Araucanian Chile, 1150–1730," *Southwestern Journal of Anthropology,* Vol. 13, pp. 103–121, University of New Mexico Press, Albuquerque, New Mexico.

Palavecino, Enrique (1948), "Areas y capas culturales en el territorio Argentino," *Gaea,* Vol. 8, pp. 447–523, Buenos Aires.

Palmatary, H. C. (1939), *Tapajó Pottery,* Comparative Ethnological Studies, No. 8, Göteborg, Sweden.

Palmatary, H. C. (1950), *The Pottery of Marajó Island, Brazil,* Transactions of the American Philosophical Society, Vol. 39, Pt. 3, Philadelphia.

Palmatary, H. C. (1960), *The Archaeology of the Lower Tapajós Valley, Brazil,* Transactions of the American Philosophical Society, Vol. 50, Pt. 3, Philadelphia.

Park, W. Z. (1946), "Tribes of the Sierra Nevada de Santa Marta, Colombia," in *Handbook of South American Indians,* J. H. Steward, ed., Vol. 2, pp. 865–886, Bureau of American Ethnology, Bulletin 143, Smithsonian Institution, Washington, D.C.

Parker, G. J. (1963), "La Clasificación Genética de los Dialectos Quechuas," *Revista, Museo Nacional de Antropología y Arqueología,* Vol. 32, pp. 241–252, Lima.

Parsons, J. J. (1966), "Los campos de cultivos prehispánicos del Bajo San Jorge," *Revista, Academia Colombiana de Ciencias Exactas, Físicas, y Naturales,* Vol. 12, No. 48, pp. 449–458, Bogotá.

Parsons, J. J. (1969), "Ridged Fields in the Guayas Valley, Ecuador," *American Antiquity,* Vol. 34, No. 1, pp. 76–80, Salt Lake City.

Parsons, J. J. and W. A. Bowen (1966), "Ancient Ridged Fields of the San Jorge River Floodplain, Colombia," *The Geographical Review,* Vol. 56, pp. 317–343, New York.

Parsons, J. J. and W. M. Denevan (1967), "Pre-Colombian Ridged Fields," *Scientific American,* Vol. 217, No. 1, pp. 92–100, New York.

Parsons, Jeffrey R. (1968), "An Estimate of Size and Population for Middle Horizon Tiahuanaco, Bolivia," *American Antiquity,* Vol. 33, No. 2, pp. 243–245, Salt Lake City.

Pascual, Rosendo (1960), "Informe sobre los restos de vertebrados hallados en la caverna de Intihuasi y 'paraderos' vecinos de San Luis," Appendix II in "La Estratigrafía de la Gruta de Intihuasi (Prov. de San Luis, R.A.), y Sus Relaciones con Otros Sitios Precerámicos de Sudamerica," *Revista del Instituto de Antropología,* Vol. 1, pp. 299–302, Universidad Nacional de Córdoba, Argentina.

Patterson, T. C. (1963 a, ms.), "A Preliminary Study of the Archaeology of Lowland South America," typescript, Berkeley.

Patterson, T. C. (1963 b, ms.), "A Preliminary Study of the Archaeology of Bolivia," typescript, Berkeley.

Patterson, T. C. (1963 c, ms.), "A Preliminary Study of the Archaeology of Chile," typescript, Berkeley.

Patterson, T. C. (1965), "Ceramic Sequences at Tierradentro and San Agustín, Colombia," *American Antiquity,* Vol. 31, No. 1, pp. 66–73, Salt Lake City.

Patterson, T. C. (1966 a), *Pattern and Process in the Early Intermediate Period Pottery of the Central Coast of Peru,* University of California Publications in Anthropology, Vol. 3, Berkeley and Los Angeles.

Patterson, T. C. (1966 b), "Early Cultural Remains on the Central Coast of Peru," *Nawpa Pacha*, No. 4, pp. 145–153, Institute of Andean Studies, Berkeley.

Patterson, T. C. (1966 ms.), "The Culture History of Central Peru," mimeogr., Cambridge.

Patterson, T. C. and R. F. Heizer (1965), "A Preceramic Stone Tool Collection from Viscachani, Bolivia," *Nawpa Pacha*, No. 3, pp. 107–114, Institute of Andean Studies, Berkeley.

Patterson, T. C. and E. P. Lanning (1964), "Changing Settlement Patterns on the Central Peruvian Coast," *Nawpa Pacha*, Vol. 2, pp. 113–123, Institute of Andean Studies, Berkeley.

Patterson, T. C. and E. P. Lanning (1967), "Los Medios Ambientes Glacial Tardio y Postglacial de Sudamerica," *Boletín de la Sociedad Geográfica de Lima*, Vol. 86, pp. 1–19, Lima.

Pereira de Godoy, Manuel (1952), "Cachimbos Tupis-Guaranís de Pirassununga," *Selected Papers, 29th International Congress of Americanists*, Vol. 3, *Indian Tribes of Aboriginal America*, S. Tax, ed., pp. 314–322, University of Chicago Press, Chicago.

Pérez de Barradas, José (1937), *Arqueología y Antropología Precolombinas de Tierra Dentro*, Publicaciones de la Sección de Arqueología, No. 1, Bogotá.

Pérez de Barradas, José (1943), *Arqueología Agustiniana*, Bogotá.

Pérez de Barradas, José (1954), *Orfebrería Prehispánica de Colombia. Estilo Calima*, 2 Vols., Banco de la República de Colombia, Bogotá (printed in Madrid).

Pérez de Barradas, José (1958), *Orfebrería Prehispánica de Colombia. Estilos Tolima y Muisca*, 2 Vols., Banco de la República de Colombia, Bogotá (printed in Madrid).

Pérez de Barradas, José (1965–66), *Orfebrería Prehispánica de Colombia. Estilos Quimbaya y Otros*, 2 Vols., Banco de la República de Colombia, Bogotá (printed in Madrid).

Pericot, Luis (1936), "América indígena," in *Historia de América*, A. Ballesteros, ed., Vol. 1, Bar-celona (see also 1962 edition).

Petrullo, Vincenzo (1939), "The Archaeology of Arauquín," *Anthropological Papers*, No. 12, Bureau of American Ethnology, Bulletin 123, Smithsonian Institution, Washington, D.C.

Phillips, Philip (1966), "The Role of Transpacific Contacts in the Development of New World Pre-Columbian Civilizations," in *Handbook of Middle American Indians*, R. Wauchope, G. F. Ekholm, and G. R. Willey, eds., Vol. 4, pp. 296–315, University of Texas Press, Austin.

Piazza, W. F. (1965), "O sitio arqueológico do Río Tavares (Santa Catarina)," *Dédalo*, Vol. 1, No. 2, pp. 53–79, Museu de Arte e Arqueología da Universidade de São Paulo, São Paulo.

Piazza, W. F. (1967), "Nota preliminar sobre o Programa Nacional de Pesquisas Arqueológicas no Estado de Santa Catarina," *Programa Nacional de Pesquisas Arqueológicas; Resultados Preliminares do Primeiro Ano 1965–1966*, Museu Paraense Emílio Goeldi, Publicações Avulsas, No. 6, pp. 39–46, Belém do Pará, Brazil.

Plafker, George (1963), "Observations on Archaeological Remains in Northeastern Bolivia," *American Antiquity*, Vol. 28, No. 3, pp. 372–378, Salt Lake City.

Poma de Ayala, Felipe Guaman (1936), *Nueva Corónica y Buen Gobierno (Codex Péruvien Illustré)*, Travaux et Mémoires, Vol. 23, Institut d'Ethnologie, Paris.

Ponce Sangines, Carlos, ed. (1957), *Arqueología Boliviana*, Biblioteca Paceña, La Paz.

Ponce Sangines, Carlos (1964), *Descripción Sumaria del Templete Semisubterráneo de Tiwanaku*, Publicación No. 2 del Centro de Investigaciones Arqueológicas en Tiwanaku, Tiahuanaco, Bolivia.

Porter, M. N. (1953), *Tlatilco and the Pre-Classic Cultures of the New World*, Viking Fund Publications in Anthropology, No. 19, Wenner-Gren Foundation, New York.

Posnansky, Arthur (1945), *Tihuanacu; the Cradle of American Man* (Spanish text in same vol.), J. J. Augustin, New York.

Prescott, W. H. (1908), *History of the Conquest of Peru*, Everyman's Library, No. 301, London and New York.

Preuss, K. T. (1931), *Arte Monumental Prehistorico*, 2nd ed., 2 Vols. (originally published in German in 1929), Escuelas Salesianas de Tipografía y Fotograbado, Bogotá.

Pride, Andrew (1926), "Un descubrimiento arqueológico en el Chaco Paraguayo," *Revista Sociedad Científica del Paraguay*, Vol. 2, pp. 28–30, Asunción.

PRONAPA (1970), "Brazilian Archaeology in 1968, an Interim Report on the National Program of Archaeological Research," *American Antiquity*, Vol. 35, No. 1, Salt Lake City.

Quiroga, Adán (1899), "Ruinas de Anfama: el pueblo prehistórico de La Ciénega," *Boletín del Instituto Geográfico Argentino*, Vol. 20, pp. 95–123, Buenos Aires.

Rauth, J. W. (1967), "Nota prévia sobre a escavação do sambaquí do Porto Mauricio," *Programa Nacional de Pesquisas Arqueológicas; Resultados Preliminares do Primeiro Ano 1965–1966*, Museu Paraense Emílio Goeldi, Publicações Avulsas, No. 6, pp. 59–78, Belém do Pará, Brazil.

Rauth, J. W. and W. R. Hurt (1960), "The Shell Mound of Saquarema, Paraná, Brazil," *Museum News*, Vol. 21, No. 9, pp. 1–7, Vermillion, South Dakota.

Ravines, Rogger (1965), "Ambo, a New Prehistoric Site in Peru," *American Antiquity*, Vol. 31, No. 1, pp. 104–105, Salt Lake City.

Ravines, Rogger (1967), "El Abrigo de Carú y sus relaciones culturales con otros sitios tempranos del sur del Perú," *Nawpa Pacha*, No. 5, pp. 39–57, Institute of Andean Studies, Berkeley.

Reichel-Dolmatoff, Alicia Dussan de (1954), "Crespo: Un nuevo complejo arqueológico del norte de Colombia," *Revista Colombiana de Antropología*, Vol. 3, pp. 171–188, Bogotá.

Reichel-Dolmatoff, Gerardo (1949–51), "Los Kogi, una Tribu de la Sierra de Santa Marta, Colombia," *Revista del Instituto Etnológico Nacional*, Vol. 4, Bogotá.

Reichel-Dolmatoff, Gerardo (1954 a), "A Preliminary Study of Space and Time Perspective in Northern Colombia," *American Antiquity*, Vol. 19, pp. 352–366, Salt Lake City.

Reichel-Dolmatoff, Gerardo (1954 b), "Investigaciones arqueológicas en la Sierra Nevada de Santa Marta," Pts. 1 and 2, *Revista Colombiana de Antropología*, Vol. 2, No. 2, pp. 145–206, Bogotá.

Reichel-Dolmatoff, Gerardo (1954 c), "Investigaciones arqueológicas en la Sierra Nevada de Santa Marta," Pt. 3, *Revista Colombiana de Antropología*, Vol. 3, pp. 139–170, Bogotá.

Reichel-Dolmatoff, Gerardo (1955), "Excavaciones en los Conchales de la Costa de Barlovento," *Revista Colombiana de Antropología*, Vol. 4, pp. 249–272, Bogotá.

Reichel-Dolmatoff, Gerardo (1958), "Recientes investigaciones arqueológicas en el norte de Colombia," *Miscellanea, Paul Rivet, Octogenaria Dictata*, Vol. 2, pp. 471–486, Universidad Nacional Autónomo de México, México, D.F.

Reichel-Dolmatoff, Gerardo (1959), "The Formative Stage, an Appraisal from the Colombian Perspective," *33rd International Congress of Americanists*, Vol. 1, pp. 152–164, San José, Costa Rica.

Reichel-Dolmatoff, Gerardo (1961 a), "Puerto Hormiga: Un Complejo Prehistórico Marginal de Colombia," *Revista Colombiana de Antropología*, Vol. 10, pp. 349–354, Bogotá.

Reichel-Dolmatoff, Gerardo (1961 b), "The Agricultural Basis of the Sub-Andean Chiefdoms of Colombia," in *The Evolution of Horticultural Systems in Native South America, Causes and Consequences*, J. Wilbert, ed., pp. 83–101, Sociedad de Ciencias Naturales La Salle, Carácas.

Reichel-Dolmatoff, Gerardo (1965 a), *Colombia*, in Ancient Peoples and Places Series, No. 44, G. Daniel, ed., Frederick A. Praeger, New York.

Reichel-Dolmatoff, Gerardo (1965

b), *Excavaciones Arqueológicas en Puerto Hormiga, Departamento de Bolívar*, Publicaciones de la Universidad de Los Andes, Antropología 2, Bogotá.

Reichel-Dolmatoff, Gerardo (1966), "Jungle Gods of San Agustín," *Natural History*, Vol. 75, No. 10, pp. 42–54, American Museum of Natural History, New York.

Reichel-Dolmatoff, Gerardo (1967), "Recientes investigaciones arqueológicas en San Agustín," *Razon y Fábula*, Revista de la Universidad de Los Andes, No. 2, pp. 35–38, Bogotá.

Reichel-Dolmatoff, Gerardo and Alicia Dussan de (1951), "Investigaciones arqueológicas en el Departamento del Magdalena, Colombia, 1946–1950," *Boletín de Arqueología*, Vol. 3, Nos. 1–6, Bogotá.

Reichel-Dolmatoff, Gerardo and Alicia Dussan de (1953), "Investigaciones arqueológicas en el Departamento del Magdalena, Colombia, 1946–1950. Parte III," *Divulgaciones Etnológicas*, Vol. 3, No. 4, Instituto de Investigación Etnológica, Universidad de Atlántico, Barranquilla, Colombia.

Reichel-Dolmatoff, Gerardo and Alicia Dussan de (1954), "Contribuciones a la arqueología del Bajo Magdalena (Plato, Zambrano, Tenerife)," *Divulgaciones Etnológicas*, Vol. 3, No. 5, Instituto de Investigación Etnológica, Universidad de Atlántico, Barranquilla, Colombia.

Reichel-Dolmatoff, Gerardo and Alicia Dussan de (1956), "Momíl, excavaciones en el Sinú," *Revista Colombiana de Antropología*, Vol. 5, pp. 109–334, Bogotá.

Reichel-Dolmatoff, Gerardo and Alicia Dussan de (1958), "Reconocimiento arqueológico de la hoya del Río Sinú," *Revista Colombiana de Antropología*, Vol. 6, pp. 31–149, Bogotá.

Reichel-Dolmatoff, Gerardo and Alicia Dussan de (1959), "La Mesa. Un complejo arqueológico de la Sierra Nevada de Santa Marta," *Revista Colombiana de Antropología*, Vol. 8, pp. 159–214, Bogotá.

Reichel-Dolmatoff, Gerardo and Alicia Dussan de (1961), "Inves-

tigaciones arqueológicas en la costa Pacifica de Colombia. I: El sitio de Cupica," *Revista Colombiana de Antropología*, Vol. 10, pp. 239–317, Bogotá.

Reichel-Dolmatoff, Gerardo and Alicia Dussan de (1962), "Investigaciones arqueológicas en la costa Pacifica de Colombia. II. Una secuencia cultural del Bajo Río San Juan," *Revista Colombiana de Antropología*, Vol. 11, pp. 9–72, Bogotá.

Reichlen, Henri (1940), "Recherches archéologiques dans la Province de Santiago del Estero," *Journal de la Société des Américanistes*, Vol. 32, pp. 133–225, Paris.

Reichlen, Henri and Paule (1947), "Contribution à l'archéologie de la Guyane Française," *Journal de la Société des Américanistes*, Vol. 35, pp. 1–24, Paris.

Reichlen, Henri and Paule (1949), "Recherches archéologiques dans les Andes de Cajamarca: Premier Rapport de la Mission Ethnologique Française au Pérou septentrional," *Journal de la Société des Américanistes*, Vol. 38, pp. 137–174, Paris.

Restrepo, Vicente (1895), *Los Chibchas antes de la Conquista Española*, Imprenta de la Luz, Bogotá.

Reyes, Francisco (1958), "Informe sobre construcciones en la cumbre del Cerro de Plomo (5,430 m.) y sus alrededores," *Arqueología Chilena*, No. 4, pp. 64–72, Centro de Estudios Antropológicos, Universidad de Chile, Santiago.

Richardson, F. B. (1940), "Non-Maya Monumental Sculpture of Central America," in *The Maya and Their Neighbors*, C. L. Hay et al., eds., pp. 395–416, D. Appleton-Century Co., Inc., New York.

Richardson, J. B. III (1969 ms.), "The Preceramic Sequence and the Pleistocene and Post Pleistocene Climate of Northwest Peru," paper read at 34th Annual Meeting, Society for American Archaeology, Milwaukee.

Rivet, Paul (1924), "Langues Américaines. III: Langues de l'Amérique du Sud et des Antilles," in *Les Langues du Monde*,

A. Meillet and M. Cohen, eds., Collection Linguistique Américaine, Vol. 16, pp. 639–712, Paris.

Rogers, D. J. (1963), "Studies of *Manihot esculenta* Crantz and Related Species," *Bulletin, Torrey Botanical Club,* Vol. 90, pp. 43–54 (cited from Bronson, 1966).

Rohr, Alfredo, S. J. (1960), "Pesquisas páleo-etnográficas na Ilha de Santa Catarina, No. II—1959," *Pesquisas, Antropología,* No. 8, Instituto Anchientano de Pesquisas, Porto Alegre, Brazil.

Rohr, Alfredo, S. J. (1966), "Pesquisas arqueológicas em Santa Catarina," *Pesquisas, Antropología,* No. 15, Instituto Anchietano de Pesquisas, Porto Alegre, Brazil.

Roosevelt, Cornelius Van S. (1935), "Ancient Civilizations of the Santa Valley and Chavín," *Geographical Review,* Vol. 25, pp. 21–42, New York.

Rouse, Irving (1941), *Culture of the Ft. Liberté Region, Haiti,* Yale University Publications in Anthropology, No. 24, New Haven.

Rouse, Irving (1942), *Archaeology of the Maniabon Hills, Cuba,* Yale University Publications in Anthropology, No. 26, New Haven.

Rouse, Irving (1947), "Prehistory of Trinidad in Relation to Adjacent Areas," *Man,* Vol. 47, pp. 93–98, London.

Rouse, Irving (1948 a), "The Ciboney," in *Handbook of South American Indians,* J. H. Steward, ed., Vol. 4, pp. 495–503, Bureau of American Ethnology, Bulletin 143, Smithsonian Institution, Washington, D.C.

Rouse, Irving (1948 b), "The Arawak," in *Handbook of South American Indians,* J. H. Steward, ed., Vol. 4, pp. 507–546, Bureau of American Ethnology, Bulletin 143, Smithsonian Institution, Washington, D.C.

Rouse, Irving (1948 c), "The Carib," in *Handbook of South American Indians,* J. H. Steward, ed., Vol. 4, pp. 547–566, Bureau of American Ethnology, Bulletin 143, Smithsonian Institution, Washington, D.C.

Rouse, Irving (1951), "Areas and Periods of Culture in the Greater Antilles," *Southwestern Journal of Anthropology,* Vol. 7, pp. 248–265, Albuquerque, New Mexico.

Rouse, Irving (1952), *Porto Rican Prehistory,* Scientific Survey of Porto Rico and the Virgin Islands, Vol. 18, Pts. 3, 4, New York Academy of Sciences, New York.

Rouse, Irving (1953 a), "The Circum-Caribbean Theory. An Archaeological Test," *American Anthropologist,* Vol. 55, pp. 188–200, Menasha, Wisconsin.

Rouse, Irving (1953 b), "Indian Sites in Trinidad," in *On the Excavation of a Shell Mound at Palo Seco, Trinidad, B. W. I.,* J. A. Bullbrook, ed., pp. 94–111, Yale University Publications in Anthropology, No. 50, New Haven.

Rouse, Irving (1954), "On the Use of the Concept of Area Co-Tradition," *American Antiquity,* Vol. 19, pp. 221–225, Salt Lake City.

Rouse, Irving (1960), *The Entry of Man into the West Indies,* Yale University Publications in Anthropology, No. 61, New Haven.

Rouse, Irving (1961), "The Bailey Collection of Stone Artifacts from Puerto Rico," in *Essays in Pre-Columbian Art and Archaeology,* S. K. Lothrop *et al.,* eds., pp. 342–355, Harvard University Press, Cambridge.

Rouse, Irving (1962), "The Intermediate Area, Amazonia, and the Caribbean Area," in *Courses toward Urban Life,* R. J. Braidwood and G. R. Willey, eds., Viking Fund Publications in Anthropology, No. 32, pp. 34–59, Wenner-Gren Foundation, New York.

Rouse, Irving (1964 a), "The Caribbean Area," in *Prehistoric Man in the New World,* J. D. Jennings and E. Norbeck, eds., pp. 389–417, University of Chicago Press, Chicago.

Rouse, Irving (1964 b), "Prehistory of the West Indies," *Science,* Vol. 144, pp. 499–514, Lancaster, Pennsylvania.

Rouse, Irving and J. M. Cruxent (1963), *Venezuelan Archaeology,* Yale University Caribbean Series, No. 6, New Haven.

Rowe, J. H. (1944), *An Introduction to the Archaeology of Cuzco,* Peabody Museum Papers, Vol. 27, No. 2, Harvard University, Cambridge.

Rowe, J. H. (1948), "The Kingdom of Chimor," *Acta Americana,* Vol. 6, pp. 26–59, Mexico City.

Rowe, J. H. (1949), "The Potter's Art of Atacames," *Archaeology,* Vol. 2, No. 1, pp. 31–34, Archaeological Institute of America, New York.

Rowe, J. H. (1956), "Archaeological Explorations in Southern Peru, 1954–1955," *American Antiquity,* Vol. 22, No. 2, pp. 135–150, Salt Lake City.

Rowe, J. H. (1957 ms.), "The Identification of Moche Phases," typescript, Berkeley.

Rowe, J. H. (1959), "Carl Hartman and His Place in the History of Archaeology," *Actas, 33rd International Congress of Americanists,* Vol. 2, pp. 268–279, San José, Costa Rica.

Rowe, J. H. (1960 a), "Cultural Unity and Diversification in Peruvian Archaeology," in *Men and Cultures, Selected Papers, 5th International Congress of Anthropological and Ethnological Sciences,* A. F. C. Wallace, ed., pp. 627–631, University of Pennsylvania Press, Philadelphia.

Rowe, J. H. (1960 b), "Notes and News — Chile," *American Antiquity,* Vol. 26, No. 1, pp. 141–142, Salt Lake City.

Rowe, J. H. (1961), "The Chronology of Inca Wooden Cups," in *Essays in Pre-Columbian Art and Archaeology,* S. K. Lothrop *et al.,* eds., pp. 317–341, Harvard University Press, Cambridge.

Rowe, J. H. (1962 a), "Stages and Periods in Archaeological Interpretation," *Southwestern Journal of Anthropology,* Vol. 18, No. 1, pp. 40–54, Albuquerque, New Mexico.

Rowe, J. H. (1962 b), *Chavín Art, An Inquiry into Its Form and Meaning,* The Museum of Primitive Art, New York.

Rowe, J. H. (1963), "Urban Settlements in Ancient Peru," *Nawpa Pacha,* Vol. 1, No. 1, pp. 1–27, Institute of Andean Studies, Berkeley.

Rowe, J. H. (1965), "An Interpretation of Radiocarbon Measurements on Archaeological Samples from Peru," *Proceedings, Sixth International Conference, Radiocarbon and Tritium Dating,* pp. 187–198, Washington State University, Pullman, Washington; distributed by Clearinghouse for Federal Scientific and Technical Information, United States Department of Commerce, Washington, D.C.

Rowe, J. H. (1967), "Form and Meaning in Chavín Art," in *Peruvian Archaeology, Selected Readings,* J. H. Rowe and Dorothy Menzel, eds., pp. 72–103, Peek Publications, Palo Alto, California.

Rowe, J. H., Donald Collier, and G. R. Willey (1950), "Reconnaissance Notes on the Site of Huari, near Ayacucho, Peru," *American Antiquity,* Vol. 16, No. 2, pp. 120–137, Menasha, Wisconsin.

Rowe, J. H. and Dorothy Menzel (1964 ms.), "Some Comments on *Peru,* Revised Edition, 1963, by Geoffrey H. S. Bushnell," mimeogr., Berkeley.

Royo y Gómez, José (1960), "Venezuela Note," *Society of Vertebrate Paleontology News Bulletin,* No. 58, pp. 31–32, Cambridge.

Rusconi, Carlos (1928), "Investigaciones en el sur de Villa Lugano," *Gaea,* Vol. 3, No. 1, pp. 75–118, Buenos Aires.

Rydén, Stig (1936), *Archaeological Researches in the Department of Candelaria (Prov. Salta, Argentina),* Ethnologiska Studier, Vol. 3, Stockholm.

Rydén, Stig (1944), *Contribution to the Archaeology of the Rio Loa Region,* Elanders Boktryckeri Aktiebolag, Göteborg, Sweden.

Rydén, Stig (1947), *Archaeological Researches in the Highlands of Bolivia,* Elanders Boktryckeri Aktiebolag, Göteborg, Sweden.

Rydén, Stig (1948), "Cord Impression Decoration in Chaco Ceramics," *Archivos Ethnos,* No. 1, pp. 1–6, Buenos Aires.

Rydén, Stig (1952), "Chullpa Pampa — A Pre-Tiahuanaco Site in the Cochabamba Region, Bolivia," *Ethnos,* Vol. 17, pp. 39–50, Stockholm.

Rydén, Stig (1956), *The Erland Nordenskiold Archaeological Col-*

lection from the Mizque Valley, Bolivia, Etnologiska Studier, No. 22, The Ethnographical Museum, Göteborg, Sweden.

Rydén, Stig (1959), *Andean Excavations II — Tupuraya and Cayhuasi: Two Tiahuanaco Sites,* Monograph Ser., Publication No. 6, The Ethnographical Museum of Sweden, Stockholm.

Rydén, Stig (1964), "Tripod Ceramics and Grater Bowls from Mojos, Bolivia," *Völkerkundliche Abhandlungen,* Vol. 1, pp. 261–270, Niedersächsisches Landesmuseum, Hannover, Germany.

Samanos, Juan (1884), *Relación de Los Primeros Descubrimientos de Francisco Pizarro y Diego Almagro,* Colección de Documentos Ineditos para la Historia de España, Vol. 5, pp. 193–201, Madrid.

Sánchez-Albornoy, Nicolas (1958), "Una penetración Neolítica en Tierra del Fuego," *Cuadernos del Sur,* Instituto de Humanidades, Universidad Nacional del Sur, Bahía Blanca, Argentina.

Sander, Dan (1959), "Fluted Points from Madden Lake," *Panama Archaeologist,* Vol. 2, No. 1, pp. 39–51, Archaeological Society of Panama, Balboa.

Sander, Dan (1964), "Lithic Material from Panama — Fluted Points from Madden Lake," *Actas y Memorias, 35th International Congress of Americanists,* Vol. 1, pp. 183–192, México, D.F.

Sanders, W. T. and B. J. Price (1968), *Mesoamerica, the Evolution of a Civilization,* Random House Studies in Anthropology, Random House, New York.

Sanguinetti de Bórmida, Amalia (1961–63), "Las industrias líticas de Trenque Lauquen (Provincia de Buenos Aires)," *Acta Praehistorica,* Vols. 5–7, pp. 72–95, Centro Argentino de Estudios Prehistóricos, Buenos Aires.

Sanguinetti de Bórmida, Amalia (1965), "Dispersión y características de las principales industrias precerámicas del territorio Argentino," *Etnía,* Vol. 1, Nos. 3–4, Museo Etnográfico Municipal "Dámaso Arce," Buenos Aires.

Sanoja, Mario (1963), "Cultural Development in Venezuela," in *Aboriginal Cultural Development*

in Latin America: An Interpretative Review, B. J. Meggers and C. Evans, eds., pp. 67–76, Smithsonian Miscellaneous Collections, Vol. 146, No. 1, Smithsonian Institution, Washington, D.C.

Sanoja, Mario (1965), "Venezuelan Archaeology Looking Toward the West Indies," *American Antiquity,* Vol. 31, No. 2, pp. 232–236, Salt Lake City.

Sauer, C. O. (1944), "A Geographical Sketch of Early Man in America," *Geographical Review,* Vol. 34, No. 4, pp. 529–573, New York.

Sauer, C. O. (1950 a), "Geography of South America," in *Handbook of South American Indians,* J. H. Steward, ed., Vol. 5, pp. 319–344, Bulletin 143, Bureau of American Ethnology, Smithsonian Institution, Washington, D.C.

Sauer, C. O. (1950 b), "Cultivated Plants of South and Central America," in *Handbook of South American Indians,* J. H. Steward, ed., Vol. 5, pp. 487–544, Bureau of American Ethnology, Bulletin 143, Smithsonian Institution, Washington, D.C.

Sauer, C. O. (1952), *Agricultural Origins and Dispersals,* American Geographical Society, New York.

Saville, M. H. (1907–10), *The Antiquities of Manabí, Ecuador,* 2 Vols., Contributions to South American Archaeology, Heye Expedition, Heye Foundation, New York.

Saville, M. H. (1924), *The Gold Treasure of Sigsig, Ecuador,* Leaflet No. 3, Museum of the American Indian, Heye Foundation, New York.

Sawyer, A. R. (1966), *Ancient Peruvian Ceramics. The Nathan Cummings Collection,* The Metropolitan Museum of Art, New York.

Schaedel, R. P. (1957), "Informe general sobre la expedición a la zona comprendida entre Arica y La Serena," *Arqueología Chilena,* pp. 7–42 (see also Appendix No. 5, pp. 73–76, concerning terminology), Centro de Estudios Antropológicos, Universidad de Chile, Santiago.

Scheele, Harry and T. C. Patterson (1966), "A Preliminary Seriation of the Chimu Pottery Style,"

Nawpa Pacha, No. 4, pp. 15–30, Institute of Andean Studies, Berkeley.

Schiappacasse F., Virgilio and Hans Niemeyer F. (1964), "Excavaciones de un conchal en el pueblo de Guanaqueros (Prov. de Coquimbo)," in *Arqueología de Chile Central y Areas Vecinas,* Publicación de los Trabajos Presentados al Tercer Congreso Internacional de Arqueología Chilena, pp. 235–262, Imprenta "Los Andes," Santiago.

Schlesier, K. H. (1967), "Sedna Creek: Report on an Archaeological Survey on the Arctic Slope of the Brooks Range," *American Antiquity,* Vol. 32, No. 2, pp. 210–213, Salt Lake City.

Schmidt, Max (1932), "Nuevos hallazgos prehistóricos del Paraguay," *Revista, Sociedad Científica del Paraguay,* Vol. 3, No. 3, Asunción.

Schmidt, Max (1934), "Nuevos hallazgos prehistóricos del Paraguay," *Revista, Sociedad Científica del Paraguay,* Vol. 3, No. 5, Asunción.

Schmitz, P. I., et al. (1967), "Arqueología no Río Grande do Sul," *Pesquisas, Antropología,* No. 16, Instituto Anchietano de Pesquisas, São Leopoldo, Brazil.

Schobinger, Juan (1956), "Las 'clavas insignias' de Argentina y Chile," *Runa,* Vol. 7, Pt. 2, pp. 252–280, Buenos Aires.

Schobinger, Juan (1959 a), "Esquema de la prehistoria Argentina," *Ampurias,* Vol. 21, pp. 29–67, Barcelona.

Schobinger, Juan (1959 b), "Arqueología de la Provincia del Neuquén," *Anales de Arqueología y Etnología,* Vol. 13, pp. 5–231, Facultad de Filosofía y Letras, Universidad Nacional de Cuyo, Mendoza, Argentina.

Schobinger, Juan (1962), "Investigaciones arqueológicas en la provincia de San Juan, Rep. Argentina (Informe Preliminar)," *Actas y Memorias, 35th International Congress of Americanists,* Vol. 1, pp. 615–620, México, D.F.

Serrano, Antonio (1922), "Arqueología de Las Tejas (Provincia de Sante Fe)," *Revista Universitaria del Litoral,* Vol. 1, No. 12, Para-

ná, Argentina (cited from Howard and Willey, 1948).

Serrano, Antonio (1930), "El área de dispersión de las llamadas alfarerías gruesas del territorio Argentino," *Physis,* Vol. 10, pp. 181–187, Buenos Aires.

Serrano, Antonio (1931), *Arqueología del Litoral,* Memorias del Museo de Paraná, No. 4, Paraná, Argentina.

Serrano, Antonio (1932), *Exploraciones Arqueológicas en El Río Uruguay Medio,* Memorias del Museo de Paraná, No. 2, Paraná, Argentina.

Serrano, Antonio (1934), "Noticias sobre un paradero indígena de la margen izquierdo del Arroyo Las Conchas," *25th International Congress of Americanists,* Vol. 2, pp. 165–172, Buenos Aires.

Serrano, Antonio (1946 a), "The Sambaquís of the Brazilian Coast," in *Handbook of South American Indians,* J. H. Steward, ed., Vol. 1, pp. 401–407, Bureau of American Ethnology, Bulletin 143, Smithsonian Institution, Washington, D.C.

Serrano, Antonio (1946 b), *Arqueología del Arroyo de Las Mulas en el Noroeste de Entre Ríos,* Universidad Nacional de Córdoba, Argentina.

Serrano, Antonio (1946 c), "The Charrúa," in *Handbook of South American Indians,* J. H. Steward, ed., Vol. 1, pp. 191–196, Bureau of American Ethnology, Bulletin 143, Smithsonian Institution, Washington, D.C.

Serrano, Antonio (1954), "Contenido e interpretación de la arqueología Argentina: El área litoral," *Revista de la Universidad Nacional del Litoral,* No. 29, Santa Fé, Argentina.

Siegert, J. G. B. (1840), *Venezuela and Angostura,* G. H. R. Rampling and Son, London.

Silva Celis, Eliécer (1945), "Investigaciones arqueológicas en Sogamoso," *Boletín de Arqueología,* Vol. 1, pp. 36–48, 93–112, 283–297, 467–490, Bogotá.

Silva Celis, Eliécer (1964–65), "Antiguedad y relaciones de la civilización Chibcha," *Revista Colombiana de Antropología,* Vol. 8, pp. 239–266, Bogotá.

Silva, Fernando Altenfelder (1961–62), "Considerações sobre alguns sitios Tupí-Guaraní no sul do Brasil," *Revista do Museu Paulista,* Vol. 13, pp. 377–398, São Paulo.

Silva, Fernando Altenfelder (1967), "Informes preliminares sobre a arqueologia de Río Claro," *Programa Nacional de Pesquisas Arqueológicas; Resultados Preliminares do Primeiro Ano 1965–1966,* Museu Paraense Emílio Goeldi, Publicações Avulsas, No. 6, pp. 79–88, Belém do Pará, Brazil.

Silva, Fernando Altenfelder and Oldemar Blasi (1955), "Escavações preliminares em Estirão Comprido," *31st International Congress of Americanists,* Vol. 2, pp. 829–845, São Paulo.

Silva, Fernando Altenfelder and B. J. Meggers (1963), "Cultural Development in Brazil," in *Aboriginal Cultural Development in Latin America: An Interpretative Review,* B. J. Meggers and C. Evans, Jr., eds., pp. 119–130, Smithsonian Miscellaneous Collections, Vol. 146, No. 1, Smithsonian Institution, Washington, D.C.

Silva, J. E. (1964), "Investigaciones arqueológicas en la costa de la zona central Chile," in *Arqueología de Chile Central y Areas Vecinas,* Publicación de los Trabajos Presentados al Tercer Congreso Internacional de Arqueología Chilena, pp. 263–274, Imprenta "Los Andes," Santiago.

Simoes, M. F. (1967), "Considerações preliminares sobre a arqueología do Alto Xingú (Mato Grosso)," *Programa Nacional de Pesquisas Arqueológicas; Resultados Preliminares do Primeiro Ano 1965–1966,* Museu Paraense Emílio Goeldi, Publicações Avulsas, No. 6, pp. 129–152, Belém do Pará, Brazil.

Simons, B. B. (1966), "Pottery from the State of São Paulo, Brazil: A Study of Decorated Sherds and Vessels," *Actas y Memorias, 36th International Congress of Americanists,* Vol. 1, pp. 459–472, Seville.

Sleight, F. W. (1965), "Certain Environmental Considerations in

West Indian Archaeology," *American Antiquity,* Vol. 31, No. 2, pp. 226–231, Salt Lake City.

Smith, C. T., W. M. Denevan, and P. Hamilton (1968), "Ancient Ridged Fields in the Region of Lake Titicaca," *The Geographical Journal,* Vol. 134, Pt. 3, pp. 353–367, London.

Solecki, R. S. (1950), "New Data on the Inland Eskimo of Northern Alaska," *Journal of the Washington Academy of Sciences,* Vol. 40, pp. 137–157, Washington, D.C.

Solecki, R. S. (1951), "Notes on Two Archaeological Discoveries in Alaska," *American Antiquity,* Vol. 17, No. 1, pp. 55–57, Salt Lake City.

Spahni, J. C. (1964), "Le cimetière atacamenien du Pucará de Lasana, Vallée du Rio Loa (Chili)," *Journal de la Société des Américanistes,* Vol. 53, pp. 147–180, Paris.

Spahni, J. C. (1967), "Recherches archéologiques a l'embouchure du Rio Loa, Côte du Pacifique—Chili," *Journal de la Société des Américanistes,* Vol. 66, No. 1, pp. 179–239, Paris.

Spinden, H. J. (1925), "The Chorotegan Culture Area," *Proceedings, 21st International Congress of Americanists,* Pt. 2, pp. 529–545, Göteborg, Sweden.

Squier, E. G. (1877), *Peru. Incidents of Travel and Exploration in the Land of the Incas,* Harper and Brothers, New York.

Steager, P. W. (1965), "The Yahgan and Alacaluf: An Ecological Description," *Kroeber Anthropological Society Papers,* No. 32, pp. 69–77, Department of Anthropology, University of California, Berkeley.

Steere, J. B. (1927), *The Archaeology of the Amazon,* Official Publications, Vol. 29, No. 9, Report of the Associate Director of the Museum of Anthropology, University of Michigan, Ann Arbor.

Steward, J. H. (1947), "American Culture History in the Light of South America," *Southwestern Journal of Anthropology,* Vol. 3, No. 2, pp. 85–107, Albuquerque, New Mexico.

Steward, J. H. (1948), "The Circum-Caribbean Tribes: An Introduction," in *Handbook of South American Indians,* J. H. Steward, ed., Vol. 4, pp. 1–42, Bureau of American Ethnology, Bulletin 143, Smithsonian Institution, Washington, D.C.

Steward, J. H. (1949 a), "South American Cultures: An Interpretative Summary," in *Handbook of South American Indians,* J. H. Steward, ed., Vol. 5, pp. 669–772, Bureau of American Ethnology, Bulletin 143, Smithsonian Institution, Washington, D.C.

Steward, J. H. (1949 b), "Cultural Causality and Law: A Trial Formulation of the Development of Early Civilizations," *American Anthropologist,* Vol. 51, pp. 1–25, Menasha, Wisconsin.

Steward, J. H., ed. (1946 a), *Handbook of South American Indians,* Vol. 1, *The Marginal Tribes,* Bureau of American Ethnology, Bulletin 143, Smithsonian Institution, Washington, D.C.

Steward, J. H., ed. (1946 b), *Handbook of South American Indians,* Vol. 2, *The Andean Civilizations,* Bureau of American Ethnology, Bulletin 143, Smithsonian Institution, Washington, D.C.

Steward, J. H., ed. (1948 a), *Handbook of South American Indians,* Vol. 3, *The Tropical Forest Tribes,* Bureau of American Ethnology, Bulletin 143, Smithsonian Institution, Washington, D.C.

Steward, J. H., ed. (1948 b), *Handbook of South American Indians,* Vol. 4, *The Circum-Caribbean Tribes,* Bureau of American Ethnology, Bulletin 143, Smithsonian Institution, Washington, D.C.

Steward, J. H., ed. (1949), *Handbook of South American Indians,* Vol. 5, *The Comparative Ethnology of South American Indians,* Bureau of American Ethnology, Bulletin 143, Smithsonian Institution, Washington, D.C.

Steward, J. H., ed. (1950), *Handbook of South American Indians,* Vol. 6, *Physical Anthropology, Linguistics, and Cultural Geography of South American Indians,* Bureau of American Ethnology, Bulletin 143, Smithsonian Institution, Washington, D.C.

Steward, J. H. and L. C. Faron (1959), *Native Peoples of South America,* McGraw-Hill Book Company, Inc., New York.

Stewart, T. D. (1950), "Deformity, Trephining, and Mutilation in South American Indian Skeletal Remains," in *Handbook of South American Indians,* J. H. Steward, ed., Vol. 6, pp. 43–48, Bureau of American Ethnology, Bulletin 143, Smithsonian Institution, Washington, D.C.

Stirling, M. W. (1949), "Exploring the Past in Panama," *National Geographic Magazine,* Vol. 95, No. 2, pp. 373–399, Washington, D.C.

Stirling, M. W. (1950), "Exploring Ancient Panama by Helicopter," *National Geographic Magazine,* Vol. 97, No. 2, pp. 227–246, Washington, D.C.

Stirling, M. W. and Marion (1963), "Tarqui, an Early Site in Manabí Province, Ecuador," *Anthropological Papers,* No. 63, pp. 1–28, Bureau of American Ethnology, Bulletin 186, Smithsonian Institution, Washington, D.C.

Stirling, M. W. and Marion (1964 a), "El Limón, an Early Tomb Site in Coclé Province, Panama," *Anthropological Papers,* No. 71, pp. 251–254, Bureau of American Ethnology, Bulletin 191, Smithsonian Institution, Washington, D.C.

Stirling, M. W. and Marion (1964 b), "The Archaeology of Taboga, Urabá, and Taboguilla Islands, Panama," *Anthropological Papers,* No. 73, pp. 285–348, Bureau of American Ethnology, Bulletin 191, Smithsonian Institution, Washington, D.C.

Stirling, M. W. and Marion (1964 c), "Archaeological Notes on Almirante Bay, Bocas del Toro, Panama," *Anthropological Papers,* No. 72, pp. 255–284, Bureau of American Ethnology, Bulletin 191, Smithsonian Institution, Washington, D.C.

Stone, D. Z. (1941), *Archaeology of the North Coast of Honduras,* Peabody Museum Memoirs, Vol. 9, No. 1, Harvard University, Cambridge.

Stone, D. Z. (1958), *Introduction to the Archaeology of Costa Rica,*

Museo Nacional, San José, Costa Rica.

Stone, D. Z. (1966), "Synthesis of Lower Central American Ethnohistory," in *Handbook of Middle American Indians,* R. Wauchope, G. F. Ekholm, and G. R. Willey, eds., Vol. 4, pp. 209–233, University of Texas Press, Austin.

Stone, D. Z. and Carlos Balser (1965), "Incised Slate Disks from the Atlantic Watershed of Costa Rica," *American Antiquity,* Vol. 30, No. 3, pp. 310–329, Salt Lake City.

Stout, D. B. (1938), "Culture Types and Culture Areas in South America," *Papers, Michigan Academy of Science, Arts, and Letters,* Vol. 23, pp. 73–86, University of Michigan Press, Ann Arbor.

Stout, D. B. (1948), "The Cuna," in *Handbook of South American Indians,* J. H. Steward, ed., Vol. 4, pp. 257–268, Bureau of American Ethnology, Bulletin 143, Smithsonian Institution, Washington, D.C.

Strong, W. D. (1925), *The Uhle Pottery Collections from Ancon,* University of California Publications in American Archaeology and Ethnology, Vol. 21, pp. 135–190, Berkeley.

Strong, W. D. (1935), *Archaeological Investigations in the Bay Islands, Spanish Honduras,* Smithsonian Miscellaneous Collections, Vol. 92, No. 14, Smithsonian Institution, Washington, D. C.

Strong, W. D. (1948 a), "Cultural Epochs and Refuse Stratigraphy in Peruvian Archaeology," in *A Reappraisal of Peruvian Archaeology,* W. C. Bennett, ed., Memoir 4, pp. 93–102, Society for American Archaeology, Menasha, Wisconsin.

Strong, W. D. (1948 b), "The Archaeology of Costa Rica and Nicaragua," in *Handbook of South American Indians,* J. H. Steward, ed., Vol. 4, pp. 121–142, Bureau of American Ethnology, Bulletin 143, Smithsonian Institution, Washington, D.C.

Strong, W. D. (1948 c), "The Archaeology of Honduras," in *Handbook of South American Indians,* J. H. Steward, ed., Vol.

4, pp. 71–120, Bureau of American Ethnology, Bulletin 143, Smithsonian Institution, Washington, D.C.

Strong, W. D. (1957), *Paracas, Nazca and Tiahuanacoid Cultural Relationships in South Coastal Peru,* Memoir 13, Society for American Archaeology, Salt Lake City.

Strong, W. D. and J. M. Corbett (1943), "A Ceramic Sequence at Pachacamac," in *Archaeological Studies in Peru, 1941–1942,* W. D. Strong, G. R. Willey, and J. M. Corbett, eds., Columbia University Studies in Archaeology and Ethnology, Vol. 1, No. 2, Columbia University Press, New York.

Strong, W. D. and Clifford Evans, Jr. (1952), *Cultural Stratigraphy in the Virú Valley, Northern Peru,* Columbia University Studies in Archaeology and Ethnology, Vol. 4, Columbia University Press, New York.

Strong, W. D., Alfred Kidder, II, and A. J. D. Paul (1938), *Preliminary Report on the Smithsonian-Harvard University Archaeological Expedition to Northwestern Honduras, 1936,* Smithsonian Miscellaneous Collections, Vol. 97, No. 1, Smithsonian Institution, Washington, D.C.

Stumer, L. M. (1953), "Playa Grande: Primitive Elegance in Pre-Tiahuanaco Peru," *Archaeology,* Vol. 6, No. 1, pp. 42–48, Brattleboro, Massachusetts.

Stumer, L. M. (1954 a), "Population Centers of the Rimac Valley of Peru," *American Antiquity,* Vol. 20, No. 2, pp. 130–148, Salt Lake City.

Stumer, L. M. (1954 b), "The Chillón Valley of Peru: Excavation and Reconnaissance, 1952–1953, Parts 1 and 2," *Archaeology,* Vol. 7, Nos. 3, 4, pp. 171–178, 222–228, Brattleboro, Massachusetts.

Stumer, L. M. (1956), "Development of Peruvian Coastal Tiahuanaco Styles," *American Antiquity,* Vol. 22, No. 1, pp. 59–68, Salt Lake City.

Sturtevant, W. C. (1961), "Taino Agriculture," in *The Evolution of Horticultural Systems in Native*

South America, Causes and Consequences, J. Wilbert, ed., pp. 69–82, Sociedad de Ciencias Naturales La Salle, Carácas.

Sullivan, L. R. and Milo Hellman (1925), *The Punín Calvarium,* Anthropological Papers, Vol. 23, American Museum of Natural History, New York.

Swauger, J. L. and W. J. Mayer-Oakes (1952), "A Fluted Point from Costa Rica," *American Antiquity,* Vol. 17, pp. 264–265, Salt Lake City.

Tabío, E. E. and J. M. Guarch (1966), *Excavaciones en Arroyo del Palo, Mayarí, Cuba,* Departamento de Antropología, Academia de Ciencias de la República de Cuba, Havana.

Tabío, E. E. and Estrella Rey (1966), *Prehistoria de Cuba,* Departamento de Antropología, Academia de Ciencias de la República de Cuba, Havana.

Taylor, Douglas and Irving Rouse (1955), "Linguistic and Archaeological Time Depth in the West Indies," *International Journal of American Linguistics,* Vol. 21, No. 2, pp. 105–115, Baltimore.

Tello, J. C. (1923), "Wira-Kocha," *Inca,* Vol. 1, pp. 93–320, 583–606, Lima.

Tello, J. C. (1929), *Antiguo Perú, Primera Epoca,* Comisión Organizadora del Segundo Congreso Sudamericano de Turismo, ed., Lima.

Tello, J. C. (1942), "Origen y desarrollo de las civilizaciones prehistóricas andinas," *Actas y Trabajos Científicos, 27th International Congress of Americanists, Lima Session, 1939,* Vol. 1, pp. 589–720, Lima.

Tello, J. C. (1943), "Discovery of the Chavín Culture in Peru," *American Antiquity,* Vol. 9, pp. 135–160, Menasha, Wisconsin.

Tello, J. C. (1956), *Arqueología del Valle de Casma. Culturas: Chavín, Santa o Huaylas Yunga y Sub-Chimu,* Publicación Antropológica del Archivo "Julio C. Tello," Vol. 1, Universidad de San Marcos, Lima.

Tello, J. C. (1960), *Chavín, Cultura Matriz de la Civilización Andina. Primera Parte,* Publicación Antropológica del Archivo

"Julio C. Tello," Vol. 2, Universidad de San Marcos, Lima.

Terada, Kazuo (1964), "Early Subsistence, Settlement, and Architecture in the Peruvian Highlands," mimeogr. seminar paper, Peabody Museum, Harvard University, Cambridge.

Thompson, D. E. (1962), "The Problem of Dating Certain Stone-Faced Pyramids on the North Coast of Peru," *Southwestern Journal of Anthropology,* Vol. 18, No. 4, pp. 291–301, University of New Mexico, Albuquerque, New Mexico.

Thompson, D. E. (1964 a), "Formative Period Architecture in the Casma Valley, Peru," *Actas y Memorias, 35th International Congress of Americanists,* Vol. 1, pp. 205–212, México, D.F.

Thompson, D. E. (1964 b), "Postclassic Innovations in Architecture and Settlement Patterns in the Casma Valley, Peru," *Southwestern Journal of Anthropology,* Vol. 20, No. 1, pp. 91–105, Albuquerque, New Mexico.

Tiburtius, Guilherme and I. K. Bigarella (1960), "Objetos zoomorfos do litoral de Santa Catarina e Paraná," *Pesquisas, Antropología,* No. 7, Instituto Anchietano de Pesquisas, Porto Alegre, Brazil.

Toledo, Francisco de (1940), *Informaciones que Mando Levantar el Virrey Toledo sobre los Incas,* Vol. 2, Imprenta Porter Hnos., Buenos Aires.

Torres, L. M. (1907), "Arqueología de la cuenca del Rio Paraná," *Revista del Museo de La Plata,* Vol. 14, pp. 53–122, La Plata, Argentina.

Torres, L. M. (1911), *Los Primitivos Habitantes del Delta del Paraná,* Biblioteca Centenaria, Vol. 4, Universidad Nacional de La Plata, Buenos Aires.

Torres, L. M. (1922), "Arqueología de Peninsula San Blas," *Revista del Museo de La Plata,* Vol. 26, pp. 437–532, La Plata, Argentina.

Towle, M. A. (1961), *The Ethnobotany of Pre-Columbian Peru,* Viking Fund Publications in Anthropology, No. 30, Wenner-Gren Foundation, New York.

Trautman, M. A. and E. H. Willis

(1966), "Isotopes, Inc. Radiocarbon Measurements V," *Radiocarbon,* Vol. 8, pp. 161–203 (*American Journal of Science*), Yale University, New Haven.

Trewartha, G. T. (1954), *An Introduction to Climate,* McGraw-Hill Book Company, Inc., New York.

True, D. L., A. Lautaro Núñez, and H. Patrico Núñez (1970), "Archaeological Investigations in Northern Chile: Project Tarapaca —Preceramic Resources," *American Antiquity,* Vol. 35, No. 2, pp. 170–184, Salt Lake City.

Tschopik, Harry, Jr. (1946 a), "The Aymara," in *Handbook of South American Indians,* J. H. Steward, ed., Vol. 2, pp. 501–574, Bureau of American Ethnology, Bulletin 143, Smithsonian Institution, Washington, D.C.

Tschopik, Harry, Jr. (1946 b), "Some Notes on Rock Shelter Sites near Huancayo, Peru," *American Antiquity,* Vol. 12, pp. 73–80, Menasha, Wisconsin.

Tschopik, M. H. (1946), *Some Notes on the Archaeology of the Department of Puno, Peru,* Peabody Museum Papers, Vol. 27, No. 3, Harvard University, Cambridge.

Ubbelohde Doering, Heinrich (1951), "Ceramic Comparisons of Two North Coast Peruvian Valleys," *Selected Papers, 29th International Congress of Americanists,* S. Tax, ed., Vol. 1, pp. 224–231, University of Chicago Press, Chicago.

Uhle, Max (1903), *Pachacamac,* Department of Archaeology, University of Pennsylvania, Philadelphia.

Uhle, Max (1912), "Las relaciones prehistóricas entre el Perú y Argentina," *17th International Congress of Americanists,* pp. 509–540, Buenos Aires.

Uhle, Max (1913), "Die Ruinen von Moche," *Journal de la Société des Américanistes,* Vol. 10, pp. 95–117, Paris.

Uhle, Max (1919), "La arqueología de Arica y Tacna," *Boletín, Sociedad Ecuatoriana de Estudios Históricos,* Vol. 3, pp. 1–48, Quito.

Uhle, Max (1922 a), *Fundamentos*

Etnicos y Arqueología de Arica y Tacna, 2nd ed., Imprenta de la Universidad Central, Quito.

Uhle, Max (1922 b), "Influencias mayas en el alto Ecuador," *Boletín, Academia Nacional de Historia de Ecuador,* Vol. 4, Nos. 10–11, Vol. 5, Nos. 12–14, Quito.

Uhle, Max (1922 c), "Sepulturas ricas de oro en la Provincia del Azuay," *Boletín, Academia Nacional de Historia de Ecuador,* Vol. 4, pp. 108–114, Quito.

Uhle, Max (1923), *Las Ruinas de Tomebamba,* Imprenta Julio Sáenz Rebolledo, Quito.

Uhle, Max (1927), "Estudios Esmeraldeños," *Anales de la Universidad Central,* Vol. 39, No. 262, Quito.

Vellard, J. (1934), "Notes sur la céramique Pre-Columbienne des environs d'Asunción," *Journal de la Société des Américanistes,* Vol. 26, pp. 37–45, Paris.

Vescelius, G. S. (1963), "Some New Finds at San Nicolas," *Nawpa Pacha,* No. 1, pp. 43–45, Institute of Andean Studies, Berkeley.

Vignati, M. A. (1923 a), "Las llamadas Hachas Patagonicas," *Comunicaciones, Museo Nacional de Historia Natural de Buenos Aires,* Vol. 2, No. 3, pp. 18–44, Buenos Aires.

Vignati, M. A. (1923 b), "Hachas de piedra pulida provenientes de Patagonia," *Comunicaciones, Museo Nacional de Historia Natural de Buenos Aires,* Vol. 2, No. 6, pp. 61–66, Buenos Aires.

Vignati, M. A. (1927), "Arqueología y antropología de los conchales fueginos," *Revista del Museo de La Plata,* Vol. 30, pp. 79–143, La Plata, Argentina.

Vignati, M. A. (1931 a), "Datos referentes a la arqueología de Punta Piedras (Provincia de Buenos Aires)," *Notas Preliminares del Museo de La Plata,* Vol. 1, pp. 205–224, La Plata, Argentina.

Vignati, M. A. (1931 b), "Interpretación de algunos instrumentos líticos considerados como Hachas Insignias o Pillantoki," *Notas Preliminares del Museo de La Plata,* Vol. 1, pp. 173–187, La Plata, Argentina.

Vignati, M. A. (1944), "Antiguedades en la región de los lagos Nahuel Huapí y Traful," *Notas Preliminares del Museo de La Plata,* Vol. 9, Nos. 23–29, pp. 53–165, La Plata, Argentina.

Vignati, M. A. (1950), "Estudios Antropológicos de la Zona Militar de Comodoro Rivadavia," *Anales, Museo de La Plata, Sección de Antropología,* No. 1, La Plata, Argentina.

Villegas Basavilbaso, Florencio (1937), "Un paradero indígena en la margen izquierda del Río Matanzas," *Relaciones, Sociedad Argentina de Antropología,* Vol. 1, pp. 59–63, Buenos Aires.

Von Eickstedt, Egon (1933–34), *Rassenkunde und Rassengeschichte der Menschheit,* Ferdinand Enke Verlag, Stuttgart.

Wagner, Erika (1965), "Arqueología Andina Venezolano," *Revista Colombiana de Antropología,* Vol. 13, pp. 229–237, Bogotá.

Wagner, Erika (1967 a), *The Prehistory and Ethnohistory of the Carache Area in Western Venezuela,* Yale University Publications in Anthropology, No. 71, New Haven.

Wagner, Erika (1967 b), "Patrones culturales de los Andes Venezolanos," *Acta Científica Venezolano,* Vol. 18, No. 1, pp. 5–8, Carácas.

Wagner, E. R. and D. L. (1934), *La Civilización Chaco-Santiagueño y Sus Correlaciones con las del Viejo y Nuevo Mundo,* Vol. 1, Compañia Impresora Argentina, Buenos Aires.

Wallace, D. T. (1962), "Cerrillos, an Early Paracas Site in Ica, Peru," *American Antiquity,* Vol. 27, No. 3, pp. 303–314, Salt Lake City.

Walter, H. V. (1948), *The Pre-History of the Lagoa Santa Region (Minas Gerais),* Oficina Gráficas de Papelería e Tipografía Brazil de Vellosa and Cia., Ltd., Belo Horizonte, Brazil.

Walter, H. V. (1958), *Archaeology of the Lagoa Santa Region (Minas Gerais),* Sedrega, Rio de Janeiro.

Watson, Virginia Drew (1947), "Ciudad Real: A Guaraní-Spanish Site on the Alto Paraná River," *American Antiquity,* Vol. 13, pp.

163–176, Menasha, Wisconsin.

Wedel, W. R. (1953), "Some Aspects of Human Ecology in the Central Plains," *American Anthropologist,* Vol. 55, pp. 499–514, Menasha, Wisconsin.

Wendorf, Fred (1966), "Early Man in the New World: Problems of Migration," *The American Naturalist,* Vol. 100, No. 912, pp. 253–270, Lancaster, Pennsylvania.

West, R. C. (1961), "Aboriginal Sea Navigation between Middle and South America," *American Anthropologist,* Vol. 63, pp. 133–135, Menasha, Wisconsin.

Willey, G. R. (1943), "Excavations in the Chancay Valley," in *Archaeological Studies in Peru,* W. D. Strong, G. R. Willey, and J. M. Corbett, eds., Columbia University Studies in Archaeology and Ethnology, Vol. 1, No. 3, Columbia University Press, New York.

Willey, G. R. (1945), "Horizon Styles and Pottery Traditions in Peruvian Archaeology," *American Antiquity,* Vol. 11, pp. 49–56, Menasha, Wisconsin.

Willey, G. R. (1946 a), "The Archaeology of the Greater Pampa," in *Handbook of South American Indians,* J. H. Steward, ed., Vol. 1, pp. 25–46, Bureau of American Ethnology, Bulletin 143, Smithsonian Institution, Washington, D.C.

Willey, G. R. (1946 b), "The Culture of La Candelaria," in *Handbook of South American Indians,* J. H. Steward, ed., Vol. 2, pp. 661–672, Bureau of American Ethnology, Bulletin 143, Smithsonian Institution, Washington, D.C.

Willey, G. R. (1948), "Functional Analysis of 'Horizon Styles' in Peruvian Archaeology," in *A Reappraisal of Peruvian Archaeology,* W. C. Bennett, ed., Society for American Archaeology, Memoir No. 4, pp. 8–15, Menasha, Wisconsin.

Willey, G. R. (1949), "Ceramics," in *Handbook of South American Indians,* J. H. Steward, ed., Vol. 5, pp. 139–204, Bureau of American Ethnology, Bulletin 143, Smithsonian Institution, Washington D.C.

Willey, G. R. (1950), "Separate

Migrations as an Explanation of the Physical Variability among American Indians," *Journal of the Washington Academy of Sciences,* Vol. 40, No. 3, pp. 71–75, Washington, D.C.

Willey, G. R. (1951 a), "The Chavín Problem, a Review and Critique," *Southwestern Journal of Anthropology,* Vol. 7, pp. 103–144, Albuquerque, New Mexico.

Willey, G. R. (1951 b), "A Preliminary Report on the Monagrillo Culture of Panama," *29th International Congress of Americanists,* Vol. 1, *The Civilizations of Ancient America,* S. Tax, ed., pp. 173–180, University of Chicago Press, Chicago.

Willey, G. R. (1953), *Prehistoric Settlement Patterns in the Virú Valley, Peru,* Bureau of American Ethnology, Bulletin 155, Smithsonian Institution, Washington, D.C.

Willey, G. R. (1954 a), "Review of Paracas Cavernas and Chavín, by A. L. Kroeber," *American Antiquity,* Vol. 20, No. 2, pp. 184–185, Salt Lake City.

Willey, G. R. (1954 b), "Tradition Trend in Ceramic Development," *American Antiquity,* Vol. 20, No. 1, pp. 9–14, Salt Lake City.

Willey, G. R. (1955 a), "The Interrelated Rise of the Native Cultures of Middle and South America," in *New Interpretations of Aboriginal American Culture History,* 75th Anniversary Volume, pp. 28–45, Anthropological Society of Washington, Washington, D.C.

Willey, G. R. (1955 b), "The Prehistoric Civilizations of Nuclear America," *American Anthropologist,* Vol. 57, No. 3, pp. 571–593, Menasha, Wisconsin.

Willey, G. R. (1958), "Estimated Correlations and Dating of South and Central American Culture Sequences," *American Antiquity,* Vol. 23, No. 4, pp. 353–378, Salt Lake City.

Willey, G. R. (1959), "The 'Intermediate Area' of Nuclear America: Its Prehistoric Relationships to Middle America and Peru," *Actas, 33rd International Congress of Americanists,* Vol. I, pp. 184–194, San José, Costa Rica.

Willey, G. R. (1962), "The Early

Great Styles and the Rise of the Pre-Columbian Civilizations," *American Anthropologist,* Vol. 64, No. 1, pp. 1–14, Menasha, Wisconsin.

Willey, G. R. (1964), "Diagram of a Pottery Tradition," in *Process and Pattern in Culture, Essays in Honor of Julian H. Steward,* R. A. Manners, ed., pp. 156–172, Aldine Publishing Co., Chicago.

Willey, Gordon R. (1966), *An Introduction to American Archaeology, Volume 1: North and Middle America,* Prentice-Hall, Inc., Englewood Cliffs, New Jersey.

Willey, Gordon R. (1969), "The Mesoamericanization of the Honduran-Salvadoran Periphery: A Symposium Commentary," *38th International Congress of Americanists,* Vol. 1, pp. 533–542, Stuttgart and Munich.

Willey, G. R. and J. M. Corbett (1954), *Early Ancón and Early Supe Culture: Chavín Horizon Sites of the Central Peruvian Coast,* Columbia University Studies in Archaeology and Ethnology, Vol. 3, Columbia University Press, New York.

Willey, G. R. and C. R. McGimsey (1954), *The Monagrillo Culture of Panama,* Peabody Museum Papers, Vol. 49, No. 2, Harvard University, Cambridge.

Willey, G. R. and T. L. Stoddard (1954), "Cultural Stratigraphy in Panama: A Preliminary Report on the Girón Site," *American Antiquity,* Vol. 19, pp. 332–342, Salt Lake City.

Willey, Gordon R. and Philip Phillips (1958), *Method and Theory in American Archaeology,* University of Chicago Press, Chicago.

Wilmsen, E. N. (1964), "Flake Tools in the American Arctic: Some Speculations," *American Antiquity,* Vol. 29, No. 3, pp. 338–344, Salt Lake City.

Wissler, Clark (1938), *The American Indian,* 3rd ed., Oxford University Press, New York.

Wormington, H. M. (1961), "Prehistoric Cultural Stages of Alberta, Canada," in *Homenaje a Pablo Martínez del Río,* 25 Anniversario de la edición de *Los Orígenes Americanos,* pp. 163–171, México, D.F.

Xérez, Francisco de (1872), *Reports on the Discovery of Peru,* C. R. Markham, trans. and ed., Hakluyt Society, London.

Yamasaki, F., T. Hamada, and C. Fujiyama (1966), "RIKEN Natural Radiocarbon Measurements II," *Radiocarbon,* Vol. 8, pp. 324–339 (*American Journal of Science*), Yale University, New Haven.

Zevallos M., Carlos (1958), "Tecnología Metalúrgica Arqueológica, Elaboración del Alambre," *Cuadernos de Historia y Arqueología,* Vol. 6, Nos. 16–18, pp. 5–11, Casa de La Cultura Ecuatoriana, Núcleo del Guayas, Guayaquil.

Zevallos M., Carlos and Olaf Holm (1960), *Excavaciones Arqueológicas en San Pablo,* Editorial Casa de La Cultura Ecuatoriana, Núcleo del Guayas, Guayaquil.

Zucchi, Alberta (1966), "Nueva forma cerámica en la arqueológia del occidente Venezolano," *Boletín Informativo, Instituto Venezolano de Investigaciones Científicas,* No. 4, Departamento de Antropología, Universidad Central de Venezuela, Carácas.

Zucchi R., Alberta (1967), "Informes preliminares de las excavaciones del yacimiento la Betania, Estado Barinas, Venezuela," *Boletín Indigenista Venezolano,* Vol. 10, Nos. 1–4, pp. 155–168, Carácas.

Zuidema, R. T. (1962), *The Ceque System of Cuzco; the Social Organization of the Capital of the Inca,* mimeogr., Rijks University, Leiden.

Maps

550

Chronological Charts

Index

A

Abary phase, 378, 379
Abipón, 14, 453, 455
Achagua, 14, 370, 396
Achona complex, 36
Agrelo culture, 245, 246
Aguada culture, 233–235
Aija stone sculpture, 87, 89, 151
  (*see also* Sculpture, stone)
Alacaluf, 10, 12, 24, 67, 474, 500
Alaka culture, 365, 489
Alleröd (*see* Two Creeks Interstadial)
Alpaca, domestication of, 7, 17
Altoparaná complex, 37, 41, 61, 64, 461
Altoparanense (*see* Altoparaná complex)
Amahuaca, 397
Amazonian cultural tradition, 66
Amazonides, 11
Ambo site, 52
Ampajango complex, 54, 483
Ampajango site, 40, 41
Ancón Yacht Club, 93
Andaquí, 308
Andean Hunting-Collecting tradition, 31, 33, 43, 46, 48–61, 211, 246, 487, 500, 501, 503

Andirá complex, 63, 441
Apalai, 397
Araquinoid subtradition, 376
Araucanian language, 12, 22
Arawak, 14, 370, 393, 398, 496
Arawakan language, 13, 22, 23, 396, 453
Area chronologies, definition, 4
Arenal phase, 52, 57, 59, 85, 487
  (*see also* Lomas culture sites)
Aruã, 396, 409–411, 416, 417
Ashluslay, 453
Asia Valley site, 99–101
Atacameño, 12, 22, 199
Atacames, 304
Ayampitín, 46, 54, 56
Aymará, 12, 90
Aymaran language, 22

B

Bagaces, 328
Bahía phase, 290–293, 498
Ball game, 371, 389, 391–393
Barbacoa, 304
Barlovento complex, 273, 489, 490, 501
Barlovento site, 271
Barracão complex, 37, 63